BODYGUARD OF LIES

BODYGUARD OF LIES

Anthony Cave Brown

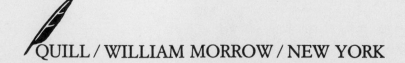

QUILL / WILLIAM MORROW / NEW YORK

Copyright © 1975 by Anthony Cave Brown

Published by arrangement with HarperCollins Publishers, Inc.

It is the policy of William Morrow and Company, Inc., and its imprints and affiliates, recognizing the importance of preserving what has been written, to print the books we publish on acid-free paper, and we exert our best efforts to that end.

Library of Congress Cataloging-in-Publication Data

Brown, Anthony Cave.
    Bodyguard of lies / Anthony Cave Brown.
        p.   cm.
    Reprint. Originally published: New York : Harper & Row, 1975.
    Includes bibliographical references and index.
    ISBN 0-688-10281-6
    1. World War, 1939–1945—Secret service. I. Title.
D810.S7B74   1991
940.54'85—dc20   90-22531
                                                                                      CIP

Printed in the United States of America

First Quill Edition

1 2 3 4 5 6 7 8 9 10

Contents

EUROPEAN THEATER OF OPERATIONS, WORLD WAR II

Allies of the Axis
Neutral Nations
Countries Occupied by Germany
Furthest German Advance into Russia
   and North Africa
The Major Cover and Deception
   Operations of Plan Bodyguard

Faroe Is.

Shetland Is.

Orkney Is.
(Scapa Flow)

NORTH SEA

NO

DENMARK

SCOTLAND

Edinburgh

FORTITUDE NORTH

FORTITUDE SOUTH

N. IRELAND

EIRE

Dublin

Coventry

ENGLAND

London

Le Havre

Hambu

NETHER-LANDS

GE

BELGIUM

Cologne

English Channel

Dieppe

Cherbourg

Paris

Frank

Nurember

Brest

IRONSIDE

ATLANTIC OCEAN

Bay of Biscay

FRANCE

Vichy

SWITZERLAND

Bordeaux

ITALY

PORTUGAL

Lisbon

Madrid

SPAIN

Barcelona

Marseilles

CORSIC

ROYAL FLUSH

VENDETTA

SARDINIA

Tangier

Gibraltar (Br.)

SPANISH MOROCCO

Oran

Algiers

MEDI

Tunis

Casablanca

Kasserine

MOROCCO
(FRENCH)

ALGERIA
(FRENCH)

TUNISIA
(FRENCH)

PART V: NORMANDY TO NEMESIS—JUNE 6
TO AUGUST 20, 1944

BODYGUARD OF LIES

Prologue

GENERAL SIR STEWART MENZIES, the chief of the British secret intelligence service (MI-6), a pale man—"pale skin, pale eyes, silvery blond hair," who was known to the Allied high command by the enigmatical cipher "C," walked past the brooding statues of Beaconsfield and Lincoln on Parliament Square and entered the narrow doorway at 2 Great George Street near Storey's Gate. With him that morning—it was in the beginning of December 1943—was Colonel David Bruce, the chief of the Office of Strategic Services (OSS) in Europe, MI-6's American counterpart. The two men passed through the sandbagged guardpost at the entrance to the War Cabinet offices, crossed a small lobby, and then went down into Prime Minister Winston Churchill's command post under the pavements of Westminster. Here, there was none of the neon-lit, Lysoled asepticism of the modern war room; the headquarters resembled the innards of some old ironclad. Menzies and Bruce stepped through a series of steel bulkhead doors, walked down corridors that were shored up with the heavy timbers of one of Nelson's ships-of-the-line, went through the map room, which was under 4 feet of concrete reinforced by old London tramrails, and finally reached their destination. It was a small conference room that looked like a wardroom—a whirring fan, a portrait of the King-Emperor, a lithograph of London Bridge, oriental carpets on the floor, comfortable furniture, a clock on the wall inscribed with the words: "Victoria R.I., Ministry of Works, 1889." Even the maps bespoke another era; one of them had been published in 1910 by the Navy League of the British Empire.

The men, and one woman, who greeted Menzies and Bruce were almost all young, and some wore the red gorgets and golden lions of the Imperial General Staff. For a few minutes they talked about the latest war news and high command gossip, standing around the old, well-polished conference table at the center of which was a small figurine—the Dancing

Faun, the Greco-Roman numen that suggested dark and evil spirits at work in tangled forests. It was the emblem of the London Controlling Section (LCS), a secret bureau that had been established by Churchill within his personal headquarters to plan stratagems to deceive Hitler and the German General Staff about Allied operations in the war against the Third Reich.

The agile, devious, elegant figurine hinted at the nature of the LCS's work. For "stratagem" is defined in the Oxford English Dictionary as: "An operation or act of generalship, usually an artifice or trick designed to outwit or surprise the enemy; a device or scheme for obtaining an advantage; cunning, used loosely for a deed of blood or violence." The men gathered around the Faun were either members of the LCS or hierarchs of other British and American secret bureaus who were responsible for the execution of their schemes. The weapons they used were called—in the British military lexicon—"special means," a vaguely sinister term that included a wide variety of surreptitious, sometimes murderous, always intricate operations of covert warfare designed to cloak overt military operations in secrecy and to mystify Hitler about the real intentions of the Allies. They were operations that, as M. R. D. Foot would observe, were "true to the tradition of English eccentricity; the sort of thing that Captain Hornblower or Mycroft Holmes in fiction, or Admiral Cochrane or Chinese Gordon in fact, would have gone in for had they been faced with a similar challenge; the sort of thing that looks odd at the time, and eminently sensible later."

Britain's experience in the use of special means was very long—longer than that of any other power. For over five hundred years her statesmen and generals had used them to establish first a kingdom and then an empire, and to defend both against their enemies. They had outwitted the Spanish, the French and the Dutch in previous centuries; and once before in this century they had been forced to fight the aggrandizement of Germany. But scarcely twenty years after the defeat of Kaiser Wilhelm II and the German Empire, a new Germany under the leadership of Adolf Hitler had risen from the wreckage of the first bitter conflict, and the world was again at war. Special means had played a role in influencing Hitler's strategy in the early years of that war. Now, Britain's experience in special means was to be harnessed to the protection of the most difficult and dangerous military operation of the Second World War—"Neptune," the code word for the invasion of the Norman coast of France in the spring of 1944.

Preparations for Neptune had already taken three and a half years, and involved the combined industrial, military and intellectual power of the British Empire and the United States. Yet not even that combined might was sufficient to assure the western powers of victory. Hitler's armies, despite the bloodletting of the campaigns in Russia, Italy and North Africa, were still immensely powerful. There were a million men in the West, entrenched behind the Atlantic Wall, a line of fortifications that was the strongest in history since the Great Wall of China. If the Germans were ready and waiting, they could pour a hail of fire into the assault forces that would destroy Neptune at the water's edge. Even if Neptune obtained a toehold in Normandy, Hitler, it had to be expected, would—and could— quickly concentrate every man and gun at the beachhead, seal it off and doom the Allies to a campaign as fruitless and bloody as those experienced by the British at Flanders and the Somme in the First World War. Not even the weather could be guaranteed to favor the assault; the English Channel was one of the world's most capricious waterways, and if only moderately heavy seas sprang up unexpectedly, they would wreck the carefully pre- pared timetables upon which the success of the invasion might depend.

As everyone knew, if the invasion failed, all else would fail. Britain would have to seek terms, for she would commit everything in her armory to this attack. The Americans, appalled by the bloodshed and the magni- tude of the disaster, would almost certainly reject President Franklin D. Roosevelt when he came up for reelection late in 1944 and seek a victory against Japan before deciding whether to attempt a second invasion. Then Hitler would be able to concentrate his entire might against Russia, with every prospect of defeating the Red Army and emerging as master of Europe.

Hitler himself was completely confident in his ability to destroy the invasion at the outset. There was not, however, complete certainty in the Allied camp that Neptune would succeed. General Dwight D. Eisenhower, who was about to become Supreme Commander for the expedition, would write in a letter to a friend in Washington: "As the big day approaches tension grows and everybody gets more and more on edge. This time, because of the stakes involved, the atmosphere is probably more electric than ever before. In this particular venture, we are not risking a tactical defeat; we are putting the whole works on one number."

It was said that Churchill had nightmares about what might happen in Normandy on D-Day. Debating Neptune's chances for success, he wrote: "It still seemed to me . . . that fortifications of concrete and steel armed with modern fire-power, and fully manned by trained, resolute men, could only be overcome by . . ."—What? He supplied the answer—surprise. Only if Hitler was surprised by the time and place of the attack would Nep- tune achieve that small advantage that might spell the difference between victory and defeat. But how was this clever enemy to be surprised? His ships, planes, radar, sentinels—all, it had to be expected, would be alert and awake. How could the presence of the greatest number of men and ma- chines in military history be concealed as they assembled in England in readiness for the invasion? The location of their encampments alone might be enough to permit Hitler to deduce that Normandy was their destination. Even if this host could be hidden in England, how could it be concealed as it left the ports of embarkation to cross the Channel, a voyage that, for some units of the invasion force, would take the better part of two days? Hitler knew that the Allies must return to Europe, and it seemed almost impossible that he would not be able to discover when and where they would attack. In all probability, he would not be caught off guard. Yet it was the responsibility of the LCS and its associated bureaus to provide Neptune with that elusive quality called surprise.

Colonel John Bevan, the chief of the LCS, called this meeting to order, and Lady Jane Pleydell-Bouverie, his personal assistant, distributed a document. It was seven pages long, and at the top of the first foolscap page were five green bars, there to draw attention to the especially secret nature of the document—so secret that its contents would not become public until December 1972, twenty-nine years later. Above the bars was the super-scription: "This document is the Property of His Britannic Majesty's Government," a warning that was reserved for the most important British state papers. And below the bars were the words: "Most Secret," "Re-stricted Circulation," and the odd code word "Bigot," which meant that the document contained information about the key secrets of Neptune. It was "Plan Jael," the "overall deception policy" of the high commands of America, Britain and Russia to mislead Hitler about Allied strategy and tactics in the months ahead, and about military operations that would include the gigantic assault on the *Atlantikwall* at Normandy. Thus Plan Jael was quite as important as the Neptune plan itself, for in its seven tersely worded pages, it outlined the deceptions and stratagems that would be used to cloak Neptune's advance across the Channel—deceptions and stratagems created by a variety of special means which, if they were successful, would give the invasion armada the essential element of surprise.

It was Churchill who was largely responsible for the central role that special means would play in Neptune. Their employment as a major weapon in the Second World War, and the creation of a central agency, the LCS, to conceive and coordinate the stratagems of special means, was probably his greatest single contribution to military theory and practice. It was a theory born of Churchill's own experience in another war with a military operation that had ended in disaster—Gallipoli. In 1915, appalled by the stalemate on the western front, Churchill sought to break the deadlock in the battles of the trenches with what he would call a "knife thrust" through the "soft underbelly of Europe." A large Allied expeditionary force was landed at the Dardanelles to create a new front that would draw German forces from France. But the knife broke, and the expedition foundered with the loss of 252,000 troops, largely through the inertia and caution of the Allied generals and admirals in command. Churchill, as the principal architect of the plan, was forced to resign as First Lord of the Admiralty—a resignation that seemed at the time to spell the end of his career as a politician and statesman. While in the political wilderness, he reflected upon the "dull carnage" in France that was wiping out an entire generation of Englishmen, and wrote an essay that was now the credo of the LCS. His main point was that

> Battles are won by slaughter and manoeuvre. The greater the general, the more he contributes in manoeuvre, the less he demands in slaughter. . . . Nearly all the battles which are regarded as the masterpieces of the military art . . . have been battles of manoeuvre in which very often the enemy has found himself defeated by some novel expedient or device, some queer, swift, unexpected thrust or stratagem. In such battles the losses of the victors have been small. There is required for the composition of a great commander not only massive common sense and reasoning power, not only imagination, but also an element of legerdemain, an original and sinister touch, which leaves the enemy puzzled as well as beaten. . . . There are many kinds of manoeuvres in war, some only of which take place upon the battlefield. There are manoeuvres far to the flank or rear. There are manoeuvres in time, in diplomacy, in mechanics, in psychology; all of which are removed from the battlefield, but react often decisively upon it, and the object of all is to find easier ways, other than sheer slaughter, of achieving the main purpose.

This philosophy, born of tragedy and holocaust in one amphibious operation, was now to be employed to prevent another, even greater tragedy and holocaust on D-Day. And it was Plan Jael that was intended to provide the novel expedient and sinister touches for Neptune. Five main arenas of secret activity were involved in the plan. The first was offensive intelligence, the business of divining the enemy's secrets. If Neptune was to succeed, it was imperative that the Allied commanders have a detailed and accurate picture of the fortifications of the Atlantic Wall, the strength and disposition of the German forces and, above all, foreknowledge of Hitler's intentions. Offensive intelligence was the responsibility of MI-6 and the OSS, and explained the presence of their chiefs, Menzies and Bruce, at meetings of the LCS.

Thus far in the course of the war, MI-6 and the OSS had achieved considerable success in discovering Hitler's secrets through conventional intelligence and espionage channels—the reports of spies and informants throughout Nazi-occupied Europe and in the satellite and neutral nations; the censorship of foreign mail; the interrogation of prisoners of war. But MI-6—and the Allied high command—had two sources of secret intelligence that were not conventional. One was called "Ultra," and it was derived from the interception and decryption of secret German wireless communications. The other was known as the "Schwarze Kapelle," or "Black Orchestra," a small group of German officers and men—among them Admiral Wilhelm Canaris, chief of the Abwehr, the German secret intelligence service—who were conspiring to overthrow Hitler and the Third Reich. Throughout the war, Ultra and—sometimes—the Schwarze Kapelle had systematically provided the Allied high command with secret intelligence of vital significance in the military operations that paved the way for Neptune. But, as all who were privy to these secret sources of information knew, ciphers can be changed, and plotters arrested, overnight. No one could be sure that Ultra and the Schwarze Kapelle would continue to provide the kind of secret intelligence upon which the success of Neptune might depend.

The second major arena of secret activity proposed in Plan Jael was counterintelligence and security, those operations that were designed to deny Hitler knowledge of the secrets of Neptune. Chief among these operations was the destruction of the German secret intelligence service; and MI-6 and the OSS were, again, charged with this task. MI-5, the British counterintelligence agency, was responsible for the liquidation of the enemy secret service in Britain, and thus far it, too, had a remarkable record. It had brought the entire German espionage network in Britain under control, and the FBI had achieved similar results in America. Once captured, however, not all enemy agents had been jailed or executed. Some were being used in a game of deception by the curiously named XX-Committee of MI-5, and by X2 of the OSS. It was a game in which, as Norman Holmes Pearson, the Yale professor who was associated with the XX-Committee, would write, "The dermal and subdermal took on new and nerve-wracking significance." It was especially nerve-wracking to the Neptune planners, for all knew that one blunder, one indiscretion could reveal the secrets of Neptune. Yet it was a game that had to be played— and won—if Neptune was to take Hitler by surprise.

The main weapons in these first two arenas of secret operations proposed by Jael were intellect and stealth, menace and deception, with only an occasional act of thuggery committed in some dark alley of Europe. It was in the third arena that violence occurred, the arena that was called, blandly, special operations. Here the agencies involved were Britain's Special Operations Executive (SOE), commanded by General Colin Gubbins, a Hebridean and an expert in clandestine warfare, and America's Special Operations branch of the OSS (SO), commanded by Colonel Joseph Haskell. Both these agencies were represented at the meetings of the LCS, for their particular task was to locate, encourage and supply the guerrilla organizations that criss-crossed all of Europe from the Channel to the Polish-Russian border, from the Lofoten Islands in the Arctic to Cairo, from Helsinki to Tangier. These organizations were called *réseaux,* from the French word for network, and their work was to attack the Nazi régime and its soldiers from behind the lines.

In the special context of Neptune, SOE's and SO's main task would be to organize, equip and control the impassioned and politically divided French resistance, and to guide those acts of sabotage and guerrilla warfare against German lines of communication and transportation that would delay or disrupt the enemy's response to Neptune. But again, there was a question in the minds of the Neptune planners. The world of special operations was one of "Proustian complexity," where even the lives of agents and *résistants* could be used as pawns. Yet Neptune, in some measure, would depend upon the loyalty and obedience of the French *résistants*—and upon their willingness to risk their lives.

The fourth arena of secret activity proposed in Jael was political warfare. The British Political Warfare Executive (PWE) and, to a lesser extent, the American Office of War Information (OWI) had been created expressly to wage, in concert with the LCS, a war of words against the Third Reich. Their credo was "to approach the German mind through a deception and through elaborately sustained fictions, calculated to throw it off its guard and to appeal to the selfish, disloyal, individualist motives in the (German soldier and citizen)." Their main weapon was rumor—the theory that you may not be able to bomb a currency but you can certainly destroy it with a whisper; and their objective was "to drive a wedge between the Nazi leaders and the people, and to create an intensification of war-weariness and defeatism by every means, open and clandestine. . . ."

But words are not bullets, rumors are not bombs, and there were few indications that the obedience of the German people to their Fuehrer was wavering, or that the German soldier was weakening in his determination to repulse an invasion. The Neptune planners knew of the serious disagreements between Hitler and his generals; many of the highest officers of the German General Staff were, in fact, members of the Schwarze Kapelle. Thus far their conspiracies had come to little, and Hitler retained his iron grip over his generals, the German people and the continent of Europe. But any maneuver, any expedient was worthy of consideration. For this was total war. The Allies had demanded, in the resounding—and some high commanders believed ill-considered—proclamation of "Unconditional Surrender," the complete capitulation of Germany. And Germany would not surrender without a monumental fight. Neptune would be the decisive encounter in a war that had to be fought to the bitter end, and the secret war that attended Neptune would be equally bitter. As Foot later wrote: "Nothing quite like it had been seen before; probably nothing quite like it will be seen again, for the circumstances of Hitler's war were unique, and called out this among other unique responses."

The most unique of those responses was the fifth arena of covert activity proposed in Plan Jael—deception, the ultimate secret weapon and the most secret of all secret operations. Deception was the province of the LCS, and its special assignment was to plant upon the enemy, along the channels open to it through the Allied high command, hundreds, perhaps thousands of splinters of information that, when assembled by the enemy intelligence services, would form a plausible and acceptable—but false— picture of Allied military intentions. The LCS had refined the arts of deception in its past operations; now Jael proposed that Hitler be led to believe that the Allies intended to attack not Normandy but elsewhere in France. It was a deception that would decide the fate of Neptune. The LCS would have to use every conduit at its disposal in a carefully conceived and timed scenario of special means to send this fiction to the desk of Hitler. Those special means would involve whispers and rumors, the services of double and even triple agents, the careers and reputations of famous generals, sacrificial military and clandestine operations, wireless games, the creation of fictitious armies and the manipulation of resistance forces and the Schwarze Kapelle. In short, nothing could be overlooked in the attempt to convince the Germans that the invasion would strike at a different time and a different place than was actually intended.

The men who had been charged with this seemingly impossible task were, of course, of several minds; but they appeared to be united by a single factor—class. Deception, like intelligence, was the pursuit of gentlemen. Colonel Bevan, the chief of the LCS, was a son-in-law of the Earl of Lucan and a grandson of the founder of Barclay's Bank. Bevan's deputy and the author of Plan Jael, Colonel Sir Ronald Evelyn Leslie Wingate, was the son of Wingate Pasha of the Anglo-Egyptian Sudan and a cousin of both Lawrence of Arabia and Wingate of Burma. The other members of the LCS and of the secret agencies associated with it included financiers, politicians, diplomats, scientists, writers, artists—men in London, Washington, the Mediterranean, India and Southeast Asia with connections and a talent for special means. Above them all was Churchill himself. As Wingate would later write: "It was Churchill who had all the ideas. It was his drive, his brilliant imagination, and his technical knowledge that initiated all these ideas and plans." Churchill delighted in examining and advising the LCS, and he was a master of what would come to be called "the game plan." It was the American member of the LCS, Colonel William H. Baumer, who would later comment upon the difficulty of the game they were playing—and its ethical implications. "Looking back on it all," he said,

> Bevan and his boys were extraordinarily clever. They knew exactly when and where to play upon Hitler's fury, and they did so knowing full well that if what they did became public property in later years they might all earn public opprobrium. But they were quite academic about this at the time. They

were playing for the highest stakes imaginable, and there was no time for squeamishness. They knew they simply could not lose because, if they did, they and Britain would lose everything. Their object was to make Hitler run about like a blue-arse fly. It was a dangerous business for they never knew from minute to minute whether they might be exposed and, thereby, expose the very matters that they were seeking to hide.

A plaque hung on the wall behind the men who were now meeting beneath the pavements of Westminster to discuss the intricacies of Plan Jael. It was placed there as if in answer to the criticisms that were, perhaps, inevitable when the existence of this super-secret agency finally became known some fifteen years after the war was over. On the plaque were the words of Sir Garnet Wolseley, a former Commander-in-Chief of the British army, who wrote in *The Soldier's Handbook* in 1869:

> We are bred up to feel it a disgrace ever to succeed by falsehood . . . we will keep hammering along with the conviction that honesty is the best policy, and that truth always wins in the long run. These pretty little sentiments do well for a child's copy book, but a man who acts on them had better sheathe his sword forever.

It was clear that Churchill and the LCS would stop at nothing to ensure secrecy and surprise for Neptune. Even Churchill's choice of code name for the cover and deception operations that would attend Neptune revealed something of their cunning, mercilessness and intent. Jael was the woman in the Song of Deborah of the Old Testament who committed one of the blackest acts of treachery in that long, dark chronicle. For the Song tells how Deborah the Prophetess plotted with Barak, the commander of the Israelite army, to defeat Jabin, the King of Canaan, and Sisera, the Canaanite commander who, with "nine hundred chariots of iron," had ruled the Israelites for twenty years. Their stratagem succeeded and Sisera was lured to battle at the foot of Mount Tabor on the Plain of Esdraelon. There was a heaven-sent rainstorm, Sisera's chariots bogged down, Barak and his men emerged from their hiding place on the mountainside, "And the Lord discomfited Sisera, and all his chariots . . . and all the host of Sisera fell upon the edge of the sword; and there was not a man left."

Sisera himself survived and fled the battlefield on foot; and as he was trying to reach Canaan, he happened upon the encampment of Heber the Kenite, who was absent that day. But his wife Jael greeted him cordially; and believing that a treaty of friendship existed between the Canaanites and the Kenites, Sisera asked for food and a place to rest. To this Jael agreed, and exhausted by battle and his flight, Sisera lay down upon her bed. Jael brought him goat's milk and promised to stand guard at the tent door; but when Sisera was deeply asleep, she took a hammer and a tent peg and "smote the nail into his temples, and fastened it into the ground. . . ."

Thus ended the Canaanites' rule of the Israelites. And thus, it was hoped, would Plan Jael help the Allies end the rule of Hitler.

The meeting of the LCS that December morning in 1943 was not a long one. Its purpose was merely to read and approve the final draft of Plan Jael before it was sent for approval to the Combined Chiefs of Staff at Washington, the highest Allied war council. It was little more than a formality, for Jael had already been agreed upon as the overall deception policy of the Grand Alliance at the conference between Churchill, Roosevelt and Marshal Josef Stalin at Teheran in November 1943. But before the meeting broke up, the question of the code name was discussed. Appropriate as it was, it was decided, reluctantly, to change the name of the plan. For only a few days before, at Teheran, Churchill, in describing the special means of Plan Jael, had made a remark that would become a classic epigram:

> In war-time, truth is so precious that she should always be attended by a bodyguard of lies.

And so Plan Jael was renamed "Plan Bodyguard," a *ruse de guerre* that would come to be compared with the Trojan Horse—a stratagem for which the totem was that graceful but wicked little sprite at the center of the LCS conference table.

The meeting adjourned and the hierarchs of the LCS's executive agencies departed to begin employing those special means that might enable the best and finest of the young men of the Allied armies to get ashore—and stay ashore—in the first tumultuous hours of D-Day. No one could predict the success of Bodyguard until Neptune actually emerged from the sea. No one could be certain that the influences symbolized by the Dancing Faun would work to achieve surprise on June 6, 1944. For as General Sir Frederick Morgan, one of the planners of Neptune, later remarked, corrupting slightly the words of Wellington after Waterloo:

> It was going to be a close-run thing, a damned close-run thing—the closest-run thing you ever saw in your life.

PART I

THE ORIGINS OF SPECIAL MEANS

1938–1942

In the high ranges of Secret Service work the actual facts in many cases were in every respect equal to the most fantastic inventions of romance and melodrama. Tangle within tangle, plot and counter-plot, ruse and treachery, cross and double-cross, true agent, false agent, double agent, gold and steel, the bomb, the dagger and the firing party, were interwoven in many a texture so intricate as to be incredible and yet true. The Chief and the High Officers of the Secret Service revelled in these subterranean labyrinths, and pursued their task with cold and silent passion.

WINSTON S. CHURCHILL

Ultra

THE SKIES over London were a brilliant, clear blue that August Bank Holiday of 1938, yet there was a sultry obscurity in the air and forecasters—political and meteorological—reported thunder and lightning to the east, beyond the English Channel. An atmosphere of foreboding hung over all of Europe, but no anxious crowds lined the pavements outside the Prime Minister's residence at 10 Downing Street—the usual sign of crisis. This was one of England's great holidays; all normal business was suspended. Huge crowds romped on the beaches, in the countryside, in the parks; it seemed as if the only sound of violence on that hot, somnolent afternoon was the thud of leather upon willow at Lords, where Cheltenham was playing Haileybury.

There were some who sensed the approaching storm, among them Winston Churchill, who was telling his constituents in Essex: "It is difficult for us in this ancient forest of Theydon Bois, the very name of which carries us back to Norman days—here, in the heart of peaceful, law-abiding England . . . (to grasp) that the whole state of Europe and of the world is moving steadily towards a climax which cannot be long delayed." He warned that "ferocious passions" were "rife in Europe," and that there were "fifteen hundred thousand soldiers upon a war footing" in Germany. Yet such was the British temperament that the Reverend J. S. Crole's failure to win the Bournemouth Open Bowls Tournament received about the same space in *The Times* as did Churchill's address and only slightly less space than the news that on Tuesday Lord Runciman would lead a diplomatic mission to Prague and Berlin in an attempt to prevent war between Germany and Czechoslovakia.

It seemed inconceivable that war might be near. But there were ominous signs that Herr Hitler, as he was being called in Parliament and the press, did indeed intend war if he could not obtain an empire in Europe by political and diplomatic means. And that Monday, while the Royal Dragoons were playing polo at Le Touquet, great brown phalanxes of German stormtroopers at Nuremburg were about to rededicate themselves with Teuton rites to the principle of *ein Reich, ein Volk, ein Führer*. Germany was resurgent, angry, menacing, implacable. What was it she wanted? What did she intend? Were the shrill proclamations of her leaders a bluff? Or was Hitler truly determined to "correct the humiliations" of the Versailles Treaty and to ensure, by force of arms if necessary, "a place in the sun" for the Third Reich? And if there was to be war, what was the reality of German power? How many divisions did she have, how many cannon, how many tanks, how many air squadrons, how many submarines? What was her oil and steel capacity? Who would be her allies? What would Russia and America do?

Not since the end of the First World War had the statesmen of England felt such urgent need of sound intelligence from Germany. That was why, that weekend, Colonel Stewart Menzies was at his desk in the headquarters of the British secret intelligence service on Broadway, a quiet side street near Westminster Abbey. Now forty-eight, Menzies was deputy chief of MI-6 and chief of the German section of Military Intelligence at the War Office. As such, it was his particular responsibility to superintend the gathering of intelligence about Hitler's intentions and the strength and disposition of the Wehrmacht, the German war machine. And the fact that Menzies was in his office at all that weekend reflected the forebodings of the times. Much—perhaps everything—hung upon the ability of MI-6 to obtain foreknowledge of Hitler's plans. A steady stream of intelligence about the military and political state of the Third Reich was reaching Menzies from a variety of sources, among them Admiral Wilhelm Canaris —the chief of the Abwehr. But gunroom gossip—for that was what much of this information amounted to—was not sufficient if the British government was to be kept quickly and accurately informed of Hitler's secret decisions. There was only one sure way to obtain the intelligence the British needed: cryptanalysis, the ancient craft of intercepting and breaking the ciphers of the secret communications of an adversary.

Britain had successfully intercepted and decrypted German military, diplomatic and commercial telegrams for many years. But Hitler knew the importance of secrecy, and in 1934 the German government began to change its ciphers to a new system. MI-6 had long been involved in a worldwide inquiry to establish the nature of that new system. Now, four years later, it seemed that Menzies had the information MI-6 had been searching for.

That search had begun when Major Francis Foley, the MI-6 resident at Berlin (known to the service as "1200"), learned that the German army was experimenting with a cipher machine called Enigma. He reported this information to Admiral Sir Hugh Sinclair, the chief of MI-6, and Sinclair gave Menzies the task of finding out what was known about the machine. Menzies's men discovered that Enigma was the invention of a Dutchman, Hugo Koch of Delft, who had patented a *Geheimschrijfmachine*—a "secret writing machine"—at The Hague in October 1919. Koch had established a company to develop and market his invention, but he had not been able to build a machine and had assigned the patents to a German, Artur Scherbius, an engineer and inventor living in Berlin. Scherbius did build a machine from Koch's plans and he called it "Enigma," after the *Enigma Variations* of Sir Edward Elgar, in which Elgar described his friends in musical cipher. Scherbius's model, a primitive form of rotor cipher machine, was exhibited publicly for the first time at the 1923 Congress of the International Postal Union. In 1924, the German post office used an Enigma to exchange greetings with the Congress; it was publicized in *Radio News* in America and in a book on cipher machines by Dr. Siegfried Turkel, the scientific director of the Viennese criminological institute. According to a brochure circulated in English, the machine was originally conceived to protect the secrets of business, not the secrets of war. The brochure claimed:

> The natural inquisitiveness of competitors is at once checkmated by a machine which enables you to keep all your documents, or at least their important parts, entirely secret without occasioning any expenses worth mentioning. One secret, well-protected, may pay the whole cost of the machine. . . .

But Scherbius's venture did not prosper and he sold the Enigma patents to another company. By that time Hitler had come to power, rearmament and reorganization of the Wehrmacht were under way, and his generals were scouring the laboratories and workshops for some new cipher machine with which to protect their secrets. The evaluation of Enigma was the responsibility of Colonel Erich Fellgiebel, who was to become the chief signals officer of the German army and of the German high command. Significantly, Fellgiebel would also become one of the most active conspirators of the Schwarze Kapelle.

Enigma disappeared from the commercial world as Fellgiebel experimented with the machine. It was found to be inexpensive, sturdy, portable, simple to operate, easy to service, and it produced ciphers in great abundance. Above all, it was pronounced secure from even the most advanced cryptanalytical attack. It was relatively unimportant whether or not the machine was captured by an enemy; it was quite useless to him without knowledge of the keying procedures. Enigma was deemed suitable in every way to the needs of the Wehrmacht.

MI-6 knew this much of the machine, but little else until Major Harold Lehrs Gibson, the MI-6 resident at Prague, reported that the Polish secret intelligence service, which worked with MI-6 against the Russians and the Germans, was also interested in Enigma. Department BS4, the cryptographic section of the Polish General Staff, had legally acquired the commercial version of Enigma; and Polish cryptanalysts, led by two leading Polish mathematicians, M. Rejewski and H. Zygalski, had managed to resolve some of the mathematical problems involved in deciphering its transmissions. Gibson's report produced immediate excitement in the British cryptanalytical service, for the Poles were noted for their expertise in cryptanalysis; their ability to read Russian ciphers had resulted in a victory for the Poles in the Russo-Polish War of 1920, a war that checked communism's first overt westward thrust after the First World War. But the Polish penetration of Enigma was mathematical, not mechanical; and they had experimented only with the commercial model, which, it could be assumed, the Germans had modified and refined for the Wehrmacht's use.

It was the French who first managed to penetrate the military version, not through the trial-and-error of mathematical analysis, but through treason. General Gustave Bertrand, a high officer of "2 bis," the French cryptanalytical bureau, would record that in the summer of 1937 a German presented himself at the French Embassy at Berne and offered to work in the service of France against the Third Reich. He was, he declared, an officer of the Forschungsamt, the Reich's main cryptographic bureau, and his motives, he said, were ideological. His offer was reported to Colonel Louis Rivet at 2 bis, and at first the French were inclined to believe that the German, who was codenamed "Source D," might be an agent provocateur sent to compromise their diplomatic status and privileges in Switzerland. But Rivet, so Bertrand would remember, declared that this might be "a chance that will never come again," and he despatched a Captain Navarre of 2 bis to Berne. After prolonged interrogation of Source D, Navarre reported that he was "a traitor acting out of avarice," but he had revealed that "German technicians have developed a coding and decoding apparatus of a completely new type." It was Enigma.

Navarre was ordered to make the German "a modest compensation with a promise of a payment on a generous scale" if he obtained some of the machine's production for their next meeting. Source D did better than that. When he later met Navarre in a small café in Brussels, he produced "a secret instruction manual on the use of the machine," as well as a cipher text and its plain text counterpart. The original of the manual was returned to the German the next day, along with part of the "generous payment" that had been promised. The rest would be sent to him through Brussels and Berne if the "French technicians charged with the examination of the data (find) them satisfactory."

Navarre then returned to Paris, and Bertrand, with the data supplied by Source D, was able to produce—using the precision-tool capacity of a

Franco-American cash register factory outside Paris—a replica of Enigma. Moreover, if French claims are correct, Source D began to send 2 bis notice of the monthly keying changes employed by the Wehrmacht to thwart cryptographic attack. In short, the French had the capacity to read the Germans' most secret ciphers—an intelligence coup of majestic importance. But they could do so only as long as Source D continued to supply the keying changes.

The British intelligence attack against Enigma took a somewhat different course. In June of 1938, Menzies had received a message that would prove to be the most important in the intelligence history of the Second World War. It came, again, from Gibson at Prague, who reported that he had just returned from Warsaw where, through the Polish intelligence service, he had encountered a Polish Jew who had offered to sell MI-6 his knowledge of Enigma. The Pole, Richard Lewinski (not his real name), had worked as a mathematician and engineer at the factory in Berlin where Enigma was produced. But he had been expelled from Germany because of his religion and had then come to the attention of the British Embassy at Warsaw. At the interview with Gibson, Lewinski announced his price: £10,000, a British passport, and a resident's permit for France for himself and his wife. He did not wish to live in England because he had no friends or ties there. Lewinski claimed that he knew enough about Enigma to build a replica, and to draw diagrams of the heart of the machine—the complicated wiring system in each of its rotors.

When the letter reached Menzies, he was both electrified and cautious. It seemed incredible that a man with such valuable information would have been permitted to leave Germany, and Menzies, suspicious that Lewinski had been sent to lure the small British cryptographic bureau down a blind alley while the Germans conducted their business free from surveillance, was not prepared to take any action without a recommendation from experts in cryptanalysis. But when they had examined some technical data sent over by Gibson and pronounced that Lewinski's information appeared to be genuine, Menzies decided to send two of the experts to Warsaw to interview Lewinski in person. They had been summoned to his office to discuss their mission; that was why Menzies was in London that August Bank Holiday weekend.

The three men met in Menzies's office beneath a portrait of his patron, the late King Edward VII, dressed in tweeds and deerstalker, a shotgun in one hand, a brace of grouse in the other, and a gun dog playing in the heather. One of his visitors was Alfred Dilwyn Knox, a tall, spare man who was England's leading cryptanalyst. His companion was Alan Mathison Turing, a young and burly man with an air of abstraction and a reputation as an outstanding mathematical logician. Briefing the men on their mission, Menzies said their task was to go to Warsaw, interview Lewinski and report upon his knowledge. If they were satisfied that it was genuine, they were to arrange with Gibson to take the Pole and his wife to Paris and place him in the charge of Commander Wilfred Dunderdale, the MI-6 resident there, known to the service as "2400." Then, under their supervision, Lewinski was to recreate the Enigma machine.

A little later Knox and Turing boarded the Golden Arrow at Victoria Station, and in forty-eight hours they were in Warsaw.

They were a brilliant but tragic pair. Alfred Knox was the senior— "tall, with a rather gangling figure, unruly black hair, his eyes, behind glasses, some miles away in thought." He was the son of the Bishop of Manchester, and his two brothers were equally distinguished: Monsignor Ronald Knox, the Catholic theologian and Domestic Prelate to the Pope, had himself been a cryptanalyst with the Admiralty in the First World War; E. V. Knox was the editor of *Punch,* a post he would hold for seventeen years. Alfred Knox had gone to Eton as a King's Scholar and became Captain of the School. He won the school's main prize in mathematics, the Tomline, and then trod the well-worn path of Etonians to King's College, Cambridge, where he became a Chancellor's Medallist and a Fellow. In the First World War he joined the new Admiralty cryptanalytical bureau, Room OB-40, and it was said that his first main success in codebreaking was to solve a three-letter German flag code while in his bath. He had also been involved in the Zimmermann Telegram episode which brought the United States into the war. He stayed in cryptanalysis after the war, transferring to the Foreign Office's Government Code and Cipher School (GC&CS), which during the Second World War would be located at Bletchley Park, a large, gloomy Victorian mansion near the London Midland and Scottish Railway just outside the town of Bletchley, about 40 miles north of London. While he was employed at the GC&CS, Knox demonstrated his pure intellectual genius; he completed the great task of his friend and mentor, the late Professor Walter Headlam, in translating the seven hundred verses of Herodas, the third-century Greek poet. Working with Headlam's manuscript and the original papyri, discovered at Fayum at the turn of the century, Knox completed the translation in eight years—an immense cryptanalytical and literary feat. It was a combination of mathematical analysis and erudition that made Knox's mind so invaluable to the recondite craft of codebreaking.

Alan Turing, his assistant, was an authentic—if eccentric—mathematical genius. He had been educated at Sherborne School in Dorset and had gone on to King's, where he took a First and Second in Mathematical Logic. He had then attended the Institute for Advanced Studies at Princeton, where he studied under Einstein; and while at Princeton he had been offered the post as personal assistant to Professor John von Neumann, the brain behind the first American computer. But instead, he returned to England to become Knox's assistant at the Foreign Office; and there, in secrecy, he began work in a trade as ancient as the hieroglyphs—cryptanalysis. He did not abandon his research. Turing was one of the pioneers of computer theory, but he had also long been toying with the notion of a "Universal Machine," not a computer, but a machine which, when supplied with suitable instructions, would imitate the behavior of another machine. Or, as Turing explained its function: "A sonnet written by a machine will be better appreciated by another machine."

His friends said that such a machine was an impossibility. It would have to be as large as St. Paul's Cathedral or the Capitol Building; it would require new universities wholly dedicated to the training of high skills to man it; it would need more power than a facility the size of Boulder Dam could produce. But Turing was not dissuaded, and he persisted with his theories. He wrote a number of papers of major importance, among them one that would give him, according to his obituary in *The Times,* "a permanent place in mathematical logic." Turing never said (outside his own tiny professional circle) how his theories could be applied to cryptanalysis. But as his mother would write in an *In Memoriam* about her son, "In answer to a question of mine regarding the application of mathematics to mundane ends, Alan referred to something he had been working on, which might be of military value. He gave no details. But as he had some scruples about the application of any such device (to military affairs), he consulted me about its moral aspects."

Yet for all his intelligence, his scruples and his dreams, Turing had a very odd, childlike side to his nature. He listened every night to "Toytown," a children's play about Larry the Lamb on the BBC, keeping the long-distance telephone line open to his mother so that they could discuss each development. While working at Bletchley, he was arrested by an officer of the Buckinghamshire Constabulary who encountered him walking down a country lane with his gas mask on. It filtered pollen, Turing explained, and he suffered from hay fever. He would convert the family money into silver ingots at the outbreak of war, bury them, and then forget where they were. He corresponded with friends in a cipher punched onto a tape which no one could read. He was a long-distance runner and would on occasion arrive at conferences at the Foreign Office in London having run the 40 miles from Bletchley in old flannels and a vest with an alarm clock tied with binder twine around his waist. He was "wild as to hair, clothes and conventions," and given to "long, disturbing silences punctuated by a cackle" that "wracked the nerves of his closest friends." But of his genius there was no doubt. Sir Geoffrey Jefferson, who would propose his membership to the Royal Society, that most august of scientific bodies, thought Turing "so unversed in worldly ways, so child-like, so unconventional, so non-conformist, so very absent-minded . . . a sort of scientific Shelley."

Such were the extraordinary minds of the two men who journeyed to Warsaw to discover how much Richard Lewinski knew about Enigma. They met him first at the Madame Curie Museum, and their conversation continued as they walked along the bank of the Vistula to Lewinski's rooms in the ghetto. Lewinski was a dark man in his early forties, thin and bent; Commander Dunderdale later said that he reminded him of a "raven plucking an abacus." Knox and Turing already knew much about Enigma; their interest lay in how the Germans had modified it, how they managed the keying procedures and which German departments used it. It was clear that Lewinski's knowledge of these questions was considerable. Knox and Turing recommended to Menzies that his bargain be accepted. The necessary arrangements were made, and Lewinski and his wife were taken by Major Gibson and two other men to Paris, traveling on British diplomatic *laissez-passez* through Gdynia and Stockholm to avoid Germany. In Paris they came under the charge of Dunderdale, who, through his connections with the French intelligence service, obtained residential papers for them without revealing what Lewinski was doing in France.

Under Dunderdale, Enigma took shape. Lewinski worked in an apartment on the Left Bank, and the machine he created was a joy of imitative engineering. It was about 24 inches square and 18 inches high, and was enclosed in a wooden box. It was connected to two electric typewriters, and to transform a plain-language signal into a cipher text, all the operator had to do was consult the book of keys, select the key for the time of the day, the day of the month, and the month of the quarter, plug in accordingly, and type the signal out on the left-hand typewriter. Electrical impulses entered the complex wiring of each of the rotors of the machine, the message was enciphered and then transmitted to the right-hand typewriter. When the enciphered text reached its destination, an operator set the keys of a similar apparatus according to an advisory contained in the message, typed the enciphered signal out on the left-hand machine, and the right-hand machine duly delivered the plain text.

Until the arrival of the machine cipher system, enciphering was done slowly and carefully by human hand. Now Enigma, as Knox and Turing discovered, could produce an almost infinite number of different cipher alphabets merely by changing the keying procedure. It was, or so it seemed, the ultimate secret writing machine. Hitler evidently trusted Enigma completely. Long, persistent and secret inquiry established that at Fellgiebel's recommendation Enigma had been adopted for use throughout the three

armed services of the Wehrmacht; it was being, or already had been, intro-
duced from the highest down to the regimental level of command. It was
used to encipher Hitler's communications and those of Field Marshal Wilhelm Keitel, the Chief of Staff of the Oberkommando der Wehrmacht
(OKW), the Supreme Command of the German armed services, and by
Keitel's chief operations officer, General Alfred Jodl, and his staff. Field
Marshal Hermann Goering used it as C-in-C of the Luftwaffe, and Admiral
Erich Raeder as C-in-C of the Kriegsmarine. And so did their staffs. U-boats
and even small ships liable to capture were equipped with the machine, for
the possession of an Enigma by an enemy was not sufficient to enable him
to read encoded traffic. Only knowledge of the keying system and procedures would permit that. As a result, Hitler had allowed Enigma to be sold
to Japan, which used it as her main cipher machine for naval and diplomatic
traffic; to Italy, whose Commando Supremo used it; and to Rumania and
Bulgaria. Most important to Menzies, Admiral Wilhelm Canaris of the
Abwehr also used Enigma for his main-line communications—particularly
those between Berlin and Madrid; and Canaris would be Menzies's principal
opponent if Britain and Germany went to war.

Clearly, Hitler's trust in Enigma was misplaced, for both the Poles and
the French had penetrated its ciphers, and the British had managed to
create a duplicate of the machine. The accuracy of Lewinski's creation
would later be confirmed when the Poles were able to obtain an actual
Enigma, which was handed over to Captain Alastair Denniston, an officer
of the British cryptographic establishment, who went to Warsaw to collect
it. But the British realized that, unlike the Poles, they could not rely solely
upon painstaking and time-consuming mathematical decryptions of Enigma
transmissions; the real value of such intelligence depended upon the speed
with which it could be deciphered and distributed. Nor, unlike the French,
could they rely upon the services of a traitor to provide the keying schedules. It had to be presumed that the Germans would guard these schedules
with the greatest of care, and if they fell into enemy hands, it would be a
simple matter to change them. Therefore the only way to penetrate the
secrets of Enigma was to make another machine that could imitate or inter-
pret the performance of each of the thousands of Enigmas that would come
to exist in the Wehrmacht. This machine would also have to extrapolate
the constant changes of keying procedure that every major German command ordered every day and every night, year in year out; and it would
have to be capable of making an almost infinite number of mathematical
calculations at speeds far beyond human ability. Such a machine existed
only in theory—the theories embodied in Turing's Universal Machine. But
could Turing and the other cryptanalytical experts build one in fact? Was
it not beyond the technology of the times?

The task of penetrating Enigma mechanically presented Knox, Turing and the other experts at the GC&CS with a towering challenge. But, while Britain had allowed many of her conventional defenses to fall into disrepair between the wars, the 1930's was a period of great technical innovation—radar, High Frequency Direction Finding (huff-duff), microphotography, advanced telecommunications and wireless, early work on the atomic bomb, primitive cybernetics. Thus the official attitude was sympathetic to the GC&CS's requirements. The Foreign Office obtained an appropriation for the machine, specifications were soon ready, and they were with the engineers during the last quarter of 1938. The contract went to the British Tabulating Machine Company at Letchworth, not far from Bletchley, and BTM assigned the task of building "The Bomb"—as the Turing engine came to be called—to its chief engineer, Harold Keen, and a team of twelve men. In complete secrecy—remnants of that secrecy were still being encountered in 1974—the machine took shape, and it was by no means as large as St. Paul's or the Capitol. It was a copper-colored cabinet some 8 feet tall and perhaps 8 feet wide at its base, shaped like an old-fashioned keyhole. And inside the cabinet was a piece of engineering which defied description. As Keen said, it was not a computer, and "There was no other machine like it. It was unique, built especially for this purpose. Neither was it a complex tabulating machine, which was sometimes used in crypt-analysis. What it did was to match the electrical circuits of Enigma. Its secret was in the internal wiring of (Enigma's) rotors, which 'The Bomb' sought to imitate."

The machine was installed at Hut 3, a large Nissen hut under the trees in Bletchley's parkland, and the time soon came to begin operational trials by feeding Enigma intercepts to "The Bomb." These intercepts were simply obtained from the string of tall-pyloned wireless interception posts which the British government had established around the world. The posts re-corded all enemy, hostile and suspect wireless traffic and radioed it to Bletchley Park, where Enigma transmissions were identified, put on tape and fed into "The Bomb." If "The Bomb" could find the keys in which the transmissions had been ciphered, the cryptanalysts at Bletchley could then "unbutton" the messages.

The experiments at Bletchley were conducted with the utmost secrecy, but even if they proved to be successful, there was a danger ahead. With the cryptographers of three nations attempting to read Enigma traffic, how long would it be before the Germans discovered that their most secret cipher machine had been compromised? And if they did, they would almost certainly replace it with a new system, or modify Enigma in a way that would negate any further penetration. To tighten the security surrounding the Enigma attack, British, French and Polish intelligence experts held a series of conferences at the Château Vignolle, about 25 miles from Paris, where the French cryptographic service worked under the code name "P.C. Bruno." The principal decision, made at the first of these conferences on January 9, 1939, was that, since both Poland and France might be overrun in any war with Germany, all vital papers, machines and personnel connected with Enigma should be concentrated in England. At a later conference at a Polish intelligence station in the Pyry forest near Warsaw, the Poles handed over to the British everything in their possession concerning Enigma, retaining only the material that was needed for operational purposes. It was taken under heavy escort to London on July 24, 1939. It proved a wise precaution. Only a month later the Germans attacked Poland, and the Second World War began. With the capture of Warsaw and the collapse of the Polish government, the key cryptographers involved in Enigma were evacuated from Poland together with the Polish General Staff and the British military mission of Colonel Colin Gubbins. They crossed the Polish frontier into Rumania, and the cryptographers were detached by MI-6 and sent—as had been agreed upon—to Château Vignolle to work with the French. But for these precautions, the Germans would almost certainly have discovered that the Poles had penetrated Enigma. Yet, mysteriously, despite their partial ability to read the German secret ciphers, the Poles had been taken completely by surprise when the Wehrmacht attacked.

Meanwhile, experiments with "The Bomb" continued at Bletchley. Its initial performance was uncertain, and its sound was strange; it made a noise like a battery of knitting needles as it worked to produce the German keys. But with adjustments, its performance improved and it began to penetrate Enigma at about the same time the Germans prepared to attack Poland. Indeed, General Sir Francis de Guingand, who was then Military Assistant to the War Minister, Leslie Hore-Belisha, would recall seeing an intercept of an Enigma-enciphered transmission obtained from Japanese wireless traffic as early as the mid-summer of 1939. "The Bomb's" initial productions seemed to have been a matter of chance rather than calculation. Nevertheless, it had proved that it was not the dream of some mad inventor. It worked. When the Germans invaded Poland on September 3, 1939, Britain and France finally declared war on Herr Hitler and the Third Reich. Britain was ill-prepared for the conflict, but "The Bomb" was operational; and it was a machine that promised to provide the most valuable intelligence material of the war—Ultra.

"The Bomb" unbuttoned its first signals of consequence from intercepts of the Enigma traffic of the Luftwaffe sometime in April 1940, as Hitler, victorious in Poland, was marshaling his armies and air forces for the invasion of the Low Countries and France. Squadron Leader Frederick W. Winterbotham, the chief of Air Intelligence at MI-6, would remember the moment vividly:

> . . . it was just as the bitter cold days of that frozen winter were giving way to the first days of April sunshine that the oracle of Bletchley spoke and Menzies handed me four little slips of paper, each with a short Luftwaffe message [on them]. . . . From the Intelligence point of view they were of little value, except as a small bit of administrative inventory, but to the backroom boys at Bletchley Park and to Menzies . . . they were like the magic in the pot of gold at the end of the rainbow.
>   The miracle had arrived.

That miracle would be codenamed Ultra, once the name of the old Admirals' Code at Trafalgar, and now used by the British (and later the Americans) to denote intelligence of the highest grade derived from cryptanalysis. The contents of these first Ultras were relatively unimportant, but their significance was immediately apparent. If "The Bomb" had penetrated Goering's traffic, how long would it be before it could decode the secret wireless communications of the other commanders of the German armed services, of Canaris and his secret intelligence service, of Hitler himself? Here was information that was beginning to flow from the very heart of the German high command. If Ultra lived up to its promise, it would surely become a weapon of great importance in the war against the Third Reich.

Menzies was now acting chief of MI-6; he had received a temporary appointment as C in November 1939 upon the death from cancer of Admiral Sir Hugh Sinclair, the submariner who had commanded MI-6 for over a decade. But his position was by no means secure; there was considerable opposition to his permanent appointment, particularly from the Admiralty. Traditionally the post of C went to a sailor and Menzies was a soldier. Moreover, he was severely criticized for his handling of the Venlo Incident in which two chiefs of MI-6 in Europe had been kidnapped by German agents shortly after the outbreak of war. It would also be said afterward that Menzies was quite without the intellectual qualities necessary to appreciate the importance of what he had unleashed that August Bank Holiday. But he was not the upper-class drone that his enemies—and there were plenty of those—thought he was. When "The Bomb" began to provide the first Ultras of consequence, not only did he understand their importance, he also perceived that the way to gain confirmation in the much-coveted post of C was to obtain control of the vital intelligence source that Ultra promised to be.

As deftly as he played bezique, Menzies set out to secure Ultra as an MI-6 province; and his first step was to establish a system to ensure its security. It was obvious that Ultra would be of use to the British only as long as the Germans remained unaware that Enigma had been penetrated. If they discovered that their secret ciphers were being read by the enemy, they had merely to change to another system which might prove even harder to crack than Enigma. The only way to secure Ultra was to limit severely its distribution and use among the members of the British high command; and Winterbotham proposed, in effect, that a new secret agency be established to handle Ultra. He suggested that "Special Liaison Units" (SLU's) should be set up by MI-6, using air force officers of proven discretion and MI-6 wireless operators and cipher clerks to handle and route the Ultra intercepts. Menzies agreed and obtained approval to set up the system of SLU's; these, under the command of Winterbotham, would prove to be so effective in guarding Ultra that it would be difficult even thirty years later to find out that this source of secret intelligence had ever existed. SLU's would eventually be established at the higher levels of all the British (and later the American) military commands, their particular function being to ensure that no general or admiral, American or British, used Ultra intelligence carelessly, ambitiously, or in such a manner that the enemy might detect that his signals were being read. These units would come to be stationed at every major Allied headquarters around the globe, employing many hundreds of the best brains in England and America; and so secure was their system of secret communication that the Prime Minister himself would use the SLU's for his own secret and personal communications. In fact, the success of the SLU's in guarding Ultra would be a triumph second only to the penetration of Enigma itself.

Menzies secured for MI-6 control over both the acquisition and distribution of Ultra, despite the opposition of the Admiralty and the Foreign Office, two of the most powerful lobbies in Westminster. But the controversy surrounding the control of Ultra did not end there. It would provoke some of the most prolonged interdepartmental warfare in the modern history of Whitehall, and it would later be alleged that Menzies had secured it by some bureaucratic sleight-of-hand solely for the purpose of furthering his own career.

Stewart Graham Menzies was born on January 30, 1890 (the same year as Eisenhower and de Gaulle), into a rich British ruling-class family that had provided courtiers for the throne for many generations. Both his parents were members of the Prince of Wales's "set"; his father's wealth came originally from whiskey and gin distilling, his mother's family owned the Wilson Steamship Company of Hull, the forerunner of the Ellerman's Wilson Line. The Menzies family seat was Hallyburton, a great estate in the Sidlaw Hills of Angus, north of the Firth of Tay in "Macbeth country." And the family crest, appropriately for a future spymaster, included a

plaque of a falcon preying upon a stork and the words: *"N'oublie pas"*—
"Do not forget."

Stewart Menzies was the second of John Graham Menzies's three sons,
all of whom became colonels of the Guards. His father described himself
on their birth certificates as a "Gentleman of Private Means," and little
could be discovered about him—except that, like all the Menzies, he spent
a great deal of time riding and fox hunting. After he died in 1910,
Menzies's mother married Lieutenant Colonel Sir George Holford, commander of the 1st Life Guards and a Silver Stick, the officer whose duties
were to "guard the very person of the King from actual bodily injury,
against personal attack, and to do so with his own hands and body."
Holford would serve the royal family as equerry for nearly thirty years,
through the reigns of Victoria, Edward VII, George V and Edward VIII,
and Menzies's mother became a Lady-in-Waiting to Queen Mary. His
stepfather was even richer than his father and the family lived in two of
England's greatest private palaces—Westonbirt in Gloucestershire and
Dorchester House in Park Lane, Mayfair, where Holford kept one of the
world's finest private art collections.

Thus, Menzies grew up among the members of the tiny, privileged and
immensely powerful élite that ruled half the globe; and in 1903, he entered
"the Blessed College of St. Mary's at Eton," not through scholarship but as
an Oppidan, the son of "noble and powerful persons, special friends of the
said college." At Eton he won the Prince Consort prizes for French and
German, and was one of the best all-round sportsmen of his generation. He
became Master of the Eton College Hunt and, more important, president
of "Pop," the Eton College Society, the oldest and most powerful of all
British schoolboy societies—a post which marked the incumbent for high
public office in later life. Moreover, Menzies attended Eton during the
school's most influential period, an era when the pupils were taught that
character was more important than intellect, that the first business of the
school was religion, and that the highest virtues were those of thrift,
discretion, truth, loyalty and service—a policy that resulted in one of the
most extraordinary records of any school in any war. In the First World
War, 5768 Etonians joined the Colours, 1160 were killed, 1467 were
wounded, 13 won the Victoria Cross, 548 the Distinguished Service Cross,
and 744 the Military Cross. It was said afterwards that Eton had produced
lions with brains, but its critics claimed that it also produced leaders who
were unscrupulous, opportunistic, and concerned only with the preservation of their class and the Empire.

Menzies did not go on to Oxford; he joined first the Grenadiers and
then the Life Guards, that small group of officers drawn from the "most
select families of competent Noblemen and Gentlemen of the Kingdom,"
whose duty it was to "guard the King's life, constantly and without inter-

mission." It was in the Guards that Menzies became a praetorian—"one of a company whose function or interest is to defend an established power or system." A splendid figure in a helmet of German silver, a white plume, a uniform of red, gold and blue, on a black horse that was elaborately decorated with expensive furniture, he rode at the side of the King—a fact that, again, marked him for high service. And in June 1911, the young Lieutenant Menzies appeared briefly in a gorgeous flash of pageantry, like a kingfisher in a gathering dusk, when he commanded the Regalia Escort— the guard on the Crown Jewels—at the coronation of King George V at Westminster.

It was this ceremony, however, that marked the beginning of the end of the world that, as Churchill would write with nostalgia, was very "fair to see." On June 28, 1914, a single pistol shot at Sarajevo ended the Gorgeous Age forever. The "marvellous system of combinations in equipoise and of armaments in equation," of which Churchill wrote, collapsed. A few weeks later war was declared, and the "great commotion" that would last thirty years began between England and Germany. The Life Guards changed into khaki, the grand uniforms were put into mothballs, and by October 29, Menzies and his regiment were at the front in Flanders near the village of Zwartelen, guarding the old city of Ypres, the gateway to the Channel ports.

In the first Battle of Ypres, the Prussian Guard managed to break the line between British and French units, and capture Hill 60, a spoil heap to the east of Ypres, and a point which commanded the entire Allied front. The Household Brigade, of which Menzies's regiment was a part, was given the critical task of retrieving the hill; and on November 6, it broke the German screen, took the village of Zwartelen, and rushed upon the hill. Most of the officers and almost all of the men were killed or wounded in the charge. With only a handful left, heavy command responsibilities fell upon Menzies, and he was among the leaders in the capture of the hill— one of the epic small unit actions of the First World War. They held it despite all the attacks of the Prussians, and by November 11 the breach had been closed—but at an appalling price. The Life Guards was all but destroyed; the young élite of England had fallen. On December 2, 1914, Menzies received the DSO from the King at a ceremony in the field, returned to the line as captain and adjutant, and later won the Military Cross. And then, on December 18, 1915, at the age of twenty-six, he joined the intelligence services.

Little would become known of Menzies's career in MI-6 during the balance of the war, save for an encounter in Spain in 1916 with a young German naval officer who had also recently joined the intelligence service of his own country—Wilhelm Canaris. Evidently Menzies displayed an ability for his work—his command of languages and his connections alone would have impressed his superiors—and he was offered, and accepted, a permanent post with MI-6 after the war. But for Menzies, as for so many other Englishmen of his generation, including Churchill, Ypres would remain an indelible memory. He knew Churchill, and when they met, he would listen with interest to Churchill's theories of indirect warfare and special means.

With the exception of the publicity concerning his divorce, when he sued his wife, the daughter of the 8th Earl de la Warr, on the grounds of adultery, seriously endangering his career as an officer in the Guards and his acceptance at Court—a scandal that was hushed and smoothed over by friends in high places—Menzies slid into almost complete anonymity and obscurity during the interwar years. His entry in *Kelly's Handbook to the Titled, Landed and Official Classes* was almost suspiciously laconic; and it might have seemed to the casual enquirer that all he did in life was to ride with the Beaufort Hunt and attend his clubs. He was, in fact, slowly rising in the hierarchy of MI-6.

MI-6 had been founded by Sir Francis Walsingham at the time of the Armada to "gather all the secrets at the girdles of the princes of Europe." But its modern form was the result of an incident on July 1, 1911, when the Kaiser sent the German gunboat *Panther* to Agadir, an old Moorish port on the Atlantic, ostensibly to protect the lives and properties of Hamburg merchants from insurgents. The Admiralty, which had been deeply alarmed by the growth in power of the German fleet—and by the Kaiser's proclamation of himself as the "Admiral of the Atlantic"—saw only the prospect of a German naval base athwart Britain's trade routes with Africa and South America. A major crisis developed and war seemed possible. The crisis finally subsided, but the Agadir Incident had revealed that the British intelligence system was largely a fiction. Awakened from the torpor of almost a century—except for the Boer War—the British government reformed, refinanced and expanded its secret intelligence service.

A one-legged naval officer who had distinguished himself on the China Station, Captain Mansfield Smith-Cumming, was put in command; and his stamp remained upon the service until its secrets were betrayed to the Russians by Kim Philby during the Second World War. It was Smith-Cumming who first called himself C; and it was he who laid it down that to be effective, a secret service must be secret. He recruited only from the Establishment; and he gave the service its air of mystery and omniscience. Its headquarters were a state secret (they were, in fact, in Northumberland Avenue between the British and Foreign Bible Society and the National Liberal Club, and George Bernard Shaw was permitted to keep the tenancy of his apartment in the block). Smith-Cumming would sometimes disconcert callers who were not aware that he had a peg-leg by stabbing a sharp desk knife into the cork in order to make his points. But for all his many eccentricities, Smith-Cumming was an able and influential administrator. It was he who established the worldwide system of "Passport Control Officers" behind which MI-6 hid and worked for so long. It was he who played a major although undetected part in seeing that the government reenacted (in 1911) the draconian Official Secrets Act of 1889, which effectively muzzled any public inquiry into the work of the service—and made it the grandest of crimes so to do. And it was Smith-Cumming who believed that the service was not only an instrument for gathering other people's secrets but also for making mischief among the King's enemies. Any act was permissible—even assassination. The only crime was to be caught. If an agent was caught, he was disowned.

MI-6 fought the First World War under Smith-Cumming's control; and he is generally conceded to have won that round. He played the game with the highest stakes—a million here, a million there—but the British victory was not decisive; the Germans merely went underground and prepared for round two of the great struggle. When, once again, the German secret service emerged as a world force, MI-6 was ill-prepared to meet it. Its appropriation had been cut drastically during the interwar years—and would not be increased substantially until 1936–37, in order to finance the attack against Enigma, and again in 1938–39, during the period of the building of "The Bomb." Furthermore, Prime Minister Neville Chamberlain and the Foreign Office were anxious not to provoke Hitler's anger by strong and aggressive secret operations against Germany. Thus, while Admiral Sinclair, the Admiralty nominee who had succeeded Smith-Cumming when he died, was personally very able and vigorous, MI-6 itself had withered to the point where its entire bureaucracy could be contained in a small townhouse in Kensington.

But in 1938, with the threat of a new war, Sinclair began to transfuse fresh life into MI-6. Eminent brains came down from the universities, from the law, from the press; the old hands of the service were moved sideways, and Menzies was appointed deputy chief. Sinclair thought highly of him—so highly, it was said, that when he learned that he was dying of cancer in 1939, he wrote a letter, placed it in his personal safe and gave his secretary instructions that it was only to be taken out and delivered—to the Prime Minister—upon his death. It concerned the succession as C; Sinclair was well aware that there would be a ferocious fight for his office when he was gone. He recommended Menzies for the post, since only he knew everything there was to know about Enigma and Ultra. And so it was; when Sinclair died on November 4, 1939, the letter was delivered to Chamberlain; and the following day Menzies's appointment was approved—but only on a temporary basis. The Cabinet could not quite overcome its suspicion that, under Menzies, MI-6 might become an agreeable club for middle-aged aristocrats who had been at Eton or in the Guards.

It was now that the controversies surrounding Menzies began. The Admiralty, seeking to defend what it believed to be its prerogatives, strongly opposed his permanent appointment. Other critics thought him unsuitable for the job. How, it was argued, could the secret service be run from the bar of White's or from the hunting field? Was Menzies not too much of a Tory diehard to command an organization that had to employ all manner of men with all manner of political beliefs? The new, young intellectuals who now crowded the lower rungs of the service, all fresh and eager from university, doubted his intellectual qualifications for such a post. Menzies, however, had influential friends, among them Chamberlain, Churchill, who was then First Lord of the Admiralty, and the sovereign, George VI, who by protocol was required to approve the appointment of a new C.

All were telling voices. But it was Lord Halifax, the Foreign Secretary, who, as Alexander Cadogan, the permanent under-secretary of the Foreign Office, would note in his diary, "played his hand well and won the trick." MI-6 was a dependency of the Foreign Office, and both Halifax, an Etonian, and Cadogan, another Etonian, much admired Menzies. At their instigation, at a Cabinet meeting on November 28, 1939, Chamberlain, Churchill and Hore-Belisha agreed to submit Menzies's name to the King. To the astonishment and anger of the Admiralty and clubland alike, he was summoned to the Palace to be confirmed and presented by the King with "The Ivory," an ivory plaque given by the sovereign only to his most trusted and indispensable servants. Its original purpose had not been corrupted by time or usage; it permitted the bearer in the event of siege or civil disturbance to enter St. James's Park through the Horse Guards in Whitehall, which was the only open gate at such times. The Ivory was given only to those officials who would have absolute need to be with the sovereign—the Keeper of the Privy Purse, the commander of the garrison defending London, the chief of the Metropolitan Police, the permanent under-secretaries of the Treasury, the Foreign Office, the army and the navy. It was also the prerogative of the Gold and Silver Sticks, the Life Guards officers responsible for the King's safety. And over the years possession of The Ivory had become as prized as any of the Honours.

Menzies moved into C's handsome office with its glorious views of Whitehall and St. James's, and its private staircase and door—a door that was built, so it was said, to allow C to come and go without danger of being observed or identified with MI-6. And since it was an offense in law to discuss his appointment in the press, and even to link Menzies and MI-6, a baffling pall of anonymity descended upon the new C. His world became a very strange one, and it would be recorded that he inhabited, in common with Freemasons and the *mafiosi,* an "intellectual twilight . . . in which it is hard to distinguish with certainty between the menacing and the merely ludicrous."

Gradually, under the pressure and magnitude of events in the war, the criticism of Menzies subsided. He would emerge as the model British bureaucrat—clever, informed, adroit, careful, loyal. He would appear to be a man who was a thoroughly trustworthy member of his class. But above all, he had Ultra, and he had set up the machinery that would guarantee its security. And Ultra, in Winterbotham's words, would soon come to provide "the unique experience of knowing not only the precise composition, strength and location of the enemy's forces, but also, with few exceptions, of knowing beforehand exactly what he intended to do in the many operations and battles of World War II."

Coventry

2

ULTRA's first major intelligence contribution in the Second World War was to warn Britain of "Case Yellow," Hitler's great offensive against western Europe. General Bertrand would later claim that, between the end of October 1939 and the middle of June 1940, the French alone succeeded in obtaining solutions to a total of 141 different Enigma ciphers; and these solutions, in turn, enabled the French and the British to read about 15,000 German messages. That information was supported by persistent warnings of the imminence of the attack from members of the Schwarze Kapelle within the German General Staff and the Abwehr, and from the Vatican. It was further confirmed in February 1940 when a German courier plane was forced down in Belgium by bad weather and the complete Case Yellow plan fell into Belgian hands. Moreover, French aerial reconnaissance revealed the immense concentrations of German armor and infantry in the Eifel region; and, so it would later be claimed, the direction and objectives of the offensive were disclosed by German intelligence questionnaires that fell into French counterintelligence hands through the work of German traitors working as French double agents. But when Hitler's armies of 2.5 million men attacked Belgium, The Netherlands and France on May 10, 1940, they achieved complete tactical surprise. It was one of the most mysterious and catastrophic failures to appreciate and act upon intelligence in history.

The Germans had also achieved surprise in April 1940 in their attack on Denmark and Norway. Worse, they had inflicted serious casualties on the Royal Navy during the Norwegian operations because they were able to read Admiralty codes and ciphers. The Chamberlain government was tottering as a result of the Norwegian campaign; with the onset of Case Yellow, it fell. At eleven o'clock on the morning of the attack, only hours after the German cannon began their opening barrage, and while German paratroopers were still dropping on key points in Holland and Belgium, Winston Churchill, the First Lord of the Admiralty, was summoned to 10 Downing Street. Chamberlain had heard the dread words of Cromwell at the Long Parliament hurled at him from his own Tory benches: "You have sat too long here for any good you have been doing. Depart, I say, and let us have done with you. In the name of God, go!" Chamberlain decided to resign, and he asked Churchill if he would accept the succession. Churchill said he would; and the summons from the King came late that afternoon as Churchill was at work behind the seahorses on the façade above the Admiralty doors.

Churchill presented himself to the King at Buckingham Palace at six o'clock that evening. There, at that hour, King George VI asked the First Lord whether he would form a government, and Churchill replied he "would certainly do so." The sovereign and the new Prime Minister talked about the situation, kissed hands, and then Churchill departed, walking backwards, bowing low. He was sixty-six years of age; and to those who knew him, it seemed that his entire life had been training for this moment. Edwardian, convinced by his aristocratic heritage of England's greatness and the primacy of his class, moody, rash, intricate, pragmatic, impossible in his hours, often as ruthless with his generals as was Hitler, poet and orator, Churchill immediately surrounded himself with a youthful, blue-blooded staff and swiftly established the apparatus with which total war would be fought. As the Germans destroyed the Belgian and Dutch armies and began the great armored operation at Sedan that would lead to the surrender of France, he founded or expanded the powers of the War Cabinet, the Chiefs of Staff Committee and the Joint Planning Staff (of which the LCS would form part). He ordered the reformation of the Joint Intelligence Committee so that, unlike Hitler, he would have available a single source of authoritative intelligence rather than several rival organizations—a key factor in the coming war of special means. Even as the British army was withdrawing toward the Channel ports, he demanded to know of the Ministry of Supply what designs existed for building landing craft and artificial harbors, making provision almost four years to the day for the equipment that would be necessary for what Churchill called a Return to Europe. He ordered the formation of "troops of the hunter class" to make " 'butcher and bolt' " raids against the enemy, an order that became a license for the creation of élitist, private armies, among them the Commandos, the Special Air Service, and the Jedburghs. He helped to create the Special Operations Executive to harass the enemy from behind the lines; and he authorized the vast expansion of Menzies's service with a memo to General Hastings Ismay on June 6, 1940—a significant date—requiring "A proper system of espionage and intelligence along the whole coasts." He sped through MI-5's authorization to found the XX-Committee, and a host of new organizations were formed under his spur: the Ministry of Economic Warfare, the Political Warfare Executive, A-Force, the Ankara Committee, Security Intelligence Middle East. It was a mobilization of the intellectual power of England that had no precedent. An industry of at least 100,000 men and women would soon come into being to gather and evaluate intelligence, to engage in counterintelligence and security, to wage political and economic warfare and to execute special operations. But for the moment none of these organizations could influence the battle being fought in France. Belgium and Holland surrendered, and the German armies advanced across Flanders toward Paris, trapping and expelling the British army at Dunkirk.

In the confusion and tumult of May and June 1940, MI-6 and Menzies were confronted with a number of urgent tasks—the most urgent of which was the security of Ultra. It was imperative to evacuate Lewinski and his wife from Paris lest they be captured by the Germans, and to remove all equipment, documentation and personnel who were in France on Ultra business. Both tasks were entrusted to Winterbotham as head of Ultra security. He ordered the secret service's pilot, Squadron Leader Sydney Cotton, a pioneer in aerial photography, to France; and on or about May 18, 1940, escorted by Spitfires, Cotton flew MI-6's duck-egg-blue Lockheed 12A to Orly to spirit the Pole to England. Escorted by Commander Dunderdale, Lewinski and his wife with all their possessions waited at Orly, which was crowded with wealthy Frenchmen trying to get themselves or their families out of France. Dunderdale, who was well known socially in Paris, was spotted by one of these Frenchmen, who, believing that a plane was coming to collect Dunderdale, saw an opportunity to get out of France. Dunderdale was approached and offered a small fortune to take the Frenchman and his family with him. Dunderdale refused. When the Frenchman saw Cotton arrive, he made a similar offer, and this Cotton entertained. Dunderdale ordered Cotton to get Lewinski away without any further delay. When Cotton demurred, Dunderdale made an urgent telephone call to London and Winterbotham threatened to have Cotton court-martialed and sent to the Tower unless he took off immediately. Lewinski and his wife boarded the Lockheed while, in a pathetic and ugly scene, Dunderdale and French police held back panic-stricken Frenchmen from forcing their way aboard the aircraft.

When Lewinski arrived in London he was given lodgings by MI-6 and a police guard. Then he disappeared. So far as was known, he made no contact with the Polish Embassy or the Polish exiles in London. There were several accounts of his disappearance. Some Poles believed the secret service had spirited him to Canada. Another Pole said he had "certain information" that he was sent to Australia, where he was rewarded with a farm. Yet another story was that he had elected to go to a religious settlement on the Roper River in the vast wilderness of the Northern Territory of Australia. Whatever happened, Lewinski left no trace.

As Lewinski was being evacuated, the French intelligence services also began to withdraw from Paris. All material relating to Enigma was sent by road under armed guard to Vichy, the fashionable resort amid the green hills of the Auvergne that would become the capital of France during the German occupation; and there it was hidden in caves near the Source des Célestins, the famous healing waters, until a felucca could be arranged at Marseilles to get it aboard a French submarine bound for England.

Neither did the British leave any trace of Ultra in France: the SLU at British headquarters was flown out with Lord Gort, the British C-in-C. The Germans seized all the French and British communications intelligence they could find, intelligence that might have thoroughly compromised the security of British military cryptosystems in the months ahead had not new systems been introduced on an emergency basis. But nothing remained in France to reveal that Enigma had been penetrated when, on June 21, 1940, the French received their armistice terms from Hitler in the railway carriage of Marshal Foch at the Forêt de Compiègne—the same carriage in which Germany had surrendered her sword at the end of the First World War. One week later, the German army reached the Spanish frontier and so presented England with a new front that stretched from the North Cape in the Arctic Circle to the Pyrenees.

Hitler entered Paris in triumph; his men had defeated the mighty French army—it was stronger than Germany's both in men and matériel, but not in spirit nor in daring and skill—in just forty-two days. Back in Berlin he offered to make peace. He did not want a long war with England; he thought the war was over. Churchill disdained even to reply, and for a few days there seemed to be a pause in the onrush of events. What would Hitler do next? Would he invade the British Isles? The Joint Intelligence Committee (JIC) tried to divine Hitler's intentions, but the intelligence resources left to Menzies on the continent were small; MI-6's networks had collapsed and their staffs had been evacuated to England. The few agents who remained behind were in hiding and some did not have any means of communication, or if they did, dared not use them. The British were forced to rely on aerial reconnaissance and wireless intelligence supplied by the Y service, which attempted to determine the strength and dispositions of the enemy from the pattern of his wireless communications. The evidence available to the JIC was, in consequence, slender. Aerial reconnaissance showed that Hitler was indeed massing divisions and shipping suitable for invasion at the Channel ports; the Y service reported that behind the

Channel ports there were very large assemblies of follow-up troops and equipment. That, virtually, was all. It was not sufficient to determine what the Germans really intended to do.

Not before in British history—at least not since the Armada in 1588—had good intelligence been so important if Britain was to survive. The predicament of the islanders was very great, for, after Dunkirk, the British army was in disarray; the Royal Air Force, while of high quality, was all too small; and the Royal Navy, although still one of the world's largest fleets, was seriously extended in its operations to patrol the Channel and to keep open the supply routes from America and the Empire. In order to use such forces as she had to repulse an invasion, Britain was compelled to begin a campaign of bluff and stratagem—bluff to fox Hitler about the reality of British strength on the islands, and stratagem to obtain fore-knowledge of his intentions. It was now, toward the end of July or the start of August, that Ultra began to realize its early promise.

Hitler issued his first orders for "Operation Sealion"—the invasion of England—on July 2, 1940. Further, more detailed orders went out on July 16. Then, on August 1, Hitler issued a directive entitled "Conduct of Air and Sea Warfare Against England," with instructions that it was to be put into effect immediately by the Luftwaffe in order "to establish the necessary conditions for the final conquest of England." The overall purpose of Sealion was, as Hitler wrote, "To prevent England from being used as a base from which to continue the war against Germany." Thus was the Battle of Britain proclaimed, a battle that Churchill, in a secret session of the Commons on June 20, 1940, even before the fall of France, had led his countrymen to expect. "All depends," he had said, "on winning this battle, here in Britain, this summer."

The Battle of Britain began with massed aerial attacks by the Luftwaffe to bring the RAF Fighter Command to battle and destruction. In obedience to Hitler's orders, Goering sought control of the British skies as an essential precondition to invasion by a land army. And from the beginning of its campaign, Churchill and the Air Staff were informed, through Ultra, of most, and often all, the Luftwaffe's plans, targets and tactics. This fore-knowledge enabled RAF tacticians to assemble their fighter squadrons at the right place, the right time and the right altitude, concentrating their main defenses against the main attacks, rather than expending the RAF's slender reserves of strength and vitality chasing across the skies after myriad red herring attacks.

Even so, good intelligence does not win battles, and the RAF, after more than two months of fierce aerial combat with the Luftwaffe, was nearing exhaustion. Then Ultra came through with decisive intelligence. Goering proclaimed Eagle Day for September 15—that day when the Luftwaffe would mount a mighty, final onslaught to destroy the RAF. If

Eagle Day was successful, Hitler would invade; if it failed, Hitler would not invade. Fully informed of the Germans' intentions through Ultra, Churchill went to the BBC microphones and declared: "We must regard the next week or so as a very important period in our history. It ranks with the days when the Spanish Armada was approaching the Channel and Drake was finishing his game of bowls; or when Nelson stood between us and Napoleon's Grand Army at Boulogne."

Early on September 15, Churchill drove from Chequers, the official country residence of Prime Ministers, to the RAF fighter control room at Uxbridge in the outer London suburbs. There II Group, which was responsible for defending London and southeast England, had its operations center. It was known that the tides, moon and weather were all favorable to a large-scale crossing of the Channel by the German armies. It was also appreciated that if they did not come now they would not be able to come at all this year; the equinoctial gales would set in. The only force that barred their way was the badly weakened RAF. But forewarned of Eagle Day by Ultra, Air Marshal Sir Hugh Dowding, the C-in-C of the RAF Fighter Command, was able to position the remnants of his squadrons at the places where they could rise and intercept the German squadrons to the maximum advantage of the RAF. All radar and flak defenses were at optimum alert.

From his seat in the circle overlooking the large horizontal map table, Churchill watched the Luftwaffe assemble over the Channel ports. He watched the RAF coming into corresponding states of readiness. The target was London; and it would be attacked by 1000 bomber and 700 fighter sorties. Of this intention, Ultra had told all. The odds were great, the margins small, the stakes infinite. Like some croupier, Squadron Leader the Lord Willoughby de Broke ordered his squadrons about the skies of southern England, from square to square, as if he were attending a roulette board. And on the other side of the Channel, in a pure white uniform with gold furniture, Reichsmarshall Goering watched the battle from an eyrie on Cap Gris-Nez. The brilliant blue skies were laced with contrails, the silence of the still, hot day broken by the howl of overtaxed aero engines or superchargers cutting in, and the deadly little rattle of machine-gun fire at very high altitude.

By one o'clock the skies of southeast England were aflame with battle as twenty-five squadrons of Spitfires and Hurricanes engaged the first Luftwaffe fleets. But by teatime the RAF had broken the German lance. The Luftwaffe had not met the essential precondition for the invasion. The RAF still controlled the skies of England.

Two days later, on September 17, "The Bomb" decrypted a signal from the German General Staff relaying Hitler's authorization to dismantle paratroop air-loading equipment at Dutch airfields. It was a signal of great significance, and when it was sent to Churchill, he called a meeting of the Chiefs of Staff that evening. Winterbotham would recall that memorable meeting: "I was struck by the extraordinary change that had come over these men [the Chiefs of Staff] in the last few hours. It was as if someone had suddenly cut all the strings of the violins in the middle of a dreary concerto. There were controlled smiles on the faces of these men." In the opinion of the Chief of the Air Staff, the signal meant that Hitler had abandoned his plans to invade, at least for the year; and with that news, "There was a very broad smile on Churchill's face now as he lit up his massive cigar and suggested that we should all take a little fresh air."

Ultra had become, even at this early stage in the war, a major strategic advantage. The Battle of Britain was unquestionably one of the finest hours in British history; but it would appear that, through the foreknowledge of Hitler's intentions provided by Ultra, Britain's position in the summer of 1940 was not as perilous as Churchill led the world to believe. In fact, at the height of the invasion threat, Churchill ordered sizable armored, infantry and naval forces to the defense of the Suez Canal and to help General Charles de Gaulle plant his standard at Dakar—forces that would have been essential to the defense of the home islands. They were actions that seemed foolhardy until the existence of Ultra was finally revealed. Churchill knew that Hitler would not invade without aerial superiority, but he deliberately led the world to believe that Britain was in mortal peril in order to rally his own people to meet the threat and to enlist the support and sympathy of the United States. Winterbotham would later acknowledge that "It was Goering's and the Luftwaffe's careless use of Enigma that lost the Battle of Britain for Hitler—and, for that matter, the war itself." Churchill could make no such admission, even long after the war was over. To disclose the existence of Ultra would have revealed to the Russians the extent of Britain's cryptographic abilities—and it would have required much painful revision of glorious history.

Defeated in its attempt to gain aerial superiority over England, the Luftwaffe soon changed its tactics and resorted more and more to night bombing, a campaign that, while it hurt Britain grievously and destroyed large areas of many of her major cities, could not be decisive. Ultra had helped thwart a German invasion, but the time was fast approaching when Britain would have to pay a high price for "my most secret source," as Churchill called Ultra. The cost concerned a city called Coventry.

On the morning of November 12, 1940, a number of command directives began to issue from the headquarters of the Luftwaffe to the headquarters of the German air fleets in western Europe. They were quickly unbuttoned by "The Bomb" and there emerged plans for what the Germans called "Moonlight Sonata"—a raid in great strength for the night of November 14/15, 1940, against the cathedral and industrial city of Coventry. As Bletchley transmitted the Ultras through MI-6 to the Prime Minister's war bunker, it became clear that the Germans intended the same fate for Coventry as they had visited upon Rotterdam on May 14, 1940, when they attacked and razed the old inner city and killed nine hundred people. They had used only 57 Heinkel III's in the Rotterdam raid, but Ultras revealed that they would send 509 Heinkels over Coventry—and the results were expected to be correspondingly more devastating.

The Luftwaffe's target was a city of around a quarter of a million people, living in some 30 square miles of urban area about 90 miles northwest of London in the heart of the Midlands. Coventry had architectural, historical and industrial importance. It was founded in 1043 when Leofric, Earl of Mercia, and his wife Godgifu, the Lady Godiva of legend, built a Benedictine monastery there. The cathedral, St. Michael's, for which the first stones were laid in the fourteenth century, was regarded as one of the finest examples of the perpendicular style of architecture in England. There were also Grey Friars Church and the Holy Trinity Church; Ford's, an early sixteenth-century half-timbered hospital; and St. Mary's Hall, a center of civic life ever since it had been built by the Merchant Guild of St. Mary in the fourteenth century, all surrounded by a warren of narrow, ancient streets lined with timber and brick houses and shops. Coventry's industrial importance was great; it was one of Britain's main arsenals. Armstrong Whitworth made bombers; Alvis made aero engines; Daimler, Hillman, and the Standard Motor Works made armored fighting vehicles, trucks and cars. The largest machine tool works in the world at that time was also located there; and so were the Coventry Radiator and Press Company, the British Piston Ring Company, and firms producing precision instruments, electrical and telecommunications equipment, and agricultural machinery. Such was the fabric of the city whose destruction was now threatened.

The motive for Moonlight Sonata was revenge. On the evening of November 8, 1940, just at the time Hitler was to have addressed the old guard of the Nazi Party in the Löwenbräukeller of Munich to commemorate the seventeenth anniversary of the Beer Hall Putsch of 1923—Hitler's first attempt at revolution, which collapsed in a gunfight with the police—the RAF had made a small, provocative raid on Munich. Hitler was not caught by the raid; he left the Löwenbräukeller some ninety minutes before the first RAF bombers arrived. But in the attack the hall was bombed, there were a few casualties, and some slight damage was done to homes and shops around the railyards. The German communiqué on the raid alleged that the attack had been directed "exclusively against civilian

dwellings, monuments, and the civilian population," and declared menacingly: "There will be particularly heavy retaliation against England." The
retaliation was Moonlight Sonata.

The Ultra intercepts showed that, in addition to Coventry, two other
major British cities—Birmingham ("Operation Umbrella") and Wolverhampton ("Operation All-One-Piece")—were to be attacked in the moonlight period of November 1940. They also showed in some detail what
German tactics against Coventry would be. The raid was to be led by the
famous Kampfgruppe 100, a Pathfinder force based at Meucon, near
Vannes in Brittany. These aircraft were to fly to Coventry down a radio-
beam system known as the X-Gerät, and they would bomb with incendiaries to start fires that would act as beacons for the main bomber force.
This force would come from airfields at Orly, Chartres and Évreux in
France, from Cambrai, Brussels and Antwerp in Belgium, and from Eindhoven, Soesterburg and Amsterdam in Holland. The routes the aircraft
would take were all clearly specified. It is uncertain whether the Ultras
showed what armament the Germans intended to use; it is probable, but in
the event they would drop some 150,000 incendiaries, 1400 high-explosive
bombs and 130 parachute mines, bombing the fires created by Kampfgruppe 100 in order to shatter the water mains upon which the fire brigades
would depend. And then to increase the volume of fire and to make it
impossible for the fire brigades to concentrate their efforts against the main
fires, the bombers would attack in waves, using incendiary and high explosive alternatively.

Ultra gave Churchill and his advisers at least forty-eight, possibly sixty,
hours' warning of the devastating raid that was planned for Coventry.
When the Luftwaffe intercepts reached Churchill's headquarters, he gave
instructions that their contents were to be kept to the smallest possible
circle as he and his advisers debated the defense options open to them.
There were many such options available, but throughout their discussions
one factor was of paramount importance—the security of Ultra. All knew
that if any but the usual defensive measures were undertaken for the
protection of Coventry, the Germans would suspect that the British had
received forewarning of the raid, perhaps through cryptanalysis, and that
suspicion might lead them to conclude that Enigma had been penetrated
and so change to a new cipher system. How important was the security of
Ultra? Was it more important than the security of a major industrial city?
It would be for Churchill alone to decide.

While the defenses against night bombing attacks were then extremely
primitive, there were several measures that could be taken to protect
Coventry. The first was to frustrate the raid at the outset by using all
available aircraft in an operation that was codenamed "Cold Douche."
Through Ultra and the RAF Y service—the technical wireless intelligence

services—the British had accurate and detailed knowledge of the location and strength of the German air squadrons in western Europe. Cold Douche proposed, therefore, that the RAF attack the bombers when they were at their most vulnerable—as, heavily laden, they assembled and took off from their airfields. Then it was intended that the German bomber streams should be harassed all the way to the target to force them to disperse or to drop their bombs at sea or over open countryside and flee. The weather, it was estimated, would favor such operations. But in the event, as Wing Commander Asher Lee, the Prime Minister's air intelligence adviser, would later acknowledge, Cold Douche was "sadly and badly conceived." Intruder operations were undertaken, but they were so ineffective and on such a small scale that they failed to stop or to break up the German bomber formation.

Various schemes to assassinate the pilots of Kampfgruppe 100 were also considered; all were rejected because time was too short. And the organization through which the attacks could be made—the Special Operations Executive—was not yet functioning. But there was time to increase—even concentrate—anti-aircraft, searchlight and smokescreen defenses, and fire-fighting and ambulance services around the city. A combination of guns and searchlights might at least force the Germans to fly high or throw them off their aim. There were 410 mobile anti-aircraft guns then available in Britain, and any or all of them could have been speeded to the defense of Coventry. But that might compromise the security of Ultra. Coventry's anti-aircraft defenses would not be reinforced, nor those of Birmingham against the attack that Ultra had revealed would fall five days after the raid on Coventry. Only the anti-aircraft defenses of Wolverhampton would be strengthened, and as the RAF official history would later state, somewhat evasively:

> It is a striking illustration of the advantage then held by the Germans that though this information [about the raids] was in our hands, and though attacks against their airfields were duly carried out, Coventry and Birmingham were both heavily smitten within the next few nights. Wolverhampton, more fortunate, escaped. The sudden increase in its anti-aircraft defences was possibly observed by the enemy.

But if no extraordinary defensive measures could be taken to protect Coventry, might not a confidential warning that their city was about to be attacked on a large scale be given to civic authorities and to the fire-fighting, ambulance and hospital services? Should not the population of the inner city, together with the aged, the young, and those in hospitals who could be moved, be evacuated? To all these propositions, Churchill said no; there must be no evacuations and no warnings. To do so might cause panic among the population, panic that could result in far more casualties than the actual bombing; and, again, it would alert the German intelligence service to the fact that the British had foreknowledge of the raid. As Captain S. A. Hector, who was Chief Constable and chief of Civil Defence of Coventry at the time of the raid, would later confirm, no warning was received by him and no special defensive precautions were taken to defend the city. However, he would state that "all the Civil Defence units were trained and deployed in various districts in a constant state of readiness, day and night, with arrangements for calling out resting reserves and mutual aid as the circumstances warranted." But on that night, said Hector, the reserves were not called up in advance because "You will appreciate that in war information of all kinds is received, much of it false, in order to deceive. It would therefore (have been) most unwise to begin calling up reserves etc. on every occasion it was reported that a particular attack was contemplated."

It was a tragic decision for Churchill to have to make, but it was the only way to protect Ultra. Ultra had already proved to be a weapon of decisive importance in the Battle of Britain, and Churchill could not risk losing what he hoped would become—what, indeed, did become—one of the principal weapons of victory in the war. Britain had the means to protect Coventry, but its defenses were to be left as they were, and all reaction to the raid must follow a normal course.

The night of November 14/15, 1940, was brilliantly moonlit, there was little or no industrial haze, and the city of Coventry lay bathed in bright silver light. The air-raid sirens sounded at 1905 hours; five minutes later the drone of the Heinkels was heard overhead. Only then were the police, hospital, fire and civil defense teams aware that the city was to be attacked. Everywhere, the surprise was the same as that experienced at the Coventry and Warwickshire Hospital, the main casualty center for the city. Not until the staff heard the siren were any special precautions taken, and it was not until the first bombs began to fall that they were completed. Some patients were placed under their beds with their mattresses on top of them; others on the upper floors were hurriedly removed to the lower, although there were quite a few—fifteen obstetrical and a dozen fracture cases—who could not be moved quickly and had to be left where they were. Harry Winter, a young Canadian doctor, described the scene: "I switched on the yellow action station lights throughout the hospital and began to patrol the wards and corridors to see that everything was shipshape. I stepped onto the flat roof of the main building. I could hardly believe my eyes. All around the hospital grounds glowed literally hundreds of incendiaries, like lights twinkling on a mammoth Christmas tree."

During the raid, the immovable patients lay strung up in their wire frames, or in varying stages of childbirth, watching the German aircraft through a huge hole blown in one of the hospital walls. The lighting in all the operating theaters and throughout the hospital failed, and when the emergency generators came on, there was only enough power to permit surgery by the light of automobile headlamps, which had been quickly rigged up and connected to the batteries. The hospital, into which most of the casualties came, lost all power and steam; soon patients and casualties were lying head to toe on every inch of available space on the ground floor. Their treatment was carried out by the lights of hurricane lamps and torches. At dawn the hospital was a windowless ruin; it had been struck no less than five times by high-explosive bombs and hundreds of times by incendiaries.

Throughout the city it was the same story: surprise and then disaster. Defiant and Blenheim night fighters were ineffectual in dislocating the German bomber streams, and there was not enough anti-aircraft gunfire to keep them high. Within minutes of the warning, the city was showered with incendiaries, followed by the dull thud of high explosives. Moonlight Sonata was being carried out in exactly the way that Ultra had foretold, and Hitler got his revenge for minor damage to a Munich beer hall by destroying St. Michael's Cathedral.

The ravaged cathedral became a symbol of British heroism. It might just as well have been a symbol of sacrifice. St. Michael's need not have been destroyed, for the fire that attacked it was a very small one at first, and had emergency water supplies been arranged beforehand, it could have been saved. As an anonymous police sergeant recorded:

> A report was received saying that the Cathedral had caught fire and was beginning to get a hold. I went inside (the Cathedral) and saw that one corner of the roof was on fire. Firemen had arrived by this time and the hoses were connected up. We could see it would not be very hard to put out, but nothing happened when the water was turned on. The water mains were fractured and no water was coming through! Water was eventually found in Prior Street, but it was too late to save the most famous building in Coventry. The roof collapsed within two hours and by morning there was nothing left but the spire and the four outside walls.

There were hundreds of similar episodes throughout the city. Parts of Coventry were smashed as flat as Rotterdam. A total of 50,749 houses were destroyed or damaged. All that remained of Christ Church was the ancient spire of Grey Friars. The sixteenth-century half-timbered Ford's Hospital was smoldering wood. The Standard Motor Works and the Radiator and Press Company were badly damaged, together with some twelve plants associated with aircraft production and nine other factories. The disruption of public utilities made work at other factories impossible. Nearly two hundred gas mains were broken, and so were countless power lines, water supply mains, sewage disposal systems, telecommunications.

All railway lines were blocked and all roads were more or less impassable with rubble. A few fires still smoldered a week later. The destruction of some five hundred shops handicapped the distribution of food.

The raid lasted ten hours, and Moonlight Sonata accomplished its mission. A German reporter with the bombers called it "the greatest attack in the history of aerial warfare," and described the sight as he flew away from the city: "It looked as if the earth had broken open and spewed fiery masses of lava far over the land. . . . Far on the return flight there stood behind us like a beacon of ill omen the kilometer-high fiery cloud shining red in the sky. . . ." Only one German bomber was shot down by anti-aircraft fire near Loughborough as it was making its way toward Coventry. Although the RAF flew 165 sorties that night, it reported seeing only seven intruders, of which two were attacked—neither with any success.

Could more have been done to save the city? The answer is yes. More was done to defend Birmingham and Wolverhampton. In the case of the former, the RAF sent twenty-four Hampden bombers over the city to lay an aerial minefield. In the case of the latter, the raid was frustrated altogether because the Germans became aware that the anti-aircraft defenses had been suddenly strengthened—information they obtained, presumably, through their wireless intelligence service. Certainly something might have been done to bring additional civil defense and fire-fighting reinforcements into or near Coventry, but as the official history clearly stated, this was not done until dawn, when the raid was over.

The *New York Times* correspondent in London visited Coventry after the raid and reported: "Coventry is now like a city that has been wrecked by an earthquake. . . ." *The Times* (London) called Coventry a "martyred city." And indeed it was—martyred in part to Ultra. For some 554 of its citizens had been killed—150 of them buried in a common grave since it was impossible to identify the corpses—and another 865 seriously wounded. Some 4000 citizens suffered other wounds and burns, and their city lay in devastation. Such was the price paid for Ultra.

3

Special Means Operational

WHILE storms and fogs helped protect the cities of England from the Luftwaffe during the winter months of 1940–41, the British slowly but steadily regained strength. As they did so, thousands of miles away in the Libyan desert able and resourceful Englishmen demonstrated for the first time in the Second World War that with the use of special means they could outwit an army much more powerful than their own. It was a welcome victory after a long succession of defeats, and a victory that would lead to the formation of the LCS, the first bureaucracy in statehood constructed purely to deceive.

The father of the LCS was Churchill, but there were two godfathers. One was Major J. C. F. Holland, a pilot and engineer who had flown in the Near East during the First World War and in Ireland during the Troubles. When his health broke down he was made chief of GS (R)—a section in the War Office, consisting of one officer and one typist, that was responsible for conceiving irregular operations of all kinds. Under Holland, GS (R) launched the Commandos, created the escape chains down which thousands of Allied soldiers and airmen would come across enemy territory in the years ahead, founded SOE, and initiated what would come to be called the "sizeable escape and deception industries" of the Second World War.

The second godfather of the LCS was General Sir Archibald Wavell, the C-in-C in the Middle East. A product of Winchester, Wavell was a burly, one-eyed man who was in the mold of Clive of India. To the delight of the Treasury he had, during the winter of 1939–40, virtually ruled Britain's vast empire in Arabia with an agile brain, a small but clever bureaucracy, and a few battalions of good infantry held together through the heat and dust by unmatched discipline, great tradition, imposing ceremonial, a sense of duty, and the conviction that they were there not only to protect the Empire but also for the good of the natives.

Wavell had incubated his ideas about grand strategy and its ally, deception, at the precise moment that Churchill was fighting the Battle of Britain. Sir Ronald Wingate later wrote:

All his life Wavell had been not only a student of the art of modern war, but a student of the art of war throughout the ages. . . . He knew and foresaw, that the Second World War would be a world war in all its implications, controlled centrally by the two great antagonists, the Axis and the Allies. Every operation in every part of the world, however distant, and however disparate the conditions, would have its effect on every other operation. Therefore he argued that if it was possible to deceive the enemy in one theatre, that deception, especially on the strategic plane, could not be effective and might even be dangerous if its effects on operations in other theatres were not controlled.

Wavell was not alone in this theory; it was understood precisely and in all its dimensions by Hitler himself. But Hitler was an artist by nature, not a bureaucrat; Wavell was a soldier, artist and bureaucrat who perceived the necessity of forming a central bureau to control and coordinate deception operations in every theater of the war. And it was a memorandum that he had written in "the dark days of 1940" that was the catalyst for the creation of the LCS.

In his memorandum, Wavell recommended to the British Chiefs of Staff that the cover and deception plans of theater commanders must be coordinated by the Chiefs of Staff in London, so that—as Wingate continued—"they should not only have the maximum effect in their own theatre, but should fit in with the general plan of campaign of the other theatres." As for the plans themselves, Wavell wrote in his memorandum that "Practically all the ruses and stratagems of war are variations or developments of a few simple tricks that have been practised by man on man since man was hunted by man." He divided these tricks into four rough headings: "False information or disguise"; "feigned retreat," while really preparing to attack, the "encouragement of treachery"; and the "weakening of the enemy's morale." He declared that "every commander should constantly be considering methods of misleading his opponent, of playing upon his fears, and of disturbing his mental balance"; and he added that the "elementary principle of all deception is to attract the enemy's attention to what you wish him to see and to distract his attention from what you do not wish him to see. It is by these methods that the skillful conjuror obtains his results." The object of all was "to force the enemy to DO SOMETHING that will assist our operations, e.g., to move his reserves to the wrong place or to refrain from moving to the right place . . . or to induce the enemy to waste his effort."

Dealing extensively with the methodology of deception—special means that included visual, aural and even nasal ruses that could be used to distract the enemy's attention—the memorandum also discussed "signal deception," a uniquely effective stratagem. The enemy could deduce the size, nature and purpose of bodies of troops from their wireless communications, the sites of their wireless stations, the types of ciphers being used on various links, and the volume of the traffic. That being the case, the memorandum went on shrewdly to show how wireless communications could be deliberately manipulated to "ensure that the enemy obtains from his wireless intercept services the same impression as from other deception sources. . . . If signal deception is omitted, the plan is likely to fail. . . ."

Another basic factor in the success of a deception was that it be "plausible; it is unlikely to achieve its object unless the apparent intention disclosed to the enemy is sufficiently reasonable to have been included in the enemy's appreciation as one of the courses open to the British commander." The memorandum also stressed the importance of knowing the mind of the enemy commander. "The intelligence staffs should at all times be in vigorous pursuit of this class of information. It will be far more valuable to know that an opposing general is thoroughly excitable than it is to know that he graduated at some staff college in such-and-such a year."

Finally, the handmaiden of a successful deception, the memorandum emphasized, was secrecy. It was imperative to hide the deception from the enemy, for if he saw through the falsehoods, he could deduce the truth. Thus as few people as possible should know about the deception—even if it meant deceiving friend as well as foe. The memorandum noted that "In certain cases it may be essential that the commanders and troops executing a deception plan . . . understand both the real intention of the higher commander and the object of the deception plan . . . ," but "Normally, the fact that their moves . . . are being carried out purely to deceive the enemy, should not be disclosed to the troops concerned." It was a stratagem that would have peculiar—and even sinister—application among not only the troops, but also the secret agents and resistance organizations that would become involved in future Allied cover and deception operations.

There was little that was novel about Wavell's ideas; tricking an enemy is as old as war. But acting upon his recommendation, Churchill undertook to institutionalize deception both in military affairs and statehood; and that was startlingly new. In due course, the small organization that he created, the LCS, would become a large, and eventually vast, institution wholly devoted to the manufacture of stratagems. The existence of the LCS would be as carefully guarded as the experiments with the atomic bomb; indeed, the doctrines of cover and deception would remain a state secret in both London and Washington long after nuclear fission had become public property. Not until 1975 would a document come to light at the National Archives in Washington, D.C., that revealed Allied methodology in the secret war against the Third Reich. The document, a memorandum to the

Joint Chiefs of Staff dated May 14, 1945, described cover and deception operations as a "separate war" whose weapons had included all of Wavell's tricks—and much more. For his rather old-fashioned theories had been wedded to the special means of modern military technology, to the sophisticated techniques of political and psychological warfare and to the extensive use of every arm of the military services on operations intended purely to deceive. Thus, Wavell's theories would evolve into methods of waging war that were as complex and ruthless as they were secret; but it was Wavell himself who first put them to the test in North Africa. The outcome would provide a valuable object lesson in the techniques of both strategical and tactical deception for the rest of the war, for Wavell's minute fighting force was confronted by a seemingly mighty army, and like David, he would bring down the Italian Goliath.

Control of the Mediterranean was vital to Britain; through it ran the Empire's "lifeline"—the short sea route to the dominions east of Suez and to the oilfields of the Persian Gulf. But when Italy declared war on Britain on June 10, 1940, Benito Mussolini immediately began to lay his plans to cut this lifeline by two massive strokes—eastward from Libya and northwestward from Italian East Africa. He had 200,000 troops on a full war footing in Libya, and 110,000 in the Red Sea states.

Against this force, Wavell had an army of only 36,000 men, an incomplete tank division, and some small packets of troops on garrison duties in the Middle East, the Persian Gulf and East Africa. Many of these troops were either untrained, natives, or administrative personnel; none of the fighting units was ready for combat; and the prospect of rapid reinforcement was hopeless. Britain was embattled, the army in India was weak and ill-trained, the Australians and New Zealanders were just mobilizing. Yet Wavell was expected to garrison, secure and defend British possessions and interests in Egypt, the Sudan, Palestine, Jordan, Cyprus, French and British Somaliland, Iraq, Aden, the Persian Gulf states, Kenya, Uganda, Tanganyika, Syria and Lebanon.

The Italians were not the only threat to the British in the Near East. Wavell foresaw the possibility of an advance by Germany, perhaps with the Russians, into the Balkans to gain control of the northern shores of the Mediterranean; and he also had to consider the possibility of a move by Russia against the Iraqi and Persian oilfields. Only one factor existed to assist Wavell; neither the Germans nor the Italians knew how strong—or how weak—Britain was. She had taken pains to paint a picture of enormous latent strength in the area, and both the Germans and the Italians came to accept this as being probably correct—with immense consequences both for the present and the future. However, menace alone was not enough to meet the Italian threat. Wavell—who had learned the art of deception under Sir Edmund Allenby at the Third Battle of Gaza in 1917, when the British destroyed the Ottoman Empire with a trick—had to use craft and cunning.

A remarkable officer had joined Wavell's staff from London. He was Brigadier Dudley Wrangel Clarke, then forty-one, a peacetime solicitor and a student of the tactics of the Boer and Irish rebels. Clarke had been responsible for the memorandum that led to the creation of the Commandos—élite, well-trained and well-armed raiding forces formed especially to keep German troops awake at night along the Channel coast. He would now employ his agile mind, and his lawyer's arts and crafts, in helping Wavell fox the Italians. His operations were the embryo of A-Force, the immense British (and later Anglo-American) deception industry in the Near East and the Mediterranean that would work in close cooperation with the LCS.

The Italians had opened their campaign in Africa with an attack on the British from Libya, and Marshal Rodolfo Graziani's army entered Egypt on a narrow front along the coast on September 13, 1940. The British fell back, and it seemed improbable that Wavell would be able to halt Graziani further west than the outskirts of the great British naval base at Alexandria. Reinforcements for Wavell's tiny army were en route from England —reinforcements that would be essential to repel a German invasion, or so it seemed at the time to those who were not privy to the secrets of Ultra—but it was imperative to deceive the Italians about Wavell's military strength.

Under Clarke, teams of men were assigned that task. Using hundreds of cruiser tanks made of rubber which could be packed into a cricket bag and then taken out and blown up like balloons, field guns which fitted into biscuit boxes, and 2-ton trucks and prime movers that when deflated were no larger than an ammunition case, they fabricated a powerful force. In an elementary tactical deception, Clarke's engineers laid dummy roads and tank tracks to the south of Sidi Barrâni, where Graziani's men were resting. Then they brought in crowds of Arabs with camels and horses, and dragging harrow-like devices behind them, they raised great clouds of dust which, when observed from the air, resembled large tank columns on the move. The Italians flew over to photograph the area, but anti-aircraft fire kept them at high altitude, thus preventing them from detecting what was going on below. When the photographs were processed, Graziani had evidence of what appeared to be formations of powerful tanks and guns on his right flank—tanks and guns more numerous than his own. With that evidence, and with intelligence reports that reinforcements were on the way, Graziani, fearing that he might be attacked in the flank and cut off by the tank force, gave orders to his columns to dig in and create fortified positions along the Alexandria road.

Wavell and Clarke kept these tactics up long enough for the British forces to concentrate for an attack, and to receive the reinforcements from England. Wavell moved up in great secrecy and then, on December 9, 1940, he struck. Graziani's forces were still vastly superior, but the attack was one of the most daring campaigns of the war. With the Italians in full retreat, Wavell's men advanced 650 miles into Libya, and by February 7, 1941, had taken 130,000 prisoners, 400 tanks and 1290 guns, although at no time did Wavell's commander have more than two divisions of "Desert Rats"—as the British troops in the desert had come to be called. Wavell's losses were 500 dead and 1400 wounded, with 55 missing and believed prisoners of war. At the same time—at a cost of 135 men dead, 310 wounded and 52 missing—Wavell's tiny force in Italian East Africa captured 50,000 prisoners of the army of the Duke of Aosta in another daring offensive. The Italians' dream of an empire in Africa was shattered, as were their armies.

The impact of these British victories was very considerable. The Italians never recovered their spirits, and the Germans were forced to come to their rescue. The war had taken a new turn, strategic and tactical deception had proved its special value, and the Chiefs of Staff Committee established the LCS at Churchill's headquarters in April 1941 under the chairmanship of Colonel the Honourable Oliver Stanley, a leading Tory minister and blueblood. From now on, throughout the world, every British (and later American) war planning staff would have a deception section—a "Committee of Special Means"—linked directly to the LCS. While each of these secretariats was small, their power and influence would become very large. To them would come the sum total of all intelligence, and they would influence the Allied commanders in the scope, timing and direction of their operations. They would even prevent some operations from being under-taken if they appeared to compromise other, larger, more important operations. The Germans, while extremely wily and clever at deception, would have nothing comparable, and the LCS and its associated agencies would contribute handsomely—even decisively—to victory.

Within a few weeks of the Coventry disaster, events began to vindicate Churchill in his decision to accept all risks to protect Ultra. For Ultra revealed a startling fact; Hitler, abandoning his plans to invade Britain, was moving his best troops, tanks and air squadrons out of France toward the Balkans and back into Poland. As the evidence mounted that he intended a campaign in the East, Churchill and Britain were able to draw breath. Although there was no possibility that the British could take advantage of Hitler's weakened position in France to recross the Channel, the intelligence enabled them to change their industrial program from a heavy emphasis on defensive weaponry to offensive arms—another important Ultra contribution with long-range strategic implications.

In the middle of March 1941, Ultra also provided intelligence that contributed to Britain's first fleet action victory in the Second World War: the Battle of Cape Matapan. Penetrating the Enigma traffic of both the Luftwaffe and the Italian fleet, the Turing engine revealed that the Germans and Italians planned a large-scale attack on British convoys in the Mediterranean. It even revealed the date of the attack: March 27, 1941. Alerted by Ultra, Admiral Sir Andrew Cunningham, the C-in-C of the Mediterranean fleet, at anchor at Alexandria, ordered the British squadron there—three battleships, an aircraft carrier and nine destroyers—to raise steam. To disguise the squadron's intentions from Axis agents who might be on the waterfront, Cunningham came ashore in civilian clothes, carrying his golf clubs. He returned just after dusk, secretly and without ceremony. Then, to make the Italians believe that aerial reconnaissance and not cryptanalysis was responsible for the detection of their sortie from Naples, he sent up a Sunderland flying boat to scout the flagship of the Italian fleet, the *Vittorio Veneto*.

Cunningham set sail, and on the 28th, joined by four cruisers and four destroyers, the British squadron engaged the Italians off Cape Matapan. The Luftwaffe failed to come to the assistance of its allies, and a large part of the Italian fleet was either sunk or badly damaged. Ultra had again provided the British with an important strategic advantage. As Churchill would write, "This timely and welcome victory off Cape Matapan disposed of all challenge to British naval mastery in the Eastern Mediterranean at this critical time."

But Churchill and the Chiefs of Staff could not always take advantage of the foreknowledge provided by Ultra. It was not the fault of "The Bomb." Rather, it was the result of a poverty in military resources. One such case was "Operation Mercury," the German airborne and seaborne invasion of Crete. The Germans had invaded Yugoslavia and Greece in April; Crete was the next logical step. Hitler intended to eject the British air and naval forces operating from Cretan bases and use the island as a base from which to conduct his own operations in the eastern Mediterranean.

Ultras, almost entirely derived, once again, from Luftwaffe traffic, revealed Hitler's plans in detail. Churchill and the Chiefs of Staff knew when, how and where the Germans would attack the island. Aware that the British position in the Middle East and North Africa would be fundamentally disadvantaged if Crete fell, they decided to strengthen the defenses of the island. The available troops were stationed in those areas where the British knew from Ultra that the German airborne assault would land; and the Royal Navy, also armed with Ultra, positioned powerful forces to thwart the seaborne phase of the attack.

It was to no avail. The British took a bloody toll of the German invaders, but they were finally overwhelmed by the sheer weight of the attack. The casualties on both sides were high, but such was the severity of the German losses that Hitler would not again mount an airborne assault of comparable magnitude. Hereafter he would use his airborne troops as infantry. Had they remained intact as an organic unit and been used elsewhere—in an invasion of Britain, a drop on Alexandria or in Normandy during the D-Day period—the results might have been decisive. Once more Ultra had played an important role, not in winning a battle this time, but in forcing Hitler to change his tactics to, as events would show, the Allied advantage.

Time and time again that winter and spring, Ultra gave Churchill forewarning of Hitler's intentions. It revealed the ebb of German forces away from the English Channel into Poland and the Balkans, and the formation of the Afrika Korps under the command of General Erwin Rommel to aid the beleaguered Italians in North Africa. Intelligence derived from Ultra revealed Hitler's plans to capture Malta, the lynchpin of Britain's position in the Mediterranean—intelligence that, in the long term, enabled the RAF and the Royal Navy to thwart those plans. Through Ultra, MI-6 was able to frustrate Abwehr operations in Spain, Morocco, Persia and Iraq. Ultra continued to provide the most detailed intelligence about the order of battle of the Luftwaffe, as well as a fairly detailed portrait, when allied to other intelligence, of the order of battle of the German army. Above all, perhaps, the existence of Ultra was a source of comfort to Churchill, for it permitted him to employ British military and industrial strength with economy and steer a much safer course than might otherwise have been possible.

But Britain still stood alone in the conflict, although it now appeared that Hitler was preparing to invade Russia. America, too, was gradually being drawn into the war. Stunned by the velocity of events in the summer and autumn of 1940, President Roosevelt had authorized the United States army to begin building up its field forces. He had been reelected to the presidency the week before Coventry, and when Churchill informed him that "We are entering upon a sombre phase of what must evidently be a protracted and broadening war," Roosevelt declared America to be "the arsenal of Democracy." He ramrodded Lend-Lease through Congress—a method to supply arms and munitions to Britain in return for only a nominal payment; and in March 1941, aircraft, ships, guns, tanks, trucks and munitions began to flow across the North Atlantic in ever-increasing weight. Americans, too, began to appear in London, men in civilian clothes whose job it was to study how the Germans—and the British—were fighting a war which, all knew, America would be fighting herself before long.

Supplies from America and the Empire were essential to Britain's survival, and if she was no longer under the threat of a land invasion in the spring of 1941, a new threat began to emerge on the high seas. To cut Britain off from her sources of supply, German U-boats ranged the Mediterranean and North Atlantic trade routes, exacting a terrible toll of British shipping. It was Hitler's intention to strangle Britain into submission, and Churchill immediately recognized the gravity of this threat. At a meeting in March 1941 with Admiral Sir Dudley Pound, the First Sea Lord, he declared: "We have got to lift this business to the highest plane, over everything else. I am going to proclaim 'the Battle of the Atlantic.' " No battle would be more important to ultimate victory over the Third Reich.

The tumultuous ocean now became a vast battlefield, but in that battle Ultra initially played no part. For reasons that are not clear, the Turing engine did not function well against the Kriegsmarine's Enigma-enciphered signals, or if it did the Admiralty took no action upon the Ultras. Winterbotham alleged that "an Admiralty muddle" was responsible for the failure of Ultra at this time, an allegation for which there is no support. Muddle or not, all arms of the services were employed with great boldness to improve Bletchley's knowledge of Enigma and the system employed by the Kriegsmarine in its use.

Ever since they had flashed the War Telegram to all warships and merchantmen flying the British flag on September 3, 1939, the Lords of the Admiralty had sought to take a U-boat as prize and obtain the communications, tactical and technical procedures of the German wolfpacks. At last the time for such a capture arrived, and the consequences would be far-reaching. In the first days of May 1941, a British convoy of thirty-eight merchantmen, carrying troops, cannon and tanks to Egypt and large quantities of whiskey and general merchandise to the United States, steamed into the Atlantic north of the Hebrides. It was a tranquil departure, with the merchantmen in three lines abreast, protected by an escort of destroyers and flower-class corvettes. But on May 7 the tranquility was ruptured. A German U-boat had picked up the convoy's scent. It was the U-110, one of the Kriegsmarine's newest and best submarines, commanded by one of its boldest and most daring skippers, Kapitänleutnant Fritz Julius Lemp, the man who sank the liner *Athenia* on the first day of the war with the loss of 112 passengers and crew members, including 28 Americans.

Lemp claimed two victims in his first attack, and two days later he struck again as the convoy passed within sight of the coast of Greenland. Two more merchantmen were hit, and Lemp stayed at periscope depth to watch the consequences. His curiosity sealed his fate. His periscope was sighted by a corvette which pounded the area with a ten-charge pattern. Moments later, the U-110 broke surface, and its hull, gun and tower were raked with shot from destroyers and corvettes. Commander John Baker-Cresswell aboard his destroyer, *Bulldog,* was about to ram the U-boat when he noticed the crew jumping into the water. It was an extraordinary moment in the history of the Battle of the Atlantic, for Baker-Cresswell realized that he might be able to capture the U-boat intact.

A boarding party from *Bulldog* found that the U-110 had been completely abandoned and no attempt made to destroy its wireless equipment, its code and cipher books, the sheaves of signals that had been sent and received, or the technical charts and handbooks. Above all, there was the Enigma, complete with its operating instructions, manuals, keying tables and spare wheels. The U-110 was taken in tow, and informing the Admiralty by the highest-grade cipher in his possession that he had captured the submarine, Baker-Cresswell headed for Iceland. But by May 10 it was clear that the U-110 was shipping water fast and would not make port. That evening it suddenly reared its bow into the air, the towline was slipped, and the U-110 sank. To some it seemed that a disaster had occurred; in fact, all the U-boat's secret equipment and papers were safely stowed aboard *Bulldog.*

Bulldog returned to the great fleet anchorage at Scapa Flow in the Shetlands two days later, flying her battle pennant to indicate that she had sunk—not captured—a U-boat. Cipher and anti-submarine warfare experts were on hand to meet her, and honors would be showered upon all the protagonists of the operation. But no word of the capture was allowed to leak out. Not until 1966 did the Admiralty permit an account to be published. Only then was it officially acknowledged, with justification, that the capture of the U-110 was the most important and far-reaching success achieved by the British anti-submarine forces during the whole course of the war.

Significant operational consequences immediately began to flow from the capture of the U-110's Enigma and secret books, among them the destruction of the sea element of the Etappendienst, the super-secret intelligence and supply organization of the German fleet. The Etappe had been refounded after the First World War by Wilhelm Canaris, now the chief of the Abwehr, as a means to provide German ocean raiders and submarines with intelligence, victuals and fuel during wartime. Its representatives throughout the world were men and women who either used German consular cover or were employees of German shipping lines; and by 1941, the Etappe had a number of large, fast and modern supply ships at sea to sustain the powerful German surface battle fleet in major marauding operations across the North Atlantic supply lines. These operations were due to begin in late spring of 1941, spearheaded by the great German battleship *Bismarck* and two heavy battle cruisers, *Scharnhorst* and *Gneisenau.* If the Germans could supply these warships on the high seas—*Bismarck* was more powerful than any single battleship in the British fleet—it would be quite possible for them to stop all shipping movements between England and America, a blockade that might force Britain to seek terms.

Such was the strategic situation when the U-110 was captured; the secret materials aboard, when related to intelligence derived earlier from Ultra, gave the Admiralty the key to the whereabouts of almost all Etappe's supply ships. Again taking every precaution to protect the source of their information, British cruisers and destroyers were despatched to the supply ships' cruising areas to find and destroy them—with dramatic results. Between June 4 and June 23, 1941, the British captured, sank or caused the crews to scuttle ten German supply ships.

The Battle of the Atlantic had been joined, and although that battle was far from over, the destruction of the Etappe's fleet was one of the turning points of the war at sea. Its consequences were not confined to limiting the operational capacities of the German surface and submarine fleets. It was also a significant moment in the unremitting struggle to deny to the Germans that most necessary of all intelligence—meteorological information. Few military operations can prosper without dependable weather intelligence; with the destruction of the Etappe's fleet, the Germans would be deprived of an important source of that intelligence.

But it was Ultra's triumph against *Bismarck* herself—a triumph which was the climax of one of the epics of naval intelligence—which showed all concerned that such sacrifices for Ultra's security as Coventry were fully justified. It occurred even before the destruction of the German supply ships at a time of terrible news for England. Rommel had humbled Wavell in the Western Desert; the Germans were occupying Greece, and the British were forced to evacuate with the loss of some thirty ships. Then *Bismarck* was detected making her way into the Atlantic. Accompanied by the powerful new cruiser *Prinz Eugen,* she sailed into Norwegian waters from the Baltic at breakfast time on the morning of May 20, 1941.

The movement was reported by a contact in the Swedish navy at Stockholm to the British naval attaché, Captain Henry Denham, who, in turn, signaled the Admiralty. But the Admiralty had already obtained some forewarning of the sortie through Ultra. The Luftwaffe had been making special surveys of the weather situation in the Denmark Strait between Iceland and Greenland, Ultra had intercepted its signals and the Admiralty had alerted the Home Fleet at Scapa Flow.

Bismarck and *Prinz Eugen* were picked up and shadowed by patrol aircraft of Coastal Command as they entered Korsfjord in Norway on May 21; and then British agents at Korsfjord reported that the two great ships had sailed into the North Atlantic. By that time the Home Fleet was at action stations in the Denmark Strait; and in the early hours of May 24, the Germans were intercepted by the battle cruiser *Hood,* the battleship

Prince of Wales, and the cruisers *Suffolk* and *Norfolk.* The battle was joined and *Bismarck* was hit; but at six o'clock that morning *Hood*—the pride of the British fleet—was struck by one of *Bismarck*'s salvos. *Hood* exploded and all but 3 of the 1500 men aboard were lost.

It was yet another devastating blow to British pride that made *Bismarck*'s destruction an imperative. Worse was to follow; the bridge of *Prince of Wales,* one of the most modern British battleships, was shattered in the encounter, she was holed beneath her waterline, and the captain was forced to break off the action. But *Bismarck,* too, had been seriously damaged; and as the German ship made off with oil trailing behind her, shadowed by *Suffolk* and *Norfolk,* the Admiralty in London summoned all forces to intercept and destroy her.

That same evening, at about ten o'clock, *Bismarck* was struck by a torpedo from an aircraft launched by the carrier *Victorious.* Her performance was further reduced, and hopes were now very high at the Admiralty and Churchill's office that *Bismarck* would be caught. But these hopes were broken when, at about three o'clock on the morning of May 25, the *Suffolk* lost her. For some thirty hours, *Bismarck* was loose in the Atlantic. So confident was her captain that he had shaken off his pursuers that he sent a long signal to Berlin to report the situation. The time was eight minutes before nine o'clock on May 26. The signal was intercepted by British wireless intelligence stations and *Bismarck*'s position was fixed; but owing to an error, it was incorrectly charted when received aboard the British flagship. *Bismarck* was, in fact, 200 miles south of her charted position, steaming to safety.

But then the Germans blundered. Someone at German headquarters in Berlin, for reasons that are not clear, sent a series of wireless messages, one of which instructed *Bismarck*'s captain to proceed with all speed to Brest. The signal was intercepted by the British, it was relayed to Knox, and he succeeded in breaking its contents with speed and accuracy. It was relayed to the Operational Intelligence Centre at the Admiralty; and from this information—coupled with Ultras that showed unusual Luftwaffe activity in France, presumed to be operations to give *Bismarck* aerial protection—it was possible for the OIC to predict the rough course *Bismarck* must take to get to Brest. Coastal Command patrol aircraft were launched from Lough Erne in Northern Ireland, and one of them located *Bismarck* on course for Brest about 700 miles from that port. Then two Swordfish torpedo-carrying aircraft from the carrier *Ark Royal* picked her up. And from that moment onward, *Bismarck* was doomed. Swordfish and British battleships pressed the attack. *Bismarck* was stricken; at about 10:40 A.M. on May 27, a flaming and smoking ruin, she turned over and sank, taking with her nearly 2000 men. Only 110 of her crew were picked out of the water.

The sense of relief and victory was very great as Churchill was able to announce her destruction at the morning session of the Commons that same day. The disaster was, however, too much for Grand Admiral Raeder, the C-in-C of the Kriegsmarine. The destruction of *Bismarck,* and later of the Etappe's supply ships, was too striking to dismiss the possibility that the Kriegsmarine's ciphers had been broken, or that there was a traitor somewhere in the Kriegsmarine's command organization. But in all cases, a Board of Inquiry dismissed the belief that Enigma had been compromised. "It is not necessary," the German board concluded its report, "to put the blame on a breach of security as regards the code and cipher tables." Instead, the board preferred to place the blame upon the ubiquity of MI-6 and upon the probability of a traitor at Kriegsmarine headquarters. The report noted that the navy's telephone lines between Berlin and Paris ran through boosters that were not always manned by Germans. Therefore, the tapping of those lines by British agents was very probable. It was the same story throughout the war; the Nazis feared their own traitors more than enemy cryptographers. "They had," noted one British naval intelligence officer, "more confidence in their own efficiency than in the loyalty commanded by their political system." For that arrogance, the Third Reich would pay the ultimate price.

At three o'clock on the morning of June 22, 1941, an event occurred which would have massive implications for British strategy. German armies of 3 million men swept across the Russian border on a 2000-mile front, taking the Russians by surprise. It was no surprise to Churchill; Ultra had foretold the event for many months, and although Churchill had once dismissed communism as "foul baboonery," he had sought to alert Stalin in a series of dramatic telegrams sent to Moscow through conventional diplomatic channels. He made no mention of the source of his information. In fact, Stalin would not be told about Ultra throughout the war.

Stalin had not acted upon the warnings he received and Churchill would later remark that "so far as strategy, policy, foresight, competence are arbiters, Stalin and his commissars showed themselves at this moment the most completely outwitted bunglers of the Second World War." Would Churchill, the arch anti-Communist, seek an alliance with the Soviet Union? He would welcome it, for he at last saw an opportunity for the employment of his theories of peripheral warfare. Recalling that the Russian collapse in the First World War had freed German armies for service in France, the Balkans and Arabia, Churchill was determined to keep the Kremlin from yielding or making terms. Great convoys began to sail from British ports bearing armaments to sustain the Red Army in battle, even though those armaments were needed by British forces at home, in North Africa and in the Far East. Russia must be kept fighting, whatever the cost.

Churchill feared and distrusted the Communists, but as he remarked to his private secretary, "If Hitler invaded Hell I would make at least a favorable reference to the Devil in the House of Commons."

Churchill did more than that; he wasted little time in making a pact with the devil. It concerned cooperation between the secret services of Britain and Russia—those ancient enemies—and it was negotiated by Anthony Eden, the Foreign Secretary, and Cadogan. The two men sailed from Scapa Flow aboard the cruiser *Kent* on December 7, 1941, the day the Japanese attacked Pearl Harbor; they reached Murmansk en route to Moscow on December 12, the day upon which Britain lost its Far East squadron—the battleships *Prince of Wales* and *Repulse*—and Japan obtained full command of the Pacific Ocean and the China Sea; they arrived in Moscow the day the German invaders penetrated the city's western outskirts. As Cadogan's editor would write: "The prospects for these talks in Moscow did not look unpromising."

Stalin opened their first meeting at the Kremlin by stating that he did not want mere words of mutual sympathy—"algebra," as he called it. He wanted an agreement—"practical mathematics"—to cover wartime collaboration and postwar reconstruction. Stalin also raised for the first time, but by no means the last, the question of the Return to Europe. He accepted the fact that Britain could not open an invasion at this stage of the war, but he left no one in doubt that he expected one in 1942. The talks continued, and on December 16 Cadogan met the menacing person of the head of the Russian secret services, Lavrenti Beria. Beria asked what plans Britain had for supplying arms to the resistance forces in Hitler-occupied Europe, and Cadogan, who was one of the founders of the organization, told him about the Special Operations Executive and its objectives. Beria said that he was forming a similar organization to operate in eastern Europe. Cadogan replied that he hoped the two organizations would not find themselves in conflict; Beria said he hoped as much as well.

The negotiations of the British and Russian delegations finally led to the MI-6–SOE–NKVD pact of December 20, 1941. Among the Russians, only Stalin, Beria and Vyacheslav Molotov, the Foreign Minister, knew of the pact, and the men who actually negotiated the agreement with Cadogan did their own typing. The pact provided for an exchange of both countries' secret intelligence about Germany, an agreement which, despite Britain's precautions and fears for Ultra and Russia's belief that MI-6 was, in reality, an instrument designed to destroy bolshevism, was subsequently honored. The second part of the pact was less effective. It provided that both sides would supply arms, money and equipment to anyone in Nazi-occupied Europe who was prepared to fight Hitler. In theory, the intention was admirable. It would not work out in practice, for while the British supplied everyone from Communists to Catholics with munitions and money, the Russians would see to it that only Communists got their guns. Even though confronted with utter defeat, Stalin had his eyes on the future.

By the time the secret pact with Russia was negotiated, Britain had another ally in the field—the United States. And again, months before America declared war on the Axis powers, there were subtle indications of the intentions of her enemies. This time the intelligence came not wholly through Ultra, but from another source—the XX-Committee. For in June 1941, six months before the Japanese attacked, an XX-Committee double agent provided information which showed that the Germans, working on behalf of the Japanese, were displaying a sinister interest in Pearl Harbor.

The XX-Committee had been created expressly to control captured German agents in Britain (and, later, overseas), until then a ramshackle, uncoordinated business in which private enterprise played a leading role. But with the formation of the XX-Committee (so called because the Roman numerals XX also represented the double-cross), it would evolve into an especially effective weapon of war. A dependency of MI-5, the committee held its first meeting on January 2, 1941, at MI-5 headquarters in St. James's Street. It was controlled by a Seaforth Highlander, Lieutenant Colonel Thomas Robertson; and John C. Masterman of Oxford University, a tall, reedy don of fifty with Gladstonian eyes—clear-blue and sly—who had been a First Class Modern History Scholar at Oxford and a student, lecturer and Censor of Christ Church, was among its earliest members.

Masterman would later become the official chronicler of the XX-Committee's wartime activities, and he would outline its special purpose and objectives. The first was to apprehend all enemy agents and either put them out of business or induce them to change their allegiance and work for Britain by supplying their former masters with information provided by the committee. The latter course was considered preferable, if possible, for as Masterman later wrote, ". . . if the Germans are receiving an adequate service of news from our controlled agents they will not expend a great deal of time and effort to establish another system as well." An agent under the committee's control, without the knowledge of the Germans, could also provide information that would lead to the capture of other agents and reveal the personalities, working methods, and code and cipher procedures of the enemy. And through a double agent, the committee could obtain important information about the enemy's intentions; as Masterman put it, the Germans "will not ask a number of questions about the defence of southeast England if they intend to invade in the southwest." Finally, and perhaps most important, a double agent could be used to supply the Germans with *false* information in reply to their questions, information that might "influence and perhaps change the operational intentions of the enemy." In this area of their activities, the members of the XX-Committee would come to work closely with the LCS to spread its deceptions to the desk of Hitler himself.

By the spring of 1941, a steady stream of German spies—European Nazi idealists, British traitors, adventurers—had passed through the XX-Committee's interrogation center at Latchmere House, a former convalescent home for shell-shocked British army officers on Ham Common near the Royal Borough of Richmond in Surrey. In the main they had been betrayed either by Ultra's ability to read the Abwehr main-line traffic between Berlin and Madrid or by agents who had preceded them into England and capture. A few were located by radiogoniometrical—wireless location—processes. A few more, usually the best for the purposes of the XX-Committee, had surrendered for ideological reasons and willingly offered their services to the British. Almost all were rejected by the XX-Committee as insufficiently intelligent and not worth the time and expense of employing as double agents; a few—a very few—were diehards who were handed over to the law and, usually, thence to the executioner. But the best, after careful interrogation, were kept for service with the XX-Committee to play what was called "the great game"—deceiving their former German masters.

One of the XX-Committee's first and most important double agents was a thirty-year-old Yugoslav businessman named Dusko Popov. A member of a well-to-do royalist family, Popov had been approached by the Abwehr at the outbreak of the war with the suggestion that his family's political ambitions might be enhanced if he worked for Germany as a spy against the British. Popov agreed—and promptly informed the MI-6 representative in Belgrade of his Abwehr connections. He arrived in England on December 20, 1940, and made a "most favorable impression" when closely questioned by the British secret intelligence services. He was then passed on to the XX-Committee and rechristened "Tricycle," and he opened up secret communications with the Abwehr in Lisbon. He established himself as a highly placed agent in England; and in the next several months, he supplied the Abwehr with a great deal of information about the size of the British armed forces after Dunkirk—information fabricated by the XX-Committee that beclouded all German estimates about British strength for the remainder of the war.

Then in June 1941, the Abwehr, pleased with Tricycle's performance in Britain, instructed him to go to America on an espionage mission to investigate in detail, among other targets, the air, military and naval installations at Pearl Harbor, which the Japanese had asked the Abwehr to reconnoiter because of the difficulties that ethnic Japanese agents in Hawaii were encountering. Popov informed the XX-Committee of his assignment and, through the American Embassy, the XX-Committee informed the

FBI. The Abwehr questionnaire, which was designed to guide Popov in his reconnaissance, was also passed on to the FBI. But shortly after Popov arrived in the United States by Pan American Clipper from Lisbon on August 24, 1941, he encountered the full wrath of the director of the FBI, J. Edgar Hoover. Hoover did not want agents of any foreign power working in America. At their only meeting, he treated Popov with disgust, and declared that—according to Popov—"I can catch spies without your or anybody else's help." He accused Popov of being "Like all double agents. You're begging for information to sell to your German friends so that you make a lot of money and be a playboy." Popov, who had taken a woman friend to Florida for a holiday, would find himself threatened with prosecution under the Mann Act, and agents of the Internal Revenue Service were also set on him. Britain's early attempts to embroil the United States in XX-Committee operations were not a success. The situation would improve only much later on—with enormously important consequences for the outcome of the war.

Popov's questionnaire concerning Pearl Harbor was not, apparently, interpreted correctly. The British extricated him lest his presence in the United States cause a rupture in relations between the British and American intelligence communities (he left with the IRS hot on his heels, a predicament which forced the British Embassy to meet his obligations), and the Japanese attacked at Pearl Harbor. Although the American government had some foreknowledge from other intelligence sources of the impending attack, notably from its naval cryptanalytical bureau in Room 1649 of the Navy Department on Constitution Avenue in Washington, when the attack came that calamitous Sunday of December 7, 1941, the surprise was complete. The American Pacific Fleet was dealt a blow from which it would take many months to recover.

The United States declared war upon the Axis powers, and for Churchill, America's entry into the conflict was the answer to a constant prayer. He recalled the words of Edward Grey more than thirty years before—that the United States was like a " 'gigantic boiler. Once the fire is lighted under it there is no limit to the power it can generate.' " His joy was boundless, his confidence in victory now unextinguishable. He would later write:

> . . . we had won the war. Britain would live; the Commonwealth of Nations and the Empire would live. . . . Once again in our long Island history we should emerge, however mauled or mutilated, safe and victorious. . . . The British Empire, the Soviet Union, and now the United States, bound together with every scrap of their life and strength, were, according to my lights, twice or even thrice the force of their antagonists. No doubt it would take a long time (but) . . . united we could subdue everybody else in the world. Many disasters, immeasurable cost and tribulation lay ahead, but there was no more doubt about the end. . . .

The Search for a Strategy

ALMOST immediately after the attack on Pearl Harbor, Churchill and a large British delegation arrived in Washington to integrate their interests and operations with those of the American government and armed forces. It was the first of the great conferences of grand strategy of the Second World War. A number of remarkable agreements were struck between Britain and America—two of the four great powers that Churchill would call "the Grand Alliance." It was decided that Germany would be the first major enemy to be tackled and defeated before the alliance turned its full might upon Japan; and the Combined Chiefs of Staff (CCS) was established to provide the higher command apparatus necessary for the gigantic military and industrial deployments that a global conflict would demand—deployments that would exhaust the riches of England and transform America from a somnolent continent into a world superpower. It was also agreed, in fact as well as spirit, that the British Empire and the United States would undertake complementary industrial programs, concert military policies and plans, and share all their secrets. Rarely before in history had two major powers, motivated in the long term by nationalistic interests, entered into such a close alliance in an effort to defeat their enemies.

In the beginning of the new alliance, the United States would be almost wholly dependent upon the British for intelligence. If Britain's dilemma in 1941 lay in not always being able to take military advantage of the intelligence supplied by Ultra, America found herself in an equally singular predicament. Even as she was slowly being drawn into the war, she had only the most rudimentary military intelligence services, and no functioning secret service whatsoever. America was, in fact, the only major nation in the world not to possess such a service.

There were those in Washington, however, who had recognized a grave national deficiency; and to correct it, General William J. Donovan had been nominated by executive order to form the organization that came to be called the Office of Strategic Services. Donovan, an Irish-American born in Buffalo in 1883, had returned from the First World War as the most decorated man in American military history. Between the wars he became deeply involved in international politics as a lawyer, and was a friend and confidant of both Churchill and Roosevelt. Ordered in 1941 to set up a central agency for gathering and evaluating secret intelligence, he began to recruit his men from the world of what he described as "a blend of Wall Street orthodoxy and sophisticated American nationalism." Colonel David Bruce was a characteristic choice. Married to the daughter of Andrew Mellon, he was a lawyer, a politician and a diplomat before he became OSS chief in Europe. After the war, he would become the American ambassador to Britain, France, Germany and China. A second—and important—Donovan recruit was Allen Welsh Dulles, a prominent lawyer who would serve as OSS chief in Berne. Later he would become chief of the Central Intelligence Agency, the postwar successor to the OSS.

At the highest levels of command—between Menzies and Bruce, for example, two men who had much in common—there would be both cooperation and admiration between the OSS and MI-6. But at the lower levels, there was often scorn and rivalry. The Americans, new to the game of intelligence, were regarded as amateurs by the seasoned professionals of MI-6, and in some cases agents of MI-6 and the OSS in the field would find themselves in conflict for nationalistic or ideological reasons. Nevertheless, the two agencies would come to work together in a pattern of reserved cooperation, although the OSS would not play a major role in the secret war against the Third Reich until after D-Day.

In another sphere of the secret war—cryptanalysis—the relationship between Britain and America began on a tenuous note. Like the Poles, the French and the British, the Americans had shown an early interest in the Enigma machine. In October 1923 the military attaché at the American Embassy in Berlin wrote to General Marlborough Churchill, the Chief of Intelligence of the United States Army, to report that he had "witnessed a demonstration with a working model" of Enigma. The man who had demonstrated the machine was Artur Scherbius, the Berlin engineer who had assumed the patents from its inventor, Hugo Koch. Scherbius, it seemed, was showing Enigma to every Entente embassy in Berlin. Enclosed in the report to Churchill was a prospectus about the machine, which stated in part:

> For the protection of secrets or reports two basic conditions must be satisfied: The dependability and efficiency of the persons entrusted therewith and an absolutely dependable coding system for letter and telegraphic communications.

Enigma, the prospectus claimed with monumental irony, was that system. It was capable of producing 22 billion different code combinations. "If one man worked continuously day and night and tried a different cipher-key every minute," the prospectus continued, "it would take him 42,000 years to exhaust all combination possibilities."

Given the state of the craft of cryptology in the 1920's, these were bold and exciting claims; but the intelligence section of the American army, one of the most impoverished of all government agencies in those days, took no action to find out more about the machine for three years. Meanwhile, Scherbius had, evidently, reassigned the patents of his machine to Alexander von Kryha, a Ukrainian engineer doing business in Berlin; and an article about Enigma in a German journal in 1926 aroused the interest of the Signal Corps of the United States army. Again General Marlborough Churchill was petitioned to investigate the possibilities of the machine. Inquiries were made through the military attaché at Berlin, and the "Kryha Coding Machine Company" sent a representative to New York to demonstrate the machine to American cryptanalytical experts.

At that time, William Frederick Friedman was one of America's leading cryptanalysts, the counterpart of Alfred Dilwyn Knox of England. Born in Russia in 1891, he had come with his family to America a year later, and was graduated from Pittsburgh Central High School, Michigan Agricultural College and Cornell University. A geneticist, he had attracted the attention of a rich textile merchant, George Fabyan, who was interested in cryptology and was also trying to prove that Bacon wrote Shakespeare's plays. Fabyan gave Friedman a job as a cryptologist, stirring his dormant interest in that field, and during the First World War he was employed by the American military. His first "target" was the cipher of a group of Hindus who were agitating in America for Indian independence. His work resulted in mass arrests and trials of the agitators for illegally trying to purchase arms. By 1921, Friedman was in the employment of the War Department, devising cryptosystems. He wrote a standard work on the craft, *Elements of Cryptanalysis,* and in 1922 he was appointed Chief Cryptanalyst of the Signal Corps. As one of the world's leading authorities on cryptology, Friedman came to the public's attention in 1924 when he testified before a Congressional committee about some coded messages that had been exchanged in the Teapot Dome Scandal.

It was Friedman who went to see Kryha's representative in New York. He was evidently impressed with the performance of Enigma, for on January 15, 1927, the Chief Signals Officer of the United States decided to order one each of two models of the machine. However, such was the parsimony of the Treasury that before the order could be placed, the Signal Corps needed to know the exact cost of the machines and the charges for packing, freight and export duties. Letters flowed between

Washington and Berlin for over a year. Prices were quoted and then raised, one of the models of the machine was discontinued, but finally the contract was signed and the machine was shipped in February 1928. Then another snag developed. The Kryha Company had not paid the freight and import charges, as it had agreed to do, and the Signal Corps had no appropriation for such payments.

The shipment was not released from the warehouse until April 5, 1928, when the charges were finally paid. More than four years had elapsed between the time that Enigma was first offered for sale and Friedman was able to begin the task of penetrating its secrets. His work, however, received another setback in 1929 when Secretary of State Henry L. Stimson withdrew his department's support for the "Black Chamber"—as the United States cryptanalytic services were called—on the ground, so it was said, that gentlemen do not open each other's mail. Friedman was appointed Chief of the Signals Intelligence Service in 1930, but his staff, it appeared, consisted of three young cryptanalysts and two clerks. Nevertheless, by 1934 he had succeeded in thoroughly penetrating the Kryha Enigma; and when he learned that the Japanese had purchased an advanced model of the machine, he turned his attention to the Japanese rather than the German cryptosystems. So successful were his efforts that, by 1942, the United States was reading the Enigma traffic of both the Japanese navy and Foreign Office; and these intercepts, which were essentially the American counterpart of Ultra, were codenamed "Magic."

With America's entry into the war, the advantages to the Allies of sharing their Ultra and Magic intercepts were obvious. But the British, apprehensive about America's ability to keep such an important secret, were at first reluctant to disclose the full range of their cryptanalytical activities at Bletchley. Their apprehensions stemmed, at least in part, from two serious scares that had threatened the security of Ultra in its earliest days, one of which was traced to the Russians and the other to the Americans.

For quite some time before Britain declared war on Germany and Italy in 1939, the Foreign Office, MI-6 and MI-5 had been conscious of serious leakages of information about secret British policy, most noticeably in the declarations of Mussolini and Stalin, who was then an ally of Hitler. It seemed to Foreign Office analysts of the two dictators' utterances that they knew altogether too much about British intentions. Where could the leak be? At first, attention fastened upon the British Embassy in Rome. Mussolini, it was discovered, had two agents in the entourage of the ambassador, Lord Perth. One, a chauffeur, gave himself away by stealing Lady Perth's tiara. He was dismissed, but the leaks continued. Then the second agent was discovered. He was an Italian clerk who was in the habit of rifling the rickety old safe which contained the "print," the Foreign Office's term for the file of cables between London and all important embassies.

The clerk, one Segundo, was also discharged; and thereafter Mussolini's statements revealed that his sources of secret information had dried up.

Stalin's statements, however, continued to show signs of access to British secrets; and in September 1939, acting on a tip from the British Embassy in Washington, MI-5 began a surveillance of Russians in London. It was discovered that a member of the Soviet Trade Delegation, A. A. Doschenko, was in the habit of taking a train to the market town of Leighton Buzzard. No one could imagine what legitimate business a Russian diplomat might have in such a sleepy little place; but when he took a walk down the Grand Union canal, he was joined by a second man. This man was followed back to Bletchley Park, which was only a few miles from Leighton Buzzard, and which housed the Foreign Office's Communications Department as well as the GC&CS. The man worked at Bletchley Park, handling Foreign Office cipher traffic. He was arrested on September 27, 1939. Apparently the victim of a blackmail operation, he confessed that he had been supplying the Russians with secret information and material for years; and some of this material, the security authorities learned, had enabled the Russians to read British diplomatic traffic.

The man was tried and sentenced to ten years' hard labor, Doschenko was expelled, and Stalin's intelligence source was plugged. But had Ultra been compromised? It was established that the man at Bletchley Park had not had access to, and apparently knew nothing of, the most secret activities going on in Hut 3. But with the security of Ultra uppermost in their minds, the British introduced for the first time the process that would come to be called "positive vetting"—detailed and deep security checks on all personnel handling secret materials; and it was this process, in part, that would ensure the remarkable fact that the secret of Ultra would be kept for thirty years.

In the early months of 1940, another serious security breach was discovered—this time at the American Embassy in London. The trail was convoluted, but it eventually led to Tyler Gateswood Kent, who had arrived at the embassy in October 1939 from Moscow, where he had served since 1936 as a State Department code and cipher clerk. A pleasant, tall and studious young man, Kent was the son of an American consul in China, the scion of an illustrious southern family, extremely well educated, fluent in German, Russian and the main Latin languages, and a student of history and political science. Aged twenty-nine, he was a man destined for the highest places in the State Department—except that he had formed some singular theories about the turbulent world of the thirties, among them the belief that international Jewry was propelling the world into war in order to obtain hegemony out of the ruins. Nevertheless, Kent was trusted completely and was assigned to the code room, where he handled the most confidential communications between the embassy and the State

Department. He had access to Ambassador Joseph Kennedy's correspondence with Roosevelt and Cordell Hull, the Secretary of State, as well as to the despatches of Ambassador William Bullitt in Paris and of American envoys in other parts of Europe who used the London embassy as a message center. Moreover, Kent handled the Gray Code, a cipher system that the State Department thought to be unbreakable; and it was in this code that Churchill, even before becoming Prime Minister, was corresponding with Roosevelt.

Ultra was just then beginning to flow across Churchill's desk from Bletchley; and without disclosing the source of his information, he passed naval intelligence derived from Ultra to Roosevelt. Roosevelt passed Churchill some Magic intercepts in return, again without disclosing their source. The object was to permit the two leaders and their naval staffs to make sensible dispositions of their fleets in both the Pacific and the Atlantic. But Churchill had another motive; he was frankly trying to enlist American sympathy and support for the British cause. Kent handled some of their messages in the solitude of the embassy code room, brooding about their meaning and portent.

It became apparent to the British security authorities that there was a leak somewhere when Hans Mackensen, the German ambassador in Rome, made a number of public declarations about Anglo-American naval policy which revealed that he was in possession of part of the information in the Churchill-Roosevelt communications. Suspicion fastened upon an assistant military attaché at the Italian Embassy in London, Don Francesco Maringliano, the Duke of Del Monte. He was shadowed by Special Branch officers of Scotland Yard, and they discovered that Maringliano occasionally went to a Russian tea room in London owned by a czarist admiral named Wolkoff. They also discovered that Maringliano had formed an association with the admiral's daughter, Anna Wolkoff, a naturalized British subject who made her living as a dressmaker and was known to be a "virulent anti-Semite" and Fascist sympathizer. Her file at Scotland Yard showed that she was a prominent and active member of the "Right Club," a nest of anti-Jewish right-wingers headed by Captain Archibald Ramsay, a distant relative of the royal family and an MP. The Special Branch put Miss Wolkoff under surveillance (she was detected pasting up "sticky backs" on bus stops, telephone boxes and the walls of dark streets, announcing that this was a "Jew's War"), and the trail led to the studio of a photographer named Nicholas Smirnov. It was found that Miss Wolkoff and Maringliano met at the studio. It was also found that Miss Wolkoff was in surreptitious contact with Kent. The British security authorities informed the Foreign Office and, with the knowledge and permission of Kennedy, it was decided to move in on Kent.

At 10 A.M. on May 20, 1940, four men—two Special Branch detectives, an MI-5 counterespionage officer, and a second secretary from the American Embassy—raided Kent's apartment. They found some 1500 documents stuffed into various suitcases and cupboards, a few of Miss Wolkoff's "sticky-back" posters, some photographic negatives and a set of keys that enabled Kent to get into the embassy code room and the safe where Kennedy kept his most secret papers. Kent was taken to the American Embassy and there confessed to Kennedy. He explained that during his Moscow tour he had become dissatisfied with American foreign policy. It had been his intention, he said, to bring the stolen documents "to the attention of the Congress of the United States in time to prevent America's involvement in a war that was being fomented by his own President and the man who was soon to become the Prime Minister of Great Britain." He had been unable to find a means of submitting the documents to Congress—but then he met Miss Wolkoff. She persuaded him to show samples of the documents to Captain Ramsay, and from there, unknown to Kent, they had found their way to Rome and Berlin.

Kent denied that he was a spy. Nevertheless, he was dismissed from the Foreign Service; and with his immunity gone, he was tried, convicted, sentenced to—and he served—seven years in the most grim of British prisons, Dartmoor. The consequences of his actions, however patriotic he thought them to be, were grave. The Gray Code was compromised and all diplomatic communications from American embassies and missions throughout the world were blacked out for weeks until a new system could be established. Furthermore, the documents he had leaked revealed that Roosevelt had abandoned a positive neutral stance, a disclosure that aggravated both the Germans and those in America who were opposed to any involvement in the war. And Kent's treachery had been detected at the very moment when the British were expelled from Europe, France fell, and Hitler began to contemplate an invasion of Britain.

Apparently Kent had not compromised Ultra; a check of the Churchill-Roosevelt Gray Code correspondence would show that neither man had referred to Ultra or Magic. But it had been a severe fright, and British security authorities questioned the wisdom of disclosing the secrets of Ultra to anyone, including the Americans. For that reason, the first agreement to share Ultra and Magic was a limited one. Shortly after Pearl Harbor, Admiral John Godfrey, the director of naval intelligence of the Admiralty, and his personal assistant, Lieutenant Commander Ian Fleming, the future author of the James Bond novels, flew to Washington to arrange a pact to share only British and American naval intelligence. But in February 1942, after assurances were sought and given that neither Britain nor America would employ Ultra-Magic intercepts in circumstances that might cause the enemy to suspect that his secret communications were being read, the pact was extended to include army, air force and diplomatic intelligence. The British would concentrate on penetrating German ciphers, while the Americans concentrated on the Japanese; and to hide the existence of Ultra, it was also agreed that all Ultra signals disseminated for operational purposes should be called Magic. Thus, if the Germans became suspicious through American leakages that their secret cipher system had been penetrated, they would conclude, hopefully, that it was the fault of the Japanese, not their own, and continue to use Enigma. For all practical purposes, Ultra became Magic, and was rarely referred to by its real name, at least in the United States. Furthermore, in Europe, whenever material derived from Ultra was circulated to levels lower than commanding generals, it was often referred to either as "Zeal," or as "Pearl" or "Thumb," two code names that were, in reality, those for low-level cryptographic and wireless intelligence intercepts. So successful would these disguises be that, until the secret of Ultra finally became known, the Germans and the Japanese would believe that the source of their historic discomfiture had been Magic.

When the Ultra-Magic agreement was reached, Turing journeyed to the United States to show his American counterparts how his machine worked. The Americans, in turn, brought to England a copy of the machine that had helped penetrate the Japanese system, and American cryptographers and cipher clerks began to swell the population at Bletchley. Even so, the British remained apprehensive about the agreement, for America, with its vast population and land area, and its aggressive and unbridled press, could not enforce the same degree of security that was possible in Britain. Nor did America have a centralized bureau, like the LCS, to orchestrate cover and deception operations. Both deficiencies were remedied by the creation, in May 1942, of a new secret service, the Joint Security Control, a dependency of the Joint Chiefs of Staff. Its founding charter directed the agency "to prevent the leakage of information in connection with military operations, to devise measures to deceive the enemy in connection therewith, to coordinate all security measures within the armed forces, and to act in an advisory capacity on security for all other government agencies that have direct or indirect activities bearing on military operations." Somewhat later, the Joint Security Control would extend its sphere of operations to cover cryptanalytical security as well. The Americans, with the British as a model, were gearing up for a war of special means. But it was a concept of warfare that was antithetical to the ideas of many; secrecy and deception were European characteristics that had no place in American public life. Cooperation between the press and the government, and even between the various arms of the military services, would be difficult to achieve—as difficult as the unreserved cooperation between the governments and military services of Britain and America. The agreements reached between the two powers in the months after the Pearl Harbor attack hung on a slender thread of trust, and while that thread would fray dangerously on a number of occasions in the years ahead, it would ultimately hold.

It was in a similar atmosphere of trust tinged with suspicion that American and British high commanders began to plan their strategy; and for all the agreements in detail that had been reached between the two powers, it was immediately evident that there was a serious disagreement about how the Third Reich was to be attacked and defeated. Both partners recognized that an invasion of the continent of Europe across the English Channel was probably inevitable. But the British believed that the Third Reich was immensely powerful, and that before such an invasion could be launched there would have to be a long, hard, bloody struggle to disperse Germany's forces and sap her strength. Therefore, they advocated a stealthy, patient, indirect strategy—a strategy of superior wits and special means.

The Americans, on the other hand, believed that the Third Reich could be defeated only with the tactics that the British were determined to avoid—an immediate frontal attack from England against Germany through the coast of northwest France. While the British sought victory through subtle and less costly stratagems, the Americans saw the war as a battle between well-armored and well-nourished juggernauts, with laurels going to the side which could survive a duel of strength. The difference between the two concepts was as fundamental as the difference between British cricket and American football. Winston Churchill and General Sir Alan Brooke, Chief of the Imperial General Staff, fighting the war with the specter of Ypres at their shoulders, could see only catastrophe in the American conception; together they would maneuver to retain strategic control of the war and persuade the Americans to accept the British design for victory. Consequently, the alliance was not six months old before the gravest dispute threatened its integrity.

At the center of this dispute was a plan conceived by General George C. Marshall, Chief of Staff of the United States army, and by the unknown and untested Chief of the War Plans Division in Washington, D.C., Major General Dwight D. Eisenhower. The plan, codenamed "Sledgehammer," provided for an invasion of northwest France in the late summer or early autumn of 1942, an operation that had already been rejected by the British because the overwhelming strength of the Wehrmacht in France would certainly result in disaster. British maneuvers to circumvent Sledgehammer would contribute to one of the war's most melancholy and mysterious operations, the large-scale raid in August 1942 on the Channel port of Dieppe.

When Brooke became Chief of the Imperial General Staff in the winter of 1941, he brought to that supreme military post within the British

Empire a new application of a traditional British military principle: never attack the enemy frontally if that is where he is strongest, and only engage him in mass and concentration when he has been weakened by attacks against his leadership, his morale and his economy. Brooke's strategy for the Second World War was to secure command of the seas and drive the Germans and Italians from North Africa. This first phase would restore British naval superiority and compel Hitler to garrison the entire Mediterranean coast of Europe from the Spanish frontier to the Turkish border at the expense of his Western and Eastern frontiers. At the same time— Brooke's design went on—Germany was to be weakened by day and night bombing and economic blockade, rendered uncertain about Allied intentions by unrelenting stratagem, and remorselessly attacked from within by Allied-nourished rebellions and political warfare. Finally, when the Wehrmacht showed all the signs of disintegration and distension, but not before, the Allies would cross the Channel to invade France and the German heartland. Under certain circumstances, Brooke believed, the Wehrmacht might even be compelled to withdraw from France by the combined weight of these pressures; and in that event it would not be necessary to undertake the vast task of invasion at all.

General Marshall and General Eisenhower contested this strategy. On April 1, 1942, convinced of the strength of America and the weakness of Germany, they presented President Roosevelt with Sledgehammer, which visualized cross-Channel operations to secure a beachhead in northwestern France that year, from which full-scale military operations, codenamed "Roundup," might be conducted in 1943. The objective of the 1942 operations was to relieve the Red Army, which appeared in Washington (but not in London) to be in danger of collapse, and to keep the Soviet Union in the war. The President approved Sledgehammer and decided to send Harry Hopkins, his adviser, and General Marshall to London to press the plan upon Churchill and Brooke. Sledgehammer, Roosevelt wired Churchill, "has my heart and *mind* in it."

The debate over the contesting strategies opened at 10:30 A.M. on April 8, 1942, at the War Office, and General Marshall faced a powerful and experienced opponent in General Brooke. A tough, shrewd and choleric Orangeman, Brooke had distinguished himself in action in both world wars and would soon become a field marshal and the most decorated British soldier since Marlborough, Wellington and Frederick Sleigh Roberts. He was not only a brave fighting man and staff officer; he was a military scientist and strategist of high competence. But so reserved and awkward was his personality that he was virtually unknown to the public; he was, indeed, better known as a student of birds and a zoologist than he was as a soldier.

A slightly stooped, aquiline man of fifty-eight, Brooke greeted Marshall under a heroic oil painting of Kitchener's expedition against the Mahdi. Marshall was a quiet, courtly Virginian, sixty-one years old, more experienced in military politics than in waging war. From the beginning, these two officers, whose opinions would be decisive in planning and executing the strategies of the alliance, regarded each other with reserve and, on occasion, irritation. Brooke regarded American generals as both short-sighted and incompetent. Moreover, from a tactical viewpoint Marshall could not have come to see Brooke at a less favorable time. Both England and America faced defeat on every front, and the American army was quite unready to carry out an operation like Sledgehammer. As Field Marshal Sir John Dill, the senior British military representative in Washington, wrote to Brooke: "This country is the most highly organised for peace you can imagine. . . . At present this country has not—repeat not—the slightest conception of what the war means, and their armed forces are more unready for war than it is possible to imagine. Eventually they will do great things, but . . . (at the moment) the whole organisation belongs to the days of George Washington."

The Americans thought even less of British fighting forces. Donovan, after a trip to Britain early in 1942, reported that the British had been "totally unprepared" for German methods of attack, and that after the severe mauling the army had received at the hands of the enemy, it seemed fit only for defense, not offense. In Donovan's opinion, the British army was not strong enough, confident enough, or well enough equipped for a major offensive in Europe at this stage of the war. Yet Marshall proposed that on or about September 15, 1942, using England as the springboard, six divisions, to be followed by twelve more, would cross the Channel and storm the French shore. The operation would be supported by 5800 aircraft, 2550 of which would be British, and by a fleet that would be, inevitably, British. The American troop contribution could be, said Marshall, only three infantry and two armored divisions; but America would send 100,000 men per week until a force of 1 million Americans, or thirty divisions, had been built up. Thus almost the entire assault force would be British. And what of the German force? As Brooke pointed out, there were twenty-five German divisions in the western European group of nations and, in all respects, they were superior to the best that was available to both America and Britain at that time.

Marshall's and Eisenhower's plan was not only thought to smell of the lamp, it was also considered extremely dangerous. And Brooke said so. In an exasperated moment after the meeting with Marshall, he noted in his diary, "Whether we are to play *baccarat* or *chemin-de-fer* at Le Touquet . . . is not stipulated." The Grand Alliance was only "hanging on by (its) eyelids," everywhere, and therefore "In the light of the existing situation (Marshall's) plans for September of 1942 were just fantastic." Marshall was, he noted, "a good general at raising armies . . . but his strategical ability does not impress me at all. In fact, in many respects he is a very dangerous man whilst being a very charming one. . . ."

The conference ended in a cloud of ambiguity and misunderstanding. The Americans returned to Washington in the belief that Churchill and Brooke had agreed to undertake Sledgehammer. In fact, Roosevelt cabled Stalin with the news that the Anglo-Americans would invade France in 1942. But Churchill and Brooke had agreed only that planning should start for a possible emergency landing if the Russians appeared to be collapsing, and that planning should also begin for the American build-up in Britain for a cross-Channel attack in 1943. Churchill and Brooke recognized the necessity of luring the Luftwaffe into a large-scale battle, and of leading Hitler to believe that there would be an invasion that year, thus forcing him to garrison France at the expense of his fighting front in Russia. But they proposed to do that in quite another way—with a campaign of false rumors of an imminent invasion to draw Hitler's attention to the French Channel coast. To give substance to those rumors, as well as to put to the test of fire the tactics and equipment that would be necessary for an actual invasion, "Operation Rutter"—the old German name for a horse soldier—was being conceived. It would be an attack on Dieppe, and the largest amphibious operation since Gallipoli. But it was planned as a raid—*not* an invasion.

Into this confusion of plan and counterplan there now bounded a new, fresh, vigorous, likable figure: the author of Sledgehammer, General Eisenhower, who, less than eighteen months before, had been a lieutenant colonel and who had never commanded even a battalion in action. His academic and military career had been undistinguished, he had been to Europe only once before to write a guidebook to American war monuments, and at the time of Pearl Harbor he thought so little of his chances for promotion that he accepted command of a tank regiment in an armored division commanded by General George S. Patton, Jr. Eisenhower had come to London as the commanding general of the European Theater of Operations, U.S. Army (ETOUSA), to supervise the buildup for Sledgehammer-Roundup operations. And he had come in the belief that "at long last, and after months of struggle (with the British) . . . we are all definitely committed to one concept of fighting!" He was soon to report that the British were not committed to Sledgehammer at all.

Eisenhower quickly became familiar with the intricate machinery that propelled British strategy, including the LCS, the agency expressly formed to deceive the Germans about British intentions. Colonel the Honourable Oliver Stanley was its chief, and his aristocratic origins—son of the 17th Earl of Derby, grandson of the 7th Duke of Manchester, son-in-law of the 7th Marquess of Londonderry—proclaimed the principle that deception was like intelligence: it was the business of gentlemen. A High Tory intellectual, Stanley had held a number of Cabinet posts, including that of the War Ministry in 1940. When the Chiefs of Staff established the LCS, Stanley, who was known as "The Fox" at MI-6, was asked to head the bureau and, despite his antipathy for Churchill, accepted. And from its inception, the LCS under Stanley had been busy sowing rumor and misinformation in widely separated parts of the world more or less simultaneously. When all the fragments were assembled by the German intelligence evaluators they formed a single picture—but a false one—of British strategy which was close to what the Germans themselves thought logical and probable and were therefore disposed to believe.

At first, Eisenhower was puzzled by the artful dodgers of England, the LCS. A plainsman born and reared in the infinite clear horizons of Kansas, he did not appreciate, or like, the world of the well-born alley cat. It was too intricate for him, as London in wartime was too intricate for many Americans. When the time came for him to judge the achievements of the LCS, he would write:

> In the early days of the war, particularly when Britain stood alone in 1940 and 1941, the British had little with which to oppose the Germans except deception. They resorted to every type of subterfuge . . . in order to confuse the Germans as to the amount of military strength (they had) and, more important, its disposition. Out of this was born a habit that was later difficult (for them) to discard.

When Eisenhower was introduced to the LCS, Colonel Stanley was playing his first great game. His agents were filling the whispering gallery of Europe—and the world—with suggestions and rumors of an imminent invasion by the Allies of northwestern France. Eisenhower was not impressed; it was, he said, difficult to see how, in the long run, a war of words could be a substitute for metal and powder. He may have been correct. Nevertheless, this war of words, combined with a series of sharp Commando attacks along the Norwegian and the French Channel coasts—one a raid against Bruneval, where the British stole a new German radar set and discovered the secrets of the electronic defenses of Hitler's Europe, and another at St. Nazaire, where they destroyed the only drydock installation in Europe outside Germany that was capable of handling the Kriegsmarine's largest warships—had compelled Hitler to promulgate Directive 40 in March 1942 which ordered the construction of the Atlantic Wall, the German coastal defenses for western Europe.

Conceived as one of the great engineering projects of history, and executed as such, the Atlantic Wall would require a vast diversion and dispersal of German resources. In response to LCS deception operations and the host of pinprick Commando attacks, Hitler, convinced that his empire was vulnerable at almost every point, stretched his fortifications from the North Cape to the Spanish frontier. Thus he played into the hands of British strategists, for while the Atlantic Wall would be a formidable barrier—both physically and psychologically—to an invading Allied army, Hitler, in an attempt to be strong everywhere, would not be strong enough at the point and moment of an actual invasion. Like the Great Wall of China, the Atlantic Wall would prove to be largely useless.

As the strategical debate on Sledgehammer continued, and as Eisenhower integrated himself into wartime London in a mood of increasing skepticism and disappointment at what he thought to be the caution of British strategy, plans for Rutter were completed and troop training began. It was to be a frontal attack—the most dangerous of all assaults—from the sea against Dieppe, undertaken by two brigades of the Canadian Second Division, supported by Commandos and a battalion of twenty-eight new Churchill tanks. The naval forces would consist of some two hundred ships, including destroyers to provide bombardment. The troops were to get ashore and stay ashore for two tides, capture the port and certain German installations, take some prizes (including an Enigma if one could be found), infiltrate some agents, and then withdraw. Some fifty-six squadrons of RAF fighters—more than existed at the time of the Battle of Britain—would engage the Luftwaffe and provide aerial support.

The Rutter planners, who were commanded by General Sir Bernard Montgomery, demanded two prerequisites for the raid: secrecy and surprise. The Chiefs of Staff approved the overall strategy on May 13, 1942, force commanders were appointed and detailed planning started. But at almost the same time Colonel Stanley began to direct deception operations that were designed to rivet German attention on the very stretch of the French coast where Rutter was to go in. Thus from the outset Rutter was in jeopardy because, so it seemed, the right hand did not let the left hand know what it was doing. This might possibly be explained by the fact that the Rutter planners were separated from Churchill's headquarters geographically, but it is not likely. It might also be explained by the fact that the LCS worked in conditions of super-secrecy and that few of the Rutter planners would even have been aware of its existence; but this, too, is hardly tenable since the Chiefs of Staff were responsible for coordinating all acts of war. Finally, it might be explained by the fact that Rutter was intended as a sacrificial operation from the very beginning—an operation to give the appearance of truth to the LCS's deception. But now high politics intervened to complicate the reasons for the Dieppe raid.

In Washington, where Marshall was setting "Bolero"—the code word for the American build-up in Britain—in motion, it soon became apparent that Churchill and his Chiefs of Staff were sidestepping Sledgehammer and now favored "Torch," the invasion of North Africa. Marshall, alarmed at the situation in Russia where the German offensive had reopened with a drive on the Caucasian oilfields, was equally determined upon Sledgehammer. The Red Army had just lost 250,000 men in the great battles of May and June for the Crimea and once again seemed about to collapse. If Russia was to remain in the war, Marshall believed that Sledgehammer must be launched without delay. A great clamor for a Second Front arose in England and America, and the Soviet Foreign Minister, V. M. Molotov, arrived in London to demand a positive commitment for an invasion of France in 1942.

Brooke did not share Marshall's view that the Russians were played out; on the contrary, he considered that the Germans were in a serious predicament, despite the successes of their summer offensive. He rejected American pressure for an early invasion of France to help Russia on the grounds that ". . . a premature Western Front (can) only result in the most appalling shambles which must . . . reduce the chances of ultimate victory to a minimum." But he also wrote, ominously for Rutter, "We discussed [at a Chief of Staff meeting] the problem of assistance to Russia by operations in France, either large raid or lodgment. Decided only hope was to try and draw off (Luftwaffe) from Russia and that for this purpose raid must be carried out on Calais front."

At Brooke's insistence, Churchill, briefing Molotov on British plans, assured him only that "We are making preparations for a landing on the Continent in August or September 1942," and that if conditions for an operation appeared "sound and sensible, we shall not hesitate to put our plans into effect." But in Washington, where Molotov went next in an attempt to get from Roosevelt what he had failed to get from Churchill, the attitude toward the invasion was quite different. The plight of Russia, as described by Molotov at the White House, made a profound impression upon Roosevelt; after consulting with Marshall, he authorized Molotov to inform Stalin that he expected the formation of a Second Front in the current year. D-Day for Sledgehammer, Molotov was told, would be during the month of August 1942—not more than ten weeks off.

Roosevelt's promise was embodied in a telegram that was sent to both Stalin and Churchill, but when Molotov returned to London, Churchill told him once again that the British government could give no assurance that Sledgehammer-Roundup would be undertaken that year. What Churchill had in mind—Rutter apart—was a large-scale deception operation of a type not hitherto attempted. Nevertheless, a public statement, approved by both Roosevelt and Molotov and broadcast to the world, declared that "full understanding was reached with regard to the urgent task of creating a second front in Europe in 1942." "There could be no harm in a public statement," Churchill would later write, "which might make the Germans apprehensive and consequently hold as many of their troops in the West as possible."

Meanwhile, Churchill had sent Admiral the Lord Louis Mountbatten to Washington to explain the British position; but Marshall, backed by Secretary of War Henry L. Stimson, continued to insist that Sledgehammer be launched to save Russia. A crisis was looming in Allied affairs. Churchill resolved to go to Washington himself and take Brooke with him. "Roosevelt," said the Prime Minister, "(is) getting a little off the rails."

On June 17, 1942, Churchill and Brooke departed for the United States by Pan American Clipper and landed on the Potomac River. They found Marshall in a stubborn and ominous mood, still dangerously optimistic about the ability of raw American troops to land from the sea and defeat a superior and veteran German army. He was completely backed by Secretary of War Stimson who, on the morning of the arrival of the British party, warned Roosevelt that Churchill and Brooke had come to "wheedle" the President into the "wildest kind of diversionary debauch"—as Stimson called Torch. That was, indeed, Churchill's intention. In a memorandum to Roosevelt he stated:

> We hold strongly to the view that there should be no substantial landing in France this year unless we are going to stay. . . . But . . . what else are we going to do? Can we afford to stand idle in the Atlantic theatre during the whole of 1942? Ought we not to be preparing within the general structure of "Bolero" some other operation by which we may gain positions of advantage, and also directly or indirectly to take some of the weight off Russia? It is in this setting and on this background that the French Northwest Africa operation [Torch] should be studied.

On June 21 Churchill, the President, Marshall, Brooke, Field Marshal Sir John Dill and Harry Hopkins met at the White House until 4:30 P.M. to discuss plans. But with appalling suddenness disaster intruded; an aide entered the room and handed Roosevelt a flimsy. The President read it and then handed it to the Prime Minister. It announced the fall of Tobruk. General Rommel was on the rampage in North Africa, and Britain's 8th Army was streaming back into Egypt in the wildest disorder. The sting of the moment lay in Tobruk. At Churchill's command the little port had been transformed into a fortress and, during an earlier battle with Rommel, it had held out for thirty-three weeks. This time it had collapsed in a day. It appeared that there was now little to stop Rommel from marching into Egypt and taking Cairo and the great naval base of Alexandria.

Churchill was stunned by the news, partly because he had learned it from the President rather than from his own sources. He said afterward that he felt it was the most mortifying experience suffered by an Englishman in America since General Burgoyne. Defeat, said Churchill, was one thing; disgrace another.

The disaster weakened the authority of Churchill's and Brooke's arguments over those of Marshall and his supporters. In the short time left for discussion, Churchill invoked visions of Passchendaele and Ypres in the First World War to warn the President against the foolhardiness of Sledge-hammer. He was opposed to a sacrificial landing on the coast of France to save Russia, and said that if such an expedition was attempted the Channel would become a "river of blood." He reminded the President of the British belief that the Second World War should not become a "war of vast armies, firing immense masses of shells at one another," and said that he believed that sea and air power *"plus superior wits"* would accomplish Hitler's defeat. It would be a long time before the American army was battle-worthy, and he insisted that the only way America and Britain could lose the Second World War was by suffering a disastrous defeat on the French shore. He had, he said, a healthy respect for the German army.

Even so, the Military Conclusions of the meeting of June 21, 1942— the day upon which the news of the Tobruk disaster reached Churchill— stated in part:

> Operations in France or the Low Countries in 1942 would, if successful, yield greater political and strategic gains than operations in any other theatre. Plans and preparations for the operations in this theatre are to be pressed forward with all possible speed, energy, and ingenuity. The most resolute efforts must be made to overcome the obvious dangers and diffi-culties of the enterprise. If a sound and sensible plan can be contrived we should not hesitate to give effect to it. If, on the other hand, detailed exami-nation shows that, despite all efforts, success is improbable, we must be ready with an alternative.

On that note of uncertain accord, Churchill sped home to face what the American press described as his "supreme political crisis," for following the collapse of the 8th Army in North Africa, a vote of no confidence had been introduced against him in the House of Commons. Churchill survived the vote by a wide margin on July 2, the same day that the 8th Army finally stopped Rommel at El Alamein. His political future was saved.

Less certain was the future of the American alliance, for despite his political predicament the Prime Minister lost little time in debating the wisdom of Sledgehammer anew with his Chiefs of Staff. On July 8 he made his final decision: Britain would *not* support Sledgehammer. He tele-graphed the President accordingly on that day. "No responsible British general, admiral, or air marshal is prepared to recommend 'Sledgehammer' as a practicable operation in 1942," his signal read. "The Chiefs of Staff have reported, 'The conditions which would make "Sledgehammer" a sound, sensible enterprise are very unlikely to occur.' "

On that same day, the Rutter raid was abandoned. It was to have been launched on July 4, 1942; a small armada had assembled and was loaded with troops, guns and tanks. All the aircraft had been made ready. But quite suddenly the weather turned bad in the Channel, there was no hope that it might improve, and there had been disturbing news from France. The 10th Panzer Division had moved into the area of Dieppe, which seemed to indicate that the Germans had some foreknowledge of the raid. Moreover, German aircraft had attacked some of Rutter's ships and must certainly have observed the assembled convoy. Accordingly, the troops were disembarked and returned to their camps. The planners considered that Rutter was now wholly compromised and, they recommended to the Chiefs of Staff, it would be lunacy to remount the operation. Their recommendation would not be heeded.

In Washington, meanwhile, strong tensions were growing over the Prime Minister's telegram of July 8. They were increased by another telegram from Churchill on July 14, in which he said:

> I am most anxious for you to know where I stand myself at the present time. I have found no one who regards "Sledgehammer" as possible. I should like you to do (Torch) as soon as possible, and that we in concert with the Russians should try for "Jupiter." Meanwhile all preparations for "Round-up" in 1943 should proceed at full blast, thus holding the maximum enemy forces opposite England. All this seems to me as clear as noonday.

When Marshall realized that not only were the British resolved to abandon Sledgehammer but they were also proposing to embark upon "Jupiter"—the code name of a plan for an invasion of northern Norway—he concluded that Churchill's and Brooke's words could no longer be trusted. Twice, he believed, they had agreed to Sledgehammer, and twice, he believed, they had reneged on that agreement. Dill, whom Marshall did trust, warned Churchill of the approaching storm. On July 15 he telegraphed the Prime Minister that Marshall, Admiral Ernest J. King and Harry Hopkins were coming to London for what would be a major showdown. His message read in part: "Unless you can convince (Marshall) of your unswerving devotion to (Sledgehammer) everything points to a complete reversal of our present agreed strategy and the withdrawal of America to a war of her own in the Pacific, leaving (Britain) with limited American assistance to make out as best we can against Germany."

Not before, and not again, would the Grand Alliance be in such danger; not before, and not again, would Hitler appear to be so close to victory—for that must have been the consequence of an Anglo-American split. It was a moment of great peril. Clearly Marshall was not used to, and neither could he tolerate, the special language of English negotiations. He was chief of the army of a nation that believed there was no enemy, no problem that could not be overcome by determination, energy and, if necessary, force. On the other hand, the British, with their greater experience in the strategies of diplomacy and war, believed that the Wehrmacht could not be defeated as easily and simply as Marshall supposed. But Churchill could not now persuade the Americans by the power of his personality or the prestige of the British army, for both were suspect. He would write: "The fall of Tobruk, the political clamour at home, and the undoubted loss of prestige which our country, and I as its representative, suffered from this disaster had rendered it impossible for me to obtain satisfaction." How could Churchill convince the Americans that Sledgehammer would be a disaster? On July 15, 1942—three days before Marshall was due in London for the showdown—he directed that Rutter should be resurrected, although all the Rutter planners and the force commanders warned that to do so would probably mean the destruction of the force.

At first Churchill demanded that a full-scale raid be undertaken against the French coast at a place other than Dieppe. When the Chiefs of Staff explained that there was no time to plan and remount another big raid, Churchill was adamant. He explained his reasons later:

> However, I thought it most important that a large-scale operation should take place this summer, and military opinion seemed unanimous that until an operation on that scale was undertaken, no responsible general would take the responsibility of planning for the main invasion. In discussion with Admiral Mountbatten it became clear that time did not permit a new large-scale operation to be mounted during the summer, but that Dieppe could be remountĕd . . . within a month, provided extraordinary steps were taken to ensure secrecy.

At the time this explanation may have been sufficient for the Chiefs of Staff; as Englishmen they knew the perils of those unruly Narrows. Who would dare undertake the invasion of a hostile shore to engage a seemingly invincible army without, first, having made a reconnaissance in force? Yet time and history would contest Churchill's statement as being the only reason for the raid on that old pirate port. It would be alleged that Churchill repudiated his conscience and reordered Rutter to show the Americans that Sledgehammer would be a disaster. It would also be alleged that, in the sure knowledge that a tragedy would occur, he was prepared to sacrifice 5000 men in order to shake the Americans away from an infinitely more dangerous course: an invasion that might cost the western powers 500,000 men, all their matériel, a large part of their navies and air forces—and the war.

From the beginning of "Jubilee" (as Rutter came to be called from this point), all planning was done in the atmosphere of a plot. Churchill directed that steps should be taken for which, so far as is known, there was no precedent. He ordered that nothing was to appear on paper about Jubilee at meetings of the Chiefs of Staff. All planning was to be confined to a small cabal of men of proven discretion. The troops' commanders were not to know what their mission was until they were actually sealed in their ships. To conceal the movements of the Canadians, all were to be told they were going on exercises. Not even the First Lord of the Admiralty was to be told what the planners required 250 ships for. There were to be no rehearsals and no concentration of shipping; the expedition was to sail in bits and pieces and rendezvous out in the Channel. Finally, there was to be no cover and deception. This order was particularly mystifying, for it suggested that Churchill and the Chiefs of Staff did not want the Germans to be distracted.

At the same time the LCS, whose campaign of rumor that Europe would soon be invaded through the Channel coast was at its height, was not directed to cease the campaign, or to divert German attention elsewhere. More mysteriously, the XX-Committee received instructions *not* to use double agents to feed their German controllers with misinformation about the purpose and destination of all the shipping gathering at the British Channel ports. The XX-Committee had proposed such an operation, but it was vetoed by Combined Operations headquarters. As Masterman wrote later: "It is sad, but interesting, to speculate whether the Dieppe raid might not have been more successful, or at least less costly, if it had been effectively covered."

One man at least found the situation intolerable: Colonel Stanley, the chief of the LCS. A man of towering anger—had he not blackballed the Aga Khan at the Turf?—he resigned abruptly. Having been responsible for the 1942 campaigns to persuade Hitler that the Allies *would* invade in the West that year, and having seen Hitler's reactions through his access to Ultra, he knew better than most men how prepared the Germans were for any expedition across the Channel and, with his experience in the trenches during the First World War, he knew what the butcher's bill would be for Dieppe. He could no longer be a member of an entourage that would sacrifice or risk 5000 loyal Empire troops to keep Russia in the war. As one of his friends would later explain his position: "A man whose ancestors had put the Tudors on the throne saw no reason to bow low to foreign potentates." Stanley departed, and was succeeded after the Dieppe raid by Colonel John Bevan. But Stanley did not go into the wilderness; he went to be Minister of the Colonies.

As the operational planning for Jubilee proceeded in circumstances of abnormal secrecy, even for those days, at the headquarters of Combined Operations in Richmond Terrace, where Mountbatten, the chief, presided over a sort of private fiefdom, the American delegation—Marshall, King and Hopkins—arrived at Prestwick Airport in Scotland. The British had made arrangements for a private train to take them to a stop near Chequers. But the members of the delegation insisted that the train take them straight to London. This, undoubtedly, was a personal and a diplomatic affront to Churchill. But the Americans were in no mood for protocol.

The conference began the following day, July 20, and the American delegation, which now included Eisenhower and the American ground, air force and naval commanders, pressed for an immediate Sledgehammer. Only Admiral Harold R. Stark, the naval commander, was opposed; as a sailor he knew that in a few short weeks the French Channel coast would have become a dangerous lee shore. The British voted against the operation to a man. By July 22 the two sides were deadlocked and Hopkins, in a note to Marshall across the table in the Cabinet Room of 10 Downing Street, wrote: "I feel damn depressed." Hopkins then declared that he and the U.S. Chiefs of Staff would have to consult the President, and this they did. The President telegraphed a reply immediately; the U.S. Chiefs were to seek an alternative operation against the Germans that would involve American troops offensively in 1942.

Churchill and Brooke finally got their way; on July 24 the Americans agreed to launch Torch. This invasion of French Northwest Africa would have an American Supreme Commander—Eisenhower—and a combined Anglo-American staff. The long and dangerous verbal battle over Sledgehammer was at an end; yet it was not wholly a triumph for British strategy. Eisenhower's nomination was of high political importance, although no one cared to acknowledge it at the time; it marked the beginning of the end of Britain's domination of the strategy of the war—and her position as a first-rank world power. But Churchill was, for the moment, content. He would write: "All was therefore agreed and settled in accordance with my long-conceived ideas and those of my colleagues, military and political. This was a great joy to me, especially as it came in what seemed to be the darkest hour." In a talk with his friend Sir Robert Boothby, however, he would later reconsider these words and, in a rather despondent mood, remark that the final verdict of history would take account not only of the victories achieved under his direction, but of the political results which flowed from them. And, he said, "Judged by this standard, I am not sure that I shall be held to have done very well."

Yet the Grand Alliance had survived a critical test, and as Roosevelt wrote to Churchill: "I cannot help feeling that the past week represented a turning point in the whole war and that now we are on our way shoulder to shoulder."

The decision for Torch removed the political need for the raid on Dieppe; it was no longer necessary to show the Americans the danger of a premature invasion. It might seem that Churchill and the British Chiefs of Staff would, therefore, have canceled Jubilee. But they did not. Its objectives—to lure the Luftwaffe to battle, to action-test the new theories of triphibious warfare, and to try to take some of the weight off the Russians —remained. And now a new factor emerged. In a message to Roosevelt on July 27, 1942, Churchill proposed that Jupiter (the plan for an invasion of northern Norway) and Sledgehammer should be used to deceive Hitler about where the Torch convoys were bound. Churchill wrote:

> All depends upon secrecy and speed. . . . Secrecy can only be maintained by deception. For this purpose I am running "Jupiter" and we must also work up "Sledgehammer" with the utmost vigour. These will cover all movements in the United Kingdom. When your troops start for "Torch" everyone except the secret circles should believe that they are going to Suez or (the Persian Gulf), thus explaining (the Torch troops') tropical kit. The Canadian Army here will be fitted for Arctic service. Thus we shall be able to keep the enemy in doubt till the last moment.

The U.S. Chiefs accepted this proposition; the raid on Dieppe would be launched to give teeth to "Overthrow"—a deception campaign to suggest that part of the forces in Britain would do what the LCS had been trying to convince the Germans all summer that they would do: invade France. Whereas before the forces of Jubilee might have been offered up to the gods of grand strategy and high politics, they were now to be offered up to the gods of grand strategy and deception.

The deception and political warfare campaign that climaxed in Overthrow and Dieppe had been going full-blast ever since the late spring. It began with an alarming BBC proclamation to the French nation, and particularly the French on the Channel coast, in what was an early example of the manipulation of the French—and the BBC—for the purposes of deception and political warfare. "The coastal regions of occupied France are likely to become more and more a theatre of war operations. . . . They will inevitably bring with them the gravest dangers for the civilian population," the BBC warned. This broadcast, in concert with the announcement that Britain and Russia had reached a "full understanding . . . with regard to the urgent task of creating a second front in Europe in 1942," created exactly the climate of expectancy that the LCS intended— and that would precipitate Stanley's resignation.

As speculation about an invasion began to mount in the press and on the radio in both Britain and America, the Political Warfare Executive (PWE) and British and American diplomatic agents throughout the world began to spread rumors in a "sibs" campaign (so-called from the Latin *sibilare,* to hiss) to support the fiction. The Vatican "learned" that large-scale operations would take place in the region of the Pas de Calais,

Flanders, Normandy and the Cherbourg peninsula, and was urged to safeguard religious treasures in those zones. MI-6, SOE and the XX-Committee primed their agents with similar reports, while small, fast naval craft and the Commandos made "reconnaissance missions" and actual raids up and down the French coast. Time and time again the BBC went on the air to warn the French against uprising in support of an invasion before they received instructions from London. And all that summer the RAF trailed its coat across the skies of France and Belgium, seeking to bring the Luftwaffe to battle and to give the impression that it was engaged in preparatory operations for an invasion. Altogether the RAF flew a total of 43,000 missions over France and Belgium, and 73,000 missions over England and the Channel—and lost a total of 915 aircraft.

All this activity—tragically for Jubilee—had brought the Germans into a high state of readiness and expectancy when, on the afternoon of August 18, 1942, the troops were embarked. Jubilee had been launched despite all warnings that it would end in disaster. Air Vice Marshal Trafford Leigh-Mallory, of Fighter Command's II Group, the air commander for the operation, warned the planning syndicate: "The troops will be pinned down on the beaches at the very beginning. They'll never get going again, mark my words."

Just before nightfall the Jubilee force slipped its cables at moorings in the small ports along the English coast and headed for the rendezvous where, after dark, it would assemble and make way for Dieppe. As the half-moon rose in the purple of the darkened Channel, over 6000 men in 250 ships considered the single question: Did the Germans know they were coming and did they know where they were to land? Indeed, how much had the Germans learned of the raid on Dieppe?

On July 9, 1942, Hitler, who was directing the summer offensive on the Russian front at his command post in the East Prussian forests, issued a new directive that concerned France. "As a result of our victories, so swiftly achieved," he declared, "England may be faced with the choice either of immediately mounting a major landing in order to create a Second Front or of losing Soviet Russia as a political and military factor. It is highly probable therefore that enemy landings will shortly take place in the areas of C-in-C West." Then Hitler went on to detail where he supposed these landings might occur: ". . . in the first place, the Channel coast, the area between Dieppe and Le Havre, and Normandy, since these sectors can be reached by enemy fighters and also because they lie within range of a large proportion of the invasion craft."

How had the Fuehrer made this surprisingly accurate deduction? He specified three main sources: from agents' reports and other intelligence; from the heavy concentration of invasion craft on the south coast of

England; and from reduced activity by the RAF. Hitler drew the conclusions that any strategist would draw, and impelled by the LCS deception campaign, he assigned very large new formations to the defense of the West—at a time when he was short of men and matériel on the Russian front and needed every German soldier for the campaign there. Thus Overthrow achieved one of its primary objectives by relieving some of the pressures on the Red Army.

But two can play the game of deception, and to deceive the British about the strength of the forces that guarded Dieppe, Field Marshal Gerd von Rundstedt, the C-in-C West, launched "Porto II"—an operation to mislead agents into reporting that the Dieppe area was held by only 1400 low-grade troops of the 110th Infantry Division, a unit that had been weakened in Russia and was resting and refitting on the Channel, when in fact the area was held by the very powerful 302nd Infantry Division—of the same series that would almost decimate the Americans at D-Day on Omaha beach. Moreover, Dieppe itself was not garrisoned, as Porto II said it was, by a mere battalion of raw troops, but by a complete infantry regiment of some 5000 riflemen, some 250 artillerymen and ancillary troops; and immediately available as reserves were no less than three battalions of infantry, an artillery battalion, a tank company, and an entire panzer division six hours' march distant.

Porto II was, apparently, accepted as fact by MI-6. As Churchill wrote: "From available intelligence Dieppe was held only by German low-category troops amounting to one battalion with supporting units making no more than 1400 men in all." Thus MI-6, which was responsible for the reconnaissance, was not only badly tricked but was also badly served by its field agents, who were mainly French. It was not until after the war that Menzies learned how the Germans had managed to deduce that Dieppe was at least one of the targets. The deduction was made as a result of information obtained by Captain Heinz Eckert, an Abwehr counterintelligence officer with special responsibility for penetrating enemy secret services. Eckert was in contact with two French traitors. One was Raoul Kiffer ("Kiki"), a former British agent and member of Interallié, a large and important MI-6 *réseau*, who had been "turned" by the Abwehr; and the other was André Lemoin, a French marine painter whose code name was "Moineau." There was evidence that Kiffer had betrayed British intentions in the earlier combined operation against the great gates of the drydock at St. Nazaire.

Through Kiffer and Lemoin, Eckert was introduced to Madame Jeanette Dumoulins, a member of a Gaulliste *réseau* in the Norman village of Veules-les-Roses about 16 miles from Dieppe. Madame Dumoulins believed Eckert was a Canadian agent—he was introduced as "Mr. Evans"—and she told him she had heard a *message personnel* on the BBC from her husband who had escaped to England. The message was: "Georges will very soon embrace Jeanette." Unsuspectingly, Madame Dumoulins asked Eckert whether he knew the exact time and place of her husband's arrival. Eckert promised to make enquiries in London. Then Madame Dumoulins revealed that the commander of the *réseau* was in touch with an officer of the Organization Todt—German paramilitary construction engineers and workers. This officer, who had an important position at Dieppe, was a fervent anti-Nazi, and was supplying London through the *réseau* with specially requested information on Dieppe's docks, installations, fortifications, the position of shore batteries and the deployment of German units. Eckert now had two important clues: "Georges will very soon embrace Jeanette," a message which he knew was intended to alert the *réseau* to the imminence of a landing operation; and the special request for Dieppe intelligence, indicating that Dieppe might be the target.

That, then, was the Jubilee security situation on the evening of August 14. Jubilee had already been thoroughly compromised. But then a tiny episode occurred to bring the German forces at Dieppe into a state of highest expectancy. It began on the evening of June 22. Two Organization Todt workers attached to the small German garrison around the Barfleur lighthouse on the tip of the Cherbourg peninsula were set upon in a dark lane by assailants as they staggered home to their quarters, three sheets to the wind with calvados. Their throats were cut. Then, at 0340 hours on August 15, four days before the Dieppe raid, a sentry on a light machine gun at a defense post near the Barfleur Light, in the same area where the Organization Todt men had been murdered, heard a movement in the undergrowth. He demanded the password and was greeted by five hand grenades and seventeen rounds of submachine-gun fire. Patrols saw a motor torpedo boat standing offshore, lights signaling, and they discovered the footprints of six pairs of British Commando boots in the sand, together with the scrape marks of a pneumatic assault boat. It had been nothing more than a typical small irritation raid. No one was hurt and the MTB got under way and disappeared—leaving the Germans even more suspicious and alert all the way from Cherbourg to Antwerp.

The timing of this raid would remain a mystery. The British must have known that it would alert the Germans on the very eve of Jubilee. But unless there was a blunder—which was not likely—is it not possible that the British *wanted* the Germans to be alert and nervous along the Channel coast? That, too, was one of the primary objectives of Overthrow; and if it was the reason for the raid (which, curiously, was never made public), it achieved the desired results.

That same day, August 15, the German wireless intelligence service noted a change in the pattern of wireless traffic in southern England, followed by a highly significant wireless silence, and this, it was known from a long study of British wireless behavior, sometimes presaged an attack. At the same time the B-Dienst, the German naval cryptanalytical bureau, broke one of the Royal Navy ciphers in use at Portsmouth and obtained intelligence that indicated the imminence of a large-scale naval movement. Finally, as if to ensure the doom of Jubilee, a German coastal convoy accompanied by sub-chasers was spotted by shore radar in England as the attack force made its way across the Channel, and warnings were flashed to the Jubilee commanders. The messages were received satisfactorily but not in time to prevent one of Jubilee's convoys from colliding with the Germans. A fire fight broke out and the German commander managed to send a message to his headquarters that resulted in a "battle imminent" alert being passed to the garrison commander at Dieppe about forty-five minutes before the first waves of Canadians were due to land.

The troops at Dieppe had been in a high state of alert ever since August 1; and at one of the key beaches to be crossed by the Canadians, they were sleeping in position in their clothes. Sappers had laid 14,000 new mines along the beach and esplanade, and buildings had been razed to give guns better fields of fire. Other buildings, including the famous Casino, had been wired for demolition in the event of a landing, and all telephone switchboards and communications points were being manned by officers (as was usually the case at times of maximum alert) to ensure rapid transmission of information and orders. The Gobes—ancient cave dwellers' homes in the cliffs at both ends of the town—concealed scores of machine-gun and anti-tank gun nests that had not been detected by aerial reconnaissance, and all were in readiness. Disaster was compounding itself, as it so often does once set in motion.

At sea, the forces of Jubilee—the old Jewish word for a time of rejoicing and celebration announced by the sound of a ram's horn—felt their way through a minefield. It was a starlit night, the sea was smooth and the air calm; it was one of the finest nights of the summer. But, as the records show, there was a feeling of certain doom among the Canadians. "Even before we put to sea," wrote a Canadian newspaper correspondent, Ross Munro, "some had an ominous feeling about what was ahead of them on the other side of the Channel. Nobody said anything but many were wondering how the security had been . . . since (Rutter's abandonment). Did the Germans know the Canadians were going to France and were they waiting? This was the question being asked in many minds. They were puzzled, too, why the raid had been decided upon so suddenly." Another correspondent wrote: "One question worried all of us in those last silent twenty minutes after the long, cramped voyage in the starlight. Would the Germans be ready for us? Thinking of it made my stomach flutter. I remembered that old R.A.F. saying, 'I had kittens,' and suddenly knew what it meant. But I hung, in my rising funk, on to the thought that 'the other bastards' were twice as scared as me."

In the chill pre-dawn twilight off the Dieppe coast, the infantry ships lowered their boats, which were filled with the finest men of the finest regiments of Canada. Munro recalled that one sailor leaned over the side "and in a stage whisper said, 'Cheerio, lads, all the best; give the bastards a walloping.' " The sea was glossy with starlight, wrote Munro, and as the assault craft began their run in, they left a "phosphorescent wake that stood out like diamonds on black velvet." At the exact instant and in the exact place the landing craft touched down on the beaches, the machine guns and artillery in the Gobes opened fire. Munro recorded: "We bumped on the beach and down went the ramp and out poured the first infantrymen. They plunged into about two feet of water and machine-gun bullets laced into them. Bodies piled up on the ramp. Some staggered to the beach and fell. . . . They had been cut down before they had a chance to fire a shot."

At this moment the awful reality of Sledgehammer was apparent. Generals in air-cooled offices might conceive plans, syndicates might refine those plans, but here was the moment of truth. With a shattering roar the Casino was blown up; Churchill tanks rumbled out of the LST's and, with but one exception, dug themselves fast into the shingle and were then destroyed by anti-tank guns on the promenade. Most of the 6000 men never got beyond the sea wall; many never disembarked at all before they were killed. The greatest battle since 1940 roared in the clear, clean air overhead; "the whole sky and sea had gone mad with . . . confusion," wrote Munro. A Ju-88 dropped a heavy bomb on the destroyer *Berkley*. It struck slightly forward of amidships and broke her back; the first American ground casualty of the European war—Lieutenant Colonel L. B. Hill-singer—was blown off the bridge onto the forward deck. He lost a foot which, with the shoe still on it, floated alongside the sinking destroyer.

The remnants of the Jubilee force quickly withdrew, and by 5:40 P.M. Rundstedt was able to telegraph Hitler that "No armed Englishman remains on the Continent." The raid was a failure—not even a glorious failure. And the losses were frightful. Of the 6086 men involved in the land operation, 3623 (59.5 per cent) became casualties; of the 4963 Canadians who went in, 3367 (68 per cent) were killed, wounded or captured. Some of the Canadian regiments were virtually wiped out. The RAF suffered 13 per cent casualties and lost 106 planes against German losses of 46; Jubilee's attempt to bloodlet the Luftwaffe had failed. The navy lost a destroyer and 33 landing craft of a fleet that totaled 252 vessels of all sizes, and a total of 550 officers and other ratings were killed, wounded, captured or missing.

German losses were very light. In all the Wehrmacht suffered 591 casualties, of whom 297 were actually killed. And at his headquarters Rundstedt sent in a report on the action to Hitler that ended with the words: "They will not do it like this a second time!" Indeed, they would not.

The Germans were exultant. Dr. Josef Goebbels, the German propagandist, using photographs of the mounds of corpses and the carbonized hulks of the tanks, the lurched artillery and the back-broken hulls of the ships—all reminiscent of Dunkirk—proclaimed a picture of *Festung Europa,* the impregnable Fortress Europe. The German Radio Service, in a broadcast to the United States, announced: "In London they appear to have held as a bluff the German statements about an unbroken defense front along all the coasts of the European continent from North Cape to Biscay. How cruelly then the English had deceived themselves is shown by the miserable outcome of their attack."

For the British, Dieppe was just one more in a long string of defeats. But the Prime Minister, who bore executive responsibility for the disaster, took a more optimistic view. When the raid was repulsed, he and Brooke were in Cairo to shake up the Near East command. In a report from Egypt to the Deputy Prime Minister, Clement Attlee, Churchill wrote on August 21, 1942: "My general impression of Jubilee is that the results fully justified the heavy cost. The large scale air battle alone justified the raid." And later he recorded:

> Looking back, the casualties of this memorable action may seem out of proportion to the results. It would be wrong to judge the episode solely by such a standard. Dieppe occupies a place of its own in the story of the war, and the grim casualty figures must not class it as a failure. It was a costly but not unfruitful reconnaissance-in-force. Tactically it was a mine of experience. It shed revealing light on many shortcomings in our outlook. It taught us to build in good time various new types of craft and appliances for later use. We learnt again the value of powerful support by heavy naval guns in an opposed landing and our bombardment technique, both marine and aerial, was thereafter improved. Above all it was shown that individual skill and gallantry without thorough organisation and combined training would not prevail, and that team work was the secret of success. This could only be provided by trained and organised amphibious formations. All these lessons were taken to heart.
>
> Strategically the raid served to make the Germans more conscious of danger along the whole coast of Occupied France. This helped to hold troops and resources in the West, which did something to take the weight off Russia. Honour to the brave who fell. Their sacrifice was not in vain.

When Brooke heard the news of the extent of the casualties at Dieppe, he grunted—according to Lord Moran, Churchill's personal physician and confidant, who was with the Prime Minister and Brooke in Cairo—"It is a lesson to the people who are clamouring for the invasion of France." Later he was more critical. "This bloody affair," he wrote, "though productive of many valuable lessons, ended the summer's attempt to draw off planes from Russia by trailing Fighter Command's coat over northern France—a gesture that had cost Britain nearly a thousand pilots and aircraft." The British high command had involved an important part of the RAF in diversion and deception for the first, but not the last time. At least the raid served to quench American insistence on a direct, frontal assault against Hitler's Fortress Europe. Of the American high command reaction, Brooke wrote: "Several of the less rigid military planners had been profoundly shaken by the Dieppe casualties, and . . . considered that it would not now be . . . possible to stage any large-scale cross-Channel operation before the summer of 1944." Eisenhower, sadder and wiser about the perils of a headlong leap across the Channel, made the single comment that the Dieppe raid did not promise any easy conquest of the Norman beaches. He was to recall those words on the evening of June 5, 1944—the eve of D-Day.

When the time came to assess the disaster of Dieppe, the debates were full of anger, distress and recrimination. There were those who alleged that the raid had proven nothing more than the dictates of common sense. Yet, for all the intrigue that attended Jubilee and Rutter, some extremely significant lessons were learned, and not the least of these was the effect that Jubilee had upon later thinking by the Germans themselves. Hitler's fears of an invasion of France were reawakened, and despite the bloodbath at Dieppe, he was convinced that the Allies would try again. He ordered work on the Atlantic Wall speeded up, with particular attention paid to the region between the Seine and the Scheldt known as the Pas de Calais. It was, Hitler believed, the most logical point of attack, and the strongest and most numerous of the new defense posts were built there, while OKW was directed to concentrate its most powerful army, the 15th, in the same region. Hitler and OKW were also convinced that the Allies would go for a large port in the initial stages of an invasion, and this wrong conviction colored all their planning. They concentrated their main forces and fortifications in and around Channel ports, leaving only holding forces—albeit formidable holding forces—along the shores between. But Dieppe taught the Allied military strategists that a frontal attack upon a well-defended port was not a feasible act of war, and it was decided that such an operation should not be tried again—not even on D-Day.

Allied military strategists also realized that no invasion of France could be attempted without complete and accurate intelligence of the enemy's defenses, and without complete secrecy surrounding Allied intentions. Hitler must be surprised, and surprise would depend upon successful deception and special means. Furthermore, Dieppe demonstrated the enormous strength of German forces in the West. An invasion could succeed only if Hitler was compelled to disperse his armies throughout Fortress Europe. And that objective could be achieved only through strategy and stratagem.

The disaster at Dieppe proved that there was no shortcut to victory. Churchill's and Brooke's advocacy had been correct; the war would be long and hard, and the march to Berlin would have to begin at the outer reaches of the Nazi empire. For Britain that march would start on the hard, stony Libyan Desert alongside the Mediterranean about 70 miles west of Alexandria. There, at a railway halt for Senussi traders called El Alamein, strategy and stratagem, cryptanalysis, deception and special means would all combine to confound the man who had come to symbolize the seeming omnipotence of Hitler—Erwin Rommel.

5

Alam Halfa

GENERAL ERWIN ROMMEL arrived in North Africa for the first time in mid-February 1941 to form the right claw of a gigantic pincer movement with which Hitler hoped to establish a German empire in the Near East, and to rescue the Italian army from General Sir Archibald Wavell. Ultra revealed Rommel's arrival, as it would reveal his order of battle and his intentions throughout much of the North African campaign. But it did Wavell no good to know what his enemy planned; his armies were too weak. When Rommel's Afrika Korps launched its initial attack on March 24, 1941, he won the first of the victories that made him the legendary "Desert Fox." His panzers destroyed the British 2nd Armoured Division in detail, captured the port of Benghazi, overran and destroyed an Indian Motor Brigade, surrounded the 9th Australian Division in the port of Tobruk, sent the rest of the British army flying in disorder, and, by May 30, Rommel stood at the frontier wire of Egypt.

This defeat, when coupled with the disaster to British arms in Greece and Crete, resulted in Wavell's dismissal from command. He was replaced by General Sir Claude Auchinleck, another highly regarded British soldier; and Rommel's victory caused Churchill to rise in the Commons and declare: "We have a very daring and skilful opponent against us, and, may I say across the havoc of war, a great general."

Little was known about Rommel when Ultra reported his arrival as the C-in-C of the Afrika Korps. Who was this general who, with a mixture of cunning, tenacity, daring and skill, would almost destroy the British in North Africa, defeat an American corps at Kasserine, and defend Normandy against invading Allied armies on D-Day? He was Hitler's most popular and trusted commander, but he would become, in the end, one of his most determined enemies.

Erwin Johannes Eugen Rommel was a Württemberger, born on November 15, 1891, at Heidenheim, a small town on the Swabian Mountain Road near Hellenstein Castle. His father was a schoolmaster and mathematician and his mother was a daughter of the president of the Government of Württemberg. Rommel inherited his father's mathematical ability and showed an early interest in a career in aviation; but his father opposed the idea and, although there was little military tradition in the family, Rommel chose a career in the army. On July 19, 1910, he joined the infantry as an officer cadet and was commissioned without distinction in January 1912. He was a small man, silent, sober, shrewd, businesslike, careful, and had a hard streak in him. At once he showed himself interested in the minutiae of military organization, and, with "a jubilant shout of German warrior youth," he went off to war with the infantry on August 1, 1914. His biographer, Desmond Young, wrote: "From the moment that he first came under fire he stood out as the perfect fighting animal, cold, cunning, ruthless, untiring, quick of decision, incredibly brave." After a stunning victory over the Italians in 1917, the propagandists began to sing his praises and it was said that "Where Rommel is, the front is." He was reputed to possess *Fingerspitzengefühl*—intuition in the fingertips, or a sixth sense—was always "trying to minimise losses by tactics," and was a man who "was body and soul in the war." Rommel was, indeed, a war-lover— exultant in battle, uninterested in all literature save military works, Spartan, celibate, indifferent to food, wine, theater, the pleasures. He was narrow, completely dedicated and apolitical.

At the end of the war Rommel rejoined his regiment at Weingarten, became a member of the 100,000-man Reichswehr permitted Germany under the Versailles Treaty, married, and by 1933 was a major in command of a mountain battalion. He remained apart from the political events that brought Hitler to power and had little to do with the Nazis until he was posted to the War Academy at Potsdam in October 1935. Then he was offered and accepted the job of training a unit of the Hitlerjugend, the Hitler Youth; but he resigned in protest against the creation of "little Napoleons." He returned to normal duties, was promoted to colonel in command of the War Academy at Wiener Neustadt, and, during the occupation of the Sudetenland in October 1938, was appointed by Hitler to command the army battalion responsible for the Fuehrer's personal safety. The reason for Hitler's interest in this unknown officer, who was not a member of the Nazi Party and would not become one, lay in a booklet by Rommel on infantry tactics entitled *Infanterie greift an*. Hitler read and admired it, and Rommel entered the Fuehrer's official family.

At first Rommel saw much that was admirable in Hitler; the Fuehrer was without fear, his capacity for military matters seemed close to genius, and he had a magnetic, even hypnotic power. His memory was remarkable—whole pages and chapters of books, once read, were etched upon his mind—and his grasp of statistics was particularly strong. For his part, Hitler admired Rommel for his loyalty and his ruthless execution of every order. Hitler found him refreshingly direct after dealing with the slippery generals in the German General Staff. Consequently, he promoted Rommel from colonel to—within a few months' time—general, and rewarded him with the Knight's Cross of the Iron Cross for his victories during the battle for France. In that campaign Rommel had commanded the 7th ("Phantom") Panzer Division and had captured the Admiral of the French Navy (North), four other admirals, one corps commander, four French divisional commanders and their staffs, 277 cannon and 64 anti-tank guns, 458 tanks and armored cars, some 5000 trucks, 2000 horse and mule wagons and 400 buses; his men had taken 97,468 prisoners, shot down 52 aircraft, captured 15 more on the ground and destroyed 12 others. Incredibly, Rommel's casualties were only 48 officers killed and 77 wounded, 526 other ranks killed and 1252 wounded; three officers, 34 sergeants and above and 229 other ranks had been reported missing, and he had lost only 42 tanks. Now he wore the copper-brown insignia of the Afrika Korps—a palm tree on a swastika—and his mission was to conquer Cairo and take the Suez Canal.

His initial drive for the Valley of the Nile sent the British into full retreat, and all during the summer of 1941, Rommel stood at the Egyptian frontier, awaiting permission from the Fuehrer to march on Cairo. But the order never came and the summer passed quietly. The British, meanwhile, were planning "Crusader," a counteroffensive against Rommel to begin November 18, 1941, which Churchill hoped would become a victory comparable to both Blenheim and Waterloo. Crusader was to open with a murder—Rommel's murder. The British intention was to destroy Rommel's main force of panzers, relieve Tobruk—the cluster of white houses and sheds that had become a British fortress at Rommel's rear—and wrest Libya and Tripolitania from the Italian empire. Then, the Army of the Nile, having ejected the Axis from Africa, was to march east and north to guard the Levant against a German drive upon Arabia through the mountain passes of Russian and Persian Caucasia. The forces on both sides were more or less evenly matched, with armored superiority lying with Rommel and air superiority with Auchinleck. Auchinleck's only hope of achieving this new Waterloo was surprise; if he could assassinate Rommel, the chaos in the Axis command would give the British that surprise. It was the first of the British attempts to murder Rommel; it would not be the last.

One night that October, a Wellington bomber flew out across the silvered Mediterranean, and then turned toward Cyrene, the old city of Hannibal. Once overland, the captain let his undercarriage down to slow his airspeed and into the night leaped a British intelligence agent, J. E. Haselden, an Arabist in the mold of Lawrence. Haselden, who could speak the dialects of the Senussi as well as he could speak English, buried his parachute in the camel-scrub desert and put on the *galabieh,* the Senussi's robes. He dyed his skin nut-brown, and then, after daybreak when the camel trains were on the move again, walked into Beda Littoria. It was here that Rommel was reported to have his headquarters. Posing as a trader in ostrich feathers, Haselden spent several weeks in the vicinity of a large, white-walled villa which was obviously a German command post. He watched Rommel go in and out in his armored cabriolet. There was a large signals detachment in the grounds beneath the cypresses and a heavy guard around the villa. The activity, the comings and goings of officers and despatch riders—all suggested that this was Rommel's headquarters. Haselden wirelessed his reports to Cairo.

There, on the basis of Haselden's reports, the Director of Military Intelligence, General Francis W. de Guingand, planned a raid on the villa with Colonel R. E. Laycock, the Commando chief in the Middle East. Their plan was for six officers and fifty-three Commandos to land near Beda Littoria from two submarines, the *Torbay* and the *Talisman.* They had four missions: to kill or capture Rommel; to attack and destroy the Italian army headquarters at Cyrene; to attack and seize the papers and ciphers of Italian intelligence headquarters at Appollonia and kill the staff; and to cut all telephone and telegraph communications with these targets and seize all Enigma-related material.

The submarines surfaced off Beda Littoria in driving rain and rough seas after dark on November 17. On the beach Haselden made light signals in the darkness to guide the Commandos' rubber boats to the shore. They formed up on the beach, sodden with rain and spray, and moved up to a ridge overlooking the villa. There, at half-past ten that night, they rested while a sapper destroyed telephone lines leading down to the villa. Then, led by Lieutenant Colonel Geoffrey Keyes, a three-man assault team pushed through a hedge at the back of the villa into the garden. Moving silently and quickly—the rain muffling their sounds—they went to the front of the villa, ran up the steps and pushed open the door. Almost immediately they were confronted by a German officer in a steel helmet and overcoat. Keyes menaced him with his tommy gun but the German seized the muzzle and tried to wrest it away. Keyes drew his knife to kill the German silently but one of his men shot him with a revolver as they wrestled between the first and second doors of the entrance. The three men then rushed into the hall, which was dimly lit, and saw another German running down the stone staircase. One of the Commandos directed a burst of fire at him, which missed, and the German ran back up the stairs. Then Keyes noticed a light beneath a door. He flung it open, saw some ten Germans putting on steel helmets, fired two or three shots from his pistol into them, and a Commando threw a grenade. But at that moment, one of the Germans fired and a bullet struck Keyes just over the heart. He fell and died as he was carried out through the front door and laid in the wet grass. One of the other would-be assassins was shot in the leg by a Commando in the shadows who was playing covering fire on the door.

Both this and the other connected raids were failures. The only casualties inflicted upon the Germans were three supply colonels and a soldier killed at the villa. The targets at Cyrene and Appollonia were not attacked, and the only damage done was to a petrol supply point, which was blown up. The entire British party was lost, except for Colonel Laycock and a sergeant, who lay up in a wadi until they were rescued by the spearheads of Crusader. As for Rommel, the gloomy villa among the cypresses had only been his temporary headquarters and he had moved some weeks before to another headquarters at Gambut, about 100 miles away down the coast. The Commandos could not have caught the Desert Fox even there; he was celebrating his birthday with his wife and some friends at Rome when the Crusader counteroffensive began—the first of three curious absences from his command posts on each of three major British attacks during the course of the war. When he returned to meet Crusader, despite his anger at discovering that none of his would-be assassins wore any insignia that identified them as enemies, he directed that Keyes be given a Christian burial with full military honors and ordered his chaplain to make a thirty-six-hour journey for the ceremonial. He had one of his carpenters make crosses of cypress to place on the graves of the British and German dead and also ordered some young cypresses planted as memorials. As a last gesture, he instructed that photographs be taken of the ceremony and of Keyes's grave and sent to the young Commando's parents. This chivalrous act marked Rommel's entire conduct of the war in the desert, and did not go unnoticed by his adversaries.

Crusader lasted until December 20, 1941. The fortress of Tobruk, which had become a symbol of British resistance, was relieved, and Rommel was driven back to the point where he had started his offensive in March—El Agheila, on the Gulf of Sidra. But in January 1942 he attacked again, and by June, despite the significant success of Crusader, British troops in the desert had become so mesmerized by Rommel that Auchinleck felt compelled to issue this edict to his commanders:

> There exists a real danger that our friend Rommel is becoming a kind of magician or bogey-man to our troops, who are talking far too much about him. He is by no means a superman, although he is undoubtedly very energetic and able. Even if he were a superman, it would still be highly undesirable that our men should credit him with supernatural powers.
>
> I wish you to dispel by all possible means the idea that Rommel represents something more than an ordinary German general. The important thing now is to see that we do not always talk of Rommel when we mean

the enemy in Libya. We must refer to "the Germans" or "the Axis powers" or "the enemy" and not always keep harping on Rommel.

Please ensure that this order is put into immediate effect, and impress upon all Commanders that, from a psychological point of view, it is a matter of the highest importance.

No sooner had Auchinleck issued his command than Rommel struck again, an attack that destroyed Auchinleck's career and dangerously embarrassed Churchill. It was a disaster for which the Ultra security precautions bore much responsibility.

In the fluidity of desert fighting, and the omnipresence of wireless intelligence eavesdroppers, it was decided that none of the generals at the front would be allowed to see, possess or even know of Ultra; the danger that they might be captured was too great. Within GHQ Middle East near Cairo only three men were allowed to read Ultras—Auchinleck, the theater commander; his Director of Military Operations; and de Guingand, the Director of Military Intelligence. General Sir Neil Ritchie, the commander of the 8th Army, was not allowed to see Ultras; if the contents of an Ultra were of importance to his battle planning, either Auchinleck acquainted him with the intelligence in a personal letter, which did not reveal the source and which was accompanied by instructions to destroy by fire after reading, or de Guingand flew to the army commander's headquarters to brief Ritchie personally, again without mentioning Ultra. This procedure was, under the circumstances, the only one possible at that time, but it carried with it the danger that Ritchie might reject the information in the belief that his own, local intelligence was better and more up to date. And that, precisely, was how Britain lost her armored army in the desert between May 28 and June 13, 1942, while Churchill was at the White House debating Sledgehammer and the future conduct of the war with Roosevelt.

Ultra had given Auchinleck and Ritchie ample knowledge of Rommel's intention to attack, and of his objectives. On the eve of his offensive, Rommel issued an order of the day to all forces under his command in which he revealed that it was his intention to destroy the British armored army of some six hundred tanks, capture Tobruk, and then deliver a decisive attack upon the 8th Army. As Auchinleck cabled Churchill: "We had foreseen this attack and were ready for it." When Rommel's panzers struck across the camel-scrub desert by bright moonlight, Ritchie's armor and artillery inflicted such losses upon them that Auchinleck, after a week of the most ferocious fighting between British and German forces so far in the war, radioed Ritchie with an order to destroy Rommel and his army. But Rommel got away, regrouped and crouched for a second engagement. This time, however, he did not propose to attack but to lure the British armored army, which now had some 325 tanks left, into an ambush.

He laid his 88-mm cannon among the ridges around the little desert township and airfield of El Adem, and then adopted the old tactic of Jem Mace, the great pugilist: "Let 'em come to ye, they'll beat theirselves."

Rommel committed his plan to a signal of information to OKW which he did nightly, the signal was unbuttoned at Bletchley and was flashed by Winterbotham's SLU to GHQ Cairo. Auchinleck read it and ordered de Guingand to fly to Ritchie's headquarters and warn the army commander. He arrived on or about June 11, and, according to de Guingand, relayed the Ultra to Ritchie without revealing the source, as was usual. Ritchie, who had been deputy Chief of Staff to Auchinleck at GHQ, should have guessed that it derived from cryptanalysis, although he had not been privy to Ultra at GHQ. Whatever the case, he did not act upon de Guingand's information, possibly because he thought that Rommel's deception and cover operations had influenced Auchinleck. On what became known as "Black Saturday"—June 13, 1942—Ritchie ordered some 300 of his tanks to attack; they ran straight into Rommel's ambush and within half a day the 88-mm cannon had wiped out 230 of them. The battle was lost in those few hours.

Rommel's panzers then leaped forward, knifed through the British positions, captured the fortress of Tobruk together with its garrison of 33,000 men, and turned eastward toward the Egyptian frontier. In what was nothing less than a flight, the 8th Army withdrew in disorder to El Alamein. In all, Rommel inflicted 75,000 casualties upon Ritchie's army, Ritchie was relieved of command, and the few tanks of the armored army that were left withdrew into Egypt. At Cairo, British government offices burned their secret paper in such quantities that the day became known as "Ash Wednesday," the British fleet prepared to withdraw into the Red Sea, and Mussolini arrived in North Africa with a white horse, bands, and the Sword of Islam, ready to make a triumphant march into Cairo. Hitler made Rommel, "beloved of the nation," the youngest field marshal in German history. OKW struck campaign medals for the occupation of Egypt and Suez, German propagandists prepared the Egyptian people for their "liberation," and the Reichsbank printed vast quantities of occupation currency. It was one of the most staggering defeats suffered by the British army in its modern history.

The British rout in North Africa marked the lowest ebb in the tide of Allied military misfortunes. Although Rommel was finally stopped at El Alamein, the threat to Egypt and the Suez Canal remained; while all along the Russian front, the Wehrmacht, in a sweeping and powerful summer offensive, was once again on the move. It was left to Churchill to restore the confidence of the Grand Alliance and, at the same time, to press for cooperation in the pursuit of his strategy for turning defeat into victory. He had succeeded in persuading the Americans to abandon Sledgehammer in favor of Torch; but securing Stalin's cooperation was another matter. The Russians believed that they had been promised a Second Front in 1942; and of what use to them was an invasion of North Africa? The Germans were besieging the city of Leningrad, were only fifty miles from Moscow, had crossed the Don, were standing at the gates of Stalingrad.

On August 12, 1942, Churchill, with Cadogan, Brooke and the other Chiefs of Staff, flew to Moscow to explain why the western Allies could not invade Europe in 1942, and to brief Stalin on Torch and its strategical implications. It was the first time the two men had met, and it was bound to be a disturbing and even dangerous encounter. Stalin was not likely to forget that Britain had sent troops to Russia after the First World War to put down the Bolshevik revolution, or that a British agent, Robert Bruce-Lockhart, had been involved in an attempt to assassinate Lenin. Moreover, Stalin was convinced that Britain and America were conniving to let Russia and Germany bleed each other into exhaustion before they attempted to invade the continent. Churchill, for his part, was as much preoccupied with informing Stalin as he was with deceiving the Germans, for he knew that links existed between the Russian and German general staffs, and believed that if it was to Stalin's advantage, the plans of the western Allies would almost certainly reach Hitler.

The two men met in a bare room at the Kremlin beneath the state portrait of Lenin; and Stalin, who wore a lilac-colored tunic with his trousers stuffed into the tops of his boots, was cold, crude and calculating. Colonel Ian Jacob, one of Churchill's military secretaries, would note in his diary: "I should say that to make friends with Stalin would be equivalent to making friends with a python." He asked through his interpreter why Britain was "so afraid of the Germans," and Churchill, bristling at this oblique accusation of cowardice, rose to the defense of his strategy. The Russians had *not* been promised a Second Front in 1942, he explained; Britain was making plans for a diversion that year—the Dieppe raid—not an invasion. If the western powers were to land in France, they must do so with the intention of staying, and that would be impossible in 1942. But, Churchill went on, America and Britain were preparing "for a very great operation in 1943." He did not say what this operation was, but he did leave Stalin with the impression that it would be a cross-Channel attack. Churchill was dissembling; the western powers had made no such agreement. But perhaps, with his penchant for the use of stratagems and special means when military might was not available, he was trying to plant the seeds of a major strategic deception scheme which the LCS would execute in northern France in 1943 to draw off German strength from Russia and Italy—a scheme to be called "Cockade."

Churchill then turned to the operation which the Allies did intend for 1942—Torch. The western Allies would land in North Africa, he explained, while holding the Germans in France by deception. Torch, he said, must be considered in conjunction with the 1943 operation. Stalin appeared interested, and when the meeting ended, Churchill had the impression that "at least the ice was broken and a human contact had been established"; he felt that he had, as Cadogan would write, "cast off the millstone of (Roosevelt's) half-promise of a Second Front in 1942." He was wrong. At their next meeting the following evening, Stalin renewed his attack and directly accused the British of cowardice. It was too much for Churchill. He "burst into a torrent of oratory," speaking so rapidly that the interpreters could not keep up with him. The meeting ended abruptly when Stalin held up his hand and declared: "I do not understand the words, but by God I like your spirit!"

The following day was taken up by an exchange of memoranda between the two leaders, and the debate continued with written rather than spoken words. Churchill would not budge and once again explained his stand; ". . . all the talk about an Anglo-American invasion of France this year has misled the enemy, and has held large enemy forces on the French Channel coast," he wrote. Such an invasion was impossible, but the threat must be maintained; "The wisest course is to use 'Sledgehammer' as a blind for 'Torch,' and proclaim 'Torch' when it begins as the Second Front. This is what we ourselves mean to do."

Churchill was anxious to be off; he saw little hope of winning Stalin over to his point of view. But when he called on the Premier the evening of the 15th, intending only to say goodbye—he was to fly to Cairo at dawn the next morning—Stalin extended an invitation. They went to his flat in the Kremlin and, while Stalin's red-haired daughter, Svetlana, served them dinner, talked for the next six hours. Stalin now spoke favorably of Torch and agreed to cooperate with Jupiter, Churchill's pet project to invade northern Norway. Churchill, in return, said he felt able to *promise* an invasion of northern France in 1943; and Stalin said he would hold him to that promise. Was Churchill still dissembling to win Stalin's cooperation, or had Stalin, using food, wine and cajolery where insult had failed, exacted an unwise, and unauthorized, concession from the Prime Minister? In either case, the consequences would be serious, for Stalin would be forced to employ even more devious means in the future—including an apparent attempt to betray Torch and maneuvers to drive a wedge through the Anglo-American alliance—to get around the clever and stubborn Churchill.

With dawn not far away, Churchill left the Russian leader, and after a short rest, boarded his aircraft to fly to Cairo. He had persuaded his allies that the road to Berlin must begin in North Africa, and it was his intention to give the battered British army in Egypt the biggest shaking up in its modern history. Another blow to British pride would reach him in Cairo— news of the disaster at Dieppe; but for the moment his primary concern was Rommel. At a conference at GHQ he walked up and down the room, declaiming: "Rommel, Rommel, Rommel! What else matters but beating him!" He sacked Auchinleck and most of his staff, except de Guingand, and then appointed two of Brooke's favorite generals to replace Auchinleck and Ritchie. The C-in-C of the Middle East became General Sir Harold Alexander, and General Sir Bernard Montgomery was made C-in-C of the 8th Army. They were an outstanding, beautifully matched pair: Alexander, the strategist and the Cavalier; Montgomery, the tactician and the Roundhead. Their objective, the Prime Minister told Alexander and Montgomery at a meeting beneath the Great Pyramid at Giza, where GHQ was located, was not to hole the Desert Fox but to kill him. That, they knew from Ultra, would be less difficult than the British public supposed, for when Rommel arrived at the frontier wire his army was exhausted and he had only twelve tanks left, while nearly one thousand of the most modern tanks were on the high seas en route to the 8th Army.

During the conference at Giza, Churchill and his commanders debated the reasons for Rommel's success, his audacity and personal courage apart. He had never had a superiority of force, although his tanks were better than Britain's. At most, he had commanded fewer than 100,000 men, of whom about half were Italians of varying courage and fighting ability, while British forces in the theater numbered some 750,000 men in uniform. What were the secrets of Rommel's victories?

Colonel Frank Bonner Fellers was the American military attaché at Cairo whose mission it was to inform Washington of British military and diplomatic plans and operations in the Middle East. Fellers was privy to almost all the information he required; he was a frequent visitor to GHQ and to British field units, where he was received with cordiality and trust. But when—after Tobruk—the British started to investigate the security of their wireless communications to establish whether any of their ciphers had been compromised, attention began to fasten upon Fellers. The colonel was punctilious about security; he always filed his messages to Washington in the "Black Code," a cipher used by American military attachés throughout the world and thought to be quite secure. But a small attack on a German wireless post at Tel-el-Eisa in July 1942 revealed that the Black Code was thoroughly compromised by both the German and Italian cryptographic services. In the raid, documents were obtained which showed that the Black Code had not been penetrated by cryptanalysis but by theft. An Italian working at the American Embassy in Rome, who was an agent of SIM (the Italian secret service) and an expert in lockpicking, had managed to get into the safe of the U.S. military attaché, Colonel Norman E. Fiske, in August 1941. He obtained the Black Code, photographed it and then returned it. SIM's chief, Cesare Amé, provided the Abwehr with a copy and thenceforward the Germans were able to read much of the military traffic throughout the world, including that of Colonel Fellers.

It had been a valuable harvest. From about late September of 1941 until August of 1942, Fellers had transmitted to Washington an almost daily report on British strength, reinforcements, equipment, morale and plans not only in Egypt and Libya but also throughout the eastern Mediterranean and the Middle East command. His reports had included studies of commanders' abilities, reputations, tactics; the movements of convoys and warships; the locations, equipment and serviceability of tank and air squadrons. He delivered these reports each day to the Egyptian Telegraph Office in central Cairo; and each day, as they were flashed through the ether to Washington, every cipher group that was legible was taken down, transcribed and then passed to Rommel and OKW. David Kahn, the American historian of cryptography, wrote: ". . . what messages they were! They provided Rommel with undoubtedly the broadest and clearest picture of enemy forces and intentions available to any Axis commander throughout the war."

When Fellers was informed, as he was in August 1942, that his traffic was being read by the Germans, he was deeply upset. The U.S. cryptographic agency provided him with a new cipher (as it did with all military attachés using the Black Code), but at the request of the British he used this cipher only for his most secret traffic. He continued to transmit information of a less secret nature in the Black Code. For the British saw in this channel of communication a means for passing deceptive information to the enemy.

In the same raid on the German wireless outpost at Tel-el-Eisa that had disclosed the penetration of the Black Code, the British discovered another of the secrets of Rommel's desert victories—wireless intelligence, the whispers of modern war. Throughout the desert campaign both British and German commanders relied heavily on wireless communications; the great distances involved, combined with the high mobility of the battles, made wireless—and particularly voice communications—an essential weapon of desert warfare. But both sides were sometimes careless in the use of this vital yet vulnerable communications system. And both sides could often tell with great accuracy what the enemy was preparing from chatter on the radio telephone. Captain Alfred Seebohm was the commanding officer of Rommel's Horch—wireless intelligence—Company, and he had become particularly proficient in listening to wireless whispers from the British camp. He had developed an extremely sharp sense of what was normal and what was abnormal from listening in to the pattern of British wireless traffic. A snatch of radiotelephony here, some high-speed Morse there; tank commanders talking between themselves on the radio here, an artillery commander speaking with his gunpits over there; military policemen directing traffic here, RAF ground liaison officers calling up for air support there—all served, when sifted and evaluated, as an extremely accurate portrait of British plans and the order of battle on the front lines and, frequently, far to the rear. The weakness of wireless intelligence, however, lay in the expertise of the eavesdroppers themselves; if one of them was ill, on leave, or a battlefield casualty, it took many months of training to replace him. It followed, therefore, that if Seebohm's company could be destroyed as an entity, then for most practical purposes Rommel would be without reliable wireless intelligence.

The British wireless intelligence system, known as the Y service, located Seebohm's post on the El Alamein front in a group of sun-blasted hills overlooking the Mediterranean at Tel-el-Eisa, "the Hill of Jesus." It had not been possible to locate the company precisely, the precondition for an aerial attack. Therefore a ground assault was necessary and the task fell to the 2/48th Battalion of the Australian 9th Infantry Division, commanded by Lieutenant Colonel H. H. Hammer, a sheep farmer from Victoria, South Australia, who was known as "Hard-as-nails Hammer."

The assault was set for July 10, 1942, and it would be part of a much larger attack in which two divisions with tank and artillery support were to clean the enemy out of the high ground of the Tel-el-Eisa area. With great stealth and all possible silence the assault force moved into position. Seebohm's company was thought to be located in the vicinity of a hill that was called "Trig 33" on the military maps; and to surprise the 100-odd men thought to be with Seebohm, Hammer had ordered that there be no preliminary artillery barrage.

The silent advance began at 0340 A.M. on July 10. It was an intensely dark night, but suddenly an aircraft dropped a parachute flare immediately over the heads of the assault force. The night was lit like day. The men froze, expecting a terrific outburst of fire. But none came: the 7th Bersaglieri Regiment of the Italian army, which was holding the perimeter around Seebohm's company, was asleep. The Australians, who had shod their boots with sacking to muffle any noise of movement, worked their way along a ridge on either side of the crest of "Trig 33." And when at dawn the artillery opened a drumfire in support of the Australians, the Bersaglieri found themselves surrounded. Their commanding officer was captured and some of the prisoners taken were still in bed.

The Australians came across Seebohm's company on Tel-el-Eisa itself. Seebohm and his men were not surprised. Alerted by the bombardment, they had formed a defensive perimeter around their vehicles—armored command trucks stuffed with wireless equipment and mounted with antennae. The Australians charged with fixed bayonets out of a smoke screen laid around the site by the artillery, and the post was captured only after very violent hand-to-hand fighting. Seebohm and his men had made some attempt to destroy their equipment, but they had not succeeded; the Australians' charge had been too sudden. When the battle was over, some one hundred of the highly trained men of Seebohm's company lay dead among the rocks. The others were captured, including Seebohm himself, who had gone down fighting and was badly wounded. He was taken to Cairo where he died, silently, having resisted all attempts to make him talk.

Experts made their way to the site to examine the captured material. It was quite the most important intelligence coup of the entire North African campaign. All Seebohm's records fell intact into British hands, including much detail about the penetration of the Black Code and the security leak in Cairo through Colonel Fellers, which was quickly plugged. But even more important, the documents found at Tel-el-Eisa revealed that a great deal of the foxiness of the Desert Fox was due entirely to good German wireless intelligence and poor British wireless security. The British had given much of their operational planning in the forward areas away to Rommel themselves. It was a significant discovery. As Brigadier Walter Scott, the wireless expert who was in charge of the intelligence party that examined the captured documents, recalled: "The consequences of this capture were very far-reaching, for the rest of the North African campaign, for the Sicilian and Italian campaigns, and then for the invasion. It enabled us to build powerful forces at all points thereafter without giving the fact away, which we had done in the past."

Scott called for widespread reforms in wireless security, and he was heeded. New disciplines were imposed for the use of radiotelephones, call signs, cryptographic procedures, voice codes, wireless silences for units on the move; all the sources of intelligence that had hitherto provided Rommel with the stuff of victory were now frozen in a wall of silence and discretion. The British formed new companies to monitor the security procedures of their own troops, and severe disciplinary action was taken against offenders. But above all, the discoveries on "the Hill of Jesus" made Rommel very vulnerable to wireless deception. When the new Horch Company arrived, it had neither the ability nor the experience to separate truth from fiction. Thus the hunt for the Desert Fox began to turn in favor of the British as they took care that Rommel heard only the whispers they wanted him to hear.

Booty captured in the raid on Seebohm's company revealed that Rommel had yet a third source of battlefield intelligence: the Kondor mission— two German spies and a string of curious sub-agents whose activities centered around a houseboat on the Nile. And when the British security authorities moved in to put a stop to those activities, they would uncover an overripe Durrellian melodrama.

The Kondor mission was headed by John Eppler, a twenty-eight-year-old Abwehr agent born of German parents at Alexandria, a young man who had made the Haj and was therefore a Muslim. His mother married an Egyptian lawyer when his father died. Eppler had grown up as a rich Cairene, while keeping his allegiances to Germany. He was recruited into the Abwehr just before the outbreak of the Second World War by a Vietnamese prostitute in Beirut, the famous Su Yan; and having served at the Tirpitzufer on a number of schemes to raise a Jihad—a Holy War— against the British in Arabia, he was selected for the Kondor mission when Rommel asked for a team of dependable German agents with knowledge of Cairo to go to the Egyptian capital to spy.

Eppler arrived at Tripoli in April 1942 on the first stage of his journey to Cairo, bringing with him two American Hallicrafter transceivers and £50,000 in British five- and one-pound notes. He also had a copy of *Rebecca,* for the Kondor mission's cipher was based on the Daphne du Maurier novel. The cryptographic principle involved in the use of the novel was not a new one, but it was simple and impenetrable—unless the attacker knew the system. In the case of Kondor, Eppler would base his cipher on the prearranged use of certain pages of the novel on certain days. His listening posts, including Seebohm's Horch Company, would use similar copies in their possession to decipher it.

The second member of the mission was Peter Monkaster, a tall, slim, blond German oil mechanic who had spent much of his life in East Africa. The two men left for Cairo on May 11, 1942, from the Oasis of Gialo, traveling by captured British vehicles across the naked desert. They had an Afrika Korps escort, and their navigator was the Hungarian Arabist Count Ladislaus de Almaszy, an explorer who had spent many years in the Libyan Desert looking for the long-lost Oasis of Zerazura—the place toward which the Army of Cambyses, 10,000 men strong, had marched westward from the Nile Delta never to be heard of again. Almaszy knew the route across the 2000 miles that the Kondor mission would have to take to infiltrate Egypt and Cairo from the south. The vehicles and men were disguised as a British reconnaissance unit, in case they were spotted by a British patrol or aircraft; and about three weeks after leaving Gialo— around the end of May or the beginning of June—the Kondor mission was in British territory. The count and the Afrika Korps escort turned back, Eppler and Monkaster changed into civilian clothes and entered Assyut, a town 300 miles south of Cairo that was only lightly guarded by the British and Egyptian authorities. Although they were stopped, both could speak English—Eppler as an Egyptian and Monkaster as an American. After examining their papers, which showed Eppler to be an Anglo-Egyptian merchant and Monkaster an American oil-rig mechanic, a British patrol allowed them to proceed to the railway station. They caught the evening train to Cairo and there they employed an Arab to carry their suitcases, containing the money and the wireless sets, through the Anglo-Egyptian checkpoint at Cairo Station.

Once in Cairo, Eppler and Monkaster settled into a small *pension* in Garden City, a suburb, and Eppler immediately began to seek friends he could trust. Among those he found was Hekmeth Fahmy, one of Egypt's leading *danseuses du ventre*—belly dancers. Fahmy, who was violently anti-British and an Arab nationalist, lived on a houseboat on the Nile at Zamalek; and it was there that she and Eppler went when she had finished her night's work at the Kit Kat Cabaret.

Mlle Fahmy soon revealed that she was a spy working against the British for the Muslim Brotherhood and the Free Officers' Movement of the Egyptian army, and that her main source of information was a "Major Smith" of British GHQ in Cairo—her lover. In turn, Eppler told her that he was a German agent working for Rommel. At this revelation, Mlle Fahmy arranged to let him see the contents of Major Smith's briefcase while she and Smith were in bed. She also agreed to put Eppler in touch with a friend, General Aziz-el-Masri, a powerful and passionate anglophobe who had been relieved as Chief of Staff of the Egyptian army at British insistence.

Eppler and Monkaster rented another houseboat close to Fahmy's, hid one of the Hallicrafters in a church run by an Austrian priest at Zamalek, installed the second on the houseboat, and then went to work. Fahmy was as good as her word; when Major Smith visited her, generally in the afternoons, Eppler and Monkaster read the contents of his briefcase and learned much about British strength, disposition and intentions. Then, using the *Rebecca* cipher, they reported either to Seebohm's wireless intelligence company or to the Wehrmacht's listening post at Athens, each night around midnight.

Eppler met General Aziz-el-Masri by appointment at a dentist's surgery, and the general, impressed by the mission's credentials, intelligence, money—and the fact that Eppler and Monkaster worked for Rommel—listened to their proposals for espionage against the British and their plans to raise a Jihad when Rommel launched his great offensive to take Cairo and Alexandria. Aziz-el-Masri agreed to cooperate. He arranged a meeting between the Kondor mission and Sheikh Hassan-el-Banna, the watchmaker-turned-prophet who had founded the Muslim Brotherhood and was now known as the Supreme Guide. A strange, possessed figure who wore a long red cloak that hid all of his face but his eyes, the sheikh is said to have made 1500 speeches a year in proclaiming the mission of the Brotherhood, demanding that all true Muslims abandon material possessions, adhere strictly to the Koran, and engage in exercises to obtain moral and physical perfection and the regeneration of the Muslim society. He wrote patriotic poetry, campaigned against the unveiling of women, went from door to door before dawn rousing people for prayer, and established branches of the Brotherhood throughout Egypt to build mosques, give courses in physical training, and to study eschatology, the science of the four last things—death, judgment, heaven and hell.

By the outbreak of the war the Brotherhood had become an organization of patriots possessed by a fanatical religious ardor who wanted to expel all foreigners—particularly the British—and establish a theocratic state. They took their initiates' oath with the Koran in one hand and a pistol in the other, swearing to be loyal, obedient and secret. Gradually Sheikh Hassan-el-Banna had attracted to his banner Muslims from all classes, and the Brotherhood had also been infiltrated by the Free Officers' Movement, an anti-British nationalist conspiracy within the Egyptian army headed by two young officers, Gamal Abdel Nasser and Anwar el-Sadat. Both were to become Presidents of Egypt after the group they led overthrew the monarchy of Farouk and, in June 1953, established the Egyptian Republic.

It was Sadat who met Eppler and Monkaster. "We examined their documents," wrote the future President of Egypt, "which proved beyond doubt that they were what they purported to be." The three men spent several hours discussing how a successful revolt of the Egyptian army might be raised. Sadat said to Eppler: "Now is the time to strike. We can turn the Delta into a blood-bath if we rise now. Please tell that to your superiors, and urge them to be ready to back us." So confident were the conspirators that Rommel would soon be in Cairo that Sadat found him a conqueror's residence—an imposing mansion on the rue des Pyramides, close to the Mena House Hotel.

It was now about the middle of June 1942, the 8th Army had retreated into Egypt, and the conspirators prepared for their Jihad as the smoke of "Ash Wednesday" hung over Cairo. But the British security authorities learned that a Jihad was planned, and embarked on a large security operation to prevent it. It was a time of extraordinary tension when suspicions were high everywhere.

Eppler now made a mistake. It was not a very serious one, and but for the tensions of the times it might not have been noticed. Dressed in the uniform of a British captain, he went to the Turf Club for a drink—and to get the latest gossip. But he had run out of the Egyptian pounds that he had brought with him, and believing that English currency was still the legal tender it had been when he was living in Cairo, he paid for his drink with a British pound note. The bartender accepted the note, for it could be exchanged at the British Paymaster's Office for Egyptian currency. After his drink at the Turf Club, Eppler went on to the bar on the roof of the Metropolitan Hotel, the haunt of newspaper correspondents. There, again, he paid for his drinks with British notes. He also picked up a bar girl, who called herself Yvette, and bought her a considerable amount of expensive champagne—once again paying with British currency. Then he took her back to his houseboat for the night. In the morning, he paid her £20 in British five-pound notes, and asked her to come and see him again. She agreed, and then left.

Eppler had made his second mistake; Yvette was an agent of the Jewish Agency, which then worked with MI-6. She reported the encounter to her employer and said she thought Eppler was a German because he spoke "with a Saarland accent." She also thought he was a spy because "he is very nervous and he has too much money." Her employer told her to keep in touch with Eppler, and made arrangements with MI-6 to keep the houseboat under surveillance. An Egyptian dressed as a beggar came to squat in the dust at the end of the towpath, and it was this beggar who noted Fahmy's visits to Eppler's houseboat, as well as the visits of a British army major in uniform to Fahmy's houseboat.

Two or three days after their first meeting, Yvette called on Eppler again. There was no reply at the saloon door when she knocked. But the door was open and she went in. The room, she noted, was littered with bottles, full ashtrays, stale food and dirty dishes—the remnants of a party. Both Eppler and Monkaster were fast asleep in their cabins. Yvette then began to look the boat over, and in a small room she found a desk with a book and some notepaper on it—no more. But she noticed the book's title—*Rebecca*—and saw that the notepaper was covered with gridded squares and six-letter groups. Yvette knew enough about espionage to realize that this might be some form of cipher, and suspecting that Eppler and Monkaster were spies, she let the pages of the book fall open, noted the numbers of the "used" pages, and took down the first of the cipher groups on each line of the notepaper. Then she left—to be arrested and taken to a police station for questioning; the beggar who had been watching the boat had signaled her departure to some policemen and they, not knowing that she had connections with MI-6, detained her on suspicion.

Meanwhile, two prisoners of the raid on Seebohm's wireless intelligence company had arrived in Cairo. Their names would be given as "Aberle" and "Weber"; and in their kit was another copy of *Rebecca*. It immediately raised the suspicions of their interrogators, for what would a German be doing reading such a book in English? Moreover, both men behaved uneasily when they were questioned about where they had bought the book. A careful examination revealed that it had almost certainly been purchased in Portugal; someone had rubbed the penciled price—50 escudos—off the flyleaf. Fairly sure that the book might be the basis of some cipher, MI-6 at Cairo cabled MI-6 at Lisbon to make inquiries about whether anyone had recently bought two or more copies of *Rebecca* at any of the bookstalls there. Since there were only a few English-language bookshops in Portugal, it was a relatively easy matter to visit them all. Within the week, the inquiry showed that the wife of the German assistant military attaché had bought six copies of the work at a bookshop in Estoril on April 3, 1942.

It was now quite evident that *Rebecca* was indeed the basis of a cipher, but who was using it? Aberle and Weber could not be persuaded to talk, but the British Paymaster provided another clue. He had become suspicious of the new British pound notes that were turned in to him for exchange. He notified Major A. W. Sansom, the chief of Field Security at Cairo, and it was discovered that the pound note that the "British captain" had used to pay for his drinks at the Turf Club was an extremely clever forgery which was known to be German. The discovery left little doubt in the mind of Major Sansom that he was dealing with a resolute and well-equipped German mission.

But if the mission was resolute, it was also careless—more notes turned up when a Greek provisions merchant on Zamalek Island brought £300 to the Paymaster's Office opposite the Kasr-el-Nil barracks for exchange. The large sum attracted the attention of the teller, and Sansom was informed. He went to see the merchant, who told him that he had sold a quantity of luxury goods to two young men living in Zamalek, and that he had also delivered them to their home—a houseboat on the Nile. A quick check showed that these notes, too, were forgeries; and now Sansom had little doubt that Eppler and Monkaster were the men he was looking for.

At five o'clock during the afternoon of August 10, Sansom struck. He stationed river boats a discreet distance from the houseboat, set up roadblocks, ringed the area with armed troops, and blocked either end of the towpath. Having given instructions that the suspects were to be captured, and that even if they opened fire they were to be taken alive, he crept up the gangplank with an armed party and smashed in the door of the houseboat. Both suspects were on the boat, but they had a plan for just such an eventuality. As the British party came across the deck, Monkaster dived into the bilges, opened a trapdoor and dumped one Hallicrafter, the copy of *Rebecca* and all the mission's back traffic into the Nile. He attempted to escape by the same route, but was caught by one of the river boats when he surfaced, hauled aboard and handcuffed.

On deck, Eppler had held the boarding party off by rolling socks into tight balls and throwing them at the men who were making their way across the deck. The British thought they were hand grenades and dived for cover, giving Monkaster just enough time to complete the job of getting rid of the communications equipment. Then Eppler leaped straight into the crowd of Britons shouting: "Go on, shoot me! You won't! You want me alive!" It was quite true, but he was laid out with a blow from a rifle butt to the kidneys, handcuffed and, together with Monkaster, placed under arrest.

The raiding party searched the boat for the wireless and the cipher. They found nothing. The belly dancer Hekmeth Fahmy was also arrested, her boat was searched, and again nothing was found except some uniforms and clothing belonging to her lover, Major Smith. Eppler, Monkaster and Mlle Fahmy were then taken for questioning to the British Combined Services Detailed Interrogation Centre (CSDIC) at Maadi. The Germans refused to talk, but Fahmy told the British all she knew. She revealed her liaison with Major Smith and the means by which she and Eppler read the contents of his briefcase. She told Sansom where Eppler's Egyptian contacts were to be found, and Sadat and several others (but not Nasser) were arrested immediately, as was the Austrian priest who had hidden the mission's second Hallicrafter behind the altar of his church. Then by a stroke of luck the first Hallicrafter was found. After Monkaster left the door open to the bilges on the houseboat, it had slowly scuttled itself. But the boat was raised, and the Hallicrafter was discovered underneath it in the mud of the Nile. The mechanism was unusable, but it was still set to the frequency for the mission's last transmission to Athens.

However, further clues to the mission's cipher could not be found; its back traffic and the copy of *Rebecca* had disappeared. The cipher was all-important to the British, for the surprise raid on the houseboat and the determination to capture Eppler and Monkaster alive were designed to achieve a single goal. The British hoped to impersonate the Kondor mission's transmissions and send false and misleading information to Rommel. They had Eppler and Monkaster in custody, they had the wavelength to the listening post at Athens—but they did not have the cipher, although they suspected it was based on *Rebecca*. Eppler and Monkaster knew the importance of the cipher and refused to talk. Then Monkaster tried to kill himself. He cut his throat with a luncheon knife, but he was rushed to the hospital and his life was saved.

The interrogators now concentrated on Eppler, and when he still refused to discuss the cipher, he was taken—so he said afterwards—to a clinic where a drug was administered to make him talk. Evidently he said nothing of importance while under the drug, and so, after a week of the most intensive interrogation, the British tried their ace psychological trick in breaking prisoners down. They staged an elaborate mock court-martial. Charges were read out against Eppler; witnesses, including Mlle Fahmy, were called to testify; he was found guilty and the sentence of death was pronounced. As he waited in his cell for the firing squad, he was visited from time to time by his inquisitors. Still he refused to talk.

The British appear to have tried one last trick to get the cipher. According to Sadat, in his memoir *Revolt on the Nile,* "It happened that Winston Churchill was passing through Cairo and he said he would like to interrogate the spies himself. Brought before Churchill, the spies at first persisted in their silence, but when the Prime Minister promised that their lives would be spared, they changed their minds and talked." It is possible that Churchill did indeed interrogate the Kondor mission, but the British did not obtain the *Rebecca* cipher in that manner. They obtained it from Yvette, the bar girl who was an agent of the Jewish Agency.

Yvette had been in police hands throughout the period of Eppler's and Monkaster's interrogation, but she was finally released when her employer contacted a friend in MI-6. While they were going through the technicalities of her discharge, Yvette mentioned to the MI-6 officer that she had been on Eppler's houseboat the afternoon she was arrested. Only by chance, the officer asked her whether she had seen a book lying around. In a flash, Yvette realized the importance of the copy of *Rebecca* that she had discovered on the houseboat, and she revealed that she had noted down the page numbers and some of the leading cipher groups that Eppler and Monkaster had used for their transmissions. While incomplete, her notes enabled British cryptographers to establish the sequence of pages and paragraphs on which the cipher was based. The *Rebecca* cipher was broken.

The British now had all they needed to impersonate Eppler and Monkaster and resume transmissions to Athens. And this they set out to do. Thus it was that the third of Rommel's sources of secret intelligence was effectively plugged. But more important, the Kondor mission's channel of communication remained open—and Rommel would continue to trust it. It was a mistake that would alter the course of the war in North Africa.

In the first week of August 1942, Rommel began to plan his next offensive against the British. German and British forces were still stalled along the El Alamein front, but the 8th Army was quickly rebuilding its strength, and Rommel knew that he would have to move quickly if he hoped to conquer Egypt. His mobile headquarters was drawn up in an airless defile near the coast, and there he devised a plan to penetrate the El Alamein line, destroy Montgomery's army and then march to Cairo. His battle maps and intelligence files told him that the British defenses at the southern end of the El Alamein line were thin. Here, then, was the place to attack. He would move the Afrika Korps in great secrecy from the northern to the southern end of the line; and when all units were in place, he would burst through the British defenses, strike north toward the sea, trap and destroy British troops in the El Alamein "box," and then turn eastward to the Nile Delta.

It was a practical, clean, simple plan, and one with a reasonable chance of success—provided it was kept quite secret. By night and with stealth, Rommel moved his units to the south, leaving dummy vehicles and trucks behind so that their departure would not be spotted from either the ground or the air. All units kept total wireless silence to prevent the British wireless intelligence services from detecting the southward move. But Rommel made two mistakes. To obtain maximum air support he informed the Luftwaffe of his plan; and to obtain the maximum amount of petrol, ammunition and other supplies from Italy, he wirelessed his intentions to Rome and Berlin. Through Ultra, his plan was on the desks of Montgomery and Alexander almost as quickly as it reached the Germans.

Montgomery disposed his troops with speed and secrecy to meet Rommel's attack, and Churchill, who visited the front, would later write: "I was taken to the key point southeast of the Ruweisat Ridge. Here, amid the hard, rolling curves and creases of the desert, lay the mass of our armour, camouflaged, concealed, and dispersed. . . . Montgomery explained to me the disposition of our artillery of all natures. Every crevice of the desert was packed with camouflaged concealed batteries. Three or four hundred guns would fire at the German armour before we hurled in our own." But even with foreknowledge, as Churchill reported to the War Cabinet from Cairo on August 21, "The ensuing battle will be hard and critical." For the German forces were formidable, and Churchill later commented: "At any moment Rommel might attack with a devastating surge of armour. He could come in by the Pyramids with hardly a check except a single canal till he reached the Nile." How, then, could he be stopped?

It was at the Pyramids, where Alexander had made his forward headquarters, that a remarkable discussion took place. Alexander, Montgomery, Churchill and various staff officers, including General de Guingand, who was now Montgomery's Chief of Staff, looked over the maps of the area of the Ragil depression where Rommel was expected to make his attack. It was de Guingand who noticed, from a set of maps captured earlier, that Rommel had very little knowledge of the actual terrain conditions around the Ragil. In certain places in the area, the sands were deep, shifting and treacherous—definitely not the sort of terrain where the German panzers could operate. Furthermore, aerial reconnaissance would almost surely fail to correct that lack of knowledge. The way to stop Rommel, then, was not to prevent the offensive, but to encourage him to attack through the Ragil.

To achieve that objective, the sources of battlefield intelligence that had served Rommel so well were now turned against him. De Guingand sent for Colonel Dudley Clarke, who had become chief of A-Force, the Middle East branch of the LCS, and together the two men laid plans to lure Rommel into a trap. The first of these plans involved the Kondor mission. Clarke was in charge of the operations to impersonate the mission's transmissions, and it was decided to send a message stating that the British were prepared to resist any attack at the southern end of the El Alamein line at Alam Halfa ridge, but that their defenses were weak at the moment, and if Rommel attacked now he might easily achieve a breakthrough. The actual message read:

> Condor calling. Have confirmed message from reliablest source Eighth Army plan to make final stand in battle for Egypt at Alam Halfa. They are still awaiting reinforcements and are not yet ready for more than make-shift defence.

Then followed some information about reinforcements and supplies arriving at Port Said, and it is known that Rommel received and read the message, for when it was later captured, it had his mark on it.

A few nights later, Kondor came up with another message, this time a report on the British order of battle along the Alam Halfa ridge. The message caused Rommel to slap "his thighs with joy." He declared: "our spy in Cairo is the greatest hero of them all," and asked OKW to award him the Iron Cross. He would not have been so pleased had he known that the British were deliberately luring him into the shifting sands of the Ragil.

To make sure that Rommel swallowed the bait, the British devised another plan. De Guingand directed his cartographers to make a map of the Ragil showing that the area was "hard going," a condition favorable to panzers. Then the map had to be played into Rommel's hands in such a way that his suspicions would not be aroused. "Major Smith" was the man chosen for the job. The major had been under arrest ever since his liaison with Hekmeth Fahmy had come to light, and now he was compelled to take a scout car into the desert near the German lines, carrying the false map with him. The Germans saw him coming; suddenly they heard a loud explosion and saw the scout car leap into the air. They sent out a patrol and found the major's corpse—and the false map. As Churchill would later write with satisfaction, "this false information had its intended effect. Certainly the battle now took the precise form that Montgomery desired." Rommel decided to use the trails marked "hard going" for his attack.

On the night of August 24, 1942, Rommel notified Berlin that he would begin his offensive on the night of August 30/31. Within hours, Alexander was reading the signal in Cairo, and he informed Churchill in London: " 'Zip' [the prearranged code word for Rommel's offensive], now equal money every day." Just after dawn on September 1, he sent a clear-the-line cable to the Prime Minister. It carried the single word *"Zip."* Rommel's attack had begun, but Montgomery was ready for him. Sappers had laid a new minefield at the exact point where the Germans' main force made its thrust. When German engineers were ordered into the minefield to clear a path, the night sky became alive with British aircraft; the first wave dropped parachute flares to illuminate the long columns of armor, and it was followed by bombers that drenched the area with high explosive.

At dawn, Rommel had failed to obtain a single objective. He had planned to advance 30 miles to the east by moonlight and then turn and strike north toward the Mediterranean. As Rommel recorded: "The assault force (was) held up far too long by the strong and hitherto unsuspected mine barriers, and the element of surprise, which had formed the basis of the whole plan (was) lost." Should he abandon the attack? He decided to continue eastward when he received a report that a path had been cleared through the minefield. Then a new difficulty arose. Rommel had been informed that the sector was defended by a single armored division. His intelligence was not correct. Montgomery had secretly reinforced the area with three armored divisions. To meet this development, Rommel ordered the Afrika Korps to turn north sooner than had been planned. He had fallen into Montgomery's trap, for ahead lay the treacherous sands of the Ragil and the Alam Halfa ridge, whose defenses were now formidable.

Soon after Rommel's advance resumed, the Afrika Korps began to run into soft sand. Tanks, armored cars, half-tracks, trucks by the score found themselves floundering on what was marked as "hard going" on the false British map. As their crews got out to try to free the vehicles, squadrons of RAF fighters swept in to bomb and machine-gun them. Disaster piled upon disaster that day. The petrol Rommel had been promised for his offensive had not yet arrived. What had become of it? Rommel was not aware that Ultra had revealed the dates and times of the departures of his supply ships, and the RAF and British navy had sunk three tankers as they crossed the Mediterranean from Italy. As nightfall came, the desert was littered with hundreds of burning German vehicles. Long columns of black oil smoke drifted into the rose-red sunset. There was no escape, and no cover.

On the morning of September 3, three years to the day after Britain had declared war on Germany, Rommel went to the battlefield to see what he could do. Six times in two hours his vehicle was attacked by low-flying fighters, and once he was almost hit by a piece of red-hot metal 8 inches long. Swarms of fighters attacked again and again, and for every shell the Germans fired, the British, as Rommel reported, responded with ten. Finally, on the morning of the 4th, he ordered a general retreat. He retired behind a screen of 88-mm anti-tank guns, as he always did, hoping to lure the British armor onto the screen. Montgomery stood fast—too many generals had lost too many tanks in the past to that ruse—and Rommel retreated behind his own minefield.

The Battle of Alam Halfa was over—with only a small proportion of the British armor and no infantry ever having been involved. Nevertheless, the British lost 1640 men killed, wounded and missing, along with 68 tanks and 18 anti-tank guns. When Rommel looked at his casualty returns, he found he had lost 4800 men, 50 tanks, and 70 guns. In a battle of attrition where he could not expect reinforcements as quickly as the British, these were very serious losses. Rommel's last chance of taking Cairo was gone. The Desert Fox had been outfoxed, and already ailing and wearied, Rommel began to lose heart. He knew that he had been tricked, for he would write, ". . . the British command had been aware of our intention to attack." How they had known, how he had been tricked, Rommel never learned. Neither would he ever realize that his Enigma had been penetrated, and that his espionage net in Cairo was under British control. As for Montgomery, he left Rommel alone during the weeks ahead. He did nothing to straighten the front, or to take back any of the terrain he had lost. He considered that he had Rommel exactly where he wanted him, and he returned to his headquarters to "proceed methodically with my own preparations for a big offensive later on." That offensive would become known as the Battle of El Alamein.

El Alamein

FOLLOWING his victory at Alam Halfa, Montgomery began to plan "Lightfoot," the offensive that with Torch (the Anglo-American invasion of French North Africa) was intended to drive the Axis out of Africa and create a new front in southern Europe along the entire length of the Mediterranean—a front that Hitler would be compelled to defend. Deception would once again play a crucial role in Montgomery's plans, and throughout September and the first weeks of October 1942, as a prelude to Lightfoot, the wireless set commandeered from Eppler and Monkaster, the Black Code conduit, and the "first violins"—a group of German agents in the Middle East and in Britain who were under British control—were orchestrated to persuade Rommel and OKW that, for political and military reasons, the 8th Army would not be able to mount a major offensive before mid-November at the earliest. In fact, Montgomery intended to attack on the night of the October full moon, the 23rd. This cantata was again conducted by Colonel Dudley Clarke until he was sent to Washington with Colonel John Bevan of the LCS to brief the American Chiefs of Staff on British deceptive practices in September 1942. His baton was then taken up by Colonel Noel Wild, a clever Hussar.

Clarke and Wild wrote their scores at their headquarters, a former brothel near Groppis, the famous Cairene restaurant on the Kasr-el-Nil. But the genius then—and later in Plan Jael—was Clarke, an artful, baffling man and an expert in unorthodox warfare and clandestinity. Noted for his mysterious journeys, "He was," recalled Marshal of the Royal Air Force Sir John Slessor, the former C-in-C of the RAF in the Mediterranean theater, "forever buzzing about Istanbul in mufti." The facility of his organization, A-Force, for creating divisions and armies of men that did not exist was considered amazing, and on at least one occasion he would succeed in persuading Eisenhower that Britain had two armies in reserve— the 9th and the 10th—in the Levant. At a time when the Italian campaign was going badly through lack of infantry, Eisenhower was not pleased to learn that they were paper armies. Yet it was Clarke's work on "Bertram" —the code name for the cover and deception operations for Montgomery's Lightfoot offensive—that would serve as the prototype for the cover and deception operations for D-Day.

Clarke surrounded himself with a motley crew that included a merchant banker, a chemist, a music-hall conjurer, a film scenario writer, an artist, intelligence men, a don or two, and Noel Wild, who had left his regiment, the élite 11th Hussars, to join Clarke and A-Force. It seemed that there were men ready to do Clarke's business for him everywhere from Baghdad to Gibraltar, and for the purposes of Bertram he worked closely with Montgomery's Chief of Staff, de Guingand. At their first planning meeting in de Guingand's caravan on the sands beside the Mediterranean at Burg-el-Arab, de Guingand outlined Montgomery's plans. The El Alamein front stretched 40 miles from the shore of the Mediterranean to the Qattara Depression, the great, impassable inland sea of sand. The only practical method of attack was a frontal assault in the area of the northern sector, and Rommel knew this. Therefore Montgomery would attack in the north, but he wished to conceal the preparations there and to suggest instead that the attack would be mounted in the south. But since a build-up in the north could not be concealed indefinitely, he also wished to minimize its apparent scale and to organize the preparations so that when everything was in fact ready for the attack, Rommel would believe that the British were not ready at all and that he had a week or two before the attack could begin.

So simply expressed, the problem did not seem as large as it was. The desert around El Alamein was a plain of hard sand, stone outcroppings and camel scrub with few features—in general, easily visible from Rommel's positions. Yet somehow A-Force had to camouflage Montgomery's immense force, which included 1000 tanks, 1000 guns and 81 battalions of infantry, and several thousand vehicles with many tens of thousands of tons of war stores. In all, perhaps 150,000 men and 10,000 vehicles had to be moved across an empty plain without Rommel's knowledge; everything had to be concealed or revealed according to a plan that required the artifices of a master conjurer or a Chaldean. It was, or seemed to be, an almost impossible task. For if the enemy—and he was clever—became suspicious that offensive preparations were taking place in the north, all he had to do was set a tumbler on a rock and put his ear to the tumbler. The rumble in the ground would tell him all he needed to know—and explode Bertram. Yet it had to be done if Montgomery was to achieve surprise. As de Guingand said to Clarke: "Well there it is. You must conceal 150,000 men with a thousand guns and a thousand tanks on a plain as flat and as hard as a billiard table, and the Germans must not know anything about it, although they will be watching every movement, listening for every noise, charting every track. Every bloody wog will be watching you and telling the Germans what you are doing for the price of a packet of tea. You can't do it, of course, but you've bloody well got to!"

Clarke conferred with Lieutenant Colonel Geoffrey Barkas, a film set designer, and Major Jasper Maskelyne, a conjuror, his two main camouflage experts. Within two hours, working at an ancient and gritty typewriter in the third-class waiting room of the Alamein railroad station, they arrived at a plan that was essentially taken from literature; the only way to hide the army, they decided, was to do what Malcolm had done at Birnam Wood—move forward under camouflage so gradually that the enemy's sharpest eyes and lenses would fail to perceive the movement.

As Clarke conducted his strange intelligence chorus—the score was the language of the Middle Orient and the choristers were Euphrates tribesmen in kaffiyehs and agals, Jews in ringlets and caftans, Egyptans in fezzes, Kurds in high felt hats, Sunni townsmen in astrakhan caps—Barkas prepared what would become one of history's most remarkable conjuring tricks. His men started with the 6000 tons of stores in the north which had to be concealed within 5 miles of the front, most of them in the region of Alamein station. But where could they be hidden without blasting and significant engineering? Barkas and his other principal assistant, Major Michael Ayrton, an artist, found a large complex of slit trenches lined with masonry which had been there for a year. Ayrton, his eyes trained to the nuances of light and shade, lined one of the trenches with cans full of petrol and then flew over to see whether the internal shadows of the trenches, which showed on aerial photographs, were changed. He took some photographs and when they were examined he found that the shadow forms were not changed. Within three nights some 2000 tons of petrol were brought in and hidden. The British wireless intelligence service, listening in to the German front-line wireless traffic, found no evidence that the movement had been detected.

Now Barkas and Ayrton turned to the question of caching the war stores. Their answer was a masterpiece. In another three nights 4000 tons of stores were brought in and stacked in such a way that, when covered with nets, they resembled 10-ton trucks, and overflows were built to resemble soldiers' bivouacs. The artillery also had to be concealed, for Montgomery planned to open Lightfoot with a barrage in the north from some 1000 guns, and he required that this concentration be totally camouflaged not once but twice: first in the assembly area and then again in their barrage positions. The task was of exceptional difficulty because both the gun and the prime mover had distinctive shapes. Yet again the solution was relatively simple. By backing the prime mover and the gun, it was possible to get both under a dummy of a 3-ton truck. By dawn in one night 3000 pieces of equipment—guns, limbers, movers—were in position but resembled 1200 trucks, which was not an uncommon concentration on the desert. On the eve of Lightfoot, they would be moved forward into their barrage positions, and 1200 more dummy trucks would be quickly erected to conceal the fact that the original trucks had moved. But how to conceal the forward movement of an entire armored corps? Again the camouflage men came up with a plan. The soft-skinned vehicles of the corps—trucks and the like—were taken into the attack area quite openly three weeks before Zero Day so that, as Barkas later wrote, "the enemy would become accustomed to seeing (the concentrations) and, when nothing further seemed to happen, might be expected to relax his vigilance." That is exactly what happened; the Germans observed these new concentrations but, when confronted with acceptable evidence of a major attack force being assembled in the south, they concluded that all the new vehicles were merely supplies for the front-line infantry.

However, the armored fighting vehicles—720 tanks, self-propelled guns, armored cars, weapons carriers—also had to be moved to the assault area, and they presented Barkas with his greatest problem. It was overcome by holding the armor well to the rear of the front line in three staging areas—Murrayfield (North), Murrayfield (South), and Melting Pot—which were chosen because they stood astride a system of conspicuous tracks. These tracks tended toward the southern sector; but slightly to the west, there was a second series of tracks that led toward the north. When Rommel's aerial reconnaissance detected the armor, it was concluded that they were bound for the south. But at night just before the attack, the armor would move out, proceeding south at first and then doubling back to the north. There, in an area called Martello, each tank would slip in beneath a "sunshield"—a structure resembling a 10-ton truck—which had been there for a week to lull the enemy further. To hide the fact that the armor had moved from the Murrayfield-Melting Pot areas, Barkas's engineers would build dummies of the armored force—with plaited panels of split palm which the natives used as beds—and they would obliterate the tracks of the armor's northern movement by literally sweeping the desert clean. By dawn Murrayfield and Melting Pot would look exactly as they had the night before: a huge armored force awaiting orders to move to the south.

While all these deceptions were going on in the north, Barkas's and Ayrton's men were being equally artful in the south. To mislead the Germans about the location of Lightfoot's spearhead early on—so that Rommel would have time to move some of his divisions to the south to meet the threat—the camouflage men began to build, on September 27, a 20-mile stretch of what appeared to be a new water pipeline; but, in fact, it too was a dummy. The scheme was codenamed "Diamond." A trench was dug by Pioneers in the normal way, in stretches of 5 miles at a time, and a 5-mile length of dummy pipeline fashioned from old 4-gallon petrol cans was laid alongside the trench's parapet. Then, after dark, it would be moved forward while the trench was filled and a new trench started. The rate of progress was controlled so that it conformed exactly to the rate at which an actual pipeline would be built; and from every indication it could not be completed until at least forty-eight hours *after* Zero Hour, to deceive the Germans further about the time of the attack. Three dummy pump-houses were constructed, and "overhead tanks" and "can-filling stations" were built together with a shallow "reservoir." "Vehicles" were dotted about near the watering places, "men" could be seen from the air filling their cans, and enough actual traffic was diverted along the "pipeline" to give life to the fiction.

Obviously an attack could not be launched from the south without a vast supply of stores. So at the southern end of the "pipeline," a 9-square-mile patch of desert, codenamed "Brian," was selected as a "supply dump" and 700 "stacks" were built, creating the illusion that 9000 tons of ammunition, petrol and oil, food and engineer-ordnance stores had been put down. Then engineers moved in three and a half "regiments" of "field artillery"—telegraph poles put in gunpits under the cover of camouflage netting. But here Bertram called for a double bluff. The camouflage was allowed to rot so that the enemy would detect that they were dummy positions and would therefore take no notice of them. Then, again just prior to the major assault, the dummies would be whipped out and real guns and real crews put in. For a whole day they would lie still and silent, but when Montgomery initiated a small attack in the south to substantiate Bertram, the guns which the Germans had ignored would suddenly speak.

Plan Bertram was executed without a serious hitch. In the southern sector the "pipeline" was not yet completed, and since to all appearances the assault forces were still in the Murrayfield-Melting Pot staging areas, poised for an attack to the south, the Germans could assume that no attack was imminent. All that was visible in the north was a heavy concentration of 3-ton and 10-ton trucks. Yet an armored corps lay there silently, crouched to spring, while the infantry strike force lay doggo beneath the blistering sun. The only bleats of wireless communication, the only dust storms raised by speeding tanks, occurred in the south.

Along with this miasma of physical deception was spread an equally impenetrable fog of verbal deception. Wild had systematically built up the prestige and reliability of the German agents under his control by permitting them to transmit to their German controllers a careful selection of valuable facts. The Black Code conduit transmitted to Washington perfectly true reports of the arrival of convoys together with their manifests, and perfectly true political reports about British preoccupations with civil disturbances in India. But along with these true reports the fictions of Bertram were also transmitted to draw Rommel's attention to the southern sector of the Alamein front.

By October 21 Bertram had been completed. Had it worked? From all indications it had, for Ultra and the British Y service showed that Rommel was uneasy but suspected nothing. His Chief of Staff, General Fritz Bayerlein, would later comment on the success of the stratagem. Crediting Montgomery with superb coordination in his use of a mass of ingenious devices to dupe the Germans into believing that the attack would come from the southern sector while he prepared for his assault in the north, Bayerlein would remark that German intelligence was so thoroughly deceived that the high command had no advance warning of either the time or place of the attack.

If the Germans were in the dark about Montgomery's intentions, Rommel's intentions were bathed in the glare of Ultra, which kept Montgomery and A-Force fully informed about how he was reacting to Bertram —and much more. Ultra had now reached a very high degree of proficiency, for all Rommel's communications with OKW and the Commando Supremo in Rome were of necessity conducted by wireless in Enigma-enciphered messages. If the German and Italian high commands had laid a cable to North Africa, the story of Alamein might have been decidedly different; but they did not and the telephone lines that the Italians had laid on the seabed in peacetime had been dragged up and cut. Ultra gave Montgomery the most detailed picture of the enemy that a general had so far had in the war. He and his intelligence and operational staffs knew the state and disposition of the Afrika Korps, its supply position, the times and dates of departure—and the routes they were to take—of Rommel's supply ships, together with their manifests, the strength and state of repair of his panzers, the state of his air arm, and even the details of Rommel's health and state of mind.

Thus, in the long run, it was Ultra—not Bertram or Lightfoot—that would be the deciding factor in the Western Desert. Although the Afrika Korps was no longer the élite unit that it once had been, it was still strong enough to inflict severe casualties, and perhaps even defeat, upon Montgomery's army. Its greatest weakness lay in its supply link to Italy, and Ultra revealed all the British needed to know to cut that link almost completely. With the approval of Churchill, who had the last word in all Ultra matters, Montgomery requested and received an unprecedented air and naval campaign against Rommel's shipping. It was an effective campaign: in August, 30 per cent of Rommel's supplies were sent to the bottom; in September, another 30 per cent went the same way; in October, the figure rose to 40 per cent. Troops, tanks, guns, ordnance, trucks, food, medical supplies, and above all petrol were sent to the bottom of the

Mediterranean in an ever-growing crescendo of destruction. Mussolini, who was responsible for supplying Rommel, said in a memorandum a little later on that if the sinkings continued at the present rate—55,000 to 80,000 tons a month—all that Italy would have left within six months in the way of a mercantile marine would be her fishing fleet.

The consequences for the Afrika Korps were catastrophic. An Ultra dated October 19, 1942—four days before Zero Day for Lightfoot—revealed that Rommel's tanks had only about a week's supply of petrol. It also revealed that there was sufficient bread for only three weeks at the current ration of 1 pound per man per day; and tires and spare parts were so short that about one-third of all Rommel's vehicles were in workshops for up to two weeks. While the fighting strength of the 8th Army was assessed at 195,000 men, all that Rommel could muster was 50,000 Germans and 54,000 Italians—well below strength. Moreover, the sick rate was very high, and finally there was enough ammunition of all types for only nine days' heavy fighting.

The British had received even more telling confirmation of the desperate plight of the Afrika Korps—and of the success of the deceptive operations that surrounded Lightfoot—a month before when Rommel decided to leave the Alamein front and return to Germany to argue his supply position with the Fuehrer in person and to undertake some needed medical treatment. In making this decision, he had relied heavily on the forecasts of Fremde Heere West (FHW). The chief of that intelligence gathering and evaluation agency had sent an officer to Rommel's headquarters to assure him that intelligence from all sources showed that the 8th Army would not be capable of launching any major attack for several weeks. Only with that assurance did Rommel leave his command post—for the second time just before a major attack. But FHW had misinformed him, and not for the last time. The behavior of that organization—which was as vital to Hitler in the successful conduct of the war as it was to his generals—would come in for very close scrutiny by the Gestapo; and some of its officials would be hanged for high treason. But high treason was not, at this moment, the cause of FHW's misinformation. It was due to the deception campaigns of A-Force and the LCS.

FHW was one of the most vital services within the Wehrmacht—and the most vulnerable to deception. Indeed, it had been created to guard the German high command *against* deception. To that group of desks at German army headquarters in the larch plantations at Zossen, which lay about forty minutes by car from the center of Berlin, came the quintessence of that vast and expensive industry, the German intelligence services. Much of OKW's planning depended upon the accuracy of FHW's opinions; and if FHW was deceived, it was possible that the entire German high command might be deceived. It was the job of FHW to distill the most profuse, complicated and fragmented intelligence into a few coldly written paragraphs of information; even more important, its evaluators had to sift the truth out of the mass of deceptive fictions that surrounded them every hour of their working lives.

In the late summer of 1942, FHW was confronted by an intelligence problem of great complexity: what were the British and Americans up to in Africa? From a score of different sources, there was evidence that the British would strike westward from El Alamein while the Americans appeared to be preparing for an invasion of the North African coastal ports. That was indeed the Allied plan; and during the early stages of the operation, the breaches of security were so gross that it seemed incredible that FHW had difficulty figuring it out. To the dismay of high commanders on both sides of the Atlantic, the imminence of a major Allied amphibious enterprise was common gossip in Washington; and in what was the OSS's first major mission, scores of American agents, thinly disguised as "consuls," "embassy clerks" and "legation guards," were arriving by ship and plane to reconnoiter, in full view of agents in the pay of the Germans, every North African port and capital from Dakar to Tunis. Even worse, on or about October 2, 1942, a German wireless intercept station monitoring radio telephone calls collected a conversation *en clair* between a Gaulliste intelligence officer in London and a Free French diplomat in Washington which revealed that, after an operation called Torch, the Allies intended to establish a headquarters in Algiers. If that was not bad enough, another Gaulliste intelligence officer, one Clamorgan, was killed on a flight from Lisbon to Tangiers when his aircraft crashed into the sea off Cadiz. His body was washed ashore, documents which he was carrying were seized by Spanish intelligence authorities, who passed them to the Germans, and they, too, indicated quite clearly that the Allies were focusing their attention on Algiers.

Torch, at least at first, had all the earmarks of another "Menace"—the ill-fated British expedition to take the port of Dakar. But in a curious way, that operation, in combination with a host of cover and deception schemes to protect the secrets of Lightfoot and Torch, thoroughly befuddled FHW. Reports were circulated that neither the British nor the Americans had the manpower or the matériel for such expeditions. Montgomery could not attack without heavy reinforcements, which had not yet arrived. Moreover, Churchill appeared to be more concerned with a rebellion in India and with German threats to Britain's oil wells in Persia and Iraq than with renewed offensive operations in North Africa; and there was some evidence that large British forces had been moving eastward through Jordan in recent weeks. But perhaps the Allies were just strong enough, so the rumors went, to leap across the Atlantic and the Bay of Biscay to take Dakar, which was occupied only by a few French colonial troops. The Americans, it was reported—accurately—were spending forty million francs on subversive and propaganda activities in Senegal, far more than they were spending anywhere else in Africa. More agents were going into Senegal than elsewhere, and the wireless traffic between America and Senegal was rising with suspicious rapidity. Had not the British attempted to take Dakar once before? Even the Kriegsmarine had planned to seize the port at one time. As for all the clandestine activities in the other North African ports, it seemed to the intelligence experts at FHW that these were the deception operations, not the flurry of activity in Senegal; and the documents found on the body of Clamorgan might well have been deliberately planted. Furthermore, there was no indication of any preparations for offensive action on the El Alamein front. FHW was convinced that the British would probably not be capable of anything more than aggressive defense in the Western Desert until November or December, and then the winter rains might delay operations until spring.

Such was the intelligence evaluation that FHW conveyed to Rommel, and the field marshal weighed the issues. He was uneasy; his *Fingerspitzengefühl* told him that something was afoot, but he could not be sure what it was. Accordingly, he made a major—and fatal—mistake; he split his armored forces, which consisted of four divisions with five hundred tanks between them. He kept the 15th Panzer Division and the Littorio Armored Division in the north opposite El Alamein station, and sent the 21st Panzer and the Ariete armored divisions to positions directly opposite the axis of the false threat in the south. He disposed the German 90th Light Division and the Italian Trieste Division somewhat to the rear of the northern sector, and then handed over his command to General Georg Stumme, an elderly panzer general with a weak heart. Rommel himself was in such a bad state of health that he had to be lifted in and out of his vehicles, and so great was his pain that he could not sleep. Even so, he would surely have stayed at Alamein if he suspected that a British attack was imminent. But he did not; he left Africa with "a heavy heart" on September 23—exactly one month to the day before Zero Hour for Lightfoot.

His first stop was in Rome, where he saw Mussolini and declared that "unless supplies were sent to us at least on the scale I had demanded we should have to get out of North Africa." Then he flew on to Führerhauptquartier at Vinnitsa in Russia. Rommel arrived at a moment when Hitler was firing his generals right and left for what he considered their failures to obey his order in the Caucasus. Just as the British were holding the Germans at El Alamein, so the Russians were holding them at Stalingrad. Hitler was ill with high blood pressure and diarrhea, and the euphoria of his conviction that the Red Army was finished was beginning to dissipate as the Russian winter gathered over the Aral Sea. Nevertheless, he was cordial enough in his greeting of Rommel.

Hitler, who suffered from a form of far-sightedness, put on spectacles to examine the maps as Rommel explained his situation at El Alamein. Then he turned to the question of supply; and this, Rommel said, was little short of disastrous. In the first week of September alone, the British had sunk seven supply ships, including three tankers. Rommel was suspicious that Italian traitors—or Italian security leaks, which amounted to the same thing—were responsible. Dwelling upon the state of his supply of petrol, ammunition and fresh troops, Rommel said quite frankly that he was in a desperate position and that only adequate and uninterrupted supplies could save him.

Hitler did not react angrily to this statement, as well he might have. Instead he declared: "Don't worry, I mean to give Africa all the support needed. Never fear, we are going to get Alexandria all right." He spoke at length of new ferries that would speed Rommel's stores to him, of new fighter aircraft, new tanks, new multi-barreled mortars—all arms that were superior to anything the British had. He also mentioned a new secret weapon which had such explosive power that the blast would "throw a man off his horse at a distance of over two miles." He was referring to the atomic bomb.

Rommel's meeting with the Fuehrer ended and Hitler begged him to have a good rest. Rommel flew to Wiener Neustadt in Austria, and from there he was driven into the mountains at Semmering for his health cure. He arrived at Semmering on October 6, 1942, still, quite evidently, unaware of the imminence of Lightfoot. But as his cabriolet climbed the alpine road, Rommel made a remark that seemed to indicate that he no longer completely trusted Hitler. "I wonder," he said to his wife, "if (Hitler) told me all that to keep me quiet." For his part, Hitler remarked that he was dissatisfied with Rommel's apparent defeatism. "But really," said the Fuehrer, "I think one shouldn't leave a man too long in a position of such heavy responsibility. Gradually he loses his nerve. . . . That's Göring's impression too. He says that Rommel has completely lost his nerve." The Hitler-Rommel relationship was beginning to deteriorate.

The evening of October 23, 1942, came with a burst of gold in the western sky, and then a deep purple cloak settled over the desert. It was intensely silent along the front at El Alamein, as it almost always was in the early evening, with only an occasional *pi*-dog yapping or the sizzle of a flare going up. At German headquarters in a defile west of Tel-el-Eisa, there was not the slightest indication that the British attack would come that night. General Stumme was dining with his staff at a trestle table. The meat was tender; someone had shot a gazelle that day.

At exactly 2140 hours the eastern sky was lit by the biggest tornado of fire that had occurred so far in the war; and within a few seconds first the rumble and then the breeze caused by the muzzle reports and exploding shells reached Stumme's table. Lightfoot had begun. The very intensity of the fire indicated that this was no ordinary artillery bombardment; several thousand shells were falling every minute. Stumme was shocked and surprised, as were all his divisional commanders and his intelligence officers. There had not been a shred of evidence that the British had managed to assemble and hide such a powerful concentration of artillery in the north; there was little real evidence to show that an attack was imminent anywhere, including the south. But within a few minutes of the opening of the bombardment in the north, the commanding general of the 21st Panzer telephoned to state that the British had also launched a major attack—or what appeared to be a major attack—in the south. Other reports reaching Stumme confused the issue of where the spearhead was even further; the barrage had opened along the entire front but was gradually shifting in weight to the northern sector.

Another threat materialized when coast-watchers on the Mediterranean shore just behind the German front line called to report that warships, supported by strong bomber forces, were bombarding the sector of the 90th Light Division between El Daba and Sidi Abd el Rahman. British heavy artillery had opened up on the German positions, motor torpedo boats were racing back and forth along the shore laying down a smoke screen, and from the smoke screen—so the coast-watchers reported—were coming the sounds of what seemed to be a major amphibious attack: the noise and smell of engines, the rattling of anchor chains, the voices of men shouting over loud-hailers, a shower of flares to illuminate the beaches. Stumme reacted immediately; he ordered bombers and fighters into the air and directed the 90th Light's reserve regiment to the area to repulse what appeared to be an attempt to land behind the German line. Artillery and tanks began to rake the sea with fire; but when the smoke screen finally lifted, all that was visible were a few rafts bobbing on the sea. It had been a feint; the British had unveiled a new weapon in their armory of special means—sonic and nasal deception. The noises of battle had come from recordings played over sound amplifiers brought in close to the beaches by MTB's. The flares had been fired into the air automatically; the smell of engines had come from cannisters on the rafts. It was a stratagem that the British would use again and again, and of its effectiveness there could be little doubt. Stumme had been tricked into sending an important segment of one his best divisions out of the main battle.

At dawn, Stumme's headquarters still did not know what the British intended. Artillery fire had destroyed the German communications network; and to find out for himself what the situation was, Stumme set out in an armored half-track for the headquarters of the 90th Light Division. He never arrived. In the region of Hill 21 in the north, he was ambushed by British anti-tank and machine guns, fell from his half-track, and died from a heart attack. The Afrika Korps was now without a commander. By noon, at almost the same time that OKW had been informed, Montgomery, while sitting in his caravan beside the clear blue sea at Burg-el-Arab just to the rear of El Alamein, received an Ultra telling him of Stumme's death. Bertram—and Ultra—had triumphed.

At Semmering, high in the Austrian Alps, the telephone rang in Rommel's chalet in the pinewoods. Field Marshal Keitel was on the line from Führerhauptquartier, which had just moved back to Rastenburg in East Prussia. Keitel announced that the British had launched a major attack at El Alamein and that Stumme was missing, believed dead. Would Rommel be fit enough to return to his command immediately? A Heinkel III would be ready for him at Wiener Neustadt from two o'clock onwards. Rommel replied that he was willing to leave within the hour. Keitel asked him to await a further telephone call. At midnight, the telephone rang again. Hitler came on the line and asked Rommel if he felt fit enough to return to Africa. Rommel said he was perfectly fit. The Fuehrer then said he felt obliged to ask Rommel to fly back to Africa and resume command.

By noon on the 24th Rommel had landed at Ciampino Airfield outside Rome. He was aware that none of the new weapons promised by Hitler had gone to Africa, and he knew that supplies had fallen far short of the minimum demands he had made at OKW and the Commando Supremo. But just how bad the situation really was he had yet to learn. At Ciampino he was met by General Enno von Rintelen, the German military attaché at the Quirinale, who reported that the British attack was still in progress, and only three issues of petrol remained for each vehicle in the entire theater. Rommel was bitterly angry; without the necessary supplies, his army was lost. He demanded that Rintelen spare no effort to ensure that ships began to run petrol and ammunition to North Africa that night. Then he climbed into the Heinkel and took off for Derna in Libya.

Back in Rome Rintelen went immediately to Field Marshal Albert Kesselring, the German Commander-in-Chief in the Mediterranean and southeastern Europe. Kesselring sped to his task; he called Mussolini. Il Duce telephoned the Commander-in-Chief of the Italian navy. All available supply ships must be loaded with petrol and ammunition without delay and ready to sail as soon as possible. Then Kesselring sent a long wireless report to Rommel, informing him that a small convoy of five ships carrying ammunition and petrol could be expected at his supply ports within seventy-two hours. In the signal he pointed out that with a little good fortune these ships should get through; there was heavy sea fog all the way across the Mediterranean from Sicily to North Africa. The Turing engine decrypted Kesselring's signal and it was on the desk of F. W.

Winterbotham in London at about the same time that Rommel received it in Africa.

Throughout the Lightfoot period Winterbotham had remained on duty to ensure that, despite the urgency of the hour, Ultra's security procedures were maintained; in the heat of battle there was a risk that commanders might waive the conditions under which Ultra could be used. Now Ultra revealed the boldest attempt of the campaign so far to get supplies to Rommel, and it was evident that they must be stopped. But Winterbotham quickly recognized a danger in this particular intercept. It was a standing order that no enemy ship could be attacked on the basis of Ultra alone; before an attack was mounted, an aircraft must be sent to the ship to make a visual report. In that way, the enemy would be led to believe that aerial reconnaissance—not cryptanalysis—was the method by which the British were managing to intercept Axis vessels with such accuracy and frequency. Clearly, if five ships in five different locations were all attacked in fog, Ultra would be endangered. Might it not be better to let the ships go? But if they reached Rommel, he might be able to make a stand and blunt if not destroy Lightfoot. Only one man could decide which course of action to take. That man was Churchill.

It was just after midnight on the night of October 26/27. Churchill was at Chequers and, from experience, Winterbotham knew that the Prime Minister would still be up. He put in a call on the scrambler telephone and explained the dilemma to Churchill: which was more important, defeating Rommel or protecting Ultra? Churchill hesitated for an appreciable period as he weighed the alternatives. Then he ordered that the ships were to be attacked and sunk. This time Churchill was willing to risk Ultra.

Within an hour command instructions were on their way to Malta, and just after dawn on the 27th, twenty Beauforts and Bisleys took off from Luqa and Halfar airfields and caught the first of the Italian ships, *Proserpina,* at sea in fog off Tobruk. She was under heavy escort and in the battle the RAF lost six of the twenty aircraft—but the *Proserpina* was sunk. RAF Wellingtons then caught the tanker *Tripolino* by the light of flares in a mist to the northwest of Tobruk. She was sunk. Her companion, *Ostia,* was torpedoed at dawn on the 28th. That same dawn Beauforts found *Zara* about 60 miles north of Tobruk. She was sunk with torpedoes. Her companion, *Brioni,* managed to get into Tobruk, but she was sunk by American Liberators before she could unload her cargo of petrol.

The explosion from Rommel was inevitable. While his forces were locked in the gravest battle of the campaign, the British had wiped out his supplies almost overnight. How—Rommel demanded to know—had the British managed to find those ships in conditions of heavy sea fog? He was deeply suspicious. On November 1 he sent a long telegram demanding that Kesselring investigate all possible sources of leakage—wireless indiscretion, Italian treachery *and* the security of the Enigma system, which he had hitherto accepted without question. The message was intercepted and placed before Winterbotham in London; what he had feared might happen had indeed happened.

Menzies and Winterbotham watched the rising threat to Ultra with concern. Could anything be done to divert German suspicions? It was Winterbotham who offered the only possible solution. He suggested that MI-6 in Cairo send a signal in a cipher which the Germans would be able to read to a phantom group of agents in Italy, congratulating them on their information concerning shipping movements from Naples and promising a pay rise. Menzies agreed, the message was sent on or about November 2, and at about the same time a monitor of communications between Kesselring and Rommel showed that the signal had been intercepted by the Germans as planned and that inquiries had begun. Ultra seemed safe.

From the start of the Battle of El Alamein Rommel's army was doomed. Confronted by bigger, better-equipped Imperial forces, his supply arteries all but cut, denied accurate intelligence, bombed and harassed by day and by night, betrayed in every major move he made by Ultra, Rommel was a general without hope. In a series of signals to Hitler—all of which were read by Montgomery through Ultra—he warned that he had no petrol to permit the withdrawal of two German and four Italian nonmotorized divisions, and that most would be taken prisoner. There were only nominal reserves of ammunition, and even the tanks could not retreat very far with their present petrol supply.

Montgomery had Hitler's reply more quickly than Rommel himself; Rommel's Enigma was defective—some sand had got into the mechanism. Rommel's signals officer asked OKW for a retransmission, which came in two hours later. By that time the Turing engine had unbuttoned Hitler's reply and it was received at Montgomery's headquarters about an hour before Rommel got his copy. It read:

> To Field Marshal Rommel:
> In the situation in which you find yourself there can be no other thought but to stand fast and throw every gun and every man into the battle. The utmost efforts are being made to help you. Your enemy, despite his superiority, must also be at the end of his strength. It would not be the first time in history that a strong will has triumphed over the bigger battalions. As to your troops, you can show them no other road than that to victory or death.
> Adolf Hitler

Rommel read the communication and put it aside in despair. As he would write, even the most devoted soldiers can be killed by bombs. Arms, petrol, aircraft, fresh troops—all would have helped. But not words. "An overwhelming bitterness welled up in us when we saw the superlative spirit of the army." It was being crushed and, as he wrote to his wife: "At night I lie open-eyed, racking my brains for a way out of this plight for my poor troops. We are facing very difficult days, perhaps the most difficult a man can face. The dead are lucky, it's all over for them."

On the afternoon of November 4, 1942, the catastrophe he expected occurred; Montgomery finally broke the Axis front. By November 5 Rommel's command was in confused general retreat. Its vehicles and men jammed the road for the 60 miles between El Alamein and the new position in Fuka. The night was extremely dark but the RAF kept it light with thousands of flares that hung over the desert like descending chandeliers. At dawn on the 7th, Rommel's headquarters found itself at the wire around Fuka Airfield and, looking back, there was a great wall of dust as a sandstorm advanced across a scene of devastation: tanks, trucks, tents, armored cars, ambulances—all burning from the air raids of the night before. Columns of tens of thousands of men dragged themselves along on foot; the petrol supply had all but dried up, and for most of the troops there was no choice but to march out of the cauldron of fire and dust. According to reports Rommel received that morning, of the more than five hundred armored vehicles that he once commanded, only twelve were left. There was nothing else; the rest lay blackened and smoldering where they had been hit, or trackless in the minefields, or simply abandoned through want of petrol.

By November 15 Rommel realized that the Axis position in Africa was hopeless. While he had succeeded in extricating his panzer remnants from total annihilation, his supply ships continued to be sunk. Moreover, the Allies had invaded North Africa in Operation Torch. Proceeding to Brooke's grand strategic design, a largely American army traveling aboard a largely British naval force had occupied Casablanca, Algiers and Oran. Under the command of Eisenhower in the first field captaincy of his career—a matter that caused Brooke serious misgivings—the invasion had taken Hitler totally by surprise. But he reacted with characteristic speed and restored the strategic position of the Axis in North Africa by establishing a large Italo-German bridgehead in Tunisia to which Rommel could withdraw.

As for Rommel, he had come to inflict a new Cannae upon the British; and Montgomery had inflicted a new Cannae upon him. The prizes of Alexandria and Cairo lay far behind him and his losses had been enormous. Some 59,000 men had been killed, wounded or captured, 34,000 of them German. He had lost five hundred tanks and four hundred guns, and when the 21st Panzer, his favorite unit, ran out of petrol at Mersa Matruh and formed a hedgehog to make a last stand, the crews abandoned their tanks and walked out of the trap. Angry and disillusioned with the Fuehrer,

Rommel decided to leave his command without authorization and fly to Führerhauptquartier to compel Hitler to agree either to reinforce and supply his troops properly or to evacuate them before they were trapped and destroyed. Rommel wrote in a letter to his wife: "Whether I survive this defeat lies in God's hands. The lot of the vanquished is heavy."

Rommel arrived at Rastenburg in East Prussia on the afternoon of November 28 and was summoned to see the Fuehrer at five o'clock. They met in a conference room buried deep under the turf, a dank and airless place from which Hitler ruled almost the entire continent of Europe. The meeting was quite different in atmosphere from the one just before the British attack at El Alamein. "There was," Rommel recorded, "a noticeable chill."

Rommel began by describing his position in North Africa at that moment and then turned the discussion toward the future. He did not mince words; if the German army remained in North Africa, it would be destroyed. Hitler exploded. "The mere mention of the strategic question worked like a spark in a powder barrel," Rommel recorded. Hitler accused him of defeatism, his troops of being cowards, and as his fury rose, he warned Rommel that "Generals who had made the same sort of suggestion in Russia . . . had been put up against a wall and shot."

Rommel was not daunted by Hitler's anger. He protested the allegations and stated that it was quite impossible to judge the battle of North Africa from East Prussia. Then he further infuriated the Fuehrer with the suggestion that either he or Keitel and Jodl go to Africa to inspect the position for themselves. This was too much, evidently, for Hitler. According to an OSS secret intelligence report, he turned upon Rommel contemptuously and said: *"Herr Generalfeldmarschall,* capitulate if you want to—that's what you are a field-marshal for. If you, as a field-marshal, think that you can no longer carry on (in Africa), then there was no point in my making you a field-marshal. Now get out!"

At that, Rommel saluted, turned on his heel and left the room. But as he closed the door, it flew open again and Hitler came out and put his arm on Rommel's shoulder. "You must excuse me," he said. "I'm in a very nervous state. But everything is going to be all right. Come and see me tomorrow and we will talk about it calmly. It is impossible to think of the Afrika Korps being destroyed."

The next day Rommel presented himself again at Führerhauptquartier and Hitler announced that he would send Goering to Rome to straighten out the question of supplies. The two men left Führerhauptquartier for Rome in Goering's private train, there to demand action from Mussolini and the Italian army. But when they arrived, Goering spent most of his time looking for pictures and sculptures with which he hoped to fill his train. He appeared at a party dressed in a toga with bejeweled sandals, rouged cheeks, and scarlet-painted toenails. He did not, Rommel complained, try to see anyone on business. After three days Rommel decided that, for all the good he was achieving in Rome, he would be better off in North Africa. He was, he said, disgusted with Goering, who was quite mad, and Hitler was not much better. "Flying back to Africa," he wrote, "I realised that we were now completely thrown back on our resources and that to keep the army from being destroyed as a result of some crazy order or other would need all our skill."

Rommel did his utmost to avoid defeat. As Alexander's army advanced from the east, and Eisenhower's advanced from the west, he retreated skillfully into Tunisia, and his prestige was soon restored with the Fuehrer. The Desert Fox showed a flash of his former abilities when he came bounding out of the scrub at Kasserine and gave the American troops a nasty scratch that might have turned into a running sore. The Americans were caught off guard partly because of poor generalship (Eisenhower relieved one corps commander—General Lloyd R. Fredendall—and one divisional commander), partly because they were "green" and no match for the veterans of the Afrika Korps. American wireless security was also poor, but for a change, Rommel's was not. He ordered complete wireless silence before his attack; and Eisenhower's chief of intelligence, Brigadier E. T. Mockler-Ferryman, and his staff assumed that because there was no Ultra there would be no attack. For that error of judgment Mockler-Ferryman was dismissed and sent back to London, to be replaced by Brigadier Kenneth W. D. Strong, of the Royal Scots Fusiliers, a former military attaché at Berlin and a man with a close connection to the conspirators of the Schwarze Kapelle. Strong would remain at Eisenhower's side for the rest of the war.

Kasserine seriously damaged Eisenhower's reputation, and provided a dramatic illustration of the dangers of overdependence on Ultra—a mistake that the Allies would make again in northwest Europe. Rommel withdrew from Kasserine in good order; he would try once more to fight his way out of the Allied trap. At Médenine in Tunisia on March 5, 1943, he assembled his beloved 15th and 21st Panzer divisions (which had been rebuilt after the disaster of November) and struck Montgomery a sharp blow. Montgomery, alerted by Ultra's forewarning, heard him coming, assembled a powerful anti-tank screen, and shattered the attack before Rommel could make a dent in his lines. Rommel withdrew, leaving 52 of the 140 tanks with which he had started on the battlefield.

It was Rommel's last battle in Africa. On March 7, 1943, he left his command at the orders of Hitler. The Fuehrer received Rommel on the afternoon of March 10 at Rastenburg. "I should have listened to you earlier," he said. "Africa is lost now." "Do you really think we can have the complete victory we aim at?" Rommel asked, and Hitler replied: "No!" "Do you realise the consequences of defeat?" Rommel said. "Yes," Hitler replied, "I know it is necessary to make peace with one side or the other, but no one will make peace with me." With that remark—and convinced now that in defeat Hitler would bring Germany down with him—Rommel left the Fuehrer.

On May 7 the 11th Hussars, the original "Desert Rats" of the 8th Army, entered Tunis, and the remnants of Army Group Afrika—some 220,000 Germans and Italians—surrendered with all their commanders. The war in Africa was over. It had cost the Axis over 600,000 men, 8000 aircraft, 6000 guns, 2500 tanks, 70,000 trucks and 2.4 million tons of shipping, against Allied losses of about 70,000 men. It was a stupendous victory that would be the prototype for future Allied joint operations. Several of the major preconditions for invasion laid down by Brooke—the opening of the Mediterranean to safe shipping, the establishment of a new front along the shores of southern Europe, and the creation of new air bases from which to attack the German industrial war machine from the South as well as from the West—had been obtained. Brooke had been proven right, Marshall had been proven wrong, Eisenhower had been found wanting. But in the euphoria of the moment all this was obscured. Nine months ago, the Allies had been on the brink of defeat; now they could anticipate victory with assurance—unless something went dreadfully wrong on D-Day.

Rommel watched the end in North Africa from his mountaintop villa at Semmering, and grief-stricken at the destruction of the men and the army he had genuinely and deeply loved, he realized that Germany faced ruin. At about this time he received his friend, Dr. Karl Stroelin, the Oberbürgermeister of Stuttgart, and he heard, possibly for the first time, of the existence of the Schwarze Kapelle.

PART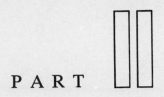

THE ROOTS OF CONSPIRACY

1934–1943

GEHLEN: Don't you think that treason decided the outcome of the Second World War?

SIBERT: I think there was another factor which was more important. We were reading your command cipher traffic, you know— the British were reading it from the beginning. The conspirators got blamed for a great deal they did not do; we used them to provide cover for Ultra.

GEHLEN: If that was the case, we hadn't a Chinaman's chance.

A CONVERSATION BETWEEN GENERAL REINHARD GEHLEN AND GENERAL EDWIN L. SIBERT

Canaris

REAR ADMIRAL WILHELM FRANZ CANARIS, the director of the Abwehr, spent the first weekend of September 1939 in his office at 76/78 Tirpitzufer, overlooking the beautiful chestnuts and limes of Berlin's Tiergarten. On Sunday morning, the 3rd of September, he rose at dawn to read the tele-printer reports that came in from the chiefs of his intelligence stations throughout the world. He then made ready for the day and went for a stroll in the Tiergarten with his deputy, Colonel Hans Oster, walking beside the bridle paths where they encountered several members of the German General Staff who, looking like lords of creation, were taking their morning rides. The two men spoke of the world crisis that was at hand—for within three hours Britain's ultimatum to Germany, demanding that Hitler with-draw his forces from Poland, would expire. What would the Fuehrer do now that his bluff had, at last, been called? He had bellowed at a visitor to the Chancellery on Friday evening: "If England wants to fight for a year, I shall fight for a year; if England wants to fight two years, I shall fight two years. . . . If England wants to fight for three years, I shall fight for three years. . . ." But, so the visitor had noticed, Hitler's bellicosity was super-ficial; he was obviously nervous and deeply apprehensive. Canaris, too, was apprehensive. He and Oster continued their walk into the Rosengarten with its great marble statue of the Empress Auguste Viktoria, and there they met the Spanish military attaché. "Naturally," said the Spaniard from his horse, "Germany has calculated this war out to the last detail of ultimate victory." Canaris replied: "Calculated nothing at all."

The headquarters of the Abwehr occupied two former townhouses, served by a creaky old elevator which rattled and swayed up the well. Canaris's office was on the fourth floor and resembled, some visitors said, the study of a slightly untidy and preoccupied don. There was an old Persian carpet, which Canaris had refused to have replaced; his nineteenth-century desk was ornately bound in bronze but ink-stained and unpolished.

The cot in the corner of the room was piled with army blankets, and was a favorite spot of Seppl—Canaris's dachshund and his constant companion. On the desk was a model of the light cruiser *Dresden* and a letterpress mounted with the insignia of the Abwehr—three brass monkeys, one cupping its ear and listening, the second looking sharply over its shoulder, and the third with its hand over its mouth. The shelves were cluttered with the latest books and magazines; on one of the walls was a picture of the devil—a gift from the Japanese ambassador—and on other walls were portraits of Canaris's predecessors. Behind his desk was a photograph of Hitler boarding Canaris's former command, the old battleship *Schlesien*. It was from this room that Canaris controlled the immense espionage organization which provided Hitler, the Supreme Command (OKW), and the General Staff with foreign military, political, economic and diplomatic intelligence—and a counterespionage organization to confound Germany's enemies.

At ten o'clock, shortly after he returned from his walk, an aide brought Canaris a message. The British secret intelligence service (MI-6) had issued a code word to all its stations. That word was "Halberd"—an ax for smashing helmets—and from this Canaris concluded that the British considered war inevitable. The minutes ticked by, and at noon Canaris went to his high-domed Telefunken wireless set, tuned in to the BBC in London. At 12:15 precisely, Prime Minister Neville Chamberlain's thin, sad voice came through the ether:

> I am speaking to you from the Cabinet Room at No. 10 Downing Street. This morning, the British Ambassador at Berlin handed the German Government a final note, stating that unless the British government heard from them by 11 o'clock that they were prepared at once to withdraw their troops from Poland, a state of war would exist between us. I have now to tell you that no such undertaking has been received, and that consequently this country is at war with Germany. . . .

Canaris switched off the wireless and gave Oster the order to issue the War Telegram that would inform the 3000 men and women on his staff that a state of hostilities existed between Germany and Great Britain and France. Then he summoned a *Kolonne*—a staff meeting—and after reviewing the Abwehr's dispositions for war, Canaris uttered some singular words about the British secret service, his main adversary in the conflict he now faced:

> I must warn you about them for several reasons. Should you work for them it will most probably be brought to my notice, as I think I have penetrated it here and there. They will want to send messages about you in cipher and from time to time we can break a cipher. Your names would appear in files and registers. That is bad, too. It would be difficult in the long run to over-

look such activities. It is also my knowledge that the (British) secret service will requite you badly—if it is a matter of money, let me tell you, they do not reward services well, and if they have the least suspicions, they will not hesitate to betray you. . . .

It was a needless warning; the Abwehr executive was absolutely loyal to the little admiral. But where did Canaris's loyalty lie? It was a strange but legitimate question, for after warning his *Kolonne* about the British secret service, Canaris added a fateful corollary to a few intimates who remained behind. He said that he felt a defeat for Germany in this war might be disastrous, but that a victory for Hitler would be a catastrophe. Therefore, the Abwehr must *do nothing that would prolong this war by a day*.

It was an astonishing remark for the commander of the secret intelligence arm of the German Supreme Command to make. But, in fact, Canaris had long been a member of a group of military men who were opposed to Hitler and his messianic ambitions for the Third Reich. As Hitler tightened his grip upon the German people and led them ever closer to a new world war, this group had evolved from passive dissidence to active conspiracy against the Fuehrer and the Nazi Party. It would come to be known as the Schwarze Kapelle, and Canaris was among the leaders of the conspiracy. Indeed, as a man who was privy to the deepest secrets of the Third Reich, and who directed its intelligence and counterintelligence activities, he was in a position to do fundamental damage to Hitler and his policies. Thus it was that, when the war with Britain was scarcely six hours old, Canaris authorized what was clearly an act of treason. He permitted Oster, who was also a member of the Schwarze Kapelle, to send a young assistant, Major Fabian von Schlabrendorff, to the Hotel Adlon where, Canaris knew, the remnants of the British diplomatic mission were assembling for repatriation. There, Schlabrendorff sought out the British military attaché, Colonel Dennis Daley, and found him with MI-6's station chief in Germany, Major Francis Foley. Schlabrendorff informed the wary Englishmen that the German military opposition to Hitler would shortly endeavor to open a line of communication to the British government through the Vatican. He also warned them that Hitler would make a big bombing raid on London to mark the outbreak of the war. Daley thanked the German, wished him good fortune, and then hastened away to inform London.

That same Sunday morning, radar in the Thames Estuary picked up an aircraft that should not have been there. Just as the Prime Minister was finishing his declaration of war upon Nazi Germany, the air-raid sirens sounded, the great balloon barrages rose into the skies, and crews manned the anti-aircraft guns. All London went to the air-raid shelters. It was a false alarm. The aircraft was identified as a French courier plane coming to London on unannounced business. No German planes flew over Britain that day, and when Schlabrendorff's warning reached London, it was interpreted by MI-6 as a trick—one of many threats and counterthreats that had been traded between the German and the British secret services in the psychological warfare that preceded the declaration of hostilities. It would not be until the end of the war, when General Alfred Jodl, Hitler's chief operations officer, was being interrogated, that the truth became known. Hitler had indeed intended to launch a bombing raid against London on the first day of the war. But Jodl had dissuaded him; the raid, Jodl had said, would achieve nothing and would invite retaliation. Canaris had, it emerged, warned the British in all good faith.

Canaris had been appointed to the command of the Abwehr during the last days of 1933, and formally took office on his forty-seventh birthday, January 1, 1934. He was a small and secretive man, nervous and intense in disposition. He had a slight lisp, a melancholic expression, and walked with a stoop, his hands clasped behind his back. His manners were those of the Wilhelminians: courteous, sincere, benevolent, watchful and tough; his eyes were like a basilisk's, piercing and blue. An educated and well-traveled man, he could speak the languages of Germany's potential enemies —England, France and Russia—almost as well as those of her potential friends—Spain and Italy. His hair was quite white when he assumed his post at the Abwehr. And from that moment on he began an odyssey of intrigue with few, if any, parallels in modern history.

A decade later he was dead, and his world had been consumed with the German phoenix. All that was left were men who could not—or would not—talk, rumor, half-fact, a few documents of state, his daughter, and his silent widow Erika, living her final years in deep mourning in exile in Spain, with a villa provided by General Franco and a pension supposedly arranged by Allen Dulles, the head of the Central Intelligence Agency. Canaris had been determined to confound history with mystery.

There were as many opinions about him as there were men employed by Menzies to assess his peculiar, elusive and complicated behavior—opinions ascribing it to everything from homosexual anglophilia to Jesuitical russophobia. Colonel Samuel Lohan, as spokesman for the secret agencies of England, dismissed Canaris as an "inefficient, intriguing, traitorous, lisping queer." Professor Sir John Wheeler-Bennett described him as the "grey fox with a lair on the Tirpitzufer." General Louis Rivet, Canaris's main French adversary, called him a "trapeze artist," adding somberly that "even the best trapeze artists get killed." General Efisio Marras, the Italian military attaché at Berlin for much of the Second World War, saw him as an "extraordinarily intelligent man [who is] quite without scruples." Ernst Kaltenbrunner, the chief of the Sicherheitsdienst (SD), the security service of the Schutzstaffel (SS), the élite military order that functioned as Hitler's personal army, and the deadly rival of the Abwehr, cried from the dock at his trial: "I have ascertained the high treason of Canaris to a most terrible degree." Otto Skorzeny, a leader of the SS, denounced him with the words: "Canaris betrayed his country's military secrets to Britain directly and wittingly from the beginning of his career to its end." Jodl would inform the International Tribunal at Nuremberg that Canaris had "served the enemy for years." Allen Dulles would describe him as "one of the bravest men of modern history—a gentleman, a patriot, and a visionary of a United States of Europe led by England, France and Germany." Even one of the sourest critics of the Schwarze Kapelle, General Reinhard Gehlen, the wartime chief of Fremde Heere, Hitler's intelligence evaluation section, and, virtually, Canaris's successor as chief of the postwar German intelligence service, would concede that while Canaris's character was "shrouded even now in mists of ill repute," he was "endowed with intellectual traits not seen in officers since the first half of the nineteenth century. . . ."

What was the truth about this mysterious man? Among the Germans, Ernst Baron von Weizsacker, the State Secretary of the German Foreign Ministry and an occasional member of the conspiracy, perhaps approached it when he wrote:

> He is one of the most interesting phenomena of the time, of a type brought to light and perfected under dictatorship, a combination of disinterested idealism and shrewdness, such as is particularly rare in Germany. As wise as serpents, as pure as doves. . . . Whether he had Greek blood I do not know; but, at all events, he passed for a cunning Odysseus. This much even Hitler must have recognized; otherwise, he would have hardly entrusted his whole military intelligence to a sailor. But he had not seen into his heart. Even the Gestapo . . . did not know what kind of man he was. Canaris had the gift of getting people to talk, without revealing himself. His pale blue eyes did not uncover the depth of his being. Very seldom, and only through a narrow crack, did one see his crystal-clear character, the deeply moral and tragic side of his personality.

And among the British, only Menzies—with Prime Minister Churchill and his Foreign Secretary, Anthony Eden—would at last penetrate the mystery. But Menzies would be very guarded in his remarks about his old adversary, save to say that Canaris was "damned brave and damned unlucky."

There were several striking similarities between the lives and careers of Menzies and Canaris. Both were born into the élite of an age of intense national dynamism and ambition, and twice within their lifetimes, their countries would be driven to settle their dynastic differences in war. Both men would serve in the first great conflict; both would rise to head their governments' secret intelligence agencies in the second. Canaris was three years older than Menzies, born on New Year's Day of 1887 in a large, walled villa on a cobbled road in the Dortmund coal-mining suburb of Aplerbeck. His father, like Menzies's, was a wealthy man, a chimney baron who owned pits and forges in the region. His mother was a daughter of the Master Forester of the Frankenwald estates of the Dukes of Saxe-Coburg-Gotha. Italian in origin, the family had arrived in Germany as migrants from Sala on Lake Como during the sixteenth century, and had settled as vineyard workers at Bernkastel, the great wine center on the Mosel. It was not an undistinguished family; one of the Canarisi was said to have provided a forebear for Napoleon, another for Konstantin Kanaris, the Greek admiral whose fireships destroyed the Turkish squadron of Kara Ali at Chios and so liberated Greece from Ottoman rule. By 1789, Franz Canaris was Chamberlain at the Court of the Elector of Trèves, one of the capitals of the Holy Roman Empire, an intricate court where "spies and assassins, double-dealers and feline deceivers marched four abreast down the long ramps of dynastic religious or political machinations." In the early nineteenth century, the family abandoned Catholicism for Protestantism when one of its members married into an evangelist family; it also abandoned the wine trade. The family moved north and Canaris's grandfather became *königlicher Bergrat*—royal mine master—to the dukedom of Hesse. They prospered with the Kruppsian boom, entered industry on their own account, and by the time of Canaris's birth they were wealthy, influential bourgeois.

There was no military tradition in the modern family. But young Canaris, after attending the Realgymnasium at Dortmund, elected to join the navy; and on April 1, 1905, he entered the Naval Academy at Kiel. In late 1906 he served before the mast on a training ship in Mediterranean waters, and when he had completed his training, he was appointed to the light cruiser *Dresden,* a modern ship that was sailing for duty in the South Atlantic. *Dresden* was coaling at St. Thomas in the Danish West Indies at the outbreak of the First World War. She slipped the harbor and embarked on a naval saga that had few comparisons for seamanship, courage and endurance. For 214 days she was a gray wolf in the southern oceans, sinking merchantmen on the beef and nitrate routes from South America to England. *Dresden* was present at the Battle of the Coronel in October 1914 when Admiral Graf von Spee destroyed the British battleship squadron of Rear Admiral Sir Christopher Cradock, the first major defeat suffered by the Royal Navy in over a century; and she was the sole German survivor of the British victory at the Battle of the Falkland Islands. *Dresden* escaped and managed to elude her pursuers for almost 100 days, but finally she was trapped by three British cruisers under the sheer face of a black lava island off the east coast of Chile.

When the British cruisers opened fire and *Dresden* was damaged,

Canaris, who was flag and intelligence officer, put out from his ship to HMS *Glasgow* to protest the engagement on the grounds that *Dresden* was in neutral waters and was therefore noncombatant. In reality he had come to gain time to allow his captain to evacuate the crew and scuttle the ship before the British boarded and captured her. The British captain rejected Canaris's protest; he said he was under orders neither to proffer nor to accept any terms other than unconditional surrender. Thirty years later Canaris would once again hear those fateful words. Suddenly an explosion holed *Dresden* and she began to sink. Canaris saluted his adversary and left *Glasgow* to rejoin *Dresden*'s crew, which was now assembled ashore, singing the German national anthem as the cruiser, her battle flag still flying, settled upon the bottom of the bay.

Dresden's crew was interned by the Chilean government on an island 500 miles out in the Pacific, but Canaris was not there long. He bribed the captain of a fishing boat to take him to the mainland and went to the German Embassy at Santiago, where he was given papers that declared him to be an Anglo-Chilean named Reed-Rosas. He then set out by car for Osorno, and from there, disguised as a mestizo, he made his way through the Andean cordillera in mid-winter. When he reached Neuquen, a small town in the mountains, he took a train to Buenos Aires, where passage was arranged for him aboard the Dutch steamer *Frisia* bound for Rotterdam.

On September 17, 1915, Canaris arrived at the Admiralstab in Berlin, a ghost of a man. Ill and drawn, he had contracted recurring malaria and enteritis, and he was generally exhausted. His private saga did not go unrecognized. Kaiser Wilhelm bestowed upon the young lieutenant the Iron Cross; and after a period of leave and recuperation, Canaris was promoted to captain and joined Captain Kurt von Krohn, the chief of the Etappe in Spain—the German fleet's secret supply and intelligence organization. Early in 1916, he found himself in Madrid; his long career as a secret agent—and his entanglement with the British secret intelligence service—had begun.

It was a time when the secret war between Britain and Germany was being fought for huge stakes and single lives were of little account. The prizes were command of the Mediterranean and of Suez, control of the great Arabian and Persian oil basins and—for Britain—communication with her Empire east of Suez. German submarines operating from the Austro-Hungarian port of Pola in the Adriatic were reaping a dreadful harvest of Entente shipping, much of which was sunk as the result of Canaris's work among the wharfingers of Cartagena. Thus in the summer of 1916 Captain Menzies of MI-6 was sent to Spain to "kill or capture" the young German. It was to be their first and only encounter in the field.

Canaris was not well that summer. His malaria had returned and his many months of hardship and clandestinity were taking a severe toll.

Captain Krohn decided that he should return to Germany for rest and medical treatment. Accordingly, dressed as a monk and posing as a pilgrim bound for the shrine of St. Francis of Assisi, Canaris crossed into France and made his way to Italy. But instead of going to Assisi he went to Domodossola, the border town for Switzerland. There, the Entente counterintelligence forces caught up with him, and he was jailed and told to expect a trial as a German spy. He managed to stave off trial by faking tuberculosis; he bit his tongue to create bloody mucus. Then he was released. Powerful Spanish friends, including a young officer named Franco, heard of his arrest, made representations to the Italian ambassador at Madrid, strings were pulled and Canaris was spared the firing squad.

He was back in Madrid in August of 1916 and Menzies quickly picked up his scent. Krohn wirelessed the Admiralstab for a U-boat to collect his sick assistant, but the exchange of signals was intercepted by the Admiralty's cryptanalytical agency and a trap was laid at Cartagena for both the U-boat—which was under the command of Captain Arnauld de la Perière, the German U-boat ace in the Mediterranean—and Canaris. The rendezvous was in Salitrona Bay off Cartagena. Pursued by Menzies and an Entente counterintelligence team, Canaris arrived there and took sanctuary aboard the interned German steamer *Roma.*

Menzies soon found out where his quarry was hiding. His informant was Juan March, a young Jew who controlled the Cartagenan waterfront and who would come to control the economy of Spain. With the help of March, Menzies ringed *Roma.* At sea lay the French coastal submarines *Topaze* and *Opale,* ready to put torpedoes into the U-35 that was coming to Salitrona Bay to rescue Canaris. If they failed, three surface vessels and a squadron of torpedo-carrying float planes were standing by to attack.

The night was dark on the Cartagenan waterfront when Canaris and two other German agents slipped aboard a small fishing boat and left the harbor among the Spanish mackerel fleet. Menzies learned of his escape and signals were sent to the French submarines and the surface vessels that were stationed along the line on which Canaris would rendezvous with the U-35. But by then scores of fishing boats had gathered along that line, any one of which might have had Canaris aboard.

The U-35 glided into Salitrona Bay and laid up off Tinoso Beacon at 0230 on October 1. Captain Arnauld de la Perière put up his periscope and saw that he was surrounded by bobbing fishing boats. His instructions were to look out for a vessel that flashed the Morse letter "M" from its masthead; but all the fishing boats carried masthead lamps, and all appeared to be blinking as they rose and fell on the gentle swell. The sun was rising, and in the east the dawn was a thin sliver of blood red between the black glassy sea and the sky. It was at that time—0632, according to Canaris's report to the Admiralstab—that de la Perière saw a smack flying a red pennant and flashing the signal "M." It was Canaris. De la Perière brought the U-boat almost alongside the smack, and broke surface very gently. Canaris and his companions leaped aboard and disappeared into the submarine through a deck hatch. Then the U-35 submerged and ran fast and deep for Pola in the Adriatic. The commanders of *Topaze* and *Opale* had seen nothing, although their periscopes were up; they had been blinded by the rays of the rising sun. Canaris had won the first round of his contest with Menzies.

In 1917, after prolonged medical treatment, Canaris joined the U-boat service as a captain and sank some eighteen ships in the Mediterranean. At the end of the war, he returned to a defeated Germany. The Kaiser had gone into exile aboard his cream and gold train, the monarchy had collapsed in Bavaria, the Communists had seized the royal palace at Potsdam, and the smoke of civil war hung over Berlin. The victorious Allies imposed merciless terms upon the vanquished; the Weimar Republic was established and under Paul von Hindenburg, not so much a hero as a monument, ruled uneasily from the seat of the grand dukes of Saxony. For Germany, the night seemed very dark, and the dawn very distant.

In the 1920's, Canaris played politics and would be accused of aiding in the murders of the socialist revolutionaries Karl Liebknecht and Rosa Luxemburg, as well as conspiring against the Weimar Republic to restore the Kaiser to the throne. His activities came to the attention of the U.S. Office of Naval Intelligence in 1928, when he was suddenly detached from duty as a liaison officer at the Admiralstab and sent abroad. Curious, the American naval attaché at Berlin began an investigation and discovered a murky intrigue concerning Canaris that would never be fully explained. At the end of the First World War, the German government had been permitted to keep intact a section of the Admiralstab known as the Marine Transport Abteilung which became, in secret, the cover organization behind which the Etappe was reestablished. But who was funding the organization? The Entente attachés, who kept a close watch on the German budget, could not find out—until the "Phoebus Scandal" broke. Then it emerged that Canaris and other officers in the Abteilung had been investing certain Admiralstab monies in private companies to provide cover and funds for their intelligence activities. Among these companies was a film production organization called Phoebus, which went bankrupt for a total of 26 million gold marks. Its creditors sued the company's principals and they, in turn, sought to remove the responsibility to the Abteilung. Canaris and a certain Captain Lohman were named in the German press, but they were sent abroad before they could be brought into court and compelled to make statements implicating the German government in illegal offensive intelligence operations.

During this same period, the late 1920's, Canaris also had some part in founding an embryonic intelligence network in central Europe and the Balkans, and cooperated with at least one Entente intelligence agency— most probably the British—against Communist agents who had begun to flood into western Europe to provoke revolutions in support of the Kremlin. Yet all his official records showed was that he served in turn as first officer of the cruiser *Berlin,* first officer of the old battleship *Schlesien,* and Chief of Staff of the North Sea station. Finally, in 1933, he became commanding officer of the naval depot at Swinemünde on the Baltic. And there his career might have ended if the fates—and Hitler—had not intervened.

Canaris was not a member of the inner circle around the C-in-C of the Kriegsmarine, Admiral Erich Raeder, nor was he a member of the Nazi Party. But traditionally, the post of Abwehr chief was a naval preserve, and when that post fell vacant, Raeder recommended him. He was summoned to the Fuehrer's office at the Reichskanzlei "What I want," said Hitler at an early meeting, "is something like the British Secret Service—an Order, doing its work with passion." On New Year's Day of 1934, Canaris, now an admiral, became the new chief of the Abwehr.

Canaris was an unlikely choice to fill such an important and sensitive post. He was, it was said, "untransparent"; moreover, he belonged to that freemasonry of aristocrats and plutocrats that Hitler called "The Blue International," a group which Hitler himself both feared and detested. Perhaps he thought he could manipulate a naval officer more easily than the stiff-backed Prussian militarists of the German General Staff; and from the first, Hitler set out to court his new spymaster. To all appearances, relations between the two men were cordial, although Canaris would never become a member of that quintessential group of Nazi leaders to whom the Fuehrer confided his most private thoughts. But he would have access to the deepest secrets of the Third Reich, secrets upon which the fate of the new Germany and of Hitler himself would depend. From Hitler's point of view, the choice of Canaris was not only unlikely; it was unwise. He would have cause to regret it.

In the light of his future course of action, however, it is difficult to determine why Canaris accepted the Abwehr post in the first place. Here ambition may have played a part. Or Canaris may have thought that he could exercise some restraining influence over the erratic Fuehrer; he was once heard to say that Hitler was "reasonable and sees your point of view, if you point it out to him properly." (*"Man kann mit ihm reden"*—"You can tell him things.") Equally, Canaris may have accepted the post in the belief that Hitler was a turbulent but useful ally who, if handled with cynical realism, could be manipulated to the profit of the cause of German conservative reaction. But by far the most probable reason was to work for the overthrow of the Nazi régime from within.

Evidence on this critical point would come to light after the war when

Captain Franz Maria Liedig, an official in the naval branch of the Abwehr, and one of Canaris's least known but most trusted confidants, would tell American military intelligence interrogators that Canaris began to work against the régime from the moment he was accepted into it. "The 'Canaris group,' i.e. a circle within the Abwehr," stated Liedig, "was the first united military clique working against Hitler with any semblance of a planned programme. . . . This feeling of rebellion existed for many years before the war; it actually began in 1934, when Admiral Canaris was put in charge of the Abwehr." Not for many years, however—and certainly not until after war had begun—would it become apparent to such men as Menzies what Canaris was really after. Germany was a potential enemy, and as the good wizard said of the bad wizard in *The Lord of the Rings:* "It is difficult with these evil folk to know when they are in league, and when they are cheating one another."

The Schwarze Kapelle

WHILE Canaris founded the Schwarze Kapelle in everything but name—the SD and the Gestapo would give it that—the organization was powerless to mount a rebellion against Hitler without the cooperation of the German General Staff. But throughout its life, not more than a very few of the more progressive, enlightened and intelligent German officers supported the conspiracy—or, indeed, were even aware of it. Between 1934 and 1938, most of the generals and colonels who were thought to be involved were little more than aging grumblers complaining at the Herrenklub—the central citadel of German military and conservative power—of the intrusion of the "gutter" into affairs of state. If they viewed with distaste the hypnotic Bohemian corporal who ruled (and eventually destroyed) them, they were prepared to tolerate him as long as he continued to provide order and a sense of national purpose to the Reich. Moreover, Hitler proclaimed that the army was the "sole bearer of arms in the Reich"; he continued to treat his generals, overtly at least, as the watchdogs of the nation; and he was busy restoring to them their flags, their bands, their brigades and divisions, their rituals. Why should any of them conspire against him?

There was another powerful factor that kept most of the high officers of the German General Staff loyal—a factor apart from the difficulties of plotting under the watchful eye of the Gestapo in a system riddled with informers. Tradition and training made them totally obedient to the civil authority. For the General Staff, absolute and unquestioning obedience was a rite carried to lengths that were incomprehensible elsewhere in the world. It was the secret of German military power. As Major Milton Shulman, an intelligence officer with the Canadian army, would put the situation:

> Orders of a superior were to be obeyed without question, and any break from tradition was seriously frowned upon. Not only was their military life

strictly supervised, but their personal life was also subject to an unrelenting social code . . . these automatic and impersonal creatures of the officers corps were so obsessed with the omnipotence of authority that they were hypnotized by its very presence. To live was to obey. There was no other end in life.

The result was certain: "To challenge the Supreme Commander of the armed forces, Adolf Hitler, was unthinkable."

There were, however, a few men who were prepared to challenge the unlimited authority of the man who would come to be called *Der Führer,* among them the Chief of the German General Staff, General Ludwig Beck. Beck, who in 1934 was fifty-four, was regarded at home and abroad as the most efficient and humane soldier of his generation. But while he held the most powerful post in the German armed forces, he was not a scion of the Junkerdom that Frederick the Great had molded into a coldly proficient and haughty military aristocracy; his father was a scientist and ironmaster in Hesse, his mother the daughter of lawyers. He was born in 1880, attended the Humanistic Gymnasium at Wiesbaden, joined the 15th Field Artillery Regiment as an officer-aspirant in 1898, and fought in the First World War as a member of the staff of the army group of Crown Prince Rupprecht of Bavaria. He stayed with the army after the Armistice, and when his wife died in bearing their only child, a daughter, he devoted himself totally to his career. That devotion, and his extraordinary gifts as a soldier and a man, were rewarded by his appointment as Chief of the General Staff—on the same day that Canaris became chief of the Abwehr.

Beck, a conservative German nationalist, distrusted his new masters, Hitler and the Nazis. He had already clashed fundamentally with Hitler when, late in June 1934, two events occurred that turned his opposition— and that of Canaris—into implacable conspiracy. At a meeting with Hitler the afternoon of June 29, Beck informed the new Chancellor that he had not accepted his high office to build an army for the purposes of foreign conquest; his purpose was to build an army that could defend the Reich. Hitler rejected his words with the ominous statement: "General Beck, it is impossible to build up an army and give it a sense of worth if the object of its existence is not the preparation for battle. Armies for the preparation of peace do not exist; they exist for triumphant execution in war." But Beck reminded Hitler of the vow that he had made to Hindenburg that he would not lead Germany into another war. And before taking his leave, he also reminded Hitler, prophetically, that another war would become a multi-front conflict which Germany could not survive.

Beck returned to the great marble hall on the Bendlerstrasse that housed the headquarters of the General Staff, and there he received a telephone call from Canaris warning him that Hitler was about to embark on a purge to destroy all sources of opposition to his régime. Among the marked men were General Kurt von Schleicher, Hitler's predecessor as Chancellor and a slippery kingmaker who was an apostle of the "Black Broth of Sparta" (as the Prussian militarist ethic was called), and Schleicher's friend and assistant, General Kurt von Bredow, once a high official in the Abwehr. Canaris said that Hitler believed that Schleicher and Bredow were conspiring with the French ambassador, André François-Poncet, to restore the Hohenzollerns to the throne of Germany. Beck knew that the allegations were not far from the truth, and he had to act quickly. He sent a friend to warn Schleicher of the danger; but the general, who had just returned from a honeymoon with a new, young wife, seemed unconcerned. God, he said, had discouraged his further involvement in political activities.

Just after twelve o'clock on June 30, there was a ring at the Schleichers' garden gate. Unsuspectingly, the cook pressed the button that released the lock and went into the garden to see what the caller wanted. Five men came up the path, brushed her aside and entered the villa. They went to the study, where Schleicher was at work on some papers, and asked him whether he was General Kurt von Schleicher, the former Chancellor of Germany. Half-rising, the general said that he was no other, and at that the men drew pistols and shot him. Frau von Schleicher, who had been in another room arranging flowers, hastened into the study with a basket of roses on her arm and gardening gloves on her hands. She, too, was shot.

That same afternoon General Kurt von Bredow was at the Hotel Adlon taking tea with friends. A messenger from the Bendlerstrasse brought him an envelope containing the news of the death of Schleicher, and Bredow turned to the French diplomat with him and murmured: "I wonder why the pigs haven't killed me yet." The diplomat, hoping to remove Bredow from danger at least for the time being, invited the general to his home for dinner, but Bredow declined and left the hotel. He was in uniform and, because it was summer, a white linen tunic. Just as he was getting into a taxi, a young colonel of the General Staff came up. "They have assassinated Schleicher," Bredow said. "He was the only man who could have saved Germany. *He* was my leader. There is nothing for me now." Then Bredow got into the taxi, closed the door and was driven off to his home. At about five o'clock that afternoon, there was a ring at his front door. Bredow, who was still in his white tunic and field-gray breeches with their claret stripes, answered the door. He was shot in the chest and killed.

There were many other murders that night and during the days that followed. Agents of the SS scoured all of Germany, killing anyone whom Hitler considered a threat to his assumption of complete power. It was a spasm of ambition and revenge that would go down in history as the "Night of the Long Knives," and the murders would affect Canaris profoundly. Captain Liedig would later testify: "The events of 30 June 1934 proved to Canaris that Hitler was and would remain a confirmed revolutionary to whom the exploitation of trust, decency and truth was a mere instrument of policy." From that moment onward, Canaris would engage in what Liedig called "adroit intrigue" to "influence and ultimately convince other military organisations, high commands and so on of the danger of the Hitler regime and the necessity to remove it." And the Abwehr became "the centre of gravity for all anti-Hitler activities within the armed forces."

Neither for the first nor for the last time Hitler had gambled dangerously, for it was conceivable that, immediately following the "Night of the Long Knives," the General Staff would rebel. In the event, all the senior members of the caste did was to protest. Field Marshal August von Mackensen, a revered general of the First World War and the commander of the élite Death's Head Hussars, called upon Hitler to demand the reestablishment of decency in public life and in the conduct of the state's business. Ashen-faced and intense, Hitler was silent for a moment. Then he said: "It may be as you say, but I cannot help myself."

Powerful forces within the General Staff now began to range themselves against Hitler and the Nazis. The War Minister, General Werner von Blomberg, ordered that the dead generals were to be regarded as traitors and that no General Staff officer should attend their funerals. Defying his order, Mackensen, Beck and Oster, newly appointed as Canaris's deputy at the Abwehr, gathered behind the cortège. Dressed in full uniform and carrying Schleicher's medals on crimson cushions, they followed the black horses with the black plumes and the cart of the dead to the cemetery. But there, at the gates, the cortège was stopped by men of the SS in midnight black and silver uniforms.

Outraged, Mackensen called a meeting of the Schlieffen Society, an organization within the General Staff. Four hundred officers gathered at the Zeughaus, the old armory in the center of Berlin, and there beneath the great sculptures of "The Masks of the Dying Warriors," they resolved unanimously that Schleicher and Bredow were not traitors but men who had "Fallen on the Field of Honour." The resolution was, according to the code of discipline by which the Officer Corps lived, tantamount to rebellion. Then Mackensen and thirty officers of the Society wrote a letter to President von Hindenburg, setting down the details of Schleicher's and Bredow's "executions," and requesting that the President demand the restoration of their names to the Roll Call of Honour of their regiment— the Third Foot Guards, Hindenburg's own regiment—from which they had been struck by Blomberg on Hitler's order.

The letter was dated July 18, 1934, and was sent to the President's estate on vast hazy plains of East Prussia at Neudeck on July 20. But if the letter ever reached him, he could not have read it. Hindenburg lay near death on the old camp bed he had used in his tent at Tannenberg, his hands clasping a Bible, his rheumy old eyes fastened on Valhalla. He died at nine o'clock on August 2, 1934, and, stricken by grief, Mackensen put the matter of Schleicher and Bredow aside. Beck and his generals became involved in the planning and execution of the obsequies. Hitler planned a *coup d'état.*

At three o'clock on the afternoon of Hindenburg's death, the War Minister, Blomberg, ordered the General Staff to parade at the foot of the Siegessäule—the Column of Victory, a great tower of sandstone surrounded by rows of captured French cannon. All over Germany the Wehrmacht gathered for similar ceremonies. That same afternoon, Hitler proclaimed himself Fuehrer and ordered the armed forces to swear an oath of allegiance to him—to him alone, and not to a nation nor to a constitution.

The saluting cannon fired in honor of the dead President. The band played the mournful Song of Remembrance: *"Ich hatt' einen Kameraden!"* There were two minutes of silence. Then Blomberg stepped forward to take the *Fahneneid*—the blood oath of the Teuton knights. General Werner von Fritsch, the C-in-C of the army, and Beck followed, each holding the flag of the Third Reich in one hand and the Bible in the other and reciting:

> I swear by God this holy oath, that I will render to Adolf Hitler, Führer of the German Nation and People, Supreme Commander of the Armed Services, unconditional obedience, and I am ready as a brave soldier to risk my life at any time for this oath.

The rank and file of the General Staff recited the same oath. Until that moment they could have discarded Hitler. But now they had made a blood pact with him; they had sworn to obey the new Fuehrer without question for the rest of their lives.

Walking with Fritsch back to the Truppenamt under the line of statues of the rulers of Germany along the Siegesallee, Beck stopped beneath that of Otto the Indolent and declared: "This is a fateful hour. (This oath) means physical and moral suicide." A little further on Beck stopped again and said: "He took us unawares. I did not realize that we were swearing a completely new form of oath." From that moment until he finally paid the price of the oath with his own life, Beck never ceased to brood that he had taken the *Fahneneid* to Adolf Hitler.

3

Friend or Foe

HITLER gave Canaris almost unlimited authority and unlimited funds with which to rebuild the German secret service. Canaris favored executives in his own mold—quiet, orderly, orthodox Wilhelminians of good birth and private incomes—and with such men he built with rapidity an intelligence and counterintelligence service that embraced the world. He was particularly successful in establishing a large *réseau* in Spain, a *réseau* that would become the cornerstone of his secret empire. But MI-6 was also active in that turbulent land, and it was through its contacts in Spain that Menzies first learned of Canaris's growing disaffection for the Fuehrer and his new Germany.

The information came from Don Juan March, the illiterate fisherman's son from Majorca who had assisted Menzies in the attempt to capture Canaris at Cartagena in 1916, and whose riches had now elevated him to the Spanish nobility. So powerful had March become, however, that he was above allegiance to a single nationality. As Spain moved toward civil war, he maintained his close ties with Menzies and MI-6; but at the same time he was in contact with Canaris and the increasingly powerful forces advocating German intervention in the troubled Spanish political scene.

Germany feared a Communist government in Spain, and when the Civil War broke out, Canaris crisscrossed the Pyrenees in his personal Ju-52, organizing arms shipments, finance and intelligence for the Fascist revolutionary forces of General Franco. It was during meetings with men like March at this time that Canaris made a remarkable admission. In due course, March communicated that admission to Menzies in London, and brought him the first news of the conspiracy that came to be called the Schwarze Kapelle. Canaris, March reported, had displayed considerable reserve about Hitler's military intentions. Canaris "does not love nor trust his new masters," March related, and added: "He is our best ally in Europe at the moment." A little later, in another report, March warned Menzies that Canaris was "a man to be watched, cultivated and possibly won over . . . 'as a sleeping partner of British espionage.' "

It was an intriguing possibility to Menzies—that the new chief of a rival secret intelligence service might be prepared to work with MI-6 against Hitler. But was it true? Could Canaris be trusted? These questions deeply divided the small group of officers in command of MI-6. As one would write:

> At best it seemed to be a wildly optimistic gamble that might come off; at worst it could be an invitation to walk into a well-laid trap with disastrous consequences. Those who saw Bolshevism as the main enemy naturally tended to take more notice of the optimistic reports on Canaris. They pointed out that if the British Secret Service could come to an understanding with Canaris, it might be possible to pool information on the machinations of international communism. But those who regarded Germany as Britain's potential enemy were highly suspicious. Canaris' whole career was one which did not suggest he was any better than a good German patriot, and in some respects he was a downright scoundrel.

Yet during the years just prior to the war, everyone conceded that Canaris had attempted to open up lines of secret communication between the German and British governments. Was he acting on the orders of the Fuehrer, or was he pursuing some covert purpose of his own? To MI-6, either or both seemed quite possible.

From the first Hitler counseled Canaris to be cautious in any offensive intelligence operations against England. The Fuehrer gave him the strictest instructions that, since he was hopeful that the Third Reich might be able to form an alliance with Great Britain, the Abwehr must do nothing to provoke the fears or suspicions of the British. Hitler permitted Canaris to establish agents in Britain, but not for the purposes of espionage; they were to act as a channel for confidential communication between the two governments. Such instructions had their precedent; Major Waenker von Dankenschweil, one of Canaris's predecessors, was given identical authority by Chancellor Leo von Caprivi in 1889. Thus, in what was one of Canaris's earliest dispositions, he ordered Captain Robert Treeck, a Hannoverian cavalryman, to England in 1935 to make contact with Menzies. Treeck became Menzies's neighbor at Luckington, the small village in the Wiltshire Hundreds between Bath and Chippenham where Menzies had his country house, Bridges Court. In the spring of 1935 a caravan of pantechnicons and horse boxes arrived at Luckington Manor, the home of Mrs. Dody Hartmann, a London socialite who had rented the house to Treeck. The movers deposited Treeck's possessions and his horses, and then Treeck himself arrived with a mistress, Violetta Baroness de Schroeders, a Chilean. With Treeck came a chef, a stud groom, a butler and a valet, and he employed locally a footman, a housekeeper, two undercooks, three maids, two grooms and three gardeners.

It was evident that Treeck was socially acceptable from the moment of his arrival, an acceptability that suggested the cooperation of Menzies himself. He joined the Beaufort Hunt, of which Menzies was a leading member. The Beaufort was so exclusive that it had its own livery—blue and buff instead of pink and black—but its activities were not confined to the pursuit of the fox. It was one of the most influential political groups in England. Treeck announced that he had been born in Latvia and had served with the Uhlans in the First World War. The Communists had dispossessed his father of the family estates and, during the family's escape to Germany, Treeck said he had been shot by the Communists in the throat—which accounted for a pronounced scar. He never revealed that he was a member of the Abwehr, although the probability that he was a German agent was discussed in the village. And it emerged that he had rented other expensive homes in England. They included 12 Cheyne Place, London, a quarter much favored by British politicians, editors and wealthy members of the squirearchy, and Guilsborough House, a small estate with a master's house of twenty-one rooms in the heart of Northamptonshire hunting country. There he joined the Pytcheley, a hunt which was only a shade less exclusive than the Beaufort. He married the Baroness de Schroeders quietly on April 27, 1938, in a civil ceremony at the Chelsea Registry Office, declaring on his wedding lines that he was forty-one and a "gentleman of private means." His bride declared herself to be thirty-eight, also of private means, and her identity was given as "Violetta Cousino, otherwise de Schroeders." Their witnesses were two friends, Connor Carrigan, an Anglo-Irish sportsman, and Mrs. Pearl Balfour, a society woman, of Smith Street, Chelsea.

Treeck had been sent, evidently, to cultivate the British branch of "The Blue International"—that small, closely knit political and merchant aristocracy that held the true power of Europe. With that class's passion for horses and hunts, nowhere could "The Blue International" be met—and penetrated—more easily than on the hunting field, and at the social functions that followed. The hunt—and particularly the Beaufort, whose Master was the Duke of Beaufort, the Master of the Horse at Buckingham Palace—was as much a political conspiracy as a sport. Hitler, for all his scorn of aristocracy, listened carefully to the opinions of the British upper classes. They ruled a world empire.

Treeck's choice of Luckington Manor as his country residence was not a coincidence. It was well known to anyone who studied *Kelly's Handbook to the Titled, Landed and Official Classes* where Menzies was to be found on a Sunday morning. But just how far Treeck managed to insinuate himself into Menzies's cabal will not be known. Only a yew hedge separated their grounds, but if Treeck ventured across, Menzies never said so; no one was better at keeping secrets than "the Colonel." At the hunt Menzies would cry *"Deutschland über alles!"* somewhat contemptuously at Treeck as their horses thundered over stone walls in pursuit of the fox. But in private their transactions, if there were any, were very discreet. All that is known is that Treeck made a formal approach to Menzies on one occasion while taking sherry after a meet. It happened on the terrace of Badminton, the Duke of Beaufort's palace. Treeck asked Menzies if they might have a few words, and Menzies agreed. They walked together for some time across a greensward beneath the great cedars, and Treeck— according to Menzies—said that Canaris had required him to make contact with Menzies and act as a liaison in "such matters as might concern us both." Menzies said afterwards that he did not reject the overture. He replied merely that he would not make Treeck's task in England difficult, provided he did nothing illegal.

Treeck remained at Luckington and Guilsborough until the outbreak of war. Then he went to Germany. He left much property behind him, including some of his horses, his Krupp sporting guns, a collection of Dresden porcelain, some good wines and a wardrobe of hunting and sporting clothing. They were placed in the care of the Custodian of Enemy Property and later sold at auction. One channel of confidential communication from Canaris was closed. He would open up others with Menzies before and during the war, but the question would always remain: Could Canaris be trusted? It is a question that was not easily answered.

If there always remained some doubt about Canaris, there was never any question about the motives and loyalty of Germany's other secret intelligence chief, Reinhard Heydrich. On the surface at least, the two men were friends, but Heydrich's sudden rise to power, and his ruthless exercise of that power, were in part responsible for Canaris's disenchantment with Nazism. Canaris served the German General Staff; Heydrich, as chief of the Sicherheitsdienst (SD), served the Nazi Party and the SS, which the puffy, bespectacled Heinrich Himmler had fashioned into a secret, fanatical military order that combined the rites and customs of romantic Teutonism with cold-blooded power politics. Inevitably, Canaris and Heydrich were rivals, as the German army and the SS were rivals, although both were ostensibly engaged in similar activities in support of the secret interests of the Third Reich. But their curious relationship would go much deeper than that.

Reinhard Tristan Eugen Heydrich—his father was an opera singer and his mother was an actress, and he was named after characters in Wagner's operas—was born in 1904 at Halle, a small town of steep-roofed, half-timbered houses in the Teutoburg Forest. He joined the navy in 1922 and in 1923 was sent to the training cruiser *Berlin,* where he met Canaris, then first officer of the ship. Tall and blond, Heydrich seemed to excel at everything he did. He was a capable officer, a first-class signalsmaster, an outstanding sportsman—the apotheosis, even then, of the Nazi doctrine of Nordic racial supremacy. He passed his examinations into the naval intelligence service with honors, showing first-class abilities in English, French and Russian; and he would become a good fighter pilot. It was his exquisite playing of the violin that brought Heydrich into Canaris's household. His tone was mellow and delicate, his fingerwork beautiful; and when Frau Canaris heard him play one evening at a concert in the wardroom of *Berlin,* she invited him to join the little chamber music concerts which she gave at her home on Sunday evenings after croquet. Doubtless Canaris came to regret that he had ever had the man in his house.

Heydrich might have reached the highest ranks within the navy but for his ungovernable sexual appetite. In 1929, he became signals officer aboard the Baltic fleet flagship *Schleswig-Holstein,* and met a nineteen-year-old beauty, Lina Mathilde von Osten, the daughter of a schoolmaster on the Baltic island of Fehmarn. Heydrich rescued her when her boat overturned during an evening's sailing and, in December 1930, they became engaged. At the same time he was seducing the daughter of a director of the IG Farben-industrie, the great chemicals corporation that did much business with the Kriegsmarine. She became pregnant and her father demanded that Heydrich marry her, but he refused with the words that he could never marry a girl of such easy virtue. Incensed, her father took the matter to the Kriegsmarine's Commander-in-Chief, Admiral Erich Raeder. Raeder saw Heydrich and advised him to marry the girl, and when he again refused, Raeder had no alternative but to order him to appear before a Court of Honour. The court gave Heydrich another chance to marry the girl and save his career; instead, he accused her of lying, suggested that another was responsible for her condition, and stated arrogantly that he would not marry her even if the price was his naval career. The court reacted strongly; Heydrich was cashiered in April 1931 with the fearful words "Dismissal for impropriety" stamped on his documents.

Heydrich was now an outcast in a nation of outcasts. It seemed that he was ruined. Miss von Osten, who was as resourceful and influential in the Nazi Party as she was beautiful, came to his rescue. She arranged for Heydrich to meet Heinrich Himmler, who was forming the SS as the imperial guard of the New Germany. The two men met at Himmler's chicken farm at Waldtrudering, near Munich, on June 14, 1931, and Himmler was immediately impressed by Heydrich's intelligence. He gave Heydrich twenty minutes to write a plan for the formation of what would become the Nazi Party security and intelligence service, approved the plan, and then assigned Heydrich the task of building the new intelligence machine. On October 5, 1931, Nazi Party headquarters at Hamburg received this telegram:

> Party Member Reinhard Heydrich, Hamburg, Membership Number 544916, will, with effect from October of this year, be carried on the strength of Party headquarters as a member of the staff of the Reichsführer SS Himmler with the rank of Sturmführer SS.

With this signal, Europe's newest secret intelligence service was born.

Heydrich rose quickly in the councils of Nazi power, his strength, according to Brigadeführer SS Walter Schellenberg, one of his deputies, being his "incredibly acute perception of the moral, human, professional and political weaknesses of others. . . ." He and Canaris were, presumably, friends, and when Canaris came to Berlin as chief of the Abwehr, he was seen frequently in Heydrich's company. The two men resumed their dainty intercourse—croquet and chamber music at the Canaris home on Sundays; Berliners saw them eating together at Horchers and riding together in the Tiergarten. When Canaris took a house in the Dollestrasse of Südende, a Berlin garden suburb, Heydrich, who had married Miss von Osten, took a house in the same street. When Canaris moved to the Betastrasse of Schlachtensee, another exclusive garden suburb, Heydrich followed six months later. But all the time the two spymasters were conspiring against each other. Heydrich assigned SD agents to spy on Abwehr agents and had microphones placed in Canaris's office. In turn, Canaris procured Heydrich's *Ahnenliste*—the "ancestry list" that was kept on all members of the Nazi Party. For Canaris suspected that Heydrich—the man whose orders would later result in the murder of 6 million Jews—was himself partly Jewish. If that was not enough to hang a man in the Third Reich, it was also suspected that Heydrich had homosexual predilections. Then, having compiled a dossier, Canaris sent it for safekeeping to a friend in Switzerland with instructions that it was to be given to the *New York Times* if he or any member of his family suffered any "untoward experience." With that, Canaris informed Heydrich of what he had done; and Heydrich, aware that publication of the dossier would ruin him, did nothing against his rival. Canaris was playing a dangerous game with Heydrich and the other Nazi hierarchs, perhaps motivated by the Machiavellian principle that:

> Where the very safety of the country depends upon the resolution to be taken, no considerations of justice or injustice, humanity or cruelty, nor of glory or of shame, should be allowed to prevail. But putting all other considerations aside, the only question should be, What course will save the life and liberty of the country?

The Plot Begins

WHILE it was the "Night of the Long Knives" that awakened men of conscience like Canaris and Beck to the criminality of Hitler and his régime, it was a conference held late in 1937 that started the Schwarze Kapelle on the road to outright treason. At 4:30 P.M. on November 5, 1937, Hitler gathered with a group of the most powerful men in the Reich at the fireside of the Little Cabinet Room at the Reichskanzelei on the Wilhelmstrasse. Present at the secret meeting were the Foreign Minister, Baron Konstantin von Neurath; the War Minister, Field Marshal Werner von Blomberg; the C-in-C of the Luftwaffe, General Hermann Goering; the C-in-C of the army, General Werner Baron von Fritsch; and the C-in-C of the Kriegsmarine, Grand Admiral Erich Raeder. When the men were settled in the big club chairs under an oil portrait of the Iron Chancellor, Bismarck, Hitler first swore them to secrecy and then, as a wintry gloom descended on Berlin outside the French windows, he uttered the words that spelled doom for a continent and for the German General Staff itself.

Hitler, now forty-eight and slightly stooped with the onset of kyphosis of the spine, gave expression to a startling policy; he was, he said, determined to begin without delay the acquisition of *Lebensraum*—living space for the German people. For the next four hours he spoke of his decision, whether general war was the outcome or not, to annex, either by diplomacy or force, Austria, his birthplace; Czechoslovakia and Poland; and finally, when the Wehrmacht was ready, he would take Russia. He declared that his decision was final, predicted that the Anglo-French powers would not interfere, demanded unconditional obedience, and directed that the operations begin in 1938 and end in 1943.

The enormity of Hitler's decision, so quietly and firmly expressed, had a terrible effect upon most of those present. Both Fritsch and Blomberg declared with passion that the proposals meant war with England and

France—a war, they said, that the Wehrmacht would not win. Neurath, in protest, reminded Hitler of his pledge to Hindenburg that he would spare Germany another war. Raeder declared that the navy was not ready—and would not be ready for at least a decade—for such a war. Only Goering spoke in support of Hitler. To all the arguments, Hitler countered that England and France were too decadent and weak to oppose him, but even if they did so he was still determined to proceed. The "Teuton furore" had begun.

Deeply disturbed by the meeting, Neurath and Fritsch broke their vow of secrecy and conferred with Beck about how Hitler might be stopped. They would go to him and prove that his proposals were both impractical and dangerous. But if the three men thought they could change the Fuehrer's mind, they were quite wrong. Not only would Hitler not listen, he refused to see them at all. At that point, Beck decided that the western powers should be informed of Hitler's intentions and consulted Canaris about the means. Canaris said there would be no difficulty.

Canaris probably had Major Francis Foley in mind. MI-6's man at Berlin from 1920 until the outbreak of war between Britain and Germany in September 1939, Foley was a former infantry officer who, it was said, had the appearance of a clerk, the mind of a divorce lawyer, and the manner of a Somerset livestock dealer. Working in offices at the British Consulate General, and operating under the title of "His Britannic Majesty's Passport Control Officer"—the cover for MI-6 officers attached to British embassies—Foley had been reporting the secrets of the strange men and queer events that had dominated Germany ever since the end of the First World War. His mission was no secret to Canaris, however, and he was undoubtedly permitted to remain in Berlin because Canaris found him a useful contact with the British. Now, largely through Foley, the British would learn of the struggle that was developing between Hitler and the General Staff—a struggle on which the peace of Europe, and of the world, would depend.

Hitler realized that war was the last thing his generals wanted. At every point in his political career there had been a general to oppose him. At every turning there had been one of those field-gray cardinals watching and waiting for a moment to restore the Hohenzollerns or to make politics with the Russians. Now he was being opposed in one of the boldest conceptions in modern German history. If he was to carry out his plans, he would have to rid himself once and for all of his opponents on the General Staff and replace them with men who would do his bidding without argument or discussion.

Blomberg was the first to feel his sting. In December 1937, Blomberg, fifty-nine years old and a widower, asked the Fuehrer's permission to marry a twenty-six-year-old typist. Hitler wished the field marshal every happiness and even attended the ceremony as a witness. But no sooner had the bride and groom left for a honeymoon on Capri than rumors began to circulate that the new *Feldmarschallin* was a "sister of joy" with police convictions for prostitution and petty fraud. Goering was the man behind the whispers. Blomberg, Goering demanded, must go. He obtained the *Feldmarschallin*'s docket from Himmler and presented it to the Fuehrer. Here was evidence that the rumors were true and Hitler professed to be greatly distressed. He immediately ordered Blomberg to return from his honeymoon, and when the field marshal refused to divorce his wife, Hitler stripped him of his command.

Who should succeed Blomberg? The logical choice was Fritsch. But Goering, who aspired to the post of War Minister, was in a position to dispose of that candidature; he placed Fritsch's SD file on Hitler's desk. It told a dismaying story; Fritsch had been accused by a man called Otto Schmidt, who was at present in police hands, of committing a homosexual act with a male prostitute known as "Bavarian Joe" in the *Privatstrasse* of the Wannsee railway station. When Fritsch learned of the allegation, he demanded that the Fuehrer hear him out in person. Hitler agreed, but unknown to Fritsch, he arranged to have Otto Schmidt present at the interview. Schmidt repeated his accusations, and although Fritsch denied them, Hitler declared that he must consider himself relieved of his duties.

Other than the doubtful word of Otto Schmidt, there was no proof of the charges against Fritsch. It was a plot engineered by Goering, Himmler and Heydrich to blacken the name of a blameless officer, and although the Gestapo sped to all parts of Germany and East Prussia to interview Fritsch's "military family," no one was prepared to testify that Fritsch was homosexual. Nevertheless, trial papers were drawn up while Hitler planned the reconstruction of the Wehrmacht in such a manner that the General Staff would be compelled to carry out his war policy without argument.

With the assistance of General Wilhelm Keitel, a stiff fellow with a monocle who was one general known to be *"führertreu,"* Hitler founded the Oberkommando der Wehrmacht (OKW), the Supreme Command of the German armed services. All staffs, including the General Staff, would be subordinate to OKW, and Hitler himself would become Supreme Commander, with Keitel his Chief of Staff and General Alfred Jodl his Chief of Operations. Hitler considered replacing Beck with General Franz Halder, but stopped short when he realized that Halder was a Bavarian and a Catholic, and that neither had ever before been a Chief of the General Staff. Hitler, who disliked Bavarian Catholic generals as much as Prussian Protestants, kept Beck. By January 30, 1938, he had completed his plans and listed his victims; and on February 4, in what was nothing less than another *coup d'état,* he was ready to act.

That morning "radio wardens" hurried from door to door throughout

Germany to see to it that the *Herrenvolk* were at their *deutscher Kleinem-pfänger*—cheap, state-manufactured wireless sets. By one o'clock most of the 23 million households and 40 million adults were listening attentively when the "Eroica" began to blare, as it always did at such moments. Then came the word. The nation listened with astonishment, all Europe with apprehension, as famous name after famous name toppled. The War Minister and the C-in-C of the army had retired on grounds of health. General after general had retired or been demoted—in all, thirty-five of Hitler's most illustrious generals were sacked. Joachim von Ribbentrop replaced Neurath as Foreign Minister; General Walther von Brauchitsch replaced Fritsch as C-in-C of the army; Goering became a field marshal; the ambassadors at Rome and Tokyo were superseded; and replacing Blomberg, Hitler himself assumed the title of War Minister. The diplomatic and press corps darted for their cableheads and the news flashed around the world. That same evening, Hitler summoned his three hundred generals (there had been only twenty-three in 1923) to the Reichskanzlei to hear his version of Fritsch's and Blomberg's frailties. The generals listened in silence, and then left. Hitler said afterwards that he had feared they would either resign *en masse,* or arrest him. They did neither, and when Hitler relaxed later that evening with some old Party cronies, he declared that now he knew that every general was either a coward or a fool.

As for the generals, they put silk handkerchiefs over their knees to protect their creases, crossed their legs, sipped wine in their messes and clubs, and decided that all that had happened was a reshuffle in the high command. They did not realize that, finally, Hitler had broken the last conservative bastion—the generals themselves. They did not see that Hitler was now what he had intended to become: the sole master of the Reich.

The time came to try Fritsch. A brave man, Ruediger Count von der Goltz, stood before Fritsch's court-martial and its president, the new Field Marshal Goering, and tore the evidence of the Gestapo to shreds. He proved that there had been a plot against the C-in-C, and that Schmidt had been induced by the plotters to give perjured evidence. Goering, unable to convict his victim, acquitted him; it was ruled that Colonel General Baron von Fritsch was innocent on all counts. Fritsch was able to walk away a free man, his honor, but not his career, restored. Schmidt was shot, and Himmler and Heydrich disappeared on staff business in remotest Germany—for, as they said, they expected that the army would march, and that if it did not do so now, it never would. History would prove them correct.

But if Hitler had succeeded in evading an overt military rebellion, covert opposition to his rule began to crystallize. Liedig would testify:

> Hitler's criminal procedure against . . . Fritsch . . . had a profound effect upon the Wehrmacht and the Abwehr. The result of this event was to split

army opinion, and the systematic organisation of associations among Hitler's opponents began at this point. The final decision to work for the regime's overthrow, which was initiated originally by the Canaris-Oster group, was then made. It was our belief that the eyes of even the military specialists would be opened by the vile and deceitful treatment of von Fritsch. Henceforth there was a systematic and continuous campaign to recruit leading soldiers for the anti-Hitler campaign.

Throughout this period, General Beck remained sphinxlike, although he remarked later that the Fritsch-Blomberg affair was the prelude to world war. And Hitler, who had said that war was not the last expedient of statehood, but its essence, now had an instrument, OKW, to execute his designs. Yet he had only one wholehearted supporter among the departmental heads of the OKW—Hermann Goering. All the rest, including Canaris, were ranged against him. The top-level officers of OKW were quite isolated in their opposition, however, for Hitler had the unquestioning love and trust of the people, and the support of the rank and file of the army, industry and the Luftwaffe. Any plot against him would result in nothing short of civil war. The conspirators of the Schwarze Kapelle were not yet ready to take that risk.

The men who dared oppose Hitler gathered around Beck; and at first their opposition took a form that marked German military planning from that time forward. Whenever they received an order from Hitler and OKW to plan for some military adventure, the group around Beck faithfully carried out its orders, but at the same time drew up a counter-plan to show that Hitler's intentions were dangerous and impracticable. The dissidents first applied this tactic in "the Battle of Flowers"—the invasion of Austria. But the Fuehrer was now in a position to ignore his generals, and with a young colonel called Erwin Rommel in command of his bodyguard, he made a triumphant entry into Vienna on March 13, 1938, thus taking the first fateful step in his quest for *Lebensraum*.

Hitler's sense of personal triumph was very great, for it was in Vienna that he had begun his political life as a youth, earning his livelihood with crudely drawn picture postcards and advertisements for "Teddy Perspiration Powder" and of Santa Claus selling colored candles. It was in this aristocratic, baroque city that, without money or a job, Hitler had stayed from 1909 until 1913 as, so he wrote himself, an art student earning "my daily bread, first as a casual labourer, then as a painter of little trifles." It was here that he had lived, dreamed and conspired as the occupant of a bed in a dosshouse behind the Meidling railroad station, or at 27 Meldemannstrasse in the 20th *Quartier,* a hostel for working men established by a charitable foundation. It was here that, wearing an old, lice-ridden overcoat given to him by a Hungarian Jew, and presenting the "apparition of a man such as rarely occurs among Christians," Hitler had first displayed the qualities of violence, argument, exuberance, denunciation and despondency that marked his life as the Fuehrer. Now he had incorporated Austria into the Reich. He was master of the city that had once rejected him.

But when he came to survey the efficiency with which the occupation had been carried out by the army, Hitler was appalled. The General Staff had failed to execute the mobilization plans, the road to Vienna was littered with broken-down tanks and trucks, and the muddled way in which the generals handled the armored columns bespoke sabotage. That element was certainly present; and as Canaris said to General Erwin Lahousen, chief of intelligence in the Austrian General Staff, "Why didn't you people shoot? Then the Corporal would have known that things can't go on like this for ever. However else is the man to learn any sense?"

The Fuehrer was now ready for his next move. With fulsome assurances to the Czechs that he had no designs upon their nation, Hitler proceeded with "Case Green"—the plan for the occupation, by force or by trickery, of Czechoslovakia. But when orders for Case Green came down from OKW to the General Staff, Beck again resolved to frustrate them as best he knew how: by pointing out in a parallel appreciation for Hitler's consumption that an attack upon Czechoslovakia would provoke war on several fronts and would bring in not only France and England but also, eventually, the United States. Hitler was not to be dissuaded. He demanded that preparations for the invasion of Czechoslovakia proceed and, at the same time, sought to placate his generals' fears.

On April 1, 1938, he called a meeting to announce the "rehabilitation" of General von Fritsch, but he also declared his "unshakeable determination" to eliminate the "threat" of Czechoslovakia. In return, realizing that Hitler was ignoring the warnings of the General Staff, Beck called upon the Fuehrer at the Reichskanzlei to demand "specific guarantees" that he had no intention of starting a new general war. Hitler, like a fox in a hen run, assured Beck that he had no such intention, but at the same time somewhat menacingly reminded the Chief of the General Staff that the army was the instrument of statesmen, and that its duty was to find ways of carrying out the tasks with which the statesmen charged it. It was not the army's duty, said Hitler, to question its orders. Beck replied courageously and directly— for he was inviting even worse treatment than had just been visited upon Blomberg and Fritsch by expressing any opposition to the Fuehrer's plans —that he would not execute orders of which he did not approve. With that remark, Beck departed from Hitler; his career, he knew, was ended.

Beck had no alternative but to resign. But before he resigned he would do one more thing; he would try to provoke the generals into a mass resignation in protest against Case Green. He directed General Karl-Heinrich von Stuelpnagel, his friend and the heir to one of the great names of Prussia, to "examine the possibilities of supporting collective action . . .

by military means"—a judicious circumlocution that meant revolution. Stuelpnagel spoke with the commanding generals at the Herrenklub. But, so the generals argued, Beck's proposition required of them action that was completely contrary to their military training—to engage in politics against the civil power. If anyone was to turn Hitler out, they said, it was the German people who had elected him. So they returned to their *Kirschwasser,* their cards—and their doom.

Beck, whose health was in ruins through the intrigue, resigned. All his plans had failed. Before he left his office at General Staff headquarters, he called his colleagues together and told them that Hitler was like Charles XII of Sweden, the monarch who had led his army from one military adventure to another until at last it perished on the Russian steppes. As he spoke, Beck's face was very tranquil—and extraordinarily like that of the Elder Moltke, the founder of the General Staff whose portrait gazed down on the somber scene. He concluded his remarks with a note of warning: "A war begun by Germany will immediately call into the field other states than the one she has attacked, and in a war against a world coalition she will succumb and for good or evil be put at that coalition's mercy."

With that statement, Beck bowed slightly in the German manner to the small group present and walked out of his office. His staff was left with the somber thought that an act of great historical moment had occurred; and indeed it had, for the last force of restraint upon the Fuehrer had departed for the wilderness of power peculiar to fallen generals. As General George C. Marshall would later report to Congress: "The elimination of Beck constituted the elimination of the last of the effective conservative influences in German foreign policy."

Hitler accepted Beck's resignation with some relief. As he said during the Fritsch affair: "The only one (of my generals) whom I fear is Beck. That man would be capable of undertaking something." Hitler was wrong, for there were other men who believed as Beck believed, and who would eventually risk even treason in their opposition to him. One was Canaris, who would seek to reveal Hitler's secret political and military plans to Germany's enemies as the best means to thwart them. Another was Oster, Canaris's deputy at the Abwehr and a man who, with Canaris's knowledge and often at his order, would betray Hitler's secrets again and again in an effort to destroy him. A third was Stuelpnagel, one of Beck's quartermasters; and a fourth was General Erich Fellgiebel, the chief of the Signals Department of OKW. There was also General Erwin von Witzleben, the commander of the Berlin military district, an eagle-faced Prussian with heavy-lidded eyes whose family had provided members of the General Staff since the reign of Frederick the Great. These men would not forget Beck's last words, and they would come to form the nucleus of a much more active and determined conspiracy.

As for Beck, he would remain the spiritual leader of the conspiracy. The afternoon he left his office at General Staff headquarters, he made his way to the Mittwochgesellschaft—the Wednesday Club—there to deliver to a small group of intellectual friends a lecture about Marshal Foch. Then he went home to a widower's dinner at 8 Goethestrasse, not far from where Schleicher and Bredow had been murdered. He was a sick man, worn by moral conflict, afraid of the future; but from that moment forward he would devote himself to the activities of the Schwarze Kapelle.

Beck's successor as Chief of the General Staff was General Franz Halder, a small man with the drawn face of an evangelist and the manner of a science master. Hitler ordered him to continue to work on Case Green, and with calm precision he and his staff took over Beck's labors. At the same time, with Halder's uneasy cooperation—for he knew all about the conspiracy—the members of the Schwarze Kapelle for the first time undertook to prepare a positive plan for a *coup d'état*. Hitler was to be seized in Berlin, but it was not the Schwarze Kapelle's intention to kill him; he would be placed on trial before the German people, the procedures for which had been worked out by Hans von Dohnanyi, a lawyer who was about to become Oster's deputy at the Abwehr. Oster had obtained the medical case history of Hitler's service in the army in the First World War—which revealed that he had gone mad as a result of being gassed— and a panel of psychiatrists was secretly investigating his mental fitness. At his trial, Hitler was to be exposed as criminally irresponsible and unfit to hold the offices of Fuehrer and Chancellor. Then a civilian of prominence and respectability was to form a government. The moment to strike would be the moment Hitler gave the final order for Case Green to proceed against Czechoslovakia.

The plan for the Schwarze Kapelle's seizure of power was comprehensive. At the proper moment, Fellgiebel would cut all communications throughout Germany, and Berlin was to be occupied by troops under the command of Witzleben. Hitler, Himmler, Heyrich, Goering—all were to be arrested and taken under the strongest guard to a castle in Bavaria. Hitler's bodyguard—the SS Leibstandarte at Munich, a brigade of the best-trained and best-equipped troops in Germany—was to be surrounded and compelled to surrender by the Wuppertal Panzer Division of General Erich Hoepner, the German panzer theorist who was with his troops in the Thuringian Forest. Troops were also available to put down the SS. The plan was worked out down to the last detail, but one important question remained: Would the British and French oppose an invasion of Czechoslovakia? If the western powers took a stand against Hitler, the invasion could probably be prevented, and the revolt against a humbled Fuehrer would have every chance of success.

It was now mid-August, and as the intolerable tensions that marked that high, brilliant summer of 1938 were beginning to build in Europe, a Junkers tri-motor arrived at Croydon Airport near London and Ewald von Kleist-Schmenzin, a Pomeranian gentleman-farmer and a secret envoy of the Schwarze Kapelle, disembarked. Herr Kleist had come to London with an offer and a warning. It was a bold journey to undertake, for Kleist risked arrest and indictment—and certain death—at the hands of the Gestapo, and indiscretion or outright betrayal by the British. Nevertheless, as Ian Colvin, then a young British reporter in Berlin who acted as an occasional intermediary between Canaris and the British, would write, Kleist had been instructed by Beck and Canaris to tell the British that "through yielding to Hitler the British Government will lose its two main allies here—the German General Staff and the German people. If you can bring me positive proof that the British will make war if we invade Czechoslovakia, I will make an end to this regime." And what would Beck regard as positive proof? "An open pledge," Beck had told Kleist, "to assist Czechoslovakia in the event of war."

Evidently—probably through Colvin and the British Embassy in Berlin—Sinclair, the chief of MI-6, and Menzies knew that Kleist was coming. Special precautions were taken at Croydon Airport to see that he passed into England without difficulty from customs, immigration, or security controls; and an escort of MI-6 men took him to the Hyde Park Hotel, where he was visited first by Lord Lloyd of Dolobran, a man with close connections with Menzies and in the government and at the Palace. The president of the Navy League of the British Empire, chairman of the British Council and a former High Commissioner in the Anglo-Egyptian Sudan, Lord Lloyd dined alone with Kleist in a private room at Claridge's. There Kleist committed one of the Schwarze Kapelle's first acts of obvious treason. He said: "Everything is decided, Lord Lloyd. The mobilisation plans are complete, zero-day is fixed, the army group commanders have their orders. All will run according to plan at the end of September, and no one can stop it unless Britain speaks an open warning to Herr Hitler."

Then, as Lord Lloyd served the German from a dumbwaiter, Kleist revealed all he knew about the state of affairs in Germany. He told of the plans for a *coup d'état* and the inadequacy of the German army to wage war against a coalition of powers; and he said that if Britain, along with France and Russia, took "a firm and positive stand" against Hitler, "there was a good hope that the commanding generals would arrest him if he persisted in his war policy and would thus put an end to the Nazi regime." There were, Kleist added, powerful friends of Britain in Germany, among them Canaris and Oster. Lord Lloyd listened very carefully and was deeply impressed by the intelligence, sincerity and courage of the emissary.

The next morning Kleist met with Sir Robert Vansittart, the British government's adviser on foreign affairs, and speaking with the "utmost frankness and gravity," he went over the same ground as he had done with Lord Lloyd. Vansittart listened attentively, but he was uneasy. Kleist wanted to make deals about Germany's frontiers after a successful revolt against Hitler; and Britain would make no concessions at others' expense in return for peace. Then, as later, it was the Schwarze Kapelle's attempts to strike a bargain that cost the conspiracy much support in Britain.

Kleist's next call was upon Churchill at his country house deep in the Kentish Weald. There, on August 17, 1938, he asked Churchill for the desired pledge, and Churchill went to his desk and wrote as "a personal opinion" that:

> I am as certain as I was at the end of July 1914 that England will march with France and certainly the United States is now strongly anti-Nazi. It is difficult for democracies to make precise declarations, but the spectacle of an armed attack by Germany upon a small neighbour and the bloody fighting that will follow will rouse the whole British Empire and compel the gravest decisions. Do not, I pray you, be misled upon this point. Such a war, once started, would be fought out like the last to the bitter end, and one must consider not what might happen in the first few months, but where we should all be at the end of the third or fourth year.

When he had finished, Churchill is supposed to have told Kleist: "You can have everything, but first bring us Hitler's head." It was the first occasion on which Churchill, in the interests of British policy, incited the Schwarze Kapelle to rebel. The next would not occur until after D-Day in 1944.

Kleist returned to Berlin as secretly as he had come. He lunched first with Colvin and then walked to Canaris's office at the Tirpitzufer. To Canaris, alone, Kleist reported: "I have found nobody in London who wishes to take this opportunity to wage a preventive war. I have the impression that they wish to avoid war at almost any cost this year. . . . They say that it is not possible under the British Constitution to commit themselves on a situation that has not yet arisen."

Churchill's letter fell far short of the open declaration that Beck and Canaris needed. Nevertheless, the Schwarze Kapelle continued its preparations for a coup. On September 8, 1938, Stuelpnagel arranged to have Hitler's final orders for Case Green available to the plotters five days before they were to be executed—to enable them to make their arrangements for the seizure of power. At the same time the General Staff did nothing to oil the wheels of movement for Case Green. There arose a shortage of rolling stock, and of petrol; and the secret mobilization of soldiers worked in a slovenly fashion as if the posts and telegraphs did not exist. It was noted by OKW that the Officer Corps had no enthusiasm for its task.

As the Czechoslovak crisis deepened, the British government made no move to discourage Hitler, or to encourage the Schwarze Kapelle. On the contrary, the forces of appeasement were at work. After deliberating at length, Chamberlain decided to fly to Berchtesgaden to seek a peaceful solution to the problem. Canaris was at dinner with his staff when he heard of Chamberlain's mission. He laid down his knife and fork, complained that the news had destroyed his appetite, and spluttered: "What he—visit that man!" As Colvin recalled:

> He muttered the words blankly at first as if he scarcely understood. Then he repeated them to himself and got up from the table, walking about the room. He was utterly distracted and ate no more dinner. . . . The Admiral excused himself to his heads of departments and went early to bed. Had he been mistaken in opening his hand to the British? . . . Maybe they had not believed that his advice was anything more than mischief and deceit.

Kleist's impression that the British wished to avoid war at almost any cost proved correct; the cost was the partition of Czechoslovakia. Appeasement made it impossible for the conspirators of the Schwarze Kapelle to act. The Czech state was dismembered and the revolution collapsed. How could they arrest Hitler and try him as a war criminal when he had just won a completely bloodless victory? Not again—at least not until 1943—would the conspirators have such well-laid plans for a *coup d'état*. Not again would they be so apparently united in their resolve to rid themselves of the Fuehrer. Liedig would state that from thenceforward all plots were riddled with "rivalries, prejudices, wishful thinking, the weakness of human character" that inhibited positive and determined action. For that reason, almost certainly, it was at this point that Canaris decided to act alone, or in concert with only the smallest group of generals whom he really trusted. Hitler had not been challenged at the most vulnerable moment in his career either by his generals or by the world's statesmen. Now he was, as Beck was said to have declared, "Germany's destiny for good or evil."

The Outbreak of War

IN TRYING to assess the purpose of Canaris's activities during the last months of 1938 and the first half of 1939, Britain was confronted with ambiguity from every side. It seemed that Canaris was playing three hands at once. He was endeavoring to infiltrate agents into Britain, or to suborn men and women who might be useful to the Abwehr; his agents sought to inflame the world situation with rumor and counter-rumor; and still more agents arrived in London for the ostensible purpose of building a secret bridge between the Abwehr, the German General Staff and the British government. Only in the afterlight of those furious months would Canaris's true motives finally emerge.

It was a period of unprecedented tension in the affairs of Britain and Germany. The Germans and the Italians announced the Pact of Steel, and Mussolini appeared ready to invade the Balkans. In March of 1939 German troops completed the occupation of Czechoslovakia and Hitler proclaimed the "Protectorate of Bohemia and Moravia." Chamberlain accused Hitler of breaking his word that he would not invade the rest of the Czech state; Hitler rejected the Anglo-French protest notes. Chamberlain announced British and French guarantees to Poland and ordered military conscription. The world staggered under the blow and counter-blow of this diplomatic battle of wills. The preparations for war were everywhere, and in London that Easter, the fluctuating, high-pitched moan of sirens was heard for the first time as Britain tested its air-raid defenses.

Although Ultra was not yet operational, the British government was well informed of Hitler's intentions, both through its own intelligence sources and through the continuing stream of emissaries from the Schwarze Kapelle. A procession of Germans with illustrious names came secretly to London at the behest of Canaris, Oster and Beck to try to get Chamberlain and the British government to block Hitler's next move—"Case White," the invasion of Poland—among them the young Major Fabian von Schlabrendorff and Helmuth Count von Moltke, the great-great-nephew of the venerated field marshal who had helped found the German General Staff. No state secrets in history were as badly kept as Hitler's that last year of the peace, and the persistent warnings were not ignored. Although the British made no overt military move to oppose Hitler, the Committee of Imperial Defence, virtually Britain's supreme war council, accelerated its preparations for war, including the defense of the realm against air attack. The production of military aircraft was stepped up from 250 to 600 units a month—and that precaution, when combined with intelligence that derived from Ultra, would cost Hitler the Battle of Britain. Thus Canaris and the other conspirators of the Schwarze Kapelle had, at least indirectly, accomplished a part of their goal. They would not succeed in preventing a war, but they would help ensure that Hitler could not win it.

The British government was as well-informed about Hitler's moods as about his intentions. In January 1939 Cadogan had warned the government that ". . . Hitler's mental condition, his insensate rage against Great Britain and his megalomania, which are alarming the moderates around him, are entirely consistent with the execution of a desperate coup against the western powers." Moreover, he had added, ". . . the authorities in Germany whom we have consulted including anti-Nazi Germans of sound judgement are agreed that Hitler's orders would be carried out and that no revolt can be anticipated at all events during the initial stages of the war."

Perhaps in response to this appreciation and other warnings of the state of affairs in Germany, the British government considered a scheme to assassinate Hitler. Menzies would later state that he was in sympathy with the plan, which was suggested by General Sir Mason-MacFarlane, the military attaché at the British Embassy in Berlin. MacFarlane, a clever man (he would go secretly into Rome to negotiate the Italian surrender in 1943), whose occasional red-faced bluster concealed a natural clandestine's mind, proposed that Hitler should be shot with a high-powered marksman's rifle equipped with a telescopic sight from an apartment in Berlin overlooking the Chancellery. According to an article in the German magazine *der Spiegel,* published in 1971 on the basis of what it described as a note on the proposition found at the Imperial War Museum, MacFarlane's conclusion was that "Hitler's death at that time could have led to the overthrow of national socialism and that millions of lives could have been saved." But, said the magazine, the British government vetoed the scheme on the grounds that it was "unsportsmanlike," and that there was "antipathy on principle against murder in democratic states." Later, the British government would be somewhat less concerned with scruples.

Soon after the invasion of Czechoslovakia, when, as Cadogan would write, "We were being swept along on a rapid series of surprises sprung upon us by Hitler with a speed that took one's breath away," Canaris attempted another strategy. On April 3, 1939, he planted a report that the Luftwaffe might make a surprise attack on the British fleet. A second such report warned that German submarines were patrolling the English Channel and the Thames Estuary. The Cabinet believed these reports and met; that same day Lord Stanhope, the First Lord of the Admiralty, boarded the aircraft carrier *Ark Royal* to announce that "Shortly before I left the Admiralty it became necessary to give orders to man the anti-aircraft guns of the Fleet so as to be ready for anything that might happen." The world reverberated with the announcement. The powerful British fleet was ready for immediate and determined action; war, it seemed, was imminent and unavoidable.

Like an earlier warning, which probably also originated with Canaris, that Hitler planned to bomb London in March of 1939, these reports proved to be false. And in planting them, so it appeared at the time, Canaris had overplayed his hand. It was generally believed that they were part of Hitler's clever, unending war of nerves, and Canaris was blamed for con-cocting elaborate rumors and deception schemes to trouble the security of the western powers. His credibility was destroyed. But in the light of his future actions, his campaign of scare tactics might be traced to an entirely different motive. Disappointed by the failure of the British to respond to the warnings of his emissaries, he wanted to frighten them into taking some positive action that would deter Hitler. All he succeeded in doing was to make the British doubt his sincerity.

Yet again, the flood of rumors and reports that inundated the British government that spring and summer would eventually work to the benefit of Canaris and the Schwarze Kapelle, and to the detriment of Hitler. Most of these rumors and reports were found to be, after the fact, quite accurate; the surprises of which Cadogan wrote were surprises only because the British were ill-equipped to assess the truth of the intelligence that they had gathered from a wide variety of sources. Part of the problem lay in the very nature of some of those sources. The emissaries of the Schwarze Kapelle could be considered, at best, disgruntled monarchists and, at worst, traitors—neither a very reliable source of the truth. Canaris himself seemed little more than an agent provocateur. But just as their warnings had induced the British to strengthen their military defenses, so they also led to the strengthening of the British intelligence apparatus. A new organization, the Situation Report Centre, was created, and a Foreign Office man, Victor Cavendish-Bentinck, a relative of the Duke of Portland and a product of Wellington and the Grenadier Guards, was put in charge. Thereafter, the other intelligence organizations would report to him and a committee made up of the directors of the army, navy and air force intelligence services, which would be responsible for the collation, assessment and dissemination of all intelligence, whatever its source. Gradually Cavendish-Bentinck, a man of exceptional perception and a wide knowledge of Germany, would expand his sphere to control all intelligence work—offensive, defensive, secret, technical, subversive and political; and the Situation Report Centre would be the forerunner of the Joint Intelligence Committee, also headed by Cavendish-Bentinck and the organization with which Britain would conduct its triumphant intelligence operations during the Second World War.

In the final moments of peace, Canaris and his group made one last attempt to avert the looming catastrophe. An officer of the German General Staff was sent to London overtly as a military observer, but covertly to make contact with "officers of the military and of British intelligence." He was Lieutenant Colonel Gerhardt Count von Schwerin, chief of the English section of the department that would become FHW, an important intelligence arm of OKW and, in 1943 and 1944, a major center of conspiracy against Hitler. Schwerin's visit appeared to have been the outcome of an intrigue between General Ulrich Liss, the chief of FHW, and his friend the deputy British military attaché at the embassy in Berlin, Major Kenneth W. D. Strong, the man who would become, for D-Day, chief of intelligence to General Dwight D. Eisenhower, the Supreme Allied Commander.

The count's stay in London was not a secret matter for either the Germans or the British; it was customary even at this moment of European history for the German and British general staffs to exchange observers; Liss himself had been in Britain a few months earlier. Schwerin, a panzer specialist, took no pains to disguise himself or his overt mission. He took a flat in Piccadilly and behaved like a German aristocrat. He had calling cards printed and distributed them wherever he went. He was to be seen riding in Rotten Row, practicing the *haute école* of a German gentleman. He appeared at Ascot, Sandhurst and the Guards' Ball. But few except Strong and the director of naval intelligence, Admiral John Godfrey, knew the true purpose of his visit. On March 28, 1939, he had warned the British Embassy in Berlin that "Hitler had decided to push his eastern expansion policy" that year; he was in Britain now to warn that Hitler had declared on May 23, 1939, that he was determined to "attack Poland at the first suitable opportunity." Under Godfrey's "management," Schwerin met "a careful selection of Foreign Office and intelligence officials and MPs." To all he carried the same message; the only way to prevent the attack on Poland was for Britain to "impress Hitler both with its strength and determination."

On July 14, 1939, Schwerin was a guest at a dinner party at Godfrey's flat in Cadogan Place. Present were General Sir James Marshall-Cornwall, an old MI-6 hand who had been military attaché in Berlin from 1928–1932 and was now Vice Chief of the Imperial General Staff, Cadogan, Menzies and the directors of the military intelligence services. There was, Marshall-Cornwall would record in his diary, "a good deal of good champagne consumed," and Schwerin reiterated his message. Marshall-Cornwall would record:

> Count Schwerin wanted Britain to make a series of gestures on the Continent. He told us that Hitler would attack Poland but that he might be restrained if, in the first place, Britain made a powerful naval demonstration —something like a squadron of battleships, he proposed—in the Baltic. He also suggested we should station a group of heavy bombers in France, and send to France the two fully-equipped divisions that we had at that time. The next day we forwarded Schwerin's proposals to the various interested authorities, including the Prime Minister, and Schwerin returned to Germany with an expression of cordiality from Menzies to Canaris. But, alas, Schwerin's proposals fell upon poor soil.

Prime Minister Chamberlain and Lord Halifax made it known that Britain would do nothing at this stage; if she did so, the statesmen averred, such demonstrations would serve only to provoke Hitler.

Hitler did not require provocation; on August 22, 1939, the highest commanders of the Wehrmacht were ordered to report for a conference at the Adlerhorst (the Eagle's Nest), the Fuehrer's eyrie on a mountaintop in the Obersalzberg of Bavaria. Their stream of staff cars purred along the white concrete autobahn through the mountain valleys, into the village of Berchtesgaden with its sixteenth-century houses, and out toward the Hohergoll. They climbed up the winding Kehlsteinstrasse until the road ended abruptly in the side of the Kehlstein Mountain. Two great bronze doors opened at the touch of a button from SS guards and, leaving the valleys in bright sunshine below, the procession entered a long, marble-walled tunnel lit by bronze lanterns. The chauffeurs parked the cars in the large underground garage and the commanders walked through a short and smaller tunnel to the big, copper-lined elevator outfitted with deep leather seats. They were whisked up a shaft bored through the heart of the mountain for 400 feet, and when the doors opened they found themselves at 6184 feet in the Eagle's Nest.

Hitler kept his generals and admirals waiting for a few minutes in the anteroom where he displayed his collection of Nymphenburg and Frankenthal porcelain. Then, at a signal from the blond giant who was chief of Hitler's SS bodyguard, they entered the Fuehrer's salon for the conference. The view from his wide panoramic window was Wagnerian: the Untersberg, the highest mountain near Salzburg, where the Emperor Frederick Barbarossa, according to legend, awaited the call to rise and restore the glories of the German Empire; the steeples and hills of Salzburg itself, where Mozart was born. The commanders settled themselves into large rustic furniture in a room that was dominated by a massive clock crowned by a bronze eagle and a bronze bust of Richard Wagner. The walls were covered with large oils, including a nude that was said to have been painted by

Titian, two soft and haunting tapestries, a landscape by Spitzweg, some Roman ruins by Pannini and a structure by Eduard von Steinle that resembled an altar.

Hitler began to speak: "There will probably never again in the future be a man with more authority than I have. My existence is therefore a factor of great value. But I can be eliminated at any time by a criminal or a lunatic. . . . There is no time to lose. War must come in my lifetime."

Displaying unbounded self-assurance, Hitler then announced that Ribbentrop had signed a Treaty of Friendship with the Soviet Union and that, whereas previously he had believed that an attack upon Poland would mean war with England and France, now he was certain there would be no war. "I have," Hitler declared, "struck this instrument [assistance from Russia] from the hands of the western powers. Now we can strike at the heart of Poland. To the best of our knowledge the military road is free."

His declarations drew considerable surprise from his audience. The Fuehrer continued with a statement that he thought no British statesman would risk a long war with Germany while Russia remained out of the conflict. As for France, he said that she had been dragged along against her will by England and could not afford a long and bloody war without the help of Russia; French casualties in the First World War had seen to that. Moreover, he believed that "Our enemies are little worms: I saw them in Munich." And he added, "I am only afraid that at the last minute some *Schweinhund* will produce a plan of mediation."

Hitler spoke with such great force that all those present were silent. Why must there be war, he asked? "We have nothing to lose; we can only gain." He reviewed the tense world situation and concluded:

> All these fortunate circumstances will no longer prevail in two or three years. No one knows how long I shall live. Therefore war is better now. Hannibal at Cannae, Frederick the Great at Leuthen, and Hindenburg and Ludendorff at Tannenberg—they took chances. So now we also must take risks which can only be mastered by iron determination.

With that the gathering broke up for a late lunch. According to an account in a Nuremberg document, Goering, beside himself with excitement, jumped onto the long table in the salon and gave "bloodthirsty thanks and bloody promises. He danced around like a savage." When the conference resumed, Hitler continued his harangue, exhorting his commanders to "Have no pity! Brutal attitude. Eighty million people must get what is their right." And then the Fuehrer announced that Case White was to be put into effect immediately. X-Day was August 26, 1939; Zero Hour was 0430. The object of the operation: "The destruction of Poland."

In the main Hitler's commanders favored his decision; had not the Wehrmacht swept through Austria and Czechoslovakia virtually unopposed? But several men—Halder, Witzleben, Stuelpnagel, Fellgiebel, Canaris—kept silent. In their view, war was inevitable if Hitler was allowed to proceed. But how could he be stopped? Once again Canaris saw an opportunity to frustrate Hitler's plans, and he took it. He drove from Berchtesgaden to the Hotel of the Four Seasons in Munich, and there he made some notes and handed them to his deputy, Oster. Oster took the night express to Berlin, and shortly after the train left the Munich station, he met a man in civilian clothes in the corridor outside his sleeper—Major Gijsbertus Jacob Sas, an assistant military attaché at the Dutch Embassy in Berlin, who had been a friend of Oster's for many years. Oster gave him Canaris's notes and by the evening of August 23 a report of Hitler's speech was on the desk of Major Foley in Berlin, just as it was on the desks of all other intelligence services friendly to the Dutch.

The leakage was effective, for it reached both London and Paris. The French reaction was immediate and drastic; Premier Édouard Daladier gave the *Alerte,* the signal that put the Maginot Line on a war footing. The British government also took precautionary measures. Orders were issued for key parties of the coast and anti-aircraft defenses to assemble, and for the protection of vulnerable points. Telegrams sent to the dominions and colonies warned that it might be necessary to enter a precautionary stance for war, the Lord Privy Seal was authorized to bring all civil defense and evacuation procedures to a war footing, and the Admiralty was given Cabinet authority to requisition twenty-five merchant ships for conversion into armed merchant cruisers. The Admiralty issued warnings to all merchantmen, all leave was stopped throughout the armed services, the anti-aircraft defenses were fully deployed, and reservists were called up in large numbers.

Such was the effect of Canaris's warning. On August 25, OKW and army headquarters at Zossen received a signal. Case White was to be postponed. Hitler had been informed that, the Nazi-Soviet Pact notwithstanding, if Germany attacked Poland, Britain and France would declare war. And to show the Fuehrer it meant business, the British government had announced through the Foreign Office that an alliance had just been concluded with Poland. In Rome Mussolini, who had received his own copy of Hitler's address, declared that Italy could not support Germany in a great war without substantial assistance in war materials and military supplies.

At Abwehr headquarters Canaris and Oster were jubilant. The man who claimed to be the "greatest strategist of all times, a war lord of a new kind," and who had issued orders to attack one minute and canceled them the next, could not be taken seriously by the generals. Oster said there was no longer any reason for a coup; Hitler would now fall through his own actions. And at the *Kolonne* the next morning the little admiral declared: "Peace has been saved for the next twenty years."

It was not to be. Hitler was determined to proceed. He told Brauchitsch at the Reichskanzlei that he was to regard X-Day as September 1, 1939. He would, he said, if he was pushed to it, wage a two-front war—the one type of war that all German strategists in modern history had declared Germany could not win. When Canaris heard the news, he faced the future with a shattered spirit. Across the years to come he saw in prospect the defeat and dissolution of all that he and many of his co-conspirators held dear: the Reich, the existence of the armed forces, the Officer Corps, power, privilege, position—all would go.

In the predawn twilight of September 1, 1939, 1600 aircraft of the Luftwaffe opened the bombardment of Poland, and at five o'clock that same morning five German armies crossed the frontier. On September 3, the British and the French declared war upon the Third Reich.

Conspiracy at the Vatican

THE GERMAN *Blitzkrieg* in Poland—the Wehrmacht shattered an army of 800,000 men and conquered a nation of 33 million people in just twenty-seven days—raised Hitler to a new pinnacle of popular admiration. His triumph splintered the hopes of the Schwarze Kapelle that the Wehrmacht would come to support a rebellion against him. His commanding generals could not argue with success. Yet dark events now intruded to drive a new wedge between Hitler and the General Staff. The SS began to exterminate the Poles—the aristocracy, the intelligentsia, the priesthood and the Jews. It was the start of Himmler's campaign to create out of the Slavic lands a new fiefdom of Teutonic knights, and Heydrich was the man in charge of the job.

It was not long before Canaris, ever alert for information about the criminal activities of the SS and the SD, learned of the mass executions. On September 8, 1939, only seven days after the Polish invasion, he flew to the Fuehrer's special train near Illnau to lodge a protest with Keitel. "One day the world will hold the Wehrmacht responsible for these methods since these things are taking place under its nose," he warned. But his protest made no impact upon Keitel; he said merely that if the army did not want to do "these things," it must not complain when the SS and the SD undertook the work.

Back in Berlin, almost overcome by sorrow, Canaris began an inquiry into the Polish atrocities. When it became too ghastly a task, he created an Abwehrkommando to continue the investigation, and, steadily, the dossier thickened. He and Oster saw to it that all of Hitler's commanding generals were informed of SS activities in Poland, and reports were also smuggled to the Vatican and to Berne for dissemination to MI-6 and the Deuxième Bureau. They could do no more, for in spite of the protests of his generals, Hitler removed Poland from army jurisdiction and put it under the rule of the SS. The army might have been expected to oppose this dissolution of its powers, but it did not; and the one man who held out against the Fuehrer, General Johannes Blaskowitz, was relieved of his command and placed in a reserve of general officers. His example was not lost on Hitler's other generals; if they cherished their careers, they would follow his orders, whatever those orders were. Once again the conspirators of the Schwarze Kapelle despaired of fomenting a revolution between the Fuehrer and the General Staff.

On October 9, 1939, Hitler, having fleshed his sword on Poland, offered his generals fresh conquest—and provided the Schwarze Kapelle with a fresh pretext for revolution. He ordered "Case Yellow," the military operations for the invasion of The Netherlands, Belgium and France. It was to be a *Blitzkrieg* campaign conducted by the entire might of the Wehrmacht, and it would commence at a place and time when the western powers would least expect it—in the Ardennes during the winter solstice.

The General Staff and the army commanders, already appalled by the Polish murders, reacted with vehemence. With their memories of Ypres in 1914, Loos in 1915, the Somme in 1916, and Passchendaele in 1917, when winter campaigns had foundered in a sea of blood and mud, Case Yellow filled them with the specter of Flanders. With few exceptions they denounced the operation as lunacy. But Hitler was not to be deterred and, refusing the advice of his best generals, ordered the campaign to be ready within one week from November 5. The generals were thunderstruck, and the Schwarze Kapelle entered a second phase of the most determined intrigues to rid Germany of the Fuehrer before he succeeded in destroying the country. Canaris, Oster, and the rest of the Schwarze Kapelle, which now commanded a degree of support from Halder, the Chief of the General Staff, decided to resort to the only weapon left to them if they wished to prevent what they considered would become a new German tragedy. That weapon was treason.

The Schwarze Kapelle's plot fell into two spheres: one internal, the other external. In the first instance, the conspirators planned a march upon Berlin to capture Hitler and overthrow the Nazi Party. Two panzer divisions en route from Poland to the western front would be ready to turn back to Berlin and secure the city against the SS. The Fuehrer was to be indicted for crimes against humanity, declared insane and unfit to stand trial, and confined to an asylum. Beck was then to be proclaimed Regent, the army would provide a provisional government supported by all political parties, and a Hohenzollern would be invited to return to the throne. It was a neat, clever, workable plan, drawn up according to the best principles of the General Staff by Lieutenant Colonel Helmuth Groscurth, an officer of the Abwehr. There was to be no shooting, no barricades, no wild outbursts, only a quick and orderly return to the governmental methods of the

German Empire—legality and order, Christianity and calm. And what would happen if Hitler, Goering, Goebbels, Himmler, Heydrich and the others resisted? They would be shot and responsibility for their deaths laid at the door of the SS.

The success of the coup, however, depended upon its reception by Germany's enemies, for it was the Schwarze Kapelle's intention to seek first a cease-fire and then an armistice. Thus it was essential to determine those conditions that would be acceptable both to Britain and France, and to Germany. Canaris was given responsibility for the external sphere of the conspiracy, and he turned to Oster to open a secret line of communication with the British government.

Oster was the sword arm of the conspiracy. As chief of Department Z, the headquarters staff and central registry of the Abwehr, he possessed the bureaucracy and communications that enabled him to run the affairs of the Schwarze Kapelle under the disguise of normal intelligence operations. A Saxon horse gunner who was at once elegant and arrogant—over his desk was the Saxon proverb: "An eagle hunts no flies"—Oster was openly contemptuous of Hitler and the Nazis. He had made it his business to procure Hitler's military, police and medical files, and the only thing that saved him from the Gestapo or the SD was the iron wall that Canaris built around the Abwehr. With Hitler's agreement, Canaris established with Heydrich that the Nazi's forces of surveillance and inquiry had no jurisdiction on Abwehr territory.

The Abwehr provided Oster with an ideal cover for his intrigues. His office was a beehive of strange activities and even stranger people. One historian would write:

> One grew used to seeing the most extraordinary figures in a wild variety of dress and appearance. Anyone working in that uncanny hum had to have many faces or one quite impenetrable one. His right hand never dared know what his left was up to. His element was a game, the stakes were life and death, his daily task to catch without being caught.
>
> Oster, teetering often on the very edge of the abyss, worked for years in that surrealistic atmosphere. Anyone who saw him trembled at the artistry, especially if he knew that Oster was working for both sides at once—the regime and its opposition. He had four secret telephone lines and it was a terrifying experience to watch him speaking to four unseen agents, giving different instructions, without batting an eyelid. All this took place in an atmosphere where high treason and espionage were no longer distinguishable.

Oster had already committed treason against the Third Reich in betraying the secrets of Case White. Now he set the wheels in motion for another act of treachery: his object the subversion of Case Yellow. He believed that if Case Yellow were destroyed by the western powers at the outset, or rendered impossible, it would also destroy Hitler's reputation for invincibility, and lead not only to his removal but also to an early peace. From the military point of view, he was convinced that the possible sacrifices which his betrayal of Case Yellow might cost his own people bore no comparison to the suffering of the hundreds of thousands of victims and the incalculable destruction that the war would bring to the other peoples of Europe —a war which, because of the rival strengths, could never be won by Germany.

For the work of contacting the British Oster selected, and summoned to his office, Dr. Josef Mueller, a lawyer from Munich. Mueller, a Catholic, was known to and favorably regarded by Pope Pius XII. He was also a friend of Monsignor Ludwig Kaas, the Keeper of the Fabric at St. Peter's, and of Father Robert Leiber, the Jesuit who was the archivist at the Vatican and a confidant of the Pope. These connections were invaluable to the Schwarze Kapelle, and Oster, who knew of Mueller's opposition to the Nazi régime, asked him if he would undertake to establish a line of communication between the Schwarze Kapelle and the British government through his friends at the Vatican. Without hesitation, Mueller agreed to accept the assignment. Then Oster explained that having made contact through the Vatican, Mueller was to inform the British of Case Yellow and determine what terms they would accept to bring about an armistice after Hitler's removal or assassination. Mueller understood the dangers of his task and, before leaving Oster, he agreed to this compact: "It is Hitler or we!" If he was caught he would go to the axman alone and silent. The two men shook hands on this brave pledge, and Mueller departed, riding down to the lobby of Abwehr headquarters in the ancient elevator and stepping away among the dead leaves along the side of the Landwehrkanal. Two weeks later he met Monsignor Kaas in secret at a wine garden near the Quo Vadis Chapel off the Appian Way.

By the first fortnight of October 1939, Mueller was able to report to Canaris and Oster that the Pope had consented to serve the Schwarze Kapelle as intermediary with the British government in the person of Sir D'Arcy Osborne, the British ambassador at the Holy See. His Holiness, Mueller reported, had accepted with the words: "The German Opposition must be heard in Britain," and he would be its voice. The objective of the Pope's intercession would be a peace based upon the proposition that Britain and France would not attempt to take advantage of the disturbance that would follow the deposition of Hitler to invade and occupy Germany. Mueller informed Canaris and Oster that the Pope had not consented to receive him personally on the grounds that his visits were bound to be observed and reported. The Schwarze Kapelle's proposals would therefore be conveyed to the Pope by Father Leiber and Father Kaas, both of whose discretion could be trusted absolutely. On the other hand, the Pope would receive Sir D'Arcy because it would be perfectly natural for him to do so.

Mueller informed his principals that the Pope was now in contact with Sir D'Arcy to obtain Britain's cooperation in the exchanges.

Mueller's report gave the conspirators of the Schwarze Kapelle new hope; all contact had not been lost with the British through the outbreak of war. As Helmuth Groscurth noted in his diary on October 20, 1939: "The Pope is very interested and holds an honorable peace to be possible. Personally guarantees that Germany will not be swindled as in the forest of Compiègne. With all peace feelers one encounters the categorical demand for the removal of Hitler."

Then, on or about October 27, Mueller received a message to meet Father Leiber after dark at the priest's quarters in the Pontifical University of the Gregorians on the Piazza Pilota. There, Father Leiber revealed that the Pope had received a message from Sir D'Arcy declaring that Lord Halifax, the British Foreign Secretary, had given his consent for Sir D'Arcy to take part in the exchanges. The time had come, said Father Leiber, for Mueller's principals to present their proposals for an armistice. At precisely that moment, the Schwarze Kapelle was struck by another misfortune.

The great Benedictine abbey of Beuron stands proudly isolated like a secular palace in rolling countryside in the Swabian Mountains beside the Danube. Here, for over eight hundred years, the black-clad monks followed the teachings of St. Benedict and made their lavish devotions, praying seven times during the day and once during the night. Heydrich had seen the importance of infiltrating this splendid, baroque center of Jesuitical learning and had recruited as an informant Hermann Keller, an exceptionally intelligent, restless, erratic and ambitious monk. For years Keller had tried to remove the Arch Abbot, Rafael Walser, and was said to have rigged charges of foreign currency manipulations against his superior. The accusations had left Keller in virtual charge of the monastery until the Primate of the Benedictines, Fidelis von Stotzingen, had asked Dr. Josef Mueller to investigate. Mueller was able to prove that Keller had invented the charges and he was deprived of his priorship and exiled to the Benedictine abbey on Mount Zion in Palestine. There, Keller had succeeded in ingratiating himself with the Grand Mufti of Jerusalem, an association that resulted in his recruitment first to the Abwehr and then to the SD.

Through the offices of the SD, Keller was restored to his priorship at Beuron and the new Arch Abbot, Benedict Bauer, employed him in confidential Jesuit work that made him especially valuable to the SD. Now he would have an opportunity to settle his account with Mueller. Heydrich was suspicious of Mueller and gave Keller the task of reporting his movements at the Vatican. For Heydrich was aware of the conspiracies and intrigues that were going on at the Holy See.

In October 1939, presumably by design, Keller traveled to Basel where, at a bar on the banks of the Rhine, he met a Berlin lawyer, Dr. Hans Etscheit, who was an Abwehr agent and had introduced Mueller to Canaris. Etscheit knew Keller and spent the evening with him, during which both men drank a great deal of wine. Keller, who was in monk's habit, engaged Etscheit's confidence and Etscheit, assuming that because Keller was a Jesuit he was anti-Nazi, informed him of the Schwarze Kapelle's plot for the removal of Hitler. At that moment, in fact, said Etscheit, Mueller was at the Vatican contacting the British. It was a most convivial evening, and when Etscheit departed, he gave Keller, whom he supposed to be a poor monk making a humble pilgrimage in sandals and cowl to St. Peter's, 100 Swiss francs to make his journey across the Alps more pleasant.

Keller hardly needed the money; he sped in the opulence of a wagon-lit to Rome to see what Mueller was doing. At the Vatican he approached Father Augustin Maier for information. He told Maier that he had heard that Mueller was engaged in treasonable talks with the British, that this action would endanger the neutrality of the Vatican, and that he was afraid Mueller was trying to compromise him personally yet again. Did Maier know anything of such matters? Maier said he did not, but once Keller had left his cell, he went immediately to speak with his friend Mueller at his hotel, the Albergo Flora on the Via Veneto, which was used exclusively by Abwehr personnel. Mueller listened coolly but anxiously; and when it became clear that Keller had embarked upon a personal vendetta that might implicate the entire conspiracy, he left Rome for Berlin to warn Canaris and Oster. At the same time Keller hastened to Stuttgart to inform his SD controller and to write a preliminary report for Heydrich, dutifully making a copy for Canaris in his capacity as an Abwehr agent.

When Mueller arrived at Abwehr headquarters in Berlin, he was met by Oster and his principal deputy and co-conspirator, Hans von Dohnanyi. They handed him Canaris's copy of Keller's report to the SD with the somewhat humorous remark that they had not expected to have to protect Mueller from his own kind. Mueller read the report, which was based exclusively upon Etscheit's story and which admitted that no confirmation of the allegations could be obtained at the Vatican. Nevertheless, the allegations were grave enough to hang the conspirators if Heydrich could get more information.

The gravity of the situation intensified when the conspirators learned that Heydrich had summoned Keller to Berlin, and Keller had told him, embellishing his original report, that Mueller was engaged in some Jesuitical plot against Hitler. Keller then went to see Oster and Dohnanyi and told them that Heydrich regarded Mueller as a traitor whose arrest was imminent. The entire conspiracy was clearly endangered; everyone knew that the Gestapo had the means and the will to make men talk, even men as stout and as brave as Mueller.

Oster informed Canaris of this new threat, and Canaris acted. Meeting with Mueller in his office, he asked him to dictate a report to his confidential secretary. In the report Mueller was to say that before the war he had learned that some of the generals had planned a *coup d'état* to forestall a conflict. He was not to mention the names Beck or Halder but rather General von Fritsch, the former C-in-C of the army whom Hitler had dismissed in 1938 for trumped-up homosexual activities and who had sought, and found, a soldier's death in Poland. Canaris also directed Mueller to include the name of General Walther von Reichenau, a man whom Hitler admired and trusted and would soon make a field marshal. Puzzled, Mueller went away to dictate the report which, when it was finished, he handed to the admiral.

Canaris took the report to the Reichskanzlei to inform the Fuehrer in person. He told Hitler that he considered the allegations of great gravity, although he stressed that the most diligent inquiries by both the Abwehr and the SD had not been able to produce any substantiation. Hitler read the report with interest and concern—until he came to the name Reichenau. Then he threw it aside with the single word *"Schmarren"*—nonsense. Canaris apologized to the Fuehrer for having wasted his time, and withdrew with the assurance that he was convinced the report was inaccurate.

That evening Canaris went to Heydrich's home to discuss the affair. "Just imagine," he said to Heydrich, "here I thought I was bringing the Führer something really important in the shape of a report from Dr. Josef Müller, my ace man in the Vatican, about plans for a military coup. Then, when he finished reading it, the Führer threw it down and cried, *Schmarren.*"

The maneuver effectively quenched, for the moment, Heydrich's inquiries. But they were revived when a Swiss newspaper published a report that high officers of the General Staff were involved in a plot against Hitler. Always on the alert, Heydrich once again sent Keller to the Vatican; and once again all Keller's reports about Mueller reached Canaris at the same time as they reached Heydrich. Unfortunately, Keller's activities acted as a brake upon the Vatican negotiations, in which time was of the greatest importance if an understanding was to be reached with Britain *before* the start of Case Yellow.

Finally, Keller went too far. He was reported to have boasted to a contact at the Vatican (who was also an Abwehr agent, although Keller was not aware of it) that he was on a special mission for the Abwehr to investigate a plot against the Fuehrer. Canaris went to Heydrich and complained that Keller's clumsiness was disturbing his cover and deception plan for Case Yellow. At a time when absolute discretion was needed if the plan was to succeed, here was a drunken monk proclaiming his trade and his mission in—of all places—the Vatican, which was neutral territory. And if Keller was embarrassing Abwehr operations, Canaris said, might he not also be embarrassing SD operations? Heydrich, no doubt with some suspicion, agreed that it might be better if Keller were transferred to duties where his tongue might not be quite so dangerous. Canaris informed Heydrich that he had no further use for Keller's services, and recommended that Heydrich dismiss him as well. But Keller, with his special knowledge of the Jesuit world, was far too valuable to Heydrich. He was retained by the SD and would later go to Paris with the occupation forces to keep an eye on the Jesuits in that city.

The Schwarze Kapelle had escaped by a whisker. Still the conspiracy did not prosper; for while it had powerful support, the plotters found it almost impossible to communicate with each other as the forces of security and surveillance, always quickened when military action was imminent, worked to protect the secrets of Case Yellow. No telephone line, no teleprinter line, no letter could be regarded as secure. Hitler himself was a hard man to find; he changed his schedules and itineraries daily for the very purpose of preventing any action against his person—for he was not unaware of the discontent of his generals. And as the plot wavered upon the brink of collapse, and as Hitler ordered and reordered Zero Day for Case Yellow with bewildering frequency, even Halder was prepared to condone murder. "Cannot someone finally put an end to this dog!" he grumbled to Canaris and Oster. He took to carrying a pistol with him when visiting Hitler. But always, when the impulse was strongest and the opportunity present, his courage failed him. He could not, he said, bring himself as a "human being and a Christian to shoot down an unarmed man."

There seemed to be no other way to avert Case Yellow. When, on November 5, 1939, Brauchitsch, the C-in-C of the army, went to the Fuehrer to make a final appeal against launching the offensive, Hitler flew into a rage against his generals and threw him out of his office. Threatened by the specter of another bloodbath like the "Night of the Long Knives," Halder declared that no further action must be taken to resist Case Yellow and ordered the destruction of all plans and documents relating to the conspiracy and the coup. The Schwarze Kapelle had wound the clock of revolution, but the bell would not sound. "We have no one who will throw the bomb," Oster announced, "in order to liberate our generals from their scruples." And then, as if the fates intended to bury the Schwarze Kapelle for good, there occurred the Venlo Incident.

7

The Venlo Incident

THE WAR was two months old when, in November 1939, Sinclair died suddenly of cancer and Menzies was appointed acting chief of MI-6. Ultra was not yet operational and it was imperative to cultivate all possible sources of intelligence about the Third Reich, including the Schwarze Kapelle. It was intriguing to believe that the German General Staff might itself overthrow Hitler and restore the peace; even more intriguing was the possibility that Canaris was a member of the conspiracy. Yet Menzies's attitude toward the Schwarze Kapelle was like that of the British government: alert for mischief but prepared to listen. So it was that as the Vatican negotiations ran their troubled course, a second line of communication appeared to have opened up from Berlin to The Hague.

On October 30, 1939, the two most senior MI-6 officers on the continent—Major S. Payne Best and Captain R. Henry Stevens—awaited "emissaries of the German General Staff" at the small Dutch city of Arnhem. Menzies had warned the British agents that this new overture might be a trap engineered by Himmler and Heydrich to compromise the British intelligence system, or part of some large deception scheme to conceal German military intentions. Instructed to proceed with caution, Best, who had close connections with the Dutch intelligence chief, Colonel van de Plassche, arranged that the emissaries be detained and investigated by the Dutch border police before their meeting. Lieutenant Dirk Klop, the Dutch intelligence officer assigned to Best and Stevens to arrange the interrogation, established that the emissaries' papers showed them to be who they said they were—Captain Schaemmel, of the transportation corps, and Captain Hausmann, of the army medical corps.

The interrogation and a baggage search revealed nothing to alarm Best and Stevens and they signaled Klop to release the emissaries. They came out of the police station into the sleet-driven street, entered Best's blue

Buick, and were driven to Amsterdam for their meeting. Neither Best nor Stevens had any reason to suspect that the emissaries were, in fact, Brigadeführer SS Walter Schellenberg, the chief of the foreign intelligence section of the SD, and a friend whose appearance and manner suggested an upper-class Austrian officer of the Wehrmacht but who was Professor Max de Crinis, a psychologist at Berlin University and the Charité Hospital. The mission of Schellenberg and de Crinis, as assigned them by Himmler and Heydrich with the knowledge and approval of Hitler, was to open negotiations with the British and attempt to establish the nature and extent of other conspiracies against the Fuehrer.

The meeting with Best and Stevens took place at MI-6 headquarters at Niewe Uitleg 15, the offices of the "Continental Trading Corporation" on a cobbled street beside one of Amsterdam's canals. At the end of the meeting, which lasted until after dark, an *aide-mémoire* was produced, the text of which, according to Schellenberg, read:

> The political overthrow of Hitler and his closest assistants was to be followed immediately by the conclusion of peace with the Western Powers. The terms were to be the restoration of Austria, Czechoslovakia and Poland to their former status; the renunciation of Germany's economic policies and her return to the gold standard. The possibility of a return to Germany of the colonies she had held before the First World War was one of the most important subjects of our discussion.

When the *aide-mémoire* was completed, Stevens left the room and spoke on the telephone with Menzies in London. Menzies recalled later that he was "encouraged" by the results of the exchange but warned Stevens that he had no authority to proceed further until the opinion of Lord Halifax was known. Menzies also warned Stevens to "watch out for yourselves," and said he would telephone instructions that evening. Best and Stevens entertained the emissaries at dinner. During the course of the meal—at which Best served the most "marvellous oysters" that Schellenberg could remember and at which the conversation included Dutch painting and German violin music—Best suggested that the emissaries might be provided with a small wireless transceiver and a cipher with which to communicate with the British. But first, said Best, he would have to await further instructions from London.

The dinner party ended when Schellenberg complained of a headache. He was shown to his room by Best who, after having obtained some aspirin for the German, went to his office to take Menzies's call. According to Menzies, he warned Best that, while the terms of the *aide-mémoire* were interesting, they did not correspond with the terms being offered by German negotiators elsewhere—presumably at the Vatican. This did not automatically mean that this new overture was a trap, but the discrepancy had caused nervousness in London. Best asked for permission to supply Schaemmel with a wireless set and a cipher, to which Menzies agreed, and then Best was told that he would receive appropriate communications procedural instructions by the morning. Best also stated, almost as an afterthought, that Schaemmel and Hausmann had suggested that their principal, a "general," might be prepared to fly to London so that further discussions might take place "on the highest plane." Menzies agreed to talk with Halifax to see whether such a meeting was desirable. With that, the call ended.

After breakfast on October 31, Best showed Schaemmel a wireless set—an early version of the "suitcase wireless"—and gave him a cipher with operating instructions and a transmission and reception schedule with MI-6's wireless station in the Chiltern Hills about 40 miles north of London. Best assigned Schaemmel the call sign ON-4, showed him how to work the wireless, and then set out in the Buick to return the emissaries to the German border. There, the Germans disappeared into the sleet mist.

A few days later, on or about November 4, ON-4 came up with a signal that the "general" would be available to fly to London on November 9, and asked for instructions about the means of transportation and the point of departure, and for guarantees about the security of the party and the complete secrecy of the mission. Shortly thereafter Best received instructions from Menzies that Cabinet approval had been received for the "general"—who was not named throughout the discussions but whom Menzies thought at first might be Beck—and the emissaries to come to London by air from Copenhagen on November 9. An RAF Anson courier plane of the King's Flight would make the journey. Best, Stevens and Schaemmel had a brief meeting on the border on November 7—the day of Sinclair's funeral—despite Menzies's *direct order* to Best that no further meetings were to take place on the frontier and that if the Germans wished to talk they must do so at The Hague or in Amsterdam. Nevertheless, the men met, Schaemmel was informed of the travel arrangements and a rendezvous was fixed for November 9—at the Café Bacchus at Venlo, a town on the Dutch-German border.

Schellenberg, a sure-footed young SS intellectual who had been recruited by Heydrich personally for the SD, returned to his headquarters at Düsseldorf, where he went over the plan with the "general." The identity of the "general" has never been revealed, nor is it known whom he was supposed to impersonate or how he proposed to convince the British of his bona fides. But it does seem that until the eve of their departure for Venlo and London, Schellenberg and his party intended to make the journey.

Schellenberg retired early in the evening of November 8 and took a sleeping pill. He was in a deep sleep when, sometime after midnight, his bedside telephone rang. Schellenberg struggled to clear his mind, lifted the receiver, and heard the unmistakable voice of Himmler. As Schellenberg wrote afterwards, Himmler announced that during the evening of the 8th an attempt had been made on Hitler's life. A bomb had gone off in the Bürgerbräukeller at Munich just after Hitler had finished making his annual speech to the Nazi old guard. "Several old Party comrades have been killed," Himmler declared, "and the damage is pretty considerable." It was then that Himmler gave new orders concerning Schellenberg's mission. "There's no doubt that the British Secret Service is behind it all," Schellenberg recorded that Himmler stated. "(Hitler) now says—and this is an order—when you meet the British agents for your conference tomorrow, you are to arrest them immediately and bring them to Germany."

A bomb had indeed gone off at the Bürgerbräukeller in Munich, and its seismic effect would be felt all the way to MI-6 headquarters in London. Hitler had arrived at the beer cellar at 8:07 P.M. to address the Nazis who had supported him during the 1923 Putsch—his first attempt to seize power that had ended in a hail of police bullets and a term in jail. At 8:12 P.M. he began a violent speech—primarily against Churchill and England —that lasted until 9:08 P.M. At 9:22 P.M. Hitler left the cellar with all his lieutenants, rather earlier than had been programmed, and at 9:30 P.M. a bomb exploded with great violence. It killed six of the old guard and wounded some sixty others.

The outcry was immediate and ferocious, particularly against MI-6. The German press uniformly accused the "British Secret Service" of the attack and announced a reward of $200,000 for information leading to the arrest of the "assassins." In fact, the attack had nothing to do with MI-6, much as that organization might have wished for the Fuehrer's death. A crazed German carpenter, Georg Elser, was eventually arrested on suspicion when a photograph of the cellar, with an X marking the spot where the bomb had been planted, was found in his luggage as he attempted to cross the Swiss border. But Hitler, when he was informed of his narrow brush with death, was in a mood for retaliation. He had had reservations about Schellenberg's mission and had more than once indicated that it was too dangerous to proceed with and should be called off. Now he ordered that the British agents be kidnapped and brought to Berlin.

On November 9, Schellenberg rose with the dawn to brief his plain-clothes bodyguard, which was under the command of an expert SS officer, Alfred Naujocks. Schellenberg told Naujocks of Himmler's orders, and the two men agreed upon a plan. Then the party set out from Düsseldorf. At two o'clock that afternoon Schellenberg and the "general" crossed into Holland at Venlo and went to the Café Bacchus, an ordinary frontier café with candy-striped awnings and a small children's playground. Everything appeared normal, but out of sight on the German side of the border, Naujocks and his SS men awaited their signal.

At 2:08 P.M. Best's blue Buick edged its way down the narrow street and stopped as someone put his head round the corner. There were four men in the car—Best, Stevens, the driver and Lieutenant Klop—and clearly they were suspicious, but the car turned the corner at slow speed and approached the Café Bacchus. At that moment three Mercedes crashed through the pole dividing Germany from Holland, and an SS man fired his machine pistol into the air to scatter the Dutch border guards. One of the Mercedes came down the street at high speed and blocked the Buick. Naujocks and a party of four SS men leaped out and seized and handcuffed the two Britons. As they were bundling them—and their driver—into the Mercedes, Naujocks saw Klop draw a pistol. He shot and killed the Dutch agent. The Mercedes did not turn around; it roared its way backwards up the street and across the border into Germany. The operation was all over in the twinkling of an eye, and Best and Stevens, two of MI-6's most important agents in western Europe, were rushed to Berlin where they were clapped into a cell in the basement of SD headquarters at 8 Prinzalbrechtstrasse, a former art school. Hitler, jubilant at the coup, received Schellenberg, Naujocks and the SS men at the Reichskanzlei and presented each with the Iron Cross.

For Menzies, the Venlo Incident proved an inauspicious beginning of his career as C, and his critics did not hesitate to use the blunders of Stevens and Best as a weapon to try to remove him. The Foreign Office, suspecting further treachery, broke off the Vatican talks, but Menzies did not allow the incident to rupture whatever contact existed between him and Canaris. He may not have trusted the little admiral or the conspirators of the Schwarze Kapelle, but they were a line of contact that might prove invaluable later on. Moreover—as Menzies said later—there was some evidence that the Abwehr had not taken part in the Venlo Incident and that Canaris was not aware of the operation. This was true, for Canaris was aghast when he heard of the kidnapping.

The conspirators of the Schwarze Kapelle also suffered a severe setback. Clearly, the incident would make the British even more cautious in dealing with them, and generals who might have been expected to join the conspiracy dived for cover as the Gestapo investigated every shred of evidence about a plot. The most serious threat was the possibility that the Gestapo would make Best and Stevens talk. How much did they know of the Vatican exchanges? They knew nothing, and under interrogation—in the best traditions of the service—they would not say anything that was either useful or true. But the conspirators could not take that chance.

Finally, the Venlo Incident marked a turning point in the secret war between Britain and the Third Reich. It was a strange fact that in the opening rounds of that war both sides had gone about their business with relative gentility for fear that violence would provoke the enemy into violent retaliation. The kidnapping of Best and Stevens served to remove that restraint. The white kid gloves were off, and henceforward the secret war would grow increasingly violent until, as General Gubbins of SOE later remarked, it became "bloodier than the Somme."

"Adroit Intrigue"

THE VATICAN talks hung fire for over a month, and were only resumed when the Pope vouched for the bona fides and honesty of Mueller. With that assurance, made personally by Pius XII in a communication to Lord Halifax, the conversations reopened with a meeting between the Pope and Sir D'Arcy Osborne, which took place—according to the British Cabinet Minutes—at the Vatican on January 12, 1940. To all appearances, their conversations were a most important step toward an armistice before Case Yellow began. The Pope warned Sir D'Arcy that he had information that a "violent, bitter and unscrupulous offensive" against Holland was being prepared by Hitler for mid-February; and he went on to declare that "the generals" were prepared to act to forestall this offensive if "they could be assured of peace." Sir D'Arcy seems to have been acquainted with the MI-6 evaluation of the Schwarze Kapelle's seriousness and ability of purpose at this time; MI-6 thought, rightly enough, that a German military revolt might succeed, but the Foreign Office "doubted" if any of "the generals" had it in them to "take the initiative." As a result, Sir D'Arcy told the Pope that he considered their approach "so vague as to be useless." And at that, if the Cabinet Minutes are accurate, the Pope tried to withdraw from the conversations.

However, at a further meeting with the British ambassador on February 7, the Supreme Pontiff returned to the matter, although, as Sir D'Arcy reported, he did so "with reluctance." The Pope said that he had new information that "part of the army was prepared to act, even at the risk of civil war, if they could be reassured that the territorial integrity of Germany together with Austria would be respected." Sir D'Arcy, in a telegram to Lord Halifax, now reported himself "impressed" by this new approach. And so apparently was Lord Halifax. On February 17, Halifax instructed Sir D'Arcy that Britain could not act without France. But in that same communication, Halifax indicated that Britain would be prepared to offer terms to "the generals," provided they proposed what Halifax called "a definite programme authoritatively vouched for." This program was to include, again according to the Cabinet Minutes, reparations for Germany's neighbors and firm guarantees for security and freedom of choice for Austria. Those, so far as the Minutes show, were the only conditions the British made.

But—if Mueller is to be believed—the British in fact demanded a great deal more in return for an armistice. Shortly before February 1, 1940, Mueller brought to Berlin what would be called "the long-awaited British answer on which rested the final hopes of the German Opposition in the Twilight War." This answer, according to Mueller, was written by Father Leiber on a single sheet of paper. It was dictated to him by the Pope and contained details about the peace Britain would negotiate with a post-Hitler government. According to Sir John Wheeler-Bennett, a high officer of the Political Warfare Executive, the paper was the Pope's personal stationery and to it Father Leiber affixed his own calling card.

With the arrival of the paper by the hand of Mueller in Berlin, Mueller and Dohnanyi wrote a report of the Vatican dialogue in German military terminology. This document, which embodied Leiber's transcription of the Pope's statements, ran to twelve pages and came to be called the "X-Report," after Mueller, who was known as "Agent X" at the Abwehr. Leiber's note appears to have led off with the categorical phrase: *"Conditio sine qua non:* constitution of a government capable of negotiating." This, in turn, formed the premise for the X-Report. But Mueller and Dohnanyi appear to have changed the wording slightly but significantly: *"Conditio sine qua non:* removal of the National Socialist regime and constitution of a government capable of negotiating."

After the war, the nine survivors of the Schwarze Kapelle who saw the X-Report were unanimous in stating that it "contained a broad hint from London on the form the new (German) state should take." It referred to a "decentralized" Germany—presumably a federation of states. The future of Austria was to be decided by plebiscite, and it "contemplated" what the British called "a certain restoration of Czechia"—Czechoslovakia, which was taken to mean the reunion of Czech and Slovak territories. The Sudetenland of Czechoslovakia was to remain with Germany. Here, however, the unanimity of recollection ends. In regard to Germany's eastern frontiers, Halder insisted that they were to be restored to what they were in 1914; according to Leiber, the state of Poland was to be restored completely. Mueller himself recalled that areas opting for Germany were "to remain with the Reich."

On balance, the X-Report seems to have been a protocol for a treaty; not the treaty itself. But the Schwarze Kapelle appears to have accepted the document as something more than a mere protocol. On April 3, 1940,

Canaris and Halder discussed the report at Zossen, and immediately there-after Halder undertook to present it to the C-in-C, Brauchitsch, presumably with the intention of fostering some new action by the generals against Case Yellow. He gave the report to Brauchitsch to read overnight and, when he returned in the morning, he related that he found the Commander-in-Chief in an "unusually serious mood." Brauchitsch declared:

> You should not have shown this to me. What we face here is pure na-tional treason (*Landesverrat*). That does not come into question for us under any conditions. We are at war. That one in time of peace establishes contact with a foreign power may be considered. In war this is impossible for a soldier. Moreover, in this case it is not a matter between governments but of a decision between philosophies of life. The removal of Hitler would therefore be useless.

Brauchitsch turned upon the Chief of the General Staff. His agony of conscience was clear; but he could not and would not compromise the ancient General Staff belief—that if the nation had come to war the thing to do was to win it, not discuss its morality. Like Beck, he believed that Germany was not equal to a major war of long duration; but it does not follow that men in high places have great moral courage. Brauchitsch was a case in point. Who, he demanded to know, had brought this document to Zossen? He must be arrested and the document sent to OKW or to the SD for investigation. At that, Halder, who was never far from a nervous collapse as he planned Case Yellow on the one hand, and intrigued against the Fuehrer on the other replied: "If there is anyone to be arrested, then please arrest me." Brauchitsch said no more about treason, and Halder said no more about rebellion.

Halder, whose family had given Germany soldiers for three hundred years, a quick, shrewd and witty man, was a Bavarian, and a Bavarian, as Bismarck remarked, was "a cross between a man and an Austrian." Caught between two fierce fires, his caste training and his Catholic morality, Halder now more or less withdrew from the Schwarze Kapelle. For him, the flames of treason were too hot. As for the X-Report, it went into the big safe manufactured by Pohlschroeder of Dortmund where the Abwehr kept its most secret papers in a bunker at Zossen, and there it remained like a time bomb. In effect, Brauchitsch had dashed the sword of rebellion from the hands of the conspirators within the army high command. But elsewhere, the flames still flickered.

At the Vatican, on April 3, 1940, Sir D'Arcy Osborne was back in Pius XII's study but, as the Supreme Pontiff announced, he feared that the *démarche* had come to an end. In fact, conscious of the dangers it was running, the Vatican had lost confidence in the negotiations. Some of the men around the Pope had tried to establish the identities of Mueller's principals; and when they failed, they began to wonder about Mueller's authority. Certainly no attempt had been made to overthrow the Nazi régime. In fact, within a few short days, the Fuehrer, bolder than ever, would order the surprise invasion of Denmark and Norway. But Beck was not yet ready to give up. He realized that the Allies must conclude that the Vatican talks were another Venlo if something was not done, so he decided to make an attempt to reopen the negotiations.

Once again Mueller set out on the road to Rome to warn the world of Case Yellow—the gravest act of *Landesverrat* so far. For if he succeeded, and Case Yellow was repulsed, how many German soldiers must perish? The message he brought with him had been "carefully formulated" at Abwehr headquarters on the basis of Beck's advice. It contained, as Mueller recalled afterwards, an "indignant repudiation of the approaching attack on the Low Countries," and the statement that "Hitler will attack and this action lies just ahead." Mueller handed this warning to Father Leiber, and then went to the home of Abbot General Hubert Noots, the head of the Premonstratensian Order, and a Belgian. Noots knew—and trusted— Mueller of old, and Mueller gave him a "detailed picture of the situation and prospects as he saw them." There were two such meetings; and then Mueller, aware of the great personal peril in which he now stood, returned home on May 4. He purchased, with some cigars and a lighter, a frontier entry and exit stamp from an Italian immigration official; and with this stamp he proceeded to make unrecognizable in his passport the dates on which he had entered and left Italy.

Mueller's warning circulated through the Vatican, and it seems certain that Sir D'Arcy was aware of it. But when it reached London, it was treated as if it was part of some large-scale deception by the SD to cover Hitler's attack plans. The specter of Venlo was not easily forgotten, and the Vatican negotiations themselves were referred to in the British Cabinet Minutes as attempts to "wangle a botched-up peace."

The matter did not end there, however, for the conspirators of the Schwarze Kapelle would come dangerously close to paying the ultimate price for their treason. Father Leiber, having delivered Mueller's warning to the Pope, went to inform a Jesuit priest, the Reverend Theodor Monnens, a colleague at the Gregorian University. Monnens took the warning to the Belgian ambassador, Adrien Nieuwenhuys, who brushed it aside with the angry words: "No German would do a thing like that." But on the heels of Monnens there came another more impressive informant—Abbot General Noots. Before the week was out, said Noots, the Germans would invade the Low Countries with tanks, infantry, paratroopers and aircraft. This time Nieuwenhuys listened and, on May 2, 1940, he sent a warning telegram to the Foreign Ministry in Brussels.

Alarmed, Brussels asked for more, and on May 3, Nieuwenhuys sent further details of Mueller's warning. But he—and the Belgian government—was disinclined to believe it. Like the British government, they interpreted it as part of the war of nerves of the period. It seemed incomprehensible that higher motives than treachery were involved in the Schwarze Kapelle's actions.

But as the ambassador's two messages were transmitted to Brussels, the Forschungsamt was listening. The Forschungsamt tapped telephones, opened letters, solved intercepted ciphered telegrams and maintained a close relationship with the SD, supplying it, at least in the early days of Nazism, with most of its external intelligence. Its productions were printed on brown paper embossed with the Reich eagle and were, as a result, known as "brown birds." The Forschungsamt intercepted both of Nieuwenhuys's telegrams, they were quickly deciphered, and equally quickly reached the desks of Heydrich, Himmler—and, presumably, Hitler. Astounded that there was a traitor in his entourage, Hitler ordered a full-scale investigation.

News of this investigation leaked to Canaris and Oster; and Mueller, who was now at home in Munich, was ordered to report to Berlin—covering his tracks as he came. Worried by the urgency of his orders, Mueller set out by car and went as instructed to Oster's home. There, Oster told him that they were both "deep in the ink," and reminded Mueller of their pledge that, if one of them had to go to the gallows, he would do so alone. Then Oster instructed Mueller to go without delay to Abwehr headquarters and see Canaris. Mueller met the little admiral in the corridor of the executive floor, and Canaris stopped and lisped, as he often did when he was agitated: "The brown birds! Have you seen the brown birds?" When Mueller shook his head, Canaris told him to go to Dohnanyi's office and read and consider the contents of "the brown birds."

When Mueller saw "the brown birds," he realized immediately that they were the texts of Nieuwenhuys's messages of May 2 and 3. As he had feared, he was being labeled a traitor or an agent provocateur. Finally Canaris came into the room and asked: "Is that you?" Mueller responded: "Admiral, I cannot be sure; it can be, yes and it can be, no." His composure so impressed Canaris that he laid his hand on Mueller's shoulder and declared: *"Unser ruhende Pol in der Erscheinung Flucht"*—"Our calm pole in the flight of events." Then Canaris asked Mueller: "Are you prepared to receive an order from me?"—for the terms of Mueller's employment provided that he could accept or reject any order. Mueller replied that it would depend upon its character.

Its character was astonishing and illustrated what Liedig would mean by "adroit intrigue." Canaris asked Mueller to go to Rome to investigate the Case Yellow leak for which he alone was responsible. It was preposterous: Mueller ordered to Rome to be—as he himself put it later—"his own gendarme." Yet he agreed to go. Canaris told him that he must leave immediately, and that he must call from Berlin to Munich to arrange to have his baggage waiting for him at Munich Airport when his personal plane landed. As soon as he had taken off again, Canaris would order all frontier controls lifted for his flight to Italy—to frustrate Heydrich and prevent Mueller from getting caught up in the SD's net. Further, Colonel Hans Helferich—Canaris's representative at SIM, the Italian secret service, and the Abwehr chief at Rome—would be informed that Mueller was arriving on a special mission to investigate the leakage of state secrets, and he would be instructed to give Mueller unreserved assistance. Helferich would also be told that the investigation must take precedence over rank, and that control must remain with Mueller.

Mueller departed, and Canaris went to see Hitler to tell him that he had ordered the strongest possible inquiry into the leakage of Case Yellow at Rome. He informed the Fuehrer that he had instructed his special agent, Josef Mueller, to proceed there without delay. Hitler gave his assent to the inquiry. It was a stroke of pure genius.

Mueller arrived safely at Rome and immediately called upon Father Leiber. He told Leiber that Ambassador Nieuwenhuys must leave the Vatican without delay, so that "he could not easily be got at." Leiber agreed to do all that he could to protect Nieuwenhuys, but it would also be imperative to protect the identity of Abbot General Noots, who had passed the Case Yellow leak to the Belgian ambassador, and to disguise the role that Mueller himself had played.

Mueller now called on Helferich and asked to see his file on the leak in order to acquaint himself with what had so far been done. Then, in order to impress Helferich, he called Canaris on the A-Net, the Abwehr's most secret telephone system. In Helferich's presence, Mueller announced calculatingly that he had had a "very satisfactory conversation" with Helferich, who, he said, had conducted the investigation with great skill. Helferich, who was a lazy, agreeable man, was flattered by this report; he was also grateful that the extra work involved in the investigation had been taken out of his hands.

Early the next morning Mueller and Leiber met again and, as he recalled later, Leiber revealed that he had had a brainwave: "One of our fathers, a Belgian, has left for the Congo and is well beyond reach. Why not shove everything onto him as the 'compatriot' referred to by Nieuwenhuys? That should serve to draw attention away from Noots." According to the OSS man who later investigated the whole of this incident, Harold C. Deutsch: "There evidently was a trace of elfin mischief in this usually so austere member of the Society of Jesus." Mueller agreed to the plan and returned to Abwehr headquarters to announce that a Belgian Jesuit had left

Rome suddenly and quite obviously was the compatriot to whom Nieuwen-huys had referred in his two telegrams.

There remained a final problem: How had the information reached Rome in the first place? With the help of Abbot General Noots, whose sense of intrigue was as sharp as Leiber's, Mueller concocted a story that he knew Himmler would like to believe: that Count Galeazzo Ciano, Mussolini's son-in-law and the Italian Foreign Minister, whom Himmler detested, had ferreted the information out of persons in Ribbentrop's entourage—for Himmler also detested Ribbentrop. Thus fact and fiction were so interwoven as to be indistinguishable—and to be acceptable to the SD's prejudices.

Both Canaris and Mueller had played their hands cleverly, and the investigation was closed for the moment, although Heydrich was growing deeply suspicious that Abwehr headquarters was a nest of traitors. Unfortunately, the Vatican talks were also closed. Had it not been for the Venlo Incident, an agreement might have been struck with the British. At the very least, Britain and her continental Allies might have given greater credence to the Schwarze Kapelle and the peril they faced with the onset of Case Yellow. But they did not. Truth and treason are unlikely companions.

The Vatican was not the only channel of communication that the Schwarze Kapelle used to try to confound Hitler in the anxious months between the fall of Poland and the start of Case Yellow. Very early in the morning of November 4, 1939, the guard at the British Embassy at Oslo was making his rounds in a snowstorm when he found a parcel on the stone ledge by the porter's lodge. It was half-covered with snow and had it not been found then might not have been discovered for weeks. It was about 3 inches thick, the size and shape of a block of legal-size pads, and it was addressed to the British naval attaché. When the attaché came on duty, he opened the parcel and found a note signed by a "well-wishing German scientist." There was no explanation for the parcel's contents. It contained documents in German together with diagrams of a nature that clearly indicated weaponry.

The parcel was sent in the diplomatic bag to London and found its way to the desk of Dr. R. V. Jones, who was a member of the scientific and technical department of MI-6. Jones was 28, a tall, solemn product of Wadham and Balliol, and of the Clarendon Laboratory. A physicist, natural philosopher and astronomer, he had joined MI-6 in September 1939, and his first task was to examine MI-6 files on German weaponry and make a report. Thus acquainted with the sum total of the knowledge available to Britain of German weapons programs, Jones was in a position to study and evaluate the "Oslo Report," as the contents of the parcel came to be called, with less political skepticism than his superiors.

It was a startling document. Among a mass of technical information, there was data on a new torpedo that homed onto its target acoustically, a new system to permit the Luftwaffe to bomb blind, and German progress on two radar systems—Würzburg and Freya. There was much else besides, but Jones was particularly intrigued by what the report described as the Aggregatprogramm—the rocket program. According to the report, the Germans were test-firing large long-range rockets at a place called Peenemünde on the island of Usedom in the Baltic.

It was obvious from the report—were it true—that a wholly new dimension of warfare was beginning to unfold. The ingenuity of German scientists was well known, and as the U.S. General Board recorded later: "Tremendous strides in rocket development (had been) made and it is not hard to visualize what could have been in store for the Allies had the Germans been given time to complete the development." But at this early stage of the war, no one was in a position to determine the validity of the Oslo Report. Not until the existence of the X-Gerät—the blind bombing device that enabled the Luftwaffe to zero in so accurately on British cities, Coventry among them—was confirmed, and not until a Würzburg radar was "pinched" in a Commando raid against the French village of Bruneval, did the scientific intelligence authorities accept the truth of the report. But that was not until 1941–42.

The source of the Oslo Report was perhaps the chief reason it was greeted with incredulity. Who was the "well-wishing German scientist," and was the report valid or just another of Hitler's scare tactics? For many years the hand behind the report defied identification—until Canaris's methodology became known. In evaluating the report, both Dr. Jones and Dr. Robert Cockburn, the chief of the radar countermeasures section of the Telecommunications Research Establishment (TRE), debated at length who in the German hierarchy was so highly placed that he could obtain what seemed to be the entire German secret weapons program. There were many scientists who might be privy to part of the program, but none would, it was reasoned, have access to the whole. Only men such as Canaris would have this kind of access, and, as important, only men such as Canaris would have had the means to evade Gestapo surveillance and spirit the package abroad for delivery. The Oslo Report might well have been another "leak" similar in purpose to his many proven activities on behalf of the Schwarze Kapelle. As Cockburn said later: "It seemed quite possible that the Report was Canaris's doing. But we never found out. And we never discovered who else but Canaris or his agent could have done it."

While the belief that the Oslo Report was the work of Canaris is only speculation, there were, at other times, comparable acts that were beyond question the work of the Schwarze Kapelle. Among them were such episodes as the 1943 "Lisbon Report," which contained more very valuable information about the German rocket program in addition to political information of the highest importance; the 1943 "Istanbul Report," which provided MI-6 with the Enigma keys for the Abwehr's signals trunk routes; and the 1942–43 "Berne Report," which revealed to the OSS all that was important in the German Foreign Ministry signals file for a period of nearly two years. But a mystery similar to the one surrounding the Oslo Report will probably always remain around the greatest intelligence triumph of the war in Europe—the evolution of Ultra.

To produce Ultra, the Turing engine at Bletchley was designed to duplicate, at least to a certain degree, and thus to unbutton the secret ciphers of the German Enigma machine. But because the machine was capable of an almost infinite number of ciphers, depending upon the keying procedures that were being used, knowledge of those procedures facilitated the use of the Turing engine and was of the utmost importance to British cryptanalysts. Part of their knowledge would later be derived from the Enigma machines captured, in some cases along with their keying procedures and transmission schedules, on the battlefield. And the capture, in May of 1941, of the Enigma machine and related material on the U-110 added immeasurably to Britain's understanding of just how the German secret ciphers were keyed. But there is also some reason to believe that the Enigma's keying procedures were systematically and regularly transmitted to MI-6 from a fairly early stage in the war by the conspirators of the Schwarze Kapelle. The intention behind this betrayal was, it can be assumed, to expose Hitler's plans in his own words (for he used Enigma for his secret signals) so that the Allies might take suitable military and diplomatic action to counteract them. Why should the Schwarze Kapelle not betray the Enigma keys? They had betrayed more or less all of Hitler's secrets since he announced his decision to make war on November 5, 1937. To give Britain the Enigma keys would surely be the fastest and, for the conspirators, the safest way of revealing Hitler's intentions.

The supposition is not improbable. But again the question must be asked: Who among the conspirators had both the motive and the opportunity to betray Enigma? Suspicion falls upon General Erich Fellgiebel, the signalsmaster of OKW who was finally executed by the Gestapo for grand treason, and upon his deputy, General Fritz Thiele, who was also executed. Hitler himself was quite certain that Fellgiebel and Thiele were in contact with the British and even went so far as to state in a conversation with Albert Speer, his Minister of Munitions and Armaments Production, that Fellgiebel had a direct telecommunications line to the British in Switzerland. Certainly, Fellgiebel did arrange to lay secret telephone and teleprinter lines between his headquarters and the outposts of the conspiracy across hundreds of miles without the knowledge of either OKW or the Gestapo.

There are other even more telling reasons to suspect Fellgiebel. He was the man who was in charge of experimenting with the Enigma machine, and it was upon his recommendation that Enigma was introduced for use throughout the Wehrmacht. Further, Fellgiebel and Thiele, who were close friends, advised upon and controlled all OKW and army communications, and had much to do with the signals arrangements not only for the other two armed services but also for the Abwehr and the SS. Between them they almost wholly controlled cipher creation and distribution, as well as wireless security and wireless intelligence; and what they did not control in the world of secret communications was, with few exceptions, controlled by the Abwehr. Finally, both men were members of the Schwarze Kapelle, Fellgiebel since its inception at the time of the murders of Schleicher and Bredow.

But why should Fellgiebel have drunk from the poisoned chalice of conspiracy? He was an especial friend of Beck, and like most of the early conspirators a Wilhelminian and a soldier of the old German Empire. Born in 1886 in Silesia, the son of a landowner, he was a gifted and intelligent man: a classicist, scholar, technician and horseman. His antipathy for Hitler sprang not only from social or moral reasons, but also from his belief, as a member of the General Staff, that Hitler's military policies were strategical lunacy that would destroy Germany. He is said to have declared, as did Canaris at the outbreak of war, that he would do everything within his power to frustrate Hitler's plans. He was perhaps in the best position of all the conspirators to sabotage those plans; he had the means for illicit communication by wireless with the British, and only he had access to all the Enigma ciphers, keying procedures and transmission schedules in use by Germany. Why, therefore, should he not use wireless—the science he knew best—as the weapon for Hitler's ruin? In the recondite world of communications most things would be possible to the man in command.

Whatever Britain's source of information about Enigma, however successful she would eventually become in reading the secret signals of the Wehrmacht, the Turing engine was only partially operational as Case Yellow loomed. Yet the British did not lack for warning. Quite apart from Mueller's Vatican leak, all through the autumn, winter and spring of 1939 and 1940, Oster also attempted to alert them to Hitler's plan to overrun the Low Countries and France.

Oster was deeply troubled by his part in the conspiracy. He was as loyal to the Fatherland as any officer or man, and he sought to quell his conscience with Talleyrand's famous statement: *"Trahison est une question du date."* Yet he could not deny that he was committing the worst crime in the law of the German soldier. As early as October 1939 he had admitted his disquiet to his friend Liedig. Walking together through the woods around the Potsdamer Lake, Oster remarked:

> There is no going back for me anymore. It is much simpler to take a pistol and shoot someone down or to run into a machine gun burst when it is done for a cause than to do what I have determined. I beg you to remain after my death that friend who knows how things were with me and what induced me to do things which others will perhaps never understand or at least would never have done themselves. . . . One may say I am a traitor to my country but actually I am not that. I regard myself as a better German than all those who run after Hitler. It is my plan and my duty to free Germany and thereby the world of this plague.

Oster might as well have saved himself from his agony of spirit; his warnings were neither believed nor heeded, and were repeatedly dismissed as "deceptions" and "psychological warfare." In all, Oster passed, or authorized the passage of, some fifteen of the twenty-eight different dates for the start of Case Yellow; but each time—save the last—Hitler postponed the invasion on account of the weather, which was peculiarly capricious that winter and spring. Most of these warnings were given to his friend Major Sas, who was acting as his principal informant to the West. Sas relayed them to the Dutch and Belgian intelligence authorities; and they, in turn, passed them on to Menzies. But as one "Zero Day" after another came and went, everyone wearied of this continual crying wolf. Gradually, Oster's credibility diminished with the Dutch and the Belgians until he was considered unreliable and, possibly, a dangerous agent provocateur. As a result of this loss of faith, Oster's final warnings were not relayed to the British secret service.

As for Sas, he became a prophet without honor in his own country. He dutifully passed Oster's warnings to his government, including the information that Holland would not escape invasion as she had in the First World War, and that plans for an invasion of Belgium were being made. But his superiors received his information skeptically from the first, and finally he was considered to be a victim of a clever war of nerves being conducted from Berlin by the Abwehr.

Meanwhile, the weeks and months ticked by. Then suddenly, in April 1940, Hitler diverted his attention momentarily from the Low Countries and France to invade Denmark and Norway. At Canaris's instigation, Oster once again passed a warning of the attack to Sas, the object of which was, as Liedig would remember, "to cause the British navy to make a demonstration in Norwegian waters to force Hitler to cancel his plans." Once again the warning was ignored by the Dutch, the Danes, the Norwegians—and the British. The Allies were dealt another stunning blow, but strangely, even this did not seem to add credibility to the imminence of Case Yellow. Yet Oster and Sas persisted. On the evening of Monday, May

6, 1940, Oster informed Sas that Zero Day for Case Yellow was now set for the 8th, and that it might be preceded by an extremely short ultimatum. Sas enciphered the facts in a telegram to the Dutch Foreign Office, but it proved to be another false alarm. The 8th came and went and Case Yellow did not begin. But that same day Oster called Sas and informed him that Thursday, the 9th, had been earmarked by Hitler as the day upon which "final orders" were to be issued for the attack. If by 9:30 P.M. on the 8th no counter-order had been issued, the Wehrmacht would move.

Oster and Sas met for dinner that evening at Horchers, where the placid and faithful Herr Haeckh, the manager, hung solicitously over their table. They had to be careful for—as Oster knew well, for he employed them—the Abwehr had deaf-mutes there regularly to lipread the conversations of powerful persons. It was, Sas told a Netherlands Parliamentary Tribunal after the war, a "funeral banquet." At 9:30 P.M., having dined, Oster and Sas walked around to the OKW office in the Bendlerstrasse. Sas waited for twenty minutes in a taxi. When Oster emerged he spoke these words: "My dear friend, now it is really all over. There have been no counterorders. The swine has gone off to the Western Front. Now it is definitely all over. I hope we will see each other again after the war." Oster then took his friend by a coat button and added: "Sas, blow up the Meuse bridges for me."

They said their last farewells and Sas hurried to the Dutch legation to telephone the War Ministry at The Hague. He passed Oster's information in code to a naval lieutenant, and then went to work with his colleagues burning confidential paper. At about midnight, Sas received a telephone call from the man who had refused to believe him in the past, Colonel van de Plassche, the chief of the Dutch intelligence service. "I have such bad reports from you about the operation on your wife," announced the colonel. "What is her trouble? Have you consulted all the doctors?" Outraged at the carelessness of van de Plassche, Sas replied angrily: "Yes, but I do not understand how you can bother me in such circumstances. You know it now. There is nothing to change about the operation. I have talked with all the doctors. Tomorrow at dawn it will take place."

At three o'clock the following morning the first Stukas appeared over the fair tulip fields of Holland. The bridges over the Meuse had not been blown. The panzers began to roll across Germany's western frontier at dawn, and within four days the old port of Rotterdam lay smoldering and destroyed. Despite the repeated warnings of the Schwarze Kapelle, despite the information revealed by Ultra that Hitler was assembling vast forces behind the Siegfried Line—information confirmed by aerial reconnaissance—the Wehrmacht obtained what Churchill would call "complete tactical surprise . . . in nearly every case." It took Hitler only fifty-two days to become the conquerer of all of western Europe save the neutral states.

Canaris at Work

On July 19, 1940, at the Kroll Opera House in Berlin, Hitler stood at the lectern in a simple uniform of dove-gray with an Iron Cross on the left breast of his tunic—the Iron Cross he had won in 1914 at Ypres, the same action in which Menzies had won the DSO. "I . . . appeal once more to reason and common sense in Great Britain," he declared, and offered the island peoples a conqueror's charity. "I consider myself in a position to make this appeal since I am not the vanquished begging favours, but the victor speaking in the name of reason. I can see no reason why this war must go on."

Great Britain ignored Hitler's appeal, even as the German nation and armed forces celebrated his new military victory and the conspirators of the Schwarze Kapelle once more despaired of mounting a successful revolution. Yet, incredibly, at that very moment of seeming invincibility a new phase of the conspiracy against Hitler was beginning to take shape in a suite at the Hotel Meurice in Paris. There, several members of the conspiracy met for the ostensible purpose of planning the Fuehrer's triumphant entry into the French capital. They included General Karl-Heinrich von Stuelpnagel, General Eduard Wagner, the chief of the OKW economics branch, General Erich Fellgiebel, and two colonels whose names may be remembered—Henning von Tresckow and Klaus Count von Stauffenberg. When the meeting ended, the conspirators went to Stuelpnagel's room, where they agreed that Hitler's victories had crushed all hope, for the moment, of a rebellion. The thing to do now was to plan for a *coup d'état* along General Staff lines. And it was during these bold and dangerous conversations that Stauffenberg uttered singular words. Hitler, he said, was not a great general. All the great generals of history had also been great lawmakers. But Hitler was not a lawmaker; he was not a Charlemagne, a Justinian, or even a Napoleon. He was a man possessed with a lust for nihilistic power and a passion for cruel display, and therefore, said

Stauffenberg, he must be removed. The idea of tyrannicide, so long rejected by Beck and only indirectly considered by Canaris and Oster, was beginning to occur to Stauffenberg.

Count von Stauffenberg, now thirty-three, was the son of a Swabian nobleman whose family traced its line back to 1262. He was born at the Castle Greiffenstein, a fortress which had long been the seat of the nobility of Württemberg. His father had been Senior Marshal and Lord Privy at the Court of Wilhelm II and his mother was a granddaughter of Field Marshal August Count Wilhelm Neithardt von Gneisenau, one of the founders of the General Staff. The family—including Stauffenberg—was Catholic. Having attended a school for the sons of noblemen at Stuttgart, Stauffenberg at first elected to become an architect, then a cellist, and finally a soldier. He was commissioned into the 17th Cavalry at Bamberg, an élite regiment, and married Nina Baroness von Lerchenfeld, the daughter of a Bavarian diplomat. It was an orthodox progression for a member of his caste and class. Less orthodox was his opinion of the Fuehrer. Stauffenberg's moral opposition to Hitler and the Nazis began to grow with the "Night of the Long Knives" in 1934 and then with the *Kristallnacht* in November 1938 when Hitler launched the pogrom. By the time he entered the War Academy, Stauffenberg had come to regard Hitler with profound distaste.

At the War Academy, he showed a capacity for military science, history and economics that marked him down as a future Chief of the General Staff. Extraordinarily handsome—even beautiful, some said—he was tall, noble in appearance and build, intelligent, and vital. He joined the 6th Panzer Division and fought in Poland and France and then, on the eve of France's surrender, was ordered to the General Staff. With the staff, Stauffenberg began to travel between all headquarters of the Wehrmacht, and he learned of the SS's work in Poland. It was the mass extermination of the Polish aristocracy and Jews that finally launched him on the road to tyrannicide. And Stauffenberg, as a fighting soldier, was not deterred by the burden of the *Fahneneid* or the Christian belief that a new state cannot be founded upon assassination.

For the most part, however, the older and more conservative members of the conspiracy continued to reject the idea of tyrannicide on religious and moral grounds. Instead, they sought the assistance and encouragement of Britain, and to that end, Ulrich von Hassell, a member of the Schwarze Kapelle, of the Wednesday Club, and the former German ambassador at the Quirinale, had composed a memorandum at the request of General Beck for transmission through secret channels to London. The memorandum repeated the Schwarze Kapelle's intention to overthrow Hitler and the Nazi Party and establish a constitutional monarchy based on British principles. Beck would head a Regency Council during the transitional period, but who was to be the new Kaiser? Would the British accept a restoration of the Prussian monarchy? With little more than a straw to grasp at, the conspirators studied old political pronouncements and drew comfort from statements made in the early 1930's by Churchill, who had declared that a Hohenzollern restoration would be a comparatively hopeful event when measured against the growing dominion of strident Nazism. They were statements that had lost all relevance; yet the conspirators, with the fervor of the lost, resurrected the Hohenzollern name and fastened their hopes upon Prince Louis Ferdinand of Prussia, the grandson of the Kaiser. Would this amiable playboy assume the dangerous role of Pretender? Yes, said Prince Louis through an intermediary, he would.

The conspirators accepted Prince Louis, despite the notoriety attending his name. He had sown more than his share of youthful wild oats, notably with the film actress Lily Damita, who had jilted him first for the Duke of Kent and then for Errol Flynn. There were rumors about his conduct; worse, he was said to have expressed intense dislike for his royal cousins in England. But he had other important connections. He had married the former Grand Duchess Kira of Russia, and in America he counted among his friends both Henry Ford and President Roosevelt.

With the Hassell memorandum and the Hohenzollern restoration, the conspiracy took on—for the moment—a weird, fairyland air of unreality. Who but desperate men would seriously believe that at this catastrophic moment in their history the British, whose army had been humiliated by the Wehrmacht, would contemplate an alliance with a group of latterday Jacobites? Brave though they were, they should have realized that the British were now fighting a total war, and that the Schwarze Kapelle would be considered merely as another weapon in that war. Nimble minds in Britain were indeed quick to perceive that a strategic advantage could be derived from these dissident Germans. Sefton Delmer, a high official of the Foreign Office department responsible for political stratagem—the Political Warfare Executive—would write: "(If we could) trick the generals into action against the supreme war-lord, I was going to have no regrets. A coup by the generals, whether successful or not—even so much as the suspicion of an anti-Hitler conspiracy among them—would help to hasten Hitler's defeat." ". . . All they had to do," Delmer continued, "was overthrow Hitler for us to be ready to start peace negotiations." But the British had not the slightest intention of making peace; their intention was to foment maximum suspicion and trouble between Hitler and his generals.

The Hassell memorandum eventually found its way to London through contacts that had been established between MI-6 and the Abwehr in Belgium. It would be among the first of the vehicles used by the British to sow dissension in the German ranks; but it would not be the last, for the Schwarze Kapelle would put forth new proposals through other secret channels as the war progressed. Whether they greeted these proposals with feigned interest or with indifference, the British were careful to keep such channels open. Those conspirators who were willing to betray the secrets of the Third Reich to demonstrate their good faith might serve as a source of useful intelligence, and, in turn, might be fed false intelligence about Allied intentions. There was also the possibility that the British, by leaking news of the conspirators' activities, could further irritate Hitler and the Nazis. But primarily the Schwarze Kapelle was seen from the first not as a means to end the war by negotiation but as a means to subvert the Third Reich from within.

Thus the stage was set, even in the early months of the war, for the deliberate and cynical manipulation of these well-intentioned and desperate men. It was a policy that was bound eventually to cause a massacre among the conspirators, for they risked not only the wrath of the Gestapo but also betrayal by those whose help they sought. That massacre would occur when the Schwarze Kapelle attempted—unsuccessfully—to assassinate Hitler on July 20, 1944, at a time of maximum advantage to the Allied armies in France. But it would cause few regrets. As Delmer wrote: "I am sorry the generals ended their lives on Hitler's meat-hooks. But I cannot say that I have any compunction about having raised false hopes in them."

While other members of the Schwarze Kapelle contemplated a *coup d'état* and an end to the war through political negotiation, Canaris sought to check the ambitions of the Fuehrer through more subtle and realistic means. With the collapse of France and the withdrawal of the British army from the continent in the summer of 1940, Hitler ordered his staff to plan for "Operation Sealion," the code name for the invasion of England. Accordingly, Canaris began an intelligence attack against the British Isles to provide the Wehrmacht with the information it needed for the battle and the occupation. But General Ulrich Liss, the chief of FHW and the man who was responsible for preparing intelligence dockets from Canaris's raw material, would note something unusual about the manner in which the admiral went about his task:

> You know, I saw Canaris frequently during *Case Yellow* and the intelligence planning for *Sealion* . . . I came to the conclusion during *Case Yellow* that his offensive intelligence operations against the French, Norway, Belgium and the Low Countries were all models of efficiency. But the same could not be said for his *Sealion* operations. I thought then that, while he appeared to be trying to be efficient, he was not doing his job against England with conviction. We never quite got the intelligence from England that we needed to make correct estimates of England's strengths and dispositions on the ground.

If anything, Liss's remarks were too generous, for in the main, the Abwehr's intelligence effort against England was erratic, jejune and, on several occasions, tinged with absurdity.

Canaris's resident agents in England were quite numerous but far from impressive. In general, they were a second-rate crowd of adventurers, dissidents, misfits, failures, fantasts, and the venal—usually half-trained, if at all, in the crafts of espionage. Most, if not all, were known to MI-5 and the Special Branch of Scotland Yard, and were quickly scooped up in a security net at the outbreak of war; few, if any, were possessed of the high intelligence and deep conviction of either the members of the Schwarze Kapelle or the mainstream of British and American agents that were sent into the field after 1942. Typical of the lot was Dorothy Pamela O'Grady, a short, dark, greedy woman who ran a cheap boardinghouse at Sandown, Isle of Wight, for summer visitors, and spent her winters making crude plans of defenses, cutting telephone wires, and scribbling her information to an address in Portugal in elementary secret ink—crimes for which she would be sentenced to death in December 1940, but later reprieved. The only German agent of any real importance at this stage of the secret war was a man known as "Snow," whom Masterman later described as the *"fons et origo"* of all future XX-Committee operations.

Snow was a Canadian electrical engineer whose real name was Alfred George Owens. As early as 1936, he had offered his services as a spy first to British naval intelligence, then to MI-6 and, finally, in a neat about-face, to the Abwehr. But MI-6 quickly uncovered his Abwehr connections, and although Snow was permitted to run for several months, he was arrested by the Special Branch on September 4, 1939, one day after war was declared. He was liable to the hangman, but at the "suggestion" of MI-6, the transmitter that he had been provided by his Abwehr controllers was brought to him in his cell at Wandsworth Prison, and on September 5 he opened up communications with the Abwehr in Hamburg, sending—significantly—false meteorological intelligence based upon true data that was known to the Germans. The Abwehr was unaware that Snow had been "turned"; in succeeding months he was evidently regarded as "the lynchpin" of German intelligence activities in Britain. He continued to transmit to Hamburg, and later to Iberia, and from the instructions he received in return, the British were able to apprehend all of the Abwehr agents who came stumbling into England from July 1940 onwards. Equally important, Snow's ciphers and the intelligence questionnaires he was sent enabled the British to deduce the exact nature of German intentions during the tense months when the home islands lay under the threat of invasion.

The Abwehr's activities in connection with Sealion were scarcely less inept. Although the Case Yellow directive clearly specified the British Isles as the ultimate target, Canaris had not evidently made any real preparation for a major intelligence operation against England. And when he received his orders from Keitel on June 21, 1940, to launch that operation, which was codenamed "Lobster," he hardly applied himself diligently. He merely gave his station chief at Hamburg, Captain Herbert Wichmann, instructions to set the operation in motion—a matter that he might have undertaken himself if he had been wholeheartedly loyal to Hitler and regarded his orders with the gravity they deserved. Then he turned his own attentions elsewhere.

All Wichmann had available for Lobster were fifteen ill-trained, low-grade agents to undertake the vast task of Gondomar:

> . . . Pray, what use
> Put I my summer recreation to,
> But more to inform my knowledge in the state
> and strength of the White English kingdom?

The first four sailed from Le Touquet on the afternoon of September 2, 1940: Carl Meier, a twenty-five-year-old Dutchman of German birth; Charles van der Kieboom, a twenty-six-year-old Eurasian with markedly oriental eyes; Sjord Pons, a Dutch army nurse of twenty-eight; and Rudolf Waldberg, the one member of the party who could speak English. All were less than half-trained in wireless, elementary cryptography, and in British military matters. They landed at dawn in the general area of Hythe and Dungeness, suffering from serious hangovers, and Meier and Pons were immediately arrested by an astonished private of the Somerset Light Infantry who came across them sitting behind a sand dune attacking a German sausage. Waldberg managed to send a single brief message to Germany, and then, thirsty, he went into the small town of Lydd. Ignorant of British laws prohibiting the sale of liquor before 10 A.M., he asked an innkeeper for a quart of cider—at 9 A.M. The innkeeper told him to go look at the village church and come back in an hour; when he did so he was arrested by two local policemen on bicycles. Kieboom was also caught within twenty-four hours and all but Pons were later executed. Pons persuaded the court that he was, in reality, a Dutch patriot who had joined the Abwehr to get to England and serve Prince Bernhard of The Netherlands. The first stage of Lobster was a failure; the second, in which eleven more agents crept ashore in widely separate parts of the islands, was no more successful. All were caught, and most were hanged or given life imprisonment at hard labor. Two, whose code names were "Tate" and "Summer," were turned into special agents of the XX-Committee and would later play major roles in British deception schemes.

Certainly, Canaris's task against England was extremely difficult. First there was the Channel itself, and British control of the sea and sky, which made the job of infiltrating agents and exfiltrating intelligence one of great complexity—but not of such complexity that it was beyond the powers of the Abwehr to undertake if it had been determined to do so. Canaris had achieved notable results elsewhere, but as Hitler and OKW laid their plans for Sealion, they were confronted by an almost complete intelligence vacuum—a vacuum which the British deception agencies, even though they were only a shadow of what they would later become, had the means to fill with false information showing that Britain was much stronger than was the case. In consequence, FHW was not able to assess with certainty the fighting capabilities and locations of the British defensive forces. Jodl, Hitler's operations officer, expressed the opinion on July 31, 1940, that "the German forces need to reckon only with a poor British army, which has not had time to apply the lessons of this war." But Hitler, bedeviled by the absence of accurate intelligence, disagreed; he believed that "a defensively prepared and utterly determined enemy faces us," a view supported by Canaris, who reported to the Fuehrer that in his opinion "even the Dunkirk combatants are not inclined to peace." On September 2, when actual British strength on paper was twenty-nine divisions, Canaris followed through with a report that there were thirty-seven divisions, equipped, eager, trained and determined to repulse an invasion. Determined they were, but they were far fewer and less well equipped than Hitler was led by Canaris to believe. It was too much for Hitler; he began to use his preparations for Sealion less as the basis for an actual operation and more as a strategic deception to cover his plans and intentions in the East. Eventually, he would abandon Sealion completely.

If Canaris's operations in England were unsuccessful, his attempts to set up intelligence centers in "Mackerel"—the Abwehr's code name for Eire—were ludicrous, even though he could and did enlist the assistance of the IRA. The Abwehr's attempt to infiltrate Ireland began on January 28, 1940, when Ernst Weber-Drohl, an aging Austrian acrobat, arrived by U-boat to arrange a treaty with the IRA. Of all the agents of the Second World War, Weber-Drohl was the drollest. He had appeared in circuses throughout Europe as "Atlas the Iron Giant" and "Drohl, the World's Strongest Man"; and he was quite well known in Ireland, for he had appeared in music halls there as a wrestler and weightlifter. He hoped his Irish "relatives"—two illegitimate children by a mistress some thirty-three years before—would help him set up his cover as a chiropractor, but he was soon arrested by the Irish police, fined £3 and released when he promised not to undertake any activities inimical to Eire. He finally found his "relatives," but they refused to have anything to do with him. And so, penniless and without a job, Weber-Drohl elected to work for England against Germany. The XX-Committee had a new agent.

Weber-Drohl was followed by Hermann Goetz, a Hamburg lawyer turned spy who the Abwehr thought could find his way about enemy territory "with the certainty of a sleepwalker." He would prove to be less sure-footed than that; in fact, he would be described as "the most inept and, even worse, the unluckiest of all spies in history." Goetz, a gentleman with fine instincts, landed by parachute (on his third try) from a Heinkel III, on a mission that "had some connection with an unpractical plan, codenamed Kathleen, for a German invasion of (Eire); this had been submitted to the Abwehr in Hamburg by an emissary of the IRA." His misfortunes began immediately. He landed not in Eire but in Ulster, and he could not bury his Luftwaffe uniform because he had lost his spade—along with his wireless—in the drop. Still in uniform, he set out to walk the 70 miles across wild country to the point where he should have landed, but the batteries of his flashlight, which was marked "Made in Dresden," soon gave out, and while he carried a good deal of money—an OSS report said the equivalent of $200,000 in British and Irish notes—he went hungry because he was not aware that both were currency in Eire and Ulster. He was then compelled to swim the Boyne "with great difficulty since the weight of my fur combination exhausted me," he wrote afterwards, adding plaintively: "This swim also cost me my invisible ink." He finally discarded his uniform and "I was now in high boots, breeches and jumper, with a little black beret on my head. . . . I kept my military cap as a vessel for drinks and my war medals for sentimental reasons." Peter Fleming would later write of this episode: "The lonely, brave, baffled figure trudging across the empty Irish landscape in jackboots, with a little black beret on his head and a pocket full of 1914–18 medals, is a reminder of how far the German intelligence effort fell short of those standards of subtlety and dissimulations which were expected of it. . . ."

Eventually, Goetz found himself at a safehouse in Dublin owned by Stephen Held, an IRA figure who was, at the time, believed also to be in Menzies's service. But a few days after Goetz's arrival, the house was raided by IRA men who stole all his money. On May 22, 1940, the house was again raided, this time by the police. Held was detained and Goetz vanished over the garden wall into Dublin, leaving behind what remained of his espionage equipment. The police—possibly at British instigation—put £3000 on his head, and he was betrayed by the IRA, caught and jailed. As he was about to be handed over to the British, he bit into the last remnant of his Abwehr equipment—a cyanide capsule—and died complaining that the IRA was "rotten to its very core."

Was the IRA as ill-disposed toward Germany as it had been toward Goetz? A confidential U.S. report would state that it had up to 5000 members throughout Ireland, and "German agents have been in Ireland and IRA agents have been in Germany." The report added, "while it has been reported that the German agents have been dismayed by the loose state of organization in the IRA," the "Germans are attempting to exploit (it) both as sabotage and espionage agents." In fact, the relationship between the IRA and the Abwehr was closer and more dangerous than was known at the time. Sean Russell, a former Chief of Staff of the IRA and its link with the Clann na Gael in the United States, had been recruited by the Abwehr as an agent; and with another prominent IRA man, Frank Ryan, he had gone to Berlin just before the outbreak of war to offer his services to Germany in the cause of a United Ireland. He had been accepted, as was Ryan, and both had been exceptionally well trained when, on August 8, 1940, they set out from Kiel aboard a U-boat with a small group of Irishmen who had been recruited from prisoner-of-war camps to synchronize IRA activities with the forthcoming invasion of England.

But Canaris was no more fortunate in his choice of Russell than he was with either Goetz or Weber-Drohl. Russell collapsed and died of a heart attack while at sea in the U-boat, and the party returned to Germany and was disbanded. Yet the British, and later the Americans, would have cause for real concern about the German presence in neutral Eire, and about the loyalties and activities of the Irish. That concern would grow over the next four years until finally drastic and unprecedented action was taken to protect the secrets of D-Day from the IRA and from SD and Abwehr agents who had infiltrated the country.

As Sealion lolled indecisively upon the French coast that hot summer, Canaris's main interests were centered in Spain and Gibraltar. The Abwehr was strongest in Spain; some said it ran the country. Canaris's influence upon Franco was great; it was greater still in the Foreign Ministry, the Armada, and the security service, the Dirección General de Seguridad. Had not "M. Guillermo"—Canaris's code name for himself—arranged German military, financial and economic assistance for Franco during the Civil War? Franco had good reason to be grateful to Canaris for past favors, and now he would have an even better reason for gratitude.

On June 30, 1940, Jodl presented the Fuehrer with a strategic survey of the war, pointing out that if the primary objective of Germany was the defeat of Great Britain, the way to achieve that defeat was the seizure of Gibraltar. This, Jodl argued, would cut England's links with her Empire in the East, and destroy the bond of encirclement that Britain would inevitably throw around Germany as soon as she was strong enough. All that was necessary, Jodl warned, was a quick decision, for the passage of each day worked against Germany and in favor of the recovering British forces. But Hitler, apparently incapable of rapid thought, retreated to Berchtesgaden to contemplate. Not until July 13 did he voice the opinion that Britain might be coerced into making terms by the seizure of Gibraltar and an invasion of French Northwest Africa. With that declaration Jodl took the initiative and assembled a reconnaissance group for duty in Spain. The party would be led by Canaris.

Canaris and the other members of the group left Berlin in civilian clothes bearing false passports. Traveling by separate means and different routes, they arrived at Madrid and made contact with the Abwehr's station chief, Wilhelm Leissner. Leissner commanded the entire Abwehr operation in Iberia and Morocco, using the *nom de guerre* "Gustav Lenz" and the cover of the "Excelsior Import and Export Company," traders in lead, zinc, cork and mercury. Leissner had been a colleague of Canaris's in the Mediterranean during the First World War and was described as a "strange old buzzard" in an "exotic aviary." Wearing "conservatively-cut, ill-fitting, sombre dark-grey suits and white shirts with high starched collars, and sporting carefully-groomed handlebars, he looked like the man in the old ads selling pomades for moustachios." But his organization was not to be underestimated, for he had 717 full-time officers and agents and over 600 part-time employees in Spain; and according to an instruction issued by Franco on September 6, 1940, he could depend upon the services of all Spanish consuls in England for his intelligence inquiries.

Canaris despatched his experts to reconnoiter various parts of Spain. On July 27, 1940, when they had reassembled in Madrid, he wrote a report that was a masterpiece of calculated discouragement. No, there could be no question of a surprise attack on Gibraltar; the gauges of the French and Spanish railways were different and German forces would have to change trains at the Spanish frontier, where they would be seen and reported. Worse, only a single road led directly to Gibraltar, and the Germans would have to use that. The British were aware of the threat to the fortress; a sizable reinforcement of the garrison had taken place while Canaris was in Madrid. Moreover, the geography of the fortress confounded accepted military principles. The steep slopes, the turbulent wind currents, the limited landing sites—all ruled out glider or parachute operations. The British had mined the narrow peninsula connecting Gibraltar with the mainland and their guns controlled the strip from several angles; any ground troops would have to cross that strip and the casualties would be high. Rail and road routes were not in good repair; they would not sustain large-scale movement without frequent repairs, and these the Spaniards would not be able to undertake without German assistance. The probabilities of reducing the garrison by direct air attack before invasion were not hopeful; the British anti-aircraft defenses were too strong. The garrison might be reduced by artillery but the attackers would need eleven or twelve regiments of artillery, with at least sixteen 380-mm guns and another sixteen 210-mm assault cannons—which, as Canaris well knew, the Wehrmacht could not spare at that time. A limited-scale operation by sea and air could not succeed without surprise and this, as Canaris had pointed out, was out of the question. What was more, if such an attack was contemplated, the assault forces would require the use of the African port of Ceuta. But, unfortunately, the cranes there were inadequate to the task of unloading heavy field pieces in the time available. Finally, Canaris reported, no attack of any sort could succeed without the approval and assistance of the Spanish government. Would that be forthcoming? Canaris took steps to see that such help was not available.

When Serrano Suñer, Franco's brother-in-law and Spain's Foreign Minister, arrived on business in Rome, he was approached by and received Dr. Josef Mueller, who had survived all Himmler's and Heydrich's assaults and was still Canaris's representative at the Holy See. "The admiral asks you to tell Franco," Mueller whispered to the Spaniard, "to hold Spain out of this game at all costs. It may seem to you now that our position is the stronger. It is in reality desperate, and we have little hope of winning this war. Franco may be assured that Hitler will not use the force of arms to enter Spain." In Madrid Canaris told Franco to ask Hitler for ten 15-inch guns for "Felix"—as the assault on Gibraltar was now codenamed—knowing, of course, that such heavy guns did not exist and would therefore have to be manufactured, which would take a very long time. Canaris continued his strategy of subtle discouragement in Berlin, and when Suñer came away from a visit there to discuss Spanish-German cooperation, he reported to Franco that he "perceived in Berlin that anything to do with Spanish affairs was utterly confused," adding that "one of the reasons for this confusion was the somewhat singular role played by Admiral Canaris."

Then, on October 23, 1940, Hitler himself traveled across Europe by train to Hendaye in the foothills of the Pyrenees to speak with Franco about Felix. The little Spanish general arrived some two hours late for the meeting. Hitler "sought to overbear Franco," and for nine hours there was that "suffocating flow of language with which he habitually stupefied his victims, like a boa constrictor covering his prey with saliva before devouring it." Hitler described the might of the Wehrmacht, the effect of the bombing of London, the U-boat war at sea, the predicament of the English. But Franco, affable, dignified and quite uncowed, made no commitment to Felix. There were, he said, certain problems—problems of artillery, problems of petrol from America if he joined the Axis, problems of grain, even problems of telecommunications, for the Americans owned Spain's telephone lines. Nothing was settled and the two dictators parted. Hitler had clearly been out-maneuvered, but later he demanded that Franco make a statement of his position and, on February 6, 1941, wrote to him of the urgency of Felix. When Franco finally replied on February 26, he began: "Your letter of the sixth makes me wish to reply very promptly . . ." Franco had been informed by Canaris that Hitler would not invade Spain if she remained neutral; and Franco, whose country had not yet recovered from the ravages of civil war, was not about to embark upon an adventure that might deny him the assistance and markets of America and the British Empire.

This quaint story of medieval guile fizzled out as Hitler turned his attentions upon Russia. "I would," the Fuehrer said to Mussolini of negotiations with Franco, "rather have four teeth out than go through that again." With the clever assistance of his old friend Don Juan March, Canaris had administered to Hitler his most serious diplomatic defeat so far. As Ian Colvin, another of Canaris's go-betweens in the prewar period, later wrote: ". . . in Spain [Canaris] had achieved something lasting. He had saved this mysterious land from prolonged torture." He had also done Britain a notable favor. Had Hitler's intentions in Spain and Gibraltar been translated into successful military action, he might have brought Britain to her knees with a blockade of food and oil from the outposts of the Empire.

By the late winter of 1941, the mighty Wehrmacht was stalled in the West at the English Channel and at the Pyrenees, but Hitler had already begun secret preparations for "Barbarossa"—the invasion of Russia—and for a German conquest of North Africa to pursue his dream of empire in the Middle East. Essential to the success of both operations were the countries of the Balkans, particularly Bulgaria, that tiny nation whose collapse in 1918 had heralded the defeat of Germany. Unlike Franco, Czar Boris of Bulgaria, a ruler whose main occupation seemed to be driving railway engines at high speed, could not resist the Fuehrer's blandishments. He joined the Axis, Rumania and Hungary soon followed suit, and gradually, relentlessly, the field-gray tide spread over the ocher lands of the Balkans toward the Bosporus. As the panzers rolled across the Danube, other German forces began landing in Libya and it seemed that Germany could not be stopped.

Yugoslavia and Greece now lay under the threat of German attack, but suddenly, Prince Paul of Yugoslavia agreed to become Hitler's ally and the pact was signed on March 24, 1941. Churchill's reaction was vehement and immediate. On Menzies's orders, British agents at Belgrade, who had provided support for General Bora Mirković, the commander of the Yugoslav air force, detonated a rebellion. At dawn on March 27, pro-British revolutionaries seized all key points in Belgrade, including the palace. The King, Peter II, was placed in the care of resolute officers, and General Dušan Simović, whose office at the Air Ministry was the center of opposition to German penetration of the Balkans, took over the government in his name. Prince Paul, who as Regent had negotiated the pact with Hitler, was arrested along with the two other Regents and sent into exile in Greece. By nightfall, without bloodshed, the coup had been accomplished, and there were scenes of great rejoicing. English and French flags appeared everywhere, and the German minister was publicly insulted by Serbian mobs who spat on his car.

Hitler was infuriated. He summoned OKW and gave orders to "destroy

Yugoslavia militarily and as a national unit. . . ." He directed that the Luftwaffe bomb Belgrade with "unmerciful harshness" in continuous day and night air attacks. In movements that Ultra revealed, Hitler upset all the carefully laid timetables for the preparatory moves of his invasion of Russia; and on the morning of April 6, 1941, in an operation codenamed "Punishment," the Luftwaffe struck Belgrade. Flying from bases in Rumania and Bulgaria, the Germans methodically destroyed the capital from rooftop height in an action that lasted three days. When silence finally came, some 17,000 citizens were dead or lay under the debris.

The sight of the devastation had the direst effect upon Canaris, who arrived at the capital by air as soon as invading German troops had secured the city. The admiral was after intelligence booty to assist the Abwehr in its campaign to infiltrate Turkey and the Near East. But in the ruins of Belgrade he saw the consequences of his powerlessness to thwart the vengeful will of the Fuehrer. Although Canaris had learned of the attack and had passed a warning to the Yugoslav authorities in Berlin, a warning which had resulted in the capital being declared an open city on April 3, he realized that his action, which again constituted treason, had been useless. After spending the day touring the city, he withdrew to a hotel in the hills, unable to stand the sight and stench of death any longer. Then he flew to Spain, arriving at Madrid on April 11. There, it appears, he suffered a form of spiritual collapse from which he never really recovered.

The Assassination
of Heydrich

CONSISTENTLY, cleverly and with determination, Canaris sought to frustrate the Fuehrer's grand designs everywhere. Yet Hitler's confidence in the little admiral was not diminished by 1942. The rapid conquest of western Europe was due in part to the excellence of the work of the Abwehr. Britain had not come to terms, but that could not be attributed solely to Canaris's service; and if Spain had not elected to join the Axis, the Abwehr was thoroughly entrenched at every level of the Spanish government. The Swedish intelligence service was so heavily penetrated by German agents that it was for all practical purposes under German control, and the Abwehr had access to most, and sometimes all, Swedish diplomatic reports from London and Washington. In Switzerland, a powerful Abwehr force existed as the harbinger of occupation. In France, the forces of resistance were being effectively neutralized by the Abwehr counterespionage service. Canaris's work in the Balkans had also been remarkably successful while Egypt, Turkey, Iraq, Persia, Syria and Lebanon were riddled with German agents. Within the Fatherland itself, the Abwehr was so efficient that it was virtually impossible for any foreign agent to flourish.

But if Hitler had reason to be pleased with Canaris, there were others in the Nazi hierarchy who viewed him with suspicion and distrust, chief among them Reinhard Heydrich. The two men remained on the friendliest of terms, but Heydrich continually sought the means to displace Canaris and absorb the Abwehr into the SD, thereby creating a single intelligence empire under his control. In the spring of 1942, Heydrich finally found the weapon he needed; he uncovered indisputable evidence of grand treason by a high officer of Canaris's staff. The man in question, whose code name was "Franta," was one of the senior executives at the Abwehr's headquarters in Dresden, where Canaris conducted operations into southern Russia, the Balkans and the Near East.

The Franta case began on the evening of April 5, 1936 when Major Josef Bartik, chief of the counterintelligence section of the Czech secret service (the best of the intelligence services in central Europe), got out of his car near a village on the frontier between northern Bohemia and Germany. Bartik, a friendless man with a limp, walked beneath the poplars lining the lane, and as the church clock at the nearby village of Neugeschrei chimed 8:30 P.M., he arrived at a crossroads between a steam mill and a warehouse. He waited for a moment and then a figure in a long dark coat and a beret, carrying a haversack, stepped out of the darkness into a pool of light cast from a street lantern. It was Franta, and he gave the password *"Altvater"*—German for patriarch—and the German greeting *"Grüss Gott!"* The two men walked back to Bartik's car and, in the back seat, Franta produced a bundle of documents. Upon later examination, these documents proved to be the order of battle of the Abwehr, the organization of the SD in Saxony and its operational responsibilities, and a description of the network and responsibilities of German frontier agencies. This intelligence was of considerable importance to the Czechs—and to MI-6, with which the Czech secret service had an alliance—and Franta was paid 3000 Reichsmarks and 200 Czech crowns for the material. He gave Bartik a poste restante address through which they could continue to communicate; and then Franta got out of the car, walked the 50 yards to the German frontier and disappeared. Bartik drove back to Prague and within a few days received the chief of MI-6 at the Czech capital, Major Harold Lehrs Gibson.

From that moment until Heydrich became Reichsprotektor of Bohemia and Moravia in 1941 Franta continued to pass to the Czechs, who in turn sent copies to Gibson, what amounted to OKW's operational orders and material that would be described as "secret documents prepared for the personal attention of Admiral Canaris." He also revealed in great detail the Abwehr's and SD's organizations in Finland, Latvia, Estonia, Rumania, Bulgaria, Yugoslavia, Hungary, Greece, Turkey, Persia and Egypt; and much about the SD's work in Sweden, Holland and Belgium. It would be claimed that his warnings permitted Gibson and the Czech government and intelligence hierarchy to escape to London a short step ahead of the German occupation forces when they moved into Prague in March 1939; that he warned of Hitler's plans to occupy Poland and to invade Norway, Denmark, Holland, Belgium and France; and that his information permitted the British to bring out—before the Germans could capture them— the Queen of Holland, Wilhelmina, and the King of Norway, Haakon. He also warned the "Three Kings"—the chiefs of the Czech intelligence service's stay-behind agency in Prague—of Wehrmacht operations against Greece, Yugoslavia, Bulgaria, Rumania, Hungary and Russia, information that was communicated to London by the "Three Kings' " wireless posts at Prague—Sparta I and Sparta II.

Who was Franta and what were his motives? It seemed possible, at first, that he might be part of some scheme to penetrate the British secret intelligence services and plant false information; but almost invariably, when compared with other intelligence sources such as Ultra, the great wealth of Franta's material proved to be true. Could he be playing Canaris's and Oster's other game by revealing Hitler's and OKW's plans so that Britain could take steps to frustrate them? That, too, seemed possible, for no one, except operational and intelligence chiefs, would have access to such detailed information. Franta, quite simply, knew too much for one man.

Then, early in 1941, Heydrich moved in to destroy the Czech underground. German wireless intelligence had uncovered UVOD, the Central Committee for Internal Resistance, a virulent and efficient espionage organization in Prague with links to London. It was the organization controlled by the "Three Kings." On April 22, 1941, the Gestapo captured the first of the "Three Kings," a lieutenant colonel of the Czech army called Balaban, in a raid on an apartment. In another raid on May 13, the Gestapo captured the second of the "Three Kings," a lieutenant colonel of the Czech army called Masin. The Germans broke into an apartment as Sparta I was in the act of transmitting intelligence to London. The third of the "Three Kings," Captain Vaclac Moravek, was also in the apartment supervising the transmission, and while Masin engaged the Gestapo in a gunfight, Moravek—the only man who knew who Franta was—escaped with Sparta I, the wireless operator. Masin shot down three Gestapo agents on a staircase before he tripped, fell, caught his leg in a bannister, and broke it. The Gestapo pounced on him but did not kill him; it wanted prisoners for interrogation. Masin died silently before a firing squad after much torture. Moravek and Sparta I escaped by tying the aerial of the wireless to a sofa in the flat and sliding down into the street 45 feet below. Sparta I was captured almost immediately, and he died quite as silently as Masin. But Moravek, one of his fingers sheared by the wire and hanging on by a thread of sinew, got away. He cut the finger off with a razor blade, flushed it down a toilet, and then made his way to the Sparta II wireless post. There, he reported to London that the Gestapo was closing in on both Franta and himself. In fact, Heydrich's agents had identified Franta as a "Dr. Paul Steinberg," but they knew that it was not his real name, and they had no address for him.

London reacted strongly to Moravek's warning; at the request of the Czech government-in-exile, the Joint Intelligence Committee authorized an assassination mission to fly to Prague and kill Heydrich. The mission was codenamed "Anthropoids"; and the gunmen landed by parachute in Czechoslovakia in December 1941. By then Heydrich had learned the true identity of "Dr. Steinberg." He was Paul Thummel, a Saxon who was a member of the Nazi old guard, held the Gold Party Badge, and was employed by the Abwehr in Prague as the chief of "the section dealing with Czechoslovakia, the Balkans, and the Near East." Thummel was arrested; and again London reacted strongly. The Anthropoids were authorized to postpone the task of killing Heydrich to rescue Thummel, if it was feasible. The operation was to be controlled by Moravek; and Franta was to be brought to England. Clearly, Thummel was something more than a mere spy; spies were usually expendable once they were exposed—unless their services had been so important to England that they warranted saving for other tasks.

On February 22, 1942, Thummel was taken to Gestapo headquarters with some courtesy; his rank and eminence in the Nazi Party were too high to permit rough treatment. There, at a court-martial, he explained that he had been trying to penetrate UVOD through Moravek, with a view to collapsing the entire *réseau*. He had, he complained, been on the point of achieving this when he was arrested. But he denied being Franta. The case was referred to Himmler who, at a meeting with Canaris, accepted Thummel's story and directed that he be released. This was done on March 2. But Heydrich was not satisfied, and Thummel was permitted to return to his apartment only if a Gestapo agent lived there with him.

Meanwhile, London expressed great anxiety to Moravek about Franta's fate. But before Moravek could reply—or launch the Anthropoid mission to get Franta out of the country—he himself was caught. On the evening of March 22, Thummel was re-arrested and the Gestapo learned that Moravek was to meet a UVOD agent in a little park alongside the Convent of Loretta in Prague. At seven o'clock that evening, an invisible cordon of Gestapo surrounded the park with Moravek inside, sitting on a bench awaiting the UVOD agent, Stanislau Rehak, known as "The Dandy." When "The Dandy" approached at 7:10 P.M., the Gestapo pounced. Rehak was captured, handcuffed, and dragged from the park. Moravek leaped into some bushes and, a gun in each hand, opened fire. The Gestapo returned fire and Moravek was shot in the leg. He was able to run, however, and tried to get out of the park in the vicinity of Prague's Military Academy, an area that he knew from his youth. But he collapsed before he could escape; the bullet in his leg had severed the main artery. When the Gestapo came up, one of the agents put a pistol to Moravek's temple and fired. Moravek, the last of the "Three Kings," was dead. Not satisfied, the Gestapo man fired his remaining bullets into his neck.

UVOD was shattered, the Anthropoids went to ground. Thummel was held on suspicion of grand treason—and Heydrich had the evidence he needed to move against Canaris and the Abwehr. But Canaris was not easily outmaneuvered; he came to Prague in person to defend himself and his service against Heydrich.

The two men met on May 21, 1942, at Heydrich's headquarters in the Hradcany Castle, the great Gothic edifice on a hill's peak overlooking Prague and the Moldau. There, in an ornate salon, Canaris, the "cunning Odysseus," faced Heydrich, the proponent of medieval brute force. The record shows that Heydrich accused the Abwehr of "political unreliability"—a charge akin to the capital crime of treason in the Third Reich. Heydrich then declared, almost apologetically, that "at certain levels" of the Abwehr there was "unfortunate inefficiency." He "commended" to Canaris that the SD should assume responsibility for counterintelligence, and he also "commended" the wisdom of relaxing the ban that prevented the Gestapo and the SD from making investigations and conducting interrogations on military property. As nimble and equivocal as ever, Canaris accepted the wisdom of the first "commendation" while eluding discussion and commitment on the second—which would have permitted the Gestapo and the SD to interrogate Abwehr men whom they suspected of belonging to the Schwarze Kapelle.

At their meeting, the two German spymasters hammered out what became known as "Heydrich's Decalogue"—an agreement that provided for a division of intelligence and counterintelligence labors. The agreement went some way toward conceding to the SD a part of the Abwehr's sovereignty in the intelligence world, even though the moment the meeting was over, Canaris quietly gave his lieutenants verbal orders that the agreement was to be ignored. But if he had thwarted Heydrich, at least momentarily, he was in grave trouble for the first time from an even more powerful corner—the Fuehrer himself.

Canaris and the Abwehr, by the terms of the directive from their employer, OKW, had been charged with the tasks not only of extracting the enemy's secrets but also of protecting Germany's secrets from the enemy. And until the winter of 1941–42, Hitler had few causes for complaint. But by then a new element had entered into the secret war: the Commandos. These élite uniformed troops, employing every art of hand-to-hand combat known to the Boer, the Iroquois or a Chicago gangster, had been raiding German outposts—preferably lonely outposts—with ever-greater audacity and viciousness. The ordinary German soldier standing guard over the walls of Hitler's new empire had come to dread these attacks, in which the knife and the garrote played the deadliest part. They infuriated Hitler who, even when he was planning and conducting the great campaigns on the Russian steppes that involved millions of men, often spent much of his noonday conferences with OKW discussing the secret war. Curiously, Commando attacks had an effect upon Hitler that was out of all proportion to the number of men and casualties involved. He could accept the loss of 10,000 men in Russia with near-equanimity, but when the Commandos struck he was reduced to a quivering mass of anger.

Then, on the night of February 27/28, 1942, British paratroopers struck at a lonely outpost at Bruneval, a bold cape with a lighthouse on the English Channel not far from Le Havre. The raid was intended as more than mere harassment, for Bruneval was the site of an important German Würzburg radar installation. Ever since the fall of France, British radar scientists had been studying the performance of German radar in order to evolve some form of radio or electronic countermeasure—a new dimension in the war of wits—to protect British bomber fleets raiding Europe and, as important, to blind or mislead Hitler's radar defenses when the time came for an invasion. Aerial reconnaissance had located the Würzburg installation on top of the 600-feet-high cliffs at Bruneval, and the paratroopers, dropping behind the installation, succeeded in dismantling the key parts of the equipment. Under heavy gunfire, they scrambled down the cliffs to the beach, where they were met by boats and sped back across the Channel. The Würzburg had been "pinched."

The sense of triumph in high circles in England was very great; the Germans had lost the key to their electronic defenses of Europe. At Führerhauptquartier the reaction was quite different. Hitler, in a great rage, demanded to know why "the British secret service" could make these raids, but the Abwehr could not. Canaris had formed a special unit of shock troops, the Brandenburg Division, for the purpose of making Commando-type raids. Where was it? Why did it not raid the British coast in retaliation? The English Channel was but a ditch, the Fuehrer stormed, but it might as well be as wide as Asia for all the intelligence the Abwehr managed to get out of England! It was time intelligence was taken out of the hands of these General Staff officers and given to a reliable party organization such as the SD. What did Canaris know of British radar? Hitler demanded to see the file, and when he was told that the Abwehr knew little or nothing about such technical matters, he became enraged anew. He sent for Himmler and directed that the work of acquiring technical information be carried out in future by the SD.

It was the beginning of the end of Canaris's complete autonomy in the field of foreign military intelligence. It was also, as Brigadeführer SS Walter Schellenberg noted, the beginning of the end for Canaris. For when Heydrich, stimulated by the Thummel affair, conceived a plan to unify the Abwehr and the SD, Hitler was disposed to listen. A blueprint for the immense bureaucratic task was drawn up, and it would have been implemented—but for Heydrich's murder.

On all counts, the Anthropoid mission was an extremely risky one. Its objective, the assassination of Heydrich, would gratify the Czechs, for as Reichsprotektor of Bohemia and Moravia, Heydrich had earned a reputation for ruthlessness and brutality that eclipsed even Hitler's. The British, too, viewed him as an especially malevolent enemy; the SD under Heydrich's command had become an all-too-efficient weapon of terror in the secret war. But the murder of one of the most powerful men in the Third Reich was certain to evoke mass retaliation among the Czechs, and this had to be an important consideration for Menzies. MI-6 was running the intelligence game in Czechoslovakia, and MI-6 was certain to suffer the consequences. But perhaps there was another consideration. With Heydrich out of the way, Menzies may well have reasoned that Canaris and the other conspirators of the Schwarze Kapelle would have somewhat greater freedom of movement. Significantly, Menzies went to considerable lengths to frustrate British plans to assassinate Canaris, who was, Menzies would state, much more valuable alive than dead. But with no compunctions he signed Heydrich's death warrant when he agreed to allow the Anthropoids to remount their mission. If the British had once had scruples about political assassination, those scruples were now gone.

The Anthropoids were Czechs—Jan Kubis and Josef Gabcik—both of whom carried British army paybooks. Accompanied by a wireless and cipher team of three more Czechs led by a Lieutenant Bartos, they had parachuted from an RAF Halifax into the Bohemian hills near a village called Lidice by the light of the December half-moon in 1941. All had landed safely and had quickly submerged into the Czech underground. There they remained for six months, awaiting their opportunity to strike. It proved impossible for them to rescue Thummel, but patiently and stealthily, with the help of UVOD and through visual observations of Heydrich's movements, they built up a fair picture of their target's daily activities.

Then by a stroke of fortune, the Anthropoids learned exactly where Heydrich would be on May 27, 1942. Four days before, an antique clock in Heydrich's office gave trouble and his secretary called in a Czech repairman to put it right. Josef Novotny set the clock on Heydrich's desk, and as he was taking the back off, he noticed a piece of paper with Heydrich's itinerary for the 27th typed on it. Novotny took the paper, screwed it into a ball and threw it into the wastepaper basket. Having repaired the clock, he left and minutes later one of the cleaners, Marie Rasnerova, entered Heydrich's office and emptied the wastepaper basket into her sack. Within a few hours the itinerary was in the hands of Kubis and Gabcik, and to their dismay they discovered that Heydrich was leaving Prague permanently on the 27th. They had little time to plan their attack. But they did know in detail where Heydrich would be on that day and which routes he would take. They decided to make the attack in the Prague suburb of Holesovice, where the Dresden-Prague road traces a hairpin bend down to the Troja Bridge. This was the road Heydrich would take from his villa in Panenske-Breschen to Hradcany Castle. Heydrich's car, which was only rarely escorted, was compelled to slow down at this point in order to negotiate the bend.

At 9:30 A.M. on the morning of the 27th, Kubis and Gabcik were in position with submachine guns under their raincoats and some grenades. With them were two other gunmen, and they distributed themselves around the bend. The plan provided that Rela Fafek, Gabcik's girlfriend, who owned a car, should precede Heydrich's car and if he was unescorted she would wear a hat. A fifth man was positioned in a hedge around the bend to signal with a mirror when Heydrich's Mercedes was actually approaching. As Heydrich entered the bend, Gabcik was to kill both him and the chauffeur with the submachine gun, while Kubis snatched Heydrich's briefcase.

At 10:31 Rela Fafek drove round the bend wearing a hat. Seconds later the mirror signal came. Gabcik stepped into the road and aimed at the bend. Heydrich's Mercedes came into view and Gabcik pulled the trigger. But the gun jammed—some grass had got into the breech. Kubis drew a bomb and threw it at the car as both Heydrich and his chauffeur rose and shot Gabcik. The bomb exploded near the car, shattering the door. Heydrich dropped his pistol. Kubis was hit by shrapnel and debris in the face and eyes but managed to get onto his woman's pedal cycle and ride off. The two other gunmen also got away.

Heydrich staggered a few paces from the car and then collapsed. He was taken to a hospital, and there, at first, it was thought his wounds were not serious; an X-ray revealed a broken rib and some fragments of cloth and metal in his stomach. Pieces of burned leather upholstery and uniform cloth were buried near the spleen, and other small fragments embedded in the pleura. But on June 4 Heydrich died—not of his wounds but of gangrene. The dark rituals of mourning now began. Heydrich's corpse was dressed in the midnight black and silver ceremonial uniform of the SS, placed in a coffin of gunmetal and silver and taken on the breech of a cannon to the forecourt of Hradcany Castle. There it was guarded by the SS until the time came for the remains of the lord of the German terror system to be taken by a black-crêped train to Berlin.

The Anthropoids had succeeded in their mission, but the Germans exacted a high price in revenge. In Prague, a *ratissage* (literally a "rat-hunt," Gestapo vernacular for a man-hunt) was unleashed upon the

Czechs. Over 10,000 were arrested and at least 1300 executed. The worst of the reprisals occurred at Lidice, a small mining village of sandstone and red-tile houses nestling on a hillside around an old baroque church, whose citizens the Gestapo believed—wrongly—had harbored the Anthropoids. The SS and the army descended upon the village at night and, by the light of the glow of blast furnaces at nearby steel mills, gathered the entire population in the village square. All males between sixteen and seventy were taken to a field and summarily shot. The women and children were carried away in trucks and, with few exceptions, were not heard of again. Then the village was leveled by fire and powder.

The Anthropoids went into hiding in the crypt of the Karel Borromaeus Greek Orthodox Church on Ressl Street in the Old Town of Prague. Using the narrow niches in the stone walls (which had been built to hold the corpses of monks) as their hiding places, they waited there as members of the Czech underground made a plan for their escape into the Moravian Mountains, whence they could be evacuated to England. The plan was to stage a mass funeral of some of the victims of the Gestapo purge at the church, and then spirit the Anthropoids away in coffins. The wireless and cipher team, Bartos and his assistant, a man called Potuchek, was still in communication with London, and June 19, 1942, was selected as the day upon which the Anthropoids would be evacuated from the church into the mountains. But before they could be moved, they were betrayed by a Czech, Karel Curda, who was covetous of the Gestapo's bounty of 10 million crowns (£125,000 or $600,000). Curda took the Gestapo to Bartos's safehouse in the town of Pardubice. Bartos was not there, but in the house the Gestapo found his war diary, which contained copies of all his communications with London. This led them to one of Bartos's assistants, Atya Moravech. The Gestapo tortured the nineteen-year-old boy, who was said to have broken down when his interrogators produced his mother's severed head, and revealed where the Anthropoids were hiding.

When the funeral cortège in which the Anthropoids were to be evacuated drove into Charles Square, the pallbearers found the area sealed off by Gestapo and SS. They were turned back. Within the hour, shock troops of the SS moved against the church; they captured the sexton and compelled him to take them into the church by a side door. But as the SS troops made their way through the pews, they were met by a hail of gunfire from the choir loft, where Kubis and some other men were hiding. Kubis was killed with a hand grenade; Bartos took poison and in the instant before the pill killed him, shot himself through the temple. The SS men tried to get into the crypt and lifted a flagstone—to be met by another hail of bullets. The Gestapo then called in the fire brigade to flood the cellar. Down to their last cartridges, the men shot each other one by one until the only man left shot himself. The battle of the catacombs was over. But the reprisals were not; 115 people were killed that day, including the former Prime Minister of Czechoslovakia. Only Potuchek, the wireless operator, still survived. He was in hiding in the village of Lezhaky. He sent a message to London on June 26 warning of the disaster and arranging to make a further transmission at 2300 hours on June 28. But he did not make the transmission. He was caught and shot, and with his death the Anthropoids' mission closed.

When Heydrich's coffin reached Berlin, it was taken under escort of the Leibstandarte SS "Adolf Hitler"—the Fuehrer's personal guard—on the breech of a rubber-tired cannon to the Reichskanzlei on the Wilhelmstrasse for the state obsequies. Hitler wore a black band on his dove-gray uniform coat and, laying a wreath of orchids beside the corpse, pronounced that Heydrich "was one of the greatest defenders of our greater German ideal, . . . the man with the iron heart." Himmler assembled the Knights of the Order—the Obergruppenführer SS—at the side of the catafalque, and made a speech concerning the obligations of the SS leaders to the memory of "your murdered chief." It should, said Himmler, induce them to give the best of themselves in their conduct and in their work, particularly in the area of secret intelligence operations abroad. He told the Obergruppenführer that their achievements in this "special sector still could not compare with those of the British Secret Service." The corpse of Reinhard Heydrich was ample proof of that. Himmler then made a few remarks concerning Brigadeführer SS Walter Schellenberg, whose powers as chief of the foreign intelligence branch of the SS must now be extended as the result of Heydrich's assassination. He was, said Himmler, "the Benjamin of our leadership corps," and he directed the Obergruppenführer to support him despite his youth. Schellenberg, the son of a Saarland piano manufacturer and the man who had engineered the Venlo Incident, was just thirty-two when he began to take over where Heydrich left off in the intelligence world.

The cortège moved off to the cemetery. On the swastika-draped bier rested Heydrich's death mask, a creation that revealed "deceptive features of uncanny spirituality and entirely perverted beauty, like a Renaissance Cardinal." Among the large number of Reich potentates at the graveside was Canaris. His vivid blue eyes brimmed over with tears and, his voice "choked with emotion," he said to Schellenberg: "After all, he was a great man. I have lost a friend in him."

The German intelligence services would never really recover from the murder of Heydrich. In the long term, it was a *coup de main* with important consequences; for if Heydrich had survived and had succeeded in eliminating Canaris, the intelligence story surrounding the Allied invasion of France might have been very different. Heydrich was about to go to Paris as head of the SS in France when he was killed. Schellenberg, whose "almost feminine sensibility made him as moody as a film star no longer sure of success," would prove to be a less dangerous enemy both to the Allies and to Canaris. For the moment, Canaris was a man reprieved.

Heydrich was, perhaps, the most noteworthy victim of the relentless war between the British and the German secret intelligence services, but he was by no means the only one. In Britain alone some thirty German agents were executed by hanging. Others died mysteriously, like Ulrich von der Osten, a senior Abwehr agent. Osten had landed at Los Angeles in March 1941 with false papers proclaiming him to be "Don Julio Lopez Lido"; he checked into the Taft Hotel in New York City on the 16th of that same month, and within two days was a corpse in Bellevue Hospital. His movements had been shadowed by the FBI and the British Security Coordination, the MI-6 organization in North America with headquarters in Rockefeller Center; and when he left the hotel to dine at Child's Restaurant in Times Square, he was hit and fatally injured by a taxicab. Another equally mysterious death involved Jan Villen Ter Braak, a man whose true identity was never established. He was found shot to death on the grimy concrete floor of an air-raid shelter in Cambridge, England, his suitcase wireless set beside him. Whether it was suicide or murder would never be known.

There was nothing mysterious about Heydrich's death; it was an outright political assassination. In general the British were opposed to the execution of lesser German agents unless no other course was possible; for, as Masterman would write: "A live spy . . . is always of some use as a book of reference; a dead spy is of no sort of use." And while several schemes were considered to assassinate the Allies' arch-foe, Hitler, all, for a number of reasons, were eventually discarded. But Heydrich had been a marked man ever since he assumed control of the SD. He could not be permitted to live; he was too dangerous to Menzies, to the Allied cause—and to Canaris.

Operation Flash

CANARIS had opposed Barbarossa—the invasion of Russia. Planning the campaign at Führerhauptquartier in the Forest of Görlitz near Rastenburg in East Prussia—a silent, wooded, remote place that resembled the setting for some mystical Teutonic folk play—Hitler, General Ulrich Liss would recall, was shrewd, lucid, untiring, confident of success. Canaris had declared that he could not share the Fuehrer's confidence. Liss would remember how Canaris had described the great imponderables of an attack upon Russia. Her strength might be relatively superficial on the frontiers; she might even be weak in the interior. But in the great equation of strategy—space equals time—she had inexhaustible reserves. No one knew how many troops Russia might be able to raise; no one had been able to assess accurately the power of her industrial base.

Canaris had not yet been discredited—the Bruneval raid and the Franta affair were yet to occur—and the high commanders at Führerhauptquartier were still disposed to listen to him. And listen they did when he questioned Hitler's demand that the German armed forces must crush Soviet Russia in a quick campaign. It might be possible, Canaris conceded, but what if the campaign was not so quick? What if it went on into the winter—the fearful Russian winter? For once, Canaris was not indirect in his criticism of the Fuehrer. He spoke openly, even to the man who was soon to become his chief rival, Walter Schellenberg. Schellenberg would remember that Canaris damned Barbarossa in "the strongest terms." He accused the Wehrmacht commanders of being "irresponsible and foolish" in imagining, as they did, that Russia could be defeated within three months. Schellenberg would write:

> He would not be a party to this (he said), and could not understand how the generals, von Brauchitsch, Halder, Keitel and Jodl, could be so complacent, so unrealistic, and so optimistic. But any attempt at opposition was useless;

he had already made himself unpopular by his repeated warnings. . . .
Keitel had said to him, "My dear Canaris, you may have some understanding of the Abwehr, but you belong to the navy; you really should not try
to give us lessons in strategic and political planning." When Canaris repeated such remarks he would usually . . . look at me with wide eyes, and
say quite seriously, "Wouldn't you find all this quite comic—if it weren't so
desperately serious?"

Canaris, however, had been unable to frustrate Hitler in the grand
design. At dawn on June 22, 1941, the Wehrmacht struck Russia's borders
from Finland to the Black Sea. The Russian defenses collapsed like glass-
houses in a typhoon; in the first phase of Barbarossa, the Red Army lost 3
million men, 22,000 guns, 18,000 tanks and 14,000 aircraft. But, delayed
by Menzies's diversionary *coup d'état* in Yugoslavia, the campaign did not
achieve a decisive victory before the great, mysterious ice clouds of the
Russian winter gathered behind the Aral Sea and sped across the steppe
with mounting violence. Even as the German armies approached Moscow
and Leningrad, and dug deeper into the vastness of the Ukraine, Hitler's
generals began to realize that Russia could not be conquered that year.
They began to argue, even to plead, with OKW. Their armies must go to
winter quarters; they were not equipped as were the Russians for operations
in the darkness, the snow and the mud. They reminded OKW of Napoleon's
fate in 1812. But their protestations were as useless as their recommenda-
tions. Just like Napoleon, Hitler, now wavering between moods of optimism
and pessimism, permitted the golden days of autumn to pass away before
he ordered the German army to capture the Russian capital. The prodigies
of courage were the same; and so were the consequences. But there the
similarities ended. For the winter that defeated Napoleon was early and
mild; the winter that confronted Hitler would be early and brutal.

At Führerhauptquartier, the old quarrels between Hitler and his generals broke out anew; and in quick succession, all the men who commanded army groups in Russia resigned or were dismissed, including
Rundstedt and Stuelpnagel. With Field Marshal Guenther von Kluge now
in command of an army on the Moscow front, it seemed at first that his
march would end in the capture of the capital. During the short afternoon
light of December 2, 1941, an officer of the 258th Infantry Division
wirelessed Kluge that he "could see the towers of the Kremlin reflecting the
setting sun." His men, he said, were now fighting for possession of the last
station on the Moscow Underground. That was as far as the *Feldgrau*
got.

On December 6, in an impenetrable blizzard, one hundred new Russian
divisions struck the German army with fearful force. By the end of the day,
the Red Army was in general counteroffensive; and for the next one
hundred days the *Feldgrau,* half-drunk on the schnapps they had been

given to keep out the cold, stricken by the tens of thousands by frostbite, motivated only by their fanatical belief in the Fuehrer, fought like few armies in history.

Hitler took personal charge of the battle from Rastenburg, broadcasting his commands by wireless and voice radio. With a will bordering upon dementia, he ordered his armies to stay where they were and roll themselves up like hedgehogs around defensive positions. The *Feldgrau* obeyed; they grouped around villages and small towns and, even as temperatures dropped to 50 below zero and the breeches of their rifles froze, they fought on blindly. Habit and discipline alone kept them alive; and in the end they blunted the Russian attack. Their allegiance to the Fuehrer had prevented disaster; and as a result Hitler finally obtained a moral ascendancy over his generals that he never lost.

Suddenly, as suddenly as the winter came, the spring arrived, and the thaws stopped all movement—Russian as well as German. Exhausted, the two armies glowered at each other over the sunlit, blasted steppe, while at Führerhauptquartier, Hitler began to humiliate the generals who, he said, had betrayed him. Four field marshals were relieved of command and retired; two army commanders and thirty-five other generals were dismissed; and he fired the C-in-C, Brauchitsch, with the words that he had had enough of these "vain, cowardly" generals. Hitler assumed the position of army C-in-C himself; he was now the Supreme Commander in fact as well as in title. The process that had begun with the assassinations of Schleicher and Bredow was now complete. It was the final consummation of his military triumph over his generals and the Officer Corps. Not since the Fritsch-Blomberg affair had there been such a devastating purge of the German army. Wheeler-Bennett would write: "Gone were the days of privilege and security enjoyed by the Generals; gone the respect which was automatically rendered by those who wore the claret-coloured trouser stripe of the General Staff. The wages of prostitution, which are so often power without responsibility, were (now) for them degradation, hopeless servility, and the disdain of their master."

The abasement of the General Staff and the Officer Corps reawakened thoughts of treason and rebellion among some of Hitler's generals, but while the Schwarze Kapelle was dusting off its plans, on June 7, 1942, like a thunderclap, Hitler launched his summer offensive. The German armies, recovered and refurbished, fanned out through the steppe grass and corn stubble toward Caucasia and the precious oilfields; and General Friedrich von Paulus led the 6th Army toward Stalingrad, creating an enormous dust cloud that, with the flame and smoke from burning villages and cornfields, could be seen 40 miles away.

Everywhere that summer the Axis was triumphant and Allied fortunes were at their lowest ebb. The newest member of the alliance, the United

States, was still staggering from the surprise attack at Pearl Harbor. And while Japan crippled both the American and British fleets in the Pacific, Rommel's Afrika Korps pursued Britain's 8th Army to El Alamein. But even in victory, the Fuehrer was not content. He moved his headquarters from Rastenburg to Vinnitsa, about 100 miles east of the old Polish-Russian border; and there the animosity that had been simmering between Hitler and Halder at last came to the boil. Halder was once again counseling caution on the Russian front. But Hitler finally turned upon the Chief of the General Staff and declared: "Half my nervous exhaustion is due to you! It is not worth it to go on!" He ordered Halder from OKW and from the army—and later gave Himmler instructions to see to it that he found himself at Dachau, the pleasant old town north of Munich that had become the most fearful of all the Nazi concentration camps.

In Halder's stead, Hitler appointed General Kurt Zeitzler, a former Chief of Staff to Field Marshal von Rundstedt at C-in-C West, and an officer who had played some part in inflicting the Dieppe disaster upon the Canadians. But Zeitzler would be responsible only for the command of operations on the eastern front. Hitler reserved for himself and OKW the overriding power of decision there and total command of operations on all other fronts—including those in the Balkans, Sicily, Italy, North Africa and, when the time came, France. It was a change in operational responsibility that would have fateful consequences, for OKW had neither the power nor the numbers to deal adequately with so many diverse commands. Nor could one man, whatever his abilities as a military strategist and tactician, master the challenges of a multi-front conflict that would be fought with every weapon in the arsenal of total war. Vivid confirmation of the inadequacies of both Hitler and OKW was not long in coming.

It was through the Fuehrer's iron command and personal mystique that Germany had been established as a geopolitical force stretching from Cap de La Hague at Cherbourg to Stalingrad on the Volga, from the North Cape of Scandinavia to the Elburz Mountains almost at the Persian frontier, and from Hendaye on the Spanish-French border to El Alamein on the Libyan-Egyptian frontier. But in October of 1942, the limits of Hitler's empire were reached. The monstrous war of movement was coming to an end; and Hitler, accustomed to thinking in terms of miles, would now have to fight for every inch. Paulus's 6th Army had swept across the Ukraine and had entered Stalingrad, but the Germans had succeeded in capturing only that part of the city that lay on the west bank of the Volga. Rommel had been stopped at El Alamein, and suddenly, on October 23, 1942, Montgomery launched the Lightfoot counteroffensive that took the Germans completely by surprise. Then on the last day of the month, the Kriegsmarine reported that very large Allied troop convoys had been spotted in the Atlantic. Where were they bound? No one at Hitler's headquarters knew. But that report signaled another significant change in the Fuehrer's fortunes, for Torch had been lit.

A week later, Hitler was aboard his private train, rumbling through the hills of Franconia on his way to Munich, where he was to attend the nineteenth anniversary of the Beer Hall Putsch of 1923. It was November 7, 1942, and from dawn onwards, teleprinter reports had reached the train that a mighty Allied armada of transports and warships was now passing through the Strait of Gibraltar into the Mediterranean. Still no one knew its destination. "On the basis of somewhat vague reports," announced Jodl, "there are indications that the Anglo-Saxons intend multiple landings in West Africa." All the available evidence pointed to Dakar. The ships that had passed through the Strait, Jodl thought, were destined for Malta; but, he said, there was no clear evidence about where the Allies were going or what they intended.

That evening, as Hitler went to bed in his coach beneath the Beerberg, the Torch invasion fleets began to disembark troops in a vast arc from Casablanca to Bougie. It was not until two o'clock in the morning of November 8 that he knew for sure what the Allies intended. At that hour he was awakened with a report that they were landing in French North Africa; and as he would exclaim even eighteen months afterwards: "We didn't even dream of it."

The Fuehrer was clearly astounded. Torch had achieved absolute surprise, despite a rash of early security leaks and the fact that no expedition was more vulnerable to detection—if the enemy had been able to obtain reliable intelligence. As Lieutenant Commander Donald McLachlan, a naval intelligence officer connected with the LCS, would describe the situation:

> To land first 90,000 men, and later another 200,000, with all their supplies and weapons, on probably unfriendly territory, across 1,500 miles of sea from Britain and 3,000 miles from America, within easy range of German and Italian air reconnaissance from Sicily and with convoys forming up and aircraft being assembled under the eyes of the Spaniards [and, he might have added, German agents] in Gibraltar—this was possible only if the enemy were left guessing up to the last moment about the ultimate destination of these Mediterranean-bound forces. That they were there or going there could not be concealed; but what was the objective?

Indeed, what was the objective? Hitler knew only that this vast force was assembling for some expedition, and to intercept it he had stationed wolfpacks totaling forty U-boats between Gibraltar and Dakar. But, mysteriously, the Allied convoys had eluded the German U-boats and entered the Mediterranean; and of all the possible targets there—Malta, Sicily,

Sardinia, central Italy, southern France—French Northwest Africa seemed the least likely. How had Hitler been so thoroughly deceived?

The Allies had learned well the lessons of the desert campaigns and the disaster at Dieppe, for Torch was cloaked with clever cover and deception plans, and concealed in deep security. The LCS and its associated secret bureaus, including the XX-Committee, opened their deception campaign by suggesting, in the plan codenamed "Solo I," that the forces assembling in Britain were destined for Norway, or, in Plan Overthrow, for a cross-Channel invasion of France. When those deceptions were no longer tenable, "Solo II" came into being to suggest that the Allied convoys assembling in the Atlantic were bound for Dakar in French West Africa. Their actual destinations were a carefully guarded secret, and nobody talked. As Masterman would put it: "The real triumph of TORCH from our angle was *not* that the cover plans were successfully planted on the Germans but that the real plan was not disclosed or guessed. In other words, it was a triumph of security."

Even so, the Germans might have deduced the truth had it not been for several other factors that were operating in favor of the Allies. First, there was the progressive dislocation of the Abwehr. Canaris and his service had failed to provide any intelligence that contradicted the LCS fabrications; and Jodl would exclaim, even before the Torch expedition began to land, "Once again, Canaris has let us down through his irrationality and instability." Moreover, the B-Dienst, the German counterpart of Bletchley, had also failed to come up with any cryptanalytical intelligence disclosing the secrets of Torch. The reason was quite simple: the British, who were largely responsible for the naval movements connected with Torch, imposed baffling and completely effective wireless security over the expedition. Finally, there was Ultra, which was now fully functional. Through Ultra, the Allies knew what the Germans knew and how they obtained their information; and Ultra had revealed that they were totally ignorant of Torch.

What of "an element of legerdemain, an original and sinister touch, which leaves the enemy puzzled as well as beaten"? Had Torch employed any of those? The wolfpacks patrolling the approaches to the Mediterranean had suddenly left those waters to pursue a convoy of empty ships homeward bound to England from Sierra Leone. No one would be more surprised than the commodore of the convoy, Rear Admiral C. N. Reyne. The U-boats detected the movement of his convoy, SL125, off Madeira, and in a week-long battle thirteen of its ships were sunk. But as the official British naval historian would write: "Had the enemy not been thus engaged he might well have detected the great movement of (Torch) troop and supply ships, have attacked them or guessed their purpose and destinations, and so deprived our landing forces of the important advantage of surprise." Admiral Reyne would remark that it was the only time he was congratulated for losing ships.

Was the fate of convoy SL125 a fortunate accident or a strategic sacrifice? The truth will not be known, although the Admiralty was at pains to state afterwards that "the ill fortune which overtook this convoy appears to have benefited the Allied cause, quite unexpectedly. . . ." Because the Germans were busy sinking empty ships, the great Torch convoys—there were more than 1500 ships crowding the approaches to the Mediterranean—reached their destinations with only one being torpedoed, and without loss of life. Torch was indeed a triumph, and its combination of imaginative deception and good security would serve as a model for the Allied assault on Normandy.

The Fuehrer had been starved for accurate intelligence about Torch, but apparently there were others in the German intelligence system who were better informed. After the war, it was discovered that Captain Herbert Wichmann, Canaris's station chief at Hamburg, whence the Abwehr conducted its main operations against the United States and Great Britain, had obtained an accurate and timely report from an A1 source showing that French North Africa was *the* target. He had, Wichmann protested, sent the report to OKW under the speediest priority and the highest security classification—a priority and a classification that must have ensured it would have been seen at least by Keitel. What had become of the report? No one knew. No doubt Canaris remained impassive, as he did when he was challenged.

The German high command was beginning to believe that it was being badly served by Canaris. But if OKW did not yet suspect that he was actually working against Hitler, there were those on the Allied side who did. The clearest evidence of sympathy for Canaris in London would come at the time of Torch when he arrived at Algeciras, the town in Spain next door to Gibraltar where the Abwehr had one of its main bases. MI-6 at Gibraltar learned of his presence, and a plan to kidnap Canaris and fly him to London was formulated with the approval of the Governor of Gibraltar, General Mason-MacFarlane, the former British military attaché at Berlin whose proposal for the assassination of Hitler in 1938 had been turned down by the Foreign Office. But as Ian Colvin, the London journalist who first asked questions about Canaris's loyalties, wrote: "Gibraltar received a message from London cancelling the operation." Colvin's informant told him that the message did not state exactly: "Leave our man alone." What the signal said was that "(Canaris) was far more valuable where he was."

Even though Torch caught Hitler off guard, he reacted with great speed and foresight. He ordered signals to be sent to Field Marshal Albert Kesselring at Rome to speed the best available German troops to create a bridgehead in Tunisia. This Kesselring did—and among the troops was a young colonel of the General Staff, Count von Stauffenberg. These forces would delay an Allied victory in North Africa for many months; but Hitler quickly became less concerned with events in that theater of the war. His attention was riveted on Stalingrad, where the struggle had become titanic and personal. The Luftwaffe had burned the city to the ground, and little parties of soldiers met each other in hand-to-hand combat in the giant petrified forest of blackened chimney stacks. They fought for meters of ground through factories and offices, in sewers, into and out of houses. The battle would rage for eighty days and eighty nights, and an officer of the 24th Panzer Division would write: "Stalingrad is no longer a town. By day it is an enormous cloud of burning, blinding smoke. . . . And when night arrives, one of those scorching howling bleeding nights, the dogs plunge into the Volga and swim desperately to gain the other bank. . . . Animals flee this hell; the hardest stones cannot bear it for long; only men endure."

To Hitler, Stalingrad was not just a city; it was an obsession. Like Leningrad, it was not only a military but a psychological objective; he was convinced that once these two cities, named after the twin heroes of the revolution, had fallen into his hands, the political régime of Russia would collapse. Stalin was equally obsessed with determination to hold Stalingrad. He had given his name to this great industrial city. Thus the battles of Stalingrad and Leningrad were a personal contest between the two dictators.

The battles now joined in North Africa and on the Russian front would become the Jena and Auerstadt of the Third Reich. And as it grew apparent that the Allies were beginning to prevail, the deep gloom of defeat began to spread over the Reich. It was a spirit in which a revolution might flourish, and early in 1943, with Hitler's grand strategy threatened or collapsing everywhere, Beck observed to Canaris that the decisive hour for the Schwarze Kapelle was at hand. The German General Staff, he said, would never overthrow the Fuehrer while he was victorious; only when he and the army were in defeat would the fighting generals and colonels back a conspiracy. He was correct. With every defeat, the Schwarze Kapelle gathered new recruits and rapidly became much more than a few white-haired moralists seeking the restoration of a lost era. The questions of conscience—the *Fahneneid,* assassination, removing the head of state and of the army while the nation was in mortal peril—no longer troubled the plotters to the same extent as in the past. If Germany was not to be destroyed, most agreed, the only thing to do with Hitler was to kill him.

The Schwarze Kapelle was no longer a few scattered seeds of discontent, each seeking to survive the purges of the Gestapo and the SD. The conspirators were still playing with their lives, but now there was a central command and its tentacles were in contact with all other headquarters of consequence from Paris to Smolensk. Equally important, they had conceived a plan to assassinate Hitler—"Operation Flash"—as well as a plan to seize power if the assassination was successful. All that remained to be decided was *when* and *where* the attack upon Hitler should be made; the question *if* was no longer a factor.

The instrument with which the conspirators proposed to seize power after Hitler's assassination was "Case Valkyrie." In the late spring of 1942, Canaris had told the Fuehrer that there were some 4 million foreign workers in Germany and that this number would rise to 8 million by 1944. Canaris drew Hitler's attention to the dangers to the Reich of such a large number of foreign workers and advised him to command that a plan be made to deal with them in the event they rioted or revolted. Hitler agreed and issued a directive for Case Valkyrie to be drawn up by the C-in-C of the Home Army, General Friedrich Fromm. The actual task of writing the plan was given to General Friedrich Olbricht, the Chief of Staff, and by October 13, 1942, it had been completed and issued as a most secret matter of state to the commanders of the Military Districts. Olbricht, a watchful, shrewd, precise and affable man, was one of the most determined members of the Schwarze Kapelle, and in preparing Case Valkyrie he saw instantly that, if written appropriately, it could be used by the conspiracy as the instrument for the seizure of power and the neutralization of the Nazi Party, the SS and the SD.

The plan visualized a sudden state of disorder among the foreign population at a time when the Fuehrer was at some distant headquarters conducting his campaigns and not immediately available to take personal command of the situation. Therefore, the plan invested executive power in the army, and specifically in the person of General Fromm—an officer whose political allegiance to Hitler was, as events would show, ambiguous. Fromm was considered by the conspirators, and particularly by his Chief of Staff, to be an upright and decent man who would support the conspiracy if Hitler were dead. Moreover, he was a lazy man who was constantly off hunting—leaving Olbricht with authority to sign his name on documents and orders of the highest state importance.

Armed with this authority, Olbricht introduced clauses and appendices to Case Valkyrie in Fromm's name that had nothing whatsoever to do with the suppression of internal disturbances; they dealt with the seizure of power and the neutralization of the party base upon which Hitler's power rested—not only in Berlin and other principal centers, but throughout the Reich. Olbricht had only to issue the Valkyrie code word and all army units in the Reich would instantly spring to the "protection" of government and party offices and officials, signals and postal services, newspaper and radio offices, railroads and public transportation systems. Olbricht had the power to impose martial law and curfew, to suspend all private travel and telephone and postal services, and to order drumhead courts-martial and immediate executions without appeal. Valkyrie gave the army complete authority over all the other armed services, including the SS, and it provided for the despatch to all main population centers of special liaison officers whose duty would be to see that Valkyrie orders were obeyed without question or delay. In short, Valkyrie provided the Schwarze Kapelle with the power to control every aspect of German life and, as important, military units to enforce that control—for Olbricht's plan resulted in the formation of regiment-sized Valkyrie battle units at every key point in the Reich. These men were armed, trained and positioned so that they were a match for anyone—including the SS.

This time the Schwarze Kapelle was better prepared than ever before to attempt a *coup d'état.* The conspirators had, they believed, established channels of communication with the Allies through which they could negotiate a political settlement of the war. They also believed they had enlisted the sympathies and cooperation of a man who was both a favorite of the Fuehrer and a hero of the German people. That man was Field Marshal Guenther von Kluge.

Kluge, the C-in-C of the army on the Moscow front, did not love the Fuehrer, and neither was he blinded by the *Fahneneid,* at least not to the same extent as most of his fellow marshals. His devotion was to Germany and to himself; and when either was threatened, he toyed with treason. A brave soldier and a decisive and capable general, Kluge was commanded by the Prussian soldier's ethic he had learned as a cadet. "Gentlemen," his tutor had said, "you have the highest aim in view. We teach you now to fulfill this aim. You are here to learn what gives your life its real meaning. You are here to learn how to die!" The heroics of this doctrine dominated Kluge; he was to be found constantly flying low over the battlefield in his Fieseler Storch, directing the panzers, and he is said to have become exultant when watching the power and majesty of massed tanks and guns on the move across the Russian steppe. Now just over sixty—he was born at Posen in western Poland in 1882, the son of one of the Kaiser's cannoneers—Kluge and his commands had spearheaded the Fuehrer's armies in every major campaign in the war. In 1939, his army had occupied the Sudetenland of Czechoslovakia, and helped in the destruction of the Polish army and the subsequent capture of Warsaw. In 1940, his command drove the Belgian army into surrender, surrounded the British Expeditionary Force at Dunkirk, broke the last organized resistance of the French army at Rouen, captured the Cherbourg and Brittany peninsulas, and advanced as far south as the Bay of Biscay. In Russia his 4th

Army had captured corps after corps of the Red Army in the panzers' drive upon Moscow, and helped cut off and capture an army group of 600,000 men at Briansk. It was Kluge's troops who had reached the outer limits of the Moscow Underground in December 1941, and had then taken the brunt of the Russian counteroffensive. In consequence his authority with Hitler was very great; time after time, when Hitler telephoned with some new tactical idea, Kluge would respond: "But, my dear Führer, what you suggest simply is not practicable; you must come down out of *Wolken-kuckucksheim* (cloud-cuckoo-land)."

Kluge's weakness was his political ambiguity. He was not a Nazi general; he was the Kaiser's man, and, while he had done nothing to frustrate Hitler and the Nazis when they grabbed power, he was never quite able to accept the new revolutionary system. He recognized the régime as the lawfully constituted government of Germany and swore the *Fahneneid* to the head of that government, but when the wisdom of taking this oath was challenged by his Chief of Staff, General Henning von Tresckow, who had considerable personal influence over the field marshal, he toyed with his Knight's Cross and responded: "I am a soldier, not a politician." Because of this lack of commitment, the field marshal's loyalties had become the objective of both the Fuehrer and the Schwarze Kapelle.

Beck believed that Kluge's royalist origins and his sense of Prussian honor would, when Hitler's military policy finally showed itself in disaster, lead him to become the most powerful of the Schwarze Kapelle's allies among the field generals. Hitler believed that batons, medals and cash gifts could purchase the loyalty of his senior commanders, and on Kluge's sixtieth birthday, he gave the field marshal a present out of his privy purse of 250,000 *Reichsmark*—a small fortune for an officer of limited means and a salary of 60,000 *Reichsmark* a year. Kluge had purchased an estate at Rathenow; and against all the dictates of his Officer Corps training, which stressed the necessity of an officer's independence of the civil power, he accepted Hitler's gift. He also accepted a building license and a license for materials at a time when every brick was needed for the repair of bomb damage. In doing so Kluge compromised himself irretrievably with the men of his own "official family," and played his person firmly into the hands of Tresckow, one of the most active members of the younger generation of the Schwarze Kapelle.

Then just forty-one, Tresckow had been born in Wartenburg on an estate in the beautiful countryside of the Harz. He joined the 1st Prussian Foot Guards and in 1932 entered the Military Academy, where his reports described him as "a man far above the average," and "a soldier of quite considerable stature." A born *grand seigneur*, Tresckow saw Hitler as a military amateur whose delusions and obstinacy threatened to entomb the

German army in Russia forever. He had gone to war with the intention of removing Hitler the moment the opportunity presented itself. That moment, he believed, had come.

A man with a gift for making other men admire and follow him, Tresckow had surrounded himself with other conspirators, among them Major Fabian von Schlabrendorff, a lively and determined young officer who had long been a Canaris man. For many months the two men had discussed plans to seize, try and execute Hitler on the Russian front, but they had come to nothing because of the extraordinary measures the Fuehrer always took to protect himself and conceal his movements. Only if a man close to Hitler could be persuaded to join the conspiracy would any attempt on his life have a chance of success. That man was Kluge.

Both Tresckow and Schlabrendorff were serving on Kluge's staff at his headquarters in the Forest of Smolensk during the summer of 1942, and there they began to put pressure on the field marshal to become a party to their plot to assassinate the Fuehrer. Using Hitler's gift to Kluge as a weapon of blackmail, Tresckow persuaded the field marshal to receive Karl-Friedrich Goerdeler, the former Oberbürgermeister of Leipzig and the shadow chancellor in Beck's regency. In October 1942, the gaunt old economist, who called himself Pastor "Pfaff," appeared out of the gloom of the thick woods dressed as an itinerant preacher come to spread the gospel among the *Feldgrau*. He had, in fact, come to spread the gospel of revolution, and what he had to say to Kluge, in a conversation that lasted several hours, was of extraordinary interest.

Goerdeler told the field marshal that in April of 1942 he had traveled to Stockholm (on exit permits supplied by Canaris and Oster) to explain the objectives of the Schwarze Kapelle to Jacob and Marcus Wallenberg, the Swedish international bankers whose business took them frequently to both Germany and England, where they were known to Churchill and Menzies. Goerdeler met Marcus Wallenberg secretly in an old, drafty house at Styrmans-gatan, a place chosen deliberately to enable Goerdeler to lose any followers in the cold, thick Baltic mist which shrouded this dockland tenement area. Goerdeler told Wallenberg of the Schwarze Kapelle's plan to assassinate Hitler and asked what terms for an armistice, if any, would be acceptable to the British and Americans if the plan was successful. Wallenberg, who had just come from London where he had talked with Churchill, was not encouraging. He said that from his knowledge neither the British nor the Americans would make promises in advance which would bind them in their future policy toward Germany. If the conspirators succeeded in ridding their nation of the Nazis, well and good; but they must act first and seek terms afterwards. Wallenberg, however, was sympathetic and anxious to help, and assured Goerdeler that once Hitler was disposed of he would get in touch with Churchill immediately. With that assurance, the meeting ended and Goerdeler had flown back to Berlin to report to Oster.

Goerdeler revealed all this to Kluge as the two men walked together through the dark woods that surrounded the field marshal's headquarters at Smolensk. Would Kluge lend his authority to the conspiracy? Kluge hesitated. Ever since the near-collapse of his army outside Moscow during the winter of 1941–42, he had perceived that Hitler's strategies must eventually bring ruin to the Reich. But the field marshal was a circuitous man. While he recognized the desirability of ending the war, he could not, he told Goerdeler, act until Hitler was dead. But if someone were to pull the trigger, he would take action once the word was given by Beck. It was a momentous agreement. The Schwarze Kapelle had, or thought it had, a major ally in Kluge, and an important power base on the Russian front. Now all that was needed was an opportune moment to assassinate the Fuehrer.

That moment came when at last, on February 2, 1943, disaster fell upon the Wehrmacht at Stalingrad. Paulus, whom Hitler had made a field marshal, surrendered the 6th Army with 24 generals, 2000 officers and 90,000 ragged and bearded men to the Red Army. The enormous battle had claimed another 175,000 German dead and wounded, and the Fuehrer alone was responsible. But Hitler reacted predictably to the defeat; he blamed Paulus and declared that he should have killed himself rather than be taken alive by the enemy. The disaster bred another crisis of command; and aware of the anger of Hitler's generals, Beck lit the fuse of "Operation Flash," a fuse that led to Kluge's headquarters at Smolensk.

Kluge, acting at the suggestion of Tresckow and Schlabrendorff, invited Hitler to visit his headquarters and, to the surprise of all, Hitler accepted. It was the opportunity the conspirators had been waiting for; and Canaris and Oster, pretending that they were visiting Kluge's headquarters on Abwehr business, flew immediately to Smolensk to make the final arrangements for Flash. The plan was quite simple; a bomb would be hidden in the Fuehrer's private plane, set to go off on the return trip from Smolensk. Oster had obtained some British-made plastic explosive and fuses for the bomb—captured SOE stores held by the Abwehr at the Satory barracks in Paris.

Tresckow and Schlabrendorff made the bomb. They fashioned packages of the explosive into a parcel that resembled two bottles of Cointreau, the only liqueur sold in squarish containers. The wrapping was arranged so that the fuse could be triggered from the outside without disturbing the package; all that was required to set the bomb running was to depress a small trigger which broke a bottle of corrosive acid onto a wire holding back the detonating pin. Meanwhile, in Berlin, everything was being made ready for the seizure of power. Olbricht would issue the Valkyrie orders upon receipt of the single word "Flash" from Kluge's headquarters, while agents of the Schwarze Kapelle in neutral capitals were preparing to talk with the Allies.

At noon on March 13, 1943, the Fuehrer's Focke-Wulf-200 transport came out of the clouds above Smolensk attended by an escort of Me-109 fighters. It landed at the headquarters airstrip and Hitler disembarked, accompanied by a party of about thirty staff officers, his physician, and his personal chef with his special food supplies. Kluge and Tresckow were at the strip to meet him. They exchanged Roman salutes and were driven to Kluge's quarters where they debated the situation on the Russian front. Then Kluge took Hitler in to lunch. Schlabrendorff recorded the scene:

> As always, Hitler was served a special meal prepared by the cook he had brought along, and the food had to be tasted in his sight by his doctor. Watching Hitler eat was a most disagreeable experience. He shoveled in the food, consisting of assorted vegetables, with his right hand. However, he did not lift his hand to his mouth, but kept his mouth down over the plate. Now and then, he drank various nonalcoholic beverages that were arranged at his place. By his order, there was no smoking after the meal.

During the luncheon, Tresckow approached Colonel Heinz Brandt, a member of Hitler's entourage, and asked him casually whether he would be good enough to take along a small parcel containing two bottles of liqueur for General Helmuth Stieff in Berlin. Brandt readily agreed. With the bomb in Brandt's charge, Schlabrendorff then went to a telephone and placed a priority call to Captain Ludwig Gehre at Abwehr headquarters at Berlin. In the course of their conversation, Schlabrendorff mentioned that the Fuehrer had appeared to enjoy his visit and that he liked the apricots that had been provided for him—the code words. When the call ended, Gehre went down the corridor to Oster's office, and Oster telephoned Olbricht, who ordered the preliminary alert orders for Valkyrie. They were transmitted to all commands within thirty minutes, and this preliminary alert had the effect of bringing the staffs of the commanders of the military districts throughout the Reich to an interim state of alarm.

At Smolensk, the Fuehrer talked with Kluge for an hour after lunch and then prepared to return to Rastenburg. As he boarded his aircraft, Schlabrendorff started the mechanism of the bomb which was set to explode after thirty minutes when the FW-200 was at 8000 feet near Minsk. He handed the package to Brandt, who took it with him and placed it in the luggage compartment in the tail of the aircraft. With a final wave from the Fuehrer, the plane rumbled down to the end of the runway and took off, attended by the fighter escort. Schlabrendorff returned to headquarters to telephone Gehre with the report that Hitler's plane had left for Rastenburg.

Three hours later a teletype message reached Kluge announcing Hitler's safe arrival. Dumbfounded, Schlabrendorff hastened to Rastenburg to retrieve his package before someone else opened it and discovered it was a bomb. In a sleeping car on his return journey, he unwrapped the package and found out what had gone wrong. The fuse had worked and the acid had begun to seep onto the detonator wire; but before the striker was freed the acid had frozen. It was not until later that Hitler's pilot explained that he had run into some clouds and turbulence and, to spare the Fuehrer any discomfort, had taken the aircraft to a higher altitude. The temperature in the luggage compartment of the plane, where Brandt had put his kit, had dropped rapidly, freezing the acid.

The failure of the fuse—the failure of Flash and Valkyrie—was a grave blow to the Schwarze Kapelle, and particularly to Canaris, for he realized that when one of the Schwarze Kapelle's plots failed, the conspirators lost credibility in the Allied camp. But if their credibility was in question, as indeed it was, perhaps the greatest enemy of Canaris and the conspirators was time. Time had not waited for their decision to act; and with the failure of Flash it would not wait for them to devise some new plan. The high commanders of Great Britain and the United States had met at Casablanca to formulate plans of their own. They had not contemplated a political settlement to end the war. The end they foresaw was the complete destruction or the complete surrender of the Third Reich.

PART

HIGH STRATEGY AND LOW TACTICS

1943

"Cover" was carried
to remarkable refinements
as we became more experienced
and wily.

WINSTON S. CHURCHILL

Casablanca

THE MIDDLE ACT of the war between the Grand Alliance and the Third Reich began on January 13, 1943, when President Roosevelt and Prime Minister Churchill, with their staffs, met at Casablanca to chart the course of their operations for the coming year. As they conferred at the Anfa Hotel overlooking a sparkling blue Atlantic, it seemed that the tide of battle had turned in favor of the Allies—but only just. Hitler's 6th Army was being put through the Russian meat grinder of Stalingrad, and his Italian, Rumanian and Hungarian allies were proving unreliable. Field Marshal Rommel was withdrawing to Tunisia to join the army of General Juergen von Arnim and the battle was stalemated; but as Montgomery's 8th Army closed from the east and Eisenhower's Anglo-American army came up from the west, there were few who doubted that, once the spring campaign season opened, the Axis would be completely ejected from Africa. In England, air fleets of ever-growing might were beginning the Combined Bomber Offensive against German cities and industry. But at sea, the tale was one of unrelieved disaster. Through the combined operations of the Axis navies in 1942, the Allies had lost 1665 ships totaling almost 7.8 million tons; and most of these ships were sunk in North Atlantic waters—the lifeline of the Grand Alliance. Hitler had been stopped on land, but the battle for the supremacy of the sea was yet to be decided.

The purpose of the Casablanca Conference was to formulate a common strategy for the defeat first of Germany and then of Japan. But even as prospects of victory seemed brighter, the British and the Americans still did not agree about how and when to launch a cross-Channel attack. While the bloodbath at Dieppe had profoundly shaken some of General Marshall's planners, he came to the conference table determined to force the acceptance of an invasion of Europe through northwestern France in 1943. Equally, General Brooke was determined to prevent such an adventure until all his preconditions had been met. To ensure backing for his arguments against an invasion of France that year, Brooke obtained the use of the 6000-ton former liner *Bulolo,* now a communications ship for Combined Operations, and staffed it with all the principal figures at Churchill's war headquarters in Storey's Gate, near Westminster. Whereas Marshall and his team arrived with only essential documents for their proposals, Brooke had a contingency plan for every eventuality, with experts and intelligence to back him. The *Bulolo,* which also brought to the conference every Ultra so far produced, was anchored under heavy naval guard at the port; and its presence impressed the Americans. General Albert C. Wedemeyer, chief of the Strategy and Policy Group of Marshall's staff, would write:

> They swarmed down upon us like locusts with a plentiful supply of planners and various other assistants with prepared plans to ensure that they not only accomplished their purpose but did so in stride and with fair promise of continuing in their role of directing strategically the course of this war . . . if I were a Britisher I would feel very proud. However, as an American I wish that we might be more glib and better organised to cope with these super-negotiators. From a worm's eye viewpoint it was apparent that we were confronted by generations and generations of experience in committee work and in rationalising points of view. They had us on the defensive practically all the time.

The British had yet another advantage at the conference table. Ralph Ingersoll, an intelligence officer with the American delegation, would write: "In matters touching the European Theater, the British had a 100 per cent airtight, hermetically sealed monopoly on intelligence about the enemy. . . . They were the sole and *unquestioned* authority, first, because we had no military Intelligence on the Continent worthy of the name and, second, because the British had—and an excellent one, too." Ultra was at the heart of the British intelligence system, and Ingersoll would claim that the British concealed much from the Americans, or, it might be presumed, revealed only the intelligence that supported their strategical arguments.

Brooke stated his proposals on January 16, 1943, and by all accounts it was a masterful and enthralling performance. In fast, clipped speech that irritated Marshall, Brooke argued first, for the defeat of the U-boat to enable the Allies to build up the strength in England necessary for an invasion; and second, for offensive operations in the Mediterranean to compel Hitler to garrison his southern and southeastern fronts at the expense of his garrisons in France. His arguments were long, detailed and, with the knowledge within *Bulolo*'s files at his instant disposal, irrefutable. Marshall, although he believed that the Mediterranean was a "kind of dark hole, into which one entered at one's peril," yielded. He agreed to support operations against southern Europe, but warned Brooke that he was "opposed as much as ever to interminable operations in the Mediterranean." He also made it clear that the U.S. Chiefs of Staff would agree to support further Mediterranean operations only as "an expedient action dictated by current circumstances."

The Military Conclusions of the conference conformed exactly to Brooke's advocacy:

1. To defeat the U-boat, the first charge upon the resources of the western powers.
2. After the destruction of the Axis forces in Africa, to attack Sicily.
3. To create a position of Allied strength in the Mediterranean that would undermine the Axis in the Balkans, remove Italy from the war and bring in Turkey with her forty-four divisions on the side of the Allies.
4. To develop and sustain the heaviest possible air campaign against German cities.
5. To assemble the largest possible American forces in England without delay for a large-scale invasion of western Europe in the late spring of 1944.
6. To continue and expand a campaign of political warfare, subversion, economic warfare, and deception in order to undermine the German will and ability to fight and pin down forces wherever they might be found.

It is said that high strategy and low tactics walk hand-in-hand; and from the last of these Military Conclusions there would follow a series of operations that were the equal of any in the long, dark catalogue of subterfuge.

The Casablanca Conference came to an end. But before the statesmen and high commanders returned to their desks, Roosevelt and Churchill called a press conference, and Roosevelt made a statement that reverberated around the world. He announced that he and the Prime Minister were determined to accept nothing less than the unconditional surrender of Germany, Japan and Italy. Churchill was taken completely by surprise. He would later explain to Robert E. Sherwood:

> I heard the words "Unconditional Surrender" for the first time from the President's lips at the Conference. It must be remembered that at that moment no one had a right to proclaim that Victory was assured. Therefore, Defiance was the note. I would not myself have used these words, but I immediately stood by the President and have frequently defended the decision.

Roosevelt himself would later state that he had had no time to prepare for the press conference, and "the thought popped into my mind that they had called Grant 'Old Unconditional Surrender' and the next thing I knew, I had said it." But once said, and defended, the proclamation would cause widespread dismay. Many Allied generals would protest that it gave the Germans no other choice but to fight. Eisenhower would be quoted as saying: "If you were given two choices—one to mount the scaffold and the other to charge twenty bayonets, you might as well charge twenty bayonets." Marshal of the Royal Air Force Sir John Slessor would agree that "its effect was . . . unfortunate," and Menzies would warn the Prime Minister that unless the terms were softened, the German army would fight with what he called "the despairing ferocity of cornered rats."

There were other grounds for Menzies's disapproval of the proclamation. It eliminated the possibility of a political settlement to end the war. With no hope of terms other than Unconditional Surrender, what reason would the conspirators of the Schwarze Kapelle have to maintain their clandestine contacts with Allied agents, contacts that were useful in obtaining Germany's secrets and in planting deceptive information within the German high command? And if the Allies refused to consider a political settlement, what reason would the Schwarze Kapelle have to kill Hitler and overthrow the Nazi Party? In a subtle attempt to circumvent the policy of Unconditional Surrender and keep open his lines of communication with the conspirators, Menzies invited Dusko Popov, the Yugoslav double agent who had been christened Tricycle by the XX-Committee, to spend a weekend at his country residence. In reality, Tricycle served two masters—the XX-Committee and MI-6—for he had valuable connections within the Abwehr; and at an earlier meeting with Menzies, he had been commissioned to find out what he could about the men who formed the nucleus of the anti-Hitler conspiracy in the German secret intelligence service—Canaris, Oster and Dohnanyi.

Popov accepted Menzies's invitation and he would write that during their meeting Menzies declared:

> There is much talk—you probably have heard it—of unconditional surrender. I personally dislike it. A phrase. It means nothing. . . . But that is official Allied policy, and I can do nothing to change it. There is something else, however, that we may do. It would be . . . uh . . . beneficial if certain individuals in the right places in Germany were given to understand the proper meaning of that phrase. . . . One should assure the proper-thinking Germans—and I think they will understand—that we do not mean to blot Germany from the map. That would be contrary to the ideal of freedom for which we are fighting.

Menzies, who could only have been acting with the authority and knowledge of Churchill, then revealed that he was assigning an agent who would act as a postbox and adviser in Popov's contacts with the Abwehr hierarchy, and who "can be of great help to all those who want to eliminate Hitler and start talking peace." Popov would write that:

> Menzies was no longer as optimistic as he had been about arriving at a peace by circumventing Hitler. My impression was that he felt such a peace might have been feasible, particularly now that the tides of war were going against Germany, were it not for the "unconditional surrender" motif. . . . Still, the idea of ending a war a few years earlier was too attractive a goal for him to drop even if it had only the flimsiest chance to succeed.

In Berlin, upon hearing of the proclamation of Unconditional Surrender, Canaris turned to General Erwin Lahousen, one of his deputies and confidants, and remarked:

> You know, my dear Lahousen, the students of history will not need to trouble their heads after this war, as they did after the last, to determine who was guilty of starting it. The case is however different when we consider guilt for prolonging the war. I believe that the other side have now disarmed us of the last weapon with which we could have ended it. Unconditional surrender, no, our generals will not swallow that. Now I cannot see any solution.

The proclamation was heard like a thunderclap of doom by the other conspirators of the Schwarze Kapelle. After the twin defeats of Alamein and Stalingrad, Germany was ripening for revolution, but as Witzleben declared: "Now no honorable man can lead the German people into such a situation (as surrender)." And with the failure of Operation Flash, hopes for the overthrow of the Nazis and a political settlement to end the war seemed all but extinguished.

Only the Nazis rejoiced at the proclamation. Six days after the Casablanca Conference, Hitler and Dr. Josef Goebbels, the Reich Propaganda Minister, made a proclamation of their own—"Total War." In a speech on January 30, Goebbels called upon the German people to rally to meet the "extraordinary dangers of the military situation," warning that since the enemies of Germany were fighting to "enslave the German nation," the war had become an urgent struggle for national preservation in which no sacrifice was too great.

Exhorted to believe that they were the new Spartans at Thermopylae, the German people sprang to their tasks, and the *Feldgrau*—the "sledgehammer of God," as the Kaiser once called his army—were convinced that they would finally triumph. The Allies, too, entered this new phase of the war with high resolve, but as one historian recorded:

> To compel a powerful enemy to accept unconditional surrender will require every weapon in the arsenal, and the enemy in turn will be forced to resort to the most desperate form of warfare to resist. . . . The cost in

added intensity of resistance, in lives of political prisoners, and in the unmeasurable factors of social cohesion, moral values, and cultural monuments can only be guessed.

Roosevelt had given his generals—and the generals of Great Britain—no choice but to plan and then embark upon that most feared of all military enterprises: D-Day.

The Battle of the Atlantic

In ACCORD with the Combined Chiefs' decision that the defeat of the U-boat must be first charge upon the resources of the Allies in 1943, the Atlantic became a vast battleground in which the dominant elements were, Churchill would write, "groping and drowning, ambuscade and stratagem, science and seamanship." Naval warfare of unprecedented scale and violence developed between the North Cape and Cape Hatteras, between Cape Charles and the Cape of Good Hope, between the Western Approaches and Tierra del Fuego, as the Allied navies sought to clear the seas of U-boats and secure the sealanes along which might flow the men and matériel for the invasion.

Even as the Prime Minister and the President met at Casablanca, and as the North Atlantic trade routes were struck by particularly violent tempests, the battle for primacy was joined. It was a battle of ships, aircraft, radar, wireless, tactics, seamanship—and cryptanalysis. The Germans were reading the British convoy ciphers with devastating consequences; the British were reading the German U-boat ciphers through Ultra with equally devastating results. Both sides were fairly evenly matched during the early months of the year; and so at first the battle was a curious, deadly waltz in which the Allies swung their convoys one way to escape the submarine wolfpacks and the Germans swung their wolfpacks another way to bring the convoys back within torpedo range. Neither side, at least in the first ninety days of the battle, seems to have been aware that the other was reading its secret cipher communications. But victory was assured to the side that could continue to unbutton enemy traffic—and had the will and stamina to sustain the ferocious conflict.

Here, Britain, which bore the brunt of the battle, was disadvantaged. Alfred Dilwyn Knox, her chief cryptographer, and, with Alan Turing, the man who had first penetrated the mysteries of Enigma, was dying of cancer. The illness was first discovered before the war when he was slightly injured in a crash with a baker's van in a country lane while riding to Bletchley on his motorcycle. At the time, he underwent surgery and, it was thought the malignancy had been removed. But the condition reappeared in 1941. Knox was soon confined to his bed at his home in Hughenden in the Thames Valley, but he kept himself at work although he was weak and in pain. It is said that he exhausted himself further by the huge intellectual effort that had been required to track the battleship *Bismarck* in May of 1941. And—his family was told afterwards—it was his deathbed crypt-analytical exploit that had enabled the Admiralty to locate and sink the great battleship. Knox, propped up in bed by several pillows, used paper and pencil to attack the special battleship cipher being employed by *Bismarck* to communicate with the Admiralstab. Although he failed to crack this cipher (which was not cracked by any other agency either), he did manage to unbutton Luftwaffe and diplomatic orders associated with *Bismarck*'s sortie. It was these orders that had revealed *Bismarck*'s position on the night of May 26/27, 1941, after she had escaped her shadowing cruisers and her location was unknown at the Admiralty.

For his part in this great naval victory, Knox was made a Companion of the Order of St. Michael and St. George. But he was too ill to go to Buckingham Palace to receive the honor from King George VI, and the King sent an emissary to Knox's home. Although he was clearly a dying man, Knox insisted upon getting up. He appeared on the balcony overlooking his drawing room, fully dressed and looking—as his son recalled—"dreadfully emaciated," with his clothes "hanging dreadfully from his frame." He managed to descend the staircase for the ceremony, at which his family was gathered, and then, when the Saxon blue and scarlet ribbon with its gold and white star was placed around his throat, he returned to his room.

The Prime Minister, who was fully aware of Knox's importance in the war, intervened in an attempt to restore him to health. At a time when every ship was needed to fight in the Battle of the Atlantic—and, for that matter, every other ocean—Churchill offered Mrs. Knox the services of a destroyer to take her husband to the warmth of the Caribbean. But Knox was too ill to be moved. Churchill then obtained special medical treatment for him through his own physician, Lord Moran, the president of the Royal College of Physicians, and also arranged with the United States Embassy in London to obtain supplies of fresh tropical fruit, a rarity in wartime England for which Knox had cravings. But all was useless, and he died on February 27, 1943, having worked almost up to the end of his life on the U-boat ciphers. Churchill declared that his death was a "national calamity," but such was the wartime necessity for secrecy in these matters that it went unreported and unacknowledged. The only public tribute made was in the report of his death to the Fellows of King's College, Cambridge, which was read with solemnity by the president at one of their periodic meetings. Part of this eulogy said: "The service he so generously gave was of a kind few others could have given, and has proved vitally important in the present crisis. His labours were exacting and his keen sense of responsibility, which would not let him rest . . . impaired his health."

Although Ultra had become a major industry by 1943, employing some 6000 people to unbutton some 2000 signals a day, great new burdens now fell upon Turing, whom Knox had taken the trouble to train as his successor. Turing was a man of enormous intellect but, by then, few reserves of nervous energy. He was nearing the end of his tether as he coaxed his battery of engines at Bletchley to penetrate Enigma-enciphered U-boat communications and pinpoint the movements of the fearful enemy. As the Battle of the Atlantic approached its climacteric, he began to show signs of extreme mental fatigue. In a rare act of generosity, the Foreign Office, Turing's employers, gave him £200 ($960), provided him with a car and petrol, and instructed him to take a holiday. This he did, climbing Snowdon, the highest peak in Wales. Then he was sent to the United States by sea to exchange more knowledge about Ultra for Magic. When he returned, however, he had not really recovered; his brain was the equal of the ruthless mental struggle against the ever-changing U-boat ciphers, but apparently he was also fighting some private battle of his own. He became progressively more eccentric—noticeably so, even in the weird world of Bletchley. Obsessed that someone was using his tea mug, he spent many hours of exacting mental work to find a way of chaining it to the wall in Hut 3 with an unbreakable cipher lock. His landlady informed the medical authorities at Bletchley that he muttered abstractedly for hours at a time in his room at the Crown Inn at Shenley Brooke End. He allowed his hair to become long, dirty and wild, and his clothes were often soiled and holed. But still he continued to perform his intricate work in Hut 3.

The battle now to be decided had already lasted forty-five months, and it had not gone well for England. In 1940, Britain lost 4 million tons of shipping through war action—mainly to U-boats. In 1941—when, briefly, Ultra's success made it seem possible that the U-boat had been defeated— German war operations destroyed yet another 4 million tons of shipping. Then came 1942—the year of the greatest disaster of the war in terms of merchant shipping. The losses shot up to nearly 8 million tons, most of them off the east coast of the United States. Until then, the Germans had been sinking ships in all waters at the rate of two and a half merchantmen a day; now perhaps five a day were being lost, and it seemed that the war itself might be lost. Goebbels proclaimed: "German heroism conquers even the widest oceans!" Grand Admiral Karl Doenitz, the C-in-C of the U-boat fleet, declared: "Our submarines are operating close inshore along the coast of the United States, so that bathers and sometimes entire coastal

cities are witnesses of that drama of war whose visual climaxes are constituted by the red glorioles of blazing tankers." The triumph of the U-boat
crews was captured by this rhyme which Kapitänleutnant Jochen Mohr, the
skipper of the U-124, wrote and wirelessed to Doenitz while operating off
what the Kriegsmarine called "the American front":

> The new-moon night is black as ink.
> Off Hatteras the tankers sink.
> While sadly Roosevelt counts the score—
> Some fifty thousand tons—by
> 　　　　　　　　Mohr.

The year 1943 opened with more German submarines in Doenitz's fleet
than ever before; he had about 400, of which about 110 were in the
Atlantic at any one time—against the 57 he had had at the outbreak of the
war. In January, a month of severe storms that inhibited U-boat operations, they sank thirty-seven ships of 203,000 tons; but in February, the
toll rose to sixty-three ships of 360,000 tons. The reason for these losses
would be traced, at least in part, to the fact that both the United States and
Great Britain used their respective cryptanalytical services—Magic and
Ultra—with considerable caution lest their enemies detected that their
ciphers were being read. This, apparently, led the Allies to accept casualties in the merchant marine rather than divert convoys around wolfpacks—
and perhaps betray their secret knowledge.

It was later suggested that the Americans had gone too far in sacrificing
ships for cryptanalytical security. In fact, if the allegation was true, it was
the fault of the British. The Americans advocated the abandonment of
many of the precautions for the security of Ultra in order to locate, sink
and destroy the submarines that were threatening to cut the Old World off
from the New. Time and again the British had to intervene to prevent the
Americans from attacking U-boats on the basis of Ultra intelligence alone,
which would, the British believed, cause Doenitz to conclude that Enigma
was no longer inviolate. As Air Marshal Sir John Slessor, who commanded
much of the air force engaged in the Battle of the Atlantic, reported
afterwards: "American impetuosity in the use of Ultra gave us near heart
failure. We had so little with which to fight the Germans and the Japanese.
How much worse off we all would have been had we not had Ultra and
Magic!"

It was a point well taken, for in March the Allies sustained the greatest
losses in any one month of the war—108 ships of 627,000 tons. With the
Canadians, the Admiralty was responsible for the security of the North
Atlantic trade routes, and for many other theaters of the U-boat war. And
that war still hung in delicate balance—a balance that could be tipped in
either direction by the security of Ultra. Early in 1943, Ultra had revealed

that Doenitz was becoming uneasy about the security of his ciphers and communications; the tenor of his signals to his U-boat captains showed clearly that he believed the British had some form of inside knowledge about the Admiralstab's submarine warfare plans. Time and again, quite suddenly and for no other reason than the possession of good intelligence, the Admiralty would suddenly divert a convoy out of the way of a wolf-pack. The Admiralstab, which was reading some of the Admiralty's ciphers, wondered how the Admiralty knew where the wolfpacks were. But once again an Admiralstab investigation had concluded that the diversions were either the work of traitors in the Kriegsmarine's communications, or of British wiliness in the Submarine Tracking Room, or both. The investigation cleared Enigma.

The Admiralty did not clear its convoy ciphers, however. Certain from Ultra that the Germans had, once again, penetrated the ciphers, as they had done in 1940 with catastrophic consequences, the Admiralty began to change its systems in March of 1943. Such changes could not be made overnight, involving as they did ships on every ocean and every sea. They were not completed until May, and by then German victories at sea had forced other changes in the strategies used to defeat the U-boat—including a relaxation of the restrictions surrounding the tactical use of Ultra. Once before, in intercepting and destroying the ships supplying Rommel in North Africa, it had been decided that the stakes were high enough to risk the security of Ultra. The stakes were even higher in the Battle of the Atlantic.

The necessity for a change in strategy became shockingly apparent with the huge shipping losses sustained in March, and particularly with the fate that month of the great convoys HX229 and SC122. The Germans decrypted a signal in convoy cipher from the SS *Abraham Lincoln,* in which the commodore of HX229, a convoy of some forty ships under heavy escort, informed the Admiralty Trade Division in London that it had departed America for England on March 8, 1943. Other signals revealed to Doenitz where the ships were bound: the ports of the Mersey, the Clyde, Belfast, Loch Ewe. They revealed the dainty names of the escorts: *Chelsea,* USS *Kendwick,* HMCS *Frederiction* and *Oakville, Volunteer, Abelia, Pennyworth, Sherbrooke, Anemone, Beverley, Highlander.* The signals also told Doenitz in some detail what the ships were carrying: bombs and ammunition for the air war on Germany, petroleum, tanks and armored fighting vehicles, aircraft, food, rifles and machine guns, cannon and boots, tires and bandages, tank tracks and Spam. Doenitz knew when the convoy would enter the seas west of England; he knew its speed, course and the weather. All this information was weighed and discussed, and strategies and tactics were laid and communicated to the U-boats through Goliath, the great U-boat transmitter at Frankfurt an der Oder. The signals crackled across the ionosphere, and far away at sea, off the outer limits of the

Greenland icepack, the U-boats of the *Stürmer* Wolfpack—the "dare-devils"—moved across HX229's path.

But at the same time, Ultra was reading the Admiralstab's signals and the intercepts were quickly sent to the Admiralty's Submarine Tracking Room at The Citadel, the ivy-covered fortress beneath Admiralty Arch at the other end of The Mall from Buckingham Palace. Here, Captain Rodger Winn, the chief of intelligence in Room 39, worked with his assistants in what resembled a large billiard room. The light—day and night—was focused on a table of some 8 feet square upon which lay a chart of the North Atlantic. Flags, pins and symbols represented the locations of the Allied convoys and the German wolfpacks; red arcs radiating from Coastal Command and USAAF bases in Wales, Scotland, Ireland, Newfoundland and Iceland showed the ranges of the planes available for sorties. From this room, into which poured the sum total of all naval intelligence, emanated the instructions upon which the convoy commodores made their diversions. Winn had much freedom of discretion in the use of Ultras that gave warning of U-boat moves and plans; but, at the beginning, he used the intelligence to steer convoys clear of submarines only if it would not compromise the system—except in cases where U-boats were lying in wait for fast ships like the *Queen Elizabeth* and the *Queen Mary,* which were carrying large numbers of American troops or important figures such as Churchill.

Winn gave instructions for HX229 to change course. But at about that time Doenitz obtained intelligence on a second convoy, the SC122. It was a group of some sixty-six ships, also heavily escorted; and when the signal reached Doenitz, he responded by ordering the *Dränger* Wolfpack—the German word for "force" and "storm"—across the route of SC122. When Ultra intercepted Doenitz's signal in turn, Winn sent out a warning to SC122, which changed course. And so the battle of wits began as the two convoys maneuvered across the sea, sometimes in thick fog, sometimes in bright moonlight, sometimes in a snow storm, sometimes amid icebergs, sometimes in an ice pack—steaming for England at 10 knots, the crews sounding their ships' bottoms to make sure the ice had not torn holes. Gradually, HX229 and SC122 closed ranks and formed a large mass of shipping in a relatively confined space of ocean. The *Stürmer* and *Dränger* wolfpacks moved in on their targets.

At the Hotel-am-Steinplatz in Berlin, and at The Citadel in London, Doenitz and Winn watched the deadly moves of the game on their charts; Winn and his staff seemed to know the captains of the U-boats almost intimately, even though they had never met. They knew how each of *Stürmer*'s and *Dränger*'s boats would perform; from their nightly reports they knew almost as much as Doenitz did about their state of repair, the morale and health of their crews, how much fuel and how many torpedoes they had left, their positions, courses and speed, when and how they proposed to attack. Winn telephoned Coastal Command at Pembroke Dock in Wales and at Oban in Scotland; tenders leaped away from the piers to take aircrews out to the white, stately Sunderland flying boats lying at rest in the lee of the low hills. From USAAF bases on Iceland and Greenland, at Halifax and Rhode Island, Liberators lumbered down the runways and became airborne to join the air cover for HX229 and SC122, which were now steaming east in eleven majestic columns. Agile escorts whooped and darted about the column, their watches clad in oilskins, the white spray dashing up over the open bridges, the blowers and compressors screeching for all their worth. The aurora borealis flicked across the northern sky and the moon washed the convoys with silver. And then, at 0201 exactly on March 17, sea state 14, visibility good, the U-boats struck. In that minute four ships—*Kingsbury, King Gruffyd, Aldermine* and *Fort Cedar Lake*—were torpedoed and the night sky was rent as their petrol and ammunition exploded.

At first it was thought this was the beginning of the main attack. But it was not; possibly a U-boat had seen the green bow light of *Losada,* which inexplicably had been left burning, and, attracted by the light, sighted the merchantmen outlined by the moon and the aurora. The escorts sprang into action, performing "snowflakes" and "half-raspberries"—various forms of search and attack—but the U-boat had run deep and silent. As dawn broke, huff-duff located six U-boats within 20 miles of SC122. The Liberators arrived and began "cobra" patrols. But suddenly *Granville* was struck; she exploded and sank, trucks and tanks from her deck cargo hurtling into the sky. Again and again the U-boats evaded detection to claim other victims. That day, SC122 lost seven ships, and the HX229 ten; by the time the two convoys came within sight of the Scottish shore in the region of the Outer Hebrides, they had lost five more. One in every five ships that had sailed from New York had been sunk. It was, as the official historian noted, "a serious disaster to the Allied cause." As bad, only one U-boat had been destroyed.

In all, the Allies lost ninety-seven ships in the first twenty days of March 1943, and the month was not yet over. What made the sinkings more serious was that two out of three were lost in convoy—and the convoy was considered to be the main answer to the U-boat threat. The Admiralty was compelled to conclude that "the Germans never came so near to disrupting communications between the New World and the Old as in the first 20 days of March, 1943"; and, "It appeared possible that we should not be able to continue (to regard) the convoy as an effective system of defence." But if the convoy had been proven ineffective, where else could the Admiralty turn? "They did not know," wrote the official historian, "but they must have felt, though no one admitted it, that defeat stared them in the face."

Not even Ultra had permitted the Admiralty to triumph—at least not in the way that the Submarine Tracking Room had used it. It was clearly not enough to know where the wolfpacks were located, and to rely on maneuver, the convoy's escorts and air cover to drive them off. They had to be destroyed before they closed in on their targets. And so in April, when Ultra revealed the ominous news that, like a shoal of great sharks, ninety-eight U-boats were streaming into the Atlantic—the most Doenitz had ever sent out at one time—it was imperative to effect a change of strategy. The restrictions surrounding the tactical use of Ultra were relaxed, cautiously. Allied losses decreased as the Admiralty risked Ultra to swing convoys boldly this way and that through the four wolfpacks of sixty submarines that Doenitz had stationed across the North Atlantic trade routes. The strategy was only partially successful. Doenitz lost seven of his U-boats, but his wolfpacks claimed fifty-six ships of 330,000 tons.

The turning point in the Battle of the Atlantic finally came in May. Until that month, much had worked in favor of the Germans. They could read the convoy cipher. They had "Metox," a device that detected approaching aircraft through radar emanations and enabled the U-boats to dive and escape attack. And the Allies were not as strong in escorts and aircraft as they were to become. But now, each of the German advantages was chipped away. In the first place, convoys were protected by more escorts and aircraft. In the second, by May the British had replaced the compromised convoy cipher. In the third, there was H2S, the first 10-centimeter radar that employed a revolutionary valve called the magnetron. It had exceptional range and precision; and the fact that it was centrimetric radar meant that it could not be detected by Metox. And last there was Ultra. The Turing engines were performing better than ever against the Kriegsmarine's signals. Moreover, Churchill had directed that even Ultra must be risked if it meant the destruction of Doenitz's U-boat fleet. All commands, British and American, were advised to sink any U-boat no matter in what circumstances it was located. Unleashed from the shackles that had attended Ultra, aircraft captains were told where the U-boats were by wireless from the Submarine Tracking Room. Then, using the H2S, they were able to pinpoint the U-boats, even at night, and attack.

The consequences were immediate and devastating. In the first twenty-one days of May, Doenitz lost forty-one U-boats and Allied shipping losses were down to about 200,000 tons. Doenitz was forced to order the withdrawal of his wolfpacks from the North Atlantic until he had established what means the Allies had used to locate U-boats. But in June seventeen more U-boats were destroyed in other theaters of operation while the Allies lost only 22,000 tons of shipping. The U-boat had been defeated in the "month of the thunderbolt," as May of 1943 was called, and for Doenitz it was a personal tragedy; he lost two of his own sons in his U-boats.

As June passed into July and August, it was clear that the Allied victory in the North Atlantic was more than a temporary reversal in the fortunes of war; for in those three months, in all waters excluding the Mediterranean, the Germans sank no more than fifty-eight Allied merchantmen, totaling 323,000 tons, and lost seventy-two U-boats doing so. Doenitz immediately initiated an inquiry which revealed that no less than fifty-eight of those U-boats had been sunk by air attack. How had this come about? Suspicion fell upon the security of Enigma, but as the official British historian would note: "After examining all the possibilities they concluded that there was no evidence of treachery and that their ciphers were secure." Again, Ultra had made a major contribution to a strategic victory in the German war. It had been instrumental to victory in the Battle of Britain, to victory in North Africa, and now to victory in the Battle of the Atlantic.

The repercussions of that last victory were widespread. The morale of the U-boat crews was devastated, and Doenitz had to abandon wolfpack tactics and rely on single boats whose chances for attack were rare. As a result, not one American soldier lost his life through enemy action in the North Atlantic during the build-up for the invasion. Moreover, in direct relation to the invasion, Allied supremacy both on and over the seas would contribute to a significant tactical advantage. The Germans would form a screen of U-boats stretching from Norway to the Spanish border to warn of the approach of an Allied invasion armada, and U-boats would be stationed in Norway and in the Breton and Biscayan ports, armed, fueled and fully ready on six hours' notice to create havoc among seaborne invasion and supply fleets. But the German submariners would discover that it was not possible to run intelligence patrols in the narrow, shallow waters of the Channel and the Western Approaches. The enemy seemed to know exactly where they were and attack the moment they put their periscopes above the waves.

The Admiralty, which was largely responsible for victory in the Battle of the Atlantic, would never state directly how it had been achieved. The official British historian would credit "the combination of the intuition of certain experienced individuals with the most modern technical resources," and although intelligence was also cited, there was no mention of what sort of intelligence it was. Even as late as 1959, when Doenitz published his memoirs, he still refused to believe that his ciphers had been compromised. He attributed the calamity that befell his U-boats to the excellence of British radar. In fact, radar was only part of the story. In the "month of the thunderbolt" and throughout the rest of the war, Ultra intelligence guided

Allied warships and aircraft to the locations of the German U-boats, radar pinpointed their exact positions, particularly at night or in fog as they lay on the surface taking in air, and newly developed tactics of attack and destruction, coupled with violent new weapons, did the rest. The Allies once again dominated the seas, one of Brooke's primary preconditions for D-Day had been met, and Hitler himself was compelled to acknowledge that Germany's first line of defense had been destroyed.

With the eclipse of the U-boat, the attention of Allied naval commanders turned to the remaining German naval menace—the powerful surface squadron positioned under the black, bare mountains of Alta Fjord in north Norway. This squadron consisted of the formidable battleship *Tirpitz,* the battlecruiser *Scharnhorst,* the cruiser *Lützow,* and a congregation of destroyers that often numbered ten; its existence posed a threat both to the North Atlantic trade routes and to the Murmansk run. The Allies were compelled to dispose powerful formations of heavy warships, including aircraft carriers, in and around the great British naval base at Scapa Flow in the Orkneys to prevent the German squadron from breaking out into the North Atlantic, and for a time, the convoys taking war supplies to Murmansk were stopped completely. Until this squadron, and *Tirpitz* in particular, was rendered incapable of offensive action, no convoy, no invasion of Europe, could be deemed a safe operation of war.

As spring of 1943 gave way to summer, the Admiralty intensified its search for a means to immobilize or destroy the German squadron. All the plans, however, were considered impracticable. The ships could not be attacked from the sea, at least by any conventional means, for their lair was impenetrable. They could not be attacked from the air because, at that time, they were 900 miles from the nearest British air base, beyond the range of any aircraft then available. As a result, the British were forced to resort to unconventional means—a midget submarine called the X-Craft, a "descendant of the Elizabethan fireship" that had wreaked such havoc with the Spanish Armada.

The X-Craft, which would play a most important part in the intelligence operations for D-Day, and would help guide the invasion force to the beaches, was 51 feet long, weighed about 35 tons, could dive to 300 feet, and traveled at 6.5 knots on the surface and 5 knots beneath it. Its crew consisted of three officers and one engine room artificer, and its weapons were two detachable mines, each containing 2 tons of explosive. The mission of the machine and its crew was to penetrate the minefields, antisubmarine nets and boom defenses that guarded the German squadron's lair, position the mines under the keels of the heavy ships, and then depart—leaving the mines' clockwork time fuses to do the job of blowing up their quarry. Throughout the summer of 1943, the crews of six such X-

Craft were trained for just such a mission on Loch Cairnbawn in Argyll-shire. By September 10, the craft were ready to be towed by conventional submarines to a point about 150 miles off Alta Fjord. There they would slip their tows, make their attack, and then return to the parent sub-marines. Three X-Craft were to attack *Tirpitz,* two *Scharnhorst,* and one *Lützow.*

The midgets were towed from Loch Cairnbawn between September 11 and 12, but only two of them—X6 and X7—reached the fjord. It was then discovered that *Scharnhorst* had left her anchorage for exercises; but X6 and X7 set out to attack *Tirpitz.* They crossed the minefields successfully on the night of September 20/21, but misadventures befell X6 and only X7 remained. More trouble lay ahead. X7 became entangled in the anti-submarine nets, lost control and broke surface only 30 yards from the great hull of *Tirpitz.* But it managed to dive, struck the hull, and then planted one of its mines. Working its way further aft down *Tirpitz's* keel, it planted the second charge and made a run for it. But again X7 became entangled in the nets, lost control, broke surface under heavy gun and grenade fire, and then sank. Two of the crew survived, two lost their lives. But the attack succeeded; the mines exploded and caused "the whole great ship to heave several feet out of the water." The explosions put all three main turbines out of action; *Tirpitz* was immobilized and British agents and Ultra soon confirmed that she was no longer seaworthy. The cost had been severe—none of the midgets returned home—but the exploit was termed "one of the most courageous acts of all time."

At the Admiralty, it was decided to resume convoys to Russia, even though *Scharnhorst* and *Lützow* still lurked in the northern seas; and the U.S. squadron at Scapa Flow was released for other urgent duties. Such were the operational benefits that flowed from the brave midget submarine attack. Then the attention of the Admiralty turned to *Scharnhorst,* which had been left alone off northern Norway when her companion, *Lützow,* returned safely to home port.

Scharnhorst's fate was sealed on Christmas Day 1943 when the 32,000-ton battlecruiser with a crew of 2000 sailed with five destroyers to intercept two convoys totaling 41 ships bound for Murmansk. Her departure was detected more or less immediately; *Scharnhorst* sailed at approximately 7 P.M. on Christmas Day and a British heavy squadron built around the battleship *Duke of York* was warned at 0339 on December 26 that she was "probably" at sea.

Later in the morning of that same day, *Scharnhorst* was detected on radar by the cruiser *Belfast* between the North Cape and Bear Island, and the battle was engaged in the weird twilight of the Arctic winter. The cruiser *Norfolk* fired starshells to illuminate the magnificent ship and managed to get in at least one, possibly two, hits. *Scharnhorst* put on 30 knots and plunged away. She disappeared for a time but was soon relocated by *Belfast*'s radar. *Scharnhorst*'s guns struck and damaged the pursuing cruisers *Norfolk* and *Sheffield,* and then she sped away again, without knowing it, directly for *Duke of York.* In the meantime, *Scharnhorst*'s destroyers obeyed an order to return home, and the great ship was left like a stag ringed by hounds. At 4:17 P.M. that afternoon, she was spotted on *Duke of York*'s radar at a range of 22 miles to the north northeast.

As snow storms swept across the heaving sea, *Duke of York* pursued her prey; and when starshells illuminated *Scharnhorst* at 4:50 P.M. and heavy gunfire started pouring into her at 12,000-yard range, the German commander was, apparently, completely surprised. "I noticed," recorded an officer on the destroyer *Scorpion,* "her turrets were fore-and-aft; and what a lovely sight she was at full speed. She was almost at once obliterated by a wall of water from the *Duke of York*'s first salvo. . . ." With that salvo the Royal Navy began to settle a particular score with *Scharnhorst.* For, on February 12, 1942, with her sister battlecruiser *Gneisenau,* she had escaped from Brest at the Fuehrer's command and, while the Royal Navy slept, made a run through British home waters—the English Channel—to Germany. The dash caused a public and private storm around the Prime Minister, and *The Times* declared: "No more mortifying an episode has occurred in 300 years of British seapower."

Scharnhorst did not recover quickly from the surprise of finding herself under the guns of a British battleship, and the *Duke of York*'s 14-inch shells pounded her mercilessly. In all she received at least thirteen hits from the *Duke*'s heavy guns, at least twelve from the lighter guns of the cruisers, and eleven torpedoes from the destroyers. The sky was lit with the glow of her fires and internal explosions. At 7:45 P.M. on Boxing Day, in a position of 72 degrees 16 minutes North 28 degrees 41 minutes East, *Scharnhorst* sank beneath the icy waters. Before she went down, her captain signaled the Fuehrer: "We shall fight to the last shell." He did so; and when the seas closed over her, the North Atlantic was finally an Allied maritime dominion. Only thirty-six of *Scharnhorst*'s crew, which had included some forty naval cadets on their first voyage, survived. At the Admiralty debate on her fate, it was noted with satisfaction that it was "accurate intelligence which made all else possible." That intelligence was, again, derived from Ultra.

As the battle proceeded for mastery above and below the sea, Ultra was making another major contribution to victory over the Third Reich— the destruction of the German weather intelligence gathering and reporting system. Both the Allies and the Germans recognized that attack as well as defense along that most treacherous of Europe's waterways, the English

Channel, would be influenced to an important extent by the weather. Cloud cover, wind velocity, tides, wave heights—all could affect, seriously disrupt, or even prevent the complex land, sea and air operations of an assault on France. As Eisenhower would write, perhaps recalling the fate of the Spanish Armada in the Channel in 1588: "If really bad weather should endure permanently, the Nazi would need nothing else to defend the Normandy coast!" Accurate weather forecasts, therefore, were vital to the Allied command and the Germans alike, and it was imperative to deny the Germans as much weather information as possible. Thus a series of systematic and unsung battles were fought between the Allies and the Germans in the remote latitudes of the North Atlantic where the Channel's weather was made. They were battles as fierce and violent as those fought in any other sphere of action; they began the moment the war broke out, and they ended only when the war itself ended.

The first operation in the "weather war" occurred on May 10, 1940, when Major General Robert Sturges, of the Royal Marines, landed at the Icelandic capital of Reykjavik with a mixed party of Marines and troops from the cruiser *Berwick* to arrest the German consul-general, round up spare U-boat crews who were stationed there, establish a coast-watching service, remove German weather-reporting stations, and generally pave the way for a British occupation of the island. His mission was accomplished in a swift, gentlemanly manner, and Iceland became first a British and then an American base for ships and aircraft fighting the Battle of the Atlantic.

Having secured Iceland, the British moved against other weather-reporting stations in the northern seas. The first to be taken were the Norwegian stations on Jan Mayen, a lonely, rugged island deep in the Arctic Ocean which, in a meteorological sense, was regarded as one of the key points of the Arctic. It was invaded and occupied by a party of Danes under British orders in October of 1940. German-occupied Norwegian and Danish stations on Greenland were also destroyed and British stations established in their place.

Deprived of land-based stations, the Kriegsmarine attempted to establish a network of weather-reporting trawlers in the northern seas. But they were detected by cryptanalysis and huff-duff, and in April 1941, the Admiralty directed that the network, which worked the area Greenland–Iceland–Jan Mayen–Faroes, be dismantled. Three cruisers and four destroyers were sent to search a line northeast of Iceland and roughly halfway between the Faroes and Jan Mayen. On May 22, 1941, the German trawler *München,* a vessel of 1200 tons, was caught and sunk by HMS *Edinburgh*. The squadron then turned to the pursuit of *Lauenburg,* another specially equipped vessel. She was caught on June 25, 1941, by the cruiser *Nigeria* and three destroyers as she lay beneath the 8000-foot Beerenburg on Jan Mayen Island. Although *Lauenburg* was in thick fog, her wireless emissions had betrayed her, and *Nigeria*'s radar plot completed the job of locating her. *Nigeria*'s instructions were to give the *Lauenburg*'s crew no time to destroy its wireless or Enigma equipment; after a few practice 6-inch shells had frightened the crew over the side, a party from the destroyer *Tartar* boarded her. *Lauenburg*'s Enigma and all her wireless equipment and secret papers were captured intact.

In quick succession Commandos and sailors destroyed weather-reporting stations at Spitzbergen, Vaagö (where another Enigma was taken from the armed trawler *Krebs*) and the Lofotens. But Greenland posed a somewhat more difficult problem, for the United States had made the island an American protectorate on April 9, 1941. Thus, by agreement with the British, although she was not yet at war, the United States assumed the responsibility for patrolling the seas around Greenland to keep the Germans from returning to the island. On September 13, 1941, the United States committed one of her first acts of war against the Third Reich when the U.S. Coast Guard cutter *Northland* arrested the weather-reporting trawler *Buskoe* off southeast Greenland. Camouflaged with swatches of white and ice-blue, *Northland* had lain silent and almost invisible under a *storis*—one of the giant icebergs floating in a belt along the Greenland coast—watching *Buskoe* butt her way through the growling ice. *Northland*'s captain, Commander Edward "Iceberg" Smith, saw through his binoculars that *Buskoe* was carrying an array of aerials that denoted she was equipped with powerful modern wireless equipment—much more powerful and modern than that usually carried on trawlers. He decided to arrest the trawler as potentially hostile and ordered his gun crew to fire a shot across her bow. As the blast echoed among the icebergs, and the reverberations of the shot split great chunks of rotting ice off the *storis,* a plume of sea-green water shot up ahead of *Buskoe*. She hoisted a signal announcing that she had stopped engines and *Northland* sprang from the shadow of the iceberg to come alongside. A party of men boarded *Buskoe* and reported that there were twenty-seven men and one woman aboard, whose papers showed them to be Danish "hunters" and Norwegian "trappers." But their radio equipment bespoke a technical operation such as espionage and weather reporting. Moreover, one of the crew admitted that they had put two parties ashore, both equipped with wireless, near the entrance of Franz Josef Fjord. With that information, Smith ordered *Buskoe* to proceed to McKenzie Bay, a spot under the 15,000-feet-high sierras of Greenland. She was under arrest.

When Smith boarded *Buskoe* in McKenzie Bay, it was clear that this was no hunting and trapping expedition. The ship was equipped with better wireless than *Northland;* she had a main transmitter, a portable transmitter, a main receiver, a portable receiver, a portable engine generator, and a control panel. Smith informed the Dane who was commanding

Buskoe that *Northland* would leave a prize crew aboard. Then he sailed south to Franz Josef Fjord to apprehend the men put ashore by *Buskoe*. A landing party discovered a shack with antennas, and at about midnight on September 14, 1941, the shack was surrounded and the door broken down. Inside were three men who proved to be Germans. They surrendered without a fight.

In the next twenty months, the U.S. Coast Guard concentrated large forces in the Greenland seas to keep the Germans out, while ashore Danes and Eskimos were employed to patrol the moraines and eskers of the island. It was a strange battlefield, lit by the flames and rayed arcs of the aurora borealis. It was so cold that it hurt to inhale and, when a man exhaled, beads of ice formed in large clusters on his beard. Storms with wind velocities of 150 mph swept the area constantly as Coast Guard patrols worked across the Greenland Ice Cap from Cape Farewell in the far south, along the Denmark Strait to Scoresbysund, up the 15,000-foot sierra of the Greenland Sea littoral, and even as far north as Peary Land, a place where few human beings had ever been.

Time after time the Coast Guard caught German parties trying to set up weather bases. Many planes and many lives were lost on that inhospitable battlefield, and at least one ship disappeared without a trace. On December 17, 1942, the armed USCG trawler *Natsek,* commanded by Thomas S. LaFarge, an artist and grandson of the noted painter John LaFarge, sailed from Narsarssuak in Greenland for Boston with a crew of twenty-seven men in company with the converted trawler *Nanok* and the USS *Bluebird,* a minesweeper. The little procession entered Belle Isle Strait. Snow soon began to fall, and *Bluebird* lost contact. *Natsek* took the lead because *Nanok*'s fathometer was unserviceable, but the weather thickened and visual contact was soon lost. As they moved out beyond Point Amour Light, the weather cleared but the wind quickly reached gale force. It was then that black ice began to form—a phenomenon that spelled doom to many a trawler in the Arctic. Wind whipped up the sea spray and sent it over the superstructure of both *Natsek* and *Nanok,* where it froze into layers of ice that soon weighed scores of tons. Threatened with capsizing, the crews fought the black ice for three days and three nights, attacking the accumulation with picks and chisels. Steam was useless; no sooner had it been played over the ice than the steam itself froze. Miraculously, *Nanok* made it; but somewhere LaFarge lost his battle with the ice. It built up until *Natsek* became top-heavy, turned over and sank. In those seas no man could survive for more than five minutes unless he was in a boat, and even then he could not live through the night unless he was rescued quickly. For the *Natsek,* homeward bound, there was no rescue.

The Germans suffered even greater casualties in this brutal war whose dimensions were not measured in hours or miles but in months and degrees of longitude and latitude, and whose victories were reflected only by the curious symbols used on weather maps. Time after time German teams were picked off as they landed on or moved across the icy terrain, their aircraft were lost in wild Arctic storms, their ships trapped in heaving icepacks. Hundreds of men froze to death, but throughout 1942 and well into 1943, the Germans persisted—such was their need for accurate weather intelligence. But the Americans also persisted. Using Magic, sharp-prowed icebreakers, sledge patrols and lumbering Catalinas that were sometimes torn apart by Arctic storms, they searched out and destroyed German trawlers and land-based stations wherever they sprang up until, finally, the Germans admitted defeat.

The weather war was not confined to the Arctic seas. It was fought wherever the Germans attempted to obtain weather data outside the frontiers of the Axis empire. Nor were the weapons of the battle confined to guns, ships and aircraft. The subtler weapons of wireless were used to seek out and jam those stations which were beyond the range of capture; and when weather stations were found to be sited on neutral territory—as was the case with a weather and intelligence station in the Spanish colony of Ifni, Morocco—the Allies employed the blunt instruments of economic and diplomatic sanction. The OSS launched a small but thorough intelligence operation against the Ifni station, and armed with this intelligence, the American ambassador at Madrid, Carlton Hayes, took his complaint—and threat—to the Spanish government. Spain was particularly dependent on American oil, and so the Germans lost another weather station.

The destruction of the Etappe's fleet and the U-boats in the North Atlantic also served to deprive the Germans of weather intelligence, and for this, too, Ultra deserved much of the credit. As significant was the fact that, from the earliest days of the war, the Turing engine enabled the British meteorological service to read German weather reports. It was extraordinarily important intelligence for a number of reasons. From those highly secret reports, the Allies knew with some precision when and where the weather over the continent would favor an aerial attack. They knew what the Germans knew of weather over the British Isles, and that intelligence enabled them to launch aerial operations when the Germans did not expect them because of unfavorable conditions. Much could also be deduced about German intentions from the intensity of their interest in the weather over certain areas. But most important of all, in the context of the invasion, the ability to read German weather reports would enable the Allied high commanders to know when the Germans were expecting an attack because of weather conditions and when they were not. Their meteorological code had been an extremely difficult one to break; but in 1943, after many changes and variations, the Germans in the West standardized their cryptosystem. They would not change it until after the invasion.

There were many queer twists in the weather war, for not only were the Germans deprived of accurate weather intelligence, a campaign was also launched to provide them with false and misleading forecasts. The campaign began the moment the war broke out when the double agent Snow broadcast from his jail cell false reports of the weather over London to throw Hitler off if he decided to commence hostilities with a Luftwaffe attack on the British capital. It continued when German agents trying to infiltrate the North Atlantic islands to set up weather-reporting stations were captured, "turned" and began to supply Berlin with false weather data. XX-Committee double agents in Britain also supplied their controllers with false weather intelligence.

As a final consequence of the deception campaign, tricks of technology and the savage little war within a war, the Germans would have to depend for their intelligence of the weather over the British Isles, the Atlantic and the eastern seaboard of the Americas upon a statistical process based on weather patterns in the English Channel over the past fifty years, random and isolated U-boat and Luftwaffe reports, data supplied by stations on secure German territory, intercepts of Allied meteorological reporting units—and what they could see outside their windows with their own eyes. The Allies, on the other hand, had detailed meteorological intelligence at their disposal; and of all the natural factors, of all the schemes of men, that would influence the success of the invasion, Allied knowledge—and German ignorance—of weather conditions on the eve of D-Day would prove to be the most important.

The LCS and Plan Jael

By THE SPRING of 1943, all Allied secret agencies were fully operational and another dimension of the great conflict—the secret war—was rising in tempo and violence. Deception would soon come to dominate this labyrinthine war; and the LCS—the inheritors of that ancient British faculty that made Louis XIV's philosopher, Jacques Bénigne Bossuet, exclaim: *"Ah! la perfide angleterre!"*—began to weave a complex series of stratagems that, for their cunning, had no discernible parallels in English—or, for that matter, American—history. If there were parallels, they could be found in the precepts of Sun Tzu, the conqueror of Ch'u, Ch'i and Ch'in in 600–500 B.C., who was writing the world's first textbook of military theory when London was still a prehistoric swamp. Sun Tzu had provided an exact definition of the tasks of the LCS and its associated agencies in the months ahead: "Undermine the enemy first, then his army will fall to you. Subvert him, attack his morale, strike at his economy, corrupt him. Sow internal discord among his leaders; destroy him without fighting him."

The purpose of all deception from now on was to render Hitler and OKW "puzzled as well as beaten" about "Overlord," the code word for Allied strategical intentions in northwest Europe in 1944. And the main target was the mind of Hitler himself, for he was the German Supreme Commander. Ranged against that brilliant autodidact was a group of men who represented the aristocratic cream of a caste of blood, land and money, and who now dominated the British secret agencies. They were descendants of that self-perpetuating cabal that had created and ruled a world empire for over two hundred years; and they had at their disposal a wealth of experience in stratagem and special means. These men approached their tasks with zest and dedication—and with a malevolence perhaps born of the realization that, if they failed, their class would not survive. They came to the gaming table in the spirit that this was Britain's last, great throw, and they began to play their cards as Châteaubriand had done when his class was being extinguished in the French Revolution, guarding that "strong love of liberty peculiar to an aristocracy whose last hour has sounded."

At Storey's Gate, Churchill's bunker beneath the pavements of Westminster, "The Controller of Deception"—as the chief of the LCS, Colonel John Henry Bevan, was called, as if he were a character in Kafka—typified these clever, menaced British aristocrats. Quite unknown publicly, for he was a very silent man, Bevan was at the center of financial power in London. A grandson of one of the greatest of the British bankers and the son of a leading London stockbroker, Bevan was himself an important stockbroker in peacetime and would later advise the royal family on its investments. He would become a Privy Councillor, one of the sovereign's advisers, and his appointment as The Controller of Deception was in the tradition of the post—it was an aristocrat's job. For the LCS had, in turn, been headed by a son of the Earl of Derby, by a brother of the Earl of Scarborough, and now by Bevan, who was by marriage a member of the family of the Earl of Lucan and connected through his mother with the Viscounts Hampden and the Dukes of Buccleuch.

Bevan had been at "The Blessed College" of Eton (with Menzies) and had gone on to Christ Church, the richest of the Oxford colleges, where the burden of the curriculum was aimed at teaching intelligent undergraduates whose social position might enable them to obtain high office in the public service. It was a world within a world whose members knew each other intimately long before they ever got to Westminster, an admirable background for a man whose work in deception would demand the confidence and close cooperation of the politically powerful.

Bevan's stay at Christ Church was cut short by the First World War when he was commissioned into the Yeomanry, the Hertfordshires. He won the Military Cross and, toward the end of the war, was appointed to the staff of Field Marshal Lord Haig, the British C-in-C in France. After the war he returned to the City and married Lady Barbara Bingham, whose ancestor, Lord Lucan, commanded the Cavalry Division in the charge of the Light Brigade at Balaklava, and whose brother-in-law would become Field Marshal Lord Alexander, the future Supreme Commander in the Mediterranean during the Second World War. At the outbreak of the Second World War, Bevan rejoined the Hertfordshires and became intelligence officer at Western Command headquarters in Chester. When the LCS was established, its first chief, Colonel Stanley, brought him south to become his staff officer and, soon after Stanley resigned, Bevan was appointed Controller.

By this time deception had been successfully tested as a weapon of strategic warfare, but under Bevan the LCS's stature would increase in the military hierarchy to a point where it came to control many of the activities of other British secret agencies. The Americans conceded British expertise in the game in European, Near Eastern and Indian Ocean theaters; and bureaus were established at Washington, Cairo, Algiers, Delhi and, eventually, Trincomalee. Thus Bevan's arena was global and his authority, when he cared to use it, was also global, although in practice it worked none too well in the theater commanded by General Douglas MacArthur; like the representatives of Ultra in MacArthur's command, the LCS men found themselves up against the general's antipathy for all things British. But when necessary, Bevan had the authority to direct any government department in London and, through the Joint Security Control, in Washington, to perform according to the LCS's score. He had powers without precedent and on occasions even Roosevelt and Churchill made their personal movements and statements conform to the dictates of deception. In consequence, Bevan came to be regarded at Storey's Gate as the British regarded their public executioner: with curiosity, even admiration, but at all times with caution and respect.

To those outside Storey's Gate, including army commanders, Bevan and the LCS were viewed as clever, mysterious men whose precise duties and activities must not be inquired into. Even the most recalcitrant socialists in Churchill's government—notably, Herbert Morrison, the Home Secretary, who was not an easy man to control—found it prudent to conform. So did the trades unions; "difficult" organs of public opinion such as the *Daily Mirror* and the *New York Times;* even the BBC and the Church. Those who had frequent contact with Bevan were often left with the feeling that they had dealt cards with an enigma. "Colonel Bevan played his games with great skill," recalled General John R. Deane, the chief of the U.S. Military Mission to Moscow, "and never let his left hand know what his right hand was up to. After a time I became aware that not even his own staff knew everything he was doing." Like Canaris, Bevan was determined to confound history with mystery; when he talked about his role years later, he said in the opulence and privacy of his apartment in St. James's: "I do not think I should say what I did. I do not think Governments should admit to such matters, even if they were done in wartime."

Bevan himself enjoyed the complete confidence of Churchill and, through him, of Roosevelt, for the President took no less delight in deception than did the Prime Minister. There was no reason to doubt the statement that Churchill spent as much time with Bevan cooking up plots over good brandy with majestical flights of late-night imagination as he did with any of his other bureaus. "Bevan and Churchill," one LCS officer remembered, "sparked each other off and pulled out what were all the old tricks of Eton and Harrow and polished them up for the task at hand."

Bevan's "annexe" was his club, an institution which in Britain often illustrated the character of a man. In this case, it was Brooks's, according to George Trevelyan, the "most famous political club that will ever have existed in London." It was also famous for its gamblers and eccentrics; Charles James Fox lost £154,000 there in a month or so, and Sir Edward Elgar used to telephone his home in distant Worcestershire to hear his dogs bark. It was at Brooks's, in the bar, beneath the portrait of Spencer Perceval, the only British Prime Minister ever assassinated, that Bevan met the man who became his deputy at LCS—Wingate. Of Bevan's subordinates, only Wingate knew The Controller's activities in all their dimensions.

Lieutenant Colonel Sir Ronald Evelyn Leslie Wingate was a shortish, myopic man with black hair carefully brushed straight back. It was once said of him that he could "think nine ways at once." Certainly of formidable intellect, he was also a classicist, a clubman, a fly fisherman whose favorite ghillie was a bishop, and it seemed as if his entire career had trained him for his brief occupation as the sorcerer's apprentice.

Wingate was born on September 30, 1889, the eldest son of Wingate Pasha of Egypt and the Sudan—General Sir F. Reginald Wingate, a fierce Victorian who was among the Empress's most decorated soldiers. General Wingate came from a family of impoverished Lowland lairds who had served the crowns of Scotland and England, mainly as soldiers, for nine hundred years. As Kitchener's intelligence officer, he was one of the men who destroyed the Mahdi and Mahdism in the Sudan in the late nineteenth century, and added some 30 million people in that vast territory to the Empire, the second largest possession of the Crown after India. And by 1917, General Wingate was the most powerful man in Arabia. Colonel Wingate's uncle had added the Aden Protectorate to the Crown; another uncle was Governor of Malta; his godfathers were Field Marshal the Lord Kitchener of Khartoum, and Field Marshal the Earl Roberts of Kandahar. His mother came from a long line of captains and admirals. Lawrence of Arabia was related from the wrong side of the blanket; Wingate of Burma was a cousin. It was an Imperialist family in an Imperialist age, a family whose ties led to the remotest corners of the Empire.

Wingate went to a public school, Bradfield, near Rugby, and then to Balliol, Oxford, an institution "preoccupied not so much with scholarship as with success," which gave the impression of being "more of a cult than a college." He came to speak beautiful French, Greek, Urdu and Arabic, married the daughter of Professor Paul Vinagradov, the former head of Moscow University, and became an Assistant Commissioner at Sialkot in the Punjab of Kipling's India. In the First World War he had served as a political officer in Mesopotamia, where he helped destroy the eastern marches of the Ottoman Empire to ensure that Britain obtained the oilfields of the Karun. He learned the lessons of intrigue from such tutors as Sir Percy Cox, the great Arabist; G. E. Leachman, the explorer and ruler of the Anaizeh tribe; E. B. Sloane, the British agent who spoke five dialects of Kurdish and Persian, and conspired against the Turks in Kurdistan dressed as a cheese-seller; Gertrude Bell, the extraordinary Englishwoman who spent her life in the Arabian deserts and was the only woman officer in the British army. Wingate had been involved in the attempt to bribe the Turkish army commander who had cut off a British expeditionary force on the Tigris at Kut—with £1 million. He was at the capture of Basra, in the march upon Baghdad, and helped fight it out with Turkish and German agents in the alleys of the great cities of the Hittites and the Babylonian, Assyrian and Sassanian empires. But his great triumph in Arabia had been to help deny the Turks the Holy City of Najef, the Muslim shrine where Ali, son-in-law of the Prophet, was assassinated.

Between the wars Wingate became, in turn, Political Agent at Muscat and Oman, where he brought the tribes firmly under British control; secretary to the Agent of the Governor-General of Rajputana; Political Agent of Quètta; Joint Secretary and Acting Political Secretary in the Government of All India; and finally, Revenue Commissioner and Agent to the Governor-General of Baluchistan. Like his father, his entire career was spent in the service of the Crown and, again like his father, he developed a belief that nine-tenths of humanity were not worth saving—unless they were citizens of the Empire. Beneath his great charm and diplomacy, he was shrewd and hard. Above all, his intellect had been sharpened by his decades in India and the Middle East—settling quarrels, collecting revenues, improving communications, holding court in Hindi, Urdu or Arabic, watching out for (and countering) Russian subversion, clipping the claws of the moneylenders, keeping the Muslims apart from the Sikhs, the Dogra from the Jat. There was, in consequence, an almost Armenian streak to his mind; and when he came to the LCS—having taken part in "Menace," General de Gaulle's 1940 expedition to Dakar, and in various operations to secure from the Germans the gold deposits of Belgium and Poland— Wingate had already dealt, successfully, with some of the most politically deft and devious people in the world. By the standards of ordinary men, his experience in intrigue had been endless and severe. Now, with Bevan, whose mind had been polished by his career in the upper reaches of finance in the City of London, he applied that experience to conceiving the stratagems of the LCS. Both men, through their connections with many prominent members of government, officials of the Empire, soldiers, politicians and leading journalists, were able to reach out and place their ideas into a much wider framework than that of the ordinary bureaucrat.

Around Bevan and Wingate was a small bureau of ingenious men. There was the first member of the LCS, Wing Commander Dennis

Wheatley, a leading British novelist and a student of crime and black magic whose best-sellers included *The Eunuch of Stamboul, The Golden Spaniard* and *The Haunting of Toby Jugg*. There were George Mallaby, who became High Commissioner in New Zealand; Harold Peteval, a millionaire soap manufacturer in peacetime and a leading intelligence officer in wartime; Derrick Morley, a financier and shipowner; James Arbuthnott, a luminary in the tea business. Then there was Professor Edward Neville da Costa Andrade, one of Britain's most illustrious scientists, and a man whose passion was, he said, "collecting old scientific books and useless knowledge." He had dreamed up the little crickets that Allied paratroopers would use to identify friend from foe in the dark, and his special sphere of interest was in using the tricks of science to deceive the enemy.

Sir Reginald Hoare, a banker as well as diplomat who knew most of the back streets of central and eastern European capitals, served as the LCS's link to the Foreign Office. The representative of the Pentagon was Lieutenant Colonel William H. Baumer, of Omaha, Nebraska, a product of Creighton and West Point. At Cairo, the LCS's interests were managed by Brigadier Dudley Clarke, the wealthy London solicitor whose work on Bertram had contributed to Rommel's defeat at Alamein. At Washington there were Lieutenant Colonel H. M. O'Connor, who was well known in Ireland as a racehorse owner, and Major Michael Bratby, the artist; and in India and Southeast Asia there was Colonel Peter Fleming, the author, journalist, ornithologist, and brother of Ian Fleming, the espionage novelist.

From this nucleus of men radiated connections to all the main military, intelligence and policy centers in the joint Anglo-American high commands. At COSSAC, the newly established planning headquarters for the invasion, deception was the responsibility of the Committee of Special Means, or Ops B, a subsection of the operations department. The chief British agencies which executed LCS stratagems were MI-6, MI-5 and the XX-Committee, PWE and the intelligence departments of the three main services. In the United States and in the American sphere of influence, the main agency used by the LCS and the CSM was the Joint Security Control, which in turn controlled the OSS, the FBI, the various American information agencies and the State Department. Thus, the structure of the LCS was such that a stone cast at Storey's Gate rippled in ever-widening circles—political, financial, civilian, diplomatic, scientific, military—until it became, according to Helmuth Greiner, OKW's historian, "waves of confusing deceptions." The LCS also had the means, when necessary, to place a deceptive message directly on Hitler's desk within one half hour of its origination at Churchill's headquarters—and it would do so on one memorable occasion during the invasion period.

In particular, the banks and the City of London played a definite if imperceptible role in both intelligence and deception; and Bevan and

Menzies were placed well by class and family to use the immense but largely secret world of finance to the advantage of Allied strategy. Hitler, it was reasoned, was a revolutionary whose word could not be trusted and whose policy and actions boded no good—and much bad—for the institutions of world trade. With their centuries of experience, their belief that it does not matter *what* a man knows but *whom* he knows, with their myriad invisible connections linking the City and Wall Street with every capital in the world, with their interlocking families, committees, religions, with the very power and velocity of money and financial information on the move, the hierarchs of the financial world provided Bevan and Menzies with seductive conduits to the halls of rule in Berlin.

Perhaps the most important of the LCS's lines of influence, however, was through General Sir Hastings Ismay, Churchill's Chief of Staff and the Military Secretary to the Prime Minister, the War Cabinet and the Chiefs of Staff. Ismay was a friend of both Bevan and Wingate, and he and Wingate had grown up together in the service of the Crown in India. The son of the chief judge at Mysore, Ismay became a lieutenant with the 21st Cavalry, an expert in Arabic and Persian, a champion pigsticker, a veteran of small frontier wars, and a polished military diplomat. When Wingate became Political Secretary to the Viceroy of India, Ismay was Military Secretary. And when Ismay became a Secretary to the Committee of Imperial Defence, and then Churchill's Chief of Staff, he arranged for Wingate to come into the LCS. Ismay was, said Lord Moran, the Pepys at Churchill's court, the "perfect oil-can."

The members of the LCS were not concerned with the tactics of the war, nor with the execution of their deception schemes. Their task was wholly strategical, and their textbooks were the classics of history rather than of military science. Adam Smith was more frequently consulted than Vegetius; Procopius was their guide, not Frederick the Great. They had about them a certain Edwardian arrogance; they were men of intellect, charm, determination, ruthlessness and ambition. Their power was very great, as those who crossed them discovered, and above all, they were secretive. They did not intend that their existence or function should ever become known. In this, of course, they failed, just as they would fail to survive as a class. But for the time being they, like Churchill, exerted an extraordinary and powerful influence on the direction of the war. Indeed, if Churchill had not been Prime Minister, he would have been a member of the LCS.

In the early months of 1943, the LCS was fully occupied with a major cover and deception operation. It was Plan Jael, Bevan and Wingate were its principal authors, and the object of the plan was "to induce the enemy to make faulty strategic dispositions in relation to operations by the United

Nations against Germany" prior to D-Day. There were two major components of the plan, both of which had been decided upon at Casablanca. The first, "Cockade," was intended to "contain the maximum enemy forces in western Europe and the Mediterranean area and thus discourage their transfer to the Russian front." The second was "Zeppelin," whose objective was to deceive Hitler into believing that, at the end of the Tunisian campaign, the Allies would *not* invade Sicily and Italy (the evident next step in Allied strategy) but rather would invade Greece and southern France. What, in effect, the Anglo-American high command required was that from Storey's Gate the LCS should conceal the movements of armies and fleets that existed in fact, and, at the same time, invent the movements of armies and fleets that did not exist at all.

Immense as this task would be, it was made simpler by several factors. First, it was evident from Ultra that the Germans did not have accurate knowledge of the strength and dispositions of the armies of the British Empire, although they knew much about those of the United States. OKW consistently overestimated British strength by as much as 20 to 30 per cent, and gave credit to the British for two armies in the Near East—the 9th and the 10th—that were little more than brigades. Second, from intelligence gained through Ultra and MI-6, through statements made by emissaries of the Schwarze Kapelle to the American and British governments, and through Russian estimates of Germany's order of battle, the strength and dispositions of the German armies were known in the greatest detail. These same sources also revealed how sensitive Hitler was to threats against the fringes of his empire: Norway; the Balkans and its "armpit," the Ljubljana Gap through the Julian Alps at the top of the Adriatic; the Aegean Islands, which Hitler regarded as the barbicans of southeastern Europe; and Turkey, who might abandon her neutrality in favor of the Allies. As important, it was soon realized at the LCS that Hitler's concept of military strategy made him especially vulnerable to feints. His whole thinking was geared to the principle of the territorial imperative; if he perceived a threat growing up at any point around Fortress Europe, his reaction was to speed reinforcements from his reserves. Thus, he might be lured into offending a fundamental military law: to try to be strong everywhere is to be weak everywhere.

Yet Hitler was not a strategical innocent. He was extraordinarily quick to spot a trick, but the LCS was aware that he was being badly served by his intelligence services. After his initial successes of 1940 and 1941, no potentate in history had more fallible "eyes and ears" than the Fuehrer. By 1943, the combined Anglo-American secret agencies had largely muzzled the Abwehr and the SD outside the borders of the German Empire. Hitler's cryptographic wireless intelligence services still worked well—in some cases, extremely well, particularly in the naval sphere. But superior Allied wireless security systems, first introduced to hide the El Alamein offensive, successfully denied him an accurate and coordinated picture of Allied strengths and intentions. Further, his aerial reconnaissance services were, more often than not, restricted through Allied air superiority. As for his intelligence evaluation services, they were skilled and perceptive, but they suffered from two major defects; their sources of intelligence were unreliable and inaccurate, and even when they did manage to promulgate correct evaluations, Hitler tended to disregard them in favor of "trustworthy"—party—assessments. Nor did the German diplomatic services serve the Fuehrer well. Whatever sources of information he had in Britain and America were invariably under firm MI-5 or FBI control. And finally, there was always Ultra, which could be used to detect Hitler's reaction to any leak from the Allied camp.

The LCS had another major factor in its favor: the excellence of Britain's system of commercial, military and diplomatic communications. These global nets would enable the LCS to transmit its instructions on a fast, secure, reliable and synchronized basis. This meant, for example, that a story planted in diplomatic circles in Lisbon could be substantiated by a political move in Washington, a newspaper story from Stockholm, a military action along the Syrian-Turkish border, a calculated leak at Madrid, a rumor at Cairo, and the statement of a high commander at Delhi. Through these communications—communications constructed to control the Empire—Bevan had the means to ring his carillon at will.

But Bevan and the men of the LCS knew that their stratagems would work only if there was watertight security on the Allies' own secrets. It was fundamental to successful deception that there be discretion and consistency in everything that was said and done. An impetuous statement, a wrong move, a penetrated cipher—any one of a number of errors might serve to unmask a deception. If that occurred, the Germans could determine the truth from the substance of the falsehood, make a correct disposal of their forces and surprise the Allies. To ensure security, the truth of Allied intentions could only be made known to an extremely small group of Allied commanders. In short, it would sometimes be necessary to mislead a friend in order to deceive the enemy.

The success of a deception also demanded the most meticulous obedience to the LCS's directives by all the personalities and agencies involved; and this, the LCS would find, was not so easily achieved, particularly with the Americans. On several important occasions, Americans, who could sometimes be told nothing of the reasons for their orders, questioned and even ignored them. It was a problem that would most often occur with American field operatives on the lower rungs. Although at the top the executives of the Allied secret agencies were united in the single objective of defeating the German secret agencies, at the lower levels they were sometimes at dangerous odds. There were, in some cases, intense rivalries between the secret agents of different governments, and even between operatives of the secret agencies of the same government.

Agents were sent into the field to serve not only the general interests of the Allies, but also the special interests of their governments. More often than not—particularly where British and Russian agents were embroiled— these interests did not coincide. Nowhere was this conflict more pronounced than in the Balkans and the Middle East, particularly in Turkey, where the British and Russian governments had been at odds for centuries. It was in this area that the main stratagems of Zeppelin would be played out—at the very moment when British agents were struggling to preserve British hegemony in the area, and Russian agents were intriguing to destroy that influence and supplant it. At the same time, British agents of left-wing convictions worked with the Russians against the Americans while American agents worked with the Russians against the British. And in one singular instance a British agent was discovered to be working with the Germans against the Russians *and* the Americans—a lonely man fighting the lost cause of old Europe. In all, the LCS acknowledged that it was dealing with a snakes'-nest world where the safest policy was secrecy and silence.

Thus, the LCS began the extraordinarily dangerous and intricate game called Plan Jael. Essentially, it was a very British game—seeking great victories with small means and good brains. The object of the game for the LCS, and particularly for men like Bevan and Wingate, was not only the defeat of Hitler; it was also the preservation of the Empire and of Britain as a world leader. Who could foresee that in winning a great victory over the most proficient military machine in the world, the LCS and the secret bureaus of England would be unable to preserve the very entity they were sworn to maintain—the power of London? That was the vast irony of the secret war.

Mincemeat

ON MAY 23, 1943, Hitler directed that a map of the Balkans be laid out on the map table at Führerhauptquartier at Rastenburg and, putting on his presbyopic spectacles, declared: "One has to be on the watch like a spider in its web. Thank God I've always had a pretty good nose for everything so that I can generally smell things out before they happen." Then he added: "It is really of decisive importance that we hold the Balkans: copper, bauxite, chrome and most important of all to ensure that . . . we don't have what I would call a complete crash there." Pointing to the Golden Horn, the narrow Turkish waterway linking the Black Sea to the Mediterranean and dividing Europe from Asia, Hitler declared: "Here is where the decisive events will take place." And, he said, "If the worst comes to the worst," OKW "must milk" the Russian front of "even more" divisions to prevent a successful Allied invasion in the area.

What was there about the Balkans—a name derived from the Turkish words for "the mountains"—that transfixed Hitler? There was, of course, the ancient and recurrent German dream of *Drang nach Osten*—an empire in Arabia and beyond into Africa and India. Of more immediate importance were the raw materials of the area, Rumania's oil in particular. And there was the historical pattern of British strategy. As Major F. W. Deakin, a British agent in the Balkans during the Second World War and later the Warden of St. Antony's College, Oxford, would observe:

> . . . the shadow of the Dardanelles and the Macedonian campaign lay heavily across (Hitler's) thinking. It was inconceivable to him that Churchill could not be obsessed by the desire to prove in 1943 the validity of his grand strategy of 1915, of a decisive assault against enemy occupied Europe from the South-East. This was the central fear of the Fuehrer, which now coloured his planning against the Western Allies, often in defiance of the appreciations of his military experts.

Allied strategists were aware of Hitler's fears for the Balkans. But, by the time the Axis armies in Tunisia surrendered to the Anglo-American armies in May of 1943, it had already been decided at Casablanca that the next step toward Europe would be Sicily. And when, on June 11, 1943, the Allies captured the small island of Pantelleria, it might have seemed at OKW that the Allies' intentions were crystal clear. As Churchill said: "Anybody but a damned fool would *know* that it was Sicily." What could be done to mislead Hitler? There was, it was decided, only one thing to do: play upon his probable conviction that Sicily was *too* obvious a target and that the Allies were planning extensive landings on other parts of the southern littoral of Europe. To cloak "Husky," as the invasion of Sicily was cryptogrammed, Hitler must be led to believe that the Allies intended to invade two places: Greece in preparation for a thrust through the Balkans, and Sardinia as a jumping-off point for an invasion of southern France. Thus the LCS began to plan a deception campaign to make it appear that Churchill's strategy in 1943 would be the same as it had been in 1915—the Allies were indeed raising a knife to slide through "the soft underbelly of Europe." When its plans matured, as they did in June 1943, the LCS had produced a ruse that was the equal of any of the great stratagems of history. It was codenamed "Trojan Horse," after the most famous of history's great deceptions, and its main component was called "Mincemeat."

When the war was over, Mincemeat would become celebrated as one of the most ingenious and original stratagems of the war. Ingenious it was, but, in essence, the idea behind Mincemeat was merely a variant of an old device: playing false papers into the enemy's hands in order to lead him to do something to his own disadvantage. The same game has been played in war and peace for centuries, but it achieved one of its greatest successes at the hands of Colonel Richard Meinertzhagen and Brigadier Archibald Wavell during the British campaign in Arabia against the Turks and the Germans in the First World War. And its success had consequences that would ultimately shape the course of the second great world conflict. Churchill's interest in the stratagem had led him to study deception as a practicable instrument of modern warfare. It had also inspired Wavell, who would rise to the highest ranks of the British military hierarchy, to write the memorandum to Churchill that resulted in the formation of the LCS. Moreover, its memory would lead Wingate, whose father had been one of the men behind Meinertzhagen, to recommend that a similar ruse be tried in the case of Husky, and Mincemeat would bear many striking similarities to the Meinertzhagen operation. But its influence did not end there, for it was the prototype for the deceptions used by Wavell against the Italians in North Africa, and for Plan Bertram, which gained surprise for Montgomery at El

Alamein. To a certain extent, it would also be the model for the cover operations for D-Day itself.

When General Sir Edmund Allenby became C-in-C of the Imperial army in the Sinai Desert in 1917, the front had been stalemated. Commander after commander had tried to break the Turco-German line on the stony and waterless desert at Gaza, but all attacks had failed. Allenby decided to attempt what he knew the German commander of the enemy forces thought to be impossible: envelop the enemy with a cavalry sweep launched through the Turco-Germans' lightly defended inland flank at Beersheba, where the going for cavalry was so daunting that neither friend nor foe had tried it. Meinertzhagen was an intelligence officer on Allenby's staff, Wavell was on the General Staff of a cavalry brigade, and it was their task to provide cover for this operation. Their first move was to liquidate the Germans' espionage system in the desert and prevent all Turco-German aerial reconnaissance of the front. This they did successfully. Then, to persuade the German commander, General Kress von Kressenstein, that Allenby would attack again at Gaza, and that all movement in the area of Beersheba was only a feint, Meinertzhagen planned his *ruse de guerre*. Here, the tasks were twofold: to play contrived documents into the enemy's hands to support this stratagem and then, in the second stage, to provide the enemy's cryptanalytical section with corroborative evidence.

Meinertzhagen decided to plant the documents himself, and he compiled a false staff officer's notebook to suggest that the Beersheba movements were only a feint, and that D-Day for the attack at Gaza would be some weeks later than the date actually set for the offensive. The notebook was placed in a haversack together with £ 20 in notes—a tidy sum in those days—to give the impression that its loss was not intentional. And to give additional credence to the "plant," Meinertzhagen had a letter written purporting to have come from the officer's wife announcing the birth of their son. A second letter suggested correspondence between two British staff officers complaining about Allenby's rudeness and ambition—and revealing that the original plan for an attack against Gaza at the end of October, the actual D-Day, had been replaced by a new plan for an offensive in mid-November. Meinertzhagen also falsified an agenda of a GHQ conference that tended to confirm this gossip, and finally he included a fairly valuable cipher in the haversack. In all, the documents were of a type that a staff officer on reconnaissance might easily carry.

On October 10, 1917, Meinertzhagen, carrying the haversack, rode out into no-man's-land between the British and German lines in search of a Turkish patrol. He soon found one, and when he came under fire, he dropped the haversack and made off back to his own lines. He also dropped his field glasses, water bottle and rifle to make it appear that his flight had been disorderly, and as an extra touch, to suggest that he had abandoned the haversack because he was too weak to carry it further, he had previously stained it with blood let from one of his horse's minor veins. The Turks retrieved the haversack and it quickly found its way to German headquarters. .

Then Meinertzhagen played his second card. He assumed that the enemy would use the cipher discovered in the haversack to decrypt traffic from the British wireless station, which was mounted at the top of the 450-foot-high Khufu Pyramid at Giza. This is exactly what happened and Meinertzhagen began systematically to feed the enemy false information. First he arranged for a signal to be sent from GHQ ordering a most urgent search for the lost haversack. He arranged for another signal complaining about his lack of care in losing the haversack and demanding his immediate court-martial. Then he sent a third signal in the planted cipher ordering "Colonel R. Meinertzhagen, Desert Mounted Corps, to report to GHQ for a court of inquiry. This officer will be returned to duty in time for the attack on *November 14, 1917*." Finally, other signals were exchanged in the cipher suggesting that no offensive could be undertaken before November 14—the false D-Day—because Allenby had gone on leave and would not return until the 7th. And again, as an extra touch, the C-in-C of the Desert Mounted Corps and his staff were invited to a race meeting in Cairo on the 14th. To give credence to this last signal, posters were put up all over Cairo announcing the race meeting, the *Egyptian Gazette* published the form, and marquees were erected on the course.

Meanwhile, British wireless intelligence showed that the enemy was accepting the *ruse de guerre* and was making new dispositions. It was time for Meinertzhagen's trump card. Aware that the Turks were extremely short of cigarettes, he had manufactured some 120,000 packets that contained opium. While Allenby secretly and silently transferred his cavalry from Gaza to Beersheba—leaving behind 15,000 "horses" of straw and canvas, and creating wireless traffic to make it appear that the cavalry was still at Gaza—the Royal Flying Corps dropped the cigarettes over the enemy lines. When the dawn bombardment opened up at Beersheba on October 30, 1917, and 15,000 cavalrymen rose out of the wadis and attacked the city, the Turks were sound asleep. They were too doped to destroy the Beersheba wells, and the Imperial cavalry turned their line and rolled it up into the sea toward Gaza. Then Allenby attacked at Gaza, the Turks collapsed, and by November 15, the Imperial army was in the Judean Hills marching upon Jerusalem. On December 9, 1917, as Meinertzhagen recorded, Allenby marched into Jerusalem, "once and for all to evict the Turk from the sacred places of Christianity."

Such was the ingenuity of Meinertzhagen's stratagem. But a generation later, for the purposes of Mincemeat, it had to be considerably refined. It was proposed, first of all, to conceal an "obvious" offensive, not an "impossible" one—a much more difficult task. And in the second place, in modern warfare the means that can be used to separate fact from fiction had become extremely sophisticated. Any false information planted on the enemy would have to be resistant to the most penetrating forensic inquiry. This time a bloodstained haversack would not suffice; the vehicle for the deception had to be authentic.

The solution to this last problem was originally suggested by Lieutenant Commander Ewen Montagu of Section 17F at the Admiralty—the department of naval intelligence responsible for maintaining liaison with the deception agencies. Montagu was the son of Lord Swaythling, one of the British Jewish banking barons. He had received an international education at Westminster, Harvard and Trinity, he was a King's Counsel, and would become one of England's great jurists: Recorder of Devizes, Judge Advocate of the Fleet, Bencher of the Middle Temple, Recorder of London, chairman of the Hampshire Quarter Sessions. And he was one of the best fly fishermen in the realm. It was through a discussion between Montagu and Squadron Leader Sir Archibald Cholmondley, an expert in antiques who was Montagu's counterpart at the Air Ministry, that a new element was added to an old stratagem, an element worthy of Meinertzhagen himself. As Montagu later proposed to the XX-Committee: "Why shouldn't we get a body, disguise it as a staff officer, and give him really high-level papers which will show clearly that we are going to attack somewhere (other than Sicily)."

Thus was born the idea of "The Man Who Never Was." And after many meetings the plan was finally approved by Churchill, Eisenhower, the Combined Chiefs at Washington, and the Chiefs of Staff at London. The object of the plan was to plant a briefcase containing documents on the Germans that would lead them to conclude the Allies intended to invade Sardinia and Greece, not Sicily. A corpse would be the vehicle for the deception; and it would be set adrift from a submarine near Huelva in Spain, where the Abwehr was known to have an agent with good connection with the Spaniards. There was much in favor of the plan. The German intelligence network in Spain was known to be hasty and superficial in its operations. The documents found on the body of the French officer Clamorgan had, for example, been rushed to Berlin with only a cursory investigation of their authenticity. But there were serious risks, too. The Germans had discounted the Clamorgan documents as fakes even though they, and the circumstances of Clamorgan's death, were real. Might they not do the same, no matter how cleverly the deception was fabricated? Or if they saw through the deception for some other reason, the Germans might establish the truth by reading the evidence in reverse. In that case, they might assemble all available strength to repulse the Sicilian attack, or cause the Anglo-American high command to abandon Husky altogether. Deception, while an intriguing weapon, was also a double-edged one.

The XX-Committee, however, decided to take the risk and began to look for the corpse of a man who had died from pneumonia and would have water in his lungs. Thus if a postmortem were performed on the body it would appear to be the victim of drowning at sea. Such a corpse was soon obtained from Mr. Bentley Purchase, the Pickwickian coroner for London, although with less ease than might be thought in wartime. It lay in the mortuary in Horseferry Road, around the corner from MI-6 headquarters, a chapel-like building designed in the "Victorian–Early-Christian–Byzantine" style, reeking of Lysol, embalming fluid, and death.

The parents of the dead man were then approached and, although they were not told why the corpse was wanted, their permission to use it for "special medical purposes" was obtained. The parents made only one condition: that the name of the corpse must never be revealed. This led to considerable speculation about the family's identity. While Wingate would later say that he believed the corpse to have been that of a derelict alcoholic who had been found beneath the arches of Charing Cross Bridge dying from pneumonia, Brooke said he believed the corpse was that of a professional gardener. Another story was that he was the wastrel brother of an MP. All Montagu, who had charge of the corpse, would say was that "the body was that of a young man in his early thirties. He had not been very physically fit for some time before his death, but we could accept that for, as I said to a senior officer who queried the point, 'He does not have to look like an officer—only like a staff officer.' "

The corpse was packed in dry ice, placed in a cylinder, and taken by van to the XX-Committee's offices over a music publisher's in Regent Street. The Committee gave it a name: "Captain (acting Major) William Martin, 09560, Royal Marines, a staff officer at Combined Operations Headquarters." But a name was not enough; Martin had to have an identity—and a personality. And so the XX-Committee fabricated both, using the same device Meinertzhagen had used, personal letters. Martin had an overdraft at his bank, and a politely dunning letter from Lloyds Bank was obtained and included with his other papers. He had just become engaged and carried a bill for the ring, purchased on credit from S. J. Phillips, the international jewelers of Bond Street. And to prove that a fiancée really existed, a woman secretary on Montagu's staff provided the corpse with two "love letters."

Additional letters were fabricated from Martin's father and from the family's solicitors, all carefully dated and each confirming details mentioned in the others. Equal care was taken with the items that would be found on Martin's person, with special attention paid to the dates on receipted bills and ticket stubs. The corpse was to sail on April 19, 1943, and was due to be launched into the sea off Huelva on April 29–30. But since Martin was supposed to have gone down in an airplane, and because the XX-Committee wanted the Germans to think the body had been floating at sea for four or five days—to cover the degree of decomposition by this time—bills and ticket stubs indicated that he had not left London until April 24.

These small deceptions, however, were only to give credence to the major deception: the documents that Martin would carry which revealed that the Allies were indeed preparing for an invasion of Sicily—but *only* as a cover for invasions of Sardinia and Greece. The most important of these was a falsified personal letter from General Archibald Nye, the Vice Chief of the Imperial General Staff, to General Sir Harold Alexander, the commander under Eisenhower who would execute Husky. This and other letters and documents that tended to support the fiction were put in Martin's briefcase.

As a final consideration, it was certainly possible that the Germans would wonder why a man who was only an acting major would be entrusted with such important papers. Martin had to be given a credible status, and here Lord Louis Mountbatten made the subscription. In a personal letter to the C-in-C Mediterranean, Admiral of the Fleet Sir Andrew Cunningham, which was also put in the briefcase, Lord Louis declared that Martin was an expert in the employment of landing craft, and: "He is quiet and shy at first, but he really knows his stuff. He was more accurate than some of us about the probable run of events at Dieppe and he has been well in on the experiments with the latest barges and equipment which took place up in Scotland. Let me have him back, please, as soon as the assault is over." Then, with a little hint of the bogus target, Sardinia, Mountbatten concluded: "He might bring some sardines with him. . . ." They were, said Mountbatten, rationed in Britain. Altogether, it was a pretty trick; every clue was neatly in place. But would the Germans fall for it?

At six o'clock in the evening of April 19, 1943, operation Mincemeat got under way. Major Martin left his homeland aboard the submarine HMS *Seraph,* and just before dawn on April 30, off the Spanish coast at Huelva, an old Moorish fishing town in the Gulf of Cadiz, *Seraph* surfaced. Major Martin, still in his container, was brought up on deck as the submarine heaved in the gentle swell. The container was opened and the corpse was removed; the briefcase containing the falsified documents had been securely attached to the body by a chain. A crewman blew up Martin's lifejacket and the corpse was put gently into the water. The wash of the screws drove the body toward the shore as *Seraph* made out to sea. The container was sunk with a burst of machine-gun fire at close range, and then the submarine submerged.

Major Martin was found floating just after dawn that same day. A fisherman saw the corpse, hauled it aboard his little craft, and took it into the port. The briefcase was still attached to the body by its chain, and the corpse was placed in the care of the Armada. A little later, the British vice-consul at Huelva, who knew nothing of the plot, was informed by the Spanish naval office in the town. In turn, the consul telephoned the news to Captain J. H. Hillgarth, the British naval attaché at Madrid, requesting instructions. Hillgarth, who had been informed of the stratagem, asked the vice-consul to be sure that the briefcase was retrieved unopened and intact. When the vice-consul asked the Spaniards for the briefcase, he was told that it had been retained for judicial purposes. But the leak had already begun, for at the same time the Spanish informed the British, the local Abwehr official was also informed. While a Spanish doctor examined the corpse and certified that it was that of a British officer who had died by drowning after an air crash, the Abwehr official busied himself photocopying the documents.

From Madrid, with carefully calculated insistence, Hillgarth increased his pressure for the return of the briefcase—a fact that was reported to the Abwehr. And in London, the Casualty Section of the Commissions and Warrants Branch of the Admiralty posted among others killed in the period April 29–30, 1943, the name of "Temporary Captain (acting Major) William Martin, Royal Marines." Major Martin's death was also included in the casualty list published in *The Times* on June 4—a list that, by chance, contained the names of two officers who had actually lost their lives in an air crash at sea in the same area.

Meanwhile at Huelva, Major Martin was buried with full military honors. His "fiancée" sent a wreath to the funeral, with a heartbroken card of remembrance, and the British vice-consul sent Major Martin's family some photographs of the Spanish naval party firing a salute at the graveside. Eventually, a tombstone, of plain white marble, was put up by the vice-consul. Its inscription read:

> WILLIAM MARTIN
> Born 29th March, 1907
> Beloved son of John Glyndwyr Martin and
> the late Antonia Martin of Cardiff, Wales
> *Dulce et decorum est pro patria mori*
> R.I.P.

The Abwehr representative in Huelva lost no time in notifying Berlin of his lucky find; and in cooperation with the Armada, he practiced a small deception of his own. The letters and documents were carefully returned to the briefcase in their original condition, for if the British suspected that they had fallen into enemy hands, they would surely alter or postpone the operations that had been revealed. The briefcase was eventually returned to the British through the Spanish Foreign Office. But photocopies of the documents were sent to Berlin for evaluation and the Abwehr representative was queried for further details. Since the Turing engine could decrypt at least part of the Abwehr's traffic, much of the signals flow was read by the Chiefs of Staff and the LCS. It must have been read with gratification, for the Abwehr representative reported in detail on the contents of the briefcase and their condition, but did not question their authenticity. He read the clues of the receipted bills and the dated letters exactly as the Mincemeat planners hoped he would, and as far as he was concerned, all the pieces fitted together perfectly. He added, however, that the Armada was making further inquiries about the pilot of the downed aircraft and the fate of any other passengers.

Mincemeat was off to a good start. But further evaluation was in the hands of Colonel Baron von Roenne, chief of Fremde Heere West. Roenne, too, was convinced of the authenticity of the documents, and his appreciation of their contents followed the false information contained in Nye's letter to Alexander almost to the word. The Allies were preparing major operations against Sardinia and the Peloponnesus, combined with a feint against Sicily. There followed a series of further reports and evaluations, and while some concern was expressed that the loss of the documents would cause the Allies to change their plans, all agreed that it seemed quite certain that they intended to move in force against targets in the eastern and western Mediterranean—not against Sicily. Major Martin had done his work well. Mincemeat was a success.

Just how successful the deception was would be revealed by later events. The false documents began to infect Hitler's strategical thinking—for he had not the slightest doubt that they were genuine—at a time of great crisis in the affairs of the Pact of Steel. The Anglo-American armies had begun their final offensive to destroy Heeregruppe Afrika in Tunisia and would soon be ready for their next offensive. But where? And as the corpse of Major Martin floated ashore, Hitler was preparing for what would be the greatest tank battle in history—the Battle of Kursk. After the holocaust of the winter of 1942–43, he had only just enough panzer power left for the Kursk offensive, without having to face a new threat along the southern walls of Fortress Europe. He could not spare a single man or a single tank from the Russian front, yet he was convinced by the Mincemeat documents that he was confronted with a perilous situation in the Mediterranean—and particularly the Balkans. He had voiced his concern in a letter to Mussolini in which he said he was not worried about a Second

Front in the West in 1943. He was troubled about the Balkans. There, he said:

> 'I regard the situation . . . with the gravest concern.' This was the historic invasion route into the heart of Europe. . . . An enemy landing in the area, backed by local nationalist and Communist uprisings, might lead to . . . the worst nightmare of all, to the exposing of the German southern flank in the East and an eventual gigantic turning movement—a joint Anglo-American-Russian enterprise—into Germany itself.

Until now, the Balkans had been mainly garrisoned by Italians. The Italian high command maintained thirty-three divisions to keep Greece, the islands, Yugoslavia, and Albania secure; while German forces in Greece and Yugoslavia, as of December 1, 1942, consisted only of one corps of six divisions, including the élite 7th SS Prinz Eugen Mountain Division, and a paratroop division in "Fortress Crete"—the island dominating the Aegean. But how dependable was Italy as an ally? The SD had just uncovered evidence of a royalist plot in Rome to overthrow Mussolini and surrender to America and Britain. The discovery caused a major crisis in Hitler's strategical thinking at the very moment he was balancing the needs of the Kursk offensive against those implied by the threats in the Mincemeat papers. If Italy did surrender, Hitler would have to find fresh forces to replace the thirty-three Italian divisions in the Balkans theater—to say nothing of the ten Italian divisions in Russia.

As Hitler and OKW debated the problem, the LCS added to their apprehensions with other deceptions. A second corpse was washed up on the seashore near Cagliari, the main town on Sardinia, and was found to carry documents indicating that the man, who was in British Commando uniform, had been part of a small unit reconnoitering the Sardinian coast. The corpse was another "plant," carried out by submarine to reinforce the Sardinian threat contained in Major Martin's letters.

The LCS did not, however, rely solely on corpses to spread misinformation. For some time, LCS agents had been planting false intelligence about Allied plans and military movements on the Spanish ambassador at London, Jacobo María del Pilar Carlos Manuel Fitz-James Stuart, 10th Duke of Alba. The sixty-five-year-old Spanish grandee was an anglophile and a member of the London Establishment who was very closely connected with the Prime Minister and his entourage. The same claim could not be made for the Spanish Foreign Minister, Count Francisco Gómez Jordaña, who regularly submitted the ambassador's reports on the British scene to the German ambassador at Madrid. This fact was known to MI-5 and to the LCS, and they did not hesitate to use this conduit into the heart of the German Foreign Ministry for deceptive purposes. So it was that the German ambassador at Madrid, Hans Heinrich Dieckhoff, warned Berlin that the Allies were preparing to attack Greece, not Italy. His information came from "a wholly reliable source"—Jordaña.

Hitler was at last compelled to act. In a directive dated May 12, 1943, he ordered measures that were virtually a summary of the Mincemeat documents:

> Following the impending end of fighting in Tunisia, it is to be expected that the Anglo-Americans will try to continue the operations in the Mediterranean in quick succession. Preparations for this purpose must in general be considered concluded. The following are most endangered: in the Western Mediterranean, Sardinia, Corsica, and Sicily: in the Eastern Mediterranean, the Peloponnese and the Dodecanese islands.
>
> I expect that all German commands and offices which are concerned with the defences in the Mediterranean will co-operate very closely and quickly to utilize all forces and equipment to strengthen as much as possible the defences in these particularly endangered areas during the short time which is probably left to us. *Measures regarding Sardinia and the Peloponnese take precedence over everything else.*

OKW quickly attended to the despatch of commanders and units to the threatened areas. Field Marshal Rommel was sent to Athens to form an army group there. The Reichsführer SS Brigade was sent to Sardinia, and one panzer division was detached from the German army in France and sent in 160 trains on the 7-day journey to Greece. Hitler also sanctioned the withdrawal of two panzer divisions from the Russian front and their preparation for the 320-train, 9½-day journey to Greece. Again the Fuehrer had been let down by his intelligence services at a decisive time in the history of the Third Reich. The rivalry between the Abwehr and the SD made the cool, logical appreciations which help win battles and wars quite impossible. Moreover, to add to the confusion generated by the Mincemeat papers, there occurred, at precisely the moment when they were found, a catastrophe at Abwehr headquarters. The Abwehr's treachery, so long suspected by the SD, was suddenly proven. Part of the Abwehr executive was swept away into jail, leaving that vast organization in confusion at a time when Hitler needed every ounce of good intelligence he could get. With the Abwehr floundering, the SD was not, as yet, geared properly for large-scale foreign intelligence activities, and its appreciation of Allied intentions in the Mediterranean served to aggravate Hitler's fears for the Balkans. Had the Abwehr been fully operational, and not watching over its shoulder for signs of the Gestapo, Mincemeat and the other deceptions surrounding Husky might have been detected or, at the least, suspected. But they were not.

As Field Marshal Rommel established his headquarters in Greece, so the Allies, on the night of July 9/10, 1943, landed in Sicily. Again surprise was complete at Hitler's headquarters. Sicily was quickly conquered by the armies of Montgomery and General George C. Patton, and the traditional nightmare of the German General Staff—the encirclement of the Reich so that no one could be sure from which point the Fatherland's enemies would strike next—was at hand. The Allies had not invaded the Balkans . . . this time. Might they not do so in the future? The lesson of Hitler's compulsive response to Mincemeat was not lost on the Allied planners, and maintaining realistic threats against "the soft underbelly of Europe" would become a cornerstone of the cover and deception plans surrounding D-Day. Mincemeat was only one of those threats, and its ingenuity and later fame would tend to obscure other no less ingenious stratagems that were devised to lure German forces into the Balkans—stratagems that would deceive not only Hitler but history itself.

5

Quebec

As the Allied armies moved to complete the conquest of Sicily in August of 1943, General Brooke and General Marshall met in the Château Frontenac at Quebec for another serious confrontation. It was the third such conference in 1943—the first at Casablanca in January, the second at Washington in May—and still the Allies had not agreed upon a strategy for the invasion and liberation of Europe.

The war in the West was going well for the Grand Alliance. The Germans had been badly tricked by Mincemeat over Sicily; Mussolini had been arrested and Italy seemed about to ask for terms; the Germans were on the retreat in Russia; the Combined Bomber Offensive mounted in power and violence each day; the U-boat had been defeated in the North Atlantic. But for all the satisfaction at these victories, the Americans and Britons who gathered at the conference table in the great Gothic-style hotel overlooking the St. Lawrence had yet to resolve a basic difference in their concepts of waging war.

Brooke continued to insist that an invasion across the Channel was not an intelligent act of war until Germany's strength was dissipated by indirect strategy and tactics—peripheral warfare, bombing, economic and political warfare, subversion, sabotage, deception, and the generation of revolution within the Nazi empire. Marshall, on the other hand, still believed as he had done before Dieppe that the only way Germany could be defeated was by a power punch across the Channel, the direct engagement by the Allied armies of the German army in a massive battle, and the destruction of that army in detail. But behind the strategical disagreements a fundamental political controversy had emerged; it was the question not only of *how* the war should be fought and won, but also *why*.

Ever since the earliest days of the war, Marshall and his advisers had tried to establish why Churchill and the British Chiefs of Staff appeared to accept their demands for a cross-Channel attack, and then, through clever diplomacy, talked them into operations in the Mediterranean that could only delay that attack, while the burden of the land battle in Europe was left to the Russians. Among Marshall's most influential advisers was General Stanley D. Embick, the former Chief of the War Plans Division and former Deputy Chief of Staff of the United States Army. An elder statesman and kingmaker in the American military hierarchy, Embick, both in person and through his son-in-law, General Albert C. Wedemeyer, the Chief of the U.S. Strategy and Policy Group, was a powerful voice in shaping American military plans; and in November 1942, he undertook the task, with Wedemeyer, of assessing the truth behind the rococo personality and oratory of Churchill. In a paper that was at once ugly and cynical, Embick wrote that the British had not deviated in more than a century from their efforts to maintain the balance of power in Europe; and he contended that it was Britain's intention "to delay Germany's defeat until military attrition and civilian famine had materially reduced Russia's potential toward Europe." Extended operations in the Mediterranean served the treble purpose of marking time with a minimum expenditure of British resources, of dispersing and diverting German forces, and of ensuring British presence in the area in the postwar world. In short, Embick, Wedemeyer and many other Americans believed as Stalin did: that Britain, whatever the cost to the Grand Alliance, was fighting primarily for the preservation of the Empire.

It was an assessment that may have been close to the truth. But, in fact, the American policy makers were far from unanimous in their commitment to the rapid defeat of Germany. American troops and shipping scheduled to arrive in Britain for the pre-invasion build-up were being diverted to the Pacific. A plan was afoot to present MacArthur to the American electorate as a presidential candidate in 1944, and victories in the Pacific were required to increase his stature to the point where he would be uncontestable. There was the ever-present danger that America might decide to abandon the "Europe first" policy of the Grand Alliance and seek the defeat of Japan, while in Europe, Britain, Germany and Russia were left to slug it out alone.

At the Trident Conference at Washington in May, Brooke and Marshall, as the spokesmen for conflicting strategies that could be traced beyond their own personal views to a divergence in the political aims of their separate nations, had once again tried to iron out their differences. They had achieved a compromise. America had renewed its commitment to the early defeat of Germany, Britain its commitment to a cross-Channel attack in the spring of 1944. But the question of further operations in the Mediterranean, after the invasion and conquest of Sicily, was left in doubt. Also unanswered was the question of which of the two military leaders—Brooke or Marshall—would be chosen as the Supreme Commander for the great expedition—and which of their governments would thereby lead the postwar world. Brooke, testy, birdlike, quick, the staff college professional, was probably the more clever; and it was this very cleverness that rankled Marshall. He was aware that Brooke was usually able to outwit him, and he had recently heard Senator Arthur Vandenberg state before a Senate subcommittee that he and some of his fellow senators were "disturbed" because the Americans were "not as united" as the British, and because the British "usually ended up on top"; Vandenberg was uneasy "about *who* makes our decisions and *how,* and about the British dominion." Although at this stage of the war the armed forces of Great Britain in the European and Mediterranean theaters were stronger and larger than those of the United States, it could not be long before American strength became preponderant. Since it was a general rule that the nation which supplied the most troops also supplied the command and the policy, Marshall was resolved to make an end to British domination of the conference table—and of the war.

When Churchill and Brooke arrived at Halifax, Nova Scotia, aboard the *Queen Mary,* they brought with them 250 delegates, advisers, typists, clerks, a portable map room, and the Special Information Centre in which there were, as at Casablanca, British position papers for every contingency and intelligence, including Ultra, to back those papers. The British, as usual, had come well prepared, but to their surprise, upon reaching the Château Frontenac, they found an almost identical number of Americans similarly well equipped with position papers and intelligence. Had the Americans mastered the tactics of strategic planning and salesmanship? That remained to be seen. Certainly the mood of the American delegation was less amiable and more businesslike and determined than it had been at Casablanca. As the American official historian, Maurice Matloff, would state: "In preparing for the meetings with the British, American military planners as well as their chiefs had carefully studied British preparations, representation, and techniques in negotiations at past conferences and had taken steps to match them."

The Americans were committed to Overlord and wanted no more adventures in the Mediterranean (and especially not in Italy), adventures which would surely be the outcome of defeat at this conference table. Roosevelt's position on Overlord was somewhat vague, save for his wish for a preponderance of American force to be "able to justify the choice of an American commander for the operation." He was strongly supported in this wish by a memorandum from Henry L. Stimson, the Secretary of War, presented on the eve of the conference. Stimson wrote:

> We cannot now rationally hope to be able to cross the Channel and come to grips with our German enemy under a British commander. His

Prime Minister and his Chief of the Imperial Staff [sic] are frankly at variance with such a proposal. The shadows of Passchendaele and Dunkerque still hang too heavily over the imagination of these leaders of his government.

The British, said Stimson, rendered "lip service" to Overlord, but, he declared: ". . . their hearts are not in it and it will require more independence, more faith, and more vigor than it is reasonable to expect we can find in any British commander to overcome the natural difficulties of such an operation carried on in such an atmosphere of his government."

Stimson declared devastatingly—for the British—that the difference between the two powers was a "vital difference of faith," and that only by massing the entire youth and industry of the two nations could Germany be defeated. The Germans would never be defeated by "pinprick warfare." His letter—one of the most dramatic of the war—went on to say:

I believe therefore that the time has come for you to decide that your government must assume the responsibility of leadership in this great final movement of the European war which is now confronting us. . . . Nearly two years ago the British offered us (the post of Supreme Allied Commander). I think that now it should be accepted—if necessary, insisted upon.

And who should this Supreme Commander be? Stimson concluded that the time had come to put "our most commanding soldier in charge of this critical operation at this critical time." That man, he said, was Marshall.

The President read and approved each of Stimson's advocacies, and when Churchill arrived at Hyde Park for a private meeting before joining the conference at Quebec, his mind was made up. His resolve, he said to Churchill, was to concentrate every available soldier in England for a cross-Channel attack in 1944. He wanted to abandon all further Mediterranean operations, and he announced that he wished that Marshall would command Overlord. It was the second of the major decisions that wrested strategic command of the war from Britain; the first had been Eisenhower's appointment as C-in-C of Torch. With those two strokes the President effectively destroyed Britain's position as the principal Anglo-Saxon power in the world.

Churchill was put in an awkward position; he had already promised the post of Supreme Commander to Brooke. But wily as ever, he heartily agreed with Roosevelt's proposal. The Americans would furnish most of the troops after the assault; why, therefore, should the command not go to an American? On the other hand, since the Mediterranean was now relegated to the position of a secondary theater, should not the supreme command there go to a Briton? Roosevelt saw no reason why not—provided Britain stuck unequivocally to Overlord as *the* maximum effort. Of course, of course, purred Churchill.

While the President and the Prime Minister talked at Roosevelt's estate beside the Hudson River, the military delegates had begun their talks beside the St. Lawrence; Roosevelt and Churchill planned to join them when the donkeywork was done. The delegates settled down at the conference table in fresh uniforms and sparkling insignia. But all knew that there must be a serious collision over Overlord; and it was not long in coming. While the secretaries would carefully filter out all the fumes and anger of debate, referring only occasionally to a point being "forcefully made," the meeting of the two staffs on August 15, 1943, was stormy. Admiral Ernest J. King, the Chief of Naval Operations, was said to have employed "very undiplomatic language, to use a mild term," in responding to Brooke's points. It was as cold and bleak inside the conference room as was the weather outside.

Marshall "took the offensive" immediately by opening with the proposition "forcefully" that the British must now give the cross-Channel strategy overriding priority over all other operations in Europe in 1944. Brooke replied equally forcefully; he declared that the British Chiefs of Staff agreed with Marshall. Overlord should be the major Allied operation in 1944, *but* . . . It was this "but" that angered the Americans; it was always there. Brooke then stressed the "necessity of achieving the three main conditions on which the success of the *Overlord* plan was based": (1) the reduction of the strength of the Luftwaffe; (2) the restriction of German strength in France and the Low Countries and of German ability to bring in reinforcements during the first two months after the invasion; (3) a solution to the problems of supplying the invasion armies across the beaches. And how might a situation favorable to Overlord be obtained? By invading Italy to contain the maximum German forces and by air action from Italian bases to reduce the German air forces.

There it was again, the apparition of Marshall's that the British were seeking to drag America into extended operations "in that dark hole"—the Mediterranean. Marshall was quite convinced that this constant British pressure for a Mediterranean strategy had to do with Churchill's desire for postwar control of Arabia—the region he had once called the "belt buckle of the Empire." He may not have been wrong; but self-sufficient in oil and only indirectly dependent upon the Suez Canal, America considered the Middle East of little strategic importance at that time, and Marshall was well prepared for Brooke's stand. Unless Overlord was given absolute priority, and unless the British honored the agreements made at Casablanca and Washington, he said, the "entire US–UK strategic concept would have to be revised." It was a veiled threat, for he implied a "reorientation of American offensive efforts towards the Pacific." In that event, the British army would, more or less, have to fight Germany without the American army. America and Britain, said Marshall, would have to rely upon airpower to destroy the Reich, for the United States army would leave behind only a reinforced corps for an "opportunistic" cross-Channel operation.

By now the sun was going down over the St. Lawrence, and the two sides adjourned. It had been, wrote Brooke in his diary, a "gloomy and unpleasant day." It was "quite impossible to argue with (Marshall) as he does not begin to understand a strategic problem. . . . The only real argument he produced was a threat. . . . We parted at 5:30 p.m., having sat for three very unpleasant hours." Later that evening, Field Marshal Sir John Dill, whom Marshall admired greatly, went to see him in the hope that he might be able to reconcile the two. But he could not. According to Brooke, Dill found Marshall to be "most unmanageable and irreconcilable. Even threatening to resign if we pressed our point." "This had indeed been a black day." There was worse to come for Brooke.

Churchill and Roosevelt arrived at Quebec; and there, on the Plains of Abraham where Wolfe, in 1759, had destroyed Montcalm's army and added a territory to the British Crown that was larger than Europe, the politicians joined the generals. Churchill took Brooke for a walk on the terrace of the château and informed him of the decision that had been made concerning the post of Supreme Commander. Brooke was stunned. He would write:

> I remember it as if it was yesterday as we walked up and down on the terrace . . . looking down on to that wonderful view of the St. Lawrence River and the fateful scene of Wolfe's battle for the Heights of Quebec. As Winston spoke all that scenery was swamped by a dark cloud of despair. . . . Not for one moment did he realise what this meant to me. He offered no sympathy, no regrets at having had to change his mind, and dealt with the matter as if it were one of minor importance.

It was a bitter pill, and the morrow would make it even more bitter. For it had been learned that an Italian general had contacted Eisenhower's headquarters to discuss the surrender of the Italian empire and the proposal that, immediately thereafter, the Italians join the Grand Alliance against Hitler. This was splendid news; but there was better yet. Ultra revealed that very large German army and air forces were gathering in the Alps, presumably to begin the occupation of northern Italy and Italian positions in the Balkans. Thirteen divisions of Germans were now in Italy, when they might have gone either to France or Russia. Brooke's pre-invasion strategy—to disperse the enemy—was becoming a reality.

This was no time for niceties; the Axis was crumbling fast. Brooke hastened to the conference table and told Marshall that America and

Britain must take advantage of the Italian collapse and begin preparations for an invasion of Italy immediately. "Our talk was pretty frank," Brooke wrote. "I opened by telling them that the root of the matter was that we were not trusting each other." Then Brooke again went into the whole question of his Mediterranean strategy, particularly in the light of the Italian proposals. It was now possible, he said, to suck not only divisions but whole German armies into the areas which had previously been garrisoned by Italians—armies that would not therefore be available to Hitler for deployment to either France or Russia. After three hours of brutal conference, wrote Brooke, "To my great relief they accepted our proposals . . . so that all our arguing has borne fruit. . . ." Marshall agreed to the immediate invasion of Italy. Montgomery's 8th Army was to cross the Straits of Messina within fourteen days, and the embryo of a new American army, the 5th, under General Mark Clark, was to land at Salerno a week later to begin the march upon Naples. The possibility of dropping an American airborne division on Rome was also discussed. In the moment of his greatest despair, Brooke's policies had triumphed.

That evening, news arrived that Sicily had been conquered with a loss to the enemy of 250,000 men, 65,000 of them Germans, against a loss of 31,000 Allied troops. It was a stunning victory. But what had become of Overlord? A compromise was reached in which the British agreed to Marshall's demands that Overlord be the main operation of 1944, and a target date was fixed—May 1, 1944. General Frederick Morgan's overall conception for Overlord was approved and orders were sent out to London to begin the detailed planning for the mighty endeavor. The invasion would take place upon the beaches of Normandy, the same beaches from which Duke William had sailed in 1066 to conquer England. Deception and massive air attacks would be used to deflect and delay the arrival of Hitler's panzers, the greatest threat to the success of the invasion. As part of that deflection, Marshall agreed that Naples, Rome, Sardinia, Corsica and, if possible, the Dodecanese Islands should be occupied. Heavy bomber bases should be established at Foggia and in Campagna to bombard central Germany from the south. The Balkans guerrillas were to be nourished by the Allies wherever they were to be found. And to settle Brooke's worries about supplying the armies across the invasion beaches, two artificial ports called "Mulberries," each with the capacity of Dover, were to be built, towed across the Channel, and anchored off the Norman shore.

The greatest military undertaking in history had been agreed upon, and Marshall returned to Washington to speed up the industrial effort that would establish America as the world's supreme power. For Brooke, it was a personal triumph. But he was left dispirited, disappointed and, in his own words, "feeling the inevitable flatness and depression which swamps me after a spell of continuous work and of battling against difficulties, differences of opinion, stubbornness, stupidity, pettiness and pig-headedness." But what of Churchill? Had he really been converted to Overlord? Or had he agreed to the invasion only to obtain time to exploit the situation caused by the Italian surrender? He would later write: "I knew that (an invasion of France) would be a very heavy and hazardous adventure. The fearful price we had had to pay in human life and blood for the great offensives of the First World War was graven in my mind. . . ." In short, his views had not changed. And as if to remind the Allies of the fearful price they might have to pay on D-Day, there occurred the near-disaster of the amphibious forces that landed at Salerno in Italy on September 9, 1943.

Just before dusk on September 8, 1943, as the great Salerno task force sailed across the Tyrrhenian Sea with all the stately majesty peculiar to massed fleets of warships and merchantmen, a signal broke out from the masthead of the flagship, the USS *Alcon:* "Italy has surrendered." As the word spread, wild bursts of cheering echoed from ship to ship. It put the men who would land at Salerno at dawn into great heart. The first Allied invasion of the European continent might, they thought, be unopposed. As one of the troops recalled: "I never again expect to witness such scenes of sheer joy. We would dock in Naples harbor unopposed, with an olive branch in one hand and an opera ticket in the other." The fleet steamed on as Ultra crews scanned the German wireless spectrums; there was nothing to indicate that the operation had been detected.

Aboard the *Alcon,* General Mark Clark, the commander of the U.S. 5th Army, waited expectantly in the operations room. The army—one American corps and one British—prepared to land on a 36-mile crescent of beaches extending from the Sorrento cliffs to Paestum. On the northern skyline the undersides of wadded clouds glinted with splinters of fire from a naval bombardment. Then the troops began to waddle down the nets into the assault boats. Guided by small inshore submarines flashing colored beacons, the assault boats formed up into great Vs and made for the silent shore. It was the same at all the beaches; the approach was unopposed. At Paestum, where the Doric columns of an ancient Greek temple formed the landmark, assault parties of the U.S. 36th Division were put ashore in waist-deep surf. But at that moment, as elsewhere, brilliant flares shot up and illuminated the assault boats. A few seconds later came a storm of machine-gun fire and the *whoomp* of 88-mm cannon. At Paestum, as everywhere, the beaches were turned into a bedlam of fire and confusion. Clark had not obtained the quality of surprise; the Germans, through wireless intelligence and aerial reconnaissance, knew he was coming.

By nightfall on the British beaches, the troops were at best only 2 miles inshore, none of the Anglo-American beachheads had joined up, and the

Allies were confronted by an entire German panzer division. Then the crisis worsened. The Luftwaffe began to make heavy airstrikes using a new weapon—wireless-controlled, rocket-propelled, armor-piercing bombs known as FX1400's. The British had learned of the FX1400 from the Oslo Report in November 1939, but this was the first time it had been used. The bombs ripped into the invasion fleet, and the first to suffer were the U.S. cruisers *Philadelphia* and *Savannah*. A shower of bombs hit the British cruiser *Uganda,* which was badly holed, and sank five transports, a hospital ship, and eight landing ships. The great British battleship *Warspite* was shaken from stem to stern by two near-misses, and then a third bomb hit her in the boiler room and almost sank her. At the same time, the German commander, Field Marshal Albert Kesselring, counterattacked with six divisions and almost drove the Americans into the sea. The Allied situation was now described as desperate, and Clark directed that arrangements be made for the evacuation of the American forces into the British beachheads, where the situation was somewhat easier. They held on until the arrival of massive reinforcements, supported by superb naval gunfire. Finally, on September 16, 1943, the German front crumbled and the invading forces began to move inland.

When Churchill heard the news of the near-disaster, he was particularly disturbed. He later wrote:

> Evidently a most critical and protracted struggle was in progress. My concern was all the greater because I had always strongly pressed for this seaborne landing, and felt a special responsibility for its success. Surprise, violence, and speed are the essence of all amphibious landings. After the first twenty-four hours the advantage of sea-power in striking where you will may well have vanished. Where there were ten men there are soon ten thousand. My mind travelled back over the years. I thought of General Stopford waiting nearly three days on the beach at Suvla Bay in 1915 while Mustafa Kemal marched two Turkish divisions from the lines at Bulair to the hitherto undefended battlefield.

What had gone wrong? The Germans had, like Mustafa Kemal, deployed an army to the beachhead with great speed—while the U.S. corps commander, General E. J. Dawley, hesitated. Clark removed Dawley from command—the second U.S. corps commander to be relieved in the face of the enemy in less than a year. The whole operation demonstrated, once again, the perils of amphibious warfare and the fact that, whatever the intelligence estimates said, the Wehrmacht was still the most efficient, mobile and battleworthy army in the world. Moreover, German "secret weapons" could no longer be regarded as mere propaganda.

The lessons for D-Day were obvious: the necessity of diffusing German forces at the point of attack and of slowing down the mobility of reinforcements; the importance of massive aerial and naval bombardment; a reduction in the strength of the Luftwaffe; and above all, the imperatives of secrecy and surprise. When the casualties at Salerno were counted, the Allies discovered that they had lost 15,000 of their best men—when it was thought they would lose only a small fraction of that number. The Germans lost fewer than 8000 men, and far from the swift occupation of Naples, that prize was not seized until October 2, 1943, twenty-three days after the landing. Churchill's apprehensions about the invasion of France were confirmed. If this was the price of a comparatively small operation, what would be the price of D-Day?

The Schwarze Kapelle, 1943

THE FORTUNES of the Schwarze Kapelle did not prosper with the collapse of Operation Flash in March 1943. The will to rid themselves of Hitler existed with the conspirators, as did the means and the men. Nor was it ineptitude that confounded their plans. They were hampered by sheer misfortune and the fact that they sought to remove a man who commanded perhaps the most expert and vigilant police state the world had known. There were, within the Reich, well over 100,000 agents of various internal security organizations at work to uncover precisely what it was the Schwarze Kapelle was doing—plotting against the régime. The axman's shadow was omnipresent as they worked in circumstances of hideous danger from a ruthless and clever security system; and, unlike every other resistance movement throughout the world, they received neither help nor encouragement from America or Britain. Indeed, every overture to the Allies was treated with silence and official indifference; no one came forward from the highest places to challenge the wisdom of that messianic proclamation of vengeance, Unconditional Surrender.

Yet, in the midsummer of 1943, many portents in London pointed to the possibility of the imminent collapse of the Third Reich, and accordingly the Allied high command—COSSAC—made a series of military plans known as "Rankin" to prepare for this contingency. The most important of these plans was "Rankin Case C," a large-scale Anglo-American–Canadian operation to land in and bring order and sustenance to all of Europe as far east as the Oder in the event of a Nazi collapse. The Allies were prepared, then, to take full and immediate advantage of an anti-Hitler revolution, although they were still unwilling to aid the men who might bring it about. But the plans did reflect a new British belief in the efficacy of the conspiracy, even without Allied help. This belief stemmed from intelligence reaching Menzies—who was now a general and a Knight of the Order of St. Michael and St. George—that seemed to indicate not only that the

Schwarze Kapelle had revived after the failure of Flash, but that a fresh, clever and determined leadership had sprung up out of the German General Staff around Colonel Klaus Philip Maria Count von Stauffenberg. Stauffenberg, it seemed in London, had taken the reins of conspiracy at the very moment when, through the series of Wehrmacht disasters, the Nazis were in eclipse. Would he succeed where his predecessors had failed?

Stauffenberg had not lessened in his detestation of the Fuehrer, nor in his resolve to remove him. But his plans had been dislocated when he was transferred from his post in Berlin to the 10th Panzer Division in Tunisia; and with his transfer he was, effectively, removed as a potential leader of the Schwarze Kapelle. But then, the misfortunes of war restored him to the conspiracy. While supervising the withdrawal of a battalion of the 10th Panzers in the Tunisian *jebel,* he had been caught in the open by a pair of American Thunderbolt fighters. Machine-gun fire took his right arm and the third and fourth fingers of his left hand; his left eye was destroyed, his right eye badly damaged, his trunk and one of his knees were riddled with flying metal fragments and stones, and the explosions impaired one middle ear.

Stauffenberg was taken to the German military hospital at Carthage, beside the site of the Temple of Aesculapius, where it seemed that he would die. His head and body were swaddled in bandages, he was deeply sedated and in traction, and temporarily blind. But he recovered sufficiently to be moved to Germany, and there he made two remarks through the bandages that covered his face. He said to his uncle, Count von Uxkull: "Since the generals have so far done nothing, the colonels must now go into action" against Hitler. And to the son of Professor Sauerbruch, the eminent German surgeon who was a member of the Schwarze Kapelle and was working on Stauffenberg, he said: "I could never look the wives and children of the fallen in the eye if I did not do something to stop this senseless slaughter."

As spring gave way to summer, Stauffenberg gradually regained his strength. He taught himself to do his own toilet and to dress himself, using his teeth, his toes, and the remnants of his left hand. When Professor Sauerbruch counseled leave and rest in the cool of the Bavarian woods, Stauffenberg replied that he had no time to rest; he had urgent work to do. He had learned, while on a visit to Berlin to have an artificial hand fitted, that Oster and Dohnanyi, hitherto the sword-arms of the conspiracy, had been accused of treason by the Gestapo; Oster was under house arrest and Dohnanyi was in prison. Moreover, Beck had been operated on for cancer and had not yet sufficiently recovered to resume his post as head of the conspiracy. Canaris had gone to ground for the moment, trying to rebuild the Abwehr executive after its decapitation.

What circumstances had led to this new disaster for the Schwarze

Kapelle and for "Belinda"—the code name for Abwehr headquarters? It was a convoluted story that began in April of 1942 when German guards at Cehba on the Czech frontier stopped and searched a Jewish family. Their baggage was found to contain a sum of dollars, and when the family was questioned about where they had obtained the money—for major foreign currencies were the subject of the most strict controls—they declared it had been provided by Dr. Wilhelm Schmidhuber, a Munich businessman who was also the honorary Portuguese consul in the Bavarian capital and confidant and agent of Canaris. In fact, Schmidhuber had been involved in "Operation 7"—a plan conceived by Canaris and executed by Dohnanyi to exfiltrate a group of Jews from Germany to Switzerland disguised as Abwehr agents. Canaris had told Heydrich of the employment of the Jews as "agents," and Heydrich had become suspicious; but he had not been able to prove conspiracy against the Abwehr by the time he was assassinated by British agents at Prague in May of 1942. The case had hung fire at Gestapo headquarters at Prinzalbrechtstrasse—until the arrest of the Jews at Cehba. Now the Gestapo had the substance of capital charges against the Abwehr executive.

Schmidhuber, a flabby, greedy man, was arrested and taken to Gestapo headquarters in Berlin. But he had managed to get a message to Canaris; if Canaris did not invoke the Abwehr's protection for him—the Gestapo had no jurisdiction over Abwehr personnel—and obtain his release, he threatened to tell the Gestapo all that he knew about the conspiracy against Hitler. He knew about a great deal, including Dr. Josef Mueller's activities at the Vatican. His threat was taken so seriously by Oster that he considered having Schmidhuber assassinated. But before anything could be done, the Gestapo, acting swiftly to protect its catch, had him beyond the reach of the Abwehr, at least for the time being, in one of the cells in the basement of Gestapo headquarters. There, in the belief that he had been betrayed by Canaris and Oster, Schmidhuber talked. He revealed enough about the Vatican negotiations to justify the Gestapo intruding into Abwehr headquarters and forcing an interview with Oster and Dohnanyi in Canaris's presence. A pebble had caused a landslide.

On April 5, 1943, Dr. Manfred Roeder, an army investigator, and Gestapo Commissioner Sonderegger appeared at Abwehr headquarters. It was the beginning of the end of the Abwehr. Canaris received the inquisitors in his office, alone. They made an astounding allegation; they stated that Dohnanyi, in league with his brother-in-law, Dietrich Bonhoeffer, the distinguished theologian, was a spy plotting with the British secret service to overthrow the régime. Their charges were, in part, true. Dohnanyi had long been active in the Schwarze Kapelle; and Bonhoeffer had made several journeys to neutral capitals on behalf of the conspiracy.

Producing a warrant, Roeder demanded of Canaris the right to search

Dohnanyi's safe and, with Oster and Canaris present, he and Sonderegger did so. The precise allegation against Dohnanyi was that he had been taking bribes for smuggling Jews from Germany into Switzerland—an echo of the Operation 7 investigation. When the contents of his safe were placed on the desks in the office, Roeder came across some slips of paper which were known within the Abwehr as "playing cards." These cards contained information and instructions for secret intelligence missions, and one of them suggested that Bonhoeffer was to go to Rome with Mueller to explain to the Vatican why Operation Flash had failed. Dohnanyi saw the playing card before Roeder did; and realizing that it might hang them all, he passed it to Canaris with the observation that it was a super-secret operation proceeding at that time and should not be seen by any unauthorized person. Canaris gave the card to Oster, who attempted to slip it into his coat pocket, but Sonderegger saw him and told Roeder. It was fatal. Roeder demanded that Oster hand over the card; Oster denied that he was concealing anything. The fate of the Schwarze Kapelle hung on a sleight-of-hand. Finally, Oster gave him the card and was ordered to go to his own office and remain there.

Roeder also found evidence linking Dohnanyi to Operation 7 and further documentation implicating both Bonhoeffer and Mueller in a possible conspiracy. Despite Canaris's protests, Roeder announced that he had the authority to arrest Dohnanyi. He was taken to the Wehrmacht prison at 64 Lehterstrasse in Berlin, where Mueller also found himself within a few hours. Oster was placed under house arrest in Dresden, but Bonhoeffer was accorded no such concession. Arrested and jailed at Tegel Prison, he was placed in the reception cell where he "could not bring himself to use the blankets of the plank-bed, as he could not stand the stench that rose from them." In the morning, dry bread was thrown to him through a crack in the door and the warder called him a *"Strolch"*—blackguard. When he had been processed, he was kept in solitary confinement until he emerged, hand-cuffed, to attend his first hearing before the Reichskriegsgericht—the Reich War Court.

Roeder conducted the hearing, and thus began an eighteen-month drama in which Bonhoeffer wove a complicated mesh of camouflage over his activities as an Abwehr agent. But the chief accused—for this was a contest between the Abwehr and the SD—was Dohnanyi. His prosecutors sought to strike through him at the whole of the Abwehr, while Canaris attempted to protect the Abwehr by explaining to Roeder that he was shocked by the possibility that Dohnanyi had been engaged in fraud, and anxious that the charges against his lieutenant be thoroughly and quickly examined.

Hitler himself was informed of the interrogations; but Roeder found no easy victim in Dohnanyi. Both were able lawyers; Dohnanyi proved the abler. Roeder insisted that Dohnanyi was guilty of high treason; Dohnanyi insisted that his activities at the Abwehr were ordinary operational matters. He managed to prove that Bonhoeffer's journeys were intelligence missions launched as a "counter-espionage" operation to establish the mood of the enemy. As for Operation 7, Roeder could present no evidence that Dohnanyi had lined his pockets—as, indeed, he had not.

Then Canaris made his move; he complained to Keitel that Roeder was activated by a desire to besmirch the good name of the army by proving treason against the Abwehr. Keitel responded appropriately; he dismissed Roeder from the case and appointed in his stead a less vindictive and ambitious official. Under this official—a certain Kutzner—the case against the accused gradually ran out of steam, and Roeder was finally ridiculed when he called the Brandenburg Division, Canaris's private army, a "Drones Club." The divisional commander heard of the allegation, called on Roeder, boxed his ears and then challenged him to a duel.

For the moment it appeared that Dohnanyi was safe, but the strain of jail and trial had a serious effect upon him. He developed an inflammation of the veins in both legs. The malady grew more serious; his speech and vision became disturbed and it was found that he was suffering from a brain embolism. Arrangements were made to transfer him to Professor Sauerbruch's clinic (where both Beck and Stauffenberg were undergoing treatment). He was admitted, but Roeder and the Gestapo had not given up yet. Roeder confronted the professor and demanded that Dohnanyi, who was now outside army jurisdiction, be handed over. Sauerbruch refused and declared that Dohnanyi was in peril of his life and could not be moved. Roeder ceased to be a threat when he vanished into the legal wilderness of the Balkans judge advocate's office, but the Gestapo persisted. A few weeks later, Gestapo officers arrived at the clinic with an ambulance, but Sauerbruch again refused to let the authorities see or obtain the person of his patient. This battle of wits continued for many months until, finally, the Gestapo won. On January 22, 1944, while Sauerbruch was absent, a Gestapo doctor appeared in Dohnanyi's sickroom and he was removed to an SS clinic at Buch. There he was examined by Professor Max de Crinis, Schellenberg's accomplice in the Venlo Incident, who pronounced that Dohnanyi would be fit to testify in eight to ten days. Once again Canaris and the Schwarze Kapelle were in dire danger.

The only way that Dohnanyi could prevent the Gestapo from interrogating him was to make his sickness a weapon. In a letter smuggled out of the prison clinic to his wife, he made a bizarre request:

> The only thing to do is gain time. I must make sure that I'm unfit to be tried. The best thing would be for me to get a solid attack of dysentery. A culture must be available for medical purposes in the Koch Institute. If you wrap up some food in a red cloth, and also put an ink-mark on the

glass, then I'll know that it contains a decent infection that'll get me to hospital. . . .

Frau von Dohnanyi managed to obtain the culture and smuggle it to her husband, but it did not work. Then Dohnanyi asked her to get him a diphtheria culture. In another letter he wrote:

> You can scarcely imagine the excitement when I saw a glass covered with red in the case . . . I'm not frightened of any infectious illness. I know very well that I would lie down with the feeling that it would not only save my life, but that of many others also, whose situation is bound up with mine. . . . Naturally I put the diphtheria culture in my mouth immediately and chewed thoroughly, but for practical reasons it wasn't possible to do it until half past seven at night. . . . And it seemed to me that the cotton wool had become quite dry. Now I'm eating the sweets as quickly as possible, I've heard that diphtheria bacilli are not very volatile, but can't stand dryness, needing moisture to keep alive. Incubation period is three to eight days. I'm afraid I may be immune and won't get anything.

It did not work the first time, but he ate a second culture and the infection took hold. He developed a grave case of diphtheria that not only kept him out of court but also, during the danger period, prevented the Gestapo from attempting further interrogations. Eventually, the Gestapo lost patience with him. He was taken from jail and on a nearby pile of bomb spoil was shot to death. With him was Dietrich Bonhoeffer.

As the Gestapo proceeded with its attack on the Abwehr, Schellenberg and the SD uncovered evidence of Canaris's direct involvement in treason. "During the years 1941–1942," Schellenberg would later write, "the greater part of the work of my organization was concerned with silencing treacherous informers in Italy." The SD evidently believed that it was Italian treachery, not British cryptanalysis, that had been responsible for the loss of so many of Rommel's supply ships, and Schellenberg formed the impression that the Abwehr—which was in charge of counterespionage activities within the Wehrmacht—was not prosecuting its mission with sufficient energy. In particular, he formed a deep suspicion of the relationship between Canaris and General Cesare Amé, the head of SIM, the Italian military intelligence and counterespionage service. To establish what Amé was up to, Schellenberg's agents in Rome succeeded in compromising his chauffeurs, both of whom were homosexuals. The two men eavesdropped on Amé's and his staff's discussions and reported what they heard to the SD in Rome; and their reports, in turn, implicated Canaris in what Schellenberg would call "a matter of serious sabotage in Italy."

It began in July 1943 when Marshal Pietro Badoglio, the former Chief of the Italian General Staff, arrested Mussolini and, assuming power in the

King's name, secretly opened a channel of communication with Eisen-hower's headquarters to obtain surrender terms. The possibility of an Italian defection was of fundamental concern to Hitler. He warned that he would occupy Italy if Badoglio contemplated surrender. But despite the fact that, as Schellenberg would write, "All the reports received by our Military and Political Intelligence Services pointed clearly to the imminence of such a change," Canaris's reports to Keitel "were reassuring." Keitel trusted Canaris, but Hitler was not satisfied with this opinion. It was decided to send Canaris to Italy. Schellenberg would continue: "At Keitel's suggestion Canaris was sent to discuss the situation with General Amé—a suggestion which was probably Canaris's own in the first place."

Canaris and Amé met at Venice, and Amé asked Canaris to do his utmost to prevent any action that would forestall Italy's withdrawal from the war. Canaris agreed, and the two men, talking privately in the back of Amé's car, decided to hold a full-scale official conference which would be attended by the executives of the Abwehr, the SD and SIM in Italy. When the conference convened, Canaris posed the questions which Keitel had instructed him to ask. Amé, with an impressive display of feigned outrage for the benefit of the SD officers present, declared emphatically that there was not a word of truth in the suspicions that Hitler harbored against Badoglio. Badoglio, he said, was determined to continue the struggle side by side with Germany until final victory was won. The conference ended with an inspired and enthusiastic declaration by Amé of Badoglio's friend-ship for Hitler and regard for the Axis alliance.

On his return to OKW, Canaris submitted a report of the conference to Keitel—taking care that the signature on the report was that of a subordi-nate. Keitel accepted the report and assured Hitler that Italy had no intention of defecting. Although Hitler was suspicious, the only action he took was to order plans drawn up to control and disarm the Italian armed forces and to reinforce the German troops protecting the Alpine communi-cations. He did not execute his intention to occupy Italy and he did not attempt to arrest Badoglio. Thus Badoglio was able to negotiate a sur-render to the Allies without interference from Hitler or the Wehrmacht. The surrender was signed secretly on September 3, 1943, and became effective on September 8.

Hitler was taken completely by surprise. But when the Italian fleet, which still included six modern battleships, fled, he reacted with ferocity. As it was steaming down the Sardinian coast, the fleet was attacked by German aircraft using the HS.293 wireless-controlled glider bombs. The flagship *Roma* was hit and blew up with very heavy loss of life, and a second battleship was badly damaged. Nevertheless, the main body of this still powerful and valuable force soon arrived at Malta. On the morning of September 11, Admiral Sir Andrew Cunningham, the British C-in-C, was able to send the precise and splendid signal to the Lords of the Admiralty: "Be pleased to inform their Lordships that the Italian Battle fleet now lies at anchor under the guns of the fortress of Malta."

Canaris's part in the intrigue to conceal Italian intentions was one of the cleverest moves he had made. Through his efforts Italy had surrendered, Hitler lost the Italian fleet, and Rome—which Hitler had threatened to destroy as he had destroyed Belgrade as punishment—was spared. But time was closing in on Canaris. Schellenberg would later claim that, through the suborned chauffeurs, he had learned the truth of the Canaris-Amé talk, and "I was able to present Himmler with a dossier which included absolute proof of Canaris's treachery." Himmler's only reaction was to "nervously tap his thumbnail against his teeth," and to instruct Schellenberg to "Leave the dossier here with me. I will bring it to Hitler's attention when the right opportunity arises." But Himmler did nothing with the dossier. Schellenberg would offer a reason: "I am certain that at some time or other Canaris must have got to know something incriminating against Himmler, for otherwise there is no possible explanation of Himmler's reaction to the material which I placed before him." Canaris remained in office, and he would succeed in deceiving Hitler once again.

The arrests of the Abwehr executive staff were a grave blow to the Schwarze Kapelle. With Beck still hospitalized with cancer and Witzleben incapacitated with piles, it was without effective leadership. But all was not lost. Field Marshal von Kluge, at his headquarters in the central sector of the Russian front, was still approachable, and it was to him that Karl-Friedrich Goerdeler wrote an eloquent appeal to rejoin the conspiracy. Goerdeler had been successful in securing the field marshal's tacit support for Operation Flash, but with the failure of that plot, Kluge's confidence in the conspirators had been badly shaken. Goerdeler's efforts on behalf of the Schwarze Kapelle had not flagged in the intervening months, and when he returned from a tour of the devastated cities of the Ruhr, he once again attempted to enlist Kluge's support.

It was a moving letter. "You would be as shocked as I was," wrote Goerdeler. "The work of a thousand years is nothing but rubble. . . . Furthermore, nothing can be done with these ruins. They are heaps of debris, concrete and iron. Reconstruction will take generations." He spoke of the flight of the population of the German cities, of the grave decline in industrial production, of the collapse of honor and morality among both civilians and soldiers.

In view of this national disaster which is now becoming obvious and into which we have been led by an insane and godless leadership which disregards human rights, I take the liberty of making a last appeal to you, Field

Marshal. . . . The hour has now come at which we must take the final decision on our personal fate. . . . German interests must once again be represented with force and reason by decent Germans. . . .

The letter reached Kluge at an opportune moment; the Wehrmacht in the East had just suffered an even greater defeat than Stalingrad—"Citadelle," the Battle of the Kursk salient. The purpose of the battle was to regain the initiative on the Russian front, but the attack had been betrayed by pro-Russian army officers of colonel rank, by information from the British that had derived from Ultra, and by the Russians' own wireless intelligence. Stalin's cannon, cleverly sited and concealed, were waiting for the gigantic attack and Citadelle was smashed. The Germans suffered unheard-of casualties; Hitler lost 70,000 men, 3000 tanks, 1000 guns, 5000 motor vehicles and 1400 planes—all in eleven days. The defeat was decisive; it ended German mass attacks in the East, the panzer divisions were virtually destroyed, and it was questionable whether they could be rebuilt in time for deployment against Russia in the spring of 1943 or against the western Allies during the invasion.

Kluge's response to Goerdeler's letter would be crucial to the conspiracy. Tresckow, his Chief of Staff, had tried in vain to enlist the support of other generals on the Russian front; Goerdeler's emissary to Field Marshal von Rundstedt in Paris had been rebuffed. Only Kluge was left. And it seemed that he, too, was ruled out when he replied to Goerdeler that he was "not interested." But he was more interested than he would admit. In due course, after he learned that Stauffenberg had recovered sufficiently to become the operational head of the Schwarze Kapelle, he gave Tresckow extended leave on medical grounds to go to Berlin and begin the new régime's plotting on secure, reliable and practical General Staff lines; and he agreed to meet the Schwarze Kapelle's new leaders in Berlin.

The meeting took place in September 1943 at the home of General Friedrich Olbricht, the Chief of Staff of the Home Army, whose headquarters on the Bendlerstrasse had become the center of the new plot. Beck, Olbricht, Tresckow and Goerdeler discussed the situation with Kluge. In a spirit of confidence and optimism, Goerdeler told of the Schwarze Kapelle's lines of communication to the Americans and British. He tried to calm Kluge's fears that the British would demand the total destruction of German power and industry by pointing out that it was in Britain's interest to keep a powerful Germany as a bulwark against Russia. Finally, Kluge was convinced and said that Hitler "must be removed, by force if necessary, in the national interests." He declared himself for the *coup d'état,* and, understandably, the conspirators were jubilant. At last they had a fighting marshal to follow. But their jubilation was short-lived. Not long after the meeting Kluge was badly hurt in a motor accident when his chauffeur hit a tank on the Orscha-Minsk road. The fates were never very kind to the Schwarze Kapelle.

With Kluge's accident, Witzleben became C-in-C of the army in Beck's regency. The accident was a hard blow to the conspiracy, but its power center remained intact within the department of General Friedrich Fromm, the C-in-C of the Home Army, and it would be in his name that Valkyrie orders—for the plan was kept both as an instrument of state and of the conspiracy—would go out to the subordinate commanders. The new leaders of the plot—Stauffenberg, Olbricht, Tresckow—remained vigorous and dedicated; and about this time, the Schwarze Kapelle enlisted the support of a group of important figures at Zossen, among them—and most important of all—Colonel Alexis Baron von Roenne, the chief of FHW and a man whose intelligence appreciations carried much weight with Hitler and OKW. Somewhat less insistent than their predecessors upon Anglo-American declarations of support, the conspirators decided upon two fundamental policies in regard to the Allies. If no declarations were forthcoming by D-Day—and all knew that day must come—the Schwarze Kapelle would see to it that the Allies were fought at the water's edge in the hope that heavy casualties would compel them to seek an armistice. But if declarations were forthcoming, arrangements would be made to open up the Channel front to the invading armies and facilitate their march across western and central Europe to the Elbe before the Russians arrived. It was in this spirit, therefore, that the Schwarze Kapelle's emissaries traveled to Stockholm, Berne, Lisbon and Madrid to recommence negotiations with Allied diplomatic and secret agents.

The new round of approaches to the British and American governments had begun soon after Stauffenberg assumed operational leadership of the Schwarze Kapelle, and would last until the eve of D-Day. In August 1943 at Berlin Goerdeler once again saw Jacob Wallenberg, the Swedish banker. It was their sixth meeting since the outbreak of war, and Goerdeler told Wallenberg, altogether too optimistically, that preparations were ready for a coup in September and that, when it took place, arrangements had been made to send Fabian von Schlabrendorff, the young officer who had been one of the two would-be assassins in Flash, to Stockholm to treat with Anglo-American agents. Goerdeler asked Wallenberg "to persuade the British to send a suitable contact man to meet Schlabrendorff." Wallenberg replied that "I should be glad to do this as soon as the coup occurred and that I would inform the Allies that a German, representing the new leaders, was in Stockholm not to negotiate but merely to obtain Allied advice as to how the new government should go about obtaining peace." Wallenberg relayed Goerdeler's information to his brother, Marcus, who in turn, "passed (it) on to the British."

The two men met for the last time at Berlin in September. Goerdeler had prepared a memorandum, at Wallenberg's request, on the Schwarze Kapelle's intentions for transmission to Churchill. The memorandum outlined the conspirators' plans for the overthrow of the Nazis and again requested some indication of British support: ". . . the group's leaders wish to clarify whether, in accordance with earlier assurances on the part of the British government, it will be possible to initiate negotiations for a peace treaty immediately after the establishment of a German government that has rejected national socialism." The memorandum then set forth the Schwarze Kapelle's conception of what the terms of the peace should be; and incredibly, the conspirators believed that they could set their own terms if they agreed to open up the Atlantic Wall. Goerdeler did not receive a reply from the British.

At Berne, however, Hans Bernd Gisevius, the former Gestapo lawyer who was, under German diplomatic cover, the Schwarze Kapelle's emissary to Allen Dulles, appeared to be a great deal more successful. Gisevius and the British had long since ceased to trust each other when Dulles arrived at Berne as the OSS station chief in Switzerland with the express mission of making contact with the Schwarze Kapelle. A lawyer (Donovan favored lawyers as Menzies favored bankers), Dulles was not new to espionage or to Switzerland; in the First World War he had worked there as an American agent against the German and Austro-Hungarian empires. Then, as later, he felt that an Anglo-German–American rapprochement was the surest guarantee of peace. Between the wars, Dulles had met the élite of German industry and banking through the Berlin office of Sullivan and Cromwell, the New York law firm for which he worked; and through his friend, Hugh Wilson, who became Roosevelt's ambassador at Hitler's court, he was well informed about the German political situation.

When America declared war on Germany, Dulles joined Donovan's organization and formed a committee of experts on German affairs; and in the autumn of 1942, as Colonel David Bruce began his journey to London to become chief of OSS in Europe, Dulles took up his post in Berne. There, in his offices at Herrengasse 23, he established an American espionage network in Europe that, extraordinarily well financed, extended from London to Prague. Dulles's main recruit, and the man who became his personal assistant, was Gero von Schulze Gaevernitz, the son of a leading Berlin economist and liberal whom Dulles had known ever since the First World War. Gaevernitz, who had married into the Stinnes family of Rhenish industrialists, made his home in Switzerland at the outbreak of war, probably with the help of Canaris or Oster; and it was through Gaevernitz that Dulles met Gisevius.

The British had dismissed Gisevius as a German deception agent; and as Dulles did not wholly trust the huge, 6-foot-4-inch Prussian, the two men first met under cover of darkness on the steps of the World Council of Churches building. They hammered out a means of communication that would avoid Gestapo surveillance, and then Dulles arranged with his control at Washington for a special distribution system for his intelligence cables about the Schwarze Kapelle, which he codenamed "the Breakers," to ensure that they were read only by those in the highest places. These cables were known as "L-Documents" and their distribution was extremely narrow; they went only to Roosevelt's White House map room; to the Secretary of State, Cordell Hull; to the U.S. Chiefs of Staff intelligence center; and to Fletcher Warren, a Texan with ambassadorial status who was executive assistant to the Assistant Secretary of State. In all, between March of 1943 and May of 1944, Dulles would send about 145 Breakers cables to Washington. In addition, he sent a number of letters and at least one large package—the manuscript of Gisevius's history of the Schwarze Kapelle, a document that was both compelling and some 200,000 words long. Therefore, Washington was, if it chose to read Dulles's correspondence, at least as knowledgeable about the Schwarze Kapelle as was Churchill through his own and Menzies's sources.

Dulles came to believe, however, that his Breakers cables had not been distributed, and would theorize that a Russian agent in Washington had blocked their circulation to prevent an accord between the Schwarze Kapelle and the western Allies. That theory proved to be wrong; nevertheless, not one of his cables would appear in the records of the Combined or Joint Chiefs of Staff, nor was any overture by the Schwarze Kapelle considered in the secret correspondence between Roosevelt and Churchill. Indifference, not treachery, was at the root of America's attitude toward the conspiracy.

Such was not the case in British secret circles. Postwar events would reveal that someone had blocked from general circulation intelligence concerning the Schwarze Kapelle. His name was Harold "Kim" Philby, whose desk at MI-6 headquarters was just down the corridor from Menzies. Philby, who was regarded as the best type of intelligence officer, had risen in the hierarchy of MI-6 to become, by 1943, chief of the Iberian subsection of Section V, a vital department that dealt with MI-6 counterespionage operations in Spain and Portugal. Menzies, who was directly responsible for Philby's appointment and for promotions, trusted him completely. But there Menzies made the major mistake of his career, a mistake that would kill him in the end, for Philby was a particularly intelligent and insidious Soviet agent.

During the war, as the authors of *The Philby Conspiracy* would write, "Philby's job as a Soviet agent in Britain was . . . blindingly clear: to resist, in every way, the growth of feeling in Britain that there was any practical way of dealing with the Germans—short of destruction. . . ."

Thus, in addition to betraying to the Soviet Union all the secrets of MI-6, as well as such state secrets of England and America as he could get his hands on, Philby attempted to halt or question the credibility of any reports crossing his desk that suggested the possibility of treating with the Schwarze Kapelle.

While Philby unquestionably did the conspiracy great damage, he was not completely successful in blocking its overtures to London; and he played no part in Washington's attitude. Through Dulles, Washington was well informed, and if his cables did not make the impact that he expected, it was not the consequence of pro-Russian treachery in the American capital; it was the consequence of the American hierarchy's belief that the German General Staff must be eradicated if there was to be a durable peace in Europe. Moreover, Gisevius was distrusted as a reliable source. Had he not been a Gestapo official?

No such taint stuck to Dulles's most important contact in Berlin. On August 23, 1943, a German doctor named Kochertaler called upon Count Vanden Huyvel, the MI-6 station chief in Switzerland. The count listened to what the man had to say—and threw him out of his office. The doctor then went to Gerald Mayer, an official in the Office of War Information, the American equivalent of PWE, and said he represented an official in the military liaison section of the German Foreign Ministry. Could Mayer arrange a meeting for this official with Mr. Dulles? Mayer was skeptical; nevertheless he arranged the meeting, and after dark that same evening, at Herrengasse 23, Fritz Kolbe arrived at Dulles's office. He was forty-two, a short, wiry man with a halo of blond hair around a bald pate. Kolbe revealed that he was the special assistant to Ambassador Karl Ritter, a man who undertook important diplomatic missions for the Wehrmacht. In this position, Kolbe said, his job entailed screening the diplomatic "print"—all the diplomatic correspondence and wireless traffic—to keep Ritter informed. There was very little concerning the Wehrmacht's plans and policies that did not, therefore, come to Kolbe's desk.

Kolbe, who was a practical man as well as an idealist, made Dulles a very tempting offer. He would, if Dulles wished, supply the United States government regularly with a selection of Ritter's most secret correspondence. Was Dulles interested? At this point, Kolbe presented an amazed and thoroughly uneasy Dulles with 186 contemporary German diplomatic documents extracted directly from Ritter's "print." Dulles asked Kolbe for time to examine the documents, arranged a further meeting, and then Kolbe departed. The documents, which came to be called the "Berne Report," were quite breathtaking, for they consisted of most secret reports of German diplomatic missions in some twenty countries.

Dulles had no doubt that the documentation was genuine; and when the report was later compared with Ultra intercepts of the past few months, it was found to be identical in substance and terminology. "And what a yield it was!" Dulles would remember. Before him were spread the innermost secrets of the German war machine, a savage testament to all the power—and all the weakness—of the Reich. Dulles cabled both Bruce in London and Donovan in Washington with a digest. One of his cables to Washington read in part:

> Sincerely regret that you cannot see at this time Woods [Dulles had assigned Kolbe the cover name of "George Woods"] material as it stands without condensation and abridgment. In some 400 pages, dealing with the international maneuverings of German diplomatic policy for the past two months, a picture of imminent doom and final downfall is presented. Into a tormented General Headquarters and a half-dead Foreign Office stream the lamentations of a score of diplomatic posts. It is a scene wherein haggard Secret Service and diplomatic agents are doing their best to cope with the defeatism and desertion of flatly defiant satellites and allies and recalcitrant neutrals.
>
> The period of secret service under Canaris . . . is drawing to an end. . . . The final death-bed contortions of a putrefied Nazi diplomacy are pictured in these telegrams. The reader is carried from one extreme of emotion to the other as he examines these messages and sees the cruelty exhibited by the Germans in their final swan-song of brutality toward the peoples so irrevocably and pitifully enmeshed by the Gestapo after half a decade of futile struggles. . . .

But if Dulles expected his eloquence to be heard at Washington, he was mistaken; unlike London, where reports like Kolbe's gave rise to new strategic thinking such as the Rankin plans, they were received in Washington with what Dulles later described as shoulder shrugs. Who cared? However, the importance of the Berne Report did not lie in its actual contents; while Dulles did not know this, it merely, in the main, duplicated intelligence already derived through Ultra and Magic. But it did reveal just how far some Germans would go toward betraying their country in a desperate hour for purely personal ideological reasons. Kolbe's actions were, in effect, a continuation of the policy laid down by Canaris at the outbreak of war, carried on by the revelations contained in the Oslo Report and Oster's betrayal of Case Yellow in 1940, and, most probably, by Canaris's conduct of critically important intelligence operations ever since.

Lisbon, like Berne and Stockholm, was a main junction in the Schwarze Kapelle's lines of communication to the Allies; and in July and August 1943, at the direction of Stauffenberg, Otto John, a Lufthansa lawyer and a member of the conspiracy, traveled to both Madrid and Lisbon to find out whether rapid communications could be established to Washington and London. At Madrid, through the American *chargé d'affaires,* Willard L. Beaulac, John met Colonel William Hohenthal, the American military attaché, at a private dinner party. According to John's own account, he told Hohenthal that

> . . . the Wehrmacht could fight for seven years before it was totally exhausted . . . unless we first contrived to end the war earlier "through a change in régime." . . . I said, without giving names, that "we" intended to make an attempt "to change the régime," before Christmas (1943). For this purpose the outside support we needed was a declaration by the Allied High Command promising our field marshals the same treatment as had been (given Italy) . . . could we remain in touch? (Hohenthal) willingly agreed, gave me his secret telephone number in the American Embassy and promised the strictest secrecy.

With that assurance, John went to Lisbon where, he hoped, he might talk to an MI-6 contact. It was not until the turn of the year 1943–44 that a meeting was arranged in a parked car in a dark Lisbon side street. When John got to the rendezvous he found a woman, a "Miss Rita Winsor"; but as they drove through the town, according to John's account of the meeting, "she told me that strict instructions had been received from London forbidding any further contact with emissaries of the German opposition. (She said) the war would now be decided by force of arms." The Schwarze Kapelle had been rebuffed once again, probably through Philby.

John was not the Schwarze Kapelle's only representative in Lisbon, however. During the summer of 1943, Baron Oswald von Hoyningen-Huene, the former secretary to Hindenburg and now ambassador in Portugal, sent an invitation, through an intermediary, from Canaris to Menzies for a meeting on neutral territory to discuss an alliance between the Schwarze Kapelle and MI-6. Menzies received the invitation favorably, and would have met Canaris. But Anthony Eden, according to Menzies, ordered him not to accept or to reply. If the Russians learned of such a meeting, they might believe that the British were toying with considerations of making a separate peace with the Germans.

At about this same time, the Schwarze Kapelle made another overture to MI-6 at Lisbon. An Abwehr agent turned over a dossier that came to be called the "Lisbon Report." It reinforced the gesture implicit in the Berne Report and was, many Germans believed afterwards, the most damaging betrayal suffered by the Third Reich. Among a mass of technical detail, the Lisbon Report revealed that the German missile research and development program was being conducted at Peenemünde on a secluded island in the Baltic some 70 miles from Stettin. The report confirmed the information contained in the Oslo Report of 1939 and may have been intended as an indication of good faith to encourage Menzies to accept Canaris's invitation. He did not accept, but eleven days after the report was handed over, on the night of August 17/18, 1943, the RAF obliterated Peenemünde.

Again, the conspirators of the Schwarze Kapelle had demonstrated their willingness to betray the Third Reich's most important secrets; yet while the Allies were quick to take advantage of their treason, they continued to ignore the motives behind it. The American attitude toward the conspiracy had set fast, and it would not change. The Third Reich was to be destroyed by a direct confrontation in battle; there was no room for political settlements of any sort. On the other hand, Churchill's attitude became somewhat ambivalent. Fearing the bloodbath that might occur on D-Day, he was prepared to hear suggestions about how the Germans might be defeated without actually fighting them—Sun Tzu's old principle. His reasoning was, then and later, that military operations might come to an end if the conspiracy was successful and Hitler and the Nazis were overthrown. But when Churchill raised the question of the Schwarze Kapelle at the White House in May 1943, perhaps contemplating the manipulation of the conspiracy in much the same way that Britain was using the various resistance movements of Europe for the purpose of weakening or destroying Nazism from within, the President replied very sharply. As Robert E. Sherwood noted: "There is no doubt that Roosevelt never took this possibility very seriously as a solution to the problems of achieving total victory."

Yet Goerdeler, Gisevius, John—all had spoken the truth about the conspiracy's renewed determination. For between September and December 1943, the Schwarze Kapelle made no less than four attempts to kill the Fuehrer. Each attempt was carefully planned, and each time the preliminary messages for Valkyrie were issued in what were represented as "tests" for an actual emergency. General Helmuth Stieff, a little hunchback, undertook the first attack on Hitler at Führerhauptquartier; but the explosives to be used went off prematurely and the consequent security precautions around the Fuehrer made a continuation of the plot impossible. The second attempt was made by a young staff officer who had access to Hitler in the Berghof at Berchtesgaden. This officer, whose name has not been made known, proposed to smuggle a pistol into Hitler's office at a staff meeting and shoot him at point-blank range. The plot failed because the officer was of junior rank and he was placed at the back of the large room where, finding himself next to an SS bodyguard, he could not have produced a handkerchief, let alone a pistol.

In November 1943, a third opportunity arose. A young officer, Axel Baron von dem Bussche, was to model a new army greatcoat for Hitler. His plan was one of high courage and self-sacrifice; he was to hide two bombs on his person and when Hitler approached he would pull the pins and blow them both to eternity. But a sudden Allied air raid caused the demonstration to be postponed and, when it was to be resumed, it was found that the greatcoat had been destroyed in the attack. Then Stauffenberg stepped forward to undertake another attempt. Although a man with one eye, one arm and only three fingers could hardly be expected to manipulate a bomb, he volunteered to do so when Hitler called a manpower conference for December 26, 1943. Stauffenberg managed to get as far as the anteroom to the meeting, with the bomb in his briefcase. But there he was informed that the meeting had been postponed. Hitler's evil guardian angel—or perhaps an SD informer within the Schwarze Kapelle—worked well on his behalf. Thus the conspirators entered the new year of 1944. Their crime, until now, had been failure, but their misfortune was Ultra. Time and again, the conspirators attempted to barter the secrets of the Third Reich to gain support and win concessions favorable to a Germany rid of Hitler and the Nazis. But the Allies did not have to make dangerous secret deals, for the conspirators could tell them little or nothing that Ultra was not revealing. Ultra—so decisive in the defeat of the Third Reich—may in this way have postponed Hitler's personal destruction.

7

Starkey

IN PREPARATION for D-Day, an Anglo-American headquarters was established in London in the middle of 1943. Its chief was General Frederick Morgan, a forty-nine-year-old artillery and tank man who was noted for his somewhat jolly courtesy, his urbanity, and his liking for, and admiration of, Americans. He was known as COSSAC—from the initial letters of his command, Chief of Staff Supreme Allied Commander (designate)—and his headquarters were at Norfolk House in St. James's Square, a pleasant backwater off Piccadilly where George III was born, where Josiah Wedgwood had his famous showroom, and where the Norfolks, the premier Dukes and Chief Butlers of England, had their residences. Norfolk House was very convenient to the Army and Navy Club, and so the planning conferences for COSSAC's first operation—the major strategic deception campaign called "Cockade"—were held at both places. "There was a certain piquance," recalled Wingate, "about planning deception over brandy and soda beneath the nude portrait of Nell Gwynne which then hung in the club." The consequences of Cockade were less agreeable.

Cockade—one of the operating moves in Plan Jael—was the outcome of the realization at Casablanca by the Combined Chiefs of Staff that it would not be possible for the American and British armies to invade Europe across the English Channel in 1943; the men, ships and aircraft needed for such a gigantic enterprise would not be available in England. But, as the Prime Minister had advised the conference, it was of the utmost importance that the weakness of the Allies in England be concealed from the Germans. To do that, preparations for an invasion of France could be simulated, and these, it was hoped, would prevent Hitler from transferring idle divisions in France to Russia and Italy, where they were badly needed. The Allied high command also hoped that a new series of feints at the Pas de Calais in particular would help increase Hitler's fears for the security of that sector and, at the expense of the fortifications in Normandy, where the

Allied invasion would actually occur, compel him to build his strongest defenses along the shores of the Pas de Calais. The other primary purpose of Cockade was to force the Luftwaffe into a battle of attrition with the RAF and the USAAF. Accordingly, a directive had reached Morgan requiring him to prepare plans for "an elaborate camouflage and deception scheme extending over the whole summer of 1943 with a view to pinning the enemy in the west and keeping alive the expectation of large-scale cross-Channel operations in 1943."

Cockade's main component was "Starkey," a deception operation that was defined as "An amphibious feint to force the Luftwaffe to engage in intensive fighting over a period of about 14 days, by building up a threat of an imminent large-scale British landing in the Pas de Calais." Cockade also included two other, smaller deceptions: "Tindall," to suggest an Anglo-Russian invasion of north Norway; and "Wadham," to suggest that the American army in Britain was about to descend upon Brittany. The entire stratagem was to be supervised by The Controller of Deception, Colonel Bevan, with an LCS officer, Major Derrick Morley, representing LCS interests on the planning syndicates. Planning was put in the hands of Morgan, as COSSAC, but command responsibility for Starkey rested with the C-in-C Fighter Command, Air Marshal Sir Trafford Leigh-Mallory, because the primary purpose of Starkey was to lure the Luftwaffe to battle and destruction. The weapons of Cockade would be those of feint, guile and menace, a troop movement here, ships sailing there, an air squadron in flight, an "accidental" whisper in the ether, a hint in the press, a radio broadcast, the despatch of a spy, unrest in France—a multitude of fragments that, when assembled, would appear to the German intelligencers as a picture of imminent invasion of France.

From the start, the planning syndicates were confronted with a fundamental problem. How could a convincing invasion threat be mounted when there were fewer offensive troops in Britain in the summer of 1943 than there were at the time of the Dieppe pinprick in 1942? It was appreciated at COSSAC that the Germans might know—or guess—that the vast forces necessary for an invasion did not exist in the British Isles at that time. The only thing that could be done, COSSAC decided, was to try to inflate, through deception, Allied strength in England, to augment that deception with rumors of an invasion in the press and on the radio, to stimulate the British civilian population into reacting as if vast military preparations were going on in its midst, and to launch a campaign among the resistance organizations in France, Belgium and Holland to suggest that there would be an invasion in September 1943.

It was in this last decision that the great moral and political dangers lay, for the War Cabinet recognized that the *résistants* might actually believe that an invasion was at hand, rise, reveal themselves, and be destroyed by the Germans. Nevertheless, it was perceived in London that unless the *résistants* were stirred into assisting "the deception by producing the symptoms of underground activity . . . which the enemy would naturally look for as one preliminary of a real invasion," Starkey would "lack the full colour of authenticity." Accordingly, the two British agencies involved in resistance operations, the Special Operations Executive (SOE) and the Political Warfare Executive (PWE), were required to prepare a plan; and this, on July 18, 1943, they submitted to the Chiefs of Staff.

How did SOE and PWE propose to endow Starkey with the "full colour of authenticity"? The agencies recommended (and the Chiefs of Staff accepted) that:

> The method would be by rehearsing, well in advance of *D* minus 7 day, a number of Political Warfare and Subversive Operations. These would have to be on a scale sufficient to disturb and confuse the enemy, but would be so devised as not to provoke premature uprisings or to squander any stratagems or devices needed in connection with a real invasion.

Among these operations would be attacks on rail targets and German headquarters, murder sorties against German personnel and the destruction of telecommunications and certain industrial targets—all designed to suggest that invasion was imminent and that the *résistants* were preparing for their part in that operation. But the planners hoped, perhaps optimistically, that the *résistants* would go only so far and no further.

There was another danger inherent in this kind of deception. In a grim but humane appreciation of "The Problem," the SOE/PWE plan warned:

> These operations will be taking place on the eve of the most desperate winter of the war and will be directed towards territories where the expectation of early liberation is at present the main sustaining factor in resistance. The effect of these operations will be to heighten to flash-point expectations of relief before the winter, and then at the very onset of the winter to disappoint (the population of western Europe).

But the plan went on to envisage, again optimistically, that this disappointment would be acceptable to France and western Europe if operations elsewhere—notably in Sicily and Italy, which were to be invaded at about the same time as Starkey—were successful. As the plan said: "In these circumstances, the peoples of the west will be prepared to accept Starkey as a justifiable diversion and their morale will be sustained by the proofs and the hopes of success elsewhere." These were dangerous, cynical words.

Safeguards were built into the plan, however, to prevent, it was hoped, the *résistants* from erupting into open warfare. The plan proposed:

> (I) That strict orders should be broadcast to these armies, over a period prior to D-Day [for Starkey] to hold their hand until they receive from

London a direct injunction to rise. (II) That from about *D* minus 7 to D-Day leaflets and propaganda should be dropped addressed to the patriots telling them that the forthcoming activity is only a rehearsal.

These precautions, it was felt, would have the "double advantage of misleading the enemy at the time, and of maintaining the confidence of the patriots in the accuracy of our instructions and so persuading them to pay strict regard to any future instructions." These proposals, too, were approved. But it was evident from the start that the Starkey planners were playing with unstable gelignite: the French resistance movements.

Equally explosive were the special means that were to be employed to manipulate the *résistants*. It was recommended, first of all, that the BBC should be used as "an unconscious agent of the deception, *i.e.* that it should react to the news and inspired leakages created by the forthcoming operations in a normal and uninformed way until, like the press, it is allowed to know that they are a 'rehearsal.'" But the BBC occupied a special place in the world of communications. Its august reputation was built wholly on telling the truth; it was not an organ of propaganda for the British government. And it was this reputation that made it the most widely respected and listened-to radio service in the world, at a time when radio was the dominant means for the dissemination of information. At great peril to themselves, most people with a radio set in Europe listened in each night to the calm, factual, forthright newscasts from London; and they invariably respected and obeyed what they were told. Yet the Starkey planners proposed to use the BBC for the purposes of creating the symptoms of a national uprising in support of what was a military deception, and that proposal was approved.

It was also proposed that the BBC be used in a second way to manipulate the patriot forces. Quite early in the war, the BBC had undertaken to act as a channel of communications between London and the resistance forces of Europe. A system of messages known as "Avis" was devised, and the messages, which were called "idioforms" or *"messages personnels,"* were broadcast in the appropriate language in two parts. The first was known as the "A" or the "alert" message, and its function was to alert a *réseau* to prepare to carry out an assigned task. The second part, known as the "B" or the "action" message, was the order to execute that task. In theory at least, the meaning of each was known only to the leaders of the *réseau* to which the pair of messages was allocated and, of course, to the SOE operations section.

The *messages personnels* were broadcast by the European division of the BBC from Bush House in the Strand each night at 7:30 and 9. They were introduced by the first measure of Beethoven's Fifth Symphony—V-for-Victory—they usually lasted between fifteen and twenty minutes, and they began with the words: *"Voici quelques messages personnels."* The actual messages followed: *"Le chat a neuf vies,"* and then, at dictation speed, *"Le . . . chat . . . a . . . neuf . . . vies."* There would be a pause and then, *"Bénédictine est une liqueur douce"*—*"Bén-é-dict-ine . . . est . . . une . . . li-queur . . . douce." "La vache saute pardessus la lune"*—*"La . . . vache . . . saute . . . par-dessus . . . la . . . lune."* To most of the world, these words were meaningless; but to the informed few they meant, for example, prepare to blow up a railway line at Périgord, or stand by from midnight on to receive an incoming agent at Angers. *"La lune est pleine d'éléphants rouges"*—and a power plant at Clermont-Ferrand would be blown up. Or *"Romeo embrasse Juliette"*—and a busload of Luftwaffe personnel at Orly would be machine-gunned.

The system had worked satisfactorily in the past; it was important that it continue to work in the future. But the Starkey planners proposed that it be used, not for the purposes of command, but for deception. "A" messages would be broadcast to all resistance groups in France just prior to the D-Day set for Starkey, but the "B" messages were not to be sent. Thus there would not be a premature uprising of the resistance groups—*if* they were obedient to their orders from London.

Finally, the SOE/PWE plan provided for another potentially explosive move. Ever since the fall of France, SOE agents had been sent out from London to organize the French resistance movement into an underground army. These men, and some women, brought instructions with them, organized and trained the patriot armies in the crafts of clandestinity, operated the wireless posts that maintained contact with London, arranged for paradrops of incoming arms, ammunition, explosives, money and other agents, and participated in a host of clandestine activities—all at great personal risk. Up until now SOE agents had done a remarkably successful job in directing the scattered and often disorganized French *réseaux,* and rarely had they—or the *réseaux* they controlled—been used for the purposes of deception. For the purposes of Starkey, however, certain key agents already in the field, as well as agents sent to France during the pre-Starkey period, were not to be told beforehand that Starkey was a rehearsal. They, too, would be "unconscious" agents of the deception, and would be instructed to carry out their assigned duties as if Starkey were a real invasion. The Starkey planners thought that this would add to the "full colour of authenticity," and it was hoped, again optimistically, that these agents would go so far, and no further.

In all, Starkey was a highly dangerous operation for the French underground movement and its Anglo-French leaders, since the Allies intended to goad the Germans into reacting to the "invasion," and part of their defensive reaction would inevitably be a strike at the resistance. It was this possibility that concerned Jacob L. Devers, the American commanding general in England. He wrote to General George V. Strong, the chief of army intelligence in Washington, to protest that ". . . the PWE plan for Starkey . . . (may) bring about a general uprising, jeopardizing the entire resistance organization." But Strong, as a member of Joint Security Control, had in the past sanctioned the manipulation of the French—and especially the Gaulliste—resistance movements for the purposes of deception.

Despite the risks, the plan was approved, D-Day for Starkey was set for September 9, 1943, and the operation got under way. SOE organizers had already been parachuted back into France to begin preparing for the "invasion." And in late July, on the English side of the Channel, troops marched about the countryside, tank columns began to roll toward the south coast, holiday resorts were suddenly closed to visitors, mail and telephone calls from the "invasion zones" were intercepted, RAF fighter groups darted about the skies of France in provocative fashion, and the press and the radio were encouraged to speculate that, at last, the invasion was at hand.

But then, the scenario of the deception started to break down. Even those in on the operation became confused; Morgan himself grumbled: "Will someone kindly tell me what I am to say, when I am to say it, and to whom I must say it?" And stimulated by calculated leakages from PWE, correspondents and broadcasters did more than speculate about an imminent invasion. The United Press told the world: "An unofficial source states that the Allies will move against Germany by the autumn and the race for Berlin is on with Anglo-American forces poised to beat the Russians. Signs multiply that the Allies may land in Italy and in France within the next month." Tens of thousands of similar words were cabled from London by newspapermen to their editors throughout the world. The French were brought to a high pitch of readiness and expectation by this announcement, broadcast by the BBC on August 17, 1943:

. . . the liberation of the occupied countries, has begun.

We are obviously not going to reveal where the blow will fall. The people of the occupied country that is to be the first to welcome the armies of liberation will be notified at the last minute.

Pending the hour when we will be in a position to enlighten you on this crucial point, we are today addressing a preliminary appeal.

It is time for you to prepare all your actions, to perfect your preparations. All those elements that are to contribute in any way whatsoever to the success of operations on French metropolitan territory must be fully equipped to carry out their task.

You must prepare yourselves, day by day and week by week, for the role that you will have to play at a future date, which may be near, in the liberation of your country.

The Associated Press and Reuters picked up this broadcast and made it world news. Accordingly, the French Committee of National Liberation warned all patriot forces to stand by for an Allied invasion that "may come any day now." The United Press fanned the flames by announcing from London: "French underground leaders were revealed today to be confidently expecting an early invasion of France, and coincidentally there was widespread speculation in Great Britain that zero hour for the assault on western Europe is approaching. . . ." At the same time the Home Secretary, Herbert Morrison, ordered the drafting of large bodies of firemen into southeastern England, the Archbishop of Canterbury called upon the nation to pray for those "about to invade the Continent of Europe," and from Quebec, in a broadcast to the Canadian people, Churchill promised that Europe would be invaded "before the leaves of autumn fall"—without saying from which side.

The Allies added to the feeling in France that great events were at hand by making over 3000 air raids in 20 days in the area of the Pas de Calais. And ignited by this kind of "invasion fever," the fires of insurgency began to rage all over northwestern Europe. In one week, de Gaulle's headquarters reported, French gunmen in France killed over five hundred *Feldgrau*. A bomb made of *plastique* killed twenty-three German officers in a Lille restaurant; saboteurs derailed a troop train in Dijon, killing and wounding 250 soldiers. In Holland, Hendrik Seyffardt, the only Dutch general to side with the Nazis, was murdered outside his house in The Hague by SOE-armed gunmen. In Belgium, *Brussellois* taunted German troops with the question, "Have you packed your bags yet? The Allies are coming!" In Denmark, a German officer was stomped to death in Odense, the Danish navy defected to Sweden, a German troop train exploded near Aalborg, the people revolted and the Germans proclaimed martial law.

The atmosphere on both sides of the Channel became supercharged with tension, while across the Atlantic on August 19, 1943, the *New York Times* proclaimed in three-deep headlines on page 1: "ARMIES READY TO GO, SAYS EISENHOWER," and "ALLIES BID PEOPLES OF EUROPE PREPARE." The world's press hinted that the Quebec Conference had been called to supervise the invasion. But from France came worrisome reports that there would be a major explosion among the resistance unless passions were quietened. Clearly, the political warfare campaign had got out of control.

Accordingly, on August 20, Bevan called a meeting of all the agencies involved in the deception, and it was decided that PWE should "discontinue" the "be ready" campaign "in view of the danger of the enemy using it as an excuse for the round-up of all resistance groups." The situation vividly illustrated the peculiar dangers in making the radio and the press "unconscious" agents of a deception, and PWE was compelled to issue a confidential advisory to all editors which read:

(A) Increased press speculation on the probability of the invasion of the Continent from the United Kingdom this summer may seriously prejudice our military intentions and may, at the same time, dangerously and prematurely raise the hopes of our own people and the people in the Occupied Territories.

(B) The facts are briefly as follows and are given for guidance in the strictest confidence:

(C) It is of the first importance to increase the general strain on the enemy this summer. Our best means of doing this is to convince the enemy that a large scale landing is imminent. In mounting this threat we must, however, avoid a premature rising in Occupied Europe and subsequent disappointment and loss of heart. It is also essential to avoid encouraging the idea amongst our own people that an invasion of Europe from the United Kingdom is practicable this summer.

(D) Our military plan this summer in the United Kingdom involves all three services on a large scale. We must, however, do all in our power, while achieving the desired results from these operations, to avoid premature expectations by the Allied peoples of an actual landing on the Continent. It is essential, therefore, to damp down comment on this subject.

With that injunction, press and radio speculation in Britain ended abruptly. But America was another matter. By August 28, the situation in France had become so grave that PWE in London instructed its representative in Washington, David Bowes-Lyon, son of the 14th Earl of Strathmore, a relative of the Queen and an associate of Menzies, to present OWI with a directive that "suggested" that: "In view of accumulating evidence from France of expected invasion in the very near future, use special care to avoid aggravating this tension." OWI was advised to "avoid all speculation concerning invasion possibilities" prior to D-Day for Starkey; and, after D-Day, to "give fullest possible publicity to official explanation of purpose of operation and of results achieved."

Clearly, London had failed to appreciate the vigor of the American media, and the virulence of the hatred of the French for the Germans. But how could "invasion" rumors be defused without revealing to the Germans that Starkey was a hoax, or, for that matter, without destroying the trust of the resistance movements and the credibility of the BBC? General Dallas Brooks, the Royal Marine in charge of Cockade political warfare deceptions at PWE, cabled Bowes-Lyon with the answer: blame the Germans. Thus, this broadcast went out on all media outlets controlled by PWE and OWI:

Be careful of German provocations. We have learnt that the Germans are circulating inspired rumours that we are concentrating armies on our coasts with intentions of invading the Continent. Take no notice, as these provocations are intended to create among you a situation where you may be caught. Lay low! Be careful! Do only what you are told to do by the BBC.

Meanwhile, the rest of the operation lumbered on. An "invasion fleet" was assembled on the Channel coast, but even as D-Day approached, the Germans showed no signs of taking the bait. When the RAF and the USAAF launched 3215 fighter and bomber sorties in support of the "invasion," the Germans responded with only 362 sorties. On the eve of the "invasion," the Luftwaffe made only six aerial reconnaissance flights over the Channel and England, and on D-Day itself there were only eight reconnaissance missions—less than usual. Nor did Starkey provoke any bombing of note; during the night of September 8/9, only ten German bombers flew over eastern and southeastern England and scattered their loads haphazardly upon such small villages as Snailwell, Thetford, Stanton, Hepworth, East Winch and Palling. Only one harbor was attacked by one bomber—Hastings. As for the "invasion fleet," only four German planes flew over it.

In France, the Luftwaffe reacted in what the Starkey after-action report described as a "disappointing manner." On September 9, the U.S. 8th Air Force launched 1208 aircraft against German targets on the French coast to give the appearance of truth to the Starkey feint. No great air battles developed; only during the attacks on the Hispano-Suiza aero-engine factory and the Beaumont-sur-Oise fighter airfield, both near Paris, did the Luftwaffe respond in strength. The battle was left to anti-aircraft artillery defenses, and while the 8th Air Force claimed 16 German fighters, the Allies lost 5 bombers and 2 fighters, with another 129 bombers suffering battle damage, mainly through flak. It was a high price to pay for a deception. Field Marshal von Rundstedt, the German C-in-C West, was so certain that this was not a real invasion that the Luftwaffe was kept only in a state of secondary alert. The primary objective of Starkey—to lure the Luftwaffe into an extended aerial battle—had not been achieved. As the Starkey planners noted:

> During the period of the operation no German attacks were made upon land targets connected with its preparation or performance. . . . Having appreciated the nature of *Starkey* . . . (the Germans) presumably made the further inference that to attack targets connected with it would be to attack at a point of the enemy's choosing. This is contrary to German tactical teaching. . . . This policy is explicable as an economy measure and a further refusal to be hoodwinked into fighting on our terms.

Further, the Admiralty reported only the slightest Kriegsmarine reaction to Starkey, noting a concentration of offensive E-boats at Ostend and Le Havre and defensive R-boats at Dunkirk and Boulogne. But, the Admiralty assessment warned, this concentration might just as easily have been routine redeployments. As for German coastal defense activity, the only enemy gunfire came on September 7 when minesweepers appeared to cut a passage through German minefields to Starkey's "invasion beaches." One minesweeper was damaged. And although it was expected that the German coastal guns would open fire on D-Day, they did not. Like the Luftwaffe, they played canny. The Starkey after-action report noted:

> Their silence is not easy to explain, unless the Germans think that the position of possibly all their batteries is not accurately known to us, and that consequently they would be giving away their position by opening fire. A possible explanation may be that they did not wish to divulge their operation role, accuracy, and fire effect, nor encourage retaliatory bombing. The silence of the coastal batteries is in keeping with the German doctrine of not opening fire prematurely.

It was the same with German ground movements. The after-action report observed:

> Beyond movements of flak, there was no enemy military reaction in terms of movement detectable during the operation. No rail or road movement which could be judged significant was seen. Headquarters and defence sectors were not noticeably active. Enemy signals gave nothing noteworthy away, and betrayed no unusual symptoms.

And if enemy wireless activity was an indication of the Germans' response to Starkey, it was apparent that they scarcely reacted at all that hot, balmy summer. In fact, there was a *reduction* of wireless traffic on D-Day. British wireless intelligence maintained an intense surveillance of the German wireless net and intercepted only one significant message. A German observer on the cliffs overlooking the "invasion fleet" exclaimed over his radio, "What is all the fuss over there?"

The report on Starkey summed up the whole operation with the words:

> . . . it would appear that the Germans appreciated the true nature of the operation. Their reaction was, accordingly, to avoid compromising their anti-invasion arrangements by employing them without real justification and thus playing the British game . . . they took the minimum "insurance" steps to cater for the possibility of a raid.

It was an oblique manner of stating that Starkey had been a complete failure. Afterwards, Rundstedt gave the reason why. "The movements (the British) made," he said, "were rather too obvious—it was evident (they) were bluffing." In fact, Hitler was so certain the Allies were bluffing that he was actually *withdrawing* over two-thirds of his army in the West. Between April and December 1943, a total of twenty-seven divisions of the thirty-six in the western command were pulled out for service in Russia, Sicily, Italy and the Balkans—a compliment to A-Force's Zeppelin operations in the Mediterranean at the expense of the LCS's Cockade operations in London. This huge withdrawal consisted of five panzer, two motorized and twenty infantry divisions, and their replacements were lesser-grade divisions of limited immediate fighting value. In Brittany, in whose great Atlantic ports most of the operational U-boat fleet had its lairs, there had been four infantry and two panzer divisions before Cockade; but during Wadham (the component of Cockade aimed specifically at Brittany), the Germans had been so disdainful of the deception that they transferred to other fronts the equivalent of one panzer and two infantry divisions and cannibalized the remaining garrisons of tanks, guns and combat men.

The effect of the Brittany withdrawals was to create a situation where, as Marshall had predicted as early as 1942 in the fierce Anglo-American debate on Roundup and Sledgehammer, German forces were so reduced in strength that an invasion, or at least an operation to secure a bridgehead from which a full-scale attack could be launched in 1944, would have been feasible in 1943—a point that Brooke and Churchill had bitterly fought. Indeed, the Allies, even with the limited manpower and shipping available in England in the summer of 1943, might literally have walked ashore in Brittany where the German garrisons had been, as a final report on Starkey acknowledged, "practically denuded."

The LCS survived the failure of Cockade and its component deceptions, but its reputation was damaged, particularly among the American planners at COSSAC, who would succeed in destroying the LCS's original cover and deception plan for the invasion. At the inevitable inquest, it was acknowledged that Cockade had not worked; but it was also acknowledged that it had demonstrated one important factor—the patriot armies of France could be brought to "flashpoint" without exploding. There had been, in general, considerable discipline among the *résistants;* they had accepted orders from London, and if their confidence could be maintained, and if they could be armed and trained, they might be counted upon to play a significant part when the time came for the Allies to embark on a real invasion. This was not to the credit of the LCS, however; it was due to the work of SOE. But ironically, it was SOE that would pay the steepest price for the failure of the deception. For even as Starkey unfolded, messages began to reach London that spoke, uniformly, of disaster among some of the main SOE *réseaux.* If the Germans had been indifferent to the threats of Starkey, they had not been indifferent to the menace of the French resistance. And when the leaders of the resistance were stirred into activity in support of Starkey, the Germans had reacted with savagery and cunning to destroy certain key clandestine organizations in France. Thus it was that Starkey became something more serious than a "balls-up," as Morgan later described it. A deception operation that might otherwise have been written off as a rather muddled rehearsal for a performance that was still many months in the future had been transformed into a tragedy.

Prosper

GENERAL COLIN MCVEAN GUBBINS, a Hebridean who wore the whortleberry and boxwood tartan of the Clan MacBain, a sept of the MacKintoshes, hailed a taxi outside the headquarters of SOE at 64 Baker Street, close to the fictional address of Sherlock Holmes. In September 1943 he had just succeeded Sir Charles Hambro as "D"—the cipher for the chief of SOE—and he was going to the Prime Minister's bunker at Storey's Gate to report to the Chief of the Imperial General Staff, General Brooke, on the disaster that had struck his secret organizations in France during Starkey. The dimensions of that disaster were large, for "Prosper" —the great network of *réseaux* which SOE was building out of the French resistance to rise against the Wehrmacht on D-Day—had been destroyed; "Scientist," another great network stretching from Paris to the Pyrenees, was toppling; and a score of smaller secret operations had collapsed or were crumbling in a major German *ratissage* involving all of northwest Europe. It was a dark hour for SOE.

Gubbins was forty-seven, the son of a diplomat and a graduate of Cheltenham. Born in the Outer Hebridean island of Obbe, he was of illustrious Scots ancestry. For nearly a thousand years his clan had produced some of Scotland's leading soldiers. One of his forebears, Major Gillies MacBain, filled the breach in the wall at Culloden and, before he was killed by a ball in the head, slew fourteen Hanoverians; another, Major General William MacBean, of the 93rd Foot, won a Victoria Cross for a similar act of bravery at the breach of the Begum Bagh at Lucknow in 1858.

Gubbins himself was a gunner who had become a "modern" general, one of the few high commanders to appreciate that the wars of the mid-twentieth century would be fought as often and as fiercely in the underground as on the battlefield. He had spent most of his military career involved in the warfare of special means—a combination of guerrilla tactics, political warfare, sabotage, deception, and systematically applied violence of every description. In 1919 he had served in North Russia against the Bolsheviks; in 1921–22 he had fought with the Irish guerrillas; in 1925–28 he had wrestled with Indian insurgents. He had worked extensively in MI-R, the War Office's branch for unorthodox warfare; he had been chief of the British military mission at Warsaw at the outbreak of the war, and when Poland surrendered, he had virtually walked from Warsaw to Bucharest with the Polish General Staff, bringing with him much to do with the Polish attack on Enigma. He had led a Commando group to Norway during the German invasion in 1940; he was put in command of the British guerrilla organization laid down to fight the Germans if they invaded and occupied the British Isles. He had helped found SOE and before becoming its chief had commanded its London Group, the branch that had controlled and executed operations in western Europe during the past two and a half years.

Gubbins had also made extensive contributions to the technical literature of clandestine warfare. His booklet *The Art of Guerrilla Warfare* arose from his impressions of the weakness "of formed bodies of troops faced by a hostile population that was stiffened by a few resolute gunmen. . . ." His *Partisan Leader's Handbook* advised how to lay road ambushes and derail locomotives. Another booklet, *How to Use High Explosives,* fell into the wrong hands after the war and caused British—and other—colonial authorities much trouble. Gubbins's theories were blunt and practical. "Guerrilla actions will usually take place at point blank range as the result of an ambush or raid. . . . Undoubtedly, therefore, the most effective weapon for the guerrilla is the sub-machine gun." The thing to do with an informer, he advised, was to kill him quickly.

As a man, Gubbins blended Celtic charm and stealth with English pragmatism. He understood thoroughly the close relationship between ideological and orthodox warfare; and he knew how to inspire, lead and control the idealists, eccentrics, hotheads and psychopaths who crowded the guerrilla scene. Within his own organization, and in his dealings with the men and women who worked for the Allies in enemy territory, he was an officer of unusual honesty, intelligence, justice and humanity. His men were completely loyal to him, as he was completely loyal to them, and he was much admired by the Allied military hierarchy.

Gubbins was not alone when he arrived at Storey's Gate. With him was the executive of F section, the SOE branch concerned with British special operations against the Germans in France and French territories. Each country in which SOE functioned was represented at headquarters by what was called a "country section," and the chief of F section was Colonel Maurice Buckmaster, a former manager of the Ford Motor Company in Paris and a man of great administrative ability whose job was to make the turbulent army of the shadows in France conform to the general Allied strategy. His operations officer was Major Gerry Morel, a former insurance broker in Paris and a first-class linguist; and the fourth man was Major Nicholas Bodington, a former Reuters correspondent in Paris and now an important member of F section.

The news they brought to the Chiefs of Staff at Storey's Gate was grave. Through the Prosper disaster, F section had lost not only Prosper himself and his small team of organizers, wireless operators and couriers, but also some of F section's main agents, perhaps 1500 of their sub-agents, and almost all the arms, ammunition and explosives that had been flown to and hidden in northern France ready for use by the French underground in support of D-Day. This was serious enough; worse—as Gubbins reported —was the fact that the disaster was having even wider repercussions. The French were beginning to lose confidence in F section, and their growing suspicion and distrust of SOE might severely hamper future operations.

The tragedy was the latest setback suffered by F section in a long serpentine catalogue of misfortunes that had plagued SOE ever since it was founded by Churchill in 1940 with the command: "And now set Europe ablaze." Such disasters were, at least in part, due to the nature of SOE itself. It had been formed to harness to the Allied cause the forces of idealism, patriotism and hatred in occupied Europe; its purpose, as M. R. D. Foot, SOE's official postwar historian, wrote, was to make "stabbing attacks . . . between the chinks of the enemy's military and economic armour," in order to "induce in him a feeling of insecurity, and to weaken him strategically; both directly by material loss, and obliquely by dispersing his forces on to police tasks." The tactics were those employed by Hera when she sent the gadfly to madden Io. For, as Foot remarked, "unsettling the minds of enemy commanders could be of critical importance. If they were unsettled enough, commanders would lose their grip on the main battle, lose the campaign, even lose the war."

But as Gubbins knew well, SOE's strength was also its weakness. F section had recruited anyone prepared to kill Germans—a ragged underground army of Catholics, Communists, capitalists, princes, Protestants, artisans, factory workers, syndicalists, synarchists. The French underground movement was a ragamuffin army like the Sinn Feiners of Ireland, the Spanish insurgents in the Napoleonic and Civil wars, the Maoist guerrillas in China, the Afghan frontiersmen, the American colonialists, the Russian revolutionaries. Few among the French partisans had the innate sense of security which guerrilla warfare demanded; they were, in the main, ordinary people who barely knew how to fire a pistol or lay a charge of *plastique*. They were as liable to penetration from without as to treachery from within. Yet Gubbins believed they might be of use to the Allies on D-

Day—if they were given time to form, train and learn the crafts of clandestinity.

At great cost, F section had begun to do this, sending many scores of agents, wireless operators and couriers—and many tons of supplies—into the field to organize, train and equip the *résistants*. But now F section's work in the Paris region lay in ruin, and Gubbins and Buckmaster feared that many of the most important French *réseaux* might not be operational again in time for D-Day. What had happened? It was too early, Gubbins reported, to make a complete assessment, but the damage was very great. The true extent of that damage, however, and the reasons behind it, would not emerge until long after the war. Even then many of the facts would remain so obscure that one historian would describe the Prosper disaster as "a skein so tangled, a story so convoluted, attitudes of mind so Byzantine as . . . to have defied rational analysis." That story began with Prosper himself.

On the afternoon of October 1, 1942, Major Francis Suttill, the most important F section agent yet to go to France, was preparing for his mission in a Nissen hut on the edge of Manston Airfield in Kent. He was to leave that night. Colonel Buckmaster was with him, and together they made a final check to ensure that there was nothing on his person to reveal who he really was—an Anglo-Frenchman, born at Lille in 1910 of a French mother and English father; a lawyer called to the bar at Lincoln's Inn; educated at Lille and Stoneyhurst; a commissioned officer in the East Surrey Regiment; and now an F section agent with seven months' training. His mission would be to establish *réseaux* in northern, central and eastern France and bring them under his personal control in Paris, and he now assumed his cover identity: "François Desprée," traveler in agricultural produce, Belgian, born at Lille in 1910 of a French father and Belgian mother. He also assumed his F section cryptonym—"Prosper," from Prosper of Aquitaine, the fifth-century Christian writer and disciple of St. Augustine, who preached grace and predestination.

As a personality, however, Suttill did not change; he was a "brave, ambitious man of strong character, with marked gifts of leadership and charm," and "the nimble wits common in his profession. . . ." He had had no previous connection with the secret services of any nation, but his training reports spoke of his unusual coolness and natural ability as a clandestine. No mention was made of his weaknesses, for Suttill would also emerge as a man with a special, heavily camouflaged loneliness and a conviction that he was to become the seed of a French revolution against the Nazis. But that, F section considered, was the stuff of a good clandestine—an intelligent, controlled, political passion.

There was nothing about Prosper to show that he had ever been in England. His clothes, shoes, hat, cigarettes, money, personal furniture, papers, haircut, toilet equipment—all bespoke a gentleman of Lille. As the check progressed, a Lysander took off from F section's secret airbase at Gibraltar Farm, near Tempsford in Buckinghamshire, about 40 miles north of London, gathering height over the flat fields of sodden kale and the *buhr* where the children of Alfred the Great slew the Danish King of East Anglia, Guthrum II. The aircraft was a unit of one of the RAF's "Moon Squadrons"—so-called because they usually operated only when the moon's position favored clandestine missions into Europe. By D-Day, the unit would have made 2562 sorties into enemy territory, flying in 1000 British agents, bringing out some 2000 men and women wanted in London on secret business, and delivering a total of 40,000 containers of war stores to various underground organizations.

The Lysander landed at Manston and taxied over to the little compound where F section prepared its agents for their missions. Buckmaster—"F"—made Prosper a small farewell present, as he usually did when seeing agents off: gold cufflinks for the men, gold powder compacts for the women. They were a token of his high regard for them, and also, as he said, if they ran into trouble and needed some money in a hurry, the gift could be pawned or sold. Prosper waddled out to the aircraft in his parachute, and a little later the Lysander took off for France. Just after midnight, Prosper leaped out of the plane, his parachute billowed open, and he landed in a meadow near Vendôme, the old walled city about 110 miles south of Paris where Richard the Lionheart had vanquished Philippe Augustus. Prosper had arrived.

The dangers ahead were formidable, both from within and without, but Prosper soon began to build his organization. As Foot described his task: "The persevering efforts (Prosper) put into clandestine recruiting, grouping, organization of future insurgents, were a sort of Penelope's web, continually unpicked by the Gestapo, of which the bloody threads were obstinately re-knotted night by night." Nevertheless, in a remarkably short time Prosper had gathered together the nuclei of what would become important *réseaux,* including "Physician," "Donkeyman," "Bricklayer," "Chestnut," "Butler," "Satirist," "Cinema," "Orator," "Surveyor" and "Priest." He established communications, *courrier* (secret mail), intelligence, action, finance, and medical branches, and his organization began to grow. Before long he would have some 10,000 clandestines working for him. But among them were German double agents; and soon, the Abwehr and the SD learned that Prosper was in France, Prosper learned that they knew, and a deadly *pas de deux* began.

The Germans' knowledge of him was not due completely to the work of double agents; Prosper's own sense of security was not all that it might have been. He needed companions and sometimes dined publicly with his staff—an unwise practice in a world where informers flourished. Moreover, he had a streak of bravado, a carelessness commonplace in men experiencing great power for the first time. On one occasion it was reported to F that Prosper had been seen showing a Montmartre nightclub audience how a Sten submachine gun worked. On another, he entered into negotiations with the SD for the release from jail of two female members of his *réseau*. He paid 1 million francs for them (£5,000 or $24,000) and was dismayed to find two elderly whores waiting for his men when they got to the rendezvous.

Prosper's task soon became too large for him to handle without a deputy. He badly needed a wireless operator upon whom he could depend; he also needed a friend and confidant. Accordingly, believing himself to be relatively safe, he sent for Major Gilbert Norman, who arrived by parachute near Tours on the night of November 1/2, 1942. Norman would become the second central figure in the Prosper tangle. Aged twenty-eight, he had been born at St. Cloud, near Paris, of a French mother and an English father who was a senior partner in a firm of international chartered accountants and a former president of the British Chamber of Commerce in Paris. Educated in France and England, Norman was articled to the London office of his father's firm, and joined the British army in 1940. He was commissioned into the Durham Light Infantry, served as a liaison officer with General Sikorski's Polish army headquarters, and volunteered for SOE early in 1942. His code name was "Archambault," but he was known in the field more generally as "Gilbert." This would lead to confusion with another "Gilbert" who was the third central figure in the web, Henri A. E. Dericourt.

Of all the characters in that weird cavalcade, Dericourt was the most obscure. A Frenchman by nationality, he had been an airline pilot with Air France, working between Paris and Berlin. A man of exceptional intelligence and nerve, he was engaging, persuasive, handsome and skilled at creating a good first impression. When he arrived in London from Paris on September 8, 1942, he was greeted at the railway station by André Dewavrin, the chief of de Gaulle's intelligence bureau, the Bureau Central de Renseignements et d'Action (Militaire) (BCRA), and was taken immediately for interrogation and security clearance by MI-5 to their center in Battersea, the Royal Victoria Patriotic Asylum for the Orphan Daughters of Soldiers and Sailors Killed in the Crimean War. There, he told his interrogators that at the outbreak of the war he had been with the French Air Force at Aleppo. He was, he said, a captain, and had been a transport and test pilot. When Syria was overrun by British Imperial forces he had volunteered his services to a British airline, was accepted, and had worked in the Middle East until the beginning of 1942. Then he decided to return to Paris; he told his interrogators that he wished to marry. He did so, moved his wife into an apartment, gave her a large sum of money, and then arranged his passage to England, traveling over a British escape route through Spain and Portugal. Then Dericourt lied. His interrogator asked him whether he had been in contact at any time with the intelligence service of any power. Dericourt replied firmly that he had never had anything to do with secret service. But Major Bodington of F section had known Dericourt in Paris before the war, and knew that he had done some work for "at least one continental secret service." But which one: the British, the French, or the German? Dericourt himself said it was *not* a German service.

The security authorities would not give Dericourt a clean bill of health. He was too facile, his wife was still in France and he was therefore liable to pressure from the Gestapo. At any time in his long journey to England he could have been suborned by the enemy, he appeared to have too much money, and he had lied about his prewar involvement in espionage. There was also evidence that he might be well disposed toward BCRA, which the British security authorities found undesirable. Yet Dericourt was a first-rate pilot with 4000 hours' experience, he knew what there was to know about the ground handling of aircraft and F section badly needed a skilled air movements officer in France. His British employers testified to his ability, Bodington spoke highly of him, Dericourt expressed no desire to work for the Gaullists, and so he was taken on by F section. His training reports—he underwent only parachute and Lysander training—confirmed the good impression Dericourt had created, and on the night of January 22/23, 1943, he was parachuted into France near Pithiviers, north of Orléans.

Dericourt made his way to Paris and lived quite openly with his wife, Janine, at 58 rue Pergolèse, near the Avenue Foch and the Avenue de la Grande Armée—Gestapo territory. He lived under his own name; he was, he said, too well known to use another. And he explained his absence to his friends by saying he had been on business in Marseilles. It was only a dangerous coincidence that Dericourt's next-door neighbor was the redoubtable Hugo Bleicher, one of the most celebrated of the Abwehr's counterespionage officers in France. Their paths crossed, but not in such a manner that treachery was implied. Bleicher knew who Dericourt was and what he was doing in France, but such was the rivalry between the Abwehr and the SD that Bleicher did nothing to expose Dericourt, for the moment. Dericourt also knew who his neighbor was, but he had friends in the German intelligence hierarchy who were more powerful than Bleicher. For shortly after his return to France, Dericourt dined with Hans Boemelburg, a homosexual and alcoholic Bavarian who was a high officer of the SD in France, and with the SD's wireless expert, Josef Goetz. It later emerged that Dericourt had known Boemelburg before the war when Boemelburg was the SD police attaché at the German Embassy in Paris. Whatever the nature of their wartime association, Dericourt was listed on the SD's files as "V-mann BOE-48"—a confidential agent, the forty-eighth in the employment of Boemelburg. In due course, Boemelburg handed Dericourt over to Standartenführer SS H. J. Kieffer, the chief of the SD's counter-espionage service in France. And Dericourt, it was later revealed, accepted from Kieffer about 4 million francs (£20,000 or $80,000) in cash to buy a farm in the south. From every standpoint it was a sinister association for one of F section's key agents.

Dericourt's mission was among the most important of all British (and Allied) agents in France. As air movements officer for the Paris region, he sought out secret landing fields for the RAF's "Moon Squadrons," laid flarepaths for their landings and organized their takeoffs. He received incoming agents and helped them on their way to their destinations; and he arranged hiding places and transport for those agents on their way to England. He and his circuit—codenamed "Farrier"—were responsible for the security of the landing fields, and for keeping them clear of the very real hazards of such obstacles as herds of cattle or angry bulls. He was also responsible for all communications to and from London relating to air movements, and to do his work he needed a very wide knowledge of, and range of contacts in, the secret world.

Nominally at least, Dericourt was connected to Prosper, and each knew a good deal about the other's programs and assignments. This presupposed a relationship of trust between the two men, but did Prosper know that Dericourt was wining and dining with the enemy? And if he did, did he know why? The answer was no. Prosper knew nothing of Dericourt's association with the SD for many months; and when he suspected that some sort of connection did exist, it was, for Prosper, too late. But from the late spring of 1943 onwards, Prosper began to grow increasingly uneasy about Dericourt, without saying why to anyone in the field, and it became evident later that his uneasiness had to do with Dericourt's handling of the secret mail.

The efficiency of the German wireless detection service made it dangerous for SOE wireless operators to spend more than a few minutes on the air at any one time. Therefore F section agents often sent their longer reports and documents to London in the form of air mail, while London, in turn, used the *courrier* extensively to communicate its instructions to the field. The handling of this *courrier* became Dericourt's responsibility; and at length, Prosper began to suspect that he was showing it to the SD. His suspicions were well founded, for Dericourt had established the practice of taking the mail to Kieffer and leaving it with him long enough for the SD to read or copy it. Dericourt's only explanation for this apparent act of treachery was made very much later; he did it, he said, because he did not think the mail was really very important, and for showing it to the Germans he was permitted by Kieffer to conduct his air movements without German interference.

It was an ingenious explanation, and, in part, true. The Chiefs of Staff did not, at that time, rely upon communications from SOE agents in the field as a valuable source of intelligence about the Germans; the material was too often found unreliable or misleading, for it often reflected deception schemes. They preferred to depend upon MI-6 for their intelligence, and in really important matters there was often Ultra. But the *courrier* did contain a good deal of information about the personalities and politics of SOE sub-agents and *résistants*. Thus, in a sense, it was of more interest to Berlin than to London; and from it, the SD and the Abwehr could learn much about the structure of the various *réseaux*. As for communications from London, they, too, might prove of great value—unless London was aware that the Germans were reading the *courrier*. In that case, there could be other more devious reasons why Dericourt would permit them to see it.

It would later emerge that London was aware of Dericourt's association with the SD, just as the SD was aware that he was working for SOE. What, therefore, was Dericourt's game? Was he an SD man who had penetrated F section, or an F section man who was penetrating the SD? Or was he in reality working for another British secret agency and using F section as a cover? If so, did F section know and approve of activities on his part that might endanger its other agents in France? The conjugations were many, and the possibility of some such intrigue was the first of Prosper's strange bedfellows.

There was a second—carelessness. By the late spring of 1943, Prosper's network had become the largest of any agency of any power in France. It stretched from the old battlefields around Sedan, through Paris, across the majestic wine and châteaux country of the Loire, and down to the beaches at Nantes. At Paris, it was linked with a second major circuit—Scientist—and its affairs were connected with those of a large number of smaller *réseaux*. In all, Prosper came to control and supply no less than sixty large and small *réseaux*—a network that was far too large for safety. Its leaders, Prosper included, had become over-confident, and the French *résistants* displayed a native unawareness of the dangers of gossip in clandestinity. They were good at conspiracy but poor at silence. In consequence, as one British agent reported: "95 per cent of the people arrested were caught simply because their friends had been incapable of keeping their mouths shut."

Nevertheless, the *résistants* were unremitting in their campaign of violence against the conquerors. And the British stepped up their supplies of arms, ammunition and explosives. The RAF, in May 1943 alone, dropped 240 containers to Prosper. These were large drops to a single *réseau* at this stage in the war, for each container held 6 Bren light machine guns with 1000 rounds per gun, 36 rifles with 150 rounds, 27 Stens with 300 rounds per gun, 5 pistols with 50 rounds per gun, 52 grenades, 156 field dressings, 6600 rounds of 9-mm parabellum, and 3168 rounds of .303 rifle ammunition. The miracle was not that these drops were successful but that the Germans took so long to find them. They were parachuted in the dead of night from noisy aircraft in remote areas where sound carried for miles and where every hue of German agent abounded. And they were collected in an atmosphere of carnival by men who behaved as cheerfully and as exuberantly as if they were at market. As one agent would write home:

> There was nothing either quiet or clandestine about my first encounter with what the French call *"un parachutage."* Once the containers were released there was considerable drama. *Albert* began the proceedings by shouting "Attention everybody, the *bidons* descend!" Everyone present repeated this, adding advice to *Bobo, Alphonse* and *Pierre,* or whoever was nearest to "have a care that the sacred *bidons* do not crush thee." Once the containers had landed the parachute stakes were on. The winner was whoever could roll and hide away the most parachutes before being spotted by someone else. The bullock carts then came up with much encouragement from the drivers such as "But come, my old one, to the *bidons* advance!" Then began the preliminary discussions as to how the first container would be hoisted on to the cart, and who should have the honour of commencing. I found I had to go through the actions of beginning to hoist one end myself before, with loud cries of "But no, my captain, permit me" or, for example, "My captain! What an affair!" my helpers would then get on with the job.

Under the circumstances, it is not surprising that the Germans' store of knowledge about Prosper, his lieutenants, his sub-agents and his *réseaux* began to expand. Casualties in his network started to rise sharply, and those arrested were forced to talk under the brutal inquisitions of their captors. The Germans, controlling every aspect of French life from the purchase of wine to the burial of the dead, countered violence with violence. Hitler had become disturbed by the rising tempo of espionage and disorder in the western marches of his empire, and on his personal orders, the SD and the Abwehr launched "Operation Donar," named after the German god of thunder, to destroy all the forces of resistance, sabotage and espionage in France and northwest Europe. Patriot after patriot was rounded up to face an SD firing squad, and the blood on the execution ground of Mont Valérien in the Paris suburbs stained the earth ever more deeply. More and more *résistants* found themselves bent at dawn beneath "the widow"—the guillotine. The prisons were crowded, and French youth began to flee into the hills and mountains to form the *maquis*.

As each side turned the screws of vengeance and retribution, F section tried to impose discipline and order upon the *résistants* against the day they could be used as patriot armies in the German rear. But it was not easy; the French underground had never been so independent, prickly and xenophobic, so determined and impetuous. Nor had the Germans ever been so thorough and ruthless. It was in this explosive atmosphere that the fuse of Cockade and Starkey was lit—the third of Prosper's strange bedfellows. Trying to convince the Germans that an invasion of France was near could only inflame their determination to stamp out the forces of resistance wherever they appeared. And under the impression that liberation was at hand, the *résistants* themselves could only step up their campaign of sabotage and murder, and thus risk exposure and capture. Moreover, the SOE/PWE plan for Starkey made provision for deliberately misinforming F section agents in the field; even before that plan had been approved by the Chiefs of Staff and become fully operational in mid-July 1943, certain key F section agents were flown to London for "invasion" briefings, and others sent to France with instructions to carry out "pre-invasion" activities. They were to be informed, at the proper moment, that Starkey was only a rehearsal; but by then, for some of them—including Prosper—it would be too late.

Were F section agents deemed expendable? And if so, by whom? In the early stages of the preparations for Starkey, there was evidence that F section itself was misinformed. According to a statement made by Buckmaster after the war: "In the middle of 1943 [i.e., the period that Starkey preparations were being made] we had had a top secret message telling us that D-day might be closer than we thought. This message had been tied up with international politics on a level far above our knowledge and we, of course, had acted upon it without question." His orders, as he remembered them in a memorandum to the Foreign Office dated November 11, 1964, had been to "accelerate his section's preparations to support an invasion, in case it turned out possible to mount one after all later in the year"—despite the fact that the Combined Chiefs of Staff had already decided at Casablanca that no invasion from England would be possible until 1944. It may well have been, then, that F section acted in good faith, and that the organization, both in London and in France, was being used, to some degree at least, as yet another "unconscious agent" in the Starkey deception.

Prosper himself was among the first of F section's agents to be warned to expect an invasion that summer. He arrived in London, on a flight handled by Dericourt, about the third week of May 1943, and at his briefings he was instructed to have all his men and plans ready. He was also given, as Foot would record, "an 'alert' signal (for the invasion), warning the whole circuit to stand by." All this was, of course, highly misleading, and it must be presumed that Prosper—and perhaps his briefing officer—were deliberately primed with misinformation designed to support Starkey. But at the same time he was given the strictest instructions to keep a firm grip on the *résistants;* the British government wanted no bloodbaths.

During his meetings at London, Prosper at last mentioned his fears about the reliability of Dericourt. He was the chief of his circuit and his opinions should have been valued. But they were ignored—an indication that Dericourt's mission, whatever it might have been, was considered more important than the secret *courrier,* the security of the Prosper circuit and even the life of Prosper himself. Before his return flight to France, Prosper asked to be received by Pierre Culioli, one of his own sub-agents in the Sologne, rather than by Dericourt. But Culioli had warned London— through Dericourt—that the Germans were making a massive *ratissage* in his area. There is no evidence that this warning ever reached London; but if it did, it, too, was ignored. Prosper was received by Culioli on June 12 and eluded the *ratissage.* But two more F section agents, John Macalister and Frank Pickersgill, who parachuted into the same area three days later, were not so fortunate.

"Suttill," wrote Foot, "returned to clandestine duty in the belief that an invasion was probably imminent"; but back in Paris he began to display profound unease. He moved his safehouse suddenly, without telling anyone his new address, and went to ground in the maze of ancient streets near the Porte St. Denis, where he found an old workingman's hotel in the rue Mazagran. He never discussed the cause of his unease. Perhaps he suspected that he was in danger from the SD; perhaps he suspected that he was being used as a pawn in some deception scheme. Whatever his fears, he was absolutely convinced that the Allies would invade France that summer, and he behaved accordingly, preparing himself, his lieutenants and his *réseaux* for a general outbreak of guerrilla warfare in concert with the landings. He had been encouraged to put his head up when he should have kept it down—and the Germans cut it off.

On the night of June 22/23, 1943, fifteen SD officers swarmed into Prosper's dingy little hotel. Prosper was not there; but when he returned to his room the following day, he found himself looking down the barrels of four Walther pistols. He was seized, overpowered, handcuffed, and carted off to SD headquarters on the Avenue Foch where, within the hour, he was on Kieffer's well-known lavender carpet, under a great chandelier. Prosper was certain he had been betrayed, for he had moved to the hotel only two or three days before without telling anyone his new address. It was alleged after the war that he had given it to F while he was in London and that he had been betrayed by "London" directly by wireless to SD headquarters, but there was not a scintilla of evidence to support that charge. It would also be alleged that Kieffer obtained the address from Dericourt's *courrier*, but that explanation seemed as unlikely as a betrayal from London, for Prosper had not told Dericourt of his new address, nor had he committed it to the *courrier*. Kieffer may have shadowed Prosper to the hotel, or he may have obtained the address from Gilbert Norman, who was captured just before Prosper was taken. Foot would advance another possibility: that Prosper was betrayed by Roger Bardet, the deputy chief of Prosper's Donkeyman circuit south of Paris and a man who had survived an earlier *ratissage* by agreeing to work for the Germans. But how did Bardet know where Prosper was hiding?

Whatever the reason for his capture, Prosper now began his Calvary. He had no hope of hiding behind his cover; Kieffer knew exactly who he was and what he had been doing. But he did not know the locations of the stores of arms and ammunition that had been dropped to the *résistants*. Prosper's first interrogation lasted sixty-four hours, during which time he was allowed no rest, food or water, and was kept standing at attention. What did he know of the invasion plans? Where and when would the Allies land? What was the subject of his conferences in London? Where were the arms dumps? Where were his wireless posts? His interrogators did not try torture, yet; they were merely relentless. But Prosper told them nothing of value.

Several other of Prosper's lieutenants—Gilbert Norman included—had been taken prisoner and were also under interrogation. But Kieffer suspected that Norman might be the weak link. He was correct. Norman finally broke down. But he was not as cooperative as Kieffer thought him to be. He tried to alert London to his capture by inserting a warning in a wireless message that he was forced to send, and he tried to escape. He almost succeeded and was stopped only when he was shot by one of the guards. But he did begin to reveal the locations of the arms dumps, and Prosper, suspecting that the Germans would soon have all the information they were after, decided to try to use the whereabouts of the armories as bargaining counters for the lives of his men.

It was Kieffer who proposed a pact to Prosper and Norman. He said that if they revealed the locations of all the dumps, he would guarantee that none of their colleagues who had been, or might later be, captured would be killed or ill-treated. At Prosper's insistence he sent to Himmler for the authority to enter into such a pact, and although Prosper thought the guarantee would be rendered worthless the moment he delivered up the arms, he agreed to the bargain.

Prosper was then taken to the Gestapo headquarters at Prinzalbrecht-strasse in Berlin, leaving Norman to execute the pact. Armed with maps and letters supplied by Norman, and sometimes accompanied by Norman himself, the SD sped to all parts of Prosper's territory to confiscate some 470 tons of arms and stores. Then the SS came back to arrest hundreds of his sub-agents. But the Germans did honor their pact; the SD spared many lives, although not usually those of the principals. Prosper and his lieutenants went quickly to their deaths. Norman was kept alive for a time, but the rest were shot and cremated. Of all the members of Prosper's lieutenancy, only Culioli survived. After the war, he came back a wraith to face, tragically enough, a French military tribunal which tried to fasten upon him some of the responsibility for the Prosper tragedy. The charges failed.

The collapse of the Prosper network generated shockwaves far beyond its own boundaries, and F section knew almost immediately that its outposts in France had been struck by a cyclone. It also knew of the suspicions attaching to Dericourt in the affair. But nothing was done to bring him home or to liquidate him; on the contrary, it was decided to entrust Bodington to his care. To find out how far the disaster had spread, Bodington was authorized to fly into France to a Dericourt reception—a sure sign that F section still trusted Dericourt, despite all the allegations.

Their trust was well placed; Bodington went in and was received by Dericourt. Kieffer heard that he was in the country and demanded his address from Dericourt, but Dericourt said he did not know it. Bodington went to ground with a price of £10,000 on his head—a tribute to his value to the SD, for the going rate for a live F section officer was £5,000. Dericourt did not try to collect. Bodington was eventually evacuated safely, but not before SOE was confronted with a new specter—the burning of Scientist, the great F section circuit which stretched from the foothills of the Pyrenees up the Biscayan coast to the Vendée, and then turned east to join hands with Prosper in Paris. It was a pyre only a shade less furious than Prosper's; and the flames, like Prosper's, had been ignited by a fuse that seemed to lead directly to London and Starkey.

"Scientist" was Claude de Baissac, a London-trained F section officer of Mauritian origins. He was thirty-five, a man of "exceptional character," who "produced results of exceptional merit." He had landed near Nîmes, dropping blind with a wireless operator, on July 30, 1942, and he began to build Scientist with such efficiency that F soon sent him reinforcements, notably his sister Lise, who was also a London-trained officer and who became his liaison with Prosper—Baissac and Suttill were close friends. The affairs of Scientist were extremely complex; and like Prosper, it soon grew too big for safety. But F thought so highly of Scientist that the RAF was commissioned to fly to him in one month no less than 120 heavy aircraft loads of war stores—over 2000 containers, more than Prosper ever received.

There was, however, a motive other than admiration to explain London's massive generosity. "Evidently something powerful was building up," wrote R. A. Bourne-Patterson, the Scotsman who was F's deputy. Something was—and the Germans, too, perceived it. In fact, they were intended to perceive it. The LCS and A-Force, working together on a joint Cockade-Zeppelin strategic deception—their grandest so far—were seeking to distract OKW's attention from the Allied invasion of Italy at Salerno on September 9, 1943, the same day as D-Day for Starkey. The object of the stratagem, as far as Scientist was concerned, was to make it appear to OKW that the Allies would not only land in the Pas de Calais for Starkey, but also in the general region of Bordeaux. OKW was extremely sensitive to the possibility that the Allies might try to seize the great port of Bordeaux, and panzer units and several good infantry divisions were stationed in the region to contest any such invasion. The LCS hoped to induce Hitler to keep those divisions where they were, thus removing them from service in Italy, and to achieve that, it relied on the known indiscretion of Scientist sub-agents.

Arms and stores were poured into Scientist's circuits to simulate a pre-invasion build-up; and twice that summer, Scientist, who controlled over 10,000 armed men—a very useful force indeed, particularly since many of them were formidable Gascons—was ordered to stand by for operations through the BBC's Avis service. As the LCS intended, Scientist sub-agents gossiped, the gossip reached the SD in the area, and the SD, which had been pursuing Donar in a more leisurely fashion than Kieffer in Paris, reacted vigorously. Perhaps the Germans would have lashed out anyway, but just as Starkey inflamed the SD in the Paris region, so the threat of invasion precipitated new efforts to crush the resistance forces in the Bordeaux region. The Germans struck and arrested and deported—or executed—some three hundred leading Scientist *résistants*.

The downfall of the Prosper and Scientist networks had undoubtedly been caused, in part, by carelessness and lack of security among the *résistants* themselves, and, in part, by the diligence of the German counterespionage authorities. But to many Frenchmen involved in the affair, it seemed that both networks had been deliberately compromised by the British solely for the purposes of deception. The charges leveled against the British secret agencies, even long after the war was over, were various and grave. It was alleged not only that *résistants* had been encouraged to undertake clandestine operations in support of an invasion that would not take place—operations that cost some of them their lives—but also that

Prosper and other resistance leaders had been primed with misinformation about an invasion in the certain knowledge that they would be caught, break under interrogation and tell the Germans what they thought to be the truth: that an invasion was, in fact, imminent. Dericourt's activities, in particular, came under heavy suspicion, for it seemed that in showing the Germans the secret *courrier*—either with the permission of the British or because he was actually working for the Germans—he had directly contributed to Prosper's capture and the collapse of his circuit.

For a time all these charges went unanswered, in spite of persistent questions raised in Parliament, the press and in various British and French histories. The traditional *omertà*—the conspiracy of silence that shrouded most of Britain's secret wartime activities—enveloped the affair. But such ghosts were not so easily laid, and conscious that there was an undercurrent of suspicion in his dealings with French leaders, several of whom were involved in the resistance and could now make or break Britain's attempt to enter the European Common Market, Harold Macmillan as Prime Minister, whose name appeared on the distribution lists of many A-Force operational documents, eventually did what no Prime Minister had ever done before; in the early 1960's he commissioned an official history of the operations of a British secret service. The result, Foot's book, *SOE in France,* was admirable and invaluable, but incomplete. Foot himself explained that he was considerably disadvantaged in his research because a fire had consumed much of SOE's central registry just after the war, and what remained was in a state of what he called "authentic confusion." Some papers were, Foot would admit, probably falsified, others deliberately destroyed. All F section wireless messages had vanished, and they would have explained much. Morcover, Foot said he did not have access to any documents regarding large-scale deception operations. Nevertheless, he sought to rebut the charges leveled against SOE in the Prosper and Scientist affairs. He scoffed at the notion that the British had deliberately betrayed Prosper. "An assertion," he declared, "as absurd as this last one calls to mind the Duke of Wellington's reply to the man who called him Captain Jones: 'Sir, if you can believe that, you can believe anything.' " He also denied that Prosper and other F section organizers were primed with false information which, when they were captured and interrogated, they would reveal to the Germans. Citing Mincemeat as an example of how cleverly that kind of deception was practiced, he commented:

. . . . to send a few S O E agents into France primed with rumours that France was going to be invaded in 1943, on the off chance that some of them would fall into German hands and pass the rumours on, would have been a project lacking alike in bite, finish, and viability. Besides, it is undoubtedly the case that no use was made of S O E's work in France for any purposes of deception, then or later: no one trusted the agents enough for such delicate tasks.

So much, in the official view, for the allegations that Prosper and Scientist were used as pawns in a deception. But at the time that Foot was researching and writing his book, the LCS and strategic deception were still highly classified matters. Foot did not acknowledge the dominant role that deception had played in British military operations in the summer of 1943, either because he had not seen the pertinent documents or because he prudently adopted the then official line that deception, which, during the cold war, was still being practiced on a large scale, simply did not exist. Thus, Foot made no mention of Cockade or Starkey, yet, contradicting himself, he confirmed the role that deception had played in the collapse of the Scientist circuit. Writing that the BBC, as part of the deception plan that covered the surrender of Italy and the Salerno assault, twice alerted every active SOE circuit in France to expect an invasion—alerts that were intended to reach German ears through the known lack of security of the Scientist circuit—he commented that: "The staff concerned with deception relied on indiscretion, and might have thought more about safety."

Finally, when late in 1969 the LCS found it could no longer conceal its existence, Sir Ronald Wingate was authorized to speak on behalf of Bevan and his colleagues. But he, too, stated that there was no connection between the LCS and SOE. With a politician's skill in the precise use of words, he made a point of stressing, in the special context of the French resistance, that "We never used SOE for the purposes of deception; they were far too amateurish. We used the professionals." The "professionals" were, of course, MI-6 and, to a lesser extent, the Foreign Office and the Political Warfare Executive; but Wingate would not discuss what connection these LCS executive agencies had with SOE and the resistance movements. It was a fine distinction that was soon lost, for in 1972 documents began to come to light at the National Archives in Washington which showed beyond doubt that SOE itself had actively prepared and executed plans in support of LCS schemes, generally in concert with PWE.

The first of these documents was the SOE/PWE plan for Cockade and Starkey. The second was a note, dated September 3, 1943—six days before D-Day for Starkey—which proved conclusively that SOE was involved in the deception right through to the end on September 9. And it showed that F section agents in the field had been intentionally misinformed about the true nature of the operation. The note, initialed "C.A.B.," was from the Intelligence Section to the Operations Section of COSSAC, which was stage-managing the physical movements of troops, ships and aircraft involved in Starkey; and it read:

In the *Starkey* plan, it was laid down that SOE should communicate with their contacts in occupied territories D–9 to D–7 [nine to seven days before D-Day] informing them that *Starkey* was a rehearsal. SOE have been ordered to hold their hand until Saturday morning. . . . Although all is quiet at present, Colonel Rowlandson [of SOE] could give no guarantees and he would like to be able to give his boys a line as soon as possible.

Here was a clear and undeniable link between the LCS, COSSAC, SOE and F section. The French were correct in their belief that strategic deception had contributed to Prosper's downfall. For Prosper was briefed in London to prepare for a real invasion, and when he returned to the field, he was obedient to his orders. He took chances that, had he known Starkey was a ruse, he might not have taken, and the Germans struck him down, along with every other element of the French underground they could find.

Thus Starkey played a major part in the disaster; but where did Dericourt fit into the puzzle? Was he, in fact, working for the Germans, and had he betrayed Prosper to his SD contacts? Or if someone in London had authorized those contacts, were not the British a party to Prosper's betrayal? What *was* Dericourt's game and where did his loyalties lie? Foot's explanation was curiously incomplete:

The truth is that his only unswerving loyalty was to himself; he was trapped by circumstances between the upper millstone of loyalty to workmates in S O E and the nether millstone of inextricable entanglements with the Gestapo, and did what he could to serve both sides at once.

The truth—or as much of it as will ever be known—would prove to be more complicated than that.

Despite the fact that Prosper and countless other *résistants* fell before the German *ratissage,* Dericourt survived. He continued to operate as air movements officer in the Paris region, although the SD knew all about him and F section had been warned that he was a traitor. However, when allegations that he had changed sides persisted, it was decided to investigate him, and "Operation Knacker"—a man who buys and slaughters useless horses for their meat and bones—was launched to fly him out of France. Dericourt was instructed to meet a Hudson near Angers on the night of February 3/4, 1944, but he was not told that Major Morel would be aboard the plane with orders to bring him to London, at the point of a pistol if needs be.

Dericourt met the plane, and brought with him six agents, all of whom were on the run. As the agents and their belongings were being loaded, Morel told Dericourt that he, too, must go to London. Dericourt said it was quite impossible; the field had to be cleared of bicycles by dawn if it was not to be blown. Morel accepted this explanation when Dericourt promised to be ready to leave for London from the field near Tours on the night of February 8/9. The plane returned without him.

It would now have been possible for Dericourt to seek the sanctuary of the SD had he been a German agent. But he did not, even though he knew that London distrusted him—he could tell that by Morel's manner—and that he would probably not be allowed to return to the field. If that was the case, he was not prepared to leave France without his wife. He adored her and if he left her behind she would certainly be arrested by Kieffer. However, Dericourt saw Kieffer and Goetz before he left Paris. He asked them what service he might perform for the SD when he was in London, and Kieffer told him to find out the date and place of the invasion. It is possible that Kieffer or Goetz also gave him some means—a cipher or secret ink and a postbox—by which to communicate. At any rate, Kieffer must have been fairly certain that Dericourt could still be useful to him even though he was in London; he would never have allowed him to leave France otherwise.

When Dericourt and his wife arrived in Britain, F section handled them with courtesy and respect. Dericourt was not, as might have been thought, held under close arrest. He was put up at the Swan Hotel in Stratford-on-Avon, and then brought to London with his wife and given a room at the Savoy. No one could complain about the comfort of those two hotels; and F section paid the bills. Rarely was F section so generous or so concerned about the comfort of an agent, and this bespoke powerful friends for the suspect Dericourt.

A secret tribunal to investigate Dericourt's activities convened on February 11, 1944, at Northumberland Avenue, near the War Office and convenient to the cells at Scotland Yard. The interrogations were handled by Air Commodore Archibald Boyle, SOE's director of intelligence and security, and H. N. Sporborg, the vice chief of SOE; and at the outset Dericourt's record as air movements officer was the subject of the investigation. It was an impressive record. Between his first operation on March 17/18, 1943, and his last on February 8/9, 1944, he had handled a total of seventeen Lysanders and eight Hudsons in which forty-three agents arrived in France and sixty-seven left for London. He had supervised, without casualties to aircraft or air crews while on the ground, about one-fifth of all secret British air movements into France during that period—including some of MI-6's. This evidence did much to earn him the favor of Sporborg, who could see little direct proof that Dericourt had betrayed any agents to the SD, or that he had changed sides. Air Commodore Boyle, however, delivered the equivocal opinion that "The fact that casualties do not appear to have occurred does not necessarily disprove his treachery."

The tribunal was aware that Dericourt had contact with the SD, and when he undertook to explain how it had come about, he said that shortly after his return to Paris early in 1943, two Lufthansa pilots whom he had known before the war called on him at his flat. They invited him to go out for a drink, he accepted and they left the flat together. Outside, sitting in a car, was a third man—Josef Goetz. Goetz recounted Dericourt's career in detail, Dericourt told his interrogators, and invited him to work for the SD. Dericourt said he felt that it would be useless to refuse; he decided to collaborate. But when he came to London at Easter, he reported his contact with the SD and was, he said, directed to maintain it.

Who in London had given him this direction, and why? At this point the only extant account of the interrogation—Foot's official history—goes silent, discreetly and not unexpectedly. But Bodington later testified that this statement was true. Moreover, there appeared on Dericourt's personal file the penciled note by Bodington: "We know he is in contact with the Germans and also how & why."

The investigation then turned to the question of the secret *courrier,* but, evidently, not with any great anxiety. When Dericourt was challenged about this, he "made the evasive reply that even if he had made correspondence available to the Gestapo, it would have been worth it for the sake of conducting his air operations unhindered."

Buckmaster, Morel and Bodington all testified to Dericourt's fidelity and extraordinary courage and capability in the Allied cause. In this they were supported by Brigadier Eric Mockler-Ferryman, a veteran intelligence officer who had been Eisenhower's G2 in Tunisia and now held Gubbins's former post at SOE—chief of the London Group. Buckmaster offered the powerful testimonial that ". . . when—if ever—the clouds are blown away, I am prepared to bet a large sum that we shall find him entirely innocent of any voluntary dealing with the enemy." Only MI-5, the counterintelligence service that also took part in the investigation, found against Dericourt, and its opinion was hardly an indictment for treachery: ". . . we should, if the decision were entirely (ours), regard the case against him as serious enough to prevent him undertaking any further intelligence work outside this country."

MI-5 had the last word. Dericourt was not allowed to return to the field; but neither was he indicted, jailed or quarantined. It appears that he went back to the Savoy for a time, and then moved into a flat in London with his wife—possibly to communicate with his German contacts, at the direction of the XX-Committee. Whatever his activities, he disappeared from view until after the invasion.

F section was not pleased with the tribunal's ruling. Buckmaster wrote a series of irritable notes about "interference with one of his best circuits by people who did not understand conditions in the field." Morel protested that he was "absolutely revolted" by the ruling. Moreover, Dericourt retained the highest regard of some of the most important and influential intelligence officers in London. Mockler-Ferryman put him in for the Distinguished Service Order, describing Dericourt's "great ability and complete disregard of danger" and, in a direct hint that Dericourt had been something more than an air movements officer for SOE, that he had performed "in 'particularly difficult and highly dangerous' circumstances" that "involved 'keeping up many very dangerous acquaintances, particularly with pilots of the Luftwaffe and Lufthansa.' " Significantly, the DSO was the medal that Menzies most often arranged for those senior agents who had rendered MI-6 important and courageous service; it was a decoration that could not be given to, or retained by, anyone convicted of crime.

When Dericourt reappeared in September 1944, it was, again significantly, as a Spitfire pilot. If he had been an SD agent, if he had betrayed Prosper and everyone else, if he had rendered the Allies some grave disservice, he would never have been allowed to fly again, and certainly not in a high-performance aircraft. He could have defected too easily. But he did not defect; behaving with great courage, he was shot down on operations over France and badly burned. His own country rewarded his exploits as a fighter pilot with the Croix de Guerre, and at the end of the war he returned to live in Paris with his wife, again working for Air France as a pilot.

Yet the cloud of suspicion around Dericourt did not disperse. Was he a hero or a traitor? No one knew. During the period of vengeance in French national life that followed the war, when thousands of people were tried and executed for collaborating with the Germans, every attempt to indict him for grand treason was defeated. But if Dericourt had enemies in France, he also had powerful friends in Britain, and they demonstrated their friendship in arranging an accommodation with an English court on what was clearly a major indictment.

The indictment arose out of an incident that took place on April 11, 1946, when, just as he was about to take his Dakota airliner to Paris on a routine commercial flight, Dericourt was challenged by a customs officer at the old international airport at Croydon. The officer searched his valise and discovered that he was carrying platinum valued at £3158, gold valued at about £1500, and banknotes to the value of £1320; another £100 in notes was found on his person. He was accused of smuggling and found himself liable for fines totaling £18,000 and jail for up to five years. He appeared on remand before the Croydon magistrates on April 12, but, significantly, the case was adjourned on his own assurance that he would return and plead on April 23. He had to fly his aircraft back to Paris, he explained.

As good as his word, Dericourt returned to England, and when he came before the magistrates, his defense was in the hands of Derek Curtis

Bennett, an eminent King's Counsel, and two juniors. Such a formidable team could only have been assembled by somebody with considerable influence and means, which Dericourt did not have. Bennett told the court that Dericourt was carrying the consignment of platinum, gold and banknotes for "the British secret service in France." Then he eloquently described Dericourt's wartime career, and the court was impressed. Dericourt was found guilty, but was fined only £500—a sum that was paid by an unnamed acquaintance. Clearly, matters had been arranged with the court. No one asked what business "the British secret service" might have in peacetime France, and Dericourt did not go to jail. He returned to France, but soon his powerful friends had to come to his defense again—this time when he went on trial for his life.

By 1947, the British and American secret services had finished with their investigation of the former SD executive body in France, including Helmuth Knochen, the chief, and they were handed over to the French. Through interrogation, the French managed to build up what appeared to be a formidable case against Dericourt and a massive indictment for treason was filed against him. The main charge was that he had extracted from the *courrier* some 250 *messages personnels* and had shown them to the SD; from these messages, it seemed to the French, it would have been possible for the Germans to deduce how the various stages of the invasion would unfold. Dericourt was arrested and spent almost eighteen months in Fresnes Prison while the evidence was being assembled. Finally, he came to trial on June 7, 1948.

As was customary, Dericourt was given a choice of trials. He could have a civilian trial, in which case he had the right of appeal if he was found guilty. Or he could elect to go before the Tribunal Militaire Permanent de Paris, a panel of officers, some expert in intelligence matters, whose judgment was absolute. If they found Dericourt guilty, execution was inevitable; there could be no clemency and no appeal. Dericourt, apparently confident of the outcome, elected to face the TMP. He appeared at ten o'clock that morning in a room at the Neuilly Barracks; and as one chronicler noted: "(he was) dressed in a dark blue suit with a discreet white stripe . . . he had had the good taste to remove the *Légion d'Honneur* from his buttonhole. His gaze was direct and his personality commanded instant sympathy. . . ."

When Dericourt presented himself for examination, he did not deny having contact with the Germans. He told the president of the tribunal, M. Dejean de la Batie, the same particulars of how that contact had been established that he had told the SOE inquiry in London. He also told the court that he had informed the British of the contact, that he had received their instruction to continue it, and that, accordingly, he had feigned "to work for them (the Germans) in order to keep the contacts for future exploitation." Dericourt again admitted that he had been a double agent; but for the first and only time he also described his *modus operandi:*

> So as not to awaken their suspicions that I was playing them a double game I gave them the locations of eight airfields I was using in Touraine—eight out of 14. The information which I gave them was of no consequence. I threw sand in their eyes. The eight airfields which I disclosed to them had not been formally accepted by London and I knew that no aircraft would land on them. The resistance did not suffer.

M. Batie exclaimed: "What a dangerous game!" Dericourt retorted: "The more my merit!"

Then the court called the German witnesses. All seemed reluctant to say anything that might convict Dericourt—a reluctance that was interpreted by the French press as a sign that the "British Intelligence Service" had put pressure upon them to keep silent. Cross-examined by Dericourt's famous and expensive attorney, Maître Moro-Giafferi, the Germans were as one in their statements that it was likely that Dericourt had only pretended to work for them, that he had, in fact, told them nothing of value, and that he had interested them only inasmuch as they hoped he might one day be able to tell them the date and place of the invasion. And what of the 250 *messages personnels?* Had Dericourt given them over? Yes, he had, declared Knochen, but they proved useless. They would, said Knochen, have proved of use only if the Allies had landed at the Pas de Calais.

Then came testimony on Dericourt's behalf. Out of the shadows stepped Bodington, whom the newspapers described as "very mysterious" and a member of the "(British) Intelligence Service." When asked if he would employ Dericourt under the same circumstances again, Bodington said yes, he would; if he had had the task of starting F section all over again, he would do so with Dericourt—and without any hesitation whatsoever.

It was powerful testimony. The judges were deeply impressed. No less impressive was the succession of high-ranking Frenchmen called to back Dericourt and Bodington. All claimed to have been handled safely by Dericourt when he was air movements officer. One was General Henri Zeller, a leading member of the resistance, who walked across the courtroom to shake Dericourt by the hand; others included M. Roualt, the Director of the Préfecture de Police, and M. Livry-Level, a deputy for Normandy. A score of people gave evidence of Dericourt's bravery; and another score sent testimonials to the court. When their evidence was done, Moro-Giafferi rose and cried: "If he is guilty of treason, there is still death and the firing squad for traitors. If he is innocent, give him back his honor!"

The judges retired for two minutes, and returned with a unanimous verdict for acquittal on all charges. There was a roar of applause, and the Commissaire du Gouvernement formally discharged the prisoner. He announced that Dericourt was permitted to wear again the rosette of the *Légion d'Honneur,* his medals and his uniform, and Dericourt walked out of the barracks a free man.

The trial had shed some light on Dericourt's wartime mission; under the cover of an SOE agent, he had, apparently, been authorized to penetrate the SD. The suspicion remained that in carrying out that mission he had betrayed other F section agents in the field and had endangered the lives and safety of countless French *résistants*. If he had, who had allowed him to do so? It seemed to many Frenchmen that Dericourt's trial had been rigged. Who was protecting him, and why? Were Dericourt's friends interested merely in rewarding him for his services to the Allied cause? Or were they attempting to conceal an operation that, however inadvertently, had resulted in the loss of a large number of British agents and their comrades in the French underground?

No one was more interested in discovering the answers to these questions than a crusading writer, Miss Jean Overton Fuller, who was investigating the mysterious fate of her friend Princess Noor Inayat Khan. Princess Noor, an SOE agent who had been sent to France in the summer of 1943 to a Dericourt reception, had subsequently been captured and killed under circumstances that seemed, to Miss Overton Fuller, directly linked to the collapse of the Prosper network and Dericourt's ambiguous contact with the SD. She wanted to know who had authorized that contact and why, and cornering Dericourt, she forced from him a series of short statements that further illuminated the nature of his wartime mission. Dericourt told her that not only had he been authorized to maintain contact with the SD, but he had also been given special orders in its handling that involved a "strategic sacrifice." He said he thought Prosper had been the victim of that sacrifice. Miss Overton Fuller then declared: "You believe, then, that the whole 'Prosper' (organization) was sacrificed." Dericourt replied: "My theory—I won't tell it to you—is not so crude as yours. I knew and I reported on my visit in Easter 1943 to London that (Prosper) was penetrated from a very early stage. . . . Prosper's chiefs knew that and they handled it in their own way." Adding that Buckmaster knew nothing of his "other duties," Dericourt said: "I reported to an officer of much higher rank." According to Miss Overton Fuller, Dericourt "did not . . . believe that it was from within SOE that the decision to make a maneuver of the kind he was inclined to credit had been taken." The officers from whom he had received his orders, he said, had been "animated by honest motives," and it was "they" who had helped defend him at both the Croydon and Paris trials. But he refused to tell Miss Overton Fuller who "they" were, the names of the men who had given him his special orders or, for that matter, what those special orders were. "He could reveal nothing more of his instructions," she wrote, "except that they related to the Intelligence side."

Dissatisfied, Miss Overton Fuller went after Dericourt again. He refused to answer any more questions, but in a brief personal statement he wrote:

> . . . I can sleep in peace because I know that I was not responsible for the arrest of *Prosper* . . . or any others. But seeing things now through the eyes of different people, and in a different perspective, I realise they can look different from what they were in truth.
>
> I, like any other British, German or French agent, have to recognise that we could have been abused. We were blind fighting in darkness. To be successful in the missions for which we were responsible, we had often to clear from our way possible causes of nuisance. We used to risk our lives every day, three times a day, with no rest or encouragement. We were rich in what we had in our hearts and in our minds. Today I am rich in the friendship of the people who know what I did.
>
> I can't and won't say more.

There *l'affaire Dericourt* might have ended. But just after the war, suspicious that those in London who had authorized Dericourt's mission were responsible for the collapse of both the Prosper and Scientist networks and other smaller *réseaux* to which they were related, as well as the virtual obliteration of F section operations in and around Paris in the latter half of 1943, the Gaullistes had initiated an investigation of their own. They concluded that it was MI-6 that had directed Dericourt to maintain his contact with the SD, and in order to ingratiate himself with the Germans, he had been authorized to show them the *courrier*. The purpose of such a statagem was relatively simple; once Dericourt had earned the trust of his German contacts, he acted not only as a straightforward penetration agent, but also as a means through which deceptive intelligence was planted upon the enemy.

In the light of Dericourt's own remarks about those "higher up" and the "Intelligence side," there seems no reason to doubt that the French investigation's conclusions were generally correct; and in the light of events in his postwar career, it would appear that Dericourt had rendered both SOE and MI-6—and the Allied cause—a valuable service. How else to explain the intercession of powerful friends at the Croydon and Paris trials? Moreover, it would appear that his mission was somehow connected not only with Cockade and Starkey but also with the cover and deception plans for D-Day, for he was withdrawn from the field in February 1944 and not allowed to return until September. The French investigation concluded that Dericourt was withdrawn from France not because the British were suspicious of him, but because his French comrades no longer trusted him and he was in such peril from the resistance that he might have been forced to seek the protection of the Germans. If that had happened, Dericourt might have revealed to the SD the truth of his mission—and that, in turn, might have imperiled the cover and deception plans for D-Day.

Again, the investigation's contentions seem to have been generally correct. But what was the nature of the deception that Dericourt planted upon the Germans? The report concluded that it concerned the 250 *messages personnels* which he was alleged to have betrayed to the SD. The *messages personnels* were the means by which London communicated its instructions to the European resistance movements, and they would prove to be of extreme importance on D-Day when the French *résistants* would be ordered to undertake clandestine activities in support of the invasion. Thus, if the Germans knew what these messages meant and to whom they were directed, they could deduce the time and place of the invasion—the most critical intelligence of the war. But ever since the decision was taken to invade Europe through Normandy, the Allied secret agencies and deception organizations had sought to persuade the Germans that their armies would invade anywhere *but* Normandy, and in particular, the Pas de Calais. Cockade and Starkey were among the first of the deceptions to rivet German attention on the Pas de Calais; the Dericourt stratagem was another. It was reasoned in London that if the Allies were detected in communication with *réseaux* in the Pas de Calais, the Germans would conclude that the invasion was coming in that region—and would take defense precautions there at the expense of Normandy.

To make such a stratagem work, a false set of *messages personnels* had to be devised and planted on the Germans—while the true set was sent into France along channels about which the Germans were ignorant. Here was where Dericourt and the secret *courrier* were involved. Buried in the *courrier*, in such a manner that the Germans would come across them piece by piece, were *messages personnels* directed to *réseaux* in the Pas de Calais, *réseaux* that, in many cases, simply did not exist. It was hoped that the Germans would gradually assemble these *messages* and, when they were broadcast during the D-Day period, conclude that the invading Allied armies were calling for support from the resistance, not in Normandy, but in the Pas de Calais. Such was the nature of the stratagem. The British successfully planted a false set of *messages personnels*—communications that Allied Supreme Headquarters would term "dummy" messages—on the Germans through the aegis of Dericourt and the secret *courrier*. It was a superb trick, one of historically important consequences to the outcome of D-Day.

But the question remains: Did Dericourt betray Prosper as part of the preliminaries to establish himself with the SD? The answer is no. The French investigation could not find evidence to indicate that the SD obtained through the *courrier* any information about Prosper and his lieutenants that it did not already know or might not have obtained elsewhere. Moreover, it seems quite clear that Dericourt showed the Germans only what he, or his British controllers, wanted them to see. The reasons for Prosper's downfall lay elsewhere. By the spring of 1943, London knew that his network had been gravely penetrated, largely due to the carelessness of the *résistants* themselves. Even so, SOE had no choice but to send Prosper back into the field after his "invasion" briefing in June of 1943. His participation in Starkey was essential, and Prosper himself insisted upon returning. SOE took a gamble and lost. Prosper and his lieutenants were not betrayed by London or by Dericourt. They were captured as a result of the lack of security that attended their activities—some of which they had been instructed to undertake in support of Starkey—and the diligence of the SD.

Nothing could be done to prevent Prosper from burning, but might not a major strategic advantage be wrought from the fire? If so, that may well have been the nature of Dericourt's special orders that involved a "strategic sacrifice"—a sacrifice that Dericourt himself said he thought involved Prosper. Dericourt may have been instructed to lead the Germans to believe that he was somehow instrumental in Prosper's capture, thus further ingratiating himself with the SD. Such a supposition must remain speculative, however, for Dericourt would say no more about his mission. After his acquittal at the hands of the French tribunal, he went back to flying and was, the French press later recorded, killed in an air accident in Laos on November 20, 1962. The intricacies of his role as a double agent, and the men behind it, will never be known. But did the stratagem in which he was involved work? When he returned to London in February 1944, it was still too soon to tell. Only events on D-Day and the days that followed would prove the success or failure of his mission. But without question, it was one of the most ingenious and dangerous stratagems of the war—and one of the most Machiavellian. And it was Machiavelli who wrote:

> Though fraud in other activities be detestable, in the management of war it is laudable and glorious, and he who overcomes the enemy by fraud is as much to be praised as he who does so by force.

The Intelligence Attack

ON NOVEMBER 3, 1943, Hitler issued the second crucial directive for the war in the West. It was number 51 and it laid down for the C-in-C West, Rundstedt, the Fuehrer's plans for repulsing an invasion. Hitler had not feared a major Allied landing in the West in 1943. He and his commanders had been openly disdainful of the Cockade and Starkey deceptions, and he had stripped his Channel garrisons to meet more pressing threats on the Russian and Mediterranean fronts. But 1944 was another matter, and in Directive 51, he wrote:

> All signs point to an offensive against the Western Front of Europe no later than spring, and perhaps earlier. For that reason, I can no longer justify the further weakening of the West in favor of other theatres of war. I have therefore decided to strengthen the defences in the West, particularly at places from which we shall launch our long-range war against England. For those are the very points at which the enemy must and will attack; there— unless all indications are misleading—will be fought the decisive invasion battle.

The places to which Hitler referred were chiefly in the Pas de Calais. As the shortest cross-Channel route, it was the logical site for the invasion; and judging from the accelerating tempo of Allied air and reconnaissance operations, that was the area in which they intended to land. By "our long-range war," Hitler meant the V1 jet-propelled pilotless bombers which carried 1½ tons of very high explosive to their targets at a speed faster than any Allied fighter, and the V2 rockets which, virtually undetectable and uninterceptible, carried a 1-ton warhead.

Directive 51 went on to warn Hitler's commanders to expect diversionary attacks on other fronts; and he ordered a new, massive program for the strengthening of the Atlantic Wall. But he was interested, in particular, in directing how the battle was to be fought. "Should the enemy force a landing by concentrating his armed might," wrote Hitler, "he must be hit by the full fury of our counterattack." In the first instance, Rundstedt was to destroy the invasion at the high-water mark; but if he failed to do so, there must be ready "first-rate, fully mobile general reserves" to "prevent the enlargement of the beachhead and (to) throw the enemey back into the sea." Hitler further directed that at sea and in the air all Allied attacks must be "relentlessly countered" by the Luftwaffe and Kriegsmarine "with all their available resources." He then directed the immediate reinforcement of all arms of the Wehrmacht in the West, if necessary by stripping units in less threatened areas. And finally, he specified that strong concentrations of U-boats be positioned in southern Norway, ready to strike south at the invasion fleets. Hitler demanded a fight without restraint or mercy.

Although Directive 51 was issued in only twenty-seven copies, it was on Menzies's desk at Broadway within three weeks, reaching him through at least two separate cryptanalytical channels. Ultra provided a digest, as it often did with Hitler's directives, but a fuller version came from an American source. The intercept originated from the American Signals Intelligence Service post at Asmara in Ethiopia, and the sources of its information were extremely important to the "Martians," the code name of the large intelligence industry created by the British with headquarters in a requisitioned department store in London's Oxford Street to keep the Allied commanders informed about the Wehrmacht.

When Hitler declared war on the United States, he signed a treaty of mutual assistance with the Japanese which provided for a full exchange of information between the two nations. The large Japanese missions in Germany and other European countries were duly notified about German operations, politics, economics, industry and weaponry throughout the Nazi empire, and the offices of the Japanese ambassador at Berlin, General Hiroshi Baron Oshima, became a vast clearinghouse of intelligence on Nazi-occupied Europe. The most important of this intelligence was transmitted to Imperial Headquarters at Tokyo over an Enigma-tized high-speed radio-teleprinter link from Berlin; and when this flow was detected by the Allies, the Americans, in accordance with the hemispheric deal in regard to cryptanalysis, built an intercept station at Asmara and staffed it with a team of three hundred men.

Upon acquisition at Asmara, the raw intercepts from Berlin were enciphered on an on-line radioteleprinter to Colonel W. Preston Corderman's Signals Security Agency (SSA) at Arlington Hall, a mansion 3 miles from central Washington, and at Vint Hill Farms, an old estate in the Virginia horse country about 50 miles from the capital. When the intercepts had been unbuttoned by SSA, they were retransmitted across the Atlantic to the American signals center 100 feet below the Goodge Street tube station near the British Museum. From there, they were circulated according to a very strict procedure which ensured that probably not more than twenty men in all London knew what the material was and how it had been obtained. For military intelligence purposes connected with Overlord, they went to COSSAC's operational intelligence branch at Norfolk House, a small team of trusted officers with the highest security clearances built around one Briton, Brigadier E. J. Foord, and one American, Colonel James O. Curtis, Jr. From the Asmara intercepts—and from all other sources of intelligence, including Ultra—they and the officers around them produced a daily intelligence bulletin entitled *Neptune Monitor Report,* a fuller and more considered weekly *Theatre Intelligence Report,* stop-press bulletins when something noteworthy developed, and frequent full-length articles on German military, technical and staff developments. These were then circulated with great care to COSSAC and all those directly involved in the planning of Overlord.

Asmara's version of Directive 51 contained some important observations by Baron Oshima, who was as skilled a soldier as he was a diplomat. In October 1943, he had toured the Atlantic Wall from the Skaggerak to the Spanish frontier and reported in radiograms of between 1000 and 2000 words twice a week on the state of the defenses. He received a long briefing from Rundstedt, who told him what he had already told Hitler: that the line of coastal defenses facing England was very thin compared to the defenses on the Russian front; that almost all his divisions were under-strength and their armament, particularly anti-tank weapons, badly needed modernization and reinforcement; and that there was a serious lack of motorized transport and an overdependence upon horse-drawn vehicles. Dutifully, competently, and in the best flat General Staff terminology, Oshima reported all this information, and a great deal more, through his embassy to Tokyo; it was intercepted at Asmara and at about the same time it arrived in Tokyo it also arrived in Washington and London.

The Asmara intercepts were proven by the Martians—for who could tell whether Rundstedt was not misleading Oshima?—against Ultra, whose productions were, by mid-1943, considerable—2000, 3000 and, on occasions, 4000 top secret German signals every day. Among these signals were Rundstedt's and the other western commands' daily and weekly returns, which consisted of reports of the strengths and equipment states of all units in the West, often down to companies. Dull stuff, but some of the most priceless intelligence of the war, for it showed generally where each German division was and what its capability in battle would be. Gradually, the Martians were able to build up a complete picture of the German order of battle in the West; seldom, if ever, in history had a planning staff been better informed of its enemy. Ultra also revealed that Rundstedt, like Hitler, believed that the Allies would invade the Pas de Calais; and the basic stratagems of the invasion would be devised to bolster up this mistaken belief. Thus, by late 1943, Ultra was not only dictating or shaping the strategy and tactics of the invasion, it was also influencing the deception operations that would be used to cover it.

Ultra and the Asmara intercepts were not the only sources of high-grade intelligence available to COSSAC; the machine had not wholly replaced the spy. From its inception in March 1942, the Atlantic Wall had been a primary target for MI-6 and its associated organizations, particularly SOE; for SOE, while it had no intelligence acquisition responsibility, did supply very large quantities of information about the Wehrmacht. Most of this information was acquired by French *réseaux,* notably on the Channel coast by the right-wing "Century" organization; and the officer mainly responsible for handling the vast quantities of material gathered by Century was Commander Wilfred Dunderdale, a career MI-6 officer who had been born at the Russian Black Sea port of Nikolaev. A wealthy man, short and powerfully built, Dunderdale was fluent in Russian, French and German, and had a working command of Greek and Turkish. After serving in the First World War with a British cruiser squadron in the Black Sea and the Mediterranean, he began his MI-6 career at the British legation in Istanbul. There, he made a significant friendship with a pharmaceutical opium dealer named Georges Keun, a Sephardic Jew with a Danish passport. Then in 1926, Dunderdale was sent to Paris and remained there, latterly as the MI-6 liaison officer with the French secret services, until the fall of France in 1940. It was under Dunderdale's direction that Richard Lewinski had reconstructed the Wehrmacht's Enigma.

Soon after Dunderdale arrived at Paris, his friend Keun built a villa, the Taneh Merah, at Cap d'Antibes, and Dunderdale became a frequent house guest. Keun was a leading light in that curious interwar society which Scott Fitzgerald described. He married a relative of Sarah Bernhardt and of Georges Feydeau, the man who wrote *La Plume de Ma Tante;* various brothers and sisters married into the Borghese family of Italian princes and into the Chilean plutocracy. Keun's son, Philippe, went to Downside, the Catholic college in England, and to the Collège Stanislaus, a leading French school for the sons of wealthy and influential Catholics. But at an early age, Philippe Keun rejected Catholicism for communism; those were the days of the Front Populaire and violent social unrest, and the workers often found sympathy and support among the youth of the French ruling class. Appalled by the violence and turbulence around him, young Keun left Paris to work as a laborer in Turkey and, being a clever linguist, he began to translate parts of Shakespeare into Turkish. At the outbreak of the Second World War he returned to France, fought in the French army at Sedan, was captured, escaped, and made his way to Bordeaux. There, through his Catholic connections, he met a Jesuit who had served in the French secret service against the British and now served the British against the Germans. This man was the formidable "Colonel Claude Ollivier," whose real name was Arnould and who was posing as a coal merchant. Ollivier was founding an MI-6 *réseau* that would come to be called "Jade Amicol," a spy organization with strong connections with the Jesuits and the railways. When Ollivier requested permission from London to employ Keun as his deputy, Dunderdale approved.

By 1943, Jade Amicol—MI-6 *réseaux* took their names from precious stones combined with the code names of their leaders, and since Ollivier was known as "Le Colonel" and Keun was called "L'Amiral," the first syllables were joined to form "Amicol"—was MI-6's largest circuit in Paris and northern France. It had over 1500 sub-agents, many of them Jesuits, railwaymen and former French army officers; and, although it was hunted with great savagery by its enemies and suffered many casualties, it survived. During the Donar *ratissage,* Ollivier had a close call. He was badly wounded when he was ambushed by SD men on the stairs to an apartment near the Étoile. Bullets shattered his right arm and severed the brachial artery but, while literally bleeding to death, he escaped back down the winding staircase and out into the street. Fortune was with him; he found a horse-drawn taxi immediately, leaped into the back, told the driver to take him to the Champs-Élysées and, as the old carriage swayed and thundered, found a piece of wire in the seat. He made a tourniquet, saved his own life, and then leaped out and vanished in a crowd around Fouquet's.

Apart from Ollivier's resourcefulness and courage, the reason his *réseau* survived was because the Germans never located its main safehouse. This Jade Amicol had established in the convent of the Sisters of St. Agonie, a branch of the Lazarites, a religious and military order founded in Jerusalem about the middle of the twelfth century. The convent was at 127 rue de la Santé, a scabrous old building situated under the walls of the lunatic asylum of Sainte-Anne. With the nine sisters and the Mother Superior, Madame Henriette Frede, acting as couriers, the convent became Menzies's chief radio center in Paris and also the center for the collection of MI-6's secret mail for London. A transceiver was secreted in a small loft over the sacristy, and there were wireless outstations in various parts of Paris—including one in the loft of the Hotel Scribe.

Here, Ollivier and Keun began to acquire intelligence about the Wehrmacht, in particular its order of battle and information about military railway movements. Keun became a master of disguise, a skillful and trusted agent, and when he was not spying he was often to be found in the sacristy's loft at work translating parts of Shakespeare into Bulgarian. It was through Keun that MI-6 established a new contact with the

Schwarze Kapelle, which in Paris was centered around General Karl-Heinrich von Stuelpnagel, the elegant and cultured Military Governor of France, and his office at the Hotel Meurice. But again MI-6 was chiefly concerned with using the conspiracy as a source of intelligence, and Keun's main channel of information was through a disaffected Austrian Catholic official on Stuelpnagel's staff—a channel that existed, most probably, with the general's knowledge. The official had access to the Military Governor's safe and turned over copies of many valuable documents in the gloom of Notre Dame to one or another of the Lazarite sisters. But Keun's primary mission by May of 1943 was to find out all he could about the Atlantic Wall.

The operation to secure the secrets of the wall began well through a stroke of good fortune. Early in May 1943, outside the *mairie* at Caen, a notice appeared inviting tenders for some minor housekeeping tasks at the headquarters of Organization Todt, the German paramilitary engineering concern which was responsible for building the fortifications. René Duchez, a painter who was a member of Century (which had links to Jade Amicol through a clandestine organization of former French army officers known as "Sosies"), read the notice and decided to offer his services; it would give him an opportunity to get inside Todt headquarters and look around. He discovered that one of the tasks available was to put up new wallpaper in the Bauleiter's office at the Todt technical headquarters on the Avenue Bagatelle in Caen. He went there, asked to see Bauleiter Schnedderer, the chief, and Schnedderer, who wore the silver-encrusted uniform of a Todt employee, expounded at length on the patterns he would like to see on his wall. Blue Norsemen carrying flags on a light yellow background would be most handsome, but he also fancied silver cannon on a background of navy blue. The two men riffled through Duchez's pattern book and then Schnedderer asked Duchez to come back the next day, by which time he would have made up his mind. When Duchez did so, he found the Bauleiter at his desk, and on the desk were some maps. Duchez could see that the top map was of the Normandy coast from Le Havre to Cherbourg. It was printed by the diazo system of duplicating on blue cartographic paper stamped with the words SONDERZEICHNUNGEN, STRENG GEHEIM—Special Blueprint, Strict Secret. When Duchez's tender—attractively underpriced at 12,000 francs—was accepted and Bauleiter Schnedderer had selected the paper, the German said he had to go to a meeting. He left Duchez to begin the preparatory work. Duchez leaned over the desk to look at the map and words such as *"Blockhaus"* and *"Sofortprogramm"* (highest priority construction) caught his eyes. In a flash, he knew what it was: the blueprint for fortifications between Le Havre and Cherbourg. He took the map, folded it carefully, and hid it behind a 2-foot-square mirror in the Bauleiter's office. Almost immediately afterwards Schnedderer came back and said it would be convenient for Duchez to start work on the following Monday.

When Duchez returned with his paper, pails, brushes and paste that Monday, he discovered that Schnedderer had gone to St. Malo and that nobody at the Avenue Bagatelle knew anything about wallpapering his office. He was refused permission to begin work and told to return in a week. Duchez began to protest, loudly, and another Bauleiter, whose name was given as Adalbert Keller, came out of an office to see what the fuss was about. Duchez explained that he had been commissioned to paper Schnedderer's office, and if Keller would let him get on with it, he would paper Keller's office for nothing. Beaming at the prospect of brightening his dingy room, Keller agreed and at 8 A.M. on Wednesday, May 13, 1943, Duchez moved in and began to work. At the end of the day, he retrieved the map, which was still behind the mirror, rolled it up in some wallpaper and, with all his equipment, was waved through the guards. By the end of the week it was at Sosies headquarters in Paris. There it was copied and the master was taken to Notre Dame where it was passed over to one of the Lazarite sisters. She took it to the convent and arrangements were made for Keun to fly it to London, rather than entrusting it to the secret *courrier*. The copy was kept in France as the basis for a full-scale Century mapping operation of the wall from Cherbourg to Trouville—the area upon which, although neither Century nor the Sosies knew it, the Allies would descend.

In such a bold, quaint manner did the Martians begin to acquire the innermost secrets of the Atlantic Wall, which was, for all its faults and weaknesses, the most formidable barrier that the invading Allied armies would encounter. But by December 1943, intelligence and aerial reconnaissance material about the wall was available in such great detail and volume that Allied planners were as well informed about the enemy's fortifications as they were about his order of battle. There were, however, gaps in their knowledge that would cause near-disaster on D-Day. The Germans, as events would show, were capable of some clever deceptions of their own.

Another target of a concerted intelligence attack was Field Marshal Rommel, who had been sent by Hitler first to inspect the Atlantic Wall and then, on December 31, 1943, to command the two German armies—the 15th in the Pas de Calais region and the 7th in the invasion area—on the Channel coast. It was a significant reappearance, for wherever Rommel went, he stirred up a whirlwind of defensive preparations, and it was imperative to know where he was concentrating the burden of his efforts. If the Martians' studies showed that the Pas de Calais was receiving priority, it could be deduced that OKW expected the main Allied landings there. But if they showed that Rommel was concentrating on Normandy, it could be deduced that OKW had appreciated the truth of Allied intentions and the advantage of surprise might be lost on D-Day. Every available source of intelligence was studied most carefully—particularly aerial reconnaissance photographs—for signs of what Rommel was doing; and when, during the winter of 1943–44, it was apparent to the Martians that he was still concentrating his main efforts around Calais, the Allied high command could view the future with some hope.

But now, with shocking suddenness, a new element began to intrude on the preparations for D-Day. For all the excellence of Allied intelligence, the "Far Shore"—as the invasion beaches were called in conference, for security reasons—was a mystery to the Overlord planners. It lay across the Channel like some Lorelei, beckoning but menacing; for most of the Martians were convinced that Hitler was keeping some secret weapon for employment on D-Day, a device that would shatter the sea and air fleets and cut down the invaders in great writhing mounds. No one knew what this weapon might be, but few doubted that Hitler had one—or more. The gunrooms of Europe echoed with debates about what they were, and every prediction was made from long-range rockets to lethal rays and "radioactive dust." Speculation grew until it bordered on an actual neurosis, and Hitler cleverly fed that neurosis with all manner of rumors and deceptions until his secret weapons became a scare to rank with Sealion and the Spanish Armada.

Allied fears deepened when Hitler used a rash of wireless-controlled, rocket-propelled bombs against the invasion fleet at Salerno; and then his new HS293 wireless-controlled glider bombs began to take a heavy toll of Allied shipping in the Mediterranean. Even more unsettling was the sudden appearance of vast concrete installations at a number of little villages along the Channel coast in the Pas de Calais. Apparently these encrustations housed some form of long-range artillery capable not only of bringing new devastation to English cities but also of causing great damage to the enormous concentrations of Allied shipping and matériel that would assemble in southern England for D-Day. But what would their warheads carry: explosives, glider or rocket bombs, some instrument of chemical or bacteriological warfare, the atomic bomb? MI-6 and SOE strained every channel of information to find out what these secret weapons were, where they were manufactured, where they were emplaced, and how they could be destroyed.

As it happened, MI-6 and the Allied high commanders already knew something about two of Hitler's secret weapons—the V1 and V2 rockets. The intelligence attack by MI-6 on the German missile program had begun on March 22, 1943, when two generals of the Afrika Korps, Thoma and Cruewell, met for the first time since their capture in the "London Cage," a mansion in Kensington Palace Gardens where the British interrogated high-ranking German prisoners. Until that time, MI-6 only suspected that the Wehrmacht was developing such weapons, a suspicion in which the Oslo Report had played a key part. Although other revelations in the report had been proved true, there was a tendency at Broadway to believe that it and several other reports of missile research and development were attempts by the Germans to send the intelligence and aerial reconnaissance services off on wild, expensive, time-consuming chases for mares' nests. But when the two generals met and began to talk, in a room that was wired to record their conversation, that belief ended. For Thoma "expressed surprise that London was not yet in ruins from a rocket bombardment," and described what he had seen when he visited a firing range in Germany where giant rockets were being tested. When this information reached Dr. R. V. Jones and his colleague, Dr. F. C. Frank, at MI-6, they related Thoma's statements to other data and concluded that reports of German rockets were not just a propaganda scare; they actually existed.

On April 11, 1943, Menzies presented the Vice Chief of the Imperial General Staff, General Sir Archibald Nye, with a memorandum setting out all the various intelligence reports about German missiles that had been received by MI-6 since December 1942. The memorandum went to Churchill on April 15, 1943, in the form of a minute by General Ismay in which he wrote: "The Chiefs of Staff feel that you should be made aware of reports of German experiments with long-range rockets. The fact that five reports have been received since the end of 1942 indicates a foundation of fact even if details are inaccurate." Ismay advised the Prime Minister that the Chiefs of Staff recommended that a single investigator be appointed to head the intelligence attack. He should be, they suggested, a man with the authority to be able to call upon such members of the scientific and intelligence communities as appropriate. Churchill agreed and nominated as the investigator his son-in-law, Duncan Sandys, the Joint Parliamentary Secretary to the Ministry of Supply, a product of Eton and Magdalen College, Oxford, of the Diplomatic Service, and a young Establishment figure who had commanded Britain's first anti-aircraft rocket regiment.

Under Sandys, the investigation intensified, particularly in the field of aerial reconnaissance. Information about the German rocket program began to flood in, much of it concerning activities at Peenemünde, on a small island in the Baltic. Agents were infiltrated into the area and Peenemünde was photographed from the air, but it was still thought possible that the installation was a hoax until a clever piece of scientific deduction—and Ultra—revealed otherwise. A clerk in the German Air Ministry sent revised instructions for applying for petrol coupons to all German experimental stations, listing them on the circular in the order of their importance. Peenemünde was at the top of the list, and when the circular fell into the hands of R. V. Jones, as he would write, "The petrol instructions, to my mind, finished the case. They showed that Peenemünde was genuine. . . ."

Another piece of corroborative evidence was provided by Ultra. Jones believed that the Germans would use radar to plot the experimental flights of their test rockets, and he alerted the cryptanalysts at Bletchley to look for any signals to indicate that German radar companies were being moved up to the Baltic coast. Such a signal was soon forthcoming. Moreover, the company which began to track the missiles broadcast its plots in a simple code that was also intercepted. From those intercepts Jones was able both to pinpoint the location of the launch sites and to obtain detailed information on the performance of the missiles themselves.

Intelligence gathered from other sources provided more information about where German missiles were being manufactured, and the purpose of the peculiar installations in the Pas de Calais. Then came the Lisbon Report and all the pieces of the puzzle began to fit together. Although it has never been revealed who handed the report to the MI-6 station chief at Lisbon, its source was almost surely Captain Ludwig Gehre, an officer of the Abwehr and a prominent member of the Schwarze Kapelle. It was a document of immense value to the Allies, for it described Hitler's V-weapons program in some detail and reported that:

> Hitler and members of his Cabinet recently inspected both weapons [the V1 and V2] at Peenemünde. About 10th June, Hitler told assembled military leaders that the Germans had only to hold out, since by the end of 1943 London would be levelled to the ground and Britain forced to capitulate. October 20th is at present fixed as Zero Day for rocket attacks to begin. Hitler ordered the construction of 30,000 *A-4* [the original nomenclature for the V2] projectiles by that day; this is, however, beyond the bounds of possibility. Production of both weapons is to have first priority and 1500 skilled workers have been transferred to this work from anti-aircraft and artillery production.

The report confirmed intelligence derived from agents in the field, aerial reconnaissance and Ultra, and the information it contained was so alarming that it was decided to launch an all-out attack against every known site connected with Hitler's V-weapons program. Throughout the late summer and autumn of 1943, the British and American air forces bombarded every factory, every concrete plant, every launch site, every suspect train that they could find. But by far the most spectacular, and most decisive, raid occurred on the night of August 17/18, when the RAF mounted a cunning and ferocious operation codenamed "Hydra."

It was the end of a day over Europe during which the Luftwaffe and the 8th U.S. Air Force had engaged in the most violent daytime aerial fighting of the entire war so far—the battles over the Messerschmitt factories at Regensburg and the great ball-bearing works at Schweinfurt. While the last American bombers were landing in England, the first RAF bombers were taking off as part of the day and night campaign ordered at Casablanca to bring the Luftwaffe to battle and destroy it. Stepped-up aerial activity was also closely related to the Cockade deception which was then under way. But that night the RAF had a special destination—Peenemünde.

The Germans knew the raiders were coming; the Luftwaffe's cryptanalysts had penetrated a low-grade Bomber Command cipher some time before, and that day the cipher had been used by Bomber Command to warn the east coast defenses of England that large numbers of British bombers would be leaving and entering the defense zones. The Luftwaffe cryptanalytical experts at Paris unbuttoned the message and were able to warn the Reich Air Defense Command headquarters that a large force of RAF bombers would attack a target in northern rather than southern Germany that night. By early evening the Reich air defenses were alerted and standing by, even though almost the entire Luftwaffe in Germany was exhausted after the heavy air battles during daylight. But the advantage the Luftwaffe might have derived from this intelligence was neutralized by Bomber Command's strategy for Hydra.

For many nights in the past, the C-in-C of Bomber Command, Air Chief Marshal Sir Arthur Harris, had been sending a few fast high-flying bombers to raid Berlin. Each night the bombers—Mosquitoes, one of the best and fastest aircraft of their type, perhaps because they were made of specially toughened wood—flew the same northerly track to the capital, dropped a few bombs, and then departed. The track took the Mosquitoes near Peenemünde and air-raid sirens there always sent the scientists and their work forces to the shelters, but after a time the Peenemünde defenses became more relaxed. The Reich air defense commander also considered Peenemünde an unlikely target; he thought these pinprick attacks were the prologue to some devastating main raid on the capital. But Bomber Command had other plans. To prevent the German radar system from giving an early warning about the approach of an air armada in the region of Jutland, the fleet was to cross the North Sea at a very low altitude, creep under the horizon of the German radar screen, and then rise in mass to 7000 feet to make its bombing runs. Shortly before the main force began to cross the North Sea, however, the usual small party of Mosquitoes would attack "Whitebait"—the RAF's code name for Berlin. They were to drop marker flares as if they were laying out the target for the main force. Then having alerted, it was hoped, the Reich air defenses to the fact that Berlin would be the target for the main force, the Mosquitoes were to switch on their radar decoy equipment and further confuse them with a false electronic scent. By this time, Harris estimated, the Luftwaffe would have congregated in full strength over Berlin—as Bomber Command devastated the Peenemünde research establishment in a raid that was intended to last only forty-five minutes.

As part of this cover plan, the 4000 men in the raid were not told why they were attacking this remote target; it was explained to them at their briefing that they were after a new form of radiolocation (i.e., radar) equipment that "promised greatly to improve the German night fighter organisation." As the intelligence officer of one of the squadrons said: "In order to retard the production of this equipment and thereby help maintain the effectiveness of Bomber Command's offensive, it is necessary to destroy both the experimental station and the large factory workshops, and to kill or incapacitate the scientific and technical experts working there."

It was a glorious night on the Baltic. As the private secretary to Professor Wernher von Braun, the chief scientist of the V2 program on Peenemünde, described the scene:

> This evening nobody else seems to be in Block Four—absolute silence all around me. Shortly before 11 o'clock, I close the steel safe and walk out of the Block. Outside, a milky white landscape lit by the light of the full moon. Sunk deep in my own thoughts, I stroll slowly along the short path between the tall Scots pines and the shrubbery, past the tennis courts and up to Schlempp's construction office. At that moment the air raid sirens sound . . . there's no hurry, this is not the first time it's only been a warning. . . . (I) pick up a book and drape a bathing-wrap round my shoulders in case it gets too cold. . . . The bunker in front of Block Four is almost empty, a few people clustered outside it. Most of them are going back to bed. I find a seat on the bench, and start to read my book. I become completely absorbed in it, and don't look up from it even when a low roar, a rumble, starts way off in the distance.

Except for its flak and searchlight defenses, Peenemünde was practically an open target when the first RAF Pathfinders marked the dark with red flares. Pricked into action by the Mosquitoes, the Luftwaffe night fighters that might have rushed to its defense were circling Berlin awaiting an attack that never came.

But another mysterious factor contributed to the secrecy and surprise that cloaked the raid. Command of this air battle had been vested in General Josef Kammhuber, the C-in-C of the 12th Air Corps and the Reich's leading air defense expert. He had his headquarters in Holland, and orders to his air divisions were transmitted over a teleprinter link that fanned out from the Luftwaffe signals center at Arnhem-Deelen. Just as the raid on Peenemünde began, this cable was cut and Kammhuber found himself without contact with any of the ground control or command posts. At an inquiry afterwards, both Goering and Kammhuber declared that they were certain the cable had been cut by agents of the "British Secret Service" as part of Hydra's cover and deception plan. As David Irving, a British historian and student of the V-weapons story, wrote:

> It seemed particularly regrettable to (Kammhuber) that communications should have broken down through Deelen on the one night when RAF Bomber Command stood to lose so much. After the war Kammhuber was informed by British officers that two Germans employed at the Arnhem-Deelen operations room were, in fact, British agents, and they may well have been briefed to sabotage the defence effort on that one night, if on no other.

Were British agents responsible? It was not improbable. Such a tactic had been used before and would be used later, particularly when MI-6 wanted to force the Germans to employ wireless so that an Ultra could be obtained. It was a normal operation of the complicated and recondite wireless war that went on behind the main battle. But whatever the truth, Kammhuber was cut off from the Peenemünde raid throughout that night; it was not until noon the following day that he discovered what had happened.

Alarmed and mystified by the silence from Kammhuber's post, and certain that the RAF main force was making for Berlin, General Joachim Junck, the Luftwaffe commander at Metz in eastern France, assumed command of the air battle. He ordered all fighters to make for Berlin, apparently confusing the radar decoys used by the Mosquitoes with the RAF bomber stream. The fighters did as they were told; some 55 single-seat day fighters and 158 twin-engine night fighters made for the capital. But the day fighters were not practiced in night-fighting tactics and began to attack all aircraft with twin rudders in the belief that they were British. They were, in fact, the German night fighters. Hearing the air battle going on overhead, the capital's 89 heavy anti-aircraft batteries opened fire with a barrage of 12,000 shells against the fighters. And then the German fighters began to run out of fuel, just as they sighted fires and flares burning 100 miles away to the north—the Hydra attack going in on Peenemünde. But despite this information from the air, the Berlin ground controllers refused permission to those aircraft with sufficient fuel to leave the capital, for Berlin was out of touch with Kammhuber because of the cut cable and they could not tell whether the Peenemünde attack was the main raid or a diversion. This confusion persisted for some time, certainly until the second of the three waves of the RAF force was beginning to make its bomb run.

New squadrons were now scrambled for Peenemünde, but again they were misled. They expected to intercept the RAF main force at its normal operating altitude for a night like this, 18,000 feet. But, in fact, the bomber stream was below at 7000 feet. While the Luftwaffe fighters were sorting themselves out, the second RAF wave had departed and the third was arriving—54 Halifaxes and 126 Lancasters. It was already a terrifying sight below; the establishment seemed to be on fire from end to end. Peenemünde's 12,000 scientists, technicians and workmen huddled together as the last of the night's 1593 tons of high explosive and 281 tons of fire bombs rained down upon them. Then there was silence, except for the sirens of the all clear, the ambulances, and fire brigades.

The raid was one of the most decisive air operations of the war. Over 730 people connected with the various secret weapons programs were killed, among them two scientists—Thiel and Walther—who were key personnel. But also among the dead were several MI-6 agents who had infiltrated the establishment as laborers from Luxembourg. In all, the RAF lost forty-one bombers. But Harris's strategy had prevented heavier casualties since about 203 German fighters had been lured away by the deception plan. The Luftwaffe reported afterwards that but for this deception and the ensuing chaos, it would have shot down two hundred British aircraft on such a brilliant and clear night. Moreover, the Luftwaffe lost nine fighters in the air, and at one airfield alone—Brandenburg—over thirty fighters crash-landed and had to be written off. The effect of the raid on Hitler and Goering was such that the full brunt of their rage fell upon General Hans Jeschonnek, the Chief of the Air Staff. Jeschonnek shot himself in his office the morning after the raid.

Hitler ordered the evacuation of all important activity and production from Peenemünde. The main new proving ground was established on a former Polish army firing range at Blizna, between Cracow and Lvov—in the heart of a territory that was heavily infiltrated by Polish intelligence agents controlled by London. To escape the devastation of the raids on German industrial sites, the manufacture of missiles was transferred to a plant in the Harz Mountains called the "Central Works," the code name for the largest underground factory in the world—two parallel tunnels under the Kohnstein Mountain, each 1¼ miles long, ¾ of a mile apart, and linked by forty-six galleries. Here, 16,000 slave laborers and 2000 German technicians—and some MI-6 agents—recommenced work on the weapons with which Hitler hoped to destroy London and terrorize the Allies into making a disastrous—for themselves—invasion at Pas de Calais.

Hitler had another secret weapon that posed a vague and frightening threat to the Allies—the "London gun," a strange device which the Fuehrer called the V3. It was perhaps the most extraordinary weapon of the Second World War, excluding the atomic bomb. There were to be fifty London guns, each with a barrel 416 feet long. Through the ignition of explosive charges set at intervals up the barrel, the guns fired shells carrying 55 pounds of high explosive across ranges of up to 100 miles.

Their rate of fire was six hundred shells an hour, and their range was such that they could easily deluge London with a hail of high-explosive and incendiary warheads.

Hitler had approved the weapon after the great raid on Hamburg in July 1943, work had begun immediately on the construction and testing of three of the guns, and nearly 5500 engineers, technicians and miners had been sent to a little French hamlet called Mimoyecques, just behind Calais and 95 miles from London. There, installations for two batteries with twenty-five guns each were being built underground, protected by an 18-foot-thick concrete roof. The barrels of the guns were to be buried on the incline, with only the tips of their muzzles above ground; and 8-inch-thick steel moving doors were to be built to slide across the muzzles during air raids. 100 feet below the surface there was to be a warren of galleries serving as magazines, quarters for the firing crews, a railway line, and unloading bays for the ammunition; and 350 feet below that were the housings for the breeches. Each gun would have its own electrical hoists and elevators; and negotiations had been opened with the Société Électrique du Nord-Ouest to supply the batteries with enough power for a town of 50,000 people.

Early experiments had convinced Speer, Hitler's armaments chief, that the gun would work, and it warranted a high priority in manpower, concrete, steel and explosive. On October 19, 1943, firing trials began with one gun at Hillersleben on the Baltic, while a second was being built at Miedzyzdroje, a Baltic island. The first tests were relatively successful; the gun achieved sufficient muzzle velocity to get the shells two-thirds of the way to London. In the meantime, work continued at Mimoyecques.

While most of the construction at Mimoyecques was underground, it generated what were, in effect, two huge molehills. In late May or June MI-6 had learned of the Germans' negotiations with the Société Électrique du Nord-Ouest for power, and of the construction of cross-country power lines. This raised suspicions, but, since Mimoyecques was fairly close to Watten, where the Germans were building their missile-launching installations, it was thought at first that the molehills were associated with rockets. Then a photographic reconnaissance flight noted that all the shafts were exactly aligned on central London. And so, in November 1943, Bostons and Baltimores of the U.S. 9th Air Force raided the sites. The damage caused was serious, and the Germans decided to abandon work on one battery of twenty-five guns, and concentrate all their men and materials on the completion of the other which was, alone, capable of firing one shell into London every twelve seconds.

As the year ended, Hitler's V-weapons program had been severely dislocated, but it had not been stopped. The manufacture of missiles and the construction of launching installations continued. It was considered unlikely that they would be put to use in the near future, but D-Day was still six months away, ample time to perfect the weapons. At COSSAC, Morgan, who was involved in the detailed planning for Overlord, was asked to evaluate what effect they might have on the invasion. He did so on December 20, 1943, warning the Combined Chiefs that if they thought it necessary to shift the main concentrations of troops and stores into the west country of England, where they would be more or less out of range of such weapons, it must be decided upon immediately. The Combined Chiefs decided against the move. It would be a vast task, involving not only the movement of millions of men and millions of tons of equipment, but also the recasting of the entire strategy for the invasion—including the cover and deception plans. Plainly such an alteration of strategy, and such a movement, would concede more power to these weapons than they warranted, and might have a grave effect on the morale of the fighting men.

Not a single V-weapon had been fired, but Hitler's scare campaign was having the desired effect. While the intelligence attack against the V-weapons had been extraordinarily successful, the massive air strikes against missile manufacturing and launching sites proved to be a significant diversion from targets more directly concerned with D-Day, and Allied anxiety about the true capabilities of these weapons remained. But that scare campaign had a curious corollary, for the Fuehrer had come to believe his own propaganda. He was convinced that the mere threat of secret weapons sites in the Pas de Calais was having a profound influence on Allied strategy. If there was to be an invasion of Europe at all, the Allies *must* attack the Pas de Calais. And that was precisely what the Allied secret agencies had been laboring so diligently to make the Fuehrer believe.

In spite of their preoccupation with V-weapons, the Allies had not ignored the possibility that the Germans might possess the war's one decisive weapon—the atomic bomb. Would Hitler be able to unleash an atomic bomb on, or even before, D-Day? No one in London or Washington really knew. It was theoretically possible; the Germans were known to be advanced in nuclear fission; in 1939 they had begun a vigorous program to build such a weapon. At the same time, British intelligence undertook a vigorous program of its own to discover the nature and extent of German research, and to look for the means, if possible, to neutralize it. There was an extreme urgency to MI-6's task, and the way in which it was performed would become one of the most remarkable feats of the war.

The first "break" for MI-6 came in 1939 when the Oslo Report revealed that the Germans were, in fact, actively engaged in atomic research. Then it was discovered that their research was dependent upon the use of heavy water—deuterium oxide, which required enormous amounts of electrical power to make, and was being produced only at the Vemork plant at Rjukan, a small town under the Hardanger plateau of south Norway. With the conquest of Norway, the Germans had taken possession of the plant and gained easy access to its production of heavy water.

Menzies and his service had little technical knowledge of the eerie subject of atomic physics, save that it might breed the deadliest weapon the world had ever known. But if there was a weak link in the Germans' research and development program, it was in Norway. Therefore, Menzies put Lieutenant Commander Eric Welsh, the chief of the Norwegian country section of MI-6, in charge of the intelligence attack. Welsh was an officer with a considerable layman's knowledge of science, and he had an even greater knowledge of Norway. He had managed a chemicals and paint factory there for several years and had married a Norwegian. He knew the geography of Rjukan, he knew many of the personalities there, and in his mind's eye he knew how men might be got in to blow the place up.

The need for an attack became acute when, in October 1941, the "Princes"—the underground secret intelligence service in Denmark—sent a telegram to MI-6 saying that Niels Bohr, the Danish physicist who was something of a confessor to the international scientific fraternity engaged in atomic research, had received a visitor from Germany. Professor Werner Heisenberg, a leading figure in the German program to develop the atomic bomb, had come to ask Bohr a very difficult question. Was it morally correct, Heisenberg wished to know, for a physicist to engage in the construction of such an absolute weapon, even in wartime? Bohr responded with a question of his own. Did Heisenberg mean to imply that the Germans believed such a weapon to be feasible? Heisenberg said, sadly, that such was the case. The conversation left Bohr deeply shocked; he warned the Princes and they warned London. He was, said Bohr, convinced that Germany was on the threshold of obtaining the atomic bomb, and that belief was sufficient to compel London to take decisive action.

MI-6 turned to Professor Lief Tronstad, a chemist in his late thirties who had helped build the heavy water plant at Rjukan. Tronstad had become chief of the Norwegian government-in-exile's Section IV—the secret service—and under him there was an agent who was a native of Rjukan, Einar Skinnerland. On March 29, 1942, Skinnerland was parachuted onto the wild and desolate Hardanger plateau above Rjukan to establish an intelligence post. He soon made contact with the Vemork plant's chief engineer, Jomar Brun; and Brun reported that the Germans were increasing the plant's production of heavy water. Skinnerland transmitted that information to London by secret writing through Stockholm, and he was then instructed to obtain detailed drawings and photographs of the plant, together with the surrounding countryside. With Brun's help, he gathered the necessary information, microphotographed it and smuggled it out in a tube of toothpaste to Stockholm. When it reached London it was carefully studied at MI-6, and Menzies approached the Joint Intelligence Committee with a proposition that the Vemork plant be destroyed as a matter of urgency. The JIC agreed, and plans were made for what came to be called "Operation Freshman."

It was a bold operation. Two teams of paratroopers—forty men in all—were to land by gliders on the Hardanger plateau, and from Skinnerland's base, they were to storm and destroy the Rjukan plant in a swift and violent *coup de main*. Freshman's advance party landed as planned on October 18, 1942, just as Brun arrived in Britain after a fugitive's journey from Rjukan to Stockholm, where he was hidden in the bomb bay of a Mosquito and flown to London. He gave the Freshman teams a personal briefing on the weather, the German guards, the positions of the machine-gun posts, and the best routes down from the plateau into the gorge where the Vemork plant sat on an outcrop over a deep and powerful stream. But the Freshman teams would never reach the plant. Their gliders crash-landed in heavy weather over Norway. The survivors were quickly rounded up by German ski patrols, the injured were killed, and the rest, after interrogation, were shot, although they were in British army uniform. The Germans realized that the paratroopers' target was the heavy water plant at Rjukan. The result was inevitable; defenses were strengthened around the plant.

There was considerable despair in London at the failure of Freshman. But the plant could not be left intact; its destruction was an imperative, and Colonel Jack Wilson, the chief of SOE's Norwegian country section, was authorized to mount a second attack—"Gunnerside." The operation was well planned; from Brun's data, a large model was built not only of the plant but also of the surrounding terrain. Wilson selected his men from among volunteers from the Royal Norwegian Army. Their training was lengthy and thorough, and to ensure that none but the principals knew about Gunnerside, the men practiced at Station 17, a special training school in Scotland which had been cleared of all other agents. Their main target would be the eighteen stainless steel high-concentration cells at the Vemork plant, and the plan called for the Gunnerside party to land to a reception by the "Swallows"—the new code name for the team that had preceded Freshman. But the condition of the Swallows was not short of desperate. They had gone to ground on the Hardanger plateau—an area of inaccessible terrain, mountain peaks, grinding glaciers, precipices, marshes, swamps, impassable streams—after the Freshman fiasco. They had long since exhausted their food; severe storms made it impossible for the RAF to parachute supplies, and the deep snow made it unusually difficult to live off the land. Yet Gunnerside could not succeed without the Swallows.

Gunnerside was launched on February 16, 1943, although no one was sure what the men would find when they were parachuted in near Skrykenvann, about 28 miles across country from the Swallows' hideout. The party landed safely, and at first the weather was in their favor; the squalls, which could lift men from their feet and hurl them bodily across the frozen snow, had died down. Then a blizzard broke out and delayed their progress, but finally, as they approached Lake Kalungsjå, they sighted two of the Swallows. They looked like the men in the famous painting of Scott's last march through the Antarctic; and their condition was not so very different. Their long ragged beards were hung with icicles, the cold had made deep splits in their skin, they could barely hobble with frostbite—but they were alive.

The men holed up in the Swallows' hideout, and by the late afternoon of February 26—a Friday—the Gunnerside party had moved forward to take up position in two woodsmen's huts on a hillside just north of Rjukan. From there, they planned their attack. It was decided that the only way to get into the plant without alerting the guards was to descend into the gorge below the lip of the plateau, cross the swollen and semi-frozen torrent in the bed of the gorge, and then climb the 500-foot face of the outcrop on which the heavy water plant had been built—a formidable physical feat.

The following evening the attack party skied to the lip of the plateau, and began the descent into the gorge. The night was filled with the hum of the plant's turbines; and this, together with a rising wind, muffled the sounds of the snow slides and rockfalls the men caused as they made their way to the bottom of the gorge. They crossed the stream, began the difficult climb up the other side, and finally reached a ledge about 400 yards from the plant. Threading through a minefield and staying out of sight of the German sentries, they found a basement door; two men got into the factory through a cable duct which Brun had described, unlocked the door and let the rest of the party in. They detained the only workman in the plant that Sunday morning—a Norwegian. Then they laid the charges on all eighteen cells which helped produce the heavy water.

By 1 A.M. Gunnerside had finished its work; the fuses had been set and started. The men told the Norwegian workman to find a place of safety on one of the upper floors; and then they withdrew, scrambling down into the gorge and crossing the stream. As they began the climb on the other side, the charges exploded, and the Germans woke up to the noise of the blast and the wail of an air-raid siren. Not a shot had been fired; the Germans never saw the Gunnerside attackers, who melted into the darkness and would escape on a 250-mile march across the Hardanger plateau into Sweden. But each one of the cells had been blown up and almost a ton of heavy water had been destroyed.

When the results of the attack were analyzed in London, it was predicted that the German production of heavy water would be delayed by two years. As it was, the plant was restored by April of that same year, and toward the end of 1943 the Germans were again able to begin tapping heavy water. By that time Niels Bohr was in London. He had been spirited away from Copenhagen by MI-6 with the aid of the Princes, and he again warned of the dangers of a German atomic bomb. On November 16, 1943, the American high command ordered the 8th Air Force to make another attack on the Rjukan plant. Over seven hundred 500-pound bombs rained down upon the target, and while the plant escaped, sufficient damage was done to the power system to make further production of heavy water impossible for some time. With that, Goering, who was the minister responsible for the German atomic program, decided the time had come to evacuate the Vemork installations to Germany.

News of the decision was quickly in London. On November 30, 1943, Einar Skinnerland, SOE's principal agent in Norway, radioed from his base at Telemark that Vemork was to be evacuated to Germany. When this intelligence was examined at a meeting in London, it was decided that because Germany's available hydroelectric power was so limited and costly, the evacuation of the plant would present no immediate danger to the Allies. But there would be danger if the Germans successfully evacuated their existing stocks of heavy water. Skinnerland was instructed to make developments at Vemork his primary target.

At the end of January 1944, Skinnerland was able to wireless that the heavy water consignment was ready for shipment to Germany. There were 14 tons of fluid and 613 kilograms of heavy water in various stages of concentration; the Germans had drawn off the lot and stored it for shipment in thirty-nine drums stenciled with the words "Potash Lye." Moreover, Skinnerland reported, the consignment and the route over which it was to be shipped were being guarded by special squads of *Feldgrau* and SS. London wirelessed back to enquire about the opportunities for preventing the shipment. But Skinnerland replied that if the British intended to do anything militarily they would have to act quickly; he had heard that the heavy water was to begin its journey from Rjukan in seven days. SOE acted hurriedly; Knut Haukelid, a member of Gunnerside who had remained behind in Norway, and Skinnerland were instructed to attack and destroy the shipment.

By February 9, Haukelid and Skinnerland had decided that a direct attack upon the Vemork plant was out of the question. The only way to destroy the heavy water was to destroy it in transit; but that might provoke reprisals, and Skinnerland wirelessed London for the permission of the Norwegian government-in-exile. It was granted—reluctantly, because the American bombing in November had caused many deaths among the Rjukans, and much ill-feeling in Norway as a whole. Haukelid then went to Rjukan to see the plant's chief engineer, Alf Larsen, who had succeeded Brun. How could the heavy water be destroyed? Larsen thought it would be vulnerable to attack at only one point. The Germans, he revealed, intended to transport the heavy water in railway wagons from the plant down to the rail-ferry that crossed Lake Tinnsjö to Tinnoset. There, it would proceed by rail and road to Heröya for loading onto the ship for Germany. The lake was particularly deep—1300 feet at one point—and if the ferry was sunk, the cargo could never be salvaged. Larsen agreed to arrange it so the heavy water would be ready for shipment only in time to catch the ferry on Sunday morning, February 20, a day when it would be less crowded with Norwegian civilians than at any other time in the week; and Haukelid agreed to help Larsen escape to avoid certain execution for his part in the conspiracy.

When Haukelid and his men began to reconnoiter their target, they discovered that the ferry which would be working that Sunday morning was the *Hydro,* an old, screw-driven boat with a funnel on either side of the main deck. Railway trucks from Rjukan were shunted on at one end and shunted off the other when the ferry reached Tinnoset. Haukelid made a trial journey aboard the *Hydro* and noticed that the ferry entered deep water about thirty minutes after sailing. He concluded that if the ferry's bottom was holed by an explosion exactly forty-five minutes after departing, she would sink in deep water—even allowing for some unpunctuality. He also decided to place the charges in the bow; he wanted the ferry to sink bow-first, which would send the screws and rudders in the air and leave the boat helpless. There would be no chance for the captain to run her aground and save his cargo. The explosion had to be big enough to sink the ship, but not so severe as to cause casualties among the passengers and crew. Haukelid calculated, therefore, that he would need 18 pounds of *plastique* shaped into a sausage 12 feet long. This he made, and put it into a sack. He also made two fuses with ordinary alarm clocks, tested one, found it worked, and then he and his men retired to their mountain hideout.

Meanwhile, both London and Berlin were taking extraordinary steps, the former to make sure that the heavy water did not reach Germany, the latter to see that it did. SOE wirelessed a second group in Norway, "Chaffinch," to attack the consignment if it got as far as Heröya. The RAF was ordered to lay on a mission to sink the ship taking the heavy water across to Germany—if the consignment got that far. At the same time an SS police company was moved to Rjukan, a squadron of Fieseler Storch reconnaissance aircraft was sent from Himmler's Special Air Group to fly anti-ambush patrols, and a large army detachment was assigned to guard the heavy water during its journey. SD agents detected that some plan was afoot to destroy the consignment; but they were not sure how and where the attack would be made. In consequence, the Germans decided to mount a special guard from Vemork down to the lake and, when the *Hydro* reached the far side, to split the shipment into two halves and send them by different routes and methods. Oddly, they undertook no precautions of a special nature aboard the *Hydro* itself.

At 11 P.M. on February 19, the night before the consignment was to arrive, Haukelid and two of his men went down to the quay and boarded the *Hydro;* the boat was alongside overnight and her crew was having a party. There were no German guards aboard, but there were Norwegian watchmen. One of them stopped Haukelid and his companions as they entered the passenger saloon, but Haukelid explained that they were on the run from the Gestapo and asked for his help. The watchman showed them the door into the bilges, and Haukelid went down with one of his men, leaving the other to guard the door. Once in the bilges, they made their way along the flat bottom to the bow, and there, deep in filthy water, they laid the charge with an electric detonator and timed the fuse. By 4 A.M. that morning the job was finished, and Haukelid and his men left the *Hydro*. If all went well, at 10:45 the following morning the *Hydro* and its cargo would be on the bottom of Lake Tinnsjö.

Haukelid collected Larsen and the two men immediately began their flight, traveling by car and skis to Kongsberg, where they would board a train for the first stage of their journey to Sweden. Just as they were buying their tickets, the train from Oslo pulled in and the SS police chief of Rjukan, a certain Muggenthaler, stepped out. He had been called back from a weekend in the capital to superintend the movement of the heavy water.

At 8 A.M. that Sunday—February 20, 1944—the ferry train left the Rjukan sidings with two wagons laden with drums containing the heavy water. Guards were posted at 30-yard intervals on either side of the track, and the Fieseler Storchs flew overhead. The train itself was guarded by SS men, and Muggenthaler rode on the locomotive. By 10 A.M. the wagons had been anchored to the *Hydro*'s deck, and the ferry set out on schedule with fifty-three people aboard. Then, exactly at 10:45 A.M., the ferry shuddered under the impact of a violent "knock." The exploding *plastique* ripped a hole in the *Hydro,* and it began to settle by the bow. Seconds later, the railway wagons broke loose and plunged through the bow doors into the depths of Lake Tinnsjö. Within five minutes the *Hydro* had sunk, with the loss of twenty-six passengers and crew, all of whom were drowned. Only three of the heavy water containers were ever salvaged.

With that explosion, Germany's hopes of building an atomic bomb in time for use in the Second World War ended. It was a major triumph for Britain in the secret war. For as Dr. Kurt Diebner, one of the main figures in the Reich's research and development program, acknowledged after the war, ". . . it was the elimination of German heavy water production in Norway that was the main factor in our failure to achieve a self-sustaining atomic reactor before the war ended." The Allies had knocked out one potential threat to the success of D-Day and even to the eventual outcome of the war, although that fact would not become known for many months. But these special operations would have another repercussion on D-Day. They reaffirmed Hitler's conviction that Norway was an area of special danger to the Reich, and he would continue to pour more men, guns, concrete and steel into Norway than into Normandy.

Teheran

AT WASHINGTON, on the site of the old Government Experimental Farm alongside the Potomac, a huge five-story building of five concentric rings had sprung up, so it seemed, almost overnight. It was the Pentagon and from it General Marshall, as Chief of Staff of the United States Army, was directing the mighty American military effort that would be launched against Germany on D-Day. On the eve of the Cairo and Teheran conferences in November 1943, Marshall was approaching the pinnacle of his power and influence, for he and his staff had forged, in under two years, the largest, best-fed, best-clothed, best-equipped military machine in the world. Its lavish provision of armor and transport, of aircraft and ships, was the envy of all other generals; and American industry not only supplied its own armed forces but also provided much of the weaponry for its Allies. But more than machinery was being manufactured; a new world order had been created, and the Pentagon would become a monument to Marshall's achievements, to the military and industrial effort involved in D-Day, and to that new world order.

The building was a modern marvel—like Big Ben when it first chimed. At the Pentagon, there was none of the damp, monkish atmosphere of Hitler's headquarters, nor the wardroom air of Churchill's. Here everything was impersonal and aseptic, busy, purposeful and air-conditioned—a portent of America's future. But in Marshall's offices, overlooking the Pentagon's greenswards and the Potomac, there were reminders of her past. His desk was an antique first used by General Philip Sheridan, a Union hero of the Civil War, the victor of the battles of the Yellow Tavern and Dinwiddie Courthouse. Across the room was a long conference table, also a relic of Sheridan. On one wall hung an oil painting of a scene on the Meuse-Argonne battlefield, the American offensive that made inevitable the defeat of the German army in 1918; and on another there was a picture of some American soldiers singing hymns around an organ in a shell-shattered church in France. Dominating the room was a large, somber portrait of John J. Pershing, the commanding general of the American Expeditionary Force to France and the great American hero of the First World War.

Would Marshall become the Supreme Commander of the Allied Expeditionary Force in the Second World War? As he prepared to travel with the President and the Chiefs of Staff to Cairo and Teheran, Marshall was under the impression that he would be appointed to that post; Mrs. Marshall was packing for London and the general had even given instructions for his favorite desk set to be sent to U.S. headquarters there. But the President had not yet made up his mind. As for Eisenhower, he was so convinced that Marshall would be made Supreme Commander that he wrote to him asking for an appointment as an army group commander in Overlord. There were rumors that Eisenhower might succeed Marshall as Chief of Staff, but he also wrote, "I do not think I would be a success in your job. I understand so little about politics, and dislike them so much."

On November 11, 1943, in great secrecy, Marshall and the U.S. Chiefs of Staff embarked upon the new American battleship *Iowa* to cross the Atlantic for the last of the great conferences of grand strategy of the Second World War. It would be, the Americans intended, a final showdown with the British. For despite the solemn commitment made by Churchill and Brooke to Overlord at the Quebec Conference, the British seemed, once more, to be wavering in their preparations for what would be the decisive action of the war. Marshall and his staff were determined to accept no further delay. Morgan, after a visit to Marshall and the President in Washington, had warned Brooke that the fight at Cairo and Teheran was going to be tough; in comparison, that at Quebec might be considered "child's play."

Roosevelt and his adviser Harry Hopkins came aboard the *Iowa* and the squadron's pennants streamed in the stiff breeze as the battleship plunged into the Atlantic rollers for Gibraltar and beyond. At about the same time, Churchill and Brooke were at sea off Trafalgar aboard the British battleship *Renown*. Those who looked for symbols saw in these majestic warships the altered status of the two powers. *Iowa* was new, sparkling with fresh paint, steel, brass and wood, manned by young sailors untested by war, only just ready for a great voyage. *Renown* was old, mauled in battle, salt-stained, magnificent but weary.

Relations between Marshall and Brooke, while outwardly courteous, had not improved as both men journeyed to the conference. Neither trusted the other; and Brooke pronounced in his diary: "I wish our Conference was over. I despair of getting our American friends to have any strategic vision." At the root of his despair was his belief that "Anvil," the invasion of the Riviera proposed by the Americans to split the German armies on D-Day, was totally unnecessary. With his confidence in the skills of the LCS unshaken by the Cockade fiasco, Brooke believed that the German army in southern France could be tied down by feint, menace and deception. A vast military expedition such as the Americans envisaged need not be mounted at all, and the forces they proposed to use in Anvil could more profitably be used to strengthen the Italian campaign and back diversionary operations in the Balkans. Moreover, these forces would ensure a postwar Allied military presence in southeastern Europe and the Middle East.

But Marshall did not see the war's strategy this way. He insisted that full American power could be deployed in France only if the port of Marseilles was secured, arguing that the Germans would certainly destroy Cherbourg before it was captured. He refused to accept as wisdom Brooke's advocacy and complained that Brooke was acting in "a most underhand" way in trying to engage the United States in what Marshall believed would be a costly and indecisive campaign in the Balkans and the eastern Mediterranean. He swore that he would resign rather than commit America to land operations in that region. Another Anglo-American confrontation was in the making as the two ships steamed toward Cairo. But at Teheran a third party would join the discussions—Premier Josef Stalin. His weight would tip the scales decisively—but in which direction?

General John R. Deane, the chief of the U.S. military mission in Moscow, wirelessed *Iowa* to warn that he had information that the British and the Russians would "gang up" on the United States to force her to engage in Italian and Balkans operations. The U.S. Chiefs of Staff had not prepared for the possibility of an Anglo-Russian entente, although they had position papers for every other contingency. The main paper was a document of thirty-eight pages designed, in particular, to provide answers to "probable British proposals . . . regarding changes in the specific operations planned to implement our strategy in Europe." The document reflected the fact that England and America held markedly different opinions about the state of affairs in Germany at this juncture in the war. In the American view, the British believed that Germany was weakening so rapidly that she might simply collapse, in which case Overlord would prove unnecessary; the Allies had merely to await that collapse and then move unopposed through the French ports and occupy Europe up to the line of the Oder. All that had to be done to bring about this collapse—according to the American appreciation of the British view—was to put additional pressure on the Third Reich with continued bombing, blockade, subversion, sabotage and deception. The Americans, however, did not share this belief. Conceding that such a collapse was possible "even within the next three months or so," the paper nevertheless went on to state:

> . . . we estimate the odds are greatly against its occurrence at so early a date. . . . The British take, or are prepared to take, a more optimistic view.

We are not cognizant of the information from which they drew their conclusions. If, however, they can present factual data which (is) convincing,
we should be prepared to change our view.

Were the Americans really "not cognizant" of the information from
which the British drew their conclusions, or had they not paid sufficient
attention to their own? For at the root of this disagreement were differing
views as to the efficacy of the Schwarze Kapelle; and the Americans,
through Dulles at Berne, should have been at least as well informed about
the conspiracy as the British. Churchill and the British planners, with their
emphasis on indirect tactics, had come to regard the conspiracy as one of a
group of potential means of destroying Hitler, means that would cost the
Allies far less in lives and treasure than Overlord. But Roosevelt and his
planners still preferred to employ American might. And here lay both the
greatness and the tragedy of the war, for the entire military, industrial
and intellectual might of the Anglo-Saxon world was being committed to
end a government and an ideology when a single pistol shot might have
achieved just that.

In pre-conference sessions aboard *Iowa,* the American planners drew
up their strategy of battle, not against the Germans, but against the British.
Marshall recommended that Roosevelt adopt a "very cautious stand" on
any British proposals for operations in the Balkans—a recommendation to
which the President replied: "Amen!" The British, Marshall further
recommended, should be compelled to honor their agreements at Washington and Quebec to Overlord; the only diversionary action in the Mediterranean should be Anvil. Roosevelt's advisers pressed him to nominate
Marshall as Supreme Commander. But, the President wished to know, did
the Americans now have sufficient power to enable them to take charge in
so arbitrary a manner? Yes, they did, said Marshall. On January 1, 1944,
United States forces overseas would consist of 10.7 million men and
12,500 aircraft against Britain's 4.4 million men and 9000 aircraft. These
figures so impressed the President that, in Marshall's presence, he declared
that "General Marshall should be the C-in-C against Germany and command all the British, French, Italian and U.S. troops involved in this
effort."

Marshall, however, in his conviction that Churchill and Brooke would
try to "wash out" on Overlord and advocate instead expanded operations
in the Mediterranean, was seriously misled, or had himself failed to understand, the British advocacy. It was true that the British were wary of a
cross-Channel attack and had repeatedly insisted that certain preconditions
must be met before the invasion took place. But as Brooke and Churchill
had also insisted, it was never Britain's intention not to invade Europe
from England, nor to abandon Overlord for the Balkans. It was Britain's

intention to suck German forces into that mountain wilderness by diversionary operations, indirect tactics and special means—deception, political warfare, the use of agents, Commandos and resistance forces—so that they would not be available in Normandy on D-Day or the weeks that followed. That, in a nutshell, was the reason for Plan Jael. Was Marshall himself being misled by Jael? It was possible, for it was sometimes difficult, particularly from Churchill's statements, to distinguish between the deception strategy and the actual military strategy of the British.

On November 22, 1943, the President and Marshall, having left *Iowa* at Oran, landed at Cairo Airport in the President's airliner, the *Sacred Cow*. A squadron of Buicks drove them to their quarters, a group of villas standing amid tamarind and eucalyptus beneath the great Pyramid of Cheops. There, under the scrutiny of Brooke and of the Great Sphinx, they were greeted by Churchill. He wore a white duck suit, a white Panama hat and white shoes, and he carried a little gold-topped ebony cane. He looked like a butterfly hunter. But for all his bonhomie, Churchill was deeply worried. Lord Moran, who again attended the Prime Minister, noted that he had been gravely disturbed by the events at Salerno, which had served to confirm his forebodings over D-Day. "On the way here," Moran observed, "it became plain that he (was) brooding on the extraordinary difficulties of this 'prodigious undertaking.' He has grown more and more certain that an invasion of France as planned must fail."

When the conference opened, it was immediately apparent to the British Chiefs of Staff what the Americans intended to do. They were going to wait until Teheran to learn the Russians' position on Overlord and the Balkans before showing their hand. Warily, all parties sat around the conference table in the handsome Mena Palace Hotel. Both sides were beautifully prepared; but instead of discussing Overlord, the Americans grasped the initiative by announcing that they wished to consider the problems of the war in the Orient. General Chiang Kai-shek—"a formidable-looking ruffian, with a square jaw, carelessly shaven, dressed in a black robe like a monk"—had been invited to the conference; and to the annoyance of Churchill, the General and Madame Chiang were permitted to attend some of the key sessions.

The Americans advocated an operation to assist Chiang by landing British and American troops on the Andaman Islands in the Bay of Bengal. Churchill and Brooke were impatient to discuss similar operations in the Aegean to divert German strength from Overlord. Tempers began to fray as Marshall insisted that the Andaman operation be authorized, and Brooke declared that it was a waste of time and effort. Finally, the explosion came; it was one of the worst recorded rows between the British and the Americans. General Joseph W. Stilwell, the American commander in Southeast Asia, recalled that "Brooke got good and nasty and King

(Admiral Ernest J. King) got good and sore. King almost climbed over the table at Brooke. God, he was mad! I wish he had socked him!"

Subsequent meetings tottered along in an atmosphere of disappointment and perversity on both sides, and when the conference broke up to make ready for the long flight to Teheran, storm signals were flying. Moran wrote in his diary: ". . . I have noticed lately a certain hardening of purpose in the American camp. . . . There is an ominous sharpness in their speech when they say that they are not going to allow things to be messed about in this way indefinitely." He would also record that Harry Hopkins told him quite frankly: "Sure, we are preparing for a battle at Teheran. You will find us lining up with the Russians." And of this remark, Moran noted: "What I find so shocking is that to the Americans the P.M. is the villain of the piece; they are far more sceptical of him than they are of Stalin."

Both Roosevelt and Churchill arrived in Teheran as suitors, the object of their attentions the inscrutable Stalin. The President could state his case from a position of strength; in return for Russian support in demanding from Churchill an unequivocal commitment to Overlord, Stalin could expect the full force of American power on the long-awaited Second Front. Churchill's position would be much more difficult. He knew that Russia was in trouble. The British military mission in Moscow had reported that in twenty-nine months of war, Russia's casualties were approaching 7 million dead soldiers, over 10 million dead civilians, and about 12 million wounded. Much of her industry and agriculture was in ruins. The Red Army was so war-weary and bloodlet that it might be in the same temper as Czar Nicholas's army after the Brusilov Offensive of July 1916, when Russia shot her bolt against the Kaiser—and made the Bolshevik revolution inevitable. Might not the brave and stoic Russian *moujik* rise up and revolt against Stalin? Under these circumstances, Churchill thought that Stalin would be willing to make a deal. In return for a British commitment to Overlord, he would attempt to win Russian support for expanded operations in the eastern Mediterranean and the Balkans to divert German strength from the Normandy beaches.

But Stalin was in no mood for deals. He came to Teheran not to be chosen, but to choose. And the object of *his* attentions was Roosevelt. Clearly, much more was at stake than Overlord. The invasion was inevitable; it was now a question not of how the war would be fought, but how it would be won—and the shape the world would take afterwards. Roosevelt wanted a quick and decisive victory to present to the American electorate the following year, a victory that would ensure American mercantile hegemony throughout the postwar world. It was Britain that seemed to stand in the way of both objectives, and despite the long antipathy between capitalism and communism, Roosevelt was willing to cast his lot with Russia. Churchill, too, sought victory, but a victory that would not sap the last ounce of Britain's strength and leave her a second-rate world power. His concern for the eastern Mediterranean was not only to ensure the success of Overlord, but to maintain Britain's influence in the area and preserve her lifeline to her Empire in the East. And what of Stalin? His choice was not difficult. He thought Churchill's intention was to permit the Germans and the Russians to bleed each other into exhaustion, and so leave the Anglo-American alliance the world's most powerful force when the guns went silent. If he could drive a wedge through that alliance, so much the better; the Cold War had begun. Moreover, Stalin had his own political interests in the eastern Mediterranean, and he would do what he could to forestall any interference in the Balkans and to undermine British influence in the Mideast.

Stalin made his first move to court Roosevelt the moment the American party landed. The U.S. legation in the capital was over a mile away from the center of the city where the British and Russian embassies were to be found side by side. As a result, Roosevelt would have to travel each day through bazaars and crowded streets that were, Stalin told him, dangerous. The Russian intelligence service, said Stalin to Roosevelt shortly after his arrival, had obtained information that the SD was planning to assassinate him. A Russian agent, one Nikolai Kuznetzsov, had discovered that an operation codenamed "Long Pounce" had been mounted by Brigadeführer SS Otto Skorzeny, the German stormtrooper who had just rescued Mussolini from his captors at Gran Sasso in the Abruzzi Mountains of Italy. Six agents were known to have landed in the foothills of the Elburz Mountains around Teheran; they were, Stalin said, the advance party of Long Pounce. Might it not be wiser for Roosevelt to take one of the comfortable villas within the Russian Embassy grounds? Although the British warned the Americans that Long Pounce might be a Russian trick to get Roosevelt into Stalin's pocket—as Brooke put it—he accepted Stalin's invitation. He moved to the Russian villa and, the moment he had settled in, Stalin called upon him. The two leaders talked at length—alone. "This conference," observed Brooke when he heard of the meeting, "is over when it has only just begun."

The first plenary session of the conference opened in the Russian Embassy, and the protagonists were, predictably, Churchill, the son of an aristocrat, and Stalin, the son of a cobbler. The eloquent, florid and calculating Prime Minister offered a dramatic contrast to the blunt, almost rude, but equally calculating Georgian marshal. When he was asked what Russia would like to see the western Allies do, Stalin needed no position papers to answer the question. Although it was true, he said, that the Germans would resist there most desperately, the logical invasion point was north or northwest France. Churchill agreed but advocated diversionary operations launched either through the Ljubljana Gap or through the Balkans. Stalin responded by asking about Anvil. That, he said, with an eye to keeping Anglo-American troops out of eastern Europe, would be the only sensible operation. Overlord should be the main attack in 1944, he said, with Anvil as the diversionary assault.

The Americans were jubilant at Stalin's pronouncement; the British were not. It was at this point that Marshall revealed, despite his utter conviction that Overlord would succeed, that he, too, was gravely concerned about the problems of the cross-Channel attack. He said across the conference table to Marshal Klementi Voroshilov: "The difference between a river crossing, however wide, and a landing from the ocean is that the failure of a river crossing is a reverse while the failure of a landing operation is a catastrophe." He also admitted his lack of expertise for such an operation with the words: "Prior to the present war I never heard of any landing-craft except a rubber boat. Now I think about little else." It was a telling admission for a man who, the western powers believed, was about to be appointed the Supreme Commander of an unrepeatable operation across one of the trickiest waterways in the world.

The next day, Churchill, who had learned of Roosevelt's and Stalin's talk, sent a note to the President. Would he care to come over for lunch? Roosevelt replied that he had an engagement with his staff. In fact, he lunched briefly with members of his suite and then, again alone, saw Stalin. They talked for about fifteen minutes, and then adjourned to the main hall of the Russian Embassy to attend a ceremony in which Churchill was to present to Stalin—as the representative of the Russian people—a sword of honor marking their heroism at Stalingrad.

It was a weapon of exceptional beauty, fashioned of gilded bronze with a pommel of flawless crystal and silver, and encased in a scabbard of scarlet and gold. It was brought to Churchill by a guard of honor of British infantrymen who carried it on a cushion of Persian lambskin and crimson velvet. Beneath a huge tapestry of Napoleon's retreat across the Borodino, Churchill unsheathed the weapon for all to see, and it glinted and flashed in the weak sunlight of a Persian winter's day. Then he handed it to Stalin with the words:

> I have been commanded by His Majesty King George VI to present to you for transmission to the City of Stalingrad this sword of honor, the design of which His Majesty has chosen and approved. The sword of honor was made by English craftsmen whose ancestors have been employed in sword-making for generations. The blade of the sword bears the inscription: "To the steel-hearted citizens of Stalingrad, a gift from King George VI as a token of homage of the British people."

Stalin was visibly moved, and he replied briefly:

On behalf of the citizens of Stalingrad, I wish to express my deep appreciation for the gift of King George VI. The citizens of Stalingrad will value this gift most highly, and I ask you, Mr. Prime Minister, to convey their thanks to His Majesty the King.

Stalin kissed the hilt, and with that, handed it to Roosevelt to examine. Its 50 inches of tempered steel flashed again, and the President's hands looked small upon the hilt. "Truly they had hearts of steel," he murmured. With a ring, the sword was returned to its scabbard and Stalin handed it to Marshal Voroshilov. But, to the dismay of all, Voroshilov fumbled and the sword dropped with a noble clatter on the marble floor. As a Russian soldier hastened forward to pick it up, Stalin's eyes did not move from the face of Churchill. The accident—if it was an accident—reflected the indifference of Stalin to any British stratagem. He was interested only in winning the war, and then the peace.

The ceremony over, the triumvirs and their staffs resumed the great debate, and once again, Stalin challenged Churchill's position. The Russians, he said, needed help, urgent help, and that being the case, there were only three matters of concern to the Red Army: the date of Overlord, which must be in May and no later; Anvil; and the appointment of a Supreme Commander. Both Roosevelt and Churchill assured him that the Supreme Commander would be named within a fortnight. But with an eye to security—for if the Russians had spies in high places in Berlin, might not the Germans have spies in high places in Moscow?—they were evasive about the date of Overlord. Churchill once again attempted to advocate diversionary operations in the Balkans, but Stalin was impatient with these involved discussions. He addressed Churchill with what he called a "very direct question." "Do the Prime Minister and the British Staff really believe in 'Overlord'?" Churchill replied: "Provided the conditions previously stated for 'Overlord' are established when the time comes, it will be our stern duty to hurl across the Channel against the Germans every sinew of our strength."

The meeting adjourned to allow those present to prepare for a dinner at which Stalin was to be the host, and again Churchill was in a grim mood. As he dressed for the party, he muttered to Moran, who had come to spray his throat: "Nothing more can be done here." When Churchill had stumped off, muttering a "bloody" or two about the situation, Moran went to dinner with the British Chiefs of Staff—and found them in a similar temper. Brooke turned to him and said: "I shall come to you to send me to a lunatic asylum. I cannot stand much more of this. Seven hours' conference today, and we are not an inch further." The British staff was in a mutinous mood, not because of any fear of Overlord but because of their inability to persuade the Americans that Stalin's rejection of diversionary operations in the eastern Mediterranean had political rather than military objectives. The British high commanders also discussed the possibility that Germany might break, and "the crack," in Moran's view, "may appear at the top." But while the British hoped to derive some advantage from the disaffection of Hitler's generals, the Premier of the Soviet Union was proposing another way to deal with the entire German General Staff.

Stalin's dinner party was an endless succession of snacks and toasts that climaxed in a giant ice-cream cake modeled after an ornate Persian lantern, a work of art that was melting when it arrived and was spilled over Stalin's interpreter, who continued his translation "without the slightest pause." When the vodka began to take hold there was some merciless leg-pulling of Churchill by Stalin and Roosevelt. Uneasily, the Prime Minister sparred with humor and restraint—until Stalin suddenly grew serious and, in his quiet Georgian growl, said that after the war the German General Staff must be liquidated. Hitler's armies depended upon about 50,000 officers and technicians, Stalin went on, and if these were "rounded up and shot . . . German military strength would be extirpated." Churchill, his mind only barely dulled by his consumption of champagne, responded very sharply. He rose from the table and, pacing the dining room, retorted: "The British Parliament and public will never tolerate mass executions. Even if in war passion they allowed them to begin, they would turn violently against those responsible after the first butchery had taken place. The Soviets must be under no delusion on this point." Stalin was unmoved; he reiterated that "Fifty thousand must be shot." Churchill retorted, very red in the face: "I would rather be taken out into the garden here and now and be shot myself than sully my own and my country's honour by such infamy." Then Roosevelt intervened with a compromise—not fifty thousand, only forty-nine thousand must be shot.

At that moment, the President's son, Colonel Elliott Roosevelt, who had joined the party as an uninvited guest, rose unsteadily. He announced that he was in agreement with Stalin's proposal and that he was sure that the United States army would support it. With that, Churchill, who disliked young Roosevelt, got up from his place a second time and walked out. He found a deserted anteroom and sat down to brood. Stalin followed, and without warning or noise, he entered the room and put his hand on Churchill's shoulder. He was, said Stalin, merely joking, and asked Churchill to come back to the party. Churchill agreed and the two returned to the dining room. Stalin, who was grinning, said to Churchill: "You are pro-German. The devil is a communist, and my friend God a conservative." The conversation ended in a convivial embrace. But as Churchill wrote later: ". . . I was not then . . . fully convinced that all was chaff and there was no serious intent lurking behind. . . ." Jest or not, the exchange over the fate of the German General Staff showed clearly to Churchill that, whether he wished to make an arrangement with the Schwarze Kapelle or not, such a settlement would be no more acceptable to his Russian than to his American Allies.

The conference met for the last time on November 30, 1943, Churchill's sixty-ninth birthday. The day began with Churchill seeking a man-to-man meeting with Stalin, without Roosevelt or the triumvirate's staffs. The reason for the meeting was, as Churchill wrote later, "I felt that the Russian leader was not deriving a true impression of the British attitude. The false idea was forming in (Stalin's) mind that, to put it shortly, 'Churchill and the British Staffs mean to stop "Overlord" if they can, because they want to invade the Balkans instead.' " In other words, Stalin, like Roosevelt and Marshall, had come to believe that the activities attending Plan Jael were symptoms of actual British policy rather than dissimulation. It was, as Churchill said, his duty to remove these misconceptions. The two men met, and Churchill presented a lengthy exposition of the British case. Stalin was friendly, but firm; he was interested only in Overlord and Anvil. It left Churchill with one last recourse. If he still wished to employ indirect tactics and special means to limit the casualties that Britain would suffer on the Far Shore on D-Day, his only hope was to get all parties to accept and work together on Plan Jael itself.

That afternoon, at the third and last plenary session of the conference, Jael was the topic for discussion. And here Churchill was faced with a difficult decision. Jael could not succeed without Russian support, but the British and Russian secret agencies that would be largely responsible for implementing and disseminating the plan were long-standing enemies. Before, during and since the Russian revolution the two services had fought each other with ferocity—the Russians to supplant the British Empire, the British to destroy the Bolshevik revolution and restore to Russia a more congenial government. This clandestine, muffled struggle had not stopped at murder, nor at abduction and blackmail; it had only temporarily subsided because of the mutual need of Westminster and the Kremlin to defeat Hitler. When the world war was over, the Russo-British secret war could be expected to begin again with the same old savagery and determination—as, indeed, it did. Strategic deception would be an important, perhaps decisive weapon in that struggle; if Churchill revealed to the Russians how he proposed to make Jael work, the Russians would surely adapt these new concepts to their own needs when the secret war with Britain resumed.

Yet, Churchill did not hesitate. For the moment, nothing was more important than the success of Overlord. In that spirit, he outlined Jael and, to a certain extent, British methods of deception. In order to deflect Hitler's armies from Normandy, he explained, it would be necessary for Britain, the United States and Russia together to carry out a wide variety of diplomatic and military maneuvers to suggest that the three powers would conduct major invasions in Scandinavia and the Balkans. Russia would also be required to infect the German intelligence services with the belief that, by agreement at Teheran, the western powers would not invade France until after the Red Army had launched its main offensive for 1944, an offensive that the Germans were to be led to believe would not begin until July. By these and other misrepresentations of Allied strategy, it was to be hoped, said Churchill, that the Germans would keep their armies in place until after the main Allied force was ashore in France. Churchill then concluded with the proposal that representatives of the Anglo-American deception agencies fly to Moscow to discuss and integrate their plans with the Russian General Staff so that the Germans would behold a common, impenetrable front of deception concerning the military intentions of the Grand Alliance. Without such a front, Churchill warned, surprise might be denied the Allies and Overlord itself might fail.

Stalin, himself a master of stratagem and its value in war and politics, listened intently. But when he spoke of some of the deceptive tactics practiced by the Red Army—dummy tanks and planes, mock airfields and misleading wireless activity—it was evident that Russian methods were quite orthodox. Stalin had much to learn of the art of strategic deception on a global scale; and because he was well aware of what might befall the Red Army if Overlord failed, he agreed immediately to Churchill's proposal. "Military diplomacy must be used for military purposes," Stalin is supposed to have said, "and I would treat with the devil himself, and his grandmama, if it would help me defeat Hitler."

It was then, with a hint of rascality, that Churchill remarked: "In wartime, truth is so precious that she should always be attended by a bodyguard of lies." The remark was translated for Stalin, who chuckled. But with those words a unique alliance was struck; the British, American, Russian—and, to some extent, the German—secret services would now be united in a plan to rid the world of Hitler. The alliance was written into the Military Conclusions of the great conference:

> Agreed that the military staffs of the three Powers should henceforward keep in close touch with each other in regard to the impending operations in Europe. In particular it was agreed that a cover plan to mystify and mislead the enemy as regards these operations should be concerted between the Staffs concerned.

The three leaders placed their signatures upon the document. Plan Jael had become an act of statehood.

The conference was over, and the next day Churchill and Roosevelt flew back to Cairo. There, alone, Roosevelt began to deliberate upon who should be the Supreme Commander for Overlord. The choice could no longer be delayed. Finally he made his decision "against the almost impassioned advice of Hopkins and Stimson, against the known preference of both Stalin and Churchill, against his own proclaimed inclination to give to George Marshall the historic opportunity which he so greatly desired and so amply deserved." On Sunday morning, December 5, 1943, as they were driven out to look at the Pyramids, Roosevelt mentioned to Churchill that he felt that Marshall was both "invaluable, and indispensable to the successful conduct of the war" and that he could not spare him from Washington. Would the British accept Eisenhower? Churchill replied that it was a question which the President alone could decide, but that "we had also the warmest regard for General Eisenhower, and would trust our fortunes to his direction with hearty good will."

It would later be alleged that the British had pressured Roosevelt into appointing Eisenhower to the Supreme Command. They were looking, according to Ingersoll, for a "front man" to placate the demands of American public opinion, a man to handle "the hot political pokers" and take "the bows," while British commanders actually ran the show. They had found such a man in Eisenhower, Ingersoll would contend, and "It was confidently expected by London that he would repeat his Mediterranean performance, stick to politics and leave the management of the war in the field to those with more experience while reaping the appropriate rewards and elevations in the public's eye." There may have been some truth in these charges, although there was no evidence of how, where, when or by whom any such pressure was put on Roosevelt. Whatever the case, the Grand Alliance had at last agreed upon a strategy—a direct, triphibious assault against a heavily fortified and defended coastline. The American advocacy had prevailed, and an American would command this most complex and dangerous of all military operations. It was a daring strategy; some thought it foolhardy. But no one doubted that, win or lose, D-Day would be the conclusive action of the war.

Cicero

In the last quarter of 1943 and first quarter of 1944, neutral Turkey was a crucible of the secret war against the Third Reich. Turkey's great twin cities, Istanbul and the capital, Ankara, were a stew of plot and counter-plot of all descriptions as ambassadors and agents of every power, every cause and every faith intrigued beside the Golden Horn or down Boulevard Ataturk, the 3-mile street of acacia that was the main thorough-fare of Ankara. Britons, Germans, Americans, Russians—representatives of a host of nations—jostled each other, spied upon each other, compromised each other, subverted each other, bribed each other, deceived each other in Serge's, the Phaia, the Station Restaurant, Papa Karpic's; and the boulevard came to be called "The Rat Run." All sought alliances and deals; and all, whether allies or enemies, operated against each other without remission, often without remorse, in the cause of their special interests. It was Hobbesian war of every man against every man.

At this stage in the war, Britain's main game in Turkey was Plan Jael and its Mediterranean component, Zeppelin, to suggest that the Allies would make their major strike against the Third Reich somewhere along the rim of the great crescent between Trieste and Istanbul. As the British Joint Intelligence Committee appreciated in the preface to Plan Jael:

> . . . the enemy will do his utmost to hold southeast Europe, though limited withdrawals from the (Aegean) islands and southern Greece might be undertaken. Provided that we can persuade the enemy to believe that considerable forces and landing craft are being concentrated in the Eastern Mediterranean it should be possible to contain enemy forces in the Balkans. Our chances of success would be increased if Turkey joined the Allies, but even if she refused we might still induce the enemy to fear the results of our continued infiltration.

That was the intention of this phase of Plan Jael and the British were prepared, in order to further the stratagem, to accept heavy losses in men and matériel. To give substance to the deception, they began a series of Commando, secret intelligence and orthodox military operations in the Dodecanese, the group of islands in the Aegean that guarded Turkey and the Levant. The object was to display Allied power in the Mediterranean so forcibly that Turkey would be persuaded to join the Grand Alliance. And when Italy defected, Churchill wirelessed the British C-in-C in Cairo, General Sir Henry Maitland Wilson: "This is the time to play high. Improvise and dare. . . . This is the time to think of Clive and Marlborough, and of Rooke's men taking Gibraltar."

The British did play high; a brigade of 6000 men was risked to take the Dodecanese. Between September and November 1943, Wilson landed troops on Cos, Samos and Leros, but the Wehrmacht reacted with the ferocity of a power whose major interests were being gravely endangered, the Americans refused to send aircraft to Britain's assistance on the grounds that they were opposed to British adventures in the Eastern Mediterranean, and the British forces in the islands were compelled to surrender. The losses were grave—over 5000 men. Six destroyers and a submarine were sunk, four cruisers and six destroyers were damaged, and over one hundred aircraft were destroyed.

Such was the price Britain was willing to pay for the success of Jael. The defeat—the first since Tobruk in June 1942—resulted in a serious loss of prestige for the British and gave the Germans new confidence. The Americans were even more convinced of their wisdom in keeping out of the Mediterranean. And the Turks, who had been on the brink of joining the Grand Alliance, saw the havoc caused by German air and naval forces in the islands, considered what the Wehrmacht might do to Istanbul if they joined the Allies, and got back up on the fence. But at the same time, the violence of the German response confirmed her special sensitivity to the region as a whole, and at OKW the situation maps showed an Imperial tide creeping ever closer up the Aegean to the shores of southeastern Europe.

The main Jael game was played at Ankara, however, and the central figure at the table was His Britannic Majesty's Ambassador Extraordinary and Plenipotentiary, Sir Hughe Montgomery Knatchbull-Hugessen, Knight Commander of the Most Distinguished Order of St. Michael and St. George. A remnant of the stately world of British Imperial power, Sir Hughe lived in vice-regal splendor at the British Embassy at Ankara, a calm, cool place of green lawns and frangipani. There, "Snatch"—as he was known within the Foreign Office—sought to destroy German power in Turkey and bring the country into the war on the side of the Grand Alliance. He had been at Eton (with Menzies and Bevan) and at Balliol (with Wingate), he was the son of a leading divine who had married the daughter of a leading general, and he was fastidious, ducal and clever. Before this appointment he had been British ambassador to China and

British minister first to the Baltic States and then to Teheran. His relaxations were the piano, which he was said to have played very badly, and the composition of witty couplets about Foreign Office procedures. And he had aspirations to authorship; he had already written an elegant little book about the Knatchbulls of Mersham Hatch and was, while in Turkey, at work on a memoir to be entitled *Diplomat in Peace and War*. Sir Hughe seemed to have a curious love and sympathy for the plumply comfortable world of the old Ottoman Empire, with its musk and manners; but he was much trusted by Anthony Eden, whom he had known at Eton and at Oxford. As a result, he was carefully briefed on most (and sometimes all) the major British and Allied decisions of foreign policy. In particular, he was kept very fully informed on all the great conferences of 1943—and there lay both the opportunity and the danger.

Among the other residents at the embassy, there was another singular man—Elyesa Bazna, Sir Hughe's valet. It was a mutual love of German lieder that brought them more closely together than is usual for a master and his servant. For Bazna had some training as an opera singer; and so, usually after lunch, Sir Hughe would play the piano in his drawing room while Bazna, his plump hands clasped together, would sing those mournful ballads with a powerful tenor voice that the whole residence could hear. Soon, Bazna had ingratiated himself to such an extent that Sir Hughe elevated him from purely household duties to a position of some power within the residency and embassy. He dressed him in an imposing blue uniform, gave him a peaked cap, and used him as a guard to the door of his study, where Bazna excluded visitors when Sir Hughe was thinking or napping. For ceremonial occasions, Sir Hughe dressed him in richly embroidered brocade, shoes with turned-up toes, a fez with a tassel, gave him an immense scimitar, and placed him on the main door. Sir Hughe also paid him more than the 100 Turkish *lira* that was standard for a valet, and quietly turned a blind eye to the fact that Bazna was having an affair with Lady Knatchbull-Hugessen's handmaiden in the servants' quarters. In this manner did one of the oddest espionage cases of the Second World War commence. It was a case upon which great issues revolved; and there was much more to it than the British government, and Sir Hughe, would later admit.

Bazna, a dark, insolent man with considerable peasant cunning, was born in 1904 at Pristina, near Belgrade, at the time when Yugoslavia was part of the Turkish Empire. He said later that his father was a *mullah,* a Moslem holy man, that his grandfather was one of Ataturk's "Young Turks," Tahir Pasha the Brave, and that one of his uncles was Major General Kemal, another "Young Turk." Bazna also claimed that he had begun his education at the Fatih Military Academy in Turkey with three cousins, all of whom became prominent in the Turkish administration, one the Mayor of Ankara in the period 1960–62. Bazna admitted that he had been removed from the academy and, during the British occupation of Istanbul in 1919, began a life of petty crime. He said that he had been sent to a penal camp at Marseilles for stealing British army property and that his father had been shot by an Englishman in a hunting accident in Albania—two incidents that, said Bazna, made him hate the British. Upon his release from the camp at Marseilles, he worked at the Berliet motor factory, where he said he learned the locksmith's trade. In 1925, he returned to Istanbul to work in the transportation department of Istanbul Corporation, and then he moved to Yozgat to become chief of the fire brigade. Shortly before the Second World War, he came back to Istanbul as a taxi driver, and when he failed at that, he became a *kavass*—the Turkish name for a personal manservant in a diplomatic household. Before he was employed as Sir Hughe's valet, his credentials showed that he had served, not always satisfactorily, in the households of a Yugoslav ambassador, a British counselor, an American military attaché, and a German minister.

Bazna came to Sir Hughe in September 1943, a time when the British were heavily engaged in seducing Turkey; and he soon discovered that the ambassador was in the habit of bringing his telegrams and documents— most of them highly secret—to the residency to read in the afternoons and overnight. With a skill that bespoke a trained spy rather than an oppor- tunist, Bazna made a wax imprint of Sir Hughe's key to the red and black despatch boxes in which the documents came over from the chancellery, and had a key made from the impression. On or about October 20, 1943, he removed some of the documents, took them to his quarters beneath the stairs, photographed them with an old 35mm Leica, and then returned them. On about October 26 he went after dark to the house of the German minister, Albert Jenke, whom he had served previously as *kavass,* and offered to sell the photographs.

Jenke, who was the brother-in-law of Germany's Foreign Minister, Joachim von Ribbentrop, was incredulous and suspected that Bazna, whom he had neither liked nor trusted, was an agent provocateur sent by an enemy to compromise his diplomatic status. He said he also suspected that Bazna had had training as a professional spy. Nevertheless, Jenke asked Bazna how much he wanted for the film, and Bazna replied that the price was £20,000 ($80,000) for the first roll of fifty-two exposures and £15,000 ($60,000) for each roll thereafter. Jenke declared, with reason, that he was even more startled by Bazna's price; he had no authority to make such transactions, but he continued the negotiations only because Bazna said that he would take the material to the Russians if he found he could not do business with the Germans. At that, Jenke asked Bazna to wait a minute; he left the room and returned with the chief of the SD in Turkey, Ludwig Moyzisch.

Moyzisch would later record of this first encounter with Bazna that his "dark eyes kept darting nervously from me to the door and back again"; but he was intrigued by Bazna's air and by the size of the financial demand. If Bazna's claims were genuine, it was evident that he had access to the "print"—the Foreign Office term for the incoming and outgoing signals file at British embassies. Moyzisch proposed an arrangement whereby Bazna would hand over the first roll of film at 10 P.M. on October 30 at the toolshed in the embassy garden. He would remain while the film was processed and examined and, if Moyzisch was satisfied, he would be given the £20,000. Bazna agreed and left Jenke's house.

The next morning, Moyzisch saw Hitler's ambassador at Ankara, Franz von Papen. The wiliest of German foxes, Papen expressed considerable unease about Bazna but authorized Moyzisch to go ahead. Moyzisch also thought it might be a trick, but over Papen's signature, he and Jenke sent this telegram to Ribbentrop in Berlin:

> To the Reich Foreign Minister, Personal. Most Secret. We have offer of British Embassy employee alleged to be British ambassador's valet, to procure photographs of top secret original documents. For first delivery on October 30th twenty thousand pounds Sterling in bank notes are demanded. Fifteen thousand pounds for any further roll of films. Please advise whether offer can be accepted. If so sum required must be dispatched by special courier to arrive here not later than October 30. Alleged valet was employed several years ago by First Secretary otherwise nothing much known here.

In addition to Ribbentrop, the telegram was seen by Schellenberg and by Ambassador Ritter, the diplomat who looked after Wehrmacht matters and whose assistant, Fritz Kolbe, was Dulles's spy in the Reich's Foreign Ministry. Schellenberg, too, was suspicious of a plant. He recounted later: "At first glance the whole affair seemed quite staggering. . . . But in the course of my Secret Service work I had frequently faced equally risky decisions and had developed a certain intuitive feeling." He suggested that Bazna's offer be accepted, Ribbentrop agreed and Papen was informed by telegram:

> To Ambassador von Papen. Personal Most Secret. British valet's offer to be accepted taking every precaution. Special courier arriving Ankara 30th before noon. Expect immediate report after delivery of documents.

At the appointed hour Moyzisch and Bazna met at the embassy garden toolshed and there Bazna handed over a roll of 35mm film. Moyzisch then went to a cellar where he had a darkroom and the film was processed. A quick examination showed that the photographs appeared to be highly secret British diplomatic documents and telegrams. At that, Moyzisch returned to a room where Bazna was waiting and handed over the £20,000, which was wrapped up in a copy of the French-language newspaper *La République*.

Before Bazna left, Moyzisch asked him some technical questions about the method he had used to photograph the material. Bazna said he had constructed a tripod and photographed the documents by the light of a 100-watt bulb. He said the whole operation—from the time he removed the documents from the ambassador's room until he returned them—took only three minutes; and in reply to a direct question from Moyzisch, he said he worked quite alone. These statements made Moyzisch very uneasy, for Bazna told him that it was some distance from the ambassador's rooms to his own quarters, where he did the photography. Perhaps it was a slip or a boast, or both, but it seemed to Moyzisch that Bazna could not possibly have removed the documents, taken them perhaps 200 yards down several flights of stairs, photographed them, and then returned them—all within three minutes.

But Moyzisch's alarms were quieted when he studied the photographs. As he would write:

> My astonishment grew. It seemed almost beyond the realms of possibility. Here, on my desk, were most carefully guarded secrets of the enemy both political and military and of incalculable value. There was nothing suspect about these documents. These were no plant. There could be no shadow of a doubt that these were the real thing. Out of the blue there had dropped into our laps the sort of papers a secret service agent might dream about for a lifetime without believing that he could ever get hold of them. Even at a glance I could see that the valet's service to the Third Reich was unbelievably important. His price had not been exorbitant.

The documents, according to Moyzisch, were signals passed between the Foreign Office in London and the British Embassy in Ankara, none more than a fortnight old, and all marked "Top Secret" or "Most Secret." But as he read their contents, Moyzisch was struck by another thought. He wrote:

> They clearly showed the determination as well as the ability, of the Allies utterly to destroy the Third Reich. . . . Chance, combined with the obscure motives of (Bazna) had presented us with evidence which made it perfectly clear that Nazi Germany and its leaders were heading for absolute destruction. . . . This was not propaganda. . . . The power of the Allies was so enormous that more than miracles would be needed if Germany was to win the war.

Dawn broke over the German Embassy, and as Moyzisch read on he remembered "wondering whether the leaders of Germany, far away in Berlin or at the Führer's headquarters would grasp the full significance of what was here revealed. If they did then there was obviously only one course left open to them."

Moyzisch showed the documents to Papen, who also expressed astonishment at their contents. Giving Bazna his code name, "Cicero," Papen sent the documents by special courier to Berlin for evaluation. At the same time, he also sent a series of signals about the Cicero consignment, which, once more, came to the desk of Kolbe. At Berlin, Schellenberg's immediate reaction was disbelief; the documents were simply too good to be true. He suspected they had been planted and called Moyzisch to Berlin to report. But for all his suspicions, he directed that, through Himmler, they should go to Hitler.

Moyzisch arrived in Berlin "in the first week of November 1943," and after conferring with him, Schellenberg wrote in his diary:

> . . . we sought to analyse 'Cicero's' possible motives. At this time, nothing final could be said about the validity of the photographs, but both Moyzisch and I agreed that the tremendous expenditure had been justified; for even if the material should later prove to have been a deception by the enemy's Secret Service, such knowledge would have considerable value in itself, for it is most important to know by what means your enemy tries to mislead you.

Schellenberg and Moyzisch were concerned both about Bazna's credentials and his working method. There was little they could do at that point, however, to check either; and Moyzisch returned to Ankara with authorization to continue dealing with Cicero. But he soon discovered that, among other discrepancies in Bazna's accounts of himself, he had lied about his ability to speak English. Schellenberg informed Himmler of this lie, Himmler informed Hitler, and Hitler was convinced the whole thing was a British plant. Whether he accepted the documents as genuine would never become clear. Schellenberg believed that the documents themselves were not fakes, but he continued to speculate about what might lie behind the affair and whether or not Bazna worked alone. His suspicions were further aroused when, late in November, something occurred to show beyond doubt that Bazna was *not* working alone. On one of the photographs he passed to Moyzisch there appeared two of Bazna's fingers, and clearly visible was a distinctive signet ring which he always wore. With that discovery, Schellenberg sent an SD photographic expert to Ankara to establish positively, if possible, how Bazna worked.

Moyzisch asked Bazna to come to his office and there, with a tape recorder working and the expert hiding behind a curtain, he was induced to explain his methodology. On the basis of his statements, the expert concluded that "there might just be a ghost of a possibility that he works alone. I would put the odds against it at about a thousand to one." He found additional evidence to discredit Bazna's story in the photographs themselves. They were taken, the specialist reported, with a small stop to ensure perfect sharpness, through a very strong lens at a distance of about 4 feet. Furthermore, the photographer had used photo-floodlamps which appeared to have been mounted in a portable reflector—not a 100-watt bulb. And while the negatives were found to be uniformly slightly underexposed, all were perfectly focused. This would have been impossible had Bazna taken the photographs as he claimed, holding the camera in one hand and releasing the shutter with a single finger—or even using an improvised tripod. The expert concluded that whoever had taken the photographs was in a hurry, but was a skilled photographer—a good deal more skilled than Bazna claimed to be. Moreover, the documents themselves had been selected with care and precision; and it appeared unlikely that Bazna, whose English was limited and who had little experience in British diplomatic language and procedures as well as in the intricacies of the politics of the Grand Alliance, could have made such a selection.

The SD concluded that Bazna was not all he said he was. He was either a trained agent or was working with a trained agent. But the documents themselves could not be questioned; they were authentic and very high-grade papers indeed. On that basis, the SD continued to deal with Bazna until the beginning of March 1944, but at no time, before or after, did the value of the documents approach the rich harvest contained in the consignments from Cicero immediately following the Teheran Conference. Sir Hughe was kept fairly fully briefed on the course of these meetings, and through Cicero the Germans were also kept informed. It was well worth the more than £300,000 ($1.2 million) the SD paid Bazna for his services.

On or about April 20, 1944, at his own request, Bazna resigned as Sir Hughe's *kavass* and left the British Embassy. He was a rich man and he founded a company of building contractors to construct a luxury hotel in Turkey. He prospered until the Turkish banks became uneasy about the large numbers of sterling notes that were flooding the market. They traced some of the notes to Bazna, and a police investigation showed that almost all his money was forged—part of the large amount of sterling printed by the SD to finance its espionage activities and to shake the pound. As Bazna himself said, "the bank-notes . . . were not worth even the price of the Turkish linen out of which they had been manufactured." Bazna barely escaped going to jail for fraud, but he was bankrupt and spent his last years in penury, living in a tiny flat on a steep blind alley, dealing in used cars and giving singing lessons to pay his creditors. Some years after the war he brought a lawsuit against the West German government, demanding restitution. But the Germans mocked his claim; and in 1971 he died at Istanbul, virtually a pauper and still complaining about the iniquities of governments.

That, then, was the end of Cicero. But it was not the end of the story. Several years after the war, various people, including Papen, Moyzisch—and Bazna himself, who published a book about his activities—claimed to have obtained information from Sir Hughe's files that might have gravely jeopardized the security of Overlord. It was also alleged that through the Cicero papers the Germans had obtained an insight into the strategy of the Grand Alliance that might easily have wrecked it; and Sir Hughe, and the British, were accused of shocking negligence in protecting such vital secrets. The only thing that had saved them was Hitler's conviction that the Cicero papers were a plant; the valuable information they contained could only be a British deception, and he refused to act upon it. Stalin, who was now locked in the Cold War with his former friends, had another interpretation. He charged that the whole Cicero affair was a British plot to sabotage Overlord by revealing the intention, if not the substance, of the plan. In spite of the gravity of these charges, the British government maintained an official silence—with the exception of a single, brief, inconclusive reply to a question raised in the House. It was thought at the time that the silence was due to acute embarrassment. Or was there something more to the Cicero story that the government did not care to reveal? Had Bazna done what he, and others, claimed he had done? Had he been used by the British to sabotage Overlord, an operation to which they were opposed? Or was there yet another explanation for this curious case?

The truth behind Cicero must come from an examination of three important questions: Had Bazna worked alone or was he under British control; what was the nature of the documents he handed over to the Germans; and what was the German reaction to those documents? Did they work, in the long run, to the advantage of the Germans—or of Plan Jael? It was, in the first place, technically and physically impossible for Bazna to have worked alone, or for that matter, to have worked undetected —at least for long. For all Sir Hughe's grandeur, he was not a fool. He was very well aware of the extreme sensitivity of his post and the importance of the documents that passed through his hands. Even if the ambassador had nodded momentarily, there was another man on the embassy staff whose job it was to keep his eyes and ears open. That man was Lieutenant Colonel Montague Reaney Chidson, the former chief of MI-6's continental secret service, the post that Major Best held when he was kidnapped at Venlo, and now a high executive of the British secret service in Turkey, working at the embassy as "Assistant Military Attaché."

At fifty-one, Chidson was one of the most experienced officers in MI-6, having served it ever since the end of the First World War in a number of key posts—Gibraltar, Vienna, Bucharest, Budapest and The Hague. During the Battle of The Netherlands in 1940, he penetrated the vault of the Amsterdam diamond mart, the center of the world's diamond trade, spent twenty-four hours fiddling with the combination of the great safe, opened it and, as the Germans were occupying the building, escaped with the entire reserve of Dutch industrial diamonds. He got the diamonds—which were of enormous value to an industrial power at war—to London, and returned to organize the escape of Queen Wilhelmina, her family, Prince Bernhard, and members of her government to England. For that exploit Chidson was awarded, at Menzies's instigation, the Distinguished Service Order.

Then Chidson was posted to Ankara. Among his duties there was to check and observe embassy personnel, and a man such as Bazna could not have escaped his attention. When Bazna came into Sir Hughe's employment, Chidson ran a security check on the new *kavass* and discovered some disconcerting matters. Not only had Bazna once worked for the Germans, but it seemed likely that he had received some intelligence training from the Italian secret intelligence service, SIM. This would explain much, for as Dunderdale later stated, "We always thought Cicero was an Italian agent because of his modus operandi—they gave their agents special training in locksmithery and in infiltrating diplomatic households." In short, Chidson probably caught a whiff of a very familiar odor: the odor of a man who, if he was not already an enemy intelligence agent, had every potential for becoming one. What, therefore, did Chidson do? In all probability, Bazna ran undetected for a short time. But then, possibly without Bazna's knowledge, Chidson brought him under indirect control, permitting him to photograph only those documents which suited Chidson's brief. However, in light of the evidence of Bazna's fingers on one of the frames, it is also possible that Chidson confronted Bazna and brought him under direct control. There was no way of telling; Chidson said nothing about the affair before he died in 1957.

When this explanation for Bazna's espionage activities was first proposed, it was received skeptically by General Sir Colin Gubbins of SOE and by Sir John Lomax, who had been an economic warfare agent in Turkey and was one of the few survivors of Sir Hughe's régime at Ankara. While Gubbins would not have known of all MI-6 activities, and Sir John would most certainly not have been privy to any deception scheme such as Jael, both denounced the explanation as an attempt by Menzies to "whitewash the stupidity of his service at Istanbul and Ankara." In particular, Sir John declared that Cicero was not detected until one of his own agents, a Turk working close to the Turkish president, Ismet Inonu, warned him that a spy named Cicero was working in the British Embassy and supplying Papen with Sir Hughe's most secret papers. In fact, this warning came only just before Bazna resigned—long after warnings from other sources that

Cicero was a spy. And these warnings lead to the conclusion that Bazna was indeed under British control within a short time after he started to photograph the documents.

Early in December 1943, when Bazna had been working for the Germans for just over a month, Moyzisch lost his secretary's service when she hurt her fingers badly in slamming shut Moyzisch's safe. She was sent to Germany for medical treatment and was replaced by a German woman, Cornelia Kapp. Miss Kapp was the daughter of a German diplomat and, while working at Sofia, met and fell in love with a young American on the staff of George Earle, the former Governor of Pennsylvania who was serving as an emissary from President Roosevelt to Czar Boris III. Earle's mission was closed down when Bulgaria declared war on the side of Germany, and he was transferred to Ankara as military attaché. His assistant was also posted to Turkey, as an agent of the OSS; upon Miss Kapp's arrival at Ankara, under the escort of another OSS agent, Ewart Seager, she made contact with her lover and, subsequently, they were married. She later stated:

> I knew about *Cicero* before it became my task to open the mail that arrived in the German embassy every evening by courier from Berlin. I had plenty of time to copy out documents from Berlin which made it clear that *Cicero* was to be sought in the British embassy itself. I handed over the copies to the Americans every evening. . . . The Americans had known for some time that a man known as *Cicero* really existed. . . . It was my task to establish his identity.

This was fairly good evidence that the Americans at least knew that Bazna was a spy. And if they knew, presumably they informed the British at the meetings of the Ankara Committee, the Anglo-American inter-service intelligence, counterintelligence, political warfare, sabotage and deception coordinating organization in Turkey. But there was other, better evidence which indicated the British knew about Cicero even before the Americans. First, Dr. Erich Vermehren, an official of the Abwehr at Istanbul, defected to the British with his wife, the former Countess von Plettenberg, in February 1944. Vermehren was a member of the Schwarze Kapelle and had been in contact with "Tricycle" of the XX-Committee for many weeks before his defection. Tricycle claimed later that Vermehren's mother warned him of Cicero's existence through a colleague when they met in Portugal during the last weeks of 1943, and that he warned his British controllers immediately. Then there was Ultra, which at this time was at the height of its powers, reading not only much of the Abwehr's main-line traffic but also part of the German diplomatic traffic as well. Further, it was clear that somebody in Papen's personal entourage was supplying the OSS with the most intimate and secret information at this time, for the OSS

Turkey file at the National Archives would show precisely how much Papen was spending, what he was spending it on, and details of his foreign exchange and bullion deals.

The most telling evidence in support of the belief that Bazna was known to the British—in fact, under British control—came from Allen Dulles. Dulles would state in his memoir *Secret Surrender* that, in perhaps the second week of December, Fritz Kolbe, his informant in the German Foreign Ministry, arrived with a consignment of ministry telegrams which revealed that the Germans had two spies in the British command apparatus. One was Josephine in Stockholm, the other was Cicero in Turkey. Dulles wrote:

> Of direct practical value of the very highest kind among (Kolbe's) contributions was a copy of a cable in which the German Ambassador in Turkey . . . proudly reported to Berlin (in November, 1943) the acquisition of top-secret documents from the British Embassy in Ankara through "an important German agent." This was, of course, the famous Cicero. . . .

Kolbe gave Dulles three telegrams, two of them dated November 3, 1943, and the third dated November 4, 1943; and "Since a leak in British diplomatic security at such a sensitive post as Ankara could have hurt the Allied cause everywhere," Dulles remarked in an interview, "I gave my British colleague [Count Vanden Huyvel] a copy of Kolbe's telegrams." The two men, said Dulles, met at a small *rasthaus* at Bollingen, just outside Berne, and both agreed that London must be informed so the leakage could be blocked. But three days later, Dulles continued, a "rather breathless Vanden Huyvel came to my office and quite literally begged me to forget about the telegrams and to take no action whatsoever about the Cicero case, particularly with Kolbe. Count Vanden Huyvel said London was 'aware' of the case and, while Vanden Huyvel did not say so, it was obvious to me that the British were playing some sort of game with Cicero."

What sort of game were the British playing with Cicero? And why? The facts suggest that Cicero was indeed "an extremely clever trap," as Papen himself feared, a deception that was part of the stratagems of Plan Jael. It was significant that Bazna was permitted to walk away from the British Embassy a free man. But even more significant was the nature of the documents that he "betrayed" to the Germans. Having permitted Bazna to establish himself with Sir Hughe's "print"—a commonplace tactic in deception and one similar to the role of the *courrier* in the Dericourt stratagem—it was then possible to feed the SD information that, while it was of some value to the Germans, was of even greater value to the British in support of Jael.

Of considerable value to the British were the psychological and political warfare aspects of the Cicero documents. By showing the Germans incontrovertible evidence of the strength and determination of the Grand Alliance, by revealing that there was no hope that the alliance would fall apart, the documents presented a picture of certain doom that shocked the Nazi hierarchy. Himmler, for example, authorized Schellenberg to reopen negotiations with the OSS in Stockholm with a view to obtaining a peace agreement based upon the removal of Hitler. Thus the Cicero documents had an important effect upon Nazi attitudes about the war. But, as important, they also affected Nazi military decisions. While they did reveal to Hitler that the Allies would invade northwest Europe from England in 1944—the probability of which he had already expressed in Directive 51 in November—they did not permit him to conclude that the Allies would *not* invade the Balkans, a conclusion that would have allowed him to thin the very large garrison he had in southeastern Europe at the year's end. Had the Cicero documents induced Hitler to make that decision, their theft would have been a major disaster to the Allied cause. But as it was, they compelled him not only to keep his garrison intact in southeastern Europe but also to *reinforce* it—which was exactly what Jael was intended to achieve.

In evaluating the success of the Cicero deception, however, it is necessary to establish what, if anything, was gained by the Germans through access to Sir Hughe's "print." It was true that they obtained the code word Overlord from the Cicero documents. But by the turn of the year, the possession of this code word was of far less importance and value than it had been. Until September 1943, Overlord stood for the plan of the invasion operations; but after September, at British insistence, significantly, and for "security reasons," it became the general code word for Anglo-American strategy in northwestern Europe. The code word for the invasion itself—the vital code word—became Neptune. Thus, through possession of the code word Overlord, the Germans could have learned nothing about the key secrets of D-Day—where and when the Allies would land in France. This fact, in itself, would seem to prove the lie to Stalin's charge that the British had attempted to betray the invasion. It was also true that the Cicero papers included the most detailed briefs of the main political conference of 1943. But while these briefs were of enormous interest to the Germans, they were not of enormous importance. They simply revealed that the Allies intended to destroy the Third Reich, not how they intended to do it. The possession of that type of information does not permit governments to win battles or wars.

Finally, it was also true that from the Cicero documents the OKW did obtain forewarning of some secondary Allied military operations. A case in point was the Allied intention to bomb Sofia on January 15, 1944. In the event, the Germans took no action upon this forewarning, perhaps because they were convinced that Cicero was a plant, and no casualties were caused by the leak. But would the British deliberately reveal such information even at their own expense? The answer is yes, they would and did. Deception demanded that, on occasions, information concerning Allied operations be played into enemy hands in order to deceive Hitler about other, more important operations. Only the details of the deception were new; the principle was well established—a bloodstained satchel in the case of the Third Battle of Gaza, a floating corpse in the case of Mincemeat, the Dericourt stratagem and now a Turkish *kavass*. The British accepted that casualties—even quite serious casualties—might result from such *ruses de guerre;* as Masterman remarked of similar XX-Committee operations: "The greater the advantage the greater the price." The price paid for the Cicero stratagem was nominal. The British gave the Germans no intelligence which they would not obtain from other sources, or which they could not have obtained from accounts in the Allied and neutral press. And for those who still insisted that Cicero was a gigantic British blunder, the last word must come from Menzies, who snapped, long after it really mattered what Bazna had or had not done, "Of course Cicero was under our control."

If that was indeed the case, then Cicero was the supreme triumph of Jael. Reading a distinct Allied threat to the Balkans in the Cicero documents, and hearing British saber rattling outside the walls of his southeastern bastions, Hitler began to pour in what became, by D-Day, a total of twenty-five German divisions, including SS, parachute, mountain warfare and two panzer divisions. There they remained remote from the main battles, riveted in place by tricks, threats and the irksome activities of the Balkans partisans, also nourished by the British. With the eighteen infantry, SS and paratroop divisions, and seven more panzer divisions, pinned down in Italy, Hitler was deprived of the services of a total of fifty divisions, including nine of the feared panzer units. The magnitude of this dispersal of strength becomes apparent when measured against the number of German divisions in France on D-Day. There Hitler would have fifty infantry and parachute, and ten panzer divisions. The forces he was compelled to commit to the Balkans and Italian theaters represented one-sixth of his total strength; and any one of the SS, paratroop or panzer divisions might, had it been available in Normandy on D-Day, have made the difference between Allied success and Allied disaster.

If any evidence was needed to prove the efficacy of Plan Jael—and of the Churchill-Brooke strategy—there it was. At year's end, the shriveling Axis empire was vulnerable to attack from every side. But after months of maneuver and countermaneuver, it had been decided that the main thrust would be launched through Normandy. Hitler had deduced, as any clever strategist might, that northern France would be the scene of the war's most decisive battle, and he was reinforcing the area. Yet, through Plan Jael, he could not be certain where along the Channel coast the blow would fall. Nor, again through Jael, could he risk denuding the Balkans to strengthen his defenses in the West. He was being compelled to defend every perimeter of his empire, and his dilemma was reflected by the entry Jodl made in his diary on New Year's Day:

> Enemy intentions for 1944—
> the Atlantic Wall or the Balkans

PART

COVER AND DECEPTION

JANUARY TO JUNE, 1944

My Christmas message to you is one of greater hope than I have ever had in my life before. There is a spirit abroad in Europe which is finer and braver than anything that tired continent has known for centuries, and which cannot be withstood. . . . It is the confident will of whole peoples, who have known the utmost humiliation and suffering and have triumphed over it, to build their own life once and for all. . . . There is a marvellous opportunity before us—and all that is required from Britain, America and Russia is imagination, help and sympathy. . . . Four years of nazi occupation have made the issues in Europe very clear . . . 1944's going to be a good year, though a terrible one.

MAJOR FRANK THOMPSON, an SOE agent in Bulgaria, in a Christmas letter to his parents written just before he was arrested and executed.

Eisenhower, Supreme Commander

THE MILITARY TRAIN stopped at a coal siding near Primrose Hill in London. It was January 15, 1944, near midnight, and there was dense fog. General Dwight D. Eisenhower, the Supreme Commander for D-Day, stepped off the train, and a group of gangers around a brazier saw some vague figures salute each other beside an American staff car. Then the car, like the train, disappeared into the fog. That was all; there was no ceremony. But with Eisenhower's arrival, Supreme Headquarters, Allied Expeditionary Force (SHAEF), became a reality, and the paramount reasons for its existence—Overlord and Neptune—began to dominate every other consideration in the war against Germany.

The Supreme Commander was driven to his quarters at Hayes Lodge in Mayfair, and the fact of his arrival was kept a strict secret, except to the tiny politico-military hierarchy of the western powers. The American and British public would not know where Eisenhower was for several days. Yet, such was the curious and complicated intelligence ethic of the times, the Abwehr was informed of his whereabouts almost immediately. Even as Eisenhower settled down for a nightcap in the drawing room of Hayes Lodge, "Tate," a German spy under the control of the XX-Committee, reported to his controller in Hamburg that the new Supreme Commander had arrived that night in London. The objective was deception: to show the Germans that Tate had important connections at SHAEF, and thus to enhance his standing and credibility against the day when he would be given an important lie to transmit.

England was a strange, moving place to be in the early months of 1944. The spirit was one of hope, high courage, extraordinary endeavor and, above all, expectation. Only a few men under the pavements of Westminster really knew what was afoot. Still, this *had* to be the year of the invasion, though one could only guess when and where it would occur. The atmosphere of secrecy, the omnipresence of security, intensified the peculiar mood—a mood that was both fearful and carefree, as it was said to have been at the Guards ball before Waterloo, or as it was in the flight lines during the Battle of Britain.

To magnify the feeling that great events were imminent, hundreds of thousands—millions, eventually—of American soldiers came pouring out of the Atlantic ports into southern, southwestern and western England. They came singing such strange new battlesongs as "Hut-Sut Rawlson on the Rillera"; and they brought with them a new kind of fighting man's culture: Ramses and Camels, Sinatra and Grable, K-rations, Cola and carbines. With all the other forces involved in the invasion, they made England, and much of Scotland, Wales and Ulster, into one great military cantonment, crowding into places with enchanted names like Marston Magna, Sandford Orcas, Purse Caundle, Weston Zoyland and Kingston Bagpuize. They were accompanied by 6.5 million measurement tons of equipment and war stores—3.5 tons per man on D-Day. Between January and March 1944, no less than 3360 merchantmen crossed the North Atlantic to supply them. Only three ships were lost, while thirty-six U-boats were sent to their graves. Through Ultra and improved methods of anti-submarine warfare, the Atlantic had become an Allied lake.

The British countryman, xenophobic, narrow and suspicious of strangers, regarded this amiable host uneasily, at least at first. It was noted that the Americans walked with their hands in their pockets, chewed gum, did not salute officers, and wore medals they had not fought for. They were extremely rich by British standards, their field kitchens served ice cream, and it seemed that much of their free time was spent in doorways with their girls. And so the querulous jibe began to spread: "They're over-paid, over-fed, over-sexed, and over here." There were the inevitable brawls in public houses and reports of a rash of more serious crimes, including desertion, which were uncommon among the British rank and file. Yet no one could doubt the good will of the Americans and all welcomed the enormous power at their command: the great fleets of silver bombers that went out almost every morning just after breakfast; the unending convoys of fighting vehicles and artillery on once quiet country roads; the armadas of ships and assault craft that crammed the ports, the rivers and the creeks of England.

The new Supreme Commander seemed to personify the best of the American invasion; he made an extraordinarily good first impression. As Group Captain John Stagg, RAF, who became the Supreme Commander's chief meteorologist, would write of Eisenhower's first appearance at conference at Norfolk House, SHAEF's original headquarters: "With a broad smile, an athletic movement like a gymnastic instructor about to give his first lesson and in a trim, well-tailored battledress with well-ironed creases all in the right places he looked in first-class mental and physical condition." Eisenhower's grin, they began to say, was worth an army.

But there were many who doubted his qualifications and experience for command of the largest and most dangerous military operation of the war—perhaps of any war. Popular reserve about an American general who was being accorded more power over ordinary life in England than any other foreigner since the Battenbergs was gradually overcome by a skillful campaign directed by the British propaganda agencies to "sell" Eisenhower to the people. But in the chambers of the Imperial General Staff overlooking the Horse Guards there remained an influential body of opinion that regarded Eisenhower as a man who had risen to his position of eminence through politics, chance and good fortune, not through the tempering fires of war. General Brooke was his most powerful opponent. Still brooding over his "betrayal" at Quebec, Brooke would write such remarks as: "It must be remembered that Eisenhower had never commanded a battalion in action when he found himself commanding a group of armies in Africa," and, "I had little confidence in his ability to handle the military situation confronting him, and he caused me great anxiety . . . tactics, strategy and command were never his strong points."

In a series of barely perceptible maneuvers, Brooke, just as he had done in North Africa when he inserted General Sir Harold Alexander into command of actual operations, conspired to ensure that as little operational responsibility as possible was vested in Eisenhower during the assault and build-up phases of Neptune, the most dangerous stages of the invasion. He succeeded in surrounding Eisenhower with a wall of British commanders. The first airman and deputy Supreme Commander, Air Marshal Sir Arthur Tedder, was a Briton; the first sailor, Admiral Sir Bertram Ramsay, was a Briton; the first soldier, General Sir Bernard Montgomery, was a Briton; the commander of the tactical air forces, Air Marshal Sir Trafford Leigh-Mallory, was a Briton. Much of the operational planning for the invasion was also in British hands, as were almost all the intelligence, security and special operations.

British domination of the highest ranks of SHAEF provoked sharp criticism in Washington and posed a threat to the fragile alliance of generals upon which SHAEF was based. Recognizing the need for subtlety in dealing with the British, General Walter Bedell Smith, whom Eisenhower made his Chief of Staff over the objections of both Brooke and Churchill, who wanted Morgan in the post, issued a SHAEF directive that overrode all previous command directives. His purpose was to ensure that Eisenhower was Supreme Commander in fact as well as name. Confirmed by the Combined Chiefs of Staff in Washington, the directive vested in Eisenhower complete authority over the invasion and, while the force commanders did the actual planning for Neptune, they did so according to directives from Eisenhower and approved by the CCS. Further, Eisenhower would also coordinate and control the execution of the cover and deception plans that supported the invasion, and, in conjunction with the LCS and the War Office, implement those plans by a variety of special means. In short, nothing could be undertaken without Eisenhower's knowledge and approval. He bore executive, operational and moral responsibility for the invasion plans in all their dimensions, and he took pains to ensure that he was kept fully informed of anything that was done in his name.

Nevertheless, gossip persisted that Eisenhower was a mere figurehead, and the difficult decisions were being made by others. Extremely sensitive to such a suggestion, Eisenhower wrote in a memorandum for inclusion in his diary: ". . . it wearies me to be thought of as timid, when I've had to do things that were so risky as to be almost crazy—Oh hum!" After the invasion, Smith, who was better aware of the extent of Eisenhower's responsibilities than any other man, would state in a secret memorandum:

> The planning stages of (Neptune) presented the Supreme Commander some of the most important decisions of the war, and placed on his shoulders the burden of carrying on prolonged arguments when his views did not coincide with those of the U.S. Chiefs of Staff, the British Chiefs of Staff, or both. . . . I never realized before the loneliness and isolation of a commander at a time when (momentous decisions have to be) taken by him, with full knowledge that failure or success rests on his *individual judgment.*

It would also fall largely to Eisenhower to weld the brotherhood of arms upon which the success of the planning stages of Neptune—and indeed the expedition itself—might depend. With the growth of American military power and the decline of that of the British Empire, the old, almost traditional rivalries which had created the revolution of 1776 seemed to rear up again to plague the Supreme Commander. An analysis of Anglo-American attitudes prepared for Eisenhower before Torch had noted a degree of friction "much more marked than in World War I." Many Americans were contemptuous of the long string of defeats suffered by the British before America entered the war, while the British, for their part, were growing increasingly sensitive to American criticisms. As a result of this study, a joint committee had been established in Washington to advise the three governments—America, Britain and Canada—on ways to counter the hostility between their armies and the Axis propaganda that sought to take advantage of it. The commission had been only partially successful; and by the time Eisenhower arrived in London to assume his new post, American antipathy, matched only by British condescension, surfaced everywhere from the clubs and conference rooms of the high commanders to the pubs and dance halls frequented by the ordinary soldier.

It was a serious situation. Much would depend upon the character, personality and conduct of the Supreme Commander himself; and to Eisenhower's credit, Supreme Headquarters soon became an effective working coalition. Rarely did the clamor of national or personal rivalries reach the inner sanctum; SHAEF was a calm place, without the frenetic babble of previous international commands. It functioned with all the clinical efficiency of the head office of a large multinational corporation. And so it had to be; for Neptune was an operation so intricate, so huge, so bold, so vulnerable, so unrepeatable that even Stalin would be forced to declare with admiration: "My colleagues and I cannot but admit that the history of warfare knows no other like undertaking from the point of view of its scale, its vast conception. . . ."

Neptune justified Stalin's breathless telegram. Under Eisenhower's executive command and Montgomery's fighting command, an entire army—eight sea- and airborne divisions totaling about 200,000 men—was to be flung ashore at Normandy on D-Day. Three more divisions—perhaps 90,000 men—were to follow with 19,000 vehicles, all poured ashore from H-Hour just before the dawn twilight until midnight eighteen hours later. They would come in from an armada of 5000 assault ships, 1300 merchantmen, 1100 transport aircraft and 800 gliders. The entire force would be protected by over 1200 warships, including 7 battleships and monitors and 23 cruisers, and over 10,000 heavy and medium bombers and fighters. In all, over 4 million men and women would be directly involved in some way or another in the great expedition. And the invasion would be only the spearhead of an expeditionary force that would, with air, naval and supply forces, come to total some 6 million men.

Its size apart, Neptune would be, without question, the most complicated, difficult and dangerous military operation of the war in Europe. For as large and powerful as the invading armies would be, Hitler had the strength to repulse Neptune, unless the Allies could disperse his forces, take him by surprise on D-Day, and confuse and delay his reaction to the assault. Only then would it be possible to build up a force strong enough to withstand the inevitable German counterattack. But how could the Allies hope to achieve surprise? The time of the invasion would be determined by the weather, and as unpredictable as Channel weather could be, the conditions favorable for Neptune would be as evident to the Germans as they were to the Allies. Further, the topography of the French Channel coast would permit a seaborne assault the size of Neptune in only certain places which were, again, as well known to the Germans as they were to the Allies.

There were other factors that seemed to rule out surprise. Was it realistic to suppose that such a gigantic operation could be kept secret? The slightest indiscretion in the press or by a public figure might give away the principal secrets of Neptune. Even if those secrets were kept, how would it be possible to conceal from the Germans the locations of the assembly areas in Britain, the massing convoys prior to the Channel crossing, the crossing itself—all of which would clearly point to the beaches of Normandy? Cover and deception might work for a time, but as the most influential of the appreciations of enemy reactions to Neptune—that of the 21 Army Group on March 15, 1944—would warn: ". . . whatever further assaults our cover plan may lead him to expect elsewhere and however effective our windowing of his radar, his appreciation that we are going to assault the Neptune area will harden until about H-1 he will be certain."

This somber document also drew Eisenhower's attention to the single most prevalent fear in the minds of the Neptune planners: the German armored divisions in France. As the author of the appreciation put it neatly: "I am certain that when you carry out Neptune you will have against you more panzer divisions than you will find comfortable." Without surprise, these powerful and highly mobile units would be lying in wait for the Neptune invaders. Even with surprise, in a very short time Hitler might be able to concentrate a massive armored force at the point of attack and throw the Allies back into the sea.

Neptune would also be particularly vulnerable to detection—and destruction—from the air. Indeed, as a result of the experience at Salerno, where the assault forces had been badly mauled by German planes, the Allied high command recognized as the principal operational necessity of the coming months the need to destroy the Luftwaffe *before* the invasion. That need would give rise to the most ferocious and costly air battles of the war. But the panzers and the Luftwaffe were known threats to Neptune. What of the unknown threats—Hitler's secret weapons?

Three days before the President's decision to appoint Eisenhower the Supreme Commander, there had occurred an action in Italy that aggravated Allied fears both about the Luftwaffe and about the most insidious weapon of war—poison gas. On December 2, 1943, one hundred Ju-88 medium attack bombers of the German air force in Italy wrought appalling havoc on the port of Bari in the Adriatic, the main supply point for the Allied campaign in Italy. Seventeen ships carrying a total of nearly 90,000 tons of war supplies were sunk, and eight others were seriously damaged. In all, over 1000 Allied men and Italian civilians were killed. It was the worst seaport disaster since Pearl Harbor.

There was cause for even greater concern when it was reported that many of the casualties of the raid were suffering from some mysterious malady. Investigators were sent to the scene and it was discovered that they were victims of mustard gas poisoning. At first it was believed that the Germans had dropped mustard gas bombs on Bari and a wave of shock swept the Allied high command. Hitler had been warned that any use of poison gas would invite immediate and massive retaliation, and it seemed that the war would move into a new and horrible dimension. But further investigation revealed that the mustard gas bombs had been stored as secret cargo in the holds of some of the American supply ships in the harbor. Allied high commanders were relieved. With Bari fresh on their minds, however, the Neptune planners could not discount the possibility that Hitler might use poison gas—or some other fearful bacteriological or chemical agent—against the invasion.

To Eisenhower it seemed that the only way to overcome the multiple hazards of the Far Shore was by overwhelming force. He would rely on massive naval and aerial action to reduce the strength of the German garrisons, destroy the Luftwaffe and delay the movement of enemy reserves to the beachheads. He doubted that the truth of Neptune could be concealed from an enemy that practiced the dictum of its hero, Frederick the Great: "It is pardonable to be defeated, but never to be surprised." No, said Eisenhower, Neptune must be planned on the basis that there might not be surprise. But at the same time he would give the forces of security, deception and special means all the power they needed at least to try to baffle the enemy and dislocate his reactions. He also directed the force commanders to draw up contingency plans for evacuating the beachheads if disaster occurred. And whenever he contemplated that possibility, Eisenhower's diarist would record, the Supreme Commander's face became very gray.

Churchill was no less anxious about the outcome of the invasion. He minuted on January 25, 1944: "It is to my mind very unwise to make plans on the basis of Hitler being defeated in 1944. The possibility of his gaining a victory in France cannot be excluded. The hazards of the battle are very great." But what, at this stage of the war, were the alternatives? The British Joint Planning Staff and the Pentagon's Strategy and Policy Group had considered that question; and on November 4, 1943, a paper was promulgated in which they discussed the options that would be left open to the Allies in the event that "Germany will be capable of concentrating sufficient forces in France and the Low Countries to make the undertaking of this operation unacceptably hazardous."

The British and American strategists had examined three "alternate routes of approach to the European Continent." The first was an old favorite of Churchill (and the LCS): Norway. It was within the capability of the Allies to land in Norway, they decided, but the operation would require as much force as an invasion of Normandy, and might involve a war with Sweden. Moreover, the Allies would have to operate over sea lanes that were highly vulnerable to submarine operations, there would be inadequate fighter coverage, and the peculiar terrain and weather conditions of the area would necessitate the use of specially equipped and trained troops which were not available in sufficient numbers at that time. Since such an operation could not, in the opinion of the strategists, exert a conclusive influence on the course of the war, and since "It is apparent that the Russians would not consider this operation a suitable substitute for a landing in northern France," Jupiter—as the operation was still called—was ruled out.

A second alternative was another favorite of Churchill: the Balkans. But an even earlier appreciation by General Embick's Joint Strategic Survey Committee, in May of 1943, had pointed out the hazards—both military and political—of that operation. The committee had noted that while a Balkans strategy had certain advantages that made it "attractive at first sight," it would be virtually impossible for the western Allies to land and supply forces sufficiently large to cross the mountains into the Hungarian plain and attack the Reich from the southeast. Further, Embick's committee believed that the Russians would not favor any Allied adventure into the Balkans. Their resentment might lead them to seek a separate peace with Germany; and if they suspected that America was backing England in a policy of containment, it would have dangerous consequences in the postwar world. It was an appreciation that was dramatically confirmed by Stalin's maneuvers at the Teheran Conference.

A third alternative that had been considered by British and American strategists was an invasion of the southern coast of France. Such an operation would be possible to mount and maintain, and the Russians would accept it as a satisfactory substitute for Overlord. But if the Germans learned that the Allies had abandoned their plans for a landing in northwest Europe, they could concentrate their forces for a defense of southern France and make such an invasion even more hazardous than Neptune. The Russians had, in fact, approved an Allied attack against the Riviera coast—"Anvil"—and plans were underway to launch the assault, but only in conjunction with Neptune, not as the main thrust against the continent. In short, given the political and military imperatives, there appeared to be *no* alternative to Neptune, however great the risks. It was a grim prospect to the British and American planners, to Churchill, and to Eisenhower. And they could take little encouragement from a battle being fought at a small port on the Tyrrhenian Sea called Anzio. Anzio was Neptune in miniature, and it might be Neptune's fate.

The main strategic purposes of the Allied campaign in Italy were to bleed the still formidable reserves of German power, and to lure German divisions away from France and Russia into the tangled mountains south of Rome where they might be destroyed by the American 5th Army under General Mark Clark and the British 8th Army of General Sir Oliver Leese. The campaign was a sacrifice on the high altar of Overlord. But by January 1944, the Allies were halted at the German Winter Line—the "Gustav," a name with connotations of steely invincibility. The Germans were neither defeated nor demoralized, and the Allies could neither advance nor retreat. The Italian campaign was in a stalemate.

Churchill, with the sharp eyes of the opportunist, looked at the maps and conceived a stratagem. On his way home from the Cairo and Teheran conferences, he was tired and became ill with pneumonia; but as he recovered, he summoned the American and British high command to Carthage and presented his proposition at a time when the generals and admirals were least likely to oppose him. To end the stalemate on the Gustav and leave the way open for the capture of the Eternal City, Rome, he proposed a large-scale landing of an Anglo-American force 30 miles south of Rome at Anzio and Nettuno, two pretty little ports used by the Romans as holiday resorts. The operation also had a larger strategic purpose. Churchill would write:

> As I saw the problem, the campaign in Italy, in which a million or more of our British, British-controlled, and Allied armies were engaged, was the faithful and indispensable comrade and counterpart to the main cross-Channel operation. . . . Either they would gain Italy easily and immediately bite upon the German inner front, or they would draw large German forces from the front which we were to attack across the Channel. . . .

Churchill had not abandoned his advocacy for major diversionary operations in the Mediterranean—a strategy that had been summarily defeated by Stalin and Roosevelt at Teheran; and in a series of astute wrangles, he obtained approval for his scheme. It was codenamed "Shingle," and orders were given to General Sir Harold Alexander, the C-in-C of the army group in Italy, to plan the operation. Alexander wrote a directive which came down to Clark, and the conditions were created for a severe crisis in the Allied high command. It would revolve around the very attitudes that Eisenhower was trying to bury at Supreme Headquarters— the clash of personal ambitions and nationalistic aims among the alliance of generals that could spell disaster for Neptune.

In his directive to Clark, Alexander was crystal clear in what he required of the 5th Army. It was to attack the Gustav by crossing the Rapido and Garigliano rivers, and draw upon itself the German reserves positioned on the Tyrrhenian coast around Rome. When it was established that these reserves had been committed, Clark was to land the U.S. 6th Corps, an Anglo-American force, at Anzio and Nettuno. The corps was to strike out and *take* the Alban Hills, 5th Army was to break through the Gustav, join up with the corps, and in capturing Rome the Allies were to cut off and destroy the German 10th Army. The entire operation was, grandiosely, called the "Battle for Rome." But Clark was skeptical of Alexander's orders; he remembered Salerno. Accordingly, he instructed the commander of the 6th Corps to "advance on"—not take—the Alban Hills; and before doing that, he was to "secure a beachhead," and "advance as soon as he felt himself able to do so." There was no order to exploit the landing rapidly; the semantic difference between "advance on" and "take"—a mere three words—would deprive the Allies of a force of 300,000 men.

In a very real sense the Shingle landings were a dress rehearsal for D-Day, and the same threat existed in both cases: that the Germans would be able to build up their forces around the beachhead faster than the Allies could secure it, given all the problems implicit in landing and supplying troops from the sea. Secrecy and surprise would be essential—just as with Neptune—and everything would depend upon the close cooperation of Allied land, sea and air forces, as well as upon the skill and daring of the Allied commanders, in blunting the German reaction.

Why, then, had Clark diluted his orders? The British later theorized that he wished the corps—not the army—to draw the German reserves upon itself so that his 5th Army would have an open road to Rome. Whatever the reason, tragedy lurked around the corner for General John Porter Lucas, the commander of the 6th Corps. Lucas's mettle had been tested in North Africa where he had served alongside Eisenhower as the "eyes and ears of Marshall." He had been given first a division and then a corps to command and was a candidate for Clark's job in Italy. He had shown himself cool and capable at Salerno, where he had replaced the corps commander, General Ernest J. Dawley. And everyone seemed to admire him. He was conservative, intelligent, humane and reassuring as he smoked his corncob and contemplated his maps and graphs. He had seemed to know what he was doing during the campaign in the icy hills of the Campagna.

In fact, Lucas was an exhausted, troubled man, sick with worry about the consequences of his actions upon his men. "I am far too tenderhearted ever to be a success at my chosen profession," he would write in his diary. He doubted the wisdom of Shingle from the outset, and when he emerged from a planning session at Alexander's headquarters in the royal palace at Caserta on January 9, 1944, he wrote in his diary: "I felt like a lamb being led to the slaughter. . . . The whole affair has a strong odor of Gallipoli and apparently the same amateur (is) still on the coach's bench"—a reference to Churchill's part in that First World War disaster.

The first phase of the "Battle for Rome" opened on January 12, 1944, when the French penetrated the Gustav. It was a good beginning; and then, on January 17, the British attacked across the lower Garigliano. By dawn the following morning there were ten battalions of British infantry across the river. The Germans reacted as had been predicted; Field Marshal Albert Kesselring, the German C-in-C, saw a dangerous breach opening up in the Gustav and sent his reserves—two panzer divisions and elements of the Hermann Goering Division—into the line. Their departure from the Rome area (noted by Ultra) left the coast at Anzio wide open to Lucas's attack.

Now the third phase of the campaign began. Clark tried to force the Rapido on the night of January 20—the same night that Lucas sailed aboard the USS *Biscayne,* his command ship, with an armada of 250 ships of all classes heading for Anzio. Lucas was at sea when disaster struck Clark. The march down the mountains to the Rapido and the American attempts to cross were a nightmare. By 4 P.M. on the 22nd, Clark had lost nearly 2000 men and the Gustav remained intact; indeed, it would not be broken until May. Yet even as Clark withdrew, Lucas's task force had landed on the beaches of Anzio, 60 miles behind enemy lines, and Clark would not be able to get through the mountains to relieve him.

Lucas's force had arrived off Anzio and dropped anchor just after midnight on January 22. By dawn, some 50,000 troops were ashore with some 5200 vehicles; and as the American 3rd and the British 1st Divisions fanned out and took Anzio and Nettuno, they encountered little resistance. A single panzer grenadier battalion was quickly overwhelmed. Lucas's losses were astonishingly light: thirteen dead, ninety-seven wounded, forty-four missing. No one, particularly Lucas, had dared hope for such an easy victory. A-Force's cover and deception operations were, in part, responsible. It had employed what was by now a familiar trick: wireless broadcasts to resistance forces and agents in Italy using a cipher it was known the Germans could read. To cover the fact that German reconnaissance aircraft might sight the invasion fleet, the signals warned the recipients that an invasion was imminent not at Anzio, but at Civitavecchia, a town on the coast north of Rome. But this may not have been the whole story. A familiar figure had appeared in Italy on January 21, 1944, the eve of the landing—Admiral Canaris.

At Kesselring's headquarters, Canaris was presented with the evidence that seemed to indicate there would be a landing at Civitavecchia. General Siegfried Westphal, Kesselring's Chief of Staff, would recall:

(Canaris) was pressed to communicate any information he might have about the enemy intentions in regard to a landing. In particular we wanted to know about the positions of aircraft carriers, battleships, and landing craft. Canaris was unable to give us any details, but thought there was no need to fear a new landing in the near future. This was certainly his view. . . .

The extent of the paralysis of the German intelligence system—a paralysis that boded well for Neptune when much else boded ill—was reflected in Westphal's next remark: "Not only air reconnaissance, but also the German (intelligence), was almost completely out of action at this time." The true destination of the Shingle task force went undetected; and Westphal would add: "A few hours after the departure of Canaris the enemy landed at Anzio."

Kesselring had already moved his reserves to the Gustav and the road to Rome was open. Nothing stood between Lucas and the Eternal City. Much worse for the Germans—for Rome was but a hollow political prize—was the prospect that, if Lucas moved out of his beachhead and took the Alban Hills, the 10th Army on the Gustav would be cut off. But Lucas did not move. He did what Clark had ordered him to do; he built up his beachhead so that he would be strong enough to meet Kesselring's counterattack. Lucas's action would seem all the more inexplicable when it was learned that Ultra had revealed that there were no strong German formations within forty-eight hours of his beachhead, and that not only the Alban Hills but Rome itself were clear of strong enemy forces.

If Lucas did not act boldly, Hitler and Kesselring did. They dragged forces from everywhere, formed the 14th Army around the beachhead, Lucas was surrounded, and quite suddenly Anzio became a psychological crisis of the first magnitude. Both Hitler and Churchill recognized what was at stake. Churchill saw his political future in danger once more. He later said to Lord Moran: "Anzio was my worst moment in the war. I had most to do with it. I didn't want two (Gallipolis) in one lifetime." Hitler and Jodl saw the landing as a "first attempt on the part of the Allies to weaken and disperse the German reserves by minor attacks on the periphery of occupied Europe preparatory to the main attack across the Channel." And, said Hitler: "If we succeed in dealing with this business down there, there will be no further landing anywhere."

Lucas did not launch a major assault until January 30. It failed; and when Churchill learned that Lucas was completely sealed off, he wirelessed Dill in Washington: "We should . . . learn a good many lessons about how not to do it which will be valuable in 'Overlord.' " The fighting at Anzio was brutal; even more menacing in the context of the Normandy invasion was the power, determination and mobility of the Germans. As Churchill noted: "The ease with which they moved their pieces about on the board . . . all seemed to give us very adverse data for 'Overlord.' "

Anzio, once so full of promise of glory and political victory, became a dull, relentless, murderous battle of attrition. Allied soldiers were shot or otherwise wounded at the rate of 2000 men a week—a staggering price for a piece of drained marsh. German artillery deluged the small, crowded beachhead, firing over open sights. For the concentration of men and matériel was so great that it was almost impossible for a shell not to find a target. Another Verdun began to take shape as the Luftwaffe rose in all its strength and fury to attack the supply ships with its entire armory of powerful weapons, new and old. "I had no illusions . . ." wrote Churchill afterwards. "It was life or death."

For Alexander, Britain's most able general, the situation was too much. After a visit to Lucas at his headquarters, he sent a telegram to Brooke in London which reflected the disenchantments among the alliance of generals in the Mediterranean. A copy of the signal was sent to Eisenhower, and Eisenhower immediately recognized that a grave command problem was at hand. For Alexander stated that he was disturbed about Lucas's leadership, and sought to replace 6th Corps headquarters with a British corps headquarters, or to seek another American commander to replace Lucas. On February 18 Eisenhower sent Alexander's message to Marshall, taking unprecedented security and handling precautions to prevent the crisis from becoming widely known in Washington, and stating that he was opposed to replacing Lucas with a Briton. ". . . It is absolutely impossible in an Allied force to shift command of any unit from one nationality to another during a period of crisis," he wrote. He recommended that the problem be settled between the British and American commanders in the Mediterranean, but he added that he would be willing to send Patton "to take command of the forces in the beachhead temporarily and until the crisis is resolved."

The problem was now in Marshall's hands, and his predicament was serious. In two previous major battles with the Wehrmacht, he had had to relieve American commanders: General Lloyd Fredendall after Kasserine in Tunisia in February 1943, and General Dawley during Salerno. He knew that if he complied with the British demand to replace Lucas, it would be interpreted as the gravest reflection upon American generalship as a whole. But Marshall moved swiftly to avert wider repercussions in the Anglo-American alliance. On February 18, the same day that he received Eisenhower's message, he signaled General Jacob L. Devers, now the chief American commander in the Mediterranean and Alexander's deputy, that "Washington estimates also . . . that the drive and leadership of the (VI) corps and its commanders appeared below the stern standards required in the existing situation." And Marshall advised Devers: "Let nothing stand in the way of procuring the leadership of the quality necessary."

While this exchange was taking place, the Germans launched another major counterattack to drive the Allies into the sea. It was, probably, the most furious battle between German and Anglo-American forces so far in the war. Both sides fought with desperate courage for three days; but finally Lucas broke the attack, and his victory seemed to vindicate his early caution. If he had not built up his beachhead at Anzio, he would never have been able to resist that almost overwhelming onslaught. But the laurels of this epic victory—one of the greatest and most significant of the war—were too late to save Lucas and his career. Clark relieved him of command on February 22, 1944, exactly a month to the day since the landing—and an hour or so after Clark had signaled Eisenhower triumphantly: "The Boche has shot his wad today."

Lucas left the beachhead a broken man, but Clark's action—as inevitable as it was—did little to strengthen the alliance of generals. Nor did it augur well for Neptune. In a month of fighting, the Allies had suffered 19,000 casualties; there were 2000 dead, 8500 wounded and 8500 missing. The Luftwaffe had inflicted great disorder on the concentrations of troops and shipping on the beachhead; the panzers had assembled quickly in a ferocious counterattack; the *Feldgrau*, particularly the paratroopers, had fought with skill and tenacity. Might not the same thing occur in Normandy?

Yet in another dimension of the war—the strategy of dispersing the armies of Hitler—the expedition at Anzio had been a singular success. As Churchill said in the Commons on February 22, 1944, Hitler had resolved to defend Rome with the same fury he had shown at Stalingrad. And his decision to "send into the south of Italy as many as eighteen divisions involving, with their maintenance troops, probably something like half a million Germans . . . is not unwelcome to the Allies." In January 1944, OKW had intended to transfer five of its best divisions in Italy to the Channel coast. But when Lucas landed at Anzio, the reverse occurred and Hitler reinforced the Italian front. By the end of March 1944, he would have two armies of twenty-four divisions in Italy—half the number he had in France at that time, and three times the number he had in the 7th Army on the Normandy coast. Of particular importance was the number of panzer, panzer grenadier and paratroop divisions in Italy. When Rome finally fell two days before D-Day, Hitler would have no less than nine such divisions in Italy—as many as he had in all western Europe. If just one of those panzers or paratroop divisions had been positioned on the coast of Calvados on D-Day, then, as events would prove, the invasion would almost certainly have foundered.

The German Supreme Command

At 12:52 P.M. on January 30, 1944, the big recorders that monitored Nazi broadcasts from Berlin began to turn in their cabinets at the headquarters of the Foreign Broadcasting Intelligence Service (FBIS) in Washington, D.C. It was a major moment in world affairs; Hitler was to speak publicly on the state of the war for the first time in many months. When his voice came on the air, the monitors at FBIS listened closely for clues to the Fuehrer's mental and physical condition. But they heard nothing they could consider encouraging. His voice had lost none of its old passion, intensity and menace as he exhorted the German people to victory—a victory that he believed to be inevitable "in spite of all the deviltries of our opponents." When the broadcast ended, analysts at Washington and London probed the speech for hidden meanings. They could conclude only that Hitler was as powerful as ever in his homeland, that the Wehrmacht was still loyal and obedient to him, and that the German nation, 90 million people backed by immense military, industrial, material and economic resources, would only be defeated in battle. No political end, no sudden collapse, appeared possible.

Hitler's state of mind was of extreme importance to the Allies, for he alone ruled the Third Reich and its Wehrmacht. His reactions to the stresses of the next several months, his orders, his senses, his moods, his working habits, his mental and physical health—all could be decisive factors in the outcome of the invasion. Hitler's doctors saw their Fuehrer with his health, resilience, inner fire, stamina, intellectual powers—and his ability to bewitch his officers and men even as they stared at a cataclysm—undiminished. Although he was suffering from what would be diagnosed as a "rapidly progressive coronary sclerosis"—a condition that was kept secret from him—his doctors said, and believed, that he was in remarkably good condition for a man of fifty-five who had suffered so much. He was, in fact, in far better health than his enemies Churchill and Roosevelt. But Speer, the most intelligent and perceptive of the Fuehrer's inner circle, considered that through the savagery of his political and military defeats, the monkish world in which he lived and worked, and his conviction that he was surrounded by defeatists and traitors, Hitler had suffered a "spiritual derangement." Speer saw Hitler withdrawing more and more from his "soul-destroying entourage," and deliberately choosing his companions "so as not to remind him of his grave and by then insoluble problems." Speer would tell his American interrogators after the war: "(Hitler) came to despise people and often said as much. As he would put it, only Fräulein (Eva) Braun [Hitler's mistress] and his Alsatian dog (Blondi) belonged to him and were loyal to him."

Furthermore, Speer believed that Hitler was allowing himself to become "overwhelmed by work." He had no deputy and ignored suggestions that he should take one. His decision-making processes were turned into "uncertainty and tortured indecision," for according to Speer, Hitler, who had hitherto acted intuitively, now acted rationally—a method of reaching conclusions for which he was "not mentally well equipped or trained." What had been the main strength of his character, his intellectual capacity to surprise and mesmerize his friends and his enemies, "appeared to be switched off and extinguished." In Speer's view, the Fuehrer was a burned-out case.

But if Hitler had suffered a "spiritual derangement," it was well concealed; for in his attitude toward the war he was utterly convinced, at least outwardly, that he would ultimately wring victory from his long succession of defeats. He had the utmost contempt for the unity of the Grand Alliance, and he almost always referred to the western Allies as "the British" or the "Anglo-Saxons"; seldom did he speak of "the Americans." Although he had great respect for the British fighting man, he was scornful of the American army because it had such a small professional core and so little military tradition or experience. As Speer remarked to his postwar interrogators, "Hitler always argued that (the Americans) were not a tough people, not a closely-knit nation in the European sense. If put to the test, they would prove to be poor fighters." He would not change that opinion until after the invasion.

There were other reasons, equally strong, for Hitler's faith in victory. He was certain that he could repel the invasion. He had over 10 million Germans under arms, supplied by an armaments industry that, despite the Allied bombing campaign and the shortages of manpower and certain types of essential raw materials, seemed inexhaustible. In simple terms of production figures, the Third Reich's industrial output was staggering. In 1940, for example, German armaments factories had produced 865,000 metric tons of ammunition; in 1943, they had produced 2.25 million metric tons. In 1940, Germany had manufactured 5500 pieces of artillery; in 1943 that figure had reached 27,000. In 1940, 1359 tanks were built; in 1943, 11,897. In 1940, 8070 aircraft were constructed; in 1943, 22,050. In general, Hitler's land weapons were superior to anything in the armories of the Grand Alliance—except, possibly, the Russian T-34 tank. In the field of advanced weapons, the Wehrmacht was in the process of being reequipped with new, fast, silent, long-range, air-breathing submarines which, Hitler said, would cut Britain off from America. Jet-propelled aircraft were coming into service to destroy the massed Allied bomber fleets over Germany and to deliver bombing attacks that could not be intercepted by any aircraft on Allied airfields. The V1 and V2 missiles were now in a form of mass production and, Hitler hoped, would turn London and southern England—where the troops were concentrating for the invasion—into a ruin. There were new types of sea and land mines, aerial bombs, explosives. And behind the Wehrmacht and the Reich industrial base was all of Europe—that enormous land mass of 4 million square miles and 500 million people. Hitler was still master of the continent and everything therein, and it was protected by what he believed to be the most impregnable system of fortifications in history—the Atlantic Wall.

But for all his power, Hitler had an Achilles heel: his own personality. He was aware of the conspiracies against him, and fearing assassination and treachery he began to withdraw from all normal intercourse with the world. With his isolation came an increasing unreality about the truth of the war. Hitler knew that an invasion was inevitable, but he did not know where or when the Allies would invade. At a meeting at the Berghof on March 20, 1944, he told Field Marshal Gerd von Rundstedt, Admiral Theodor Krancke, and Field Marshal Hugo Sperrle (the Wehrmacht commanders in the West):

> It is evident that an Anglo-Saxon landing in the West will and must come. How and where it will come no one knows. Equally, no kind of speculation on the subject is possible. Whatever concentrations of shipping exist, they cannot and must not be taken as any evidence, or any indication, that the choice has fallen on any one sector of the long Western front from Norway to the Bay of Biscay, or on the Mediterranean—either the South coast of France, the Italian coast, or the Balkans.

Hitler was well aware that systematic attempts were being made in London to mislead him about Allied intentions. He was also aware that the Allies were attempting to disperse his strength before the invasion. The landing at Anzio had reawakened his old predictions that the main Allied thrust would be preceded or attended by other major landings, and he was convinced that it was essential to keep his armies where they were until the reality of the Allies' principal intentions appeared through the fog of deception, rumor and diversionary operations. Then, and only then, would he concentrate his forces at the main point of attack. He was further convinced that the Allies would try to seize a large port at the outset of the invasion. As a result, he had issued orders that all major ports in the West be designated "fortresses," which must be held "to the last round of ammunition, the last tin of rations, until every last possibility of defence has been exhausted." Plainly, Hitler knew nothing of one of the main intentions of the Allies—the decision, born at Dieppe, not to attack a port frontally but from the rear, and to bring their ports with them. He had been shown aerial reconnaissance photographs of the huge concrete caissons being assembled on the south coast of England. They were the breakwaters for the Mulberry harbors, but Hitler thought they were self-propelled quays to replace those in the French channel ports which his engineers were under orders to destroy at the moment of invasion.

As confident as he was that he could crush the invasion, Hitler had no doubts about the gravity of the moment. "The destruction of the enemy's landing attempt means more than a purely local decision on the Western Front," he said. "It is the sole decisive factor in the whole conduct of the war, and hence in its final result." He stressed that "the enemy's entire landing operation must under no circumstances be allowed to last longer than a matter of hours or, at most, days." And he added:

> Once the landing has been defeated it will under no circumstances be repeated by the enemy. Quite apart from the heavy casualties he would suffer, months would be needed for a renewed attempt. Nor is this the only factor which would deter the Ango-Americans from trying again. There would also be the crushing blow to their morale which a miscarried invasion would give.
>
> It would, for one thing, prevent the reelection of Roosevelt in America and, with luck, he would finish up somewhere in jail. In England, too, war weariness would assert itself even more greatly than hitherto and Churchill, in view of his age and illness and with his influence on the wane, would no longer be in a position to carry through a new landing operation.

"Thus," Hitler concluded, "on every single man fighting on the Western Front . . . depends the outcome of the war and with it the fate of the Reich."

But *when* would the enemy come? Discovering that, Hitler said, was a matter of good intelligence—particularly good weather intelligence. Hitler knew the importance of weather intelligence. As early as 1941 he had demanded that there be a new service, manned by men "gifted with a sixth sense, who live in nature and with nature. . . ." It did not matter whether one of them had a "humpback," another was "bandy-legged" and a third "paralytic" if he was a man "who understands the flight of midges and swallows, who can read the signs, who feels the wind, to whom the movements of the sky are familiar." But even if such men did populate the Reich's weather-reporting service, Hitler was told that he was not getting good weather intelligence, for the Allies were systematically destroying its reporting centers.

And *where* would the enemy come? Like the Allied invasion planners, Hitler knew that the weather, the tides and the topography of the Channel coast would permit a large-scale seaborne assault at only a few places and a few times of the year. Despite what his generals called the imperfections of his judgment, Hitler named Normandy as a possible point of main attack, although he conceded that "At no place along our long front is a landing impossible, except where the coast is broken by cliffs." He continued to regard the Pas de Calais as the most logical invasion site, but wherever the Allies landed, he would be there to meet them; it was, again, a matter of good intelligence. How could he be surprised or deceived about the time and the place of such a major military expedition?

Field Marshal von Rundstedt, the commander of the Wehrmacht in the West, was not as young as he used to be, either in years or in spirit. By nature a *grand seigneur,* he was now sixty-nine, was said to drink more champagne than was good for him, and he no longer conducted himself in the exact, stiff, cold manner that had characterized the General Staff of Imperial days. His face was thin, austere and sad, and he had the air of a weary man who had seen and done most things in a soldier's life—as, indeed, he had. For Rundstedt had fought more campaigns, had more rows with Hitler, been dismissed from his command and then rehired more often than his staff could remember. He had never believed that Hitler was a military genius; and he despised the shrill, fanatical world of the Nazis. All he really wished to be was Commander-in-Chief of the German army; all he really wished to do was attend the great ceremonies of state and ride his horse in Potsdam. Why, then, did he continue to serve the régime? "The Fatherland is in danger," he once explained to his Chief of Staff, General Guenther Blumentritt. "And like an old cavalry horse, if I stayed at home I should feel ashamed." Money? "That is immaterial to a true Prussian!" Honor? "It cannot be won any more!" Decorations? "Everyone already has them!" Rank? "One cannot be more than a field marshal!" No, Rundstedt's predicament was—as Blumentritt would say—that of Martin Luther at the end of his great speech to the Diet of Worms in 1521: "Here stand I, I can do no other. God help me. Amen!"

Rundstedt's antipathy for Hitler was personal as well as professional.

What did "the Bohemian corporal"—for it was he who had given Hitler that contemptuous title—know of high command? And Rundstedt had long since realized that the war was lost. As he said to Blumentritt after the twin defeats at Alamein and Stalingrad: "It may go on but ultimately we must lose it. It will mean the end of Germany as we know it, which we represent, and of which we are part." But, while he knew something about the Schwarze Kapelle, he would take no part in conspiracy himself; the bond of the *Fahneneid* was too strong. That did not mean, however, that he would not permit anyone on his staff to try to end the holocaust. As he said on this subject to Blumentritt: "I now advocate *Westgedanken*"—western thought. And, he had gone on, "I would not be opposed to anyone getting in touch with the British to see what they will accept, what they want in the way of terms."

Despite his defeatism, Rundstedt was still Germany's finest and most respected soldier, "the last of the German knights." He was a master of strategy and tactics, as the Poles in 1939, the French and the British in 1940, and the Russians in 1941 had discovered. But he no longer wished to fight for a Fuehrer who was leading the nation to destruction; and he complained that he had so little actual command of his armies that he had to ask Hitler and OKW if he wanted to change the guard outside his command post. He could have retired long ago, but he did not. He remained at his headquarters at St. Germain-en-Laye in a state of moral decline, waiting for the defeat he thought inevitable.

Yet Rundstedt's armies—on D-Day there would be five that included 1.5 million men, 350,000 of them SS, grouped into ten panzer, two paratroop, 17 first-line and 31 ordinary infantry divisions—were far from weak. It was true that the army in France had become a convalescent home and nursery for the Wehrmacht in Russia; but the belief that it was a pathetic shadow of itself because some divisions were immobile, had only horsedrawn transport, or were heavily diluted with foreign conscripts, was often Allied propaganda to calm the fears of their troops about what they would encounter in France. The fact was that, if things went right for the Germans and wrong for the Allies, Rundstedt's armies were still capable— more than capable if they were deployed quickly and correctly at the right place and the right time—of overpowering the Allied invasion.

The man who would be mainly responsible for that deployment was Rundstedt's commander on the Channel coast, Erwin Rommel. Rommel took command of Army Group B—the 7th Army in the general area of Normandy, the 15th Army on the coast between the estuary of the Seine and the Zuider Zee, and the Army of The Netherlands—at about the same time that Eisenhower became Supreme Commander. When he arrived in France at the turn of the year, it seemed that the Desert Fox had recovered, both physically and psychologically, from his defeats in North Africa. Certainly his reputation had survived; he was still the darling of the German public. And apparently once again in the favor of the Fuehrer, he had been given some major commands since his hurried evacuation from Cape Bon in May 1943. He had been C-in-C of the Wehrmacht in north Italy with the task of securing the Italian industrial base and the Reich's alpine frontier. Then he had been ordered with all speed to Greece to organize the defenses of the Balkans—dancing, although he did not know it, to Mincemeat's tune. When this proved a false alarm, he was sent to France in November 1943 to inspect and report to Hitler on the strength of the Atlantic Wall. Finally, on December 31, 1943, Hitler ordered him to command the Channel coast.

But, as both Hitler and Jodl detected, Rommel had become a pessimist—a dangerous, even fatal, state of mind in the Third Reich. He was, in fact, no longer convinced that Hitler would obtain the decisive military victory for which he worked, and he had told him so. He had also come to believe that Hitler should abdicate some of his military powers and allow his generals to try to fight the enemy into a position whereby a political settlement could be reached to end the war. But Hitler was prepared neither to hand over any of his supreme authority nor to permit a withdrawal of his armies into a shorter, more defensible perimeter around Germany. Hitler, Rommel had said, would defend everything; and therefore he would lose everything. This was not treachery, it was professional criticism. Rommel would become a conspirator only later.

When he assumed his new command, Rommel began to dash about the Channel coast at all hours, in all weathers, in a ferocious display of energy. He was everywhere in his heavy 2.3-liter Mercedes 230 cabriolet, talking with generals, laying out fields of fire, directing the installation of artillery, reorganizing the defensive positions of troops, supervising the construction of beach defenses, watching his men lay minefields. He was making the Channel coast into what he called a "devil's garden." But to what purpose? Montgomery, Rommel's adversary in the desert and now commander of the invasion forces, would remark at a Neptune briefing in London that: "He will do his level best to 'Dunkirk' us." Certainly the overt evidence indicated that Rommel intended to destroy his enemy at the high water mark—as Hitler had commanded. The energy with which he was strengthening the Atlantic Wall, the skill with which he was positioning his mobile and panzer divisions, the imagination he was showing in landscaping his "devil's garden"—all were proof of his determination to defeat the Allies in battle *if* they came. But there was more to Rommel's intentions than battle; he had taken the first steps toward joining the Schwarze Kapelle.

Soon after he assumed command of Army Group B, Rommel visited two friends who were determined and veteran conspirators. One was the Military Governor of France, General Karl-Heinrich von Stuelpnagel, and the other was the Military Governor of Belgium, General Alexander Baron von Falkenhausen. During these visits Rommel expressed his concern for the Reich, and revealed that he was in sympathy with what was known as "an independent termination of the war"—an armistice with the West, with or without the knowledge and approval of Hitler.

No doubt either Stuelpnagel or Falkenhausen remarked on Rommel's ambivalence toward Hitler; for in February 1944, he received his first direct communication from the Schwarze Kapelle. Dr. Karl Stroelin, a comrade in the First World War and now the Mayor of Stuttgart, and a conspirator in the mold of his colleague Goerdeler, called on Rommel while the field marshal was on leave at his home in the Swabian Hills near Ulm. Stroelin outlined the conspirators' plans—a new "Valkyrie." But seizing Hitler, Stroelin warned, might well result in civil war, particularly between the SS and the army, unless "some figure of outstanding eminence appeared immediately to dominate the situation." That figure, said Stroelin, was Rommel. Stroelin told him "that he was our greatest and most popular general and more respected abroad than any other. 'You are the only one who can prevent civil war in Germany. You must lend your name to the movement.'" Rommel thought deeply for a while. Dare one risk a civil war while the German people were engaged in a life struggle with their enemies? It was an awful dilemma. Not only had he taken the *Fahneneid,* not only had he commanded Hitler's bodyguard, he owed his career and eminence to the Fuehrer. But it was Hitler himself who had once said: "When the government of a nation is leading it to its doom, rebellion is not only the right but the duty of every citizen." Recalling these words, Rommel turned to Stroelin and said: "I believe it is my duty to come to the rescue of Germany."

With that statement, Rommel committed himself to the aspirations of the Schwarze Kapelle; and in the weeks ahead, his plans took on a new shape. In concert with the other conspirators in the West, he would try to get in touch with either Montgomery or Eisenhower, in the belief that the Allies would leap at the chance to end the war without having to run all the risks of invading the continent. When an agreement had been reached, Rommel also believed that the western Allies would join with Germany to hurl back the Russian hordes that were advancing toward the frontiers of the Reich. But if the western powers would not come to terms and did invade, then Rommel would do everything in his power to oppose them and inflict a defeat that would make them more reasonable.

With that strategy, as one of Rommel's biographers later wrote, the field marshal would be "in perhaps the most extraordinary position in which any general ever found himself":

On the one hand he was the chosen defender of the Atlantic Wall, entrusted by Hitler with the task of defeating the invasion on the beaches. . . . On the other hand he was convinced that the invasion could not, in fact, be defeated and was secretly committed to proposing an armistice to Generals Eisenhower and Montgomery when it succeeded. . . . By a remarkable feat of mental balance Rommel contrived to ride these two horses together. As a soldier he did his utmost to arouse the sleeping army of the West and to inspire the troops with the determination to prevent a landing. . . . He thus kept faith, professionally, with the Führer. He also kept faith with the Army. There was not a hint of irresolution in his leadership. . . . At the same time he (began to fulfill) the conditions he had made at his meeting with Dr. Strölin in February.

The success of Rommel's strategy depended, however, upon some knowledge of the time and place of the Allied invasion; and like Hitler and Rundstedt, he acknowledged that all signs, all reason indicated that the Allies would land in the Pas de Calais. But with his memories of Montgomery's skillful stratagems before Alamein, he could not quite rid himself of the thought that the Allies would *never* attempt a frontal attack at the point where his army group was the strongest—at the Pas de Calais. Surely Montgomery was too wily, too casualty-conscious for that! And so Rommel would stand over the horizontal maps at his headquarters and jab at the area between Cherbourg and Le Havre. If he were Montgomery, *he* would invade the Calvados, using his armor to split the 7th and 15th armies and move on Paris. Then with a pair of calipers he would draw arcs from the main air bases in southern and southwestern England—arcs that described the ranges of the enemy's Spitfire and Mustang fighter force. Rommel knew that whatever else they did, the Allies would never land except at a point where their air forces could be deployed to maximum effect. But those arcs embraced all of the beaches of Normandy, as well as the Cherbourg and Breton peninsulas. In short, Rommel did not have the slightest idea where or when the Allies would land.

Bodyguard

EISENHOWER WAS BRIEFED on the cover and deception plans for Overlord and Neptune at a staff study conference in the second week of January at Norfolk House. Those present included Morgan, the author of the original Overlord plan, Bevan of the LCS, and Colonel Noel Wild, the Hussar who had stage-managed Bertram and who was now the chief of the Committee of Special Means (CSM), or Ops B, the SHAEF department responsible for the execution of cover and deception plans. "Bodyguard" was the chief of those plans. It was, in essence, Plan Jael renamed in deference to Churchill's remark to Stalin at Teheran about the importance of hiding the truth in war; and as Bevan explained, Bodyguard was not a deception operation in itself. Rather, it was the overall strategy for a number of cover and deception operations—a "game plan" to mislead the enemy about, and to obscure the truth of, Allied intentions in northwest Europe in 1944.

Standing before a large wall map of Eurasia, Bevan told the Supreme Commander that Bodyguard's objectives were twofold. Through a coalition of intrigues, it was designed in the first place to continue to compel Hitler to disperse his forces throughout Europe so that he would not have sufficient strength in Normandy to defeat Neptune; and in the second place to delay his response to the invasion by confusing and disrupting the entire German signals, intelligence, supply and administrative systems. To achieve those objectives, Bevan explained, Bodyguard proposed to fabricate a war plan that was just close enough to the truth to seem credible to the Fuehrer, but would mislead him completely about the time and place of the invasion.

In the main, Bodyguard would attempt to persuade Hitler to believe six strategical considerations which would, in turn—if he accepted them as true—influence his preparations for, and his response to, D-Day.

1. The Allies believed that the Combined Bomber Offensive (Pointblank) against Germany was so seriously affecting Germany's war potential, that, if continued and increased, it alone might bring about Germany's total collapse. Consequently, reinforcement of the United Kingdom and the Mediterranean by long-range American bombers had been given such a high priority that the build-up of ground forces in the United Kingdom for a cross-Channel attack in the spring of 1944 had been delayed. This meant that if the Allies intended to invade at all in 1944, they would not be able to do so until July.

2. To prevent the Germans from withdrawing their garrisons in any part of western Europe, and from reinforcing endangered areas at the expense of less threatened sectors, they were to be persuaded that, while the Allies would not be able to make a full-scale invasion until July, there were balanced forces ready in England to take advantage of any weakening of German garrisons.

3. The Allies proposed to open land warfare in the spring of 1944 with a joint Anglo-American-Russian attack on various parts of Norway. One of the objects of these attacks would be to compel Sweden to enter the war on the side of the Grand Alliance and, when she had done so, use her ports and airfields to cover an Allied landing in Denmark from Britain in the summer.

4. To keep the German armies in southeastern Europe in place during Neptune, the Germans were to be led to believe that, since no large-scale cross-Channel operation would be possible until late summer, the main Allied effort in the spring of 1944 would be against the Balkans. These operations would consist of (a) an Anglo-American assault against the Trieste coast, (b) a British assault against Greece, and (c) an Anglo-Russian landing on the Black Sea coast of Rumania to threaten the Germans' main supplies of natural oil at Ploesti. Turkey would be invited to join the Allies to provide bases for operations against the Aegean Islands and the invasion of central Europe through Greece. Anglo-American operations in Italy would be continued and, in order to hasten their progress, amphibious operations would be conducted, in much the same way as Salerno and Anzio, against the northwest and northeast coasts. If these were successful, the Allies would advance on Vienna and Munich through the Ljubljana Gap.

5. The Russians would not begin their summer offensive before the end of June, a stratagem designed to make Hitler uncertain of his priorities and prevent him from withdrawing forces from the Russian front to reinforce France.

6. In view of the formidable character of the German coastal defenses and the present enemy strength in France and the Low Countries, the Allies considered that a total force of fifty divisions would be required for a

cross-Channel assault. These forces would not be trained and ready—and neither would the naval forces be available—until the summer. In any event, the western powers would not launch the invasion until after the Russians had opened their main summer offensive.

Those, then, were the broad strategic deceptions of Bodyguard, a scheme that had no less than thirty-six subordinate plans and scores of associated stratagems. Those that pertained, in particular, to southern and southeastern Europe were grouped under the continuing phases of "Zeppelin"; and those that were intended to disguise Allied intentions in northern and northwestern Europe, and to conceal the secrets of Neptune itself, were codenamed "Fortitude." But as many and various as these operations would be, all were designed to convince the German high command that the Allies would continue to pursue the peripheral strategy of 1943, and that a cross-Channel attack could not possibly be made before July of 1944.

The special means that were to be used to plant these deceptions, Bevan explained, would chiefly concern the number, the location, the state of training and the equipment of the Anglo-American forces assembling in Britain for the invasion—a word, incidentally, that Eisenhower disliked; in his view, it implied aggression against the territory of Allied states and, therefore, he asked that Neptune be called a "liberation." The Germans, at least at first, would be led to underestimate the number of divisions in Britain, and overestimate those in the Mediterranean and Near East. The state of training and battle experience of the divisions that would make the Neptune assault were to be misrepresented as inadequate, their movements and concentrations were to be carefully concealed, and the Germans were to be induced to believe that the special equipment needed for a large expedition from England, particularly landing craft, would not be available in sufficient numbers before July.

These stratagems were designed to conceal the time of the invasion. But, Bevan continued, it was also imperative to conceal the place. Although the Allies were preparing to invade France, Hitler must be convinced that they had the means and the intention to mount other invasions around the periphery of his empire; and he must be misled about where in France the Allies would land. Thus Fortitude included elaborate deceptions that were designed to threaten Norway, the Pas de Calais, and the Biscay and Mediterranean coasts of France, their object being, in conjunction with continuing threats to the Balkans and the military operations in Italy, to tie down German forces in those areas before, during and after Neptune.

In addition to these stratagems, Bevan went on, Bodyguard proposed to mount a large diplomatic and political offensive to induce, or at least suggest the possibility of, defection among Hitler's allies—Finland, Hungary, Rumania and Bulgaria—in the hope that he would be compelled to strengthen his garrisons in those countries and further disperse his forces on police tasks. A similar campaign, which would also include economic warfare, would be launched to "persuade" the neutrals—Sweden, Turkey, Portugal and Spain—to enter the conflict on the Allied side, or to compel them to cut their links with Germany, thus surrounding and isolating the Third Reich from the rest of the world. And finally, a massive campaign of political warfare would be directed at the occupied countries and the Third Reich itself to undermine the will and unity of the Wehrmacht, to encourage dissension between Hitler and his generals, and to convince the *Feldgrau* and the German people of the futility of further resistance.

In the context of D-Day itself, Bodyguard further proposed "To complete the process of enlisting, preparing and mobilising the Peoples of Occupied Countries for action within the framework of United Nations plans in such a way as to render maximum assistance to Overlord. . . ." It was a potentially explosive proposal, for in this sphere of operations, the political warfare agencies intended, subject to the Supreme Commander's approval, to "stimulate . . . strikes, guerilla action and armed uprisings behind the enemy lines . . ." all of which would surely imperil the lives of peoples and resistance forces friendly to the Allied cause. Yet the authors of the plan, perhaps remembering the fate of the resistance forces involved in Starkey, were aware of the dangers of that kind of deception, for they warned that it might "create premature action before D-Day or discredit authentic instructions at D-Day," and that "A deception plan based upon purely military considerations might prove to be a boomerang from a morale point of view."

Thus Bodyguard envisioned an arena of operations that would extend from the halls of power of Allied, Axis and neutral nations to the hearts and minds of all their people. Its sphere of operations would be the world itself—and a part of the heavens, too. But the command structure for deception was such that, while Eisenhower would bear executive responsibility for the plans, and would monitor all that was done in his name, operational responsibility would remain with Bevan and the LCS, and with the CSM. Under Bevan the LCS would see to it that all British military, civil and political agencies conformed to the requirements of the various plans. It would be Bevan, for example, who would advise the Cabinet against the Archbishop of Canterbury's suggestion that there be a national day of prayer on D-Day on the grounds that it would reveal to the Germans that D-Day for Neptune was *the* D-Day; and it would be Bevan who would advise the Prime Minister what to tell Parliament, and when. His position was unique, his powers unprecedented.

Bevan would also be responsible for synchronizing what was officially said and done in America concerning actual Allied strategy and tactics as well as their cover plans. His representative in the United States was Colonel H. M. O'Connor, who was attached to the British Military Mission at Washington and worked through the Pentagon's Joint Security Control (JSC), a section of the Joint Chiefs of Staff. The JSC was made up of the directors of intelligence of the American army, navy and air force, and its tasks were manifold. Like the LCS, it would be responsible for spreading the deceptions of Bodyguard and Fortitude, and for supervising the activities of civil, political and military agencies to make sure they said or did nothing to compromise the security of Neptune. Thus the LCS had an influential—and effective—partner in the United States.

At the same time, the LCS had A-Force in the Mediterranean, and similar bureaus in the Near East, India, and Southeast Asia to plant its fictions. The contributions of the Russian government to Bodyguard and Fortitude would be arranged by the British and American military missions in Moscow. When their services were required, all MI-6, OSS and SOE agents in the field were also available to the LCS, as were the deception sections in the Allied army groups, the various British and American economic and political warfare agencies, the British Foreign Office and the American State Department. In short, deception had become a major industry; and, together with the CSM, Bevan would have "musicians and choristers"—as Wingate called them—in all parts of the world who could, and would, sing the songs of Bodyguard and Fortitude.

In all, the plans were clever, logical, plausible; but on paper they were about as exciting as a large-scale corporation fraud, which, in a sense, they resembled—a skillful juggling of the facts by one group of experts to deceive another group. The intrigue would come in the way the deceptions were perpetrated. As Bevan pointed out, masses of misinformation could not simply be handed over to the Germans. It would have to be "leaked" in bits and pieces in indirect and subtle ways from places far from where the main battle would be fought. No one knew better than Bevan that intelligence easily obtained was intelligence readily disbelieved; it was the cardinal rule of deception. The Germans would be made to work for the "truth," and once they had pieced it together, after much labor and cost, a convincing whole would emerge—a strategy that approximated their own appreciations of Allied intentions. But, Bevan warned, if Bodyguard and Fortitude were to have a chance of success, the strictest security precautions must be observed; it was, he said, as important to conceal a lie as it was to protect the truth. No matter how convincing the misrepresentations of Bodyguard and Fortitude, no matter how ingenious their special means, even the smallest rent in the curtain of deception would be enough to reveal the truth.

Eisenhower's opinion of Bodyguard was succinct. "I like all this," he wrote on his copy of the plan. And there was some evidence to show that-

Bodyguard—under its previous code name, Jael—was proving effective. Of Hitler's estimated 302 divisions in the field in January 1944, some 179 were in Russia, 26 were in the Balkans, 22 in Italy, 16 in Norway and Denmark, and 59 in France. This dispersal of force revealed that while Hitler was certainly providing for a major assault in France, he had not ruled out the possibility of Allied expeditions in the Balkans and Scandinavia. But would Fortitude be as effective? Eisenhower was skeptical, for it was almost impertinent to imagine that the LCS might outfox the most proficient military organization in history—the German General Staff—in every operational theater of the war throughout the three most crucial periods of Neptune—before, during *and* after the assault. As preparations for the invasion accelerated, it would be increasingly difficult to divert Hitler's attention from the Channel coast, let alone to disguise the time and place of the assault. It seemed an impossible task and the best that could be hoped, said Eisenhower, was that Fortitude would tie down one or two panzer divisions for one or two days. Yet he knew as well as everyone else that if Fortitude failed, Neptune itself might founder.

Were the LCS and the CSM being unrealistic in their objectives? The U.S. Joint Chiefs of Staff thought so. In the summer of 1943, Wingate had presented an early draft of Plan Jael at a meeting of deception experts in Washington called the "Washington Anglo-American Cover and Deception Conference." The conference had established the "necessary organization for global cover and deception," and the plan was submitted to the U.S. Joint Chiefs for approval. They declared that "we find ourselves in general agreement with the plan," but they sounded a note of warning:

> We feel that the over-all deception policy in Plan Jael is so ambitious as to be the subject of some question as to its general plausibility. It is our view, however, that a maximum of success may be forthcoming if a considerable degree of reserve characterizes its execution. We feel, in brief, that it could easily be overplayed.

The deception agencies were aware of that danger. They shared Eisenhower's appreciation of the difficulty of their task; and what was more, they proposed to employ many of the same tricks to deceive the Germans that had already been used not only in this war but also in the First World War. Upon analysis, however, the deception agencies decided that their strategy had a fair chance of success. In the first place they knew—from Ultra, and, particularly, from the intercepts of Baron Oshima's traffic— what Hitler expected the Allies to do. He expected them to land at the Pas de Calais, which he considered the logical point of attack, as indeed it was. Secondly, as Oshima's traffic had also revealed, Hitler did not dare ignore the possibility that the Allies might launch other invasions in support of the Channel crossing. Bodyguard and Fortitude had only to convince the Fuehrer that he was quite correct in his assessment of Allied intentions.

The greatest danger to the plans, of course, lay in the ability of the German intelligence services to divine the truth behind their elaborate lies. But here, again, there were reasons for optimism at the LCS. Most of the LCS stratagems, along with the invasion itself, were being launched from Britain, an island base where secrets could be kept by an alert, suspicious and security-conscious population. It would be extremely difficult for Hitler to discover the exact nature of the military preparations being made there. All of his agents in England had been apprehended, several were operating under XX-Committee control and others were being impersonated—without, Ultra was revealing, Hitler's knowledge. The XX-Committee would be working closely with the LCS to spread the deceptions of Bodyguard and Fortitude through these double agents.

Without reliable sources of information from Britain, the German intelgence services would be almost wholly dependent upon wireless intelligence and aerial reconnaissance—or upon some Allied blunder—to discover the secrets of Neptune. The German wireless intelligence service still operated effectively, but the British were most proficient at wireless deception. They knew what the Germans would be looking for in the ether— a knowledge originally derived from the capture of Seebohm's wireless intelligence company just before Alamein—and they had the means and the ingenuity to provide it. They also knew what the Germans would be looking for from the air. But there were ways to deceive even a camera, and Allied aerial superiority would help ensure that the Germans photographed only what they were supposed to see. Thus, the LCS hoped, they would be peculiarly susceptible to plausible deceptive information because they had no means to verify it—an essential to correct intelligence evaluation.

As for the German intelligence services themselves, their operations lay largely exposed to Allied scrutiny through Ultra; and as a result of internal rivalries and of the Allied policy of "active pursuit and liquidation of the enemy intelligence services wherever they may be found," the eyes and ears of the Third Reich were already severely handicapped. There were rumors that Canaris had fallen from the Fuehrer's favor, and it was well known that the Abwehr was riddled with men who, for personal or ideological reasons, were conspiring to bring about Hitler's downfall. Time and time again, the Abwehr had failed to provide the Fuehrer with reliable intelligence about major Allied military and diplomatic operations. The LCS was confident that it would fail once more. The men of the SD were loyal to their Fuehrer, but they had proved to be far more skilled at police work than at gathering reliable intelligence. Hampered by a lack of such intelligence and the means to verify it, FHW might also fail to discern the truth behind the smoke screens of Bodyguard and Fortitude.

And so, sure of their prowess but aware that a single false step could expose the secrets of Neptune for all to see, the deception agencies prepared for the final innings of the great game against Hitler. Morgan would later recall the object of that game—and the spirit in which it was played:

> . . . there was always the necessity to do everything possible to induce the enemy to make faulty dispositions of his . . . reserves, to strive if possible to have him at a disadvantage. Damned unsporting, of course, but that is the way in real war. . . . There are times when it pays to dilate upon and encourage the allegedly traditional Anglo-Saxon sporting spirit and all that. But the fact remains that, if you can sneak up on the enemy from behind and catch him unawares, preferably asleep, the knife goes in with far less fuss and bother and his reactions are apt to be, if any, comparatively innocuous. . . . One bogus impression in the enemy's mind had to be succeeded by another equally bogus. There had to be an unbroken plausibility about it all, and ever present must be the ultimate aim, which was to arrange that the eventual blow would come where the enemy least expected it, when he least expected it, and with a force altogether outside his calculations.

The complex deceptions of Bodyguard had little chance for success without the active cooperation of the Russians. Churchill had asked Stalin for that cooperation at Teheran, and Stalin had agreed. But among those responsible for the fine art of strategic deception in Britain, there was doubt, first about the wisdom of revealing to the Russians just how they proposed to implement their strategies, and second about the kind of cooperation they were likely to receive. The Russians were bloodlet and exhausted from years of total war; how much time and patience, how many resources, would they be able to devote to deception? Bevan and his American assistant at the LCS, Colonel Baumer, were about to find out.

In the early evening of January 29, 1944, Bevan and Baumer left London for Moscow to discuss Russian participation in Bodyguard with the Red Army General Staff. With them on the long and dangerous flight over Scandinavia and the Baltic was the British ambassador at Moscow, Sir Archibald Clark Kerr, who was returning to his post from the Teheran Conference. They flew together in the bomb bay of a Liberator 24D, a long-range bomber converted for passengers.

The Liberator took off from Prestwick Airport, near Glasgow, circled the Grampians to gain altitude, and the pilot closed down the flame dampeners on the engine exhausts to make his black-painted aircraft less visible to any prowling German night fighter. He then set course for Jutland and Stockholm and so up the Baltic. As St. Elmo's fire flickered off the wing tips and high-velocity winds made the 30-ton plane shudder, the passengers swaddled themselves in their sleeping bags and settled down for the long flight. Bevan soon went to sleep; Baumer and Kerr amused themselves by discussing the differences of language between the Americans and the British. "He seemed to have them all memorised," Baumer wrote in his diary. "Such old clichés as the expression in English of 'knock me up at seven o'clock' and 'fanny' being equal to 'bum.' " But soon the roar of the four Pratt and Whitneys drowned all conversation, and Kerr and Baumer tried to get some sleep in the blue-lit bomb bay. They were awakened briefly by what appeared to be some sharp jolts in the airframe which Baumer thought might have been due to anti-aircraft gunfire from a flak ship in the Baltic. Then they dozed off again.

When the emergency came, it came as it so often does—suddenly. The passengers had been wearing oxygen masks for some time, and all at once Bevan began to struggle. His kicks awoke Baumer and the ambassador and both became conscious of a sense of being slightly drunk—a sign of oxygen starvation. Bevan's struggles grew more violent, and Kerr and Baumer quickly disconnected their masks, reconnected them to some portable oxygen bottles, and crawled on their hands and knees (they were capable of doing no more) to see what they could do for Bevan. Baumer later described the scene:

> I became very anxious indeed about Bevan. He was the lynchpin of everything at the LCS. If he had released all of Bodyguard to someone at the LCS like Wingate, I would still have been anxious, although only for his life. But I knew Bevan had not told anyone everything about the plan; he was not that sort of man. The plan could have been put together again, but probably not as well. And here we were, with Bevan unconscious, the British ambassador kneeling on his chest, and me fiddling around to try and get some oxygen to him.

Baumer's fingers were numbed by the freezing temperature of the bomb bay, but after a struggle that seemed like an hour—in fact it was only a few minutes—he managed to get Bevan's mask back on and regulate the oxygen pressure. Bevan revived somewhat and complained of feeling extremely ill. But it was not until the plane got to Moscow and landed on the snow-covered airfield that everyone realized how ill he was. Baumer wrote: "We lumbered out of the aircraft in our huge suits. It was cold and we were hungry and sick. With a member of the crew, we helped walk John Bevan about a half-mile to an administration building. . . . John looked awful."

The ordeal was not yet over. Nobody in Bevan's party spoke adequate Russian and none of the Russians spoke adequate English. The result was that the Russians thought Bevan had been drinking. He was, in fact, very near to collapse. After much telephoning and examining of passports and credentials, the party was taken to a Russian mess for "breakfast." As Baumer recalled:

> . . . we sat down to a typical banquet table, with me on the left of the ambassador and a Russian general on the right. The ambassador whispered to me to go easy on the vodka. We began toasting in vodka and cognac and before one's glass was empty the Russian officers would lean over and fill it. There was smoked herring and lots more vodka—we could not make anybody realise that Bevan was not drunk but ill, and we could not leave. The ambassador told me how the Russians liked to get their visitors stinko.

The party finally broke up when the ambassador's ancient Rolls-Royce arrived with the British minister at the embassy, John Balfour. He rescued the three men and took them to the embassy, a large former merchant's mansion across the river from the Kremlin.

Bevan soon recovered, but the Russians seemed to be in no hurry to see their visitors. Bevan and Baumer were kept waiting for a week, probably because, as a security precaution, they had not brought a copy of the Bodyguard plan with them. It was received on January 31 by signal which was transmitted laboriously—it was ten foolscap pages long—in the virtually unbreakable one-time pad cipher the British reserved for their most sensitive traffic between London and Moscow. It was then translated into Russian and presented by Kerr to Foreign Minister Molotov, a sign of the signal importance with which the document was viewed. Even so, it was not until February 7 that the Russians notified the British and American military missions that they were ready to talk.

A line of cars came to collect the delegates to the conference. Then, traveling at high speed, they were driven through the ice- and snow-bound Muscovy streets (with the blinds drawn, to protect them, they were told, "from sunburn") to some offices of the Red Army in Karl Marx Place. There, in a dingy room lit by a single naked bulb, they met the Russian delegation. It was headed by General Feodor Kuznetzov, a compact Slav with a flat face. Neither Bevan nor Baumer knew who he was or what he did; the interpreter merely referred to him as *"Excellenz."* With Kuznetzov was a formidable-looking man who was introduced as "General Nicholas Slavin," the personal assistant to the Chief of Staff of the Red Army and the officer responsible for deception in the Russian military. A third member of the delegation was an official of the Foreign Ministry who was introduced only as "Monsieur Dekanosov."

The American delegation was led by General John R. Deane, the chief of the U.S. Military Mission at Moscow; British military interests were looked after by Colonel R. G. Turner, and representatives of both the Foreign Office and the State Department were also present. They were received with cordiality but reserve. Bevan opened the first meeting with a long briefing on Bodyguard. But he dissembled about the methods and means that would be used to disseminate the various aspects of the deception, and in an effort to tell the Russians no more than they needed to know to understand what their part in the plan would be, he succeeded only in confusing them. They were further confused when the complicated if vague terminology that Bevan used was filtered through an incompetent interpreter.

Thus the plan reached the Russians in an utterly muddled state and the conference got off to a bad start. Moreover, the Russians were deeply suspicious that at Teheran the western Allies had tried to trick them into opening their grand offensive in May 1944. Churchill and Roosevelt had both assured Stalin that the target date for Overlord was May 1, 1944; but now it was revealed that this date could not be met and that the new target date—"Y-Day"—was June 1, 1944. The postponement had been dictated solely by the availability of certain types of landing craft, but the Russians believed that the Americans and Britons had never intended to invade in May and had pressed the Red Army to open its offensive then solely to draw off the German panzer divisions from France. In the Russian view, Bodyguard might prove to be another trick to deceive Russia as well as Germany. They were quite wrong, but the language difficulties and Bevan's anxiety to tell the Russians no more than they needed to know only intensified their suspicions. As Baumer wrote: "Naturally, the special language used to describe our business completely floored the Russians when it reached them." Accordingly, Deane took over the meeting. But in all, three long meetings were necessary to explain the plan.

Deane was a frank admirer of Bodyguard—too frank, as it happened, for when he later wrote of the subtlety and skill with which Bevan had developed the plan, the British, angered by the revelation of who was responsible for strategic deception in Britain, demanded his court-martial. Proceedings were actually under way when Eisenhower intervened on the grounds that the resulting publicity would be even more illuminating than the original remark. Deane was, however, successful in conveying the details of Bodyguard to the Russians, much to his own surprise. He later wrote: "I thought Kuznetzov a mental giant when, in spite of the difficulties, he appeared in a very short time to have mastered the intricacies of Bevan's plan."

The part that the Russians would play in Bodyguard and its components was comparatively simple. First, they were to deceive the Germans into believing that their major offensive on the eastern front could not be launched until July, just as the western Allies would deceive them into believing that the invasion could not be launched until after the Russians had attacked, pinning down German reserves on the eastern front. In fact, the invasion would be launched in the first week of June, before the Russian offensive opened ten days later. But in the meantime, the Russians, in cooperation with the British and Americans, were to suggest that joint Anglo-Russian invasions were being mounted against both Norway and the Bulgarian and Rumanian coasts of the Black Sea. The specific target in Norway was in the region of the Petsamo nickel ore mines, the target in the Balkans the great Ploesti oilfields, both essential to the Wehrmacht. Hitler was to be persuaded by a variety of special means—double agents, suggestive wireless traffic and naval, air and ground movements—to believe that both invasions would be launched in May or early June, and thus would be compelled to maintain his garrisons at these vulnerable points at the expense of his eastern and western frontiers.

It was all very neat and logical, and at the end of the three meetings, according to Deane, Kuznetzov became "very enthusiastic over Bevan's plan. He and his colleagues proposed a great many changes, many of which were accepted by us after an exchange of cables with our Chiefs of Staff. Representatives of the Soviet Foreign Office were called in to discuss the diplomatic aspects of the matter with representatives of the British and American Embassies." Then, according to Deane, "suddenly the lines went dead. Nothing was heard from the Russians for several weeks, and during this time Bevan, Baumer, and I were unable to contact them to see what was wrong."

It is probable that the Russians were debating the implications that the plan would have both in their present situation and in the postwar world. The complexities of Balkan politics—and Stalin was looking ahead to Russian domination of the Balkans—were not such that quick decisions could be made. There were men and parties whom Stalin wished to support or to destroy; and to be seen cooperating with the western powers might damage his long-range intentions in that turbulent region. Moreover, if the Russians were to cooperate in the operational aspects of the Scandinavian and Balkan "invasions," it would entail a considerable amount of actual and fake movement of their military forces, as well as a considerable rearrangement of their own plans for the coming summer offensive. Perhaps the Red Army commanders did not wish to involve themselves in such troublesome strategical deceptions, when they undoubtedly had large-scale tactical deceptions designed to cover their own operations. They were already badly overtaxed and, for example, the amount of wireless equipment necessary to sustain the fiction of these deceptive assaults might well burden their capabilities more heavily than they were prepared to accept. They probably also wished to consider what sort of special means they would use to plant this false strategy upon OKW. That they had the means, there was little doubt; it was later said by General Reinhard Gehlen, the chief of Fremde Heere Ost (the intelligence evaluation section on the Russian front), and later chief of the postwar German offensive intelligence agency, the DNB, that Martin Bormann, Secretary of the Nazi Party, was in fact a Communist agent.

Bevan and Baumer were in a hurry; they had to get back to London to take over the execution of Bodyguard, which was being managed in Bevan's absence by Wingate. Thus the Russians' silence was at first puzzling, then worrisome, and finally exasperating. It became evident that they were playing for time. Their representatives explained they could do nothing without Stalin's approval—and he was either at the front, ill, or "considering the issues." In all, the Bodyguard delegation would spend a total of thirty-two vital days waiting for the Russians to decide what they could and would do.

Then, on February 23, Bevan, Baumer and Deane were invited by the Soviet General Staff to a party at 17 Spiridonovskaya, a magnificent mansion with gold ceilings and brocaded walls where the Russian government entertained foreign guests. They arrived as the Honored Artists of the Soviet Union Orchestra played minuets in a corner of the reception hall. They were received by Marshal Voroshilov and Foreign Minister Molotov, and the splendor of the banquet made it hard to believe that Russia was involved in the greatest war in her history. Deane would remember:

> I had never before seen such an elaborate table service. The centerpieces were huge silver bowls containing fresh fruit specially procured from the Caucasus. It was only at such functions that one saw fresh fruit in Moscow. Beautiful cut glass ran the gamut from tall thin champagne glasses, through those for light and heavy red and white wines, to the inevitable vodka glass, midway in size between our liqueur and cocktail glasses, without which no Russian table is set. There were bottles the entire length of the table from which the glasses could be and were filled many times. Interspersed among the bottles were silver platters of Russian *zakouska,* including fresh large-grained dark gray caviar, very black pressed caviar of the consistency of tar, huge cucumber pickles, raw salmon and sturgeon. . . . Knives, forks, and spoons were of gold, and service plates of the finest china heavily encrusted with gold. The whole spectacle was amazing and called to mind the banquet scene in Charles Laughton's movie *Henry VIII.*

After the dinner, and a little unsteady from his consumption of vodka, Baumer went in search of Kuznetzov. That bonze-like Russian was in a little antechamber with two other Russian officers: General P. M. Fitin, the chief of the external intelligence service of the Russian secret service; and General A. P. Ossipov, chief of the Russian secret service department conducting subversive affairs against the Reich. They were three of the most important—and the most formidable—men in the Soviet secret apparatus. Emboldened by vodka, Baumer demanded to know what was going on, why they were being held up in Moscow, and why the Russian government would say neither yes nor no to the plan. When he got only courtesies in reply he staggered off and was embraced by Marshal Semën Budënny, a venerated Russian general with a vast mustache who was one of Stalin's archons. Both Baumer and Bevan would acknowledge, "We felt no pain that night."

But the politics of vodka seemed to work. For at 10:30 P.M. on the evening of March 1, without any prior notice, the Russians moved. The telephone rang at a cocktail party in Deane's quarters, and an English-speaking Russian officer announced that Kuznetzov would hold a meeting at 1:30 that morning—not an unusual hour for the Russians to call a meeting because, mysteriously, the Kremlin's office hours seemed to be from 5 P.M. to 5 A.M. When Bevan and Baumer arrived, as Baumer recorded in his diary, "they put us back on our heels with the announcement that they accepted our plan lock, stock and barrel, and would work to execute it. We did not know whether to shout or be suspicious." Kuznetzov then declared that a protocol would be available for signing on March 3, Baumer and Bevan, amazed at the Russians' hours and system, returned to their quarters at 2:15 A.M.

At 4 P.M. on March 3, the Bodyguard delegations assembled at Karl Marx Place to sign the protocol. But neither Bevan nor Baumer would sign it because the copies did not list the signatory nation's name first. It was a fine point. Baumer found a battered old Remington and, while the other delegates discussed the plan and methods of maintaining communication between Moscow, Washington and London, he typed the short protocol on a sideboard. Baumer recalled that it was "loaded with crossings out and misspellings, all of which had to be initialed by each of the delegates. The ribbon jammed, the letter 'l' had broken, I was trying to listen in to the conversation about Nazi intelligence as I was typing. All in all it was, in appearance, the most extraordinary document ever to find its way into the State Department archives."

The protocol was finally signed, and Bodyguard was now more than a strategical plan; it was an international agreement. On March 6, as that agreement was sent by special courier to London and Washington, Bevan and Baumer left Moscow. It had been a remarkable conference, made all the more remarkable because the Russian, American and British secret agencies were now committed to working together to bring down Hitler and the Third Reich. It was an alliance that could not, and did not, last; but while it did, it provided history with some of the most bizarre and significant episodes of subterranean warfare.

The Balkans

As BEVAN AND BAUMER negotiated Russian participation in Bodyguard at Moscow, the plan was already at work in the Balkans, playing
upon Hitler's beliefs about the importance of the region in his scheme for
empire. The Iron Gates, the Danube rapids in Rumania, were the true eastern frontiers of the Reich, he had declared, and Germany would never relin-
quish her claim to them. But in 1944 there were more immediate, more
practical reasons for his interest in the region. Not only did it supply the
Wehrmacht with the most valuable raw materials, particularly oil, but the
armed forces of his allies there—the Nazi elements of Hungary, Rumania
and Bulgaria—numbered hundreds of thousands of men, among them
some of the sturdiest soldiers in the world.

Hitler's dependence upon the Balkans was well known to the LCS
strategists, and the area had often been a target for their amalgam of
diplomatic, political and psychological warfare. A-Force had engineered
the early stratagems of Zeppelin under Plan Jael, and in the late summer of
1943, as if to assist Zeppelin, there occurred one of those mysterious
Balkans tangles that aggravated Hitler's fears for the area. Czar Boris III,
the Great Unifier of Bulgaria, collapsed and died in his palace at Sofia. He
had been, the evidence suggested, assassinated. But whether it was an
assassination or an accident, his death added an unexpected dimension to
the stratagems of Jael and, later, Bodyguard.

Czar Boris, it seemed, had been toying with the idea of surrender. But
after a stormy session with Hitler at Berchtesgaden, Boris had agreed to
remain with the Axis. A few days later, on August 28, 1943, he was dead
as a result (so Goebbels said) of some obscure poison such as snake
venom. It hardly seemed a coincidence, but if he had been murdered, who
had committed it: the Bulgars, the Germans, the Russians, the Americans,
the British? To Hitler, the Czar's death posed such a severe threat to his
Balkans strategy that an "enemy plot" was the only logical explanation—a

plot masterminded by the British and executed by some member of the Czar's entourage. In the uneasy weeks that followed, Hitler tried to shore up the faltering Bulgarian government and hold it to its military commitments, which he succeeded in doing for almost another year. But the British saw an opportunity to inflame the already volatile Bulgarian situation, and they took it. British and Communist agents began immediately to stir the nation into an anti-Hitler revolution, and whether or not an agency such as SOE or the OSS had had a hand in the Czar's death, PWE made capital of its consequences. Political warfare broadcasts and news stories kept the rumors of regicide alive and leveled accusations of their own—against the Germans—with excellent results. In the months ahead, Hitler would be compelled to strengthen his military presence in Bulgaria, further scattering the Reich's dwindling manpower reserves.

Italy's defection from the Axis, just a few days after Czar Boris's death, opened another dangerous breach in the Axis defenses of the Balkans; and A-Force, authorized by the "PWE/OWI Outline Plan for Political Warfare," a major component of Bodyguard, to "cause the peoples of the Satellite Countries to sabotage the German war effort, bring pressure upon their governments to get out of the war, or overthrow their governments if they resist such pressure," soon embarked upon a new campaign that was at once ruthless and cynical. It set out—in collaboration with PWE, SOE, the OSS and the Anglo-American diplomatic services—to encourage dissension and defection among Hitler's Balkans allies, not with the objective of making peace but of forcing Hitler to strengthen his defenses in the area.

In 1944, Hungary became a prime target for the strategies of Bodyguard. The mercantile aristocracy of Great Britain and the United States had long regarded Hungary with a condescending but affectionate air; and Hungary, with her whiff of the plumy courts of the Emperor Franz Josef, looked to the West as her natural ally. The Regent of the Kingdom of St. Michael—as Hungary's ruler, Admiral Nicholas Horthy, called himself—was not a wholly unpopular figure in the West. The trouble with Horthy and Hungary was that they had always backed the wrong horse: the Kaiser, and now the Fuehrer. Anxious to regain the territories Hungary had lost to Rumania through the First World War, Horthy enlisted his country in the Axis in 1941 and sent the 1st and 2nd Hungarian armies into Russia on a "holy crusade" with the Wehrmacht. But when Hitler failed to conquer Russia by the winter of 1941, as he intended, Horthy began to feel he had made an error of judgment; and in the early spring of 1942 he asked Nicholas Kallay, a landowner and politician with "beautiful instincts" who was reputed in his youth to have been one of the best duelists in central Europe, to become Prime Minister. Kallay was known to be an anglophile, and when he announced at an early Cabinet meeting that his task "was to carry Hungary through this crisis . . . with as little loss as possible to her moral and spiritual forces," the political climate for Bodyguard was set. Hitler realized that he had not a friend but an enemy in power in Hungary, and he immediately ordered his planners to produce "Case Margarethe I," an operation for the invasion and occupation of Hungary if she tried to defect—an operation that would, since the Hungarians were reputed to be violent defenders of their homeland, require sizable forces. While they were about it, the planners also produced "Case Margarethe II," an operation to occupy Rumania if she tried to do likewise.

Hungary took yet another step toward defection when the 1st Hungarian Army was almost destroyed by the Red Army during the battle for Stalingrad, and Kallay began to lobby the West for a separate peace through the Department of Extraordinary Affairs at the Vatican. Hitler heard of the communications and denounced Kallay as a "political adventurer" and "enemy number one of the German people." But if Kallay expected any support from the western powers, he got none. When the British government learned of his intention to defect, the BBC Hungarian Service started a campaign of menace and intimidation, warning that, through the capture of Sicily, "the Allied bombers have come much nearer to Central Europe and thus also to Hungary."

Kallay, thoroughly alarmed but still convinced that his friends the British would talk peace if they received the correct representations, played an interesting card. For some time he had been holding, in both comfort and secrecy, a British colonel, whom Kallay named as Charles Telfer Howie, a man who had escaped from a German prison camp in Silesia. Kallay installed Howie in the royal palace at Budapest, provided him with a wireless, a cipher and an operator, and asked him to get in touch with the Royal Navy at Malta. Through Howie, Kallay hoped the British could be persuaded to receive a Hungarian emissary, Andrew Frey, a Budapest journalist, with the proposition that Hungary desert the Axis, and when the Allies had landed an airborne force near Budapest, join in an attack against Germany through Vienna.

The proposition arrived at a convenient time for A-Force, which was busily engaged in trying to persuade the Germans that the Allies intended to march on Germany through the Ljubljana Gap and that the U.S. 7th Army under Patton was preparing to land near Trieste. Agents were at work at Gorizia and in the Gap itself to make it seem that the Allies were reconnoitering the terrain and recruiting the partisans to support such an operation. This activity alone had caused such disquiet at Hitler's headquarters that, for a time, Rommel had been in the region to organize the defenses of the Dolomites and the Julian Alps, and a number of divisions, including the very powerful Hermann Goering Division, which had been under orders to go to France, were stationed in the general area in case the Allied threat materialized. With the Kallay proposition, A-Force quickly recognized that new substance could be given to that threat if Hitler heard that Hungary was again wooing the Allies.

Frey was received by the British in Cairo, but in a signal to Kallay they responded merely: "We propose that the Hungarian government send to Istanbul, as soon as possible, two senior Hungarian officers to discuss details of the proposal received." The message nominated a man of Hungarian extraction, George Paloczi-Horvath, to deal with the Hungarian delegation. Both the telegram and the nominee distressed Kallay, for the British made no mention of political discussions and Paloczi-Horvath, Kallay believed, was in reality an agent of the Russians. He was distressed even further, a day or so later, when an article appeared in *The Times* which stated, as Kallay recounted, "that certain states, including Hungary, should not fancy that they could save themselves by their belated efforts to escape from the sinking ship." Kallay believed that the article was a design by the British secret service to cause trouble between Hitler and himself. As he would write, coming closer to the truth than he perhaps realized:

> What appalled us was not the stupidity of the article but the proof that some official indiscretion had taken place. The slipup not only made the success of the whole plan problematic, but it also seemed bound to provoke a reaction from the Germans, and it is not impossible that that was the purpose of the indiscretion.

Nevertheless, Kallay declared that he was willing to proceed with the discussions if a go-between other than Paloczi-Horvath could be found. But when Frey raised the point in Cairo, he was told by Paloczi-Horvath's superior in SOE (for Paloczi-Horvath was an officer of that organization) that Paloczi-Horvath might well be an agent of Moscow but that it did not matter; he was "not there to make politics but to create the maximum of confusion behind the enemy front." The hands of the LCS and A-Force were clearly at work.

Complaining of the perfidies of modern Albion, Kallay withdrew the Frey mission. But on August 17, 1943, another Hungarian V-mann, Ladislas Veres, an employee of the press section of the Hungarian Foreign Ministry and a man who "possessed English connections," was sent to Istanbul. He was received by J. C. Sterndale Bennett, the British minister to Turkey, and on September 9 the two men sailed secretly aboard the embassy's old steam-driven yacht in the Sea of Marmora. Here, Veres announced that Hungary accepted the principle of Unconditional Surrender and proposed to implement it when the Anglo-American armies reached the frontiers of Hungary. Bennett, in return, said he was empowered by the

United States and British governments to state that Hungary's capitulation, when confirmed, would be kept secret until both parties agreed that the surrender should be made public. On this issue, according to Kallay's account of the meeting, it was agreed that "publication shall in no case occur before the Allies have reached the frontiers of Hungary." But, of course, the western powers had no real intention, then or later, of even approaching the Hungarian frontier.

There were a number of other clauses in the agreement; Hungary was progressively to reduce her support for Germany, resist any German attempt to occupy the country, and at the given moment place her entire military and civilian resources at the disposal of the Allies. Hungary also agreed to receive an Anglo-American mission that would come in by parachute to "make the necessary advance preparations in connection with Hungary's surrender."

Veres was given a wireless and a cipher by the British, and when he returned to Budapest with the agreement, Kallay was euphoric. He would write:

> By concluding that agreement I thought I had brought my nation into safe harbor. I hoped that the relationship would grow more intimate as time went on. In our struggle to hold our own we had a safe backing, whatever happened. We enjoyed British protection in which we could trust. From that moment we were struck off the list of enemies and enrolled, if in disguised form, in the ranks of the resisting nations.

But Kallay was quite wrong; he should have known that surrenders are made at conferences, not aboard steam yachts.

Kallay's disillusionment came soon. An Anglo-American team did in fact arrive outside Budapest by parachute. But the team was not what he had hoped it would be—"a small, secret diplomatic mission, collaborating with our government and keeping their own government constantly informed." Neither did it prove to be "a watchtower," "established in the heart of Germany's power sphere." It was, Kallay complained, a group of "secret agents charged with the task of organizing conspiracies . . . and causing disturbances." When he realized that, he ordered the mission out of Hungary. But in the meantime, or so Kallay would allege, the British had revealed, through their secret contacts with the Germans, much of what had transpired between them and the Hungarian government. Kallay soon saw what was going on, and he wrote eloquently of his predicament: "With deep consternation I saw that as warfare was becoming mechanised, a parallel process had taken place in politics. Politics, too, had become rationalised and mechanised, and it had adopted the leitmotivs of war."

There was every reason to suppose that the British had deliberately tipped Kallay's hand, and their revelations had the desired effect in provoking the Fuehrer's wrath. Drawing the only conclusions that he could from news of Hungary's approaches to the western powers, combined with the activities of parties of secret agents at both ends of the Ljubljana Gap and in Hungary herself, and with intelligence reports that a fleet of tank landing ships originally intended for an amphibious operation in Southeast Asia were now being held in readiness for an assault by Patton's 7th Army against Trieste, Hitler ordered Case Margarethe I prepared for execution. Patton had no army—the 7th Army no longer existed except for the purposes of deception; the LST's were being held ready for the Anzio landing; and the reports of an imminent invasion of Trieste were merely a clever utilization of an abandoned plan for operations against the Dalmatian coast. The British, whose sense of economy was very pronounced, disliked wasting anything, including old plans.

By mid-February 1944, Case Margarethe I was fully prepared in all respects, except that there were no German troops available to bring Hungary back into line. For just at that moment Hitler was establishing the Anzio front with a reserve of five divisions which had been intended for France; he was fully extended on the Russian front, where a mighty battle was in progress; and reserve forces in Germany consisted only of some regimental combat groups there ostensibly to protect the Reich against the insurrection of foreign workers, but covertly ready to support the Schwarze Kapelle in its plan to seize power. OKW was able to scrape together a few divisions from Hungary's neighbors, who were anxious for spoils. But there was no armor—unless Hitler took it from the Atlantic Wall. And that was what he did.

On March 19, 1944, Hitler, finally exasperated by the fictions of Bodyguard and by the very real threat of a revolution in Hungary, invaded the country in great strength from three sides. There was little or no fighting; it was, the Germans claimed, another "Battle of the Flowers." The government fell and Kallay fled into the Turkish Embassy, where he was given sanctuary. There he remained for many months, the SS waiting for him in the street outside. He wrote a book in which he lamented: "Fate has willed it that I should live on, to see my country, which I loved like a mother, a wife, a child, die in my arms. I must be the mourner, I dig the grave." He went on living at the embassy, to the growing embarrassment of the Turks, until, as a result of an ultimatum implying that the SS would come in to get him if he did not come out, Kallay opened the wrought iron gates of the embassy at four o'clock in the afternoon of November 19, 1944, surrendered, and found himself, eventually, digging coal at Mauthausen concentration camp. He survived the war, and died an exile. He had little to comfort him except that, during his odyssey of acrobatic diplomacy, he had not been alone. Hungary's hated enemy, Rumania, had tried much the same thing, and had suffered much the same fate.

For nearly a century, Rumania's history as a Hohenzollern kingdom had been blood-violent, tragic, ludicrous, corrupt and explosive—a typical Balkans tangle. Now, in the early months of 1944, Rumania, as a satellite of Nazi Germany, was in another tangled upheaval. She, too, wished to desert her pact with Germany. But if Hungary was important to Hitler, Rumania was vital; over one-third of all Germany's oil was coming from Rumania, and to ensure that it continued to flow, Hitler paid for it in gold. When the air fleets of Pointblank—the Combined Bomber Offensive—began to attack Germany's petro-chemical industries, the great oilfields and refineries of Rumania became even more essential to Hitler. It was Bodyguard's intention to stir up trouble between Rumania and the Third Reich, putting additional pressure on Hitler to weaken his forces on the eastern and western fronts.

Rumania was already infiltrated by British (and American) troublemakers, among them Colonel Gardyne de Chastelain, a member of a French Huguenot family long settled in England. Before the war, Chastelain had been sales manager of the Phoenix Oil and Transport Company at Bucharest, and had been close to the throne of Carol II. Indeed, he had been present in September 1940 when Carol and his mistress, Madame Lupescu, fled Bucharest aboard the royal train. He was said to have helped the King load the train with 3 handsome motor cars, 4 dogs, 152 trunks, the palace's gold plate, some Rembrandts, a supply of gold ingots, his Treasury of $4 million, the couple's great wardrobes, and valises containing the deeds to several châteaux, mansions and vineyards in France and Portugal.

Chastelain left the country at the same time and, when Rumania joined the Axis, he became an adviser in several early British schemes to block the flow of oil to Germany, including a plan to blow up the cliffs on the Yugoslav side of the Danube, another to buy all the oil barges on the river, and a third to block the Iron Gates with a scuttled steamer. All these schemes came to nothing, except to alert Hitler to the fact that the British had their eyes on his oil. Then, on the night of February 22/23, 1944, Chastelain returned to Rumania on an expedition connected with Bodyguard. With two other British officers he was dropped to a reception committee that consisted of the guns, beaters and carriages of a nobleman's hunting party. It was admirable cover but, unfortunately, the police had got wind of the mission and captured Chastelain as he was getting out of his parachute shrouds. The British officers were not treated as spies, however; Marshal Ion Antonescu, the Rumanian leader, had other plans for them. They were kept under house arrest in a villa on the outskirts of Bucharest, were fed well, were permitted to go for walks, and had servants. And then, in a scheme to which King Michael, Carol's son and successor, was a party, Chastelain was invited to use his wireless operator to get in touch with the British and arrange a reception for a Rumanian peace emissary.

The time had come for Rumania to leave the Axis; the Russian army was closing in on the Carpathians, and the Balkans were alive with whispers that the Russians were about to launch an amphibious operation against the Rumanian Black Sea port of Constantsa, about 150 miles from the capital. This report was another Bodyguard deception arranged by Bevan and Baumer with the Russians in Moscow; but the people of Bucharest were thoroughly alarmed. Chastelain made the necessary arrangements, and the elegant figure and personality of Alexander Cretzianu, the former secretary general and political director of the Rumanian Foreign Ministry, was sent as a "swallow"—secret service parlance for a peace emissary—by his uncle, Prince Barbu Stirbey, to Ankara as Rumanian ambassador with instructions to inform the British and the American diplomatic missions that "everything was in readiness for an Allied landing in the Balkans. In Rumania, public opinion was anxiously awaiting the event; a new government had been agreed upon; and the military stood ready to give every assistance." King Michael, who was under a form of house arrest, blessed the mission, and there were indications from the Vatican that Rumania could expect favorable terms. But as Cretzianu would write of his reception in Ankara: ". . . my stay in Turkey started out with disappointments, the forerunners of far more cruel ones to come." The Cretzianu mission failed, and Prince Stirbey attempted to negotiate peace terms with the British in person. But after journeying in secret to Cairo in March 1944, he was dismayed to learn that both his whereabouts and his mission were being revealed on Allied newscasts. Bodyguard was at work again. Just as Hitler had been informed of Hungary's peace feelers, so he now knew (if he had not known before) that Rumania was seeking terms. Negotiations with Rumania dragged on for months, as Chastelain and other secret agents attempted to incite a revolution, and the Allies continued to disturb the Fuehrer's sleep by reconnoitering both ends of the Ljubljana Gap, recruiting anti-Nazi elements throughout the Balkans, and threatening invasion from the Adriatic, the Aegean and the Black seas.

The very real threat of revolution necessitated the invasion and occupation of Hungary, while diplomatic intimidation wedded to a formidable show of armed force was sufficient to keep Rumania and Bulgaria in line, at least until September 1944. But to arrest the rot in his eastern allies and guard against an invasion that never came, Hitler "milked" his garrisons in France of an excellent infantry division and the assault guns of four more first-rate infantry divisions, the powerful Panzer Lehr armored division, and finally the entire 2nd SS Panzer Korps—the 9th and 10th

SS Panzer divisions. In return, he sent to the West only two new and understrength infantry divisions. Moreover, Ultra detected the eastward movement of the 2nd SS Panzer Korps, and to ensure that wherever it went, it would never again be quite the same élite, full-strength fighting force, Bomber Command, on the night of March 29/30, 1944, attacked an assembly point of the 10th SS Panzer Division at the Vaires railway junction near Paris. Some of the bombs fell upon a train loaded with sea mines, and six days later German burial parties had collected the identity discs of more than 1200 *sturmtruppen*. Almost all of the division's administrative personnel, and many of its technical personnel, had been killed. Such men were not easily replaced, and there would be several hundred fewer sea mines for the Allied navies to sweep just before D-Day.

Bodyguard had done its work well. An after-action report of cover and deception operations in the European theater would note with satisfaction that Hitler, confronted with the task of collecting forces to keep his Balkans allies in line and avert a major disaster on the Russian front, had "elected to strip his garrison in France of three of its best divisions, while making no demands on four mobile divisions in reserve in Italy." And Hitler himself would admit on August 31, 1944, that "if I had had (the SS Panzer Korps) in the West (on D-Day) this affair (the invasion) would probably have never occurred."

In all, the Balkans operations orchestrated under Bodyguard were a major triumph for the LCS. But as convincing as its deceptions were, there was another factor that played a part in their success. The only antidote to good deception is good intelligence, and with good intelligence Hitler might readily have seen through the stratagems of Bodyguard. But for a variety of reasons he was not getting the intelligence upon which so much depended, and for a variety of reasons he was only rarely disposed to believe what he did get. At the root of this situation was the downfall, at long last, of the Abwehr—for petty political reasons. An astounding occurrence had taken place in February 1944 to deprive the Reich of its established intelligence service at this most critical time in German history. Canaris may not have been the best and most devoted intelligence man in the world, but he was the best that Hitler had. And just when he had the most need of his services, the Fuehrer fired Canaris.

With singular skill, over a period of nine years, Canaris had shuffled up and down the back stairs of history and politics, sometimes helping the Fuehrer in his bid for world conquest but, more often, conspiring to frustrate him. For years those who knew him wondered how he had survived; but now the master of the *Fuchsbau*—the "fox's lair," as the Abwehr staff called its headquarters—was gone. He had been dismissed by the Fuehrer, but not for any act of gross treachery. The lisping, singular, gentle admiral was fired through some gossip at a tea party in Berlin. It was a minor, involved affair; but it shattered the Abwehr—Hitler's most reliable source of military intelligence.

In September 1943, Schellenberg, whom Himmler had called the Nazi Benjamin, became suspicious of a small group of Germans of high social rank who met for tea and talk once a month in the home of Frau Hanna Solf, the widow of Dr. Wilhelm Solf, former Minister of the Colonies in the Kaiser's day and the last Foreign Minister in the Cabinet of Prince Max of Baden. It seemed to be a harmless gathering, but the Gestapo, which was ever vigilant about such meetings, noted that among the guests were Ludwig Gehre of the Abwehr, Otto Kiep, the former consul general at New York, and Count Helmuth von Moltke, a high administrative official at OKW—all of whom were suspected of being, or known to be, connected with treasonable groups. In fact, Gehre was the man who was probably the originator of the Lisbon Report; Moltke was in contact with Lionel Curtis, a Fellow of All Souls at Oxford who had connection with Menzies; and Kiep was an early member of the Schwarze Kapelle who was in touch with Dulles.

All this was unknown to Schellenberg when he decided to infiltrate Frau Solf's tea parties, using Dr. Joachim Reckzeh, a Swiss of good appearance and manners who was on the staff of Professor Max de Crinis, the principal of the Berlin Charité Hospital and Schellenberg's collaborator in the Venlo Incident of November 1939. Reckzeh was invited to tea at Frau Solf's and there he heard some startling statements. Otto Kiep denounced Hitler, Frau Solf asked him whether he could deliver a letter for her to friends in Switzerland, and Fräulein Elisabeth von Thadden, the headmistress of a girl's school, hinted that General Franz Halder, the former Chief of the General Staff, had been mixed up in a plot to remove Hitler. Gradually, Reckzeh uncovered what was, by the standards of the Reich, a treasonable conspiracy. A less paranoid society would have dismissed the *Solf Kreis*—as the Gestapo came to call the tea-party group—as self-important windbags. But Reckzeh informed Schellenberg, Schellenberg informed Himmler, and Himmler, ever anxious to indict and swallow the Abwehr, acted. He arrested Otto Kiep, which he had wanted to do for some time.

Kiep's arrest had immediate reverberations within the Abwehr overseas, for Kiep, through Canaris, had sponsored a number of young men with British and American connections for posts overseas, so that he might have channels of communication with London and Washington. One of these men was Dr. Erich Vermehren, an Abwehr agent at Istanbul who was in such close contact with MI-6 that he was known to the XX-Committee, as the double agent "Junior." On hearing that Kiep had been arrested, and fearing that he would be implicated in his interrogation, Vermehren and his wife, the former Countess Elisabeth von Plettenberg, asked MI-6 for "protection." It was granted and they were "evacuated" from Turkey to Egypt early in 1944, perhaps taking with them some secret material that included documents concerning Cicero. Before they went over to the other side, Vermehren, who had been at Oxford as a Rhodes Scholar and was passionately pro-British, warned two other German intelligence agents in Turkey that they, too, might be caught up in the affair. Both these agents, one the son of Fritz Hamburger, an Austrian tycoon, and the other a Munich journalist called Klecykowski, also defected to the British, taking more secret knowledge with them. In quick succession, probably through Kiep's interrogations, a number of other Abwehr agents defected at Lisbon, Stockholm and Casablanca.

The British saw another opportunity for political warfare against the Reich and gave Vermehren's defection wide publicity, hinting that he had brought over detailed information about the entire Abwehrkriegsorganisation and the German diplomatic cipher. Himmler, who had recently been embarrassed by a minor defection of his own, drew Hitler's attention to the treachery within the Abwehr, and Hitler demanded an immediate investigation. He was not pleased by what he discovered. On February 20, 1944, an investigator reported that Vermehren did indeed know a great deal about secret German activities in Turkey, and all of this information was now presumably in British hands. It was improbable, the investigator declared, that he had been able to betray the German code. But even the suspicion that his most secret ciphers were compromised sent shudders through the Fuehrer.

Himmler saw his opening. For years he had conspired to bring the Abwehr under party control, and now he did so. But he did not seek Canaris's head; Canaris knew too much about him. Instead he went to the Fuehrer and suggested, gently and carefully, that the gravity of the times demanded a single intelligence service placed in the hands of men who were ideologically dependable—men, said Himmler, such as Kaltenbrunner and Schellenberg. Hitler agreed; Canaris would be fired. But no Gestapo thugs came to pick him up at dawn as a common traitor. Rather, the Reich's two leading soldiers—Keitel and Jodl—called on him at Belinda, the Abwehr headquarters at Zossen, thanked him for his services to the Reich, announced that he was to receive the *Deutsches Kreuz ein Gelt,* invited him to take some leave, and asked if he would care to take over the Reich's economic warfare unit—a sinecure if there ever was one, for the Reich was hardly in a position to wage economic warfare. Canaris accepted, and so went into the bureaucratic wilderness. The fact that he had failed in every major task he was given against the western powers from 1940 onwards was not mentioned.

With the authority of an order from the Fuehrer, Himmler then called an intelligence conference at Salzburg. Ernst Kaltenbrunner, forty-one, Heydrich's successor as head of the SD, a lawyer with the build of a woodchopper and a paternity of "farmers and scythemakers," was appointed de facto chief of the new intelligence service. The working head was Schellenberg, who was only thirty-four but who had been a Nazi agent ever since his university days at Bonn. Thus, for all his youth, Schellenberg became one of the six most powerful men in the Reich.

Shrewd, somewhat feminine, with a hint of bodily plumpness, a good horseman, deeply interested in society espionage, intelligent, well read, difficult to catch, Schellenberg was no Nazi *Pabst*—tin god. He was able, quick and dangerous, but he was not quite as ideologically dependable as Hitler supposed. He, too, had his secret contacts with the Allies—the Americans: Schellenberg did not trust the British. His main channels of communication were with Dulles at Berne, and William Walton Butterworth of Princeton and Oxford, an economic warfare agent in Iberia. Schellenberg's go-between was Prince Max-Egon Hohenlohe-Langenburg, the most elegant figure in international espionage with the exception of Count Vanden Huyvel of MI-6. The prince was tall, slim, beautiful, diplomatic, with a good leg for a riding boot and an ancestry that had provided a German chancellor, a Prussian general, a Württemberg foreign minister, a Bavarian vice president, an ambassador to France, a prime minister of Prussia, a special envoy of Bismarck, a governor of Alsace-Lorraine, a marshal of France, a miracleworker in Hesse, a bishop of the Holy Roman Empire, an *aide-de-camp* to the Czar of all the Russias and now a secret agent for the Fuehrer. Through Hohenlohe-Langenburg, Schellenberg sought to take up where Canaris had left off. But Dulles was a fastidious man and, whereas he had considered Canaris's maneuvers as honest patriotism, he saw Schellenberg as a man out to make a deal. In consequence, Dulles would offer no special concessions to Schellenberg or his envoy.

Under Schellenberg, the Reich intelligence service was given a spiritual spring cleaning. The General Staff fought a tricky rearguard action to preserve something out of the ruin of the Abwehr, which in one form or another had been its dependency since Frederick the Great. And, to a certain extent, it was successful, for Amt Mil, the section created by Schellenberg to control the acquisition and flow of military intelligence, remained within the General Staff's province. Colonel Georg Hansen was given command of this new section, and although neither Himmler, Kaltenbrunner nor Schellenberg knew it, he was not only a disciple of Canaris but an energetic and clever apostle of the Schwarze Kapelle. Thus, all the Nazis had done at this decisive moment in German history was to exchange one fox for another.

Nevertheless, Schellenberg set about an impressive reorganization of the German intelligence system. At home there was much shifting of offices, desks, filing cabinets, telephones, equipment, secretaries; there was lengthy discussion about administrative and fiscal responsibility; pantechnicons and trucks came and went in convoys. Overseas, agents with great experience were replaced by men loyal to the SS but of limited or no experience; and whether or not Schellenberg suspected that the German intelligence system in Britain was firmly under British control, he was far more concerned with consolidating his new empire under SS hegemony than with running a fresh crop of agents into Britain. While all this was taking place, Germany was being subjected to one of the cleverest deception campaigns in history and the invasion armies gathering in Britain grew in size and strength. The collapse of the Abwehr was a major Allied advantage, for thereafter the secrets of Neptune would be much easier to keep.

Fortitude North

5

IN ITS LONG HISTORY of doom and intrigue, many fanciful figures had passed through the Portcullis Gate of Edinburgh Castle, up the carriageway past Argyll Battery and into the Barracks—Claverhouse and the Marquess of Argyll, Queen Margaret and the Duke of Gordon, Cardinal York and the Estates of the Realm, Cromwell and the Countess of Glamis. Now there was Klementi Budyenny, a Russian military intelligence officer, a bare twig of a man who had come to continue what Churchill and Stalin had begun at Teheran and Bevan and Baumer had cemented with the chiefs of the Russian secret agencies in Moscow. Within hours of his arrival in Edinburgh, the fact was known at Zossen through a transmission from a man called "Mutt," a XX-Committee double agent. Budyenny's mission—and Mutt's message—were the opening notes of "Fortitude," a major component of Bodyguard's cover and deception operations.

Fortitude's purpose was to conceal the secrets of Neptune, and the operation was born of a conference called "Rattle," which was held on June 28, 1943, at the Hollywood Hotel at Largs in Scotland, and attended by what the wits called the "Field of the Cloth of Gold." Present at Largs that blazing hot morning were no less than twenty generals, eleven air marshals and air commodores, eight admirals and twenty-two brigadiers from Britain, fifteen high-ranking Americans and five equally high-ranking Canadians. At the time, Admiral Lord Louis Mountbatten, who presided, remarked that they could hardly have chosen a less auspicious place for the meeting; half a mile from the hotel was a tall slender obelisk commemorating the defeat of the Norsemen at the Battle of Largs in 1263. The Norse invaders had been caught by a southwesterly gale and driven onto a lee shore—the same sort of shore that would hold so many terrors for the Neptune planners.

It was at Rattle that the question about where the Allies should land in Europe—the Pas de Calais or Normandy—was settled. The Allies would

) 459 (

return to Europe through Normandy. But, the conference decided, in order to disperse Hitler's forces, obtain surprise for Neptune, and delay the Wehrmacht's reaction to the invasion, the Germans must be led to believe that other parts of northern and northwestern Europe were also under direct threat of attack. The primary target of these bogus threats would be the Pas de Calais, and they would continue long after Neptune was ashore, culminating on or about July 20, 1944. By historical circumstance that would seem beyond coincidence, the Normandy battle would reach its climax at about that same time, which was also the time that the Schwarze Kapelle would attempt to assassinate Hitler.

Nine months after its conception, Fortitude had become the biggest and most ambitious of all Bodyguard operations—and the one most crucial to the success of Neptune. It was formally defined as:

A broad plan covering deception operations in the European theatre, with the objects (a) to cause the Wehrmacht to make faulty strategic disposi- tions in north-west Europe before *Neptune* by military threats against Norway, (b) to deceive the enemy as to the target date and target area of *Neptune,* (c) to induce (the enemy to make) faulty tactical dispositions during and after *Neptune* by threats against the Pas de Calais.

Again the dry language of the military obscured the elegance and daring of the scheme. For Fortitude proposed to tie down no less than ninety Ger- man divisions in areas far from the Normandy battle, together with all their air, naval and matériel support.

Fortitude was divided into two parts; the first, aimed specifically at Norway and the other Scandinavian countries, was codenamed "Fortitude North," and here the plan was to compel Hitler to keep the twenty-seven divisions he would have stationed in Denmark, Norway and Finland on D- Day idle but expectant with threats of a joint British-American-Russian invasion. There were, of course, almost no forces available in Britain for such an invasion. And so Fortitude North, in an operation codenamed "Skye," proposed to invent them. The Germans, by a variety of special means, were to be led to believe that the British 4th Army—a force of 350,000 men which did not, and would never, exist except as a deception organization of battalion strength—was assembling in Scotland; and from there, in cooperation with the American 15th Corps—a force which did exist but which belonged to another army—and with nonexistent Russian forces, it was ready to launch a full-scale assault against Norway prior to or even after D-Day.

"Fortitude South" involved an even more daring fabrication: the cre- ation not merely of an army, but of an army group—a force of fifty divisions and a million men. There were two army groups now assembling in southern and southwestern England: Montgomery's 21st and what would become Bradley's 12th. The former would go to Normandy on D-Day; the latter would go in when a beachhead had been established. But again by a variety of special means, the Germans were to be led to believe that a third force—the First United States Army Group (FUSAG) —was assembling in southeastern England to launch the main attack against France at the Pas de Calais. The strategy behind this deception, which was codenamed "Quicksilver," was quite simple, but no less ingenious for that. If the Germans could be convinced of the existence of FUSAG, they might then believe that the Normandy invasion was a diversion to lure German forces away from the Pas de Calais, and that as soon as they moved to reinforce Normandy, FUSAG would descend upon the Calais area. Hitler was already predisposed to believe that the Pas de Calais would be the main point of the Allied attack, and he had garrisoned the area with the 15th Army, the strongest force in the West. It was the objective of the Quicksilver ruse to keep that force in place.

There were other components to Fortitude. The operation codenamed "Ironside" was designed to keep the German 1st Army occupied in the region of Bordeaux during the D-Day period by threats of an invasion along the Biscay coast; and "Vendetta" was calculated to achieve the same result with the German 19th Army in the region of Marseilles. The current phase of Zeppelin would continue to put pressure on the Balkans during the D-Day period; and "Diadem" was designed to pin down Hitler's army in Italy through orthodox military operations. Finally, added to all these were scores of smaller operations with exotic code names that would, it was hoped, distract the attention of the German forces from Normandy during the actual invasion.

The Fortitude scenario was one of great complexity, with a command set-up for its operations of corresponding complexity. Bevan and the LCS (with the JSC in America) exercised overall responsibility for both Bodyguard and Fortitude; but day-to-day control of Fortitude in particular was the business of the operations staff of General Harold R. Bull at SHAEF, of which the CSM was a part. The two officers of the CSM primarily concerned with Quicksilver were Colonel J. V. B. Jervis-Reid and Colonel Roger Fleetwood Hesketh. Jervis-Reid was a sapper, a product of St. George's, Windsor, and Emmanuel College, Cambridge; Hesketh was the millionaire son-in-law of the Earl of Scarborough, Lord of the Manor of North Meols, and a future Conservative MP. But deception had become an attractive trade, and new agencies began to proliferate. Colonel David I. Strangeways commanded R-Force, the deception organization at Montgomery's headquarters; Colonel William H. Harris commanded the Special Plans Branch, Bradley's deception team. There were also "special headquarters," "special wireless units," "special research units"—all concerned with deception—to say nothing of deception organizations within MI-6, OSS, PWE, OWI, navy and air force headquarters, the War Office and the Pentagon. Baumer would comment after the war that the great number of deception agencies confused not only the Germans but also the Allied high command. There was the danger of discord between them; there was the even greater danger of inconsistencies in their operations. Only under Bevan's severe and cautious direction could they perform their parts in Fortitude with the necessary harmony.

On paper, Fortitude was a magnificent fiction with which to surprise and confound the enemy. But would its stratagems work in practice? The enemy was clever, resourceful, powerful—and schooled in the dictum of the General Staff's greatest tutor, Clausewitz, who wrote: "A great part of the information obtained in war is contradictory, a still greater part is false, and by far the greatest part is somewhat doubtful." Would the Germans remember that dictum, or could the Allied deception agencies convince them that the fictions of Fortitude were both consistent with their own strategical and tactical beliefs and true beyond a shadow of a doubt?

Fortitude North was aimed at Hitler's obsession about Scandinavia. The Fuehrer had once read an essay on naval strategy in the First World War by Wolfgang Wegener, a German admiral who believed that the Kaiser had lost that war because the British succeeded in pinning the High Seas Fleet in the German Bight. Wegener argued that if that fleet had been able to break free and roam the Atlantic, the disruption of Britain's mercantile marine would have destroyed her capacity to wage war at all. Accordingly, Wegener argued, if another war came Germany must seize the ice-free ports of Norway. That was what Hitler had done in 1940; and thereafter he remained exceptionally sensitive to any Allied threat to Scandinavia. Very strong forces of the Wehrmacht were stationed in Norway— at one time the Fuehrer had all his capital ships and most of his submarines there—and by November 7, 1943, the country was garrisoned with no less than 380,000 fighting men, a large air force, a panzer division, and over 1500 coastal defense guns and projectors. It would be Fortitude North's task to keep those forces there during Neptune by spreading the fiction that Anglo-American and Russian forces were preparing to invade Norway. That was the reason for Budyenny's presence in Edinburgh. Soon other unusual activities would be centered there.

The Allies had no intention of attacking Norway, but Fortitude North was not an idle exercise, nor an expenditure of men and military supplies that might have been better devoted to Neptune. The chief objective of the operation was to surprise the enemy and to *save* lives on D-Day. As obvious, and as essential to the success of D-Day as that aspect of the deception was, it had other more subtle ramifications that could influence the course of the war in the months ahead. By mounting a threat to Norway, the Allies also hoped to put pressure on Sweden to abandon her neutrality and enter the war on the side of the Allies. With Sweden in the Allied camp, Hitler would be cut off from the special grade iron ore without which the Bessemer process steel mills of the Ruhr would go silent, and his forces in Finland would be isolated from the European mainland. Fortitude North also meant to suggest that once Anglo-American and Russian forces had secured the Scandinavian peninsula, they would launch an invasion of Denmark, assaulting the Third Reich from the north. To counter that threat, it was hoped that Hitler would be compelled to keep his garrisons in place along the North Sea coast—and in the Pas de Calais—thus further diverting the forces that he might use against Neptune. But the most ingenious aspect of the deception involved "Skye," the creation of the fictitious British 4th Army that was to spearhead the Norwegian invasion. For not only would this force be created out of thin air, but once the invasion armies were ashore in Normandy and a convincing threat against Norway could no longer be maintained, the 4th Army would not simply vanish as mysteriously as it had appeared. The Germans were to be led to believe that it was moving out of Scotland into southern England where it would link up with another nonexistent army, the American 14th, to form FUSAG, the fictitious army group that was to invade the Pas de Calais.

The man in charge of Skye was Colonel R. M. "Rory" MacLeod, a horsegunner who had been so badly wounded on the Somme in the First World War that one-third of his skull was made of a silver plate. MacLeod had thought his military career was over until he received a telegram while umpiring war games on the wet and windy Yorkshire Moors on March 2, 1944. His early and middle years had been full of promise. He had won the DSO and the MC in the First World War, had held a number of good posts between the wars, and in the first year of the Second World War was military assistant to Field Marshal Lord Ironside of Archangel, the Chief of the Imperial General Staff and C-in-C of the army in Britain at the time when Germany seemed about to invade. MacLeod had hoped that, when his tour of duty at the Horse Guards had finished, he would be given command of an infantry division. But it was not to be; Churchill did not think highly of Ironside, he was replaced and MacLeod went into the military wilderness. Now he was fifty-two, and apparently there was no place for him in Neptune. But then someone at the CSM found a paper which MacLeod had read to the Indian Staff College at Quetta in 1933. It was about the strategy and tactics with which Genghis Khan had conquered the world between Canton and Budapest—strategy and tactics that bore a surprising similarity to the games now being played by the LCS.

The telegram summoned MacLeod to Supreme Headquarters at Norfolk House, and he went hoping for a command in the "big show"—Neptune. It would prove to be a phantom command—the British 4th Army. Brigadier Richard Barker, the signalsmaster for Home Forces, told him:

> Rory, old boy, you have been selected to run a deception operation for SHAEF from Scottish Command. You will travel to Edinburgh. And there you will represent an army which does not in fact exist. By means of fake signals traffic you will, however, fool the Germans into believing that it does exist and, what is more, that it is about to land in Norway and clear the Germans out of there. The whole thing is an important part of the coming invasion of France. You are to keep the Germans fully occupied in Norway so that they don't reinforce the units in France from there. . . . It is terrifically important that it should be a success.

Barker went on to explain that the C-in-C of 4th Army would appear to the Germans to be a former military attaché in Berlin, General Sir Andrew "Bulgy" Thorne, a distinguished officer whom the older German generals would look for in any major British campaign. Was Thorne not the former Major General of the Brigade of Guards and had he not led the British 48th Infantry Division out of Flanders in 1940 with great skill? But MacLeod would do the work, and that work would consist mainly of fabricating the wireless traffic typical of an assembling army, traffic that the Germans were meant to overhear. It would not be as easy as sending out a few random messages, however; the airwaves had to be filled with an exact and detailed simulation of the real wireless traffic of a real army, for as Barker pointed out in his briefing:

> The Germans are damn good at interception and radio-location. They'll have your headquarters pinpointed with a maximum error of five miles. And it won't take them more than a few hours to do so. What is more. they'll be able to identify the grade of headquarters—whether army, divisions, corps, or what not—from the nature of the traffic and the sets being used.

A mild man, MacLeod did not protest or intrigue; he caught the night train for Edinburgh and arrived there on March 6. He set up 4th Army headquarters in a number of rooms under Edinburgh Castle, close to the "great iron murderer" called "Muckle-Meg"—Mons Meg, a huge piece of artillery made in 1486. Here, MacLeod put together his "staff"—twenty officers who, so it had been said, "were just a little bit beyond active service." Two elderly majors and six junior officers established a "corps" at Stirling, another was established near Dundee, and since the deception involved the U.S. 15th Corps of General Wade H. Haislip in Ulster, an American liaison officer was assigned to the group. Together with wireless operators, a handful of men and women began to create the wireless traffic of an army which would have, by the time it moved into southeastern

England for the Pas de Calais "invasion," two corps headquarters with troops, one airborne division, four infantry divisions, one armored division and one armored brigade—a force of over a quarter of a million men with its own tactical air command and some 350 tanks and armored fighting vehicles.

By the end of the first week of April 1944, the air over Scotland was alive with messages in cipher, plain text or radiotelephony; "battalions" spoke to "brigades," and "brigades" spoke to "divisions," "divisions" transmitted to "corps," and "corps" transmitted to "army." What else but an invasion of Norway could the Germans deduce from messages such as these: "Captain R. V. H. Smith, 10th Cameronians, will report to Aviemore for ski training forthwith . . ." "2 Corps Car Company requires handbooks on engine functioning in low temperatures and high altitudes . . ." "7 Corps requests the promised demonstrators in the Bilgeri method of climbing rock faces . . ." "80 Div. requests 1800 pairs of crampons, 1800 pairs of Kandahar ski bindings . . ."?

Just as Barker had predicted, the Germans quickly located 4th Army's wireless station, and an aircraft zoomed over and shot it up with machine guns, startling everyone but hurting no one. The 4th Army had experienced its first—and last—combat in the Second World War. The wireless station survived and continued its transmissions. The Germans, however, were wary of this kind of intelligence; wireless deception was, after all, a familiar British trick. They needed further confirmation that some military expedition was being mounted in Scotland. The XX-Committee's double agents, "Mutt" and "Jeff," supplied it. Both men had been sent to England as spies, and both had surrendered when they waded ashore from an Arado seaplane near MacDuff, a small town of herring fishermen on the south shore of the Moray Firth, on April 7, 1941. They had been "turned" and their ciphers and schedules were now being used by the XX-Committee to communicate with their German controllers. Mutt had become a "farm manager" to a British landowner with large estates in Scotland, and Jeff was an officer in the Norwegian army there—or so their controllers believed, although Jeff was actually in jail at Dartmoor at this time for being difficult. What did they know of activities in Scotland, their controllers inquired? Mutt reported the arrival of the Russian Budyenny at Edinburgh Castle, apparently to coordinate an Anglo-Russian move against Scandinavia, and the existence of the British 2nd Corps headquarters at Stirling. Jeff, who was being successfully impersonated, reported that the British 7th Corps was located at Dundee, and when he was asked to describe the insignia of the 4th Army, he replied that it was a square, half blue, half red, with the figure eight in gold but with the lower loop missing. It resembled, he said, the Anglo-Saxon rune for the woman's name Ethel.

Calculated leaks to the press and radio amplified the deception. Local newspapers wrote of "4th Army football matches," the Scottish BBC spent a day with "7th Corps in the field." A pipe band of the "2nd Corps" beat the Retreat at Edinburgh Castle, and a "major of the 4th Army" married, said the newspapers, a member of the women's auxiliary of the "7th Corps." In the meantime, hundreds of twin-engine aircraft—wooden ones—began to appear on Scottish airfields. And hundreds of warships—real ones, part of Force "S" for Neptune—assembled under the low purple hills of the Scottish coast.

British agents in Norway were also involved in the deception. London began to make discreet, but not too discreet, inquiries about the snow levels in the Kjölen Mountains, the great spine of Norway. Would the bridge over the Rauma at Åndalsnes support medium infantry tanks? Was the 142nd Infantry Battalion of the SS Mountain Division Prinz Eugen still at Stjordalshalsen? What was the alpine component of the Hochgebirgs-jäger (the high mountain troops) of the 7th Infantry Division? Can German alpinists travel more than 20 miles a day over nève? Please report whether the German alpinists have evolved any special clothing which will increase their endurance in weather conditions such as are to be found in Finnish Karelia.

While the British controllers were asking their agents in Norway these questions, German controllers were questioning "Tricycle" and "Garbo," two spies whom they considered to be among their most reliable sources of intelligence from Britain. In fact, Tricycle and Garbo had been under XX-Committee control for many years, and both were soon on the air with reports that substantiated the deception. The Russians, acting upon their agreement with the Allied secret agencies in Moscow, had begun to play their part in Fortitude North. They were leaking intelligence to the Germans that Russian troops and ships were concentrating in the Kola Inlet for an attack on Petsamo in Norway, and that they were forming a new army for an Arctic campaign beginning in June 1944. Tricycle and Garbo confirmed these leakages from London, and Tricycle backed up a report from Mutt that a Soviet military and naval mission had established itself at Edinburgh to coordinate Russian operations with those of the 4th Army.

Neither the Russians nor the British had a battalion, let alone an army, to spare in operations against Norway. But that spring small units of British special forces, and even individual agents, made a series of daring raids against German garrisons and industrial installations that had all the earmarks of "pre-invasion" tactics, and at the same time destroyed Norwegian sources of supply vital to the Reich. In an operation codenamed "Archery," British Commandos sank 15,000 tons of shipping, destroyed an oil refinery and put much else to the fuse; in "Title," they mined the great German battleship *Tirpitz*. In "Archer," "Penguin," "Heron I" and "II," "Mallard," "Redshank," "Knottgrass," "Unicorn" and "Freshman

II" agents and Commandos attacked mines, a power station, an aluminum plant and iron ore installations. "Cartoon" struck the mine installations at Litlabo and Stord, and destroyed the means to transport some 150,000 tons of ore to Germany. "Seagull" hit the Arendal smelting works, and then flew back to put bombs in the Lysaker chemical works and the Norsk sulphur factory at Vorpen. "Granard" and "Feather II" struck the Orkla pyrite mines—after the Germans had spent four months repairing the damage from a previous attack. "Mardonius" came in with limpet mines and sank the German steamers *Ortelsburg* and *Tugela,* and the troopship *Donau* with 1200 troops aboard. "Lapwing," "Fieldfare" and "Woodpecker" blew up railways around Oslo, Bergen and Skien. "Lapwing II" blew up the Norsk Watson company, destroying the machine tabulators which the Germans were using to organize the compulsory mobilization of 80,000 Norwegians for work in Germany. And a series of Commando raids, "Vestige I" to "XIV," crept in to disturb the general peace of mind of Germans in their outposts with the knife and the hand grenade.

Other steps were taken to intensify the appearance of imminent military operations in Scandinavia. The Home Fleet sortied from Scapa Flow, and trailed its coat from the Nordkapp to the Skagerrak. The RAF and the USAAF increased their photographic reconnaissance flights over Finnmark. Russian submarines appeared to reconnoiter the "invasion coast" around Petsamo. The Norwegian section of SOE began to send blocks of false messages which seemed to the Germans in Norway to be instructions to the Norwegian resistance. Allied military wireless traffic in Iceland, the Faroes, Ulster and Bear Island began to intensify in volume, as did Russian traffic around the Kola Inlet. The SD detected an increase of instructions to "The Princes" in Denmark—the spy section of the Danish underground. Cryptic messages to "The Brewers" (which meant action against the electrical system), to "The Painters" (which directed sabotage against the railways), to "The Barristers" (in charge of action against German telecommunications) and to "The Priests" (for action against harbors) began to crowd the Danish Service of the BBC.

Neutral Sweden was also a target for Fortitude North. A British military mission was photographed as it measured the heights of tunnels on the main rail routes through Varmland from Stockholm to Oslo. The press reported that American and British military engineers were inquiring about the load capacities of Swedish rolling stock and railbeds, and hinted that these inquiries had to do with the movement of Allied armored forces from Norway down to the Baltic. British airmen were said to be inspecting the runways and hardstandings of Swedish military airfields. Parliamentary correspondents reported that the western powers were negotiating for transit rights and port facilities for Allied military forces on the islands of Gotland and Öland, which faced the German Baltic coast; and rumors began to circulate that the Allies wanted these facilities to attack Germany across the Baltic and through Denmark. The Swedish people were advised to dig air-raid shelters if they had not already done so, and to lay in stocks of food, wood, oil, medicaments, candles and electric light bulbs. The implication was that Sweden might be subjected to a siege or air raids. Apprehension was increased when it became known on the Swedish stock exchange that speculators on the London and New York markets were buying up long-moribund Scandinavian stocks; and when the British government stepped in and bought £500,000's worth of the securities, it could only mean that the Allies really intended to land in Scandinavia. In fact, Bevan had requested the Treasury to buy the stocks to heighten the tensions of Fortitude North—and, he would later claim, "they were eventually sold at a fine profit."

The atmosphere of crisis reached a climax when the Allies launched "Graffham," an operation which was defined as: "A diplomatic threat [against Sweden] to reinforce *Fortitude North,*" and "negotiations for Swedish airfields and transport facilities." The threat was direct and uncomplicated: if Sweden wished a place in the postwar council of nations— the United Nations—it would be advisable to stop trafficking with the enemy and grant to the Allies the same transportation facilities that she granted the Nazis. To give bite to the threat the Allies also launched an unprecedented campaign of economic warfare against Sweden, a campaign that included, wrote one official involved, "secret negotiations, trade concessions, economic pressure and financial skulduggery," and "made use of the power and prestige of diplomats and bankers, but was equally ready to use the reckless unscrupulousness of the wildest adventurers." The main weapons of the campaign were the British Statutory List and the American Proclaimed List—black lists comprised of the names of Axis, Allied and neutral citizens who gave undue aid and comfort to the enemies of the United States and Great Britain. According to one definition of these lists: "By law, persons on the black list were considered enemies of the United Kingdom or the United States, and were treated as economic lepers. Any of their property that came within our reach was subject to seizure; no American or Briton might deal with them in any way; and . . . they were refused facilities for passage of their persons, goods, or correspondence by any route under Allied control." Further, the ships and aircraft of nations giving aid and comfort to the enemy were liable to seizure, and could not obtain insurance, cargoes, fuel or victuals, or even landing rights in any ports under Allied control; they were doomed to wander the high seas until they either broke down, ran out of fuel, or were arrested.

The campaign also included the other neutrals, but it was especially painful to the Swedes, for Sweden and Germany were closely linked through trade, marriage and finance. Nevertheless, the Allies insisted that the Swedes put an end to German military traffic across Sweden and stop the export of iron ore, special steels and machine tools. The Allies also demanded that the Swedes refuse further credit to the Reich; and in return, they offered increased exports of petroleum products—of which the Swedes were very short. But the most important objective of this campaign of economic warfare was the denial to Germany of Swedish ball bearings, for bearings were essential in the production of German aircraft, tanks and weapons of all sorts, and their own production capacity was not sufficient to meet the needs of the Wehrmacht. Therefore they imported most of their bearings from Sweden, the country which had invented them and, through the SKF company, dominated the great bearings cartel. The Allies were determined, by whatever means possible, to cut off that supply.

At the end of 1943 and during the first half of 1944, ball-bearing factories in Germany became a prime target for Allied bombers. So important were bearings to the Wehrmacht that, as part of the air operations that preceded Neptune, the Allies were prepared to sacrifice large numbers of men and aircraft to destroy Germany's own limited manufacturing capacity—and the Germans were equally prepared to defend it. Witness the raid against Schweinfurt. On October 14, 1943, 220 bombers of the USAAF carrying 478 tons of bombs attacked the Franconian ball-bearing cities, and 300 German fighters rose to intercept the *dicken Hund* (literally, the "fat dog," German fighter pilots' jargon for the massed phalanx bomber formation which the USAAF flew). In an air battle of unprecedented fury, the Germans shot down sixty American bombers, and damaged a further seventeen so seriously that, while they managed to get back to their bases, they could not be repaired or flown again. Almost all the rest were disabled to one degree or another. It was the blackest day in the history of the American aerial campaign against Germany.

As part of Graffham and the associated economic warfare campaign, the Allies turned to other means to cut off the German ball-bearing supply. An extraordinary American, Stanton Griffis, one of Donovan's special agents, arrived in Stockholm. Griffis was chairman of the board of Madison Square Garden, the owner of the Brentano bookstore chain, a major executive of Paramount Pictures, and later American ambassador in turn to Poland, Egypt, Argentina and Spain. Surrounded by a cloud of Swedish beauties—his cover was as a talent scout for Paramount—Griffis was secretly meeting with the Stockholm business community, checkbook in hand, in an attempt to buy up all SFK's ball-bearing exports to Germany. The Swedes rejected the offer; they declared that an invasion of the continent was mere Allied propaganda and that the war would drag on for years. But their resistance was broken by what one account called "a judicious mixture of black list threats, promises of compensating Allied orders, and businessman-to-businessman persuasion." The Swedes finally came to heel. They stopped all German military traffic through Sweden. They withdrew insurance from all ships entering German ports, and supplies of iron ore were gradually halted, as were supplies of ball bearings and machine tools. German agents, newspapermen and diplomats were also prevented from entering the country, and by December 1944 Sweden had shut Germany's window to the north.

While Griffis was arm-twisting Swedish businessmen, MI-6, PWE and OSS agents were at work infecting high authorities in Berlin itself with the fictions of Fortitude North. In Stockholm, Dr. Bruce Hopper, a Harvard professor of political science, and Dr. George Brewer, a former Yale English master who had written *Dark Victory,* a Broadway hit starring Tallulah Bankhead and later a movie starring Bette Davis, Humphrey Bogart and Ronald Reagan, succeeded in making contact with Dr. Felix Kersten, a masseur who had become personal physician to Himmler. He lived in Stockholm and traveled to Berlin once a month to give Himmler's back a rub. Himmler once said that the masseur was "my only friend, my Buddha," and he trusted Kersten absolutely. To Kersten, Himmler confided every plan of Hitler's that came to his notice; and in turn, Kersten confided this information to Hopper and Brewer—not out of treachery but because he thought he could win them as friends for Himmler. Eventually the contact became so important a conduit for both intelligence and deception that it was taken over by yet another remarkable American. He was Abram Stevens Hewitt, a rich New York lawyer, a graduate of Oxford and Harvard, the grandson of a Mayor of New York, and the son-in-law of a Boston banker. While ostensibly negotiating with Himmler through Schellenberg to facilitate a plan by Himmler for a *coup d'état* against Hitler, Hewitt "accidentally" discussed commercial affairs that, so it seemed, pointed with certainty to an Allied invasion of both Scandinavia and the Balkans that year as the precursor to Neptune.

Stockholm was also the scene of another unique deception scheme. Early in his association with Allen Dulles, Fritz Kolbe, the special assistant to Ambassador Karl Ritter, the German Foreign Office representative at OKW, had noted a heavy flow of most secret intelligence traffic coming across his desk from Stockholm. All of it began: *"Josephine meldet"* ("Josephine reports"), and it frequently mentioned the code name "Hektor," a man who appeared to be in Churchill's headquarters in London and who had admission to the meetings of the Air Ministry, the Ministry of Supply, the Ministry of Aircraft Production, and the Atlantic Convoy Committee, and access to the minutes of the American War Production Board. "Beware," Kolbe told Dulles sometime in November 1943, "the Abwehr has a man close to Churchill in London." But when Dulles reported this information to his MI-6 counterpart in Berne, Count Vanden Huyvel, he was told, "Hush. We know."

In fact, the British had only recently discovered the source of the Josephine reports. He was Karl-Heinz Kraemer, a lawyer turned Abwehr agent who had long been involved in intelligence operations against the British, including the Kondor mission in Cairo in 1942, and since 1943 had been conducting his business from Stockholm. He was a clever operator, for as one who met him would write, Kraemer evolved "a novel method that would enable the Abwehr to procure the highest-grade intelligence about Britain without the need of keeping even a single of its own V-men in England, but simply by tapping the secret services of other countries which still maintained agents in Britain." Kraemer's most valuable sources were Major S. E. Cornelius and Count J. G. Oxenstjerna, the Swedish air and naval attachés in London. Both were highly qualified technical and scientific advisers who were trusted by the British and therefore enjoyed considerable access to British military establishments. Their reports were models of detail, and they would have been horrified to learn that a pro-German member of the Swedish Combined Intelligence Staff at Stockholm was surreptitiously showing them to Kraemer.

To hide the method by which he was obtaining his intelligence—from both the Swedes and from Schellenberg, who was ever alert for irregularities in the Abwehr—Kraemer invented a number of code names to suggest that his sources were in England. Among them was Hektor, the highly placed official, whom Kraemer represented as being besotted with love for "Josephine," a "London society woman" who was Kraemer's "postbox" in London. Neither of these agents existed, although Kraemer drew very large sums of money from the Abwehr imprest account to keep them operational. Nevertheless, his intelligence was both accurate and invaluable, at least at first. He reported the arrival of American convoys and the locations of arms depots, and between June and August 1943, he transmitted a very large number of long reports concerning British aircraft production and Allied bomber and general strategical policy, including information that the Allies did not intend to launch a large-scale invasion in the West until the results of the round-the-clock bombing campaign of German cities were known. It was at this time that the LCS was trying to persuade OKW that the Allies would indeed land in the West; and these revelations, when combined with the results of technical intelligence-gathering and other sources of information available to the Germans, may well have played a part in the general failure of Cockade and Starkey.

Kraemer sustained this flow of intelligence until around October 1943. Then something happened. British agents in touch with German agents in Lisbon learned of the Hektor–Josephine–Kraemer traffic. Supporting evidence was obtained through Ultra and from Dulles. But instead of suppressing the London sources of Kraemer's information—Cornelius and Oxenstjerna among them—the LCS decided to permit them to remain open, but to turn them to the use of Fortitude North. Cornelius and Oxenstjerna were not expelled; they were allowed to continue their visits to British military establishments. But at the same time their reports were deliberately seeded by LCS agents with false but plausible information designed to impress the Swedish government with the belief that the Allies would open land warfare in 1944 with a descent upon Scandinavia.

The Swedes were no less alarmed than the Germans. When he learned that a Russian mission had established itself at Edinburgh Castle to coordinate Russian naval and military operations with those of the British 4th Army, Colonel von Roenne, the chief of FHW, began to listen. But he sat up abruptly when he received a report from Josephine via Kraemer that Anthony Eden, the British Foreign Secretary, had returned to London from Moscow (he had never been there in fact) with details of a combined enterprise in Norway—Fortitude North. Roenne was not entirely convinced that the Grand Alliance intended to invade Norway, although he could not persuade the Fuehrer of that fact. But he did become convinced of the existence of the British 4th Army, the force that would shortly move south from Scotland to join the equally fictitious FUSAG in southeastern England to invade the Pas de Calais.

Fortunately for the LCS and Fortitude, Kraemer continued to be trusted by his German controllers until the late spring of 1944. Then, following Canaris's dismissal, the SD engaged in a widespread purge of Abwehr officers; among them—despite Schellenberg's opinion that he was loyal and sound—was Kraemer. He was ordered home to report and "was told bluntly that he was under investigation as a possible faker, misusing official funds by financing non-existent intelligence operations." He survived a thirty-six-hour nonstop interrogation, but he was no longer trusted. As the SD report on him said: "The evaluation of this operation by (Amt Mil) is no longer valid. The quality of the Josephine material, especially those concerning army matters, is generally inferior."

If the SD had come to that conclusion before June 1944, instead of after it, Hitler might have had 400,000 more men to fight the battle in Normandy. But in fact Fortitude North, and the diplomatic, political and economic warfare campaigns associated with it, were extraordinarily successful. The Fuehrer not only kept his garrisons in place in Norway, he reinforced them to counter the threatened invasion. By the late spring of 1944, he would have 13 army divisions stationed there with 90,000 naval and 60,000 air personnel, 6000 SS and 12,000 German paramilitary troops. His forces included one panzer division, a small but powerful squadron of U- and E-boats, and an air force—all of which would have been very useful in France. The German army would remain in Norway, more or less intact, still awaiting an invasion when the Allies finally did land . . . after the end of the war to accept their surrender.

Fortitude South

THE PILOT of General George S. Patton's C-47 transport let down on instruments and broke cloud over the gentle landscape of Buckinghamshire, sighted Ivinghoe Beacon and the violet approach lights at Traveller's Rest, and then landed at the American air force base at Cheddington. It was January 26, 1944, a dull and misty morning, and there were no bands to welcome the general; neither was there a guard of honor. Patton was met somewhat coldly at the farthest edge of the airfield by General J. C. H. Lee, the chief quartermaster of the U.S. army in England, and by Commander Harry C. Butcher, U.S.N., the Supreme Commander's naval *aide-de-camp* and diarist (who had actually come to collect Eisenhower's dog Telek). When his kit had been stowed in the boot of a Packard that bore no stars, Patton was driven into London where he was received by Eisenhower at Hayes Lodge. There the Supreme Commander gave Patton certain explicit instructions that marked the start of the key stratagem of the war in Europe.

Patton was not sure what was in store for him when he arrived in England. His flamboyance, brutality and indiscretion had all damaged his reputation and career. Yet no one could contest his ability as an army commander. He had displayed that ability during Torch when the Allies captured 1000 miles of African coast in seventy-six hours. As a result of his brilliance as a tactician and disciplinarian in Sicily, he and his armored forces had received the lion's share of the honors in a thirty-nine-day campaign which cost the Axis 167,000 casualties (including 37,000 Germans), at a price of 16,769 Allied troops. But it was the very violence with which Patton had conducted this battle that had got him into trouble; in a fit of nervous anger and impatience he had twice slapped the faces of shell-shocked American soldiers as they lay in hospital. Eisenhower wrote him a "blistering epistle" of reprimand for his "despicable" conduct. The President castigated him for his "reprehensible conduct." An angry howl of protest swept the United States, his court-martial was demanded, and Eisenhower was not able to obtain an operational command for Patton during the Italian campaign, as he had planned.

But in the strange way that bad publicity is sometimes good publicity— or can be turned to good use—the furore worked in favor of A-Force, the Allied deception organization in the Mediterranean. Aware of the German belief that Patton was certain to be in the place of main action, and looking for such an Allied field commander to give substance to the early Zeppelin schemes, Brigadier Clarke asked for and obtained the services of the flamboyant general. Suddenly, Patton appeared in Corsica to support rumors that the 7th Army was about to land in northern Italy; then he was seen at Malta, "inspecting amphibious forces"; a little later he was found to be at Cairo, "having discussions with the British about an invasion of Greece"; and at Christmas he was back at 7th Army headquarters at Palermo in Sicily, "preparing for operations in the Adriatic." Then he disappeared, and while the Abwehr and the SD scoured the Mediterranean for news of his whereabouts, he slipped quietly into England.

Despite the disgrace he was in, Patton expected to get more than he got: command of the U.S. 3rd Army under Montgomery, whom he detested, and Bradley, about whom he was patronizing. As Eisenhower told him that evening at Hayes Lodge, according to the Neptune plan, the 3rd Army, after the breakout from Normandy, would rush for and take the Breton port of Brest, which was essential as a supply base. But, Eisenhower went on, 3rd Army was still in the United States, and while it was on the high seas, Patton must lend his services to another force. Before, and even after, his own army had assembled in Britain, Patton must appear to be the commander of FUSAG, the Quicksilver force that was at the very core of Fortitude.

According to the Quicksilver scenario, FUSAG would consist of the 1st Canadian Army, which would make the assault on the Pas de Calais with one Canadian and three American infantry divisions, and one Canadian armored division. The four armored and four infantry divisions of the American 3rd Army would constitute a follow-up force, and behind them were fifty more divisions, so the story went, in the United States awaiting shipment to the Pas de Calais when FUSAG had established its beachhead. Most of these forces, with the exception of the fifty divisions in the United States, did—or would—exist; but they belonged either to Montgomery's or Bradley's commands and would invade France through Normandy. Yet this was the force that the Germans must be led to believe was poised and ready to strike the Pas de Calais. And even if FUSAG existed in name only, its commanding general had to be unquestionably real. That was where Patton came on stage. He had a reputation for daring and brilliant unorthodoxy among the Germans, just as the Americans and the British admired Rommel's tactical cunning. The Germans were sure that he would be in the spearhead of the invasion. The LCS and CSM knew that and so, once more, Patton was to be used for the purposes of deception.

As the leading figure in Quicksilver, Patton would be expected to heed one imperative: absolute discretion. From now on, Eisenhower told him, everything he did and said would have to be most carefully orchestrated to the score of Fortitude and Quicksilver. A single major blunder might—almost certainly would—destroy the stratagem, and the Germans might—almost certainly would—divine what the Allied strategy really was. But silence and discretion were not among Patton's strong points, as Eisenhower knew well. With those weaknesses in mind, he gave Patton a word of warning:

> You persistently disregarded my advice [about making statements to the press and appearances without permission], but it is not just advice any longer. Well, from now on it is an order. Think before you leap, George, or you will have no one to blame but yourself for the consequences of your rashness.

Patton, a "master of flattery," was deferential and said "he certainly would be more careful as to the place where he has a tantrum. . . ." Then he went off to his own quarters at 22 Mount Street, Mayfair, where, so it was said afterwards, he broke his undertaking to the Supreme Commander almost immediately. He took a dislike to his quarters—they were rich, ornate, and "queer"—and exploded to his aide: "Whoever picked this Goddamn place has a genius for cloak and dagger. It seems to be the ideal hideout for a fellow like me they're trying to keep under wraps." He said to a friend: "Sandy, let's get the hell out of this Goddamn crib. I'd rather be shot in the streets than spend an evening sitting around this sink of iniquity." And with that declaration—according to a biographer—he went to see Robert E. Sherwood's play *There Shall Be No Night* with Alfred Lunt and Lynn Fontanne at the Haymarket Theatre. After the show, he first visited the stars' dressing rooms to pay his compliments, then went on with the Lunts to the Savoy Hotel for a party. His presence at the Savoy was noted by the press—it was a headquarters for the American newspapers—and also came to the attention of the security authorities at Supreme Headquarters.

Patton's transgression was so flagrant that it may well have been intentional—or so it was later suggested. For Patton was not to be "kept under wraps" at all; to give substance to Quicksilver, his presence in England as an army group commander was to be brought to the attention of the German intelligence system in a variety of ways. Little or nothing was done to conceal his activities. He was constantly calling on Eisenhower and

Bradley in Grosvenor Square; he was received by Brooke and made a Knight Commander of the Most Honourable Order of the Bath; he lunched with Tedder, the deputy Supreme Commander; he went to Euston to board a special train which took him to Scotland to meet the advance guard of the 3rd Army; he paraded magnificently before a bevy of British generals and admirals at Greenock as the *Queen Mary* steamed in—thousands of American soldiers aboard the liner saw and cheered him; he inspected a German prisoner of war compound; he hobnobbed with the British gentry and nobility; he was driven in the grand manner to visit Montgomery; he occupied the pew of the Master of Peover Hall at the local church near his headquarters at Knutsford in Cheshire. In short, the only thing the CSM did not do was to announce Patton's presence in Britain in the press. A brief announcement to that effect finally appeared in the Los Angeles *Times,* but meanwhile, two XX-Committee double agents, Tricycle and Treasure, had already informed their German controllers of Patton's whereabouts, and on March 20, 1944, FHW stated in a bulletin: "It has now been clarified . . . that General Patton, who was formerly employed in North Africa and is highly regarded for his proficiency, is now in England." That same day, Eisenhower's headquarters announced vaguely that Patton had relinquished command of the 7th Army for another army command.

Patton disliked his assignment in Britain before the invasion. As one of his biographers would write: "Patton appreciated the importance of (Fortitude) but did not enjoy his role in it. He was especially chagrined that his clearly secondary—as a matter of fact, fictitious—part in (Neptune) removed him from the planning of the campaign. . . ." Moreover, Patton came to suspect that his indiscretions—of which there were several—were deliberately blown up out of all proportion to call the Germans' attention to himself and his command. Such certainly appeared to be the case in an episode that came to be called the "Knutsford Affair."

In April 1944, Patton disobeyed Eisenhower's orders not to make speeches or public appearances without permission and accepted an invitation to be the principal guest at the inauguration of the "Welcome Club," which had been established by the villagers of Knutsford, close to Patton's headquarters, for American servicemen. He was assured that he would be there unofficially and that there would be no ceremony. But when he arrived he discovered, to his dismay, that there were a crowd, a brass band, an honor guard of British women auxiliaries to welcome him—and a number of press photographers. Patton requested that no photographs of him be taken, and the photographers agreed. Told that there were no reporters present, he then proceeded to make a few bellicose remarks, among them the declaration that ". . . since it is the evident destiny of the British and Americans to rule the world, the better we know each other the better job we will do." It was that remark—an insult to Russia—which was quickly splashed across the headlines of the world press.

How the press obtained the story, and how it got out of Britain, which was under total censorship at the time, would never be clear. It could only have been accomplished through a blunder in the censor's department, which had been told to be especially alert for all news concerning Patton and to delay the transmission of all telegrams until Smith's approval had been obtained, or through some official connivance, although not necessarily the Supreme Commander's. As it happened there had been an official representative of the British government present at Knutsford; his name was Mould. It was almost certainly he who released the text of Patton's speech. But on whose authority? And for what reason?

Whatever the reason, the reaction was immediate, and Patton suddenly found himself in the center of another raging controversy. Windows began to rattle at the Kremlin, the White House and at the St. George's Hotel in Algiers where de Gaulle was quartered, but not in Britain where the statement was suppressed. The ensuing storm caught Marshall at a most embarrassing moment; he was seeking to win congressional approval to appoint a number of officers to the permanent rank of general, including Patton. As a result of his bombast, so Marshall said in a signal to Eisenhower, not only had Patton's fitness for command been brought into serious question, but he had imperiled the entire permanent promotions list.

The controversy could not be quelled, particularly in the United States; but Marshall, although he was greatly perturbed, left it to Eisenhower to decide whether or not Patton should be replaced. Eisenhower, his nerves already stretched to concert pitch over other menaces to the success of Neptune, expressed his displeasure in a personal letter to Patton: "I am thoroughly weary of your failure to control your tongue and have begun to doubt your all-round judgment, so essential in high military position." But in a signal to Marshall he admitted that Patton was indispensable to Neptune. He may have been aware that the Knutsford leak was intentional; he certainly gave orders to use Patton's name for deception purposes later on. In any case, he decided to retain Patton in command.

Patton was contrite, but he suspected that there was some other explanation for the incident. In his reply to Eisenhower's letter, he wrote: "You probably are damn fed up with me . . . but certainly my last alleged escapade smells strongly of having been a frame-up in view of the fact that . . . the thing was under the auspices of the (British) Ministry of Information (whose representative) was present." And then, expecting to be cashiered, he wrote in his diary with welling bitterness: "I feel like death, but I am not out yet. If they will let me fight, I will; but if not, I will resign so as to be able to talk, and then I will tell the truth, and possibly do my country some good." He had already ordered his batman to begin packing when the furor ended as suddenly as it had begun. Eisenhower called Patton to say that he was to keep his command. But in another entry in his diary, Patton wrote: ". . . this last incident was so trivial in its nature, but so terrible in its effect, that it is not the result of an accident. . . ."

Was the "Knutsford Affair" part of the Fortitude deception scheme? If it was, then the Allied high command had gambled not only with Patton's reputation but also with his career. They were certainly not above that kind of manipulation, but there was never any proof at the time. Only after Fortitude was buried did evidence emerge that the LCS and the Allied Supreme Command, for reasons of deception, had indeed played with Patton's reputation. But the devices used to advertise Patton would prove to be artless compared to the stratagems that were employed to create his fictitious command—the Quicksilver army group, FUSAG.

Quicksilver began where such a force would have to begin, in America, and the opening note was sounded by a double agent whom J. Edgar Hoover had christened "Albert van Loop." Described as "51, a swarthy, somewhat corpulent, shy man looking at the world with squinted eyes through thick-lensed glasses," van Loop was Dutch by nationality. But he had served in German intelligence in the First World War as a specialist in the U.S. army, and when the Americans entered the Second World War, Canaris reemployed him. After extensive training, van Loop was sent to Madrid, his mission to infiltrate the United States. He was to approach the U.S. legation and state that he had been press-ganged into the Abwehr but now wanted to offer his services to the OSS or the FBI. He was to reveal one cipher (while concealing a second) and hope that the American authorities would accept him as a defector, send him to the United States and give him a job. Then when their suspicions were relaxed, van Loop could begin his real business—reporting the movement of American divisions to Britain and the Mediterranean.

But instead of double-crossing the Americans at Madrid, van Loop, to all appearances, double-crossed the Abwehr. He announced that he really did want to go to America and work for the FBI or the OSS. To prove his sincerity he produced *both* his ciphers and *all* his transmission schedules, wavelengths, call signs and security checks. His real cipher was an ingenious double transposition system based on the Dutch prayer book, while his operating instructions were very cleverly concealed in secret ink amid the clefs and staves of the score of the Dutch national anthem.

With these revelations, Madrid decided that, whatever else he was, van Loop was a German spy, and as such would have some value to the FBI. He was sent to the United States via Lisbon and Buenos Aires, and when he reached New York the third week of June 1943, he was taken into custody by the FBI, and kept under guard—it was said—at an FBI safehouse in the Queens district of New York. His ciphers and operating instructions were taken over by an expert wireless operator on the staff of Dr. George Sterling's Radio Intelligence Service, a section of the Federal Communications Commission.

Quicksilver got under way when, acting under the general supervision of Joint Security Control, which provided supervision of the FBI, the new van Loop opened communication with Hamburg in late September 1943. Over the following weeks the RIS operator impersonating van Loop transmitted a careful blend of truth and fiction until it was apparent that Hamburg trusted him. Then in a secret ink report he explained that he had done exactly as he had been told to do—give himself up to the Americans—and that, after a period of interrogation and surveillance, he had been released and had gone to work as the "night manager" of the Henry Hudson Hotel, on West 57th Street in New York. This, he explained, was especially suited to his assignment since the U.S. army used the hotel extensively for lodging American officers going to England. He was able, he wrote, to see the lists of troopships proceeding from New York, and these, together with the lists of officers, revealed the designations of the divisions en route to Britain.

Some of the information sent in van Loop's name was accurate, for it was considered inevitable that, sooner or later, the Germans would be able to identify the real divisions for themselves, usually through the press or prisoners of war. But at the same time, information was sent about departing units that did not exist, at least on the Allied order of battle maps, in the hope that the Germans would believe that they were part of the Quicksilver assault force assembling in Britain. Did Hamburg trust van Loop's despatches? Apparently it did, if the yardstick of that trust was the amount of money he was paid. He had extracted some $55,000 from the Abwehr by February 1944.

That was not the end of the van Loop case, however. The FBI sent Hamburg a total of 115 messages in van Loop's name, but when his file was captured and examined after the war, it was discovered that the Abwehr had received 231 wireless messages from him—some of them in a cipher other than the one based on the Dutch prayer book which the FBI was using. According to Ladislas Farago, the intelligence historian who investigated the incident, van Loop had managed to outwit the FBI, whose surveillance of him was not as expert as it might have been. With a new supply of money smuggled to him by his wife, who arrived in the United States with $10,000 sewn into her girdle, he reverted to his original loyalty, made contact with another German agent in America, and through him established communications with his German controllers. Van Loop was not a double but a triple agent.

Even so, the Germans appear not to have doubted the information about Quicksilver transmitted by the fictitious van Loop, perhaps because the real van Loop was ignorant of the FBI transmissions and did not bother to inform his controllers of the possibility that he was being impersonated. The bureaucratic confusion that followed the SD's assumption of the command of the Abwehr may also have made it difficult to sort out evidence indicating which German agents in America or Britain might be under control. Whatever the case, the Allied deception agencies in dealing with double agents were treading a narrow and dangerous line throughout the Quicksilver stratagem.

When the fictitious Quicksilver forces began to arrive in Britain, the stratagem was taken over by the British deception agencies, and a series of calculated leakages began to appear in the press: "2/lt. N, of O, Falls Church, Va., on active service in England with the 9th Airborne Division, a sophomore of Johns Hopkins, has announced his engagement to Miss P of Norwich, England." Or on the radio: "This is the American Forces Network. Here is *Sweethearts' Playtime.* Private M of the 315th Reconnaissance Troop, 11th Infantry Division, on duty somewhere overseas, is twenty today; and here is *Six Lessons from Madame Lazonga,* as requested by his fiancée, Miss R, of Great Neck, New York . . ." This type of announcement was sufficient to alert FHW—whose men read and listened to everything—to the possibility that these formations really existed; but *that* trick was as old as the hills. Thus, in addition to these seemingly harmless leaks, the CSM began to generate wireless sounds that simulated the presence of an army or divisional headquarters, a regiment or an armored battalion, in the fairly confident hope that the excellent German wireless intelligence service would be listening in. Moreover, the Quicksilver army group had to be seen as well as heard. There had to be troop concentrations, tank parks, petrol dumps, hospitals, pipelines, sewage farms—all the weft and warp of life created by the existence of a million men. And so these military installations began to appear on the British landscape—fabricated, much as Hollywood might create a film set, out of lumber, rubber, wire and cardboard.

Even this, however, was not considered to be enough to fool Roenne and the other intelligence experts at FHW. This point was acknowledged by Masterman who would later write:

> Speculations, guesses, or leakages, would have little or no effect on the German military mind, for the German staff officer would make his own appreciations and his own guesses from the facts put before him. What he would require would be facts . . . (including) the location and identification of formations, units, headquarters, assembly areas and the like.

This kind of intelligence could come only from double agents under XX-Committee control, agents who were, it was hoped, trusted by the Germans.

The XX-Committee had a number of such agents they could use; early in January 1944 there was a total of twenty under British control, nine of whom had wireless, with many other similar channels open to the LCS overseas through MI-6's penetration of the Abwehr and the SD. But the committee was the first to realize that an agent was trusted by the Germans only in direct relationship to the excellence and truth of the intelligence he had transmitted in the past. Which of these agents did the Germans really trust? And could the XX-Committee trust any of them? After all, they were spies, one or two of whom had changed sides two and three times. No matter how elaborately Quicksilver was being staged, a single false note, intentional or unintentional, could destroy the illusion. Furthermore, as Masterman would note, "An agent who, in spite of all precautions on our part, turned out not to be believed by the enemy, might wreck the whole enterprise, or, even worse, his messages might be 'read in reverse' and the true target of attack be exposed instead of concealed by him."

In consequence, it was decided that the "orchestra" employed to spread the "facts" of Quicksilver would be small instead of large. The "first violins"—to use the jargon of espionage—would consist of Garbo, whom the Germans considered their best agent in England; "Brutus," a Pole who worked for MI-6 in France after the fall, and had agreed, so the Germans thought, to work for the Abwehr as an agent in Britain; "Treasure," a Frenchwoman of Russian origins; and Tricycle, the winning but weaselly Yugoslav businessman who was regarded both by the Germans and the British as the very best type of European idealist. Other agents—the "second violins"—would be used in the operation, but these four would carry the main themes of Quicksilver and its allied deceptions, particularly Skye. But as the sly men of the XX-Committee put these strange musicians to work, they would again come perilously close to disaster—for themselves, for Fortitude and Quicksilver, and for Neptune.

Garbo was a Spaniard. That was all that would be known about him personally. But Masterman later wrote: "Connoisseurs of double cross have always regarded the GARBO case as the most highly developed example of their art. . . ." He was, it was said, equally hostile to Nazism and communism, had been compelled to hide for two years in one house during the Spanish Civil War, and seemed to have had ambitions to become a professional spy for the British in either Germany or Italy. He offered his services to MI-6 at Madrid in January 1941, but his offer was rejected, and so Garbo presented himself to the Germans. He went to see Wilhelm Leissner, an old Abwehr hand who, as "Gustav Lenz," was chief of the Abwehr in Iberia; and Lenz, after what Masterman called "characteristically lengthy and involved negotiations," decided to send Garbo to England in July 1941 "with a questionnaire, secret ink, money, cover addresses, and the German blessing. . . ."

Garbo did not go to London at all; when he arrived in Lisbon he decided to stay there. And it was from Lisbon that he began to fabricate intelligence reports about the British Isles, using a few well-known guides and reference books. But such were his talents that his reports had the ring of authenticity, and in some cases came very close to the truth. The Germans grew to trust him, perhaps because he always reported what they wanted to hear. They also believed that he employed three sub-agents in various parts of Great Britain to assist him in his work. But by February 1942, MI-6 had learned of Garbo. Ultra revealed that the Germans were making preparations to intercept a big convoy which was supposed to have left Liverpool for Malta. As Masterman wrote: "Only later did we establish the fact that GARBO was the sole inventor and begetter of this convoy, and thus responsible for a great expenditure of useless labour on the part of the enemy. It became clear to us at this stage that GARBO was more fitted to be a worthy collaborator than an unconscious competitor." He was brought to England as an XX-Committee special agent.

There was no need to create a spy network for Garbo; he had already done that himself. He was also a tireless worker. Posing as the employee of a large fruit and vegetable importer who did much business with Iberia from Covent Garden market, he spent seven days a week, averaging six to eight hours a day, drafting secret letters. In all, he would compose 400 secret letters and 2000 wireless messages between Torch and Neptune; and the Germans financed him to the tune of £20,000 ($96,000)—handsome reward indeed. During 1943 he was used to pass over the greater part of Plan Starkey; and if that plan was a short-term failure, it was a long-term success, for in the course of the operation Garbo gave the Germans what was the embryo of the Quicksilver order of battle.

By the spring of 1944, Garbo had fabricated an even more extensive network in Britain; he was informing Lenz that he employed fourteen agents and eleven well-placed contacts, including one in the Ministry of Information, where most Allied secret matters were discussed at one time or another. He also had an agent in Canada, busily inflating the order of battle of the 1st Canadian Army, and another in Ceylon, spying on Mountbatten, the Allied Supreme Commander in Southeast Asia, who knew most things about Neptune. He used two wireless operators and had reporting posts all over southwestern, western and eastern Britain—handily for Quicksilver. Masterman would observe: "The one-man band of Lisbon (had) developed into an orchestra. . . ." Thus it was that agents who did not exist began to report an army group that did not exist.

Did the Germans trust Garbo? Obviously they did, for they sent him the cipher (for his own use) which they used themselves in wireless communications between Madrid and Hamburg and Madrid and Tangier. The possession of that cipher released "The Bomb" at Bletchley for other duties and played an important part in the liquidation of the enemy intelligence services in time for D-Day—at least in the Mediterranean. When the Germans changed the cipher key, as they did from time to time, they entrusted Garbo with the new one, too—and the Bletchley cryptanalysts continued their work with little inconvenience.

A character no less singular than Garbo, and no less important to Quicksilver, was codenamed "Brutus" by the XX-Committee. He was, in reality, Captain Roman Garby-Czerniawski, an officer of the Polish General Staff who, in 1940, was in his mid-thirties. A man of extraordinary abilities, he was both a pilot and an Olympic skier, and his professional mind had been sharpened by a period in the cryptanalytical service of the Polish General Staff, the service that broke the main Soviet military cipher during the Russo-Polish War of 1920 and later helped Britain obtain Enigma. With the destruction of the Polish armies by the Wehrmacht in 1939, Garby-Czerniawski made his way to Paris; and he was in the service of Polish intelligence there when the French surrendered in 1940. He then went underground, and as "Paul" founded Interallié, an MI-6 *réseau*. But in 1941 he was betrayed by his cipher clerk, Mathilde Carré, and arrested by the Abwehr while in bed at his home at St. Germain-en-Laye. His captor, Hugo Bleicher, one of the best of the German counterintelligence agents in France, had succeeded in turning Mme Carré's loyalties when she became jealous of Paul's relationship with another young woman in the *réseau*. He was taken to Fresnes Prison to await execution; but then the Abwehr conceived another use for his services, and his life was spared.

For many months Colonel Joachim Rohleder, the chief of the Abwehr department responsible for the penetration of the British secret agencies, had combed the jails for British agents who might be turned and sent to England as German agents. His attention fastened upon Garby-Czerniawski for the same reasons that he had been employed by the British in the first place; he was a first-rate intelligence officer, cool, brave, patriotic and dependable, despite his indiscretion over Carré. Rohleder presented Garby-Czerniawski with a proposition—if he would go to England as a German spy, the one hundred members of Interallié who were now under arrest would not be executed but rather treated as prisoners of war. Garby-Czerniawski considered the proposal and countered with one of his own. He demanded that, in return for his services, the Germans must promise that Poland would be granted full national sovereignty after the war. Rohleder could not give him such a guarantee, and their negotiations collapsed. Then Germany invaded Russia, and Garby-Czerniawski, calling Rohleder back to his cell, declared that he now realized that Russia, not Germany, was Poland's natural enemy, and that if the jailed members of

Interallié were treated as prisoners of war, he would go to England and, as he put it, "work for peace."

A formal contract was struck between the Abwehr and Garby-Czerniawski, who was now rechristened "Armand," and the details of his "escape" were arranged. These were put in the hands of Hugo Bleicher, who would write:

> I received a strange commission at the beginning of July 1942. I was to fetch Armand out of Fresnes prison allegedly to go to an interrogation in Paris, but I was to allow him to make an escape on the way. . . . The whole business was mysterious in the extreme. It appeared to me that Armand had a special mission from a very high quarter in German Military Intelligence Headquarters. . . . My duties had hitherto been to catch spies. Now I was to help the chief of a big spy organisation to escape. It was a grotesque situation. It had been impressed on me that this flight of Armand might become known to the French Resistance. I must also ensure that the S.D. should get no wind of it. In order that the news should reach the Resistance in the most natural manner, I took with me to Fresnes one of my agents who I knew to be working for the other side. Of course, I did not let him into the secret.

Armand's "escape" was cleverly planned. Bleicher and Raoul Kiffer, the French double agent, were to pick up Armand from Fresnes in an Abwehr car, and when the car approached a sharp bend in the road at Pont Orléans, they would see a stalled German army truck. As the car slowed down, Armand was to leap out and make off. Bleicher and Kiffer would give chase and even fire some shots, but Armand was to disregard all challenges and make for an Abwehr safehouse on the Boulevard Massena. There, if he had not already succeeded in removing them by other means, his handcuffs would be taken off, and he would be given fresh clothes, false papers representing him to be a courier of the Rumanian Embassy at Paris, some money and some travel papers. He would then go to Lyon where he would rendezvous at the Hôtel Beaux Arts with Bleicher, who would arrange his passage into Spain.

Garby-Czerniawski "escaped" on Bastille Day 1942 exactly as planned, although the Abwehr car failed to avoid a collision with the stalled truck, which added an unexpected note of authenticity. The French resistance learned of his escape, informed London and two weeks later Armand had made his way across the Pyrenees over a British escape line. He met first with a British escape line officer at Madrid codenamed "Monday," but later he met and was briefed by General Erich Kuhlenthal, the second in command of the Abwehrkriegsorganisation in Iberia. At these meetings Armand was given a list of intelligence targets to tackle when he reached England. He was instructed how to build a wireless transmitter from parts generally available in British shops; he was given a supply of *G-Tinten*

—shoulder pads impregnated with the slightly yellow secret ink made from pyramidon; and he was introduced to the *Mikropunkt* system of microphotography. He was also given an Abwehr cipher based upon *The Story of St. Michele* by Axel Munthe. Then Armand drove with Monday to Lisbon, where he was to catch a BOAC DC-3 to England. He had, of course, told Monday everything.

Armand arrived in England in January 1943 and he was taken, as was usual, to the Royal Patriotic School at Battersea for interrogation, clearance and observation. His case was then passed to the XX-Committee to see if he might be of service as a double agent. The committee hesitated to use him at first, for the Germans knew that he had once worked for MI-6 and might do so again. In that event, they might not trust Armand and read what he was sending them "in reverse." Nevertheless, it was decided to employ him, but not on operational matters, and he was given his third code name in eighteen months—Brutus. Soon, however, it became clear from the nature of the questions they sent him that the Germans did trust Brutus; and it was decided to "build him up" as a liaison officer between the Polish and the Royal Air Force—a position in which Brutus might be expected to learn much about Neptune. It was a fortunate decision, for when a disaster occurred to thin the ranks of the XX-Committee special agents, a new and greater burden would fall upon Brutus. The man whom the XX-Committee had not been inclined to trust would become the main agent for the transmission of Quicksilver.

Treasure was more appropriately codenamed than Brutus, for she added small, dainty touches of authenticity to Quicksilver. Her real name was Lily Sergeyev, she was twenty-six, a Frenchwoman of Russian origins, and she had first come to the attention of the British secret service in 1937 through her uncle, General George de Miller, the leader of the Czarist Russian exiles in Paris. In appearance Treasure would be described as having a "rough-hewn Slavic face . . . marred by a square chin but mellowed by her gently sloping brow and sensitive eyes. She wore her rich auburn hair down to shoulders that were firm and broad, giving her a somewhat masculine appearance. But Lily was all woman—tender, skittish, vital, highly-strung, and set in her ways." Judged by her German and British controllers alike as intelligent but temperamental and difficult to handle, she cared nothing for her personal safety because she believed that she was dying of leukemia. (In fact, she would still be alive in 1971.)

At the outbreak of war Miss Sergeyev was in Lebanon on the leg of a Paris-Saigon cycle ride. An anti-Communist because of her Czarist background, she decided to return to Paris and offer her services to MI-6. But before she could make contact with Dunderdale, Paris fell to the Wehrmacht, and Miss Sergeyev conceived another plan. She presented herself for employment in the Abwehr, and after much expensive wining and dining, the Abwehr agreed to take her on. But Miss Sergeyev intended to defect and was using the Abwehr only to provide her with papers and money to get to Iberia. And this, in June 1943, she managed to do.

The Abwehr refused to equip her with a transceiver and ciphers. No Abwehr female agent had been so equipped for service in the field by 1943, for Canaris disliked and distrusted women agents; he felt they were too susceptible to emotional involvement and lacked the objectivity of men. Thus Miss Sergeyev would communicate with her controllers by secret writing. But when she reached Madrid, she surrendered to the British Embassy and, unknown to the Germans, told an official of her mission for the Abwehr. She was given papers allowing her entry into England by air from Lisbon and, on her arrival, she was detained for interrogation by the security authorities at the Royal Patriotic School. Her loyalties finally established, Miss Sergeyev was offered "secret work"—XX-Committee work, although she was never told that such an organization existed or what her work would be. The Committee was somewhat uneasy about her, but they needed a female agent for the special tasks they had in mind. And so Miss Sergeyev became Treasure.

Treasure soon opened contact with her controller through a letter box in Lisbon, using a secret ink preparation. She reported that she had enlisted in the British women's army service which, in fact, she did do later on. Her credentials established, she notified her controller that she had met a staff officer of the American 14th Army at Bristol. Bristol was, in truth, the headquarters for the American assault army for Neptune, the 1st; the 14th Army did not exist other than for the purposes of deception. Treasure then reported that 14th Army headquarters had moved to Little Waltham in Essex, directly facing the North Sea and the Pas de Calais, the area in which the fictitious FUSAG was supposed to be assembling. It was a movement that pleased Treasure, she said, because now the 14th Army was close to London she would be able to see her friend more often. Treasure also reported on real American and British units which were being used to give substance to Quicksilver, but, of course, she lied about their locations, misrepresented their missions and disguised their affiliation with the army groups that would actually take part in Neptune. All this information filled in some of the details of the broader picture of FUSAG being presented to the Germans by the other members of the Quicksilver chorus; and if Treasure reported the precise location of a military unit, there was certain to be a characteristic pattern of wireless traffic coming from that area to verify her story when the German wireless intelligence service listened in.

When Ultra surveillance of the Abwehr's traffic between Madrid and Berlin showed that Treasure was in good standing with the Germans, she announced the bitter news that she had "broken off her friendship with her friend at 14th Army"; "he would be going to France soon and there would be no hope of her following." But, she announced happily a little later, she had found somebody else in the U.S. Judge Advocate General's branch at Cheltenham who was in a position to provide her with most valuable information. It appeared that it was the custom of the U.S. Army to make out monthly crime reports, division by division, which were used, among other things, as a barometer of morale and divisional efficiency. Would such reports be useful? Indeed they would, Treasure's controller replied. So the CSM arranged for the preparation of such reports that excluded the divisions about which the Germans knew nothing or which the Allies wished to conceal, and included those in FUSAG which they wished to reveal. Quicksilver was becoming a reality. But, unknown to the LCS and the CSM, there was serious trouble ahead. It involved the case of Tricycle.

Tricycle, the young Yugoslav whose real name was Dusko Popov, came to the XX-Committee by a more direct route than many of its double agents. While studying at Freiburg University before the war, he had become friendly with a fellow student named Johann Jebsen. Popov later entered the shipping business; and Jebsen, who would become a figure of importance in the Abwehr, and was, apparently, connected to it even when he was at Freiburg, made vague suggestions to his friend that he might wish to increase his income and status in Germany by spying for Germany against the British. The suggestion was repeated to Popov in 1940 when he called at the German Consulate in Belgrade to arrange some documentation in connection with the sale of two ships to Germany. But Popov's loyalties lay elsewhere. He contacted the MI-6 representative at Belgrade, and it was agreed that he should continue to appear interested in the Abwehr's approaches. Then, the Abwehr asked Popov to go to England to collect some secret *courrier* from a member of the Yugoslav Embassy in London who was in the employ of the Abwehr. He reported his mission to MI-6, which then arranged his papers, and he arrived in London on December 20, 1940. There, Masterman wrote: "He was interrogated and created a most favorable impression . . . we had in him a new agent of high quality who could plausibly meet persons in any social stratum, who was well established with the Germans at the instance of an Abwehr official [Jebsen], and who had an excellent business cover for frequent journeys to Lisbon or to other neutral countries." Menzies, too, would find Popov useful in the conduct of MI-6 business. His Abwehr connections would serve as a valuable link between MI-6 and the anti-Hitler conspirators, including Canaris, in the German secret intelligence service.

Popov was also well connected at the Yugoslav court; and when MI-6 arranged the evacuation to London of King Peter, Popov, now known as Tricycle, was able to represent to the Germans that, through the King, he had entrance into circles close to the Prime Minister. This claim, which Tricycle was able to substantiate with choice bits of information about life at Storey's Gate, including intelligence about Churchill's health, enhanced his prestige with the Abwehr enormously. His business cover required him to travel to Lisbon frequently, which the British allowed him to do, and Tricycle was soon trained and equipped to transmit intelligence from Britain to his controller at Lisbon, a certain Karsthoff, by all available means, including wireless, secret writing and microphotography. This intelligence was, of course, supplied by the XX-Committee, and enough of it was useful and true that Tricycle steadily rose in the estimation of the Abwehr.

It was in June 1941 that Tricycle was instructed by the Abwehr to go to America to report, among other matters, the defenses of Pearl Harbor. The British permitted him to go, passing his case on to their colleagues in the FBI. But Tricycle did not prosper in the United States; J. Edgar Hoover wanted no spies in America, and Tricycle returned to Lisbon in October 1942, explaining that his poor performance in America was due to the Abwehr's failure to send him adequate funds. That error was corrected when he was given a large imprest with which to return to Britain and expand his network. From that point on, Tricycle became the Abwehr's second most trusted agent, and he expanded his network in Britain as he had been asked to do. He already had "Balloon," a British army officer who had resigned because of debts, and "Gelatine," an Austrian woman expatriate in London who had worked for MI-5 and had been recruited by Tricycle as an Abwehr spy without knowing that he was working for the British. Then he added "Meteor" to his string, who was a member of King Peter's inner circle and a "Yugoslav of good family, high character, and patriotic principles. . . ."

In July 1943, Tricycle was back in Lisbon, this time to see his old friend Jebsen. Jebsen had risen in the Abwehr and had been sent by Canaris to Lisbon, possibly on Schwarze Kapelle business. During their reunion he said enough to Tricycle to indicate that he was disenchanted with Hitlerism, and Tricycle reported to the XX-Committee on his return to London that Jebsen was ready and willing to sell out to Great Britain. It was through "Artist" (as Jebsen came to be called by the XX-Committee) that Tricycle enlisted another agent in his network—"Freak." Freak was also a Yugoslav officer, and in December 1943, after he had been trained by the Abwehr as a wireless operator, he arrived in England and promptly joined Tricycle. Yet another Yugoslav from the Belgrade establishment, "The Worm," joined the network at about the same time and, during his interrogation, confirmed Tricycle's impression that both Artist —and Canaris—were wavering in their allegiance to the Third Reich. Thus, by the turn of 1943–44, the "Yugoslav Ring" of Abwehr agents around King Peter was wholly controlled by the XX-Committee through Tricycle. And this was more than fortunate for Allied security during the

Neptune period, for King Peter resided at the Savoy Hotel and was frequently to be seen at the American Bar with Allied generals and war correspondents.

Artist's usefulness to the XX-Committee was still in question, however. But when Tricycle again visited Lisbon in November 1943, Artist gave him much important information regarding V-weapons and the Schwarze Kapelle, which strengthened his belief that he might be enlisted as a resident agent in Lisbon. Two MI-5 men were sent from London to check both Tricycle and Artist, and when they returned with a favorable report, it was finally decided to enlist Artist. But an aura of doubt remained, for Artist might pose a very serious threat to the security of the "Yugoslav Ring." If his treachery was detected by the Abwehr and he was forced to talk, he might bring down both Tricycle and Garbo, for Artist believed that Garbo was a German spy in Britain, and he would naturally warn the British. Then, if the Abwehr learned that Garbo had not been arrested, it would logically conclude that he, too, was under British control. The XX-Committee was apprehensive about Artist, and for good reason; but there his case rested—for the time being.

In February 1944, Tricycle returned to Lisbon on his most important mission of the war: Quicksilver. He carried with him detailed information about the Allied order of battle in Britain for the invasion which, he informed his controller, Karsthoff, had been gathered by Balloon, Gelatine, Meteor, Freak, The Worm and their sub-agents. In fact, the information was the framework of the Quicksilver order of battle which had been fabricated by the XX-Committee. It was a bold move, for the success or failure of the Quicksilver deception now depended entirely upon whether or not the Abwehr trusted Tricycle. If it did, all the calculated leaks and the reports from other double agents under XX-Committee control would serve to enhance the deception; if it did not, Quicksilver would be revealed as a hoax before it had scarcely begun. For reasons that would not be clear, Karsthoff reacted angrily to Tricycle's intelligence, describing it as "warmed-over gossip." But Tricycle protested against the accusation and demanded that it be sent to Berlin for assessment. This Karsthoff did; and fortunately for Quicksilver, the reaction of FHW was quite different. FHW saw what the LCS and the CSM intended it to see—the embryo of FUSAG assembling in southeastern and eastern England. As Roenne would write in a bulletin to Hitler and OKW on March 9, 1944: "A V-mann dispatch . . . has brought particularly valuable information. . . . The authenticity of the report was checked and proved. It contains information about three armies, three army corps and twenty-three (divisions) among which the location of only one need be regarded as questionable. The report confirms our operational picture."

Roenne's acceptance of Tricycle's despatch was yet another major victory for the LCS and CSM strategists—one comparable to Fortitude North. If FHW continued to believe in the existence of FUSAG, it would have far-reaching consequences not only upon the success of Neptune but also upon the outcome of the war. Thus, from its very inception, Quicksilver seemed to be a success; and between February and May 1944, the LCS, the CSM and the XX-Committee, working on that assumption, leaked additional information about FUSAG through the "Yugoslav Ring," Garbo and his network, Treasure, and by a variety of other special means. But all that time, unknown to the Allied deception agencies, the entire Fortitude fabrication was dangerously close to failure.

The first near-disaster concerned the case of Jeff, the Abwehr agent who, with his partner Mutt, had come ashore in 1941 on the Moray Firth. Though Jeff had turned sour and was jailed at Dartmoor for "recalcitrancy," he had managed to get in touch by means of secret writing with one Erich Carl, warning him not only that Mutt was working for the British, but also that he was working for the XX-Committee, the existence of which was unknown to the Germans. Carl, a member of the German War Graves Commission who was being detained in Britain, was repatriated when he grew seriously ill, and returned to Germany with information that might have destroyed Fortitude. But the German secret intelligence services remained unaware that their agents in Britain were under control, perhaps because their reports were more convincing than any information to the contrary, or perhaps because of the bureaucratic chaos that followed the Abwehr's absorption by the SD. Again, Fortitude had escaped by a whisker.

A German agent in Lisbon who was not under XX-Committee control posed another threat to the deception. His name was Paul Fidrmuc, his German code name was "Ostro," and he was the Iberian representative of an American pharmaceutical firm. Like Garbo before he was recruited by the committee, Ostro had invented a string of agents in Britain and was supplying the Germans with intelligence reports that were products of his own imagination. When his activities were uncovered, the British took little notice at first; but then his reports began to come uncomfortably close to the truth. "It was not impossible," Masterman would write, "that OSTRO might by a fluke give the exact area of the attack on the Continent, and thus destroy the deception plan." It was decided that Ostro must be eliminated, but MI-5, MI-6 and SOE could not quite catch him. He continued to operate, but as imaginative as he was, he never uncovered the secrets of Neptune. He reported that the Allies would come ashore at the Pas de Calais.

Plainly, the success of Fortitude depended upon a good deal of luck, and suddenly, as D-Day neared, it seemed that luck had run out for the Allied deception agencies. The SD, as part of the *ratissages* that followed the Solf tea parties and the defection of the Vermehrens and their associates from Turkey, had grown suspicious of Artist, the weakest link in the Fortitude-Quicksilver chain. For one thing, Artist was a frequent guest of Frau Vermehren, Erich Vermehren's mother, who had her home in Lisbon; and for another he was suspected of financial irregularities. Neither at the time nor later was it clear whether the SD was aware of Artist's connection with Tricycle. In any event, its agents arrested Artist early in May at his villa among the gardens of Lapa. He was drugged, packed into a tin trunk, and taken through Spain and France into Germany as diplomatic baggage. His interrogations began at the Prinzalbrechtstrasse; and even if it seemed that the SD was chiefly concerned, at least at the start, about his association with Frau Vermehren and his financial dealings in Lisbon, under interrogation he might reveal everything he knew.

The XX-Committee soon learned of Artist's fate through Ultra, and while it appeared that his arrest had more to do with money than with treachery, this was, as Masterman wrote, "small consolation." Under the circumstances, the XX-Committee was compelled to assume that Artist would tell all. As Masterman put it: "On the most optimistic estimate . . . we had lost one of the most important cases, or sets of cases, just as D Day approached; on the most pessimistic, the whole deception through double-cross agents was in danger." Prudence dictated that Tricycle and the "Yugoslav Ring" be retired from the Quicksilver chorus, although, curiously, Garbo and his network would remain operative in the later stages of the deception, perhaps because Artist knew only that he was a German agent in Britain, not that he was under XX-Committee control.

It was now that Brutus was elevated to new importance in the deception, for the LCS and the CSM could not simply abandon Quicksilver at this late date. To have done so would have necessitated a complete revision of Allied plans, both actual and deceptive, for the Normandy invasion, and that was an operation so vast that SHAEF was unwilling to undertake it. SHAEF, however, did turn its attention to Ultra to establish, if possible, whether the truth of Neptune lay bare before the Fuehrer's eyes. If Artist had revealed that Tricycle was a double agent, the Germans could assume that all of the information he had passed to them was false, FUSAG would be exposed as a fiction, and an invasion of the Pas de Calais as an improbability. To the horror of the Allied planners, Ultra revealed that Hitler was ordering considerable reinforcements in the Normandy area, although it also showed that he was *not* reducing his garrisons at the Pas de Calais. Whether Ultra revealed the actual text of the order that led to the sudden reinforcement of Normandy would not be established. But General Blumentritt, Rundstedt's Chief of Staff, sent this signal to all commands at 8 P.M. on May 8, 1944:

> The Führer attaches extreme importance to Normandy and the defense of Normandy. In the coming enemy offensive, very strong landings by air and

heavy bombing raids, as well as the main attacks from the sea, are to be expected. . . . High Command Army Group B will report its plans for submission to (OKW).

If this signal was intercepted—and it may well have been—it might have seemed that Neptune's security had collapsed. Not until the eve of D-Day would the Allied high command be certain that Artist had not blown Quicksilver. It was, therefore, a period of extreme anxiety at Supreme Headquarters and the LCS, for no one could know that Artist would behave as he did. He was murdered soon after D-Day without revealing anything of his own or of Tricycle's connections with the British. But, ironically, even if he had, Quicksilver might still have been assured of success, not only through the skillful efforts of the Allied deception agencies but also through an intrigue at FHW that was among the most extraordinary acts of treason in the history of the Third Reich.

The man chiefly responsible for determining the order of battle of the western powers before D-Day was Colonel Alexis Baron von Roenne, a tall, slim, sarcastic and pious Junker who seemed to be a *Flügelmann* of the officers of the old German Empire. As chief of FHW, he performed his work with the fastidiousness for fact and detail, for precision and intelligent objectivity that was the hallmark of a staff officer of his age and class. He was a master of the diplomatic phraseology used by the General Staff when it studied the power of an intended victim; there was never a word too many. General Ulrich Liss, a chief of FHW during the campaign against France in 1940, would remember of him: "He was an excellent man in all respects—a man who set very high standards for himself and his men. He had also a perception of political and military matters that was akin to genius. He had a clear and realistic mind, and he was able to make decisions with the speed of lightning." It came, therefore, as a great sense of shock when, four years later, it was discovered that Baron von Roenne had cooked the books at FHW.

Roenne was of a caste which made such conduct quite incomprehensible. He came from the aristocracy east of the Elbe River that was the very spine of German military science and power. His family was one of the oldest in the Reich. They had always been King's men; they had always worn the royal cloak. Their baronetcy was bestowed upon them by Frederick the Great for the parts they had played in the battles he waged from Zorndorf to Leuthen, from Rossbach to Mollwitz. They were patricians of old Prussia, and Roenne's conduct had been molded by a social code that was so rigid that—for example—it was forbidden to talk to a jockey in public. The rules of etiquette were severe; even more severe was the code of loyalty and discipline. If an officer violated that code, far better to shoot himself than to go on living in a world that treated him as an outcast.

Roenne, in a sense the brain of the German army in the West, came to FHW in 1939, after an impeccable career. He had served with distinction in the First World War with one of the Kaiser's finest, the 9th Potsdam Infantry Regiment; Hindenburg was his colonel-in-chief. But because his family lost their estates in the Bolshevik revolution in Courland just after the war, he was compelled to resign his commission in order to restore the family's fortunes. He became a banker, but when Hitler began to rearm and a career as an army officer was attractive once more, Roenne returned to his regiment. He did well and was selected for the War Academy, a school only for those officers who were likely to reach the highest rank. After graduation—the courses were so demanding that it was said that a man who had attended the War Academy never smiled again—he was admitted to the General Staff. By the outbreak of the second great war he was chief of Group France, the branch of FHW responsible for studying the military power and intentions of the French Republic.

It was as head of Group France that Roenne's excellence as an intelligence evaluator first came to the attention of Hitler. The Fuehrer was then planning his offensive against Poland, but because the Wehrmacht was so small in 1939, it would be impossible to invade Poland and still maintain a strong defense in the West. It was imperative to know what the French and the British reaction to an attack against Poland would be. Hitler asked for a special study, the task was given to Roenne, and he wrote a report stating that in his opinion the western powers would only assemble their armies; they would not attack Germany while Germany was invading Poland. The report confirmed Hitler's own impression. He vanquished the Poles and the western powers did nothing. Roenne was proven correct and thereafter he enjoyed the favor of the Fuehrer. That favor was confirmed when, again in response to a request from Hitler for a special evaluation, Roenne predicted that if the German panzers struck across the Meuse between Givet and Sedan, the French army would collapse. Hitler attacked that sector, and again Roenne was proven correct. The fact that the French army was defeated so quickly was—as Liss would state—due in no small part to the shrewdness of Roenne's appreciations. The Fuehrer awarded him the *Deutsches Kreuz*.

When Hitler began to prepare for the invasion of Russia, Roenne, bent upon retrieving the family estates in Latvia, volunteered for service in the northern sector of the eastern frontier. He went to battle and behaved with gallantry, but was wounded badly before his regiment got to Tukkum. After spending many months in hospital, he returned to FHW; and then, in early 1943, largely as a result of Hitler's insistence, he was appointed its chief. It was a position of great influence and power, for Roenne enjoyed the complete confidence of the Fuehrer, and only he had all the facts at his fingertips. Every scrap of intelligence about the western powers poured into

FHW's headquarters at Zossen, and it was Roenne who put all the pieces together in his weekly and monthly reports for OKW and the Fuehrer. Seldom, if ever, did anyone question his authority or challenge his opinions.

Roenne's loyalty to Hitler and to the Third Reich would seem, under these circumstances, to have been above suspicion. But, in fact, he was a confirmed conspirator of the Schwarze Kapelle. Just when he set out on this dangerous path would never quite be determined. It probably began with the trap of the *Fahneneid,* the humiliation of General von Fritsch and the dismissal of General Beck. He was appalled by the SS pogroms in Poland, and he detested, as did so many others of his class, the gutter behavior of the Nazis and what the general staff considered to be their lack of military professionalism. Roenne had worked very closely with the Abwehr and had formed a high, respectful regard for Canaris, and a close friendship with Oster. Roenne and Oster were often to be seen riding together, practicing the *haute école* in the Tiergarten, the Potsdam Cavalry School and the Brandenburg woods. Gradually Roenne fell under Oster's spell, and then under the influence of Stauffenberg, whom he had known well since their days together at the War Academy. Roenne had no post in the Schwarze Kapelle, and neither did he have any tasks, except to keep the leadership closely informed with relevant political and military intelligence. He remained at FHW, in a position that enabled him to render the Fuehrer the greatest service—or disservice. For it was his job to estimate the strength of the forces ranged against Germany by the western powers, and to discern the truth of Allied intentions in Europe during 1944.

From the start of his attack on the Allied order of battle for D-Day, Roenne was bedeviled in a number of key areas of intelligence acquisition —and without good acquisition there could be no good evaluation. Ever since the British had retreated to the home islands after the debacle of Dunkirk, it had been virtually impossible for FHW to establish with certainty the strength of British forces. Now, with the build-up of forces in preparation for the invasion, it was even more difficult to obtain accurate estimates of Allied strength. Furthermore, Roenne was well aware that the Allies were systematically and on a large scale attempting to mislead OKW about their military strength and intentions. As early as Starkey he wrote in a report to the Fuehrer: "The multiplicity of the at times utterly fantastic reports about allegedly imminent operations . . . reveals an intention to deceive and mislead." Yet, Roenne and FHW had been deceived and misled by operations such as Mincemeat and by the Cicero case. But could the Allied deception agencies mislead them about the secrets of Neptune?

It seemed at first that they might not, for Roenne reported in his first major assessment of 1944 that he had conclusive evidence that the Allies would make their decisive stroke that year not in the Balkans but in

France. He followed up this bulletin with another on February 8, 1944, in which he advised that:

> In 1944 an operation is planned outside the Eastern Mediterranean that will seek to force a decision (in the world war), and, therefore, will be carried out (from England) with all available forces. This operation is probably being prepared under the codename of *Overlock* and the distribution of enemy forces and troop movements clearly point to England as a point of departure.

How, with most of the sources upon which he depended for his intelligence in disarray or under Allied control, had Roenne been able to make this excellent and—for the Allies—dangerous assessment? It was a question that would not be answered until thirty years later when documents concerning the extent to which the Germans had penetrated Allied secrets were finally declassified. These documents revealed that the omnipresent German wireless intelligence service had obtained, through a variety of eavesdropping techniques, the information upon which Roenne had based his estimate. When, late in December 1943 and early in January 1944, Allied troops and assault shipping began to move from the Mediterranean to England in preparation for Neptune, German Y service analysts noted the rising crescendo of wireless traffic in the British Isles and a decrease in the Mediterranean theater, despite Allied attempts to use false wireless traffic to conceal the movement. Clearly, all of the British Isles were becoming an armed camp.

The German Y service also detected the arrival in Britain of the élite American 82nd Airborne Division from Italy—an event that confirmed Roenne's belief that England would be the springboard for the invasion. The Y service had been listening in on the 82nd's traffic for over a year and knew intimately the pattern of its wireless nets, the characteristics of its transmissions and even the names and home addresses of its operators. When the 82nd dropped out of sight in Italy, the Germans began to look for it in England; the radio nets which the division had left behind to make it seem that it was still positioned in the Mediterranean displayed few of the characteristics the Germans had studied for so long. Such was the excellence of SHAEF's wireless security plan that the 82nd's presence in Britain was not detected upon arrival; but then, early in February, the Germans picked up a radio net in Britain that they could not identify and overheard a signal *en clair* concerning paternity proceedings instituted in the United States against an American soldier. They also collected the reply which stated that the wanted soldier was in England with the 82nd Airborne and that the lawyers could interview him at the divisional command post at Banbury. The cat was out of the bag. Nevertheless, OKW at first refused to believe the report that the 82nd was in England. One high officer of German wireless intelligence would recall that Jodl's office replied facetiously that, unless the division had been transported by submarine, then it must still be in the Mediterranean; no transports had been observed by Abwehr agents on either side of the Pillars of Hercules. The Y service responded by bringing to Cherbourg the wireless analysts in Italy who were so familiar with the 82nd's wireless traffic. They placed the net under special observation, noted exactly the same characteristics as they had noted in Italy, and were able to provide indisputable evidence that the division was indeed in England.

The German Y service would prove to be an even more dangerous threat to the secrets of Neptune in the months ahead; but while its surveillance of the British Isles indicated that the Allies were planning a cross-Channel attack, that evidence alone was not sufficient to permit Roenne to conclude that there would be no invasion of the Balkans. As a result Hitler would not be able to withdraw his divisions from the Balkans to reinforce the Channel and Russian fronts. Equally, Roenne did not have the evidence to disabuse the Fuehrer of the prospect of an invasion of Norway if he withdrew his divisions from there, or of a strike across the Adriatic and an invasion of Germany through the Ljubljana Gap if he withdrew his forces from Italy. Nor was he able to predict, in the winter of 1943–44, *where* the Allies would land in France, so that OKW was compelled to divide its forces in northwestern Europe among no less than five sectors: The Netherlands, the Pas de Calais, the Normandy-Brittany area, and the Biscayan and Mediterranean coasts of France. The stratagems of Bodyguard and Fortitude, it appeared, were having the desired effect upon Roenne.

But even the most skillful deception campaigns would have fallen far short of success had Roenne been able to deduce with accuracy the strength and location of the Allied armies in Britain. With that kind of intelligence, it would have required little more than common sense to eliminate all but the Normandy-Brittany sector as the point of the major Allied attack. Concealing the Allied order of battle from the Germans was therefore at the very core of the cover and deception plans surrounding Neptune; and Roenne's reaction to Quicksilver in particular would be of crucial importance. The carefully calculated leaks to the press and radio, the reports from the XX-Committee's double agents, were often for the benefit of Roenne. It was Roenne and FHW that must be misled if Quicksilver was to succeed. For Roenne had the Fuehrer's ear. As Colonel Anton Staubwasser, who served under Roenne as chief of Group England until he became Rommel's chief of intelligence before the invasion, would state: ". . . it is known to me that the opinions held by Hitler and *OKW* [about the invasion] were based principally on the information supplied by FHW and did not deviate from that department's ideas in essentials."

How, then, did Roenne and FHW assess the Allied order of battle? Did Roenne believe that the Quicksilver force really existed? Did he believe that FUSAG was assembling in southeastern Britain and that Patton would lead this mighty army group against the Pas de Calais? The answer would prove to be far more complicated than the Allied deception agencies could have guessed. For just as Quicksilver got under way, the stiff, proud and hitherto impeccably honest Roenne was engaged in a deception of his own—an intrigue that would have a profound effect upon the outcome of Neptune.

It began at the end of 1943 when a newcomer joined the staff of FHW—Lieutenant Colonel Roger Michel, who succeeded Staubwasser as chief of Group England. A boisterous and heavy-drinking man—FHW, for all the primness of its chief, as Gehlen would say, "had a reputation for sloth" and for "throwing drinking parties on the most tenuous of pretexts"—Michel was born at Zaalen, not far from the Swiss frontier at Lake Constance. He was the son of a south German schoolmaster and his English wife; and as Staubwasser would later state, Michel, as a young man, spent time in England as a member of the German national rugby team. According to Staubwasser, he was "tall, sporty and athletic . . . and in spite of his baldness he had a youthful manner. He had a jolly, easy, happy disposition, and was said to be a good comrade." Staubwasser would further testify to Michel's fondness for "alcohol and women," but he would also remark that "In his work he was said to be reliable and he had a quick understanding of essentials. He was above average intelligence."

Michel's area of responsibility at FHW was England, and in January 1944 he approached Roenne with a complaint that was fully justified. As part of the continuing battle between the Abwehr and the SD for command of the Reich's intelligence system, and in order to prove to Hitler that its sources, intellect and objectivity were superior to the army's, the SD had consistently *halved* Michel's estimates of the Allied order of battle. Roenne was well aware of the truth of what Michel told him; but, as he explained, he saw no way of preventing SD interference. The system required that all FHW reports be filtered through the SD in order to "ensure their accuracy" and to be certain that they corresponded with the information and evaluations of the SD.

By March the situation had become serious, for Hitler, believing that the halved estimates of Allied strength came from Roenne, whom he had had every reason to trust, was removing divisions from the West. Roenne, in fact, believed he should reinforce the Atlantic Wall; but what could be done? Since the downfall of Canaris and the dissolution of the Abwehr, the

SD had become more powerful than ever. It was Michel who proposed a solution. He suggested that from now on FHW should *double* its estimate of the number of Allied divisions in Britain. Then, when the SD halved it, which was done now almost as a routine, an estimate that was pretty near the truth would find its way to the Fuehrer's desk. Michel's suggestion was contrary to all the principles of FHW, and of Roenne himself. But the idea took hold in his mind.

When Roenne became desperate about the apparent lack of reality at Hitler's headquarters concerning the dangers from England, he approached Colonel Lothar Metz, his operations officer, about the proposal. Would Metz assist? Metz refused instantly and advised Roenne to have nothing to do with the scheme either. What would happen, he asked, if the SD accepted rather than halved the estimate? If that did happen, Metz warned, no one at OKW would be able to establish the truth of the situation in England—unless Roenne admitted what he had done. And that admission would certainly cost him his career, and probably his head.

But then Metz was transferred from FHW, and when he had gone Roenne did as Michel had proposed. He began to submit reports to Hitler that exaggerated Allied strength in Britain. This was serious enough; worse was to follow. The system required that evidence be available to substantiate the existence of divisions mentioned in FHW's estimates. But where was this evidence to be obtained? Michel had another suggestion; FHW should accept as true all of the leakages and reports about the strength of Allied forces in England. This intelligence was, of course, being deliberately fed to the Germans as part of Quicksilver, and Roenne knew very well that it might be a deception. But confident that the SD would halve his estimate, he went ahead with a major survey of Allied military strength in the British Isles. His survey was sent to the SD in May 1944; and it was then that the unexpected happened. Just as Metz had warned, the SD—possibly because the man who was doing the halving had been transferred—*accepted* and promulgated Roenne's inflated estimate. His survey reported that there were eighty-five to ninety Allied divisions assembling in Britain, together with seven airborne divisions, instead of the thirty-five (including three airborne divisions) which was the reality. This was the estimate that found its way onto all the charts throughout the Wehrmacht.

Thus, the Allied deception agencies had an unwitting ally in Roenne. For this survey of Allied strength in England prior to D-Day conformed in all respects to the Quicksilver order of battle. From May on the fictitious FUSAG became a reality to the Fuehrer and OKW, and no amount of maneuvering on Roenne's part could alter that reality. He discovered that it was much easier to put Allied divisions on an order of battle chart than it was to get them off; and indeed, as evidence continued to pour into FHW supporting the existence of eighty-five to ninety Allied divisions in Britain, Roenne himself began to believe that he might have been right in the first place. By the time the SD learned that it had been tricked, it would be too late to make any corrections; the last battle had been joined.

Roenne would pay for his intrigue with his life. But the progenitor of the scheme, Michel, escaped retribution, a fact which would lead to the suspicion in postwar Germany that he had been an agent for either the British or the American secret services. This suspicion increased when Michel was freed long before the rest of the General Staff was released from internment, appeared at Heidelburg wearing an American uniform, and announced that he was employed in the U.S. Counter-Intelligence Corps. But Michel did not remain in West Germany long. He soon fled into the Russian zone, thereby compounding a wartime mystery with a peace-time defection.

Whether or not Michel was an Allied agent is of incidental importance, just as it is useless to speculate whether Roenne's act of treachery was motivated by a desire to protect Germany or to pull the Fuehrer and the Third Reich down. Whatever the case, between them Roenne and Michel helped complete the tangled web that the Allied deception agencies spun around Neptune—a web that trapped the Fuehrer himself and would impede him in all his plans to meet the invasion.

7

Nuremberg

WHILE ROENNE'S INTRIGUE was a major factor in OKW's acceptance of Quicksilver, it was not the only one. OKW had a strong belief in the loyalty, reliability and competence of its main agents in England during the build-up for Neptune. Rarely was the intelligence gathered from these men questioned. Why did OKW not suspect that at least some of them, and perhaps even all, might be under British control?

There were several reasons: the chaos of the German intelligence services; the astuteness of Allied deception; the fact that the controlled agents generally transmitted information that conformed to OKW's own beliefs, and to military logic; and the fact that much of what agents such as Garbo and Brutus sent could be, and was, verified by aerial reconnaissance and wireless intelligence. But another reason for OKW's confidence was that its principal agents in Britain had supplied the Reich, over a considerable period, with intelligence that had proven to be correct. In short, the British high command, and later Supreme Headquarters, were often telling the Germans the truth, their motive being to establish and maintain the credibility of the agents under Allied control—"a necessary preliminary," Masterman would write, "for the passing over of the lie." The stratagem worked, for the performance of these agents had been so consistently valuable to the Germans that they came to accept as fact their information about the existence of Quicksilver and the deceptive strategy implied in Fortitude.

That being the case, what was the nature of the true intelligence the Allies—and particularly the British—were willing to reveal in order to ensure the success of Fortitude? Since the value of intelligence in war is measured in death and destruction, were the Allies willing to leak information detrimental to their own cause? Were they willing to risk or even sacrifice their own men to set up a deception scheme? Were some men and operations considered expendable in order that larger, decisive operations might succeed? After the war, Masterman deliberated these questions and replied: "We never gave the enemy information that would have cost Allied lives." But Masterman's military master for Neptune, General Sir Francis de Guingand, Montgomery's Chief of Staff and the 21st Army Group officer who ensured that deception conformed to strategy and tactics, disagreed. The British high command, he said, did indeed make such sacrifices. "On at least one occasion," de Guingand recalled, "the deception people were authorized to reveal the target of a major air attack on a German city to the Germans beforehand in order to reinforce the credibility of an (XX-Committee) agent who was to be used to mislead the German high command during Neptune." He said he seemed to remember that the city was Stuttgart, and the month in which the stratagem took place was March 1944. But he could not be sure that it was not Nuremberg in that same month. He was certain, however, that the incident took place just before the Allied heavy bomber forces were switched from Pointblank to tactical support of Neptune, which occurred on April 14, 1944.

Was de Guingand correct in his assertion? If so, the reasons for such an action might be traced beyond the demands of deception to Allied strategy governing the prosecution of the air war against Germany. Pointblank, the Allied Combined Bomber Offensive that preceded the invasion, had as a major objective the systematic destruction of the German industrial heartland. It was also the policy of the American and British air forces conjointly to compel the Luftwaffe to battle—or to force it to diffuse its strength by guarding theaters remote from France and Germany—so that it might be eliminated as a source of danger on D-Day. As the Pointblank directive said, the destruction of the Luftwaffe was second to none in priority. To obtain that objective, the USAAF in Washington instructed Wallace Carroll, chief of the European department of OWI, the American political warfare agency, ". . . to bait the *Luftwaffe*. Do *everything* you can to make the Germans come up and fight." The RAF, said Carroll, agreed with and cooperated in the policy; the purpose of this "cruel expedient," he continued, was to "save lives in the long run." " 'If the aim of the air force is achieved,' I told a meeting [of the New York office of OWI], 'the sacrifice which may now be made will mean the saving of thousands, even tens of thousands, of lives on the beaches when the Allied armies land on the Continent!' " The Anglo-American high command did not dispute the tragic logic of this policy. Eisenhower would tell Butcher: "One of the duties of a General is to determine the best investment of human lives. If he thinks expenditure of 10,000 lives in the current battle will save 20,000 lives later, it is up to him to do it."

Carroll, in accordance with his instructions, and with the knowledge and cooperation of the British, launched "Huguenot," a political warfare operation to lure the Luftwaffe into the air. It was prosecuted with great success but, as Carroll would recall, "no other propaganda campaign ever caused us so much heart-burning," because through it the Allied air forces encountered "more rather than less opposition in their raids." Propaganda was only part of that campaign, however, for Carroll wrote that U.S. heavy bomber forces were sent out "over routes which had been deliberately selected to bring out the maximum opposition from the Germans." There is no doubt that air commanders were aware of this strategy, for Eisenhower's diarist, Butcher, wrote on April 22, 1944: "General Spaatz [the commander of the U.S. Strategic Air Force in Europe] is not too crazy about it but admits that the strategic planes are supposed to draw the fire of the *Luftwaffe* over Germany." Spaatz himself would announce that he was prepared to take "more than ordinary risks to complete the task [of destroying the Luftwaffe as a prelude to Neptune], including the risk of exceptional losses."

While this strategy was a ruthless one—for American casualties were bound to increase—it was no more ruthless than the general means being used to fight a total war. However, the flight tactics of the Americans made them well able to take care of themselves. American bombers were heavily armed and armored, they flew in close formation to mass their firepower against attackers—the B17 was accurately called the Flying Fortress—and they were escorted by hundreds of long-range fighters that were the equal of most if not all the Luftwaffe's fighters. Their power was such that—as General Walter Grabmann, the commander of the German 3rd Fighter Division, would state—the Americans by the spring of 1944 no longer "had to bother about special maneuvers to mislead the defence." Moreover, just before D-Day, as Grabmann continued, "Their fighter preponderance was such that, in fine weather particularly, they could send out whole formations in advance to shatter the Germans before they were in position." The Americans, therefore, would have everything to gain by forewarning the Germans of the target for the day; such forewarning would virtually guarantee large numbers of Germans to shoot down. Even so, American casualties in the three months before D-Day were extremely heavy. The 8th Air Force lost nearly 10,000 men, 800 heavy bombers and over 500 long-range fighters. And when the losses of the other U.S. air forces involved in the enormous bombardment of Europe before D-Day were included—at times it seemed that almost the entire continent between the Channel and Potsdam was covered with the smoke, fumes, ash, sound and aircraft of war—these casualties were almost doubled.

The RAF supported, indeed it was the instigator of, Pointblank in all its objectives. But British flight tactics were different from the American. British bombers sacrificed heavy defensive armament in return for much heavier bomb loads than the Americans were able to carry; they relied upon the cover of darkness, cloud and deception to avoid heavy losses, and they usually operated without fighter protection and in streams rather than formations, which meant that, on clear nights at least, they were extremely vulnerable to attack by radar-equipped night fighters. Thus the British would have a great deal more to lose by deliberately forewarning the enemy of the target of an attack to bait the Luftwaffe or to establish the credibility of a double agent. Yet de Guingand stated that they did just that.

If de Guingand was correct—and no one in the Allied high command was less likely to be in error, or less capable of exaggeration—the raid in question must have occurred during March 1944. That month Bomber Command did indeed attack Stuttgart, the great industrial city of 400,000 people on the Neckar River in Württemberg. The city was raided on March 1/2 and March 15/16, but neither raid showed signs of German foreknowledge. In the attack on Berlin on March 24/25, German night fighters shot down 72 of the 811 bombers that took part in the raid; but the heavy casualties were probably caused by factors other than foreknowledge. Of all the raids of the period, the only one that showed signs of German foreknowledge was the attack on Nuremberg by ninety squadrons of Bomber Command on March 30/31.

The circumstances of the Nuremberg raid were most unusual, and it was suggested, both at the time and later, that it might have been betrayed. The Royal Institute of International Affairs' *Chronology of the Second World War* used the word "ambush" in its report of the attack—with all that word's connotations of lying in wait and foreknowledge. Flight Lieutenant Alfred Price, a serving officer of the RAF and the author of *Instruments of Darkness,* a study of electronic deception in the Second World War, was not prevented by the Ministry of Defence from recording: "Since the war there have been suggestions that the Germans had some foreknowledge that the night's target was to be Nuremberg and had arranged their defences accordingly." Then even the official British air campaign historians, Sir Charles Webster, the president of the Royal Academy, and Dr. Noble Frankland, a director of studies at the Royal Institute of International Affairs, found something strange about the strategy employed in the attack. "This was," they wrote in *The Strategic Air Offensive Against Germany 1939–1945,* "indeed a curious operation. . . . The plan of action . . . abandoned most of the tactical precepts which for a long time had governed Bomber Command operations. . . . The normal ruses seemed to give way to a straightforward declaration of intention and the German fighter force was presented with a unique opportunity. . . ."

What was the intention of the raid on Nuremberg? By mid-March, the Allies' daylight raids over the continent had dealt the enemy such a severe blow that they had, through actual operations and Huguenot, achieved a large measure of daytime aerial superiority over France and the Low Countries. Moreover, American long-range fighters had established an important degree of sovereignty over the daylight skies of Germany. And the combined attacks of Bomber Command and the U.S. Strategic Air Forces in Europe had compelled the enemy to concentrate upon the defense of Germany rather than the Channel countries, thus reducing the Germans' ability to defend Normandy on D-Day. But in darkness air superiority had not yet been won, and it was expected that most of the Germans' air operations against Neptune would be conducted by night air crews. Therefore, it was vital to bring on an immense night battle where the best of the German night fighters might be destroyed. That, certainly, was a principal intention of the raid.

The choice of target—Nuremberg—reinforced that intention. For while Nuremberg was an important military target (equipment for tanks, aircraft, aero-engines and armored cars was produced there), it also had a special political and psychological significance. It was at Nuremberg in 1934 that Hitler had proclaimed that "The German form of life is definitely determined for the next thousand years"; and every year since then, the Nazi hierarchy, amid a vast Teutonic ceremonial, had dedicated itself anew. A successful raid against this Nazi shrine would demonstrate the impotence and the looming destruction of the Third Reich, and the Luftwaffe could be expected to defend the city with determination. But to bait the Luftwaffe, were the British willing to expose RAF air crews to even greater dangers than those normally associated with such a raid? And to ensure that the Luftwaffe took the bait, and to establish the credibility of a double agent, were they willing to forewarn the Germans of the raid? These were the central mysteries of the Nuremberg attack.

The mystery began from the moment Air Chief Marshal Arthur Harris, the C-in-C of Bomber Command, took the chair at his routine morning conference on March 30, 1944, at his headquarters in a hillside near the Buckinghamshire town of High Wycombe. The first order of business was the weather. Mr. Magnus Spence, the Command meteorological officer, presented his forecast; and while he was hesitant about making a positive prediction, he did say enough to suggest that the weather over Germany that night might not favor Bomber Command. It might favor the defense. The half-moon might be very brilliant, high winds might break up the bomber stream, and he could not guarantee that there would be cloud to hide the bombers from the night fighters. In short, weather conditions might be the direct opposite of those in which the Command preferred to operate—pitch-black, windless, cloudy nights.

Despite this forecast, Harris proceeded to announce the target for that night: Nuremberg. His announcement caused some surprise, for Nuremberg was not one of the targets on his current directive. Moreover, it was deep inside Germany. Even if weather conditions favored the raid, the bomber stream would be over enemy territory for so long that a major air battle was almost inevitable. There was cause for even greater surprise when Harris announced the route the Command was to take to reach the target. His plan was to gather almost the entire might of the Command over The Naze, a headland in eastern England, proceed to and cross the Belgian coast near Bruges, and fly directly to Charleroi in Belgium. At Charleroi, the bomber stream was to proceed in a straight line some 265 miles to Fulda, across the German frontier near Frankfurt; and at Fulda, it was to change course again and fly directly to Nuremberg.

It was this route—and particularly the "long leg" from Charleroi to Fulda—that provoked in Air Marshal Sir Robert Saundby, deputy C-in-C of Bomber Command, what would be called his "mounting apprehension" about the raid. Harris himself had recently ordered that, because of the heavy casualties suffered in the Leipzig and Berlin raids earlier that month, bomber streams should henceforward be split up to approach their targets from different directions in order to confuse and split night fighter defenses. Now he proposed to send a single stream to Nuremberg. Moreover, it would follow a route that would take it close to the thick concentration of German night fighter bases around the Ruhr, and directly over the fighters' assembly beacons at Aachen (codenamed "Ida") and Frankfurt ("Otto"). These tactics, as well as the depth of the target, seemed to confirm that luring the Luftwaffe to battle was a primary objective of the raid. But Saundby was concerned about the extraordinary dangers of the route, and when the conference ended, he voiced his concern to Harris. Harris replied merely that if the weather did turn definitely against Bomber Command, the operation could always be canceled at the last moment.

Before proceeding with the detailed planning for the attack, Saundby telephoned Air Vice Marshal D. C. T. Bennett—the air officer commanding (AOC) the Pathfinder force, which consisted of picked crews who would lead the bomber stream to Nuremberg and then mark the target with flares for accurate bombardment—to tell him about the route. Bennett protested immediately that the long leg was inviting disaster and told Saundby he would prepare a route himself, one that would avoid, so far as possible, the night fighter beacons and bases, and which would contain the usual "dog legs" to confuse the German night fighter controllers about the destination of the bombers. Saundby agreed to present Bennett's route to Harris. But when he held his usual telephone conference with the AOC's of the bomber groups, he found that they agreed with Harris's "straight in, straight out" route. It meant, they contended, that the bombers would be in and out of Germany much more quickly than if they took the route that Bennett was proposing. It was decided that the "straight in, straight out" route should stand. Informed that his opinion had been overruled, Bennett was overheard to remark: "The blood is on their heads."

By noon, Saundby and his staff had completed the detailed planning for the raid, including diversionary operations. To turn the Germans' attention away from the bomber stream, and to pin down the 1st German Fighter Division in northern Germany, fifty Halifaxes were to fly across the North Sea, simulating the approach of a much larger force in flight to Hamburg or Berlin. Their flight would be scheduled so that they approached the German coast at the same time that the main force approached the Belgian coast nearly 300 miles away to the southeast. Then, as the main force crossed the coast, Mosquitos would fly three missions, again simulating much larger forces threatening Aachen, Cologne and Kassel.

These were usual diversionary tactics, designed to confuse the Germans for as long as possible about the actual destination of the main force, and thus split their defenses. But the plan also called for some seventy to eighty long-range Mosquito night fighters to accompany the main force to engage the German night fighters as they were taking off or landing at their bases, or as they tried to penetrate the bomber stream. These were not usual tactics, and they again confirmed that the primary purpose of the raid was to lure the Luftwaffe to battle. The British intended to tempt the Germans into the air with a stream of lumbering bombers flying a long and dangerous route, and then shoot them down with night fighters. It was a risky strategy, but the bomber stream would have the protection of the Mosquitos and, it was hoped, the weather. All those concerned with planning the raid were convinced that it would be canceled if late weather forecasts proved unfavorable.

But reports from Spence's meteorological flights that afternoon confirmed his earlier predictions. There would be no high cloud over Germany, and weather conditions were such that the bomber stream would leave contrails—those tell-tale trails of frozen vapor that would pinpoint the location of every bomber. Furthermore, over Nuremberg itself there would be thick cloud at bombing altitude, which meant that the Pathfinders would not be able to mark the city accurately, and therefore the bombers might not be able to bomb accurately. Plainly, the weather would favor the defense, and it now seemed certain that Harris would cancel the raid.

It was not canceled. At the main briefings, which took place between 5 and 6 P.M. that afternoon and were attended by all the men who would fly that night, there were general expressions of surprise—and even of dismay—when the target and the route were revealed. Perhaps because they anticipated such a reaction, or perhaps because they had been misinformed by Bomber Command, briefing officers misled the bomber crews about the dangers of the route. To explain why the bomber stream was being routed through Flak Valley, a hell-spot near Cologne where anti-aircraft defenses were very deep and effective, the crews at Coningsby bomber base were told, according to Martin Middlebrook, an historian of the Nuremberg raid, that "the Germans were known to have moved their fighters to the coast in readiness for the shortening raids of the less deep spring nights and would not be expecting a deep penetration." The crews at Lissett bomber base were told that "the defences covering southern Germany were weak and the gap near Cologne [Flak Valley] would be 'virtually unprotected.' "

Many bomber crews were also misled about the weather. Middlebrook would write that:

> . . . at station level, every effort was made to keep from crews the un-pleasant fact that they were to fly a constant course for 265 miles through a well-defended part of Germany in bright moonlight but with little chance of cloud cover. On at least eleven stations, the crews were given the specific forecasts that there would be cloud cover at operational flight on this out-ward flight.

Flight Sergeant Tom Fogaty of 115 Squadron would remark that "we were assured that there would be ten-tenths cloud cover for most of the way." The crews of 102 Squadron were told that "it should be a milk-run . . . (because) cloud and fog would completely black-out the Continent and that they could therefore expect practically no night-fighter opposition for some time (until) after they had crossed the enemy coast."

There can have been only one reason for misinforming the bomber crews; if they had been told the truth there might have been—given the heavy casualties they had suffered in recent operations—serious refusals to fly. As it was, there were further protests about the route, but they were useless. Harris, it seemed, was determined to mount the raid however vulnerable the bomber stream would be because of the route and the weather. Apparently, an attempt to destroy the Luftwaffe night fighter force warranted such risks. But did it warrant the additional risk of de-liberately forewarning the Germans of the attack? Whatever the answer to that question, the bomber crews would soon discover that the Germans were ready and waiting for them.

At about 4:30 P.M., General Wolfgang Martini, the chief of the Ger-man signals intelligence service, having examined all data from the techni-cal surveillance of the RAF's electronics traffic, sent a signal to General Hans-Juergen Stumpff, the C-in-C of the Reich Air Defense Command. Martini expressed the opinion that the RAF was preparing for a major attack that night. But he did not say what he thought the strength of the attack would be. Neither could he say where he felt the attack would be delivered. There was little that was unusual about this appreciation. Mar-tini knew Bomber Command's procedure. RAF wireless and radar equip-ment was always tested before the aircraft were loaded with fuel to prevent sparks from detonating petrol fumes. Martini's technical intelligence experts had detected heavy test transmissions that morning; therefore it could be assumed that the RAF was preparing for an attack that night. However, there was something unusual about the signal Martini sent between 5 and 6 P.M. He said he thought that between seven hundred and eight hundred bombers would attack Germany that night. How he could have been so close to the truth is not clear. It was possible, but not probable, that he deduced the number of bombers that would take part in the raid from his observations of the strength, location and pattern of British test transmissions. But he could not have deduced with any certainty that Germany would be the target that night; Bomber Command was striking everywhere from Murmansk to Milan. Had Martini made an inspired guess, or had he had some forewarning of the attack?

Whatever the source of Martini's assessment, Stumpff's headquarters at Berlin-Wannsee, the great underground command post on the outskirts of Berlin, began to prepare the crews, and arm, fuel and service the aircraft of no less than six air divisions, and to bring some of the most distant squadrons to airfields closer to Otto and Ida. Again, that was not unusual. But Stumpff's later disposition of his forces would be unusual indeed.

Shortly before 10 P.M. that night, the quiet of the English countryside was shattered as thousands of Koffmann starters exploded in clouds of acrid blue smoke; propellers began to revolve, and 898 British and 10 American aircraft connected with the raid began to move. At 10 P.M. exactly the first greens were fired from the towers and the first bombers began to roar down the runways, lifting up over the silvered countryside. Fifty-five of the aircraft soon aborted the operation through technical failure and returned to base, leaving 843 flying toward Germany. Once airborne, the main force clawed for the operating altitude and formed into the great bomber stream, Bomber Command's tactic for overwhelming each line of German defenses by a sheer profusion of targets; the bombers would pass over any given point on the ground at an average rate of forty a minute. As the bombers left the British coast on a southeasterly heading, the bomb-aimers flicked switches to arm the bombs, the gunners test-fired their machine guns, the navigators worked under the glow of amber lamps plotting the track of the planes across the pink-printed charts of northern Europe. By the time it was out over the Channel, the force occupied a volume of sky some 65 miles long, 10 miles wide and 1 mile deep—a great thundering phalanx moving forward at nearly 4 miles a minute. But there was trouble ahead. Almost immediately high winds began to disorder the stream, and the bomber crews were astounded to find that the sky was as clear as a summer's night. They were, they discovered, naked in the moonlight.

As the main force neared the Belgian coast, the fifty Halifaxes in the diversionary force approached the German coast at Heligoland Bay, feigning a raid against either Hamburg or Berlin. If Stumpff was uncertain about which of the two forces was the main one, he would be compelled to keep the two fighter divisions in northwestern and northern Europe in place and the bombers destined for Nuremberg might slip through Flak Valley into central Germany. But Stumpff knew which was the main force; his technical intelligence men informed him that the northern force was not using the H2S precision bombing radar, which was always the case with a major attack. Therefore, it was the diversionary force, and Stumpff ordered all fighter squadrons of the 1st and 2nd Fighter Divisions to rendezvous with the 3rd Division over Ida and Otto. The weather made it impossible, Stumpff reasoned, for the main force to be going anywhere other than central Germany. The Luftwaffe was concentrating almost all the fighter defenses of Germany and western Europe along the exact route that the bomber stream would fly. Was it a coincidence, or did Stumpff have some foreknowledge of the route and destination of the attack?

It was the Luftwaffe's customary strategy to intercept a bomber stream long before it reached its target, but that night the German fighters were among the stream exceptionally early. Flight Sergeant Ronald Gardner of 103 Squadron would recall:

> The fighters were waiting for us shortly after we crossed the coast, as if they already knew our target and route. And they were in force. Never have I seen so many gathered at one point during my tour of operations . . . (the sky) was full of Me-109s and 110s. . . . Normally, flying in the leading wave, we were seldom attacked by fighters until well into France or Germany. . . . Usually the fighters took at least half an hour to get amongst us.

It was now that other factors intruded to ensure the looming catastrophe. The spoof raids by Mosquitos on Cologne, Kassel and Aachen were as accurately interpreted by Stumpff as had been the Halifax feint at Hamburg and Berlin. He left the spoofs to the flak as his night fighters concentrated on the bomber stream. German ground controllers used voice radio communications to help the night fighters home in on their targets, and the RAF employed giant transmitters to jam their frequencies with sounds of ringing bells, shouts, massed bands, long speeches by Hitler and Goering, interminable passages from Goethe. More often than not, the ground controllers' orders were successfully blocked; but that night, the jamming was not fully effective. The Germans normally changed their frequencies at random to confuse the jammers, but on this occasion, as the Bomber Command signals officer would report: "The enemy displayed . . . unusual subtlety (in avoiding the RAF's jamming transmissions) in that he appeared to be making his frequency changes in step with our Group

Broadcast times. . . ." How the Germans were able to do this would remain a mystery, for it was not yet technically possible to scan and locate an open frequency automatically. Was it, again, a coincidence, or did they have some foreknowledge of the main force's signals plan?

The German night fighters also used radar to direct them to their targets, and that night, for the first time, they used a new type—the SN-2. The Mosquitos that were accompanying the bomber stream to pick off the night fighters as they rose to the attack were not able to home in on this new system. The Germans eluded them both in the air and on the ground. Few of the Mosquito attacks against the fighter bases were successful; all of the fighters had taken off by the time the Mosquitos arrived, and the bomber stream was virtually defenseless except for its own guns.

The weather completed the tragedy. The bomber stream was flying in brilliant moonlight at an altitude that produced luminous contrails. Flight Sergeant Robert Truman of 625 Squadron would recount: "You could see them clearly; the sky was full of contrails. I remember thinking that if they were so clear to us then they must be equally clear to the night fighters and that, if they were anywhere about, they could not fail to get onto us."

The night fighters were all about by the time the stream reached the first of the two beacons, Ida. Stumpff had concentrated between 200 and 250 aircraft in the area; and he had calculated the estimated time of arrival of the main force and the flight time of the fighters, which was of very limited duration, with remarkable precision. They were up in strength and "fresh"; each had a full fuel load and could stay in the stream, falling upon the bombers like falcons on disordered geese. The night sky was filled with deadly beauty as the fighters dropped their flares, which were hardly necessary in the bright moonlight, and opened fire with cannon tracer. Flying Officer George Foley, a radar operator in one of the Pathfinders, would remember: "I knew things were going very badly when I heard the captain call out over the intercom, 'Better put your parachutes on, chaps, as I have just seen the 42nd go down.' "

At RAF Kingsdown, the British wireless intelligence post in the tip of the Kentish peninsula, the operators all knew that a disaster was in the making. The German night fighters' voice radio bands were filled with the Nazi greeting *Sieg Heil!*, followed by the transmitting aircraft's call sign— the procedure for announcing a kill. By the time the main force had reached the end of the long leg at Fulda, the landscape below was marked by a necklace of fifty-nine crashed and burning bombers. Flying Officer L. Young of 103 Squadron later recalled: ". . . one could navigate on the blazing wrecks below." Flight Sergeant Ronald Holder of 460 Squadron, who had flown eighty-six missions over Germany before this one—an almost unheard-of number—recorded:

It was a story of the perfect air ambush. . . . The ground controllers had to guess where we were making for, and they guessed correctly. . . . There were enemy fighters everywhere. We were sitting ducks, with no cloud cover to shield us. . . . Before this hellish action we had bombed many big German cities . . . but this was our first real experience of encountering the full fury of the enemy's fighter force . . . and it was terrifying.

At approximately 12:45 A.M. the first Lancaster turned southeast at Fulda toward Nuremberg, which was now only 75 miles away—twenty minutes' flying time. But this course change, which was intended to fox the Germans into thinking that either Berlin or Leipzig might be the target, had seemingly been anticipated. Stumpff had scrambled fresh squadrons into this final leg before the bomb run. Moreover, Nuremberg had been warned that it might be the target shortly before midnight—some seventy-five minutes before the attack was due to start, while the bomber stream was far away and could still have gone in any direction. Shortly afterwards— perhaps forty minutes before 1:10 A.M., Zero Hour for the attack—the sirens sounded the preliminary *Öffentliche Luftwarnung*. The main alarm —the *Fliegeralarm*—was sounded at 12:38, even before the bombers reached the end of the long leg, thirty minutes before Zero Hour. Again, it seemed that the Germans had foreknowledge that Nuremberg would be the target, for normally, given RAF tactics, the Germans were able to provide their cities with only a few minutes' warning, if any at all.

There were 643 bombers left in the stream; casualties and aborts had removed one out of every five aircraft that had taken off from England. But still—if all went well—the force approaching Nuremberg was big enough to wipe the city off the map. Furthermore, the Pathfinder force and the force responsible for marking the target were virtually intact. But all did not go well. Light white clouds began to appear below, making the bombers, as one pilot put it, appear to the night fighters above like flies on a white tablecloth. By the time the marker force reached Nuremberg, the cloud cover was nearly 2 miles thick and totally obscured the city. The marker flares—red and green cascades called "Christmas trees" and huge mushrooming ground flares—disappeared into the thick cloud and could not be seen by the bomb-aimers aboard the main force. But other flares, inaccurately dropped, could be seen, and it was on these that the main force bombed. Some damage was caused to the industrial areas of the city, but in general damage to the rest of Nuremberg was slight.

Then came the flight back to England. The night fighters had shot their bolt, but they did muster enough force to catch and shoot down more bombers on the way home. How many would not be clear, for although ten heavy bombers were lost on the return flight, some were aircraft that had been disabled in attacks before they reached the target, or while they were over it. But these casualties did not mark the end of the agony that night. More aircraft were lost over the English countryside, or in the Channel, crashing either through the miscalculation of exhausted pilots or because they had been shot to pieces and simply fell apart in the turbulence. Such was the distress of the force that, as James Campbell, a British journalist, would write:

> The air over half of England that foggy dawn hummed with Mayday calls as wireless operators tapped out desperate emergency signals in the knowledge that they could not remain airborne much longer. And from control towers of fog-shrouded bases equally frantic signals flashed back to the bombers, diverting them to fog-free airfields where grim-faced controllers fought the clock to sort out landing priorities and get the flak-battered aircraft down as swiftly as possible. . . .

When the aircraft did get down, many of the crews were extremely angry, bitter and suspicious. The Pathfinder leader, Wing Commander Daniels, found Bennett, his AOC, waiting for him as he got out of his aircraft. Daniels exclaimed: "Bloody hell! Why did we have to go that way?" At the debriefings, the crews' attitudes were similar. Flight Lieutenant Stephen Burrows would recall the debriefing at Dunholme Lodge base: "It certainly appeared to me that Jerry was waiting for us, and there were rumors that the raid had been leaked. In fact, it was said quite openly during (debriefing)—with lots of derogatory remarks being made." Flight Sergeant Ronald Gardner, a Pathfinder with 103 Squadron, would recall: "Everyone I talked to after the raid was sure that it had been leaked." Pilot Officer Merril of 463 Squadron summed up the general opinion when he wrote in his debriefing report: "Fighter activity from leaving position B [Charleroi] to the target was such that enemy may have been aware of the route taken by the main force."

Now came the reckoning. The raid was a disaster for Bomber Command, yet the dimension of that disaster would remain obscure. All that was said about losses on the main BBC newscast on March 31 was that ninety-six bombers had failed to return. When two of the missing aircraft turned up, the total was reduced to ninety-four; but an official analysis would show that ninety-five bombers had been lost, a further ten were total losses upon crashing in England, one was later scrapped because of the severity of its battle damage, and seventy more sustained damage that put them out of action for between six hours and six months. Furthermore, a Halifax taking SOE agents to Belgium that night had been shot down, as well as a Mosquito taking part in airfield attack operations supporting the Nuremberg raid. That brought the known total to 108 aircraft for the entire night's operations. In all, 745 crewmen were killed or wounded and a further 159, some of whom were wounded, were taken prisoner. But that may not have been the end of the casualty list. Intelligence documents which were not intended for general circulation are said to have revealed that 53 bombers had, in fact, crashed in England, bringing the total to 160 aircraft; while yet another source, one that was only semi-official, would increase the number of crashes to 66 and the total to 178. Whatever the actual total, the RAF had suffered its heaviest casualties of the war, and the crew loss was higher than that for the entire Battle of Britain. German losses, on the other hand, totaled five aircraft, with five more damaged seriously and three less seriously. German dead, civil as well as military, totaled 129.

With the hindsight of history, it seemed incredible to the RAF and its historians that the Nuremberg raid was mounted at all. The destruction of the German night fighter force was an important military priority, and the choice of Nuremberg as a target, as well as the route and tactics employed in the raid, plainly indicated that Bomber Command was being used as live bait, just as Spaatz was using his command. But why undertake such a mission on a night when the weather promised to favor the defense? Saundby would speculate:

> . . . I always had the impression that (Churchill) exerted pressure on Harris to make the raid before Bomber Command was switched to the (*Neptune*) operations and attacks on pre-invasion targets in France. Nuremberg was the place where Hitler held his big rallies, and Churchill was persistent in that it must be bombed (now). . . .

Harris would deny, however, that Churchill demanded the city be attacked that night, adding that on one occasion the Prime Minister had told him that he did not expect Bomber Command to fight both the enemy *and* the weather. Harris would further state that it was doubtful that he would have gone ahead with the operation if he had known more accurately what the weather would be that night. He would also defend the route and tactics used in the raid:

> In sending the force in one stream to Nuremberg we thought we would fool the German night-controller, who we considered would not believe it. We had used in the past so many tactics and diversions—making out that such-and-such a city was to be the target and then heading for the real one—that we hoped that the straight run to Nuremberg would fox the Germans into thinking that we would, as in the past, suddenly turn off before the city was reached and deliver our attack elsewhere. . . .

It is certain, of course, that neither Churchill and Harris nor anyone else concerned with planning the raid intended that Bomber Command should suffer such heavy losses in the pursuit of aerial supremacy for D-Day. In fact, shortly after the Nuremberg raid, the British withdrew their support from Huguenot. Clearly, the operation had backfired. The Luftwaffe had been lured to battle, but it was the RAF that suffered the devastating casualties. The city of Nuremberg was scarcely touched. Everything, it seemed, had gone wrong: the weather, a grave miscalculation of the German reaction to the novel tactics of the raid, the ineffectiveness of the diversionary raids, the failure of the Mosquito night fighters to protect the bomber stream—all contributed to the tragedy. But what of the contention that the Germans were given forewarning of the raid? If so, would that not, above all, have sealed Bomber Command's fate?

There were several indications that the Germans knew of Bomber Command's plans in advance—the early appreciation of the size of the raid, the fact that the German night fighters were concentrated at exactly the right place and the right altitude for an ambush, the alerts passed to Nuremberg before the bomber stream turned into the final leg of its run. Moreover, British airmen who had been shot down and were being held prisoner at the time of the raid would state after the war that during the afternoon of the 30th—about five hours before the bomber stream took off—they were told by Luftwaffe intelligence interrogators at the main interrogation center at Oberursel, near Frankfurt, that the target for the raid that night was Nuremberg. At least one prisoner claimed that he saw that someone in the Luftwaffe had marked the route to be taken, with the target, on a wall map in the room where he was questioned. Prisoners taken after the raid would state that they were told by their interrogators at Oberursel that the route and target were known to the Luftwaffe at four o'clock in the afternoon on March 30.

While it was common for interrogators on both sides to claim more knowledge than in fact they had, in order to demoralize prisoners and persuade them that there was no point in keeping silent, these statements, if the prisoners concerned reported correctly, at least warranted further investigation. But neither Bomber Command nor the British intelligence authorities pursued the allegation—an odd fact in itself. A document which surfaced in the RAF archives after the war would add to the mystery. It was the Raid Plot, upon which was noted the exact crash position of each missing aircraft. It had been compiled not only from RAF intelligence and records but also from the findings of RAF intelligence teams in Germany after the war and from captured German records. The person who had investigated the raid and compiled the map had written in large capital letters on top of the document: "THEY KNEW WE WERE COMING," and "CARELESS TALK COSTS LIVES." Middlebrook would draw attention to this document in his book on the Nuremberg raid which was published in 1974; but when the Public Records Office in London was asked to supply the Raid Plot in 1975, the document with the superscription was not provided.

Few of the British principals in the disaster ever said very much about the raid. Air Vice Marshal Bennett, the Pathfinder AOC, was said to have told James Campbell, who was investigating the affair, that "It was caused, . . . and was not merely accidental." Campbell would find it "strange" that Harris made no mention at all of the raid in his memoirs after the war. He would also find it strange that Churchill dismissed it with one short paragraph in a work of six volumes. Their reticence, however, might be attributed to the fact that the raid was, by its very nature, sacrificial, just as were other British and American raids of the period that were intended to entrap the Luftwaffe. The difference, in this case, was simply the magnitude of the sacrifice. Yet the contention that the Germans were given foreknowledge of the raid as an additional incentive to come up and fight—and, at the same time, to establish the credibility of a double agent —cannot be discounted, particularly in light of de Guingand's remark.

If this was, in fact, what happened, it seems quite clear that Harris was not privy to the stratagem. It was Churchill who, again, appeared to occupy the center of the web. Harris may well have been under pressure from the Prime Minister to launch the raid, but every high commander was under similar pressure to mount extremely risky operations to obtain the preconditions of intelligence, security and safety for the invasion. Harris accepted the risks of a deep-penetrating mission even under adverse weather conditions, and he sought to counter those risks with diversionary operations and fighter protection for the bomber stream. He could not have predicted the outcome, nor could he be held responsible. But once it had been decided to undertake such an operation—and Churchill as Minister of Defence was one of two or three men who were informed of Bomber Command's targets in advance—it may also have been decided to add one of the sinister touches to which Churchill was addicted.

The dangers of forewarning the Germans of the raid were obvious, but so were the dangers of the novel tactics employed in the raid. Just as Harris hoped that the Germans would be fooled by such a "straightforward declaration of intention," so it was possible that Churchill thought that they would disbelieve, and fail to act upon, a forewarning. Furthermore, a double agent could not tell the Germans very much more beforehand than they would learn for themselves from radar and wireless intelligence once the main force was airborne. All other factors being equal, the probability was that Bomber Command would suffer no greater losses through foreknowledge than if there had been none.

The advantages of such a stratagem, however, were numerous. The Germans were keenly interested in obtaining foreknowledge of the RAF's and the USAAF's targets during this period. Any agent who could provide such information, even if it resulted in a major defeat for the Luftwaffe— which was the intention of the Nuremberg raid—would soar in the estimation of the German intelligence services. Who, in the future, would dare disbelieve reports from an agent who had warned of any of the Allies' major targets at this time? His information had merely to be true; it need not have been so detailed and specific that the Luftwaffe would be able to thwart the attack or inflict severe casualties. In fact, an agent who supplied that kind of information might be immediately suspect, for how would it be possible that he could reveal the details of one raid and of no other?

If a double agent was used to warn the Germans of the Nuremberg attack, Garbo or Brutus would have been logical choices. The Germans believed that Brutus actually served on an air staff, and that both men had sub-agents connected with Allied air headquarters. Both Garbo and Brutus were, significantly, playing central roles in establishing the deceptions of Fortitude and Quicksilver in German minds; they would also play a crucial part in a later, even more daring deception to prevent the Germans, it was hoped, from launching the massive panzer counteroffensive that the Allies expected shortly after D-Day. Because the success of military operations that involved millions might depend upon the credibility of one or two double agents, Churchill may well have considered it essential to tell the Germans the truth about Nuremberg, if only in broad outline, to prime them for the lies of Fortitude.

If the Germans had foreknowledge of the raid, and acted upon it, here was grim evidence indeed of the truth of Masterman's remark that "the larger the prize the higher must also be the preliminary stake." Miscalculation, misfortune, coincidence, perhaps even foreknowledge, had combined to provide Goering with a major victory. In an Order of the Day he proclaimed triumphantly: "The enemy has been dealt the heaviest nocturnal defeat so far in his criminal attack on our beloved homeland." The German night fighter pilots were the heroes of the hour, while among the pilots and crews of Bomber Command there was a profound bitterness against those who had planned and ordered the attack. There were too many empty seats at breakfast the morning after the raid, too many "chop girls"—the girl friends of missing airmen who were, through superstition, shunned by the survivors. There they stood, at Flying Control, at the ends of runways, in the messes, at the bars, lonely, disconsolate, silent reminders of the lives that had been lost in an operation that was intended to save lives on D-Day.

Aerial Stratagems

THE LYSANDER AIRCRAFT landed at Manston just after midnight and taxied over to the SOE/MI-6 hardstanding in the southeast corner of the field. The bulky form of Commander Dunderdale came out of the darkness to open the aircraft door and help two passengers down the steps. They were "M. Pierre Moreau," a nervous, bespectacled French railway official who had been exfiltrated earlier that evening from his home near Lyon, and his wife, who was wrapped in an old fur coat. When the trio was in the brightly lit crew room, "Mme Moreau" took the coat off, and Dunderdale noted that she was heavily pregnant. By daybreak, M. and Mme Moreau were at Brown's Hotel on Piccadilly; and there, after they had slept, bathed and eaten, Moreau received a caller. He was Professor Solly Zuckerman, a brilliant anatomist whose range of studies extended from apes to the effects of bomb blast on the human frame. Now he was concerned with another study in which Moreau would play an important part—the destruction of the French railroads.

Before Moreau arrived, a major disagreement had been raging for weeks between the Supreme Command and its airmen on the one hand, and Churchill, the War Cabinet and the Anglo-American heavy bomber barons on the other. The dispute centered upon the huge Allied heavy bomber force and how it was to be employed in direct support of Neptune. Eisenhower demanded that it must be used not only in bombing enemy cities but also in massed attacks to destroy the rail centers of western Europe— rail centers through which the panzers and German reserves must move to reach Normandy. At the request of Air Chief Marshal Sir Trafford Leigh-Mallory, the C-in-C of the Allied Expeditionary Air Force (AEAF), Professor Zuckerman had produced a plan for a ninety-day attack against eighty rail targets in western Europe. The plan went to Tedder, the deputy Supreme Commander, it was codenamed "Transportation," and it received Eisenhower's strong support. He insisted that, since the first five or six weeks of Neptune were likely to be the most critical, it was essential to take every possible step to ensure that the assault forces obtained and held the largest possible foothold in Europe, an objective that would be difficult to achieve if the Germans were able to rush major reinforcements by rail to Normandy.

The military advantages of destroying the major rail centers of western Europe were self-evident, but the political implications of the Transportation plan raised a host of objections. The War Cabinet, upon hearing that the plan might kill 20,000 and injure 60,000 Frenchmen and Belgians, took what its Minutes described as a "grave and on the whole adverse view of the proposal." Churchill supported this view and at a Defence Committee meeting on April 26, 1944, stated that if the western powers proceeded with the plan, then "we should build up a volume of dull hatred in France which would affect our relations with that country for many years to come." He wired Roosevelt to ask him to order Eisenhower to find some other means of delaying the panzers. But Roosevelt was unwilling to interfere. After consultation with the Joint Chiefs of Staff, he replied to Churchill: "I am not prepared to impose from this distance any restriction on military action by responsible Commanders that in their opinion might militate against the success of Overlord or cause additional loss of life to our Allied forces of invasion." His cable was decisive; western Europe was to be turned into a railway desert in the interests of Neptune.

M. Moreau was a man of considerable importance to that aerial campaign. As a lifelong and senior official of the French railway system, the Société Nationale des Chemins de Fer (SNCF), he knew as much as any man about the military capacity of the system, and of German plans for its use in the event of invasion. Moreau had been approached by MI-6's *réseau* in Paris, Jade Amicol, which had important connections within the executive of SNCF, and had agreed to go to England and place his knowledge and experience at the service of Neptune. He brought with him the set of three volumes which constituted the latest operating manual for the French railways, together with extensive material about German plans for their operations in the event of an invasion. And with the end of the political dispute over Transportation, he joined the Railway Research Service (RRS), which had been established to survey northwest Europe's rail yards, sidings, stations, sheds, tracks, repair shops, roundhouses, turntables, signals systems, switches, locomotive and rolling stock resources, and bridges. Moreau's particular job would be to assist the RRS in selecting targets whose destruction would have the maximum effect upon the ability of the Germans to move their reserves up to Normandy.

Moreau placed his wife in the care of an obstetrician, and then went to work. He was a nervous, sensitive man who seemed to his colleagues to be the archetype of the French civil servant—fussy in sums and in life—and it was not long before a crisis developed. Mme Moreau bore a son and Moreau, who was a Jew, insisted that since he was in England on British government business, the British government must pay all the expenses of the birth—including the circumcision. MI-6 agreed to pay the obstetrician's fees but the paymaster balked at paying for the circumcision. This, he said, should be charged against the AEAF and the RRS. But as neither had funds for such purposes, both refused to pay. Moreau reacted by stating that he would resume his work only when he was reimbursed for the expense. The world might be involved in a cataclysmic war, but the French attitude toward money had not changed, and neither had the spirit of English bureaucracy. Aware of French punctiliousness about small sums, Dunderdale decided to raise the matter at the next meeting of the Air Council. He did so, mentioning the question of the circumcision fee under the heading of "any other business," and the chairman, Marshal of the Royal Air Force Sir Charles Portal, "put his hand in his pocket and produced a half-crown. The other members of the council did likewise, and there was shortly enough to meet the bill."

Moreau resumed work, but in a state of increasing agitation. For as Transportation got under way, he began to realize that he was contributing to a national disaster in French life by helping destroy the railroads. Apparently unaware of the enormity of Allied airpower, he listened aghast to the radio stations at Paris, Vichy and Brussels which reported the casualties and damage caused by his and the RRS's work. He reacted very strongly when he heard that the French cardinals had issued an appeal to British and American episcopates to halt the campaign. And he finally stopped work altogether when, on May 23, 1944, he heard the Nazi-controlled Radio Paris describe the devastation:

> The French railway system is in complete chaos. The Allies have successfully pulverized into rubble whole marshalling yards. They have destroyed countless locomotives and have made scores of railway stations unusable. The rest of the destructive work which could not be done by the Allied pilots has been accomplished by experienced squads of saboteurs. . . . The temper of the population, especially that of Paris, is rising because no food is available, nobody can travel, and there are severe restrictions in the use of electricity. . . .

It was also reported that, by the third week of May, 6062 civilians had been killed in the campaign.

Moreau refused to do any further work for the RRS, waited in England until France had been liberated and then went home. Long after the war, Dunderdale received a letter from the SNCF stating that Moreau had retired and had applied for his pension after forty years of service. Unfortunately, the letter pointed out, there was a period of broken service in the spring of 1944 which Moreau could not explain satisfactorily. He asked that the SNCF approach the Foreign Office for the information; he could say nothing. But neither could Dunderdale. For MI-6 did not officially exist, and therefore had never employed anybody. Moreover, Dunderdale was not sure what effect his words might have upon Moreau's pension if the SNCF discovered that he had played a role in the wartime destruction of the French railways.

Transportation was only one aspect of the gigantic aerial campaign waged by the Allied air forces prior to D-Day; and just as the Battle of the Atlantic was fought to destroy the Kriegsmarine, so the prize in the air was the destruction of the Luftwaffe and, coincidentally, the obliteration of the industrial centers that supplied the German war machine. With the virtual elimination of the U-boat threat and victory in North Africa in 1943, the aerial campaign came to dominate Allied priorities, for the Luftwaffe posed a dual hazard to Neptune. Allied planners feared that even a handful of German planes might create havoc in the crowded sea lanes and beachheads of the Neptune assault area, just as they had done at Bari. And the Luftwaffe, which had at its disposal a complete paratroop army of at least five divisions, might react to Neptune by making a mass drop on the ports of southern England, on London, or on the beachhead zones. Indeed, it was discovered after the war that such a plan had been drawn up by Goering, and it might have been attempted if the Germans had been able to obtain foreknowledge of the time and place of the invasion, if the Luftwaffe had available the transport aircraft necessary to carry the paratroopers to the target—and if the Allies had not been able to achieve aerial supremacy and wipe out a paratroop armada before it reached the French bases from which it would have to operate.

Victory in the air, however, was not simply a matter of which side had the greatest number of aircraft. There were the additional imperatives of keeping Allied casualties to a minimum and, as important, of concealing from the Germans the truths about Neptune that might be deduced from the patterns and intensity of the pre-invasion aerial campaign. The German air intelligence service was large, experienced and extremely capable, and it existed for the sole purpose of confounding Allied aerial attacks. Through its surveillance of Allied tactics, formations and targets, its cryptanalytical and wireless intelligence activities, and its techniques for blinding or jamming radar systems and radio navigation devices, it had the means to predict, and perhaps even prevent, Neptune. Thus deception, and in particular the fictions of Fortitude, became the dominant influence on the pre-invasion aerial campaign. Aerial warfare itself was new, and it called forth a catalogue of stratagems as ingenious, and as ruthless, as any practiced against the enemy on land or at sea.

There were, first of all, systematic attempts to deceive the German wireless intelligence service. It was known that the Germans monitored Allied air force wireless traffic and assumed from certain characteristic patterns that a major strike was in the offing. Therefore, false wireless traffic was broadcast to keep them continuously, and needlessly, alert; and in the special context of Neptune, dummy traffic similar to the real traffic that would occur on the eve of D-Day was broadcast to coincide with large-scale pre-invasion exercises so that, it was hoped, the enemy would conclude that Neptune itself was just another exercise. Deceptive traffic was also broadcast in the clear or in an easily breakable code so that the Germans would think they had intercepted some important piece of information through a security leak. This was a familiar ruse, however, and was employed very sparingly lest the Germans see the truth behind a lie too easily obtained.

Aware that if the enemy could not see what was going on in England, he could certainly hear it, the strategists of the aerial campaign began broadcasting false wireless traffic that revealed, or so it appeared, that the main concentration of Allied air power was located on the flat fields of East Anglia—the Quicksilver area—while the real squadrons in southwestern England were kept silent or transmitted their signals by landline. American and British aircraft also flew deception missions coincidentally with real air strikes, broadcasting false wireless traffic to suggest that their point of departure and return was East Anglia. But above all, the principal stratagem in the wireless deception campaign was simply to produce so much false traffic that the German wireless intelligence facilities were completely swamped. And to add to their burden, the Allied air forces systematically attacked all the wireless stations in both the Neptune and Fortitude areas, culminating in a massed raid of one hundred Lancasters upon the headquarters of the German signals intelligence service in northwestern Europe, located at Ferme d'Urville near Cherbourg. The raid was so effective that, as a subsequent photographic interpretation report stated: "The station is completely useless, the site itself is rendered unsuitable for rebuilding the installations without much effort being expended in levelling and filling in the craters." This and other raids against German wireless stations served another purpose; they compelled the enemy to resort to hastily-built installations to restore communications, which rendered secret traffic much more liable to the depredations of Ultra. The *maquis,* meanwhile, were busy cutting telecommunications cables, again forcing the Germans to resort to wireless transmission.

The selection of targets was perhaps the most ruthless of the Allied aerial stratagems. While laying waste to western European rail centers, the Allied air forces were also dealing with the road and rail bridges. But to suggest that the invasion would occur in the Pas de Calais, only the bridges over the Seine were attacked before D-Day; those of the Loire and the other rivers were not attacked until afterwards. Thus, between April 21 and June 5, 1944, all the bridges over the Seine between Rouen and Paris were successfully sent crashing into the water. Rommel himself witnessed one such attack when 8 Thunderbolts of the U.S. 9th Air Force wrecked the 725-foot steel girder railway bridge over the Seine at Vernon with 8 tons of bombs. In all, thirty-six bridges suffered a similar fate. Coastal batteries, radar sites, airfields, tank parks, petrol and oil dumps, headquarters (but not those which were serving the purposes of Ultra), and, particularly, V-weapons sites were also devastated from the air. And since most of these targets were located in the Fortitude area, their destruction served the purposes of deception admirably. A Top Secret memorandum entitled "Cover and Deception in Air Force Operations, European Theater of Operations," would sum up the basic strategy of the campaign. Since it was "absolutely vital that neither the target date nor target area be indicated by the bombardment intensity or pattern," the memorandum stated, "the coastal defences in the Pas de Calais (the cover or fictional assault area) were attacked equally, and sometimes twice as heavily, as those in Normandy." For every pound of bombs dropped inside the assault area, two pounds were dropped outside it; and because German aerial defenses were much stronger in the Pas de Calais than elsewhere, this stratagem would result in a significant increase in casualties among the Allied air crews.

Air operations to supply the resistance movements of Belgium and northern France, as well as reconnaissance flights over enemy-occupied territory, followed a similar pattern. Throughout the pre-invasion period, supply missions flown into the Fortitude area outnumbered those into Normandy by a ratio of two or three to one, while false reconnaissance missions were flown with the same thoroughness over the Fortitude area as over the area where Neptune would actually land. The reconnaissance pilots themselves were, of course, not informed which was the cover area and which the real target, although the "Cover and Deception" memorandum indicated that they may have been led to believe that the Pas de Calais was the assault area—in case they were shot down and interrogated. It can be assumed that these operations, too, resulted in an increase in casualties, a portion of which must be charged to the Fortitude account.

How much were the Allies willing to spend in the campaign to defeat the Luftwaffe and guard the secrets of Neptune? Allied losses were particularly heavy in the raids against the rail centers of Aachen, Hasselt, Juvisy, Lille and Trappes, giving rise once again to the speculation that the Germans might have been fed foreknowledge of the attacks to induce the Luftwaffe to come up and fight. Moreover, Wingate would recall that the RAF was prepared to hand over to the Germans the latest model Spitfire fighter reconnaissance aircraft in a game of deception that was a variant of both the Meinertzhagen stratagem and Mincemeat. A German fighter pilot who was taken prisoner, a man known to be both fanatically *führer-treu* and a skilled pilot, was taken to the RAF base at Leuchars in Scotland "for interrogation." The RAF intelligence officer in charge of the prisoner excused himself midway through the interrogation to, as he put it, "see a man about a dog." A few moments later, RAF ground crews brought up the Spitfire in full view of the German. They fueled the aircraft, turned the propeller, and then with great cries of "There's the NAAFI wagon," went off for tea. The sky-blue aircraft was so beautiful in line that it was said that no real pilot could resist flying it; and that was what the German was supposed to do, for the air deception staff had planted a set of false maps in its cockpit. The cockpit hatch was left open, there was not a soul in sight. It would have been a simple matter for the German to leave the office where he was being interrogated (the RAF intelligence officer had not locked the door), climb in the cockpit and take off. But, according to Wingate, he did nothing but sit by the window looking at the Spitfire, waiting patiently for the intelligence officer to return.

It was known that the Luftwaffe had been badly beaten in the great air battles of the winter and spring of 1944. But how badly? In spite of claims to the contrary, Ultra failed at this crucial time to provide the Supreme Command with an accurate estimate of the Luftwaffe order of battle. In fact, estimates of Luftwaffe strength and capability "varied so widely," as the American official history, *Cross-Channel Attack,* would note, "that they might have been drawn from a hat." There were several reasons for this gap in SHAEF's knowledge, among them the rivalry between the American and British air intelligence services and the rigid security imposed upon the Luftwaffe intelligence that Ultra was able to provide. But the Germans were becoming more wily; the game of intelligence and counter-intelligence had gone on for so long that the Luftwaffe had learned to guard its secrets. As a result, there was a fundamental difference of opinion between the Pentagon and the Air Ministry about German strength in the air, and both, in the event, would prove to be exaggerations. Thus, as D-Day approached, the Supreme Command was infected with a profound unease that influenced all its plans. In spite of the massive pre-invasion aerial campaign, the Luftwaffe remained a grave threat to Neptune. Aerial operations, including those mounted to give truth to the fictions of Fortitude, were intensified. In all, between April 1 and June 5, 1944, the Allied air forces launched just over 200,000 missions against targets in northern France and Belgium, dropping 200,000 tons of bombs. Even before the campaign had ended, the effect was considerable. But the cost was grievous. Over 12,000 Allied airmen and 2000 aircraft were lost during those last few weeks of aerial *Blitzkrieg*. French and Belgian civilian deaths totaled some 12,000 people; and most of the Allied and civilian casualties occurred north of the Seine rather than to the south of it—in the Fortitude area. The Allies would lose almost as many men in the aerial preparations that cut a path for the invading armies as those armies would lose in the invasion of France. Was it all necessary? The Supreme Commander thought so, for he would report to the Combined Chiefs of Staff: "No single factor contributing to the success of our efforts in Normandy could be overlooked or disregarded. Military events, I believe, justified the decision taken. . . ."

A vital component of the pre-invasion aerial campaign were the attacks against German radar sites along the Channel coast, attacks which again served the interests of both Neptune and Fortitude. If the Allies were to achieve tactical surprise on D-Day, the enemy radar system that guarded the invasion area had to be seriously or completely deranged. But to conceal the particular interest of the Allies in Normandy, sites in other areas were even more heavily bombed, again increasing the human and material cost of the campaign. In all, twenty-six of forty-two radar sites were put out of action between the Channel Islands and Ostend. But in a new and sophisticated twist to the techniques of aerial warfare—and deception— several of these sites were purposely left operational. For throughout this period the Allies were testing and perfecting a unique variety of ruses that would be put to use on D-Day. All involved so-called radio or electronic counter-measures (RCM's or ECM's), which were designed specifically to trick the German radar equipment that was allowed to survive.

During April and May 1944, the final tests of a series of ECM deceptions were being made at Tantallon Castle on a headland overlooking the Firth of Forth. There, in a hut under the red ruins of the castle, electronic scientists from TRE and the American-British Laboratory 15 (ABL-15) at Harvard, led by Dr. Robert Cockburn and including Dr. Joan Curran, had assembled the latest in the German arsenal of radar equipment, "pinched" as long ago as February 1942 in the raid on Bruneval and updated by bits and pieces captured in Africa, Sicily and Italy. The group was first concerned with the ECM known as "Window."

Window was the British code name for the dipole; its American code name was "Chaff," and it consisted of strips of foil which could be unloaded in large quantities from an approaching bomber stream to create an effect upon radar screens not unlike that of a blizzard upon the human eye; it became impossible to distinguish objects. But in the simplicity of the dipole lay its vulnerability. Quite early in the war, both Britain and Germany had discovered the effectiveness of the dipole; but because both sides had radar networks upon which they depended heavily for protection, and because they were unaware that they shared the same secret, each was reluctant to use it for fear of revealing the secret and inviting retaliation.

The decision not to use dipoles had involved the highest Allied and Axis commands. Goering had ordered the technical reports describing their effectiveness destroyed by fire; Churchill was prepared to accept very heavy RAF casualties to protect British radar. But the British finally tipped their hand in the great raid on Hamburg on July 26, 1943, and had been using Window ever since to confound the German radar screens.

It was not done without reason, for the British had perfected a new weapon of electronic warfare that the Germans did not have. Dr. Curran, an outstanding radar scientist, had discovered that when dipoles were dropped from a few aircraft under calculated and controlled circumstances, they produced echoes on radar screens that resembled an entire air fleet. She had carried her experiments forward and also discovered that an electronic device, which she called "Moonshine," could be built and installed in ships or aircraft. Moonshine received the pulses of the enemy radar, and amplified and returned them to produce symptoms on radar screens somewhat similar to those produced by a large number of ships or planes on the move. In short, Moonshine could make it appear to the enemy, without his knowledge that he was being tricked, that large formations of ships or aircraft were approaching him when, in fact, only a few Moonshine-equipped craft were.

The potential of Moonshine for making feints against the Germans' coastal defenses, in order to lure their formations away from the point actually to be attacked, had been recognized immediately by Professor Edward Neville da Costa Andrade, the brilliant but quaint scientific member of the LCS. He recommended that the device be action-tested, and on April 6, 1942, nine Defiant fighters equipped with Moonshine had circled over Portland to suggest that a large group of American bombers was approaching Cherbourg. Ultra vigilance showed that thirty German fighters —the entire daytime air defense for the port—rose to meet the nonexistent threat. On April 17, 1942, Moonshine was used to lure the Luftwaffe away from an actual attack; as Moonshine Defiants circled over the Thames to duplicate the pulses created by bomber streams assembling for a raid, Ultra showed that the Luftwaffe controller launched 144 fighters to meet the deception thrust. To meet the actual attack—a raid by Fortresses of the U.S. 8th Air Force against Rouen—the controller put up seventy fighters. Its effectiveness as an airborne deception proven, Moonshine was put on ice and electronics scientists worked on further refinements for use on D-Day.

To test the results of the combined use of Window and Moonshine, Drs. Cockburn, Curran and their assistants at Tantallon required the services of a fleet of Stirlings and Lancasters, the Canadian destroyer *Haida* and a number of other sea and air craft. Stirlings flew over the test area at an exact altitude and an exact speed, dropping bundles of Window at predetermined intervals. Lancasters equipped with search radar flew above them in equally complicated patterns, while *Haida* and a small fleet of minesweepers sailed into the Firth trailing Filberts, naval balloons with radar reflectors built inside. *Haida* and the minesweepers were ordered to "Moonshine" the search radar of the Lancasters, and when they did so, the combination of Window, Moonshine and the Filbert reflectors created impressions on the scientists' scopes that resembled a vast mass of shipping which covered some 200 square miles and was approaching the shore at exactly the speed a real invasion fleet would move. The tests were a success, and "Taxable" and "Glimmer"—electronic deception operations to make it appear that two great fleets were approaching the French coast between Le Havre and Calais as the real invasion fleet steamed into the Bay of the Seine—were approved for use in Fortitude between midnight and daybreak on D-Day.

Now Dr. Cockburn, again using *Haida* and the minesweepers, tried another ruse. When the test fleet had reached a point 10 miles off the headland, it stopped and moored its Filbert floats. Then the Lancasters and Stirlings flew over the area, and all scopes and Moonshines were switched on. But this time great noise amplifiers on the boats began to make sounds like the squeals and rattles of anchors being dropped, and of landing craft being lowered. Then a number of high-speed motor launches swooped in to lay a smoke screen. Visually, aurally, electronically, and from all angles, it looked as if there was a large invasion fleet lying just offshore, engaged in all the activities that preceded a seaborne assault. It was a more elaborate version of the trick used to divert the German response to Montgomery's attack at El Alamein, and it would be used again to divert their response to the Normandy assault.

Well satisfied, Cockburn turned to his next and last electronic deception. Aircraft again flew over the area, and at an appointed time, place and altitude hundreds of dummy paratroopers were dropped through a Window screen. When they hit the ground, they exploded with the sounds of a ground battle: machine-gun fire, pistol reports, the snap of rifles. A few real SAS troopers were dropped along with the dummies, and when they landed, they switched on amplifiers and records of gunfire, soldiers' oaths, cries for help, thuds. They also unleashed a chemical preparation which, in the form of light smoke, created the smell of battle. Those tests, too, were successful, and would form the basis of "Titanic," a stratagem to attract the enemy's attention to the landing of dummy paratroop brigades and divisions, while the real airborne invaders were dropped into other areas.

The tests over, Cockburn and his team returned to London to begin work on equipping the various naval craft that would be used in these deceptions, while air crews continued to perfect the extraordinarily precise flying techniques that would be necessary—techniques that would require the installation in each aircraft of a wholly new system of automatic pilotage. The ECM deceptions had worked well in Scotland and would be employed operationally on D-Day. A new military science had been created for this moment—electronic spoofing. If it succeeded in confusing and confounding German technical defenses, electronics would be confirmed as a new dimension of war, a weapon as revolutionary as the rifle, the machine gun and the tank.

Security

The spring of 1944 was a peculiar time in the history of England. As D-Day neared and millions of strangers crowded the countryside with even stranger vehicles, a great fog descended upon the island—a fog of security, the handmaiden of deception. Never before had such extraordinary precautions been taken to protect the secrets of a military operation; never before had Britons been so suspicious, so cautious. Busybodies and informers flourished, every village bobby kept his eyes and ears open for German spies, and ordinary human indiscretions assumed the proportions of crime. The campaign which the British government had begun at the outbreak of war—"Careless talk costs lives"—was intensified to an extraordinary degree. A social historian of the times would write: "Urging others not to spread rumours became a national occupation. Newspapers harangued their readers, clergy their congregations, headmasters their pupils. Special anti-rumour rallies were even held in some places." Security became an obsession, enveloping every aspect of every life; not even the King or the Prime Minister could do or say as he pleased.

When Eisenhower arrived in London as Supreme Commander, he had used his new pro-consular powers to urge the British government to take the most extensive and unusual security precautions in its history. He wrote to the British Chiefs of Staff: "It will go hard on our consciences if we were to feel, in later years, that by neglecting any security precaution we had compromised the success of these vital operations." With that letter, Britain became, temporarily, a police state isolated from the rest of the world. Overseas cabling privileges were withdrawn from all but the most trusted newspapermen. The press growled but—with one grave exception—honored the restrictions. Churchill himself advocated the censorship of the press, for Captain B. H. Liddell Hart, the British military writer who worked for Eisenhower making assessments of the personalities and abilities of enemy high commanders, showed him that it was possible to have made reasonably accurate deductions about Allied intentions between June 1943 and February 1944 simply by reading the main British and American newspapers. At the same time, every telephone call made by a soldier or an official, every letter in every sensitive part of Britain, every telegram, could be, and frequently was, monitored. Foreign and troops' mail was delayed, travel in and out of England was forbidden to all except essential personnel, and a ban was imposed on all visits in and out of a broad swath of the British Isles from the northern tip of Scotland to Land's End.

Restrictions on the military were even more severe, and Eisenhower warned every man under his command soon after his arrival:

> The rules of security are known to us all—a guarded tongue and safeguarded documents. It rests with each of us to ensure that there is no relaxation of these rules until success is achieved. All commanders will ensure that the highest standard of individual security discipline is maintained throughout their commands, and that the most stringent disciplinary action is taken in all cases of the violations of security.

A special procedure was instituted for the protection of all documents that revealed the time and place of the invasion. This was the "Bigot procedure," which took its curious name from the stamp "To Gib" that had appeared on the papers of all officers traveling to Gibraltar for the Torch invasions. To confuse the curious, the letters had been reversed, and for Neptune the Bigot designation was retained as the highest general security classification of the times. In the main, only Bigots could see Bigot documents; and to become a Bigot was as difficult as joining a good club. The most thorough security checks were made on candidates on both sides of the Atlantic, and even after clearance a Bigot's behavior and performance in England were liable to the most intimate scrutiny. But inevitably there were security breaches, even among Bigots, some of them serious and even terrifying in their gravity.

One of the first was a mysterious affair that began late in March 1944 when General Clayton Bissell, the chief of U.S. army intelligence at the Pentagon, received information from the FBI that a package of very secret papers had broken open by accident at a U.S. army mail sorting office at Chicago. Four unauthorized persons had seen the contents of the package in the headquarters of the U.S. army post office, and another ten had seen the documents when they reached the Chicago post office; no attempt was made, it appeared, to reseal the package. The sender was "Sergeant Thomas P. Kane," a man of German extraction who was a secretary to General Robert W. Crawford, chief of the ordnance supply section at Supreme Headquarters in London. Kane had sent the package, somewhat oddly, to "The Ordnance Division, G-4," but the address he wrote was that of his sister in Chicago, who lived in a predominantly German quarter of the city.

The situation was quickly brought to the attention of General Thomas J. Betts, the assistant chief of intelligence at Supreme Headquarters. It was a serious situation indeed, for as Betts later said:

> There lurked in the background the nagging doubt as to how long this had been going on, and whether or not it was still continuing. The documents were very important, for they revealed the target date and place of the invasion and schedules for the build-up and breakout. The mercy was that we had six weeks to investigate the affair and see whether we must recommend that changes be made in the Neptune plans.

An FBI check of Kane and his family showed that, so far as anyone knew, all were perfectly loyal American citizens with no history of any connection with pro-Nazi organizations. Kane was summoned before a departmental tribunal and admitted that the handwriting on the parcel was his. But he could not explain why he had put such secret documents into an envelope and posted them to his sister except, as Butcher (Eisenhower's diarist) noted, that his sister had been seriously ill, he was overtired, and he was thinking of her. "The clumsy handling would indicate that no professional spy was involved," Butcher continued, "but nevertheless important facts, including strength, places, equipment and target date have been disclosed to unauthorized persons."

The FBI was instructed to keep all persons who had seen the documents under surveillance. A court-martial was recommended for Kane, but no action was taken, although he too was kept under observation, his telephone was tapped, and he was not allowed to leave his quarters until after D-Day. That was not the end of the episode, however, for there were security men in both London and Washington who were convinced that the leakage was in some way connected with the Chicago *Tribune,* which was regarded with extreme displeasure by the two governments for having published information that the Allies had broken the Japanese naval code. Suspicion would again arise about the paper when it was discovered that, shortly before D-Day, one of the editors of the *Tribune* had tried to leave Britain in a U.S. transport despite a total ban on all travel from Britain by any unauthorized person. But no connection between the Kane case and the *Tribune* was ever established, and the editor in question was apparently guilty of nothing more than irresponsibility.

No sooner had the Kane case ended than another security breach occurred, this time involving a friend of Eisenhower's himself. He was Major General Henry Jervis Friese Miller who, at fifty-four, was one of the U.S. army's most able officers. He had been graduated from West Point with Eisenhower in 1915, and had then advanced through the ranks of the U.S.

cavalry to become the general commanding the Air Service Command. He was now, for the invasion, the quartermaster of the U.S. 9th Air Force, and he was a Bigot.

On the evening of April 18, 1944, Miller attended a dinner party for American Red Cross nurses given by General Edwin L. Sibert, chief of intelligence in the U.S. European Theater of Operations and later G2 to Bradley's 12th Army Group. The party was held in a public dining room of Claridge's and during the conversation Miller complained of his difficulties in obtaining supplies from the United States. Then he declared to the nurses, without even gracing the secret with a whisper, that the invasion would take place before June 15, 1944. Sibert, who overheard the remark, was furious. It was a gross breach of security, and the next morning he reported the matter to Bradley. Bradley also knew and liked Miller, but as he later said: "I had no choice. I telephoned Ike . . ."

Eisenhower was quite merciless; after a quick investigation he ordered Miller to return to the United States on the next boat and reduced him to his substantive rank, that of lieutenant colonel. "There were officers," wrote Bradley, "who afterward contended that Ike had acted with unnecessary harshness but I was not among them. For had I been in Eisenhower's shoes, I would have been no less severe. . . . At the same time this punishment reassured the British that we would not tolerate any loose talk."

Miller sought the claims of friendship and wrote in a letter to Eisenhower: "I simply want to ask you to have me shipped home in my present grade [i.e., major general], there to await such action as the fates have in store for me." He also strongly protested his innocence, but to no avail. Eisenhower replied to him confidentially: "I know of nothing that causes me more real distress than to be faced with the necessity of sitting as a judge in cases involving military offenses by officers of character and good record, particularly when they are old and warm friends." But, he continued, ". . . it was because of your long record of efficient service that I felt justified in recommending only administrative rather than more drastic procedure in your case."

Almost immediately after the Miller case, there occurred another embarrassing security breach for which the British were responsible. In April 1944, a deputy to Brigadier Lionel Harris, chief of the telecommunications department of SHAEF, reported that he had lost the SHAEF communications plan for Neptune as he was going home by train via Waterloo Station. And he said he had no idea how or where he had lost it. This seemed odd, for the plan was as bulky as *Gone With the Wind;* and Harris formed the impression that the man had been drinking. But the loss of the plan was the most serious imaginable, for it contained in every detail all the wireless nets and ciphers to be used during the assault. From that information, which was priceless in itself, an experienced wireless intelligence expert could also have deduced the layout, strength and disposition of the assault forces, and something of the time and place of the invasion.

In all, the document—had it got into German hands—would have made Neptune impossible to undertake unless the American and British governments were prepared to accept defeat on the Far Shore. But just as Harris was about to go and explain the catastrophe to Smith, the lost property office of Scotland Yard called to report that it had a briefcase belonging to an officer at Norfolk House. Inside, the police officer said, were some documents marked "Bigot" and "Top Secret" which appeared to be connected with wireless, and (so the story went) some socks and a bottle of beer. The police officer asked if the documents were important, and if so, could Norfolk House send someone round for them, as he had nobody in his office to send? Harris himself hurried across St. James's Park to retrieve the briefcase. It had been found by the driver of a taxi that had dropped a passenger at Waterloo.

The documents contained in another briefcase were never found. In March and April, the Luftwaffe mounted a series of very sharp raids on the official quarter of London; and in one of these, a string of bombs landed between Norfolk House and St. James's Palace, riddling Norfolk House and its intelligence section with shrapnel. More grievously, a bomb that dropped in the street near the palace blew to pieces the officer in charge of the Fortitude and Quicksilver wireless deceptions, Lieutenant Colonel Finlay Austin. Austin was carrying his briefcase when he was killed, and in it were the master documents of the Fortitude wireless plan. They were never recovered. It was assumed—but not without extensive forensic and police inquiry—that they had simply disintegrated in the flash of the aluminum-based high explosive in the bomb. However, the Fortitude wireless game was discontinued for a short time while a new commanding officer was briefed and trained.

Only a very few weeks before the invasion, the third serious security breach occurred in the American high command. This time the offender was a naval officer, "Captain Edward M. Miles," who was an aide to Admiral Harold R. "Betty" Stark, the C-in-C of U.S. naval forces in Europe and one of the top Neptune planners. The plaintiff was Air Chief Marshal Sir Trafford Leigh-Mallory, the C-in-C of the Tactical Air Force for Neptune, who wrote to Eisenhower that Miles had revealed in public "details of impending operations to include areas, lift, strength and dates." The indiscretion had taken place at a party given by Colonel Sir William Dupree, the Portsmouth brewer, and Leigh-Mallory complained that Miles was "apparently intoxicated."

Eisenhower, on May 21, 1944, wrote to Stark to say that he was "disturbed, not to say alarmed" by the report of Miles's indiscretion, and went on: "If this report is even partially true . . . , then I must say that the greatest harm could result from this indiscretion. I know that you will take prompt and effective action. . . ." Two days later Stark replied that he was sending Miles home. "I see no alternative. He will be a distinct loss and I have no replacement at present, but that can't be helped."

Meanwhile Eisenhower had written to Marshall to say that the Miles indiscretion had given him the "shakes," and that he "would willingly shoot the offender myself." But in Washington, Miles was given the chance to redeem his career, although privately he made it known that he had been the victim of an intrigue. After a period of doldrums, he was rehabilitated, given command of a transport division at Okinawa during the assault in 1944, and awarded the Bronze Star with Combat Distinction. He also distinguished himself during the invasion of the Philippines.

The Miller and Miles cases were serious blows to Eisenhower, for they seemed to reflect upon the discretion and responsibility of the U.S. staff in London. An occasional unguarded tongue or unguarded document was perhaps inevitable in a command the size of SHAEF, but not even coincidence could satisfactorily explain a security leak that was traced to quite a different quarter. In May 1944, a British officer was traveling to work by train and, as usual, passing the time by doing the crossword puzzle in his morning newspaper, the *Daily Telegraph*. The number of the puzzle was 5775, and 17 Across asked for a four-letter word that was "One of the U.S." The answer was "Utah," and the officer, who was a senior member of the Supreme Commander's staff, was surprised to see it, for he knew most of the principal code names for Neptune, and Utah was the name of one of the two main American beachheads in Normandy. Later he was even more surprised when he was doing puzzle number 5792 and found that the answer to the clue: "Red Indian on the Missouri" was "Omaha"—the code name for the other main American beachhead. Later still, tackling puzzle number 5797, he found that the answer to the clue "But some big wig like this has stolen some of it at times" was "Overlord"—the code name for the entire Allied strategy in northwest Europe in 1944. There was even more to come, however. Puzzle number 5799 asked for an eight-letter word for "This bush is a centre of nursery revolutions." The answer was "Mulberry"—the code name for the amphibious harbors that were being built for the invasion in the greatest secrecy. And finally, a fifth code name appeared as a solution. The clue was "Britannia and he hold to the same thing." The answer was "Neptune"—most priceless of all the code names of the period, that of the invasion itself.

By this time the security authorities had already begun to look into this strange affair, but despite the most thorough investigation into the backgrounds of the compilers, nothing sinister was found. One of them was

Leonard Sidney Dawe, a schoolmaster living a perfectly respectable life in the small London dormitory town of Leatherhead. The other was his friend Neville Jones, another schoolmaster. Dawe had been the *Telegraph*'s senior crossword puzzle compiler for more than twenty years. He explained that quite often his puzzles were compiled six months ahead of publication; and if this was so, he had created the puzzles before the authorities had created many of the code words. His explanation was accepted and the case was closed. But even twenty-five years later, at a symposium to mark the 25th anniversary of D-Day, George M. Elsey, the president of the American Red Cross and a U.S. naval historian, suggested that there was more to this episode than was ever proven. "Was it really coincidence?" he asked. "Were those rustic British schoolteachers who compiled the puzzles really so naïve and innocent?" The answers to those questions will never be known.

Basic to the security of Neptune was Eisenhower's order that no one in uniform with any knowledge of the invasion be sent on operations where there was the danger of capture. But despite that order, SHAEF security learned, on the morning of May 7, 1944, that Air Commodore Ronald Ivelaw-Chapman had been lost on an RAF bombing raid against an ammunition dump at Le Mans. Since Ivelaw-Chapman held the rank equivalent to a brigadier general in the American air force, SHAEF security asked the Air Ministry to make inquiries about his knowledge of Neptune. The first part of the Air Ministry's report was reassuring; Ivelaw-Chapman was the commander of the bomber base at Elsham Wolds in Lincolnshire, and would therefore have no knowledge of the invasion plans. But the second part of the report caused a storm, for he had been on the Planning Staff at the Air Ministry shortly before going to Elsham Wolds, he had had contact with Morgan at COSSAC, and he was a specialist in paratroop movements. Ivelaw-Chapman might have some knowledge of the paratroop operational plans for Neptune. Moreover, said the Air Ministry, his presence on the raid had *not* been authorized.

Later, Ivelaw-Chapman would protest that his flight over enemy territory that night had been authorized, although he admitted that he was flying as "additional aircrew." Whatever the case, his loss was of major concern at SHAEF. Was he alive or dead? Inquiries among the crews of the fifty Lancasters on the raid disclosed that Ivelaw-Chapman's aircraft —the only one that was shot down—had been intercepted fifteen minutes from Le Mans on the homeward run. A number of the crewmen had been seen bailing out over open country, and it was probable that Ivelaw-Chapman had survived—as indeed he had. He had landed safely and was in the hands of a fragment of "Donkeyman," an F section *réseau* which operated across the Eure and the Orne. There were hidden dangers there, however, for Donkeyman was led by Roger Bardet, a Frenchman turned German agent, apparently without the knowledge of SOE.

A wireless message from Donkeyman brought the first news that Ivelaw-Chapman was alive, and SHAEF decided that every effort must be made to get him out of France. It was for this purpose exactly that the British had formed MI-9, an escape organization with lines that ran all over Europe. SHAEF contacted Lieutenant Colonel Airey Neave, and asked him to exfiltrate the missing air commodore. Neave, a peacetime lawyer who ran a section of MI-9 from the War Office, and who had himself escaped from Colditz Castle near Leipzig in January 1942 and made his way to Switzerland, contacted "Burgundy," the code name of a French agent who had established what came to be called the Burgundy Line which carried escaping Allied soldiers, airmen and agents from Paris to Douarnenez, the small port between Brest and Quimper in Brittany. Could Burgundy locate Ivelaw-Chapman and fly him out? Burgundy agreed to try and, finally, at the very end of May, he succeeded. Ivelaw-Chapman, in civilian clothes, was in hiding with *résistants* about 60 miles from Le Mans, and a Lysander was scheduled to pick him up on the night of June 8/9, 1944. But as Ivelaw-Chapman himself would state, ten hours before the Lysander was due, Gestapo agents raided the house where he was hiding and arrested him. Fortunately, he had managed to elude capture until after the invasion had begun. But curiously, Ivelaw-Chapman would recall that the Gestapo did not interrogate him about Neptune at all; they were interested only in who had given him his French identity papers. Neither did his Luftwaffe interrogation officer at Oberursel near Frankfurt ask him about anything other than the order of battle of Bomber Command. Apparently the Germans were more concerned with routine police and intelligence matters than with Neptune operational plans.

Another worry for SHAEF security authorities concerned the Supreme Commander himself. In 1942, when Eisenhower first arrived in London as C-in-C of ETOUSA, he met and formed a relationship with his driver, Kay Summersby, an Irishwoman in her early thirties who had been a model and film extra before joining the British Auxiliary Territorial Service (ATS) as a private. Mrs. Summersby was divorced from her first husband and had met and was engaged to an American colonel when Eisenhower appeared on the scene. The colonel was later killed in action in Tunisia, where Mrs. Summersby was sent when Eisenhower established his headquarters in Algiers. She became his confidential secretary, chauffeuse, hostess and companion, remaining a member of his "official family" throughout the North African campaigns.

When Eisenhower came to London as Supreme Commander for Neptune and Overlord, Mrs. Summersby followed and, although she was a

British citizen, he arranged that she be given a commission in the American Women's Army Corps. She spent much time at Eisenhower's quarters at Telegraph Lodge, was seen frequently at his side on important social occasions and in due course Eisenhower wrote to Marshall asking his advice about whether he might divorce his wife Mamie and marry Mrs. Summersby. Marshall rejected the proposition angrily, warning Eisenhower that if he persisted it would cost him his career.

Despite official disapproval and embarrassment, Eisenhower did persist in the relationship, and because Churchill especially feared the consequences if it became known to the Germans—particularly Goebbels—that Eisenhower had taken a mistress, the affair was one of the most carefully guarded secrets of the pre-invasion period. It was known to the security authorities, however, and they were concerned on a number of counts. The first was the question of Mrs. Summersby's origins; she had been born Kathleen McCarthy-Morrogh on the island of Inish Beg, off the coast of County Cork; and as an Eiranean she was technically disqualified from any contact with Bigots or with invasion secrets. Yet, as was well known, the senior staff at SHAEF discussed most secret matters quite openly in front of her; and for a time, when Butcher was posted to other duties, she kept the Supreme Commander's secret diary. Her proximity to Allied secrets was even more alarming because she was known to visit, from time to time, the American bar at the Savoy Hotel, a haunt for American foreign correspondents, and she was in the habit of dining occasionally with Frank McGee, the eminent American journalist and, later, television personality. McGee became infatuated with Mrs. Summersby and disapproved of her relationship with Eisenhower. Smith, who knew of the triangle, begged the Supreme Commander to be cautious, and he was.

The situation would have been little short of melodrama had it not been for the stakes involved. One high-ranking American intelligence officer would later remark that there was absolutely no question of Mrs. Summersby's loyalty and discretion. McGee, too, was absolutely dependable. The security authorities saw to that. But SHAEF was haunted, he recalled, by what might happen if Goebbels heard of the affair—or if Eisenhower and Summersby fell out. They did not fall out. Mrs. Summersby remained at Eisenhower's side until July 1945 when he was called back to the United States to embark upon the career that eventually took him to the White House.

Of all the dangers to the security of Neptune in the anxious months before the invasion, one of the most serious came from Churchill himself. Addicted to the telephone, he was forever calling Roosevelt from his private telephone booth, which was covered in blue damask and stood like a sedan chair outside the conference room in the War Bunker at Storey's Gate. While he was always guarded in what he said, and always used code names when discussing plans and operations with the President, much could have been deduced from Churchill's terminology. But he was sure that the connection was secure from eavesdropping. Was the line not "scrambled" by the Bell A-3 device? What Churchill did not know—until Ultra told him—was that the SD was indeed tapping the connection, and had been able to do so since September 1941.

The conversations between the President and the Prime Minister were routed through the American Telephone and Telegraph Company's switchboard at 47 Walker Street, New York, where, in a special locked and guarded room, they were mangled by the A-3 system and rendered incomprehensible, it was thought, to anyone tapping the radiotelephone link. Moreover, the operators handling the calls constantly moved the link from one radio frequency to another, more or less at random. The Germans soon learned that the A-3 existed, however, and found a means not only to unscramble parts of the conversations but also to keep track of the frequency changes. Using the technical and manpower resources of the giant Phillips electrical engineering works at Eindhoven in Holland, they established a large radiotelephone interception and unscrambling station on the Dutch coast near The Hague. From there they listened in to the conversations between the Prime Minister and the President, and for a time the operation was remarkably successful. In one call between Churchill and Roosevelt, the Germans learned for the first time that Italy was secretly negotiating surrender to the western powers. This same call also revealed that Cockade was a trick, thus adding to all the other strikes against that illfated stratagem.

The installation was still operational and effective as late as January 1944 when, as Schellenberg would write, another conversation between Churchill and Roosevelt "disclosed a crescendo of military activity in Britain," which corroborated "the many reports of impending invasion." Other conversations revealed that the western powers' main attack in 1944 would come not through the Balkans, as had been thought possible, but through France. Fortunately for Neptune, the unscrambling operation, and the other intelligence operations with which it was associated, did not permit the Germans to deduce that there would be no operations at all in the Balkans. Nor did they learn where and when in France the Allies would strike. They might well have, but American experiments had demonstrated that the Allies must regard the A-3 as insecure for half the time it was in use, and Ultra intercepts of German diplomatic traffic revealed, upon analysis by British security authorities at Storey's Gate, terminology and facts that could have been extracted only from Churchill's talks with Roosevelt. A new scrambling system was installed and in operation by February 1944; and to make certain that the Germans did not penetrate that system as well, the RAF bombed and destroyed the recovery station near The Hague late that same month. A dangerous tap on Allied communications was successfully closed.

Neptune was not merely a military operation; neither was Overlord just a strategic design. Both were the forces of destiny. Every country in the world had a stake in their outcome, and the governments-in-exile of the Allied nations, as well as the ambassadors and agents of the neutrals, were gathered at London in the months that preceded the invasion clamoring for information. London became, literally, Istanbul-on-Thames, and the ensuing bedlam posed a very serious security problem for Supreme Headquarters. What nation, if any, could be trusted to keep the secrets of Neptune?

In the first place there was the question of how much—or how little— should be told to the representatives of France and Russia. In both cases the answers were complex and dangerous. The Russians were part of the triumvirate that formed the main core of the Grand Alliance. They had undertaken to synchronize the Red Army's main summer offensive with Neptune in order to pin down as many German divisions as possible on the eastern front. Moreover, they were a party to the deceptions of Bodyguard. Yet, as the russophobes in high places in London pointed out, who could say that the Russians themselves would not betray the secrets of D-Day to the Germans? They remembered the ominous conduct of Ivan Maisky, the Russian ambassador in London, over the invasion of North Africa. As the Torch convoys were being prepared in British and American ports, Maisky, who had been told of the operation in the strictest confidence, revealed the operational plan in a conversation with two reporters. Why had he done this? He was not a man who could fail to appreciate the importance of secrecy in military operations. The russophobes—and they dominated the British military hierarchy—thought that Maisky had revealed the plan because Stalin believed that Torch could bring the Red Army no immediate relief in the desperate campaigns of late 1942 and had sought to force the western powers into an early invasion of northern France by making Torch impossible to execute.

If the British were suspicious of Maisky, they had a positive paranoia over his successor, Feodor Tarasovich Gousev, a wooden ex-butcher whom Cadogan had dubbed "Frogface." He had been a high functionary of OGPU, the Soviet secret police, and chief of the Second European Department of the People's Commissariat for Foreign Affairs. As such, the British feared, he had been unhealthily connected with the *Gesellschaft zur Forderung gewerblicher Unternehmungen,* literally the Society for the Furthering of Industrial Enterprises, the cover organization behind which the Russian and German general staffs had worked to create German arms factories and training grounds in Russia, and whose offices the German

General Staff had used to train Russian officers. It was this organization which had also enabled the Germans to perfect the techniques of *Blitzkrieg* warfare. Who could tell whether cooperation still existed between the German and Russian militarists? Who could tell whether Stalin might, if it suited him, reveal the Neptune plans just as he had done with Torch? He might well see an advantage in the failure of the invasion, for it would create a power vacuum throughout western Europe—a vacuum that only the Russians could fill. With these suspicions in the background, the decision was taken; the Russians would be told no more than the target date of the invasion. They would not be told where on the Channel coast the invaders would land. Furthermore, they would be told nothing of the Allied order of battle, and nothing of Fortitude South other than that the Quicksilver army group actually existed.

The French question was equally delicate. The confusion of loyalties among the French both inside and outside France, the conflicts between individual interests and patriotic duty, the power of the conqueror to obtain secrets from the French, the deep national sickness engendered by the calamity of defeat in 1940, the known intention of some members of the French high command to prevent the Allies from making their homeland a battlefield—all combined to compel the Supreme Command to make an incontrovertible decision. It was impossible to know which Frenchmen could really be trusted; therefore none should be trusted. As a result, all American and British officers who were connected with the French forces in Britain and elsewhere were ordered not to consult the French regarding Neptune operations of any kind. It was a decision that would create great bitterness between the French, the British and the Americans in the postwar world.

The variety of exiled kings, queens and princes that were assembled in London at this time posed another serious security problem, not because their own discretion was in question, but because they were usually surrounded by a large entourage of relatives, advisers and attendants, some of whom might well have conflicting loyalties. Like the French, the representatives of all other governments-in-exile at SHAEF were to be kept completely in the dark about Neptune.

The diplomatic representatives of the neutral nations in London presented an even more difficult security problem than exiled royalty. For they, too, moved in the highest circles and their reports to their governments could easily fall into enemy hands—and sometimes did. Further, there were men on embassy staffs and in the foreign offices of neutral governments whose particular business it was to feed information to the Germans. There was only one way to plug these potentially dangerous leaks. Eisenhower, armed with the almost absolute authority of a plenipotentiary, "requested" the complete suspension of all communications from every diplomatic representative in London excepting those of Russia, the United States, and the Dominions. It was a sign of Eisenhower's authority and Churchill's fears about D-Day that the request was granted. All embassies were notified of the suspension and were informed by the Foreign Office that in the unprecedented circumstances created by the military operations impending in the present year—a statement calculated, no doubt, to add to the uncertainty and tension of the pre-invasion period—transmission or receipt of coded telegrams was forbidden. The only exception would be most urgent matters and these were to be presented to the Foreign Office for transmission in British cipher over British systems by British personnel. The British would also be responsible for deciphering and delivering the message, and for handling any reply.

The Foreign Office note also dealt with diplomatic mail. Diplomatic bags—by tradition sacrosanct and inviolable—would be opened, their contents censored, and any material that might bring aid and comfort to an enemy removed. Incoming mail, telephone calls and telegrams would also be liable to delay and even to interception. Moreover, no member of any diplomatic or consular staff or his family would be permitted to leave the country under any circumstances. Each embassy was reminded of the law about entry into the quarantined coastal zones, and some embassies were advised that their officials were not free to travel without the permission of the Foreign Office. Finally, a total ban was placed on the use of all embassy wireless equipment; and to make sure that the ban was obeyed, the Radio Security Service extended its special watch for sounds of clandestine wireless traffic to include the embassies. The Corps Diplomatique at the Court of St. James's was now, for all practical purposes, cut off from the rest of the world. The quarantine was an unprecedented violation of the traditions of international diplomacy, yet no more severe than the restrictions placed on all military personnel and the entire civilian population of the island.

The wisdom of the decision to hobble foreign diplomats for the period of the invasion was soon made evident by a major security alarm that involved a member of that corps. On April 21, 1944, "Lord Haw-Haw," the renegade Anglo-American William Joyce, who was employed as a commentator by Berlin radio, said in a broadcast:

> We know exactly what you intend to do with those concrete units. *You* think you are going to sink them on our coasts in the assault. Well, we are going to help you boys. We'll save you the trouble. When you come to get underway, we're going to sink them for you.

No broadcast during the build-up for Neptune caused greater consternation and fear, for Joyce was clearly referring to the Mulberry harbors, one of the most carefully guarded Allied secrets.

There were two Mulberries, each of which cost some £20 millions ($96 million) to build, consumed some 2 million tons of concrete and steel, and had occupied a work force of 20,000 men for eight months. To move them at the time of the invasion would require the services of every available tug in Britain and on the eastern seaboard of the United States; a fleet of 74 merchantmen was needed to build and service them; to run them required a work force of 11,000 men; and each, floating up and down with the tide, had a capacity to handle 12,000 tons of equipment every day— the capacity of Dover or Port Elizabeth at that time. But their gigantic size and cost apart, their existence was being kept an especial secret since they were the lynchpin of the Neptune strategy.

The Germans were convinced that the Allies would land near a major port at the outset of an invasion, and then attempt to seize that port to supply the invasion forces. The Allies, on the contrary, intended to land in a part of Normandy that was without major port facilities, using the Mulberries, which were to be anchored off the invasion beaches, to supply their forces. Such a strategy had a number of advantages. The Allies would not have to undertake a frontal assault on one of the heavily fortified French Channel ports—an extremely hazardous venture, as the disaster at Dieppe had proved—the area of Normandy to be attacked was relatively lightly garrisoned, and the location of the assault would in itself contribute to Neptune's surprise. The danger of the plan was that if the Germans learned of the existence of the Mulberries, they might conclude the truth of Allied strategy. Joyce's broadcast seemed to indicate that the Germans had indeed discovered the secret of the Mulberries; and Admiral Edward Ellsberg, who was involved in the Mulberry project, would recall that the effect of the broadcast was extremely demoralizing. The men who were at work at Selsey Bill, the point off the Sussex coast where parts of the Mulberries were being assembled, became very apprehensive. Even Eisenhower himself was concerned, and acting to avoid panic, he telegraphed Washington for fifty Coast Guard picket boats to be used to rescue the crews if the Mulberries were destroyed. "Goebbels had done a first-class job on us," Ellsberg would write.

Had the Germans really learned about the Mulberries? The Supreme Command looked to Ultra for the answer. Baron Oshima had made another tour of the Atlantic Wall and had been very fully briefed by Rundstedt on what the Germans expected the Allies to do. During the briefing, Rundstedt had referred to the existence of the very large structures off Selsey Bill, but stated that he had information that they were anti-aircraft gun towers. It was this information that Oshima telegraphed to Tokyo; and when it was intercepted and decrypted, the sense of relief at SHAEF was intense. Moreover, despite Joyce's remark, there had been no changes in

German dispositions along the Channel coast traceable to knowledge of the Mulberries.

The scare died, but not before questions were asked about how the Germans had learned the structures were at Selsey Bill in the first place. It was thought possible that the man at least indirectly responsible had been Count Oxenstjerna, the Swedish naval attaché in London and the same man whose reports to his government were being shown to Karl-Heinz Kraemer, the Abwehr agent in Stockholm. The Allied secret agencies had been aware of the link between Oxenstjerna and Kraemer for some time, and while his reports were carefully monitored, he was allowed to remain at his post. But finally, early in April, he had been asked to leave the country; the Admiralty "did not quite like Oxenstierna's avid interest in the Royal Navy and the aggressive manner in which he went after sensitive information." He returned to Stockholm, unaware of why he had been expelled, and there perhaps made some mention of the structures at Selsey Bill. In that event, the information would have found its way to the Abwehr, which had thoroughly penetrated the military administration of Sweden. Whatever the Abwehr's source, the information was incorrect; and it was noticed with satisfaction that, with Oxenstjerna's recall, Kraemer's naval reports suddenly dried up.

Allied measures to protect the secrets of D-Day were not confined to England; they extended to every country of Europe and every corner of the globe where Axis agents might be at work to penetrate the screen of security that protected Neptune. Nowhere were these agents harder at work than in the neutral nations; but by the spring of 1944, the British and the Americans had trained a powerful battery of diplomatic and economic weapons on Stockholm and Madrid, in particular. Slow to respond at first, Sweden and Spain would soon find themselves bested in the battle of the chancelleries. Yielding to the formal pressure of diplomatic "grand remonstrances" and the more compelling threat of economic reprisals, they gradually began to withdraw the favors granted to the Axis governments. The ban on all diplomatic communication to and from their representatives in Britain further served to blind the Axis; but one major watchtower remained uncomfortably close to Neptune—the German and Japanese diplomatic, military and intelligence missions in Dublin.

It seemed harsh and ludicrous to level the big guns of Allied diplomatic and economic warfare on the poor, rural republic of Eire. Moreover, America had strong sentimental ties with the Irish; and Ireland, in spite of her neutrality, had permitted 165,000 of her men to leave the country and serve in the British armed forces. Several of Britain's best generals—Montgomery included—were Irish or Orangemen; and the Irish had behaved with gallantry and distinction in the Allied cause. They had won no fewer than seven Victoria Crosses and many scores of other high awards. Yet both England and America were determined to neutralize German efforts based in Dublin to discover the secrets of Neptune.

When the United States entered the Second World War, the western powers had hoped that, seven hundred years of Anglo-Irish bickering notwithstanding, the Irish Free State would abandon her position of strict neutrality and join the Grand Alliance. It was a lost cause; the Irish President, Eamon de Valera, rejected the suggestion. Irish-American relations remained correct but cool; Roosevelt, however, was particularly embittered and disillusioned by the refusal of de Valera to permit American aircraft and warships to be stationed on the west coast of Eire. Had this been possible, Anglo-American losses in the Battle of the Atlantic might have been much less severe, and the battle itself won much sooner.

Then an incident occurred that aggravated the tensions between the two countries. In April 1943 an aircraft carrying General Walter Bedell Smith crash-landed near Athenry, about 15 miles inland from Galway Bay. It had developed engine trouble and, finding an emergency airstrip near Oranmore blocked with obstacles, put down on the grounds of an agricultural school. Nobody was hurt, but Smith, his staff and his crew were quickly surrounded by courteous yet firm officers of the Irish army and held at a nearby hotel while the situation was sorted out with Irish army headquarters and the Foreign Ministry. For a time it seemed that Smith might be interned, just as the Irish had interned other combatants of the warring powers who had arrived in neutral Eire. In the event, strong diplomatic representation by the American minister at Dublin, David Gray, brought results, and Smith was taken to Belfast, British territory, to continue his journey to Washington from there.

In the early months of 1944, relations between the Allies and the Irish were jolted even more sharply when both the OSS and MI-6 reported that "a great deal of information pertaining to Allied activities in England and Ulster comes from the German embassy in Dublin. This Legation, which is heavily staffed, has succeeded in infiltrating agents into England. . . . The Germans attribute great importance (to information) obtained from Irish sources." The Irish question, which had been permitted to smolder, now blazed; and when it was learned that the Irish government had arrested two SD agents with wireless transceivers in Galway just after they had landed by parachute, Roosevelt decided the time had come to act. On February 21, 1944, after consultations with the British government, Gray presented a peremptory note to de Valera. Commenting, threateningly, that Irish neutrality "continues to operate in favor of the Axis powers and against the United Nations on whom your security and the maintenance of your national economy depend," the note demanded that the Irish close the German and Japanese missions in Dublin, seize their wireless equipment, imprison all Axis agents, and sever all relations with Berlin and Tokyo.

The chief cause of American concern was the suspicion that Axis agents were spying on the U.S. 15th Corps, which was stationed in Ulster and would soon join Patton's 3rd Army in Britain. That kind of information would have been very useful to the Germans, and very damaging to the Allies. Perhaps for that reason, Gray, finally exasperated by the Irish attitude, telegraphed the State Department to recommend that, unless de Valera quickly complied with the terms of the note, U.S. forces in Ulster should cross the frontier, arrest the Axis diplomats and close down their missions by force. It was an extraordinary recommendation to make, and one that might have involved the United States in guerrilla warfare with the IRA and, perhaps, the Irish army. News of this telegram evidently reached the Irish military authorities for, almost immediately afterwards, the army was put on a state of alert, all leave was canceled, all bridges between Eire and Ulster were mined, and all frontier posts and strategic positions manned. Whether or not Gray's recommendation was considered seriously, Irish-American relations had never been worse.

De Valera replied to Gray's note, in somewhat leisurely fashion, on March 7. Remarking on the rumors sweeping Dublin of an imminent American invasion, he reminded Roosevelt, first of all, that Eire had been assured in 1942 that the United States had no intention of violating her neutrality. He then expressed surprise at the terms of the note and assured the American government of "the uniformly friendly character of Irish neutrality in relation to the United States." But he concluded:

> The Irish government are, therefore, safeguarding, and will continue to safeguard, the interests of the United States but they must in all circumstances protect the neutrality of the Irish state and the democratic way of life of the Irish people. Their attitude will continue to be determined not by fear of any measures which would be employed against them but by goodwill and the fundamental friendship existing between the two peoples.

In short, de Valera called Roosevelt's bluff, confident that any military move against Eire would cause bad blood in the large Irish-American electorate in the United States. Indeed, when news of the American ultimatum was published, it had raised a storm of protest, and de Valera knew that Roosevelt could not back up his demands with force. The wily Irish President had won the round, although Irish Special Branch men did raid the German and Japanese missions in Dublin and seize their wireless equipment.

The United States, which had undoubtedly undertaken the negotiations because of the centuries-old enmity between Britain and Ireland, was forced to stand down. But the stakes were high, and Britain and Churchill took up where America and Roosevelt left off. On March 14, 1944, Churchill announced a policy in the Commons "designed to isolate Great Britain from southern Ireland" and also "to isolate southern Ireland from the outside world during the critical period of the war that is now approaching." He added that he much regretted, in view of the large numbers of Irishmen fighting in the British armed forces, that it was necessary to take these measures. Nevertheless, from now until further notice all Eire's ships and aircraft would be prevented from leaving her coasts for foreign ports, the telephone and air services would be cut between England and Eire, and the menace of economic sanctions would be maintained. The German and Japanese diplomats would therefore be unable to leave the country or to communicate with the outside world. These measures were immediately put into effect, and with that, Germany's western window on Neptune was shut.

Allied planners readily acknowledged that an operation the size of Neptune could not possibly be undertaken without extensive dress rehearsals. Accordingly, as the winter's storms gave way to the spring's zephyrs in the Channel, Allied forces began a series of triphibious exercises to acquaint themselves with the difficulties and dangers of combined attacks on a hostile shore. But as these exercises grew in magnitude, worries concerning the security of Neptune's secrets grew apace. Might not the enemy be able to deduce from the volume of wireless traffic and the troop movements involved in these exercises just when the invasion would take place? And since most of the activity was centered in southern and southwestern England, might he not also deduce that the assault would be launched from those areas and that the most probable target would be Normandy? Because both were very serious risks, it became necessary for the LCS and the CSM to launch a stratagem to disguise the truth of the exercises. Brutus, Tricycle and Garbo were all instructed to inform their German controllers that the full dress rehearsal for Neptune, an operation codenamed "Fabius" after the Roman general of the Second Punic War who foiled Hannibal by dilatory tactics and avoidance of direct engagements, was not the last but the first of many exercises that would be needed before Neptune could be launched around July 20, 1944. To support that *ruse de guerre,* Churchill, at Eisenhower's request, made deceptive references to "many false alarms, many feints and many dress rehearsals" in a fifty-minute review of the state of the war on March 26, 1944. His remarks were also designed to disguise the truth of the exercises from the members of the French resistance, who, if they mistook the nature of these very large and provocative operations, might rise up prematurely and be decimated. But the crisis, when it occurred, came from an unexpected quarter.

Although Allied air and naval superiority had all but immobilized the Kriegsmarine, there was one branch of the German navy that was far from inert: E-boat squadrons, the very fast torpedo boats which marauded Channel waters. E-boat squadrons were fully alert to the prospect of fat pickings along the English coast, and the nature of their forays suggested that they might be getting some good intelligence from somewhere—possibly wireless intelligence. In any case, nine E-boats sailed from Cherbourg on the night of April 27, 1944, not to maraud but with a specific objective: a convoy off Portland Bill, the easternmost extremity of Lyme Bay. Instead they intercepted Exercise "Tiger," an American dress rehearsal for the Utah assault, en route from Plymouth to Slapton Sands. What happened that night may have been purely coincidental, but even so, the curtain of deception and secrecy surrounding Neptune was seriously rent.

Slapton Sands in south Devon, a long, wide and sandy beach beneath low hills, had been chosen for Tiger because the topography resembled that of Utah beach in Normandy; and it was just after midnight on April 28 when eight 5000-ton LST's edged into Lyme Bay in Indian file. The sea was smooth, the night clear but dark, the ships blacked out and almost invisible against a quarter moon that was low and setting. As the ships approached a point 11 miles offshore, the Tiger force—the U.S. 4th Infantry Division and the 1st Amphibian Engineer Brigade—prepared for "H-Hour," that time when the troops would clamber into the assault boats for the long run in to the beach, when the Sherman amphibious tanks would rumble into the sea through the bow doors and the engineers begin to blast passages for them through the maze of obstacles, wire and mines strung along the beach.

Aboard the command ship, Commander Ben Skahill and the deputy commanding general of the assault force, General Theodore Roosevelt, were uneasy. They were in dangerous waters, they had only one escort, the British corvette *Azalea,* and both the troops and the LST's were—it was thought then—irreplaceable. Furthermore, the troops and LST's were about to rehearse for the first time the tactics they would use on D-Day. As Lieutenant Colonel Ralph Ingersoll, deputy chief of the Special Plans Branch, the deception organization at Bradley's headquarters, would explain:

> The exercise concerned was the first which involved a full rehearsal of the actual assault formation that would be employed [in Neptune]. It was complete with such secret weapons as rocket boats and (amphibious) tanks. In Africa and Sicily, and at Salerno, the engineers and infantry had had to go ashore first to make it practical and relatively safe to bring in

the armor. But in Normandy we were about to try reversing the process, sending in the armor first, self-floated.

Hence the need for a full-scale rehearsal—and the strictest secrecy.

As H-Hour approached, all crews were at General Quarters, and between decks the infantry, the engineers and the tank crews were at their assault stations, waiting for the hooter to announce the start of the exercise. Then it happened. Tracer fire was suddenly directed toward LST 507 from the port quarter, and a moment later a torpedo hit the ship. The main engines stopped, the ship began to burn as fire leaped from one fuel tank to another; then it exploded. In that moment, 94 of the 165 sailors and 151 of the 282 soldiers aboard were killed or thrown into the water and drowned. The men aboard LST 531 saw LST 507 blow up, and then their ship, too, was struck by a torpedo. It caught fire from end to end, exploded, rolled over and sank. Only 28 of the 142 sailors and 44 of the 354 soldiers aboard were saved.

Astern, aboard LST 289, Lieutenant Harry J. Mettler watched the fires directly down the path of the moonlight, but he could see no targets—only flames. Were they being attacked by E-boats or a submarine? Nobody knew and before it was possible to call the convoy commander on the radiotelephone, a torpedo was sighted coming directly toward the ship. Mettler shouted to the crew of the 40-mm cannon in the stern to try to destroy the torpedo with gunfire. Then he ordered full right rudder as the gun opened up and, for a moment, he thought he had eluded the 20-knot projectile. But the torpedo was a new type that homed onto the noise of the screws; like a shark chasing a mackerel it closed in and hit the ship in the stern. The explosion blasted the cannon and its crew over the boat davits, the stern deck plating rolled up, the screws began to race, the engines stopped, fire broke out. Mettler, displaying marvelous presence of mind, lowered five of the assault boats and they took the ship in tow. But four men were dead, eight were missing, and twenty-two were wounded or burned.

The Tiger assault force quickly called for protection, the exercise was canceled and the surviving LST's scuttled safely back to Plymouth. A major disaster had occurred. In less than ten or fifteen minutes 630 men had been killed or drowned; another 8 would die in hospital from wounds, and many more were burned or wounded. Two LST's had been sunk and a third had been crippled (leaving Neptune without a single reserve LST), a brigade of amphibious tanks had been lost, and incalculable damage had been done to the morale of the men.

When the news reached Supreme Headquarters, Eisenhower forbade any public announcement to guard the secrecy of the exercise and prevent even graver damage to the morale of the Neptune assault forces. Then it was learned that one of the German E-boats, after attacking the LST's, had turned and scanned the water with a searchlight, while others had cruised through the survivors before the entire squadron sped away under the cover of smoke and darkness. The loss of men and LST's was serious enough; but the report of searchlight activity caused profound fears at Supreme Headquarters. What had the Germans been looking for? Had they picked up any prisoners? And if so, who were they? There were Bigots aboard the LST's, and it was feared that the Germans had captured one of them and would make him talk. Never before had the security of Neptune been in such grave jeopardy.

General Betts, deputy chief of intelligence at SHAEF, and Colonel Gordon Sheen, chief of the SHAEF security branch, went among the oil-soaked survivors at dawn with a list of the Bigots who had taken part in the exercise. One by one they were all accounted for, but there were still a large number of missing men who had *some* knowledge of Neptune's secrets. What had become of them? For they, too, knew enough to be able to compromise at least part of the Allied strategy—the tactics to be employed, for example.

Betts ordered that every man who was missing must be found, every corpse must be recovered and his identity checked. Divers and frogmen swam down to the wrecks, entered the compartments, wriggled between the sunken tanks, and brought up the identity discs of the corpses they found. It would have been impossible to account for every man; the tide would have taken some corpses. But most were found, and at an Admiralty inquiry into the disaster, it was thought impossible that the Germans had captured any prisoners—a claim that was disputed by the men of the Tiger force who were still angry at the lack of escort protection for the exercise.

Had the Germans taken any prisoners? Even if they had not, what had they been able to deduce about Allied strategy and tactics from the location of the Tiger exercise and the composition of the assault force? No one knew. At Montgomery's headquarters, according to Ingersoll: "There was a whole day . . . when it was seriously contemplated trying to alter the operation [Neptune] because of the knowledge which the enemy must now be presumed to have—the detailed knowledge of almost everything we planned."

Other sources of intelligence, including Ultra, were checked in an attempt to discover if the Germans were making the sort of changes in their dispositions that might be expected if they had new information about Neptune; and to the consternation of Supreme Headquarters, apparently they were. For it was only a week after the Tiger calamity that Hitler issued his command instruction to watch Normandy. In obedience to that command, the Germans began almost to double the anti-tank and anti-aircraft defenses of Normandy, the Cherbourg peninsula and Brittany, and two new divisions especially trained to combat paratroopers were ordered to precisely the area where American airborne divisions would land on D-Day. Why had Hitler suddenly focused his attention on Normandy? Was he merely taking all possible precautions, or was Neptune's destination no longer a secret?

As the invasion neared, SHAEF anxiously examined the possible reasons for the new German movements. Artist's fate remained a major concern, or perhaps the Germans had captured American soldiers in the assault rehearsal at Slapton Sands. It was also possible that not all the German agents in England had been apprehended, or, the most frightening prospect, that some German cryptanalytical feat comparable to Ultra was laying bare the reality of Allied plans. Not until after the war was over would the Allies learn what had been behind that sudden flurry of German movement only weeks before D-Day. The reason was traced, once more, to the German wireless intelligence service, the one arm of the Reich's intelligence-gathering system that the Allies had not been able to cripple.

The German wireless intelligence and cryptanalytical service—the Funkabwehr—had been responsible for a remarkable series of triumphs throughout the war. It would claim total penetration of French codes and ciphers, including machine ciphers; and it had consistently broken into every Russian cryptosystem from the highest commands down to battalions. As for the United States, a high officer of the Funkabwehr would later claim that German wireless intelligence had had no difficulty in penetrating American radio communications because of extremely poor security. The same was not true of the British; they had learned their lesson in North Africa. The Funkabwehr official would state that British radio communications were the most effective and secure of all those with which German wireless intelligence had to contend, adding that the higher-echelon cryptosystems of the British were never compromised during the Second World War. But while the Germans had not been able to penetrate the systems, they were quite successful in analyzing the characteristic patterns of British wireless traffic—particularly the traffic of the RAF signals service. The Funkabwehr official would state that the RAF was not aware that it was responsible for revealing many carefully guarded plans of the British army and thus for many losses and casualties; and he would add that the only possible explanation was interservice jealousy, which led the RAF to overestimate the quality and security of its wireless communications and to refuse to let them be subject to the supervision of the army.

During the build-up for the invasion in England, the lid of security was clamped down even tighter on both British and American wireless units, and a crisis enveloped the entire German wireless intelligence system. Once again, it was forced to rely on an analysis of the distinctive patterns of Anglo-American wireless transmissions, and upon an occasional leak, like the one that had revealed the presence in England of the American 82nd

Airborne Division. With this kind of surveillance, the Germans were able to piece together only a very vague picture of the structure, location and strength of the Anglo-American armies confronting them, a picture that was further obscured by the false wireless traffic that filled the ether. But then, in late April, they made a simple discovery that threw a blinding light upon some of the Allies' secrets. After an intensive study of the wireless traffic of both British and American divisions, Funkabwehr analysts realized that when they heard the distinctive traffic indicating that an air liaison official had been assigned to a division to provide a link between ground and air forces, it could be assumed, first, that it was an assault division and, second, that it was preparing for offensive operations. In a relatively short period of time, the Funkabwehr heard all the divisions in southern and southwestern England broadcasting air liaison traffic, and they deduced, with considerable accuracy, that the invasion was imminent and that the axis of the attack would be in the direction of Portsmouth/Plymouth and Le Havre/Cherbourg.

That was what happened late in April and early in May. The problem then, as the Funkabwehr officer would state, was to convince Hitler that the intelligence was accurate. Hitler tended to distrust wireless intelligence as a source of information on military planning; but on this occasion, to the surprise of the Funkabwehr, he believed it. Realizing that Normandy was indeed vulnerable to attack, he ordered the reinforcements that had been noted with such concern at SHAEF. He did nothing, however, to weaken the garrisons defending the rest of the Channel coast; he was, as SHAEF hoped in its most optimistic appraisal of the reasons for the reinforcements, merely taking all possible precautions.

Unknown to SHAEF, however, the Germans had obtained a significant hint of Neptune's destination through their ingenious penetration of the wireless communications of Allied assault forces. And they had acted upon it. Also unknown to SHAEF, they had discovered an even more dangerous clue through their penetration of wireless communications of a different sort. Generals and even prime ministers might be hushed up, whole governments might be intimidated into silence, but the security of the wireless traffic between SOE and its agents in France was extremely difficult to monitor and maintain. The Germans had been quick to spot this chink in Allied armor, and while SHAEF worried about loose talk and missing Bigots, a security leak that might endanger the success of Neptune had already occurred.

The Wireless Game

THE LYSANDER PILOT picked up his landmark in the moonlight—the castle of Angers with its moats and seventeen round towers—and looked out for the silvered water at the point where the Loire joins the Sarthe. He circled the area, saw the A light flashing from the meadows below, came down to 300 feet, taking care to see that the speed of his high-winged monoplane did not drop off too much, and then put his spatted wheels down onto the meadow grass. He stopped, taxied back toward the A light and dropped the aircraft's ladder, keeping his motor turning. Three women agents of SOE—Noor Inayat Khan, Cecily Lefort and Diana Rowden—stepped out into the night to be received by Henri Dericourt. Then, having taken the secret mail aboard, the pilot pulled out his boost control override and climbed rapidly away. It was a routine mission; but it was also a mission that would have mysterious and even sinister implications. For all three women were doomed to be captured and executed by the SD; and it was later alleged that they had lost their lives through an intricate weapon of war called the wireless game.

The wireless game was quite as old as wireless itself. In its simplest form, it consisted merely of preempting one of the enemy's channels of communication, a channel that he trusted as a reliable source of intelligence, and using it to transmit false and misleading information. XX-Committee operations were a prime example of this form of the game. With the capture of an enemy agent and his wireless set, ciphers, schedules and other paraphernalia, the transmission of deceptive information could begin—with or without the cooperation of the agent—and could continue as long as the Germans did not suspect that the agent or his set were under British control.

The wireless game was not, however, a British monopoly. The Germans, who called it *Englandspiele* or *Funkspiele* (wireless game), played it, too. SOE agents and wireless posts on the continent frequently fell into

German hands, and with the captured sets and ciphers the Germans maintained communication with London, usually in the hope that they would receive instructions that would reveal something of Allied military intentions, as well as information about agents and *réseaux* that had not yet been detected, and about the time and place of the arrival of new agents and drops of stores and money.

The success or failure of these games as they were played by both sides almost always hung upon whether the players learned the system of security checks on the set they were manipulating. The British, extremely wary of wireless deception, sent their agents into the field with a "bluff" check and a "true" check, both of which usually consisted, with many variations, of an arrangement to misspell words at certain places. The assumption was that if an agent was captured and forced to reveal his "bluff" check, the absence of his "true" check in any transmission would still alert his controller that he was operating under duress. The Germans soon learned of this system, however, and once they had captured an agent, they did not stop at torture to learn his checks. But even if they did so, it was sometimes possible to tell that a set was under enemy control by the operator's "fist"—his style of transmission. Each agent had certain characteristics of transmission that were familiar to his controller, and any significant variation in the way a message was sent could warn a controller that an agent was being manipulated or impersonated.

Thus a wireless game was extremely difficult to establish and sustain even in its simplest form. But the game was capable of an additional refinement that was even more risky, yet presented an excellent opportunity to counter deception with deception. If, as often happened, the British learned that one of their wireless posts was under enemy control, they could, if they wished, continue transmission, and in so doing send instructions and information that would deceive and mislead the Germans. But the key to the success of this double game was normality; the British could in no way reveal that they knew the post was in enemy hands. They had to continue to respond to inquiries and requests from the controlled post just as they would normally, including sending in arms, ammunition, stores and money that would inevitably be captured by the Germans.

There was, however, a much more sinister aspect to sustaining this form of wireless deception. Part of the normal operation of a wireless post was to arrange for the reception of incoming agents; and if the British stopped sending agents into certain posts, the Germans would naturally suspect that they had discovered the post had been captured, and the game would collapse. On the other hand, if the British continued to send in agents to posts they knew to be in enemy hands, the agents would most probably be caught and executed. A wireless game may have been worth the loss of money and military supplies, but was it worth the sacrifice of Allied agents and sympathizers?

Such men and women could also be involved in yet another refinement to the game—the cipher trick. The object of this *ruse de guerre* was to send operators into the field with ciphers that the British knew the Germans would be able to decrypt. By establishing this kind of wireless leak, deceptive instructions and information could be passed to the agent and thence to the enemy. But again, to sustain their credibility, traffic with the agent involved must appear to be normal—and normality presupposed sending in not only arms, ammunition, explosives and money, but also other agents. And the agent using the cipher would sooner or later be detected, arrested —and almost certainly killed.

After the war, the British were accused by both the French and the Dutch of deliberately ignoring the security checks and other warnings that would indicate a wireless post was under control and then sending in agents—some seventy of them—to receptions they knew would be German, all for the purpose of maintaining a channel of communication down which, at some stage, it might be possible to pass deceptive information. The British were also accused of using women agents to play cipher tricks. Aware that the Germans might be suspicious if they were able to read too easily an exchange of ciphered signals between London and a male agent, the British—so the allegation went—used women agents for this purpose on the grounds that the Germans believed that no Englishman would be so ungallant as to involve a woman in such a maneuver.

These were ugly charges which were, of course, denied. But had the British, in their determined pursuit of surprise on D-Day, once again made a "nice assessment of profit and loss"—the lives of a few agents against the lives of hundreds if not thousands of Allied soldiers on the Norman shore? It was undeniably true that, after the collapse of the Prosper empire, SOE did not immediately shut down a number of wireless posts that had been connected with Prosper and had then fallen into German hands. As a result, large consignments of money, arms and war stores would be dropped to the Germans, not the French; and a number of F section agents would be met by German, not French, reception committees. Were the British unaware that these posts had been captured, or were they playing wireless games as a part of Fortitude's attempts to mislead the Germans about the time and place of the invasion? If the former were true, they could be accused only of making a monumentally tragic blunder; if the latter, they were guilty of trading human life for tactical advantage on D-Day. But if this was, in fact, a sacrifice the British were willing to make, what did they hope to gain by it?

The allegation that the British sacrificed their own agents in wireless games and cipher tricks centered mainly on the tragic case of a young woman called "Madeleine." Her real name was Noor Inayat Khan; Noor was her first name, Inayat her surname, and Khan denoted her high birth, for she was an Indian princess. Her father was Inayat Khan, the leader of the Sufi sect of Mohammedan mystics, and the family was a direct descendant of Tipu Sultan, the eighteenth-century Sultan of Mysore and the last Muslim ruler of southern India, a warrior and intriguer who, in the service of Napoleon, gave Arthur Wellesley much trouble. Inayat Khan and his wife, the Begum, had come to Europe to found Sufi "Lodges of Blessing," his mysticism intrigued Rasputin, and they were invited to the Kremlin. There, on New Year's Day 1914, Princess Noor was born, but riots soon forced the family to flee the Russian capital. After many adventures, they settled in Paris where the "Light of Womanhood"—which was what Noor's name meant—went to school, finished at the École Normale de Musique, and, shortly before the outbreak of the Second World War, was earning her living as a writer of children's stories for Paris radio.

Just before the fall of France, Noor came to England with her brother, Vilayat. She enlisted in the Women's Auxiliary Air Force as 424598 Aircraftwoman 2nd Class Norah Baker, and was trained as a wireless operator. Then, while awaiting a posting, she saw orders inviting personnel who could speak French and work wireless to volunteer for "special duties." This she did, and found herself in a dingy room at the War Office being interviewed by SOE for what was called "secret work." She was accepted for training and was enrolled as a "nurse" in the First Aid Nursing Yeomanry—the customary form of cover for female agents sent by SOE to the field. This, Gubbins thought, might induce the Germans to behave more tolerably toward them if they were caught. She was also given a temporary commission as a flying officer in the WAAF—again, to improve her chances if she was caught.

It was now that one of the first mysteries that surrounded Princess Noor began to emerge: why was she accepted by SOF at all? For she was, one of her training officers reported: "A splendid, vague, dreamy creature, far too conspicuous—twice seen, never forgotten." Her appearance, her accent, her bearing, all were such as to attract attention, which an SOE agent was not supposed to do. Shy, of slight build, with dark eyes set in a thin olive face surrounded by long dark hair, Noor was a gentle, graceful and charming young woman. But although in character she was said to be as "strong and flexible as a rapier-blade," her head tutor in clandestinity, Colonel F. V. Spooner, reported adversely on her because he considered her "too emotional and impulsive to be suitable for employment as a secret agent." Spooner later said that he had "really stuck his neck out and gone to considerable lengths in his endeavours to prevent (Noor) from being sent to France as an agent. Not only was she too sensitive and easily hurt, but her inexperience . . . rendered her too vulnerable from a security point of view." Further, a tutor at Beaulieu in the New Forest—where she underwent part of her tuition in clandestinity—said she had *"no* sense of security," and wrote on her training reports: "She has an unstable and temperamental personality and it is very doubtful whether she is really suited to work in the field."

In spite of these and other unfavorable comments, Noor was deemed acceptable for service; Starkey was approaching and F section was very short of wireless operators. Buckmaster wrote the single word "nonsense" on her adverse reports (he said later he was convinced of Noor's ability to withstand the dangers of the field), and she was assigned the post of wireless operator to Émile-Henri Garry, the chief of "Cinema," a *réseau* on Prosper territory near Le Mans. She and two other women agents landed in France on the night of June 16/17, 1943, and it was alleged that, with the help of Dericourt, her arrival was witnessed by the SD, whose agents were hiding behind the hedges of wild roses on the edge of the field. But, if so, the Germans did nothing except watch, for the three women made their way to Angers Station, where they split up and Noor boarded a train for Paris.

Although she succeeded in getting through the German *Feldgendarmerie* controls at the station, Noor was, it was obvious, quite lost when she arrived, late on June 17, at the home of her organizer, Garry, at 40 rue Erlanger in Auteuil, a wealthy district of Paris. She confessed that she had not eaten anything since leaving England because she did not know how to use her French ration book or restaurant food coupons. Moreover, Garry had received no instructions from London that she was coming—a dangerous omission, for lesser men then Garry would have treated her as a Gestapo penetration agent. But touchingly, Noor presented Garry and his fiancée with a bunch of carnations. Both were appalled that she had been sent on such a mission.

Nevertheless, Noor was accepted by the Prosper network and taken to its operational headquarters, the École Nationale d'Agriculture, near Versailles, the next day. She was given temporary lodgings in the home of one of Prosper's lieutenants, Professor Alfred Balachowsky, but her habits immediately betrayed her British background; her hostess noted that she put the milk in the cup before the tea, when the reverse was the custom in France—a small matter but one that would attract the sharp eyes of the SD. Then she dyed her hair blonde, which instantly called attention to her coloring; and it was soon necessary for Balachowsky to scold her for leaving her cipher on the hall tallboy.

Within a week, Noor had settled into lodgings on the edge of the Bois de Boulogne; and there again, her hostess, who was a Prosper sub-agent, had to scold her for leaving her cipher open at the day's grid. She then established a wireless post in an apartment at the rue de la Faisanderie, not far—certainly not far enough—from SD headquarters on the Avenue Foch. But for all her carelessness, she was not afraid; or rather, she was in control of her fear. She was said to have obtained the assistance of her next-door neighbor, a German, in putting up her aerial; she explained that it was a clothes line.

Noor arrived in Paris at a dangerous time. The Prosper network had begun to collapse, and she was forced to find new lodgings. But she did keep her wireless post in the rue de la Faisanderie; and through Garry, she learned of the arrests of Prosper and his lieutenants, and reported the *ratissage* to London. London responded by telling her to lie low. This she did for a week or so; but then her inexperience and carelessness showed themselves again. Wearing a navy blue scarf wrapped around her head like a turban, which emphasized her Indian features, she went on a sentimental journey to her home of the 1930's, visiting school friends on the way. Bodington of F Section, who flew to Paris to investigate the extent of the Prosper disaster, saw her briefly during this period—August 1943—and heard enough from Garry to recommend to London that she be brought home. She should have gone out on the night of August 15, 1943, when Dericourt was to handle two Lysanders to evacuate Bodington, Scientist, and some survivors of the Prosper collapse. But although everyone else went, Noor remained behind; she refused to obey her order to leave until a replacement operator had arrived.

Almost incredibly, Noor survived in Paris for another two months, although the SD knew of her existence, for in the secret *courrier* that Dericourt was regularly showing to H. J. Kieffer (the chief of the SD's counterespionage service in Paris) were letters from Noor to friends and relatives in England. But her whereabouts were unknown until Renée Garry, the sister of the Cinema organizer, sold her address to the SD for 100,000 francs (£500 or $2400). Noor was arrested in her Paris apartment on or about October 13, and within minutes found herself at Gestapo headquarters. It was another grave loss for F section, for she was the last F section wireless operator in the Paris area.

Princess Noor was calm when taken and calm when interrogated. Her SD inquisitor, Kieffer, came to admire her and spared her much. He soon lost patience with her, however, for she made not one but two escape bids while at SD headquarters on the Avenue Foch. Both times she got only as far as the street before she was recaptured; but she was becoming a nuisance, and so she soon found herself at Badenweiler concentration camp where she spent many months, most of them in chains and solitary confinement.

Noor was made of sterner stuff than her SOE instructors had realized, but she had, once again, been careless. For when she was arrested, her wireless, her ciphers and all of her back traffic with London were also seized—everything, in fact, that Josef Goetz, the SD's wireless expert, needed to play a convincing *Funkspiele* with London. Noor had recorded all her back traffic in a child's exercise book, which the SD found on her bedside table. And with this invaluable background information, Goetz, impersonating Noor, reopened the Cinema circuit and began transmissions to London. London responded, but cautiously, for her messages did not ring quite true. Goetz needed Noor's help to ensure the success of his game, but she consistently refused to give it and the game was played without her.

At Christmas, the British were still suspicious; the style of "Noor's" transmissions suggested that she was being impersonated. But Goetz pressed the game forward; he signaled London that Cinema was ready to receive an arms drop. London replied that it would send in twelve containers at a given time and place, but in the event, only one container was dropped, which led Goetz to believe that "London had twigged." Buckmaster was, indeed, nervous; he went to see France Antelme, SOE's senior French adviser, and showed him all of "Noor's" transmissions. Antelme said that on balance he thought that she was free, and by the end of the year Buckmaster was inclined to agree, even though Noor's London controller was certain that she was being impersonated. Nevertheless, F section sent in 500,000 francs to the false Cinema. Goetz was definitely encouraged. He asked for more arms and London responded with large drops. But were the British really unaware that Noor's set was under German control and that Cinema receptions were, in fact, German receptions? Or were they countering Goetz's deception with a deception of their own?

Whatever the case, Goetz's *Funkspiele* now took a tragic turn—for the agents involved. Still apparently unaware that Noor was being impersonated, the British began to send in agents—seven in all—to the false Cinema. On the night of February 7/8, 1944, the first four—all of them so inexperienced and ill-trained that their mission seemed to be sacrificial—were dropped together near Poitiers. They were R. E. J. Alexandre, a twenty-two-year-old French aircraft fitter; an American called Byerley who was his wireless operator; a Canadian, Deniset, who was to have been Noor's replacement; and Jacques Ledoux, an Anglo-Frenchman who was to have established a new circuit, "Orator," at Le Mans. All were immediately captured.

Then came Goetz's finest hour. It was the capture of Antelme himself, who was also dropped to a Cinema reception; and the circumstances of his capture were as curious as everything that had gone before. Byerley, the American wireless operator in the first drop, had been instructed by F section before his departure to send certain special messages if he landed and got away safely. This was an unusual procedure, and one used only in cases where a reception committee—in this case Cinema—was suspected by SOE of being of doubtful loyalty. In fact, Byerley's set soon came on the air—it was again being worked by Goetz—but the special messages were not transmitted. That, in itself, should have been enough proof that Cinema was under German control, and Antelme's departure should have been canceled; or at least he should have been parachuted into a circuit that was known to be safe. But, on the contrary, SOE sent him in; and the Germans knew he was coming.

Antelme, a wealthy French aristocrat of forty-three who had important connections in the French banking and industrial hierarchy, was one of F section's most valuable and valued organizers. He had already completed three dangerous missions (for which he had been made a Member of the Order of the British Empire) when, in July 1943, he was appointed an adviser to F section. His knowledge of conditions in the field, and the agents and *réseaux* there, made his opinions always important and sometimes decisive. But in February he asked to be returned to the field, and he was allowed to do so. Antelme was aware of F section's suspicions that Cinema might be under German control, but despite the clear warning implicit in the absence of the special messages from Byerley's transmission, F section sent the false Cinema a request for a reception for Antelme and his party on the night of February 28/29, 1944. Cinema replied that the reception committee would await Antelme at a ground south of the village of Poigny, five miles from Rambouillet.

Goetz was jubilant, and passed the details of Antelme's arrival to Kieffer. He, in turn, aware of Antelme's importance in the SOE hierarchy, and with one eye on his own career, invited his SS chiefs to be present at the drop. On the appointed night the entire area of Rambouillet was sealed off by SS and SD parties and a local curfew was imposed. Promptly at 10:45 P.M., the German reception committee heard a plane overhead. It circled and by quarter-moonlight a stick of three dropped first: Antelme; his wireless operator, Lieutenant Lionel Lee; and his courier, Madeleine Damerment. Then the plane came round again and dropped eight large containers of war stores and several packages of other equipment. Antelme was the first to land; he struggled out of his shrouds, found himself looking into the muzzle of a Walther pistol, and was handcuffed. In an "imperial fury" Antelme cried, "I have been betrayed!" Then he and the two others were collected and taken to the Avenue Foch, where they were placed in solitary confinement, emerging only for interrogation and torture. None spoke and all were, in consequence, handled with great brutality.

With Antelme's capture, Goetz was quick to see the potential for another valuable *Funkspiele*. After nearly a month of silence, he opened communications with London on Lee's set; and, it appeared, he succeeded in hoodwinking SOE for a time, despite the fact that Lee's special security checks were not present in the transmissions, and Goetz pretended that Antelme had been injured in the drop and could not communicate with London directly. (In reality, he was sent to Gross Rosen concentration camp and shot.)

Under the circumstances—the special imperatives of the invasion—it might be expected that SOE would have been especially vigilant for signs of *Funkspiele* over Antelme's mission; and there were indeed such signs. But not for several critical weeks did SOE detect them. Why? And again, if Noor's set and the Cinema circuit were suspect *before* Antelme was dropped, why was he sent in at all? Did SOE—at the instruction of either the LCS or the CSM—continue its transmissions for some deceptive purpose? If so, what was accomplished by it?

The games being played on Noor's and Lee's sets gradually faded out as both sides tried to trick the other. But Goetz continued to play the deadliest *Funkspiele* of all with a wireless set captured from "Butler," another F section agent who had preceded Noor into the field and who was arrested just before she was. Butler was François Garel, a veteran F section organizer who had been parachuted blind into the Sarthe on March 23, 1943, with a wireless operator, Marcel Rousset, and a courier, Marcel Fox. They were dropped badly and lost all their baggage, including Rousset's wireless set. But fresh equipment—wireless, crystals, ciphers—was dropped to Rousset and, by May 1943, Butler and his crew had formed a *réseau* and were at work selecting rail and telephone targets to be blown when the Allies invaded. Garel survived the Prosper mousetraps for a time, but the Germans were aware of his existence, and through tenacious if routine detective work, they caught him, along with Rousset, Fox and a second courier, as they lunched at a safehouse in Paris.

At first Rousset denied his identity, but when Gilbert Norman confirmed that he was Butler's wireless operator he agreed to help Goetz in a *Funkspiele*—but for a reason. He told Goetz that his wireless security check consisted of no more than an agreement with London to transmit in English for Garel and in French for Fox; in fact the reverse was true. Goetz believed him and sent a message in English in which Garel asked for funds. London did not react to the warning. Butler's London controller merely asked why he had changed his *modus operandi,* and with that piece of sleepy stupidity the *Funkspiele* began.

Rousset was taken to Ravitsch concentration camp but, in order to answer some awkward questions from London, he was brought back to Paris to help Goetz prepare the answers. He was kept at the SD offices on the Place des États-Unis but, while sweeping a corridor, he bowled his guard over, broke through a window into a garden, hopped over a wall into a convent, and used the convent's telephone to call a girl friend. She brought him clothes and documents; then he tried to find a means to warn London again that his set was under German control. But he failed, and as a result, Goetz continued to play a *Funkspiele* that would not end until noon on D-Day. In response to instructions transmitted by the false Butler, large quantities of money and stores—and a succession of agents—were sent to German reception committees; and with Butler, Goetz would obtain his major prize: one of the three secrets of D-Day—*when* the Allies would invade.

The German victory concerned the BBC *messages personnels,* the "alert" and "action" messages which were assigned to every *réseau* in preparation for D-Day. The opening lines of Paul Verlaine's poem "Chanson d'Automne," were just such a message, and they were originally assigned to Butler. The first line was the alert: *"Les sanglots longs des violins d'automne"*—and it signaled Butler's sabotage squads to stand by. The second line was the "action" message—*"bercent mon coeur d'une langueur monotone"*—and it meant that they were to begin operations at midnight on the night that they received it. From November 1943 on, however, SOE withdrew the original *messages personnels,* and under circumstances of great care and secrecy they were replaced by new alert and action messages. It was a security precaution, in case the Germans had discovered the meaning of the messages assigned to the *réseaux* that had been captured in the Prosper *ratissage*—as indeed they had in the case of the Butler circuit. It was also part of the *messages personnels* stratagem in which Dericourt participated, for the British were aware that the Germans knew of the *messages personnels* system, although they did not know what individual messages meant or to whom they were directed. In fact, some messages had been revealed to the SD by Dericourt in Prosper's *courrier,* and it was the intention to broadcast these compromised alert and action signals, as well as other dummy messages directed to nonexistent *réseaux,* during the D-Day period to confuse and mislead the Germans about where and when the Allies would invade. But one of the *messages personnels* that should have been withdrawn was reassigned to an actual circuit—"Ventriloquist," an SOE *réseau* in the Loire-et-Cher. It was the Verlaine couplet.

Why a message originally assigned to a *réseau* that had fallen into German hands was to be broadcast on D-Day as an operational instruction will remain a mystery. The Germans would suggest that it was the work of an agent of their own inside SOE headquarters, a suggestion that was investigated and not proven. It was possible that SOE was unaware that Butler was under German control, in spite of the many indications to the contrary; it was also possible that SOE was playing a wireless game with Butler. But in either case, reassigning the Verlaine couplet was probably no more than an administrative blunder. Whatever the reason, the Germans now had a means to discover when the invasion would take place.

In the event, the Germans were not sure to whom the message would be directed, nor precisely what it meant. They thought it was a general call to arms to all railway resistance squads in France to begin operations against the Wehrmacht in support of the invasion when, in fact, it was designed solely for the Ventriloquist circuit. The Germans were also uncertain about the timing involved in the broadcast of the *messages personnels,* for this intelligence bulletin, which was sent out to all commanding generals in France, Belgium, Holland, Denmark and Norway, was slightly in error:

> The first part of this signal, up to and including the word *"l'Automne,"* will be broadcast by the English radio on the 1st and 15th of given months, while the second part is scheduled to be broadcast to mean that the landings would ensue during the next 48 hours, the time counted from midnight on the day of the initial transmission of the signal.

This interpretation was not quite accurate, but it was close enough to the truth so that all the Germans had to do was wait for the second line of the Verlaine couplet to be broadcast over the BBC and they would know that D-Day was to occur within forty-eight hours. It was the gravest breach of the entire security program that attended the invasion. If the Germans had obtained nothing else through *Funkspiele,* that alone would have justified all the effort that went into the game. But what justified the efforts of the British, efforts that included thousands of pounds worth of arms, ammunition and stores that were dropped to the Germans—and, so it seemed to many Frenchmen, the deliberate sacrifice of scores of agents?

After the war, the allegations that SOE had betrayed some of its agents —and particularly the party of three women agents of which Princess Noor was a member—for the purposes of wireless and military deception received very wide circulation in Europe. But the evidence cited would never have been sufficient, or even admissible, in a court of law. In the euphoria of victory in France, and with the enormity of the problems of putting the country back on its feet, the matter got little further than heady and passionate gossip at the Brasserie Lipp, the politicians' and journalists' restaurant in St. Germain-des-Prés. In Holland, however, similar allegations were taken much more seriously, and a Royal Commission was established to investigate them. Some evidence was produced that SOE, to sustain wireless games which were intended to make it seem that the Allies would invade Holland, had indeed sent in agents in response to wireless communications from *réseaux* that SOE knew—or suspected—were in enemy hands. After much evasion, the British Foreign Office permitted Dutch investigators to interview high officers of both MI-6 and SOE who had been involved in secret operations from London into Holland. The investigation foundered without a definite conclusion; but the Foreign Office, which became responsible for settling SOE's affairs after the war (SOE was closed down by the then Prime Minister, Clement Attlee, on the grounds that peacetime Britain wanted no "socialist international"), did issue a statement. In substance, it declared that the allegations that Dutch agents had been betrayed for reasons of tactical and strategical deception were both "repugnant" and "untrue."

What therefore was the truth? In the first place, the British never denied that they countered German *Funkspiele* with wireless games of their own. Nor, to sustain those games, did they deny sending in large drops of money and stores to posts they knew were under German control. The reason was both simple and ingenious; and by way of explanation, Foot, in his official account of SOE's activities, cited R. A. Bourne-Patterson, the Scots accountant who was Buckmaster's deputy. Bourne-Patterson, in SOE's secret (and unpublished) after-action report, stated, according to Foot, that drops were made to German-controlled posts "in order to give time for new circuits to establish themselves." This, obviously, was sound and successful strategy, for the Germans concentrated on the compromised circuits while SOE set up new circuits in preparation for the invasion. Moreover, British wireless games were played chiefly with circuits in the Fortitude area between the Seine and the Scheldt, and it was in that area, which included the Pas de Calais, that the attentions of the Germans were successfully fastened, when they might have been concentrating more profitably and dangerously on the region between the Seine and the Loire, which included Normandy.

But was SOE, on its own initiative or under instructions from some other secret agency, prepared to pay for the success of its wireless games with the lives of agents as coinage? Were agents, particularly women agents, used to plant deceptive cipher traffic on the Germans at the expense of their own lives? Were men and women considered no more important than money and stores to sustain wireless games? Foot denied it. With Noor and Antelme in mind, he wrote: "It was certainly never any part of F section's intention to send them straight to their death; nor indeed were their deaths intended by anybody else on the allied side." He added: "They were unfortunates who happened to be caught on an exposed flank while it was exposed." That might suffice as a statement of position, but not as an explanation. For while SOE might have stopped short of using Noor and others to set up wireless games, it was not above taking advantage of the capture of their sets and ciphers once it had occurred. And that is, perhaps, what Henri Dericourt meant to imply when he was challenged by Miss Jean Overton Fuller, the British author who attempted to find some rational reason for Noor's fate. "The ways of headquarters were impenetrable," Dericourt said enigmatically. Pressed further by Miss Overton Fuller to say whether or not Noor was a deliberate sacrifice, he added, "My theory—I won't tell it to you—is not as crude as that."

It would have been crude indeed for SOE or any other secret agency to rely upon such unpredictable means to initiate a deception. Their stratagems were far more skillfully prepared and executed than that. And if they were willing to use a *Funkspiele* to their own advantage once it had been set up, that would explain why they continued transmissions to wireless posts that had almost surely been captured by the Germans in the wake of Prosper, and why they frequently ignored the security check systems. Colonel George Starr, the controller of a large *réseau* in Gascony, would state that at great peril to himself he had warned London on two occasions that wireless posts were in enemy hands; but he had been told to mind his own business—London knew what it was doing.

But did London know what it was doing in every case? Apparently not, unless it was conceded that the British were willing to sacrifice the lives of agents the stature of Antelme, and give away one of the secrets of D-Day to sustain wireless games.

How, then, to explain these sinister aspects of the mystery? Was it, as has been suggested, departmental muddle, overwork at headquarters, the inefficiency of wireless and security staffs, the amateurishness of SOE itself? SOE was, in fact, that sort of organization. It had been set up in haste for the purposes of war; it had no established bureaucracy; it recruited hurriedly and widely in a social range that extended from pimps to princesses. Errors and casualties were, under the circumstances, bound to occur. And that, in addition to the extreme cleverness with which the Germans played *Funkspiele,* may well have been at least one reason for the high price that SOE paid for the success of its wireless games. But there could have been another that was also related to the peculiar circumstances of the organization and the times. It is possible that SOE did indeed suspect that these posts were under German control, but was not absolutely sure. As long as only money and military supplies were dropped to suspect posts, it did not really matter. That was considered a small enough price to pay to plant deceptive information that might influence the outcome of an Allied military operation. But when it came to sending in agents, SOE, working under the extraordinary pressures of Neptune and Fortitude, was forced to gamble. Other, riskier gambles had paid off; tragically, some of the gambles taken in conjunction with the wireless games did not.

The reasons for the deaths of Noor, Antelme and others will never be known. Secret services rarely make reports that might later come back to haunt them. Who can talk to the dead; who among the living dares talk publicly? Perhaps the final judgment in this sad but heroic affair must be left to the pragmatist. These men and women had volunteered for operations in the lonely, gray outer marches of the war—a world where the only standards were survival, defeat or victory. Were they not liable to betrayal, torture and execution at any time, often for mundane reasons: dislike, jealousy, the desire to purchase the loyalties of a mistress, or even to settle an old score? It was in the very nature of their work that their lives must be considered forfeit the moment they left the shores of England. Were the secret agencies not justified in using them for any purpose, if their lives— and their deaths—served the objectives of Fortitude? What did these agents exist for, but to confound and confuse the enemy? These were, the pragmatist might argue, desperate, pitiless days that demanded desperate, pitiless action. As Baumer, the American representative on the LCS, would state after the war: "I know that the British were in a stop-at-nothing mood before the invasion. The only thing that mattered was the success of Fortitude, and it was impossible for Fortitude to have been a success without sacrifices."

Princess Noor did not survive the war. She spent months in various concentration camps, in chains part of the time. Then at Dachau, on the morning of September 14, 1944, Noor and three other women agents of SOE were taken from their cells "into a sandy yard," Foot recorded, "and told to kneel down by a wall. They saw the old bloodstains in the sand, and knew their fate. They knelt two by two, each pair holding hands; an SS man came up behind them and shot each of them dead, neatly, through the back of the neck." Their corpses were burned.

But Noor was not forgotten by England. On April 5, 1949, at Gubbins's nomination, she was posthumously awarded the George Cross for "acts of the greatest heroism or of the most conspicuous courage in circumstances of extreme danger." Gubbins also arranged to place a plaque in the wall of a church at the back of Harrods in Knightsbridge. Every year someone has left a little bunch of spring flowers at the foot of the plaque.

The French Labyrinth

In April 1944, Field Marshal Rommel and his intelligence officer, Colonel Anton Staubwasser, visited the Gothic ramparts of Mont St. Michel on the Emerald Coast of Brittany. They were not interested in the renowned antiquities of the fortress-abbey; they had spent a week in Brittany surveying the formidable defenses of the area. Brittany was in Rommel's command; indeed, it was one of his most important sectors. In it were four great ports—Brest, Lorient, St. Nazaire and St. Malo; the existence of these ports alone, said Staubwasser, was sufficient reason for the Allies to invade. There was another reason. In the Breton moors, in the hilly woodlands intersected by gorges, ravines and tumbled rocks, in the prairies of sunken fields and pollarded oaks, there lurked one of the most ardent *maquis* in France. Their secret organizations had been especially difficult for the Germans to penetrate, for the Bretons were an insular, suspicious, mystical and clannish people and their Celtic lore, their Celtic tongue, their legends of Merlin and Viviane, Tristan and Iseult, the Grail, the town of Is, their Patrons, the Pardons—all served to permit them to move and communicate in ways that were almost completely mysterious to the stolid and procedural Gestapo.

Ethnically and linguistically the Bretons—there were about 3 million of them—were closer to the West Countrymen of England and the Welsh than they were even to the French. They hated their German conquerors, and Staubwasser's intelligence bulletins were filled with reports of gunrunning and *parachutage;* of mysterious meetings in the shades of the menhirs —strange megalithic remains that rose like phalluses all over Brittany; of five and twenty ponies trotting through the dark, laden with explosives and ammunition; of agents, phantom-like, running on the infiltration and exfiltration routes to and from the Breton coves; of Lysanders coming in with mail, men and wirelesses. The BBC broadcast messages in the Breton tongue that could have no meaning except to a Breton—and Staubwasser was well aware that the resistance was at work in the peninsula to provide bases from which the Allies could gradually move against the Breton ports. Or the Allies might invade the peninsula, take the ports, and then move northeast to cut off the German troops in the Cherbourg peninsula. Whatever their strategy, Brittany was certain to play an important part in the inevitable invasion.

Across the English Channel, a SHAEF syndicate was even then completing plans for the special operations that would take place in Brittany in conjunction with Neptune. The syndicate held its meetings in Room 64 at St. Paul's School, the great red-brick Gothic building that stood beside the road to Heathrow. Montgomery had attended St. Paul's (as had Milton, Pepys, Marlborough, Judge Jeffreys, and Major John André), and it was now his headquarters. The chairman of the syndicate was Brigadier R. F. K. Belchem, Montgomery's chief operations officer and the former commander of the 1st Royal Tank Regiment. The Americans were represented by Colonel Charles M. Bonesteel III, a Virginian who had been a Rhodes Scholar and would go on to command an American army. SOE was represented by Buckmaster; and Colonel Joseph Haskell (who would become a president of the National Distillers and Chemical Corporation of New York) was there for OSS. Colonel Ian Collins, a former Commando, represented the Special Air Service (SAS), the élite *banditti* who did much work for MI-6, and had been formed in Egypt to operate in the role of uniformed guerrillas behind enemy lines. There were others—RAF and USAAF men, representatives of Combined Operations, some civilians from the political warfare agencies, a couple of naval officers. But there were no Frenchmen; while it was France that was to be invaded, and France that was to be the battlefield, no Frenchman was to be privy to Neptune operational planning.

The dominant matter before the syndicate was to devise ways and means to delay the enemy reserves—and particularly the panzer, panzer grenadier, attack and paratroop divisions—that Rundstedt and Rommel would use to launch a full-blooded counterattack in Normandy. After the assault itself, no other matter was of such importance. To blunt this counterthrust, the Neptune planners were depending heavily on the deceptions of Fortitude and Quicksilver to pin down the powerful German forces in the Pas de Calais, where, it was hoped, they would be held to oppose an invasion that would never materialize. But nothing was to be left to chance, and the Neptune planners had also devised an extraordinary program of bombing, deception, guerrilla, harassment and diversion to prevent German forces in every corner of France from assembling to counter the invasion. To keep SHAEF informed of the movements of the German armored divisions, MI-6 and OSS were now, in April, embarking on "Sussex." Over a hundred intelligence teams (the British teams were called "Brissex" while the Americans were "Ossex") were being dropped to form an arc from Avranches through Orléans to Amiens to watch crossroads and rail junctions through which the panzers must move to reach Normandy. And to slow down and disconcert that movement, SOE had already put into action a number of plans. "Vert" called for concentrated sabotage against the railroads; "Tortue," similar action against bridges and highways; "Bleu," the destruction of the Wehrmacht's electrical supply systems; and "Violet," the disruption of the Germans' telecommunications systems.

There were other plans for the sabotage of locomotives and rolling stock and of railway turntables. All bridges were being sabotaged or destroyed by air attack, as were all petrol and lubricants dumps that could be found. Scores of thousands of road mines and tire-bursters that were made of cyclonite plastic explosive and resembled cattle droppings—the invention of Julian Huxley, the zoologist—were being flown or parachuted in to resistance groups to lay in the paths of the panzer columns. F section organizers were giving courses to *résistants* on how to neutralize telecommunications lines without the Germans being able to find the breaks—a thumbtack was usually enough to short a signals cable. Others were being told that a cube or two of sugar in a petrol tank was enough to keep one Panther tank with all its crew and maintenance staff immobilized for several days. Still more *résistants* were being told which German signposts must be taken down or pointed in the wrong direction. Railwaymen were being shown how to jam points and turntables with a single steel bolt, gangers how to derail flats or jam the gates of level crossings, signalsmen how to keep signals arms at the halt when they should be at the proceed, switchboard operators how to immobilize a teleprinter circuit with a feather in an armature. As Gubbins said, it was intended that the Germans should see "the sun, moon and stars at H-Hour." In all, there were 1188 rail, 30 road and 32 telecommunications targets selected for destruction the moment London issued the *messages personnels* for H-Hour; and several hundred more were still being reconnoitered by May 1, 1944.

Sabotage, however, was only one of the roles that the SHAEF planning syndicate proposed for the French resistance at H-Hour. There was another—guerrilla. But that would pose problems of great sensitivity and complexity, as well as political dangers for the future. Should the Supreme Commander order a national insurrection by the French against the Germans at H-Hour? The arguments for such action were numerous and persuasive. For one thing, if all France broke out into general guerrilla activity, this itself would serve not only to confuse the Germans about Allied intentions but also to delay the movement of the enemy reserves. Moreover, the Germans would be compelled to detach large numbers of

Feldgrau for police actions and to protect the Wehrmacht's lines of communications, installations and headquarters. But, the syndicate recognized, such an insurrection would lead inevitably to a bloodbath and the destruction of the *maquis*. The Germans, despite their preoccupations in Normandy, would still be too strong; and the *maquis,* despite the heavy *parachutage* before D-Day, too weak. The *maquis* leadership would be exposed and decapitated, leaving the vast body of the resistance flopping around uselessly until eventually it collapsed and died.

The syndicate therefore made plans for what came to be called "bloc operations"—the calling out of the resistance zone by zone as the military need for such operations arose. There would be no national insurrection. Bloc operations would be ordered in such a manner that the Germans would not be able to deduce from the outbreaks of guerrilla where and when the Allies planned each successive military move. There would be only local insurrections; and, the syndicate decided after many meetings, the first main battlefield for the *maquis* would be the Breton departments of the Côtes du Nord and Morbihan. Here, on the night of D-Day, the *maquis,* armed and commanded by special Allied units that were to be established in the area, would cut Brittany off from the rest of France and generally harass German forces if and when they began to move toward Normandy. The second stage of their operations would begin when the Americans broke out of their bridgehead in Normandy. Neptune called for Patton's 3rd Army to burst out of the Cherbourg peninsula into Brittany to take and hold the Breton ports. But in the event that Patton's tanks moved too swiftly for the infantry to keep up, the Breton *maquis* would serve as infantry. They were to hold the towns and villages through which the tanks would pass, secure the various viaducts across the gorges on the road to Brest, guard Patton's flanks and rear, and superintend his prisoners.

The *message personnel* that would signal the beginning of general guerrilla in Brittany was: *"Le chapeau de Napoléon, est-il toujours à Perros-Guirec?"* It was a message of some significance to the Bretons since "Napoleon's hat" was the local name of a famous rose-red granite rock at the holiday resort of Perros-Guirec. But would the Bretons, or, indeed, the *résistants* throughout France, obey the *messages personnels?* The Americans at SHAEF were particularly concerned about the way the French resistance had been manipulated, and the Avis system used, for the purposes of the Starkey deception. General Robert A. McClure, who was chief of psychological and political warfare at SHAEF, wrote to General Dallas Brooks, the military chief of PWE:

> These *Avis,* as originally conceived, were an excellent device for communicating operational requirements to the French. It is a pity that during the summer [of 1943] one or more *Avis* tended towards deception rather than information, and this inevitably lowered their future credibility. This

makes it all the more important, therefore, that the *Avis* device should be repositioned in the French mind.

It was a clear rebuff to the deception agencies, and at McClure's request, the BBC broadcast this message to reestablish the credibility of the Avis:

You have always been promised that, when the time comes, you would be given clear and unmistakeable instructions as to the part which you are to play during any large-scale military operations affecting your country.

In the past you have heard *Avis* which, in the name of the Allied High Command, gave you certain warnings and instructions.

These *Avis* have not always been closely followed by the operations to which their warning in fact referred. This has led to some confusion and even misgiving as to the validity and authority of these *Avis*. It is important at this stage of the war that the greatest clarity should exist among you as to the scope and purpose of these warnings.

The purpose of all *Avis* is to coordinate, while safeguarding your interests, your activities with the military plans of the Supreme Allied Commander in whose name they will be issued.

For military reasons, it will not always be possible to give the reasons underlying the instructions contained in *Avis;* they must, however, be interpreted literally. They will mean exactly what they say and will be dictated by important military considerations.

On no account should an attempt be made to read between the lines, whatever interpretation may be placed upon them by enemy rumours and propaganda.

The broadcast stressed the importance of obedience to the Supreme Allied Commander, and therein lay another uncertain factor in SHAEF's plans for the invasion. For the *résistants* were of many stripes—Protestant, Catholic, Communist, Gaulliste, Pétainiste, loyalist, secessionist. Would they listen to London or to some other voice? It was a conundrum that might influence the outcome of D-Day—a conundrum rooted in the peculiar personality and influence of General Charles de Gaulle.

When MI-6 brought de Gaulle out of France in 1940 at Churchill's orders, the ungainly, lonely, arrogant and passionate Frenchman was to be the "Steward of France." Neither the British nor the American governments regarded him as more than the leader of the French resistance. He was an outlaw in his own country, and he would shortly be declared a traitor and deserter and sentenced to death for grand treason. But de Gaulle saw himself as the personification of the renaissance of French national, military and spiritual glory; and from the moment he arrived in London until the moment four years later when he returned to France, he never ceased to intrigue to ensure that he and his disciples were accepted as the legitimate leaders of France. His attitude and actions brought him into conflicts of ever-intensifying gravity with both Churchill and Roosevelt. Finally, Roosevelt would recommend that British troops arrest de Gaulle and hold him in exile. And Churchill would declare that "We call him Joan of Arc, and we're looking for some bishops to burn him."

Although it was MI-6 that put him in business, it was not long after his arrival in London that de Gaulle and MI-6 began to war. In an early move, he founded his own secret service, the Bureau Centrale de Renseignements et d'Action (BCRA), largely with MI-6 help and finance; but instantly de Gaulle saw it as an instrument by which he would ruin his opponents and obtain the leadership of France. He appointed André Dewavrin, a passionate, extremely literate and articulate synarchist, as the spymaster of the new France. Slim, sly, quick and bloodless in appearance, Dewavrin seemed to be the archetype of the intellectual at war—a young man prepared to stop at nothing. His enemies regarded him as charming and dangerous; and his organization would be accused of political murder in London, of using "Gestapo-like methods" in processing French exiles to ensure their allegiance to Gaullism, of intellectual thuggery, and of discriminating in the arming and supply of the French resistance to ensure that, at the moment of liberation, de Gaulle would emerge as the head of the nation.

The British secret agencies, which had centuries of experience in dealing with such men, regarded de Gaulle and Dewavrin as revolutionary exiles who would naturally maintain secret communications with their homeland. And since their homeland was dominated by a pro-Nazi puppet government, it had to be assumed that their communications would fall into the possession of the Germans. In consequence, BCRA was kept under observation, and even penetrated. De Gaulle came to believe that the British secret services suborned Frenchmen to spy upon him personally, which was probably true. It was certainly true that, from the very outset, the distrust between de Gaulle and the British was intense.

That distrust increased markedly over a question of French discretion when, in September 1940, Churchill embarked upon "Menace," the large expedition mounted at the height of the Battle of Britain to enable de Gaulle to plant his standard at Dakar, from which, it was hoped, he would raise the French African colonies to support the British. Menace was a prodigious enterprise: battleships, cruisers, destroyers, an aircraft carrier, sloops and assault landing craft. The planning was Anglo-French, and surprise was not only considered desirable for the success of the operation, it was essential. But a French diplomat betrayed the expedition to his government at Vichy, which, in turn, informed the Germans; and a month before the forces of Menace sailed, Frenchmen all over London were heard drinking toasts *"à Dakar."* The result was inevitable; everyone knew Menace was coming and the damage suffered by the task force was severe. The expedition was both a humiliation and a disaster for the Royal Navy and for de Gaulle personally. Relations between the Free French and England were severely strained, and never again would the British inform the French of any military undertaking until it was unavoidable, or until the French were in such a position that they could not possibly pass the information on.

The mutual suspicions of the British and the Gaullistes did not diminish during the middle years of the war. In fact, they intensified; and nowhere were they more pronounced—or more dangerous—than in F section operations in France. De Gaulle was convinced that SOE was no more than an instrument of British imperialism and attempted to gain control of its operations. He was rebuffed, for as Gubbins, who regarded de Gaulle as a troublemaker among the brave, wrote to a colleague on January 22, 1942: "It is clear that we cannot build up a proper secret army in France under the aegis or flag of de Gaulle . . ." Gubbins believed that Britain must support anyone who would kill Germans; and if the Gaullistes proved less effective than, for example, the Communists, then it was the Communists who must get the guns. Menzies, too, tended to back others than de Gaulle and believed, as he wrote in January 1942, that "de Gaulle had not a great following but only a symbolic value." Nevertheless, de Gaulle succeeded in winning widespread loyalty among the French *résistants,* but as Gubbins warned in August of 1942: ". . . de Gaulle is busy furthering his political ends . . . (his) agents do not appear to be making any attempt to fulfil their primary role of executing an active sabotage and subversion policy." Brooke and others in London expressed similar opinions; in their view, the Gaullistes were developing a resistance movement in France for the primary purpose not of fighting the Germans but of taking over France when the Allies liberated the country.

For their part, the Gaullistes (and particularly Dewavrin of BCRA) continually criticized SOE, alleging "bad faith and sharp practices." The collapse of Interallié (Menzies's main *réseau* in Paris after the fall) and of the Prosper network did little to cool the savage words and opinions that made life at the top of the Allied secret hierarchy tiresome and difficult. There were staff officers in both MI-6 and F section who opined that Gaulliste intrigue was involved in both disasters; while the Gaullistes accused MI-6 and F section of staffing its *réseaux* in France with Britons, Frenchmen and cosmopolitans who were there to reestablish Aquitaine when the last trumpet sounded.

Then, at a time when everyone was clearing his desk for Neptune, there occurred another of those minor contretemps which confirmed the Allies in their suspicion that the French were not to be trusted. It was called "the great coding row" and it had its origins in the fate of Jean Moulin. Moulin, who was appointed by de Gaulle as his delegate-general in France, headed the Conseil National de la Résistance (CNR), a centralized organization of Gaulliste resistance leaders. It did not last long. There was a meeting of the CNR in an apartment, a shouting match ensued, the Germans were listening nearby, somebody sold Moulin; and when the CNR next met at Caluire, a suburb of Lyon, the SD arrested a round dozen of its commanders, Moulin included. Moulin was murdered when he refused to talk and the French resistance was left leaderless. The collapse of the CNR was followed almost immediately by the collapse of Prosper, and the SOE hierarchy, realizing that unless something was done immediately the French resistance would be useless on D-Day, demanded that the Gaullistes actively decentralize their organization in France. This, of course, was not what the London Gaullistes and BCRA wanted at all; it was only by the centralization of authority over the resistance that their power could be ensured. Nevertheless, they appeared to obey SOE's demand. They handed in a telegram at SOE headquarters for transmission to the field. It was in cipher but it was accompanied by a plain-language text which showed that all BCRA had done was to split France into two zones, instead of the one that had existed under Moulin. Two resistance high commands might be better than one, but it was only a slender guarantee of security. Therefore, SOE returned the telegram to BCRA, declaring that it would not be sent until it specified distinct cellularization.

BCRA countered with a new telegram, in the same cipher, but accompanied by a new plain-language text which showed that the Gaullistes had done as they had been commanded—ordered fundamental cellularization. However, an SOE staff officer noted that there were the same number of cipher groups in the first as in the second telegram. Suspecting a trick, SOE called in its cipher expert, Leonard Marks, a Pickwickian man who was said to do *The Times* crossword puzzle in fifteen minutes, and Marks exposed the two telegrams for what they were—the same. In turn, BCRA accused Marks of having used a purloined copy of the main French cipher to unbutton the telegrams. But indifferent to the accusation, Marks said that if BCRA would care to write a telegram on any subject in the same cipher, he would break the cipher in their presence. BCRA did so; and so did Marks.

The telegram was finally sent when BCRA did what it had agreed to do. But that was not the end of the affair. The Gaullistes, and particularly Dewavrin, were incensed by the ease with which their cipher had been broken. If the British could break their ciphers, they argued, so could the Germans; and as Dewavrin would comment, "If this were true, then it was surely criminal of the British to allow us to go on using them." Tempers cooled, but inescapably, "the great coding row" infected Allied thinking about the security precautions that must be taken with the French over

Neptune. When the British, at Eisenhower's request, ordered a total ban on the transmission of all telegrams unless they were sent in British, American or Russian ciphers, no exception was made for the traffic between de Gaulle's headquarters at Algiers and its SHAEF representatives in London. Moreover, to reinforce security procedures, the Gaullistes were only allowed to send those agents to France who had been cleared by British authorities. No one else—not even the couriers of de Gaulle's mail—would be permitted to leave the country until after D-Day. But once again, the Gaullistes attempted to sidestep the Supreme Command—and this time they succeeded in a contretemps that was called *"l'affaire Socrate."*

Allied policy toward the French resistance was governed by the decision that there should be no national insurrection in France on D-Day. The maximum the Allies expected and would order was local sabotage and guerrilla. But the situation within France was so flammable that no one could be sure that the whole nation would not explode on D-Day. Therefore, and very properly, General Pierre Koenig, the Gaulliste representative at Supreme Headquarters, asked permission to send an agent to France to give the necessary instructions and advice to the leaders of the resistance movements. But SHAEF rejected the suggestion on a number of grounds: that the resistance had been and would continue to be informed by agents who were already there and were in touch with London by wireless and *courrier;* that to run an agent at this time (late April) might endanger Neptune if the agent was caught and compelled to talk; that the Germans were engaged in a major *ratissage;* and finally that the candidate who had been selected for the task of instructing the resistance, Lazare Racheline, alias "Socrate," was extremely well known to the SD—his face appeared in every wanted book in France. Therefore, SOE/OSS directed—ordered—that Socrate must not leave England, and he was refused all the necessary security documents that would (it was thought) permit him to leave the country. But BCRA ignored the order and, despite the fact that England was completely sealed off to all unauthorized travelers, prepared to run Socrate.

Socrate was an expert in exfiltration; it was he who had helped establish the *Vic* escape route from Paris across the Pyrenees to the Iberian capitals and Gibraltar. A man of steady nerves and complete discretion, he knew how to hide and how to go on the run in a state that was totally controlled by a ruthless counterintelligence service. He also knew how to elude the British security authorities, for, incredibly, he traveled to France on *Var,* the Admiralty-controlled Paris-London escape line which ran through Brittany. There would be no record that he had any of the papers necessary for such a journey; he traveled in much the same way as a man who takes a train without paying for his ticket. Somehow Socrate succeeded in insinuating himself into a party of agents who were being run from London to France. Under official escort, he was taken with the others to a hotel at Torquay, Devon; and there he was cleared for his journey by torpedo boat to Brittany by, among others, the deputy director of the Admiralty's Irregular Operations Division. He was closely checked to ensure that he neither rattled nor shined, boarded the MTB and set sail across the Channel, under Spitfire and MTB escort, in time to arrive off the Breton coast two hours after sunset. When the *Var* reception committee's papers were verified, Socrate and the other agents went ashore in a rowboat, wearing gas capes to protect them from tell-tale spray. Then they were taken up the steep path to the Maison d'Alphonse, a safehouse belonging to a fisherman called Giquel. Socrate had eluded every check, and confounded even the most practiced security authorities.

In Paris, Socrate met with leaders of the resistance and obtained their written acknowledgment of orders to launch only those operations in conjunction with the invasion that were authorized by London. News of the agreement was conveyed by wireless through SOE to BCRA in London; but SOE had not known that Socrate was out of the country. In fact, he had been forbidden to leave. As Socrate was making his way back to England over *Vic* and the Pyrenees, an almighty thunderstorm burst over the heads of the security authorities. How had Socrate got out of England? How much had he known about Neptune? How much had he seen of the invasion preparations? How trustworthy was he? How trustworthy were the resistance leaders he had met in Paris? Everyone feared that Socrate might get caught up in the *ratissage* and tell all he knew. There was some relief when SHAEF learned that he was "discretion incarnate"—as Foot would describe him afterwards—and he made his way back to London safely. Nevertheless, he was received with none of the usual courtesies granted a man returning from the field. Socrate would never reveal how he had got out of the country (it was presumed that BCRA had arranged it in some fashion) and the matter was not pursued, for D-Day arrived just as the interrogation began.

This latest Gaulliste trick strengthened SHAEF's conviction that the Free French could not be trusted, and confirmed the wisdom of the decision to tell them nothing of Neptune. The fear that the embargo would affect the Supreme Command's ability to control resistance operations was outweighed by the suspicion that the Gaullistes might take some last-minute action that would be equally detrimental to Neptune. It was, however, the reliability of the resistance itself that caused the greatest concern. SHAEF recognized that the majority of the French people were pro-Allied and detested their conquerors. It was also recognized that several hundred thousand men and women might emerge on D-Day to form what de Gaulle called "the army of the shadows." But the vast body of the resistance movement was neither experienced, disciplined, united nor armed. And the hard core of guerrillas was not thought to be strong. In February 1944, MI-6 reported that it doubted whether there was a single band of 2000 men who were prepared to act together in all France—out of a nation of 40 millions at that time. By May 1944, the most optimistic SOE/OSS report estimated that there were not more than 125,000 Frenchmen with Allied guns. The figure of 85,000 was considered to be the realistic one; and of these, not more than 10,000 were believed to have ammunition for more than a day's fighting. The only *résistants* who were experienced in guerrilla were the *réseaux* under the control of F section and the Communists; and while the Gaullistes were the most numerous, they were, with a few important exceptions, the most unreliable, the most penetrated, the most inexperienced in guerrilla, the least ideologically dedicated, and the worst equipped.

The Supreme Command—and particularly its American component—viewed Neptune as the most decisive action of the Second World War; nothing could be left to chance—although, as in all military operations, chance might be a deciding factor. But why increase the already great risks by entrusting any information or military operation to the French resistance which was so badly fractured by Gaulliste-Communist rivalry and in such jeopardy from the SD? In March 1944 the Communists had begun an all-out attack on the Gaullistes, branding their leaders as self-serving crypto-Fascists, while the Germans were using every ruse, including the circulation of leaflets and orders purporting to come from SHAEF or de Gaulle, in an attempt to make the resistance expose itself prematurely. To bring the FFI into hatred and contempt, the SD arranged the assassination of popular personalities, derailed civilian trains, disorganized the lives of whole towns—and then blamed these actions upon F section, upon de Gaulle, upon SHAEF, and upon the Communists. The Gaullistes committed similar actions—and blamed them on the Communists; and the Communists blamed such actions upon everybody. Proclamations for Gaulliste insurrections were issued by the Communists in order to make them show their hands to the Germans; and the Gaullistes did likewise to the Communists.

As seen from London—particularly by the Americans—France was a devil's brew of politics. But it was not one, the British argued, that could be ignored. If France was to reoccupy her place among the nations of the world, her people had to be given the opportunity to liberate themselves and to assist the Allies. In fact, their assistance would be invaluable to Neptune. But, factions in London argued, was it worth arming the French? They recalled Wellington's warning: "I always had a horror of revolutionising any country for a political object. I always said, if they rise up themselves, well and good, but do not stir them up; it is a fearful responsibility." It was a fearful responsibility indeed, for even if the *résistants* complied with Allied orders during the invasion, might they not use the arms and ammunition against each other after the liberation? There were the most alarming stories that the Gaullistes and the Communists had lists of 40,000–50,000 people who were to be impeached or executed. Would it not be better to instruct the French nation to lie low and use conventional means, combined with Anglo-American guerrilla forces of proven reliability, to destroy the Wehrmacht?

Churchill was adamant; the French must be allowed to play a part in their own liberation. Despite the antagonisms between the Gaullistes and the Communists, F section had succeeded in expanding its London-oriented networks. Whereas after the collapse of the Prosper and Scientist circuits there were barely thirty *réseaux* of any consequence left in all France, now, in the spring of 1944, there were sixty. Thus it was finally decided by the syndicates sitting in those high-ceilinged rooms in the order and calm of Hammersmith that the resistance would be used in conjunction with Neptune, but if it was to be effective it must be heavily reinforced with drops of arms, ammunition and supplies. Equally important, the F section and OSS organizers already in the field must be reinforced by men of judgment, tolerance, authority, bearing—and experience in the craft of guerrilla. They must be exemplary men around whom the *maquis* would rally, arm, train and then fight according to Eisenhower's orders. The men to fulfill these difficult tasks would be the "Jedburghs."

The concept of the Jedburghs—and other teams with similar missions but different names, such as "Cooneys," *"Missions Interalliés,"* and the American Operational Groups—emerged from the need to impose discipline and control upon the French *maquisards*. The Jedburghs took their name from their quarters during training: Jedburgh, a royal burgh on the Jed River in the Scots border country of Roxburghshire, a place famous for its abbey and infamous for "Jeddart Justice," in which a man was hung first and tried afterwards. Each Jedburgh was to consist of one Briton, one American and one Frenchman, lest they be accused of being agents of British imperialism. And each man was to be handpicked both for his high intelligence, his skills as a partisan, his personal courage, his ability to command respect, and his fairness—for a Jed, as they were known for short, was expected to be captain, judge, confessor, and quarter- and paymaster—to say nothing of demolitions expert, gunsmith, linguist, marksman, poacher and doctor. The Jedburgh teams were to be dropped into France by parachute from the evening of D-Day onwards, as far as possible they were to wear uniforms—although some did not and therefore risked being shot as spies—and their main task was to locate *maquis* bands, arm and equip them, and then make them conform and operate to the dictates of the requirements of the orthodox land battle. In a sense, each Jed would have to be a man much in the mold of Lawrence, able to operate behind enemy lines quietly, efficiently and impressively.

Plainly, not too many men existed with the high qualifications necessary for the tasks they had to undertake. Only the British had formed a reservoir of such men: the Special Air Service brigade, which was composed of two regiments of Britons, two battalions of Frenchmen, and one "international squadron" which was much like the Foreign Legion in its composition and the history of the men in it. The OSS provided about one hundred of its best young officers, among them Major William E. Colby, a twenty-four-year-old Minnesotan and a graduate of Princeton. Later, as a member of the CIA, Colby would become station chief in South Vietnam, head of the CIA's Far Eastern operations division, and, in 1974, director of the CIA.

All the special forces teams underwent long, intensive training in the multiple crafts of guerrilla: physical fitness, silent killing, silent movement, unarmed combat, knife and rope work, the use of both Allied and enemy small arms, fieldcraft, elementary Morse, raiding tactics, railway demolitions. About eighty Jed teams would be deployed during Neptune, and a total of about three hundred inter-Allied, MI-6, OSS, SAS, SOE, BCRA, PWE, Cooney, Brissex and Ossex teams would cast a variety of balls among the German skittles. Some twenty Missions Interalliés, each consisting of between two and twenty-five men, would go in to train and stiffen the resistance, along with four purely American Operational Groups, each of thirty-four men, assigned the same mission. In addition, no less than 2200 officers and troops of the SAS, each man superbly trained in guerrilla and clandestinity, would be dropped behind the front, sometimes equipped with armored jeeps to maraud like cavalry. In all, therefore, there would be something like 5000 agents and soldiers organizing and leading the French resistance by and after D-Day—a formidable number indeed to train, equip and maintain.

In the special context of Allied strategy, the Jedburghs' chief mission would be in Brittany, where they would attempt to tie down as many as possible of the German troops stationed there. Then they would arm and train the *maquisards* into organized battalions ready to take to the field when Patton's 3rd Army broke out of the beachhead and moved to capture the Breton peninsula. But as D-Day approached, and as the Jedburghs and other special forces teams were grouped under strict security control at Milton Hall, Castor, about 60 miles north of London, it seemed that an old concept about how they might be used to support Fortitude was being resurrected, a concept that dated from "Plan Torrent."

Torrent was Fortitude in all but name; it was first promulgated secretly by COSSAC on September 20, 1943, and even though the British had been severely criticized for using agents and the French resistance in deception schemes, it again advocated the use of F section agents and special forces teams such as the Jedburghs for the purpose of deception. In its specifications for the special means to be employed in support of Torrent, the plan included this paragraph:

> *Patriot Forces.* The general sabotage in and around the Pas de Calais-Belgium area will be increased and specially briefed organisers will be sent to this area to spread rumours [that the invasion was imminent in that area] and to initiate certain limited action by resistance groups about three weeks before the target date of *Overlord* [then the code name for the invasion].

The paragraph did add the stricture that "This action must in no way prejudice the potential value of resistance groups to Operation Overlord"; but nevertheless it was a clear declaration of the Allied intention to use—and, if necessary, to sacrifice—agents and resistance groups to support a deception.

The plan met with immediate opposition from Gubbins. In the heavily garrisoned Pas de Calais, it was all but impossible for an individual intelligence agent to operate, let alone special forces teams. The plan was discarded. But toward the end of May, some of the Jeds—particularly those to be dropped into Brittany—began to detect an attitude among their briefing officers that not only reflected the extraordinary dangers of their mission but also smacked of sacrifice.

Captain B. M. W. Knox of the OSS, the American leader of Jed team "Giles," noted that attitude as he prepared for his drop into the Breton province of Finistère. He had been fully trained in the crafts of guerrilla warfare, including the techniques of silent killing under a policeman who had learned his trade from the Tongs of Shanghai, and safe-cracking under one of England's leading country-house burglars. Knox, an outstanding classics scholar at Cambridge who would become Professor of Greek at Yale and then Director of Hellenic Studies at Harvard, recalled:

> While we were wonderfully trained in the most advanced techniques of clandestine work, we were not privy to what the high command planned. We never quite knew what our function was, beyond the mission prescribed for us in our operational orders. If we were part of some larger strategical scheme, we did not know it. Neither was it desirable that we should have known; we might have been captured and forced into talking. But it was quite clear to us that our unit commanders did not expect us to come back. But this was very carefully camouflaged; had we known perhaps some of us would have had second thoughts about going in at all. There were, at the same time, indications that we were sacrifices of some sort. You know how careful the military is in making you sign for anything of value—binoculars, prismatic compasses, special watches, rum,

wireless sets, special pistols, sovereigns, fishing gear, that sort of thing? When I went to the stores to draw my special equipment, the officer concerned said he was not too bothered about a signature as it would not mean much. That was a sign that we were regarded as lost—together with our equipment—the moment we got on the plane. But none of us had the slightest doubt that what we were doing was absolutely right and, of course, that carried us through; nobody, not one man, bugged out. They were baying to get into the field.

Strictly speaking, it was not SHAEF's intention that the special forces teams, or the French resistance itself, be used in Fortitude as live bait to attract German units away from the front during the first difficult days and weeks of Neptune. Nevertheless, the word "diversion"—a synonym for deception in the military lexicon—appeared with frequency in the Jeds' orders. The orders for one Jed team going into eastern Brittany stated: "You will go to the Morbihan, organise the resistance movement already there, and prepare that movement for the greatest possible diversion of German troops away from the lodgement area." Such instructions were, of course, a departure from the declared purpose of the Jeds, which was to help the French liberate themselves. But the effect of their missions, as well as the missions of the other special forces teams, and the activities of the resistance in areas remote from the Normandy beachhead, would inevitably serve the purposes of Fortitude. No one complained, at least among the Jeds. This was total war, the issues were too great to consider the niceties of words and intentions, and the Jeds were the first to agree that if the French were to be liberated, the enemy must be tricked.

It appeared, however, that in order to ensure the success of Neptune, the Gaullistes must also be tricked. Despite the elaborate nature of the special operations that would be undertaken in the field, Eisenhower considered the danger of disobedience among the French resistance so serious that he decided to ask his superior authority, the Combined Chiefs of Staff at Washington, for permission to take Koenig into his confidence. On May 8, 1944, he wirelessed Washington:

> In order that arrangements can be made for the coordinated action by French resistance groups, it has become imperative that General Koenig, head of the French mission here, be given certain general information in connection with forthcoming operations. It is therefore my intention to give him personally but to *no* other member of the French mission, under pledge of secrecy, the name of the country in which the main attack will take place and the month for which it is scheduled. . . . Recent restrictions on communications other than by British (cipher) are considered adequate safeguard against leakage to Algiers.

Eisenhower's telegram brought the sharpest reaction; he was to tell the French nothing of Neptune, nothing whatsoever. But Eisenhower pressed the point and sent another message in which he warned that "The limitations under which we are operating in dealing with the French are becoming very embarrassing and are producing a situation which is potentially dangerous."

Indeed, the situation was already dangerous. The specter of a national insurrection on D-Day could not be quelled, despite every Allied precaution. Moreover, there were clear signs that Eisenhower's authority over the resistance movements was being undermined, and that the Communists at least were issuing orders for an insurrection on D-Day. Some Gaulliste leaders were warning Frenchmen working for SOE/OSS that if they continued to do so they would be regarded and treated as traitors after the liberation. And the rivalry between the Gaullistes and the Communists was still so intense that it might easily lead to major civil disturbances, if not outright civil war, in the rear of the Allied armies.

Eisenhower won a small concession. After consulting with the British, Roosevelt replied personally to the Supreme Commander's plea for a more reasonable treatment of Koenig. Eisenhower could inform him of the month in which the landings would take place. But that still left the tricky question of when Koenig should be informed of the broadcast schedule for the *messages personnels,* those cryptic alert and action messages endorsed, at least in theory, by both Koenig and de Gaulle, which were designed to set in motion the selected acts of sabotage and guerrilla that would be essential to Neptune in confusing the Germans and delaying their response to the invasion. Three hundred twenty-five messages had been prepared and circulated to resistance groups throughout France, and under the original concept of bloc operations, it was intended that only a fraction of the alert messages would be broadcast, commencing June 1, with a corresponding number of action messages broadcast a few hours before H-Hour. However, as early as April SHAEF had realized that confining resistance activities to Normandy and immediately adjacent areas would not serve to delay the movement of German reserves to the beachhead from other parts of France. Moreover, the Germans might deduce from guerrilla operations concentrated in Normandy and adjacent areas that Neptune was *the* invasion and Fortitude merely a feint. It was therefore decided that the plan for bloc operations must be expanded. All of the *messages personnels* relating to the invasion phase of Neptune must be broadcast prior to H-Hour. The dangers of such a plan were obvious. Under the tensions of the moment, the resistance might boil over in a general insurrection. SHAEF could only hope that the *résistants,* under the direction of orders from London and the leadership of the special forces teams, would do precisely what their messages instructed them to do, and if the rest of France kept calm, there would not—could not—be an uprising.

Gubbins, Bruce and Mockler-Ferryman, the chief of the London Group of SOE, were informed of the change of plans; but Mockler-Ferryman would not accept verbal orders. He insisted upon having them in writing, for there was a SHAEF-Gaulliste accord that the Supreme Command would do nothing to provoke a general uprising in France in support of Neptune, and Mockler-Ferryman was wary of the possibility that increasing the number of *messages personnels* broadcast prior to D-Day would be tantamount, in the eyes of the French, to calling for an insurrection. He received his orders in a letter issued by the operations staff of SHAEF. In the event, Mockler-Ferryman's apprehension was well founded, for both SOE and the Supreme Command would later be accused of triggering a French revolution in support of Neptune and Fortitude, and of sacrificing the lives of thousands of ill-armed, ill-trained Frenchmen to save the lives of American and British fighting men.

Koenig must be told of this change of plan—but when? There could be no doubt that he would know that all of the *messages personnels* were being broadcast. A Gaulliste officer had been made responsible for writing the messages, he knew roughly what each meant and the areas of France to which they applied, and undoubtedly he had given Koenig this information. If Koenig thought that SHAEF was ordering a general insurrection, betraying its agreement to the contrary, he would almost certainly try to stop or countermand the instructions being sent out to the field.

Two courses of action were, therefore, open to SHAEF. The first was to tell Koenig well in advance. But this was contrary to Eisenhower's orders from the Combined Chiefs and from the President and Prime Minister; and with this kind of advance information, Koenig would be able to deduce where and when the invasion would take place, and would inform de Gaulle in Algiers. The SHAEF security staff suspected that de Gaulle's Algiers headquarters was infiltrated by the German intelligence services—as indeed it was. The first course of action was ruled out as too dangerous, and it was decided to inform Koenig only a matter of an hour before the action messages were to be broadcast. Gubbins and Bruce would undertake the task personally, and it was hoped that Koenig's soldierly good sense would prevail, that he would see that the Supreme Command had no choice in the affair, that he would issue orders to the resistance to obey SHAEF's commands, and only those commands, and appeal to the rest of France to keep calm. This last hope was a fragile one, for not all Frenchmen had civilian wireless sets on which they could listen to the BBC and receive Koenig's orders. SHAEF recognized the grave moral and political consequences that might arise if, as a result of this second course of action, the French nation rose up en masse. But once again, the security of Neptune was more important than any other consideration.

The question of when de Gaulle was to be informed of the invasion was even thornier. The Supreme Command felt that he must be invited to

Britain prior to D-Day, if only to broadcast an appeal for calm in France during the invasion period. But when should he come? If he came too soon he might learn too much and inform Algiers—and so the Germans. If, on the other hand, he came too late, he would certainly consider it an offense to his personal dignity and the honor of France. Churchill and Roosevelt conferred and the decision was taken; de Gaulle was to be kept at Algiers until a day or two before the invasion. Then he would be invited to London by Churchill personally, who would send a government minister and his private York to fetch him. But on his arrival, Eisenhower would tell him only enough about Neptune to permit him to conclude that it was not *the* invasion, but only its start. Moreover, his communications with Algiers would be strictly controlled by the British after his briefing so that neither he nor his staff might slip any information out of the country. The self-proclaimed leader of the French nation was to be treated not as a statesman, but as an ambitious and untrustworthy general.

De Gaulle would never forget, or forgive, this final insult. But at the end of the war, when the Allies captured the SD archives, it was discovered that the only entirely accurate report that the SD had received about Neptune was from a colonel on de Gaulle's staff in Algiers. How had he obtained this intelligence, which was dated June 4, 1944? Was it a shrewd guess, or had de Gaulle, who was the only Frenchman who knew the Neptune plan in any detail before D-Day, managed to find a way of circumventing the controls on his communications from London? The answer will never be known; but mercifully for the Allies, the report, which was, in fact, circulated by the German command to its army on the invasion front, had then been filed away and forgotten among the dross of 250 other, less accurate intelligence reports that the Germans received about Neptune just prior to the invasion.

12

Canaris's Last Throw

FIELD MARSHAL ROMMEL's headquarters were at the Château de La Roche Guyon, the sprawling home of the ducs de la Rochefoucauld in the steep hills beside the Seine more or less midway between Paris and Rouen. Nearby was the village of La Roche Guyon, little more than a group of cottages, shops and an inn clustered around the fifteenth-century church of St. Samsom; but the area was extremely heavily guarded. Sentries were everywhere, pillboxes were set in the chalk outcroppings, there were numerous anti-aircraft guns, and Rommel's bodyguard commander had sited an observation post in an old tower on the highest hill above the château. But on the evening of April 15, 1944, Rommel was not concerned with his personal safety; he was concerned with politics. He sat in his office on the ground floor of the château, his back to the rose gardens and the French windows, his feet under a massive Renaissance desk. On one wall there was an old Gobelin tapestry. On another, the hooded, ironic face of François duc de la Rochefoucauld, the seventeenth-century writer of maxims, and an ancestor of the present Duke. Facing Rommel was his new Chief of Staff, General Hans Speidel. It was a most important encounter in the history of the Schwarze Kapelle. For Speidel was a dedicated and veteran member of the conspiracy; and Rommel, who spoke with despair of the military and political policies of the Third Reich, now authorized Speidel to arrange a meeting with the other German conspirators in the West.

The meeting took place a month to the day after Rommel's conversation with Speidel in a lodge deep in the Forêt de Marly, where the Sun King had hunted. The site was surrounded by Rommel's bodyguard of grenadiers of the 21st (Africa) Panzer Division stationed near Caen, men who were the remnants of the Afrika Korps and had sworn to defend their beloved marshal even unto death. Overtly the meeting was called to discuss measures for the defense of the Channel coast. But covertly, as Speidel would write, it was a "comprehensive conference on the necessary measures for ending the war in the West and overthrowing the Nazi régime." Present, in addition to Rommel and Speidel, were General von Stuelpnagel; General von Falkenhausen; General Heinrich Baron von Luettwitz, the commander of the 2nd Panzer Division; and General Gerhardt Count von Schwerin, the commander of the 116th Panzer Division—the army's two most powerful panzer divisions in the West. Schwerin was the general staff intelligence officer who came to London on the eve of war to see Menzies, Godfrey and Cadogan. The meeting at Forêt de Marly was a solemn one, for the 5th and 8th armies of the Allies had just broken through the Gustav Line in Italy and the German 10th Army was in the process of being surrounded and, it was feared, annihilated. The news from the Russian front was equally bad, and to the generals it was a signal of the beginning of the end for the army and the Reich.

The Marly meeting was concerned primarily with the steps the Schwarze Kapelle was prepared to take to achieve an armistice with the Allies, steps which included: (a) the evacuation by German forces of all territory in the West; (b) the arrest of Hitler by the army, to be followed by a trial by the civilian judiciary; (c) similar trials for all political criminals; (d) a continuation of the fighting in the East on a shorter line; (e) a revolution to overthrow the Nazi government before the invasion began, by mid-June 1944 at the latest; and (f) the promulgation of a temporary government under the leadership of Beck. Rommel was said by Speidel to have accepted the role of leader of the rebellion as he was the only one who had the "undisputed esteem" of the people and the armed forces; and he undertook, with the Allies, to keep order after the revolution. It was also agreed that, so far as possible, the 2nd and 116th panzer divisions should be held in Rommel's command and kept out of military operations in the West so that they would be available to the conspirators to put down any resistance from the SS. There was only one strong area of disagreement between Rommel and most of the other conspirators; it was on the question of assassinating Hitler. Rommel believed that to kill Hitler would be a mistake. It might create a martyr out of him and make the possibility of civil war a probability. Furthermore, it was the duty of the people who had elected him to try, convict and punish him.

This disagreement had not yet been resolved when a third meeting took place at Speidel's home in Freudenstadt on May 28, 1944. Rommel was not present at the meeting for security reasons; he was too well known, and if he was seen going to Speidel's home with men who were suspected conspirators, he too might become suspect. The purpose of this meeting was to integrate the activities of the western conspirators with those of Stauffenberg in Berlin and Tresckow in the East—for Tresckow was, despite the failure of Flash, still very active. And since the Flash conspiracy, the Schwarze Kapelle had become a fundamental if covert part of the German military-political scene. Stauffenberg's organization had representatives in every important command center in the German army, as well as adherents at all the major intelligence, signals, operations and supply centers, in the military governments of the occupied territories, and in all German *Wehrkreise* or "military districts" into which the Reich had been divided for the purposes of administration, mobilization and industry. The main axis of the conspiracy, however, was Paris-Berlin-Smolensk, and would remain so; and the original Valkyrie plan to seize all key points in Germany had been retained and polished.

The conspirators' contacts with the western powers were now, so the Schwarze Kapelle believed, well established. Gisevius, stationed in Switzerland as a vice consul, was in constant and apparently trusted communication with Dulles; and Otto John was able to travel, apparently at will, between Berlin, Madrid and Lisbon to keep in touch with the OSS and MI-6. A third channel had opened up through a senior staff officer with the German Foreign Trade Commission in Paris who was in contact with Colonel William Hohenthal, the American military attaché at Madrid, baiting his opening gambits with a diagram of the German command structure and order of battle in the West. A fourth and most significant channel was also in the process of being created: General Ulrich Liss, the former chief of FHW, now an infantry division commander in the East who was in Berlin recovering from mortar shell wounds, was under the instruction of Colonel Hansen, the chief of Amt Mil, to be ready to fly to Stockholm and from there make contact with his old friend General Kenneth W. D. Strong, who was about to become Eisenhower's chief of intelligence in London. Hansen himself had a fifth channel through a British agent in southern France; while a sixth contact existed between a German officer, Theodore Steltzer, and a British agent with the Norwegian resistance movement. And above all there was Canaris—a man with several channels to London.

The main task of the Freudenstadt conversations was quickly accomplished. The plotters worked out a system of communications among the major centers of the conspiracy—communications which only the conspirators would use and which were designed to prevent the SS and SD hierarchy from communicating with each other. At the plot's command center at the great offices of the Home Army on the Bendlerstrasse, the C-in-C, General Fromm, continued his tacit support for the plot; while Olbricht, his Chief of Staff, was about to be appointed his deputy, and Stauffenberg was about to be appointed Olbricht's successor—an appointment that would give him direct and personal access to the Fuehrer. The Valkyrie plans were amended and placed in Olbricht's safe. All proclamations and orders to the public and the army were reviewed, approved, or sent back to small planning syndicates for further study and development. Trusted panzer and cavalry units were selected by the Schwarze Kapelle to seize the key power centers—Berlin, Paris, Munich, Hamburg, Dresden, Frankfurt, and the like. And the police and detective services of Count Helldorf, the police president of Berlin, were employed to watch and report the movements of the Nazi hierarchy. In short, the Schwarze Kapelle was prepared to move swiftly and ruthlessly. There must be no regard for matters of conscience such as the *Fahneneid*. Even high treason was now justified.

The conspirators were working under circumstances of the greatest danger, for Himmler and the Gestapo were aware that there was a massive plot against the Fuehrer. During a conversation with Canaris in late May or early June, Himmler declared that he knew all about the Schwarze Kapelle, and he knew how to deal effectively with such malcontents as Beck and Goerdeler. Canaris relayed this grim warning to the conspirators, but they took little heed. Artur Nebe, the chief of detectives and one of the hierarchs of the Gestapo, was still a member of the Schwarze Kapelle; and he kept the conspiracy informed of what the Gestapo knew and intended. Moreover, Nebe recognized that Himmler, who often intimated that he might become head of state in any post-Hitler government, was curiously ambivalent about the Schwarze Kapelle. Much that was enigmatic was concealed behind those thick, powerful pince-nez; in a world of rapidly changing loyalties it was not impossible that Himmler, the Schwarze Kapelle's second deadliest enemy after Hitler, might become the conspirators' best friend—which, if it was known in London and Washington, could not have done the conspiracy much political good.

In fact, Himmler knew less than he claimed about the composition of the plot, but a good deal more than the plotters themselves would have wished. In March, the Gestapo had arrested Captain Ludwig Gehre, the Abwehr officer who was probably responsible for organizing the passage to MI-6 of the Lisbon Report. By watching Gehre's home, the Gestapo had also obtained a lead to John; and shortly, Kaltenbrunner would issue warrants for the arrest of both Gisevius and Goerdeler. However, these arrests did not mean that the central citadel of the conspiracy—the Home Army and its links with the commands—had been penetrated; and in late spring 1944, the Schwarze Kapelle appeared to stand well and firm.

Rommel would surely become the conspiracy's greatest asset. His stature was such that his determination to seek a political settlement of the war would command obedience at home and respect abroad. But the Schwarze Kapelle could not know to what end the Allies intended to put their respect for the field marshal. The British were even then laying plans for "Gaff," an operation to confuse the German army in the West during the opening stages of Neptune by murdering or kidnapping Rommel. It was one of the more ironic situations of the Second World War; at the precise moment that Rommel was making plans to surrender, provided honorable terms could be obtained and, if possible, before D-Day, the Allies were planning to assassinate him. This was not the only irony in the situation. The conspirators had determined to launch their revolution *before* D-Day because they considered that to do so after the Allies had landed would lessen their bargaining power; and from the best information at their disposal, they had scheduled the *coup d'état* for mid-June, expecting the invasion after that date. The Schwarze Kapelle's plans had been infected by Fortitude, just as it was infecting the military planning of the entire German high command. The grand deception operation that had been conceived to save life on D-Day was now contributing to the certainty that D-Day would, in fact, take place.

In pursuing its plans for revolution, the Schwarze Kapelle believed that the western powers, and particularly the British, were weakening in their insistence that they would neither offer nor accept any terms other than those of Unconditional Surrender. Were London and Washington, confronted as they now were with Neptune's inevitable cost in lives and treasure, prepared to modify the stringent terms of that declaration? The situation on the eve of the invasion was a curious one.

Throughout the winter and spring of 1944, there had been a prolonged debate about the wisdom of the doctrine of Unconditional Surrender between the soldiers and the politicians. In general, the former advocated a redefinition of Allied terms on the grounds that Unconditional Surrender was stiffening German resolve and so making the tasks of the fighting men more difficult. However, many of the latter insisted that any abatement of the terms would be taken as a sign of Allied weakness and would be exploited by the German propagandists to make their men fight even harder. But as the invasion neared, it became clear that this political belief was largely confined to the White House, and, fearing a holocaust in France on D-Day, powerful factors in both London and Washington sought a modification of Roosevelt's policy. The British Joint Intelligence Committee had asked its American counterparts what were called "pertinent questions" about the wisdom of Unconditional Surrender. The questions stirred new inquiries into the doctrine among the Pentagon's highest committees and divisions; and after much discussion the Joint Chiefs of Staff submitted a memorandum to the President on March 25, 1944, which read in part: "The Joint Chiefs of Staff are of the opinion that a restatement of the formula of unconditional surrender should be made . . . at an early date so that it may establish a favorable condition precedent to *Overlord*."

The Joint Chiefs, the highest U.S. military authority under the President in his capacity as C-in-C, then submitted to Roosevelt a draft of what he should say to the German army and people. In essence, the JCS proposal reiterated demands for the Unconditional Surrender of the Nazis and the Wehrmacht, but at the same time it gave the German people and ordinary soldiery some hope. The key parts of the memorandum read: ". . . it is not our purpose to extinguish the German people or Germany as a nation. . . . It will be a main task of Allied military occupation to create the conditions for the rebirth of a peaceful German society. . . . Only unconditional surrender can provide the necessary basis for a fresh start." What the JCS sought to achieve was a differentiation in the doctrine between the German people and their "gangster overlords," and to reassure the German people that the Allies had no intention of destroying the German nation, but only the Nazis and the Wehrmacht. The State Department also thought that the doctrine could usefully be modified in its application toward Hungary, Rumania, Bulgaria and Finland to induce them to surrender. And General Frank N. Roberts, chief of the Strategy and Policy Group of the Pentagon's Operations and Plans Division, the man chiefly responsible for executing the Americans' contributions to Bodyguard and Fortitude, saw the proposed proclamation of a modified formula for Unconditional Surrender as a "psychological blockbuster" that should be "keyed to (Neptune)" in order to "reduce German resistance to the cross-Channel attack."

Even Eisenhower had bitten the bullet. At the surrender of the German army in Tunisia in 1943, he had declared that he would never receive a German general, except for the purposes of intelligence, nor would he give enemy commanders the honors of war. But now, perhaps under the influence of Smith, he modified his view and accepted the advocacy of his propaganda chief, McClure, that the policy of Unconditional Surrender be "restated" shortly before D-Day so that the *Feldgrau* would see that it was "good business" to surrender rather than fight.

For a few days both the JCS and SHAEF awaited the President's reply in a mood of hopefulness. Might it not be possible, after all, to *walk* ashore instead of fighting ashore? Surely Roosevelt would not turn down such a powerfully backed suggestion? But on April 1, 1944, the President, in a reply that rang with vengeance, moral cleansing and cynicism about the intentions and capabilities of the Schwarze Kapelle, did reject the proposal. He declared:

> The trouble is that the reasoning of the (JCS) memorandum supposes a reconstitution of a German state which would give active cooperation apparently at once to peace in Europe. A somewhat long and personal experience in and out of Germany leads me to believe that German Philosophy cannot be changed by decree, law or military order. The change in German Philosophy must be evolutionary and may take two generations.

To assume otherwise is to assume, of necessity, a period of quiet followed by a third world war.

I think that the simplest way of approaching this whole matter is to stick to what I have already said, (a) that the United Nations are determined to administer a total defeat to Germany as a whole (b) that the Allies have no intention of detroying the German people. Please note that I am not willing at this time to say that we do not intend to destroy the German nation. As long as the word "Reich" exists in Germany as expressing a nationhood, it will forever be associated with the present form of nationhood. If we admit that, we must seek to eliminate the very word "Reich" and what it stands for today.

The President's declaration surprised even Marshall, who remarked to Dill that "they were up against an obstinate Dutchman who had brought the phrase out and didn't like to go back on it." Roosevelt's reaffirmation of the harsh doctrine of Unconditional Surrender made the invasion an inevitability. But Eisenhower, fully aware of the hazards of both the invasion and a prolonged battle on the European mainland, made one last attempt to get for the Germans what his diarist called a "white alley": a route down which the enemy could surrender with honor. On April 14, 1944, he received Edward R. Stettinius, of U.S. Steel, who was shortly to become Secretary of State, and Eisenhower asked him to cable Cordell Hull about the Supreme Command's views. This Stettinius did, stating:

In conversation this morning with General Eisenhower and General Smith they raised with me and expressed the considered opinion that the term "unconditional surrender" should be clarified by announcing the principles on which the treatment of a defeated Germany would be based. This seemed to them highly desirable in view of the accumulated evidence that German propaganda is interpreting the words "unconditional surrender" to strengthen the morale of the German army and people. In order to offset this the generals thought it very necessary to create, if possible, through our own propaganda (a) a mood of acceptance of unconditional surrender in the German army such as would make possible a collapse of resistance similar to that which took place in Tunisia; and (b) to create a mood in the German General Staff as a result of which necessary political steps might be undertaken by a German "Badoglio" [i.e., the Italian field marshal who led the Italian nation out of the war by revolution against Mussolini] for unconditional surrender.

Stettinius's telegram went on to reveal that "General Smith rather than General Eisenhower" recommended that, after this governmental announcement, the Supreme Commander should call upon the German commander in the West to surrender. This call, Smith had evidently suggested, should be "recited in soldierly terms," and should be made *after* the bridgehead had been established. Finally, Stettinius's cable declared:

General Smith expressed the opinion that from all available evidence, in default of such declarations, it would be impossible to exploit the crisis in the German army which will undoubtedly arise immediately after a successful Allied landing.

SHAEF was obviously well informed, through MI-6's special contacts with the enemy, of the state of mind of the German generals. On May 23, 1944, an important report was circulated to all SHAEF's commands which said in part:

> In the German Army, as in German political life, authority is exercised at the top and almost always obeyed at the bottom. For that reason, political trends among the generals in the German Army are of great significance. Should the *Wehrmacht* suffer severe setbacks [through Neptune] the generals may play a decisive role in determining the future. There has been some evidence of friction between Hitler and his higher commanders as a result of German retreats . . . when the generals recognize defeat as inevitable, they may be unwilling to fight on until Germany is reduced to chaos. The generals are likely to believe themselves in a position to get better terms from the conquerors than the nazis. . . . If the first weeks of invasion indicate that the (Allies) cannot be stopped, high-ranking officers of the German Army, recognizing the war-weariness of the German people, may act quickly against Hitler. Politically and psychologically that would be the moment for them to stage a coup. To a majority of German general officers the future of Germany is more important than the future of Hitler. . . . Trends among the German generals during the first weeks of successful invasion will (therefore) merit the closest analysis. . . .

The report amounted virtually to a prophecy, and as such must have been of immense importance and encouragement to Eisenhower. A revolt against Hitler led by his own generals, even if it was unsuccessful, would dramatically disconcert German opposition to the invading Allied armies. If it was successful, like the revolt that deposed the Kaiser, Berlin would lie shimmering, and not far away. It was, perhaps, too much to hope, at this late stage, that such a revolt might precede the invasion and that Neptune itself would prove unnecessary. Although the Rankin contingency plans for unopposed landings on the European mainland remained in readiness at SHAEF, Eisenhower seemed irrevocably committed to launch the invasion—and Rommel irrevocably committed to oppose it. Otherwise, Eisenhower and Rommel were not far apart; both now advocated communication across the drawn lines of battle. But would Churchill or Roosevelt permit such a contact? How many lives, how many cities, how much treasure might be saved if Allied and German generals could negotiate a surrender that would be mutually acceptable? It was a moment of extraordinary opportunity.

The Prime Minister made the first move. On May 24, 1944, he rose before Parliament and spoke of the enemy less ferociously than usual, stating merely that, while Unconditional Surrender gave the enemy no rights, it relieved the Allies of none of their duties. "Justice," he declared vaguely, "will have to be done and retribution will fall upon the wicked and the cruel." McClure's Political Warfare Branch at Supreme Headquarters then prepared a statement for Eisenhower. It was touched up by Robert Sherwood, the playwright, who was an executive of the OWI, and finally polished by William Phillips, the Supreme Commander's American political adviser. The speech was to be a "fireside chat" by Eisenhower to the German soldier, broadcast *after* the Allies had secured a beachhead in Normandy. Its object was, by redefining, explaining, and making more palatable the implications to German honor of Unconditional Surrender, to weaken the determination and powers of resistance of the *Feldgrau* in France. The speech was sent to Washington, but no word of approval or disapproval came back from the White House. There was only silence. Roosevelt did, however, yield to pressure for modifications of Unconditional Surrender so far as it affected Rumania, Hungary, Bulgaria and Finland—but not Germany. Further than that the President would not and did not go. But there was no explosion, as might have been expected— for the Supreme Commander, who was but an instrument of Anglo-American political policy, had no right or power to influence or change that policy. He had greatly exceeded his powers in even permitting such an address to be written without the express, written authority of London and Washington. The explosion came from Churchill on May 31, 1944.

The Prime Minister, already concerned about the extent of the powers that Eisenhower had assumed, particularly those related to security, wrote an angry letter accusing him of "begging before we have won the battle." "This is a matter which really must be dealt with by Governments, and cannot be made the subject of fireside talks," Churchill wrote. "I never read anything less suitable for the troops (on the eve of battle)."

The contretemps with Churchill on the eve of Neptune was one of Eisenhower's earliest lessons in statesmanship. He had trodden where wise men fear to tread—into the area of coalition politics. He did not try again. Unconditional Surrender remained in force, unmodified, for Germany. Nevertheless, the political climate and the inclination—to say nothing of many opportunities—for secret contacts between the Supreme Command and the Schwarze Kapelle continued to exist on both sides of the English Channel. And as if to confirm that these contacts might yet be exploited, a familiar figure was at work behind the scenes. Admiral Canaris reappeared once again at a critical moment in the history of the Third Reich.

In preparing the plans for Neptune and allied operations, the SHAEF syndicates enjoyed a unique advantage. They had before them detailed intelligence about German strength, dispositions, fortifications, supply and telecommunications routes, morale and much else that was, with a few important exceptions, almost complete. No military commander in history would be better informed than Eisenhower on the eve of D-Day, and for that information, at least in part, he could thank Canaris.

Canaris's role in, once again, betraying top-level German secrets to the Allies during the pre-Neptune period would remain obscure. But there can be little question about his involvement, for it would be affirmed by men who were in a position to know of it, among them General James O. Curtis. From late February to early May 1944, Curtis, then a colonel, was the senior American intelligence evaluator in the Operational Intelligence Centre of the Supreme Command. Colonel E. J. Foord was the chief of the section, and the other members of OIC included Major John Austin, an Oxford don in peacetime and a future professor of metaphysics, and Colonel Eric Birley, another don who used to spend his leaves establishing the order of battle of Caesar's 10th Legion in Britain. Together these men were responsible for much the same tasks as those of FHW, sifting the nuggets of truth from the dross of hundreds of thousands of bits of intelligence that arrived each month that spring. And when the nuggets had been weighed and analyzed to establish their substance and value, they were incorporated into the intelligence bulletins known as Neptune *Monitors*. But from the beginning of his involvement in operational intelligence, Curtis, who prided himself on the excellence of his relations with the British, felt that he was not wholly trusted by them. His job demanded skepticism and thoroughness, and he was not disposed to accept the authenticity of material placed before him until he knew more about its origins. Curtis said later that he was well aware that the British had most secret sources of intelligence, but he felt that he could not advise the U.S. army commanders with absolute confidence unless he knew as much about the sources of the material reaching his desk as did his British counterparts.

For that reason, Curtis decided to ask Foord where so much intelligence of the highest grade was coming from. According to Curtis, he heard nothing from Foord about his demand for a day or two; and then Foord, after a meeting at Norfolk House, took him into an anteroom. There, he revealed what Curtis had already guessed: that much of the high-grade intelligence was obtained through Ultra intercepts of OKW's and Hitler's own wireless traffic. But to the revelation concerning Ultra, Foord added the astonishing information that some of the material reaching Curtis was coming from Canaris. Curtis would later elaborate in a witnessed statement:

> I first heard the name Canaris in February 1944. My duties required me to check the authenticity of certain information reaching my desk. We had a system of grading information at SHAEF which ranged from A1 to F6, so

that the highest grade and most authentic information was graded A1 while the lowest grade and the least authentic information was graded F6.

It is not usual to get large amounts of A1 but I noticed that a surprising amount of A1 information was coming through. It was necessary for me to know the source, and so I inquired at a meeting of the Order of Battle intelligence section. A British officer, E. J. Foord, took me quietly on one side [Curtis here inserted, "Just two in the room"] and said that the source was Canaris personally. Foord said: "The only reason that I am telling you this is that we want you to regard this information as being priceless and copper-bottomed." The source, said Foord, was known to only a few men—men like Roosevelt, Churchill, Ike, Montgomery, etc.

His most important service was to give us substantially the complete order of battle plans for the German Army, together with the plans they had worked out for coping with the invasion.

Curtis would remember, even after twenty-three years, how surprised he was at hearing this information. "I was, at first, afraid to go to sleep in case I talked in my sleep," he said. He would add that Canaris sent this intelligence by courier to the Iberian capitals and, on occasions, even directly by wireless to the MI-6 wireless station—using, he thought, a trusted Abwehr wireless operator. For, as Curtis would continue: "Canaris had a code name and this appeared at the top of all intelligence emanating from him—it was a naval term." Could it have been Dreadnought? Curtis thought so. Equally, the code name Albatross rang a bell. But he was certain that Foord had told him that "to all intents and purposes Canaris was in the service of the Allies, not as an agent but in the same way that statesmen confide secrets to each other if it will bring them advantages at the bargaining table."

Foord's statement to Curtis would be supported by de Guingand, who knew more about Allied secret affairs as a whole than almost any other man. He would state:

I distinctly remember being told that Canaris was the source of some of our most secret intelligence. Whether Canaris transmitted this material to us deliberately. or whether we obtained it through our ability to read his command instructions, I did not know at that time. I had no reason to know. But after the war, I was told not once but several times at the highest level that, for ideological and political reasons, Canaris imparted high-level German command decisions to us.

And what was Canaris's motive? De Guingand thought: "Canaris was more afraid of the Russians than he was of us and, presumably, he wanted us to get ashore with the minimum of loss so that we would be able to bring the maximum power to bear upon the Russians and keep them out of Germany."

Further confirmation would come not from the Allied side but from one of Canaris's own compatriots, General Reinhard Gehlen, the man who had once been Roenne's chief and chief of intelligence at Fremde Heere Ost, and then became chief of the DNB, the postwar successor to the Abwehr. Gehlen stated that he was sure that Canaris had had "contact with the British secret service" and was not in the least surprised about the fact. He further remarked:

> I myself had contact with that organization. As chief of (Fremde Heere Ost) in 1944 I told a subordinate to communicate by wireless to the British secret service at Istanbul our appreciations of the Red Army's order of battle, and my appreciations of their strategic aims and intentions. The British were exceedingly grateful to me.

Gehlen would also write in his memoir, *The Service,* that MI-6 and the British military mission in Moscow passed his agents there material about the Russians. In particular, Gehlen would claim that he received through MI-6 "by devious means" an appreciation by Churchill of Russia's postwar intentions in Europe. These were surprising admissions, if Gehlen's story was true, for they showed that there were secret lines of communication between the British and German General Staff. It also gave rise to the speculation that if Fremde Heere Ost could transmit and receive from the British, Roenne and Michel at FHW might have been able to do likewise. As for Canaris, a man even more determined in his efforts to wreck Nazism, his years of service as chief of the Abwehr, his close association with the conspirators of the Schwarze Kapelle, and his myriad contacts in the world of secret intelligence, including his curious relationship with Menzies at MI-6, put him in an even better position to maintain, and use, secret channels of communication with the British.

In revealing the German order of battle before D-Day, Canaris would have attempted to do no more than he had done in the past: to thwart Hitler. But as winter gave way to spring, and the inevitable invasion neared, he would attempt an even bolder move. Abandoning the caution and indirection that had always characterized his clandestine activities, he would make a last, desperate, personal appeal to save Germany.

After his dismissal as chief of the Abwehr, Canaris had gone even deeper into the shadows of the Third Reich. There were reports that he was under house arrest at the Castle Lauenstein in Franconia; but they proved to be untrue. The castle was, in fact, the headquarters of the German economic warfare department and Canaris was its chief. His old enemies, Kaltenbrunner in particular, seemed to have lost interest in him as a quarry; the SD now saw him as an old Wilhelminian gentleman who had been put out to clover. None of the charges that had been made against him could be proven; the circumstances did not yet exist in which he might be placed in what the Nazis called "protective custody," and as far as

Keitel and OKW were concerned, Canaris was the victim of a bureaucratic reshuffle, not the perpetrator of crimes against the state. Thus Canaris could now have been even more valuable to the Schwarze Kapelle than he had been as chief of the Abwehr. He was no longer under the continual observation of the SD, and as chief of economic warfare he could still travel widely and freely.

It can be presumed that Canaris remained in touch with Beck and Goerdeler in Berlin; and it may have been on their behalf that he emerged from the shadows and traveled to Paris on the most extraordinary mission in his long career of clandestinity. None of the Schwarze Kapelle's own accounts, none of the SD's accounts, and none of MI-6's or the Allies' official accounts would record that mission. But long after the war was over, there would be the testaments of eye witnesses.

By the late spring of 1944, Jade Amicol, the MI-6 *réseau* with its headquarters in the Lazarite convent in Paris, had become Britain's most important secret intelligence organization in northern France. Its operations were not confined to military espionage against the Wehrmacht; the organization had become a clearinghouse for political intelligence of all forms. With these new responsibilities, the *réseau* seems to have split into two parts with Colonel Arnould, the founder, looking after its military aspects and his partner, Major Philippe Keun, involved in its subtler political aspects. And in addition to its many other contacts in the anti-German underground, Jade Amicol was close to the Paris faction of the Schwarze Kapelle through an Austrian Catholic who was a member of the secretarial staff in the headquarters of Stuelpnagel. Keun would not survive the war; soon after D-Day he would be sold by a Frenchman in his own organization and murdered by the SD. But Arnould did survive, and he would state, in an interview in 1969, that through this secretary Canaris was able to make contact with Keun in Paris sometime in May 1944. Moreover, Arnould would state—and he was an officer in high standing with Menzies, who would arrange for him to receive the Distinguished Service Order, normally awarded to foreigners only if they had rendered Great Britain quite exceptionally valuable and distinguished service under fire or while on active service against the enemy in special circumstances—that the May contact was not an isolated one. Keun had apparently been in contact with Canaris in April.

Arnould went on to say that when he learned of this contact, he was alarmed,

> because I feared that the whole matter might be a trick by the Germans to find our headquarters. But Keun assured me it was not a trick and that Canaris was representing a group of high-ranking Germans who were anxious to get in touch with the Allied high command in London. He told me he must get this information to London without delay. He made the

arrangements for an aircraft over our wireless set, which was hidden in the loft over the sacristy.

And, according to Arnould's recollections, ". . . Philippe flew to London on or about May 30, 1944."

That, then, was the nature of Canaris's extraordinary mission: to communicate once more directly with Menzies. But what did his message contain that warranted such grave personal risks, both on his part and on the part of Keun? Arnould said that he assumed it concerned an attempt by the military opposition to Hitler to open discussions for an armistice.

Without written records, any contact between Keun and Canaris, as well as the existence of a personal message from Canaris to Menzies, is open to question. But Keun did travel to England at this time and that fact was later confirmed by Commander Dunderdale, the liaison officer for MI-6 with the French secret services, a long-standing friend of the Keun family and Keun's sometime controller. Dunderdale said he went down to Manston, MI-6's forward airbase on the tip of the Kentish peninsula, to receive Keun personally. However, he was mystified by the story that Keun brought with him a personal communication from Canaris to Menzies. "Keun came over to receive instructions about the part Jade Amicol was to play in the invasion and had he brought a message with him I think he would have told me. Even if he had not told me I think I would have been told by Menzies. But Menzies said nothing." Nevertheless, Dunderdale agreed that he was not privy to everything that occurred between Menzies and Jade Amicol, and he confirmed that Canaris did have contacts with Menzies—as Menzies himself admitted. These, said Dunderdale, occurred at this time through Oswald Baron Hoyningen-Huene, the German ambassador at Lisbon, who was a fringe member of the Schwarze Kapelle. However, Dunderdale persisted in his objection to the story that Keun was the bearer of a message from Canaris to Menzies, observing: "It seems inconceivable that it happened this way, if it happened at all. In the first place, Canaris was far too wily an old bird to commit himself under circumstances where the messenger might very easily be captured. And Keun himself would have thought twice about carrying any message." However, Dunderdale became much less sure when he heard that, in addition to Arnould's testimony, Madame Henriette Frede, the Mother Superior of the convent in Paris, had stated that she had seen Keun walking with a man whom she later knew to be Canaris around the Lion of Belfort in the Place Denfert-Rochereau in the last week of May 1944. Finally, Dunderdale would say he was prepared to accept the story "tentatively" when he heard that Menzies had replied to the message, and that there had been a meeting between Canaris, Arnould and the Mother Superior at the convent just before the invasion. Thus it can be assumed that such a communication existed, that Keun was its courier, and that Dunderdale's objections were based on the fact that neigher Keun nor Menzies told him about its existence. But as Dunderdale would admit: "There was no earthly reason why they should. Such matters were not my concern."

Nor, in spite of Menzies's position, were they his concern. How could he respond to such a communication? It would have been unthinkable for him to have acted without the authority of the Foreign Office. When he had received similar communications before, he had always referred them to Anthony Eden, the Foreign Secretary; and Eden had always instructed him to take no action. Dulles in Berne was in a like situation; he would state that when "I received a request from Canaris for a personal meeting on the German-Swiss frontier, Cordell Hull refused permission to accept." In both cases, the reasons were much the same. There was always the specter of another Venlo; no one could forget that two of MI-6's most important agents in western Europe had been kidnapped while, they thought, they were on business concerning the Schwarze Kapelle. Even without Venlo, there would have been the specter of the Russians, who suspected that Britain was so war-weary she was ready to talk peace. In January 1944, *Pravda,* the official Russian newspaper, had reproduced a story then circulating in the neutral press that British agents had met agents of Ribbentrop in a town in the Pyrenees. The British denied the story; but they remained cautious not to give the Russians any cause to suspect that the western powers were seeking a political termination to the war that would leave the Germans free to fight the Russians, nor to give Hitler any cause to suspect that there was a split in the Grand Alliance.

If Menzies at MI-6 was powerless to respond to Canaris's appeal, there was one bureau where the news of such a communication would have been extremely interesting, and that was the LCS. Wingate would not be able to remember whether either he or Bevan ever heard of the communication. But both were aware that such appeals had been made several times before. Wingate would recall:

> We received reports frequently about the German opposition [sic]. But the political authorities decided that no reliance could be placed on these. It had been decided long since that the war could only be ended by military means. Therefore, we did ask ourselves about the use that we could make of these contacts in order to assist our strategic deception operations. We decided that such overtures were examples of defeatism and of course where you have disaffected elements they are more liable to accept information which was to the disadvantage of Hitler. Perhaps this is what Bevan meant when he told me that we had people on the German Staff (who were being used by the LCS to sow its deceptions). The ability to put a word in the ear of the German Staff was worth divisions on occasions.

Thus the fate of Canaris's final overture was already sealed. He might better have saved himself the trouble. No accommodation could be offered. There could be only Unconditional Surrender. It was in this spirit that Menzies must have settled down to write his reply to Canaris—the last communication in the long years of their peculiar association. But here was another mystery. Why should Menzies have replied at all? Was it not too dangerous? Would the letter not have been Keun's and Canaris's death warrant had it been captured? Might it not have been a most valuable instrument for the German propagandists—if it had fallen into their hands —in stiffening the resolve of the *Feldgrau* and *Herrenvolk* and in splitting the Grand Alliance? Would it not have been more prudent for Menzies to meet the overture with disdainful silence? Perhaps; but his reply may simply have been the act of a gentleman, or Menzies, ever alert for an opportunity to "put a word in the ear of the German Staff," may not have wanted to end a channel of communication that had lasted for so long. At any rate, according to Arnould, Menzies did reply, and Keun returned to Paris with his letter.

Keun arrived back at the Convent of St. Agonie at about lunchtime "three or four days before the *débarquement*," and again, the events that followed were later described by eye witnesses—the Mother Superior and Arnould. The Mother Superior answered Keun's special knock at the chapel door and then led him through the chapel into the sacristy, where Arnould was waiting for him. The two men went into the Mother Superior's private room and there Keun told Arnould that he had brought a letter from London which must be given to Canaris without delay. Arnould immediately telephoned his contact at Stuelpnagel's headquarters, and they arranged to meet at a confessional at Notre Dame. Canaris was thought to be still in Paris, and at Notre Dame that afternoon, Arnould instructed his contact to get a message to Canaris, asking him to be at the windmill beside the racetrack at Longchamps at eleven o'clock on the morning of June 3.

Just before 11 A.M. next day, Arnould cycled past the windmill, which he considered a safe rendezvous because it was close to the copses of the Bois de Boulogne and because the windmill itself stood on high ground from which all roads leading into the area could be observed. Moreover, Arnould had a safehouse in the nearby suburb of Auteil to which he could escape. At about a quarter past eleven, Arnould saw Canaris—"a short man in a dark suit, easily identifiable because of his silver hair"— climb the steps to the windmill and then begin to walk around the pebble track, as if he was looking over the racecourse. Arnould approached Canaris from behind and, ensuring there were no witnesses either in the road below or on the windmill itself, spoke to him. He introduced himself as "Colonel Ollivier," a code name Canaris knew well, and said that he had received a letter for the admiral from London. He explained that it was too dangerous to bring by hand and could not be transmitted by post. Consequently, he invited the admiral to the convent that same evening at six o'clock. And Canaris—according to Arnould's own account of the encounter—agreed to be there.

It was an incredible rendezvous, for both men were risking everything. An even more incredible encounter was to follow that evening. At six o'clock Canaris arrived at the convent and rang the bell on the old door. It was answered by the Mother Superior, who asked him what he wanted. "Canaris seemed nonplussed," she would recall, "and replied that he had come to pray." He was, perhaps, unaware that the convent was MI-6 headquarters in France, and thought that he might be given the letter in the chapel. But Arnould had told the Mother Superior who was coming, and she had taken the precaution of confining her twelve sisters to their quarters so that none might observe the important visitor. She drew the bolts and asked the admiral to follow her. They crossed the nave, passed the little spiral stairs which led to the choir loft over the sacristy where Keun had his transceiver, walked down a narrow stone-flagged passageway toward the clinic and entered her own room.

There, Canaris was again confronted by Arnould. The table was set for what the Mother Superior later described as a "simple but wholesome dinner." The two men shook hands and while the Mother Superior was out of the room Arnould produced the letter. It was an ordinary white foolscap envelope unmarked by either name or address, and it appeared—from where Arnould stood—to contain two sheets of plain typewritten letter paper with a signature at the bottom. Canaris sat down in one of the Mother Superior's easy chairs to read the letter, and there was a deep silence in the room. But when he finished it, he seemed to go quite white and give a little gasp. "This is the finish for Germany," he said. "They will not give us any terms whatsoever. There must be unconditional surrender or nothing."

Canaris put the letter in one of his inside pockets, and the two men sat for a short while without saying a word until Canaris repeated, *"Finis Germaniae!"* Arnould then offered him some calvados, which the admiral refused with thanks, but he did accept an invitation to dine. The conversation over the meal was desultory. As Arnould recalled: "It was an agonizing meal. The admiral was clearly in great despair. He said nothing about the contents, but it was clear from the nature of our conversation that he had written to General Menzies about an armistice and he had been rejected."

Shortly after seven o'clock Canaris rose, thanked Arnould for his hospitality, wished him good luck, and asked to be shown out. Arnould escorted his visitor back down the corridor into the nave, where prayers were now being held, and so into the street. Canaris walked off up the rue de la Santé, a narrow cobbled road leading onto the Boulevard Arago, and disappeared into the crowds of that sultry evening. He had failed, once again, to avert disaster for his homeland. Now no one could save Germany, for in Britain the clock had already been set ticking inexorably toward D-Day.

Vendetta

"VENDETTA," the last turn of the screw of special means during the pre-Neptune period, was issued to every Allied command at 0705 Greenwich Mean Time on May 1, 1944. It was a brief, pregnant message that read simply: "Word is Vendetta." While strictly speaking it was the code name for the threat against southern France from North Africa during Neptune, the promulgation of Vendetta would set in motion operations of an almost hemispherical nature during the month of May, all designed to produce uncertainty in the minds of the German high command and fear about their fate among the *Feldgrau*. The flames of Vendetta, fanned by the Supreme Command in London, ringed the German Empire. The Grand Alliance demanded that Turkey join "the cause"; and severe words were spoken to Rumania, Bulgaria, Hungary and Finland. In the Levant, the British 9th and 10th armies, which in fact had no more than a brigade of men apiece, appeared to be concentrating at Turkey's southern frontier, ready to march with the forty divisions of the Turkish army into Greece and Bulgaria. In the Balkans, special forces began raiding the Greek and Aegean islands with even greater frequency. In Yugoslavia, Tito's army of 800,000 partisans, now lightly equipped with artillery and tanks, intensified the volume of its aggressive defense; and the Germans retaliated with "Knight's Move," the code name of an operation to liquidate Tito and the partisan high command—an operation that almost succeeded. At the top of the Adriatic, Allied warships probed the defenses around Trieste as special agents continued to reconnoiter the entrance to the Ljubljana Gap. In January, America—Spain's only source—refused further supplies of petroleum products and Spain and Portugal were gradually being brought to heel by the increasing pressures of Allied diplomatic and economic warfare. And in Algeria, the French army, reborn and rearmed with American equipment, appeared to be mounting an invasion of the Riviera coast of France, while the *maquis* in that region began sabotage operations that seemed to be a preparation for such an invasion. On the Biscay coast, the *maquisards* undertook similar operations that seemed to portend a large-scale uprising in concert with an Allied landing. It was the same story in northern France, Belgium, Denmark, Holland and Norway, where the resistance was at work like tens of thousands of deathwatch beetles burrowing into the prow of the Reich. In Scandinavia, rumors were still rife of Anglo-Russian landings to seize the nickel ore mines at Petsamo, rumors that were aggravated by the Russians, who were playing their part in Bodyguard by simulating the preparations for a seaborne assault. At Stockholm, an Anglo-American mission continued to seek, or so it seemed, bases from which to attack the Baltic coast of Germany.

Hundreds of incidents, indeed thousands, occurred right round the rim of the war. A general was kidnapped in Crete; an SD officer was murdered at Lyon; the Greek Sacred Heart Boat Squadron attacked a radar post on Rhodes; German aircraft crashed in flames at Athens and abrasive grease was found in their engines; three German soldiers vanished in a Commando raid on Sagvaag in Norway; F section agents blew up three compressors in the liquid oxygen factory at Boulogne-sur-Seine; saboteurs wrecked the Luftwaffe repair shops at Klovermarksvej in Denmark; a German leave train was derailed in the Ardennes; 300,000 liters of petroleum products were destroyed in a suspicious fire at Boussens in France; a sabotage team gave the manager of the ball-bearing factory at Aubervilliers a choice: either he put the plant out of action or the RAF would—he chose the former. Everywhere in Europe surreptitious, nerve-racking underground warfare sought to pin down the Wehrmacht as Gulliver was ensnared by the Lilliputians.

The Germans reacted very strongly to this incessant activity, particularly in France where, time and time again, they cut down the *maquis*—only to have them spring up in even greater numbers. The nervous, hysterical tenor of their reactions was just what the Allies hoped to achieve: a fear among the *Feldgrau* that they were surrounded by enemies who were omnipresent, clever and murderous. Adding to that fear was the ominous silence on the military fronts. The fighting in Italy was in a stalemate, but the Allied armies were preparing for "Diadem," the great offensive that would lead to the capture of Rome. On the Russian front, the guns were silent; the Red Army, honoring its commitment to Bodyguard, was waiting to launch its summer offensive at a time and place that would help Neptune. And in England, the build-up for the invasion continued as hundreds of thousands of men and millions of tons of equipment assembled for D-Day. The Germans knew that the storm would soon break. But would they discover where and when the Allies would invade?

To keep the enemy mystified about these key secrets of Neptune, the Allied deception agencies were busy putting the finishing touches to Fortitude and Quicksilver. During the month of May, as Montgomery's 21st Army Group, the invasion force, was secretly and silently assembling in the Gloucester-Falmouth-Brighton triangle, Patton's virtually nonexistent FUSAG was "assembling" in the Dover-Cambridge-King's Lynn triangle. Elaborate preparations had been made to give this "concentration" of troops the appearance of a massive force, and once those preparations were complete, German reconnaissance aircraft were allowed to intrude over the FUSAG zone. There, in the creeks, harbors and river mouths of eastern England, from Lowestoft and Yarmouth down to the Norfolk Broads, the Deben River, the Orwell, at Dover, Folkestone and the Thames Estuary, they spotted 400 "landing ships"—each in reality little more than tubular scaffolding, canvas and wood floating on oil drums. They had been manufactured at the film studios at Shepperton, near London, and then brought down by road. Smoke coiled from their funnels, they were surrounded by oil patches, laundry hung from the rigging, motorboats left wakes from ship to ship, and intruding aircraft could see their crews —over-age or unfit soldiers of units such as the 10th Worcestershires and the 4th Northamptonshires. Thousands of carefully shielded truck lights indicated the presence of large convoys, and lights over "hards" gave the impression of intense loading activity after dark. And behind this "invasion fleet," which was large enough to "land" the entire 1st Canadian Army, which did not as yet exist, the fields of East Anglia and Kent were crowded with tanks, guns, half-tracks, ammunition dumps, field kitchens, hospitals, troop encampments and fuel lines.

They, too, were fakes. Farmer Sydney George Cripps, of Chaul End, a tiny hamlet in the hills just off the Watling Street, the ancient Roman road, saw a line of trucks in one of his meadows late one May evening. It was a common enough sight and he took no further notice. But at dawn the next day he saw scores of tanks in the same meadow. Afraid that they would chew up his grass, Cripps was on his way to complain to the officer in charge when he noticed that the tanks had left no tracks. The only tracks in the thick, dewy grass were being made by some American soldiers who were dragging a device across the meadow behind a truck. Then Cripps saw something even odder. A bull was loose in the meadow and charged one of the tanks; but when its horns struck the side of the tank, it collapsed with a huge hiss like a balloon. The tanks—there were more than a brigade of them—were just that: balloons. And the American soldiers were making tracks for them in case a German reconnaissance plane came over with its cameras.

Sounds as well as sights were used to complete the deception. The ionosphere over FUSAG was filled by the sporadic wireless noises made by an army group, while it was silent over Montgomery's invasion force. German wireless intelligence men across the Channel heard radio chatter that had been compiled as a scenario in a book 8 inches thick, including the classic "1/5th Queen's Royal Regiment report a number of civilian women, presumably unauthorised, in the baggage train. What are we going to do with them—take them to Calais?" To confirm all the other indications that the main troop concentrations were in the Dover and Cambridge areas, signals engineers laid lines from Montgomery's real operations headquarters at Portsmouth to Dover Castle and released his wireless traffic from there. Then, to prevent the Germans from being able to inquire too closely into the truth of the information they were getting through intercepts, and to destroy their ability to find out where the Allied armies were really concentrating through the use of wireless direction finding, a series of air attacks were mounted against their wireless stations, including their signals intelligence headquarters near Cherbourg, which was leveled in a massive raid.

Leaks to the press added to the reality of FUSAG—chaplains were announced to have joined the army group which was "preparing for the invasion of Europe across the historic plains of Flanders." And there was yet another visual illusion designed to make the Germans believe that FUSAG was destined for the Pas de Calais. Preparations were being made for Pluto—the mnemonic for "pipeline under the ocean"—to be laid between southern England and Normandy to supply the invasion armies with petrol. To deceive the Germans about where such a pipeline would start— and therefore where it would terminate—Britain's finest architect of the period had been called in to create a vast but entirely fake oil dock at Dover.

Basil Spence, Professor of Architecture at the Royal Academy, member of the Fine Art Commission, one of the creators of the Viceroy of India's residence at Delhi, architect of the British Embassy in Rome and the future Household Cavalry Barracks at Knightsbridge, consultant for the extension to the Palais des Nations at Geneva, architect for the new cathedral at Coventry—and a score of other such projects—designed and built the phony oil dock with the aid of film and theater stagehands. Made almost entirely of camouflaged scaffolding, fiber board and old sewage pipes, it occupied nearly 3 square miles of the Dover foreshore, and it consisted of fake pipelines, storage tanks, powerhouses, a fire brigade, anti-aircraft gun posts, guardrooms, lorry parks, jetties—everything that a real oil dock would have. Wind machines blew up clouds of dust to make it look as if rapid progress was being made and to hide the fact that in reality there were only a few score men at work there. The area was closely guarded by military police. The King "inspected" the dock, and so did Montgomery. Eisenhower spoke to the "construction workers" at a dinner party held at the White Cliffs Hotel in Dover; and the Mayor made satisfied remarks about the "opening of a new installation, the precise nature of which must remain secret until the war is over, but which will bring the borough material benefits of consequence." The RAF maintained constant fighter patrols overhead, as if to protect the installation; the Royal Engineers cloaked it each night with artificial fog generated from smoke pots burning crude oil; and German reconnaissance aircraft were permitted to fly over-head—but only after they had been "engaged" by the fighter patrols, and provided they were at 33,000 feet, where it was impossible for their cameras to pick out any defects in the installation. Whenever German long-range artillery batteries on Cap Gris Nez attempted to shell it, as they did occasionally, "hits" and subsequent "fires" were created from massive sodium flares.

Fakery had become an immense industry in the interests of Fortitude and Quicksilver. East Anglia resembled an enormous film lot, and no detail was spared. Livid vicars struck up angry correspondence in the East Anglia newspapers about the "moral collapse" that had occurred since "the vast number of foreign troops"—and "particularly American paratroopers and French and Polish tank units"—had "invaded the area." There was spirited discussion about the "immense numbers of-rubber contraceptives" found around "the American paratroop bases at Marham and Coggeshall." But, in essence, all this fakery was designed primarily as physical confirma-tion for the reports which the XX-Committee's double agents Garbo and Brutus had been feeding, and continued to feed, the Germans about FUSAG. On May 19, 1944, as part of the process to build him up as a replacement for Tricycle, Brutus told his controllers by wireless that he had been posted to Patton's headquarters as a liaison officer between the Polish high command and FUSAG. This mundane job had been selected deliber-ately by the XX-Committee as a post where Brutus might have access to much without access to everything, for there was the constant threat that the Germans would ask him for more information than SHAEF was dis-posed to reveal. Having established himself in his new job, Brutus each night just before midnight began to send the entire FUSAG order of battle to his controller. This was stunning information for FHW to receive; but since it corresponded both with Roenne's own rigged estimates, with the reports of other agents and with the intelligence yield of aerial reconnais-sance and wireless intercepts, Roenne had no recourse, after passing the intelligence through his analysis system, but to place the FUSAG order of battle before Hitler at Berchtesgaden.

As for Garbo, he, too, announced that he had been offered a new job—as translator by the chief of the Iberian subsection of the Ministry of Information. There, he explained, he would be privy to the secrets of a man who knew everything in Britain—Brendan Bracken, the minister and confidant of Churchill. But, as Garbo went on, he disliked very much the "idea of betraying the Führer by working for the British." Under the circumstances, since he could still obtain excellent intelligence by not working for the British, should he accept the post? His instructions came back immediately: Garbo must forget his scruples and accept the post. He did so, and a flow of even more deceptive information followed.

A feminine voice was also part of the XX-Committee chorus at this time. She was a beautiful young Argentinian whose father was at the Argentine Embassy in Vichy. In 1942, the young woman had visited her father, and while she was in France an Abwehr recruiting officer suggested that she might like to go to England (where her father had had important connections before the war) as an Abwehr agent. She accepted, but en route to London via Madrid, she went to the British and told them all. MI-6 helped her on her way and she landed in Bristol at the end of October 1942. In London, she was held by the security authorities for an extensive period; and then the XX-Committee assumed control of her at the beginning of 1943. She was codenamed "Bronx."

Bronx began as a secret ink letter writer, supplying the Germans with information supplied to her by the XX-Committee. Her work was considered so good by the Germans that they paid her a retainer of £25 ($120) a month, with expenses—a fair sum in those days—plus a number of bonuses. She corresponded with the Abwehr through the Bank of the Holy Ghost in Lisbon, which was also her own bank, and it was that connection which determined the next move in the game. Toward the end of 1943, the Germans, even then preoccupied with the invasion, provided Bronx with an interesting cipher to enable her to transmit more urgent and important information by commercial telegram. If she learned anything about the time and place of the invasion, she was to send a request to her bank along these lines: £100 indicated that the invasion would come in northern France; £125 would mean the Biscay coast; £150 would mean the French Mediterranean coast; £175 would mean the Adriatic; £200, Greece; £225, Denmark; £250, Norway; and so on. Further, if she put the purpose for which she needed the money into her telegram, it would indicate the month of the invasion.

Bronx, of course, passed the cipher on to the XX-Committee, which decided to put it to use for the purposes of "Ironside," the Fortitude operation designed to threaten the Bordeaux region and pin down the German 11th Panzer Division for as long as possible before, during and after D-Day. It was not expected in London that any stratagem would keep the division in place for very long; but then advantage was being measured in hours. Consequently, on May 15, 1944, Bronx sent this telegram to her bank through the Foreign Office (private telegrams could still be sent over commercial wires, provided the Foreign Office was allowed to handle them):

Envoyez vite cinquante livres. J'ai besoin
pour mon dentiste.

The cable meant: "I have definite news that a landing will be made in the Bay of Biscay in about one month"—around June 15, 1944, nine days after D-Day. This was just another of the "witty hors d'oeuvres" that preceded the "main course," the invasion; but as time would tell, it had a significant effect upon German reactions to Neptune.

The deception experts considered that it was not enough that the Germans learn of Allied military intentions in France only through wireless and aerial intelligence and the reports of agents whose veracity might be in question. How much better if there was someone of undoubted veracity who could report in person to the German General Staff on the enormous build-up in England for the invasion—and particularly on the existence of FUSAG. The LCS and the CSM had searched for such a man, and they found him in General Hans Cramer.

Cramer, the last commander of the Afrika Korps, had been captured in May 1943 at the Axis collapse in Tunisia. He was brought to England, and because his health had begun to deteriorate, it was decided to send him home in a repatriation program run by the Swedish Red Cross—but not before he had been of service to Fortitude. In May 1944 he was taken by road from his camp in south Wales to the "London Cage," the Combined Services Detailed Interrogation Centre in Kensington Palace Gardens. His route lay directly through the Neptune assembly area, and he was deliberately permitted to see immense build-ups of armor, shipping and aircraft. He dined with Patton, who was introduced as the "C-in-C of FUSAG," and he was received by various divisional commanders, all of whom laid emphasis on the fact that they were going to land at Calais. But what he was not allowed to know was where he had been; he was told that he had traveled through southern and eastern England when in fact he had been in central, south and southwestern England. He had no way of telling (except by the sun) where he had actually been, for ever since the Battle of Britain all signposts had been removed, and so had all place names on police stations, local government offices, shops, railway stations, and the like.

Cramer then embarked on the Swedish ship *Gripsholm* for passage to a German port and reached Berlin on May 23, 1944. He reported first to General Kurt Zeitzler, the Chief of Staff of the German army, and then to OKW at Berchtesgaden. Then, after a period of leave and a medical check, he was posted as a special adviser to the headquarters of General Leo Baron Geyr von Schweppenburg, the C-in-C of the German Panzerarmee in the West. Both at Berchtesgaden and Paris, Cramer evidently informed his superiors of what he had seen in Britain—and where he had seen it. For Goering would state after the war: "One of our generals . . . had been captured by the British and subsequently returned to us by exchange. Before his release [by the British] he was thoroughly indoctrinated by them and shown the vast stores of matériel and equipment along the southern coast of England. He came back to us with all those impressions (and) . . . a defeatist attitude." This was exactly what the LCS and the CSM had intended. The Cramer stratagem was, for all its simplicity, one of the most important instruments of corroboration for the existence of FUSAG. For who would distrust the report of a full *General der Panzertruppen* with the Knight's Cross of the Iron Cross with Oak Leaves?

Then came "Copperhead," a deception operation which was designed to reinforce the threat of an Allied invasion in the south of France. A romanticized version of the operation would become widely known after the war as the story of "Monty's Double." "The truth," according to Lieutenant Colonel J. V. B. Jervis-Reid, "was somewhat less romantic." It began on March 14, 1944, when, by chance, Jervis-Reid, the deputy chief of the CSM, happened to see a photograph of Lieutenant Meyrick Edward Clifton James, of the Royal Army Pay Corps stationed at Leicester, in the *News Chronicle.* James, in peacetime a minor actor on the English provincial stage, had appeared at an armed services theatrical show at the Comedy Theatre in London and the caption read: "You're wrong—His name is James!" For, as was quite evident in the photograph, James bore a very close resemblance to Montgomery.

Jervis-Reid conceived a scheme in which James would impersonate Montgomery. But at first the case did not look very promising; Montgomery was a strict teetotaler and James, investigation showed, suffered from serious bouts of alcoholism. Nevertheless, Jervis-Reid decided to pursue his scheme. He saw James at Leicester, gave him lunch, and explained that he wished to use him in a propaganda film to be made by the Army Kinematograph Service. James's reaction to the proposition betrayed much of the essence of his personality—a personality that was quite unlike that of Montgomery's arrogant self-assurance. As James would afterwards: "I had an imaginary pre-view of a thrilling screen drama in which a glamorous enemy spy spreads alarm and confusion by vamping a pay clerk and persuades him to falsify the accounts." That, however, was not what Jervis-Reid had in mind. Despite his reservations, he "took rather a liking to the sad little fellow," and decided that, with close supervision and encouragement, James might work out. He arranged with his commanding officer to allow the paymaster to come to London on special duties; and James soon arrived for what was intended to be the biggest performance of his career.

The Copperhead plan proposed that James impersonate Montgomery and, under the direction of the CSM and A-Force, be paraded through

Gibraltar and Algiers shortly before D-Day. The objectives were three: to lead the Germans to believe that, with Montgomery out of Britain, the invasion would not be launched across the Channel in the first week of June, as other reports and signs might indicate; to lead the Germans to believe that when the Neptune fleet sailed, it was just another exercise; and to pin down the four armored divisions (two of them SS) stationed south of the Loire by making the Germans believe that Montgomery was in command of Allied military operations from Africa and Italy against southern France.

James was separated both from his wife and from the bottle; and he was told he was impersonating Montgomery as part of training for a film production. He settled down well to the task of studying Montgomery from a distance, and then the two men were brought fact-to-face aboard the C-in-C's personal train. James would recount: "The likeness struck me as uncanny. . . . On the stage it is something if you can resemble a man after using every artifice of make-up, but in this case there was no need for false eyebrows, padded cheeks, or anything of that kind." James had lost one of his fingers; but in all other physical respects, he and Montgomery seemed to be products of the same template. Their stances, build and walk were almost identical; and James found that he could imitate Montgomery's rapid, somewhat squeaky diction without trouble. As important, Jervis-Reid saw that James could develop Montgomery's air of authority. With that, he decided to go ahead with Copperhead—but still without telling James of the real purpose of the impersonation.

The paymaster was now introduced to the minutiae of his role, especially to such cocktail party and dinner table matters as Churchill's hours, Roosevelt's health, Eisenhower's ability, Smith's ulcer, Bradley's competence, Brooke's temper. Then James was outfitted by Myer and Mortimer, the military tailors, in a well-cut battledress with the scarlet gorgets of the Imperial General Staff, epaulets that included a general's crossed swords, four rows of decorations and honors, a black beret with two badges, the heavy Veldtschoen that Montgomery wore, a gold chain and fob, some handkerchiefs with the initials "BLM," a sheepskin flying jacket and a natty little cane. A trustworthy makeup artist was called in, trimmed James's mustache a shade, brushed up his eyebrows to make them bristle like Montgomery's and applied a touch of greasepaint to make his temples appear a little grayer. Now the likeness was indeed uncanny.

James was at last told what his mission was going to be—with the news that Montgomery had insisted that if James was going to impersonate him then he must be paid like him. But this did not smother James's alarm. He was, he would write, "overcome by the worst fit of stage fright I had yet had . . . I thought I looked as much like a successful general as a hypnotised rabbit." Nevertheless, he agreed to go through with the charade; and during the late afternoon of May 25, 1944, he was dressed, his false finger was put on, his beret set at the right angle, and then, traveling in a staff car, he was taken to the airfield at Northolt. With the minimum of flourish (but enough to permit gossip to circulate that it was Montgomery going on a tour), James boarded a Liberator and took off for Gibraltar. There was only one detail that had been overlooked; James, Jervis-Reid would recall, had hidden a hip flask of gin in his handkit.

The flight was due to land at Gibraltar shortly before breakfast time on May 26; and to make sure that James was fit and fresh for the morning, he was given a sleeping draught. Then everyone settled down for the night. But James got up again, perhaps because of the extreme cold, and went to the toilet in the rear of the aircraft. He was not missed at first, but when he was, his escort went after him—and found James nipping the gin. The pint flask was half empty. Worse, through the interaction of the gin and the sleeping draught, James was noticeably unsteady on his feet. Gibraltar was now only two hours away, and unless James could be sobered up quickly, it would be quite evident to everyone—not least the Liberator crew, which was not party to the stratagem—that the whole thing was a trick. Montgomery's loathing for alcohol and tobacco was as celebrated as the two badges on his beret. It was an emergency, and James was subjected to treatment that he was not likely to forget. His body was bared to the icy slipstream coming through the plughole in one of the cabin windows, he was made to vomit, he was kept walking up and down, he was thoroughly massaged and slapped, he was doused in cold water, and he was given a shave—in case he nicked himself. By the time the Liberator landed at Gibraltar, James was quite sober and, chastened, ready to begin his performance. Copperhead had been saved—for the moment.

When James disembarked, he gave the "Monty salute" to the small but impressive reception party, some men around the aircraft shouted "Up Monty!", the Spaniards working in the area were allowed to get a good look at the general, and then he was driven away to spend the night at Government House. The Governor, General Sir Ralph T. Eastwood, a man who had been at Sandhurst with Montgomery and knew all he had to know about Copperhead in order to cooperate convincingly, greeted him and there seemed little doubt that his arrival at both the airport and Government House was observed by German agents. Further, Eastwood gave a small party that evening at which "Montgomery" was introduced to two Spanish bankers, one of whom was thought to have connections with the SD, and they overheard James talking in a loud voice about "Plan 303." To the gratification of the A-Force representative on the spot, it was not long before the local counterintelligence office telephoned to state that all

Gibraltar was abuzz with news that Montgomery was staying with the Governor, that he was talking about a "Plan 303," and that he was on his way the next morning to a conference at Algiers.

Driving back to the airfield the following morning—along a route which took the car through British engineers who were working on the roads—James was again put on public view. There were loud cries of "Good old Monty!" and "Up Monty!" as he flashed that famous salute. There were more such cries as the car swept through the main gates of the airfield, the guards gave a snappy present arms, and James got out close to his aircraft. Ceremonies were kept to a minimum, just as if a real general was traveling on active service. But to give time for a crowd to gather and observe the departure, the Liberator was allowed to develop a minor gremlin. Eastwood took James to the airport canteen for a cup of tea while the aircraft was being inspected, and there, James contrived to leave one of his "BLM" handkerchiefs for a Spanish servant to pick up, and within earshot of civilians, he again began to talk about "Plan 303." Finally, the aircraft was ready, and after a few last words with Eastwood, James boarded, the doors were closed and, within minutes, the Liberator was flying along the Queen of Spain's Chair on course for Algiers. So far, James's performance had been distinctly good, even brilliant. It seemed almost impossible for the Germans not to have known about "Montgomery's" visit; Algeciras, just across the bay from Gibraltar, was a main Abwehr outpost.

At Algiers, James was received with rather more ceremony at Maison Blanche airfield. Some French *spahis* formed a guard of honor; the huge figure of the Supreme Commander, General Sir Henry Maitland Wilson, could be seen towering like a pyramid out of the shimmering heat haze; and the British, American and French staff was formed up for James to meet. Then he was driven off to his quarters in the St. George Hotel overlooking the city. It was not long before all Algiers knew that Montgomery was in town; and from time to time his staff car, a pennant flying, outriders on both sides, was to be seen hurtling through the streets to one meeting or another. But then, the most incredible stories began to circulate at Eisenhower's headquarters in London that "Montgomery" had been seen staggering around the streets of Algiers with a cigar in his mouth. Whether or not the stories were true, "Montgomery," quite suddenly and for reasons that were never given out, vanished and Copperhead came to a rapid end.

Whatever had happened at Algiers, James was returned to a lieutenant's uniform, pay and privileges, and he was flown home not in his own personal aircraft but in the bucket seat of a DC-3 courier plane. At London, he was told that if he breathed a word of the operation he would be court-martialed; and he soon found himself back at his paymaster's desk. There, he encountered a new set of problems, for when he was unable to explain his absence, his colleagues began to gossip in the mess that he had been off on a bender, and his commanding officer wanted to court-martial him for being absent without leave. The War Office increased the confusion by telephoning James's commanding officer, who had been told nothing of the impersonation, to ask why a mere lieutenant had been drawing a general's pay and allowances. It was hinted that James had been fraudulent; and finally, a rumor spread that he had been in the Tower of London, arrested on suspicion of espionage.

It was not until the war was over that James could explain what he had done during those five weeks away from his desk. And then, in a ghostwritten memoir and a film called *I Was Monty's Double,* the most extravagant claims were made by him and on his behalf for the success of Copperhead. The facts were somewhat different. Nothing would appear in Abwehr documents captured after the war to show that the Germans had taken into their calculations the fact that "Montgomery" had visited the Mediterranean theater during this period. They were concerned about the threat of an Allied invasion in the south of France, but that concern was based on other, weightier, less melodramatic exploits—for example, the Vendetta comings and goings at Oran of the assault-trained U.S. 91st Infantry Division. But nothing was lost by Copperhead. The CSM had simply staged a performance—perhaps James's greatest performance—to an empty house.

Far more successful in aggravating German fear of an invasion of southern France was an operation called "Royal Flush." In a diplomatic maneuver conducted at the express instructions of Brooke, Marshall, Hull and Eden, the American and British ambassadors at Madrid called upon the Spanish Foreign Minister, General don Francisco Gómez Jordaña, to request the use of facilities at the port of Barcelona for the evacuation of Allied casualties in "impending operations." At the same time American and British diplomats appeared among the wharfingers of Barcelona, asking questions about the port's capacity to handle food and "other supplies," berthing arrangements and billeting facilities for surgical and nursing personnel. To all appearances, the Allies wished to turn the "Manchester of Spain" into a hospital for some great campaign shortly to be undertaken on the other side of the Golfe du Lion in southern France, a campaign that was indeed planned but for a later date. Would the Spanish government cooperate? The answer reached the Germans as quickly as it reached the Allies; yes Generalissimo Franco would be pleased to provide suitable space at Barcelona for 2000 hospitalized men and their attendants together with all dock, labor, warehouse and other facilities of the port. When this information was allied to intelligence about the activities of the American 91st Infantry Division, to the rapidly growing size of the French 1st Army in North Africa—an operation that was costing the United States $1.2

billion—and to the incessant prowling of reconnaissance ships and aircraft, OKW decided to keep its entire Army of the Riviera in place for the time being—including its panzer divisions.

Well before the Copperhead charade had run its course, Eisenhower had issued the last of a series of orders that marked the end of the Neptune preparatory period. After a long and careful study of the tides, the phases of the moon, the hours of daylight and the currents, Allied planners had agreed that only three days in early June—the 5th, the 6th and the 7th—filled all the basic requirements of Neptune. "Y-Day," that day when everything must be ready for the assault, was set for the 1st of June, and its code word was "Halcyon." June 5 was selected as the day of the assault, but the 6th and 7th would also be acceptable if bad weather interfered on the 5th. If the expedition could not sail on any one of these three days for any reason—particularly the weather—the next period during which all the natural factors would combine to favor Neptune would be between the 19th and the 22nd of June.

No one could predict what the weather might be during that first week in June. But with Halcyon set, Eisenhower ordered the great concentration of military force to begin in the counties of Cornwall, Devon, Somerset, Gloucestershire, Wiltshire, Dorset, Sussex and Surrey. On May 18, 1944, convoys—often 100 miles long—started to snake their way down quiet English roads to the embarkation points. Tanks with bridges over their turrets, and arms to lay them across ditches; tanks with trailers and strange nozzles to blast German positions with liquid fire; tanks with great bundles of wood overhead to lay in culverts and permit other tanks to move across; tanks with flails of chains to cut passages through minefields; armored cars, jeeps, ambulances, mobile headquarters, field kitchens, mobile hospitals, weapons carriers, half-tracks, Dodge and Bedford trucks by the thousands; mobile wireless and radar stations, anti-aircraft guns, self-propelled artillery, tank trucks—weapons and vehicles of every shape, every size, for every purpose, and in an abundance never before seen anywhere, advanced into the concentration areas to be loaded into the largest fleet in the history of maritime affairs. Yet such was the miasma of secrecy and deception that there were many who believed—as did Hitler—that the whole affair was mere shadowboxing. Eisenhower's diarist recorded on May 18: "Whitman [of the New York *Daily News*], a veteran war correspondent . . . told me that some correspondents believe there will not be an invasion, that talk of one is a giant hoax."

As the troops concentrated and tensions mounted, there were many portents and alarms. A Finnish professor announced that a comet would shortly appear over Europe, and Berlin radio urged the German people to ignore the old superstition that the phenomenon portended catastrophe.

The women of Caddington in the Chilterns swore they saw the Angel of Mons in the night sky, just as it had been seen before the great battles in Flanders in the First World War. They refused to believe it when they were told that the vision was no more than a combination of flares and searchlights being tested to illuminate the ground at night. The world stood still for an hour on the evening of May 27 when a woman announcer on Berlin radio interrupted a program to declare: "Ladies and gentlemen, we have sensational news. Stand by for it later in this program. . . ." But the tension eased when Berlin radio later announced: "And now to the important news. In just a few moments you will hear a very talented Berlin artist play on a violin that was made in 1626."

The fears of ordinary people were magnified by the absence of news, but apprehension was no less great among those who knew all about Neptune. The Supreme Commander told his doctor that he was suffering from an almost intolerable ringing in the ear—a sign of extreme nervous tension. His diarist wrote: "Ike looks worn and tired. The strain is telling on him. He looks older now than at any time since I have been with him." And Eisenhower himself wrote in a letter to his friend General Brehon B. Somervell, in Washington:

> . . . tension grows and everybody gets more on edge. This time, because of the stakes involved, the atmosphere is probably more electric than ever before . . . we are not merely risking a tactical defeat; we are putting the whole works on one number. A sense of humor and a great faith, or else a complete lack of imagination, are essential to sanity.

Napoleon or Wellington might have expressed himself better, but the sense would have been the same.

Only Montgomery seemed quite impervious; like a monk, he worked and prayed in his caravan, venturing forth into the sunlight to speak to his men of the "holy crusade" on which they were about to embark. Other generals were apprehensive. On May 12, 1944, Smith had expressed the view that "our chances of holding the beachhead, particularly after the Germans get their buildup, are only fifty-fifty." Fifty-fifty—and it had taken the entire military, industrial, economic and intellectual resources of the Anglo-Saxon world four years just to mount the expedition.

Apprehension was manifested in different ways among the assault troops in the tented cities on the moors and in the valleys and forests of southwestern and southern England. They were well aware of the bitter fighting and bloodshed going on in Italy. Almost 150,000 men had been killed, wounded or declared missing since September 3, 1943, when the Allies first landed there. How much worse was Neptune going to be? For the Germans in France were ten times as numerous as they were in Italy;

they had had four years since Dunkirk—four years almost to the day—in which to fortify the Channel coast. Some of the assault troops, it seemed, no longer cared what would happen to them. There were signs of severe morale problems among others, problems that would worsen if they were kept idle and waiting too long. Nor was Eisenhower always impressed by the officers he met during his visits to the assault divisions. His diarist would record: "I am concerned over the absence of toughness and alertness of the young American officers whom I saw on this trip. . . . They are as green as growing corn. How will they act in battle? . . . A good many of the full colonels also give me a pain. They are fat, gray and oldish. Most of them wear the Rainbow Ribbon of the last war and are still fighting it." Men of all ranks knew that many would be killed or wounded, burned or drowned. But if they were fearful, their mood, in the main, was one of compliance, as if the Far Shore and its dangers existed in dimensions other than time and place.

No expense or effort had been spared to ensure that Neptune would succeed. Eisenhower would command the finest expeditionary force ever to leave any shore, and he knew more about his enemy than any other commander in history. But no intelligence in war can ever be complete. There were gaps in SHAEF's knowledge, and one of them concerned the 352nd Infantry Division, a first-rate German fighting formation—despite the commanding general's claim that most of its newcomers were so undernourished that he had to build them up with special rations of Normandy buttermilk. This division had been located near St. Lô, at the base of the neck of the Cherbourg peninsula. But in May, it had inched forward and taken up a position overlooking what would become Omaha. Thus, instead of the two divisions of understrength and under-equipped infantry which the Americans believed were in the Atlantic Wall on the invasion coast of Calvados, there were three; and instead of the four battalions of infantry which the Americans expected to encounter at Omaha, there were two regiments, with a third close behind the coast in reserve. Furthermore, these men had created what an American naval historian would call "the best imitation of hell for an invading force that American troops (would encounter) anywhere." But not until the eve of D-Day would the Americans discover that the 352nd had moved up. And here was the mystery. On May 23, 1944, working with precisely the same intelligence that was available to the Americans, the British warned their forces that the 352nd might be encountered on D-Day. Then, on D−2, Brigadier E. T. Williams, Montgomery's intelligence officer, again warned in the *21 Army Group Weekly Neptune Intelligence Review,* which was circulated to the Americans as well as the British, that "It should not be surprising if we discovered that (the) 352nd Division has one regiment up and two to play." Granted the intelligence was only speculative, but it would later be suggested that it was withheld from the American commanders, with Eisenhower's knowledge and approval, in order not to increase the morale problems of the U.S. 1st and 29th divisions by informing them too far ahead that they would be facing a first-rate infantry division that had been tempered in the fires of the Russian front—as, indeed, had been the 352nd's lot before it arrived in Normandy.

Equally mysterious were the silence and inactivity of the enemy on the eve of D-Day. Where were the secret weapons? What were the Luftwaffe and the Kriegsmarine up to? The only German aerial activity just before the invasion was an occasional reconnaissance flight, the odd nuisance raid on London to keep everyone awake, and, on the night of May 30, a single attack in which a few bombs fell and caused casualties at an American ordnance base near Falmouth. Everyone assumed the Germans were saving their strength for the great contest on D-Day; and when the Allied commanders obtained information that the enemy might use gas or some bacteriological weapon, they reiterated their standing orders concerning the detection and combatting of such attacks. Here lay another task for Bronx. She was induced to write a letter to her controller stating that the Allies had very large stocks of a germ warfare agent that created conditions like the bubonic plague. This story, intended to warn Hitler that if he used gas or germ warfare the Allies would retaliate, was supported by reports from other XX-Committee agents. But the troops need not have worried; Hitler, with his personal experience in the First World War of what it was like to be gassed, had no intention of using such weapons on D-Day.

It was now—on the eve of Halcyon—time to assess the effects of Bodyguard and Fortitude. There was encouraging news from Italy. On May 23, an American patrol near Valmontone captured a German headquarters vehicle hidden in an olive grove, and papers found in armored cabinets were immediately sent to Allied headquarters at the royal palace in Caserta. When they were analyzed by G2 and A-Force, they revealed that Bodyguard was a triumph of strategic deception. For this was the German order of battle in May—and it would not change by D-Day:

Russian front: 122 infantry-type divisions, 25 panzer divisions plus one brigade; 17 miscellaneous divisions plus one brigade.

Italian and Balkans fronts: 37 infantry divisions plus two brigades; nine panzer and four miscellaneous divisions.

Western front including The Netherlands, Denmark and Norway: 64 infantry divisions plus one regiment; 12 panzer divisions plus two brigades; 12 miscellaneous divisions.

Reserves in Germany: three infantry divisions plus one brigade; one panzer division plus two brigades; four miscellaneous divisions plus two brigades.

In short, the Wehrmacht had dispersed its forces in response to Body-guard's threats, a fact that was confirmed by Ultra; and it had no worth-while reserves.

Ultra also revealed, in an intercept on the evening of May 30, that Fortitude, too, was a success—at least so far. A report of a conversation that Baron Oshima had held with Hitler at Berchtesgaden was decrypted, and it disclosed that Hitler still believed in the Fortitude and Quicksilver stories that there were eighty to ninety divisions in Britain, with seven or eight airborne divisions; and he continued to hold the view that, while the invasion might well start elsewhere, for example in Normandy or Brittany, it would culminate in a main attack against the coast between the Seine and the Somme—the Pas de Calais.

But what of the tactical situation in and around Normandy? How were Rundstedt and Rommel disposing of the forces under their command—particularly the panzers? Agents' reports concerning the 1st SS Panzer Korps Adolf Hitler, the most powerful German armored formation in the West, were encouraging. It was almost ludicrously simple to detect the movements of German divisions. As General Munro McCloskey, the com-mander of a USAAF special air squadron, would relate after the war, all that was necessary was to watch the laundry. The French intelligence serv-ice had gone into the laundry business and, through low prices and good work, had succeeded in capturing the custom of the German army. When the Germans moved, they collected all their laundry, and left behind for-warding addresses if it was not ready. The *Feldgrau* might be going to Val-halla, but they were not prepared to go without their linen. This form of surveillance revealed that, at Y-Day, neither of the corps's two SS panzer divisions, "Das Reich" at Toulouse and the "Adolf Hitler" between Brussels and Antwerp, had changed its position. This was regarded as significant in-telligence at Supreme Headquarters, for if the Germans had seen through Fortitude, these powerful units would surely be moving toward the Calva-dos coast.

On the other hand, there was disquieting intelligence from Normandy. Rommel had suddenly made new dispositions in and around the Cherbourg peninsula that showed he might at least have obtained partial knowledge of Allied intentions. The 91st Airlanding Division, specialists in fighting para-troopers, and the 6th Parachute Regiment had moved inexplicably into exactly the area around St. Mère-Église where the American paratroop divisions were to land on D-Day. This movement was reported on May 29, and Leigh-Mallory, C-in-C of the air forces that would support Neptune on D-Day and the man who had prophesied disaster at Dieppe, delivered a solemn warning to Eisenhower. The arrival of the 91st, he said, meant that Allied paratrooper formations would be cut to pieces and that perhaps 50 per cent of the air transport force involved—some five hundred planes—would be lost. Eisenhower responded that, whatever the risks, the operation must proceed; without it, Neptune itself could not succeed.

Adding to the fear that, after all, the Germans had penetrated Neptune's strategies, was an appreciation of their estimate of Allied intentions in the West. Promulgated on May 25 by the British Joint Intelligence Committee, it was so secret that it was distributed on an "eyes only" basis to the actual force commanders and, in the Mediterranean, personally to Wilson, the Supreme Commander there. This appreciation, which seemed to spell a bloodbath in Normandy, stated:

> 1. *Area of main assault.* Main assault is expected against Northern coast of France from Boulogne to include Cherbourg inclusive. Although German High Command will until our assault takes place reckon with possibility that it will come across the Straits of Dover to Pas de Calais area, there is some evidence that Le Havre-Cherbourg areas [the actual Neptune area] . . . (are) regarded as likely and perhaps even the main point of assault.

That intelligence was bad enough, but if the JIC appreciation was accurate, then it seemed that the Germans also knew when to expect the invasion. "Enemy appreciates," the JIC signaled Wilson, "that Allied preparations are sufficiently advanced to permit operations any time now and that from the point of view of moonlight and tide first week in June is next likely period for assault." Neither was the JIC any more encouraging about the effectiveness of Vendetta's threats to the French Mediterranean coast, for as the report went on: "Enemy appreciates that while raids against French Mediterranean coast are possible at any time, Allied preparations for a major attack in this area are not yet completed." Similarly, the JIC doubted the effectiveness of Ironside's deceptions to threaten the Biscay coast. Only Fortitude North's operations against Norway, so it seemed to the JIC, were proving successful.

Under these circumstances, the code word for the next phase of the invasion—Halcyon—portended not tranquility and peace but the calm before a storm. It was issued to all formations at midnight May 31/June 1. Few knew that it had been issued; fewer still knew what it meant. But its consequences were felt throughout the land. As *The Times* (London) put it afterwards: "We have been as those speaking in whispers." All the multitudes of soldiers, sailors and airmen seemed to vanish. In the Queen's Head, the George and Dragon, the Star and Garter, the Good Queen Bess, the Sir Walter Raleigh, the Crown and Anchor, the George the Third, the Royal Steamer, the Wheatsheaf—in the pubs throughout England south of the line Humber-Mersey—for the first time in over a year only the locals came in to drink mild and bitter, to play dominoes and beer skittles. Silent Rapp, Skin Walbourne, Macadoo Machado, Lightning Ruberg—all the soldiers were gone. The troopers had stopped for a while, they had refreshed themselves, and now they had remounted and clattered on.

At Berchtesgaden, Hitler still retained absolute confidence in the outcome for Germany of the invasion. He believed that the invasions of North Africa had succeeded "only with the help of traitors." There would be, he said, no traitors in the West. Yet from time to time, at his noonday conference with his staff, he displayed sudden flashes of irritation and petulance at the Allies' stratagems. Following the diplomatic quarantine, for example, he declared that Allied invasion preparations were insolent posturing, a "completely bare-faced bluff." But petulant or not, Hitler was a better general than those around him, and a better military intellect than his enemies —Allied as well as German—gave him credit for. His critics had a tendency to sneer at what had become known as "Hitler's intuition." But between February and May of 1944, that intuition was at work to sniff out the secrets of Neptune—and it succeeded in a startling and dangerous fashion.

Hitler's conviction that the Allies' main assault would be directed against the Pas de Calais remained unchanged; but just as he had planned to invade England at more than one place in 1940, so it seemed probable that the Allies would have a similar strategy for their invasion in 1944. But where would these secondary and diversionary assaults come? Considerable thought was given to this question by *der Führer und Oberste Befehlshaber der Wehrmacht des Grossdeutschen Reichs*—as Hitler was thunderously styled in law; and at one time or another he saw threats—as the LCS and A-Force intended—everywhere from Petsamo to the Peloponnesus. But in February, Hitler grew sensitive to the dangers to Normandy and Brittany. On March 4, he regarded them as particularly threatened; and on May 6, following the noon conference, Jodl telephoned Blumentritt, a call that resulted in Blumentritt advising all headquarters that "The Führer attaches particular importance to Normandy and the defense of Normandy." Having commanded, he was obeyed—in the most thorough manner possible. Work on the fortifications along the Calvados coast was intensified, and the peninsula was reinforced with the troop movements that gave Leigh-Mallory such a fright. The mighty Panzer Lehr Armored Division was brought back from Hungary, whence it had gone to put down the rebellion, and the 21st Panzer Division was moved to Caen from Brittany. These were significant changes in the Normandy sector, changes that gave Eisenhower doubts about the sanctity of the secrets of Neptune. But at the same time Hitler did nothing to weaken the Pas de Calais front.

It was from the Pas de Calais, in fact, that he intended to launch the secret weapon that the invasion armies had grown to fear. This was the V1, the ramjet 440-mph pilotless aircraft manufactured by Volkswagen at its Fallersleben plant, which cost only $600 to build and exploded with the force of a 4000-pound blockbuster bomb. The other V-weapons and the London gun had fallen short of expectations, and the production of the V1's was less than the 2000 rounds per month that had been visualized. Even so, Hitler was confident that they would turn the tide of battle, and on May 16, 1944, he issued orders concerning the bombardment of London. It was to be coordinated with heavy air attacks and an artillery bombardment of the British Channel towns by long-range conventional artillery in the Pas de Calais; and the exact time the offensive would begin was to be selected by Rundstedt, who would issue the code word "Junkroom." The 692 square miles of Greater London would be impossible to miss; the British capital would be turned into a flaming desert. Moreover, the flying bomb offensive would shatter the invasion before it had even sailed. But here again, Fortitude had infected the Fuehrer's thinking, for the V1 bombardment was tentatively scheduled to begin on or about June 16.

Hitler was less confident about the ability of another arm of the mighty Wehrmacht to repel an invasion, if and when it came. As he told Baron Oshima at Berchtesgaden on May 28, 1944, there was only one front about which he was really worried; and that was in the air. The Luftwaffe had fought the enormous air battles of the first months of 1944 with demonic energy and courage, but while the great numbers of aircraft that had been lost could be replaced, the loss of experienced aircrews left a gap in the ranks that could never be refilled. Operation Pointblank had achieved its objective. The Luftwaffe was beginning to buckle under the weight of Allied airpower. It was no longer able to defend Fortress Europe, and its aerial reconnaissance planes, which might have detected the fabrications of Fortitude and provided first warning of the approach of an invasion fleet, were rarely able to penetrate Allied defenses.

Hitler might also have been concerned about the Kriegsmarine. It, too, had been humbled by the Allied air forces—and Ultra. Yet it could at least alert German land commanders to the approach of Neptune. But Admiral Theodor Krancke, the German naval commander in the West, like other German commanders—and the Fuehrer himself—had based his counter-invasion strategy on preconceived notions of what the Allies intended to do. Krancke had made a long and thorough study of Allied amphibious warfare tactics and the natural conditions which must prevail before such a landing could take place. He believed that the Allies would attack during darkness, by moonlight, at full tide to permit the assault craft to sail in over obstacles, and in the immediate neighborhood of a large port but away from cliffs and shallow, rocky waters where currents were strong. He also believed that the Allies could and would not attack if the wind exceeded 24 knots, where visibility was less than 3 miles, and when the wave heights were higher than between 5 and 8 feet. Obedient to this philosophy, Krancke's main defensive measures—minefields and coastal artillery—were generally concentrated in areas other than those of the Bay of the Seine.

But Krancke was wrong, disastrously wrong; the Allies would attack at daybreak shortly after low tide, far from a large port, and at some points beneath sheer or high cliffs and in reefy waters where currents were strong. Moreover, the weather parameters, under certain circumstances, were wider than Krancke believed—due, doubtless, to some of the XX-Committee reports from England. As a result, the Kriegsmarine would be watchful for a different set of conditions from those which the Allies required.

Rundstedt was, by Y-Day, also uncertain about what the Allies intended, and his appreciations to OKW reflected his uncertainty. On April 24, 1944, he had written that he thought Normandy was in the danger zone; but his conception of the threatened area was very wide. It stretched about 175 miles (as the crow flies) from Caen to the mouth of the Scheldt. He had narrowed his focus by May 15 when he had stressed that the Allies "need to win large and capacious harbours"; and for that reason, he advised OKW, "Le Havre and Cherbourg are primarily to be considered for this purpose, Boulogne and Brest secondarily. The attempt to form a bridgehead rapidly on the [Cherbourg] peninsula in the first phase would therefore seem very natural." He came closer still to the truth on May 29 when, having examined the pattern of Allied air operations against the Seine bridges, he again concluded that the Allies might land in Normandy. In general, however, Rundstedt thought that the Allies might go for Cherbourg, but that their main thrust would come in the Pas de Calais.

Rundstedt's appreciations may well have been influenced by another clever stitch in the tapestry of Fortitude. Just as the Allies watched the 1st SS Panzer Korps of Sepp Dietrich because they were sure that these divisions would be committed to the Channel coast as soon as the Germans received any positive intelligence of Allied intentions, so Rundstedt had closely followed Garbo's reports concerning the location of the Guards Armoured Division, a crack British formation. His reasoning seems to have been that no general as blue-blooded as the commanding officer of the Guards Armoured, General Sir Allan Henry Shafto Adair (the 6th baronet, Harrow, Grenadier Guards, later governor of Harrow and Ensign of the King's Bodyguard of the Yeomen of the Guard), would ever allow himself to be very far from the main battle at H-Hour. But here, aware that snobbery often affected Rundstedt's judgment, the CSM played a merry ball. While proletarian armored divisions were moved into the concentration areas in great secrecy, the Guards Armoured was seen (and heard) moving from Brompton in Yorkshire to Hove on the Sussex coast as a component of FUSAG, not of Montgomery's army group. Between April 30 and May 28, 1944, in a series of reports which earned him the congratulations of Himmler, Garbo had related that there was considerable trouble in the divisional headquarters of the Guards Armoured. While on the road, the baggage had become mixed up and one unit of the division had received the mess silver of another. Moreover, to support this story, any German signaler listening in to the plain-language traffic on the division's wireless net would have heard sulphurous dialogue about the silver between generals, and triangularization would have revealed that the sharp words were coming from the FUSAG area.

Nevertheless, on Y-Day, Rundstedt's command, OB-West, considered that D-Day might be imminent, and its judgment was based on two main factors: the air battle and the state of the resistance. In the case of the former, Allied air activity had increased greatly, and the Germans detected that its main thrust was the destruction of supply lines. But the campaign was carried out in such a way that they could not deduce where the Allies would land. Resistance operations were plotted in the same way as air operations, and the parachuting of agents, weapons, ammunition and explosives at night—as well as the exchange of signals between aircraft and the ground—were extensively observed and charted. But here again, while the Germans detected an increase in these operations, they revealed nothing significant about the time or the place of the invasion. The German high command in the West was almost as ignorant about what the Allies would do as was the humblest *Feldgrau*.

Only Rommel and his intelligence officer, Staubwasser, had penetrated, but only partly, the smoke screens of Fortitude. On May 31, the two men met in Rommel's study at the Château de La Roche Guyon, and both felt sure that FHW had exaggerated its estimates of Allied strength within the British Isles. Further, Rommel was now certain that there would be only one landing, which would come either around the mouth of the Somme or of the Seine. There would not be, as OKW and OB-West estimated, "a number of major landings and diverting operations." It was also the OKW/ OB-West consensus that the Allies would attack first with airborne troops, which could land only by day or at dusk, and that the aerial assault would be followed by major seaborne landings in darkness and at high tide. But because of the nature and extent of his "devil's garden," Rommel knew that it would be necessary to land assault engineers first to cut passages through the obstacles for the assault shipping. Such sapping could take place only in daylight and at low tide. Therefore, contrary to OKW and OB-West, Rommel and Staubwasser agreed that the airborne assault would come by moonlight, and the seaborne landings would take place at daybreak, just after low tide.

But when would the invasion come? The Allies certainly had the strength to make the assault wherever they wanted, said Rommel; but they could not choose *when* they would invade. That would be determined by natural conditions. Both men agreed that the Allies would require a guarantee of at least six days of settled weather—good June weather. Rommel then declared that there were only two periods in June when the moon, daybreak and tides would all combine to favor the operation. The first was between the 5th and 7th of the month, the second between the 12th and the 14th.

Rommel planned to go see the Fuehrer on the 5th to make another appeal for control of all the Wehrmacht's armored forces in the West, some of which Hitler had retained under his own command. If Rommel was to succeed in his plan to "Dunkirk" the Allies at H-Hour, he could not wait until the enemy had already established a foothold. He would need all the German panzer units at his immediate disposal to counter the landing; requesting their use through the normal channels would mean inevitable and possibly fatal delays.

Through Ultra the Allies had been able to read Rommel's angry protests about the disposition of the panzer forces. They had followed the debate as it went up to Hitler; they read the decision when it came down. Hitler retained control of four powerful panzer divisions in the West, which would constitute a reserve and would be held where they were. As Winterbotham would recall: "This, of course, was the plum we had been waiting for; had the final decision gone the other way it would have seriously jeopardized the chances of success of (Neptune) as it then stood."

Rommel intended to reopen the debate in person when he visited the Fuehrer at Berchtesgaden. But he realized he could not be absent from his command on the 5th—unless the weather was bad. Then he would go.

The Eve of D-Day

ON MAY 29, 1944, Eisenhower joined his battle headquarters at South-wick House, a mansion amid parkland on the lip of the hills above Ports-mouth. Awaiting him was a telegram from Marshall in Washington. It announced that the American Chiefs of Staff would fly to London on June 7 "to be on hand in case major decisions by the Combined Chiefs of Staff were necessary" concerning Neptune, and to be present if "two possible eventualities" occurred which "might require action." The first was the "possible development of the situation where we have a very insecure hold on a beachhead and decision may be required as to whether to withdraw or to continue the operation." The second was that critical decisions might have to be taken "seven to eight days after D-Day, at which time a major German counterattack might be expected." For all its prosaic wording, the telegram reflected the grave anxieties of the Allied high command.

It was a Monday and the weather that weekend had been as gentle as a shepherd's call—as indeed it had been for much of the month. The skies were clear, the Channel smooth and blue, the winds calm, the moon in the right quarter. Having examined the charts for the next five days, and fairly satisfied that the weather would hold during the D-Day period, Eisen-hower directed that the signal "Exercise Hornpipe plus six" be sent to all Commanders-in-Chief. It meant that D-Day was set for June 5, 1944. Eisenhower and his meteorological staff in the office next to the opera-tions room hoped that it would stay that way. For the great machine called Neptune was beginning to turn. The troops and the vehicles of war were moving with precision down to the assault fleets, while follow-up formations were replacing them in the encampments under the woods and along the lanes of southern England. Every piece was being fitted into place for transfer across the Channel to the Far Shore. But all the schemes of men notwithstanding, one factor alone would determine when, and if, the Allied armies would arrive at their destination in good order for immediate and perhaps decisive battle—the weather. Would the weather hold? Everything depended upon the facts contained in the six-figure code groups which flooded in from the weather-reporting ships, aircraft and stations arcing from Nova Scotia through Greenland, Iceland, the Faroes, Ulster, down to the Azores and the Canaries and across to Bermuda and the Caribbean.

It was lunchtime on May 29 when a group of signals came in from an aircraft plotting weather over Newfoundland which showed that the weather was beginning to change off the east coast of America. It was almost precisely at this same time that Eisenhower authorized a second important signal to be sent—"Halcyon plus 4." The code word, taken from the name of the bird of ancient fable that could calm the winds and the waves, meant to Marshall in Washington that D-Day was still scheduled for June 5. But even as it was being punched onto tape for radioteleprinting across the Atlantic, the weathermen began to plot the great whorls of what would come to be called "L5"—a disturbance that threatened Neptune itself.

There was disquiet among the members of Eisenhower's weather syndicate as L5 began to take shape. The syndicate included meteorological officers from the air forces, the Admiralty, the Air Ministry, the British weather central at Dunstable, and the U.S. Weather Services, all of whom communicated with the director, Group Captain John Stagg, an RAF meteorologist, and his deputy, D. N. Yates, an American air force colonel, over scrambled telephone conference lines to their headquarters which had been set up under the trees near Southwick House. All members of the syndicate received the same data and were expected to provide Eisenhower with a five-day forecast. But that in itself had proved to be an almost impossible task. For as G. K. N. Douglas, the leading British meteorologist and occasionally the spokesman for Dunstable, warned Stagg: "Unless Channel weather in 1944 turns out to be wholly exceptional, the production of regular forecasts which have any true scientific validity or worthwhile dependability is likely to be out of the question for more than two days ahead, or even, at times, more than twenty-four hours." Given this difficulty, in addition to the wide range of individual interpretations and opinions that prevailed among the group, the men of Stagg's syndicate rarely found themselves in complete agreement, and their squabbles often made them sound like fishwives rather than scientists. But now, in the crucial days that preceded Neptune, Eisenhower needed not arguments and opinions but an accurate assessment of what the weather over the Channel would be. It was up to Stagg to provide it.

The first signs of a crisis appeared on Thursday, June 1, as the ships of the heavy bombardment squadrons were preparing for their departure from Scapa and the sea lochs of Ulster and western Scotland the following day. There were enough indications of disturbances forming out in the Atlantic for Stagg to warn the Supreme Command that the weather prospects for the 4th, 5th and probably the 6th were not good. But the weather centers, he reported, were not sufficiently confident about the outlook to say more. Bull, SHAEF's operations officer, made the comment: "For heaven's sake, Stagg, get it sorted out by tomorrow morning before you come to the Supreme Commander's conference. General Eisenhower is a very worried man."

Stagg spent the rest of Thursday in constant telephone contact with the weather centers, but the data coming in from the special chain of warships and aircraft out in the Atlantic became more confused. Several deep depressions were forming rapidly between Newfoundland and Ireland, and the members of the syndicate could not agree on a forecast. Some believed that there would be no bad weather over the British Isles, some that there would be bad weather but that it would not involve the Channel or the Western Approaches, and the rest that a long period of disturbed weather in the Channel was inevitable. That night Stagg and Yates "wearied ourselves with discussion into a restless sleep. . . ."

The two men were up again before first light on Friday, June 2, examining the changes that had been reported while they slept. It was clear that the prospect had darkened, and as Stagg would recall of the charts lying on the table before him: "The whole north Atlantic ocean area appeared to be filled with a succession of depressions. . . . In all the charts for the 40 or 50 years I had examined I could not recall one which at this time of the year remotely resembled this chart in the number and intensity of depressions it portrayed at one time."

At the morning telephone conference, the weathermen again engaged in their usual wrangling and failed to arrive at a unanimous forecast. Stagg and Yates tended to support the view that the Channel would not escape very bad weather, with gale force winds and low cloud. Eisenhower was advised of this forecast later that morning, but Stagg decided against warning him of the dangerous disagreements between individual members of the syndicate. The Supreme Commander had problems already sufficiently arduous without burdening him with more. But another meeting was called for 9:30 that evening, and the moment was rapidly approaching when Eisenhower must decide whether or not to proceed with D-Day on the 5th.

By the evening telephone conference, the weather experts were still divided. Part of the syndicate was not only confident but certain that no bad weather would pass through the Channel, that cloud amounts would be small, and the wind speed would not exceed Force 4 throughout the period. This situation, the optimists declared, would hold from Sunday, June 3, through to Wednesday, June 7. But other members of the syndicate, including Stagg, thought the whole situation "untrustworthy." There was the potential for calamity in this disagreement, for if he accepted the optimists' opinion, passed it to the Supreme Commander, and he gave the order to proceed, the entire enterprise might be wrecked. Of the row that marked the conference, Stagg would note in his diary:

> Had it not been fraught with such potential tragedy, the whole business was ridiculous. In less than half-an-hour I was expected to present to General Eisenhower an "agreed" forecast for the next five days which covered the time of launching of the greatest military operation ever mounted (and) no two of the expert participants in the discussion could agree on the likely weather even for the next 24 hours . . . it was a desperate quandary from which I was saved only by the clock.

Stagg ran—literally—from the telephone conference to the Supreme Commander's conference.

Present in the bare, paneled room at Southwick House were Eisenhower, the three Commanders-in-Chief (Ramsay, Montgomery and Leigh-Mallory), their Chiefs of Staff, and the SHAEF chiefs of divisions. Breathless, Stagg opened the door and was greeted by Eisenhower with the words: "Well, Stagg, what have you for us this time?" Stagg, replying that the situation was now "potentially full of menace," gave his forecast: until at least Tuesday or Wednesday, the 6th and 7th of June, there would be much cloud and westerly winds of between Force 4 and 5. Eisenhower, who was still unaware of the disputes among the weathermen, pressed Stagg for his personal opinion, and Stagg—according to Tedder—replied: "If I answered that, Sir, I would be guessing, not behaving as your meteorological adviser."

Stagg and Yates then withdrew, half expecting news to reach them in the waiting room that the Supreme Commander had decided to postpone the launching of Neptune by twenty-four hours. As he waited, Stagg was possessed of terrible self-doubts. Had he been too pessimistic? If the Supreme Commander ordered a postponement, the first squadrons of the armada already at sea would have to scatter or turn back, and if they were spotted by enemy aircraft, surprise might be lost. But shortly, Bull came out of the meeting to tell Stagg that there would be no change of plans for the next twenty-four hours.

Stagg and Yates again spent a restless night, and at breakfast time on Saturday, June 3, Bull called at their quarters to ask whether anything new had developed. Stagg told him that there was no evidence of improvement. If anything, the weather was more complex. The outlook was "knife-edge marginal," and it could still "go either way by evening." Stagg later met Morgan by the lake in the park, and Morgan called out, "Good luck, Stagg; may all your depressions be nice little ones: but remember, we'll string you up from the nearest lamp post if you don't read the omens aright." Stagg would remember: "Though I could not foresee that happening whatever I did, the image haunted me, quite irrationally, that Saturday—and to this day it still does when under strain." For that Saturday was the day of the crucial decision. All the assault troops were now loading in the invasion craft, along with their tanks, guns and transport. Some convoys must begin to sail that evening if they were to be at the beaches on time at H-Hour, which was still set for Monday, June 5.

During the day, however, Stagg's despondency decreased, for he was proven correct in giving Eisenhower an adverse forecast for the 5th. That evening, he again barely reached the Supreme Commander's conference in time; and as he went into the meeting, Admiral Sir George Creasy, Ramsay's Chief of Staff, was heard to say, "There goes six foot two of Stagg and six foot one of gloom." It was meant well, but Stagg had nothing to say that would cheer the fifteen high commanders who were present. He outlined the weather picture, and then gave as the judgment of the syndicate the forecast that from June 4 until June 7 the weather in the Channel would be cloudy and stormy with winds of Force 5. The outlook after June 7 was uncertain, but Stagg thought there would be less persistent cloud once the cold front had cleared the Channel. After much question and answer, Eisenhower asked Stagg: "Now let me put this one to you. . . . Isn't there just a chance that you might be a bit more optimistic again tomorrow?" Stagg said there was no chance.

Stagg and Yates then withdrew to the anteroom; and an hour later, Bull came out and stated that Eisenhower had made a provisional decision to postpone D-Day for twenty-four hours. But there would be a further meeting at 4:15 A.M. the next morning, Sunday, June 4, and Stagg and his syndicate must review the situation during the night and report again. Then, Eisenhower would make his final decision—to proceed or to postpone the operation.

When Stagg arrived at the 4:15 A.M. conference, he noted that the "tension in the room was palpable." The Supreme Commander was "serious and unsmiling," and at a nod from Eisenhower, Stagg informed the conference that there was no substantial change in his forecast. There was silence for a moment, and then after some discussion among the Commanders-in-Chief, the provisional decision of the night before was confirmed. Eisenhower told Smith to issue the code word to postpone D-Day by twenty-four hours—"Ripcord plus 24."

By this time, every ship (2010 in the American assault force, and 3323 in the British and Canadian) was in position, and every berth and every mooring in every port, river and creek was filled from Felixstowe on the North Sea to Milford Haven in Wales. Behind the assault forces were assembling those of the build-up, jamming the Bristol Channel, the Thames Estuary, the Humber, the Clyde and Belfast Lough—another thousand ships. Well over 2 million men—counting soldiers, sailors, airmen, and transportation and civil defense services—were in various stages of commitment to this first phase of D-Day. But now, through "Ripcord," the entire operation was placed in a state of suspended animation. It seemed inconceivable that the Germans would not detect the imminence of Neptune; it could almost be *sensed*.

Worse, major units were already at sea, including the heavy bombardment forces, the old merchantmen that would form the Mulberry breakwaters, and the seventeen convoys destined for Omaha and Utah beaches which were en route from their ports of embarkation in Cornwall and Devon. Ripcord caused little trouble to the heavy bombardment and Mulberry units; all they had to do was to mark time in the Irish Sea until they were given final orders. The danger lay with the small craft; one minesweeping force was only 35 miles from the Norman shore when it received the postponement order. It complied, and, astonishingly, the force was never detected by the Germans. Most of the convoys received the postponement order without difficulty and made about in the black, stormy night, although a number of the smaller, flat-bottomed landing craft were overturned and some lives were lost. But the message did not reach one convoy of 138 ships carrying troops of the U.S. 4th Infantry Division, and by 0900 on Sunday morning it was already 25 miles south of the Isle of Wight, steaming for the Far Shore. Unless the convoy was turned about, it would make its landfall off the Far Shore, there would be a disaster, and almost inevitably the security and surprise of Neptune would be lost.

Repeated efforts to contact the convoy by wireless had failed. Its speed was estimated at 8 knots, the sea was short and steep, and there were no naval craft in the vicinity capable of intercepting it. Aircraft were despatched, and flying at about 100 feet in fierce squalls, little Walrus pusher-engined biplanes hunted the convoy until it was spotted shortly before dark. One of the planes flew low over the commodore's ship to drop an official, signed and stamped message from naval headquarters, in cipher. But the canister missed and sank in the sea. The pilot of the Walrus scribbled a note instructing the commodore to return to anchor and refuel in Weymouth Bay, and then made a second pass. This time the canister landed on the ship. There was a danger that the commodore might ignore the message on the grounds of its informal wording, format and delivery, and for some forty-five minutes the ships steamed on. But finally the command ship ran up signals ordering the convoy to reverse. The disaster had been averted.

This was but the first of the events of that most extraordinary day in the history of the Supreme Command—Sunday, June 4, 1944. It was followed by news that Clark's army had captured Rome in what was a psychologically important but militarily hollow victory. Then Churchill's caravan of cars and motorcyclists arrived at Southwick House, filled their tanks, "diminished our supplies of Scotch like the devil," and disappeared into a storm that was, wrote Butcher, now raging in the Channel in "near-hurricane" proportions. Stagg awoke that morning after two or three hours' sleep in his tent, and as he walked over to the weather center, he noticed the clouds had thickened, the trees were swaying, and a wind of about Force 4 was running—just as he had predicted. The postponement of Neptune had been justified; but if there was no abatement in the weather, Neptune would have to be postponed again, not for one but for fourteen days. The moon and tides would then compel a fundamental change in the timing of the operation, and everyone recalled what had happened when the Dieppe raid was canceled and then remounted. Stagg knew that Eisenhower trusted him; and his forecast that day would almost certainly determine the fate of Neptune.

That morning as he examined the charts, Stagg saw that a cold front was moving toward the Channel that would pass through Portsmouth later in the day or during the night. But this was not the only portent he saw. While the general picture was extraordinarily confused, he noted that one of the depressions in the Atlantic, at that time off Newfoundland, was intensifying and deepening, thus slowing its progression toward England. Stagg and Yates talked about the development excitedly, for if their interpretation was correct, as Stagg would write:

> . . . then between the passage of the cold front and the approach of the depression there could be an interlude of improved weather, and this interlude if long enough and if it occurred at the right time might just allow the first two critical sets of assault landings to be launched, at dawn and at dusk, on the same day and that day could be Tuesday.

There was a danger that the Germans would also detect this development, but if they did not, they would surely believe that the weather would remain too disturbed to permit an invasion, and Neptune would catch them completely off guard. "Yes," Stagg wrote, "if it eventuated and if the Supreme Commander could be persuaded to take advantage of it, it might be a heaven-sent break."

If Stagg and Yates expected support from the syndicate, they were mistaken. Stagg thought that the afternoon exchange of views would be "short and happy." Instead, the conference was "the most heatedly argumentative and most prolonged of the whole series: it lasted well over two hours." The experts went back to their cubicles that evening, put on their headsets, and the scrambler was switched on to dissolve their words into what Stagg described as the sounds of a crowd of "toothless parish councillors in some outlandish corner of Indo-china." But this time the syndicate was in a sober and subdued mood. For upon the outcome of this discussion would depend whether Neptune could be launched on Tuesday morning, or whether it must again be postponed, risking all the dangers that such a delay would cause. But if the experts were calmer, they still could not agree that a ridge of fine weather would follow the storms now crossing the Channel. There was a reasonably high degree of confidence that the weather would be more favorable to Neptune from the afternoon of Monday the 5th into Tuesday the 6th. But after that there was grave uncertainty.

At 9:30 P.M., Stagg was again in the conference room at Southwick House; and it was now, measuring his words with the greatest care, that he delivered the critical forecast. The atmosphere was, Stagg would write, tense and grave as he said that—provided the forecast was correct—cloud conditions would permit the heavy and accurate aerial and naval bombardment with which Neptune would commence, and that the wind after midnight on Monday would not be so strong, nor the cloud cover so thick, as to cause disorder among the airborne troops' fleets. Station-keeping at sea would be difficult but the waves, chop and wind should not seriously disorder the naval forces. In short, Stagg's forecast indicated weather that was tolerable, but far from ideal, for Neptune to proceed.

There was a brief debate. Ramsay reminded the commanders that there was only half an hour to make the final decision; if all the assault forces were to be at their assigned stations off the Far Shore for a D-Day on June 6, the signals had to go out now. Both Eisenhower and Smith stated that they felt the operation should proceed; and Smith added that to call off the invasion now meant they would have to wait until June 19 before Neptune could be tried again. Troops would have to be disembarked with great risk to security as well as to morale; there would be no moonlight for the airborne troops; and the longer the postponement the shorter the period of good campaigning weather on the continent, and the greater the possibility that Hitler would try to wreck the invasion with his V-weapons. Leigh-Mallory, on the other hand, doubted the ability of the air forces to operate effectively in the predicted cloud conditions; and Tedder agreed that air operations were going to be "chancy."

Eisenhower rejected these adverse views. He turned to Montgomery and asked: "Do you see any reason why we should not go on Tuesday?" Montgomery replied: "No. I would say—*Go!*" It was then, at 2145 hours, with the wind and rain beating on the windows, that the Supreme Commander announced his decision—perhaps the greatest decision of his life. "I am quite positive we must give the order . . . I don't like it, but there it is . . . I don't see how we can do anything else." With that declaration, Eisenhower gave the order to remount Neptune.

There remained the possibility, however, that the weather might become worse and the decision have to be reversed. There would be a final meeting at 4:15 A.M. the following morning. Stagg would note the paradox of the situation:

> (Neptune) had been postponed when the weather overhead was calm and clear; now in a gale of wind and rain the decision had been taken to proceed. Meteorologically I hoped it could be justified but at the moment it must have appeared a little mad to some of the Supreme Commander's military company.

On his way back to his caravan, the Supreme Commander encountered Merrill "Red" Mueller of NBC, one of the four correspondents attached to his headquarters. Eisenhower said to him: "Let's take a walk, Red." The two men disappeared into the oak wood and, as Mueller would recall, Eisenhower appeared to be "bowed down with worry." It was as if "each of the four stars on either shoulder weighed a ton." His mood was still somber when the high command gathered at Southwick House for the last time at 4:15 A.M. that Monday—the start of a new working week that would be one of the most memorable in history.

When Stagg reached the conference, he noted that "All were in battle-dress uniform except General Montgomery . . . he was dressed in a high-necked fawn-coloured pullover and light corduroy trousers. Facing them General Eisenhower seemed as spruce and immaculate as ever." The rest of the high command was settled into easy chairs and sofas; "faces were grave and the room was quiet." At a signal from Eisenhower, Stagg opened his report with the words: "Gentlemen, no substantial change has taken place since last time but as I see it the little that has changed is in the direction of optimism." It was his opinion that most of Tuesday would be just suitable for launching Neptune. The weather afterwards would be a "mixed bag" but it "might not be so bad as to jeopardize seriously the important buildup stages of the operation." When he had finished his report, Stagg would note:

> . . . the tension seemed to evaporate and the Supreme Commander and his colleagues became as new men. General Eisenhower had sat, turned sideways, facing me, taut and tense. Now a broad smile broke over his face as he said, "Well, Stagg, if this forecast comes off, I promise you we'll have a celebration when the time comes."

The meeting did not last long; and within the hour, Eisenhower sent an historic signal to all commands and the Combined Chiefs of Staff in Washington, a signal as historic as Nelson's "England expects. . . ." "Halcyon plus 5 finally and definitely confirmed." D-Day would be Tuesday, the 6th of June. For better or worse, Neptune was irrevocably launched.

Another drama was being played out that extraordinary Sunday of June 4, 1944. The Prime Minister had sent for de Gaulle, who was flying in

Churchill's private plane from Algiers to London, where it was quite possible that he might be arrested the moment he set foot on British soil. Criminal charges had been filed against him by a certain Dufour, and the case, the climax of the tedious and protracted troubles between de Gaulle and the British, had been simmering ever since.

Dufour, according to the Gaullistes, was an MI-6 agent who had attempted to infiltrate the French intelligence service in London. He was found to have misrepresented himself, and he was court-martialed by de Gaulle's commanders in England, and jailed at the French detention center at Camberley, just outside London. Dufour escaped, however, and filed a complaint with the British courts against de Gaulle and other French leaders claiming that he had been mistreated at Camberley. The British government had no power to quash the charges; once filed the case had to be heard unless it was withdrawn by the plaintiff. Nor, since de Gaulle had no official status at the time as a representative of any government, could the British grant him immunity or prevent him from being arrested if he returned to England and tried on charges that, had he been found guilty, would have resulted in his imprisonment.

Notified of the charges at his headquarters at Algiers, de Gaulle was outraged at this latest attempt "to spatter me with filth." He informed the Foreign Office that he considered the affair "an infamy," and there the matter rested until March of 1944 when he was again notified that the charges were about to be brought to trial. De Gaulle countered with charges of his own. Early in 1943, a Free Frenchman, Stephane Manier, who was employed by the Gaullistes to make broadcasts to Metropolitan France on the BBC transmitter at Accra, had returned to England, and as an alien, had been detained for interrogation by the British security authorities. Manier died—the British were unaware that he was suffering either from serious mental illness or malaria, or both—and his son, de Gaulle announced, intended to lodge a complaint against all MI-6 officers on French territory, Churchill and the entire British government. If the British could arrest de Gaulle, he could arrest Churchill.

De Gaulle would claim that he never heard of the "Affaire Dufour" again. He was quite wrong; Dufour had not withdrawn his charges, and on June 1, as the western world was about to embark on the most dangerous military operation in history, the War Cabinet had to decide whether to let de Gaulle come to England at all. No one could be sure that he was not what he claimed to be—the true leader of France. No one could be sure how the French *résistants,* or the French nation as a whole, would react if de Gaulle were indicted or jailed. But it was finally decided that he should be in London at the time of the invasion, if only to add his authority to SHAEF's orders to the *résistants* and to broadcast a message to the French people to keep calm. But what to do about the Dufour case which was about to come to trial? A special emergency Cabinet committee was formed to deal with the problem; and to settle or at least delay the case, Dufour was offered £1000 to withdraw his charges. Apparently Dufour agreed to settle, for de Gaulle was not arrested when he arrived in London early on June 4.

The French leader went immediately to Southwick House where he was met by Churchill who, in describing Neptune only in its broadest outlines and forbidding de Gaulle free rights of communication with his head-quarters at Algiers, again treated him not with confidence but with suspicion. De Gaulle then met with Eisenhower, and as Butcher put it: ". . . Ike took them all on a Cook's tour of the war room, some of the really important stuff being tucked away out of sight." Eisenhower showed de Gaulle some maps and explained the Neptune plan, but he was careful to advise the French leader that the Allied landing in Normandy was diversionary in intent, and that the main landing would come in the Pas de Calais—a statement designed to give Fortitude an extra fillip.

However limited de Gaulle's role in Neptune would be, it was recognized that his was an important voice in France, and Eisenhower gave him a copy of the speech which he said he would like de Gaulle to make to the French people. Unfortunately, the speech lacked much in grandeur, and de Gaulle rejected it. He told Eisenhower he thought it stressed too strongly French obedience to the Allied command. He made similar objections to the speech that Eisenhower intended to broadcast, calling upon Frenchmen everywhere to obey the orders of SHAEF. This was too much; Eisenhower, who had other things to attend to, turned de Gaulle over to Smith; and de Gaulle, refusing an offer from Churchill to return to London by train, left Southwick House by motorcar with his own officers.

Back in London, de Gaulle was kept under a discreet but close watch by British security authorities to ensure that he kept the secrets of D-Day; and McClure, Eisenhower's chief of psychological warfare, Lockhart, the chief of PWE, and both Churchill and Eden again urged him to read the prepared speech. De Gaulle would not be budged. Eventually, he would broadcast to the French nation—but in his own words. De Gaulle's intransigence on this and other minor matters concerned with the liberation of his own country was one of the most extraordinary pieces of *folie de grandeur* in the history of the Second World War.

During the last few hours before D-Day itself, however, there was one area in which de Gaulle was acquiescent, and that was over the thorny and explosive question of the action that the French resistance would be ordered to undertake in support of Neptune. On May 30, Gubbins and Bruce had received an instruction from the Supreme Command directing them to set in motion the machinery for broadcasting all of the 325 *messages personnels* concerned with the assault phase of Neptune. Accordingly, on the evenings of June 1 and 2, the alert messages went out in their entirety; and the volume of these messages did not, it appeared from Ultra, alert the Germans to the imminence of the invasion, as had been feared. But then, on the eve of D-Day, came the difficult task of informing Koenig —and through him de Gaulle—that the action messages were also to be broadcast in their entirety.

That evening, the telephone rang at Gubbins's headquarters. It was Bull. Gubbins was to "request the approval" of Koenig to transmit all of the action messages. The request was a formality, for the messages were already being sent. Gubbins would recall his reaction: "Bull knew that this might provoke a national uprising among the French in France, to say nothing of what the French in London might do. But they had to go out. It was an operational necessity—one of those awful things that high commanders have to order in war."

With Bruce of the OSS, Gubbins made his way to Koenig's headquarters in Queen Anne Street, a quiet backwater of dainty houses round the corner from MI-6. Gravely, Gubbins explained their visit. Did Koenig object to the *messages personnels* going out en masse? Koenig, who knew that he was being presented with a fait accompli, thought for a short while. Then he said the French Committee of National Liberation could not and would not object. He would explain his reasons later: "This torrent of telegrams could have given some of the agents the impression that (the Allies had ordered) a national insurrection. But (I knew that) if the agents stuck to their orders (this would not occur)." He would go on to say that:

> . . . these orders . . . were so arranged (a) to let doubt exist as long as possible on the points where the landing would take place, and (b) to hinder to the maximum and at one blow the assembly . . . of the enemy's army, and (c) to demoralise the enemy, so that he would no longer feel secure at any point on our territory. . . .
>
> The resistance was to furnish its maximum effort during the first hours and days which followed H-Hour. That was one of its essential missions. It could not fail at the task.

In that moment of heroic acceptance, Koenig had gone a long stride toward the redemption of French honor. Gubbins and Bruce saluted and withdrew.

As the two men made their ways back to their headquarters, an announcer's curious, disembodied, almost sinister voice was reciting the list of action messages over the BBC, speaking slowly, then repeating them, and emphasizing every syllable: "The centipede is a mammal! . . . The crocodile is thirsty! . . . The doctor buries all his patients! . . . Flora has a red neck! . . . I hope to see you twice, darling, at the Pont d'Avignon. . . . Jacques needs Melpomene! . . . You may now shake the tree and gather the pears! . . . The tomatoes are ripe and ready for plucking at Perpignan! . . . The oleander is gorgeous in the Midi!" For nearly an hour, the voice droned on—and among the messages broadcast was the second line of the Verlaine couplet.

Apparently, the Germans had displayed no reaction to the alert messages; their broadcast was, after all, a fairly frequent occurrence. But how would they react to the action messages, particularly to the Verlaine? Would they put their armies on alert? Would they send up aircraft? Would they despatch the E-boats, submarines and destroyers they had assembled in French and Norwegian ports for just this moment? Would they man all their strong points? Would they begin moving their panzer reserves toward the coast? There was still time for them to prepare for the great battle now at hand. Never before had Ultra been watched so carefully.

At least one significant Ultra reached Eisenhower's headquarters in those last hours before D-Day. It was a weather Ultra, a decryption of the Luftwaffe's nightly weather report. In a long signal in a six-digit code that had been one of the toughest German codes for the Turing engine to break, the Luftwaffe predicted that disturbed weather conditions would persist in the English Channel throughout the current phase of the moon and tides. The Germans had not detected the brief interval of improved weather that Stagg's syndicate had predicted, and it was reasonable to hope that they believed the weather would preclude an attack that night.

If the weather Ultra gave the Allied high command some cause for confidence, another report from Foord's Operational Intelligence Centre created a spasm of alarm. Brissex agents watching the tank battalions of the Panzer Lehr near Orléans had seen rail activity that suggested they were preparing to move. A heavy tank train was loading at Châteaudun, and the ranks of tank flats in the yard at Orléans were "seen to be heavily loaded with AA, usually a sign of impending or actual movement," Foord noted in a hurried bulletin to Bull at Southwick House. "The evidence suggests that Panzerlehr (is) in the process of moving. . . . It is NOT clear where it (is) intended to go."

What was afoot? Had Rundstedt and Rommel got wind of something? Was the Panzer Lehr preparing to move toward Normandy? No one knew, and this time Ultra was silent. To the Supreme Command at Southwick House, and to Menzies, who spent much of the night at Broadway in the MI-6 signals center, Ultra's silence was both an encouraging and an ominous sign. If the Germans were moving to counter Neptune, the air would be crackling with signals—unless wireless silence had been imposed upon all commands.

At Storey's Gate, in the headquarters of the LCS beneath the pavements of Westminster, Bevan and Wingate talked late into the night. To relieve the acute tension, Wingate read from Churchill's *The World Crisis,* the book that had influenced British policy throughout the war to this climactic moment. His eyes fell upon Churchill's tribute to the men of the Imperial armies, "martyrs not less than soldiers," who fell by the thousands on the battlefields of the Somme in 1916. Would that holocaust be repeated on the beaches of Normandy? If Fortitude and Quicksilver were a success, there was a chance that it might not. What had they done in stitching together the cover and deception plans for Neptune that they should not have done; what had they left undone? These were the thoughts on the minds of both Bevan and Wingate; but for reasons he could not explain, Wingate would recall that he began to discuss the virtues of the gold standard.

At the Horse Guards, Brooke, the man who, perhaps more than any other, had shaped the strategy of the war, wrote in his diary that evening: "I am very uneasy. . . . At the best it will fall so very far short of the expectations of the bulk of the people, namely all those who know nothing about its difficulties. At the worst it may well be the most ghastly disaster of the whole war. I wish to God it were safely over."

Marshall's whereabouts that night would not be recorded, but Roosevelt spent the evening at the White House, where he was at last able to tell Mrs. Roosevelt that D-Day would be at dawn tomorrow. Such were the security precautions imposed upon the American press and radio that not more than ten people in a nation of 135 millions knew that the great invasion fleet had already left England from every port between Spurn Head and the Skerries.

Churchill spent the evening in his suite at Storey's Gate, drinking brandy with his secretary, Jock Colville. All who saw him that night would remember that he appeared to be brooding darkly, and was very silent.

In France, it had been the hottest Whitsun in memory. The countryside of the Île de France, with its great bend in the Seine, had been baked dry in the sunshine, and the nights had been sultry. But the weather broke in the early morning of June 4, and a storm moaned about the gables of the Château de La Roche Guyon. When Rommel rose just after daybreak, the grounds of the château were strewn with leaves and branches, and as he made his toilet the rain still beat heavily on the windows. Walter Stoebe, the Luftwaffe meteorologist, had forecast a disturbed period of weather for the next few days which, coming at a time when the moon and tides might otherwise have favored a landing, the Kriegsmarine had said would make it impossible for the Allies to undertake major combined operations for another two weeks. The storm around the château confirmed Stoebe's forecast, and Rommel decided he would go ahead with his trip to Germany the following day to see the Fuehrer about the disposition of the panzers, and to be with his wife on her birthday.

It was true that there were certain disconcerting signs from England.

For one thing, a radio silence was in progress, and Rommel knew that in the desert this had often been the harbinger of an attack. But since March there had been several such silences, and all proved to have been used for training purposes or to keep the Wehrmacht alert, anxious and away from the urgent task of strengthening the fortifications of the Atlantic Wall. In the absence of favorable weather conditions, it was dismissed as another deception.

Throughout the German high command in the West, there was a sense that great events were close but not imminent. In a report dated June 4, Krancke observed that, while air reconnaissance in May had not been sufficient to give a clear picture of Allied preparations, he considered it "doubtful whether the enemy has yet assembled his invasion fleet in the required strength." In his weekly intelligence appreciation on that same day, Rommel urged that aerial reconnaissance of England's southern and southwestern ports be undertaken immediately; but the prolonged period of bad weather predicted for the Channel would make such flights impossible for the time being. That same weather was whipping up wave heights in excess of 5 to 8 feet on the Channel—much too high, in the German view, to permit a seaborne assault. Winds of Force 6 were predicted for the Pas de Calais, and of Force 7 at Cherbourg, with a cloud base of between 900 to 1800 feet—much too strong and low to permit an aerial attack or the use of paratroopers.

And so, at 6 A.M. on June 5, 1944, Rommel went on leave. With his aide, Lang, and his operations officer, Tempelhof, he was driven by his chauffeur, the faithful Daniel, down the carriageway of linden trees that led from the château, and out through the lanes onto the main highway. As he sped toward his home near Herrlingen, his headquarters informed OKW at Berchtesgaden that the armies might be stood down in this period of bad weather to give them some rest after a long period of watchfulness. OKW was also informed that Allied air operations continued to point to the "previously assumed focal point of the major landing"—the Pas de Calais.

That same day, Rundstedt reported: "The systematic continuation and noticeable intensification of enemy air attacks indicate a more advanced state of readiness for the descent." The report went on to estimate where the descent might occur:

> The main front between the Scheldt and Normandy is still the most probable place of attack. Its possible extension along the north coast of Brittany, including Brest, is not excluded. *Where* within this entire sector the enemy will attempt a landing is still obscure.

And Rundstedt ended his report with the words: "As yet there is no immediate prospect of the invasion."

It was quite clear that nobody at OKW suspected that the invasion was at hand—least of all Hitler. His diary revealed that on June 5 he attended a conference to discuss Portuguese tungsten imports, and the noon OKW conference was almost wholly taken up with the successful withdrawal of the 10th Army on the Italian front. Hitler then had a long session with Reichsminister Speer to discuss smoke-screening the Rhine bridges, he attended another conference to discuss building diesel trucks, and he was given a fecal examination by his physician—his meteorism was still giving him trouble.

The entire German high command was unanimous in its judgment on the eve of D-Day: whatever the Allies intended, the weather was too bad to permit an invasion during the first week of June. Neither Hitler, Rundstedt, Rommel, Krancke nor anyone else had the slightest idea that the assault fleet of over 6000 ships was already at sea. Rundstedt could not know that there would be a fair interlude between the storms over the Channel just long enough to make the invasion possible, even though the weather conditions during that period would be worse than those the Germans thought necessary for a large-scale amphibious assault. Allied victories in the little heralded weather war had systematically deprived the Germans of the means to forecast such subtle changes. It was for this moment alone that the weather war had been fought.

Because of the weather, the air and sea operations that would have detected the approaching armada were called off. No one reported that one flotilla of Allied minesweepers was already at work, cutting a passage through a German minefield lying across the path of the Utah and Omaha convoys, within sight of the shore of the Cherbourg peninsula near the Barfleur Light. Because of the weather, local leave was open to officers, and a war game to be held at Rennes, which a number of army and divisional commanders from the Normandy front were to attend, was not canceled. And because of the weather, Rommel would be absent from his post, for the third time, at a critical moment in his country's history. Although the Germans were, on the eve of D-Day, gravely unbalanced by the threats of Bodyguard and Fortitude, but for the weather, they might have been alert and waiting for Neptune. But no submarine, no aircraft, no radar set—not one officer or one man of the mighty Wehrmacht—detected the advance of the biggest force of warships in history. As General Warlimont, the deputy operations chief at German Supreme Headquarters, would record: "On 5 June 1944, . . . (OKW) had not the slightest idea that the decisive event of the war was upon them."

The Germans did, however, have one forewarning that Neptune was about to begin—the *messages personnels,* and, in particular, the Verlaine couplet. They had come to attach great importance to these messages, which were considered to be indicators of an invasion—but only one of a number. Wehrmacht intelligence staffs reported the broadcast of the alert messages on the nights of June 1 and 2; and on June 2, Colonel Oskar von Reile, the chief of the Abwehr's counterintelligence department in Paris, informed OKW and all higher headquarters in the West that several times between 1:30 P.M. and 2:30 P.M. on June 1 a British radio station had broadcast the first part of the Verlaine couplet, the alert message: "The long sobs of the violins of autumn." Reile's signal was with all commands —including Hitler's, Rundstedt's and Rommel's—by 7:55 P.M. on June 2. Had OKW, OB-West and Army Group B acted upon the intelligence available to them about the meaning of the *messages personnels*—intelligence that was close to the truth and which, oddly, had originally come from Canaris just before he was dismissed in February 1944—the armies in the West would have been put on alert to meet a probable invasion. But the German high command had heard the first line of the Verlaine and other alert messages in the past, notably on May 1, 1944. It had reacted then, only to find that nothing happened. As a result, Rundstedt had reserved for himself, with the permission of OKW, the sole right to alert his armies on the basis of the *messages personnels*. He took no action when informed of the broadcasts of June 1 and 2. In the absence of weather conditions favorable to an invasion, they were considered to be another false alarm.

The action messages, however, and in particular the second line of the Verlaine couplet—"soothes my heart with a monotonous languor"—had not been heard before. It was intercepted on the evening of June 5; in fact it was broadcast a total of fifteen times that day. The sheer volume and frequency of these broadcasts might alone have roused the Germans' suspicions, even if they had not known the approximate meaning of the Verlaine message. It was still not too late to alert the German armies, but only with reluctance did General Hans von Salmuth, the commanding general of the 15th Army between the Seine and the Somme—the Fortitude area—interrupt his bridge game to place his army in a state of alert on his own responsibility. But the 7th Army—in the Neptune area—was not alerted by its commanding general or OB-West, both of which were informed of the Verlaine intercept. Why it was not put on the alert would become one of the most impenetrable mysteries of the war, a mystery that centered around OB-West.

General Bodo Zimmermann, Rundstedt's operations officer at OB-West, would later claim that all commands in the West *were* put on alert. He would tell his postwar American interrogators that:

At 2115 on 5 June 1944 (Meyer-Detring, his intelligence officer) reported the receipt of an urgent alarm message to the effect that the enemy radio had several times repeated a code word summoning the resistance movement to arise immediately throughout France. Practically, this signified the mobilisation of the resistance movement for the following night; the report was therefore taken very seriously. (Rundstedt) decided to transmit this fact, with a general warning, to all units and agencies concerned in its area.

In what amounted to legal testimony, for in certain respects his early release from Allied captivity depended upon the truth of his statements, Zimmermann then went on to say: "Army Group B, which was aware of the above report, was ordered by (Rundstedt) to comply with all the requirements of Alarmstufe II [maximum alert] throughout its entire coastal area [Wehrmacht District Netherlands, 15th Army *and* 7th Army]. . . ." Similar instructions were sent to Army Group G in the south of France, by telephone and confirmatory teleprinter signals. This process was completed, said Zimmermann, by just after midnight—*before* any reports had arrived of landings in France. Thus—if Zimmermann's version was correct—the entire German group of armies, with the navy and the air force, should have been in a state of maximum alert by the time the first Allied soldiers started to land by parachute. But this was not the case.

Colonel Anton Staubwasser, Rommel's chief of intelligence, who was on duty at Château de La Roche Guyon that night, would tell his interrogators a quite different story. "At approximately 2200 hours," Staubwasser testified,

the 3rd General Staff Officer of the 15th Army informed me by telephone that one of these code words had again been intercepted, and that the 15th Army had therefore alerted its troops independently. I reported this matter immediately to (Speidel) . . . and, considering the circumstances that Headquarters Army Group B had *no records whatsoever* [Staubwasser's italics] by which to judge the import of the code word which had just been received, he ordered me to obtain a decision from (Rundstedt's headquarters, about whether to place the army group troops and 7th Army on alert).

At that moment, Speidel was giving a small dinner party for his brother-in-law, Dr. Horst, and for Rommel's friend, Ernst Juenger, in the château. It was virtually a meeting of the Schwarze Kapelle in the West, and those present talked much about the draft of a twenty-two-page document which Juenger, a philosopher and author, had prepared, so Speidel stated, at the request of Rommel, a document that was intended to be used by Rommel as the basis for an armistice with England and America. Following Speidel's orders, Staubwasser contacted Rundstedt's headquarters, and as he told his U.S. Army interrogators: "In the course of the ensuing conversations which I held personally, a special missions staff officer—after a short while—conveyed to me, by order of OB-West, the command to desist from alerting the troops." That was the reason, at least according to Staubwasser, that no alert was sent to the 7th Army on the invasion coast, and in turn no alert was sent by the 7th Army to 84 Corps, which bore responsibility for Utah, Omaha and most of the British sector. It would not be until 0215 that 7th Army ordered its divisions into the highest state of alert—by which time the airborne assault was under way.

What explanation was there for this fundamental difference in accounts between events at Rundstedt's and Rommel's headquarters? Who, in particular, was the "special missions staff officer" who ordered Staubwasser not to alert the troops? Hitler, later, would be convinced that there were either traitors or British agents at work at OB-West, claiming to have evidence that the British had impersonated Hans Baron von Boineburg-Langsfeld, the Commandant of Greater Paris and a member of the Schwarze Kapelle, who was, apparently, on leave at the time of the invasion. Hitler would order an investigation to be made into how it was that so many staff and field commanders were away from their posts on that particular night, why a war game had been scheduled the following day at Rennes, why the 15th Army was on alert but not the 7th Army. Speidel's conduct that evening would come under investigation by the Gestapo, and he would be arrested on suspicion that he had committed high treason. It would be asked why he entertained members of the Schwarze Kapelle that most important of all nights, and it would be suggested that he had not alerted 7th Army because he wanted the Allies to get ashore and capture France and Germany before western and central Europe were destroyed in battle, and before Russia reached Germany's eastern frontier. Later it would even be suggested that as reward for his schemes the Allies—and particularly the Americans—gave him a post in the NATO high command after the war. There would not be a shred of evidence to support any of these allegations and suspicions; indeed, there would be ample evidence that Speidel was absolutely loyal to his country, if not to the Nazi régime.

Nor would there be a shred of evidence to substantiate the suspicion that a British agent had infiltrated OB-West, although a story would go the rounds that an expert in the German language and military affairs, a certain Allied agent, had undergone plastic surgery to perfect his resemblance to a German officer. It was this agent, so the story went, who told Staubwasser to desist from alerting 7th Army, was later responsible for giving the orders that sent certain key German combat forces off in the wrong direction, and even succeeded in planting a false copy of Neptune on Rundstedt, a plan revealing that the main Allied invasion would come in the Pas de Calais rather than Normandy. As unlikely as that story appeared to be, it was possible that Menzies did succeed in infiltrating the German high command in Paris at about this time. Major Alexander Scratchley, an SAS operations officer, would recall that just before the end of the war in Europe he received an order to plan the emergency exfiltration of a British agent who was in hiding in one of the Channel ports. He was in danger of being murdered by French patriots who thought he had been a German agent; he had been seen, Scratchley was told, "riding in Paris with Rundstedt and Goering and other German notables." The operation was mounted but just before take-off it was canceled. The agent had been murdered by the French.

Another explanation for the contradictory versions of the events at Rundstedt's and Rommel's headquarters might be found in communications difficulties and misunderstandings—or in the falsification of statements and documents by the officers concerned to avoid being held responsible for letting the German army sleep that night. Whatever the reason, the "sledgehammer of God"—as the Kaiser once called the German army—was without hands on the haft. The *Feldgrau* were at their ordinary posts on the Normandy front. At St. Lô, at the hour it should have been springing to arms, the staff of 84 Corps attended a birthday party for their commander, General Erich Marcks. A number of the divisional commanders in the corps were actually on the road to Rennes for the war games. At Le Mans, where the 7th Army had its headquarters, the commander, General Friedrich Dollmann, was also at Rennes, having ordered his Chief of Staff, General Max Pemsel, to *cancel* a practice alert which had been scheduled for that night because the troops, he said to Pemsel, need their sleep. Krancke was away from his headquarters in Paris, on his way to Bordeaux to inspect a submarine base. Rommel had arrived at his home in the Swabian Hills outside Herrlingen, had dined with his wife and his son Manfred, and had gone to his study for an hour to begin writing a memorandum to Hitler about the disposition of the panzers. Rundstedt had dined in his quarters and then gone to bed.

At Berchtesgaden the night was starry, the weather was calm, and, having spent part of the evening listening to some lieder with his mistress, Eva Braun, Hitler had taken a sleeping potion. He was fast asleep when Bull at Southwick House issued another historic signal—"Adoration from 0200." It was a signal in the Fortitude scenario. Wireless activity intended to make the Germans believe that major military movements were taking place in the FUSAG area opposite the Pas de Calais would commence at the same moment that the first waves of the airborne assault descended upon Normandy. The seaborne forces for the initial assault were beginning to enter the Bay of the Seine. Paratroop sky trains and bombers, antisubmarine and night fighters convulsed the silence of the skies as they made their way to the Far Shore. H-Hour for Neptune was at hand. There was nothing more the Supreme Command could do. Like Hitler, Montgomery and Eisenhower went to sleep.

PART

NORMANDY TO NEMESIS

JUNE 6 TO AUGUST 20, 1944

'Twas on a summer's day—the sixth of June:
I like to be particular in dates,
Not only of the age, and year, but moon;
They are a sort of post-house, where the Fates
Change horses, making history change its tune,
Then spur away o'er empires and o'er states,
Leaving at last not much besides chronology,
Excepting the post-orbits of theology.
'Twas on the sixth of June, about the hour
of half-past six—perhaps still nearer seven . . .

LORD BYRON, *Don Juan*

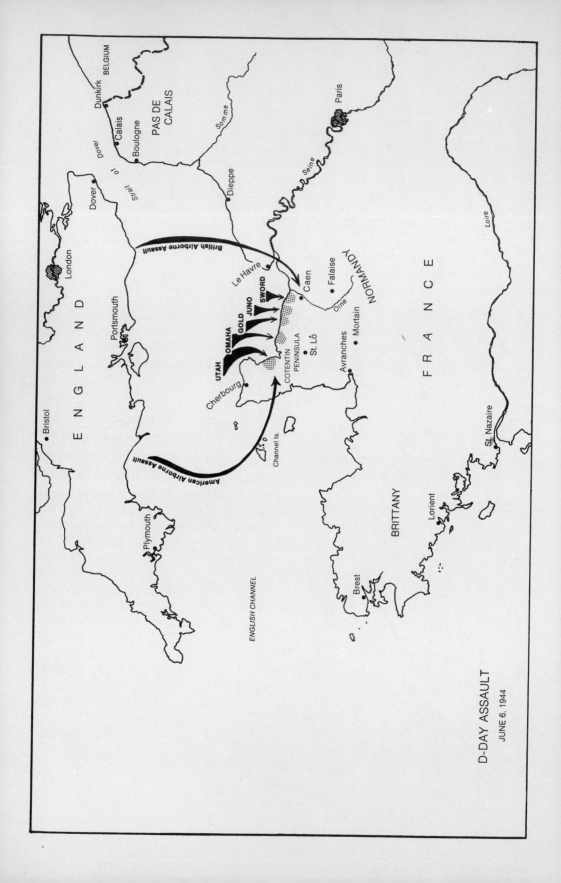

D-DAY ASSAULT
JUNE 6, 1944

D-Day

In the Bay of the Seine, in the shallows and meadows of the Norman shore, all was silent in the first few moments of June 6, 1944. D-Day began not with a cataclysmic air and naval bombardment, nor with the descent of airborne and seaborne armies. Conceived in secrecy, it commenced in stealth—with a series of deception and diversionary operations to confuse and distract the enemy.

It was eleven minutes after midnight when the first Titanic party leaped from a Stirling flying at 3000 feet above the Cherbourg peninsula. The first man away was Lieutenant Noel Poole, a Somerset bank clerk serving with the Special Air Service. Leading a party of three troopers, he jumped, struck the tail of the aircraft, fell into the scudding cloud with his parachute opening automatically, and landed—stunned—in a meadow about 5 miles due west of St. Lô on the road to Coutances. He lay in the wet grass, recovered, and then found a pigeon pannier that had been dropped with his stores. He wrote a message to London, put it in a cylinder on the bird's leg and released the pigeon. The signal read: "From Sabu 15 (Titanic 4) to HQ Airtps. NHP/1. Rang bell on leaving aircraft, received slight injuries on landing." Poole then gave a brief report on the situation. He was the first of the Allied soldiers to land on D-Day, and his was the first of the tens of millions of messages from France to England during Neptune. At 10 A.M. the following day, the pigeon was found by a village policeman fluttering on the tarmacadam of a country lane near Stokenchurch in Buckinghamshire.

A few minutes after Poole's party was dropped, a second Titanic party, commanded by Captain Harry "Chicken" Fowles, landed in the same general area, while overhead, to make it seem that these eight men were the advance party of an airborne brigade, more Stirlings flew in to drop two hundred of what the Germans would soon call "dolls"—the half-life-sized dummies of paratroopers. As the "dolls' " parachutes opened, hundreds of pintail bombs began to land and—on the principle of Roman candles— spurted parachute flares and Very lights into the sky. Thousands of rifle and machine-gun simulators dropped from the aircraft started to explode. At the same time, Poole and Fowles and their men set up boxes from which came the recorded, amplified sounds of more fire mixed with the thud of mortar bombs and soldiers' oaths and commands. Then, after about thirty minutes, silence returned to the meadows as Poole and Fowles and their men slipped away to hide up in some orchards.

Similar operations took place at Yvetot and Harfleur, near Le Havre; along the roads between Lisieux and Evreux; around the Forêt d'Écouves; near the Forêt de Cerisy; around Lessay, Villedieu-les-Poêles, and St. Hilaire-du-Harcourt. A rash of what seemed to be paratroop landings from company to brigade strength occurred in every area where sizable German mobile formations were stationed. Their purpose was to enmesh the local tactical anti-paratrooper formations in searches of the close Norman countryside as the real Allied airborne forces landed and established their airheads between Montebourg and Carentan, and astride the Orne Canal. Those "dolls" and noisemakers were to bedevil the German high command in Paris for the next few hours. In fact, Titanic would have an effect on Neptune out of all proportion to the handful of men, aircraft and technical devices used in the operation.

Even before midnight, throughout France, the men and women of the resistance gathered together, preparing to execute the acts of general guerrilla and sabotage that had been assigned to them. They had heard the call to action on the BBC; it was a moment of high emotion, a moment they had long been waiting for. In silent groups they crept from their meeting places in response to the clarion from London. Their main task, in the first few minutes of D-Day, was "Violet," SOE's plan to disrupt German telecommunications. Suddenly, all over the country, but particularly in the Neptune area between Le Havre and Avranches, the lines went dead as *résistants* dug up and spiked trunk cables and pulled down overhead wires. Operators left their switchboards, electrical power circuits fused and repeater stations exploded. From midnight on, Paris, Le Mans, Orléans, Lille, Dôle, Lyon, Tarbes, Bordeaux, St. Lô, Rouen, Avranches, Caen, Amiens—all vital German military centers—began to experience severe communications problems and sometimes total dislocation. Allied wireless and radar-jamming programs, which were carried on coincidentally with Violet, added to the chaos within the German command structure, particularly between divisions and regiments—the units that would have to fight the battle.

Other SOE plans would be put into effect in the hours and days ahead: "Vert" to sabotage rail communications and "Tortue" to disrupt German road travel, both intended to impede the rapid reinforcement of the Normandy front. All over France at shortly after midnight, aircraft approached their drop zones to spill loads of war stores and the special forces teams that would train and lead the resistance in guerrilla operations designed to harass the Germans from behind the lines. Among the most important of these teams were the French SAS troopers and the Anglo-American-French Jedburghs that were parachuted into Brittany to form a nucleus around which the sizable and brave Breton *maquis* could crystalize into fighting battalions. Lieutenant Nicholas Marienne and the men of the 4th SAS Regiment (Chasseurs Parachutistes) were one of the first special forces teams to land. At 0040 on D-Day they leaped from a Halifax into the bright moonlight over a drop zone on the moors near Vannes, hurtling past the twin rudders of the plane and arcing down through the clouds to the dark earth below, their parachutes breaking open behind them. The "Battalion of Heaven"—as the Bretons would come to call the SAS troopers—had begun to arrive.

As other Halifaxes dropped war stores, Marienne and his men landed amid the dolmens—megalithic remains similar to those at Stonehenge—and gorse of the moors. Almost immediately, they heard men nearby who were speaking an unfamiliar language. It was not French, and the men were not the *maquisards* in the Vannes area. They were probably Cossacks serving in the German army. There was a burst of machine-pistol fire and Corporal Bouetard, an SAS trooper who had been born in Brittany, was killed immediately. He was the first Allied soldier to lose his life on D-Day.

Just after midnight at Rundstedt's headquarters, a huge three-storey blockhouse in the side of a small hill on the rue Alexandre Dumas at St. Germain-en-Laye, the war room was almost silent. The duty officer sat in a little glass cubicle listening to his *deutscher Kleinempfänger*—a miniature wireless receiver. The late night Wehrmacht communiqué had been read, and it was now being followed—as it always was—with a record of Maria von Schmedes singing: "Another Beautiful Day Draws to a Close." Rundstedt had retired at eleven o'clock, as had the operations officer, Bodo Zimmermann; Meyer-Detring, the intelligence officer, had gone on local leave. The Verlaine couplet apart, it looked like a relatively uneventful night—the usual bombing raids and resistance attacks, the usual *parachutage* and prowlings of Allied ships in the Channel. That was all.

There was not the slightest doubt in anybody's mind at the headquarters that the broadcast of the second half of the Verlaine couplet was a trick; certainly nobody really believed that the Allies would begin the *Grossinvasion* that night. The tides and moon conditions might be favorable, but the weather was not—visibility, wind, wave heights, surf conditions, all were unfavorable. Moreover, there were no reports of any significant increase in resistance activities. The Kriegsmarine duty officer, entering Krancke's opinion about the Verlaine couplet in the war diary for June 5, 1944, wrote:

> Although it is hardly to be assumed that the invasion will be announced in advance [over the BBC], it must be admitted that these (*messages personnels*) would certainly cause acts of sabotage in connection with the traffic and communications network, and also insurrections, all of which would pave the way for invasion proper.

Unlike his army and navy companions, however, the air duty officer was not satisfied that all was normal. That day, the Luftwaffe Y service had detected very unusual aerial activity over England and France. First there had been massive wireless tuning—far heavier than anything intercepted before—during the morning; and that always presaged aerial operations that night. Second, the long-range forecasting station at Bad Homburg, in the Taunus, using a statistical process based on a study of Channel weather over the past fifty years, had warned that the present bad weather might clear temporarily on June 6. Third, the Y service had intercepted many American Mercury broadcasts. Mercurys were weather intelligence flights; and what made the Luftwaffe suspicious was that the Americans usually made these flights in the daytime because they only bombed by daylight. Why were Mercury flights being made at night? There could be only one explanation: the Americans were about to undertake a night-time operation. The Luftwaffe duty officer decided that the circumstances were sufficiently suspicious to warrant despatching air patrols over land as a precaution. A few night fighters were therefore scrambled and were airborne by 0034. Their activity was instantly detected by the RAF Y service at Kingsdown in Kent. It was the first sign of German reaction on D-Day. But it was not considered a significant reaction, nor one that might be dangerous; the German night fighters were being vectored between Amiens in France and Deelen in Holland. Had they patrolled 100 miles or so to the west, they might have detected that the vast Neptune fleet had already entered the Bay of the Seine. But there, save for the tail end of Stagg's storm, the skies were empty.

Three miles offshore the British sector of Normandy, two midget submarines, the X-20 and the X-23, which had been lying in 11 fathoms of water for nearly two days, surfaced briefly at about 0020 to receive a signal from the Admiralty. The code word "Padfoot" came over very faintly from the control station near Portsmouth; it meant that the invasion fleet had entered the Bay of the Seine. The X-craft crews, sickened with stale air and the hyoscine and benzedrine tablets they had taken to forestall seasickness and fatigue, gulped some fresh air, and then the submarines bottomed to wait until it was time to surface again and act as beacons for the naval assault forces.

Admiral Sir Bertram Ramsay, at battle headquarters near Portsmouth, watched the plots uneasily. The great assault convoys had reached "The Spout"—the point at which all ships converged to enter the Bay of the Seine. A minesweeper, the USS *Osprey,* had hit a floating mine and sunk with the loss of six men—the first naval casualty of Neptune. But there was not the slightest indication that the Wehrmacht had awakened, and Ramsay reported to SHAEF operations at about 0030: "The assault forces in general are conforming to the plan."

At almost precisely that moment the first American Pathfinders—paratroopers dropped ahead of the main airborne assault forces to mark the airheads for the skytrains which were now approaching the Cherbourg peninsula—were landing on the wet Norman meadow grass. Their drop was chaotic. Confused by bad weather and encountering fierce fire from the ground, their Dakotas had been forced to weave, and so many had gone off course that only thirty-eight of the Pathfinders landed accurately. Some were killed, more were drowned when they fell with their heavy loads into low-lying pasture which the Germans had flooded with river water from the Merderet. Forty miles away, the British Pathfinders were more fortunate; they had not encountered flak when they made their landfall. But in both sectors, the paratroopers ran into stiff, immediate resistance from German patrols. One party of Pathfinders landed squarely on the lawn of the headquarters of Major General Josef Reichert's 711th Infantry Division at the easternmost end of the Neptune area. They were captured immediately by Reichert's intelligence officer.

At last the Germans were beginning to react, but their reaction was that of a drugged giant. The 7th Army stirred only sluggishly; the Titanic operations, together with the widely scattered Pathfinders' drop, made it impossible for anyone to know precisely what was happening; and as the resistance, obedient to Plan Violet, disrupted telecommunications, it became difficult and sometimes impossible for the German commanders to exchange information in a situation where minutes counted.

In the main room of the operations bunker of 84 Corps at St. Lô, the birthday party for the corps commander, General Erich Marcks, ended with the loyal toast and the singing of the German version of "Happy Birthday." The cathedral clock at St. Lô struck one as the general rose and thanked his officers. But while he was making his way stiffly up the stairs—he had lost a leg in action on the Russian front—a staff officer stopped him to say that unusual air activity was being reported in the Cherbourg peninsula. Marcks turned about and came down to the operations room to study the situation maps. When the telephone rang, he picked up the receiver, and, "as he listened, the General's body seemed to stiffen." Richter, the general commanding the 716th Division on the coast at Caen, reported that British paratroopers were landing east of the Orne. The news struck the officers round the table "like lightning." Was *this* the invasion?

Although the reports were spotty and confused, Marcks acted quickly. Three of his divisional commanders were already on the road to Rennes, and he ordered the divisional command posts to get them back. Then he called General Max Pemsel, the Chief of Staff at 7th Army headquarters at Le Mans, to announce that paratroopers were reported to have landed not only east of Caen but also in the triangle Coutances-Valognes-St. Lô in the Cotentin peninsula, the area in which the Titanic parties and the American Pathfinders had indeed landed. The time was 0211. Pemsel reacted immediately by placing the 7th Army in a state of full alert at 0215—approximately five hours after the Verlaine action message had been intercepted. Then he called General Friedrich Dollmann, the 7th Army commander, with the statement: "General, I believe this is the invasion. Will you please come over immediately?"

At Château de La Roche Guyon, Speidel had been awakened at 0215 by reports of paratroop landings and had telephoned Rundstedt at OB-West. Krancke and Field Marshal Hugo Sperrle (the Luftwaffe commander) were also on to Rundstedt at about this time; and as the Kriegsmarine war diary would show, none of them believed at that moment that this was a large-scale landing. Pemsel, however, did not share the Supreme Command's view. He called Speidel at 0235 to announce that the sound of ships' engines could be heard at sea off the east coast of the Cotentin, and that naval observers were reporting the presence of ships in the area around Cherbourg. Pemsel told Speidel that in his view this naval activity, when combined with that of the paratroopers, pointed to a major operation. But Speidel rejected his opinion on the grounds that some of the paratroopers had been found to be what he called "dolls," and some of the divisional commanders thought that the fuss was to do with bomber crews bailing out or with ordinary *parachutage* to the resistance. As Speidel himself would write later on: "It was not at all clear at first whether these were airborne landings in strength or just groups of parachutists dropped to provide a link between the French resistance forces and the invasion forces."

Pemsel placed Speidel's words in the 7th Army log: "the affair is still locally confined," and the "Chief of Staff of Army Group B believes that for the time being this is not to be considered as a large operation." Nevertheless, both the 7th Army and 84th Corps were now in the highest state of alert. Officers manned all switchboards and all operations rooms; the *Feldgrau* were rousted from their beds by sergeants and rushed to their positions; mobile patrols made for crossroads and village squares ready to be sent wherever paratroopers were reported. The giant was struggling to his feet and clearing his head, but Neptune's main airborne assault phase had already begun.

As skytrains disgorged thousands of Allied paratroops onto the Cotentin and astride the Orne, thirty Lancasters and Fortresses trailed their coats between Amiens and the German border, sowing the great foil blizzards of Window that would make it seem that a large bomber stream was heading for Germany. In these same aircraft, electronic warfare operators switched on their Airborne Cigar jamming transmitters to blot out surviving German reporting stations' broadcasts over northern France, while other jamming transmitters in Britain covered such frequencies as the airborne Cigars could not tackle. At about 0230, the Kingsdown Y station intercepted a German controller ordering all fighters to scramble and those that were already airborne to vector on the ghost bomber stream. They did so and intercepted and shot down one of the Windowing Lancasters.

All but a few of the night fighters pursued the red herrings to the German border; those that were left to guard and search other areas were thoroughly confused by "Bagpipe" and "Chatter," transmitters in England which worked on the enemy's radio frequencies. Bagpipe produced sounds on the German air-ground systems that resembled those of some mad Scot playing the pipes; and Chatter passed false instructions to the German pilots, heckled the ground controllers and garbled their transmissions. Flight Lieutenant Alfred Price would recall one such operation:

> The German fighter controller recognised that fake orders were being fed into the system by the British, because of the faulty pronunciation (of the German). He warned the night fighters "Don't be led astray by the enemy" and "in the name of General Schmidt I order all aircraft to Amiens." Becoming increasingly angry, the German controller actually swore into the microphone, causing the ghost controller in England to remark: "The Englishman is now swearing!" The German controller shouted. "It is not the Englishman who is swearing, it is me!"

As the Luftwaffe prowled empty skies to the north, the great skytrains were making their way safely to the British and American airheads in Normandy. Not one of the 1100 transports or their gliders would be lost through Luftwaffe activity. But Neptune's airborne army, particularly the American divisions, encountered other difficulties. The Americans' mission was to secure the causeways leading from Utah across the swamps and flooded areas onto the hard, dry ground of the interior—causeways that the Utah forces would have to use in order to get off the beaches. But heavy flak, bad weather and the early confusion of the Pathfinders created chaos for the Americans. The 101st Airborne Division dropped over an area of 25 by 15 miles. Sixty per cent of its equipment was lost or destroyed, and by 0300 some 1500 of its men were either killed, drowned, captured, or lying about in the meadows or in the swamps, wounded, stunned or out of action with broken limbs or sprains. Nevertheless, the 101st did manage to secure two important villages and their causeways to the beaches.

If the 101st's drop was a bad one, the 82nd's, which began at 0230, was worse. Its men were scattered all the way from Valognes in the north of the Cherbourg peninsula to Carentan in the south, and from St. Sauveur-le-Vicomte in the west to St. Martin-de-Varreville in the east, an area of 35 square miles. Only one stick out of three regiments was put down accurately on the three airheads; and the casualties—particularly through drowning in the area's widespread inundations and swamps—were severe. The confusion was so great that it would be impossible to count the loss of life during the first hours of the 82nd's operations, and the division, at least temporarily, no longer existed as an integrated fighting unit. Yet the disaster was less severe in its consequences upon Neptune as a whole than it seemed. The scattered drops, when combined with surprise, the breakdown in German communications and the Titanic deception, thoroughly confused Rundstedt's, Rommel's and Dollmann's headquarters. Unable to determine, at least in the first hours of the assault, where the Americans were concentrating, they began to disperse their counterattack forces.

The mission of the British paratroopers was to establish a firm line on the Orne and secure the seaborne landings from an armored counterattack. Faring better than the Americans, they dropped well and managed to seize their objectives, even though the 21st Panzer Division was laagered but a few miles from the area. Had the panzers attacked, it might have been a different story. But they did not. General Edgar Feuchtinger, the commander of the 21st, was ready to strike, but his standing orders permitted no private enterprise. "I had been told," he would explain later, "that I was to make no move until I had heard from Rommel's headquarters." Partly due to the communications breakdown and partly due to the general confusion among the German high command, the 21st would not get into the battle until twelve hours after the airborne assault began.

At 0229, the USS *Bayfield,* an attack transport flying the two-star flag of Rear Admiral Don R. Moon and carrying the Utah beach commander, General J. Lawton Collins, arrived off Utah beach. She dropped anchor, the report, "Anchor holding, sir, in 17 fathoms," came back to the flag bridge, and the navigator announced that *Bayfield* was 11½ miles offshore. She was attended by troop transports, tank and infantry landing ships, control craft, and gunfire support ships; and the fleet had managed to get that close in without being spotted by German radar, the German navy or the Luftwaffe. At 0251 the American amphibious command ship *Ancon* anchored 11 miles off Omaha beach, again without being spotted by the German early warning defenses.

The long crossing—some ships had been at sea for two days—had been rough, but the fleet had managed to keep good station and only one of the 6100 vessels in the assault formations had been lost through enemy action. The leading ships had successfully picked up the lanes of dan buoys that marked the way through the German minefields, and as each attack transport arrived on station and anchored, it lowered the assault boats. From about 0315 onward, the troops began to file to the debarkation points as the assault boats heaved, pitched, ground and clanged against the sides of the transports. Still there was no German response. Where were the *Schnellboote,* the *Unterseeboote* and *Räumboote* that ordinarily infested the Channel, the boats that had inflicted the disaster upon Tiger? Where was the Luftwaffe? Why was there no naval gunfire? Had Neptune achieved surprise, or was this to be another Salerno, where the Germans had held their fire until the landing craft lowered their ramps into the surf? The enemy's inactivity caused much foreboding. Could the Germans be saving all their power, all their secret weapons, for one shattering counter-stroke at that time when the assault troops were at their most vulnerable—in the grounded landing craft, seasick, wet, tired, laden down with ammunition, weapons and equipment, wading through the surf toward the shore?

Off the British and Canadian beaches of Gold, Juno and Sword, where three divisions were to assault the same area from which William the Conqueror had sailed for England in 1066, the story was the same. The lack of enemy activity was disconcerting, even sinister. It seemed incomprehensible that the Wehrmacht could be unaware that fifty-nine convoys of ships were spreading out along the 60 miles of the assault area. Thousands of paratroopers were landing in France; over a thousand bombers were plastering German strong points and coastal artillery batteries right round the Bay of the Seine. But apart from Luftwaffe intercepts, Ultra revealed very little German wireless activity. In fact, there was very little activity of any sort. The thought was inevitable; had the enemy something unforeseen up his sleeve? The fearful unreality of these last moments before H-Hour was intensified by the sight of the light at Barfleur, one of the world's tallest and most brilliant beacons. The Germans had left it burning that night. Was it because they thought it would give the appearance of normality to the Bay of the Seine?

The night was very dark, although there was a full moon. Occasionally the clouds split and a sliver of moonlight outlined a warship. Its crew, with steel helmets on and dressed in anti-flash clothing, looked like pikemen of the Middle Ages—as Ernest Hemingway, who would be in the fifth assault wave at Omaha, would write. Hemingway was not alone in invoking a vision of that other great invasion in the Bay of the Seine on August 20, 1415, when Henry V sailed from England with 12,000 men to land at Harfleur and do battle with Charles VI of France at Agincourt. What was about to happen here would be more momentous than anything that had taken place before in military history. Yet many quotations from Shakespeare's *Henry V* seemed appropriate. Major C. K. "Banger" King of the British 3rd Infantry Division would remember the lines: "He that outlives this day, and comes safe home/Will stand a tip-toe when this day is named."

At Bordeaux, Admiral Krancke took a telephone call at about 0200 from the C-in-C of Naval Group Normandy, who stated that paratroopers had landed near the heavy naval battery at Marcouf. Krancke immediately telephoned his headquarters in Paris, to be informed that the radar system was almost uniformly out of action in the area between Le Havre and Cherbourg—the Neptune area. But it was, he was told, functioning spottily between Le Havre and Dunkirk—the Fortitude area. Krancke dressed and hastened across the dark courtyard to the quarters of the admiral commanding Bordeaux; he was concerned because he knew that the 15th Army had been in a state of maximum alert since midnight; and he had heard from Rundstedt that the Verlaine couplet had been broadcast.

For the moment, as he and the admiral commanding Bordeaux talked in the drawing room of quarters built for one of Napoleon's admirals, Krancke was not disposed to believe that anything major was afoot. How could the Allies invade on a night like this?—there was a Force 6 wind running in the Channel and small ships like landing craft could not navigate in such weather. But when at about 0230 Krancke's staff in Paris reported that "a fair number" of paratroop landings were taking place along practically the whole of the Normandy coast between the Orne and the Vire, he became uneasy. Together with the *Ozet* radar system, the Kriegsmarine was charged with the task of patrolling the Channel to give the alarm if an invasion fleet was approaching. The *Ozets* and patrols were supposed to be able to detect the strength and thrust of any invasion fleet and provide Rundstedt with the foreknowledge that would permit him to move his panzers toward the threatened area. But on this night Krancke had canceled all naval movements. There was not a Kriegsmarine ship at sea. Not even the Allied minesweeping activity of the night before off the Barfleur Light had alerted the Kriegsmarine. What was more, because of Fortitude all the new-type German mines available to Krancke had been laid off the ports between Le Havre and Dunkirk. The Normandy minefields were laid with old-type mines, most of which had been there for years and were so crusted with barnacles that nothing short of a direct hit with a bow at high speed would make them explode.

At 0309—according to the War Diary of German Naval Group West, if it is to be believed (there was some falsification of documents afterwards)—Krancke received a report which finally compelled him to act. The report stated: "North of Port-en-Bessin ten large craft located, lying some seven miles off the coast, thus indicating unloading activity." Now Krancke knew that a big attack was developing. At about 0400, he ordered the destroyers to sail from Royan for Brest, and sent some torpedo boats into the Bay of the Seine to see what was going on. He also began the procedure necessary for the submarine fleet to put to sea and engage the enemy. But then ECM deceptions began to cloud the picture; at 0400 the German radar chain reported enemy plots off Le Tréport in the Pas de Calais. Krancke ordered the minesweepers at Dieppe to investigate. They did so, reported seeing nothing, and returned to port. The War Diary noted: "Presumably plots were false."

The only major action between Krancke's forces and those of the Allies was fought at 0535, about an hour after the E-boats had finally managed to sail out of Le Havre. They encountered six heavy warships escorted by fifteen to twenty destroyers, but smoke screens laid by aircraft obscured the targets; the E-boats fired fifteen torpedoes, sank the Norwegian destroyer *Svenner,* and then turned for home. They were pursued by fighters which strafed them with cannon fire, and they were bombed as they entered Le Havre's inner harbor. The U-boat fleet fared no better. Just as the U-boats at Bordeaux were about to sail, their captains were told that their sortie had, for the moment, been canceled. It was possible that the Allies might land in the Bordeaux area. Ironside, the deception scheme to menace Bordeaux, had intervened.

The U-boats that did reach the Channel were quickly intercepted. For this German reaction had been anticipated by the Neptune planners and large air and sea forces had "corked" the Channel between Lands End and Ushant (the code name of the operation was in fact "Cork"). Endless chains of patrol aircraft were being flown; any aircraft making contact with a U-boat broke formation, attacked, reported the position of the craft, then rejoined the chain. "Rover" freelance aircraft collected the sighting reports, dropped beacons onto the target, and then guided in naval craft. In this manner—according to German sources—the first run of U-boats was attacked no less than fifty times. Five boats were so seriously damaged that they were compelled to put into port, and two were sunk.

Thus it was that, during the first hours of D-Day, the once mighty Kriegsmarine was not a factor. The vast Allied fleet had come through the sea and electronic defenses of one of the world's mightiest powers; and there had not been a single squeak on a radio or a blip on a cathode-ray tube to warn the Germans. Krancke later sought to explain this defeat in a report which stated: "The radar stations on the Normandy coast did not record the approaching invasion fleet because they were jammed by the enemy." But why did the jamming itself not make the Germans suspicious and cause them to send aircraft and ships to investigate? Because, said Krancke, when similar interference in the past had been investigated, it was found to be enemy deception. Once bitten, twice shy, he might have added. Finally, Krancke was compelled to admit that Allied jamming, bombing and deception measures had been so effective that it was possible to report a large fleet in the Bay of the Seine only when "the ships could be recognized by visual means."

Four minutes after the American amphibious command ship *Ancon* had anchored 11 miles off Omaha beach at 0251, when he received Pemsel's reports that engine noises could be heard out in the Bay of the Seine, Rundstedt announced that he was no longer quite so sure this was not a major operation. He told Zimmermann to get on to Berchtesgaden and tell Führerhauptquartier what was happening, and then he went to his quarters to dress. He was back in the war room, drinking black coffee, by 0315 hours—the moment when the assault boats were being lowered into the nasty chop of the Channel.

Now was the hour for Rundstedt to display that swift, formidable logic for which he was renowned. But it was not until 0415—when, still undetected, the first of the assault landing craft were leaving their mother ships for the long run into Omaha—that he made up his mind. Only then did he pronounce that the airborne landings were "definitely the opening phase of a (sea) landing to be expected at dawn." He had received no forewarning from the German radar screen, the Luftwaffe or the Kriegsmarine. But he still held one advantage: the panzers. If he was to exercise that advantage, it was imperative to order the panzer divisions to Normandy as fast as possible. If he left them until after daybreak, naval and air bombardment might seriously interfere with their movement. Furthermore, heavy ground mist would develop around dawn; and that would help hide the panzers as they closed up to the coast. But Rundstedt did not command all the panzers. Some of them were commanded by Rommel's headquarters; others were commanded by OKW and could not be deployed without Hitler's permission. After some hesitation, Rundstedt decided to act first and argue the case later. At 0430 he ordered the 12th SS Panzer Division, "Hitler Jugend" (between Paris and Caen) and the equally formidable Panzer Lehr (between Orléans and Caen) to begin to move up to the Calvados coast immediately. It was the right decision. But then Rundstedt made a mistake. He ordered General Kurt Meyer, the commander of the 12th SS, to send what was the equivalent of half the fighting force of his division to the coast north of Lisieux to deal with parachutists and a reported seaborne landing near Deauville. The parachutists were part of Titanic, and Rundstedt's orders constituted one of the early major diversions caused by the ghost airborne landings.

Rundstedt sent this signal to OKW advising of his action and requesting approval for his orders. It was a signal that reflected both his uncertainty and his concern about the situation.

> OB-West is fully aware that if this is actually a large-scale enemy operation it can only be met successfully if immediate action is taken. This involves the commitment on this day of the available strategic reserves . . . the 12th SS and the Panzer Lehr divisions. If they assemble quickly and get an early start they can enter the battle on the coast during the day.

It was *the* critical message of D-Day, for had OKW agreed to Rundstedt's action, it might have been possible for the Germans to launch an immediate, major counterattack that stood every chance of destroying the invasion at the water's edge.

When Rundstedt's message reached OKW, however, its critical nature was not at first realized. Somebody opened Jodl's door to see if he was awake, found he was asleep, and decided that the situation had not developed sufficiently for him to be disturbed. Equally, when OKW called Hitler's quarters at about 0500, nothing was said that caused instant action. The caller spoke to Hitler's naval *aide-de-camp,* Admiral Karl Jesko von Puttkamer, to say that some "extremely vague" messages had been received stating that there had been "some sort of landings in France." Puttkamer decided not to awaken the Fuehrer because "there wasn't much to tell him anyway and we . . . feared that if I woke him at this time he might start one of his endless nervous scenes which often led to the wildest decisions."

When Jodl did awake, and was told that landings were taking place and Rundstedt had ordered the panzer divisions to begin closing up to the Calvados coast, he was furious. At about 0630, the hour at which the seaborne landings were to begin, on Jodl's instructions General Treusch Baron von Buttlar-Brandenfels, the army operations chief at OKW, telephoned both Rundstedt and Speidel and objected violently to Rundstedt's "arbitrary employment" of the strategic panzer reserves. He ordered them to stop the movements and await Hitler's decision. As Zimmermann would remember: "When we warned that if we didn't get the panzers the Normandy landings would succeed and that unforeseeable consequences would follow, we were simply told that *we* were in no position to judge—that the main landing was going to come at an entirely different place anyway." Again, Fortitude was dominating the Germans' reactions.

Zimmermann tried to argue with Buttlar-Brandenfels; but the argument ended with Buttlar-Brandenfels exclaiming: "Nothing is to be done before the Fuehrer makes his decision. You are to do what you are told!" That was that; only one recourse was left to OB-West; Rundstedt must telephone Hitler. As a marshal of Germany he had the right to speak to Hitler personally at any hour if the need demanded, and by doing so at that moment he might have persuaded the Fuehrer to act immediately and decisively. But he did not, perhaps because he was somewhat hard of hearing and avoided using the telephone whenever possible, perhaps because he held the "Bohemian corporal" in such contempt that Hitler might call him, but he would never call Hitler.

At 0730, Jodl personally informed Rundstedt that the Hitler Jugend and the Panzer Lehr must not be committed without Hitler's instructions; the Hitler Jugend was to be halted at Lisieux and the Panzer Lehr was not to move at all. Thus, instead of the 500 tanks and 100 assault guns, and perhaps 40,000 panzer grenadiers as infantry that Rundstedt might have had for a three-division counterattack late on D-Day, all he would have were the 146 tanks and 51 assault guns of the 21st Panzer—and not even that division would be available for a single concerted thrust. The consequences of OKW's decision were immediately apparent to Zimmermann. He exclaimed later: "The first critical day was lost! The success of the invasion was already decided!" As for Rundstedt, he had breakfast and then spent much of the morning in his garden next door to the command post, pruning his roses.

At 0405, two hours before sunrise, the assault transports at Utah began to debark their troops into the landing craft. An 18-knot wind blew off the Cotentin peninsula to kick up the waves; the radar aboard the USS *Augusta,* General Bradley's command ship, washed in and out of the low clouds; and although the banging of the landing craft "made an ungodly racket," sailors on deck "spoke in whispers, as if the Germans could overhear." Still there was absolutely no sign that the enemy was awake. It was, all who were there would agree, quite eerie, and wholly unexpected.

At this same hour, other fleets approached other shores. Throughout the night, eighteen RAF and naval launches had been sailing at 8 knots toward the Calais coast. Each launch flew a 29-foot Filbert balloon, with a second anchored to a raft, and in each of the Filberts was a 9-foot radar reflector which gave back an echo that resembled a 10,000-ton attack transport. At a point about 15 miles off Beachy Head, the little fleet had split into two. Nine of the craft made for Cap d'Antifer, a headland north of Le Havre not far from Bruneval, where the "wizard war" of electronics had begun with the theft by paratroopers of a Würzburg radar back in February 1942. This fleet was called "Taxable." The rest of the fleet—"Glimmer"—proceeded up-Channel toward Boulogne.

At around 0100, operators in both fleets switched on their Moonshine apparatus, and at about 0200, a number of them observed signals on their green-glowing cathode-ray tubes. A German aircraft was interrogating them. They tuned in to the search signals' wavelengths and started to Moonshine the German receiver, causing echoes that resembled an immense group of warships. The wizardry had begun.

As the two fleets came up toward the French coast's horizons, each was joined by a squadron of RAF bombers; 218 Squadron flew the Glimmer spoof and 617 Squadron joined Taxable. Using special radar devices which permitted the aircraft to navigate with great accuracy, both squadrons flew the very precise patterns which had been proved during Dr. Cockburn's trials at Tantallon Castle in Scotland in May. At predetermined intervals, the aircraft dropped bundles of Window, while above them other bombers used Mandrel radar jammers. Each formation was, in essence, a giant radar reflector covering an area of 256 square miles, and it appeared on the enemy radar screens as a great mass of shipping in the Channel. To ensure that no German patrol aircraft approached too closely and saw that this "invasion fleet" consisted of little more than rubber balloons and masses of thin aluminum strips, each formation was surrounded by several scores of Mosquito night fighters.

It was a nerve-racking night for the naval and air crews. The launches pitched, heaved and rolled so violently that few of those aboard were not very seasick. As for the air crews, they had to fly exact patterns for no less than four hours in high winds and turbulence that made every airframe shudder. One of the 617 Squadron crew members would recall:

> At the time I was rather concerned about what the Germans would do when they saw Taxable. We knew that we were bait and expected just about every night fighter in creation to roll up at any moment. Our Lancaster was packed full of Window, from nose to tail. If we were forced down in the sea there would be little chance of our getting out before the aircraft sank. We finished Windowing by 4 A.M., by which time it was just beginning to get light. The sky seemed to be full of transport aircraft and gliders: the Red Berets were going in. We hoped we had made things a little easier for them.

At the first hint of daybreak the next phase of the deception began. When the two ghost fleets reached points about 10 miles offshore, the launches switched on sound amplifiers as aircraft came in to blanket the area with smoke. Any German soldier on the shore would have heard bosuns' pipes, the rattle of chain cable through hawsepipes, warships' bugle calls, commands being shouted over loudhailers, the banging of landing craft against the sides of attack transports, the squeal of steam-powered derricks at work, the sounds of laboring engines. Just as Titanic had simulated the sounds of a major airborne landing, so Taxable and Glimmer simulated the sounds of a vast invasion fleet lying off the Channel coast between Cap d'Antifer and the long, wide beaches of Boulogne.

By this time, it was quite clear to the Germans that a major attack had begun between Cherbourg and Le Havre. Yet there were also indications of another, perhaps even larger attack between Le Havre and Calais. As naval operations reported to the OB-West command center in those incredibly confused first hours: "In the main, the landings are taking place off Houlgate and north of Caen," which was correct, "and also near Octeville and Montvilliers," which was incorrect. Moreover, suspicious resistance activities were reported to be taking place between Le Havre and Boulogne, particularly in the area of Le Tréport; and reports of paratroop landings had been received from around Yvetot, Octeville, Montvilliers and Le Tréport. Any sensible man looking at the situation maps, and knowing the British, would conclude that while Cherbourg looked like the target, Le Havre was the *real* one. Was it not written in Directive 51 that that was where the main attack would come?

As a result, the Germans responded to Taxable and Glimmer more positively than they did to the great Neptune fleet in the Bay of the Seine. Warships sailed, searchlights swept the areas off Cap d'Antifer and Boulogne, and the Taxable fleet was shelled by shore batteries. No German gun fired upon the Neptune fleet before H-Hour. But by the time German warships and patrol aircraft arrived to inspect Taxable and Glimmer, there was only some smoke and the wakes of small, fast craft, bucking the sea at high speed, heading for England. The ghost fleet had vanished.

At H-Hour, the Germans were still not certain where Neptune's airborne divisions were concentrating, nor where the major seaborne assault would occur. Such was the predicament of Major Friedrich-August Baron von der Heydte, the commander of the crack German 6th Parachute Regiment, 1750 highly mobile, young, well-armed paratroopers stationed at the eastern base of the Cherbourg peninsula. His regiment, which regarded itself as "fast and lean and deadly as a whippet," was specially trained to locate and destroy any Allied airborne force. Titanic parties had landed to the south of Heydte's command post at Periers, and the drop zones of the American 101st Airborne Division were to the north; but when he called corps headquarters to learn where the paratroopers were concentrating, he could not get through. The lines had been cut by the resistance. He did not reach corps headquarters until 6 A.M., and even then he was told only that the Americans were "north of Carentan." Heydte set his battalions on the march, but as day was breaking, he was compelled to climb the church steeple at the village of St. Côme-du-mont to get the intelligence he needed to deploy his regiment. He would never forget what he saw in the gray dawn light. It was, he would say, "overwhelming." The Neptune fleet lay before him from the shore to the horizon in a panorama that was so calm it reminded him of yachts on the Wannsee Lake at Berlin on a prewar Sunday afternoon.

Neptune went in behind a hail of 10,000 tons of explosive dropped from 2500 bombers, while 7500 fighters and fighter bombers combed the area and 600 warships shelled and rocketed the beaches. The first Allied seaborne forces landed at Utah, and here the American 4th Infantry Division was virtually unopposed. Even three and a half hours later there was still no accurate enemy fire, nor was there a counterattack. All the amphibious tanks and artillery managed to get ashore, and engineers and naval demolition parties quickly cleared lanes through Rommel's "devil's garden." Then they began the march inland to link up with the American paratroopers. It was a different story on the other beaches.

At Gold, the British 50th Division, veterans of the Western Desert and the Sicilian campaign, encountered tough resistance and would fail to capture either primary target: the little port of Bessin and the small town of Bayeux. At Juno, the 3rd Canadian Infantry Division came ashore on a rough sea. Many of the German strongpoints had survived the bombing and shelling, there was deadly sustained fire, and what should have been a swift assault became a battle of infiltration. The 21st Panzer Division, which dominated a 3½-mile gap between Gold and Juno, did not attack. But primarily because the Canadians' objectives—the capture of the Caen-Bayeux road and the big airfield at Carpiquet near Caen—were over-ambitious, they were not achieved. At Sword, where the British 50th Division landed to take Caen, the key to all Allied hopes, and to link up with the 6th Airborne, the troops encountered fiercer fire and more obstacles than had been expected. The division would not reach the paratroopers, who were in an almost desperate plight, until midnight on D-Day; and Caen would not be taken for twenty-seven days. But it was at Omaha—between Utah and Gold—that the situation was most serious; and when linked with the predicament of the two airborne divisions in the Cotentin, it seemed that Neptune's right wing might collapse entirely during D-Day.

The origin of the plight of the American 1st Division at Omaha was rooted in the Allied belief that the Germans had a battery of six 155-mm coastal guns on Pointe du Hoc, a blunt, triangular cape rising sheer for 120 feet from a narrow rocky shore. It was thought that these guns would dominate the landings at both Utah and Omaha, unless they could be knocked out; but since this could not be guaranteed, Bradley had decided that the shipping assembly areas must be located not closer than 11½ miles off the beaches. This meant that the Americans would have a rougher time getting in, and the job of the amphibious tanks would be particularly difficult. The American air forces had raided the guns three times between April 14 and D-Day; but more they had not dared do, for to display closer interest in Pointe du Hoc might have revealed to the Germans that the Americans intended to land there.

The second major factor that intruded at Omaha was the American in-telligence failure to report in time that the area was defended by two com-plete regiments of the first-rate 352nd Infantry Division instead of one in-complete regiment of the inferior 716th Division. Intelligence reports had speculated on the whereabouts of the 352nd prior to D-Day, but there appeared to be no definite proof that it now defended Omaha. It was not until four hours before H-Hour that a message was flashed to Bradley, as his command ship *Augusta* entered the Bay of the Seine, warning that the 352nd had indeed moved up.

At H-Hour bad weather combined with bad intelligence to create chaos at Omaha. In the long run to the beach, twenty-seven of thirty-two am-phibious tanks sank, all the artillery was lost, and the assault itself was inadequately supported by air and sea bombardment. Due to the bom-bardiers' anxiety not to hit the approaching landing craft, few of the 1285 tons of bombs hit their targets. Throughout the run-in period, the Germans held their fire. But when the assault craft reached the shore and landings began, they opened up with every weapon in their arsenal. Mist and smoke from the naval bombardment masked the landmarks, and the troops found themselves debarking in water that was often up to their necks, laden with heavy clothing and equipment, and wading through fire that intensified as they reached the high-water mark. Many were swept away and drowned, others were cut down by the withering fire. It was Dieppe and Salerno all over again.

As the assault progressed, the black, oily smoke of burning vehicles obscured the beach and flames tinged the mist a deep red. Dead and wounded by the hundreds were washed back and forth in the bloody froth of the surf. Ammunition boxes, rifles, jeeps, tanks, bulldozers littered the sand. The scene was one of such pandemonium and carnage that, for a time, Bradley considered switching the follow-up forces to either Utah or Sword and evacuating the remnants of the American assault forces from Omaha. But then the sun and wind cleared the mist, heavy and light naval units came in closer to roast the two German regiments in the bluffs, Allied fighter bomber squadrons flew over in full strength to keep the heads of the *Feldgrau* under their parapets, and by about nine o'clock the first men had Indian-crawled across the beaches and were beginning to get up into the dead ground of the lower bluffs. Many men died, but some got through; their example was followed by the hundreds of men digging in amid the dead kelp and old wood at the high-water mark. Sections became platoons, platoons became companies, and by noon the German commanders in their post on the Pointe et Raz de la Percée overlooking Omaha (who had earlier reported to the divisional commander that the invasion had been stopped on the beaches) began to see that the Americans had not been destroyed at all, and that they could not be stopped unless reinforcements came in.

Meantime, Rangers had succeeded in scaling Pointe du Hoc, hauling themselves to the top on rope ladders fired by rocket launchers. There, later in the day, they would discover that the battery of six guns which had dictated Bradley's tactics were not guns at all. They were telephone poles. The actual guns had been pulled out following the April and May bombing raids and hidden about a mile or two away where they were found and spiked by the Rangers. A German deception had almost destroyed the assault on Omaha. And now, as if to compensate, a British deception was to contribute to its eventual success.

The 352nd Infantry Division that defended the Omaha sector was understrength, short of equipment and even food supplies. Still, it was a much stronger formation than the Americans expected to encounter. It was commanded by General Helmuth Kraiss, who was dressed and on duty when, at 0200 on D-Day, he placed his division on maximum alert in response to reports of landings by enemy paratroopers. They were, although Kraiss did not know it, the Titanic parties that had been dropped south of where the actual airborne assault would land. Task force Meyer—as the 1750 men of the division's 915th Infantry Regiment were called—was ordered to the area to counter the landings; by 0400, traveling in wheezy French-driven Otrag trucks, or by cycle, the regiment was on its way through the winding narrow lanes of the *bocage*—close country of orchards and small meadows bordered by high hedges—in pursuit of non-existent invaders. This task force was the sole main reserve for the German forces that took the brunt of the American assault at Omaha. The regiment, which was specifically charged with the task of making a counterattack if the Allies succeeded in penetrating the Atlantikwall in the 352nd's sector, would be enmeshed in the Norman countryside, "pursuing," as Foot put it, "TITANIC's spectral airborne army and a few American stragglers."

Meyer, the regimental commander, received specific instructions to keep in closest touch with Kraiss by radio in case it was necessary to order a counter-march. He drew a special radio from stores but it did not work. When the Americans touched down at Omaha and Kraiss realized that if he was to destroy the American landing he had to have the regiment back in the line as rapidly as possible, he could not get through to Meyer. It was just after 9 A.M. when Kraiss finally managed to reach Meyer with an instruction to return. At this point in the battle, it became necessary for Kraiss to order Meyer to split his force in two and send one half to Gold and one half to Omaha. Neither unit would reach its destination before late afternoon. At 11 A.M. the warmth of the sun burned off the ground mist, the sun broke through the clouds, and swarms of Allied fighters arrived to begin attacking the "very widely spaced march groups" of Meyer's task force which were now spread out over 20 square miles of countryside. The intensity of the bombardment was such that Meyer's counterattack was further delayed. Finally, at 3 P.M., Meyer reported that the enemy had anticipated his attack and was overrunning his spearheads with tanks. It was Meyer's last message; he was killed shortly afterwards.

By that time, the crisis for the Americans at Omaha was over. At nightfall they had a toehold, but it was not more than 1½ miles deep at any point. The fact that Task force Meyer was some 50 miles away from where it was needed at the critical time—at Omaha and Gold—had proved to be decisive. When it finally got back in position, it could do nothing to help repulse the assault. Titanic could be credited with the most effective tactical deception of all on D-Day.

It was not until ten o'clock on D-Day that Speidel decided the picture had cleared sufficiently to form an opinion of Allied intentions. He believed that the Normandy attack was an Allied diversion, but a situation was developing there that required Rommel's presence at La Roche Guyon. Fifteen minutes later Speidel was speaking to Rommel at the field marshal's home near Herrlingen. Speidel gave him his first complete briefing on the situation. Rommel listened, "shocked and shaken"; as one account would describe his reaction: "(Rommel) waited patiently until Speidel had finished the report and then he said quietly, with no tinge of emotion in his voice, 'How stupid of me. How stupid of me.' " He went into the breakfast room and Frau Rommel saw that "the call had changed him . . . there was a terrible tension." Rommel hurried through his breakfast and then telephoned his *aide-de-camp,* Captain Helmuth Lang, who was at his home near Strasbourg. Rommel was, Lang noted, "terribly depressed." They were due to go to Berchtesgaden that day to see Hitler and try to persuade him to allow Rommel greater control over the panzer divisions in the West. But not now. Rommel announced that he would return to La Roche Guyon at one o'clock. Later, it would emerge that he was not told that the Verlaine couplet had been intercepted.

At that same hour, ten o'clock, having wakened from his drugged sleep, Hitler was informed of the landings. Admiral von Puttkamer and General Rudolf Schmundt, Hitler's army adjutant, took a prepared situation map into his suite at the Berghof. The Fuehrer, who was in his dressing gown, listened to the briefing and then sent for Keitel and Jodl. They declared that a full report from Rundstedt had not yet been received, but it was clear that a number of major landings had taken place between Cherbourg and Le Havre, and that more landings were either expected or were occurring. Jodl explained that he had countermanded Rundstedt's orders to the

Hitler Jugend and Panzer Lehr divisions. Hitler approved and stated that, in his opinion, this might well be the opening of the invasion but that Allied intentions in Normandy were diversionary. He repeated this belief several times, and announced that any question of using the strategic reserves must await a clarification of the picture.

Hitler issued several commands that morning. He ordered Jodl to issue the code word "Junkroom," the command to begin the V1 bombardment of London, which meant little since the launch units were not ready to open fire. He gave instructions that Roenne was to make an estimate of the situation as rapidly as possible. Then he turned to the SS representative at Führerhauptquartier, Fegelein, and directed that a plan he had discussed with Himmler and Goering in April and May begin. Ever since the operations against Prosper, Hitler had taken a close interest in F section; and in his talks with Himmler and Goering, he had decided that when a major Allied landing took place in France, he would reveal to SOE that its most important circuits in Europe were under SD control. He believed it would "seriously unbalance the Allied high command to discover at this critical moment that the resistance movements they had relied on for support were penetrated by his minions." Then he went to his quarters to bathe and dress.

It was now about 11 A.M. and every panzer in the West—over 1600 of them—was fueled and armed with its crew ready to fold up the camouflage nets and begin to roll toward Normandy. The generals at all headquarters stood by their *Blitzfernschreiber* (high-speed teleprinters) awaiting Hitler's command to concentrate in preparation for an armored counter-thrust to meet and destroy the invasion. All that was needed was for Rundstedt to receive from OKW the signal that had been worked out long before—"Initiate Case Three"—and all reserves would move into the battle. But the command did not come.

At the Strub Barracks, Roenne studied the maps, the incoming situation reports and the "Arabel" file, the German code word for Garbo's mission. The chief of FHW saw the situation as Fortitude had intended that he see it. "While the Anglo-Saxon enemy landing on the coast of Normandy," he wrote in his bulletin for the Fuehrer's noonday conference, "represents a large-scale operation, the forces employed comprise only a relatively small portion of the (Allied forces available). Of the sixty large formations [i.e., divisions] held in southern England only ten to twelve divisions including airborne troops appear to be participating so far." Then Roenne warned: "Not a single unit of the First United States Army Group, which comprises around twenty-five large formations north and south of the Thames, has so far been committed. The same is true of the ten to twelve combat formations stationed in central England and Scotland [i.e., the 4th Army]." His bulletin ended with the words: "This suggests that the enemy is planning a further large-scale operation in the Channel area, which one would expect to be aimed at a coastal sector in the Pas de Calais area."

That, on D-Day at least, was the decisive appraisal, an appraisal that corresponded with what the Fuehrer believed—and therefore became fact. It was nearing noon in France, the morning haze that might have concealed the panzers' movements from the Allied air force had burned off, and marauding Allied aircraft were thick overhead, rocketing and cannoning everything that moved. It was already too late to mount an effective counterattack that day.

At around noon, Roenne telephoned Staubwasser at La Roche Guyon in response to a signal from Staubwasser pleading for his help in freeing the panzers. "My dear Staubwasser," Roenne began, "the landing operation in Normandy (will) certainly not be the only attempted major landing by the Allies. A second such attack must be expected *definitely* in the (Pas de Calais) and therefore a withdrawal of troops from that sector (to assist in Normandy) cannot be allowed." As Staubwasser would recall, Roenne went on to state that FHW had "reliable information relating to a second major landing intended by the Allies." When Staubwasser began to protest, Roenne cut him short with the peremptory statement that Rommel's head-quarters "had no data whatever to base any judgement." The two men replaced their telephones, then Staubwasser turned to an assistant and declared: "What can we do? Nothing!"

There was no noon conference at OKW that day. It was held at Klessheim Castle (distant from the command post of the entire Wehrmacht), the baroque palace under the Hohensalzburg Mountains which the Reich used as a guesthouse for visiting dignitaries. Hitler was entertaining the new Hungarian Premier, General Dome Sztójay, and he was in a sprightly mood when he met his staff and opened the conference with the words: "So, we're off." General Walter Warlimont, the deputy chief of operations, who was present, would record:

> . . . as we stood about in front of the maps and charts we awaited with some excitement Hitler's arrival and the decisions he would take. Any great expectations were destined to be bitterly disappointed. As often happened, Hitler decided to put on an act. As he came up to the maps he chuckled in a carefree manner and behaved as if this was the opportunity he had been awaiting so long to settle accounts with his enemy.

Still Hitler took no decisions about committing the strategic reserves to Normandy; he said he would think about the matter over lunch. He left the meeting and went off to brief General Sztójay in a paneled reception room. There, he exaggerated the strength of the German army in the West and the power of the secret weapons he was about to unleash against England, and he declared his absolute confidence in ultimate victory. Then Hitler led his entourage and the Hungarians in to lunch. He was still in good humor, apologized for the meatless meal, and is said to have quipped: "The elephant is the strongest animal—he also cannot stand meat!"

Just after two o'clock, Hitler suddenly emerged from the dining room and told Schmundt to inform Rundstedt that he could have control of the Hitler Jugend and the Panzer Lehr. But that was all—he must not touch any of the panzer or infantry units in the 15th Army. When the order reached the panzer divisions it was almost four o'clock. Only the lightest, fastest elements could reach Caen before darkness. The main elements would not be able to get into the battle before nightfall on the 7th, assuming that the Allied air forces permitted them to move at all.

The mighty Wehrmacht, the engine which had invented the *Blitzkrieg* and had once been powerful enough to subdue the entire continent, was sputtering along like an iron horse. This, apparently, did not worry Hitler. Later that afternoon he called at OKW on his way back to the Berghof where there was another message from Rundstedt requesting the "Case Three" reserves. But again the Fuehrer took no action except to state that he could not permit Rundstedt to use these reserves until it became clear whether the Allies intended to make a second landing. Then he took a nap.

The Deceptions of D-Day

AT FIRST LIGHT on D-Day, Eisenhower strode across the duckboards from his caravan to Southwick House. The sun was coming up in a series of pastel shades peculiar to England after a fierce rainstorm, the wind was still running high in the larches, the turf was soggy. But after the oppressive weather of the last few days, the day promised to be fresh, clear and cool. The Supreme Commander also looked fresh and cool, but he seemed to Curtis, whom he met on the duckboards, "a little rough around the edges, very much like a man who has tried to sleep all night and has failed."

News at that early hour was fragmentary. The invasion armada had crossed the Channel with virtually no interference from the enemy; all seaborne and airborne forces were ashore and consolidating. An aerial reconnaissance sweep of the panzer division assembly areas confirmed that tanks of the Panzer Lehr had been in the process of entraining on the eve of D-Day; but there was no further indication of movement. The single event that Eisenhower had once thought impossible had occurred; Neptune had achieved surprise. The stratagems of Fortitude and the well-kept secrets of the invasion itself had undoubtedly contributed to that surprise. But, in the final analysis, it was the weather that had caused the Germans to relax their vigilance. It was the weather, Stagg would record, that gave Eisenhower "the chance to get his first foothold on Europe." Eisenhower would later write to Stagg: "I thank the gods of war we went when we did."

Even with surprise, however, Neptune had gained no more than a foothold. The Germans were confused and uncertain in their reactions, but they were defending the beaches fiercely, and early reports from the American airborne divisions and from Omaha caused grave concern. Eisenhower had prepared a statement, which he carried in his breast pocket ready to issue in case the Allies lost the slight advantage they had gained. It read:

> Our landings in the Cherbourg-Havre area have failed to gain a satisfactory foothold and I have withdrawn the troops. My decision to attack at this time

and place was based upon the best information available. The troops, the air and Navy did all that bravery and devotion to duty could do. If there is any blame or fault attached to the attempt, it is mine alone.

Although it was the British who had most dreaded the hazards of a cross-Channel attack, the attitude at Storey's Gate that morning was curiously optimistic. Brooke and the British Chiefs of Staff met in the map room shortly before 10:30 to hear the Joint Intelligence Committee's first appreciation of D-Day. Menzies had provided its chairman, Victor Cavendish-Bentinck, with the night's yield of Ultra and other intelligence, and Cavendish-Bentinck declared that not only did it appear that the enemy had been taken "largely by surprise," but that he also apparently continued to "expect several landings between the Pas de Calais and Cherbourg." Then he displayed a flash of confidence that would have astounded the Americans who were fighting so desperately at Omaha. He said: "We cannot estimate precisely when Germany's resistance will collapse . . . (but) we believe that faced with the situation outlined above Germany's defeat should occur before 1945." It was this appreciation that was sent to the White House Map Room, the Combined Chiefs of Staff at Washington, and the British military missions in Washington and Moscow. Meanwhile, Montgomery, the man who would fight the battle that had as yet scarcely begun, remained at Southwick Park. Like Rundstedt, he was pruning the roses in the garden outside his headquarters before he joined his command on the Far Shore.

At the Supreme Commander's order the invasion was announced at 0917. Lance Corporal Mary Parry, of the British army, fed a tape into a teleprinter autohead and SHAEF Communiqué 1 began to tick into the newsrooms of the world's press in London. The communiqué stated: ". . . Allied naval forces, supported by strong air forces, began landing Allied armies this morning on the northern coast of France." That was all. Eisenhower also ordered "Operation Topflite" to commence; and at 0917, in London, William S. Paley, the American radio adviser at SHAEF and later chairman of the board of the Columbia Broadcasting System, lifted the Sacred Line telephone—the special line from SHAEF to the BBC that was reserved for Neptune announcements—to give the prearranged code words: "Topflite at 0930." Two minutes later the BBC broadcast news of the landings, followed at 0948 by a series of canned addresses by the exiled leaders of the peoples of Europe—specially written broadcasts to confuse the Germans about the true nature of Allied intentions in northwest Europe, and to impress upon the members of the resistance the importance of obeying their orders. Neptune was ashore, but the security of the Allied beachheads would depend, in large measure, upon the continuing success of Fortitude.

Topflite was the political warfare phase of Fortitude on D-Day, and complete calm and authority were the keynotes of these epic broadcasts. The voice of Eisenhower himself led the way at ten o'clock. In his address, he referred to the Normandy landings as an "initial" assault. He asked for "discipline and restraint" among the resistance movements, and then, speaking to the French, he declared, "A premature uprising of all Frenchmen may prevent you from being of maximum help to your country in the critical hour."

Eisenhower was followed by King Haakon of Norway who, with an eye on the dictates of Fortitude North, declared that the "initial landing" was a "link in (a) great strategic plan." He asked the Norwegians not to "allow their enthusiasm to lead them into premature or unpremeditated acts." Professor Pieter Gerbrandy, Premier of The Netherlands, warned: "The enemy will not fail to employ any means of provoking or deceiving you," and declared: "As soon as more forceful action is required of you this will be made clear from here in unmistakable fashion."

Hubert Pierlot, the Prime Minister of Belgium, one of the key areas in Fortitude, then made a speech that hinted, as was intended, that the main attack would come shortly in Belgium.

> The hour so long awaited by you is near. Preliminary operations for the liberation of Europe have begun. This first assault is the certain signal for your deliverance. You are going to undergo difficult days, in a period of anxious waiting . . . be on the alert for false orders which might be issued by the enemy. . . . The only way to check the genuineness of any news is to make sure it is issued from an Allied radio station. Above all, distrust agents provocateurs. The moment of supreme combat has not yet come.

At his own insistence, de Gaulle would broadcast to the French nation in his own way, in his own time, and with his own script. That broadcast would not begin until 6 P.M. But at SOE headquarters in Baker Street, where Gubbins had spent the night as the advance guards of the special forces teams—SAS, Jedburghs, Cooneys, F section organizers—were being parachuted into every corner of France, there were already signs that the resistance was not heeding calls for discipline and restraint. Scattered reports from the field seemed to indicate that France was catching fire from end to end. Gubbins was awaiting further reports when, at about eleven o'clock, there occurred one of those baroque moments that mark a memory forever. The controller of Station 53C, the wireless station near Bicester through which Baker Street kept contact with its staff and agents throughout Europe, called on the scrambler to advise that the SD command in Paris had come up with a signal for Gubbins from Butler, the wireless post under enemy control through which the Germans had discovered the meaning of the Verlaine poem. When the signal came through, it read: "Many

thanks large deliveries arms and ammunition . . . have greatly appreciated good tips concerning your intentions and plans."

The signal was part of Hitler's plan to disconcert the Allies by revealing, at this critical moment, that the resistance movements were heavily
penetrated. But the supreme irony of the signal was that the Germans had
not acted upon the best tip of all. They had considered the broadcast of the
Verlaine poem a deception when, in fact, it might have revealed the time
the Allies would land. Gubbins read the message, and then directed that
this reply be sent:

> Sorry to see your patience is exhausted and your nerves not so good as ours
> . . . give us ground near Berlin for reception organiser and W/T operator
> but be sure you do not clash with our Russian friends.

The exchange marked the end of German *Funkspiele,* but not the end
of British wireless games. Garbo was still hard at work in the interests of
Fortitude. Prior to D-Day, the XX-Committee and the Allied deception
agencies had conceived an ingenious stratagem. It was the "Reid Plan,"
and it called for Garbo, through Kuhlenthal, his controller at Madrid, to
inform the Germans that the opening phase of the invasion was under way
as the airborne landings started, and four hours *before* the seaborne landings began. This, the XX-Committee reasoned, would be too late for the
Germans to do anything to frustrate the attack, but would confirm that
Garbo remained alert, active and well placed to obtain critically important
intelligence.

According to the plan, Garbo was not only to reveal the fact that the
invasion had begun, he was also to report the points of embarkation of the
assault troops in England, the direction of the assault and the identities of
the units involved. All this was potentially dangerous intelligence, but the
Germans were bound to pick it up themselves within the first twenty-four
hours of the landing. What, therefore, was the reason for passing it? It was
the same as it had always been: to ensure the credibility of Garbo's future
reports. After all—it was reasoned by the CSM when it discussed the Reid
Plan with Smith and Bull at SHAEF—what would the Germans think of
an agent who had *failed* to get wind of or to report upon an operation of
the magnitude of Neptune?

The difficulty of the plan was that the German wireless station near
Madrid which corresponded with Garbo closed down each night at midnight; the operators were in the habit of going out for a late dinner when
the transmissions were finished for the day. Various tricks were employed
to induce the Madrid station to stay open on the night of June 5/6 without
alarming Kuhlenthal. All failed. The Royal Signalsman who transmitted
Garbo's messages—for Garbo himself was never allowed to communicate
personally with Kuhlenthal, nor to be close to a wireless set without an

escort—could get no response from Madrid during the early morning hours of D-Day.

Garbo was back on the air shortly before noon of D-Day. It was too late to warn the Germans of Neptune, but not too late to encourage them to believe that the Normandy landings would be followed by other assaults. To substantiate that ruse, Garbo's operator transmitted the complete text of a PWE directive (which, of course, had been manufactured for the occasion) purporting to discourage speculation about other landings. The speeches already made by Eisenhower and the leaders of the governments-in-exile, which clearly implied future assaults, seemed to contradict this directive and Garbo commented on the inconsistency. Much would depend, he said, on what Churchill said to Parliament that day. But, he warned Kuhlenthal, a PWE directive calling for caution in discussing future assaults could only mean that future assaults were, in fact, planned.

The cat-and-mouse games of Fortitude continued on D-Day in the Chamber of the House of Commons. But not even the impending announcement by Churchill about what the *Daily Mail* would call "the greatest act of war in history" could make the Speaker change the ancient rituals of the House. First, the Chaplain read the Prayer, then the Speaker announced the death of an MP during the Whitsuntide recess, from which the House had just returned. Then he announced: "I have received a telegram from the Chilean Chamber of Deputies containing a copy of a resolution of friendship towards the British House of Commons." A low, approving cheer swept the House. "It will be your desire," the Speaker went on, "that I should send a suitable reply." There were more cheers. Then, as the Order of Business required, there came an hour of questions. Were soldiers securing their voting rights? Could not cheaper houses be built if interest did not have to be paid on the loans? Why was a disabled soldier refused a permit to open a shop in Wimbledon? What were the hours of employment in service canteens? Did political considerations enter into Allied Military Government appointments? Would the War Minister authorize the issue of berets to members of the women's army service? Sir James Grigg, the War Minister, replied that this was no time for new hats in the women's services. Sir Archibald Southby rose to chide the War Minister for his lack of gallantry; even if women were in the army they were entitled to a new hat in the spring.

It was so normal, so prosaic, that it must have seemed that nothing abnormal had occurred in world history that day. Then Lloyd George tottered in, a sign that perhaps something momentous had happened after all; he came only rarely those days. Montgomery's brother who was a Chaplain to the Forces also appeared. So did Mrs. Churchill. Then, at noon precisely, the Prime Minister entered the Chamber from behind the Woolsack. The cheers that greeted him gave way to some impatient muttering as

Churchill announced: "The House should, I think, take formal cognisance of the liberation of Rome [which was captured by Mark Clark's army on June 5]." He spoke for nearly ten minutes describing this "memorable and glorious event," and then there was a pause. It lasted a few long moments before Churchill declared: "I have also to announce to the House that during the night and the early hours of this morning the first of a series of landings in force on the European Continent has taken place. . . . In this case, the liberating assault fell on the coast of France." The members assumed, as they were intended to assume, that other landings would fall on other countries, such as Belgium, Denmark and Norway. Fortitude's dissimulations had penetrated the House of Commons. Churchill went on to describe the assault and added, with Fortitude still in mind: "There are already hopes that actual tactical surprise has been attained. We hope to furnish the enemy with a succession of surprises during the course of the fighting."

The Prime Minister's canny address set the tone for the statements made by other Allied leaders that historic Tuesday. Roosevelt, speaking to the American nation of what he called "a mighty endeavor," remarked that "The Germans appear to expect landings elsewhere. Let them speculate. We are content to wait on events." So far, the LCS had stage-managed the world leaders' pronouncements with cohesion and consistency; every address that day conformed to the requirements of Fortitude—with one exception. De Gaulle, in his broadcast to the French people at six o'clock that evening, made statements that at once were an insult to the Grand Alliance, an incitement to national insurrection in France, and a declaration that this was *the* invasion.

The LCS and the Supreme Commander's political advisers knew that the Germans would listen closely to de Gaulle's broadcast for clues about how Allied strategy would unfold. That was why SHAEF had prepared a speech for him. But de Gaulle rejected it, and in his own speech made no mention of further landings in France or elsewhere. In fact, his address began with the words: "The supreme battle has begun! After so much struggle, fury, suffering, this is the decisive blow, the blow we have so much hoped for."

Worse was to follow. Despite SHAEF's anxiety not to precipitate a national uprising, de Gaulle's words to the French nation were highly inflammatory. "For the sons of France," he cried, "wherever or whoever they may be, there is a simple and sacred duty: to fight with all the means at their disposal." He instructed the resistance to obey the orders not of Eisenhower or SHAEF, but of the "French government" and of "French national and local leaders appointed by it," and it was clear that he considered himself to be the head of the French state, although he had no position in law. He made no reference whatever to Eisenhower or SHAEF.

Nor was there a single mention of America or of any of the generals, admirals, air marshals, armies, air forces, navies, industries and economies that had made this day possible. He referred to England merely as "old England." To de Gaulle, the entire affair was "France's battle," although only a handful of Frenchmen and two or three French warships were involved in Neptune. De Gaulle, alone among the Allied leaders, had refused to cooperate in Fortitude. The consequences were inevitable. Staubwasser would recall that, in combination with Allied battle plans that accidentally fell into German hands on D+1, "de Gaulle's address . . . made us all [at Rommel's headquarters] absolutely certain that this was *the* battle and that any other suggestions were tricks." What chance did Fortitude have now?

That evening Garbo was on the air to Madrid again. How was he to explain the Prime Minister's suggestion in Parliament that there would be further landings in direct contravention of the PWE directive that sought to restrain such speculations? Garbo had the answer. He told Kuhlenthal that Brendan Bracken, the Minister of Information and a friend of the Prime Minister, had tried to dissuade Churchill from telling the House that the attack was "the first of a series of landings in force upon the European Continent," but Churchill had rejected the advice, stating that in his political position he was "obliged to avoid distorting the facts and that he was not going to allow his speeches to be discredited by coming events." With that piece of subtle, brilliant dissimulation, Garbo signed off until later that evening. And quite by chance, de Gaulle's address supported the fictitious PWE directive. Only he, so it might seem to the Germans, had obeyed the ban on speculations about future assaults.

At 11 P.M. Garbo came up with another message for Kuhlenthal. He was in a "flaming fury" because he had just learned that "my important signal of June 6, 0230 hours, was not transmitted until 0830 hours." Why was Madrid not listening as it had promised on that most critical of all nights? "Were it not for my faith in the Führer and the vital importance of his mission to save Europe from the twin tyrannies of Bolshevism and Anglo-American plutocracy," Garbo went on, "I would this very day give up my work, conscious as I am of my failure." Kuhlenthal, an avuncular man who thought his entire primary network in England was about to break up, sent a long signal of explanation to Garbo which ended: "I reiterate to you, as responsible chief of the service, and to all your fellow workers our appreciation of your splendid and valued work. I beg of you to continue with us in the supreme and decisive hours of the struggle for the future of Europe."

Garbo still ranked high in the esteem of his controller, but if Kuhlenthal had thought coolly and carefully enough, there was one aspect of that day's exchange of signals that might have made him suspicious. Garbo had been on the air so long that he had given the British radiogoniometrical stations ample time on three occasions to obtain a fix on his position and arrest him. Why was he able to stay on the air so long? Did he have a charmed life? Or was he being allowed to transmit by the British for the purpose of deception? These were questions that Kuhlenthal might well have asked himself. But instead of being suspicious, he sent a message to Berlin. In it he recommended Garbo for the Iron Cross.

The day's deception campaign ended as it had begun—with menacing rumbles from East Anglia where Army Group Patton was supposed to be waiting for the Germans to move the 15th Army out of the Pas de Calais before embarking for the main attack. Hitler, the primary target for that deception, had returned that evening to Klessheim Castle for a state banquet with his Hungarian visitors which lasted until 11 P.M. At a brief OKW situation report following the banquet, he repeated his belief that the Normandy landings were a diversion and then, business over, he took his visitors to a gramophone recital of Bruckner's 7th Symphony, a work which, Hitler said, reminded him of the Tyrolean dances of his youth. He went to bed as usual at about 2 A.M. It had been a grotesque day. The Fuehrer had spent its most important hours entertaining a minor central European leader when, had he not been perfectly certain that this was not the invasion, he might have been reacting to Neptune with all the ruthless speed and command for which he was renowned.

Meanwhile, Rommel had arrived back at Château de La Roche Guyon to discover that the panzers had managed to make only one strong counterattack that day in the Calvados. General Feuchtinger's 21st Panzer Division—the remnants of Rommel's favorite division in Libya—had penetrated the spot where the Canadian and British beachheads met and had driven down to the sea at the village of Luc-sur-Mer. But just before dusk a skytrain of five hundred aircraft and gliders brought in a brigade to help the British airborne division secure Neptune's left flank on the Orne. The Germans thought, however, that it was dropping in their rear to cut them off; and the panzer thrust died in confusion and bewilderment. Feuchtinger had tried to rally his men, but it was too late; it was almost dark. All that had really been achieved was a reminder of what the panzers might have done had Rundstedt and Rommel commanded three divisions of them. But the Hitler Jugend and the Panzer Lehr, the other two divisions that might have reached the beachheads that day, had not received their movement orders until late in the afternoon. The nightfall came in suddenly, and as Chester Wilmot, a BBC correspondent with the British paratroops, would write: "This was the time for counter-stroke. The assault forces were tired and strung out in a series of hastily-prepared positions. . . . The line was thin and there were gaps which cried out for exploitation. But the Germans were not in a position to take advantage of the opportunity that was offered that night and that night alone."

By the end of the day in London, the news from the Far Shore was thin, but it was clear that, despite the difficulties of the American airborne divisions and the near disaster at Omaha, there had not been a holocaust. The casualties were heavy (12,000 men would be reported killed, wounded and missing—against the 75,000 predicted if Neptune had not achieved surprise) and the material losses had been immense. But at Storey's Gate at midnight, where Bevan and Wingate were having a drink in the mess when Menzies came in, the general feeling was that Eisenhower and Montgomery had triumphed. "There was," Wingate would remember, "cause for satisfaction. But there had been little doubt that we would get ashore. Where the doubt arose was whether we should be able to stay ashore. Since this would be decided in the next three days, we went to our beds as early as possible that night."

It was quite true. The next three or four days would decide Neptune's fate. Hitler had only to order that Case Three be put in motion, and the full weight of the German panzers and the reserves of the 15th Army would descend upon the Normandy beaches, perhaps before the Allies were strong enough to resist such a counterattack. Furthermore, news of the activities of the French resistance at the end of D-Day boded ill for Neptune. To Gubbins's dismay, the Army of the Shadows had emerged into the bright sunshine, and there was now open fighting between the *Feldgrau* and the *maquisards* everywhere from the Ain to the Hautes Alpes, from the Franche-Comté to the Dauphine and the Savoy, from the Lande to the Côte d'Or and the Bas Rhin. Discipline was breaking down in an insurrection that was not wholly the work of firebrands or the politically ambitious; it was a genuine popular uprising, as passionate and as general as the French Revolution. And as rapidly as the resistance rose up, it was being cut down ruthlessly by the Germans. How much longer could it be counted on to harass and divert the enemy from behind the lines? How much longer could Fortitude sustain the fiction of an invasion of the Pas de Calais?

3

Sword and Stratagem

HAVING ISSUED his Order of the Day to the Allied armies fighting in Normandy—it began with the words: "The Lord Mighty in Battle!"—Montgomery joined his command on the Far Shore and established his headquarters in the parkland of the Château de Creully. There, he received General Sir Miles Dempsey, the C-in-C of the Anglo-Canadian 2nd Army, and General Omar N. Bradley, the Commanding General of the American 1st Army, just after daybreak on D+1. It was the first Allied command conference in Europe, and it took place at a time when the situation within the beachheads was giving rise to "considerable anxiety."

Nowhere had Allied operations succeeded as planned. The forces at Utah had failed to link up with the paratrooper divisions in the Cherbourg peninsula. Neither the British nor the Americans had joined their beachheads into a single consolidated front. The American penetration at Omaha remained slight and insecure; all the paratroop divisions were seriously disorganized and had suffered heavy casualties. In the British-Canadian sectors, the situation was somewhat easier. But none of the final D-Day objectives—and particularly Caen, which Montgomery regarded as the gate to Paris—had been achieved. Above all, the supply situation was not far short of catastrophic, and the weather—the element which Churchill said "hung like a vulture . . . over the thoughts of the most sanguine"—was expected to worsen before the navies could get additional supplies to the beachheads.

On the credit side, 83,115 British and Canadian troops were ashore, as were some 72,000 Americans. But these forces might be dislodged if the Germans attacked in strength while they were relatively disorganized and short of supplies. At the moment, the Germans were still scattered, due largely to the surprise achieved by Neptune, and as yet they were unaware of the Allies' true intentions. But they were gathering strength with the passage of every hour; and, unknown to the commanders at the conference, they had obtained intelligence of great importance. If that intelligence was used wisely and quickly, not only would Fortitude collapse but the Germans would also have a fair chance of defeating the invasion.

Late on D-Day, *Feldgrau* of the 352nd Infantry Division, picking over the debris of the battle for loot and intelligence, came across a small boat rocking in the surf near the mouth of the Vire. In the boat they found the corpse of an American officer who had been killed in the battle at Utah, and a briefcase was attached to the corpse by a chain. The briefcase was quickly in the hands of the operations officer of the 352nd, who saw instantly that—unless the documents had been fabricated and planted, which he thought entirely possible—here were the operational orders of the American 7th Corps at Utah. Then, during the late afternoon of D+1, troops of the 352nd who had been counterattacking the Americans at the seaside village of Vierville found the operational orders of the American 5th Corps at Omaha on the corpse of another American officer.

Thus, at the outset of the battle, the Germans had in their hands "the entire scheme of maneuver and order of battle for American units in the first phase of the invasion." While the documents contained nothing about Fortitude or about British plans, when they reached Pemsel's desk at 7th Army headquarters, it was possible for the Germans to deduce from them that Fortitude was a fiction. As Pemsel would put it: "The great expansion of the American bridgehead—according to the plan as far as the inner bay of St. Malo and eastward—led to the conclusion that this operation required such a large number of American forces that a second landing at another point [Pas de Calais] was not likely at all." Pemsel's opinion was important; more important still was that of Rundstedt, who received a digest of the plans early on the morning of June 8. Blumentritt would tell his American interrogators after the war that "(Rundstedt) already had the impression on June 7 that what was going on in Normandy was the actual invasion. The operations plan of the American 5th Corps . . . brought the certainty that this was the invasion."

It would always be a mystery that the officers concerned had been allowed to take the plans ashore; each was heavily stamped with the instruction: "Destroy Before Embarkation." But fate had provided Rundstedt and Rommel with what the Abwehr and the SD had failed to get: a detailed picture of American intentions in Normandy. The Germans regarded these plans with some suspicion because of the ease with which they had been captured. Blumentritt would state that the documents might have been the product of "intentional loss and deliberate deception." However, they left neither Rundstedt nor Rommel in any doubt that Neptune was a strategic operation and not a diversion. With heavy reinforcements, they now knew exactly where to strike to disrupt the entire Neptune plan.

Rundstedt reacted accordingly; he telephoned the Fuehrer's headquarters at Berchtesgaden to request that Hitler—who had already been informed of the contents of the documents—and OKW release to him the seventeen divisions that had been earmarked in contingency planning for Case Three. As OKW deliberated, Rundstedt put into action a second plan in the event of an invasion. He replaced the Wehrmacht's field code (which he considered, with good reason, that the Allies might have penetrated) with a new system called "Rastor." Thus Montgomery was "effectively cut off from one of his most valuable sources of field intelligence," as one authority would later declare. Rastor was never really broken during the entire campaign.

Hitler approved Rundstedt's request; and so the critical moment in the history of the assault had arrived—at a time when the Allies were still ill-prepared to meet it. The situation in the British sector had improved, but the American position was still grave, although they had been given "invaluable respite" by another deception. During the late dark hours of D+1, both Rommel and Dollmann had received reports that three hundred air transports had dropped a brigade of paratroops in the Coutances-Lessay area west of St. Lô. Rommel had reacted by sending German reinforcements which were on the move to Normandy through the junction of the Breton and Cherbourg peninsulas to engage the paratroopers; and believing that the landing was the prelude to another seaborne assault, this time against the west coast of the lower Cherbourg peninsula, he had ordered "all available troops" to that area. The reports had proved to be false; it was a "Titanic" operation—another of Montgomery's master strokes based on Ultra intelligence—which had dropped more of the same dummy paratroopers that had bedeviled the Germans on D-Day. As bad, these forces, which were to be used against Omaha, as a result of a breakdown in communications had been out of contact with their higher command until daybreak on the 8th, and nearly a day was lost before they were back on the road toward the real American airheads.

German reinforcements from Brittany were also being harassed by the Breton *maquis,* and the SAS, Jedburghs and other special forces teams. Even so, the reports were ominous. Ultra showed that some six hundred German fighters and fighter bombers had been ordered from the defense of the Reich to advanced bases in Normandy, and by dawn on the 8th Rommel had three panzer divisions on the British front. Thus despite all the Allied advantages of tactical surprise, and technical ingenuity, the moment of supreme crisis was approaching with each hour. Unless Case Three could be frustrated or delayed, Neptune might yet be driven back into the sea.

Hitler's decision regarding Case Three was quickly known in London; Ultra, the Y service, aerial reconnaissance, special forces teams—all reported German moves that indicated a grand assembly of the German army in the west at Normandy. At Montgomery's, Bradley's and Eisenhower's headquarters, and at Storey's Gate, the situation was viewed with mounting concern. Marshall and the U.S. Chiefs of Staff were due to arrive in London to be present with the British Chiefs of Staff to "handle any eventuality that might arise"—a euphemism for withdrawal. The fact that this reaction had been anticipated did not lessen the tension for the Allied high command. Every weapon in the Allied arsenal—aerial warfare, guerrilla and deception—would have to be employed to prevent a rapid German assembly in Normandy. No one doubted the overwhelming might of the Allied air forces nor the determination and bravery of the French *maquis*. But the moment had now come to establish whether the German high command really believed men like Garbo and Brutus—and whether strategic deception could still be an effective weapon of war.

It was against just such a situation as had now arisen—the implementation of Case Three—that Dericourt had been used to plant the false *messages personnels* on the Germans in 1943. On June 7, the BBC had broadcast a mixture of dummy and real alert messages to the resistance groups of nothern France and Belgium. Then, on the 8th, Eisenhower, working through his former G2, General J. F. M. Whiteley, who was now a deputy chief in SHAEF operations, ordered SOE to broadcast the action messages. They went out that same day (at 2:30 P.M., 7:30 P.M. and 9:30 P.M.), as an odd, disembodied French voice in a broadcasting basement in London began apparently incoherent references to flowers and scents: carnations, violets, iris, heliotrope, jasmine. It was SHAEF's intention to order "general harassing action and guerrilla," combined with the "sabotage of specific railway, road and telecommunications targets," in northern France and Belgium, and the many well-organized *réseaux* in the Ardennes and Belgium sprang immediately to their assigned tasks. But due to the heavy concentrations of German forces in the Pas de Calais, there were actually very few *réseaux* in that area; the dummy messages were broadcast to make the Germans believe that there were a great many more pockets of active resistance than there really were. That was the purpose of the Dericourt stratagem. Both real and dummy alert messages had been broadcast in the past to deceive and alarm the Germans, for it was known that they regarded the messages as harbingers of an Allied attack. But now, to reinforce Fortitude, the action messages, both real and false, were also broadcast; and to a listening German intelligence officer, the great number of messages, combined with the activities of the *réseaux* which actually existed in northern France and Belgium, could only portend a major Allied operation in the Pas de Calais.

In a pattern of activity which was designed to be seen by the Germans as identical to that which preceded Neptune, Allied special forces and intelligence teams were parachuted into the Pas de Calais and submarines and motor torpedo boats began to appear off the French Channel beaches north of the Seine. On the English side of the Channel, the activities surrounding the fictitious FUSAG were intensified, activities that also portended a major military move. Large numbers of dummy craft, with a goodly sprinkling of real ships, particularly ships that could be used for bombardment, appeared to be gathered in great strength at ports and anchorages along the coast opposite Boulogne. The ports and "hards" were discreetly illuminated by "Paradise" lights to make it seem to German reconnaissance aircraft that the Allies were loading the ships by night. The German Y service was allowed to hear a noticeable increase in wireless traffic between SHAEF and Combined Operations Headquarters at Dover and Chatham. The wireless points of the eleven divisions of FUSAG, which, according to the scenario of Adoration, had been discreetly chattering with each other for the benefit of German ears, went silent—a sign that they were beginning offensive operations. The navies sortied to lay great smoke screens between The Wash and Dover. Minesweepers set forth to clear passages through the minefields around Calais. The ionosphere was crowded with the radiotelephone conversations of ground and air crews preparing for some mammoth operation. Allied air and naval forces began a violent bombardment of the "landing beaches" between Le Havre and Antwerp. In short, every sign pointed to an imminent invasion of the Pas de Calais.

At the same time, the Allied high command could not risk depending solely upon deception to delay a concentration of German forces upon Normandy. Powerful units were already moving toward the beachheads, and to disrupt and delay that movement Eisenhower unleashed the air forces on the French market towns and transportation centers in the Neptune lodgment area. The plan had originated with the man who now commanded the assault forces, Montgomery, its objective to create what 21 Army Group called "choke points," blocking the towns and villages through which the Germans must move with rubble and cratering. The U.S. 8th Air Force had objected to the plan; the targets were considered "unsatisfactory for air attack," and as an after-action report would state: "The stand of the 8th Air Force was based on the risks to civilian life and property." Montgomery's headquarters was adamant; the choke points must be created. But the 8th Air Force was equally adamant; it would not do the job. The case was taken to Supreme Headquarters, and the after-action report noted: ". . . SHAEF, motivated by military expediency, directed that the attack be made."

Leaflets were dropped to warn civilians to evacuate the threatened towns, but when the attacks were over, the devastation was complete. Among the towns very heavily hit was Caen, the capital of Calvados, with a population of about 52,000 and the world's main center for Norman art. Villers Bocage, the gateway to the Bocage Normand with a population of about 1500, was obliterated. The charming and serene little city of St. Lô (population about 10,000) became "the capital of ruins." Pontaubault on the Sélune, a small place with a quaint old bridge over which the Germans had to pass in order to get from Brittany to Normandy, was very badly damaged. In Coutances (6000), only the Cathédrale Notre Dame, one of the most beautiful examples of Norman Gothic art, was still standing when the dust and fire that consumed the rest of the city had settled. Thury Harcourt (1200), the gateway to the Suisse-Normande, became a lifeless ruin. The cathedral "Lisieux of St. Teresa" at Lisieux (2000) survived, but almost everything else in the quaint old city founded in Gallo-Roman days was destroyed. So was Falaise (5500), the seat of the earliest Norman dukes and noted for the horse fair held there ever since William the Conqueror. Vire (6000), the picturesque cloth-working town, was so heavily damaged as to be unrecognizable when its inhabitants returned; as was Argentan (6100), from which the four knights set out to murder Thomas Becket at Canterbury in 1107.

It was one of the most brutal uses of aerial power in history, but the campaign, when allied to the destruction of the Seine, Loire and Meuse bridges and of the French railroad system, produced a situation in which, in general, the German soldiers in troop trains moving toward Normandy would be compelled to detrain about 50 miles from the front. They would then be forced to move—usually on foot, except at night when the German truck trains could make their runs—up to the front, often under fighter bomber attack. The choke points would also prevent the rapid movement of food, fuel, arms and ammunition; and the chaos that would develop when armored and troop columns tried to move through the choke points could only be straightened out by the use of voice radio or low-grade cipher wireless traffic—time did not permit more secure enciphering. This, in turn, would enable the Allies to learn with great rapidity where most of the German formations were, and with their overwhelming aerial power to attack them again and again.

As the aerial campaign produced chaos and fear, so the deception campaign hoped to produce indecision whose effects might be as important to victory as the more tangible effects of the bombing, Allied ground operations and the activities of the resistance. To substantiate the flurry of bogus activity surrounding FUSAG, the Allied high command brought Brutus into play. In a message dated June 8, 1944, he told his controller in Paris that he had seen "with my own eyes the Army Group Patton preparing to embark at east coast and south-eastern English ports." He reported Patton as stating that "now that the diversion in Normandy is going so well, the time had come to commence operations around Calais." The King, Churchill, Eisenhower and Brooke had all visited the FUSAG command post at Dover Castle, and "General Marshall of the American army comes here from Washington on the 9th or 10th of June to see Patton and the troops off." The troops available for the assault included, according to Brutus, "at least five airborne divisions," a "sea force of at least ten divisions," and "FUSAG will have 50 divisions, some of them being here already."

This message was—Bevan would later claim—"on Hitler's desk within one half-hour of its transmission from London." Then, to support Brutus, the faithful Garbo sent a signal for Kuhlenthal on June 9 that took no less than 120 minutes to transmit. In a general review of the situation as seen by the entire Garbo mission in England, he told of the concentration of landing craft in the Orwell and Deben and of the dispositions of the Allied armies after D-Day. Like Brutus, he stressed that Neptune was a diversion and that there were still many more divisions left in England for a second strike. He concluded: "I transmit this report with the conviction that the present assault is a trap set with the purpose of making us move all our reserves in a rushed strategic redisposition which we would later regret."

Roenne, significantly, was among the first to react to the accelerating tempo of Fortitude. The mass of intelligence indicating an imminent invasion of the Pas de Calais was too credible to ignore, and after consultation with Keitel and Jodl, Roenne issued this signal from FHW to all commands in the West: "In all probability major landing by enemy on the Belgian coast is to be expected on June 10." And as the first warning to Rundstedt and Rommel that Hitler might reconsider the movement of Case Three forces to Normandy, Roenne added: "Withdrawal of our forces from 15th Army sector untenable."

Would Hitler stop the movement of the Case Three reserves? Some 500 tanks and perhaps 50,000 of Germany's élite fighting men were already on the march toward Normandy, but of those forces only the paratroop divisions in Brittany and the armored and infantry divisions in the Pas de Calais, less than a day's march away under normal circumstances, were close enough to the Normandy beachheads to pose an immediate threat to Neptune. Surely, now was the time for Hitler to display that "active and bold imagination," that "astute grasp of military matters" with which an American official study of the battle would credit him. Now was the moment for the employment of traditional German military thought and training: defeating an enemy by a decisive act rather than by a strategy of gradual and cumulative attrition. Everything would depend upon whether the Fuehrer continued to believe the fictions of Fortitude. If he did not, the Allies would be in for the fight of their lives in Normandy.

Hitler began the day of June 9 decisively enough; he ordered the 9th and 10th SS Panzer Divisions—360 tanks, including Panthers and Tigers, and 35,000 men—to France from central Poland, where they were resting after having put down the Hungarian rebellion and then destroying the mighty Russian offensive at Tarnopol. But these forces could not affect the decision in Normandy; while they had taken only a week to get from France to Hungary before the invasion, it would take them three weeks to get back. What Rommel and Rundstedt needed were the armored and troop divisions in reserve in the Pas de Calais. These divisions were now committed to the battle. But just before the OKW noon conference, Roenne telephoned Colonel Friedrich-Adolf Krummacher, Hitler's personal intelligence officer and the link between the intelligence and evaluation agencies and OKW. Speaking in his rapid, high-pitched voice, Roenne launched into an attack on OKW's decision to permit the movement of the 15th Army's panzer and infantry reserve to Normandy. He said he had definite intelligence that the enemy was about to launch a large-scale operation from the east of England; the German Y service had intercepted and decrypted a message to the Belgian resistance on the night of the 8th. This, he said, indicated large-scale guerrilla action beginning on the 9th. It would therefore be madness, he said, to permit the reserves to continue to march. Krummacher replied that he was just off to the noon conference with the Fuehrer and assured Roenne that he would "present your points with all the emphasis at my command."

At the conference, Hitler heard Jodl report Roenne's views. He was concerned, for it confirmed what had been his belief all along—that despite the information in the captured American documents, Normandy was only a diversion. But Hitler would not make up his mind about whether to issue fresh orders to the 15th Army panzers and infantry. He said he would make his final decision at the midnight conference. But before that conference, Jodl gave Hitler a message with the observation that perhaps the Fuehrer should read it in conjunction with the orders to the resistance movements and the news that Marshall was arriving shortly to inspect Army Group Patton headquarters at Dover Castle. The message was from Kuhlenthal, and it was his appreciation of Garbo's report:

> After a personal exchange of views in London with my agents . . . and after considering the massive concentration of troops in eastern and southeastern England which are taking no part in the present operations, I have come to the conclusion that the (Normandy) operations are a maneuver. Its purpose is to entice our reserves into the bridgehead in order that the decisive assault can be launched at another point. . . .

At midnight on June 9/10, Hitler pronounced: the movement of the panzer and infantry divisions from the Pas de Calais to Normandy must not only be stopped, the 15th Army must also be strengthened. The orders were with Rundstedt and Rommel during the night; and they brought both field marshals to the brink of resignation. For they recognized that with these divisions they might win the Battle of Normandy; without them they stood no chance of victory. The war, wrote Zimmermann, was lost at that point. From now onwards—at least until mid-July—Hitler, Jodl and Roenne would remain convinced that Army Group Patton was about to land at the Pas de Calais and would refuse permission to Rommel and Rundstedt to call upon the forces there to help in Normandy. The second stage of Neptune, the consolidation of the beachheads in Normandy, had ended in an Allied victory. The German Supreme Command and the General Staff had been outwitted and outgeneraled. The dimensions of that victory were soon apparent in the Martians' order of battle estimates. On D+4 it had been estimated that the Germans would have twenty-one and a half divisions in the line against an estimated sixteen of the Allies. As a result of the bombing, the destruction of the Germans' communications, resistance activity and Fortitude, they had only ten and a half divisions facing the Allies in Normandy.

Back in London, Marshall and the other American Chiefs of Staff had arrived on June 10. They gathered at Storey's Gate that day and the next with their British colleagues; and there, in an atmosphere that was "heavy with tension and pipe and cigarette smoke combined with a faint aroma of good whiskey," they watched the outcome of this critical playing of the cards. Wingate would remember:

> It was a frightful moment—there were those big red blobs on the war maps moving towards Normandy all the time. Were all the bridges out over the Seine? Had the Germans built underwater bridges? Would the tanks have to come round through Paris, where we had left the bridges intact? Ought we not to bomb the bridges over the Seine in Paris? Had Garbo overplayed his hand? That was the sort of thing that was being discussed. Then Joan Bright [a secretary who kept the most secret intelligence file] knocked on the door, came in, and said there was a message which might interest us; she had just put it in the "Black Book" [the book in which all Ultras were filed]. Brooke and Marshall went to have a look. They were all smiles. We looked at the Ultra—and there it was: Hitler had cancelled Case Three. We'd won, and what an astonishing moment that was! We knew then that we'd won—there might be very heavy battles, but we'd won. There was nobody more astonished than Bevan, for I don't think he thought that we'd really pull it off. Brooke's attitude was the oddest. He said if Hitler was such a bloody fool why had it taken us so long to beat him? Then he stalked off. The P.M. came in with Stewart Menzies and the P.M. said this was the crowning achievement of the long and glorious history of the British Secret Service— or something like that.

The French Revolt

By D+4, the Allies had completed the second stage of Neptune successfully: the consolidation of the beachheads into a single front. Now began the third stage: the battle of the build-up in which the Allies sought to bring ashore sufficient strength to break out of the beachhead while the Germans struggled to contain them and, simultaneously, to assemble the forces needed for the counter-blow that, they hoped, would drive Neptune back into the sea. Here, both sides were seriously handicapped. For the Allies, the worst summer weather since 1900 was wrecking all the carefully laid troop and supply schedules. Shortly, a severe storm would destroy one of the Mulberry harbors and sink or badly damage some eight hundred ships, landing craft, tugs and ferries—four times as many ships and stores as had been lost on D-Day. Moreover, the very shallowness of the beachhead—nowhere was it much more than 6 miles deep—made it always difficult and often impossible to bring in more troops and stores.

But if Montgomery's position was bad, Rommel's was worse. Almost immediately, he began to suffer from the effects of Allied aerial superiority, naval gunfire, and the cumulative results of the long strategical and tactical pre-invasion bombing campaign. Even without the Case Three reserves, he had the men, tanks, guns and stores to launch a great counter-strike; his problem was to assemble them in the right force at the right place and at the right time. But the railways were out and truck convoys could, generally, move only by night. Petrol, oil and ammunition shortages began to occur because, through Fortitude, the Germans had concentrated their main supply dumps in the Pas de Calais. Due to calculated attacks before the invasion against the German ball-bearing and automotive industries, all vehicles—tanks included—developed high rates of unserviceability. The infantry was compelled to move up on foot, cycles, horse-drawn vehicles, and motor transport that was in varying degrees of decrepitude; and such movement as was possible was liable to sudden, murderous air attack and disruption by the *maquisards*. The Luftwaffe might have helped protect Rommel's transport and supply routes, but for all practical purposes, like the Kriegsmarine, it had been eliminated as an effective fighting force.

The defense of the Reich was left to the army; but in addition to his other problems, Rommel's command was rapidly breaking up. Marcks, the commanding general of 84 Corps in the invasion area, was caught on the open road and killed by fighter bombers; Dollmann, the 7th Army commander, was soon to die—suicide was rumored—in the Banque Mutuelle at St. Lô. In the first stages of the invasion, six of Rommel's divisional commanders and some twenty of his other senior commanders would be killed or rendered hors de combat. All this, combined with Hitler's refusal to release the Case Three reserves, left Rommel at a distinct disadvantage. Even so, the Germans were still enormously powerful in the West. With remarkable ingenuity, Rommel was managing to get some divisions up to the line, although rarely as organic units. But if he could find the means to move them, and if he could divine precisely what the Allies intended, he had 1 million men and 1600 tanks which he could employ against the wafer-thin sliver of Europe that was all the Allies had gained in their immense attack.

Montgomery's original battle plan rested on the ability of the British and Canadian troops to break out of the beachhead, capture Caen and sweep across the flat plains of the Seine. But informed by Ultra of the Germans' gathering strength which, when combined with the lag in the Allied build-up, would probably make that objective impossible, Montgomery altered his strategy. He decided that the British and Canadians should still make every effort to take Caen, but the primary objective of their campaign would be to draw German panzer forces to the Caen sector so that Bradley's American army might have a better chance to break out in the St. Lô sector with a right hook against lesser opposition. It was a complete reversal of roles that was dictated by intelligence derived from Ultra; and this new strategy would become the basic principle of the battle in Normandy. Thus the deception agencies would be charged with an additional task. While they continued to maintain the threat to the Pas de Calais, they also had to make Hitler, Rundstedt and Rommel believe that Caen was the main Allied objective in Normandy, not St. Lô. In fact, the reverse was true.

But powder—not principles—wins battles, and Montgomery knew that he was inviting disaster by luring the panzers into the Caen sector unless their power could be severely blunted. On Rommel's orders, General der Panzertruppen Leo Baron Geyr von Schweppenburg, the former German military attaché in London and son of the Master of Horse to the King of Württemberg, had taken command of the Panzer Army in Normandy; and Ultra revealed that the German armor was beginning to concentrate.

The 17th SS Panzer Grenadier armor had moved into the woods of the Forêt de Cerisy; the 9th and 10th SS Panzer divisions—the units that Hitler had sent east to meet the threats of defection of Hungary and Rumania—had been ordered back to Normandy; the 2nd SS Panzer Division, "Das Reich," was en route north from Toulouse, and large numbers of Panther tanks at the panzer training ground at Mailly-le-Camp near Paris were being readied for the battle. The 1st SS Panzer Division was lurking east of the Seine, the 21st Panzer as well as the Panzer Lehr were already in action; and all units would come under Schweppenburg's control when they reached the front. Ultra also disclosed that he was planning a great counteroffensive in the direction of Caen that was intended to split the beachhead in two. It was imperative, Montgomery decided, to eliminate Schweppenburg. But where was he? Where was his headquarters?

The Allied wireless intelligence services had located heavy wireless signals traffic coming from La Caine, a hamlet 12 miles south of Caen. The volume of the traffic bespoke an army headquarters; reconnaissance aircraft were sent over as unobtrusively as possible, and their photo coverage showed a cluster of wireless vans, office caravans and tents inexpertly camouflaged under the trees of an apple orchard. Ultra surveillance soon revealed that it was indeed Schweppenburg's headquarters and with him as an adviser was none other than General Cramer, the officer who had been repatriated just before the invasion and who ever since his return had been busy telling everybody about Army Group Patton.

In order to confirm that this was Schweppenburg's headquarters, the RAF sent over a single fighter bomber. Flying at low altitude, and slowly, the pilot saw Schweppenburg himself with his officers, claret stripes down their trousers, watching other fighter bomber operations nearby through their fieldglasses. An hour later, on the evening of June 9, the RAF attacked and wiped out the headquarters, burying Schweppenburg and Cramer in their foxholes. All the staff officers were either killed or wounded; and the wireless vans, so essential to the command of moving panzers in close country, were destroyed. At about the same time, Lancasters plastered the tank concentrations at Mailly-le-Camp, while Mitchells and Bostons saturated the Forêt de Cerisy to knock out the 17th SS's supporting counterattack. Yet another of Rommel's hopes for a speedy panzer thrust disappeared; and Staubwasser, Rommel's chief of intelligence, would comment ruefully after the war, when he learned of Ultra: "We would have been much better off without wireless."

Meanwhile, the deception agencies spun new webs to tie down German forces in areas remote from the main battle—with varying degrees of success. Fortitude North sustained the menace to Scandinavia, but there were indications that threats to the Balkans were beginning to wear thin. Turkey still refused to join the Grand Alliance, and the stratagems of Zeppelin,

Russian maneuvers and the activities of the Balkans partisans had failed to prevent Hitler from ordering the 9th and 10th Panzer SS Divisions to Normandy. The German 1st Army, and particularly the 11th Panzer Division, continued to guard the Biscayan coast in response to the threats of Ironside; but in spite of similar threats to the Riviera coast, the powerful Das Reich panzers were moving north, while German forces that garrisoned Brittany had also been ordered to the beachhead.

Where deception failed, the Allies looked to the French *résistants,* and the special forces teams that led them, to delay and disrupt the concentration of German forces during the build-up period. But the *maquis,* disregarding orders for discipline and obedience, had, in many areas, boiled over into open rebellion. While this action would result, as an SAS appreciation for 21 Army Group noted on June 20, in delays to the Germans' movements that "have far exceeded general expectations," there was a grave danger ahead. The Germans were retaliating with such savagery that, as the appreciation went on to state:

> . . . after the initial wave of enthusiasm raised by the Allied landing, and in view of the counter-measures taken by the enemy, Resistance will tend to fall off considerably as a result of casualties unless it is wholeheartedly supported with arms and equipment and, where possible, by the presence of Allied troops. . . .

In the first few days after the invasion, the *maquis* had risen up in virtually every corner of France—uprisings that, in most cases, did little to help the Allied armies in Normandy. Just as SHAEF had feared, the rebels were ferocious, not only in their attacks against the Germans but also against resistance groups of a different political stripe, and suspected collaborators and traitors. The German reaction was equally ferocious, and the rebels were cut down wherever they could be found. The bloodshed was appalling; the casualties would never be computed with accuracy. It all added up to a single word: anarchy. Alarmed by the situation, both Eisenhower and Koenig broadcast to the French nation on June 12, stating that all that was required of the resistance outside the main areas of the battle was to *obey their orders exactly.* These orders called for limited operations, not a general insurrection. But it was too late; an unquenchable forest fire had begun.

The political repercussions were inevitable. The Gaullistes accused the high command of ordering the rebellion despite its agreements not to do so. A formal protest was lodged by the "Commandement Supérieur des Forces Françaises en Grande Brétagne et Délégation Militaire du Gouvernement Provisional de la République Française" (as de Gaulle now styled his organization) that SHAEF had issued instructions over the BBC during and after D-Day that called for a national insurrection. It was a serious charge, for unless it was answered satisfactorily, the French insurgents might turn against the Allies as well as the Germans. SHAEF ordered an investigation. General A. S. Nevins, of the G-3 operations section at SHAEF, instructed McClure, the chief of the political warfare section, to find out what had happened, and in particular to look into the activities of a certain Mme Aubrac who, de Gaulle's headquarters had claimed, had issued the instructions.

McClure quickly established that no call for a national insurrection had been made by SHAEF, by any of the American or British broadcasting authorities, or by Mme Aubrac, who was a well-known radio personality on the BBC. Moreover, his investigation showed, no such order had been issued by either the British or the American broadcasting stations in Algiers. But a check with the special report of the American Foreign Broadcasting Intelligence Service, which monitored all major radio stations' outputs, revealed that de Gaulle's own stations at Algiers and Brazzaville had made some highly inflammatory broadcasts during the D-Day period. Baron Emmanuel d'Astier de la Vigerie, a passionate Gaulliste who would become chief of de Gaulle's Service d'Action Politique en France, had gone on the air to declare that Frenchmen everywhere had "one sacred duty—the liberation of France." He had also made such statements as: "The French people will rise in their entirety to take part in the annihilation of the enemy."

The investigation cleared SHAEF of any direct responsibility for the insurrection, although the volume of *messages personnels* broadcast during the D-Day period helped spark the highly explosive atmosphere of the moment. The demands of deception also played a part in fanning the flames of rebellion; and this time, as recently declassified documents would reveal, there could be no doubt that the French resistance had been deliberately manipulated. The Fortitude after-action report would plainly state that the deception agencies sought to mislead the Germans about Allied intentions by "methods of manipulation" that included: "(1) . . . giving resistance groups intentionally misleading information. (2) . . . maneuvering resistance groups so that their observed activities will be consistent with our deception scenario. (3) . . . controlling radio traffic with groups."

But the causes of the tragedy that swept through France could not be attributed solely to SHAEF, the Gaullistes or deception. In the final assessment, they could be traced to the belief that the *messages personnels* represented a general call to arms when in fact they called for only limited action, and to the failure of the *maquisards* themselves to obey their orders precisely. Lack of security, inexperience in clandestine warfare and political rivalry among the *résistants* added fuel to the fire; and the Germans, too, were responsible in some cases for inciting open rebellion so that the *résis-*

tants could be destroyed. Thus, de Gaulle's charges were unfounded, but his bitterness over the deaths of so many of his countrymen would remain to color the relations between his postwar government and the governments of both Britain and America.

As the flames of rebellion leaped from province to province, the Allied high command watched events in Brittany with special concern, for here the *maquis* had a role that was of high importance to both Neptune and Fortitude. In support of Neptune, the Bretons were charged with cutting Brittany off from the rest of France and, in particular, with delaying the movement toward Normandy of the fighting units of the 145,000 German troops that garrisoned the peninsula. At the same time, in support of Fortitude, their activities were partly intended to make the Germans fear another major Allied invasion. While there were a number of plans for actual landings in Brittany, and at one stage Montgomery considered using one or all of them to break Rommel's stranglehold on Normandy, the Allies would not invade the peninsula from the sea. However, the Bretons would be called upon to take part in a major military action when Patton's 3rd Army moved to capture the peninsula and its valuable ports. Thus, the scope and intensity of clandestine activity were greater in Brittany than anywhere else in France.

To arm, train and lead the Breton *maquis,* scores of special forces teams had parachuted into the peninsula from D-Day onwards. Three-man Jedburgh teams went in to form a nucleus around which the *maquis* could rally. Cooneys were dropped to cut road and rail links with the French interior. F section agents came in from air and sea to try to get both left and right wings of the resistance to obey SHAEF. And the men of the SAS 4th Regiment (Chasseurs Parachutistes)—the Battalion of Heaven— landed to establish two heavily armed redoubts behind enemy lines. This flood of agents did not go unnoticed by the Germans. In a broadcast over Radio Paris, they warned the French people to beware of these "provocateurs . . . who, though outwardly polite and expressing love for our country, may be members of the Intelligence Service." "We all remember Colonel Lawrence," the broadcast continued on a somewhat hysterical note. "Who knows but that this man Lawrence, who was reputed to have been killed in a motor-cycle accident, is still wandering about the world? In any case, a large number of lesser Lawrences have descended . . . like a plague of locusts." The warning was wasted on the Breton *résistants;* they welcomed these "lesser Lawrences," particularly the men of the Battalion of Heaven, with open arms.

The moon was very brilliant in clear skies when the first men of the Battalion of Heaven arrived over the moors and copses of Brittany. It was 0045 on D-Day when Lieutenant Jules Deschamps jumped out of a Halifax, followed by his radio operator, seven SAS troopers and Jed team Frederick, their mission to establish "Samwest," one of the two Breton redoubts, near the old walled city of Guingamp in the center of heavy German paratroop concentrations. The drop was entirely successful and within hours the base had been set up in the Forêt de Duault from which special forces teams and the *maquis* were to sally forth to harass the Germans and, when they heard the action message, "Le chapeau de Napoléon est-il toujours à Perros-Guirec?", to rise up in a full-scale rebellion more or less coincidentally with the entry of the Allied armies into the peninsula. Almost immediately thousands of *maquisards* began to gather at the base, but none of the good fortune of mermaids—the heraldic symbol of the region—would attend Samwest.

The *maquisards* of the area rose exuberantly to their task, but their rivalries, lack of discipline and indifference to security caused trouble from the start. They assembled in great groups to greet new arrivals and collect drops of arms and stores; their staccato Breton chatter could be heard for miles across the moors. Jed team Frederick would report that one reception committee was "assisted by an enormous crowd of onlookers of both sexes, most of whom were smoking, which we did not consider very wise as the boches were in a town only five miles away."

Capitaine Jules Leblond, the SAS commander of Samwest, encountered similar indiscretions. As he climbed out of his harness amid the dense gorse and undergrowth of the Forêt de Duault on D+4, he was shocked by the indiscipline he found among both the troopers who had preceded him and the *maquisards* who had gathered around them. "There was," his after-action report would state, "a continual procession of visitors—sightseers and well-wishers—round the base." Leblond gave "strict orders to forbid sightseers access to the base, but these orders were indifferently carried out as the paratroops tended to fraternise with all the world, without distinction or mistrust." The result was inevitable; alerted by the crowds proceeding to Samwest, the Germans began to infiltrate the camp. Three suspected agents—two men and a woman—were arrested, and after interrogation, as team Frederick would tell Gubbins, "One woman and one man were shot and daggered respectively."

The *maquisards* at Samwest were equally brutal in their treatment of the Germans. Frederick's report would state:

> Without our knowledge some of the young patriots were armed with weapons which had been dropped the previous night to the SAS and they congregated that evening in a farm about 200 yards from the base—none of them being trained to handle a weapon like a Sten gun. As chance would have it a car containing two boche officers stopped at the farm to ask the way to Carhaix. One officer entered the room where these young patriots were having supper and quite politely asked for directions. The answer he re-

ceived was about five slugs in his belly. Holding his stomach in place with one hand he regained the car and a grenade was thrown at the patriots while the men in the car escaped.

To attack a German paratroop officer was to invite retribution without mercy. It came on June 12 when the Germans burned down a farm from which Samwest obtained all of its water and some of its food. Despite his strict orders not to come out into the open until he heard the signal "Napoleon's hat" from London, Leblond sent a party of thirty SAS troopers to the rescue of the farmers. As he put it in his report to London: "I did not want the enemy to know of our presence in the forest, but on the other hand I thought it would have a disastrous effect on morale if we let a farm be burned within a kilometre of the base without raising a hand." There was a battle between the Germans and the troopers—ten Germans were killed, two troopers were badly wounded, and the Germans withdrew. Two truckloads of Germans kept watch on the base while the third went off to find reinforcements. They returned in a convoy of thirteen truckloads, put the torch to five farms on the way (burning the two wounded SAS corporals alive in one farmhouse), and Leblond decided—as were his orders—to avoid a pitched battle and disperse the base. As the SAS troopers, the Jedburghs and the *maquisards* crept out by darkness, a sapper blew up Samwest's ordnance dump—all of which had been brought in at great cost and danger to supply what London hoped would become a redoubt of 35,000 men. The *maquis* scattered, the SAS troopers and the Jeds melted away among the menhirs, and Leblond and a small party of men, hiding on the moors by day and marching by night, made for "Dingson," the second Breton redoubt, which had been established amid the strange dolmens of the Landes de Lanvaux, a plateau outside Vannes, the first capital of Brittany. But Dingson, too, was marked for disaster.

Dingson was established at La Nouette farm near the village of St. Marcel; and when the first party of SAS troopers arrived on the evening of June 9, they discovered that the *maquisards* were already extremely well organized. Their leader had assembled sufficient cattle to feed five hundred guerrillas, together with a butchery, kitchen, bakery, electric dynamos to feed the wireless sets, a repair shop for motor vehicles, a tailor, cobblers, a small hospital, and a chit system for the purchase of wine and groceries in the village. Moreover, the *résistants'* intelligence showed that the Germans did not have the slightest idea that Dingson existed. That soon changed, again because of the Bretons' exuberance and lack of security.

On the night of June 10/11, "Le Manchot"—the one-armed man, the code name for Commandant Henri Bourgoin, the commanding officer of the Battalion of Heaven—arrived by parachute to take charge of the Dingson redoubt. He was shocked by the indiscretion of the Bretons. The base covered 1200 acres, inside 3500 men had already gathered, and Bourgoin was

> surprised by the village-fair atmosphere that reigned at la Nouette: lights on all sides, patriots coming and going feverishly in the most astonishing costumes. All the neighboring civilians were at the landing. People were everywhere—in the lofts, in the farm, in the stables, in the fields, in the woods. An extraordinary exaltation had taken hold of the *maquisards* at the sight of these men coming from the sky to arm and guide them.

There were also about a thousand Russian soldiers who had deserted the Wehrmacht, hanging about the fringes of the base begging for food. *Maquisards* en route to the base had stopped at every café for miles around for some wine, chitterlings and directions, and before long only the blind, deaf and dumb could fail to know the location of the base.

The Germans attacked Dingson in brigade strength at dawn on June 18, the same day that Leblond and his party, fleeing the destruction of Samwest, reached the redoubt. The *Feldgrau* sprayed the tinder-dry woods with tracers and started forest fires. Jed team George, which was stationed at the redoubt, radioed London on the emergency frequency, asking for air support and stating: "Dingson under attack by considerable enemy force. . . . The situation will become desperate unless a low flying attack can be made on the enemy." The attack was ordered by Montgomery's headquarters and a group of Thunderbirds streaked over from Normandy to rake the ground around Dingson with fire and bombs. They came too late. Bourgoin, realizing that he was up against a very large force of German paratroopers, gave the order to disperse. His men waited until dark, prepared the arms dump for destruction—the RAF had poured in no less than 890 containers of arms, ammunition and stores to Dingson, enough for 5000 men with part stores for another 5000—and broke camp in small parties. As they moved out across the moors, the night was lit with a terrific flash followed by the roar of an explosion. Dingson's arms dump had gone up. The destruction of the Allied redoubts in Brittany was now complete.

Bourgoin, many SAS troopers and Jed team George got away safely; but fifty troopers and two hundred *maquisards* were killed or missing. The Germans were known to have taken thirty-five prisoners, who were given collective absolution by a German priest, shot, and buried as "unknown Germans." Scores of farms were burned down and the *Feldgrau,* believing their adversaries were terrorists, spared nobody who they thought had helped the Battalion of Heaven. But like the survivors of Samwest, the remnants of Dingson re-formed in smaller groups, and under their command the Breton *maquis* again began to multiply. Soon there would be— according to British agents who were sent in to investigate the two disasters—8000 armed and 22,000 unarmed *maquisards* at work in the peninsula. The RAF, now supported by the USAAF, supplied them with hundreds of containers of fresh arms and stores. The Germans could not extinguish the fires of the Breton insurrection.

For all their early misfortunes, however, the Jedburghs, the *maquisards,* the Battalion of Heaven, and the other special forces teams had important success in delaying the movement of the Germans out of Brittany into Normandy. Rommel's strategy was to ring the bridgehead with infantry while he regrouped his panzers for a counter-thrust. But he could never quite get enough infantry when he needed it. Due to a combination of guerrilla activity and bombing in Brittany, the 77th Infantry Division took thirteen days to make a two-day journey; the 165th Infantry Division began to leave Lorient on D-Day, but was still not complete at the front by June 16; the 275th Infantry Division, which began to leave the Vannes area on June 7/8, was still arriving on the 14th, and one battalion took eight days to make a single day's journey. Parachute battalions encountered similar troubles, and these were major—if not decisive—delays. The Germans had to fight their way out of Brittany, and to greater or lesser degrees, every German division ordered to the front had much the same experience. Among them was the 2nd SS Panzer Division, Das Reich, one of the best and most formidable fighting formations in the world. Its long journey from the Périgord to Normandy would become one of the epics of guerrilla warfare.

SS Brigadeführer und Generalmajor der Waffen-SS Heinz Lammerding was the commanding general of Das Reich, one of the four SS panzer divisions in France on D-Day. Das Reich usually consisted of some 20,-000 of the most battle-hardened fighting men of the SS (almost double that of an average U.S. armored division), and its order of battle included seventy-five self-propelled assault guns, seven light tanks, fifty-seven medium tanks and ninety-nine heavy tanks. Part of the 1st SS Panzer Korps "Adolf Hitler," the division's battle honors were very long. It had helped conquer The Netherlands, had plowed through France from the German frontier to the Spanish border, and was to have been one of the spearheads of the Wehrmacht in the invasion of Britain. It had captured Belgrade, it had defeated a Russian army near Smolensk in the great battle of Yelnya in August 1941, and it was the spearhead of the German offensive south of Borodino that took the army to within a few miles of the outskirts of Moscow. It had helped prevent the Russians from recapturing the Donetz industrial basin, had led Hitler's great armored strategic counteroffensive at Kursk and had fought a hundred smaller battles. Now it was well rested and fed in the Périgord just outside Montauban, the ancient city of pink-stone arcades on the Tarn River, hated and feared by the *maquis* and very closely watched by MI-6 and BCRA agents.

It was expected at SHAEF that the Germans would rush this élite division to Normandy to meet Neptune on D+3, and the routes it would have to take to get to the beachhead with such speed were the direct rail and road routes through Brive, Limoges, Poitiers, Tours, Le Mans and Caen. It therefore became the objective of all arms—particularly F Section of SOE and the RAF—to delay the movement of Das Reich. In exactly the same way that Spanish irregulars under British control confounded Napoleon's "hurricanes" of heavy cavalry during their march on Madrid in the Peninsula War, so the descendants of the descendants of the *Grande Armée* were to confound the modern "hurricanes"—the panzers of Das Reich—on the long, hot and lonely roads through the Périgord, the Limousin, and the Dordogne.

The Allied air forces led the attack, destroying the road and rail bridges over the Loire between the Atlantic and Orléans in raids intended to prevent the German panzers in southern France from crossing the river. Then, on the evening of June 7, the RAF's 617 Squadron—the "Dambusters," who were renowned for their precision bombing and were equipped to carry the 12,000-pound "earthquake" bomb, the heaviest of the Second World War—was ordered to destroy the Saumur-Parthenay railroad tunnel under the Loire, the last main route open between the south and Normandy. The squadron was airborne at dusk, and when it reached its destination, the commander, Group Captain Leonard Cheshire, flying his Mosquito, dive-bombed his red markers from 3000 feet squarely into the tunnel mouth. Within a few minutes the earthquake bombs were streaking down in what was their first operational use. There were a series of direct hits or near misses, and one bomb bored its way through 70 feet of earth and chalk to explode inside the tunnel itself. The tunnel collapsed.

On the ground, in the first hours of D-Day, "Wheelwright" struck, and although its members came from every part and were of every faith—some with very long police records—Wheelwright was one of F section's best *réseaux*. It was controlled by George Starr, the famous "Hilaire," who was among the longest-surviving F section agents in the field; he had landed from a felucca in November 1942. He posed as a retired Belgian mining engineer who had become rich in the Congo, to explain away his odd French accent and the fact that he had very large sums of money and no visible means of support. As a man he was secure, prudent, attractive, brave and popular; and although Gascons historically had little love for foreigners, and none at all for the representatives of distant capitals, including Paris, he had become the virtual controller of all Gascony. His specialty was in cutting communications, and he and his men had caused much trouble for the *Feldgrau* in the south during 1943, frequently putting telephone lines and power stations out of order for many days. Wheelwright was based on Agen, a crossroads town in the Périgord where Starr could keep an eye on both Das Reich and the 11th Panzer Division stationed near Bordeaux; and at almost precisely the same moment that Lammerding received his orders from Rundstedt to begin moving to Normandy, Wheelwright parties blew up a large part of Das Reich's petrol dumps.

Short of fuel, Lammerding turned to the railways. But here, "Pimento" was at work. Pimento was Anthony Brooks, the youngest and also the longest-surviving F section organizer. An Englishman raised in the French cantons of Switzerland, he began clandestine life as a part-time helper on an escape line across the Pyrenees, exfiltrated himself to London, volunteered for and was taken on by F section. He was just twenty when on the night of July 1/2, 1941, he was parachuted into the Limousin to begin work with a small but skillful band of *cheminots* to interrupt rail traffic in southern France. His D-Day mission was to cut the south of France off from the rest of the country and from Italy; and at H-Hour, Pimento struck. He stopped all traffic on the line between Toulouse and Montauban, effectively halting Das Reich's supply, munitions and bridging trains—bridging trains that were now needed to cross the Loire. His men also saw to it that every single train leaving Marseilles for Lyon was derailed at least once during its journey; and this in turn made it difficult if not impossible for Das Reich to go east in order to get northwest into Normandy.

With the rail lines cut, Das Reich was forced to move out under its own power, but not before Lammerding had found enough petrol to do so. However, the line of march took the division through one of Wheelwright's sub-sectors between Bergerac and Périgueux. And there in the lovely valleys of the Dordogne, the Vézère, the Auvézère, the Isle and the Dronne, the *maquis* had set some vicious traps. Baron Philippe de Gunzbourg's *maquisards* were everywhere in the red-tiled, brown-stone villages and the granite outcrops that hung over the roads, beside old bridges and older Gallic and Roman ruins, in the caves and grottos of that part of France where Richard the Lionheart was said to have been mortally wounded. They executed some audacious ambushes, planted cyclonite landmines that looked like cow droppings, sniped at tank commanders standing in their turrets, and held up the line of march by placing upturned soup plates, which looked like the humps of buried landmines through a tank's periscope, across the roads.

When Das Reich had extricated itself from Wheelwright, it ran into "Quinine," a Jedburgh team that had been dropped into the low mountains of the Corrèze, near the village of that name close to the main road from Tulle to Clermont-Ferrand. Commanded by Major T. MacPherson, an officer of the Queen's Own Cameron Highlanders who was now working for SOE, Quinine equipped a *maquis* of "some dozen ragged ill-armed men," blew a small bridge on the main road, and then waited—for Lammerding was known to be diverting heavy units of Das Reich around the *maquis* on the normal road to Normandy. When a company of Panther tanks came into view, the twenty-seven men now in the group held the Germans at the bridge at Bicteroux for six hours. Twenty of the *maquisards* were killed. Then Das Reich ran into "Digger," an F section *réseau* in the Corrèze whose leader, Harry Peluevé, had just been caught and was in prison removing a bullet from his thigh with a spoon. Digger's men had suffered much; too much to forgive. They struck again and again in those winding hill roads; many a stormtrooper was shot, many a tank's tracks came off.

It was now D+7 and before Das Reich had even sighted the Loire it still had to deal with "Fireman," "Shipwright," "Wrestler," "Ventriloquist"—and "Bulbasket," an SAS party of fifty men and armored jeeps which had landed northwest of Limoges, the great ceramics center, at 0137 hours on D-Day. Bulbasket had been put in for just this purpose: to harass (and to help the *maquis* harass) German armor moving to Normandy from the south. Their intelligence was as good as gold; Captain J. E. Tonkin, Bulbasket's commander, learned that OB-West had sent petrol trains to provide fuel for Das Reich. When the fuel had been nicely cached at Châtellerault (between Poitiers and Tours), he radioed the target information to London and a squadron of Mosquitos came over and "secured the best petrol fire they had known." Four hundred SS men—probably of Das Reich—were detached to clean out Bulbasket; but the SAS melted into the woods, providing London with another target while on the run: an SS camp west of Limoges. The RAF came over again and, Bulbasket claimed, killed a further 150 of the stormtroopers. But Bulbasket's luck would finally run out; it was later trapped in a wood by an SS infantry battalion, some thirty of the SAS troopers were killed or captured and executed on the spot, and the rest of the team was evacuated to London by Dakotas.

By this time, the temper of the SS was dangerously frayed. As Captain C. S. S. Burt, of the Scots Guards, the leader of a team called "Dickens" which was operating in the same area, put it: "The enemy were extremely nervous." The roads were often littered with German corpses, the railway embankments dotted with locomotives and trains that had been derailed, the roads with disabled or charred German vehicles. The harassment took every form; Jedburgh team "Hamish" hijacked a truckload of butter, and twenty-eight *maquisards* held up the leading elements of "Der Führer" regiment, a unit of Das Reich, on the narrow road at the outskirts of the town of Souillac, for forty hours, while the rest of the division was bunched up on the roads around and subjected to constant air attacks and sniping.

A major explosion across the route of Das Reich occurred at Tulle, a small crossroads town on the Corrèze beneath the Plateau de Millevaches between Limoges and Clermont-Ferrand. On hearing of the actions being fought against the main force of Das Reich just to the south, the *maquisards* in and around Tulle rose and killed the German garrison in the Manufacture des Armes, the École Normale, and the Hôtel La Tremolière. Colonel Bouty, the Mayor, proclaimed the liberation of the town and set about fortifying it. But Lammerding declared that Tulle would pay with "blood and ashes" for the massacre of the German garrison. Armored vehicles fought their way into the town and SS panzer grenadiers rounded up some five hundred men and a few women. Of these, the SS commander, Sturmführer Walter, selected ninety-nine men, women and boys and hanged them from the balcony railings of the houses along the Pont Neuf. Lammerding, two or three of his officers, and a German woman secretary who had worked in the Manufacture des Armes watched the executions from the terrace of the Café Tivoli, "drinking, smoking cigarettes and listening to gramophone records."

The German reaction to another incident was even more vicious. One of Das Reich's battalion commanders, a popular man, was either sniped at and killed in his command vehicle or ambushed, taken prisoner and then shot by the *maquisards* at the village of Oradour-sur-Vayres, about 25 miles west of Limoges. The next morning, a detachment of SS troopers from Das Reich ringed the village of Oradour-sur-Glane—the wrong village but one lying in approximately the same area—and assembled the entire population in the village square. The regimental commander informed the community, mainly farmworkers, that arms and explosives were hidden in the village, and that the villagers had been harboring terrorists. He announced that an identity check would be made, and ordered the men to remain where they were and the women and children to go to the church. This, under SS escort, they did. The men were machine-gunned to death where they stood. The church door was locked and the troopers set fire to the church. Of the 652 inhabitants, 642—245 women, 207 children, 190 men—were killed. The massacre at Oradour-sur-Glane would be called "the most horrible and shameful page of the history of German war crimes," and Lammerding was branded a war criminal. He vanished after the war and was never arrested, but he was sentenced to death in absentia. Two of his unit commanders were executed by the French, and the eighteen men in the SS detachment were sentenced to prison terms of between five and twelve years. The leader of the detachment, Major Otto Dickmann, was never brought to trial; he was killed in action in Normandy a week or two later.

Das Reich continued to trudge north and finally crossed the Loire, but it still had more F section *réseaux* to fight before it got to Normandy; Ventriloquist, Headmaster and Scientist all harried it before it reached the frontline "so thoroughly mauled that when they did eventually crawl into their lagers . . . heaving a sigh of relief that at last they would have real soldiers to deal with and not these damned terrorists, their fighting quality was much below what it had been when they started." It would be correct for SOE to claim that: "The division might be compared to a cobra which had struck with its fangs at the head of a stick held out to tempt it; the amount of poison left in its bite was far less than it had been." As important was the time it had taken the division to make the march. It did not arrive until D+17; SOE would maintain:

> The extra fortnight's delay imposed on what should have been a three-day journey may well have been of decisive importance for the successful securing of the Normandy bridgehead. Affairs in the bridgehead went so badly for the allies in the first few days that the arrival of one more first-class fully-equipped overstrength armoured division might easily have rolled some part of the still tenuous allied front right back on to the beaches, and sent the whole of NEPTUNE awry.

In all, the French would claim, 4000 men of Das Reich were killed, wounded or missing in the march to Normandy from the Périgord. Moreover, several score of the pride of Krupp—the sullen *Sturmgeschütz* and broad-tracked Panthers—lay tipped on their sides, broken and burned, gutted testaments to the power of what Byron once called "the shirtless patriots" of guerrilla warfare.

Even before Das Reich was on the line, however, it was clear that the Allies were winning the battle of the build-up. Both their tactical and supply positions had improved, while the Germans were still fighting a holding battle, and the reinforcements and supplies necessary to launch a major counter-thrust had not yet arrived. The Allies had twenty-nine and a half first-rate, full-strength divisions (some were almost the size of corps) in the beachhead. The Germans had managed to bring in only sixteen and a half, and many of these were exhausted and badly chewed up when they did reach the line. Of the panzer divisions made available to Rommel, only four—the 2nd, the Panzer Lehr, the 21st and the 12th SS—were at the front more or less complete. The élite 1st SS Panzer was still being held down by Fortitude in the Pas de Calais. The 116th Panzer was in the same sector but for a different reason: Rommel's decision to keep at least one dependable army division in reserve to put down any SS opposition to his plans for "an independent termination of the war in the west." Forward elements of 9th and 10th SS Panzer divisions had reached the French frontier, but their regiments were being forced by Allied air activity to detrain at Fontainebleau and make the long march up to the front by night. Of the panzer divisions in southern and southwestern France, only Das Reich was on the move toward Normandy. The 9th Panzer was being pinned down by Vendetta on the Mediterranean coast, Ironside still preoccupied the 11th Panzer on the Biscay coast; and both divisions, along with other elements of Blaskowitz's Army Group G, would suffer the brutal and persistent harassment of *maquisards*. Key infantry units which were so badly needed if Rommel was to be able to withdraw and concentrate the panzers for a counterattack were still straggling in from Brittany. Without the forces necessary to oppose them, it would be, it seemed, only a matter of days before the Allies cracked and began to seep through the German dyke around Normandy. Deception and the war of special means had proved to be an invaluable adjunct to the methods of more conventional warfare. Yet the battle was far from being won, and Hitler had one weapon left in his arsenal that might delay and disrupt the inexorable Allied build-up. In the weeks ahead this weapon, the V1, would pose a grave threat to Neptune and Allied strategy.

Rommel

5

BY MID-JUNE, Normandy had become an immense killing ground. The Allies and the Germans were locked together among the hedgerows and orchards in what Rommel would tell his son was "one terrible bloodletting. Sometimes we had as many casualties on one day as during the whole of the summer fighting in Africa in 1942. My nerves are pretty good, but sometimes I was near collapse. It was casualty reports, wherever you went. I have never fought with such losses. If I hadn't gone to the front nearly every day, I couldn't have stood it, having to write off literally one regiment every day."

Rommel's supply position was even worse. He needed 2500 tons of food, ammunition, war stores and petrol and oil supplies daily if his armies were to be kept fighting. But through air and guerrilla operations he never received more than 400 tons of all sorts. It was, as he said to Staubwasser one evening, a preposterous situation. The army in the Pas de Calais was sitting by the seaside doing nothing, but was still receiving most of the reinforcements and stores, while his army in Normandy was rapidly being destroyed. Yet Rommel himself could not be sure that the Allies did not intend to land in the Pas de Calais. At times he said he believed that Normandy *was* the invasion, but as he had written to his wife on June 10 (even though he had only just read the captured American 5th and 7th Corps orders): "It's quite likely to start at other places soon." On June 13 he wrote again. "It's time," he said, "for politics to come into play. We are expecting the next, perhaps even heavier blow to fall elsewhere in a few days."

At the root of Rommel's predicament was Hitler's determination to command the battle in Normandy himself. "My functions in Normandy," Rommel would tell his son, "were so restricted by Hitler that any sergeant-major could have carried them out. He interfered in everything and turned down every proposal we made." Even worse for Rommel, Hitler and OKW continued to believe the fictions of Fortitude, and their command decisions reflected that belief. Apparently convinced of the veracity of reports from agents in England, mesmerized by the specter of Patton (who was reported here, there and everywhere), arrogant in the conviction that their military judgment was right and all others' wrong, Hitler and the German Supreme Command ignored the advice and pleas of their western commanders. The battle in Normandy was being fought from Berchtesgaden.

Roenne, too, remained convinced of the existence of Army Group Patton. Staubwasser would later testify that Roenne called him personally "every two or three days . . . right up to the end of July" to "emphasize" that FHW had "reliable information relating to a second major landing intended by the Allies on the west coast of France or the coast of Belgium." To support these telephone calls, Roenne sent "almost daily" teleprinter reports that the number of divisions in the British Isles ready for action exceeded the number of divisions then in Normandy, that these formations had powerful air and naval forces at their disposal, and that until they appeared in action nobody could be certain that the main blow would not fall upon the Pas de Calais. When Staubwasser, who knew something of the method by which Roenne had arrived at his estimate of Allied strength in England, challenged his figures, "Baron von Roenne insisted that the opinion held by his department was correct, emphasizing that (Rommel's headquarters) had no data whatsoever to base any judgment on in this matter, and that therefore the strengths of the Allied forces assumed by his department *must* serve as a basis for all planning carried out by Army Group B." It was very curious behavior for the man who was originally responsible for exaggerating the estimates of Allied strength. Had he come to believe his own exaggerations, or was he acting on some other motive?

As the casualties continued to mount in Normandy and the needed replacements and reinforcements did not arrive, Rommel took another step down the road to treason. Without the 15th Army, he had little hope of inflicting such heavy losses on Neptune that the Allies would be forced to seek terms, and he realized that unless he acted now he would have nothing left either to save or to bargain with in any negotiations with the Grand Alliance. Accordingly, he invited Hitler to the Château de La Roche Guyon for a conference, determined, if the Fuehrer rejected his proposals, particularly concerning the use of the 15th Army, to have him arrested by troops who were loyal only to Rommel. Hitler accepted his invitation but elected to meet at W2, an underground command post near Soissons; he was far too wily to meet Rommel at the château.

Hitler arrived at W2 on June 17, escorted by his entourage. There, under the wooded hills of the Aisne, at a post which had been built for the Fuehrer to direct the invasion of England four years before, Hitler, Rundstedt and Rommel confronted each other. The Fuehrer, pale and weary from lack of sleep, toyed nervously with his colored pencils and his spectacles as Rommel described the state of the battle. The field marshal was himself close to nervous exhaustion, for the fighting had reached a degree of ferocity that had few parallels, even in Russia. That very day American troops were penetrating the last German line of defense before Cherbourg.

For thirty minutes Rommel told how the *Feldgrau* were fighting with "unbelievable courage and tenacity," but that infantry divisions were being reduced to battalions. He spoke of the overwhelming weight of Allied firepower; of the strength of the Allied divisions in the bridgehead; of the failures of the Luftwaffe, the Kriegsmarine and the intelligence services to provide any assistance that might help the men at the front. In particular, arguing with what Staubwasser would call "a combination of strategical and intuitive reasoning," he sought to persuade Hitler that the captured 5th and 7th Corps plans provided incontrovertible evidence that Normandy was *the* invasion.

The conference was interrupted for lunch. There, moodily, Hitler played with a dish of rice and vegetables which one of his escorts had tasted first, and began a monologue that was, Speidel would write, a "strange mixture of cynicism and wrong intuition." Hitler had ordered the V1 campaign against England to begin on June 12; even as he spoke, London was being subjected to what one observer would describe as an intermittent drizzle of malignant robots that seemed harder to bear than the storm and thunder of the blitz. Hitler talked "endlessly about the V-weapons which were going to decide the war," and stated that the existence of these weapons alone would *compel* the Allies to invade at the Pas de Calais. When Rommel protested that the Norman campaign was being directed from an armchair behind the front and declared, "You are asking us to have confidence in you, but you don't yourself trust us," Hitler grew even paler. After lunch, Rommel turned upon Hitler "with complete ruthlessness" and explained what he thought about the military and political situation. He prophesied the collapse of the German front in Normandy, stated that not even the V-weapons could prevent that collapse, and ended with a bold and memorable question: Did Hitler continue to believe that this war could be won? Hitler brushed the question aside with an order: "Look after your invasion front, and don't bother about the continuation of the war."

With that remark, Hitler propelled Rommel beyond any consideration of loyalty to the régime. He was now determined to make an end to the war. Speidel would write:

Rommel was under no illusion regarding the harshness of the peace conditions which had to be expected. But he placed his hope in a modest measure of statesmanlike insight, psychological intelligence, and political planning in Allied considerations. He no longer counted on Allied sympathy or similar sentiments. But he trusted the sober brains of the Great Powers.

From now on, as Walter Bargatzky, a lawyer on Stuelpnagel's staff who was charged with the legal planning involved in the *coup d'état,* would declare, Rommel could "hardly be restrained and wanted to get things moving without delay." He received the emissary of the Schwarze Kapelle in Berlin, Lieutenant Colonel Caesar von Hofacker, a cousin of Stauffenberg's, whose assignment was to integrate the conspirators' operations with those of Rommel. Hofacker informed Rommel of the current plans to assassinate the Fuehrer, and as Bargatzky, who was a confidant of both, would state: "The (German) Army in the west was supposed to surrender at the same time." Bargatzky, who later became president of the German Red Cross and a leading official in the postwar West German Interior and Health ministries, would also reveal that Speidel had "made it his business to take all the larger SS units in France and have them engaged in battle on the Normandy front on the day of the uprising so as to protect Paris against their possible intervention." It was a statement that would bear out Speidel's contention that Rommel had planned to keep army panzer units out of the battle for as long as possible so that they might be fresh, intact and available for any counterrevolution that the SS in France might launch. Indeed, all combat arms of the SS would be deeply committed to the battle.

Rommel made plans to send six German military emissaries, including Stuelpnagel and Speidel, across the lines to negotiate an armistice, offering the complete evacuation of the occupied territories in the West and the withdrawal of the German army to the old Siegfried Line. They would ask for the immediate cessation of the bombing of the German heartland, and in return, Rommel would stop the V-weapon bombardment of London. The armistice—not Unconditional Surrender—was to be followed by peace negotiations. On the eastern front, the struggle was to be continued by a holding action along a shortened line. Rommel had no doubt, Bargatzky would state, that he could master the SS. Nor did he expect a rebuff from the Allies. He was convinced that his "friend" Montgomery would give him an armistice and a separate peace, believing completely that such matters were in Montgomery's hands.

But first Rommel decided he would give Hitler "one more chance" to make "the correct deductions of the situation." He resolved to go to Berchtesgaden to confront the Fuehrer. On June 29 he and Rundstedt arrived at the Berghof. But Hitler was in no mood to talk with his marshals. He kept them waiting for six hours; and when he received them, much was discussed yet little decided—particularly in regard to Rommel's insistence that the 15th Army must be allowed to go to the help of the 7th.

Rundstedt demanded greater freedom of action, pointing out that the high commander on the spot could take more immediate, surer action than a commander 600 miles from the front. At this, Hitler looked sharply at the old field marshal, and Rundstedt knew that his days were numbered. Rundstedt also demanded at least some of the infantry divisions of the 15th Army to form a line behind which the panzers could be concentrated for a counteroffensive. Hitler replied only that he would consider the matter and issue a new directive. In the meantime, said the Fuehrer, repeating what he had said ever since D-Day, victory was to be gained by "holding fast tenaciously to every square yard of soil." Rommel protested that such a strategy was impossible. He alluded to the fact that the Russians had opened their summer offensive, and after feinting in various directions to tie up the forty-seven panzer divisions the Wehrmacht had in the East, the Red Army had destroyed thirty divisions, torn a gap in the German lines and was about to enter East Prussia. Bulgaria, Rumania, Hungary, Finland—all were contemplating surrender. The Wehrmacht was confronted with revolution in every one of the occupied countries. The Allied breakout in Normandy was both inevitable and imminent. The skies were growing dark for Germany.

Hitler listened frostily and then replied that Rommel had not considered the fact that this was England's war and that England was being forced out of it. When that happened, through the V1 campaign and his strategy of keeping the Allies penned up in Normandy, the entire Grand Alliance would collapse and Germany would be able to consume the pieces at her will. In the meantime, Hitler ordered, Rundstedt and Rommel must hold the line. That was an imperative. Detailed orders would follow.

Rommel and Rundstedt withdrew from the meeting, the former quite clear in his own mind that Hitler's policy was insane and that, if the German army was not to suffer the fate intended for the British, Hitler must be removed and an armistice obtained. The two marshals emerged gratefully into the fresh, clean air of the alpine evening, both convinced that they would be dismissed from their commands. They made their way to OKW quarters at the Strub Barracks to bathe, dine, wine, and to talk about the gravity of the situation in the East and the West. During the conversation Rommel spoke of a remarkable similarity between the Fuehrer and King Lear. Finally, Rundstedt, the "last of the German knights," broke up the discussion with a formal bow and wandered off to bed. He had drunk a lot of champagne and was a little tipsy.

When the two field marshals returned to their headquarters late in the evening of June 30, Hitler's directive awaited them. It dealt almost wholly with detail, and said little or nothing about the use on the 7th Army front of the 15th Army's infantry divisions. This meant that the panzer divisions under Rommel's command, designed for attack, would have to be used for defense; and even if the time came when it would be possible to mount a counteroffensive, they would probably be too weak through attrition to be effective. Neither could they be replaced once they had been chewed up. Situation reports awaiting Rommel revealed that the panzers were even now in danger. The army commanders demanded an immediate evacuation of the "killing ground" of Caen, where most of the panzer divisions were concentrated, and retirement to a new line beyond the range of the naval guns which were causing appalling casualties and disruption in the assembly areas. Rommel sent the appreciations to Rundstedt that same night, Rundstedt read them, and then penned a personal signal to the Fuehrer in which he endorsed the army commanders' and Rommel's opinions. Hitler sent this reply:

> The present positions are to be held. Any further breakthrough by the enemy will be prevented by tenacious defence or by local counter-attacks. Assembly (of the armor) will continue and further mobile formations will be released (from defensive operations) by infantry divisions as they arrive.

Rundstedt's premonitions of dismissal proved to be correct. On July 2, Colonel Borgmann, one of Hitler's adjutants, arrived at Rundstedt's headquarters, gave the field marshal a letter from the Fuehrer stating that he was relieved of command on the grounds of ill-health, and handed him the Oak Leaves to his Iron Cross. Geyr von Schweppenburg had also been sacked for his defeatist attitude, and when Rommel heard of Rundstedt's dismissal, he said to Speidel, "I shall be next."

On July 3, Field Marshal von Kluge arrived to succeed Rundstedt; and at their first conference, held at the Château de La Roche Guyon, relations between Kluge and Rommel were distinctly cool. Kluge, after several weeks in the Fuehrer's presence, had taken up the appointment of C-in-C West convinced once more of Hitler's greatness. He was also convinced of his ability to eject the Allied armies and was in no mood to discuss—at least sympathetically—Rommel's ideas for an "independent termination of the war in the west." Neither was he prepared to honor any of the assurances he had previously given the Schwarze Kapelle. Shown into Rommel's study by Speidel, Kluge carried his baton and wore all his medal ribbons, which Rommel usually did not.

It was not long before the two marshals were displaying their dislike for each other. After disagreeing fundamentally about the state of the battle in Normandy, Kluge delivered a severe censure upon Rommel. He stated that the dismissal of Rundstedt was the outward sign of Hitler's dissatisfaction with the high command in the West and—according to Speidel—declared that "Rommel himself did not enjoy the absolute confidence of the Führer." Rommel, said Kluge, was "not carrying out the Führer's orders wholeheartedly." Then he became threatening: "Field

Marshal Rommel, even you must obey unconditionally from now on. This is good advice that I am giving you."

At this point Rommel flushed, and the conversation became so heated that he ordered Speidel and Tempelhof, his operations officer, both of whom were present, to leave the room. As they departed Rommel could be heard demanding that Kluge draw his "own conclusions from the general situation" and that he "withdraw his accusations at once." Rommel was heard to insist that he would set a time limit by which this must be done and he advised Kluge "not to form any opinions until he had conferred with his army commanders and with the troops and had made a tour of inspection at the front."

Kluge accepted the advice—and changed his mind about the situation in the West. He made a two-day tour of inspection and, according to Speidel, said that he had "not been able to escape the overwhelming evidence of the facts, the unanimous views of all the military commanders, and the logic of the situation; he had temporarily been bemused by Hitler's phrases. He took back all his accusations." From then on, Kluge veered closer to the conspirators' plans, tried not to interfere with control of the battle, and sought harmony with the ruffled Rommel.

Meanwhile, an eerie and remarkable incident had occurred at the front which suggested to Rommel that it might not be so difficult to get in touch with Montgomery. On July 2, as Bargatzky was actually drafting a letter for Rommel which he recommended be taken through the lines to the Allied high command by a "trustworthy German doctor," a section of German panzer grenadiers in the sector of the American 1st Infantry Division near Caumont heard with astonishment an American voice speaking German break in on their radio circuit. According to the German report of the incident, the voice called: "*Achtung! Achtung!* We call the German commander in this sector! We have important news for him!" The German commander came to the set to see what the Americans wanted, and the voice explained that they wished to repatriate a number of women, most of them nurses who had been captured at Cherbourg when that city fell to the Americans on June 26. Would the Germans take them back? After consulting with his superiors, who in turn notified Speidel, the Germans agreed to accept the nurses and suggested that a local truce be arranged to allow them to pass through the lines.

At three o'clock that afternoon, the guns went silent. Incredulous grenadiers and GI's alike, men with pink hedge roses stuck in their helmets for camouflage, rose out of their hides in meadows that were rich with clover and tall grass and saw three American officers coming down the road from the direction of the hamlet of Sept Vents. The American party was led by Captain Quentin Roosevelt, a G2 with the 1st Infantry, and Captain Fred Gercke, a prisoner of war interrogator. With them were eight

German women. From out of a hedge stepped a Major Heeren, the commanding officer of the 2nd Panzer Reconnaissance Battalion of the 2nd Panzer Division of General von Luettwitz—one of the two panzer divisions which Rommel had intended to keep out of the line to deal with "internal enemies" when the rebellion came. There was a brief conversation and the nurses were transferred at 3:10 P.M. But the guns did not begin to fire again for four hours. Why did the truce last so long? Was it the outcome of a German initiative, camouflage to conceal the passage of a letter such as Bargatzky had drafted for Rommel? The official British answer was that no communication was received from Rommel at that or at any other time.

Then, on July 9, there was a second such truce in the same area, near the hamlet of Sept Vents. Captain Roosevelt, accompanied by Lieutenant Erhardt Dabringhaus and Lieutenant Kenneth J. Calligan, having failed to raise the Germans on the wireless, proceeded from the lines of the American 26th Infantry Regiment under cover of the white flag. The guns on both sides immediately went silent as the three men walked down the road shouting "Hello"—a brave thing to do. The time was 3 P.M. A German sergeant appeared out of some bushes with two soldiers, all of whom—according to Roosevelt's report—"looked completely flabbergasted." The Americans told the Germans that they wished to hand over nine more women who had been captured in Cherbourg, two nurses and seven secretaries. The sergeant, explaining that it was his duty to do so, insisted upon blindfolding the Americans. Then a Hauptmann Branns appeared, ordered that the blindfolds be removed, and announced that he would accept the women. There was a conversation about the state of the war. The Hauptmann declared, "What a pity it is we are fighting Americans," and at that point ambulances appeared with the women inside. Two of the women gave the salute "Heil Hitler!" to the Hauptmann, who did not reply, except to make the ungallant statement, having looked the women over, that "there is not much of interest here"; the prisoners were all between forty and fifty.

The exchange completed, the envoys returned to their respective lines and the fighting resumed. But again, the truce lasted about three hours, although it had taken less than fifteen minutes to hand the women over. They had much to report about the opulence of the Americans and the excellence of their treatment; for a last lunch they had been given orange juice, pea soup, fricasseed chicken with peas and carrots, fruit cocktails, and cigarettes. This was clearly the purpose of the exchange—an attempt by the Americans to prove the truth of their propaganda claims about the handsome treatment German deserters would receive. In fact, three Germans at Sept Vents did desert. But, again, why did the truce last so long? Was there some sort of reply made to a letter sent across on July 2? Once more the official British position—for Montgomery had high command in

France at that time—was that no letters of any sort passed between the lines. All that was ever said about these incidents was a statement by Sir John Wheeler-Bennett, writing from his special place in the British secret intelligence apparatus: "With the knowledge that (a local truce) was now possible, Rommel (inspected) his frontline positions and (discussed) the position with his subordinate commanders. The outcome of his observations was embodied in a report to the *Führer* . . . couched in the terms of an ultimatum."

In the report, which was dated July 15, Rommel for the first time abandoned the careful phraseology and diplomatic niceties which had hitherto marked his correspondence with the Fuehrer. He pointed out flatly that Hitler's policies were failing. "The situation on the Normandy front is growing worse every day and is now approaching a grave crisis," he wrote. He spoke of the enemy's "enormous" concentrations of artillery and tanks, and of his own "huge" material losses. He declared that of the 97,000 men he had lost, including 2360 officers, only 6000 replacements had arrived at the front, with another 4000 promised. Against the enemy's power, Rommel wrote, "even the bravest army will be smashed piece by piece"; and drawing the Fuehrer's attention to the existence of idle divisions on the Pas de Calais front, he warned that "In these circumstances we must expect that in the foreseeable future the enemy will succeed in breaking through our thin front . . . and thrusting deep into France." He ended:

> The troops are everywhere fighting heroically, but the unequal struggle is approaching its end. It is urgently necessary for the proper conclusions to be drawn from this situation. As C-in-C of the Army Group I feel myself in duty bound to speak plainly on this point.

As protocol demanded, Rommel sent the letter to Kluge for forwarding to Hitler. But Kluge, aware that the letter might bring Rommel's relief and court-martial, held on to it for a day or two. Kluge needed Rommel in the West. For despite their intense dislike for each other, the two field marshals had agreed upon a pact. The revolution should begin not in Germany, as the Schwarze Kapelle intended, but in France. Kluge and Rommel had decided that if the opportunity arose they would open the front and permit the Anglo-American armies to march to the western borders of Germany with the assistance—not the opposition—of the Wehrmacht. The strategic objective: to allow the western powers to occupy Germany before the Russians did. Kluge had once again committed himself to conspiracy.

On the evening of the 15th—the same day that Rommel wrote to the Fuehrer—he walked with Staubwasser through the grounds of the Château de La Roche Guyon toward the two mighty cedars where there was a bench overlooking the Seine. After some long minutes of silence, Rommel said: "Staubwasser, I have given him his last chance. If he does not take it, we will act." The field marshal was silent as they walked on. But when they sat down on the bench, it was evident that Rommel was facing a personal crisis of the greatest magnitude. Suddenly he placed his head in his hands and murmured: "Oh Staubwasser! This war must be brought to an end!"

In spite of his despair, and for all the disadvantages with which he was fighting the battle, Rommel had succeeded in imposing a near stalemate upon the Allies. He had sealed off the beachhead, forcing the Allies to fight the sort of battle they feared the most—a dull killing match in country where they could not employ their armor or their airpower with decisive effect. It had become a battle that, for the British, was all too reminiscent of Flanders and the Somme.

Bradley had finally succeeded in capturing Cherbourg, fourteen days later than the Neptune plan anticipated, but twice Montgomery had tried to take the other key town in Normandy—Caen—and twice the *Panzertruppen* stopped him. Neptune was being strangled. Except in the Cotentin, the lodgment was little more than 10 miles deep. Bad weather still interrupted supply schedules and there were serious ammunition shortages. Moreover, the fierce fighting generated a crisis in the troops' morale. Eisenhower, particularly, was deeply shocked when he visited the lodgment and discovered that in one hospital alone there were over a thousand cases of SIW (self-inflicted wounds), men who had shot themselves through the foot or some other non-vital part of their bodies to get out of the firing line.

The causes of the near stalemate were many. The Allies were virtually trapped in the difficult "hedgerow country," a terrain where the normal horizon was 75 to 150 yards, where one man well dug into a hedge could hold back five, where it was impossible to use tanks, where artillery was rarely completely effective, and where the best weapons were carbines, pistols, bayonets, knives and mortars. The persistent rains prevented the Allies from using their airpower and turned the countryside into bogs. The German tanks, and particularly their 88-mm anti-aircraft artillery piece, were superior to Allied weapons. German strategy and tactics in containing the beachhead were excellent, and Rommel's armies, outnumbered and outgunned, were fighting with a stubbornness and heroism that came in part from loyalty to their commander and in part from the realization that they could not surrender.

The methods of conventional warfare alone seemed insufficient to break the German stranglehold, so the British looked anew into their armory of special means to produce, in the first place, "Hellhound." Aware (probably through Ultra) that Hitler and the German high command were directing the battle in Normandy from Berchtesgaden, the Allies prepared to launch a massive air strike against the headquarters by the U.S. 15th Air Force in Italy. Hellhound, the code name of the operation, was first mentioned in a "Redline" signal—Eisenhower's personal communication—to the Mediterranean Allied Air Force Headquarters on June 15. American photographic reconnaissance aircraft made a series of runs over Berchtesgaden during the next four days, and by June 24, intelligence mosaics had been produced and were ready for distribution for the briefing of the bomber groups. But then, mysteriously, MAAF was ordered to hold its hand. No explanation was ever given, and the operation was not mounted. Why? Only one reason appears probable; a raid against Berchtesgaden might destroy *the* key Ultra source—OKW itself—without killing Hitler.

But the British did have another plan: "Gaff," an operation that had been conceived by the special operations planning syndicates as early as March 1944, its objective to kill or kidnap the man who continued to symbolize Germany's military skill, tenacity and heroism—Rommel. The mission had not been mounted before or during the invasion, largely because of the failure to locate his headquarters accurately. But in the second week of June, Rommel's headquarters had been discovered and, with the mounting crisis over the near stalemate in Normandy, Montgomery gave his approval for the operation which, he hoped, would help break the deadlock.

Just after D-Day, Lieutenant Colonel William Fraser, of the 1st SAS Regiment, had dropped into the Morvan Mountains between Dijon and Nevers, his mission to establish "Houndsworth," another large SAS redoubt in enemy territory. Eighteen officers and 136 troopers with armored jeeps and artillery would be parachuted to the base to harass the Germans as they came up from the Côte d'Azur to Normandy. It was a bold operation, for the nearest Allied forces would be in Normandy, 300 miles away.

When Fraser and his wireless operator landed, they buried their parachutes in the thick humus, and then made their way to a thicket close to a small stone bridge over the Cure, a stream coming out of the mountains near Château Chinon, a town about 180 miles southeast of Paris. Fraser's orders were to make contact at the bridge with an F section agent, Louis, who would lead him to the headquarters of a *maquisard* called Camille. Camille was then to take him on to the Houndsworth advance party, which had gone in just after H-Hour. Intelligence-gathering formed no part of Fraser's operational orders.

At dawn, as arranged, Fraser saw a middle-aged man in a cloth cap and a baggy double-breasted suit coming down the narrow lane toward the bridge, driving some cattle. Fraser called out the passwords: *"Je cherche la maison de Charles."* The man replied: *"Vous voulez dire de Monsieur Dupont?"* It was Louis, but he demanded further evidence of Fraser's identity, and Fraser replied that he would signal London to broadcast the words *"Le médecin a les cheveux gris"* over the BBC at 1:30 P.M. the following day. Not until Louis heard those words would he take Fraser to Camille. But they began a march that lasted thirty-six hours. Finally, the men stopped by a brook and Fraser's operator tuned in to London. Fraser and Louis had spoken little until that moment; but when he heard the music of the French song *Sur le pont d'Avignon*—the idioform for the SAS in France—and the words, *"Le médecin a les cheveux gris,"* Louis broke into smiles and laughter. Three hours later they were with Camille, who, as they arrived, was trying three suspected agents of the Gestapo. One of them, a Belgian, was taken behind a clump of rhododendrons and shot.

At the base, Fraser met an aristocratic-looking Frenchman who had been staying at the nearby Château de Vermot and who introduced himself as "M. Defors, chief game warden of all the French colonies before the war," and now "the owner of an estate near the Château La Roche Guyon." What Defors had to say electrified Fraser. The château was Rommel's headquarters. Would it be possible for Fraser to go there and kill the field marshal, Defors asked, because his presence was making the local inhabitants afraid they might be bombed? Fraser determined to make the sortie, and began to gather all the data necessary from Defors. It would be, he discovered, a simple matter to approach the château, although the area was very heavily guarded by German troops. From a wood on the bank of the Seine opposite the château, a sniper could shoot at the field marshal at a range of about 400 yards, as he walked in the Italian gardens. There were *maquisards* at Vernon upon whom Fraser could rely for a safehouse, an air drop, and a landing field.

At 1645 on June 14, 1944, Fraser sent this message to London:

> From HOUNDSWORTH 102. Very reliable source states Rommel's headquarters at Chateau delaroche Guyon 50 miles W of Paris 10 miles WNW of Mantes on the right bank of Seine. Rommel there on 25 May and Staff permanently there. Rommel arrives left bank of Seine, crosses by motor launch. Walks and shoots in Foret de Moisson. Send maps from this area to area of Mantes also three snipers rifles. Would prefer you not to send another party for this job as consider it is my pigeon.

The next day at 1330 Fraser followed up this message with another:

> From HOUNDSWORTH 102. Request permission to start for Rommel's headquarters in one week's time. Have excellent contacts on route and in that area.

At Moor Park, the country mansion just outside London built by Henry VIII for Anne Boleyn which was now an SAS headquarters,

Fraser's messages were examined by Brigadier R. W. McLeod, the SAS commander, and Major Alexander Scratchley, the Duke of Norfolk's trainer and, for the moment, an SAS intelligence officer. The difficulties of the mission were obvious immediately. Fraser was more than 200 miles from the château, he would have to move through areas that were stiff with German troops and the *Geheime Feldpolizei,* and Rommel might not be there even if he succeeded in getting through. Moreover, Fraser's present assignment was too important, for Houndsworth was to cut the route the Germans were expected to use to bring the 9th Panzer Division from the south to Normandy. They wirelessed back:

> For FRASER. Regret must forbid your personal attack on Rommel. Appreciate you consider him your pigeon but your task to remain in command present area. This pigeon will be attacked by special party.

Fraser made two attempts to get McLeod to change his mind; but McLeod was adamant. He wirelessed Houndsworth: "Regret decision must stand."

There had been other indications—probably intelligence derived from the Y service—that Rommel was headquartered at the château, and RAF photo-reconnaissance planes had been prowling around the area. Additional confirmations came from F section which had a *réseau* in the vicinity; indeed, the Comtesse Y. de la Rochefoucauld, a relative of the duc, was a sub-agent. With that information, McLeod decided to go ahead with Gaff, and the plan was issued as SAS Brigade Operation Instruction 32. The orders were terse and to the point. The objective of the plan was to "kill, or kidnap and remove to England, Field Marshal Rommel, or any senior members of his staff," and while the instruction observed that "it is preferable to ensure the former rather than to attempt and fail in the latter," it also noted that "If it should prove possible to kidnap Rommel *and* bring him to this country the propaganda value would be immense and the inevitable retaliation against the local inhabitants might be mitigated or avoided."

Gaff was assigned to a specially trained party of SAS troopers—it consisted of one officer and six men—which already existed under the command of a man whose *nom de guerre* was "Raymond Lee." He was a captain in the International Squadron of the SAS, a unit made up of men of such nationalities as Algerian *pieds-noirs,* Corsicans, Sicilian *mafiosi,* anti-Communist Bulgarians and the like, which had been formed with the express purpose of committing special acts of warfare such as the assassination of enemy commanders. Evidently Lee was expert, trusted and brave; for an unspecified task while on operations in the Mediterranean he had received the Distinguished Service Order. Lee and his men were prepared for action when this letter was received by Brigadier McLeod from Montgomery's headquarters:

TOP SECRET

Copy No. .5...

HQ SAS Tps/TSB/5/G

SAS BRIGADE OPERATION INSTRUCTION No. 32

Operation GAFF - CO 2 SAS Regt

INTENTION

1.   To kill, or kidnap and remove to England, Field Marshal ROMMEL, or any senior members of his staff.

INFORMATION

2.   Recent information regarding the location and movement of ROMMEL is contained in:-

i)   SHAEF letter, 18 Jul 44, copy attached as Appendix A.

ii)   Two signals from HOUNDSWORTH dated 14 and 16 Jul stating that reliable information obtained from the owner of the estates around ROMMEL's HQ indicated that this HQ was at Chateau DE LA ROCHE, near LA ROCHE GUYON N.5572; that ROMMEL was there on 25 Jun; that his staff is there permanently; that he crosses the R. SEINE by motor launch and walks and shoots in the FORET DE MOISSON on the left bank.

iii)   A signal from HAFT dated 18 Jul saying that ROMMEL's Tac HQ is at BAGNOLES Y.9798 (HAFT has been asked for further details).

METHOD

3.   This must be left to you and you will submit your detailed proposals as soon as possible to this HQ.

4.   The following points should be borne in mind:-

   If it should prove possible to kidnap ROMMEL and bring him to this country the propaganda value would be immense and the inevitable retaliation against the local inhabitants might be mitigated or avoided.   Such a plan would involve finding and being prepared to hold for a short time if necessary, a suitable landing ground.

5.   To kill ROMMEL would obviously be easier than to kidnap him and it is preferable to ensure the former rather than to attempt and fail in the latter. Kidnapping would require successful two-way W/T communication and therefore a larger party, while killing could be reported by pigeon.

6.   The possibilities of dropping to reception arranged by SFHQ should be investigated.

   ACKNOWLEDGE.

c/o HQ Airborne Tps (Main),
APO, England.
WBKS/MDJ
10.7.44

/Distribution

Brigadier,
Commander,
SAS Troops

SAS Brigade Operation Instruction No. 32—Operation "Gaff"—the special order authorizing a plan "to kill, or kidnap" Field Marshal Rommel, an operation that was mounted even as Rommel sought to arrange an armistice and the surrender of his armies in France.

It is understood that General Montgomery has agreed to this operation and confirmation is expected shortly from 21 Army Group. Plans should therefore be proceeded with as quickly as possible.

By this time, the intelligence dossier on Rommel and his headquarters was very detailed. It described the routes that Rommel used to travel to and from the château, and noted in particular that he usually left his headquarters when going on inspection trips at between five and six o'clock in the morning, returned usually at about six o'clock, dined at about seven-thirty, and after dinner often went for a stroll in the grounds—grounds that were open to a shot from the woods on the other bank of the Seine.

On July 10, Lee and the rest of the Gaff party had been fully briefed, and were sealed in an apartment near Broadcasting House in London to await any final orders and transport to the special duties airfield at Harrington in Northamptonshire. That same day SAS headquarters reported to Montgomery's headquarters:

> SAS 116. secret. SAS ready to send party to end Rommel existence and/or any ersatz staff officer at his headquarters. Will try to arrange for his transmission to this country if you will suggest date most suitable to you for his interrogation in this country.

During the evening of July 15—the same evening that Rommel said to Staubwasser that the war must be brought to an end—the Gaff party was taken in a closed van to Harrington, for a takeoff that night. But at the last moment it was decided to postpone the mission; the weather over the drop zone near Dreux was reported bad. Lee and his men were told that they would go in when the weather cleared. Thus at the very moment that Rommel was preparing to surrender, the British were planning to kill him. Gaff was remounted late in the afternoon of July 18 and the party was parachuted into the woods between Orléans and Vernon on or about the night of the 18th or 19th. But by then it was too late. Fate had caught up with Field Marshal Rommel.

The V1

THE V1 flying bomb campaign against "Target 42"—the German cipher for London—began six days after D-Day. It did not come as a surprise to the Allied air defense authorities. There had been much physical, wireless and technical evidence that the attack was impending. Moreover, the Germans had advised their key agents in London such as Garbo to move out of the capital, and from this it was deduced that the long-awaited onslaught was about to begin.

The opening salvo in what was intended to be a mass attack of a thousand missiles was, however, as the RAF would have said, something of a fizzle. So effective had been the Allied air forces' pounding of the launch sites, supply trains and storage depots that the Germans had only ten rounds ready for launch when they received the order for the attack to begin. Of these, four crashed upon launch, two failed to hit England at all, and only four got anywhere near the aiming point—Tower Bridge in central London. The first crashed at the Thames Estuary near Gravesend, 20 miles from the bridge. The second fell even further away, at Cuckfield just north of Brighton, startling only the crows. The third fell near Sevenoaks in Kent, startling everybody. The fourth came down at Bethnal Green, one of the most densely populated quarters of London. It struck a railway bridge, killed six people and seriously injured thirteen others. They were the only casualties of the night.

The attack was hardly the holocaust that the Fuehrer demanded and desired; and it seemed to Churchill, at his Cabinet meeting the following morning, that Hitler's secret weapon was just another bluff after all. Cadogan reflected the jubilation of those present when he wrote in his diary: "Not v. impressive. Hope some will return and fall in Germany! They didn't fly higher than 8,000 ft. and only 250 mph. at most. A sitting target (for the British air defences)!" The Chiefs of Staff regarded the attack as a baffling anticlimax, for they had been expecting at least four hundred missiles—each carrying 1 ton of high explosive—to rain down upon London. But there were less optimistic counsels, among them Dr. R. V. Jones of MI-6. He thought the opening salvo was a misfire—as it was. He called Lord Cherwell, the Prime Minister's personal scientific adviser, to urge the Cabinet to be cautious. But Cherwell "exuberantly chuckled" that "The mountain hath groaned and given forth a mouse!" Jones replied: "For God's sake don't laugh this one off!" Cherwell would not listen; and neither would the Chief of the Air Staff, Portal. He decided that the 3000 Flying Fortress sorties which he had ordered against the 60-odd known launching sites should be reduced to 1000 and the balance be given to SHAEF to support the armies in France.

The jubilation had vanished when the Chiefs of Staff and the Cabinet met on the morning of June 16. The previous day seventy-three V1's had fallen on London and a new ordeal for the city had begun—at the same moment that Neptune was struggling to stay ashore in Normandy. The destruction of the missiles in flight and the bombardment of the launching sites became top priorities. Anti-aircraft equipment which was being used to protect Neptune from harassment by the Luftwaffe was withdrawn, and Eisenhower was asked to take "all possible measures to neutralise the supply and launching sites subject to no interference with the essential requirements of the Battle of France." Accordingly, on June 18, Eisenhower ordered that "Crossbow [the code name for the V1] targets would now rank higher than anything for the Allied bomber force 'except the urgent requirements of the battle.' "

That same day, a V1 hit the Guards Chapel at Wellington Barracks, only a few yards from the heart of the main nerve center of the British war machine—10 Downing Street, the Foreign Office, Parliament, MI-6 headquarters, the War Bunker at Storey's Gate and Buckingham Palace. It was a Sunday, the chapel was packed with worshipers. Elisabeth Sheppard-Jones would recall what happened just before both her legs were blown off:

> The congregation rose to its feet. . . . In the distance hummed faintly the engine of a flying bomb. "We praise thee, O God: we acknowledge Thee to be the Lord," we, the congregation, sang. The dull burr became a roar, through which our voices could now only faintly be heard. "All the earth doth worship Thee: the Father everlasting." The roar stopped abruptly as the engine cut out. . . . The Te Deum soared again into the silence. "To Thee all Angels cry aloud: the Heavens, and all the Powers therein." Then there was a noise so loud it was as if all the waters and the winds in the world had come together in mighty conflict, and the Guards' Chapel collapsed upon us in a bellow of bricks and mortar. . . . One moment I was singing the Te Deum, and the next I lay in dust and blackness, aware of one thing only—that I had to go on breathing.

In that moment of explosion, some 80 Guards officers, men and their relatives were killed and about another 120 were badly injured. Mrs. Churchill was close by, visiting her daughter Mary who was on duty with the Hyde Park flak battery; they saw the bomb descend toward Downing Street and people falling flat on their faces. Among them was Menzies, who was on his way from MI-6 headquarters to the chapel to attend the service. That day other V1's fell in Wandsworth, Croydon, Lewisham, Camberwell, Woolwich, Greenwich, Beckenham, Lambeth, Orpington, Coulsdon, Purley, West Ham, Chislehurst and Mitcham. No longer a mere threat, Hitler's secret weapon was generating a crisis of magnitude.

Churchill, who was at Chequers that Sunday, returned to the capital immediately and ordered that the House of Commons, which had been bombed out in the London blitz of 1940 but had since returned, should evacuate to Church House, "whose modern steel structure offered somewhat more protection than the Palace of Westminster." A sense akin to terror began to spread through the capital; there was little panic, but the "grating roar that resembled a badly-tuned motorcycle engine" soon dominated all life in London and southern England. As one social historian would put it:

> Of all the bombs that descended upon the British Isles between 1939 and 1945 none is remembered with more bitter loathing. The first unmanned aircraft, with its harsh-sounding engine, scuttling remorselessly across the sky like some science-fiction monster, seemed even more sinister than the bombers which preceded it . . . to have one's house wrecked or one's family killed just when this seemingly interminable war was drawing to a close seemed not merely tragic but pointless.

Churchill ordered Bomber Command to make a maximum effort against Berlin as retaliation; and on the night of June 21/22, 1944, some 2500 RAF bombers attacked the German capital in the heaviest raid so far in the Second World War. They were followed, during the daylight hours, by 1000 American heavy bombers and 1200 long-range fighters. The death and destruction in Berlin were enormous, but Hitler's V1 campaign continued.

By June 25, the Germans had launched more than 2000 bombs, hundreds of which penetrated British defenses and fell upon London and the surrounding areas. Destruction and dislocation were severe, and the government began an evacuation of women, children, the elderly and hospital patients that would total nearly 1 million people. The evacuation placed an enormous strain on roads and railways that were already carrying capacity loads to the ports for the battle in Normandy; and this, in turn, caused serious delays in the shipment of supplies that were desperately needed on the Far Shore. But more important than all else was the strain that the V1's put on the civilian population. Would it hold up under the attack? If it did not, Britain would have to sue for peace just as Hitler had predicted.

On June 27, Herbert Morrison, the Home Secretary, delivered to the Cabinet a warning that was at once more serious and somber than any he had delivered in the entire course of the war. The V1 bombardment had already destroyed or damaged over 200,000 houses, and literally millions of panes of glass had been blown out of Londoners' homes. Unless the glassmaking industry was capable of producing enough glass to replace them before winter set in, there would be disastrous losses in manpower through illnesses. Furthermore, shattered sewage systems posed the threat of epidemics, and the Ministry of Works, Morrison reported, was "finding it difficult to keep up with the damage caused." Hundreds of people were homeless and rations might have to be reduced because rail services, already overtaxed by the demands of Neptune and the evacuation, were also suffering damage. No less grave was the anxiety caused by the continual bombardment. "After five years of war," Morrison declared, "the civil population (is) not capable of standing the strain of air attack. . . ."

What was to be done? As a first step the War Cabinet ordered the mass movement of anti-aircraft artillery to the south coast—over 2000 guns and anti-aircraft rocket launchers were positioned there overnight. The second step was an intensification of Allied aerial bombardment of the launch sites and storage depots. To help the air forces, Menzies and Gubbins directed their agents in France to increase their efforts to locate the targets; and one agent in particular—"Wizard"—came through with intelligence of great importance.

Wizard was W. J. Savy, a lawyer turned F section organizer and close friend of Antelme, who had saved him from the live embers of the Prosper disaster by whisking him out of France to London aboard a Dericourt Lysander. Savy returned to France early in 1944 to act as Antelme's treasurer and quartermaster, but when Antelme was captured, he went to ground in Paris and joined another *réseau*. Savy kept his eyes and ears open and on a trip to Creil, near Paris, in March, he heard a whisper from a man who grew mushrooms in the great caves at St. Leu d'Esserent nearby. The Germans, said the mushroom man, had taken over the caves and were building a spur railway line up to them. Their roofs were being lined with concrete and shorn up with steel and wood; narrow-gauge rail tracks were being laid inside them, and anti-aircraft and machine-gun posts were also being constructed. Savy suspected, correctly, that they were to be some kind of arms dump. He flew to London just before the invasion to report and then returned after D-Day to continue his surveillance. Late in June, he discovered what the Germans were storing in the caves—2000 V1's. The intelligence was wirelessed to London in Savy's special one-time pad cipher.

Delayed by bad weather, the RAF did not find the correct conditions for a precision attack for several days. But on the night of July 4/5, 227 Lancasters carrying 4000-pound "cookies" hit the caves and the road and rail links leading into them. German night fighters rose to their defense and claimed thirteen bombers, but seventeen more Lancasters of 617 Squadron, each carrying a 6-ton earthquake bomb, slipped through. Eleven of the earthquake bombs hit the specially marked caves accurately and stove them in, while the "cookies" wrecked the gun and rail systems.

The next day, Savy's mushroom man reported that all the entrances and approaches to the caves had been blocked and that inside many of the V1's were buried in chalk, limestone and earth. Could the Germans dig them out and open up the entrances? Yes, said the mushroom man, they could—and were doing so already. Savy passed the news to London, SOE told Bomber Command, and on the night of July 7/8, 228 Lancasters came in low and buried the V1 dumps in a welter of high explosive. It was probably SOE's most important intelligence contribution of the Neptune period, for it denied to the Germans about a quarter of the missiles available to them in France.

The aerial campaign against the V1 would prove to be a costly diversion from the demands of the land battle in France. The Allies were forced to deflect a fifth of their strength in the air toward tackling the problem. It was also a costly campaign in terms of lives and aircraft; some 3000 airmen lost their lives in these operations, along with some 500 aircraft. The British were responsible for the air defense of England, and the main burden was borne by the RAF, but the dead were not only British. There were many Americans, among them Lieutenant Joseph Kennedy, of the United States Navy, the eldest son of the American ambassador in London in 1940, and the brother of future President John F. Kennedy. Lieutenant Kennedy took off from an airfield in East Anglia in a B-24 Liberator bomber crammed with 22,000 pounds of high explosives and set course for the great earthworks at Mimoyecques, a suspected rocket storage depot. Soon after Kennedy took off, a second Liberator became airborne. The plan was for Kennedy to fly to a point close to the target; then he and his co-pilot would bail out, leaving their aircraft under the radio control of the second Liberator which would direct it to Mimoyecques, where it would crash into the target. But there was an accident—the precise nature of which would never be established—and the Liberator blew up over Suffolk, killing both Kennedy and his co-pilot. Their bodies were never found.

While attack and defense measures against the V1 were being employed by the military, the British secret agencies set in motion a third measure—deception. The scheme was proposed by Dr. R. V. Jones at a meeting with MI-5 and MI-6 on July 1. The secret agencies were faced with a dilemma. Agents working for the XX-Committee were being asked by their German controllers to report the fall of the V1's, a request they could not ignore. But, said Jones, if they spotted the shots accurately, they would be giving aid and comfort to the enemy, who would continue to aim the missiles on Tower Bridge with grievous consequences to London. And if they lied, aerial reconnaissance would reveal that they had done so, and the Germans would suspect that they were under control. Furthermore, the Germans kept records of the firing time of each missile, and although they could not be certain of the location of impact, they knew the time of impact within a minute or two. Jones's scheme solved the dilemma. He proposed that XX-Committee agents report on the missiles that had fallen north of London using the impact times of missiles that had actually fallen south of the capital. Thus, Jones thought the Germans would conclude that the V1's were falling long and shorten the range by decreasing their flight times. That, in turn, would cause the missiles to fall in open country south of London.

Before the plan could be employed, approval had to be obtained. The XX-Committee took it up with Sir Findlater Stewart, the chairman of the Home Defence Executive, who was a member of the Committee and of the LCS; and he took it to Duncan Sandys, Churchill's son-in-law, the former commander of Britain's first rocket-firing regiment, and now chairman of the War Cabinet's Crossbow Committee, the organization established by Churchill to coordinate all intelligence and counteraction. Sandys took the plan to the War Cabinet, it was approved, and XX-Committee agents began to transmit the rigged fall of shot.

By a fortunate coincidence, an old friend of the XX-Committee was sent to England by the Germans at about this same time to report the fall of the V1's. His name was Edward Chapman, and his XX-Committee code name, "Zigzag," was an apt description of his career. A former Coldstream Guardsman and safe-blower, he had deserted in 1939 and had been captured by the Germans in 1940 while hiding on the Channel Islands. He volunteered for work with the Abwehr as a sabotage agent in England and, because of his knowledge of explosives, he was accepted. After extensive training at the Abwehr's espionage school in a château near Nantes, he was given a contract worth £15,000 to sabotage the de Havilland aircraft works at Hatfield in Hertfordshire. An aircraft was laid on to drop him near Ely in December 1942 but the British were waiting for him. Through Ultra, the security authorities were able to follow the movements of enemy agents, including Zigzag, well before they arrived in England. Masterman would write: ". . . we knew a great deal about ZIGZAG before his arrival, and elaborate preparations had been made with regional and police authorities to secure him quickly and without advertisement as soon as he arrived."

Zigzag was collected as he stepped out of his parachute shrouds; but upon interrogation, he proved to be on the side of Britain rather than Germany, and he agreed (in return for a pardon) to work for the XX-Committee. A violent explosion was rigged at de Havilland (together with suitable damage, arranged by some special effects and scenery experts from the Old Vic); Zigzag reported his coup (as did the British press, which was allowed to breathe fire at the ineptitude of the security services) by wireless; and then arrangements were made for him to "escape." This he did in January 1943, posing as a steward aboard the steamer *City of Lancaster,* bound for Lisbon.

Nothing more was heard of Zigzag until the middle of 1944 when, as Masterman put it, "News . . . trickled through to us of a mysterious figure at Oslo—a man speaking bad German in a rather loud high-pitched voice clad in a pepper-and-salt suit, displaying two gold teeth and enjoying the amenities of a private yacht. This we thought must be ZIGZAG, and so it was."

Zigzag returned to England out of the night sky near Cambridge at the end of June, with two wireless sets, cameras, £6000, and a contract with the Germans for £100,000 to report the fall of shot of the V1's. The XX-Committee promptly put him to work passing doctored information. But then he was overheard by MI-5 officers telling his story in a public house. His case was "terminated" and he was quietly locked up, although the XX-Committee continued to use his wireless, cipher and security checks to relay the doctored information. Zigzag did not reappear until after the war, when he was to be seen frequenting the edges of Belgravian society, and later came into the possession of a Rolls-Royce and a health farm.

The XX-Committee campaign to deflect the fall of the V1's was not entirely successful. The Germans did indeed shorten their range, but the missiles began to fall not on open country, but on the working-class quarters south of the Thames, sparing the wealthier areas north of the river. Herbert Morrison protested. He demanded that the secret agencies seek only to confuse the German's aim, rather than deflect it; and he advocated precisely what Hitler believed that the Allies must do: invade the Pas de Calais to destroy the missile launching sites. Morrison insisted that the deception campaign be stopped immediately. As an historian of the incident would write: "M.I.5 was not authorised to interfere with Providence." Morrison's protests were quietly ignored, and the deception campaign continued to the end. But Hitler's use of the V1 as a weapon of indiscriminate destruction and terror seemed, at the time, immoral in itself, and it would lead the British to consider an even deadlier form of retaliation—poison gas.

It was a trying moment in the history of the Anglo-American alliance. The battle in Normandy was going slowly and badly as the weather continued to interrupt supply schedules. The weather also provided cover for the V1's, making the job of interception and destruction by fighters extremely difficult. Churchill, under the fearful strain of events in Normandy and the accelerating V1 campaign, wanted to abandon Anvil, Marshall's plan for an invasion of southern France to open up Marseilles as a port of entry for fresh U.S. divisions and supplies. He proposed instead to strengthen the Italian campaign, which was going well, cross the Alps, and march upon Austria and Germany from the south. This suggestion brought the sharpest and rudest rejection by Roosevelt in the history of the alliance so far, a rejection that was caused in part by what the Americans regarded as Montgomery's failure to break the German front in Normandy. The American attitude was uncompromising and blunt. Anvil would proceed.

It was in this context that the British Chiefs of Staff began to consider the use of poison gas. On July 4, a note from the Chiefs of Staff Secretary to the Joint Planning Staff at Storey's Gate stated:

> At their meeting today, the COS instructed the JPS to examine the desirability and practicability of using gas as a retaliation for Crossbow attacks. The report should consider the use of gas (a) against the Crossbow area alone, (b) as a general retaliation against Germany.

While the JPS was studying the implications of using gas, Menzies brought new and serious information to Cadogan. On July 10, he reported that a German long-range rocket had fallen in Sweden accidentally, and the Germans there were attempting to recover its remains; one party had entered the area, which was sealed off, behind a funeral cart, posing as mourners. Menzies wanted permission to "buy" the rocket's remains from the Swedes in exchange for two squadrons of tanks. Cadogan agreed, so did the Swedes, and two Mosquitos were sent to Stockholm to pick up the remains. After they were examined in London, they proved beyond doubt what had hitherto been a source of argument and speculation: that Hitler had a missile even more powerful than the V1. It was the V2, a liquid-fuel rocket capable of carrying 1 ton of aluminized explosive to London; and a V2 attack would not be long delayed.

On July 13, in light of this worrying news and after studying the JPS report, Churchill sent a minute to the Vice Chiefs of Staff directing that:

> A comprehensive examination should be undertaken of the military implications of our deciding on an all-out use of gas, principally mustard gas, or any other method of warfare which we have hitherto refrained from using against the Germans, in the following circumstances:
>
> (a) as a counter-offensive in the event of the use by the enemy of flying bombs and/or giant rockets developing into a serious threat to our ability to prosecute the war; or, alternatively
>
> (b) as a means of shortening the war or of bringing to an end a situation in which there was a danger of stalemate.

The memorandum reflected the gravity with which Churchill saw the situation.

Consideration of the use of poison gas was undertaken at the highest levels and a new report from the JPS was ready on July 16. It was handed in for study as Churchill was busily promoting another deadly idea: that the RAF should select one hundred small, undefended German towns and wipe them out one by one until Hitler stopped using his missiles. The report was a chilling assessment of the advantages and disadvantages of poison gas; it stated, however, that "British use of gas in Europe would achieve an initial tactical surprise, but would thereafter restrict Allied movements." It therefore ruled out gas warfare. But it did not entirely rule out bacteriological weapons.

The JPS had studied the use of a bacteriological agent codenamed "N"—probably anthrax; and as the report stated:

There is no known prophylactic against "N." If it can be used in practise, the effect on morale will be profound. It is improbable that the Germans will initiate biological warfare. There is no evidence to show whether they are in a position to retaliate in kind, were we to initiate it. . . . There seems to be little doubt that the use of bacteriological warfare would cause heavy casualties, panic and confusion in the areas affected. It might lead to a breakdown in administration with a consequent decisive influence on the outcome of the war. . . . If the claims of N are substantiated, its use could probably make a substantial change in the war situation.

But the report concluded that "There is no likelihood of a sustained attack being possible before the middle of 1945." That was that; Churchill dropped the matter. But, for a moment at least, the almost unbearable tensions caused by the V1 bombardment and the stalemate in Normandy had weakened the war's ultimate moral restraint; as one historian of the period would point out: ". . . the possibility exists that the JPS report of 16 July might have reached a different conclusion if Britain's development of the mysterious 'N' had been a year further advanced."

Britain was forced to endure Hitler's aerial bombardment; and casualties and damage—most of them in London—were severe. In all, the Germans would launch 10,500 V1's against England, 2400 of which got through the defenses. Some 1.5 million houses were destroyed or damaged, 6,200 people were killed and 18,000 were seriously injured. But the weapon, though terrible, was not conclusive. It did not compel Eisenhower to change his plans and land in the Pas de Calais, as Hitler was convinced that it must. Moreover, Hitler had made a fundamental mistake in directing fire at London. The 630 square miles of that great city could absorb the punishment. Had the bombs been launched against the south coast ports— Dover, Folkestone, Margate, Portsmouth, Southampton—the damage and casualties would have so dislocated Neptune's supply schedules that the Germans might have regained the initiative in France. But Hitler's desire for vengeance against the Allies for the bombardment of German cities prevailed over wiser counsels. He used the V1's not to obtain a strategic advantage, but for revenge—yet another mistake that would cost him the war.

7

Goodwood

FOR ALL the flaming magnitude of the battle in Normandy, the secret war which went on behind it—the war in which the Germans sought to establish the Allied plan of campaign and strength while the Allies sought to delude the Germans on those very points—was, in manpower terms, a comparatively small affair. Yet seemingly minute incidents could—and did—provide intelligence that dictated the plans and actions of high commanders and the movements of armies and air forces. On occasions they could dictate the fate of multitudes—even the outcome of the battle for France itself. Such an incident occurred at Cherbourg.

When the SHAEF Counter-Intelligence War Room was formed behind the cover address "Post Office Box 100, Parliament Street, London, S.W.1," its chief, Colonel Dick Goldsmith White, a schoolmaster turned spymaster, issued what was known as the Detailed Counter-Intelligence Instruction No. 1, a document that became the canon for the immense counterintelligence operations that accompanied Neptune. The instruction outlined the aims of Allied counterintelligence activities, chief among them to "prevent the operation of enemy intelligence or subversive elements within the theatre." And in this area of operations, the instruction warned of a particular problem.

> The Continent of Europe has been under enemy occupation for four years and the enemy have had unrivalled opportunities for organising espionage and sabotage. There is reason to believe that the Abwehr, the (Gestapo) and the (SD) organisations will have established a co-ordinated system consisting both of individual agents and of underground German and pro-German organisations, which is designed to go into operation in the event of an Allied invasion of Western Europe. Even though the Abwehr and (Gestapo) and (SD) administrative officials will have been withdrawn and are unlikely to be captured in the advance, the system of espionage and sabotage agents will remain in the areas liberated by the Allied Forces.

) 729 (

Goldsmith White's organization thought it likely that these "stay-behind agents" (as they were called) would be especially located at ports, at villages or towns near airfields, and at the centers of road nets, their task to report by wireless the movements of Allied forces. And because they might have "submerged" themselves in their communities over a period of four years and have civilian occupations, they would be difficult to uncover. In the event, Goldsmith White's warning proved to be accurate; over 200 German stay-behind agents—often of Alsatian stock but sometimes pro-Nazi Frenchmen or women—would be detected in France, and over 1800 clandestine arms dumps would be unearthed.

The first of these stay-behind agents was detected transmitting from Cherbourg by American radiogoniometrical units shortly after the city was captured on June 26. Once a small Channel port, Cherbourg had been transformed by a succession of French monarchs of the last two centuries into a great naval base and trans-Atlantic port-of-call. Hitler had further transformed it into one of the most formidable fortresses of the Atlantik-wall; and as the Allies moved to take the city, he wired its commandant: "Even if the worst comes to the worst, it is your duty to defend the last bunker and leave to the enemy not a harbor but a field of ruins. . . ." Cherbourg fell, but not before the Germans did as they had been ordered. As Colonel Alvin G. Viney, a U.S. Army port engineer, reported after he surveyed the scene, "The demolition of the port of Cherbourg is a masterful job, beyond a doubt the most complete, intensive, and best-planned demolition in history." It would be months before the port was restored to full capacity, but it was only three weeks before the first cargo was unloaded across the beaches; the Fuehrer had reckoned without British maritime skill and American prodigies of reconstruction. The facilities of Cherbourg were soon able to compensate for the loss of one of the Mulberries, but it was important to conceal this fact from Hitler. If he believed that the Allies were having severe supply problems, it was reasoned at Montgomery's headquarters, he might continue to try to smash the beachheads by incessant counterattacks—a battle that only the Allies could win, for their manpower and supply difficulties were much less great than the Germans'.

Few German agents were so devoted to the Fuehrer that they were prepared to give their lives for him. "George," as the stay-behind agent who was discovered transmitting from Cherbourg was codenamed, was no exception. He had been captured with his set, operating codes, instructions and transmission schedules intact, and X2, the OSS counterpart of the XX-Committee, had all the necessary ingredients for a wireless game. Moreover, George's particular mission at Cherbourg had been to report to his controller in Paris on the state of the harbor and whether the Allies were able to use it as a supply base. Why should he not continue his reports? On July 25 George reopened communications with Paris, and in response to the urgent requests of his controller, began to relay messages on Allied progress in reconstructing the harbor—all carefully fabricated to make it seem that Cherbourg was not fit for a fighting and supply base, and would not be so for some time to come. Other stay-behind agents were used to play the same game. The Germans were fed deceptive information about Allied intentions, and unknowingly revealed their own intentions by the questions they put to the captured agents. With that information, combined with Ultra and the yield of the Y service, Montgomery was able to piece together an intelligence picture of remarkable accuracy. It came, it would appear, none too soon.

By the beginning of July, the Germans had succeeded in sealing off the Allied lodgment area so effectively that when Bradley began his great offensive to take the key town of St. Lô, the Battle of the Hedgerows became what the Allies feared most—a slaughter yard. Bradley finally captured the town, but his army of twelve divisions advanced only 7 miles in seventeen days and lost 40,000 men, seriously impairing the fighting capability of two-thirds of his army. So brutal was the battle that, as one American officer reported:

> Over a stretch of . . . days, you became so dulled by fatigue that the names of the killed and wounded they checked off each night, the names of men who had been your best friends, might have come out of a telephone book for all you knew. All the old values were gone, and if there was a world beyond this tangle of hedgerows . . . where one barrage could lay out half a company like a giant's club, you never expected to live to see it.

Bradley's ammunition supply became short, his supply of reinforcements worse. He was compelled to call for 25,000 infantry replacements by the fastest transportation possible. He was told they did not exist in England and therefore would have to be brought from the United States. For both the Americans and the Germans alike—as General Dietrich von Choltitz, the German corps commander around St. Lô, would state—it was "the most monstrous bloodbath, the likes of which I have not seen in eleven years of war."

Montgomery, too, was in serious trouble on the British front, and the tenuous brotherhood of arms forged for D-Day between American and British generals and fighting men began to crack. Criticism of Montgomery's command became more vocal. His own countrymen, Air Marshal Sir Arthur Tedder, the deputy Supreme Commander, and General Sir Frederick Morgan, the former COSSAC and now an assistant Chief of Staff to Eisenhower, were two of his bitterest critics. They joined the important group of Americans who openly advocated that Montgomery be replaced or, at least, that Eisenhower should take command of the battle, Montgomery be relegated to the command of the British and Canadian armies, and Bradley be given command of an American army group. To counter this criticism, Montgomery launched another attack against the Caen fortress—for the SS had turned the "Norman Athens" into a citadel—on the morning of July 8, behind a force of 467 Lancasters and Halifaxes which dropped 2560 tons of bombs. The bombardment shattered part of the German line, and on the 10th, the British and Canadians at long last captured the city. But they got no further; the bombardment had tossed about the blocks of stone with which much of Caen was built like cubes of sugar. The roads were choked with rubble, pocked with hundreds of craters, and Montgomery's attack stalled before he could get across the Orne and onto the road to Paris. The SS closed ranks and once again Montgomery was checkmated.

There was more bad news for the Allies. On June 30, Hitler had held a major conference at the Strub Barracks at Berchtesgaden to plan the long-delayed armored counteroffensive in Normandy, at last penetrating, so it seemed, the fogbanks of Fortitude. Analyzing the situation with remarkable clarity and perception, Hitler said he recognized that the Allies still retained the means to land in great strength anywhere between the North Sea and the Mediterranean coasts of Europe, and that he was "reasonably sure" that they would land on the Riviera coast—as indeed a Franco-American army would on August 15. He still believed that the Pas de Calais must be the Allies' primary objective in order to destroy the V-missile bombardment of London. But, he said, it must be remembered that the Allies had already disembarked their best troops in Normandy.

With that remark, it was clear that Fortitude was beginning to wear thin. Moreover, OKW situation reports of the next few days revealed that, while the intentions of Army Group Patton remained "the big question mark," Hitler thought "the troops in Britain were definitely second-string." Worse still for Montgomery in his present predicament, Hitler went on to state in a letter of instruction on July 8: "If they conduct a landing operation in the Pas de Calais, it (can) only be a diversionary operation." Except for Hitler's conviction that the V1 launching sites in the Pas de Calais "constituted a challenge which the Allied armies (cannot) ignore," it seemed that Fortitude was in danger of collapsing completely. The threat to Montgomery was readily apparent. If he could not break the thin German line that was holding him now, how could he hope to break it if Hitler finally agreed to let Rommel have the services of the first-rate divisions defending the Pas de Calais?

But Colonel Wild and the CSM did not intend to permit Fortitude to evaporate yet awhile. Throughout this period, Fortitude follow-through operations had been launched in quick succession to keep the deception alive. There was a British naval feint off Boulogne on June 24, intensive Allied aerial reconnaissance on either side of Dieppe that same day, and heavy smoke-screening by naval units off the southern coast of England. Resistance movements were once again alerted by a combination of real and dummy *messages personnels,* and an American staff study would note that, on the basis of those messages, and information obtained from the Belgian underground, Hitler had declared on June 30 that, since the tide and moon conditions between the 6th and 8th of July "would be like those prevailing on the night of the invasion in June," the 15th Army should receive "appropriate alert orders." The American study went on to describe the measures that had been used to reinforce this latest threat to the Pas de Calais: "As if to keep the Germans on edge during the night of 6/7 July the wire net in Belgium was disrupted; then during the night 7/8 July Third Air Fleet, which was monitoring radio channels, reported that the same picture prevailed (in Britain) as on the night of the invasion." Heavy air attacks about daybreak carried out by 2000 bombers accompanied by hundreds of fighter escorts added to and emphasized the scale of the threat.

Plainly, the LCS and CSM had come a long way since the "one-man band" operations of Garbo. When before in history had 2000 bombers with perhaps another 1000 fighters—more aircraft than existed in the entire German air force—been used solely for the purposes of stratagem? It was the most impressive display of force in support of cover and deception so far in the Second World War. But evidently it was not quite enough. For on July 8, Hitler gave orders for "Lüttich," a surprise night offensive in great strength to be launched by four SS and three army panzer divisions—perhaps 100,000 men and 500 tanks—against the British at Caen. They were to jump off without artillery preparation. Air support would be provided on the grandest scale possible, and Goering would be ordered to deploy yet another new and formidable secret weapon, the ME262 jet fighter. Hitler had been informed that the first of these jet fighters would be ready for service around July 15; many more were on the production lines, and he was convinced that with them the Luftwaffe would regain aerial superiority.

Rommel was given tactical command of Lüttich, and, expanding the scale of the attack, he envisaged using two more panzer divisions and an infantry division. This, exactly, was the magnitude of the force which the Allies had expected to meet on D+4. Moreover, to enable Rommel to pull the panzers out of the line for concentration, Hitler at long last agreed that Normandy should have the 15th Army's reserves of one panzer division (the 116th) and six infantry divisions. The first of these divisions began to move on July 13, a date that marked the beginning of the end of Fortitude's influence on the campaign.

Montgomery was soon informed of Hitler's and Rommel's intentions. Intelligence gleaned from Ultra, the Y service and the stay-behind agents under Allied control—all pointed to the looming threat. In due time, the code name and even the details of Lüttich would become known to the Allies; and with that information, it was not difficult for Montgomery to launch a series of shrewdly timed and placed attacks to throw Rommel off balance and compel him to keep his panzers on the line rather than concentrating them for a counteroffensive. But if these tactics disconcerted the timetables for Lüttich, they did not permit Montgomery to break out of the bridgehead. That he had to do at any cost before the new German infantry and armor arrived.

Throughout the brutal fighting in Normandy, and in spite of the criticisms that were being leveled against him, Montgomery, as an American official history would declare, "directed the tactical operations on the Continent with what might have seemed like exasperating calm." The reason for his calm, de Guingand, his Chief of Staff, would remember, was his belief that the Germans would soon break. The Americans were suffering heavy casualties, but they were doing what he wanted them to do: kill Germans. American casualties could be replaced; the much heavier German losses could not. Meanwhile, he was systematically destroying German armor and infantry; and once the armor had been written off, the German front would collapse with a thunderclap.

The Allied high command, however, did not share Montgomery's calm. Eisenhower, infected with the unease of a situation in stalemate, wrote Montgomery to call for a full-blooded offensive to break the deadlock. Montgomery said he had such plans in mind, and on July 10 he conferred with Bradley to lay the groundwork for "Goodwood," a mighty offensive in which the British army would attempt to crack the German lines at Caen. A few days later, the American army would attempt a similar breakout at St. Lô in an operation called "Cobra." The objective of the two-pronged attack was the encirclement and destruction of the 7th Army and the Panzer Army West. It was an ambitious plan without any guarantees of success, for Montgomery had barely managed to capture Caen, and Bradley was still battling for every mile in the difficult hedgerow country before St. Lô. But everyone recognized the imperative of an immediate offensive to shatter the German lines.

To provide full-scale cover and deception for Goodwood and Cobra, new life had to be breathed into Fortitude; and it was now that Fortitude South II, which was also known as "Rosebud," began to flower. Its object was to maintain the fiction that the million men of FUSAG still waited to invade the Pas de Calais if the Germans were unwise enough to reinforce the embattled 7th Army with idle divisions from the 15th. Rosebud was controlled not by British deception agencies this time, but by American. The man in charge was Colonel Harris of the Special Plans Branch, and it was his task to maintain the illusion that land, naval and air forces existed in England that were even larger than those of the Normandy assault. With the help of the Royal Navy and the American fleet, he was to convey to the enemy that three immense assault armadas—"Fox," "Mike," and "Nan" —were still gathering at ports and creeks between The Wash and the Thames, armadas that consisted, in reality, of immense numbers of "Bigbobs," the rubber or timber and canvas "landing ships" that had been used in the earlier phases of Fortitude South. Furthermore, he was to convince the Germans that an entirely new tactical air force—the 8th—had arrived in Britain from America for the operation, a force which, in reality, was composed of nothing more than hundreds of rubber bags that when inflated resembled, to German reconnaissance aircraft, the presence of entire squadrons of fighters. The land forces of Rosebud were but a variation of the original Quicksilver order of battle, consisting of a collection of British and American formations that existed only as skeleton units—or did not exist at all.

Rosebud got underway immediately, using the same variety of special means that had characterized earlier Fortitude deceptions—wireless chatter interspersed with ominous silences, warning reports from XX-Committee double agents, intensification of reconnaissance flights over the Pas de Calais, increased numbers of messages sent by SOE to resistance groups in the 15th Army sector, and a corresponding increase in sabotage and guerrilla activities in northern France and Belgium. At the same time, plans were laid for naval, air and military movements that would suggest large-scale assault exercises of the type that had preceded Neptune. These exercises, with code names like "Haircut," "Moustache," "Vanity I" and "II," "Jitterbug," "Filmstar," "Honeysuckle," "Viola I," "II" and "III," were scheduled to begin in the last days of July; and finally, the "invasion" itself would be launched against the Pas de Calais on August 14—almost the same time span that had occurred between the Neptune exercises and the Normandy assault.

Plainly, Rosebud was intended to create the maximum amount of anxiety within German headquarters during the period that would begin with an attempt to break the stalemate in Normandy and end with the Anvil assault across the Mediterranean beaches of France. But the deception agencies had a problem. Patton, the man who had been so conspicuously built up as the commander of the Pas de Calais assault, had arrived in France to assume command of the 3rd Army, and it would be difficult, if not impossible, to conceal his presence for long.

During the last several weeks, Patton had been extravagantly advertising himself in England. Beautifully tailored in a tight-fitting, brass-buttoned battle jacket, pink whipcord jodhpurs, gleaming riding boots with spurs, carrying a crop and accompanied by his white bulldog Willie, he had been busy delivering the same bellicose and profane speech to troop concentra-

tions throughout Britain and Ulster. In his shrill, boyish voice he spoke of
the glories of battle, of the greatness of the American fighting man, of
death, honor, duty, manhood. It was an extraordinary performance, and
one young soldier who heard him would write: ". . . you felt as if you
had been given a supercharge from some divine source. Here was the man
for whom you would go to hell and back."

Patton had moved his headquarters from Peover Hall south to the
embarkation area on the last day of June; and on the morning of July 6,
carrying with him the six volumes of Edward Freeman's *History of the
Norman Conquest* from which he hoped to learn what the roads were like
in Normandy and Brittany, he boarded his Dakota for France. He landed
at a forward airstrip just behind Omaha beach and stepped out of the
plane to be greeted by hundreds of troops. He made a speech, of course.
Standing in his jeep, he began by warning all who heard him that he was
"the Allies' secret weapon," and that they were forbidden to mention that
they had seen him in France. Then he declared:

> I'm proud to be here to fight beside you. Now let's cut the guts out of those
> krauts and get the hell on to Berlin. And when we get to Berlin, I am going
> to personally shoot that paper-hanging goddammed son-of-a-bitch [Hitler]
> just like I would a snake.

With that, he drove off in a cloud of dust to Bradley's headquarters in a
wooded field south of Isigny.

Patton had had his private D-Day. That was the trouble. The Germans
could not fail to hear that he was in France and soon they must hear that
he was in command not of an army group about to invade the Pas de
Calais, but of an army in Bradley's sector. How was the Fortitude threat to
be maintained? The answer was simple; Patton had to be "demoted." In a
letter to Smith on July 10 Eisenhower directed that it should be leaked out
that "Patton has lost his high command because of displeasure at some of
his indiscretions, and that he is reduced to army command." That, of
course, would be a serious statement to make about a general in an army
where promotions or demotions were often decided by press comment.
But, in fact, there would be some justification for spreading the story. Patton was indeed guilty of a serious indiscretion.

Ever since his arrival in France, Patton had sat fuming and restless at
his command post in an old apple orchard near the Cotentin village of
Néhou, near the Douve River. He became "obsessed with the fear that the
war would be over before he got into it"; and he worried that "all the glory
would go to others, while he was forced to sit idle watching the cider apples
growing." He began to expound a theory to newsmen that two armored
divisions, preceded by a heavy concentration of artillery fire, could crack
the German line at St. Lô, end the bloodletting, enable the Allies to get the

Breton ports and, at the same time, sweep into the center of France to surround the German army. If only "that fart," as Patton was thought to have called Montgomery on at least one occasion, was not in command.

On July 12, Bradley briefed Patton on Cobra which, curiously, called for the very operation that Patton had expounded to the newsmen: a bold, two-division attack on a narrow front preceded by a massive artillery barrage in the vicinity of St. Lô. Patton immediately did what he had promised not to do—tell his staff—and Colonel Charles C. Blakeney, his press officer, went to the correspondents' camp to announce that Patton's plan had been accepted. In consequence, the 3rd Army correspondents began to brag about their foreknowledge to their 1st Army colleagues, and they, in turn, complained to Bradley's press officer. The fat was in the fire with a vengeance; it was the grossest leakage of Bradley's operational plans, and Bradley, for a time, considered replacing Patton. But the demands of the battle made that impossible, and it was decided instead to use this indiscretion as the main reason for Patton's "demotion."

There was a second reason—and one that was less justified than the first. Shortly after the Cobra breach, word began to spread that Patton was allowing his troops to take women with them to France. The story, which caused a storm among the more puritanical of the American women's organizations, had its origins in an incident for which Patton bore no responsibility. At Omaha, on July 14, two Negro soldiers, "Pfc. Watson" and "Pvt. Dayton," were found to have smuggled a young woman from Firamsarn, Wales, to France in a DUKW amphibious truck. The two men were tried on charges of transporting the woman "for immoral purposes"; Watson was sentenced to ten years' hard labor, Dayton was found not guilty.

Patton may or may not have cooperated in his "demotion," but it soon became common knowledge among the American press corps that he had been "replaced" by General Lesley J. McNair, the sixty-one-year-old Chief of Army Ground Forces, a military establishment figure of power and influence who had built the American army from a tiny group of professionals into an immense machine of 10 million men in just over two years. McNair had graduated from West Point in 1904, eleventh in a class of 124; he had served with the Funston Expedition to Veracruz and on Pershing's expedition to the Mexican border. At thirty-five, he had been the youngest general to serve in Pershing's army in France in the First World War; he had been professor of Military Science at Purdue, had commanded an artillery brigade between the wars, had been Commandant of the Command and General Staff College at Fort Leavenworth, and was reputed to be a military intellectual. Thus the Germans, in looking at his credentials, would certainly believe that he was the sort of man who could be expected to hold high operational command.

McNair was not told what his command would be when he saw Marshall at the Pentagon shortly before his departure from Washington on or about July 12. But it was clear that he did not expect to find that he had been given command of nothing more than a paper tiger. McNair and Eisenhower met at Southwick House on July 15, and when McNair came out of the meeting, Curtis noted that "he was white with fury. I had never seen a man looking quite so angry or disappointed." Word of a "row" began to spread, but McNair acceded to his appointment, and the American press was manipulated to make it seem that he was in Europe to command an army group.

There were no stories about Patton's "demotion," but rumors abounded which inevitably reached the Germans through XX-Committee agents such as Garbo and Brutus. The Germans had indeed discovered that Patton was in France—largely through the Cobra indiscretion—and the news spread rapidly, threatening to destroy Fortitude completely, unless Brutus or Garbo could give a convincing explanation. This they tried to do between July 12 and 18. In a series of telegrams, Garbo "revealed" that FUSAG "had undergone important changes" because of the "necessity to send immediate reinforcements to Normandy." But these forces were being replaced by units fresh from the United States, and FUSAG now consisted of the American 9th Army (which existed in fact), the American 14th Army (which was bogus), and the British 4th Army (which consisted of a few second-string brigades). Brutus reported that the "milking" of FUSAG had caused a severe row between Eisenhower and Patton and that Patton had, in consequence, "been displaced as Commander-in-Chief of FUSAG by another senior General, General McNair." In a signal of elaboration he announced that "(The changes and demotion) have caused quite a stir at our headquarters."

Patton's indiscretion had clearly threatened the continuing success of Fortitude, but Roenne was not yet quite disposed to write off the story that the Allies would invade the Pas de Calais, although in weakened strength. It seemed that Hitler, too, wavered in his opinion, if only temporarily, that FUSAG would not now make a major strike across the English Channel. Thus, it was possible that Patton's "demotion" was interpreted by Hitler as a piece of what the Germans called "blossoming," their word for military deception operations. It may have appeared eminently plausible that the publicity surrounding Patton was a delicate attempt to distract the Germans' attention from FUSAG and the Pas de Calais. All in all, it was as beautiful a piece of dissimulation as there had ever been.

It was at about this same time that a new element—perhaps the most dramatic of all—entered the Allied games of deception and maneuver. Ever since April 1944 there had been rumbles of brewing revolution among the German General Staff. Now, as the Americans and British were stalled in Normandy, it seemed that an attack on Hitler might be imminent, an attack that would, even if it was unsuccessful, cause a profound dislocation among the German high command and provide Montgomery with a strategical advantage that might help break the deadlock. If it was successful and the Nazi régime was toppled, western Europe might be liberated, and Germany occupied, without further loss of blood. Surely now was the time to enter into serious negotiations with the Schwarze Kapelle; surely now was the time to soften the terms of Unconditional Surrender to encourage the conspirators to act.

The Allies were well informed about the conspiracy with intelligence derived from many sources. Dulles had filed repeated warnings to the White House and the OSS in the early weeks of July. Theodore Steltzer, a high German officer at Oslo and a member of the Schwarze Kapelle who was in close contact with Milorg, the Norwegian intelligence organization, had passed information about the plot to Milorg in mid-July and Milorg passed it to London immediately, receiving a cipher signal acknowledging receipt. Both the OSS and MI-6 had received similar reports from the Schwarze Kapelle's representative in Sweden, Robert von Mendelsohn, a German banker and an intimate of Canaris. On July 11, the British captured Joachim Count von Helldorf, an SS soldier and the son of the police president of Berlin, Wolf-Heinrich Count von Helldorf, one of the leading figures in the plot. Helldorf said under interrogation that he was to have taken part in the plot, revealed the names of the senior conspirators, and said that the execution of the *coup d'état* could not be long delayed.

There is also evidence that officers of the German General Staff were in touch with the Allies at this time. Gehlen, the chief of the Fremde Heere, would later testify that Colonel Hansen, Canaris's successor, met " 'an emissary of Churchill' on a lonely road somewhere in southern France," to discuss the "all-important question of whether the British government would be prepared to negotiate an armistice with a new German government if Hitler were overthrown." Hansen also sent Otto John to Madrid to inform his contacts that an attack against Hitler was imminent.

Then there was the curious situation of Roenne. Gehlen, Roenne's superior at Fremde Heere, would claim that: ". . . it is the duty of every sophisticated intelligence service to keep open a channel of communication with the enemy's intelligence service" and state that: "I was able to keep such channels active during the Third Reich." Is it conceivable that Roenne himself—or his assistant Michel—had these same channels available to them? Were they using them for Schwarze Kapelle business, and were the British, in turn, using them to sow the deceptions of Fortitude to FHW? It would perhaps explain Roenne's adamant conviction of the existence of Army Group Patton. There would be many indications that this was precisely what was happening during the Fortitude period, but no direct proof.

There was some proof, however, that Fellgiebel—the man who ran Gehlen's and Roenne's communications and who was now providing the conspirators with super-secret telephone and teleprinter lines to be used during the revolt—had wireless contact with the British in the period immediately before Goodwood. Fellgiebel's *aide-de-camp*, Colonel Joachim Arntz, would state at a Combined Services Detailed Interrogation Centre session in London on April 11, 1945, that Fellgiebel had told him on May 22, 1944, at Führerhauptquartier that Hitler and his staff were to be assassinated, that the German forces in France would then be withdrawn to the German frontier, the Allies were to be asked for an armistice, and that to discuss terms he had "made contact with His Majesty's Government."

Finally, at a meeting with Hansen at the end of June or the beginning of July, General Ulrich Liss, a former chief of FHW, who was at Berlin to recover from wounds he had received while commanding an infantry division on the Russian front, received instructions to be ready to fly to Stockholm immediately Hitler was dead. His job, he would state, was to get in touch with General Kenneth W. D. Strong, a British officer whom Liss had known when he was a deputy military attaché in Berlin, and who was now Eisenhower's chief of intelligence, to "arrange a channel along which most confidential communications could pass."

In short, the Allies had many reports of the imminence of a revolution in Germany. They could continue to demand Unconditional Surrender; they could agree to an armistice, if the revolution succeeded, and undertake a bloodless liberation of Europe and conquest of Germany; or they could encourage the conspirators and then attack to take advantage of the chaos that a revolution would inevitably cause in the German command structure. It seemed that the British, at least, chose the last course. For on July 6, as the Allied failure to break out from the Neptune bridgehead was reaching crisis proportions, the British government changed its tune dramatically. For the first time, it acknowledged the existence of the Schwarze Kapelle, and encouraged it to revolt. In a speech to the House of Commons that day, Clement Attlee, the deputy Prime Minister, made a declaration that was at once a fundamental change of attitude, an olive branch, and an incitement to rebellion. Attlee stated:

> So far as His Majesty's Government are concerned, it has repeatedly been made clear in public statements that we shall fight on until Germany has been forced to capitulate and until nazism is extirpated. It is for the German people to draw the logical conclusion. If any section of them wants to see a return to a regime based on respect for international law and for the rights of the individual, they must understand that no one will believe them until they have themselves taken active steps to rid themselves of their present

regime. The longer they continue to support and to tolerate their present rulers, the heavier grows their own direct responsibility for the destruction that is being wrought throughout the world, and not least in their own country.

Nothing could be clearer: kill Hitler *now* and we may be able to talk peace.

A week after Attlee's statement, the Prime Minister dropped a similar bombshell. Reminded by an MP of his advice to the Germans to overthrow "their Nazi taskmasters," and "asked what statement he could make to encourage them to do so," Churchill declared on July 12: "I am very glad to be reminded of that statement, to which I strongly adhere. I think it has been repeated in other forms by the Foreign Secretary and other Ministers. At any rate, it would certainly be a very well-advised step on the part of the Germans."

Would the Americans offer similar encouragement to the conspirators? There had been no reaction to Dulles's previous warnings when, on July 18, he sent another L-Document to the White House and the OSS, informing them that the plot had now definitely crystallized around the Home Army and Amt Mil, and reporting that the conspirators believed "that the next few weeks represent the final opportunity to initiate steps to overthrow Hitler and his organization and to set up a 'respectable government.' " Dulles's informant was Gisevius, who was even then in Berlin at great personal peril ready to open communications with Dulles if the plot succeeded. But still the Americans kept silent. Dulles would later write:

> In reviewing my notes of those days (July 1944) I find that the "Breakers" group was encouraged to proceed by a . . . statement in the House of Commons by Mr. Attlee. . . . They were also heartened by a statement made about the same time by Prime Minister Churchill, recommending that the German people should overthrow the Nazi government. I urged that some similar statement be made from America as I was convinced that whatever the result of (the revolt) might be, the fact that an attempt was made to overthrow Hitler, whether or not successfully, would help to shorten the war. Nothing of this nature was done.

In Berlin, meanwhile, Stauffenberg and Beck were indeed completing their plans for rebellion. Stauffenberg, who on July 1 had been appointed Chief of Staff of the Home Army and in this post would have direct personal access to the Fuehrer, had decided to undertake the attack on Hitler himself. Professor Sauerbruch, the German surgeon who was a friend and doctor to both Stauffenberg and Beck, advised against it; the dual role of assassin and leader of the revolt would be too much for any man, let alone one suffering from Stauffenberg's physical disabilities. Stauffenberg replied that earlier he might have agreed, but it was now too late; there would be no going back—the situation was too grave. Indeed it was, for while the German line in Normandy was groaning, the Russians had torn a huge hole in the front line in the East; the twenty-seven divisions of Army Group Center had simply disintegrated and, as bad, Army Group North was about to be cut off in East Prussia. Tresckow, the Chief of Staff to the C-in-C of the shattered army group, reported to Beck on July 8 that Russian tanks would be outside Berlin in ten days, and that a third offensive was expected against the southern part of the front. However, the conspirators in Berlin were encouraged by Hofacker's report that Kluge was now party to Rommel's schemes, although he believed that his plans to negotiate with Montgomery to end the war in the West were probably impracticable. Kluge's view was that if the war was to be ended, "action" in Berlin and at OKW was imperative. Rommel, reported Hofacker, was also tending toward this point of view, and wished to assure Stauffenberg that once action had been started in Berlin and at OKW he would give it his full support in France.

But bad luck continued to dog the conspirators. On July 11, Stauffenberg flew to a conference at Berchtesgaden, intending to kill Hitler on that day. Hitler was present, but Himmler and Goering were not; and at that stage Stauffenberg considered that the assassination of all three was necessary if the coup was to succeed. On July 13, Führerhauptquartier moved to Rastenburg; and it was there that Stauffenberg flew on July 15, again intending to assassinate Hitler. The plotters, confident of success this time, issued all preliminary signals for Valkyrie, but again, some evil providence stood at Hitler's side. Neither Himmler nor Goering was at the conference—perhaps because they, like so many others, had heard rumors of a plot—and Stauffenberg abandoned the attempt for a second time.

The day dealt the conspirators two more grave blows before it was done. Keitel heard of the Valkyrie signals and was so suspicious that it would be impossible again to camouflage Valkyrie as a "training exercise." Then it was learned that General von Falkenhausen, the Military Governor of Belgium and a key member of the Schwarze Kapelle in the West, had been suddenly relieved of command and ordered to return to OKW. Coming on top of the arrests of several important members of the Schwarze Kapelle in Berlin, and the knowledge that Himmler had issued a warrant for the arrest of Goerdeler, it was clear to Stauffenberg that there was a traitor in their midst and that unless they acted immediately there might be none of the hierarchy left.

The next day—the 16th—Stauffenberg met Beck at his home in the Goethestrasse and it was decided that he would kill the Fuehrer at the first possible moment, whether Himmler and Goering were present or not. That evening, another meeting took place, this time at Stauffenberg's home at Wannsee, and the conspirators agreed that they could not now hope to secure a modification of Unconditional Surrender. But no matter what the future might bring, Hitler must be killed "to prove to the world and to future generations that the men of the German resistance movement dared to take the decisive step and to hazard their lives upon it."

A similar urgency infected Rommel. On July 17, he toured the front, talking first to General Heinz Eberbach, the commander of the Panzer-armee on the British front, and then to General Sepp Dietrich, the commander of the 1st SS Panzer Korps, Adolf Hitler. Both assured him of their loyalty in the event of a *coup d'état*. The SS General Paul Hausser, the new commander of the 7th Army, and the SS General Wilhelm Bittrich, the commander of the 2nd SS Panzer Korps in Normandy, had also agreed to support him—an almost certain guarantee of a successful rebellion, for the prospect of civil war between the midnight black of the SS and the field gray of the army was now removed. But at this most crucial moment in the long history of the conspiracy, fate again intervened.

At four o'clock that afternoon, Rommel left Dietrich's headquarters for the Château de La Roche Guyon. With him in the car—a six-wheeled Mercedes staff car with a folding top and glass winding windows—were his aide, Lang, Corporal Holke, whose duty was to look out for maurauding aircraft, and a Major Neuhans. They were on the Livarot road approaching a hamlet with the ironic name Sainte Foy-de-Montgommery when, at about 4:20 P.M., Holke warned that two low-flying RAF Typhoons were banking toward them behind a clump of poplars. Staff Sergeant Daniel, Rommel's driver since before El Alamein, put on speed to get to another clump of poplars, there to hide until the Typhoons had passed. But just before he reached a road leading into the first houses of Sainte Foy-de-Montgommery, the Typhoons came roaring in above the tree tops, their 20-millimeter cannons spewing shells. The Mercedes was struck in the left side from the rear by the explosive shells, any one of which could wreck an armored car, and as Rommel turned round to look at the planes he was hit by flying glass and stone. He was struck in the left temple and the left cheek and was instantly unconscious. Sergeant Daniel, who was mortally wounded, lost control of the car. It hit a tree stump, careened across the road and stopped in a stormwater ditch. Rommel was thrown from the car into the road, where he was lying when another plane came in to strafe the tarmacadam. Lang and Holke ran into the road and brought Rommel, who was bleeding heavily from the wounds in his face, under cover.

When the fighters disappeared, Lang stopped a passing German car and drove Rommel, who was still unconscious, to Livarot; and there, in front of the war memorial, he met Marcel Lescene, the Mayor and chemist, who was taking his evening calvados in a café on the square. Lescene would later recall:

I saw a tank officer who was very distraught. He asked me if the village had a doctor and I said it had but I did not know where he was at this hour. I decided myself to go to the hospital and there I saw an officer whom I knew was at least a general because he wore red tabs and broad red stripes on his breeches, and because of his high boots.

I noticed he had a large open wound above his left eye and was bleeding from the ears. He was unconscious. I took his pulse, which was weak, and gave him two injections of etherated camphor. Then the commander of the German garrison hastened up and removed the seat from the back of his car, put Rommel onto the floor and drove him off to the military hospital at Bernay. I myself did not give Rommel the ghost of a chance of surviving those wounds.

His wounds were serious indeed. At the Luftwaffe hospital on the airfield at Bernay, three German doctors found that Rommel had a fracture of the base of the skull, two fractures of the left temple, and his left cheekbone had been broken in. His left eye was badly damaged, the scalp was badly torn, and he was seriously concussed.

When the news reached Rommel's headquarters and was relayed to all his subordinates, an immediate air of catastrophe and tragedy descended upon the officers and the men whom he had led. It was thought that he might die that night and Speidel would write:

Rommel was in fact eliminated in the very hour that his Army and his people could spare him the least. All those who were groping with his help to find a way to a new and better world felt themselves painfully deprived of their pillar of strength.

Ernst Juenger, the historian and philosopher who was active in the conspiracy and was a close friend of Rommel's, felt compelled to write:

The blow that felled Rommel on the Livarot road on 17 July 1944 deprived our plan of the only man strong enough to bear the terrible weight of war and civil war simultaneously, the only man who was straightforward enough to counter the frightful folly of the leaders of Germany. This was an omen which had only one interpretation.

A few hours after Rommel was struck down, the RAF delivered the mighty opening stroke of Goodwood, and Montgomery launched 1500 tanks and 250,000 men against the German lines around Caen. They jumped off into the cornfields by ghostly artificial moonlight, hundreds of powerful searchlights playing upon the undersides of the clouds. Scores of flame-throwing tanks howled and screeched as they burned the SS out of their foxholes. Preceded and attended by an aerial bombardment of un- heard-of strength—1700 heavy and 500 medium bombers dropped 7000 tons of bombs on an area of little more than 20 square miles—three tank divisions and three armored brigades moved forward behind a rolling barrage laid down by almost the entire artillery of the British 2nd Army; 45,000 shells fell upon the 2nd SS Panzer Korps alone in a few hours. Eight hundred fighter bombers took wing to give the army close support, and one RAF group alone flew 1800 rocket missions against German tanks and emplacements. It was the most concentrated and furious attack of the Second World War in western Europe.

Kluge was taken completely by surprise; misled by deceptive information supplied by stay-behind agents, he expected the attack from another direction three or four days later, and had gone to Poitiers for a conference. Even so, Goodwood was destined to fail. Montgomery's armies penetrated six of the seven deep lines of defense around Caen, and for a time it seemed that the fate of the German army in the West was in the balance. But then the British ran up against the seventh and last line of defense—the anti-tank screen guarding the entrance to the plains and Paris. The *Feldgrau* held the line until finally, on the 20th, Montgomery called the operation off. The British had lost 500 tanks and 5000 men, and all that had been captured was the industrial suburb of Caen and some 40 square miles of new territory.

The failure of Goodwood caused the most serious outcry at SHAEF so far. Tedder, believing that all the airpower used in Goodwood had been expended for nothing, declared bitterly that "we [the air forces] have been had for suckers." Morgan thought the situation "had the makings of a dangerous crisis." Cadogan snorted in his diary: "Monty . . . does a lot of publicity stuff in his sweater and beret. I don't believe he's a general at all, but just a Film Star." Eisenhower fidgeted and Churchill announced that he would go to Normandy to see what the situation was for himself.

But the commanders who were loudest in their criticism knew the least. Montgomery's tactics had forced the best of the Germans' armor and infantry to concentrate in the Caen sector, and Goodwood had torn them to pieces. Kluge realized that his armies could not withstand another such attack—an attack that he knew must come. But where—from the cornfields and hamlets around Caen, or amid the wild roses and hedgerows near St. Lô? Standing over his chinagraph maps in the Forêt d'Écouves, Kluge decided that Paris and the flying bomb launch sites must be the primary Allied objectives, and he, as well as the other German generals, considered the British and Canadian forces under Montgomery far superior to the American forces under Bradley in fighting capability. The attack would come from the Caen sector as soon as Montgomery had regrouped. But Kluge was quite wrong. The Breton ports were the main Allied objective; and the attack would come where Kluge least expected it, and where his defenses were now the weakest—from the American sector at St. Lô.

Under cover of the Rosebud phase of Fortitude, Bradley's Cobra offensive was scheduled to open on July 20, the same day that the

Schwarze Kapelle would attempt to assassinate Hitler. Was there a connection between these climactic events? The Allied high command had ample warning of the Schwarze Kapelle's intentions, and by a remarkable coincidence—if it was a coincidence—the decision to launch Cobra on the 20th was confirmed between Montgomery and Bradley on the 18th, shortly after the conspirators had decided to assassinate Hitler at the first possible moment. Had the Allied high commanders been informed of that decision; had they in any way encouraged it? If so, all of the labyrinthian strategies, stratagems and special means of the secret war against Hitler might be said to have led up to this single moment. History seldom allows for such oversimplifications; but on the evening of the 19th, as the sun went down over the Norman countryside, Montgomery did something he had never done before and would not do again. He directed his provost marshal to seal off his headquarters until further orders. No one was to be allowed in or out unless he had a special pass that showed him to be on the most urgent business. And that same evening, in Berlin, Stauffenberg took absolution from his priest and prepared for the morrow.

July 20, 1944

JULY 20, 1944, broke over Berlin in an airless, sweltering dawn. Once again Stauffenberg wrapped the British-made bomb (SOE stores captured in France) in some shirts in preparation for another attempt to assassinate the Fuehrer. He placed the package in his briefcase and then set out by car for Rangsdorf Airfield, en route to Führerhauptquartier in the East Prussian woods at Rastenburg.

For Stauffenberg, it was an ideal opportunity. All the Nazi hierarchs would be at their headquarters near the Wolfsschanze (the Wolves' Lair), on hand for a meeting between Hitler and Mussolini; only Goebbels would be in Berlin. The success of the *coup d'état* would hang upon the conspirators' ability—after Hitler was dead—to immure the Nazi high command in those thick woods far from Berlin during the first critical hours of the seizure of power; and, if everything went according to plan, it would be a relatively simple matter to prevent a counterrevolution simply by pulling the plugs on telephone, telegraph and wireless communications from the Wolfsschanze. Moreover, Hitler had moved to Rastenburg only six days before, all the communications posts there were not yet fully manned, and because the Red Army was only 100 miles away, some of the essential parts of the communications equipment had actually been dismantled ready for quick evacuation.

At about nine o'clock, Stauffenberg, who was accompanied by Lieutenant Colonel Werner von Haeften, his *aide-de-camp,* fellow conspirator and friend, boarded the special Ju-52 trimotor transport aircraft which had been provided by Eduard Wagner, the Quartermaster General of the army, to enable him to be independent of routine transportation and to get back to Berlin quickly after the assassination. Three hours later, the aircraft landed and Haeften ordered the pilot to be fueled and ready to return to Berlin at any time from noon onwards.

Stauffenberg and Haeften then left the airfield for the 10-mile drive to

the Wolfsschanze. They noticed that the security precautions, always careful, were today extremely thorough, although nobody actually searched
either of the two men, both of whom were carrying bombs. The care with
which papers and the car were searched led afterwards to the belief that the
SS may have got wind of the fact that an assassination attempt was imminent. Indeed, Schellenberg would later state that he had received "indirect
hints" of the plan. But if Rattenhuber, the chief of the SS bodyguard, had
any suspicions, he did not show them when Stauffenberg arrived at the gate
for entrance into the Fuehrer's personal compound. He asked Stauffenberg
only to hand over his pistol, probably influenced by the thought that a one-
eyed, one-armed man with three fingers would never be able to work a
pistol or a bomb with the speed and accuracy necessary to kill the Fuehrer
in a crowded room.

Stauffenberg interrupted his journey to the conference briefly at
"Anna," the code name for the army's headquarters at the Wolfsschanze,
to talk with Fellgiebel, the man who had the essential task of cutting the
Führerhauptquartier's communications after the bomb had exploded.
What they said is not known, but Fellgiebel knew precisely what he had to
do; indeed, he had planned the isolation action. With the help of his *aide-
de-camp,* Colonel Arntz, he was to cut the five communications centers at
Rastenburg, including those of the Fuehrer, the SS and Leopold (the party
communications center). The other two would be cut by the SS itself as the
result of instructions Fellgiebel would give after the attack.

Stauffenberg then called on Keitel to present a résumé of what he
intended to report to the Fuehrer. Keitel ordered Stauffenberg to be brief as
Mussolini was expected at the Wolfsschanze later that afternoon. Then,
just before 12:30 P.M. Keitel and Stauffenberg, accompanied by two other
officers, left for the map room where the conference was to be held. On the
way, Stauffenberg asked Keitel to excuse him for a moment, remarking that
he had forgotten to pick up his cap and belt. Keitel assented and Stauffenberg went into the anteroom of Keitel's suite, opened his briefcase and,
with an instrument rather like a pair of sugar tongs, squeezed and broke
the glass capsule in the fuse. At that moment the bomb was primed as a
chemical began to eat away noiselessly at the wire which restrained the
detonator. Keitel, irritated that Stauffenberg was taking so long, called to
him to hurry up. Stauffenberg emerged almost immediately and first Keitel
and then his adjutant suggested they might carry Stauffenberg's briefcase.
Stauffenberg declined with a murmur of thanks.

They entered the map room, another of those anonymous buildings at
the Wolfsschanze which caused Jodl to describe life there as a "cross
between a cloister and a concentration camp." Located in the gloomy
twilight of the forest, the map room adjoined Hitler's private quarters.
Normally, the conference would have been held in one of the concrete-

lined bunkers. But today, because of the chaos caused by preparations for an evacuation, it was to be held above ground in a large wooden hut built upon concrete and stone pillars and roofed with tarred felt. The hut had three windows, and was furnished with two small tables at either end of a large, heavily built map table covered with situation maps.

Keitel and Stauffenberg entered the room at approximately 12:40 P.M. About a score of people were present, but Himmler, Goering and Ribbentrop were not there. General Adolf Heusinger, deputy Chief of the General Staff, was reporting on the situation in the East, while Hitler, his back to the door, followed the briefing on the situation maps. He was wearing his usual grey tunic and black trousers. Keitel interrupted the briefing to present Stauffenberg. Hitler looked up somewhat sharply, cast his gaze over Stauffenberg's black eye patch and his mutilations, and said he would take his report next. Keitel moved to Hitler's side while Stauffenberg went to the corner of the table at Hitler's right. He placed the briefcase which contained the bomb on the floor close to Colonel Heinz Brandt, the man to whom Schlabrendorff had addressed the "Cointreau-bottle bomb" at Smolensk on March 13, 1943. Then he said: "I will leave this here for the moment. I have to make a telephone call." Brandt found the briefcase in his way and moved it so that it rested against the heavy, thick upright support of the table on the side farthest away from Hitler.

Stauffenberg left the hut, went to some turf at Bunker 88 about 100 yards away and lit a cigarette. Inside the hut, Heusinger was just finishing his gloomy report. Keitel looked up and said to General Walter Buhle: "Where's Stauffenberg?" Buhle went to look in the anteroom and then returned. "I can't find him," he said. "He went to make a telephone call." Keitel became irritated, for Heusinger was on the last part of his report:

> *Der Russe dreht mit starken Kräften westlich der Düna nach Norden ein. Seine Spitzen stehen bereits südwestlich Dünaburg. Wenn jetzt nicht endlich die Heeresgruppe vom Peipussee zurückgenommen wird, dann werden wir eine Katastrophe . . .*

At that moment—at the utterance of the word *"Katastrophe"*—the bomb exploded. Jodl said afterwards, "It was as if a great chandelier were coming down on your head." A thunderous bang shattered the central table, the roof fell in, the windows were blown out, and the room was filled with heavy smoke shot with orange flame. The explosion killed the official stenographer immediately, mortally wounded two generals and a colonel, seriously injured one general and one colonel, and inflicted lesser injuries on four more generals.

Stauffenberg, certain that he had killed the Fuehrer and anxious to get out of the Wolfsschanze before Rattenhuber sealed the place off, left immediately. He and Haeften were stopped at the last checkpoint by the SS guard, but Stauffenberg went to the telephone in the guardpost and got Rittmeister von Moellendorf, an officer of FHW and a fellow conspirator, on the line. Moellendorf ordered the guard to let Stauffenberg pass. He opened the heavy electrified gate and Stauffenberg swept through. Within twenty minutes he was airborne over the Masurian Lakes.

But Hitler had not been killed. The heavy upright support had deflected the blast away from him. His hair was set on fire, his right arm was paralyzed—temporarily—and both his eardrums were affected by the pressure waves. One of his trouser legs was blown off, and a weighty object had fallen across his back and buttocks. He was bruised, as he complained later, "like the backside of a baboon." Nevertheless, he behaved very calmly as he was led away from the ruin by Keitel, his right arm hanging slack at his side, his hair singed, and a livid cut across the sallow skin of his face.

Even with Hitler still alive, all was not lost. If Fellgiebel cut the communications as planned, the *coup d'état* could continue with every promise of success. This Fellgiebel proceeded to do. Almost immediately after the explosion, he ordered Arntz to see to it that all communications between Rastenburg and the outside world were cut while he found out what had happened. Arntz complied; both Anna and Leopold were shut down and the switchboards were manned, as the emergency contingency plan required, by officers of the Führerhauptquartier signals regiment. They were under orders not to complete any circuits without Fellgiebel's permission. But then, having cut two of the five communications centers, Fellgiebel's nerve failed him when he looked out of the window and saw the procession of blackened men—Hitler included—walking away from the blasted hut. He did not proceed with his plans to isolate the remaining centers, presumably because by doing so he would have implicated himself. Neither did he report to Beck or Olbricht in Berlin the outcome of the explosion, as he had agreed to do. Keitel came over to Fellgiebel's hut and told the signalmaster to resume communications; and this he did. With that action the plot began to collapse. Knowing that his part in the conspiracy would come to light, Fellgiebel declared to Arntz: "I am not going to shoot myself. One should not make these creatures think that one is afraid of them. I am going to play this game to the end, knowing that Hitler will not enjoy his triumph for long." Then, according to Arntz, they sat down together and talked at length of the immortality of the soul. Fellgiebel was arrested that same night on Keitel's orders and was subsequently hanged.

As for Hitler, he recovered with extraordinary rapidity and went to the Wolfsschanze railroad station to meet Mussolini. Surrounded by bodyguards and wearing a heavy black cloak to conceal his right arm, which was in a sling, he was in a strange, almost hysterical mood when he greeted the Italian dictator. They shook hands and embraced, and then Hitler told

Il Duce what had happened. "Duce, an infernal machine has just been let off at me," he said. The chauffeur drove them through the tall pines to the Wolfsschanze and they went straight to the wreckage of the hut. There, Hitler, amid the rubble, said to a horrified Mussolini:

> I was standing here by this table; the bomb went off just in front of my feet. . . . Look at my uniform! Look at my burns! When I reflect on all this, . . . it is obvious that nothing is going to happen to me; undoubtedly it is my fate to continue on my way and bring my task to completion. . . . What happened here today is the climax! And having now escaped death in such an extraordinary manner, I am more than ever convinced that the great cause I serve will be brought through its present perils and that everything can be brought to a good end.

Hitler, hitherto so calm, now began to speak like a prophet. He assured Mussolini of the New Roman Empire and that, the disasters of the hour notwithstanding, the Reich would live for a thousand years. Il Duce responded fervently:

> . . . you are right, Fuehrer. . . . heaven has held its protective hand over you. . . . After the miracle that has occurred here in this room today it is inconceivable that our cause should suffer from misfortune.

The two dictators then left the scene; and Hitler, who thought at first that the bomb had been dropped from an airplane or thrown at him through a window, learned that Stauffenberg had been responsible. When he also learned that the Valkyrie order had been issued by the Home Army and that war district commanders inside and outside the Reich had begun to secure the administrative and communications centers under their control, the Fuehrer realized that the attempt on his life was not an isolated incident but part of a carefully prepared *coup d'état.* Furious, he spoke again and again of the treachery of his generals and the perfidy of the British secret service. Convinced that the British were involved in the plot, Hitler ordered as retaliation a maximum V1 strike against London to begin that very night. He demanded "continuous fire at maximum tempo with an 'unrestricted expenditure of ammunition,'" and his orders were obeyed. One hundred and ninety-three rounds were catapulted during the night of July 20/21—almost twice the usual rate of fire; and a further two hundred rounds were launched the following night in the heaviest attack so far in the V1 campaign. (One missile exploded near Brooke's London home as the field marshal lay asleep; he was not harmed but the building was rocked to its foundations.) In spite of his desire for revenge, Hitler was mistaken. The British were not directly involved in the *coup d'état;* at most, they had merely encouraged the conspirators to act, possibly in coincidence with the culmination of Fortitude and the Cobra offensive. Nevertheless,

Hitler would claim that he had evidence that Count Helldorf, the police chief of Berlin, had been in league with MI-6; and he would be even more certain of British involvement when he learned that the bomb was of British manufacture.

While every one of the men in the hut had been injured by the explosion, the Nazi high command reacted with speed and efficiency to restore order and calm. Goering, Ribbentrop, Doenitz and Himmler, who were in their headquarters or personal trains nearby when the bomb went off, had rushed to their Fuehrer's side, and Hitler ordered Himmler to Berlin immediately to suppress the revolt and restore Nazi authority in the capital. Then a doctor came to examine his injuries and found that Hitler's back, buttocks and legs were peppered with wood splinters, he had slight flashburns about the face and hands, his hair and eyebrows had been singed, and his eardrums had been slightly damaged. The doctor would later report that the Fuehrer was unable to hear higher harmonics such as those in the prelude to *Lohengrin*. But oddly, the shock of the explosion had cured, although only temporarily, the palsy which afflicted his right hand and arm. Hitler said ruefully to the doctor that, while he was delighted to be rid of the affliction, "the treatment was not one that he could recommend"—a remark that showed he was a good deal less affected by the incident than his enemies would have wished. But Hitler's composure did not last long; it soon became evident that he had been badly shaken by the blast, both physically and psychologically. Eugen Dollmann, Hitler's personal representative at Mussolini's court—and the SS general who would later betray him and start the negotiations with Dulles for the surrender of the German army in Italy—would describe the Fuehrer's behavior that afternoon:

> At five o'clock there was a big tea party; it was amazingly interesting, all of them were there, in the Führer's GHQ, and over tea they all began arguing and shouting at one another, each one putting the blame on the other because the war had not yet been won! Ribbentrop raved against the generals, because they had betrayed us to England, and the generals raved in their turn against Ribbentrop and Doenitz. The Führer kept pretty quiet the whole time, and Mussolini was very reserved too . . . all of a sudden someone happened to mention the 30th of June 1934 [the "Night of the Long Knives"]. The Führer leapt up in a fit of frenzy, with foam on his lips, and yelled out that he would be revenged on all traitors, that Providence had just shown him once more that he had been chosen to make world history, and shouted about terrible punishments for (the) women and children [of the conspirators]. . . . He shouted about an eye for an eye and a tooth for a tooth for everyone who dared to set himself against divine Providence. It was awful, and it went on for half an hour! I thought to myself, the man must be mad. I don't know why I didn't go over to the Allies there and then. . . . Meanwhile more tea was served by the footmen in

white (when) a telephone call came through from Berlin to say that order had not yet been restored there. The Führer answered the call, and started yelling again, gave full powers for shooting anyone they liked. . . . Then came the lovely bit: "I'm beginning to doubt if the German people is worthy of my great ideas." At that of course there was a tremendous to-do. They all wanted to convince the Führer of their loyalty. Doenitz and Göring came out with all they had done, Doenitz told him about the blue-eyed boys in blue—damned rubbish—and Göring started having a row with Ribbentrop, and Ribbentrop shouted at him: "I am still the Foreign Minister, and my name is *von* Ribbentrop!" Göring made a pass at him with his [Reichsmarschall's] baton. I'll never forget that scene. The Führer was in a very peculiar state at that time. It was the time when his right arm began to develop a tremor. He sat there . . . eating his coloured pastilles . . . and then suddenly he'd break out like a wild animal, and wanted to get at everyone, women and children too, into the concentration camp with the lot of them, he was the one Providence had chosen, and so on.

In Berlin, at about noon, the leaders of the Schwarze Kapelle gathered at the headquarters of the Home Army on the Bendlerstrasse, prepared to issue the Valkyrie orders as soon as General Olbricht, the deputy C-in-C of the Home Army, received a telephone message from Fellgiebel telling him that the Fuehrer was dead. At the same time General von Haase, the Commandant of Greater Berlin, gave his garrison troops, which included some of the best infantry and armored units in the army, guarded preparatory orders to ensure that they were kept in their barracks ready for deployment at a moment's notice. Beck arrived and John, who was also present, would note that he was "still suffering from the consequences of a dangerous stomach operation, was then 64 years old, and looked in his brownish lounge suit more like a kind old gentleman making a social call than the man to replace Hitler as Head of the German Reich." Witzleben, who would be designated C-in-C of the Wehrmacht, entered the conspirators' room, erect, impressive, hawklike, in the full uniform and medals of a Field Marshal. Hoepner, the panzer general, was there, too, in full uniform—which he had been forbidden by Hitler to wear again—to give the orders to the Panzerarmee.

The atmosphere was extremely tense as the conspirators awaited the call, and, John would record: "The tension grew as the hands of their watches advanced from hour to hour. But the expected telephone call from General Fellgiebel did not come." One P.M., 2 P.M., 3 P.M.—the hours passed without word from Rastenburg. Then, between 3:30 and 3:45 P.M., Haeften called from Rangsdorf Airfield where he had just landed with Stauffenberg. With annoyance he demanded to know why no car had been sent to meet them. Colonel Mertz von Quirnheim, Olbricht's Chief of Staff, the plotter who took the call, asked what had happened at Rastenburg.

Was Hitler alive or dead? Haeften replied that the attack had taken place and that Hitler was dead. With that information—at about four o'clock—Olbricht issued the Valkyrie orders to all commands. In Berlin, Haase's troops prepared to march upon the government quarter, and the commanding generals of every war district in Germany and the empire were ordered to secure their headquarters and cities against "an SS revolt." The revolution had begun.

Olbricht's next move was to try to bring Fromm, his superior as the C-in-C of the Home Army, into line. Fromm had dallied with the conspiracy, and with his outright support, the plotters might obtain the services of over 3 million men in Germany who were in uniform—men on leave, garrison troops, anti-aircraft gunners, naval and air personnel, and the like. Olbricht went to Fromm's office, informed him that the Fuehrer had been murdered at Rastenburg by the SS, and suggested that he put Valkyrie into effect "in order to safeguard law and order which in view of Hitler's sudden death might be disturbed by an uprising of radical elements, particularly from among foreign workers." But Fromm was not to be rushed. He stated that as C-in-C of the Home Army he could "initiate such weighty measures only when he had assured himself personally that Hitler was, in fact, dead."

Olbricht, believing that the line to Rastenburg had been cut, suggested that Fromm ring Keitel. This Fromm did, and to Olbricht's surprise got Keitel on the line. Fromm asked him what was happening at Rastenburg as the wildest rumors were circulating in Berlin that Hitler had been killed. Keitel replied: "That is all rubbish. An attempt was made upon the Führer, but it failed. He has merely been slightly injured. He is now with the *Duce*." And, Keitel asked ominously, where was Fromm's Chief of Staff, Stauffenberg? After a few minutes of discussion, Fromm replaced the telephone and gave a direct order that Valkyrie was not to be put into effect. Incredulous at the news that Hitler was still alive, Olbricht went into his own office and found that Valkyrie orders had already gone out by teleprinter.

Just before five o'clock, Stauffenberg arrived with Haeften from Rangsdorf and was greeted by Beck. Was Hitler alive or dead? Stauffenberg, sweating heavily in the heat inside the headquarters, replied: "I saw it myself. I was standing with Fellgiebel at Bunker 88 when the explosion occurred. It was as though a fifteen centimetre shell had hit the *Barracke!* It is impossible that anyone could have survived." Olbricht then told Stauffenberg of Fromm's conversation with Keitel, and Stauffenberg went to Fromm's office. Hitler was undoubtedly dead, he announced, but Fromm countered with Keitel's report. Thereupon Stauffenberg declared coldly: "Field Marshal Keitel is lying as usual. Hitler is dead." At that moment Olbricht broke in to say that "Under these circumstances we have given the order for the proclamation of a State of Emergency to the (war district) commanders." Fromm, almost speechless with rage, leaped to his feet and roared: "What does it mean: WE? This is insubordination. Who has given such an order?" Olbricht replied that Quirnheim, his Chief of Staff, had issued the order. Fromm summoned Quirnheim to his office and declared that he was under arrest.

At that point Stauffenberg told the astounded Fromm: "Herr General-oberst, the Führer is dead. I myself ignited the bomb. No one escaped alive." Fromm gained his composure and replied: ". . . the attempt has failed. You must shoot yourself." Stauffenberg said: "I shall do nothing of the kind." Olbricht now spoke. "Herr Generaloberst, this is the last chance to take action to save our country from total ruin. If we don't strike now, all will be lost." Fromm, who had heard enough of treason for one day, glowered at Olbricht. "Are you involved in this affair?" he demanded to know. Olbricht said that he was. Fromm then declared: "You must all consider yourselves under arrest." At this, Olbricht dropped all pretenses and announced: "That is where you are mistaken, Herr Generaloberst. We, in fact, arrest you." Fromm went for his pistol and, as John recorded, "a regular rough and tumble ensued." Fromm was overpowered and, exhausted, surrendered himself and his pistol, which he had tried to use. Olbricht then declared him to be their prisoner and told him to remain quietly in the room next door. An armed officer was placed on the door, but inexplicably nobody thought to lock it.

It was about 5:30 P.M. when Stauffenberg, Olbricht and Quirnheim left Fromm to continue with the Valkyrie operations. Witzleben appointed Hoepner to replace Fromm; and for a time it seemed that the coup might succeed, especially when the Munich war district commander reported that he had the city under Valkyrie control. But in Berlin, in the hours ahead, the revolution would degenerate into an artless, inefficient mess that could have only one outcome—the firing squad and the hangman. One fact remained, however; at this critical moment in European history, the Schwarze Kapelle's two principal contacts with the Allied Supreme Command—Gisevius and John—were present as witnesses to what became the final spasms of morality and conscience of the Third Reich. John had arrived from Madrid the day before, by air, alerted to the imminence of the assassination by a code word in a letter from his brother. If the attack was successful, he had made arrangements in Madrid which would enable Hansen, the chief of Amt Mil, to get through to Eisenhower.

Gisevius had returned to Berlin on July 13, even though he knew that Himmler had placed his name on the "wanted" list. But Gisevius had powerful police friends in the Nazi hierarchy. Count Helldorf, the police chief of Berlin, and Artur Nebe, the chief of the Reich detective service, were both friends and fellow conspirators. It was still possible to hide in

Berlin, even though agents and informers were everywhere; and Gisevius did so, in the basement of the home at 31 Nuernbergerstrasse of Theodor Struenck, a captain in the Abwehr and a close associate of Oster, who was under house arrest at Dresden throughout this period.

Gisevius spent the first part of July 20 in Helldorf's office overlooking the bomb wreckage of the Alexanderplatz; Helldorf was awaiting a telephone call from Olbricht to begin operations to arrest Kaltenbrunner, Schellenberg and the chief of the Gestapo, Mueller, and to seize control of civilian life in the capital. The afternoon was sweltering, and the heat when combined with the tension made ordinary human actions all but impossible. The hours ticked past in a rising tide of anxiety and nervousness, for everyone at police headquarters knew that if the coup succeeded they would be the new rulers of Germany; if it failed they would probably be corpses by midnight.

The telephone call from Olbricht to Helldorf came at about four o'clock; and shortly afterwards Helldorf rushed excitedly into the room where Gisevius and the other conspirators were waiting and cried: " 'It's starting!' Olbricht had just telephoned him to hold himself in readiness; there would be an important message within half an hour." Just before 4:30 P.M. Helldorf reappeared. He almost shouted: "Gentlemen, we're off! Olbricht has just given me an official order to report at the Bendlerstrasse: he says the Fuehrer is dead, a state of siege has been proclaimed, and he has urgent orders to deliver to me in the name of Colonel-General Fromm."

Helldorf and Gisevius then drove to the headquarters of the Home Army; but when they passed through the guard, Gisevius became alarmed. Why was the Bendlerblock not surrounded by tanks and loyal troops of the Grossdeutschland Guard—the unit responsible for keeping order in Berlin —as had been arranged? And if they were admitted so readily, how would the SS be received if it came? Uneasily, Helldorf and Gisevius mounted the great marble staircase where they were met by Olbricht and Stauffenberg, who had just come from the airport. Of that elegant, maimed figure, Gisevius would record:

> Stauffenberg's appearance was impressive. Tall and slender, he stood breathless and bathed in perspiration. Somehow the massiveness of the man had been reduced; he seemed more spiritualized, lighter. There was a smile of victory on his face; he radiated the triumph of a test successfully completed.

Then Beck, looking very ill and drawn, joined the group. As Gisevius went on: "We greeted one another with a silent, deeply felt clasp of the hands. What could be said at such a moment?" Olbricht announced that the Fuehrer had been the victim of assassination that afternoon, the Wehrmacht had taken over the direction of the government, and a state of siege was being proclaimed. The Berlin police were hereby subordinated to the army, which was now under the command of Witzleben, and Helldorf was to carry out all army orders. Helldorf made a short, sharp bow and started to leave the room. But as he was doing so, according to Gisevius, Beck said: "One moment, Olbricht. In all loyalty we must inform the chief of police that according to certain reports from headquarters Hitler may not be dead . . ." Olbricht did not let him finish and cried: "Keitel is lying! Keitel is lying!" Stauffenberg "laughed triumphantly . . . and Helldorf, (Count) Bismarck [the deputy chief of police, who was also present] and I looked at one another in utter consternation. All at once the fiction was being torn to shreds. Suddenly we were confronted with the brutal reality of the *Putsch.*" It was Beck who now spoke. The revolution must go forward, he declared, adding: "It doesn't matter whether Keitel is lying. What is important is that Helldorf must know what the other side has asserted about the failure of the assassination. . . ." He asked that all present maintain their solidarity.

John was sitting on the stairs during this meeting, eating a plate of sausage salad, and he would report that Count Schwerin (a relative of the man whom Canaris had sent to London to see Menzies in 1939 in a last attempt to avoid war) came up and said, "We shall need every man we can get tonight." John asked when he should be able to speak to Beck or Olbricht about the memorandum to be laid before Eisenhower, and Schwerin replied: "Out of the question—useless now—wait a bit!" John insisted that Hansen and he should leave for Madrid the moment the position was clear.

The position was not clear, and at that point the revolt received another body blow. The task of General Fritz Thiele, the chief of signals at the Bendlerblock, was to ensure that only the Schwarze Kapelle's signals traffic was sent and received. But when he got no call from Fellgiebel, he telephoned Rastenburg and spoke to Arntz. Arntz reported that there had been an explosion and casualties, but Hitler was alive. Thereupon, sure that he would be among the first to be arrested and executed, Thiele tried to reinsure himself. He called his watchmasters together and, according to one who was there, gave "a spirited speech in which he pointed out how reprehensible the attempt had been, demanded loyalty to the Führer and criticised the plotters most severely." His staff interpreted his statement literally—and hurried away to cut the Schwarze Kapelle's communications. The Valkyrie orders had already gone out and Witzleben's proclamation to the Wehrmacht had been transmitted. But from about 6 P.M. on, while the plotters were given the impression that their traffic was being sent out under the highest priority to all parts of the German Empire, it was, in fact, piling up in out trays and baskets "for enciphering." The Schwarze Kapelle was, without its knowledge, effectively quarantined.

Yet the revolt might still succeed—or at least prosper—if the troops obeyed their Valkyrie orders. Goebbels, the Reichsminister for Propaganda and the only Nazi leader in Berlin that day, was at his office near the Brandenburg Gate when he saw from his window—at about six o'clock— that troops fully equipped for combat had surrounded the building and were establishing machine-gun posts and roadblocks. Goebbels knew what was afoot; he had been told of the events at Rastenburg in a telephone call from Hitler. After taking a packet of cyanide pills from his desk drawer— "just in case"—he ordered one of his assistants to go into the street and establish what the soldiers proposed. The assistant returned to report that the troops had been told that the SS had assassinated Hitler, that the army was forming a provisional government, and that their orders were to seize Radio Berlin and the Propaganda Ministry and place Goebbels in protective custody.

Albert Speer, who was with Goebbels, would record the subsequent actions of the cunning Reichsminister. Goebbels learned that the troops were under the command of Major Adolf Remer, an officer known to be ardently *führertreu* who was merely carrying out his orders in obedience to Valkyrie—no more. Goebbels sent his assistant back into the street with an invitation. Would Remer kindly come to his office to clarify the situation? The Reichsminister was confused and anxious to avoid any bloodshed. Speer described the scene when Remer came into the office, his pistol holster unfastened:

> Goebbels seemed controlled, but nervous. He seemed to sense that everything hung on this, the fate of the uprising, and thus his own fate as well. . . . First, Goebbels reminded the major of his oath to the Fuehrer. Remer replied by vowing his loyalty to Hitler and the party. But, he added, he must obey the orders of his commander. . . . Goebbels retorted with the ringing words: "The Fuehrer is alive!" Seeing that Remer was at first taken aback and then became obviously unsure of himself, Goebbels added at once: "He's alive. I spoke to him a few minutes ago. An ambitious little clique of generals has begun this military putsch. A filthy trick. The filthiest trick in history."
>
> The news that Hitler was still living was evidently an enormous relief to this perplexed young man, recipient of an incomprehensible order to cordon off the government quarter. Happy, but still incredulous, Remer stared at all of us.

Goebbels had won the first hand, and, using his mesmeric gifts, he proceeded, according to Speer, to win Remer over completely.

> Goebbels now pointed out to Remer that this was an historic hour, that a tremendous responsibility before history rested on his shoulders. Rarely had destiny afforded a single man such a chance. . . . Now the Propaganda Minister played his highest card: "I am going to talk to the Fuehrer now, and you can speak to him too. The Fuehrer can give you orders that rescind

your general's orders, can't he?" . . . Within seconds Hitler was on the phone.

Goebbels spoke to Hitler and then handed the receiver to Remer. At the precise moment that the army was occupying the government quarter of Berlin, Remer, snapping to rigid attention, took the instrument. The only hope left for the conspirators in Berlin was that Remer might conclude that the voice on the other end of the line was an impostor, and decide to carry out his orders. But as chance would have it, while thousands of majors had never exchanged a word with Hitler, Remer had met the Fuehrer; only a few weeks before he had received from Hitler personally the oak leaf cluster to his Knight's Cross of the Iron Cross. The voice cried down the line from Rastenburg: "Do you recognize me, Major Remer? Do you recognize my voice?" Remer, still standing very rigidly to attention, replied: *"Jawohl, mein Fuehrer!"* Those three words sealed the fate of the conspiracy; Remer saluted Goebbels and Speer—the latter had taken no part in dissuading him from carrying out his orders—and left the office. Obedient to the Fuehrer's command, Remer instructed his company commanders to keep the troops in their places, but to secure the government quarter *against* the conspirators. Such were the consequences of the *Fahneneid,* the strength of the Nazi faith, the belief of the ordinary German officer that an order must be obeyed without question, the magic of Hitler.

By 7 P.M., the headquarters of the Home Army was practically surrounded by Remer's men. But believing that his signals were still being transmitted to all parts of the German Empire—and that he was being obeyed—Stauffenberg continued to issue orders; and John would recall that ". . . from the telephone conversations which I overheard it seemed that everything was going forward somehow." In reality, except for a few telephone lines, the conspirators were cut off from the outside world; and when Berlin radio announced that the attempt on Hitler's life had failed, it was clear that the Nazis had managed to frustrate the Valkyrie orders and still controlled the means of public communication. The revolt in Berlin was beginning to collapse, but there was still a chance that it might succeed in the West. General Stuelpnagel had called from Paris with the most encouraging news of the day; he had, he reported, ordered the arrest of all SS officers in the West and, subject to Beck's authority, they would be executed the following morning.

Everything now depended upon Marshal von Kluge. Would he or would he not support the coup? Beck called La Roche Guyon, and when Kluge, who had been appointed C-in-C of Army Group B as well as Supreme Commander in the West after Rommel's wounding, came to the phone, he explained to him in a quiet, firm voice what the situation was. Then he said: "Kluge, I now ask you clearly: Do you approve of this action of ours and do you place yourself under my orders?" Gisevius was listening on a handset attached to Beck's telephone, and he recorded: "Kluge stammered a few phrases that were apparently the outburst of a tormented soul. It was impossible to make anything of them; yes was no and no was yes." Then Beck demanded: "Kluge, in order to remove the slightest doubt, I want to remind you of our last conversations and agreements. I ask again: Do you place yourself unconditionally under my orders?" Gisevius recounted: "Kluge remembered all the conversations, but . . . he would have to confer with his staff. He would call back in half an hour." "Kluge!" Beck exclaimed as he replaced the receiver. "There you have him!"

Nightfall had come and Berlin was in total darkness, except for some searchlights sweeping the skies. Goebbels had obtained Hitler's approval to order Remer's troops to invade the Bendlerblock and arrest the conspirators. But the situation was still confused; no one was sure who was in control of the government quarter. Against this background of doubt, a battalion of army panzers arrived at SS headquarters on the Fehrbellinerstrasse and swung its 75-mm guns almost into the windows and doors of the great, gray building. Obedient to their Valkyrie orders, the men were ready to fire upon anyone who tried to stop them from occupying the building. But then someone intervened to countermand those orders. An officer of high rank rushed up and declared:

> You're crazy. The Führer is alive. The attempt has failed. Everything has been betrayed. There's no sense in carrying on! I can give you only one piece of advice. Go back home! You can't save anything now! You can only lose your head here!

A doctor with the panzers would later testify that the officer was General Heinz Guderian, the Inspector General of Armored Forces. Guderian himself would declare that he was nowhere near SS headquarters at that hour; he was returning to his home near Deipenhof, having been out walking his dogs. Whatever the truth, the next day Guderian was appointed Chief of the General Staff in place of Zeitzler, whom Hitler had dismissed on the spot for suspected complicity in the coup. And whoever gave the panzers the order to withdraw, it was obeyed. Had they attacked SS headquarters, it would have drawn the army, including Remer's unit, into strife with the SS, and the conspirators might have had a chance to regroup and reorganize. But they did not. The last hope of the conspiracy had been extinguished.

Speer, having heard of the impending attack on the Bendlerblock, and fearing bloodshed, drove there to see if he might act as an intermediary. "In totally blacked-out Berlin," he would write, "the Bendlerstrasse headquarters was illuminated by searchlights—an unreal and ghostly scene." It "seemed as theatrical as a movie backdrop brightly lit inside a dark studio." Troops had now sealed the area off completely; their arms were drawn and loaded and they expected a gunfight. Kaltenbrunner (Heydrich's successor) and Otto Skorzeny (the Nazi commando leader) had charge of the attack operations. Speer found them standing under the trees across the road from the Bendlerblock. They "looked like phantoms and behaved as such," Speer would write. "Everything seemed muted; even the conversation was conducted in lowered voices, as at a funeral."

Inside the great building, the last drama was being enacted. Between 10 and 11 P.M., a group of officers on Fromm's staff who had remained loyal to Hitler moved against Stauffenberg. They entered his office with pistols drawn, overpowered Olbricht and wounded Stauffenberg in the back as he tried to get away through the door into an adjoining office. Fromm succeeded in overpowering the officer guarding his door and took command. All the conspirators were arrested, and at precisely the same time, troops entered the building from the street. There was no resistance; many of the conspirators who remained at large in the building had forgotten even to bring their pistols with them.

Beck was tending the wounded Stauffenberg when Fromm entered the room. According to Hoepner's testimony to the Gestapo, this conversation ensued:

Beck: I have a pistol here, but I should like to keep it for my private use.
Fromm: Very well, do so. But at once.
Beck: At this moment I am thinking of earlier days.
Fromm: We do not wish to go into that now. Will you kindly go ahead!

Beck said a few more words, put the gun to his head, and fired. The bullet grazed the top of his head, and Beck, reeling, cried: "Did it fire properly?"

"Help the old fellow!" Fromm said to two officers who were standing near Beck. "Take away his gun!"

Beck: No! No! I want to keep it!
Fromm: Take the gun away from him; he hasn't the strength.

While the two officers busied themselves with Beck, Fromm turned to Olbricht, Stauffenberg, Quirnheim and Haeften, and declared: "And you, gentlemen, if there is anything you want to put in writing, you still have a few moments." He left the room, returned five minutes later and said:

Are you finished gentlemen? Please hurry, so that it will not be too hard for the others. Now, then, in the name of the Führer a court-martial, called by myself, has taken place. The court-martial has condemned four men to death: Colonel of the General Staff Mörtz von Quirnheim, General of Infantry Olbricht, this colonel whose name I will no longer mention [Stauffenberg] and this lieutenant [Haeften].

Fromm spoke to a lieutenant at his side: "Take a few men and execute this sentence downstairs in the yard at once!" The four men were led away. Then Fromm turned to Beck and demanded: "Well, what about it?"

Beck, dazed, managed to answer: "Give me another pistol." One of the men gave him a gun and Fromm stated: "You have time for a second shot!"

Beck put the pistol to his head, fired, and again failed to kill himself. It was said that Fromm then declared to a sergeant in the room, "Give the old man a hand," and that the sergeant executed Beck with a shot through the temple. Whatever the case, there was a shot and Beck was dead. Stauffenberg, Olbricht and their comrades were taken to the cobbled yard below; and there, illuminated by the headlamps of an army truck, they faced a firing squad. In the instant before the volley, Stauffenberg was heard to cry: "Long live the eternal Germany!" Shots rang out and the four men fell dead. Later that night, their corpses, along with that of Beck, were thrown on the back of a truck. They would have no known grave. It was an inglorious end to a brave conception.

Fromm, ordered by Kaltenbrunner not to shoot any more of the conspirators, descended to the street. Speer saw "a massive shadow (appear) against the brightly illuminated background of the Bendlerstrasse. In full uniform, all alone, Fromm approached us with leaden steps. . . . 'The putsch is finished,' he began, controlling himself with stern effort. 'I have just issued the necessary commands [to cancel Valkyrie]. . . . General Olbricht and my chief of staff, Colonel Stauffenberg, are no longer living." Twenty minutes later, after a muffled conversation with Kaltenbrunner, Fromm was himself placed under "protective custody." In summarily executing the leaders of the Schwarze Kapelle, he had attempted to eliminate the witnesses to his dalliance with treason. But Witzleben and Hoepner lived to indict Fromm for complicity in the plot. He was arrested, courtmartialed and executed.

The revolution in Berlin had failed; Himmler and the SS were again in firm control. In the weeks that followed, a manhunt of unprecedented thoroughness and ruthlessness embraced all of Germany as everyone involved in the plot was arrested, tried and executed. Remarkably, both John and Gisevius escaped. Although he was being hunted by the SD, John left the country routinely by air for Iberia, survived various plots by Schellenberg to capture or kill him, and was eventually exfiltrated by MI-6 to England where Menzies got him a job in the Political Warfare Executive. Gisevius, who managed to get away from the Bendlerblock before it was surrounded, went on the run and hid in various friends' homes. Dulles would hear nothing from him for many weeks until a message arrived by the hand of a courier who was able to get to Switzerland despite the Gestapo *ratissage*. The message read:

> . . . von Kluge holds the key to the situation. . . . (He) would be ready to cooperate with the western Allies in order to facilitate a more rapid occupation [by the Anglo-American armies] if a suitable officer . . . were sent him as an intermediary. . . . The Army is deeply outraged and shocked by the events which have occurred since 20th July . . . it is only necessary now for the Allies to strike hard and the entire German structure will collapse.

This was extraordinary intelligence, but it had traveled too slowly to be of use. It was, apparently, written by Gisevius on July 25, but it did not reach Dulles until August 17. It was given special dissemination at the White House as an L-Document the following day, but by that time a tumult had struck the front in France. Gisevius remained in hiding until he was finally able to escape to Switzerland, using Gestapo documents manufactured by the OSS and smuggled to him by one of Dulles's couriers. The OSS looked after its own.

Canaris also escaped the *ratissage*—at least for the moment. In fact, he seems to have been remote from the center of the 20th of July plot. He was at home in Berlin that day, and when he was told of the attack upon Hitler, he said, "Good heavens! Who did it? The Russians?" Later he drove out to Eiche, where his economic study group met, to approve a staff telegram of congratulations to the Fuehrer on his most felicitous escape.

Hitler's escape had, indeed, been felicitous, and in the collapse of the coup the Schwarze Kapelle had suffered its greatest, and final, misfortune. It was Goebbels who delivered the epitaph to the entire conspiracy: "If they hadn't been so clumsy! . . . What dolts! What childishness! When I think how I would have handled such a thing. . . . To hold so many trumps and botch it—what beginners!"

Goebbels was quite correct. These ranking members of the German General Staff, the military clique that had conquered almost all of Europe with ruthlessness and efficiency, had failed in the simple task of seizing control of a few square miles of their own capital. Yet the revolt in Berlin had come within an ace of success. It was a different story in France. There, the conspiracy failed not because of inefficiency, but because of the ambivalence of Field Marshal von Kluge.

Kluge spent the day of July 20 conferring with his army commanders, Eberbach and Hausser, and with the corps commanders involved in repulsing Goodwood. The meeting took place in the cool woods near the Panzer

Army headquarters; Kluge wanted no repetition of the Ultra incident of June 10 when Schweppenburg's headquarters had been wiped out. According to Wilhelm Ritter von Schramm, the German military historian: "None of those present knew anything about the events (at Rastenburg) and Berlin, or of the careful preparation (for the assassination of Hitler). . . . None had any direct connection with the conspirators. None the less, even under the comforting shelter of the trees, all had the feeling of oppression and foreboding. All felt the approach of defeat. . . ."

The German commanders could not conceal their pessimism. Eberbach spoke of having lost 40,000 men and receiving only 2300 replacements. Dietrich described his orders as "mad" and "impossible," and complained of the policies from Führerhauptquartier that were causing a "mad waste of men." All present agreed that it was unlikely that the Allies would make a second landing in northeastern France; why then were three armies kept idle in other parts of France while the army group in Normandy was being "ripped in pieces like a rotten cloth"?

The conference droned on over the hood of Kluge's staff car, as did the drumfire, the sound of nemesis, from the direction of Caen. The generals agreed that the German armies must withdraw from France before they were finally destroyed. But Kluge said there could be no further retreat; the "line in the vicinity of Caen must be held at all costs." Then Kluge declared: "We will hold, and if nothing can be found to better our situation basically, then we'll die like men on the battlefield." With that, the conference ended. The generals returned to their troops and Kluge drove off to La Roche Guyon.

The severe thunderstorm of the afternoon was dying away when the field marshal arrived at the château at about six o'clock. He strode through the Hall of Arms to his study (Rommel's former office) to look at the day's message file before bathing and dining; and what he saw on his desk—a message stamped "Blitz Geheim"—was the most astounding signal of his thirty-four years as a soldier. Hitler had been assassinated and Beck declared acting Chancellor of Germany. Witzleben had issued a proclamation that he, Witzleben, had been entrusted with full powers as Commander-in-Chief of the Wehrmacht, and Kluge was ordered to eliminate the SS leadership in France.

Kluge had still not absorbed the full import of the message when Blumentritt, his Chief of Staff at St. Germain-en-Laye, was shown into the study. At that moment his telephone rang and Kluge was informed that General Fromm was on the line from the Bendlerstrasse. It was not Fromm; it was the call from Beck, who explained the situation in Berlin and asked Kluge to support the revolt and put himself under his command.

The revolt of July 20 was quite possibly the first revolution in history to be orchestrated by telephone, an instrument which all German general officers had been taught to distrust. Kluge wavered for a moment; he did not want to commit himself in a call that was perhaps being monitored by the Gestapo. Then he took the receiver, listened and in response to Beck's plea for support he replied, according to the historian Ritter von Schramm's version of the call, "I must first consult with my people here. I shall ring you back in half an hour." Kluge would not ring back.

Then the telephone rang again. It was General von Falkenhausen. He, too, had just spoken to Beck and was calling Kluge to establish what he proposed to do. Again, Kluge refused to commit himself, and Falkenhausen rang off, promising to keep in contact during the evening.

It was then that Kluge received the *Blitzfernschreiben,* a copy of Witzleben's proclamation as the new C-in-C of the Wehrmacht. It was the first official news he had received and its tone and authority had the effect of persuading him that Hitler was indeed dead and that he must join the conspiracy. Schramm recorded:

> Between 7:30 and eight o'clock Kluge was all for siding with the Berlin Resistance; he had as much as said so to Blumentritt. The obvious thing to do in the West was to try and get an armistice as Rommel had planned. But how? There was no long discussion.

Blumentritt would remember: "Kluge turned to me and said 'Blumentritt, an historic hour has come. First we must get on to Wachtel and get him to stop the V1 fire.' "

Kluge's decision to halt the V-weapons fire on London and southern England, which was reaching its most intensive stage, was the first political step of consequence he took that evening. He considered, evidently, that the cessation of the bombardment would be the olive branch to which the Allies would respond. Schramm wrote:

> . . . it was natural that Kluge should think of stopping the V-attack as the first thing to be done after Hitler's death. That would make it easier to negotiate with the Allies for a cessation of the air war, a cessation which would be the price asked for a voluntary evacuation of the occupied areas. Evacuation was the next stage; on that there was agreement.

Kluge's telephone rang yet again. It was Zimmermann from OB-West, and the message he read to Kluge shattered that moment of extraordinary relief and elation. Keitel at OKW had announced that Hitler was alive and almost uninjured after an assassination attempt and he directed all commanders to ignore any orders received from anyone but himself and Himmler. Kluge, Blumentritt remembered, looked thunderstruck as he replaced the receiver. He declared that if Keitel's message was true, there could be no thought of independent action aimed at an armistice.

Kluge turned to Blumentritt and Speidel and ordered: "Find out what is true and what is false. We must get at the facts first and until then let things stay as they are." Kluge left the room to bathe and change for dinner, and when he returned, Blumentritt was able to inform him that the Fuehrer was alive. Kluge announced that it had been a "bungled business" and poured himself a glass of sherry. He then declared to Blumentritt: "You know, or you strongly suspect, that I was in contact with 'these people.' I needn't tell you my reasons. But when I was, there was still hope. Today I am without hope, for hope is now without meaning."

Then Kluge walked toward the windows overlooking the Italian gardens and began to speak of his dalliance with treason:

> In the summer of '43 messengers from Beck and Witzleben came twice to me when I was in command of Army Group Centre at Smolensk. They tried to win me over to certain political plans. At first I spoke with them at length; the second time, I had my doubts. I broke off the conversation and asked them to leave me out of this highly dubious business. They went on to Guderian who had just been sacked. But he too turned a deaf ear. We should, of course, have reported it.

Two staff cars swept up the drive. In them were General Stuelpnagel; Colonel Eberhard Finkh, the quartermaster of the German army in the West; and Colonel Caesar von Hofacker, the principal link between the Berlin and Paris arms of the conspiracy. The three men had come from Paris, where Stuelpnagel, as Military Governor of France, had crossed his personal rubicon without hesitation. That afternoon, upon hearing of Hitler's death, he had ordered the immediate arrest of the senior officers of the SS and the SD. Having set the machinery in motion for the seizure of power in France—the first step toward an armistice with the Allies and the evacuation of German-occupied Europe—Stuelpnagel had come to the château to ensure Kluge's support.

Kluge received the three men immediately and informed them that he had heard news that the Fuehrer was not dead. The elegant Stuelpnagel seemed unfazed, and there and then Hofacker began to speak:

> Field Marshal, what has happened in Berlin is not decisive. Much more so are the decisions which will be taken in Paris. I appeal to you, for the sake of the future of Germany, to do what Field Marshal Rommel would have done, what he said he would do in the secret conference I had with him in this very room on July 9. Cut free from Hitler and yourself take over the task of liberation in the West. In Berlin power is in the hands of Colonel-General Beck, the future Head of the State; create the same *fait accompli* here in the West. The army and the nation will thank you. Put an end in the West to bloody murder; prevent a still more terrible end and avert the most terrible catastrophe in German history.

Kluge sat with an unmoved face throughout Hofacker's address. Then the field marshal rose suddenly and declared: "This is the very first I've heard about any such assassination attempt." Blumentritt's account of the events that evening follows:

> (Kluge) behaves as if he were very indignant about the whole thing. Silence. Stuelpnagel pales slightly and says: *"Herr Feldmarschall,* I thought you knew all about it." Kluge says "Good heavens, man, I had not the *slightest inkling,* otherwise I shouldn't have been out at the front. . . ."

Stuelpnagel was obviously stunned. Schramm recorded:

> (He) felt himself suffocating. He could not bear to be longer in this gloomy room. . . . He walked into the terrace garden. There were blooming the summer roses with their almost unearthly sweetness, perfuming the coming-on of night. Stuelpnagel walked past without noticing them. He was filled with one shattering thought; all was over . . . at this very moment the troops in Paris were arresting the SS and the Gestapo on . . . (his) orders.

Blumentritt's account continues:

> Then Stuelpnagel comes in from the balcony and you can see that he must have gone through a terrific mental upheaval. Then Kluge, the very figure of a country squire, says "Well Stuelpnagel, you'll stay and have a meal." We sit down to dinner—it must have been late, 9 o'clock at least. . . . During the meal Kluge talks like a book about some battle in the front line, drinks, raises his glass—"your health"—and behaves as though nothing were up. Stuelpnagel eats hardly anything and takes only a sip or two. All at once Stuelpnagel says: "But I've already taken steps. I've given the order to arrest the SD in Paris." Kluge jumps up from the table: "Heavens alive, man, you couldn't do that without my consent! Well, my dear Stuelpnagel, you'll have to save your own skin, then!" To me he said: "Ring up and see whether action has already been taken!"

Blumentritt returned from the telephone to report that the entire SS and SD hierarchy—including the Nazi ambassador Otto Abetz, and such dangerous individuals as Knochen, Boemelburg, Kieffer and Goetz—had all been arrested by picked troops of the army and were to be executed in the morning. Kluge wanted no share of the responsibility and declared: "My dear Stuelpnagel, I must ask you to give orders immediately that the SD are to be released. The best thing would be for you to get into civvies and disappear somewhere or other."

It was now nearly 11 P.M. Kluge walked with Stuelpnagel to the door of the château. "You must get back as quickly as you can to Paris and release the arrested men," he told Stuelpnagel. "The responsibility is wholly yours." Then Stuelpnagel rallied. He said: "We cannot withdraw now, Field-Marshal. Events have spoken for us." Hofacker said, "It is your honour that is at stake and the honour of the army and the fate of the nation is in your hands." Kluge replied: "It would be so if the swine were dead." But no, he could and would do nothing. He could not betray the *Fahneneid*. As the two men took formal leave of each other, Kluge advised Stuelpnagel to "Regard yourself as suspended from duty." Blumentritt, appalled that this instruction would mean Stuelpnagel's death warrant, whispered to Kluge: "We've got to help him." As Kluge and Steulpnagel went down the stone steps into the courtyard where the cars were, Kluge again advised the Military Governor of France to "Get into civilian clothes and disappear somewhere." Stuelpnagel saluted the Commander-in-Chief and was driven off into the night. They had not shaken hands.

Kluge walked back up the steps into the château, went to his study and wrote this signal:

> To the Führer and the Supreme Commander of the Armed Forces. Thanks to a merciful act of Providence, the infamous and murderous attempt against your life, My Führer, has miscarried. On behalf of the three branches of the Armed Forces entrusted to my command, I send you my congratulations and assure you, My Führer, of our unalterable loyalty, no matter what may befall us.

Then he penned an Order of the Day to the armies:

> The Führer lives! The war effort at home and the fighting at the front goes on. For us there will be no repetition of 1918, nor of the example of Italy! Long live the Führer!

He gave the order to an aide for immediate transmission, and, as a final gesture before retiring, picked up the telephone and ordered the operator to get him a *Blitz* call to Rastenburg. There he spoke to Jodl and reported Stuelpnagel's actions.

At about 0130, the field marshal slipped gratefully between the cool sheets of his bed. If he cared to, he could hear the rising fury of the guns in the distance.

The news that an attempt had been made on the life of Hitler reached Eisenhower in France where he was visiting the front. At daybreak on the 21st, Curtis was shaving in his tent after a long night's work on the order of battle estimates. He would recall:

> One of Eisenhower's aides rushed up the duckboarding as I was shaving and told me the old man wanted to see me right away. I knew from his attitude that something was up and I rushed off with the shaving soap still on my face, not even bothering to put a shirt on. Eisenhower was in the operations tent and he said to me: "Holy smoke, Curtis! There seems to be a revolt going on among the Krauts. What does it mean?" He seemed to have been taken by surprise, and I always wondered why. Dulles knew all about it, and

we got his warnings. I replied: "Sir, there have been rumors about this on and off for at least three weeks." Then I told him what I knew—stuff obtained mainly from Dulles—and he said: "Well, it looks good for Cobra!" He added a remark that I always remembered and thought important. "I wonder whether the Prime Minister knows about this."

Churchill had spent the evening of July 20 in the wardroom of the British cruiser *Enterprise,* lying off the beaches at Arromanches. The officers were singing songs and ended with "Rule Britannia." Although it is not clear whether he knew what had happened in Berlin at that hour, Churchill rose and recited one of the verses: "The nations not so blest as thee/Must in their turn to tyrants fall:/While thou shalt flourish great and free,/The dread and envy of them all."

Churchill certainly knew of the attentat on the morning of July 21, but Eisenhower made no formal pronouncements about the abortive revolt, nor did Roosevelt. And it was not until the 23rd, when Churchill was visiting a forward RAF base in Normandy, that he said anything publicly. Then, according to the *New York Times,* he remarked with "an acid grin" to a group of five hundred airmen gathered around him:

> There are grave signs of weakness in Germany. They are in a great turmoil inside. Opposite you is an enemy whose central power is crumbling. They missed the old [here Churchill used either the word "bugger" or "bastard," but the *Times* reported the word "bounder"]—but there's time yet. There is a very great disturbance in the German machine. Think how you would feel if there was a revolution at home and they were shooting at Cabinet Ministers. . . . Britain stands today as high as she ever stood in a thousand years.

Later, Churchill would admit that he had been wrong about the Schwarze Kapelle—the only resistance movement in German-occupied Europe that had not received the active support and encouragement of the Allies. The attempted assassination and *coup d'état,* even though they had failed, were "exhilarating" to the Allied high command; for they signaled the beginning of the end of the Nazi stranglehold on Germany, and could only serve to benefit the Allies in the psychological, political and military arenas of the war. But there were those, Dulles among them, who saw in the failure of the plot a greater and more far-reaching failure. Wilhelm Hoegner, one of Dulles's agents in Bavaria, who spoke with Dulles and his assistant Gaevernitz on July 21, would remember: "I never saw them so completely downtrodden. They had always hoped that through a sudden downfall of Hitler, the war would be ended before the Soviet Russians entered Berlin. A quick peace agreement with a democratic German regime would have prevented that. But now all was lost; the continuation of the war would provide the Russians with a pathway to the Elbe in the heart of Europe. American policy had suffered a terrible defeat."

The Breakout

SIMPLE SOUNDS foretold the next Allied move in Normandy: the all-night rumble of tanks here, a fragment of intercepted radiotelephony there; an artillery barrage here, a mortar-stonking there. Jays and crows cawed and hopped from bough to bough, disturbed by troops creeping up to jump-off positions in copses. The clang of a cooking pot against a spade; the sizzle of a Very light flare, fired off as patrols made their way back to their lines before dawn; a cough, a grunt, a shout in the dawn twilight—all these and a thousand other signs were the harbingers of the great battle now to be fought.

Kluge, sensing that the decisive battle was in the wind, wrote to the Fuehrer on July 21:

> I can report that the front has held . . . as a result of the magnificent valor of the troops and the resolution of the commanders. . . . However, the moment is approaching when the front will break. . . . And when the enemy has erupted into open terrain . . . orderly and effective conduct of the battle will hardly be possible.

He signed and sealed the letter and—because it was so secret and sensitive—it was taken to Rastenburg by armed guard.

The document could not have arrived at a worse moment for Kluge. As Himmler hunted down the members of the Schwarze Kapelle—Canaris, Oster, Witzleben, Tresckow, Goerdeler, Fellgiebel, Roenne, Hansen, Helldorf, Gehre, Schlabrendorff, Hofacker, Stuelpnagel, Falkenhausen were all in jail or about to be arrested—Hitler learned that Kluge *and* Rommel had been involved in plots to kill him. The atmosphere at Führerhauptquartier became pregnant with the need for cleansing and revenge. Everywhere Hitler saw traitors, particularly in his signals, intelligence and supply services; everywhere he saw connections between "blueblooded German swine" and the "international aristocracy." Yet considering that he had almost been assassinated, Hitler was remarkably calm when he read Kluge's letter. For the moment, military realities dominated his thinking; on July 23 he ordered that plans be drawn up for the withdrawal of the German army from France, and that all Todt construction workers in the Pas de Calais begin to restore the Siegfried Line, the fortifications on Germany's western frontier. This latter order was quickly decrypted by Ultra and provided Montgomery and Bradley with their first clear intelligence about Hitler's predicament after July 20.

Calamity confronted the Fuehrer from all sides. Turkey broke off relations with Germany—at long last. Army Group South was surrounded in the Ukraine. There was—again at long last—a revolution in Rumania and Hitler lost the Rumanian oilfields. Bulgaria revolted a few hours later. Bodyguard's chickens had finally come home to roost. Yet still the Fuehrer was not ready to admit defeat. He directed that the entire resources of Greater Germany be fully, ruthlessly and immediately mobilized for the defense of the Reich, and took special measures to ensure the loyalty of the armed forces. He sent an order to all fronts announcing that everyone who gave up ground would be shot. Of propositions that he should negotiate with one side or the other, Hitler declared: "Anyone who speaks to me of peace without victory will lose his head, no matter who he is or what his position."

The Fuehrer gave Germany a choice: victory or, in the event of defeat, national suttee, with himself applying the torch. He believed, with even greater intensity, that only he could save the Reich, and his behavior grew increasingly disturbed. Guderian, the new Chief of the General Staff, would write:

> . . . the deep distrust (Hitler) already felt for mankind in general, and for General Staff Corps officers and generals in particular, now became profound hatred. A by-product of the sickness from which he suffered is that it imperceptibly destroys the powers of moral judgment; in his case what had been hardness became cruelty, while a tendency to bluff became plain dishonesty. He often lied without hesitation and assumed that others lied to him. He believed no one any more. It had already been difficult enough dealing with him; it now became a torture that grew steadily worse from month to month. He frequently lost all self-control and his language grew increasingly violent.

At this conclusive moment in the war, Hitler seemed close to madness. Thus, the failure of the assassination had served the Allied cause after all; and the Allies made no attempt to kill Hitler by aerial bombardment, as might have been quite easy. There was always the possibility that among the Nazis there would be a more formidable successor. As Churchill said, while Hitler remained in power, the Allies could not lose the war.

Guderian was only one of a wholesale replacement of "unreliable" officers by those who were *führertreu*. The events of July 20 and the following days shook the German command structure severely and its morale began to crack. Cadogan would record that on July 23 he authorized the dispatch of a British agent, Colonel X, to Holland where the German C-in-C, General der Infanterie Hans Reinhard, had told another British officer of his wish to consider surrender. It was the first positive overture from a German high commander since Arnim had surrendered in Tunisia in May 1943.

But what of the commanders and the troops who still held the line in Normandy? Would they collapse, as the Allies hoped they might? In fact, they would go on fighting with all their old tenacity. Zimmermann told his American interrogators after the war:

> And now came the psychologically baffling aspect. . . . The front kept right on fighting as though nothing had happened. . . . Why did not thousands and tens of thousands lay down their arms and end the war? The answer was simple. It was because in the high emotional tension of battle, in this physical and moral over-exertion, this murderous struggle, the individual was so completely and intensely pitched to the moment of combat, to the "you or me" of fighting, that any convulsions outside the focus of this tension, no matter how strong they might be, only touched him on the fringe of his consciousness. Figuratively speaking, the combat soldier was in another world. . . . They did not have the time nor were they in a mental state to concern themselves with matters beyond the perimeter of their struggle. They saw also with their own eyes that any further attempt at a change [of government in Germany] would let loose another St. Bartholomew's massacre. So the army silently went on doing its duty, though with the bitter subconscious knowledge that an unavoidable catastrophe was impending.

Zimmermann added as an afterthought: "But for the existence of unconditional surrender, we might well have folded up right there and then." That policy had not been modified, however, and so the Germans went on fighting hopelessly—and savagely.

Kluge's attention remained firmly fixed on the Caen front. He was convinced that Montgomery would strike there; and the Allies, aware of that belief through Ultra, did everything they could to encourage it. Staubwasser would report the presence of very strong naval forces between Le Havre and Cap d'Antifer, aerial reconnaissance activity between Le Tréport and Ostend, and a "marked increase in partisan activity—attacks and acts of sabotage in Belgium and border areas of northern France." Rosebud was at work. But if it now seemed unlikely that the Allies would attempt another land assault, Staubwasser warned that the German high command had to "reckon with Allied large-scale air landings." Where? All the evidence pointed to the Caen front.

Meanwhile, Bradley prepared to unleash Cobra on the St. Lô front. The offensive, which was originally to have begun on July 20, had been postponed because bad weather prevented the massive aerial bombardment necessary to cut a path through the German lines. Cobra was rescheduled to open at midday on July 24, but bad weather forced another cancellation. That morning, Air Chief Marshal Sir Trafford Leigh-Mallory, who was at Bradley's command post, saw that the weather would still prevent the precise bombing necessary if American troops were not to be hit. He ordered a postponement, but through a signals delay his order did not reach the bomber groups until it was too late to turn back the first wave of the aerial assault. Three hundred bombers dropped 550 tons of high explosive and 135 tons of fragmentation bombs, some of which fell upon the American 30th Infantry Division, killing 25 men and wounding 131.

Cobra was off to a bad start. The morale of the Americans was badly shaken; and worse, it seemed to Bradley that the accident would alert the Germans and that he would lose the surprise he had hoped for. The Germans did respond with a large volume of artillery fire on the three American assault divisions in the area; and Kluge said to Hausser, the commander of the 7th Army on the American front, "Without any doubt, there's something new in all this air activity. We have got to expect a heavy enemy offensive somewhere." But remarkably, he still looked for the attack on the British front, and made arrangements to be there on the 25th.

The dawn broke fair that day. General Fritz Bayerlein, the commander of the Panzer Lehr Division on the American front, noticed that the heavily wadded cloud of the day before was breaking up. But except for occasional small-arms fire, the front was quiet. It remained that way until about eleven o'clock, when his scouts began to report sounds like "an orchestra of bass viols tuning up." The Cobra air armada was approaching, and within ten minutes an infernal agitation had begun.

The area to be drenched was very small: about 7000 by 2500 yards of Norman earth, bounded by the little villages of Amigny–La Chapelle–Le Mesnil Eury. But into that area in the next hour or two the Americans poured 140,000 shells, while 1800 bombers dropped 3300 tons of bombs. They were followed by 380 medium bombers which dropped over 650 tons of high explosive and fragmentation bombs; and they, in turn, were followed by 550 fighter bombers which dropped more than 200 tons of bombs and hundreds of napalm canisters. The world seemed to shake. One account of the assault noted:

The bombardment transformed the main line of (German) resistance from a familiar pastoral *paysage* into a frightening landscape of the moon. Several hours after the bombing, the village priest of la Chapelle . . . walked through the fields and thought he was in a strange world.

A thousand *Feldgrau*—one-third of Bayerlein's fighting men—were killed; the blasts destroyed or overturned so many of his tanks that only a dozen or so were left operable. Three of the Panzer Lehr's battalion command posts were destroyed. A parachute regiment attached to the division virtually vanished. Bayerlein recorded that men went mad and "rushed dementedly round in the open until they were cut down by splinters." He was among the few divisional commanders to survive. "Housed in an old Norman château, with ten-foot walls," he reported, "we were rather better protected than the others." But even so "the ground shuddered," and "quick glimpses outside showed the area shrouded by a pall of dust, with fountains of earth spewing high in the air."

The attack was devastating, but the bombardment and the power punch on land that followed merely dented the German lines; and that same evening at his command post, Bradley declared sadly that even that dent had not been obtained without grievous cost. During the aerial assault the lead bombardier of one heavy formation had trouble with his bombsight, and misjudging the intended point of impact, he dropped his bombs and a great cloud of dirt and dust obscured the red markers laid by the artillery. The rest of the formation dropped their bombs on the lead aircraft's salvo, and the ordnance of thirty-five heavy and forty-two medium bombers fell upon the 30th Infantry Division. In the second disaster in two days, the bombs killed 111 and wounded 490 men of Old Hickory.

Among the casualties of the accidental bombing was General Lesley J. McNair, who had gone forward that day to the 30th Infantry's advanced positions to watch the bombardment and the assault. Whether McNair should have been in France at all would long be debated, for during the critical breakout operations it was imperative to maintain the Fortitude threat. Eisenhower, seeking to keep Fortitude alive, cabled Marshall for a replacement, and General John L. de Witt was selected. Mrs. McNair was told nothing beyond the fact of her husband's death, and the general was buried secretly in an apple orchard near Bradley's headquarters. All news was suppressed, correspondents were not told that the most senior American general ever to be killed in action had just died, and censors were given instructions to prevent any leakages. The LCS needed time to cover its tracks, and this was done by Brutus on July 26 with a telegram to his controller that read:

I have learned that General McNair (the commanding general of First United States Army Group) has been killed in Normandy. He had gone there to consult with General Montgomery and to inspect the German coastal defences. Here at FUSAG this loss is considered very serious. It is thought that a successor will be appointed immediately to command the FUSAG operations.

Cobra struck again in the dawn mist of July 26, while Montgomery intensified his efforts to distract Kluge's panzers, praying that they might be held just a little longer around Caen—a prayer that was answered. American armor, supported by one of the greatest artillery barrages in history, was committed to the Cobra attack, and for the next two days the entire front was engulfed in "the elemental mingling of earth, air, fire and water" of an enormous battle. The troops inched forward with no time to bivouac, no time to light fires; they ate cold beans and dozed where they collapsed when the sun went down.

The *Feldgrau* fought like demons, but the dent in their lines became a bulge and, finally, on the morning of the 28th, they had had enough. In single-file, dirty, weary, they began to fall back; and the *Panzerkampf-wagen,* covered with the branches of cider apple trees, rumbled south through the seafront villages of the western Cherbourg peninsula. The German commanders had decided to make a new line along the ridges of the Suisse-Normande at the base of the peninsula. The Americans arose that morning expecting another day of bloody fighting. Units of the 30th Infantry Division, the men who had been so badly punished by their own air force's bombs, moved out; an hour passed, two, three, and there was no sign of resistance. It seemed impossible, but the *Feldgrau* had gone; the hedgerows were empty. The German line had broken.

That day, the next and the next, Americans poured into the breach; a rivulet became a stream, the stream an olive-green tide in pursuit of the retreating Germans. Kluge could not stem the flood. He reported that the front was *"eine Riesensauerei"*—one hell of a mess. In reality, there was no front, no flank but the sea. Bradley's armor rocketed south with all the velocity of a hollow-charge shell, and the Allied air forces flew a larger number of missions than had ever been flown before. Kluge commanded the tatterdemalion ruins of an army that had once been the cocks of Europe. Gone were the precise formations, the battle flags, the polished boots and pressed field gray. The 7th Army was a rabble, and Hausser and his staff only narrowly escaped capture. But despite the speed and ferocity of the American advance, the German armor, paratroopers and panzer grenadiers got away.

It was the eve of Judgment Day for the Germans in the West; and Hitler, who was at last convinced that there would be no further Allied landings along the Channel coast, gave Kluge permission to begin removing some of the infantry divisions that garrisoned the Pas de Calais—but not all. The V1 launch sites must be protected just in case the Allies did attempt another landing. Nevertheless, this decision effectively marked the end of Fortitude, which would pass into history as perhaps the greatest deception of any war. Hitler also decided that OKW should establish a command post in Alsace-Lorraine whence he would go to direct the battle in the West personally. He would tell Kluge, he announced, "only enough of future plans for the Commander-in-Chief West to carry on immediate operations." The reason, he said, was because "the broad strategic plans of the Reich . . . would be known to the Allied powers almost as soon as the details reached Paris." Hitler still suspected that traitors in his signals and supply systems were responsible. He remained in complete ignorance of Ultra. The man who had proclaimed himself to be the greatest military strategist of all time had been outwitted by the modern refinements of two of the oldest tricks in the lexicon of war—deception and cryptanalysis.

Meanwhile, in Normandy, the British and Canadians continued to slug it out around Caen like refreshed pugilists who had been too long on the ropes; and the Americans were moving so fast that at times Bradley himself knew where the spearheads were only from air reconnaissance reports of villages bursting into the red, white and blue of the tricolor—a sign that the enemy had departed. But as yet the breakout had not become a breakthrough. That could not be claimed until Bradley's army had taken Avranches, the town of Jean No-Feet and the Salt Tax Revolution of the seventeenth century.

By dawn on July 31, all attention—German as well as Allied—was focused on Avranches, a hill resort of 7000 people overlooking Mont-St.-Michel, where there was a single stone bridge over the broad estuary of the See River. If the American armor was to get into Brittany without delay, and if the Germans were not to re-form and hold a new line along the river, that bridge had to be taken undamaged and immediately. It was. Tanks of the 4th Armored Division captured and secured Avranches and hurtled on along the coast road with its constant views of the strange conical ghost of Mont-St.-Michel hanging in the mist. They approached the second town of critical importance—Pontaubault and its old, thirteen-arch stone bridge over the second river barrier, the Selune. Surely the Germans would have blown this bridge? They had not. Pontaubault and its bridge were taken by American tanks and infantry during the late afternoon of July 31. The Americans stood at the gateway to Brittany and to central France.

The stalemate in Normandy was ended, and the success of the epic charge across Normandy generated an even greater wave of relief and optimism in the Allied high command than the success of the landings. At last, Allied armor could begin to move. Eisenhower reported to Marshall: "Paris and the Seine have come within reach." Montgomery, in a directive to Bradley, announced that the destruction of the 7th and Panzer Army west of the Seine would "hasten the end of the war." Colonel

Dickson, Bradley's G2, opined of the German army that "Only discipline and habit of obedience to orders keeps the front line units fighting," and that "It is doubtful that the German forces in Normandy can continue for more than four to eight weeks as a military machine." "In the next four to eight weeks," Dickson added, "the current situation may change with dramatic suddenness into a race to reach a chaotic Germany."

For Hitler, it must have seemed that it was ten minutes to midnight on the clock of destiny. His armies were in disarray everywhere. The Russians had broken the main Finnish-German defense lines, and Finland seemed about to desert her alliance with Germany. Twenty-five of the thirty-three divisions of Army Group Center were trapped in central Russia. On the southern front, the Wehrmacht had been compelled to abandon the Crimea. In Italy, the German army was in general—although orderly—retreat to the last lines of defense in the north. And now in France, the front had burst wide open.

Yet Hitler still refused to accept OKW's advice to withdraw his armies to the German frontiers and make the nation into a fortress on easily defensible lines. He remained obdurate in his contention that the Grand Alliance was a flimsy structure which would collapse with a single massive defeat. Britain, he said, was war-weary and would seek a political settlement if he could keep France as a base for his missiles, his new jet *Blitzbombers,* and his revolutionary hydrogen-peroxide-fueled submarines. Withdrawal would mean the beginning of the end for Germany. Accordingly, he sent Kluge new orders. The front, through which at that moment a hundred American fighting battalions and a thousand armored fighting vehicles were streaming, must be restored with infantry while German armor gathered to deliver the Allies a blow they would not forget. It was Operation Lüttich again, and this time it was imperative that the tactic succeed. All he needed, said Hitler, was bad weather and good fortune.

On August 1, Bradley's new command, the 12th Army Group, was established, and Patton's army—the 3rd—was activated as the fangs of Cobra. With remarkable resource, Patton, often directing traffic personally, managed to get seven divisions across the two-lane bridge at Pontaubault in six days. The weather, which had been generally wet and cloudy ever since D-Day, suddenly turned hot and dry—tankmen's weather. One of the two combat commands of General John S. Wood's 4th Armored Division made 40 miles in an afternoon—faster than Rommel in 1940—to reach Brittany's capital city, Rennes, by early evening of August 1. Although Rennes was once described by Augustus Hare as "the dullest, as it is almost the ugliest" city in France, the cupolas of the Hôtel de Ville seen through the blood-red haze of a setting sun and the dust of a preparatory bombardment by massed Thunderbolts and Bostons were, after the maddening Battle of the Hedgerows, one of the world's greatest skylines. But the euphoria was only momentary; German panzer grenadiers stopped the advance and Wood was compelled to withdraw. He left the city to the infantry and, with orders to do so, made another dart, this time to the ancient city of Vannes, on the Golfe de Morbihan about 70 miles from Rennes. His tanks rocketed across the undulating moors of the Landes de Lanvaux and entered the town at 9 P.M. on August 5. With that stroke, Patton's army had severed the Breton peninsula—along with some 70,000 *Feldgrau*—from the rest of France. Nearly 100,000 Germans were now cut off, if the garrison in the Channel Islands was counted.

The great prize of the Breton campaign was the port of Brest, which would be used to supply the Allied forces spilling out of Normandy. While Patton turned the greater part of his army east toward Le Mans, he ordered General Robert W. Grow, the commander of the American 6th Armored Division, to take Brest. Grow was delighted; he had "received a cavalry mission from a cavalryman." But to some such an order was madness. Brest was 200 miles away and the peninsula bristled with *Feldgrau*. What kind of opposition would Grow meet on the narrow roads; was it wise to leave his flanks and rear exposed? It would depend upon the Breton *maquis*.

Since the collapse of Samwest and Dingson in June, Gubbins and Bruce had made enormous efforts to restore the clandestine situation in Brittany. They had poured Jeds into the peninsula: "Horace," "Hilary," "Felix," "Giles," "Gilbert," "Francis," "Gerald," "Guy," "Gavin." Dingson was reestablished, along with two smaller bases, "Grog" and "Wash." Nearly 200 tons of arms and explosives had been delivered by August 1. Some 30,000 Bretons were armed, another 50,000 carried grenades and acted as couriers and guides. The French parachutists of the SAS—the Battalion of Heaven—were now at work in small do-or-die bands along the two main highways that ran through the peninsula. For the moment, the entire Breton operation was commanded in the field by Bourgoin—Le Manchot, the "One-armed Man" who was so elusive that the Germans had placed a million francs on his head. Casualties had been heavy—40 per cent of his men were killed, and, in the nature of the fighting, nobody took any prisoners—but they were now an effective force that had managed, as Eisenhower would state in a special Order of the Day to mark Breton underground operations, to surround the Germans with "a terrible atmosphere of danger and hatred which ate into the confidence of the leaders and the courage of the soldiers."

At about the same time that Grow received his orders to take Brest, SFHQ wirelessed its orders to the Jeds and the other leaders of the Breton *maquis*. Now, instead of destroying, they were to preserve. They were ordered to keep all bridges open and intact, capture all German road demolition points and remove the charges, mask or mark all German artillery and anti-tank gun positions. They were to keep the roads to Brest open; and above all, the great stone viaduct at Morlaix was to be seized, held and German-laid demolition charges defused. On August 2, a hundred French SAS troopers were dropped near Morlaix, and after a brief but fierce battle, they took and held the bridge. The Germans responded, sending a battalion of the 2nd Parachute Division to retake and destroy the bridge. If they succeeded, Grow's tanks advancing on Brest would be stopped on the wrong side of the gorge.

Jed team Giles had been operating clandestinely on the Rennes-Brest highway in the Montagnes Noires ever since landing in Brittany on July 6. Now, with the receipt of the idioform *Le xérès est un vin d'Espagne,* Giles was ordered to come out in the open in support of the SAS troopers holding the bridge at Morlaix. Commanded by Bernard Knox, Giles positioned 2000 *maquisards* in the bush and hillside copses along the Rennes-Brest road between Châteauneuf and Châteaulin to intercept units of the 2nd Parachute Division moving toward Morlaix. Before dawn, they scattered hundreds of tirebursters, which resembled the little black turds of the Finistère hill sheep or the big ocher feces of the milch cows, and exploded the moment a vehicle ran over them. Giles laid on bazooka, light machine-gun and grenade parties, and then they waited.

At about ten o'clock on August 3, a battalion—perhaps a thousand German paratroopers—was discovered moving out of Châteaulin toward Pleyben, a pretty town on the Brest-Nantes canal. Giles resited some of his attack parties further to the west. And then, as the *Feldgrau* came trudging up the road behind their slow-moving motor transport and guns, Giles opened fire. Several score of the paratroopers fell in the first minutes, while trucks and trailers caught fire as the tirebursters exploded and the bazooka shells and machine-gun fire struck home. The paratroopers quickly dispersed into the countryside, where *maquisard* killing parties set out after them on what they called *"boches* hunts." In that brief moment of violence, some thirty paratroopers were killed, about twenty wounded, and some thirty captured. The wounded were killed on the spot by the *maquisards,* and the captured men were brought before Knox for interrogation. As the rest of the German battalion withdrew into Châteaulin and the villages in the area, the captured men were also shot. Knox would explain in his report to SFHQ:

> They were all from the 2nd Paratroop Division, and all of them were Hitlerites to a man. They admitted to the atrocities they had committed, refused to believe that the Americans had taken Rennes, refused to discuss the Hitler regime, and refused to explain why they had French jewelry, money and identity cards on them. They were all very young (one of the

worst was only 17) and they were all subsequently shot by the FFI. Even if
we had tried to prevent this shooting, we would have been powerless—
these men had burned farms and farmers with their wives and children all
the way along the road.

The German attempt to retake Morlaix failed, and that same day—
August 3—Giles and the other special forces teams in Brittany heard that
quaint but heroic call to arms: *Le chapeau de Napoléon, est-il toujours à
Perros-Guirec?* General Koenig came to the microphone in London and
declared:

> French people of Brittany, the hour of your liberation has come! The pro-
> visional government of the French Republic calls for the national uprising!
> French people of Brittany, workers, peasants, officials, employees! The time
> has come for you to take part, with or without weapons, in the last battle.
> . . . French people of Brittany! The whole of France salutes you! The
> whole of France will follow you in the national insurrection!

They were immortal words, not heard in France since the Revolution. They
were followed by the *Marseillaise* and—as a signal that they were also
meant for the SAS—the lilting idioform music of *Lilliburlero*.

Like their ancestors in guerrilla, the Chouans and the Companions of
Jehu, the Bretons rose almost to a man that day. The towns and villages of
the peninsula became bright with tricolors as the Jeds and the Battalion of
Heaven issued the ancient command: *Formez-vous vos bataillons!* The
Germans retreated and by the evening of August 6, Grow's armored columns were at Brest. The port would not fall for another month, but the
war of movement had ended and a flashfire of killing swept Brittany as the
maquisards, out of control, sought out individual or small parties of Germans and their collaborators and killed them in what would come to be
called "the joys of liberation."

A few days later, General de Gaulle would give the order over the BBC
for the commencement of an insurrection throughout France with the
words that it was the "simple and sacred duty" of every Frenchman to
"take part in the supreme war effort of the country." "Frenchmen!" de
Gaulle declared, "The Hour of Liberation sounds! Join the French Forces
of the Interior! Follow the directives of their leaders! The National Uprising will be the prelude of liberation! *Français! L'heure de la libération
sonne!"* The broadcast ended with massed choirs singing—and massed
bands playing—the *Marseillaise.*

With that order, the French boil burst, a rebellion began in Paris, and
the five German armies in France would find themselves in various states
of siege. It was an uprising comparable to the Commune of 1871. All were
involved—schoolteacher, postal worker, trade unionist, priest, scholar,
writer, shopkeeper, mayor, policeman, architect, cable layer, aristocrat,

hedge-dweller, vineyard worker, egg-packer, Communist, petrol pump attendant, Catholic, retired officer, rationing clerk, printer—all engaged in random but often clever actions of combined mulishness and systematic sabotage and guerrilla. Ammunition trains destined for Lyon—a classic case—found themselves at Hamburg. Locks failed to work, canal levels dropped, roadmenders pulled up paving stones in the path of panzers, trains were delayed, signals locked, points jammed, sugar got into the petrol, goods trains were improperly put together so that wagons destined for Metz were routed to Marseilles, telephone boxes became a jumble of incorrect connections, German mail addressed to Paris ended up at Turin, pylons collapsed through "frost," cows wandered in front of ambulances.

To organize roving packs of guerrillas into flank guards for Patton's spearheads, Gubbins and Bruce began to build a necklace of Jedburghs along the Loire from Nantes to Montargis, and the flames of insurrection leaped from Loire Inférieure to Anjou, the Touraine, the Sologne, the provinces of Orléans. Team "George," led by Cyr of the OSS, traveling from Brittany hidden under hundreds of lice-ridden hens in the back of a wheezy old wood-burning Renault, arrived to anchor the necklace in the woods around Ancenis. Hundreds of shirtless ones, carrying .22 rifles, shotguns and spears fashioned out of hay-knives, rallied to his command post and were sent out to watch the fords over the Loire for Germans seeking to take Patton in the side. Team "Dickens" landed near the south bank of the Loire in the province of that name; "Harold" came down in the Deux-Sèvres; "Ian" into the Vienne; "Andy" into the Haute Creuse; "Hugh" and "Hamish" in the Indre between the Creuse and the Cher; "Isaac," "Harry" and "Verveine," "Haft 105" and "Gain" landed north of the Loire; "Canelle" and "Gingembre" came down near the point where it rose.

William Colby of team "Bruce" would find himself and his two French comrades dropping into the streets of Montargis, the town due south of Paris which Hitler had ordered transformed into a fortress. He would join the SOE Donkeyman *réseau* led by the baleful figure of Roger Bardet, the most notorious double agent in France—a sinister matter that would cause the future chief of the CIA to debate thirty years later whether he had been some sort of pawn in a wireless game. A squadron of DC-3's would bring Captain Roy Farran and twenty armored jeeps bristling with machine guns to an airfield near Rennes, whence they would set forth in a great arc across France as far as the Vosges, slashing at the capillaries of the Germans' retreat routes. Ian Fenwick, the *Punch* cartoonist, landed in the gap between the Loire and the Seine to shoot up the tails of German convoys—an operation in which Fenwick would be killed and ten of his troopers caught and executed by the outraged Kieffer, an act that led, in turn, to Kieffer's execution. The culmination of the insurrection would be the liberation of Paris itself by the resistance, while throughout France many Germans would find themselves in much the same plight as did General Botho H. Elster, the officer in command of one of three columns of the German 1st Army retreating from the Biscay region. The column stretched for nearly 30 miles between Poitiers and Châteauroux: 750 officers, 18,850 men, 10 women, 400 cars, 500 lorries, 1000 horse-drawn vehicles. Harried by the *maquisards* of Jed team Hugh, Elster approached the American command and in the interests of humanity begged to be permitted to surrender to regular troops rather than to the *maquisards*. The Americans accepted his surrender. A report to the Supreme Commander of resistance operations in August would state: "The work of the resistance during the period under review has led largely to the liberation of a great portion of France." The report noted more somberly: "The achievements of the FFI have not been made without severe losses, but in almost every case these have been far lower than those of the enemy. As was anticipated . . . the value of resistance, as a strategic factor, has had a definite effect on the course of the military operations undertaken in France." As a tribute, Eisenhower agreed that *maquisards* should be allowed to paint the Allied white star on their vehicles.

In Brittany, the main battle had obscured the fact that behind the massed movements of armies, the vast comings and goings of air and sea armadas, the greatest clandestine operation in history had succeeded in diverting, harassing and cutting German forces off from the rest of France, forces that might have changed the course of the battle in Normandy. Eisenhower, in a special proclamation to the Bretons and the special forces teams, would acknowledge their contribution. The Battalion of Heaven, the Jeds and their "Groupes Mobiles d'Attaque"—as the shirtless, shoeless patriots of Brittany came to be called—had tied up countless *Feldgrau* in a bloody, interminable battle of the shadows. Then, when the breakout occurred and Grow's and Wood's tanks entered the peninsula too fast for the infantry to keep apace, the *maquisards* kept the roads open and the bridges intact, protected the Americans' flanks, acted as guides, and took care of prisoners—tasks that would have tied down tens of thousands of Patton's men and slowed down his spearheads. Finally, the *maquisards* formed themselves into infantry battalions and helped first to encircle and then to destroy the Germans holed up in the ports.

With the peninsula safe, Gaulliste bureaucrats arrived to form the first État Major on the soil of France. It was the "Mission Aloes"—a bitter plant—come to take command of Brittany from Le Manchot. The first party dropped to a Jed team Frederick reception (one of its number, an officer who would later come to be called "one of the fathers of modern Europe," refusing at the last moment to jump) on August 4, just behind Grow's tanks. Then, a few days later, ten Halifaxes towing Waco gliders appeared over the Landes de Lanvaux north of Vannes. The gliders cast off, whistling down to another Frederick reception (clandestinity was still necessary for, while the American armor had passed through, isolated pockets of Germans still fought in the rear) with their cargoes of armored jeeps, wirelesses, typewriters, mimeograph machines, heavier weapons, folding desks—equipment for the État Major du Commandement Supérieur des Forces en Grande Brétagne et Délégation Militaire du Gouvernement Provisional de la République Française. The men of the Steward of France had come to claim the keys. A new régime was established and the covert campaign in Brittany in support of Neptune was virtually over.

The État Major would give little credit to the indomitable Le Manchot and his men. The Gaullistes would give no public credit at all to the Jeds and the other special forces teams. Le Manchot would lead his Battalion of Heaven down the Champs Élysées on victory day and then go into obscurity in Brittany, honored only by the Bretons. But the Bretons would not forget the Jeds. As Knox and the men of team Giles loaded their jeep with bedding, petrol cans, wireless, guns and stores, and prepared to move off quietly from outside their safehouse at Plessis, Legal, Knox's FFI assistant, and the Communists' Groupes Mobiles d'Attaque marched up. They formed ranks around the jeep and, in the ragged manner of partisans the world over, presented arms. Then Legal stepped forward and, quite forgetting that Knox was an American, delivered a little speech.

> We regret that it was not possible to do more and do better. The lack of matériel, a certain amount of incohesion and some petty political rivalries were our handicap. Nevertheless it was with great joy that we acclaimed (you as) the first parachutists and we tried to give of our very best in assisting (you) to hunt the common enemy, "the Boches." We can never thank you sufficiently for what you have done for us and the liberation of our country. Furthermore, we regret deeply that certain untoward incidents cause a shadow on those happy days. No doubt they will be smoothed out in the near future. That is our most fervent desire, the desire of our Frenchmen of the "Resistance" who are your comrades of days gone by as well as of the future.
>
> To His Britannic Majesty, to you Sir, and to your proud warriors who were our liberators and our comrades, I and my fellow Frenchmen of the Resistance send our sincere thanks and best wishes for the good fortune and prosperity of your country—which we consider, a little, our own.

Götterdämmerung

ON August 2, 1944, the Turing engine (there were even more of them now at work) in Hut 3 at Bletchley unbuttoned a signal that would prove to be the most decisive cryptanalytical revelation of the campaign in France. It was the Fuehrer's order to Kluge to mount Lüttich at Mortain, a charming town on the Cance in the hills of lower Normandy. As the five-figure groups were first decrypted into German and then translated into English, exalted sentences began to take shape. "The decision in the Battle of France depends on the success of (Lüttich). . . . The C-in-C West has a unique opportunity, which will never return, to drive into an extremely exposed enemy area and thereby to change the situation completely." Supported by all the aircraft the Luftwaffe could scrape together—three hundred planes—the main elements of eight armored divisions were to strike through Mortain and recapture Avranches, thereby cutting Patton's army off from the rest of the American forces. An infantry division was to be put in to support the armored thrust, and the auguries were promising; only elements of one tank and one infantry division stood in the way of Lüttich. H-Hour was set for midnight, August 6.

The Ultra reached MI-6 headquarters at just about the same time that Kluge received the Fuehrer's orders at his forward command post near Alençon. It covered two whole sheets of quarto-size Ultra paper, and Winterbotham recognized its importance immediately. He placed the Ultra in a red leather Despatch Box for Churchill at 10 Downing Street, and sent a copy by teleprinter to Eisenhower's headquarters at Southwick Park. Tedder was on the scrambler line within the hour; were there any indications that Hitler might be bluffing? Winterbotham would recall that he telephoned Hut 3 "to make quite sure that the original German version was in Hitler's own distinctive style and language. They told me we had no reason to doubt it on any score, and the signal had without doubt come from Fuehrer headquarters." Winterbotham called Tedder back and told him it was "absolutely copper-bottom, gilt-edged and gold-plated."

With that, the Supreme Commander decided to fly immediately to Bradley's command post, to be on hand when the attack began.

Kluge, who was at least an excellent general, saw the dangers of Lüttich immediately and signaled Führerhauptquartier: ". . . an attack, if not immediately successful, will lay open the whole attacking force to be cut off in the west." He pointed out that in order to concentrate the necessary panzer power to attack at Mortain he would have to withdraw the armored divisions from the Caen front, thus his forces would be vulnerable to a breakthrough by the British. His signal to Hitler was decrypted by Ultra on August 3, and the debate that followed was watched with intense interest at various Allied headquarters. Winterbotham recalled: "Now the vital question was who was going to win the argument, Hitler or Kluge? My money was on Hitler. This was once again his chance to show his doubting armies that he still remained a genius and to rekindle the Hitler myth. . . . Hitler didn't keep us waiting long."

The Fuehrer replied that all risks must be taken, announcing that he would give Kluge 140 fresh tanks and some 60 armored cars, to make a rough total of armored fighting vehicles at Kluge's disposal of about 400 units—a powerful force for two American divisions to have to fight. Still Kluge protested. In a final signal to Führerhauptquartier, as Winterbotham would write:

> Kluge staked his whole career on trying to stop this attack. In his last signal he pulled no punches and boldly stated that it could only end in disaster . . . one could get a glimmer of his utter hopelessness from his signals. He must have known it was the end for him anyway.

The Fuehrer did not comment on Kluge's signal. He merely ordered him to proceed with Lüttich, an order which was known to the Allies within the hour. Then a second intelligence factor entered into the game of frustrating Lüttich and destroying the German army in the West. George, the stay-behind agent at Cherbourg, and "Mr. Desire," his sub-agent at Avranches, were ordered to report on the state of various bridges that the Lüttich force would have to cross to get to Avranches. Thus through Ultra, Montgomery and Bradley knew every detail of Lüttich, and through the questions put to the stay-behind agents, they could even deduce the time schedules for the attack.

General Leland S. Hobbs, the commander of the 30th Infantry Division, assumed command of Mortain at 8 P.M. on August 6, four hours before Lüttich H-Hour. The fifty-four-year-old infantry officer knew very little about the dispositions of friendly troops—and, for that matter, of the whereabouts of the enemy. His division was extremely tired after a long march, and it took over positions that were virtually unprepared for a major defensive battle. Fortifications and communications were inadequate, but above all the 30th had no intelligence that a major offensive was building up in the sector in front of them. The Allied high command may have known about the details of Lüttich right down to the last nut and bolt but none of this intelligence had filtered down to Hobbs's headquarters.

Hobbs's first move was to secure Hill 317, a 1030-foot peak which dominated Mortain and the countryside around it. On a clear day it was possible to see Avranches, which was just 20 miles away on the coast. As the seven hundred officers and men of three companies dug into their positions on the hill, a number of portents suggested unusual German activity in the area: odd, brief messages on German radiotelephone links; a good deal of aerial activity, the disturbed flight of crows, jackdaws and partridges in the woods to the east of Mortain; the rumble of tanks in the distance. The men on Hill 317 thought they could see the torches of military police guiding armored columns on the move. They could, but they were not American columns; they were German.

Suddenly, without preparatory artillery fire which would have alerted the defenses, the Germans attacked. Tanks carrying SS stormtroopers emerged from the woods, swept around Hill 317, entered Mortain and captured the U.S. command post in the Hôtel de la Croix-Blanche. Then the panzers fanned out through the 30th Division's defenses, one arm of the attack taking the village of Le Mesnil Adelée on the See River, while the other arm advanced on St. Hilaire on the Selune. At dawn the Germans were within 10 miles of the Avranches-Pontaubault road. At one point the panzers were only a mile from Hobbs's command post at the hamlet of La Bazoge; and at another point the 30th Division was in danger of complete disintegration. As Hobbs would report: "With a heavy onion breath that day the Germans would have achieved their objective."

But at dawn three elements intervened to blunt the attack. The first was the German failure to take Hill 317; and from their commanding view of the German assembly areas, the men on the hill could direct great volumes of artillery fire to break up the German columns. The second element was the ground mist. The Germans expected that heavy mist between sunup and eleven o'clock would give cover for their tanks from Allied fighter bombers. But the mist lifted quickly and exposed the panzers to massed Typhoon aerial rocket attacks; no fewer than ten squadrons were airborne just after 8 A.M., bombarding the panzers as they tried to shove through the *bocage*—the very country in which the Germans had stopped the Americans' armor so often before in the Cherbourg peninsula.

The third element that contributed to the failure of the initial assault at

Mortain was the curious behavior of General Gerhardt Count von Schwerin, the commander of the 116th Panzer Division, and the same officer who had tried to negotiate an understanding with Menzies, Cadogan and Godfrey on behalf of Canaris and Beck in London in 1939. Scheduled to participate in the assault, Schwerin's division had simply not appeared; and General der Panzertruppen Hans Baron von Funck, who commanded Lüttich, set out to discover what had happened to it. Where the hell had Schwerin been? Where were his panzers? Schwerin was quite indifferent to Funck's anger. He explained that he had no confidence in Lüttich; therefore he felt he could not take part in the attack. But there was more to it than that—as Funck and Kluge knew. Schwerin had lost hope of victory. Involved in the 20th of July conspiracy, he despised the régime, and Kluge in particular. Even if his neck was at stake, he was not going to have his division chewed to pieces in a lost cause far from Germany. He was going to keep it intact to defend the Fatherland.

Schwerin was guilty of flagrant disobedience and he was relieved of command at 4 P.M. on August 7. His men, who were devoted to him, began to mutter ominously; in fact, later at Aachen, they would indeed revolt against the SS. But now they did as they were told; they joined the assault. But the lead tanks were stopped when they ran into a hail of American cannon fire and RAF rocketry. The Luftwaffe got nowhere near the battle, and neither did the reinforcements that Kluge had hoped to get from the 15th Army at the Pas de Calais. Then, just before midnight on the 7th, the 1st Canadian Army struck Kluge's northern flank from the Caen sector. Spearheaded by massed formations of tanks and armored troop carriers, the great Canadian thrust penetrated the first line of the German defenses. To blast a path through the second, 1000 RAF night bombers, their targets marked for them by green flares and starshells, came over just after one o'clock. The Canadians pressed the attack, and at dawn, when Kluge spoke to Eberbach, the general commanding the panzers, his voice was heavy with anxiety. "We didn't expect this to come so soon," he said, "but I can imagine it was no surprise to you." Eberbach replied: "No, I have always waited (expected) it and looked toward the morrow with a heavy heart."

Kluge called Lüttich off, only to be blamed by Hitler for the failure of the offensive. The Fuehrer regarded Lüttich as the master stroke that would restore the German position in France. He declared that Kluge had displayed poor judgment in selecting the direction and time of the attack. He decided he could no longer rely on Kluge, and assuming command of the battle himself, he ordered a resumption of Lüttich with the words: "Greatest daring, determination, imagination must give wings to all echelons of command. Each and every man must believe in victory." Kluge foresaw only disaster, but as he told Eberbach, ". . . the order is so unequivocal that it must be obeyed."

Eisenhower, Montgomery and Bradley were informed through Ultra of the Hitler-Kluge exchange, and, like Kluge, they immediately recognized the vulnerability of the German situation. The initial thrust of the Lüttich offensive had created a dent in the Allied lines, and the Allied commanders realized that if the Germans continued to hold their present position, Bradley's forces might have time to slip around their southern flank, while Patton's armored spearheads, which were advancing toward Le Mans, might swing up from the southeast and Canadian forces descend from the north to encircle and destroy the German armies in Normandy. But the Allied commanders needed forty-eight hours to move their armies into position. How, then, could they lure the Germans into biting so deeply into the Allied front that they would not be able to escape?

Bradley, a former schoolmaster whose modesty and mildness obscured his genius as a military commander, conceived a plan to gain the necessary time. It was called "Tactical Operation B." As a rule, the Americans disliked the British practice of giving grand or symbolic code names to their special operations, but in spite of its colorless name, Tactical Operation B was the last of the great deceptions of the French campaign, a masterpiece of imaginative military thinking that represented the final flowering of one of Wavell's principal dictums of deception: feigned retreat while planning to attack. Its objective was to *encourage* the Germans to resume Lüttich or at least to delay their withdrawal from Mortain; and to achieve that, the plan proposed a "display of weakness by our forces in this area."

Montgomery approved Tactical Operation B, and Harris and Ingersoll of the Special Plans Branch, with the cooperation of Strangeways's R-Force and the XX-Committee, were given the responsibility for its execution. By August 9, Harris and Strangeways had arrived at their scenario. The "story for enemy consumption" was that:

> . . . delay on the Brest Peninsula is seriously inconveniencing us. Our growing army is straining supply on the beaches. We know that we cannot drive East beyond the Seine until we have developed the Brest Peninsula ports, and we are very chastened by the length of time it took to put Cherbourg in condition. Moreover, the commanders of both the 4th and 6th Armored Divisions at Lorient and Brest have for days been complaining that they have neither the infantry nor artillery to reduce the ports, that their supply lines are in danger, that they are short gasoline and ammunition and that their equipment is in bad shape. Both commanders *urgently* request infantry, corps artillery and supplies.

Armed with that script, a chorus of double agents, including George, Garbo and Brutus, immediately began to report to their controllers the details of the American predicament. Then they announced that:

> Faced with this situation . . . General Bradley has made a decision. It is to order the daring General Patton to clean up his situation by sending

adequate forces of infantry and artillery into the peninsula *quickly* to reduce the fortresses of St. Malo, Brest and St. Nazaire. These forces shall be
in the strength of two or three infantry plus one armored division. . . .

In short, the Germans were told that Bradley was stripping the Mortain
front; and if they believed that three or four divisions were being diverted
to the Brest peninsula, they would also believe they had nothing to fear at
Mortain.

Allied troops did begin to move into Brittany, but they were only
the 1200 men of the U.S. 23rd Headquarters Special Troops—men trained
in deception and equipped to simulate the movement of much larger
forces. Company "C" impersonated an entire armored division; Company
"A" made noises like an infantry division. Tactical Operation "Nan" simulated the westward movement of a second infantry division; Tactical
Operation "Oboe" sounded like yet a third infantry division proceeding
toward St. Nazaire. False unit insignia were painted on the vehicles and
the men wore false shoulder patches for the benefit of unlocated stay-behind
agents known to be transmitting from the Avranches, Brest and Lorient
areas. It was a movement wholly of "special effects," conducted much as
Hollywood might use a few hundred extras to create the impression that
thousands of men were on the move. Meanwhile the real divisions under
Bradley's command silently took up their positions on Kluge's southern
flank, the Canadians were poised to the north and Patton rocketed toward
Le Mans.

The effect of Tactical Operation B on the enemy can only be estimated
by subsequent events. Kluge, fearful of encirclement and annihilation, remained reluctant to remount Lüttich, but obedient to Hitler's orders, he
moved units of the 9th, 10th and 12th SS Panzer divisions away from the
British sector at Caen toward the Mortain front. Other German forces, including units of the 9th Panzer, which had finally left Bordeaux when the
Ironside threat evaporated, were moved into the area immediately behind
Mortain. Hitler appointed Eberbach to command the great new thrust and
decreed that all forces must be ready to resume the attack on August 11.
Eberbach declared that this was impossible, but Hitler demanded no further
delay and, to satisfy Eberbach's persistent requests for more forces, ordered
parts of the 11th Panzer Division, which was being held in the south to
meet the Vendetta threats and the actual menace of Anvil, to proceed immediately to the Mortain sector. But finally, on the night of the 11th, even
Hitler recognized the vulnerability of the German position. He suspended
all other orders and gave permission for the 7th Army to begin withdrawing from the Mortain area. But Bradley had gained his forty-eight hours,
and the circle around the German forces was virtually complete.

The withdrawal of the forward elements of the 7th Army brought relief
to the 30th Infantry Division at Mortain and to the defenders of Hill 317.

Of the seven hundred men who had been on the hill, only three hundred walked off. For six days and nights, they had paralyzed all German movements in the area, and over one hundred enemy tanks and self-propelled guns lay beneath them as testimony to their extraordinary tenacity and heroism. Theirs was one of the finest small unit actions of the war. In all, over three thousand Americans were killed or wounded at Mortain, but they had broken the German lance; and Hitler, contemptuous of American fighting ability, was—as with so much else—proved quite wrong.

By August 13, it was apparent that Tactical Operation B had succeeded, for on that day Kluge's nightmare of encirclement was becoming a reality. The 5th Panzer Army and the 7th Army were practically surrounded in what would come to be called the Falaise Gap—a name to rank with Stalingrad as the cenotaph of German military might. For it was here, amid the hills and valleys around the small town where William the Conqueror was born, that Army Group B met its end. In an area that stretched from Falaise to Mortain, eight German divisions with all their equipment were more or less encircled by the Americans to the south and west, and the British and the Canadians to the north and northwest—trapped like rats in a demijohn. Fighter bombers by the thousand bombarded and machine-gunned the German troops as Allied infantry and armor pressed in from all sides. Medium bombers and the shells of massed artillery increased the German agony. It was a seething, bloody cauldron which the Germans would come to call *"der Kessel von Falaise."* A British soldier, R. M. Wingfield, would write:

> Hundreds of men were coming towards me. They were German. They were from the Falaise Gap. I never want to see men like them again. They came on, shambling in dusty files. . . . They were past caring. The figures were bowed with fatigue, although they had nothing to carry but their ragged uniforms and their weary, hopeless, battle-drugged bodies.

It would be estimated that some 10,000 Germans were killed and another 50,000 captured at Falaise. Total German losses to this date would be close to 300,000 men, with a further 100,000 trapped in the Channel fortresses. Such was the price of the Normandy campaign.

On August 14, Kluge went to the front to see if he could break the Allied ring around his armies. He spent the night at Dietrich's headquarters at the castle of Fontaine l'Abbé near Bernay. Then, at dawn on the 15th— a day that would leave history with one of its most momentous mysteries— he set out to attend a meeting with two of his commanders at the village of Necy. He was to meet them in the village church between ten and eleven o'clock. With him were his son, a wireless truck, a small escort and some aides. The fact that he had taken his wireless truck—and his son—would lead to speculation that the purpose of the trip was something other than to confer with his army commanders.

The weather was hot and perfect for aerial attackers; Kluge and his party were soon under fire and two of their vehicles we~e destroyed. They tried to avoid attackers by going across country, through fields and woods, but they were again caught by *Jabos* near Ammeville. The wireless car was hit and burned, and the chief operator was killed while his assistants were all wounded. Cut off by the swarming planes, Kluge, exhausted, could go no further and collapsed into a ditch while his aide, a Lieutenant Tangermann, found a bicycle and rode to the rendezvous. When he got to the church at Necy, there was nobody there; the commanders had come and gone. Tangermann returned to Kluge but by now OKW, OB-West and Army Group B were all extremely alarmed. Kluge was declared missing and Hitler looked around for a new C-in-C West. He selected Field Marshal Walter Model, and while Model was being brought to Rastenburg for a briefing, Hitler placed Hausser in temporary command of Army Group B.

Kluge would not turn up at Eberbach's headquarters until 10 P.M. that evening. He had been missing for seventeen hours, and Hitler became convinced that he had attempted to surrender the German armies in the West to Montgomery that day. Both he and Keitel would maintain that Kluge was in radio contact with the British. Keitel would state that Kluge's wireless messages were intercepted by a special Horchkompanie set up after Hitler's suspicions were aroused by the ceasefires that accompanied the exchange of nurses early in July. At an OKW conference on August 31, Hitler would declare that "August 15th was the worst day of my life." His forces in France were crumbling; French and American armies began landing on the Riviera coast; and as Guderian would state: "Hitler was desperate . . . when Kluge had failed to return. . . . He imagined that the field marshal had established contact with the enemy." And that prospect produced one of the most violent storms witnessed since the afternoon of July 20.

Had Kluge attempted to surrender? Hitler thought so. At the staff conference on August 31 he stated:

> Field Marshal von Kluge planned to lead the whole of the Western Army into capitulation and to go over himself to the enemy. . . . It seems that the plan miscarried owing to an enemy fighter-bomber attack. He had sent away his staff officer, British-American patrols advanced, but apparently no contact was made. . . . Nevertheless the British have reported being in contact with a German general.

Time Magazine, in a report published on June 25, 1945, and obtained, presumably, from Patton, would give the following account of Kluge's missing hours:

> *The Road to Avranches*—One day last August (Kluge) suddenly left his headquarters on the Western Front. . . . With some of his staff, Kluge drove to a spot on a lonely road near Avranches in northwestern France. There he waited, hour after hour, for a party of U.S. Third Army officers with whom he had secretly arranged to discuss surrender. They did not appear. Fearing betrayal, Kluge hurried back to his headquarters.

The correspondent explained that "On the day of the rendezvous, Allied air attacks blocked the Third Army party's route to Avranches. By the time the U.S. negotiators arrived, Kluge had gone." This story—and other identical stories in the American (but not the British) press—received some confirmation from Dulles, who would later write that Kluge made "a futile attempt to surrender to General Patton's army somewhere in the Falaise Gap. . . ."

Neither Sibert, the G2 of the 12th Army Group, Strong, Eisenhower's G2, nor de Guingand, Montgomery's Chief of Staff, would provide the slightest substantiation for the story. There was, however, important evidence that surrender was on the mind of the German high command in the first and second weeks of August, despite the collapse of the Schwarze Kapelle plot. A document discovered in the OSS files at the National Archives in Washington in 1974 revealed that the German General Staff did, in fact, make at least one serious attempt at surrender during this period. The document, which was prepared by the OSS Committee on Dissemination of Intelligence and given special limited circulation on August 11, 1944, to the President, the Secretary of State and the Joint (but *not* the Combined) Chiefs of Staff, reported approaches to the OSS at Lisbon by Heinz Carl Weber, who, the report stated, was "in charge of all German mineral purchasing operations in Lisbon as representative of the *Reichswirtschaftsministerium.*" According to the report, Weber's overture had been made through a "thoroughly reliable source"—either Baron Hoyningen-Huene, the German ambassador, or one of his deputies, for there were contacts of a special nature between the English, American and German embassies in Lisbon. Weber, the report stated, had "received a message from German General Headquarters to find out how the United States would react to the following proposal: Germany would surrender unconditionally to the Western Allies and meet any industrial or territorial demands, provided the latter act at once to occupy the Reich and keep out the Soviet." The OSS document declared that "the report may merit attention in view of the channels employed and the apparent sincerity of the source."

There, then, was a chance to end the Second World War. The German army had been defeated in France and, it appeared, was willing to turn against the Nazis in the same way that the army of Italy had done. If the overture was accepted, might it not remove the need for the western powers to fight their way to Berlin, Vienna and Prague, leaving the Germans to take care of the Nazis? But if the emissary was given any reply at all—and there would be no evidence of a reply—it could only have been those fateful words that Canaris heard so many years before aboard the quarter deck of HMS *Glasgow:* "I am empowered neither to proffer nor to accept any terms other than unconditional surrender." The war was to go on for another nine months, during which time the continent would suffer more devastation than during the whole of the preceding five years.

Kluge had been able to do nothing to break the iron ring around his armies in the Falaise Gap; and on August 17, he was back at the Château de La Roche Guyon. The noise of battle was now very close as American tank columns crossed the Seine near Mantes. But Kluge appeared to care nothing for his own safety or for that of his headquarters. He was preoccupied with the signal he had received from OKW. It read: "The Commander-in-Chief West and the Commander-in-Chief Army Group B, Field Marshal von Kluge, is placed on the reserve list. At the same time Field Marshal Model is appointed Commander-in-Chief West and Commander-in-Chief Army Group B." The coldness of the signal, its very brevity, was an insult. Worse was to come. Model, a tall, monocled Nazi who had distinguished himself during the various retreats on the Russian front, arrived at the château that evening, and after exchanging formal salutes, he handed Kluge a letter. It instructed Kluge to report forthwith to Führerhauptquartier. That could mean only one thing.

Blumentritt arrived from St. Germain-en-Laye to meet the new C-in-C, and he went into Kluge's study to say goodbye. There, in the gloom, he found the field marshal bending over a map on a table. Kluge looked up, greeted his former Chief of Staff, tapped the map with his pencil, and then said: "Here at Avranches all my military reputation went. Do you remember the book which the old Moltke wrote which saved the honour of his opponent Benedek? There is no Moltke for me." It was a reference to Moltke's chivalry in protecting the reputation of the defeated Austrian general, Benedek, at the Battle of Sadowa on July 3, 1866, during the Seven Weeks' War. Blumentritt sought to console the fallen field marshal, but Kluge declared: "It's all up with me." And so it was. Hitler knew that Kluge had been involved in Operation Flash in March 1943. He had also been implicated in the July 20 plot, had lost Normandy, and now he was suspected of attempting to arrange an armistice with the Allies in the West. There was more than enough against him to warrant Kluge's arraignment on suspicion of high treason—and almost certain execution.

Blumentritt assured Kluge that responsibility for the Lüttich disaster could not and would not be laid at his door. But Kluge repeated despairingly: "No, no! It's all up with me." He prepared to return to Germany, as Model received orders that same night to begin the withdrawal of the German army from France. It was, as Sir John Wheeler-Bennett would observe, the nemesis of the power of the German General Staff, that instrument of German might which had twice in half a century brought the Reich to the verge of world hegemony. Now Germany stood on the brink of disaster. It was a process that had begun that day at the Siegessäule when the General Staff swore the *Fahneneid* to the new Fuehrer; one that ended in a botched assassination attempt at the *Wolfsschanze*.

That evening, Kluge sat down in his study to write a letter to the Fuehrer. For a man about to die, a man whose armies were destroyed and whose enemies were close to the very room where he was writing, it was an astonishing letter. Even when it no longer mattered, Kluge excused himself, his officers and his men for the German defeat. He blamed it on the insufficient numbers of tanks, anti-tank weapons, supplies and personnel available in the West—a direct tribute to the efficacy of Bodyguard. He wrote that it had been impossible to withdraw the panzer divisions in time because of the lack of infantry—a direct tribute to the efficacy of Fortitude. And then, revealing his moral ambivalence even to the end, Kluge concluded the letter with these words:

> Should the new weapons in which you place so much hope, especially those of the air force, not bring success—then, my Führer, make up your mind to end the war. The German people have suffered so unspeakably that it is time to bring the horror to a close.
>
> I have steadfastly stood in awe of your greatness, your bearing in this gigantic struggle, and your iron will. If Fate is stronger than your will and your genius, that is Destiny. You have made an honourable and tremendous fight. History will testify this for you. Show now that greatness that will be necessary if it comes to the point of ending a struggle which has become hopeless. I depart from you, my Führer, having stood closer to you in spirit than you perhaps dreamed, in the consciousness of having done my duty to the utmost.

Just before dawn on August 18, the day upon which the Germans began their retreat from France, Kluge, his *aide-de-camp* and a small escort drove down the lane of linden trees from the Château de La Roche Guyon and headed for Germany. The little column stopped briefly at the Forêt de Compiègne, where Kluge got down from his six-wheel command car to stretch his legs. Then the convoy started again and headed into the battlefields of the First World War. Near Verdun, Kluge told his chauffeur to stop for a meal. They were between Clermont-en-Argonne and Dombasle. Kluge spread a rug under a tree, asked his *aide-de-camp* Tangermann for some paper, and wrote a letter to his brother. He gave it to Tangermann with instructions to post it, and then said: "Get everything ready in about a quarter of an hour and then we'll go on."

Kluge had no intention of going on. At about 3:20 P.M. on the afternoon of August 18, 1944, Field Marshal von Kluge, the man who had almost captured Moscow and was now disgraced by a small group of Americans on a hill called 317, the man who for a few fleeting seconds might have ended the Second World War in the West, took his life. He bit into a phial of potassium cyanide and was dead in an instant.

Epilogue

THE SUICIDE of Field Marshal von Kluge marked, at least symbolically, the end of Neptune and Fortitude and, it seemed to the Allied Supreme Command, the war itself. As a SHAEF intelligence bulletin announced on August 23, 1944: "Two-and-a-half months of bitter fighting, culminating for the Germans in a bloodbath big enough even for their extravagant tastes, have brought the end of the war in Europe within sight, almost within reach. The strength of the German armies in the West has been shattered, Paris belongs to France again, and the Allied armies are streaming towards the frontiers of the Reich."

In fact, victory was still nine months away; and Neptune, one of the great acts of human courage and intellect, would deteriorate into dull carnage. Hitler had time to rally and rebuild his armies, and the road to Berlin would be a long and costly one. Conventional warfare superseded the war of special means, Eisenhower took command of the battle from Montgomery, football replaced cricket. The large-scale use of deception, in particular, ended with the success of Neptune. The Soviet General Staff formally canceled its participation in Bodyguard on September 29, 1944, a significant date in the evolution of the Cold War. The common goals and global cooperation that had made Bodyguard possible evaporated as each of the three big powers began to fight the final battles with separate political objectives.

The decline in the use of Churchill's "sinister touches" and "elements of legerdemain" was attended by a severe increase in casualties. During Neptune—when stratagem dominated—the Americans suffered 133,326 casualties (34,133 dead); the British and Canadians lost a further 83,825 men (16,138 dead). During the march to Germany—a campaign not noted for its brilliance of military thought or conduct—the casualties would number 418,791 Americans (86,000 dead) and 107,000 Britons and Canadians (25,000 dead); moreover these figures did not include air force, French or civilian casualties, all of which were immense.

So bitter and apparently interminable would the fighting become, as the Allied armies began to penetrate Germany, that Eisenhower would send a signal to the Combined Chiefs of Staff on November 22, 1944, declaring that it was of "vital importance that we should redouble our efforts to find a solution to the problem of reducing the German will to resist." The matter went to Roosevelt, who agreed and wired Churchill that a message should be broadcast to the German people defining Unconditional Surrender in kindlier terms than he had hitherto permitted, and urging them to join "in this great effort for decency and peace among human beings." It would be, by implication, an invitation to revolt. But this time it was Churchill who, after discussing the President's proposal with the War Cabinet, advised against such a broadcast. Anything which looked like appeasement, he wired Roosevelt, would "worsen our chances, confess our errors, and stiffen the enemy resistance."

Nevertheless, both Sibert and Dulles would try, through their secret contacts, to make the German General Staff revolt again. But it was too late; the Schwarze Kapelle no longer existed. With the failure of the July 20 plot, all serious resistance to Hitler and the Nazi régime ended. Everyone who was suspected of taking part in the conspiracy was rounded up and, group by group, appeared before various bloody assizes, stripped of rank, decorations, privileges, honor. Their families often disappeared in what Hitler called the *"Nacht und Nebel"*—the decree of the Night and the Fog. Wives were taken into custody, apparently to await death by execution or by malnutrition; children were given out to SS families so that the names of the conspirators would not be perpetuated. Clutching at their trousers, in crumpled and dirty civilian clothes, deprived of their belts, braces, ties, even their false teeth, lest they tried by suicide to thwart the executioner, the conspirators stood before their Nazi judges. In almost all cases, death by hanging—the ultimate insult in the German *Offizierskorps* —was the sentence.

The first hangings took place in Plötzensee Jail in Berlin on August 8, 1944, when Field Marshal von Witzleben, General Stieff, General Fellgiebel and Colonel Hansen were among those who appeared on its gallows. Erich Stoll, a film cameraman employed to record their deaths, described the scene. Each defendant came into the execution chamber and a hemp loop was placed around his neck. He was lifted up by the executioners, the upper loop of the rope was hung on what resembled a butcher's meathook, and then the condemned man was allowed to drop.

Very few of the conspirators survived. Schlabrendorff and Mueller did, even though they were arrested; a bookkeeping error is thought to have saved them. Speidel, too, survived. Both Gisevius and John escaped from Germany. Colonel Michel was never arrested, but his chief, Roenne, was. He was executed on the evening of October 11, 1944. His last act was to write a letter to his mother in which he said he would die in the spirit of the "thief on the cross at Jesus's side." The total number of people executed, or who killed themselves, in the wake of the July 20 plot will never be known; many simply disappeared or were killed out of hand by the Gestapo. The lowest estimate would be 400, the highest 7000.

After the war, an attempt was made by the West German government to honor the Schwarze Kapelle dead. Streets and squares were named after the leaders, and the 20th of July was proclaimed a national day of remembrance. But neither the dead nor the day would be really remembered. Schlabrendorff recalled that Tresckow said to him, just before he blew his head off with a grenade on the Russian front:

> Now everyone will turn upon us and cover us with abuse. But my conviction remains unshaken—we have done the right thing. Hitler is not only the arch-enemy of Germany, he is the arch-enemy of the whole world. In a few hours' time I shall stand before God, answering for my actions and for my omissions. I think I shall be able to uphold with a clear conscience all that I have done in the fight against Hitler. . . . The worth of a man is certain only if he is prepared to sacrifice his life for his convictions.

In the West, and particularly in Washington, the fate of the Schwarze Kapelle was received with indifference. Only for Rommel would there be expressions of admiration and regret. Hurriedly evacuated from France—his guards heard that both Gaff and the SS were after him—he was taken home to recover. This he did, with surprising speed. He spent his last days, his left eye covered with a black bandage, writing his version of the campaigns in Africa and Normandy. He blamed his defeat in Africa on the failure of Hitler and Mussolini to supply him adequately. He remained unaware to the end that it was Ultra that had ensured his defeat. Of the battle in France, he contended that "My functions . . . were so restricted by Hitler that any sergeant-major could have carried them out." He never admitted that he had been outwitted and outgeneraled, commenting only upon ". . . the well-thought-out, guileful method with which the Englishman wages war." And of the entire war, his last observation was that "it was all without sense or purpose."

Rommel, implicated in the Schwarze Kapelle conspiracy by Hofacker, received orders on October 13, 1944, to report to Führerhauptquartier. He refused to go, and the next day two OKW generals arrived at his house. They asked to speak to Rommel alone, and when they had done so, they went to wait outside. Manfred Rommel found his father looking pale;

Rommel said: "I have just had to tell your mother that I shall be dead in a quarter of an hour . . . the house is surrounded and Hitler is charging me with high treason." He then went on: " 'In view of my services in Africa,' I am to have the chance of dying by poison. The two generals have brought it with them. It's fatal in three seconds. If I accept, none of the usual steps will be taken against my family, that is against you. They will also leave my staff alone."

The field marshal summoned his *aide-de-camp* Hermann Aldinger, and said: "I'm to be given a state funeral. I have asked that it should take place in Ulm. In a quarter of an hour, you, Aldinger, will receive a telephone call from the Wagnerschule reserve hospital in Ulm to say that I've had a brain seizure on the way to a conference."

Rommel got into the generals' car. Twenty minutes later, the telephone rang at his villa. He was dead. Frau Rommel received this telegram from Hitler: "Accept my sincerest sympathy for the heavy loss you have suffered with the death of your husband. The name of Field Marshal Rommel will be for ever linked with the heroic battles in North Africa." Somewhat later, she received a letter from the War Graves Commission:

> The Führer has given me an order to erect a monument to the late Field Marshal, and I have asked a number of sculptors to submit designs. I enclose some of them. . . . I think that the Field Marshal should be represented by a lion. One artist has depicted a dying lion, another a lion weeping, the third a lion about to spring. . . . I prefer the last myself but if you prefer a dying lion, that, too, could be arranged.
>
> The slab can be made immediately, as I have special permission from Reichsminister Speer. Generally monuments cannot now be made in stone, but in this special case it can be made and quickly shipped. . . .

Such was the manner of the death of the modern Sisera.

Had Kluge not taken his own life, he might have suffered a similar fate, or worse—arrest, a trial and death without honor. But his suicide fore-stalled any final assessment of his part in the Schwarze Kapelle conspiracy. How much did Kluge know of the 20th of July plot? Did he attempt to surrender the German armies in the West to the Allies? These questions would remain unanswered until the spring of 1975 when the last remaining portion of the files of the U.S. War Department Historical Commission's Intelligence Branch were opened at the National Archives to reveal the existence of a sworn statement by Dr. Udo Esch, of the German Army Medical Corps, to Special Agent Montford H. Schaffner. The statement was made on October 23, 1945 and concerned "von Kluge's participation in the July 20 Putsch and his subsequent suicide."

Esch was Kluge's son-in-law and the director of a military hospital in Paris. He had been very close to Kluge, both on the Russian and French fronts, and he stated: "From my father-in-law's assertions and actions I have always taken him for an opponent of nazism." Esch also stated that he had taken part in the conference between Kluge, Goerdeler and Tresckow in Berlin in 1943, offering corroborative evidence that the meeting had occurred, and that Kluge participated in the plot. More important was Esch's testimony about Kluge's involvement in the conspiracy after he replaced Rundstedt as C-in-C West. He stated that he saw his father-in-law "almost daily" and "learned that the plot was maturing." Esch further remarked: "My father-in-law asked me to provide poison for him and the others in case the plot miscarried." He complied with the request, making up seven ampules of waterless acid cyanide in the laboratory of the University of Leipzig while on leave. When he returned to Paris, the ampules were given to the leaders of the conspiracy.

Esch's testimony revealed that both Kluge and Rommel had known that the attack on Hitler was imminent, and that Kluge had said on July 19 that it would occur the very next day. It was possibly conclusive evidence that Kluge had been kept intimately acquainted with the plans of the Schwarze Kapelle, in spite of the fact that he denied knowledge of the plot when the conspirators came to La Roche Guyon the evening of the 20th to beg for his assistance and support. But Esch stated that Kluge did, in fact, attempt to surrender to the Allies. He testified:

> After this failure (of the assassination), my father-in-law considered surrendering the Western Front to the Allies on his own authority, hoping to overthrow the nazi regime with their assistance. This plan he only discussed with me, at first, and I doubt that even General Speidel, his Chief of Staff, was informed about it. He very much doubted (that the Waffen-SS and the Luftwaffe would cooperate), but he hoped to succeed by surprise.

The means by which Kluge proposed to surrender were not revealed; Esch testified only that "He went to the front lines but was unable to get in touch with the Allied commanders." This, presumably, occurred on August 15. And what happened when he failed? Esch continued: "On his return he found Field Marshal Model as his successor and an order to report to *Führerhauptquartier.*" Esch did not see his father-in-law again. Kluge, fearing arrest if he returned to Germany, took the cyanide capsule that he had been given by his son-in-law. Esch himself was subsequently arrested as an accessory to the plot and taken to the SD jail on the Prinzalbrechtstrasse. He was placed in the cell formerly occupied by Field Marshal von Witzleben, who had just been executed, and told that he could expect death by hanging. Then, mysteriously—only he and Speidel left that terrible place alive—he was released, probably through Rundstedt's intervention. He was ordered to reenlist in the German army "owing to the lack of surgeons," and on March 30, 1945, he surrendered voluntarily to the U.S. 17th Airborne Division near Munster.

When the war finally ended, the fate of the German General Staff, once so mighty, resembled the collective fate of the Emperors of Byzantium. During his twelve years as Fuehrer, Hitler created twenty-six Field Marshals and Grand Admirals. Few escaped his own fury; and those who did survive did not escape the retribution of the Grand Alliance. All either were shot, committed suicide, were compelled to commit suicide, or were jailed by the Allies. The Chiefs of the General Staff fared no better. All suffered similar ends. Of the estimated 2500 generals of the Wehrmacht, 786 are known to have died in the war. Of these, 253 were killed in action, 44 died of wounds, 81 committed suicide, 23 were executed by Hitler, 41 were executed by the Allies for war crimes, and 326 died of other or unknown causes. Those captured by the Americans or the British were imprisoned; of those captured by the Russians, many died in jail.

The toll among the SS generals was even greater. Thirty-two were killed in action; four died of their wounds; two were executed by Hitler for treason; fourteen were executed by the Allies for war crimes; five died from unrecorded causes; nine died from natural causes while on duty; eight died in jail; four were executed by the West German government; and sixteen committed suicide. Thus ninety-four of the generals of the inner cabal of Nazidom died, from all causes, but most significant was the number of suicides—the ultimate signal of fear and despair—both in the army and the SS. Ninety-seven German generals died by their own hands. In the Kaiser's war, Germany lost 63 generals in combat and 103 through other causes; only 3 committed suicide.

The German General Staff, founded by Scharnhorst and Gneisenau as the guardians of the Reich, was extinguished, just as Stalin and Roosevelt intended. With it went Prussian militarism although, ironically, no sooner was the war over than it was revived in another form by the Americans. German generals—mostly those who had been connected with the Schwarze Kapelle—were given high and honored places in NATO councils and commands, and once again yesterday's enemies became today's friends. Stalin lived to see the destruction of one traditional enemy—Germany—and the exhaustion and bankruptcy of another—Britain. But the architect of Soviet victory and Russia's emergence as a major world power would be confronted by another power that had discovered its strength on the battlefield—America.

Stalin's hostility toward the Anglo-American bloc derived, in part, from his conviction that the western powers had deliberately contrived to let Russia and Germany fight each other into exhaustion and thereby establish world hegemony for capitalism; the war had been won, so it was said, with "British brains, American brawn and Russian blood." Hence, the Soviet Premier's belief that Britain in particular had attempted to delay, and even betray to the Germans, Allied plans for a cross-Channel invasion. Stalin was also convinced that the Allies had attempted to reach an agreement with the Schwarze Kapelle to overthrow Hitler and, with Germany, to pursue the war against Russia. In an effort to prove that suspicion, the Russians, in 1954, kidnapped one of the Schwarze Kapelle's emissaries to the West, Otto John, who had become chief of the Bundesamt für Verfassungsschutz, West Germany's equivalent of the FBI or the Special Branch. John was taken to East Berlin and then to Moscow, where he was interrogated at great length, as he explained when he subsequently escaped, about his wartime contacts with the western powers. They concentrated, John later wrote, "in particular on my knowledge of alleged secret agreements between the British government and the German Resistance in the event of a successful *coup d'état* against Hitler." But John apparently failed to convince his interrogators that he had not arranged a deal, for the Russians repeated their allegations often and publicly.

The hostility between East and West that would color the postwar decades did not diminish with Stalin's death in 1953, even though he was instantly dishonored by his successors. Of the triumvirs that had commanded the war against Germany, only Churchill now remained. Roosevelt died of a sudden, massive brain hemorrhage in April 1945, before the war was over, and the difficult business of directing America's course through the postwar world had fallen to his Vice President, Truman, and then to the obscure general Roosevelt had picked to command the battle in Europe, Eisenhower.

Of other American generals who had engineered the Allied victory, Marshall, as Secretary of State, would secure an honored place in history with the Marshall Plan, which helped restore the war-shattered economy of Europe. Bradley, retiring as chairman of the Joint Chiefs of Staff, would become the president of a watch company. Patton was relieved of command of the 3rd Army by Eisenhower just after the end of the war for stating publicly that America had been fighting the wrong enemy—Germany instead of Russia—a sentiment that many in both America and Britain would come to share. It was Patton's last indiscretion; he died shortly after of a broken neck received in a road accident.

Among the British generals, Morgan, the first planner of Overlord and Neptune, became chief of the British atomic energy authority and "father" of the British hydrogen bomb. But he would die in straitened circumstances, living in a semi-detached house in a London suburb like any low-rung civil servant. Montgomery, the master of Neptune strategy and tactics, was criticized even in retirement for his conduct of the battle, but while Ultra and deception remained highly classified secrets, he could not bring their existence to his own defense. Even so, both Montgomery and Brooke would be honored by their countrymen as the greatest generals since Wellington and Kitchener. But with peacetime and the publication of memoirs and reminiscences, the alliance of generals created for Neptune fared no better than the Grand Alliance. Eisenhower, according to Brooke, had "a very, very limited brain from a strategic point of view," while Montgomery said that "as a field commander he was very bad, very bad." Eisenhower, in turn, declared that Montgomery was a "psychopath," and "I eventually just stopped communicating with him. . . . I was just not interested in keeping up communications with a man who just can't tell the truth." Bradley remarked that "Montgomery was detestable and I never spoke to him after the war." Neither did Montgomery speak to Bradley; and with the publication of Brooke's memoirs, which were remarkably candid, Churchill refused either to see or speak to Brooke again.

The post-war squabbles of the Allied high commanders revived interest in the strategical controversies that had so often divided them during the war. Whose advocacy would history finally declare to be correct: the British or the American? D-Day was indeed "a close-run thing," and it seemed to many historians of the period that Brooke's strategy of peripheral warfare to weaken German resistance to the invasion was fully justified. Marshall was thought to have been extremely unwise in advocating such an attack in 1942 and 1943. But then, once again, documents recently made public from America's secret archives indicated that Brooke's strategy may have needlessly prolonged the war. Martian intelligence reports, declassified on April 1, 1975, revealed that on ten occasions between July 1942 and October 1943, the commanders of the German army in France, with their transportation advisers, had met with French railway authorities to discuss measures to evacuate German forces. It was known that during the summer of 1943, at the time of the Starkey feint, Hitler withdrew forces from the western front in response to the pressures on the Russian and Mediterranean fronts. The Martian reports revealed that even earlier, in July of 1943—the very time that Marshall advocated as the most suitable for a cross-Channel attack—German transportation authorities seemed to have planned for an evacuation of some 750,000 German soldiers by rail alone.

All armies have contingency plans for such operations, and the evidence is not conclusive that Hitler considered a retreat into Fortress Germany at this time. But it would seem possible that Marshall was correct in assuming that the Germans were so weakened and over-extended during the summer of 1943 that they might not have been able to resist an assault against France. The outcome of such an assault must remain a matter for conjecture, however. At best the Allies might have succeeded in capturing the Breton peninsula as a base for future operations on the continent—a strategy that Marshall had advocated as early as 1942. At worst, Hitler might have been able to push the invaders back into the sea; and Brooke was surely correct in insisting that whenever the Allies attempted to get ashore in France, they should be certain that they would be able to stay ashore.

Churchill, the champion of the British strategy, was voted out of office soon after the end of the war; but he would return to power to preside over the disintegration of the Empire and the decline of Britain's primary place in the world, both of which he had declared he would not permit. In a very real sense, he had won the battle but had lost the war. His employment of stratagem and special means was a decisive factor in the Allied victory, although in his own account of the war, and in the accounts of other writers, history would be left with the impression that the Germans had been tricked mightily, especially during Neptune; but few knew exactly how.

The mysteries that began almost immediately to surround the strategies and stratagems of Neptune originated largely with the British. While the Americans were disposed to keep few secrets about their contributions to victory, the British had their eyes on the political realities of the future. As Wingate would explain: "We wanted no articles in the *Reader's Digest* about how the Allies had outwitted the German General Staff. It was felt that we might have to take the Russian General Staff on." Yet for all the secrecy, no one doubted the importance of Jael, Bodyguard and Fortitude in the Allied strategy and tactics that led to victory in Normandy and the liberation of France. Eisenhower left several testaments to the skill, craft and malevolence of the covert war that attended D-Day. In his Report to Congress in 1945, he said that the Allied armies on D-Day "achieved a degree of tactical surprise for which we had hardly dared to hope." In a secret signal to Marshall on July 6, 1944, he declared that Fortitude and Bodyguard had been "remarkably effective," and that the deception campaign had "paid enormous dividends." Bradley, in an after-action report on Fortitude to the Supreme Commander, was moved to write more fully:

> Operation Fortitude . . . was responsible for containing a minimum of 20 enemy divisions in the Pas de Calais during the first crucial months of the invasion. The enemy was led to believe—and reacted to—a long inventory of opportune untruths, the largest, most effective and decisive of which was that (Neptune) itself was only the prelude to a major invasion in the Pas de Calais area. . . . Best testimony to the effectiveness with which this mis-information influenced the enemy's command decisions is the historic record of the enemy's committing his forces piecemeal—paralysed into indecision in Normandy by the conviction that he had more to fear from Calais.

Harris and Ingersoll of the Special Plans Branch, both of whom had been intimately involved in the strategical and tactical deceptions of Neptune, would add to the chorus of praise. In a postwar report to Joint Security Control entitled "Appreciation of Deception in the European Theater," they admitted that they had "entered deception operations in the United Kingdom with grave misgivings as to their value." They had, in fact, succeeded in destroying the first cover plan proposed for Neptune. But now they reported of Fortitude that: "There is no doubt whatever that enormous losses were avoided by the successful achievement of surprise, which was the deception's first objective." They added, however, that:

> The overwhelming success of the Fortitude operations was followed by a period of partial and/or indifferent success during the remainder of the campaign on the Continent. No over-all strategic deception was attempted. Tactical deception, despite a record of successful minor manipulations of enemy intelligence, was characterized by a succession of wasted opportunities.

With victory, the secret agencies that had engineered Fortitude—the LCS, the CSM, and the XX-Committee—were disbanded, at least officially. Bevan, however, kept the LCS alive by holding a dinner party for its members each year at his club. He also made the work of historians extraordinarily difficult by getting each member of the LCS and its satellite organizations to swear never to discuss publicly what it was they had done. Not until 1970 did this agreement begin to break down, and then only partially. Bevan returned to his job in the City and became a Privy Councillor. Wingate became chairman of the Gold Commission, a businessman and an author. But something soured him and, living peacefully in a handsome country house under the church steeple at the Wiltshire hamlet of Barford St. Martin, he remarked on occasion that "the service of the Crown is but dust and ashes." Masterman resumed his academic career and became Vice President of Oxford University, Provost of Worcester College, Governor of Wellington College, a Fellow of Eton, chairman of the Committee on the Political Activities of Civil Servants and a member of the BBC General Advisory Council. He received the Royal Order of the Crown of Yugoslavia (an odd echo of the Tricycle network), and in the early 1970's, in a complicated intrigue against the British government, his after-action report of the XX-Committee's activities was published by the Yale University Press and became a best-seller.

Of the other members of the LCS, Fleetwood Hesketh became an MP and Lord of the Manor of North Meols; Baumer retired from the army as a major general and became a successful business entrepreneur in Washington, D.C.; Wild spent his declining years at his club, the Cavalry, evading historians; Wheatley returned to writing novels about spies and black magic; Fleming died elegantly on the grouse moors; Clarke remained as mysterious and impenetrable as ever, and was rarely heard or seen outside his own small circle. Andrade, seen from time to time at one of his clubs, lectured a little dottily—so his pupils thought—about physics, mathematics and philosophy. But he would become, in fact, a director of two of the world's leading research institutes, the Davy Faraday and the Royal Institution, and a member of the Council of the Royal Society. Thus the men who had caused so much confusion and mayhem would resume their peaceful lives and, in all probability, die tranquilly in their beds. All deplored the new society they had done so much to create.

The spirit, and the methodology, of the LCS would live on, however, and return to haunt the western Allies. The British had been extremely careful to reveal to the Russians only as much of their deception machinery as was necessary to ensure their cooperation in Bodyguard. But the Russians were quick to adopt and apply this unique weapon of modern warfare. Just how quick was revealed in a reply to a letter sent by Bevan to the British Military Mission at Moscow in July of 1944 requesting the views of the mission "as to what policy (he) should pursue vis-a-vis the Russians in any large-scale cover plans which he may be called upon to prepare." Evidently the success of Bodyguard led Bevan to consider further cooperation with the Russians in this sphere of activity.

The response to Bevan's question was discouraging. The correspondent, identified only as "Bolton," Bevan's "representative at the (British) embassy," said that General Brocas Burrows, the Chief of the British Military Mission, felt that the Russians "distrusted and hated the whole thing." They had played their part in Bodyguard, but they had consistently refused to reveal anything about the special means they had used. "We know, in general," Bolton wrote, "their intelligence system is nothing like so highly developed as ours, and the impression that we derive from their treatment of *Bodyguard* is that they have no special organisation comparable with yours." He believed that Russian successes against the Germans "may have been due to careful concealment, rather than to deception." He added, moreover, that the Russians had displayed a lack of understanding of the intricacies of geopolitics and military matters, and, as important, that their machinery for the execution of global deceptions was slow and cumbersome. Bodyguard's successes, Bolton went on—ominously for the postwar world—had made "a big impression here," but he doubted that the Russians were likely "to divert brain-power to this specialised form of warfare."

In the light of later events, it would appear that Bolton was quite wrong in his assessment. If there were deficiencies in the Russian intelligence services, they were eliminated, and the Russians soon established a massive deception organization of their own. Russian intelligence and deception would work together with great effectiveness in the jousts of the postwar world, as Britain and America discovered at their own cost. It would be interesting to speculate whether Bodyguard had not been the catalyst in Russia's increased proficiency in these fields, and whether, to obtain Russia's cooperation in surprising Hitler on D-Day, the western powers had not revealed too much about their secret methodology.

Having indeed "set Europe ablaze," SOE shut up shop surrounded by a rather rascally reputation. As someone wrote in the last days, it would be "happy and handy / If Bodington baffled the coastguards / By smuggling in claret and brandy, / And super-de-luxe dirty postcards." It was a reputation that was not wholly deserved, and Churchill is said to have remarked: "we may feel sure that nothing of which we have any knowledge or record has ever been done by mortal men which surpasses the splendour and daring of their feats of arms." Eisenhower, too, commended SOE. On May 31, 1945, he wrote to Gubbins to "express my great admiration for the brave and often spectacular exploits of the agents and special groups under control of Special Force Headquarters." On the other hand, Marshal of the Royal Air Force Sir Arthur Harris, the C-in-C of Bomber Command, damned the Ministry of Economic Warfare, which controlled SOE, as "amateurish, ignorant, irresponsible and mendacious." The suspicions about sacrifice and betrayal of SOE agents persisted and there was considerable speculation about the true causes, and the reasons for, a fire which consumed many of SOE's archives just before it shut down. So persistent were the allegations against SOE, in fact, that the Foreign Office took the unusual—in Britain—step of replying publicly. They were, said the Foreign Office spokesman, monstrous and repugnant.

Rightly, no blame ever attached to Gubbins for the peculiar circumstances that often surrounded the deaths of SOE agents, or for the several thousands of their helpers who also lost their lives. After the war he disappeared from public view, only to reappear briefly as one of the men behind an Anglo-American plot to overthrow the Communist government in Albania. Then he became the chairman of a carpet factory and finally went back to where he had come from, and where he wished to die— among the crofters of the Isle of Harris in the Outer Hebrides. Buckmaster also dropped from public view, appearing occasionally at Gubbins's side at church ceremonies to honor the dead. But the mysteries about SOE and F section would linger on.

The double agents who were controlled by the XX-Committee fared better than many SOE agents. The main double agents involved in the Neptune cover plans all survived the war, and Tate, who had helped tie down some 400,000 German fighting men in Norway until the end of the war, was actually transmitting to his controller in Germany on the day the Third Reich surrendered. Garbo disappeared, with his Medal of the British Empire *and* his Iron Cross, surely the only man in history to wear the cross patonce alongside the cross-pate on the same dinner jacket. Treasure found she was not suffering from leukemia and settled contentedly in Canada. Brutus stayed in London, wrote a book and became a printer. Tricycle emerged from the shadows to publish his memoirs in 1974. But most of the double agents were like old soldiers; they simply faded away. So did their controllers and wireless men. Kuhlenthal, who did his country more damage than most men, died in his bed in 1965.

MI-6 casualties were, like those of SOE, very heavy; it lost possibly half its agents in Europe. Philippe Keun, co-chief of Jade Amicol in Paris, was sold to the Germans by a Frenchman in July 1944, and executed in a concentration camp in September of that year. Best and Stevens came back, unhonored. Stevens spent his last years on a miserable pension, trying to make ends meet by translating German books into English for London publishers. Gibson, the man whose intelligence started the main attack on Enigma, fetched up in Rome, became a local notable in commerce, and then, probably for financial reasons, killed himself. Dunderdale, a rich man, retired in the late 1960's, content, as he put it, after "40 years of legal thuggery" to spend his last years in his workshop, hand-crafting electronic devices and equipment—and going out twice each week to serve hot meals to incapacitated old-age pensioners.

The war over, MI-6 was, so it was said, all past and no future. In fact, it began rebuilding a service that would become, in other, new dimensions, the equal of the old. Its wartime staff was gradually replaced, and because of the secrecy that cloaked MI-6's work in intelligence and counterintelligence in general, and Ultra and deception in particular, the world was left with the feeling that it had accomplished little. It had accomplished a great deal; quite apart from its other triumphs, MI-6 had Ultra to its credit.

Ultra, so decisive in Neptune, continued to play an important role in the Allied pursuit of the German armies in France. The enemy generals, remaining unaware, as once was said, that "all wireless is treason," still trusted Enigma; and shortly after the breakout in Normandy, the Turing engines at Bletchley received assistance from an unexpected quarter. Toward the end of August or the beginning of September 1944, General Troy Middleton's U.S. 8th Corps was besieging the great port of Brest; and Hitler, to persuade the troops defending the city that they had not been forgotten, ordered the Luftwaffe to fly in a special consignment of Iron Crosses. The German signals corps learned of the flight and it was decided to include something else in the parcel—the Wehrmacht's Enigma keys for the coming quarter.

A Heinkel III transport flew the mission and dropped its cargo. But the parcel fell wide of the target and landed close to a U.S. battalion headquarters. An American soldier saw it coming down on its parachute in the moonlight, collected it when it landed, heard the rattle of metal—Iron Crosses—and opened it. If this particular type of consignment had been American or British, it would have burst into flames or exploded at that moment. But, despite German thoroughness and ingenuity, there was no self-destruct apparatus built into the parcel. The soldier gave the Iron Crosses to his friends as trophies of battle, and put the rest of the package—a quarter-inch file of pink and biscuit-colored documents, none of which, again, had been specially treated to self-destruct—to one side.

When the sun came up the next morning, the documents were examined more closely and were taken to a Lieutenant Finkelstein, one of the G2's on Middleton's staff. He saw instantly what they were: the *M-Schlüssel,* the German book of Enigma keys, an intelligence prize of the greatest importance. Finkelstein handed the documents over to Ensign Angus McLean Thuermer of the Forward Intelligence Unit of the U.S. 12th Fleet (and in 1974 a personal assistant to the director of the CIA), and Thuermer, in turn, took them to the unit commander. They were then rushed to London where the data was fed into the Turing engines, and Bletchley was able to decrypt the Wehrmacht's current wireless messages much faster than might otherwise have been the case.

It was an intelligence coup that enabled the Allies to score another military victory—the entrapment of a remnant of the German armies in France at the Battle of the Mons Pocket. Through Ultra, the Allies learned that the survivors of the Falaise Gap, streaming westward toward the Siegfried Line, had been formed into a provisional army near Mons. The Americans threw up powerful roadblocks across their line of retreat and the ensuing action was "like shooting sitting pigeons." Some 25,000 men, the remnants of 20 divisions, were captured, while the air forces claimed the destruction of 850 motor vehicles, 50 armored fighting vehicles, 650 horse-drawn vehicles and another 500 men. Thus, as the U.S. army's official history would state, "These potential defenders of the (Siegfried Line) were swept off the field of battle." But for the capture of the *M-Schlüssel* at Brest, the Americans might not have known of the existence of this force before it got back to Germany.

It was, effectively, Ultra's last triumph in the war in Europe. The light that it had cast for so long upon the secrets of the enemy began to dim in the fall of 1944 when the Germans finally realized that Enigma might have been penetrated—a realization that came about not through the careless use of Ultra, but through treason on the part of a member of the staff of Prince Bernhard of The Netherlands. Allied security authorities had long been concerned about Bernhard's "apparent inability to choose trustworthy and loyal advisers and assistants," as an OSS appreciation would state. The future Prince Consort and leader of the Dutch government-in-exile in London was thought to have made "questionable" and "unfortunate" selections of men for his entourage. But it was not until after the invasion that Bernhard, who as C-in-C of Dutch Forces was accredited to SHAEF, made his "worst selection," according to the report: "that of a certain Mr. Lindemans, who was accepted by the Prince as his confidential agent." The report did not exaggerate, for Lindemans was a German agent, and a very clever and dangerous one at that.

Christiaan Antonius Lindemans, then aged about twenty-seven, had been recruited as an Abwehr agent in 1943 by Lieutenant Colonel Herman Giskes, the Abwehr officer in Holland who succeeded in decimating SOE's Dutch section. He had, it appeared, offered his services in return for the release of his mistress and his younger brother, both of whom were loyal members of the Dutch resistance movement. Codenamed "King Kong" by Giskes (Lindemans was 6 feet 3 inches tall and weighed 260 pounds), he was put to work against the Dutch underground with appalling results. According to SHAEF Counter-Intelligence Report No. 4 for the week ending November 10, 1944, Lindemans was "an important agent" whose information "led to the arrest of over 250 resistance members."

The same report revealed that in late June or early July 1944, Lindemans (apparently on Giskes's orders) infiltrated the British sector of the Normandy beachhead. He was, it seemed, an ardent and knowledgeable member of the Dutch underground, and he so impressed his British interrogators that he was taken onto the staff of a British intelligence unit commanded by a Canadian captain. In due course, Lindemans succeeded in ingratiating himself with Bernhard, who now commanded the Dutch Forces of the Interior and spent much of his time with the British and Canadian forces that were nearing Holland.

On or about September 15, while with the Canadians and Bernhard's staff in Brussels, Lindemans was sent by the Canadian intelligence officer back into Holland apparently to warn Dutch underground resistance leaders not to send downed Allied pilots over the escape line from Holland into Belgium; it had been, presumably, penetrated by the Germans. Lindemans either was captured by, or surrendered to, a German patrol in no-man's-land on the Belgian-Dutch frontier near Valkenswaard. He demanded to see Giskes, and Giskes directed that he be taken without delay to Driebergen. There, Lindemans revealed all that he had learned during his brief stay on the other side of the line. He had learned a great deal. First he told of the build-up for Montgomery's great airborne and land attack to take Arnhem and cross the Rhine into northern Germany (information which, apparently, the Germans did not believe). Then Lindemans revealed the secret that the Allies, against seemingly impossible odds, had been able to keep for more than four years—Ultra.

By September 1944, the German signals security chiefs were beginning to suspect that Enigma might be a principal source of the Reich's agony. Whether traitors had revealed all his plans to the Allies, as Hitler continued to believe, or whether the Allies had in some way managed to penetrate German ciphers, the security of Enigma was in question; and possibly as a result of Lindemans's information, the Wehrmacht began late in 1944 to replace it. The task of manufacturing and distributing new machines, and of retraining the thousands of operators involved, proved to be impossible in the short time left to the Third Reich, and the Wehrmacht continued to use Enigma. However, German suspicions about its security almost certainly played a part in the extraordinary precautions which OKW adopted to protect the secrets of its Ardennes counteroffensive at Christmas 1944. When Hitler was planning the offensive, he directed that none of his orders, nor any orders relating to the attack, be sent by wireless. He was obeyed to the letter, and Ultra suddenly dried up. The Allies had obtained order of battle intelligence, as well as aerial reconnaissance and prisoner of war intelligence, all of which suggested that the Germans were preparing for an imminent offensive. But because the American intelligence staffs—and particularly Sibert's at 12th Army Group—had become over-dependent upon Ultra not only as their primary source of intelligence but also as confirmation of other less reliable and trusted sources, no action was taken. The result was, for Eisenhower and Bradley, near catastrophe. The Germans obtained complete surprise and but for the fortunes of war they might have split the American and British armies and inflicted a defeat from which the western powers would not have quickly recovered.

After Ardennes, the Germans resumed the use of Enigma on wireless, and the Turing engines were still clicking the day the Russians entered Berlin and Hitler committed suicide. The war against Germany was over, but Ultra continued to exercise a powerful, and ironic, influence in the secret war. In June 1945, before the surrender of Japan, Franco, partially in response to American economic and political pressure, decided to expel the Japanese diplomatic mission at Madrid. But the Pentagon, through Ultra, was gleaning important information from the Enigma-enciphered reports of the Japanese missions at all the neutral capitals, and its intelligence chiefs requested that the State Department do nothing to force the neutrals to terminate relations with Japan. The request was considered favorably by the "Committee of Three"—the Secretaries of State, War and the Navy, virtually the highest decision-making body under President Truman—and thereafter American policy toward the neutrals, which had been very rough, became much more benevolent.

In military operations against Japan in the Pacific, Ultra also con-

tinued to function until the war's end; and a document released by the
United States government on February 4, 1974—one of the only two documents so far discovered in the National Archives with the word "Ultra"
stamped upon it—would provide an answer to one of the most contro-
versial mysteries of the entire war: why President Truman decided to use
the atomic bomb against Hiroshima (on August 6, 1945) and Nagasaki
(on August 9, 1945) when, as many believed, the Japanese had already
notified the Allies of their intention to surrender.

So enormous were the casualties and destruction, so far-reaching the
consequences in the postwar world, that Truman was often reviled for that
decision. It was said that the Anglo-American powers wanted a quick end
to the war against Japan to prevent Russian intervention in the Far East.
Most recently, Charles Mee, an American historian and the author of
Meeting at Potsdam, would contend that Truman and Churchill "wished to
make the Russians more manageable in Europe," and that the use of the
bomb under those circumstances was "wanton murder." Truman, however,
would insist during his lifetime that he was motivated primarily by the
desire to force Japan into rapid Unconditional Surrender, and thus save
countless Allied lives. The Ultra document, a signal from Tokyo to the
Japanese ambassador in Moscow, decrypted by the American Ultra service
on July 12, 1945—twenty-five days before the first A-bomb was dropped
—substantiated Truman's claim, and provided compelling justification for
his decision to use the bomb.

The contents of the Ultra signal revealed that the Japanese Emperor
had indeed decided to surrender; but a memorandum analyzing the signal
from General John Weckerling, the deputy G2 at the Pentagon, to General
Thomas T. Handy, the deputy Chief of Staff of the United States Army,
warned that ". . . the Japanese governing clique was making a well coordinated, united effort to stave off defeat. . . ." According to Weckerling, the signal indicated that the Japanese were prepared to offer "attractive terms of peace, including withdrawal of Japanese troops from all
occupied territories to appeal to U.S. and British war weariness," and thus
prevent an invasion and occupation of Japan. The Japanese were further
prepared to block Russia's entry into the war in the Far East by "offering
renunciation of Japanese rights under the Portsmouth Treaty . . . and
concessions in Manchuria."

In short, the terms contemplated by the Japanese smacked more of a
bargain than of surrender. Still, it might be argued, was not a surrender
with strings attached morally preferable to the use of the atomic bomb?
Perhaps—if the Allies had positive assurance that the Emperor's will
would prevail. Weckerling stated in his memorandum that while the Emperor wished to surrender and had "personally intervened and brought his
will to bear in favor of peace," there were still powerful militarist elements

in the Japanese armed services who wished to continue the war with "prolonged desperate resistance." There was a danger, then, as General Clayton Bissell, the G2 of the U.S. army, wrote in reply to Weckerling's analysis, that the militarists might repudiate the Emperor's terms even if the Allies accepted something less than Unconditional Surrender. In that case, an occupation force might be ambushed, or the Japanese army might continue the battle in the remotest parts of the Pacific in order to exhaust the will to fight of the western powers.

The situation was further complicated by the inability of American cryptographers to penetrate all the Japanese secret ciphers and thus determine a full picture of their intentions. Debating this aspect of the situation, Bissell stated:

> Although some of the major Japanese Army (crypto) systems are in a stage of solution where most of the messages are solved within four to eight days after date of transmission and some are read within a few hours, there are other Army systems that are not solved and messages cannot be read for many weeks if at all . . . in view of the many unsolved Army systems, Japanese orders for general or isolated repudiation of the surrender could easily escape detection.

Given the uncertainties of the Japanese military and political situation, and the far-flung nature of their empire where a war might continue almost indefinitely, there was only one way to ensure that Japan surrendered unconditionally—the use of a weapon that would forcibly demonstrate the futility of further resistance. Truman's decision to use that weapon was the direct outcome of intelligence gleaned from Ultra; he was, as he would claim, motivated primarily by the desire to end the war, although the effect of his decision upon the Russians and, indeed, upon the politics of the postwar world as a whole, were undoubtedly secondary considerations.

Thus, Ultra made a final, grim contribution to victory in the Second World War. The teleprinters from Bletchley in Winterbotham's office went silent, and he would record that he "handed back to Stewart Menzies the key to those red boxes which had done so many journeys between my offices and No. 10, Downing Street." Winterbotham resigned from MI-6 immediately; he was honored with the rank of Commander of St. Michael and St. George, although he would not receive a knighthood. He became chief of public relations at BOAC; and then he retired to a farm in Devon where, in 1974, he completed work on a memoir about Ultra that the British security authorities allowed to be published.

Winterbotham's statements ended nearly thirty years of silence about this extraordinary intelligence victory, a silence that obscured the part Turing had played in its history. Tragically, the astonishing mental effort which resulted in the machine that broke Enigma would also break Turing.

In 1954, while working on Britain's first computer, MADAM, he began an experiment in his home at Adlington Road, Wilmslow, Cheshire, based on the supposition that he was a scientist stranded on a remote and uninhabited island with only the equipment he could build himself and the chemicals he could manufacture from what he could find. He began to make certain chemicals, among them potassium cyanide.

Why he should have chosen to make such a deadly poison would never be established; but he did, building a rudimentary electrolysis machine and scraping some gold from his fob watch to produce it. Then, again for reasons that were inexplicable, he got into bed, coated an apple with some of the cyanide, bit the apple, and died. When his housekeeper arrived for work on the following morning, she detected a strong smell of almonds—cyanide's smell—and found Turing dead in his bed, the apple beside him. The verdict was suicide. Knowing nothing of his contribution to Allied victory in the Second World War (for it was still a secret), the coroner pronounced pompously: "I am forced to the conclusion that this was a deliberate action, for with a man of this type one can never be sure what his mental processes are going to do next. Here was a brilliant mathematician with unusual mental achievements. He might easily become unbalanced and unstable." Such was the last official pronouncement upon the man who, with his colleague Knox, had enabled the Allied high command to know what the German high command was planning almost, at times, from hour to hour.

Menzies, the man behind Ultra and the chief of MI-6 who commanded much of the Allies' intelligence and counterintelligence battle with the Germans, retired after the war to his home at Luckington. But when the Cold War began to dominate the politics of the western world, he was recalled to his post by Churchill, who was back at 10 Downing Street, and remained in office until the Philby scandal broke. The discovery that there was a Russian spy in the center of Britain's secret intelligence apparatus ruined Menzies's reputation publicly. As the man who had appointed Philby in the first place, he was compelled to offer his resignation; and it was accepted. All Menzies's triumphs were largely forgotten, particularly by his enemies. Quite unfairly—for Menzies knew nothing of the affair—his reputation suffered a second major blow when one of his wartime assistants and friends was arrested on charges of major fraud.

Surrounded by criticisms that he was a "witless, upperclass snob"—criticisms that he might have countered had he been able to discuss such secret matters as Ultra and Bodyguard publicly—Menzies returned to the life of a country gentleman. He brooded upon Philby's betrayal, and as his moods became blacker and his despair greater, he eventually decided, or so it was said afterwards, to commit suicide. The story went that he shot his two gray hunters, closed the house, and went to London where he killed himself. In fact this story was quite untrue, for his death certificate read:

> Stewart Graham Menzies, Male, 78 years, of Bridges Court, Luckington, Wiltshire, Knight Commander of the Bath, Knight Commander of St. Michael and St. George, Distinguished Service Order, Military Cross, Major General: Death—1 (a) Bronchopneumonia (b) Cerebral vascular accident (c) Ischaemic heart malaise. Certified by T. G. Hudson, M.B., Date of Death 29 May 1968.

Only later would it become clear that Ultra had been Menzies's trump card. Throughout the war, it had been unnecessary for him to deploy his service conventionally in an attempt to penetrate the enemy security screens and obtain Germany's secrets. The Allies learned those secrets in large measure through Ultra and through the revelations of the conspirators of the Schwarze Kapelle. Thus Menzies was left free to deploy his men in great strength on deception operations in support of Jael/Bodyguard, and also overseas, on operations to destroy or control the enemy secret services to protect the secrets of the Allies. It is small wonder, then, that Churchill is said to have regarded Menzies as one of the men who were indispensable to victory in the Second World War. Eisenhower's career, in particular, owed much to MI-6 and the GC&CS at Bletchley Park. In a letter written to Menzies at the end of the war, he did not mention Ultra, for even the code name would remain classified until 1974, but his tribute was unmistakable.

> Dear General Menzies,
> I had hoped to be able to pay a visit to Bletchley Park in order to thank you, Sir Edward Travis, and the members of the staff personally for the magnificent services which have been rendered to the Allied cause. I am very well aware of the immense amount of work and effort which has been involved in the production of the material with which you have supplied us. I fully realize also the numerous setbacks and difficulties with which you have had to contend and how you have always, by your supreme efforts, overcome them. The intelligence which has emanated from you before and during this campaign has been of priceless value to me. It has simplified my task as a commander enormously. It has saved thousands of British and American lives and, in no small way, contributed to the speed with which the enemy was routed and eventually forced to surrender. I should be very grateful, therefore, if you would express to each and every one of those engaged in this work from me personally my heartfelt admiration and sincere thanks for their very decisive contribution to the Allied war effort.
> Sincerely,
> Dwight D. Eisenhower

Few of Menzies's principal adversaries of the Abwehr and the SD escaped Allied retribution at the end of the war. Kaltenbrunner, Heydrich's successor as chief of the SD, was hanged. Kieffer, Knochen and Goetz were all executed by the British or French for war crimes. Schellenberg served a period in prison, was released, and died in the 1950's of a liver complaint. That left only Canaris, and riddles. What was Menzies's relationship with that mysterious man? Was he, or was he not, a British agent?

Menzies pondered these questions for a long time, in the lowering gloom of a winter's day at Luckington in 1964. Then he replied:

> Canaris was never a British agent in the accepted sense of that term. The fact that I had contact with him is liable to misinterpretation, but the fact is that all sophisticated intelligence services maintain contact with their enemies. Canaris never betrayed his country's secrets to me or to anyone else on the British side, although his men did. On the other hand, he did give me assistance. For example, I wanted to get the wife of a colleague of mine out of occupied Europe; I made the fact known to Canaris through channels, and in due course she came out.

The silence in the parlor at Luckington was very intense, and Menzies, perhaps struggling with his innate belief that he should keep silent while, at the same time, wanting to say something about his old enemy, eventually went on:

> Canaris was a German patriot, a religious man, a monarchist, a conservatist, and a traditionalist. He was a man in a powerful position who wanted to do something about the situation—to save Germany and Europe from ruins. He thought I might be able to help, and he did contact me and ask me to meet him on neutral territory with a view to putting an end to the war. I spoke to Anthony Eden about it, and Eden forbade me even to reply— Venlo was still very much on everybody's mind. Furthermore, if I had gone to see Canaris the fact would soon have been known to the Russians and they would have thought that the British were dickering with a peace with the Germans aimed against the Russians. The result was that I never saw Canaris. But I did like and admire him. He was damned brave and damned unlucky.

If Canaris was not actually working for the British, it is clear that he was working against Hitler. And ironically, just as Ultra proved to be Menzies's trump card, so it was Canaris's undoing. Political considerations aside, it was unnecessary for the Allies to treat with Canaris and the other conspirators of the Schwarze Kapelle, offering certain concessions in return for useful intelligence. In almost every case, the Schwarze Kapelle could not provide any information that was not already known through Ultra. Furthermore, the existence of Ultra stained Canaris's personal reputation. As Professor H. R. Trevor-Roper, the Regius Professor of Modern History at Oxford and a wartime MI-6 officer, would explain, Ultra was *the* decisive source of intelligence of the Second World War; and in order to protect its security, it was insinuated that the material supplied by Ultra was coming "from Canaris." What better explanation for the remarkable intelligence reaching Churchill and Roosevelt and their higher commands? Thus it was that ambassadors and high administrators were led to believe that it was none other than Canaris, that "notorious right-wing intriguer," who was behind the priceless secrets on their conference tables. The *ruse de guerre* succeeded, but it also tarnished the bright and honored place that Canaris might otherwise have held in history.

For a time after the war, no one knew what had become of Canaris. Then it emerged that he had been betrayed by Hansen, who told his Gestapo inquisitors that Canaris had been conspiring against Hitler for years. Hansen also revealed that Canaris had kept diaries, volumes that covered Hitler's activities and those of the Nazis from the "Night of the Long Knives" on June 30, 1934, when Canaris, shocked by the murders of Schleicher and Bredow, first realized that Hitler was a dangerous and incorrigible revolutionary whose every activity must be watched and recorded. Anxious to find these diaries, Kaltenbrunner sent Schellenberg to arrest Canaris; and shortly after lunch on July 23, 1944, he did so. The bell rang at Canaris's home in the Dianastrasse of Schlachtensee, a lakeside colony of comfortable houses where he lived alone with his Polish cook and Algerian manservant, having sent his family into the provinces to escape the bombing. When the frail white-haired man saw who had come, he said: "Somehow I felt that it would be you. Please tell me first of all, have they found anything in writing from that fool Colonel Hansen?" Schellenberg answered quite truthfully: "Yes; a notebook in which there was among other things a list of those who were to be killed." Then Schellenberg went on: "But there was nothing about you or participation on your part." Canaris replied, still standing on the doorstep: "Those dolts on the General Staff cannot live without their scribblings." Then he invited Schellenberg and his companion, SS Hauptsturmführer Baron von Voelkersam, into his home.

Schellenberg was under orders from SS Obergruppenführer Mueller, the chief of the Special Commission ordered by Himmler to investigate the Schwarze Kapelle and the 20th of July plot, to place Canaris under honorable protective custody at the Sicherheitspolizei school at Fürstenberg in Mecklenburg. When Schellenberg had explained his mission, Canaris said with resignation:

It's too bad that we have to say good-bye in this way. But we'll get over this. You must promise me faithfully that within the next three days you will get me an opportunity to talk to Himmler personally. All the others—Kaltenbrunner and Mueller—are nothing but filthy butchers, out for my blood.

Canaris, evidently, hoped that his hold over Himmler was still strong enough to save him from investigation, trial and execution for treason. Schellenberg agreed to the request, but then, in a completely official voice, he gave Canaris the "German Chance"—the opportunity to commit suicide if he chose. Canaris refused with the words: "No, dear Schellenberg, flight is out of the question for me. And I won't kill myself either. I am sure of my case, and I have faith in the promise you have given me."

Canaris was held at Fürstenberg until Mueller sent for him. Then he was brought to Gestapo headquarters in the Prinzalbrechtstrasse in Berlin, where he was held in cells that were crammed with members of the Schwarze Kapelle. Because of his eminence, Mueller elected to interrogate Canaris personally—within the limits permitted him by Himmler. But Canaris, as eel-like as ever, was more than a match for the blunt, bullet-headed Mueller. He denied all knowledge of the 20th of July plot, but said that he had known of earlier plots because it was his duty as chief of the Abwehr to know what was happening in the Reich. He had not told Himmler of these conspiracies because he wanted to establish their extent—and had been prevented from doing so often enough by the clumsiness of the Gestapo itself.

Very cleverly, Canaris wound Mueller in a skein of half-truth. But then the interrogation was handed over to Walter Huppenkothen, the subtle lawyer from the Rhineland. Under his questioning, Canaris made the one single terrible mistake of his career. Confident that his friend and fellow conspirator, Major Werner Schrader, the Abwehr's representative at army headquarters at Zossen, had destroyed them, he admitted that he had kept diaries. They contained only personal matters and he had given them to Schrader for safekeeping at Zossen because he feared they might be destroyed in the aerial bombardment of Berlin. But Schrader had not destroyed Canaris's diaries; he had committed suicide without destroying any of the Schwarze Kapelle's archives.

Huppenkothen sent a team to Zossen, and inside a big Pohlschroeder safe, they found a mass of documentation, including a number of red, gray and black files on one of the shelves—Canaris's diaries. There, despite the orders of various high officials, including Halder, to destroy the documents, was the entire history of the conspiracy, from its inception in 1934 over the murders of Schleicher and Bredow, through the Vatican negotiations to Flash in 1943. There was much detail about Oster's betrayal of Case Yellow, and a total of fifty-two of the files contained what would be called "important military information sent in by German agents abroad, decoded and dealt with by Dohnanyi. Many of their reports had been deliberately doctored by additions and omissions before being passed on to the Wehrmacht."

It was all the evidence Himmler needed to hang Canaris and Oster; but oddly he did not do so. He used it to convict other members of the conspiracy, and then ordered the documents destroyed. As for Canaris and Oster, Himmler kept them alive. Why? It can only be assumed that Himmler feared that if Canaris was put to death, his friends would release a dossier to the world press—a dossier which, it was said, had been kept by Canaris on Himmler ever since the Nazis had seized power.

Canaris and Oster were held in various concentration camps for many months, along with such important prisoners as Halder, Best and Stevens; and as the Americans closed in on south Germany in the spring of 1945, both men found themselves at Flossenburg. Canaris spent his last days alone in a cell, reading Kantorowicz's *Friedrich II, von Hohenstauffen.* Then on the evening of April 8—twenty-nine days before the end of the war in Europe and with one of Patton's tank columns less than 100 miles away—he was taken before a "court" and was charged with high treason and conspiracy to murder Hitler. Canaris again denied all the charges laid against him, and in a final statement asked to be allowed to go to the Russian front as a common soldier. This was refused, and he was taken away for immediate execution. Oster was brought in on identical charges, and he, too, was found guilty and sentenced to death. Oster was executed in the early hours of April 9, 1945.

At some stage during the return to his cell Canaris was beaten up and his nose was broken. Alone in his cell just before his execution, using prison Morse tapped out on a pipe with a spoon, Canaris transmitted this message to Lieutenant Colonel H. M. Lunding, the former chief of the Danish secret service, who was in the next cell:

> I . . . die . . . for . . . my . . . country . . . and . . . with . . . a . . . clear . . . conscience . . . you . . . as . . . officer . . . will . . . realize . . . that . . . I . . . was . . . only . . . doing . . . my . . . duty . . . to . . . my . . . country . . . when . . . I . . . endeavored . . . to . . . oppose . . . Hitler . . . do . . . what . . . you . . . can . . . for . . . my . . . wife . . . daughters . . . theyve . . . broken . . . my . . . nose . . . I . . . die . . . this . . . morning . . . farewell.

It was, in effect, Canaris's last will and testament. Just before daybreak on April 9, 1945, Lunding, who was looking through a hole in his cell door, saw Canaris being dragged naked down the corridor of the cell block. Dr. Joseph Mueller, Canaris's secret envoy to the Vatican, who was also in the same block, later testified that an SS officer told him that Canaris was hung from the ceiling in the execution chamber by an iron collar. His executioners thought he was dead and took him down; but when they found that he was still alive, they started the execution over again. Canaris, in all, took thirty minutes to die. His corpse was then incinerated and his ashes tossed into the winds. He was given no grave and no monument. But one of his former enemies would rise in Parliament in 1947 to make a testament to Canaris and his fellow conspirators. He said of the German opposition to Hitler that it "belonged to the noblest and greatest (of resistance movements) that have ever arisen in the history of all peoples." The man who made the testament was Churchill.

Whether the conspirators of the Schwarze Kapelle were considered heroes or traitors to the German state, the fact remained that they constituted the only anti-Nazi resistance movement that did not receive the active support of the western powers. There are no documents presently available to historians to substantiate the belief, so strongly held by Stalin and by Hitler himself, that the Schwarze Kapelle and the Allied secret agencies reached some form of understanding that culminated in the climactic events of the last weeks of July 1944. But then, until quite recently, no references to Ultra could be found in the declassified documents of the Second World War, and Ultra surely existed. If evidence of a pact between the Allies and the Schwarze Kapelle does exist, it might be contained in the secret files of MI-6 and OSS(SI), which may never be declassified. If it does not—if, in fact, the Allies offered little more than verbal encouragement to the conspirators, history is left with a haunting question: Was D-Day necessary?

Charles V. P. von Luttichau, an eminent German-American military historian, would express an opinion shared by many Germans who were opposed to the Nazi regime:

> D-Day was one of the greatest political blunders of all time. If Great Britain and the United States had uttered a single word publicly of encouragement to the conspirators then Montgomery and Eisenhower would have walked ashore, and Rommel would have been there to salute them. As it was, Great Britain and the United States were determined to destroy Germany as they destroyed the Austro-Hungarian Empire in World War I; and in their blind hatred of Germany they failed to see the greater enemy beyond the horizon—Russia. Only fools could have failed to perceive that the real enemy was Russia and that one day the western powers would need a strong and democratic Germany to act as a counterweight to Bolshevism. By their actions towards the anti-Hitler conspiracy they sealed the fate of Europe and the world in a pact of blood on D-Day. It is all too hideous to look back upon, and we are paying for that blunder to this day.

Von Luttichau was both right and wrong. Certainly the course of history would have been altered if the Allies had been able to walk ashore on D-Day. But to hold the Allies solely responsible for the phenomenon of Hitler, and his continuation in power even to the moment of his suicide in a ravaged Berlin, is to absolve the conspirators of the Schwarze Kapelle, and the German people themselves, of their share of the responsibility. And if the western powers were slow to perceive a new enemy, their aid and support to the old enemy, virtually without parallel in history and motivated by both humanitarian and political aims, did result in a strong and democratic Germany.

Churchill, among the first of the western leaders to recognize the Russian menace and to regret that the Anglo-American alliance had dealt so ruthlessly with those who represented the social, political and even military conscience of Germany, died in 1965, in his ninety-first year, his reputation already beginning to suffer with hints of amoral stratagems in his conduct of the war. His part in Coventry, Dieppe, the manipulation of resistance forces, Bodyguard, Fortitude, the use of Ultra and deception and so many of the other major strategies and stratagems of the Second World War, including D-Day itself, will undoubtedly be subjects for endless debate. But in 1974, on the occasion of the centenary of his birth, the *New York Times* acknowledged his permanent place in history:

> But what a man! The familiar sound of that voice . . . reminds us again that at rare moments in history one man of courage and vision—and eloquence—can make all the difference, not merely for Britain but for the world. . . . Where and when will Britain or *any of us* again find such inspiration?

The year 1974 also marked the thirtieth anniversary of D-Day, and men in great numbers who had taken part in Neptune once again visited the Far Shore. There on the beaches of Normandy, so it is said, one can hear the sounds of old battles in the wind. It is the same phenomenon that one hears on the gentle rises at Waterloo. For those who require monuments, there are strange, rust-red shapes sticking out of the sea, looking so remote from present history that they might have been there since the days of Richard the Lionheart. They are the remnants of the merchantmen sunk as breakwaters for the Mulberry harbors. The seas wash over these relics, rising and falling with the fierce tides. But they are not destroyed. They remain as a testament to that time and place where the fates changed horses and history changed its tune.

Author's Note

Bodyguard of Lies has taken much longer to research and write than I could have expected. It was first registered at the Office of the Chief of Military History in Washington, D.C., at the time of the Cuban Missile Crisis in 1963, when I was at the Pentagon for the *Daily Mail,* London, waiting to record what we thought might be the Armageddon. I was surprised to find in that most distinguished institution of American military learning that, apart from a few references of a minor nature in its card index, there were no documents on cover and deception operations pertaining to Overlord and Neptune. One of the cards did state that there were thirty-eight cover and deception plans concerning the invasion in existence, but they were in the custody of the British Cabinet Offices in London. That seemed most strange to me for, of course, the United States armed forces had played an important part in the campaign. Moreover, I was informed in a semi-official manner at the OCMH that I would have very great difficulty in getting the materials I wanted. In its own official histories of the campaign, the OCMH itself had not been permitted to use even the term "cover and deception." General John R. Deane, I learned, had been threatened with court-martial for mentioning, in his account of his wartime assignment as chief of the U.S. Military Mission to Moscow, the names of some of those involved in cover and deception operations—proceedings that were dropped only through the direct intercession of General Eisenhower, who was then Chief of Staff of the United States Army. I also learned that two official historians, both writing on the authority of Eisenhower, had tried and failed to include chapters on cover and deception in their works. There were files concerning Bodyguard and Fortitude in the records of SHAEF and in the archives of the Joint Chiefs of Staff, I discovered, but because they were still classified even twenty years after the war, I could not see them.

In England, the situation was no more encouraging. When I approached

the Ministry of Defence for documentation in 1964, I received a letter re-
minding me of the Official Secrets Act. The Foreign Office agreed to give
me a verbal briefing, provided I submitted a list of questions beforehand;
and when I rejected the suggestion, I was advised that "The Foreign Office
will slit your gizzard if you go too far." With that it was apparent that I
would have to look elsewhere for information and I tried a fresh tack—
approaching those who had taken part in Bodyguard and Fortitude for
interviews. Again I met with a wall of silence; indeed, one man warned me
that if I persisted he would have me "horsewhipped." But General Sir
Stewart Menzies was more cordial. In two long interviews, we discussed
a number of matters, notably Canaris and Cicero, but since he had not
commanded the British deception apparatus, Menzies could not, or would
not, discuss Bodyguard and Fortitude. Nor did he mention Ultra.

There, in 1964–65, the trail seemed to end. I still knew little about
cover and deception, and I did not know that Ultra had even existed. It
was not until 1968, during a long stay at the Hoover Institution for War,
Revolution and Peace at Stanford, California, that I was able to learn
more about Bodyguard and Fortitude. Then I met General William H.
Baumer, who told me of Plan Jael. A document entitled *A Short History of
COSSAC, 1943–1944,* which, unaccountably, had been declassified, added
to my knowledge of Overlord and Neptune, and a number of histories and
memoirs began to appear that threw some new light upon the whole affair.
Finally, in 1969, as I was walking along a beach in the northeastern United
States with a distinguished military man, I heard about Ultra. "You know,"
he said, "that your people and ours were reading the German and Japanese
command ciphers for the better part of the war." It was an incredible revelation. Others almost as incredible were to follow, and gradually the story
began to fall into place.

I had learned a truth about historical research. The more you know,
the more people are inclined to talk to you. I renewed my efforts to interview men who had been personally involved in Overlord and Neptune, on
both the Allied and the German sides. I met General Reinhard Gehlen in
Washington and again, under circumstances of authentic Teutonic mystery,
at Starnberg-am-See in Bavaria. In France, I met Colonel Claude Arnould,
the former co-chief of MI-6's *réseau* in Paris, Jade Amicol. In England,
Ronald E. L. Wingate, H. R. Trevor-Roper, R. Fleetwood Hesketh and
John H. Bevan all talked to me about deception and related matters. My
knowledge of Ultra expanded considerably through meetings in Hampshire
and London with Wilfred F. Dunderdale and in Devon with Frederick W.
Winterbotham. In the United States, General Omar N. Bradley, Allen W.
Dulles, General Edwin L. Sibert and General Baumer, among many others,
contributed to my understanding of Overlord and Neptune. I am extremely

grateful to these men and the many other people who granted me the privilege of personal interviews during the course of my research. Those whose names may be used are listed below with the ranks or positions they held during the span of years covered by the book.

Although many officials involved in the invasion agreed to talk with me, I still was unable to find the necessary documentation. That, for all practical purposes, was not forthcoming until 1971–72. During that period, the American authorities at last began to liberalize their attitude toward the secret matters of the Second World War. Even so, the material available to me was but a trickle at first; and the rules were as exasperating to the many archivists, historians and librarians who attempted to help as they were to me. All of the men and women who aided my research are listed below with my thanks. Among them, Charles B. MacDonald, Charles V. P. von Luttichau and Detmar Finke at the OCMH and Robert Wolfe, George Wagner, Thomas E. Hohman, William Cunliffe, John E. Taylor and Tim Nenninger at the National Archives must be singled out for special thanks.

Almost all of the barriers finally came down in Washington early in 1975 when, ironically, work on the manuscript was virtually complete. But in the special contexts of Bodyguard, Fortitude and Ultra, it may be regarded as significant that none of the documents cited in *Bodyguard of Lies* was obtained from official British sources. Why all this secrecy both in London and Washington? I discovered the answer in the flood of documents that were finally declassified in Washington in the spring of 1975. There, in the records of the U.S. Joint Chiefs of Staff, was clear evidence of an agreement to prevent any access whatsoever to secret documents concerning cover and deception, and cryptanalytical matters, in the Second World War.

It was a complicated intercession that apparently originated with Colonel John Bevan of the LCS, who objected to the publication and distribution of a report of American authorship on Allied cover and deception operations in the European theater, submitted to the War Department late in 1944. General Clayton Bissell, the G2 of the War Department, acceded to many of Bevan's requests; all references to Ultra would be eliminated from the report. But the British sought to widen the restrictions; in a memorandum to the U.S. Joint Chiefs of Staff, dated August 5, 1945, they requested that all those concerned with compiling the official histories of the war not "be given access to any original special intelligence material." They further proposed that the British Chiefs of Staff "write up important battles, using personnel already indoctrinated," and it was this information that would be given to official historians for incorporation in their volumes. The U.S. Joint Chiefs debated the proposal; and while they doubted that such Draconian restrictions would be effective, they agreed, in a memorandum to the British Chiefs of Staff, dated September 7, 1945, that "it is desirable and necessary to take appropriate action to insure the protection of sources of signal intelligence in connection with the preparation of official histories."

At about the same time, President Truman added the weight of his authority to the restrictions surrounding Ultra. In a memorandum dated August 28, 1945, to the Secretaries of State, War and the Navy, the Attorney General, the Joint Chiefs of Staff, and the Directors of the Budget and the Office of War Information, he wrote:

> Appropriate departments of the Government and the Joint Chiefs of Staff are hereby directed to take such steps as are necessary to prevent release to the public, except with the specific approval of the President in each case, of:
> Information regarding the past or present status, technique or procedures, degree of success attained, or any specific results of any cryptanalytic unit acting under the authority of the U.S. Government or any Department thereof.

That directive muzzled all public discussion of Ultra in the United States for the next thirty years.

Meanwhile, steps had also been taken to guard the secrets of cover and deception. In a memorandum to the U.S. Joint Chiefs dated May 25, 1945, from Joint Security Control, which was working closely with the LCS, it was recommended that "The existence of a cover and deception organization, or parts thereof, must be guarded now and in peacetime at a TOP SECRET level." It was further requested that "Despatches and correspondence with respect to cover and deception plans and reports" be classified Top Secret; and equipment used in deception might only be downgraded in classification "in a manner similar to that for secret weapons." These proposals were also adopted by the Joint Chiefs, and again history was denied knowledge of the unique operations that had contributed so significantly to victory.

So rigid were the restrictions surrounding cover and deception that history would even be denied knowledge of Patton's role in these operations. Soon after his death, the Joint Chiefs of Staff seem to have tried to make posthumous amends for the way Patton's name and reputation had been used in Fortitude. Because of the agreement between the American and British governments to keep such matters Top Secret, they applied to the British for permission and the request was referred to Colonel Bevan. Speaking on behalf of Bevan, Brigadier A. T. Cornwall-Jones replied to the Joint Chiefs that although Bevan had "tried his best to produce something that would be of value," he had however "reluctantly been driven to the conclusions that it would be impossible to prepare any story which would not give away facts that the British Chiefs of Staff are particularly anxious to conceal and which the Combined Chiefs of Staff have agreed should not be revealed." Evidently Eisenhower had also been consulted on the matter, for Cornwall-Jones wrote that he "immediately understood and, I believe, satisfied the Secretary of War that publication of General Patton's activities during this period would be undesirable." But to avoid the suspicion that the British military authorities might be "trying to hide something from you," Cornwall-Jones appended what he called a "very secret account of General Patton's activities." The account, of some eight paragraphs—little more than desk diary notes—concerned Patton's role in the deception scheme to hide the Anzio landings. There was no mention of his part in Fortitude.

At the time, there seemed to be a number of sound and sensible reasons for putting such restrictions in force, notably the fear that the western powers might soon find themselves at war with the Soviet Union, and Ultra and the LCS might function as they had in the past. There may have been some hope that the Russians would adopt a cipher machine system similar to Enigma—a hope that was surely dashed when Philby revealed the existence of Ultra to the Russians—but Enigma was employed by secondary powers in the 1950's and 1960's, and the Turing engine still had its uses. Ultra, from its uncertain beginnings at Bletchley, had become a secret of the utmost importance in the conduct of international affairs.

The methodology of deception would find similar application in the postwar world, but in guarding that secret the western powers may have had their eyes on the past as well as on the future. The discovery of the uses to which resistance movements in both German-occupied countries and Germany itself were put for the purposes of deception—to mention only one of the most carefully guarded secrets of Allied methodology—was bound to generate new controversies about the conduct of the war. And, indeed, it has. Further, governments, and particularly the British government, are always reluctant to reveal their secrets, whatever those secrets may be, and the long tradition of secrecy for the sake of secrecy is difficult to break. But whatever the motives of those who attempt to conceal them, the facts of history will out; and while my research might have been made infinitely easier if the documents I sought had been available to me from the very first, I would have been denied the pleasure of searching for, and finally, finding them.

It was, however, a time-consuming task, and it might not have been completed at all were it not for the understanding, patience and support of my publishers, Harper & Row, and two of its editors, Cass Canfield, Sr., and M. S. Wyeth, Jr. There are others at Harper & Row and elsewhere to whom I am also indebted: Kitty Benedict, an editor whose early memoranda on my subject proved the spur to proceed; Florence Goldstein,

Victoria Schochet, Lynne McNabb, Harriet Stanton, Sallie Gouverneur, Anne Adelman, Stephen Hardiman, and Edmée Busch Reit. I am especially grateful for the craftsmanship of my editor, Burton Beals, who helped me across many a minefield and through many a maze. To everyone concerned with the publication of *Bodyguard of Lies* I would like to make a most sincere expression of thanks. I must also say that while no effort has been spared to ensure that the facts in these pages are accurate, the responsibility for error is mine alone.

ANTHONY CAVE BROWN

Washington, D.C., 1975

Interviews

Lieutenant Colonel Harold C. Deutsch, OSS, Chief, Research and Analysis Division, Political Intelligence Section, European Theater

Colonel Benjamin A. Dickson, G2, 1st U.S. Army

Allen W. Dulles, Chief, OSS, Switzerland

Commander Wilfred F. Dunderdale, officer of MI-6

Lieutenant Commander Ian Fleming, assistant to the Director of Naval Intelligence; Chief, Deception Sub-section, The Admiralty, London

Captain M. R. D. Foot, Special Air Service

Sister Henriette Frede (courier for Jade Amicol), Mother Superior, Convent of St. Agonie, Paris

General Reinhard Gehlen, German General Staff, Chief, Fremde Heere Organization

Father Robert A. Graham, Jesuit priest at the Vatican and editor of the *Cattolica Civiltica*

General Sir Colin McVean Gubbins, Chief of Special Operations Executive

Captain S. A. Hector, Chief Constable, Coventry, 1940

Lieutenant Colonel Roger Fleetwood Hesketh, Committee of Special Means, SHAEF

C. Holland-Martin, member of the design committee of the Turing engine

Air Commodore R. Ivelaw-Chapman, O/C RAF Station, Elsham Wolds, Lincolnshire, and member of the Planning Staff, Air Ministry, London

C. D. Jackson, Section Chief, Office of War Information, London

Lieutenant Colonel J. V. B. Jervis-Reid, Executive Officer, Committee of Special Means, SHAEF

Captain J. F. Johnston, staff member, 4th Army

H. M. Keen, designer of the Turing engine

Georges B. E. Keun, father of Major Philippe Keun

D. F. Kingston, member of the household of Captain Robert Treeck

Major B. M. W. Knox, team leader, Jedburgh team Giles, Brittany

Oliver Knox, son of Alfred Dilwyn Knox

General Ulrich Liss, German General Staff, Chief, Fremde Heere West

Colonel Samuel Lohan, Ministry of Defence, London

J. G. Lomax, agent of Ministry of Economic Warfare, Istanbul, Ankara, Lisbon, Berne

Lieutenant Commander Donald McLachlan, liaison officer between The Admiralty and the London Controlling Section

Colonel R. M. MacLeod, team leader in Quicksilver

Mrs. Lesley J. McNair, wife of General Lesley J. McNair, Commanding General, U.S. Army Ground Forces, Washington, D.C.

General Sir James Marshall-Cornwall, Vice-Chief, Imperial General Staff

Major J. C. Masterman, XX-Committee

General Sir Stewart Graham Menzies, Chief, MI-6

Colonel Lothar Metz, Fremde Heere West

Colonel Wilhelm Meyer-Detring, German General Staff, G2, OB-West, Paris

Lieutenant Colonel C. J. Moore, Royal Corps of Signals

General Sir Frederick W. Morgan, COSSAC and Deputy Chief of Staff, SHAEF

Dr. Josef Mueller, an emissary of Canaris to the Vatican

Major Airey Neave, officer of MI-9 and G.S.O. (i), 21st Army Group

Major Albert W. Norman, Historian, 12th U.S. Army Group

Dr. Forrest C. Pogue, Historian, ETOUSA

Lieutenant Noel Poole, team leader, Titanic, June 6, 1944

Flight Lieutenant Alfred Price, electronics officer, RAF Bomber Command

Colonel J. H. Randewig, Chief, Wireless Intelligence Service (West)

Colonel J. D. Ricketts, The Worcestershire Regiment (unit involved in the Quicksilver stratagem)

Major Dwight Salmon, Historian, AFHQ

Lieutenant Colonel Walter Scott, Royal Corps of Signals, Middle East and SHAEF

Major Alexander Scratchley, Special Air Service

Major General Edwin L. Sibert, G2, ETOUSA; G2, 12th U.S. Army Group

Brigadeführer SS Otto Skorzeny, team leader, SS special forces

Air Marshal Sir John C. Slessor, C-in-C Coastal Command; C-in-C RAF Mediterranean and Middle East; Deputy to Air C-in-C, Mediterranean Allied Air Forces

Colonel Anton Staubwasser, German Staff, Fremde Heere West; G2 to Field Marshal Erwin Rommel

Major General Kenneth W. D. Strong, Chief, G2, SHAEF

Dr. F. E. Terman, Director, Radio Research Laboratory, Harvard University

General Sir Andrew Thorne, C-in-C, Scottish Command

Lieutenant (jg.) Angus McLean Thuermer, Forward Intelligence Unit, 12th Fleet, U.S. Navy

Major H. R. Trevor-Roper, officer of MI-6

Major Ronald E. L. Wingate, Executive Officer, London Controlling Section

Squadron Leader Frederick W. Winterbotham, Deputy Chief of MI-6 in charge of Ultra security and dissemination

Captain Inzer Wyatt, member of a Special Liaison Unit for Ultra

Archivists, Historians
and Librarians

D. C. Allard, Chief, Operational Archives Branch, U.S. Navy, Washington, D.C.
W. Arenz, Head of Documents Center, Militargeschichtliches Forschungsamt, Freiburg
T. B. Bates, Archives Branch, Imperial War Museum, London
A. D. Bauer, Berlin Documents Center, U.S. Forces, Berlin
Magda E. Bauer, Historian, U.S. Army, Washington, D.C.
Don Chetwynd, Coventry News Service, Coventry
C. J. Child, Acting Librarian and Keeper of the Papers, Foreign Office Library, London
David L. Christensen, Research Associate, University of Alabama, Tuscaloosa, Alabama
E. S. Costrell, Chief, Historical Studies Division, Historical Office, State Department, Washington, D.C.
William Cunliffe, Acting Chief, Modern Military Records, National Archives, Washington, D.C.
B. J. Day, Naval Library, Home Division, Ministry of Defence, London
P. B. Devlin, Office of the Keeper of College Library and Collections, Eton College, Eton
Major A. J. Dickson, Curator, Household Cavalry Museum, Cavalry Barracks, Windsor
William R. Emerson, Director, Franklin D. Roosevelt Library, Hyde Park, New York
Detmar Finke, Chief Archivist, U.S. Army, Washington, D.C.
L. Fisher, Institute of Contemporary History and Wiener Library, London
E. R. Flatequal, Chief, Archives Branch, National Archives, Washington, D.C.
Oberstleutnant T. E. Forwick, Militarchiv, Freiburg
Corporal Major C. W. Frearson, Keeper, Household Cavalry Museum, Cavalry Barracks, Windsor
Lieutenant Commander J. W. Frere-Cooke, Curator, Royal Navy Submarine Service Museum, Portsmouth
Michael Garrod, Press Office, Home Office, London
Kenneth Glazier, Chief, Western Section, Hoover Institution on War, Revolution and Peace, Stanford, California

C. Haase, Niedersachsisches Staatsarchiv, Hanover
F. Hallworth, Librarian, Devizes, Wiltshire
R. Helliwell, City Librarian, Winchester
F. J. Heppner, Assistant Chief, Modern Military Records, National Archives, Washington, D.C.
Anton Hoch, Institut für Zeitgeschichte, Munich
T. E. Hohmann, Chief, Modern Military Records; Deputy Chief, Declassification and Review Board, National Archives, Washington, D.C.
F. von Hueck, Deutsches Adelsarchiv, Marburg
L. A. Jacketts, Chief, Archives Section, RAF, Ministry of Defence, London
H. John, Washington National Records Center, Suitland, Maryland
Captain Terry Johnson, Declassification Officer, AFHQ records, Washington National Records Center, Suitland, Maryland
Leo Kahn, Foreign Documents Center, Imperial War Museum, London
Lieutenant Commander P. J. Kemp, Chief, Naval Historical Branch, Ministry of Defence, London
A. G. Kogan, Research Guidance and Review Division, Historical Office, State Department, Washington, D.C.
W. Krolinski, Zentralbibliothek der Bundeswehr, Düsseldorf
Carrie Lee, Modern Military Records, National Archives, Washington, D.C.
William Lewis, General Archives Division, Washington National Records Center, Suitland, Maryland
Lieutenant Commander R. W. Mackay, Chief, Declassification Section, U.S. Navy Archives, Washington, D.C.
Bryan Melland, Historian and Archivist, Cabinet Office, London
Françoise Mosser, Archives Departmentales du Morbihan, Vannes
K. M. Murphy, Library, University College of Swansea, Wales
Abraham Nemrow, Clerk of Court, U.S. Army Judiciary, Washington, D.C.
Tim Nenninger, Modern Military Records, National Archives, Washington, D.C.
Peter Pagan, Director, Bath Municipal Libraries and Victorian Art Gallery, Bath
Edward Reese, Modern Military Records, National Archives, Washington, D.C.
W. S. Revell, Historical Section, Air Ministry, London
G. D. Ryan, Declassification Branch, Modern Military Records, National Archives, Washington, D.C.
John Saltmarsh, Historian, King's College, Cambridge
P. J. Sanhofer, Militarchiv, Freiburg
Patrick Strong, Keeper of College Library and Collections, Eton College, Eton
J. E. Taylor, Archivist in Charge of OSS Records, National Archives, Washington, D.C.
H. L. Theobald, Cabinet Office, London
D. J. Urquhart, Director, The National Lending Library for Science and Technology, Boston Spa
R. Wagner, Enemy Documents Section, National Archives, Washington, D.C.
Phillip Warner, Historian and Tutor, Royal Military Academy, Sandhurst
P. F. Whitby, Imperial War Museum, London
J. W. Willis, Imperial War Museum, London
R. Wilson, U.S. Army Records, Washington National Records Center, Suitland, Maryland

Robert Wolfe, Chief, Enemy Documents Section; Chief, Modern Military
    Records, National Archives, Washington, D.C.
Carol Zangara, Modern Military Records, National Archives, Washington, D.C.
Hannah Zedlick, Archivist, Office of the Chief of Military History, Washing-
    ton, D.C.

Glossary

Abwehr: The secret intelligence and counter-espionage service of the German General Staff

Admiralstab: German naval staff

Adoration: Code name for Fortitude South wireless deception and silence operations

A-Force: The deception organization in the Mediterranean and Middle East

Amt Mil: The intelligence acquisition section of the German General Staff, successor to the Abwehr

Ankara Committee: The Anglo-American organization responsible for intelligence in the Middle East, the Balkans and the eastern Mediterranean

Anvil: Code name for the Anglo-American invasion of southern France in August 1944 (later, Dragoon)

Avis: See *messages personnels*

Barbarossa: Code name for the German invasion of Russia in 1941

Battalion of Heaven: 4th SAS Regiment (Chasseurs Parachutistes), a force of Frenchmen trained in guerrilla warfare dropped behind German lines from D-Day onward

BCRA: Bureau Centrale de Renseignements et d'Action, the secret intelligence service founded by de Gaulle

Berne Report: German diplomatic documents leaked in 1943–44 to Allen W. Dulles, OSS chief at Berne

Bertram: Code name for British cover and deception operations to conceal Montgomery's Lightfoot offensive in North Africa in 1942

Bigot: The SHAEF code word indicating that a document contained information about Neptune and required special security handling; also used to denote an individual with knowledge of Neptune

Bodyguard: Code name for the strategic cover and deception operations to conceal Allied intentions in northwest Europe in 1944; formerly Plan Jael

"The Bomb": Engineers' slang for the machine used to decode Enigma-enciphered messages

Brissex: British secret intelligence teams dropped in France prior to D-Day

Case Green: Code name for German operations to occupy Czechoslovakia

Case White: Code name for German operations to invade Poland

Case Yellow: Code name for German operations to invade The Netherlands, Belgium and France

Cobra: Code name for Bradley's offensive to break the German lines at St. Lô in July 1944

Cockade: Code name for the LCS's major strategical deception scheme in 1943, designed to draw off German strength from the Russian and Italian fronts by threatening an Allied invasion of western Europe

Combined Chiefs of Staff (CCS): The Anglo-American supreme command in Washington, D.C.

Combined Intelligence Committee (CIC): The Combined Chiefs of Staff intelligence evaluation organization in Washington, D.C.

Commando Supremo: The Italian supreme command

Cooneys: Special forces teams trained to disrupt German communications in Brittany during Neptune

COSSAC: Chief of Staff, Supreme Allied Commander, the headquarters of the Combined Chiefs of Staff at London established in 1943 to execute Cockade and plan for Overlord and Neptune

Crossbow: Code name for the Allied aerial campaign against VI launch sites

CSM: Committee of Special Means, the SHAEF department responsible for the execution of cover and deception plans; also called Ops B

Diadem: Code name for Allied military operations in Italy in concert with Neptune and Overlord

Enigma: The name of the enciphering machine used extensively throughout the Wehrmacht, by the Abwehr and by the Axis nations

Etappe: Etappendienst, the secret supply and intelligence organization of the German navy

Fahneneid: The oath of allegiance sworn by the German armed services to Hitler

Feldgrau: The German soldier, a term derived from the field-gray color of his uniform

FH: Fremde Heere, the intelligence evaluation section of the German General Staff

FHO: Fremde Heere Ost, the section of Fremde Heere responsible for evaluating intelligence about Russia and other nations east of Germany

FHW: Fremde Heere West, the section of Fremde Heere responsible for evaluating intelligence about the western Allies

Flash: The code name of the unsuccessful operation to assassinate Hitler in 1943 by placing a bomb aboard his aircraft

Forschungsamt: The communications intelligence service of the Luftwaffe and, later, a dependency of the Nazi Party intelligence services

Fortitude: Code name for the tactical cover and deception operations to conceal the secrets of Neptune

Fortitude North: Code name for the Fortitude cover and deception operations directed at the Scandinavian countries

Fortitude South: Code name for the Fortitude cover and deception operations directed at the Channel coast of France and Belgium

Fortitude South II: Code name for the Fortitude South cover and deception operations carried on after D-Day; also called Rosebud

F section: The section of SOE concerned with special operations against the Germans in France and French territories

Führerhauptquartier: Hitler's headquarters

FUSAG: First United States Army Group, the almost wholly fictitious Allied force supposedly assembled in southeastern England to invade the Pas de Calais in 1944

Gaff: Code name for the special operation to kill or kidnap Rommel in France in 1944

GC&CS: Government Code and Cipher School, the cover-name for the main British cryptanalytical organization, a dependency of the Foreign Office located at Bletchley

German General Staff: The small, élite military hierarchy responsible for army planning which functioned under the direction of OKW

Glimmer: Code name for the deception operation that simulated the presence of an invasion fleet off Boulogne on D-Day

Goodwood: Code name for Montgomery's offensive to break the German lines at Caen in July 1944

Halcyon: Code name for Y-Day, when all preparations for the invasion of Normandy were complete

Huff-duff: High Frequency Direction Finding, a method of locating enemy ships and land stations by taking bearing on their radio traffic

Husky: Code name for the invasion of Sicily in 1943

Interallié: Early MI-6 *réseau* in Paris in 1940–41

Ironside: Code name for the cover and deception operations directed at Bordeaux and the Biscay coast; a component of Fortitude South

Jade Amicol: The main MI-6 *réseau* in Paris and northern France in 1943–44

Jael: Code name for the cover and deception operations to conceal Allied intentions in Europe in 1943; later called Plan Bodyguard

Jedburghs: Special forces teams consisting of one American, one Briton and one Frenchman trained to organize and lead the French *maquis*

Joint Chiefs of Staff (JCS): The American high command in Washington, D.C.

Joint Intelligence Committee (JIC): The name given to the highest intelligence evaluation services in both London and Washington

Joint Planning Staff (JPS): The British military planning organization, of which the LCS was a part

Joint Security Control (JSC): The American organization under the Joint Chiefs of Staff responsible for the security of military and cryptanalytical operations, and the coordination of deception operations; the American counterpart of the LCS

Jubilee: Code name for the Allied raid on Dieppe in August 1942

Jupiter: Code name for Churchill's proposal to invade northern Norway

Kondor Mission: German intelligence network in Cairo

Kriegsmarine: The German navy

LCS: London Controlling Section, the organization within the Joint Planning Staff at Churchill's headquarters responsible for devising and coordinating strategic cover and deception schemes in all theaters of war

Lightfoot: Code name for Montgomery's offensive at El Alamein in October 1942

Lisbon Report: Documents describing German rocket and missile development passed to the British in Portugal in 1943

London Group: The section of SOE responsible for special operations in western Europe

Luftwaffe: The German air force

Lüttich: Code name for the German counteroffensive in Normandy in August 1944

Magic: American code name for intelligence derived from decrypting Japanese Enigma-enciphered wireless traffic

Martians: Code name for the COSSAC/SHAEF intelligence evaluation organization in London

Menace: Code name for the unsuccessful Anglo-French operation to occupy Dakar in 1940

Messages personnels: The British system of communicating with *réseaux* in western Europe, usually by voice code broadcast by the BBC; also called Avis

MI-5: The British counterintelligence and security service

MI-6: The British Secret Intelligence Service

MI-9: A section of the War Office responsible for creating escape routes in Europe

Mincemeat: Code name for the deception operation in 1943 using a corpse carrying false documents to persuade the Germans that the Allies intended to invade Greece and southern France, not Sicily; also codenamed Trojan Horse

Moonshine: An electronic device used to amplify and return the pulses of German radar and thus simulate large numbers of approaching ships or aircraft

Mulberry: Code name for the two amphibious harbors anchored off Normandy to supply the Allied invasion forces

Neptune: Code name for the invasion of Normandy, the assault phase of Operation Overlord

OKW: Oberkommando der Wehrmacht, the German supreme command

Organization Todt: German paramilitary construction engineers and workers

Oslo Report: Documents describing German weapons development programs delivered anonymously to the British Embassy, Oslo, in 1939

OSS: Office of Strategic Services, the U.S. secret intelligence and special operations service

OSS (SI): The secret intelligence branch of the OSS

OSS (SO): The special operations branch of the OSS, the American counterpart of SOE

Ossex: American secret intelligence teams dropped in France prior to D-Day

Overlord: Code name for Allied strategic plans and operations in northwest Europe in 1944–45

Overthrow: Code name for deception operations to suggest that the Allies would invade western Europe in 1942

OWI: Office of War Information, the American political warfare agency

Pointblank: Code name for the Allied Combined Bomber Offensive against German cities and industries prior to D-Day

Princes: The underground secret intelligence service in Denmark

PWE: Political Warfare Executive, the British political warfare agency

Quicksilver: Code name for those cover and deception operations concerning FUSAG and threats to invade the Pas de Calais; a component of Fortitude South

Rankin: Code name for Allied contingency plans in the event of the collapse of Germany

Ratissage: Literally, a rat-hunt, secret service jargon for a counter-espionage manhunt

Reichskanzelei: Literally, Reich Chancellory, Hitler's headquarters in Berlin

Réseau: Literally, a nest, a term applied to clandestine intelligence or espionage organization in German-occupied territories

R-Force: The deception organization at Montgomery's headquarters

Roundup: Code name for proposed American strategical and tactical operations in France in 1942–43; *see also* Sledgehammer

Rutter: Code name for the proposed Allied raid on Dieppe in July 1942; postponed and later mounted as Operation Jubilee

SAS: Special Air Service, a British military organization trained to carry out special missions behind enemy lines

Schwarze Kapelle: Literally, Black Orchestra, the name used by the Nazi Party to describe members of the German military services and the Abwehr conspiring to overthrow Hitler

SD: Sicherheitsdienst, the intelligence and counter-espionage arm of the SS

Sealion: Code name for the German plan to invade Britain in 1940–41

SHAEF: Supreme Headquarters, Allied Expeditionary Force, acronym for the Anglo-American command established to plan and execute Overlord and Neptune under the Combined Chiefs of Staff in Washington, D.C.

SIM: Servizio Informazione Segreto, the Italian secret service

Skye: Code name for those cover and deception operations concerning the creation of a fictitious Anglo-American force in Scotland preparing to invade Norway; a component of Fortitude North

Sledgehammer: Code name for the American proposal to invade France in 1942

SLU's: Special Liaison Units, MI-6 personnel attached to all higher Allied headquarters to disseminate intelligence derived from Ultra and protect its security

SOE: Special Operations Executive, the secret British organization created in 1940 to raise, arm, fund and train patriot armies in German- and Japanese-occupied territories and nations allied to the Axis

Special Plans Branch: The deception organization at Bradley's headquarters

SS: Schutzstaffel, the political-military order of the Nazi Party through which Hitler ruled Germany and German-occupied territories

Starkey: Code name for the reception operations to lure the Luftwaffe to battle and threaten an invasion of the Pas de Calais in the summer of 1943; a component of Cockade

Starkey: Code name for the deception operations to lure the Luftwaffe to responsibility for examining and developing American military and political policies

Sussex: Code name for the operation to drop American and British intelligence teams in France prior to D-Day; *see* Brissex, Ossex

Taxable: Code name for the deception operation that simulated the presence of an invasion fleet off Cap d'Antifer on D-Day

Telecommunications Research Establishment (TRE): The British radar and wireless research and development organization

Tindall: Code name for the deception operations to suggest an Anglo-American invasion of Norway in 1943; a component of Cockade

Titanic: Code name for airborne deception operations on D-Day which simulated large paratroop landings in the Neptune area of France

Torch: Code name for the Anglo-American invasion of North Africa in 1942

Ultra: Code name for intelligence derived from decrypting German Enigma-enciphered wireless traffic

Valkyrie: Code name for the German plan to suppress internal disorders which became the instrument through which the Schwarze Kapelle hoped to seize power from Hitler and the Nazi Party

Vendetta: Code name for the cover and deception operations directed at southern France; associated with Fortitude South

Wadham: Code name for the deception operation to threaten an Anglo-American invasion of Brittany in 1943; a component of Cockade

Wehrmacht: Literally, war machine, a term used to denote German military forces

Window: British code name for the foil strips dropped from aircraft to obstruct German radar reception

X2: The counterintelligence and agent-manipulation branch of the OSS

XX-Committee: The MI-5 organization for the control and manipulation of double agents

X-Gerät: A radio-navigation device used by German bombers for blind bombing in 1940

Y service: Technical communications intelligence services of both the German and the British armed forces

Zeppelin: Code name for the cover and deception operations directed at the countries of southern and southeastern Europe in 1943–44

Sources and Notes

The names of authors cited in the Sources and Notes refer to their published works which are listed in the Bibliography.

The abbreviations listed below are used in the Sources and Notes for the names and locations of certain libraries, collections and archives; the names and locations of certain documents; and the designations of certain military units.

AFHQ	Air Force Headquarters
BAOR	British Army of the Rhine
CCS	Combined Chiefs of Staff
CIAP	Copy in Author's Possession
COS	Chiefs of Staff
COSSAC	Chief-of-Staff Supreme Allied Command
CSDIC	Combined Services Detailed Interrogation Center
DRB	Diplomatic Records Branch
ED	Eisenhower Diary, Eisenhower Library, Abilene, Kansas
EDS	Enemy Documents Section
EPF	Eisenhower Personal File, Eisenhower Library, Abilene, Kansas
ETOUSA	European Theater of Operations, United States Army
FBIS	Foreign Broadcasting Intelligence Service
FC	Fraenkel Collection, Thaxted, England
FCC	Federal Communications Commission
HI	Hoover Institution on War, Revolution and Peace, Stanford, California
IWM	Imperial War Museum, London
JCS	Joint Chiefs of Staff
JSC	Joint Security Control
KC	Karlsruhe Collection, United States Air Force Historical Branch, Maxwell Air Force Base, Montgomery, Alabama
MAAFHQ	Mediterranean Allied Air Forces Headquarters
MAFB	Maxwell Air Force Base, Montgomery, Alabama
MID	Military Intelligence Division

MMR	Modern Military Records
NA	National Archives, Washington, D.C.
OAB	Operational Archives Branch, U.S. Navy, Washington, D.C.
OCMH	Office of the Chief of Military History, U.S. Army, Washington, D.C.
OMR	Old Military Records
ONI	Office of Naval Intelligence
OPD	Operations and Plans Division
OSS	Office of Strategic Services
OUP	Of Unknown Provenance
PRO	Public Records Office, London
R&A	Research and Analysis
RUSI	Royal United Services Institute
SAS	Special Air Service
SC	Shuster Collection, Modern Military Records, National Archives, Washington, D.C.
SDA	State Department Archives
SDDLRS	State Department Division of Libraries and Reference Services, Washington, D.C.
SGS	Secretary, General Staff
SHAEF	Supreme Headquarters Allied Expeditionary Force
USDA	United States Department of the Army
USFET	United States Forces European Theater
USJCS	United States Joint Chiefs of Staff
WDGS	War Department General Staff
WDGSS	War Department General and Special Staffs
WNRC	Washington National Records Center, Suitland, Maryland

PROLOGUE

Sources

Historical Sub-Section, Office of the Secretary, General Staff, SHAEF, *A Short History of COSSAC 1943–1944,* May 1944, Center for Military Studies, U.S. Army, Washington, D.C.; SHAEF SGS 381, *Bodyguard,* MMR, NA.

Notes

page
1   "pale skin . . ." Philby, p. 78.
2   "true to the . . ." Foot, p. 12.
3   "As the big . . ." Eisenhower in a letter to Gen. Brehon Burke Somervell, April 4, 1944, ED, p. 1627.
3   "It still seemed . . ." Churchill, *The Second World War,* Vol. 5, p. 514.
5   "Battles are won . . ." Churchill, *The Great War,* Vol. 1, p. 498.
6   "The dermal . . ." Norman Holmes Pearson, in a foreword to Masterman, p. xvi.
7   "Proustian complexity," Foot, p. 12.
7   "to approach . . . SHAEF Psychological Warfare Division, Memor-

page

andum to SHAEF Ops, "Policy and Methods of Black Warfare Propaganda Against Germany," November 10, 1944, MMR, NA.

7   "to drive a wedge . . ." William J. Donovan, Director, OSS, Memorandum to the USJCS, "Over-all Strategic Plan for U.S. Psychological Warfare," February 22, 1943, Record Group 218, Records of the USJCS, JSC 385, MMR, NA.

7   "Nothing quite like . . ." Foot, p. 12.

8   "It was Churchill . . ." Wingate, p. 185.

8   "Looking back . . ." Baumer interview.

9   "nine hundred chariots of iron," *et seq.*, Old Testament, Judges 4.

10   "In war-time, truth . . ." Churchill, *The Second World War*, Vol. 5, p. 338.

10   "It was going . . ." Morgan interview.

PART I: THE ORIGINS OF SPECIAL MEANS

1. ULTRA

Sources

Information concerning Menzies was obtained from the libraries of the *Sunday Times, Sunday Telegraph,* and *Daily Mail,* London; Ellerman's Wilson Line, Ltd., Hull (M. W. Webster, Archivist); Westonbirt School (Margaret Newton, Headmistress); *Eton College Chronicles* and Eton Archives (Patrick Strong, Keeper of College Library and Collections); Household Cavalry Museum, Cavalry Barracks, Windsor (Maj. A. J. Dickson, Curator, and Cpl. Maj. C. W. Frearson, Keeper); *War Diary, 1914, 2nd Life Guards,* and an unpublished account of the charge of Zwartelen by Cpl. Maj. T. L. King, Household Cavalry Musuem, Cavalry Barracks, Windsor.

Notes

epigraph

"In the high ranges . . ." *et seq.,* Churchill, an epigraph to Hyde, *Room 3603,* p. ix.

page

13   "It is difficult . . ." Churchill, *The Second World War*, Vol. 1, p. 261.

15   "The natural inquisitiveness . . ." *Die Schreibende Enigma-Chiffriemaschinen,* undated pamphlet, cited by Kahn, p. 421.

16   "a chance that . . ." *et seq.,* Review and analysis of Bertrand in *The Rearguard,* Munich, No. 29 and 30, July 15, 1974, *et seq.*

18   "tall, with a rather . . ." Winterbotham, *The Ultra Secret,* p. 14.

19   "A sonnet written . . ." Sara Turing, citing Alan Turing, p. 134.

19   "a permanent place . . ." *The Times,* London, June 16, 1954.

19   "In answer to . . ." Sara Turing, p. 67.

19   "wild as to hair . . ." *et seq.,* Sara Turing, quoting Sir Geoffrey Jefferson, p. 58.

20   "raven plucking . . ." Dunderdale interview.

page
22 "There was no . . ." Keen interview.
24 ". . . it was just . . ." Winterbotham, *The Ultra Secret*, pp. 15–16.
26 "guard the very . . ." Standing Orders of the Household Cavalry, p. 51.
26 "most select families . . ." *et seq.*, Henry Legge-Bourke, *The King's Guard*, London: Macdonald, 1952.
27 "fair to see . . ." *et seq.*, Churchill, *The Great War*, Vol. 1, p. 62.
28 "gather all . . ." Rowan and Deindorfer, p. 70.
30 "played his hand . . ." Dilks, p. 234.
31 "intellectual twilight . . ." Page, *et al.*, p. 110.
31 "the unique experience . . ." Winterbotham, *The Ultra Secret*, pp. 2–3.

2. COVENTRY

Sources

Information concerning Ultra during the Battle of Britain and in the Coventry raid, as well as its use throughout the war, was derived in part from interviews with Frederick W. Winterbotham, and from "Results of Ultra Based on a Study of the OCMH Chronology for 1939–1944," a memorandum from Winterbotham to the author, dated June 1971, prior to the publication of his own book, *The Ultra Secret*.

Notes

page
33 "You have sat . . ." Churchill, citing the speech made by the Rt. Hon. L. S. Amery, *The Second World War*, Vol. 1, p. 594.
33 "would certainly . . ." *ibid.*, p. 599.
33 "troops of the hunter . . ." Churchill, *The Second World War* Vol. 2, p. 217.
33 "A proper system . . ." *ibid.*, p. 218.
36 "Conduct of Air and Sea Warfare . . ." KC.
36 "All depends . . ." Royal Institute of International Affairs, entry for June 20, 1940.
37 "We must regard . . ." Churchill, BBC broadcast, September 11, 1940.
38 "I was struck . . ." *et seq.*, Winterbotham, *The Ultra Secret*, p. 59.
38 "It was Goering's . . ." Winterbotham interview.
39 "exclusively against . . ." *New York Times*, November 10, 1940.
41 "sadly and badly . . ." Lee, p. 104.
41 "It is a striking . . ." *Royal Air Force, 1939–1945*, Vol. 1, p. 210.
42 "all the Civil . . ." *et seq.*, S. A. Hector, in a letter to the author, March 3, 1974.
42 "I switched on . . ." *Life*, December 23, 1940.
43 "A report was . . ." Unsigned, unpublished monograph, IWM.
44 "the greatest attack . . ." *New York Times*, November 16, 1940.
44 "Coventry is now . . . *ibid.*, November 17, 1940.
44 "martyred City." *The Times*, London, November 16, 1940.

3. SPECIAL MEANS OPERATIONAL

Sources

Führer Conferences on Naval Affairs, 1946, Naval Intelligence Division, The Admiralty, London; ONI, *Etappes, The Secret German Naval Intelligence and Supply Organization,* 1946, OAB; OSS, R&AB, *Chronology of Principal Events Relating to the USSR,* Part II: "USSR in the War, 22 June 1941–2 September 1945," September 25, 1945, SDDLRS, DRB, NA; Relevant papers of ONI and U.S. Naval Attaché at London, OMR, NA.

Notes

page
45	"sizeable escape . . ." Foot, p. 5.
46	"All his life . . ." *et seq.,* Wingate, pp. 189–90.
46–47	"Practically all . . ." *et seq.,* "Aids to Surprise with Particular Reference to Deceiving, Mystifying and Confusing the Enemy on the Battlefield," British memorandum, presumed to be War Office in origin, with an appendix entitled "Ruses and Stratagems of War," a note by Field Marshal Sir Archibald Wavell, HI.
48	"separate war," JSC, OPD, WDGS, "Cover and Deception," Memorandum to the USJCS, May 14, 1945, Record Group 218, Records of the USJCS, JCS 498/10, MMR, NA.
51	"This timely . . ." Churchill, *The Second World War,* Vol. 3, p. 194.
52	"We are entering . . ." Churchill, *The Second World War,* Vol. 2, p. 493.
53	"We have got . . ." Churchill, *The Second World War,* Vol. 3, p. 106.
53	"an Admiralty muddle," Winterbotham interview.
57	"It is not necessary . . ." McLachlan, p. 161.
57	"They had . . ." *ibid.,* p. 400.
57	"foul baboonery," Churchill, *The Great War,* Vol. 3, p. 1392.
57	"so far as . . ." Churchill, *The Second World War,* Vol. 3, p. 316.
58	"If Hitler invaded . . ." *ibid.,* p. 331.
58	"The prospects for . . ." *et seq.,* Dilks, p. 420 ff.
59–60	". . . if the Germans . . ." *et seq.,* Masterman, p. 8.
60	"most favorable impression, *ibid.,* p. 56.
61	"I can catch . . ." *et seq.,* Popov, pp. 169–70.
61	" 'gigantic boiler . . .' " Churchill, *The Second World War,* Vol. 3, p. 540.
61	". . . we had won . . ." *ibid,* p. 539.

4. THE SEARCH FOR A STRATEGY

Sources

Combined Operations Headquarters Reports C.B. 04244, "The Dieppe Raid (Combined Report), 1942," and C.B. 04244(I), "The Raid on Dieppe, Lessons Learnt," October and September 1942, OCMH; OUP, "Digest of Operation

Roundup," with "Notes on Operation Sledgehammer," June 1944, OAB; Adm. E. Weichold, "The German Naval Defense Against the Allied Invasion of Normandy," Interrogation report by ONI, undated but probably 1945, OAB; Adm. F. Ruge, "Coast Defense and Invasion," ONI Report to Chief of Naval Operations, OAB; SHAEF, "German Report on Dieppe," SHAEF/116G/4/Int, MMR, NA; Gerd von Rundstedt, *et al.*, *OB-West—A Study in Command*, Ms. No. B633, OCMH; SHAEF, "German Appreciation Cotentin Peninsula Landing of 14 Aug 42," TDS/SHAEF/86/24 February 1944, MMR, NA; SHAEF, "Cotentin Landing 14 Aug 42," Reports by the 320th Infantry Division, TDS/ SHAEF/86/24 February 1944, MMR, NA; German Admiralty, Intelligence Division, "Radio Intelligence Report on Dieppe Landing," August 19, 1942, EDS, NA; Abwehrstelle Paris to Military Governor France and C-in-C West, "Report Concerning Foreknowledge of Dieppe Raid," EDS, NA.

Additional information concerning German foreknowledge of the Dieppe raid is derived from a series of letters and articles: David Irving, *Daily Telegraph,* London, September 9, 1963; *Evening Standard,* London, October 1, 2, and 14, 1963; Capt. S. W. Roskill, *Daily Telegraph,* London, November 4, 1963; *Der Spiegel,* Hamburg, November 6, 1963.

Notes

page

63	"a blend of . . ." R. Harris Smith, p. 2.
63–64	"Witnessed a demonstration . . ." *et seq.,* U.S. Army Intelligence Division, Correspondence 1917–41, "A Cipher Machine," Record Group 165, Records of the WDGSS, OMR, NA.
67	"virulent anti-Semite," Farago, *The Game of the Foes* (New York: Bantam, 1973), p. 430.
68	"to the attention . . ." *ibid.,* p. 434.
69	"to prevent . . ." Joint U.S. Staff Planners, "Establishment of a Security Committee for Military Operations," Note by the Secretaries, May 2, 1942, Records of the USJCS, Joint Planning Staff files, MMR, NA.
71	"has my heart . . ." Churchill, *The Second World War,* Vol. 4, p. 281.
72	"This country is . . ." Alanbrooke, Vol. 1, pp. 292–93.
72	"totally unprepared," OSS, R&A Report No. 9, "Morale in the British Armed Forces," March 21, 1942, in OSS R&A files, DRB, NA.
72	"Whether we are . . ." Alanbrooke, Vol. 1, p. 358.
72	"hanging on . . ." *ibid.,* p. 357.
72	"In the light of . . ." *ibid.,* p. 354.
73	"a good general . . ." *ibid.,* p. 358.
73	"at long last . . ." Matloff and Snell, *1943–1944,* p. 13.
74	"In the early days . . ." Eisenhower, *Crusade in Europe,* p. 320.
76	". . . a premature Western . . ." Alanbrooke, Vol. 1, p. 371.
76	"We discussed . . ." *ibid.,* p. 370.
76	"We are making . . ." *et seq.,* Sherwood, p. 577.
76	"full understanding . . ." *et seq.,* Churchill, *The Second World War,* Vol. 4, p. 305.
77	"Roosevelt (is) getting . . ." Alanbrooke, Vol. 1, p. 397.
77	"wheedle," *et seq.,* Stimson and Bundy, p. 214.

page
77   "We hold strongly . . ." Churchill, *The Second World War*, Vol. 4, p. 342.
78   "river of blood," *et seq.*, Sherwood, pp. 590–91.
78   "Operations in France . . ." Churchill, *The Second World War*, Vol. 4, pp. 344–45.
78   "supreme political crisis," Sherwood, p. 592.
78   "No responsible British . . ." Churchill, *The Second World War*, Vol. 4, p. 391.
79   "I am most . . ." *ibid.*, p. 395.
79   "Unless you can . . ." *ibid.*, pp. 396–97.
80   "The fall of . . ." *ibid.*, p. 398.
80   "However, I thought it . . ." *ibid.*, p. 457.
81   "It is sad . . ." Masterman, p. 108.
81   "A man whose . . ." F. W. Winterbotham, in a note to the author, 1974.
82   "I feel damn . . ." Sherwood, p. 609.
82   "All was therefore . . ." Churchill, *The Second World War*, Vol. 4, p. 404.
82   "Judged by this . . ." Liddell Hart in Taylor, *Churchill Revised*, p. 225.
82   "I cannot help . . ." Alanbrooke, Vol. 1, p. 430.
83   "All depends upon . . ." Churchill, *The Second World War*, Vol. 4, p. 405.
83   "The coastal regions . . ." *New York Times*, June 9, 1942.
83   "full understanding . . ." Churchill, *The Second World War*, Vol. 4, p. 305.
84   "The troops will . . ." Robertson, p. 144.
84   "As a result of . . ." *Führer Order*, OKW/WFSt, 551213/42, EDS, NA.
85   "From available intelligence . . ." Churchill, *The Second World War*, Vol. 4, p. 457.
87   "Even before we . . ." Flower and Reeves, citing Munro, p. 443.
87   "One question worried . . ." *ibid.*, p. 447.
88   "and in a stage . . ." *et seq.*, *ibid.*, p. 443.
88   "We bumped on . . ." *ibid.*, p. 444.
88   "the whole sky . . ." *ibid.*, p. 446.
88   "No armed Englishman . . ." Report of the German C-in-C (Rundstedt), "Dieppe Raid," September 3, 1942, issued by the Canadian General Staff Historical Section (GS), November 1946, Army Headquarters, Ottawa.
89   "They will not . . ." *ibid.*
89   "In London they . . ." Germany to North America, August 29, 1942, FBIS, FCC, NA.
89   "My general impression . . ." Churchill, *The Second World War*, Vol. 4, p. 467.
89   "Looking back . . ." *ibid.*, p. 459.
89   "It is a lesson . . ." Moran, p. 73.
90   "This bloody affair . . ." Alanbrooke, Vol. 1, p. 488.
90   "Several of the . . ." *ibid.*, p. 541.

5. ALAM HALFA

Sources

Reports of the U.S. Military Attaché at Moscow, in Records of the USJCS, JSC 381, MMR, NA; Reports of the Military Attaché at Cairo, OMR, NA; R. P. Serle, ed., *The 2/24th Australian Infantry Battalion*, Melbourne: Jacaranda Press; Maj. Gen. R. F. H. Nalder, *The History of the British Army Signals in the Second World War*, London: Royal Signals Institution, 1953.

Notes

page
92   "We have a . . ." Churchill, *The Second World War*, Vol. 4, p. 69.
93   "a jubilant shout . . ." Desmond Young, citing Rommel, p. 15.
93   "From the moment . . ." *ibid.*, p. 16.
93   "Where Rommel is . . ." Desmond Young, citing "Hauptmann Hartmann," p. 23.
93   "trying to minimise . . ." *et seq., ibid.*, pp. 23–24.
96   "There exists . . ." Desmond Young, p. 7.
97   "We had foreseen . . ." Churchill, *The Second World War*, Vol. 4, p. 320.
98   "beloved of the . . ." Germany to North America, July 21, 1942, FBIS, FCC, NA.
99   "I should say . . ." Alanbrooke, Vol. 1, p. 471.
99   "so afraid . . ." Churchill, *The Second World War*, Vol. 4, p. 431.
99   "for a very great . . ." *ibid.*, p. 430.
100   "at least the ice . . ." *ibid.*, p. 435.
100   "cast off . . ." *et seq.*, Dilks, p. 471.
100   ". . . all the talk . . ." Churchill, *The Second World War*, Vol. 4, p. 442.
101   "Rommel, Rommel, Rommel . . ." Alanbrooke, Vol. 1, p. 450.
102   ". . . what messages they were!" Kahn, p. 473.
104   "The consequences of . . ." Scott interview.
107   "We examined . . ." Mosley, citing Sadat, p. 82.
107   "Now is the . . ." *ibid.*
108   "with a Saarland . . ." *et seq., ibid.*, p. 86.
110   "It happened that . . ." *ibid.*, citing Sadat, p. 161.
112   "I was taken . . ." Churchill, *The Second World War*, Vol. 4, p. 464.
112   "The ensuing battle . . ." *ibid.*, p. 467.
112   "At any moment . . ." *ibid.*, p. 468.
113   "Condor calling." *et seq.*, Mosley, p. 167.
113   "this false information . . ." Churchill, *The Second World War*, Vol. 4, p. 490.
113   "*Zip* now equal . . ." *ibid.*, p. 489.
114   "The assault force . . ." Rommel, p. 277.
115   ". . . the British command . . ." *ibid.*, p. 284.
115   "proceed methodically . . ." de Guingand interview.

6. EL ALAMEIN

Sources

U.S. Naval Institute Proceedings, *The Italian Navy in World War II*, Annapolis: U.S. Naval Institute, 1957; C-in-C U.S. Naval Forces, Northwest African Waters, to C-in-C U.S. Fleet, "Recommendation for Special Organization for Deceptive Warfare," with staff memorandum re "Special Operations" and "Organization and Function of 'A-Force,' " in Records of the USJCS, CCS 434/2, MMR, NA; Documents relating to the security of Torch, Record Group 218, Records of the USJCS, CCS 334, JSC, NA; Sundry documents in The Goodfellow Papers, an OSS collection, HI.

Notes

page
116 "He was . . ." Slessor interview.
117 "Well there it is." De Guingand interview.
119 "the enemy would become . . ." Barkas, p. 202.
124 "a heavy heart," *et seq., Rommel*, p. 293.
125 "Don't worry . . ." *et seq.,* Desmond Young, pp. 147–48.
125 "But really . . ." Warlimont, p. 298.
129–30 "To Field Marshal Rommel . . ." *et seq., Rommel*, pp. 320–21.
131 "Whether I survive . . ." *ibid.,* p. 363.
131 "There was . . ." *et seq., ibid.,* p. 365.
131 "Generals who had . . ." Bullock, p. 689.
131 *"Herr Generalfeldmarschall* . . ." L Document 44499, August 17, 1944, OSS German Section, MMR, NA.
131 "You must excuse me . . ." Desmond Young, p. 155.
132 "Flying back . . ." *Rommel*, p. 369.
132–33 "I should have . . ." *et seq.,* Desmond Young, pp. 161–62.

PART II: THE ROOTS OF CONSPIRACY

1. CANARIS

Sources

Items from the OSS file on Canaris, CIA Headquarters, Langley, Virginia; *Log of the Coaler* Baden (companion to *Dresden*), OUP, in English, perhaps a translation by The Admiralty, IWM; "Extracts from the Log of the *Dresden*," with "Comments," *Naval Review*, undated, IWM; Oberstleutnant-zur-See Canaris, "Aktenvermark," October 5, 1915, a personal report of the *Dresden* engagement and escape from South America, Box 431 PG75155, Kriegsmarine Archives, Freiburg; Account of the ambush of U-35 by Commandant Pradeau, in *Les marines, sociaux et politiques d'un ancien Officier de Marine*, OUP, undated, FC; Adm. Arnauld de la Perière, "Account of the Ambush of U-35," FC; Lt. Cdr. Arnauld, "Transfer of Lt. Commander Canaris off Cartagena," OUP, 1916, Kriegsmarine Archives, Freiburg; "Bericht Kapitänleutnant Canaris über Abholung durch 'U-35,' von Trefflinie bei Cap Tinoso," a signed report of his escape from Cartagena by Canaris to the Admiralstab, undated, Box 161 PG61579, Kriegsmarine Archives, Freiburg; H. B. Gisevius, "Admiral Canaris, die Sphinx der deutschen Spionage," *Weltwoche,* March 1, 1946; Helmut Krausnick, "Aus den Personalakten von Canaris," Vol. 10, No. 3, July 1962, Institut für Zeitgeschichte, Munich; *Outbreak of Hostilities Between Britain and Germany,* British Blue Book, London: HMSO, 1940; ONI, "Reports on Lieutenant Commander Wilhelm Canaris," a file of attaché reports dated April–July 1928, Record Group 38, Records of the Office of the Chief of Naval Operations, OMR, NA.

Notes

epigraph

> "Gehlen: Don't you think . . ." A conversation between General Reinhard Gehlen and General Edwin L. Sibert, Room 303, Army and Navy Club, Washington, D.C., November 1968.

page

137 "If England wants . . ." Bullock, p. 548.
137 "Naturally . . ." Colvin, *Canaris,* Maidstone, U.K.: George Mann, 1973, p. 95.
138 "I am speaking . . ." *The Times,* London, September 4, 1939.
138 "I must warn you . . ." Colvin, *Master Spy,* p. 55.
140 "inefficient, intriguing . . ." Lohan interview.
140 "grey fox . . ." Wheeler-Bennett, *Nemesis of Power,* p. 598.
140 "trapeze artist . . ." Louis Rivet, "L'énigme du service renseignements allemands sous le régime hitlérien," *Revue de Défense Nationale,* July 1947, Paris.
140 "extraordinarily intelligent . . ." Marras interrogation, OSS Bern, February 7, 1945, in OSS file on Canaris, *op. cit.*
141 "I have ascertained . . ." Colvin, *Master Spy,* p. 256.
141 "Canaris betrayed . . ." Skorzeny interview.
141 "served the enemy . . ." Colvin, *Master Spy,* p. 256.
141 "one of the bravest . . ." Dulles interview.
141 "shrouded even now . . ." Gehlen, p. 27.
141 "He is one . . ." Zeller, p. 24.
141 "damned brave . . ." Menzies interview.
142 "spies and assassins . . ." Rowan and Deindorfer, p. 62.
143 "kill or capture," Menzies interview.
146 "What I want," Fleming, p. 194.
146 "reasonable and sees . . ." Colvin, *Canaris, op. cit.,* p. 39.
147 "The 'Canaris group' . . ." Interrogation of Franz Maria Liedig, an extract from *Interim* (British army intelligence review), "The German Intelligence Branch and 20th July," No. 14, December 17, 1945, in the private collection of a former MI-6 officer.
147 "It is difficult . . ." J. R. R. Tolkien, *The Lord of the Rings,* London: Allen & Unwin, 1966, p. 171.

2. THE SCHWARZE KAPELLE

Sources

In addition to the sources cited in the Bibliography, information concerning the Schwarze Kapelle in this chapter and throughout the book has been derived from: Interrogations by U.S. Army Historical Section, Germany, of Leading

German Generals, SC; SHAEF Counterintelligence Sub-Division, G2, Evaluation and Dissemination Section Report No. 12, "Anti-Nazi Groups in Germany and Austria," February 6, 1945, MMR, NA; Albert Speer, Interrogation Report 19, "Politicians and Politics in Nazi Germany," U.S. Group Control, Office of the Director of Intelligence, Field Information Agency (Technical), January 1946, MMR, NA; Otto A. W. John, "Some Facts and Aspects of the Plot Against Hitler," undated memorandum, OUP, HI; Berlin District Interrogation Center, Consolidated Interrogation Report, "The Political and Social Background of the 20th July Incident," September 10, 1945, *World War II, Underground Movements, Germany,* OCMH; Gen. Georg von Sodenstern, *Events Leading Up to 20th July 1944,* Ms. No. B499, undated, OCMH; Günther Blumentritt, *20 July 1944,* Ms. No. B272, circa 1946, OCMH; Rudolph von Gersdorff, *History of the Attempt on Hitler's Life,* Ms. No. A855, circa 1946, OCMH; Erich Zimmermann and Hans-Adolf Jacobsen, eds., *Germans Against Hitler, 20 July 1944,* Bonn: Press and Information Office of the Federal Government of Germany, 1960; Franz von Papen, "The Schwarze Kapelle and 20th July as Seen from the German Diplomatic Service," OUP, no date but circa 1945–46, located in an MI-6 collection, CIAP; Walter Huppenkothen, "Chief SS Interrogator's Report on the Aims, Connections and Personalities of Members of the Plot Against Hitler," OUP, no date, possibly an MI-6 interrogation, CIAP; F. L. Belin, "Hitler's Generals," OSS promulgation, November 10, 1942, MMR, NA; Johannes Blaskowitz, "Strife Between German Military and Political Powers," State Department Interrogation Report, OSS German Section, MMR, NA; Horace Schacht, "How Hitler Came to Power," "Schacht's Attempt at Putsch," "Failure of the German General Staff to Keep Its Oath and Curb Hitler," State Department, Special Interrogation Report, September 25, 1945, OSS German Section, MMR, NA; OSS Switzerland, Report No. 34495, "Background of Attack upon Hitler," OSS German Section, MMR, NA; *Documents on German Foreign Policy, 1918–1945,* Series D, Vols. 4 and 8, 1951 and 1954, Washington, D.C.; "Judgment in the Trials of Walter Huppenkothen," Bavarian Landesgericht, February 1951 and November 1952, HI; OSS R&A Report No. 2458, "The Process of the Collapse of the German Armies," August 29, 1944, SDDLRS, NA.

Sources pertaining to this chapter in particular include: Hans Speidel, *Beck Against Hitler,* an undated monograph, OCMH; Fabian von Schlabrendorff, "Gestapo Report of the Investigation into the Indictment of Fritsch," Appendix, Schlabrendorff, *The Secret War Against Hitler;* Office of the U.S. Chief of Counsel for War Crimes, Sundry testimonies, interrogation summaries and interrogation reports of W. Schellenberg, November 1945–January 1947, MMR, NA.

Notes

page
148   "sole bearer of . . ." Wheeler-Bennett, *Nemesis of Power,* p. 334.
148   "Orders of a superior . . ." Shulman, pp. 9, 11.
149   "General Beck . . ." Liedig interrogation, *op. cit.*
150   "I wonder why . . ." *et seq.,* attributed to Bredow in O'Neill.
151   "The events of . . ." *et seq.,* Liedig interrogation, *op. cit.*
151   "It may be . . ." Goerlitz, p. 289.
152   "I swear by God . . ." Wheeler-Bennett, *Nemesis of Power,* p. 339.
152   "This is a fateful . . ." Gisevius, p. 279.

3. FRIEND OR FOE

Sources

Walter Tachuppik, "Canaris und Heydrich," *Die Zeitung,* November 7, 1941.

Notes

page
153–54   "does not love . . ." *et seq.,* Deacon, pp. 272–73.
156   "such matters as . . ." Menzies interview.
158   "Party Member Reinhard . . ." Höhne, p. 192.
158   "incredibly acute . . ." Schellenberg, p. 30.

4. THE PLOT BEGINS

Notes

page
162   "Hitler's criminal procedure . . ." Liedig interrogation, *op. cit.*
163   "my daily bread . . ." *et seq.,* Bullock, pp. 32, 34.
164   "Why didn't you . . ." *et seq.,* Goerlitz, p. 326.
165   "A war begun . . ." *ibid.,* p. 339.
165   "The elimination of . . ." Report of Gen. George C. Marshall, Chief of Staff, United States Army, to the President of the United States, November 6, 1945, Library of Congress, Washington, D.C.
165   "The only one . . ." Deutsch, p. 90.
167   "through yielding to . . ." *et seq.,* Colvin, *Master Spy,* p. 67.
167   "Everything is decided . . ." *et seq., ibid.,* p. 70.
168   "utmost frankness and . . ." Wheeler-Bennett, *Nemesis of Power,* p. 411.
168   "I am as certain . . ." *ibid.,* p. 412.
168   "I have found . . ." Colvin, *Master Spy,* p. 72.
169   "What he . . ." *et seq., ibid.,* p. 75.
169   "rivalries, prejudices . . ." Liedig interrogation, *op. cit.*

5. THE OUTBREAK OF WAR

Sources

Reports of the U.S. Military Attaché at Berlin, 1929–41 OMR, NA; Reports of the Director of Military Intelligence to the Chief of Staff of the U.S. Army, 1919–1939, OMR, NA; Statement by G. J. Sas to Deinstag, Report 2128/58, March 16, 1948, Institut für Zeitgeschichte, Munich.

Notes

page
171   ". . . Hitler's mental condition" *et seq.,* Dilks, pp. 141, 143.
171   "Hitler's death . . ." *et seq., The Times,* citing *Der Spiegel,* London, August 5, 1971.
171   "We were being . . ." Dilks, pp. 166–67.

page
172   "Shortly before I . . ." McLachlan, p. 245.
173   "officers of the military . . ." The diary of General Sir James Marshall-Cornwall, excerpts provided the author by Marshall-Cornwall.
173   "Hitler had decided . . ." *et seq.*, Aster, pp. 235–36.
173–74   "a good deal . . ." *et seq.*, Marshall-Cornwall diary, *op. cit.*
175   "There will probably . . ." Shirer, *The Rise and Fall of the Third Reich*, p. 41.
175   "I have struck . . ." Wheeler-Bennett, *Nemesis of Power*, p. 446.
175   "Our enemies . . ." *et seq.*, Bullock, p. 526.
175   "bloodthirsty thanks . . ." International Military Tribunal, Document No. L-3 PS 798, NA.
175   "Have no pity . . ." *et seq.*, Bullock, p. 527.
176   "greatest strategist . . ." H. R. Trevor-Roper, "The Mind of Adolf Hitler," in Hitler, p. xxv.
177   "Peace has been . . ." Wheeler-Bennett, *Nemesis of Power*, p. 451.

6. CONSPIRACY AT THE VATICAN

Sources

Reports of the U.S. Military Attaché at Rome, 1939–41, OMR, NA; George O. Kent, "Pius XII and Germany: Some Aspects of German-Vatican Relations 1933–43," *American Historical Review*, 70 (1964); Dr. Josef Mueller, Sundry statements re Canaris and Heydrich, OUP, undated, Vols. 14B, 15, 16A, 17, 18D, Dr. Mueller, FC.

Notes

page
178   "One day . . ." International Military Tribunal, Document No. 3047–PS 769, NA.
178   "these things," Liedig interrogation, *op. cit.*
180   "An eagle hunts . . ." *et seq.*, Boveri, p. 248.
181   "It is Hitler . . ." Deutsch, p. 117.
181   "The German Opposition . . ." *ibid.*, p. 121.
182   "The Pope is . . ." *ibid.*, p. 120.
184   *"Schmarren,"* *et seq.*, *ibid.*, p. 134.
185   "Cannot someone put . . ." *ibid.*, p. 196.
185   "human being and . . ." *ibid.*, p. 197.
185   "We have no . . ." *ibid.*, p. 224.

7. THE VENLO INCIDENT

Sources

MID Papers, WDGS, German Section, 1939–41, OMR, NA.

Notes

page
187   "The political overthrow . . ." Schellenberg, p. 89.
187   "encouraged," *et seq.*, Menzies interview.
187   "marvellous oysters," Schellenberg, p. 90.

page
 188 "on the highest . . ." Menzies interview.
 189 "Several old Party . . ." *et seq.,* Schellenberg, p. 94.
 191 "bloodier than the Somme." Gubbins interview.

   8. "ADROIT INTRIGUE"

Sources

 Command and Commanders in Modern War: Harold C. Deutsch, "The Rise of the Military Opposition in the Nazi Reich," with commentary by Charles V. P. von Luttichau and Peter Paret; and Walter Warlimont, *et al.,* "The Military View," Proceedings of the Second Military History Symposium, USAF Academy, May 2–3, 1968. Also Karl Brandt, "The German Resistance in American Perspective," an address at the memorial convocation for the dead of July 20, 1944, July 20, 1954; S. J. Sas, "Het hegon in Mei 1940," *Der Spiegel,* Hamburg, October 7 and 15, 1953; General Adolf Heusinger, "Military Participation in the Conspiracy of 20 July 44," Final Interrogation Report No. 30, January 10, 1946, HQ USFET Military Intelligence Service Center, SC.

Notes

page
 192–93 "violent, bitter . . ." *et seq.,* Donald Watt and Ian Colvin, "1940s Anti-Nazis Who Never Were," *Daily Telegraph,* London, January 1 and 2, 1971.
 193 "the long-awaited . . ." Deutsch, p. 289.
 193 *"Conditio sine qua . . ." et seq., ibid.,* pp. 294–95.
 193 "contained a broad . . ." *et seq., ibid.,* pp. 296–98. Mueller's recollections of his negotiations at the Vatican were related to the author in an interview before the publication of the Deutsch account.
 194 "unusually serious . . ." *ibid.,* citing Halder interview, p. 312.
 194 "You should not . . ." *et seq., ibid.*
 195 "carefully formulated," *et seq., ibid.,* pp. 336–37.
 195 "wangle a botched-up . . ." Watt and Colvin, citing Cabinet Minutes, *op. cit.*
 195 "No German . . ." Deutsch, citing Leiber interview, p. 340.
 196 "deep in the ink," *et seq., ibid.,* pp. 343–44.
 196 "his own *gendarme," ibid.,* citing Neuhausler interview, p. 344.
 197 "he could not . . ." *et seq., ibid.,* p. 345–46.
 198 "well-wishing German . . ." R. V. Jones, "Scientific Intelligence," *Journal of the Royal United Services Institute,* February 19, 1947.
 199 "Tremendous strides . . ." General Board, U.S. Forces, Europe, "V2 Rocket Attacks and Defenses," a report on the characteristics and effectiveness of the German A-4 (V2) long-range rocket, Antiaircraft Artillery Section, 1945, OCMH.
 199 "It seemed quite . . ." Cockburn interview.
 202 "There is no . . ." Deutsch pp. 99–100.
 202 "to cause . . ." Liedig interrogation, *op. cit.*
 203 "funeral banquet," *et seq.,* Deutsch, pp. 328–29.
 203 "complete tactical surprise . . ." Churchill, *The Second World War,* Vol. 2, p. 30.

9. CANARIS AT WORK

Sources

OSS Dublin Reports Nos. A2630-1-2-3-4-5, March 11, 1943, MMR, NA; OSS Report No. N5400, "German Espionage in Ireland," March 16, 1944, MMR, NA; Military Intelligence Division, War Department General Staff, "Ireland," a report by the Military Attaché, Dublin, July 26, 1944, MMR, NA; OSS file on Canaris, *op. cit.;* Gen. Walter Warlimont, "The Führer's Headquarters," Interrogation Report No. 9, October 24, 1945, HQ USFET Military Intelligence Service Center, SC.

Notes

page
204   "I appeal . . ." *et seq.,* Bullock, p. 592.
206   "(If we could) . . ." Delmer, *Black Boomerang,* p. 137.
207   "I am sorry . . ." *ibid.*
207   "You know . . ." Liss interview.
208   *"fons et origo,"* Masterman, p. 36.
210   "the German forces . . ." *et seq.,* Fleming, p. 179.
210   "with the certainty . . ." *et seq.,* Farago, *The Game of the Foxes,* p. 223.
211   "had some connection . . ." *et seq.,* Fleming, p. 182.
211   "rotten to its . . ." Farago, citing Goetz's "testament," *The Game of the Foxes,* p. 224.
211   "German agents have . . ." OSS R&A Report No. 2087, "An Introduction to the Irish Problem," May 23, 1944, MMR, NA.
213   "strange old buzzard" *et seq.,* Farago, *The Game of the Foxes,* p. 513.
214   "The admiral asks . . ." *et seq.,* Colvin, *Master Spy,* p. 149.
214–15   "sought to overbear . . ." *et seq., ibid.,* p. 151.
215   ". . . in Spain (Canaris) . . ." *ibid.,* p. 155.
215–16   "destroy Yugoslavia . . ." *et seq.,* Bullock, p. 635.

10. THE ASSASSINATION OF HEYDRICH

Sources

Files of the Personal Staff of the Reichsführer SS, Group T-175, NA; General Files, SS, Koblenz and Freiburg; Berlin Documents Center, Microfilm Groups 580–611, NA; Ernst Kaltenbrunner, "The Kaltenbrunner Report," edited by the Archiv Peter für Historische und Zeitgeschichtliche Dokumentation, Stuttgart; Sundry interrogations of W. Schellenberg, *op cit.*

Notes

page
218   "secret documents prepared . . ." Amort and Jedlicka, Introduction.
220   "the section dealing . . ." *ibid.,* p. 122.
221   "political unreliability," *et seq.,* Walter Schellenberg, *War Room: 14.8.45 Brigadeführer SS Schellenberg, Autobiography, Compiled*

page

          During His Stay in Stockholm June 1945, OUP, in the collection of a former MI-6 officer.

221   "Heydrich's Decalogue," Amort and Jedlicka, p. 147.

226   "was one . . ." Manvell and Fraenkel, *Himler,* pp. 139–40.

226   "your murdered chief," *et seq.,* Schellenberg, p. 336.

226   "deceptive features . . ." Höhne, citing Dr. Bernard Wehner, p. 560.

226   "choked with emotion," *et seq.,* Schellenberg, p. 338.

226   "almost feminine . . ." Alan Bullock, citing "Herr Harprecht, a young German journalist," in the Introduction to Schellenberg, p. 15.

227   "A live spy . . ." Masterman, p. 54.

11. OPERATION FLASH

Sources

CSDIC, Report SRGG 1347, "A Conversation Between General Eberbach and General Blumentritt," August 19, 1945, in a private collection, CIAP; *Field Marshal Günther von Kluge,* Form 201, OCMH; European Command, United States Army, Ethint 5, "An Interview with General W. Warlimont, Circumstances of the 20th July Incident: Was Von Kluge a Traitor?" August 3, 1945, MMR, NA; "Statement by M. Wallenberg," *Svenska Dagbladet,* Stockholm, September 4, 1947; Hans-Adolf Jacobsen, ed., *July 20, 1944, The German Opposition to Hitler as Viewed by Foreign Historians,* Bonn: Press and Information Office of the Federal Government of Germany, 1969; Charles de Cosse-Brissac, "Collapse of the Wehrmacht," *Revue de Défense Nationale,* Paris, March 1946; Martin Blumenson and J. Hodgson, "Hitler Versus His Generals in the West," *United States Naval Institute Proceedings,* 82: 1036–1287; Gen. Rudolph Baron von Gersdorff, "Events Leading Up to Planned Attempt on Hitler's Life on 15 March 1943," Intermediate Interrogation Report No. 34, HQ USFET Military Intelligence Service Center, SC.

Notes

page

228–29   "the strongest terms," *et seq.,* Schellenberg, p. 198.

229   "could see . . ." Alan Clark, *Barbarossa,* p. 206.

230   "vain, cowardly," Goebbels, p. 92.

230   "Gone were the days . . ." Wheeler-Bennett, *Nemesis of Power,* p. 526.

231   "Half my nervous . . ." Halder, p. 57.

232   "On the basis . . ." Speer, pp. 325–26.

232   "We didn't even . . ." *ibid.*

232   "To land first . . ." McLachlan, p. 82.

233   "The real triumph . . ." Masterman, p. 110.

233   "Once again . . ." Speer, pp. 325–26.

233–34   "Had the enemy . . ." *et seq.,* Roskill, Vol. 2, p. 213.

234   "Gibraltar received . . ." Colvin, *Master Spy,* p. 187.

235   "Stalingrad is no longer . . ." Alan Clark, *Barbarossa,* p. 269.

237   "Gentlemen . . ." Rundstedt, *et al.,* Ms. No. B633, *op. cit.,* Annex II, Part 2.

page
238   "But, my dear Führer . . ." *ibid.*
238   "I am a soldier . . ." *et seq.,* Moll, p. 73.
241   "As always, . . ." Fabian von Schlabrendorff, "Our Two Tries to Kill Hitler," *Saturday Evening Post,* July 20, 1946.

PART III: HIGH STRATEGY AND LOW TACTICS

1. CASABLANCA

Sources

Anfa Reports and Minutes in CCS/JCS files, MMR, NA; Reports and Minutes of the 55th–60th meetings of the Combined Chiefs of Staff, MMR, NA; USJCS, draft history, *The War against Germany,* Part 3, "Casablanca through Trident," Record Group 218, Records of the USJCS, MMR, NA; Report by Joint Strategic Survey Committee, "German Strategy in 1943," February 10, 1943, Record Group 218, Records of the USJCS, JSC 214, MMR, NA; "Germany (12-10-42)," Sec. I, Record Group 218, Records of the USJCS, CCS 381, MMR, NA.

Notes

epigraph
       " 'Cover' was carried . . ." attributed to Churchill.

page
246   "They swarmed down . . ." Matloff and Snell, *1943–1944,* p. 107.
246   "In matters touching . . ." Ingersoll, p. 71.
246   "kind of dark . . ." Alanbrooke, Vol. 1, p. 540.
247   "opposed as much . . ." *et seq.,* Matloff and Snell, *1943–1944,* p. 25.
247   "I heard the words . . ." *et seq.,* Sherwood, p. 696.
248   "If you were given . . ." R. E. Dupuy, *Men of West Point,* New York: Sloane, 1952, p. 324.
248   "its effect was . . ." John Slessor, "Grand Strategy and the Second World War," *The Listener,* London, November 22, 1956.
248   "the despairing ferocity . . ." Menzies interview.
248   "There is much . . ." *et seq.,* Popov, p. 245.
249   "can be . . ." *et seq., ibid.,* p. 246.
249   "You know, my dear . . ." Colvin, *Master Spy,* p. 193.
249   "Now no honorable . . ." Armstrong, p. 133.
249   "extraordinary dangers," *ibid.,* p. 162.
249   "To compel . . ." *ibid.,* p. 167.

2. THE BATTLE OF THE ATLANTIC

Sources

"Report of the Proceedings of Convoy SC122," OAB; "Report of the Proceedings of Convoy HX229," OAB; "Reports of Commander Task Force 24," U.S. Atlantic Fleet, April 13, 1942, OAB; "Report of the Flag Officer, *Newfoundland,*" to the Secretary, Naval Board, Ottawa, OAB; A collection of signals from C-in-C Western Atlantic to escorts, 1943, OAB; Excerpts from the *History of the U.S. 21st Weather Reporting Squadron,* USAF Historical Branch, MAFB; Intelligence Division, Chief of Naval Operations, "Ifni Radio Station Intelligence Reports," June 28, 1943, MMR, NA; OSS Collected Reports on German Radio and Weather-Reporting Stations, October 1, 1942, to February 5, 1944, MMR, NA; *The U.S. Coast Guard in World War II,* Washington, D.C.: Government Printing Office, 1944–53; C-in-C Allied Naval Expeditionary Force, "Operation Neptune Weather Criteria," OAB; Gen. R. E. Lee, U.S. Military Attaché, London, "Interception of Axis Weather Reports," Report to the MID, Washington, D.C., May 31, 1941, Record Group 165, Records of the WDGSS, OMR, NA; Canadian Intelligence Service, "Meteorological Security," with "Report on Arctic Operations," Record Group 218, Records of the USJCS, CCS 385, MMR, NA; Office of Naval History, *A History of Etappes,* OAB.

Notes

page
251   "groping and drowning . . ." attributed to Churchill.

252   "dreadfully emaciated," *et seq.,* Oliver Knox interview.

252   "national calamity," Wingate interview.

253   "The service he . . ." "Report on the Death of A. D. Knox to the Fellows of King's," King's College, Cambridge (John Saltmarsh, Historian).

253   "German heroism . . ." Germany to North America, November 20, 1942, FBIS, FCC, NA.

253   "Our submarines . . ." Flower and Reeves, p. 418.

254   "The new-moon night . . ." Wolfgang Frank, p. 116.

254   "American impetuosity . . ." Slessor interview.

257   "a serious disaster . . ." Roskill, Vol. 2, p. 366.

257   "the Germans never . . ." *et seq., ibid.,* pp. 367–68.

259   "After examining all . . ." *ibid.,* p. 364.

259   "the combination . . ." *ibid.,* Vol. 3, p. 16.

260   "descendant of . . ." *ibid.,* p. 64.

261   "the whole great . . ." *ibid.,* p. 68.

261   "one of the most . . ." *ibid.,* p. 69.

262   "I noticed . . ." *ibid.,* p. 86.

262   "No more mortifying . . ." *The Times,* London, February 17, 1942.

262   "We shall fight . . ." Roskill, Vol. 3, p. 87.

262   "accurate intelligence . . ." *ibid.,* p. 88.

263   "If really bad . . ." Eisenhower, *Crusade in Europe,* p. 240.

3. THE LCS AND PLAN JAEL

Sources

R. E. L. Wingate, A memorandum to the author on the history, structure, authority, responsibilities and working methods of the London Controlling Section; SHAEF SGS 381, Pre-Invasion File, MMR, NA; SHAEF, *A short History of COSSAC 1943–1944, op. cit.;* Plan Cockade, SHAEF G2 202BX/2/Int, in SHAEF Pre-Invasion File; Plan Zeppelin, SHAEF 18209/Ops (b), in SHAEF Pre-Invasion File; Helmuth Greiner, The Greiner Series: "OKW World

War II," Ms. No. C-065b, SHAEF Historical Division, OCMH; JCS Memorandum, "Deception Policy 1943 Covering Germany and Italy," March 22, 1943, Record Group 218, Records of the USJCS, CCS 184/1, MMR, NA; "Deception Policy 1943 (Germany and Italy)," (Final), April 3, 1943, Record Group 218, Records of the USJCS, CCS 184/3, MMR, NA; William J. Donovan, Director, OSS, Memorandum to the USJCS, "Overall Strategic Plan for U.S. Psychological Warfare," *op. cit.;* OSS, Psychological Warfare Analysis, January–September 1943, OUP, Record Group 218, Records of the USJCS, MMR, NA; Col. H. D. Kehm, memorandum for the Assistant Chief of Staff, OPD, WDGS, "Conference on Deception," May 29, 1943, Record Group 218, Records of the USJCS, MMR, NA; OUP, possibly OPD, Memorandum to the USJCS, "Final Report for the Washington Anglo-American Cover and Deception Conference, June 2, 1943," Record Group 218, Records of the USJCS, CCS 385, MMR, NA; Gen. A. C. Wedemeyer, for JSC, "Deception Planning and Execution," Record Group 218, Records of the USJCS, MMR, NA.

Notes

page
270   "Colonel Bevan played . . ." Deane interview.
270   "I do not think . . ." Bevan interview.
270   "Bevan and Churchill . . ." Baumer interview.
271   "most famous political . . ." Charles Graves, *Leather Armchairs,* New York:Coward-McCann (1964), p. 13.
271   "think nine ways . . ." Baumer interview.
271   "preoccupied not so much . . ." *et seq.,* Sampson, pp. 202, 203.
273   "collecting old scientific . . ." *Who's Who,* London: A. & C. Black, 1970.
273   "waves of confusing . . ." Greiner, *op. cit.*
274   "perfect oil-can," Moran, p. 121.
274   "to induce the . . ." SHAEF, *A Short History of COSSAC, op. cit.*
275   "contain the maximum . . ." Plan Cockade, *op. cit.*

4. MINCEMEAT

Notes

page
278   "One has to be . . ." *et seq.,* Warlimont, pp. 326–27.
278   "Here is where . . ." *et seq., ibid.,* p. 341.
278   ". . . the shadow of . . ." Deakin, p. 176.
279   "Anybody but a damned . . ." Wingate interview.
281   "Colonel R. Meinertzhagen . . ." Wingate interview.
281   "once and for . . ." Richard Meinertzhagen, *Army Diary 1899– 1926,* London: Oliver & Boyd, 1960, p. 224.
282   "Why shouldn't we . . ." Montagu, p. 25.
283   "the body was . . ." *ibid.,* p. 30.
284   "He is quiet . . ." *et seq., ibid.,* p. 65.
287   "I regard the situation . . ." Deakin, p. 194.
288   "a wholly reliable . . ." *ibid.,* p. 347.
288   "Following the impending . . ." *ibid.,* p. 348.

5. QUEBEC

Sources

CCS Trident Meeting, *Official Trident Conference Book,* MMR, NA; CCS Quadrant Meeting, *Official Quadrant Conference Book,* MMR, NA; Gen. Thomas T. Handy, "Conduct of the War in Europe," Memorandum to the USJCS, Record Group 218, Records of the USJCS, MMR, NA.

Notes

page
291 "to delay Germany's . . ." CCS 135/1, 135/2, CCS 134, January 4, 1943, Record Group 218, Records of the USJCS, MMR, NA.
292 "disturbed," *et seq.,* Pogue, *George C. Marshall,* Vol. 3, p. 187.
292 "about *who* . . ." Arthur H. Vandenberg, Jr. (ed.), *The Private Papers of Arthur H. Vandenberg,* Boston: Houghton Mifflin, 1952, pp. 48–49.
292 "In preparing for . . ." Matloff and Snell, *1943–1944,* p. 217.
292 "able to justify . . ." *ibid.,* p. 216.
292–93 "We cannot now . . ." *et seq.,* Stimson and Bundy, pp. 436–38.
294 "very undiplomatic language . . ." Leahy, p. 175.
294 "took the offensive," *et seq.,* Quadrant Conference Book.
294 "belt buckle . . ." Morgan interview.
294 "entire US-UK strategic . . ." *et seq.,* Matloff and Snell, *1943–1944,* p. 221.
295 "opportunistic," Quadrant Conference Book.
295 "gloomy and unpleasant . . ." *et seq.,* Alanbrooke, Vol. 1, pp. 705–7.
296 "Our talk was . . ." *ibid.,* p. 708.
296 "To my great . . ." *ibid.,* p. 710.
296 "feeling the inevitable . . ." *ibid.,* p. 718.
297 "I knew that . . ." Churchill, *The Second World War,* Vol. 5, p. 514.
297 "I never again . . ." MacDonald, p. 178.
298 "Evidently a most critical . . ." Churchill, *The Second World War,* Vol. 5, p. 126.

6. THE SCHWARZE KAPELLE (1943)

Sources

Sundry interrogations of W. Schellenberg, *op. cit.;* A collection dealing with various aspects of the plot against Hitler, including CSDIC reports, reports by various agencies including OSS and MI-6, almost wholly immediately postwar in origin, OUP, possibly MI-6, CIAP; State Department Special Interrogation Report, "Conversations of Fritz Kolbe with Harold C. Vedeler: Activity as an Allied Agent During the War, Personalities and Agencies in the Foreign Office, Activities of Sofindus," September 23–24, 1945, Wiesbaden, SDA, NA; OSS Report No. A27627 Concerning Baron Hoyningen-Huene, April 11, 1944, MMR, NA; "Peace Overtures," a collection of documents relating to anti-Nazi peace gestures, Record Group 218, Records of the USJCS, MMR, NA.

Notes

page
301   "Since the generals . . ." *et seq.*, Kramarz, p. 122.
303   "could not bring . . ." Bethge, p. 704.
304   "counter-espionage," *ibid.*, p. 713.
304   "Drones Club." Bartz, p. 125.
304–5 "The only thing . . ." Bethge, p. 815.
305   "During the years . . ." Schellenberg, pp. 407–8.
305   "a matter of serious . . ." *et seq.*, *ibid.*, p. 406.
306   "were reassuring," *et seq.*, *ibid.*, p. 407.
307   "Be pleased to . . ." Alanbrooke, Vol. 1, p. 726.
307   "I was able . . ." *et seq.*, Schellenberg, p. 407.
307–8 "You would be as . . ." Wheeler-Bennett, *Nemesis of Power*, pp. 570 ff.
308   "not interested." *ibid.*, p. 574.
308   "must be removed . . ." attributed to Kluge in Zeller.
309   "to persuade . . ." Dulles, citing a memorandum from Jacob Wallenberg, *Germany's Underground*, p. 142.
309   "I should be glad . . ." *et seq.*, *ibid.*
310   ". . . the group's leaders . . ." Liedig interrogation, *op. cit.*
311   "Philby's job . . ." Page, *et al.*, p. 159.
313   "And what a yield . . ." Dulles interview.
313   "Sincerely regret . . ." Dulles, *Secret Surrender*, p. 23.
314   ". . . the *Wehrmacht* . . ." *et seq.*, John, p. 128.
314   "she told me . . ." *ibid.*, p. 134.
315   "There is no doubt . . ." Sherwood, p. 791.

7. STARKEY

Sources

SHAEF G2, SHAEF/201DX/3/Int, *Enemy Reactions to Tindall*, MMR, NA; COSSAC/44DX/Int, *Enemy Reactions to Wadham*, MMR, NA; COSSAC/41DX/Int, *Enemy Reactions to Starkey*, MMR, NA; HQ 12th Army Group, *Operation Wadham*, in SHAEF SGS 381, Pre-Invasion File, *op. cit.;* SHAEF G6, *BBC Warnings to Resistance Groups*, File No. 000.77-I, MMR, NA; Intelligence Branch, COSSAC 182X, in SHAEF SGS 381, Pre-Invasion File, *op. cit.;* Gen. J. E. Upton, Deputy Chief, Theater Group, OPD, WDGS, Memorandum to Gen. Handy and Gen. Hull, "Tactical Report on Air Operations from Great Britain, September 1943," October 10, 1943, OPD (Great Britain) file, MMR, NA; Memorandum from London, CM-In-7887, to OPD, WDGS, "8th Air Force Operations during 9th September 1943, Dispatched in Support of Special Operation Starkey," September 10, 1943, OPD (Great Britain) file, MMR, NA; OPD (France), Record Group 165, Records of the WDGSS, MMR, NA; Selected AFHQ Records, WNRC.

Notes

page
317   "There was a certain . . ." Wingate interview.
318   "an elaborate camouflage . . ." *et seq.*, SHAEF, *A Short History of COSSAC, op. cit.*

page
319–20   "the deception by . . ." *et seq., Operation Cockade,* PWE Plan, COS (43) 384 (o) July 18, 1943, in COSSAC/41DX/Int, *op. cit.*

322   ". . . the PWE plan . . ." Jacob L. Devers, in a letter to George V. Strong, August 24, 1943, in COSSAC/41DX/Int, *op. cit.*

322   "Will someone . . ." Frederick Morgan, a note in HQ 12th Army Group, *Operation Wadham, op. cit.*

322   "An unofficial source . . ." Director of Press and Publicity, War Office Report, August 19–25, 1943, in Intelligence Branch, COSSAC/182X, *op. cit.*

322   ". . . the liberation of . . ." *New York Times,* August 19, 1943.

323   "may come any day . . ." *et seq.,* Press Digest, in COSSAC/41 DX/Int, *op. cit.*

323   "before the leaves . . ." Director of Press and Publicity, War Office Report, *op. cit.*

323   "ARMIES READY . . ." *New York Times,* August 19, 1943.

323–24   "discontinue," *et seq.,* in COSSAC/41DX/Int, *op. cit.*

324   "suggested," *et seq.,* Brig. H. Redman, British Joint Staff Mission, Offices of the CCS, Washington, D.C., to Gen. John R. Deane, "Cockade Directive," Record Group 218, Records of the USJCS, CCS 385, MMR, NA.

325–26   "disappointing manner," *et seq.,* in COSSAC/41DX/Int, *op. cit.*

326   "What is all . . ." Delmer, *The Counterfeit Spy,* p. 87.

326   ". . . it would appear . . ." in COSSAC/41DX/Int, *op. cit.*

326   "The movements . . ." Liddell Hart, *The German Generals Talk,* p. 231.

327   "practically denuded," in COSSAC/41DX/Int, *op. cit.*

327   "balls-up," Morgan interview.

8. PROSPER

Sources

Maj. Gen. Sir Colin Gubbins, "Resistance Movements in the War," Lecture to the RUSI, January 28, 1948; William J. Donovan to Brig. Gen. John R. Deane, "A Proposal to Make Use of Certain Facilities and the Services of Certain Persons in France and America with a View to Aiding the War Effort," February 20, 1943, Record Group 218, Records of the USJCS, MMR, NA.

Notes

page
329   "of formed bodies . . ." *et seq.,* Foot, p. 4.
330   "And now set . . ." *ibid.,* p. 11.
330   "stabbing attacks," *et seq., ibid.,* p. 12.
331   "a skein so . . ." Deacon, p. 344.
331   "brave, ambitious . . ." Foot, p. 198.
332   "The persevering efforts . . ." *ibid.*
334   "at least one . . ." *ibid.,* p. 290.
336   "95 per cent . . ." *ibid.,* p. 121.

page
337   "There was nothing . . ." An unsigned, undated note in the SAS Operations and Intelligence Section files, CIAP.
338–39   "In the middle . . ." *et seq.,* Foot, p. 308.
339   "Suttill . . ." *ibid.,* p. 309.
341   "exceptional character," *ibid.,* p. 199.
342   "Evidently . . ." *ibid.,* p. 178.
343   "authentic confusion." *Ibid.,* p. 449.
343   "An assertion," *ibid.,* p. 307.
343   ". . . to send a few . . ." *ibid.,* p. 308.
344   "The staff concerned . . ." *ibid.,* p. 278.
344   "We never used . . ." Wingate interview.
345   "In the *Starkey* . . ." in COSSAC/44DX/Int, *op. cit.*
345   "The truth is . . ." *et seq.,* Foot, p. 290.
346   "The fact that . . ." *ibid.*
347   "We know he is in . . ." *et seq., ibid.,* p. 303.
347   ". . . when—if ever— . . ." *et seq., ibid.,* p. 301.
348   "great ability and . . ." *et seq.,* Foot, p. 299.
349   "the British secret service . . ." Fuller, *Double Webs,* p. 215.
349   "(he was) dressed . . ." *France-Soir,* Paris, June 8, 1948.
349–50   "to work for them . . ." *et seq.,* Fuller, *Double Webs,* p. 67.
350   "very mysterious," *et seq., France-Soir,* Paris, June 9, 1948.
351–52   "strategic sacrifice," *et seq.,* Fuller, *Double Webs,* p. 208.
352   "He could reveal . . ." *ibid.,* p. 210.
352   ". . . I can sleep . . ." *ibid.,* p. 246.

9. THE INTELLIGENCE ATTACK

Sources

Foreign Office citation of Sister Henriette Frede, CIAP; A Report of Operations, The Enemy Terrain and Defense Section, G2, HQ 12th Army Group, June 2, 1945, provided the author by Gen. E. L. Sibert; US Strategic Bombing Survey, "V-Weapons (Crossbow) Campaign" and "V-Weapons on London," USAF Historical Branch, MAFB; MI-6 Interrogation Report of Otto John, CIAP; Jeremy Bennett, *British Broadcasting and the Danish Resistance Movement 1940–45: A Study of the Wartime Broadcasts of the BBC Danish Service,* Cambridge: Cambridge Univ. Press, 1966; Erik Lund, *A Girdle of Truth,* Denmark: Institute of Communication Research and Contemporary History, Arhus University, 1970; Cecil von Renthe-Fink, German Minister to Denmark, Final Interrogation Report, OI FIR 36, Military Intelligence Service, USFET, MMR, NA.

Notes

page
355–56   "All signs point . . ." *et seq.,* Harrison, Appendix D.
363   "expressed surprise . . ." Irving, *The Mare's Nest,* p. 35.
363   "The Chiefs of Staff . . ." *ibid.,* p. 38.
363   "The petrol instructions . . ." Jones, "Scientific Intelligence," *op. cit.*
364   "Hitler and members . . ." Irving, *The Mare's Nest,* p. 89.

page
    366   "promised greatly . . ." *et seq., ibid.,* p. 91.
    366   "This evening nobody . . ." *ibid.,* p. 104.
    367   "It seemed particularly . . ." *ibid.,* p. 114.
    376   ". . . it was the elimination . . ." *ibid.,* p. 211.

10. TEHERAN

Sources

CCS, JCS and COS Minutes and Documents Concerning the Cairo-Teheran-Cairo Conferences, MMR, NA, and HI; State Department Minutes and Documents Concerning the Cairo-Teheran-Cairo Conferences, SDA, NA, and HI; Valentin Berezhkov, "The Teheran Meeting," *New Times,* Moscow, June, July, and August 1948; Reports of the U.S. Military Mission to Moscow, November 1943–June 1944, MMR, NA; JCS 533, 127th Meeting, "Reaffirmation of Over-All Strategic Concept and Basic Undertakings," undated, MMR, NA; JCS 606, "Collaboration with the USSR," Note by the Secretaries, November 22, 1943, MMR, NA; CCS 586, "Information on Overlord for Soviet General Staff," June 2, 1944, MMR, NA; Gen. Sir Hastings Ismay to Joint Staff Mission, Washington, D.C., "Cover and Deception Plans 1944, Teheran Agreement with Soviet Union," January 21, 1944, Record Group 218, Records of the USJCS, MMR, NA; Charles E. Bohlen, *The Bohlen Minutes,* SDA, NA; Dr. Forrest C. Pogue, chapter notes for *The Supreme Command* (Pogue study), OCMH.

Notes

page
    379   "I do not think . . ." ED, p. 988.
    379   "child's play." Matloff and Snell, *1943–1944,* p. 335.
    379   "I wish our . . ." Alanbrooke, Vol. 2, p. 74.
    380   "a most underhand," Pogue study, *op. cit.*
    380   "probable British proposals . . ." *et seq.,* JCS 533, 124th Mtg., Item 3, "Recommended Line of Action at Next US-British Staff Conference (European-Mediterranean Strategy)," undated, MMR, NA.
    381   "very cautious stand," JSC 533, 123rd Mtg., November 15, 1943, MMR, NA.
    381   "Amen."JSC 533, Mtg. with President, November 15, 1943, MMR, NA.
    381   "General Marshall . . ." Matloff and Snell, *1943–1944,* p. 330.
    382   "On the way here . . ." Moran, p. 141.
    382   "a formidable-looking . . ." *ibid.,* p. 139.
    382   "Brooke got good and nasty . . ." Pogue, *George C. Marshall,* Vol. 3, p. 305.
    383   ". . . I have noticed . . ." Moran, p. 141.
    383   "Sure, we are . . ." *et seq., ibid.,* p. 142.
    384   "This conference . . ." *ibid.,* p. 143.
    385   "The difference between . . ." *et seq.,* Sherwood, pp. 783–84.
 385–86   "I have been commanded . . ." *et seq.,* Roosevelt, pp. 181–82.

page
386 "very direct question," *et seq.*, Churchill, *The Second World War*, Vol. 5, p. 329.
386–87 "Nothing more can . . ." *et seq.*, Moran, pp. 148–49.
387 "without the slightest . . ." Dilks, p. 581.
387 "rounded up . . ." *et seq.*, Churchill, *The Second World War*, Vol. 5, p. 330.
387 "You are pro-German . . ." Moran, p. 152.
387–88 ". . . I was not . . ." *et seq.*, Churchill, *The Second World War*, Vol. 5, p. 330.
389 "In war-time . . ." Churchill, *The Second World War*, Vol. 5, p. 338.
389 "Agreed that . . ." Bohlen, *op. cit.*, November 30, 1943.
389 "against the almost . . ." Sherwood, p. 802.
390 "invaluable, and indispensable," *et seq.*, Churchill, *The Second World War*, Vol. 5, pp. 369–70.
390 "front man," *et seq.*, Ingersoll, pp. 76–78.

11. CICERO

Sources

Christopher Buckley, *Five Ventures—Iraq–Syria–Persia–Madagascar–Do-decanese*, London: HMSO, 1954; Sir John Lomax, "The Legend of Cicero," a letter in the *Daily Telegraph*, London, no date; Miscellaneous Collection of German Foreign Ministry Documents by Franz von Papen and Ludwig Moyzisch Concerning Cicero, EDS, NA; State Department Special Interrogation Report, "Conversations of Fritz Kolbe," *op. cit.*

Notes

page
391 ". . . the enemy . . ." SHAEF SGS 381, *Bodyguard, op. cit.*
392 "This is the time . . ." D. N. Brunicardi, "Aegean Enterprise," *An Cosantoir*, Dublin, no date, HI.
395 "dark eyes kept . . ." *et seq.*, Moyzisch, p. 31.
395 "At first glance . . ." Schellenberg, p. 388.
395 "To Ambassador . . ." Moyzisch, p. 43.
396–97 "My astonishment grew," *et seq.*, *ibid.*, p. 54.
397 ". . . . we sought to . . ." Schellenberg, p. 391.
398 "there might just . . ." Moyzisch, p. 135.
398 "the bank-notes . . ." Bazna, p. 196.
399 "Assistant Military Attaché." "Obituary of Montague R. Chidson," *The Times*, London, October 4, 1957.
400 "We always thought . . ." Dunderdale interview.
400 "whitewash the stupidity . . ." Lomax interview.
401 "I knew about . . ." Bazna, p. 109.
402 "Of direct practical value . . ." Dulles, *Secret Surrender*, p. 24.
402 "Since a leak . . ." *et seq.*, Dulles interview.
403 "security reasons," Harrison, p. 485.
404 "The greater . . ." Masterman, p. 9.
404 "Of course Cicero . . ." Menzies interview.
405 "Enemy intentions . . ." Warlimont, p. 401.

PART IV: COVER AND DECEPTION

1. EISENHOWER, SUPREME COMMANDER

Sources

Neptune Monitor Daily Intelligence Reports January 1, 1944–June 5, 1944, MMR, NA; Counter Intelligence Corps (US) School, *History and Mission of the CIC in World War 2*, OCMH; SHAEF 2DX/12/Int, *Overlord, Disruption of Enemy Lines of Communication*, MMR, NA; SHAEF 2DX/16/Int, *Overlord, Enemy Reactions*, MMR, NA; "Planning for Deception Plans for Cross-Channel Operation," Vols. 1 and 2, Record Group 218, Records of USJCS, CCS 385, MMR, NA; "Outline Plan for Political Warfare—Overlord," Record Group 218, Records of the USJCS, CCS 385, MMR, NA; CCS, "Memo on Friction Between Members of the U.S. and British Armed Forces," OPD, WDGS, Records of the WDGSS, MMR, NA; Special Plans Branch, 12th U.S. Army Group, "Report on Operation Fortitude and Cover and Deception in the European Theater of Operations" (the "Harris Report"), a collection of reports prepared by Col. William A. Harris and his staff, Record Group 319, Records of the (US) Army General Staff, MMR, NA.

Notes

epigraph

"My Christmas message . . ." T. J. T. and E. P. T., *There Is a Spirit in Europe, A Memoir of Frank Thompson*, London: Gollancz, 1947, fly-leaf.

page

410   "They're over-paid . . ." OWI Bureau of Special Services, "A Pilot Study of American Sentiment Toward the British," March 29, 1943, NA.

410   "With a broad smile . . ." Stagg, p. 17.

411   "It must be . . ." *et seq.,* Alanbrooke, Vol. 1, p. 527–28.

412   ". . . it wearies me . . ." ED, p. 1063.

412   "The planning stages . . ." Gen. W. B. Smith, "Document for Inclusion in Historical Records Concerning General Eisenhower's Critical Decisions," a memorandum to Historical Section, SHAEF, February 22, 1945, OCMH.

412   "much more marked . . ." CCS Study, "British Reaction to U.S. Troops in the United Kingdom," August 24, 1942, MMR, NA.

413   "My colleagues . . ." Churchill, *The Second World War*, Vol. 6, p. 8.

414   ". . . whatever further assaults . . ." *et seq.,* 21 AG/00/Int/1101/15, "Reaction to Overlord of Enemy Land Forces in the West based on Intelligence up to March 8, 1944," in SHAEF 2DX/16/Int, *op. cit.*

415   "It is to my . . ." Churchill, *The Second World War*, Vol. 5, p. 602.

415–16   "Germany will be capable . . ." *et seq.,* Strategy and Policy Group, WDGS, "United Nations Course of Action in Europe in the Event Overlord is Canceled," in American-British Conversations (ABC Papers), USJCS file, MMR, NA.

page
416   "attractive at first . . ." Joint Strategic Survey Committee, WDGS, "Probable Russian Reaction to Anglo-American Operations in the Aegean," in ABC Papers, USJCS file, MMR, NA.
417   "As I saw the problem . . ." Churchill, *The Second World War,* Vol. 5, p. 377.
418   "advance on," *et seq.,* Jackson, p. 170.
418   "eyes and ears . . ." Blumenson, citing Lucas, *Anzio,* p. 89.
418   "I am far too . . ." *ibid.,* p. 91.
418   "I felt like . . ." *ibid.,* p. 93.
419–20   "(Canaris) was pressed . . ." *et seq.,* Westphal, p. 240.
420   "Anzio was my . . ." Moran, p. 202.
420   "first attempt . . ." Warlimont, p. 410.
420   "If we succeed . . ." *ibid.,* p. 411.
420   "We should . . ." Churchill, *The Second World War,* Vol. 5, p. 431.
420–21   "The ease with . . ." *et seq., ibid.,* p. 432.
421   ". . . It is absolutely . . ." *et seq.,* ED, February 18, 1944.
422   "The Boche has . . ." *ibid.,* February 22, 1944.
422   "send into the south . . ." Churchill, *The Second World War,* Vol. 5, p. 434.

2. THE GERMAN SUPREME COMMAND

Sources

Gen. Hans Speidel, OCMH Ms. No. B720, *Reflections and Views of General-feldmarschall Rommel, C-in-C Heeresgruppe B,* March 31, 1945, MMR, NA; Speidel, Ms. No. B721, *Background for July 20, 1944, Ideas and Preparations of GFM Rommel for an Independent Termination of the War in the West and for Putting an End to Nazi Despotism,* OCMH; Field Marshal Karl Rudolph Gerd von Rundstedt, Special Interrogation Report, February 1, 1946, Historical Section, Canadian Army, SC.

Notes

page
423   "in spite of . . ." FBIS, FCC, Daily Reports, January 1, 1944–September 1, 1944, NA.
423   "rapidly progressive . . ." "Hitler as Seen by His Doctors," OUP, undated, presumed to have originated with U.S. Group Control Council (Germany), Office of the Director of Intelligence, located in an MI-6 file in private hands.
424   "spiritual derangement," *et seq.,* "Special Interviews of A. Speer by O. Hoeffding," U.S. Group Control Council (Germany), Office of the Director of Intelligence, located in an MI-6 file in private hands.
425–26   "It is evident . . ." *et seq.,* Rommel, p. 465.
427   "gifted with a . . ." *et seq.,* Hitler, p. 52.
427   "At no place . . ." Rommel, p. 465.
427–28   "The Fatherland . . ." *et seq.,* Rundstedt, *et al.,* Ms. No. B633, *op. cit.*
429   "devil's garden." *ibid.*

page
429 "He will do . . ." Pogue study, *op. cit.*
430 "an independent . . ." Speidel, Ms. No. B721, *op. cit.*
430 "some figure . . ." Wheeler-Bennett, *Nemesis of Power,* p. 606.
430 "that he was . . ." Desmond Young, pp. 196–97.
430 "When the government . . ." Hans Speidel, *Invasion, 1944,* New York: Henry Regnery, 1950, p. 71.
430 "I believe it . . ." Desmond Young, p. 197.
430–31 "in perhaps . . ." *et seq., ibid.,* pp. 200–201.

3. BODYGUARD

Sources

SHAEF SGS 381, *Bodyguard,* and SHAEF SGS 381, *Fortitude,* MMR, NA; Plan Zeppelin, Plan Vendetta, Plan Ironside, SHAEF G3, SHAEF/18209/ Ops (b), June 3, 1944, MMR, NA; Plan Zeppelin, Intelligence Section, Office of the Director of Operations and Intelligence, MAAFHQ, WNRC; Deception Plans, S (B) 641/Int, Intelligence Section, Office of the Director of Operations and Intelligence, MAAFHQ, WNRC; Vendetta Conference Minutes, April–June 1944, MAAFHQ, WNRC; Relevant documents in the "Harris Report," *op. cit.;* Relevant documents in Record Group 218, Records of the USJCS, MMR, NA; OSS, *The PW Weekly, Psychological Warfare Analysis,* Printed for the Planning Group, OSS, R&A files, DRB, NA; Relevant documents in the files of the U.S. Military Mission to Moscow, Record Group 334, MMR, NA; Relevant documents in Record Group 226, Records of the OSS, MMR, NA; War Cabinet, London Controlling Section, "Report by Colonel John H. Bevan (Britain) and Lieutenant Colonel W. H. Baumer (America) Regarding Their Visit to Moscow," LCS (44) 10, April 2, 1944, and "Brief of Report by Colonel J. H. Bevan and Lt.-Col. W. H. Baumer Regarding Their Visit to Moscow in Connection with Plan Bodyguard," April 26, 1944, in Strategy and Policy Group files, OPD, WDGS, MMR, NA.

Notes

page
435 "To complete . . ." *et seq.,* "PWE/OWI Outline Plan for Political Warfare, including Joint PWE/OWI and SOE/OSS (SO) Political Warfare Plan," August 12, 1943, Record Group 218, Records of the USJCS, CCS 385, MMR, NA.
436 "musicians and choristers," Wingate interview.
436 "I like all this," Note by Eisenhower on a Bodyguard memorandum, in SHAEF SGS 381, *Bodyguard, op. cit.*
437 "necessary organization . . ." "Final Report of the Washington Anglo-American Cover and Deception Conference," with annexes, Record Group 218, Records of the USJCS, CCS 385, MMR, NA.
437 "we find ourselves . . ." *et seq.,* "Plan Bodyguard, Report by the Joint Staff Planners"; and "Plan Bodyguard, Memorandum from the United States Chiefs of Staff," Record Group 218, Records of the USJCS, CCS 385, MMR, NA.
438 "active pursuit and . . ." 21 AG, Counter-intelligence Instruction No. 1, April 1944, CIAP.
439 ". . . there was always . . ." Morgan, p. 239.

page
440–42   "He seemed to . . ." *et seq.,* The personal diary of Maj. Gen. William H. Baumer, copy provided the author by Gen. Baumer.
442   "I thought Kuznetzov . . ." Deane, p. 147.
443   "very enthusiastic . . ." *ibid.,* p. 148.
443   "suddenly the lines . . ." Deane interview.
444   "I had never . . ." Deane, p. 14.
445   "We felt no . . ." Bevan and Baumer interviews.
445   "they put us . . ." Baumer diary.
445   "loaded with crossings out . . ." Baumer interview.

4. THE BALKANS

Sources

"German Anti-Guerrilla Operations in the Balkans, 1941–1944," USDA Pamphlet, 1954, OCMH; S. G. Walker, "Imperial Strategy and the Middle East," lecture, RUSI, March 1949; OSS R&A Report No. 2458, "The Process of Collapse of the German Armies," August 29, 1944, SDDLRS, NA; Military Intelligence Service, Washington, D.C., Italian Air Attaché Reports, Turkey, OSS files, SDDLRS, NA; Intelligence Division, Office of Chief of Naval Operations, Report on German Activities in Turkey and the Balkans, May 27, 1944, OSS R&A file, MMR, NA; OSS R&A Report No. 1742, "The Anti-German Opposition in Bulgaria," February 29, 1944, U.S. Board of Economic Warfare, NA; U.S. Joint Intelligence Committee Middle East, OSS Reports on Bulgaria, Nos. 6283-4-5-90-91, August 14–September 9, 1943, OSS files, MMR, NA; OSS dissemination No. A-18720, "Reactions of Bulgarian Officers," January 17, 1944, MMR, NA; The Foreign Service of the United States, U.S. Consulate General, Istanbul, "An Analysis of the Situation Following the Death of King Boris 3," to Secretary of State, Washington, D.C., September 6, 1943, OSS files, MMR, NA; Helmut Heiber, *The Death of Czar Boris,* Institut für Zeitgeschichte, Munich, 1964; *Germany and Her Allies in World War II,* Vols. 1 and 2, Ms. No. P108, OCMH, MMR, NA; Maj. E. W. Sheppard, "The Eastern Mediterranean in British World Strategy," *The Fighting Forces,* London, February 1948; OSS R&A Report No. 1502, "The Role of the Local Dynasties in the Balkans," April 1944, SDDLRS, NA; Gen. Edgar Feuchtinger, *History of the 21st Panzer Division,* OCMH Ms. No. B441, circa February 1947, MMR, NA; Gen. Sylvester Stadler, *Combat Reports of the 9th SS Panzer Division,* OCMH Ms. No. B470, March 30, 1947, MMR, NA; Ambassador Frohwein to Reichsminister Ribbentrop, Report on the Vermehren Affair, February 20, 1944, in *Auswärtiges Amt, Büro des Staatssekretärs, Akton, Turkei,* November 1, 1943–April 30, 1944, CIAP; OSS Switzerland, Background Story on German Occupation of Hungary, April 4, 1944, in OSS R&A file, MMR, NA; SHAEF Theater Intelligence Section Martian Report No. 88, "The Move of the 9th SS Panzer Division Hohenstaufen from the Amiens Area (18–24 February 1944)," March 15, 1944, OPD files, MMR, NA.

Notes

page
447   "cause the peoples . . ." "Outline Plan for Political Warfare," *op. cit.*
448   "was to carry . . ." Kallay, p. 78.

5. FORTITUDE NORTH

Sources

Earl F. Ziemke, "The Northern Theater of Operations, 1940–1945," USDA Pamphlet, December 1959, OCMH; Plan Fortitude (final), February 23, 1944, in SHAEF SGS 381, *Fortitude, op. cit.;* C-in-C Home Fleet to The Admiralty and SHAEF, "Naval Plans for Operations in Support of Fortitude North," April 2, 1944, in SGS 381, *Fortitude, op. cit.;* COSSAC to All Commands, "Notes on Wireless Deception and Silences," December 9, 1943, in SGS 381, *Fortitude, op. cit.;* COSSAC, "Early Plans for Mespot (later Fortitude)," July 22, 1943, in SGS 381, *Fortitude, op. cit.;* Sir R. E. L. Wingate, a note to the author on Plan Fortitude, July 1971; Col. R. M. MacLeod, a note and letters to the author on the activities of the British 4th Army, 1963–64; Jeremy Bennett, *British Broadcasting and the Danish Resistance Movement 1940–45, op. cit.;* A collection of German Foreign Office telegrams, September 1943–June 1944, *Auswärtiges Amt file Büro England,* EDS, NA; Testimony of Walter Schellenberg taken at Horsbruck, Germany, by Lt. Col. Smith W. Brookhart, Jr., IGD, May 8, 1946, OUP but presumed to be depositions for International Military Tribunal (Nuremberg), MMR, NA; Relevant documents in the "Harris Report," *op. cit.;* Relevant documents in Record Group 218, Records of the USJCS, MMR, NA.

Notes

page
469 "a judicious mixture . . ." *ibid.*, p. 90.
470 "my only friend . . ." Höhne, p. 13.
470 "Beware . . ." *et seq.*, Dulles interview; Kolbe conversations, *op. cit.*
471 "a novel method . . ." Farago, *The Game of the Foxes*, p. 543.
472 "was told bluntly . . ." *et seq.*, *ibid.*, p. 553.

6. FORTITUDE SOUTH

Sources

J. L. Hodgson, R Study, "Fear of Allied Intentions," OCMH; Plan Quicksilver, Plan Skye, SHAEF/18209/Ops (b), in SGS 381, *Fortitude, op. cit.*; Relevant documents in the "Harris Report," *op. cit.*; Documents relating to Gen. George S. Patton, Record Group 218, Records of the USJCS, MMR, NA; BAOR, Intelligence Review, File on Colonel "M," March 1946, Bundesarchiv, Koblenz.

Notes

page
473 "blistering epistle . . ." Farago, *Patton*, p. 343.
473 "reprehensible conduct." *ibid.*, p. 356.
474 "inspecting amphibious forces," *et seq.*, Metz interview.
475 "You persistently . . ." Farago, *Patton*, p. 376.
475 "master of flattery," *et seq.*, ED, p. 1017.
475 "Whoever picked . . ." *et seq.*, Farago, *Patton*, pp. 386–87.
476 "It has now . . ." *ibid.*, p. 407.
476 "Patton appreciated . . ." *ibid.*, p. 400.
476 ". . . since it is . . ." *ibid.*, p. 417.
477 "I am thoroughly . . ." Eisenhower letter to Patton, April 28, 1944, EPF.
477 "You probably were . . ." *et seq.*, Farago, *Patton*, pp. 421–22.
478 ". . . this last . . ." *ibid.*, p. 423.
478 "51, a swarthy . . ." J. Edgar Hoover, "The Spy Who Double-Crossed Hitler," *American Magazine*, May 1946.
480 "2/lt. N, of . . ." *et seq.*, Johnston interview.
480 "Speculations, guesses, . . ." Masterman, p. 146.
481 "An agent who, . . ." *ibid.*, p. 147.
481–82 "Connoisseurs of double . . ." *et seq.*, *ibid.*, p. 114.
482 "Only later did . . ." *ibid.*, p. 116.
482 "The one-man . . ." *ibid.*, p. 142.
484 "I received . . ." Bleicher, pp. 58–59.
485 "rough-hewn Slavic . . ." Farago, *The Game of the Foxes*, p. 619.
486 "broken off . . ." Johnston interview.
487 "He was interrogated . . ." Masterman, p. 56.
488 "Yugoslav of good family, . . ." *ibid.*, p. 138.
489 "A V-mann dispatch . . ." Delmer, *The Counterfeit Spy*, p. 156.
490 "It was not . . ." Masterman, p. 151.
491 "small consolation," *et seq.*, *ibid.*, p. 154.

page
491–92   "The Führer attaches . . ." Blumentritt to all commands, letter, May 8, 1944, with note of conversation with Jodl on May 6, 1944, CIAP.
492   "He was an . . ." Liss interview.
494–95   "The multiplicity . . ." *et seq.*, FHW *Lagerberichte,* October 1943–February 1944, EDS, NA.
496   ". . . it is known . . ." Staubwasser, Ms. No. B782, *op. cit.*
497   "had a reputation . . ." Gehlen, p. 44.
497   "tall, sporty . . ." *et seq.*, Col. Anton Staubwasser, in a letter to Gen. E. L. Sibert concerning Col. Michel, March 1972, CIAP.

7. NUREMBERG

Sources

1st Air Corps (Luftwaffe) *War Diary,* and scattered associated documents, KC; "RAF Bomber Command Intelligence Narrative of Operations No. 774," PRO, London; RAF Bomber Command, "Report on Night Photographs No. P1," Air 24/268, PRO, London; RAF Bomber Command, "Casualty Report, Nuremberg, Night, 30/31 March 1944," Air 14/2674, PRO, London.

Notes

page
500   "a necessary preliminary," Masterman, p. 9.
501   "We never gave . . ." Masterman interview.
501   "On at least . . ." de Guingand interview and letter to the author, April 26, 1970.
501   ". . . to bait the . . ." Carroll, p. 217.
501   "cruel expedient," *ibid.,* p. 221.
501   "One of the . . ." ED, p. 1600.
502   "no other propaganda . . ." *et seq.,* Carroll, p. 221.
502   "General Spaatz . . ." ED, p. 1219.
502   "more than ordinary . . ." Craven and Cate, p. 31.
502   "had to bother . . ." *et seq.,* Becker, p. 353.
503   "ambush," Royal Institute of International Affairs, p. 243.
503   "Since the war . . ." Price, pp. 198 ff.
503   "This was," Webster, Vol. 3, p. 207.
504   "The German form . . ." Shirer, *The Rise and Fall of the Third Reich,* p. 287.
505   "mounting apprehension," Campbell, p. 8.
505   "The blood is . . ." *ibid.,* p. 158.
507   "the Germans were known . . ." *et seq.,* Middlebrook, p. 106.
507   "we were assured . . ." Campbell, p. 21.
507   "it should be . . ." *ibid.,* p. 62.
509   "The fighters were . . ." *ibid.,* p. 65.
509   "The enemy . . ." RAF Bomber Command, Minutes from Chief Signals Officer, "Report of Operations Night 30/31 March 1944," PRO, London.
510   "You could see . . ." Flight Lieutenant Alfred Price, "The Greatest Air Disaster Ever—Black Friday," a memorandum to the author.

page
510 "I knew things . . ." *ibid.*
510 ". . . one could navigate . . ." Middlebrook, p. 158.
511 "It was the story . . ." Campbell, p. 103.
512 "The air over . . ." *ibid.,* p. 126.
512 "Bloody hell!" *ibid.,* p. 132.
512 "It certainly appeared . . ." *et seq., ibid.,* p. 130.
512 "Fighter activity . . ." Middlebrook, p. 250.
513 ". . . I always had . . ." Campbell, p. 152.
513 "In sending the . . ." Campbell, p. 178.
514 "THEY KNEW . . ." RAF Bomber Command, "Raid Plot, Nuremberg, Night, 30/31 March 1944," Air 14/3221, PRO, London.
515 "It was caused . . ." Campbell, p. 157.
515 "strange," *ibid.,* p. 147.
516 "the larger the prize . . ." Masterman, p. 9.
516 "The enemy has . . ." Goering Order of the Day, KC.

8. AERIAL STRATAGEMS

Sources

SHAEF SGS 373, *Military Objectives for Aerial Bombardment,* MMR, NA; W. Gaul, "The German Air Force and the Invasion of Normandy, 1944," ONI, OAB; "Effect of Enemy Air Raids Before and During the Invasion," a Luftwaffe intelligence report, OUP, USAF Historical Branch, MAFB; Col. T. G. Lanphier, deputy for Air G2, "Axis Air Forces, Strength and Disposition," and documents concerning French civilian casualties, in OPD files, MMR, NA; Minutes of the 6th Meeting of the Scientific Advisory Committee on Radio Aids, Countermeasures Against Enemy RCMs and Jamming, London, April 20, 1944, CIAP; Joint Board on Scientific Information Policy, Electronics Warfare, a Report on RCMs, November 19, 1945, Washington, D.C.; Radio Research Laboratory, Harvard University, "The Operational Use of RCM in the ETO," 1945, in the private collection of Dr. F. E. Terman; Office of Scientific Research and Development, "History of the Radio Research Laboratory, March 21, 1942–January 1, 1945," in the private collection of Dr. Terman; Lt. Col. Combaux, "Communications—a Weapon of War," *Revue de la Défense Nationale,* Paris, October 1946; Sir Robert Cockburn, a letter to the author, January 4, 1970; Omar N. Bradley, "Effect of Air Power on Military Operations, Western European," Report of Air Effects Committee, 12th Army Group, U.S. Army, Wiesbaden, July 15, 1945.

Notes

page
518 "grave and on . . ." ED, April 3, 1944.
518 "we should build . . ." EPF.
518 "I am not prepared . . ." memorandum for the prime minister, Record Group 218, Records of the USJCS, CCS 385, Section I, MMR, NA.
519 "put his hand . . ." Dunderdale interview.
519 "The French railway . . ." *New York Times,* May 24, 1944.
521 "The station is . . ." Herington, p. 36.

page
522 "absolutely vital . . ." "Cover and Deception in Air Force Operations, European Theater of Operations," Informal Supplementary Report to Joint Security Control, the "Harris Report," *op. cit.*
523 "varied so widely," Harrison, p. 179.
524 "No single factor . . ." Report of the Supreme Commander to the CCS on Operations in Europe of the AEF, June 6, 1944, to May 8, 1945, EL.

9. SECURITY

Sources

SHAEF SGS 380.01/4, *Security for Operations,* MMR, NA; "Bigot Procedure," in OPD files, MMR, NA; T. Hughes, Cabinteely, County Dublin, Eire, letter to U.S. ambassador, Dublin, March 1961, concerning the crash of Gen. Smith's aircraft, in Composite Accessions, 1970, Box 1, EL; OSS R&A Report No. 30131, "The Attitude of the Eire Government on Various Points Connected with the War," March 11, 1943, Record Group 226, MMR, NA; OSS R&A Report, "An Introduction to the Irish Problem," May 23, 1944, Record Group 226, MMR, NA; Lt. J. F. Murdock to Secretary of the Navy, Report of the Loss of LST 531, May 2, 1944, OAB; Lt. H. A. Mettler to C-in-C U.S. Navy, Action Report Concerning LST 289, May 2, 1944, OAB; Ens. D. G. Harlander to Secretary of the Navy, Report of the Loss of LST 531, May 2, 1944, OAB; Lt. J. F. Murdock, *Film Record Report of the Loss of LST 507 in Normandy Invasion Exercises,* Film Record No. 263, OAB.

Notes

page
528 "Urging others . . ." Norman Longmate, *How We Lived Then,* London: Hutchinson, 1971, p. 95.
528 "It will go hard . . ." Eisenhower letter to British Chiefs of Staff, March 6, 1944, in SGS 380.01/4, *op. cit.*
529 "The rules of . . ." Eisenhower letter to Montgomery, Bradley, Ramsay, Leigh-Mallory, February 23, 1944, in SGS 380.01/4, *op. cit.*
530 "There lurked . . ." Betts interview.
530 "The clumsy . . ." ED, p. 1160.
531 "I had no choice." Bradley interview.
531 "There were officers . . ." Bradley, p. 224.
531 "I simply . . ." Miller letter to Eisenhower, April 25, 1944, EPF.
531 "I know of . . ." Eisenhower letter to Miller, April 27, 1944, EPF.
532–33 "details of impending . . ." *et seq.,* Eisenhower-Stark correspondence, May 21 and 23, 1944, OAB.
533 "shakes," Eisenhower letter to Marshall, May 21, 1944, EPF.
534 "Was it really . . ." Eisenhower Foundation, *D-Day: The Normandy Invasion in Retrospect,* University Press of Kansas, 1971, p. 170.
534 "additional aircrew." Ivelaw-Chapman interview.
537 "disclosed a crescendo . . ." Schellenberg, p. 366.
540–41 "We know exactly . . ." *et seq.,* Ellsberg, p. 155.

page
    542   "did not quite . . ." Farago, *The Game of the Foxes,* p. 549.
    543   "a great deal of . . ." OSS Report A22884A, "Ireland as a Source of Information to the Germans," March 16, 1944, Record Group 226, MMR, NA.
543–44   "continues to operate . . ." *et seq.,* The U.S. Government to the Irish Prime Minister, February–March 1944, Documents on American Foreign Relations, NA, pp. 625–26.
    545   "designed to isolate . . ." *New York Times,* March 15, 1944.
    545   "many false alarms . . ." *New York Times,* March 27, 1944.
    546   "The exercise concerned . . ." Ingersoll, p. 103.
    548   "There was a whole . . ." *ibid.,* p. 104.

10. THE WIRELESS GAME

Sources

"Use of Intelligence in Cover and Deception," "Enemy Source of Information," and "Methods of Manipulation," the "Harris Report," *op. cit.*

Notes

page
    553   "nice assessment . . ." Masterman, p. 10.
    554   "A splendid, vague, . . ." Foot, p. 337.
    554   "strong and flexible . . ." *ibid.,* p. 336.
    554   "too emotional . . ." Fuller, *Double Webs,* p. 25.
554–55   "really stuck . . ." *et seq.,* Foot, p. 337.
    557   "London had twigged." *ibid.,* p. 341.
    558   "imperial fury," *ibid.,* p. 342.
    561   "The first part . . ." Staubwasser, Ms. No. B782, *op. cit.*
    562   "in order to . . ." *et seq.,* Foot, p. 328.
    563   "The ways of headquarters . . ." Fuller, *Double Webs,* p. 208.
    564   "I know that . . ." Baumer interview.
    564   "into a sandy . . ." Foot, p. 429.

11. THE FRENCH LABYRINTH

Sources

Coordinator of Information, "French Attitudes Toward the British (Spring 1942)," July 20, 1942, Record Group 226, MMR, NA; HQ Airborne Troops, selected files in a private collection; HQ 21st Army Group, Minutes of a Conference on Destruction of Enemy Telecommunications, May 16, 1944, CIAP; Capt. D. A. Bayly Pike, A Report on Destruction of Overhead Telephone Lines, May 19, 1944, CIAP; "Telecommunications Targets for Destruction at H-Hour," OUP, no date, CIAP; 21st Army Group, Memorandum on SAS Tasks for Inclusion in 21st Army Group Plan for Delaying of Enemy Reserves, May 10, 1944, CIAP; SAS Brigade Operations Instructions, CIAP; "Organization and Command of SAS Troops for Special Operations," December 1943, CIAP; Appreciation on Control of Resistance in France, no date, HQ Airtps/TS/25006/0/Liaison, CIAP; Appreciation of Employment of SAS Troops in Overlord, no date, HQ Airtps/MS/2500/40/G, CIAP; Notes of a Meeting Held at 21st

Army Group to Consider the Various Roles of SAS, SOE and PWE in Overlord, March 1, 1944, CIAP; A Memorandum on Factors Affecting SAS Operations, May 1944, CIAP; Brig. R. W. MacLeod, "Appreciation of the Tasks Which Should Be Undertaken by SAS Troops in Overlord," March 14, 1944, CIAP; Col. I. Collins, "Delaying Enemy Reserves in Invasion Battle," June 27, 1943, and "Uniformed Airborne Guerrilla Force," August 1943, CIAP; B. M. W. Knox, "After-action Report of Jedburgh team Giles," CIAP; OSS, "Performance and Potential of French Resistance," Memorandum from Donovan to Marshall, July 9, 1944, Record Group 165, Records of the WDGSS, MMR, NA; U.S. Joint War Plans Committee, "French Collaboration in the Invasion of Europe," JWPC 229, in CCS 350.05, MMR, NA; Sundry documents concerning the rearmament of French military and resistance forces and security in Algiers, OPD 336, Security Section 1, Cases 1 through 17, Record Group 165, Records of the WDGSS, MMR, NA.

Notes

page

567 "the sun . . ." Gubbins interview.

568 "These *Avis* . . ." *et seq.,* in *BBC Warnings to Resistance Groups, op. cit.*

570 "We call him . . ." R. Harris Smith, p. 68.

570 "Gestapo-like methods," OSS R&A Report No. 2553, "The Organization of the French Intelligence Services," January 11, 1945, MMR, NA.

571 "It is clear . . ." *et seq.,* Foot, pp. 231–32.

571 "bad faith . . ." Foot, p. 232.

572 "If this were . . ." Deacon, p. 347.

574 "discretion incarnate," Foot, p. 364.

578 *"Patriot Forces . . ."* *et seq.,* Plan Torrent, in SHAEF SGS 381, Fortitude, *op. cit.*

578 "While we were . . ." Knox interview.

579 "You will go . . ." HQ Airborne Troops, Jedburgh file, in a private collection.

579–80 "In order that . . ." *et seq.,* EPF.

12. CANARIS'S LAST THROW

Sources

General Leo Baron Geyr von Schweppenberg, "Reflections on the Invasion," *Military Review,* 1961; Peter de Mendelsohn, "Speidel's Story," *New Statesman and Nation,* London, October 29, 1949.

Notes

page

584 "comprehensive conference . . ." *et seq.,* Speidel, Ms. No. B721, *op. cit.*

587–89 "pertinent questions," *et seq.,* USJCS and the Joint Intelligence Committee (US), "Effect of Unconditional Surrender Policy on German Morale," memorandum and associated documents, February 10, 1944, JIC 159/JCS 718 Series, MMR, NA.

page
589   "they were up . . ." Dilks, p. 620.
589   "white alley," ED, April 16, 1944.
589–90 "In conversation . . ." *et seq.,* JIC 159/JCS 718 Series, *op. cit.*
590   "In the German . . ." SHAEF intelligence digest, located in U.S. 1st Army After-Action Report, HI.
591   "Justice . . ." *Hansard,* London, May 25, 1944.
591   "begging before . . ." *et seq.,* Churchill letter to Eisenhower, in SHAEF SGS 380.01/4, *Security for Operations, op. cit.*
592–93 "I first heard . . ." *et seq.,* Gen. James O. Curtis, Jr., memorandum for the record of conversations with the author, witnessed by Luther Nicols, Berkeley, California, May 16, 1968, original in author's possession.
593   "I distinctly remember . . ." *et seq.,* de Guingand interview.
594   "contact with . . ." *et seq.,* Gehlen interview.
594   "by devious means," Gehlen, p. 103.
595–96 "because I feared . . ." Arnould interview.
596–97 "Keun came over . . ." *et seq.,* Dunderdale interview.
597   "I received . . ." Dulles interview.
597   "We received . . ." Wingate interview.
598   "three or four . . ." *et seq.,* Arnould interview.
599   "Canaris seemed . . ." *et seq.,* Frede interview.
599   "This is the . . ." *et seq.,* Arnould interview.

13. VENDETTA

Sources

Allied Forces Headquarters, Information and News Censorship Branch, *Plan Vendetta,* WNRC; Air Vice Marshal Sir T. Elmhurst, "The German Air Force and Its Failure," *Journal of the Royal United Services Institution,* November 1946; Col. R. M. Adams, Historical Office, Royal Signals Institution, London, letter to Brig. W. Scott re Lt. Col. F. K. Austin, November 11, 1970, CIAP; letters and documents concerning Quicksilver, Big Bob and Flake from Robert Shearer, Lt. Col. G. A. C. Danby, A. C. Walsh, P. M. Kemp, and excerpts from *The History of the Northamptonshire Regiment* (p. 321 ff.) and "Firm," Activities of the 10th Worcestershire Regiment, 1944, CIAP; JSC, *Plan Royal Flush,* with State Department, SHAEF and Joint Chiefs signals and annexes, May 26, 1944, OPD 381, MMR, NA.

Notes

page
604–5 "1/5th Queen's Royal . . ." *et seq.,* Johnston interview.
605   "idea of betraying . . ." Delmer, *The Counterfeit Spy,* p. 178.
607   *"Envoyez vite . . ."* Masterman, p. 161.
607   "One of our . . ." Special Staff, U.S. Army, An interview with Reichsmarshall Hermann Goering, Eucom:HD:OHGB:Ethint 30, July 1, 1945, MMR, NA.
608   "The truth . . ." Jervis-Reid interview.
608   "I had an imaginary . . ." James, pp. 5–6.
608   "took rather a . . ." Jervis-Reid interview.

page
609   "The likeness struck . . ." *et seq.,* James, p. 88.
613   "Whitman . . ." ED, p. 1265.
614   "Ladies and gentlemen . . ." *New York Times,* May 29, 1944.
614   "Ike looks . . ." ED, May 12, 1944.
614   ". . . tension grows . . ." Eisenhower letter to Somervell, April 4, 1944, E PF.
614   "our chances . . ." ED, May 24, 1944.
615   "I am concerned . . ." *ibid.,* April 28, 1944.
615   "the best imitation . . ." Morison, p. 115.
615   "It should not . . ." *21 Army Group Weekly Neptune Intelligence Review,* June 4, 1944, OPD 315, MMR, NA.
618   *"1. Area of main . . ." et seq.,* MAAF, Intelligence Section, Office of the Director of Operations and Intelligence, "Enemy Appreciations of Planned Intentions," May 25, 1944, Record Group 331, AFHQ microfilm, WNRC.
618   "We have been . . ." *The Times,* London, June 7, 1944.
619   "only with the . . ." Wilmot, p. 143.
619   "completely bare-faced bluff." Warlimont, p. 408.
619   "The Führer attaches . . ." Blumentritt to all commands, *op. cit.*
621   "need to win . . ." Rundstedt, *et al.,* Ms. No. B633, *op. cit.*
622   "a number of major . . ." *ibid.*
623   "This, of course . . ." Winterbotham, *The Ultra Secret,* pp. 127–28.

14. THE EVE OF D-DAY

Sources

Phillip M. Flammer, "Weather and the Normandy Invasion," *Military Review,* June 1961; ZY Detachment, 21 Weather Squadron, 9th USAF, The Albert F. Simpson Historical Research Center, MAFB; J. M. Stagg, "Meteorology in War," Meteorological Office Library, Bracknell, Berkshire, England; Memorandum on weather forecasts, May 26, 1944, in SHAEF SGS 000.91, *Meteorological Matters,* MMR, NA; Air Marshal Sir Trafford Leigh-Mallory, *Despatch,* Supplement to the *London Gazette,* December 31, 1946; SHAEF G2 (Int), Daily Intelligence Digests, June 7, 1944–May 1945, MMR, NA; Gen. Walter Bedell Smith, "Eisenhower's Six Great Decisions," *Saturday Evening Post,* June 8, 1946; RAF Kingsdown, Y Service Report, June 5/6, 1944, OUP, OCMH; SHAEF, Office of the Chief of Staff, memorandum on the events of June 5/6, 1944, Document for Inclusion in Historical Records, February 22, 1945, OCMH; Col. Anton Staubwasser, "The Alert Problem during the Night of the Invasion (June 5–6, 1944), "a memorandum to Gen. Speidel with a copy to Gen. E. L. Sibert, CIAP; Staubwasser, "The Enemy as Seen by Oberkommando of Heeresgruppe B Before the Invasion (Time: End of May–Beginning of June 1944)," Ms. No. B675, OCMH.

Notes

page
624   "to be on hand . . ." *et seq.,* Memorandum for the Record, Office of the Chief of Staff, May 31, 1944, MMR, NA.
624   "Exercise Hornpipe . . ." in SHAEF SGS 380.01/4, *Security for Operations, op. cit.*

page
625   "Halcyon plus 4." in SHAEF SGS 380.01/4, *Security for Operations, op. cit.*
625   "Unless Channel weather . . ." Stagg, p. 38.
626   "For heaven's sake . . ." *ibid.,* p. 69.
626   "wearied ourselves . . ." *et seq., ibid.,* p. 80.
626–27   "untrustworthy." *et seq., ibid.,* p. 86.
627   "Well, Stagg . . ." *et seq., ibid.,* pp. 87 and 88.
627–28   "knife-edge marginal," *et seq., ibid.,* p. 90–91.
628   "There goes six . . ." *et seq., ibid.,* pp. 96 and 98.
628   "tension in the . . ." *et seq., ibid.,* p. 102.
630   "diminished our supplies . . ." ED, June 4, 1944.
630   ". . . then between . . ." *et seq.,* Stagg, pp. 107 and 108.
630   "toothless parish . . ." *ibid.,* p. 40.
631   "chancy." *et seq., ibid.,* p. 114.
631   "I am quite positive . . ." Ryan, p. 58.
632   "(Neptune) had been . . ." Stagg, p. 115.
632   "Let's take a . . ." *et seq.,* Ryan, p. 55.
632   "all were in . . ." *et seq.,* Stagg, p. 116.
632   ". . . the tension . . ." *ibid.,* p. 118.
632   "Halcyon plus 5 . . ." in SHAEF SGS 380.01/4, *Security for Operations, op. cit.*
633   "to spatter . . ." de Gaulle, *War Memoirs,* Vol. 2, p. 244.
633   "an infamy," *ibid.,* p. 246.
634   ". . . Ike took them . . ." ED, June 4, 1944.
635   "request the approval," *et seq.,* Gubbins interview.
635   "This torrent of . . ." *et seq.,* Gen. Pierre Koenig, Memorandum on Matters Concerning *Messages Personnels* on the Evening of June 5, 1944, copy provided the author by Robert Aron.
636   "seen to be . . ." *et seq.,* SHAEF G2 Daily Intelligence Digest, June 7, 1944.
637   "martyrs not less . . ." Churchill, *The World Crisis, 1916–18,* Pt. I, New York: Scribners, 1927, p. 197.
637   "I am very . . ." Alanbrooke, Vol. 2, p. 206.
638   "doubtful whether . . ." *et seq.,* Ellis, p. 129.
639   "On 5 June . . ." Warlimont, p. 422.
640–41   "At 2115 on . . ." *et seq.,* Rundstedt, *et al.,* Ms. No. B633, *op. cit.*
641–42   "At approximately . . ." *et seq.,* Staubwasser, Ms. No. B675, *op. cit.*
643   "riding in Paris . . ." Scratchley interview.

PART V: NORMANDY TO NEMESIS

1. D-DAY

Sources

HQ German 7th Army, *War Diary,* IWM; Assessment of the Luftwaffe on the night of D-Day, a Luftwaffe report, OUP, no date, USAF Historical Branch, MAFB; Robert Cockburn, The Moonshine Operations of June 6–7, 1944, a memorandum dated June 13, 1944, in Cockburn's private collection; RAF Kingsdown Y Service Report, in 8th USAAF After-Action Report on Chronology of Developments in Normandy, Intelligence Section, USAF, OCMH; Lt. Col. Charles A. Taylor, "Omaha Beachhead," 1946, OCMH; R. G. Ruppenthal, "Utah Beach to Cherbourg," 1947, OCMH; J. W. Arnold, USNR, "NOIC Utah," *U.S. Naval Institute Proceedings,* Annapolis, 73 (June 1947): 671–81; Lt. Cdr. L. Ware, Special Historical Observer for the Commander, U. S. Naval Forces, Europe, Vol. 1: *Planning the Invasion,* Vol. 2: *War Diary, Naval Force "U,"* OAB; Commander, U.S. Naval Forces, Europe, "Plan Neptune," Sections 1–32, OAB.

Notes

epigraph

" 'Twas on a summer's . . ." Byron, *Don Juan,* Canto IV.

page

647 "From Sabu 15 . . ." HQ Airborne Troops, Titanic file, CIAP.
650 "Although it is . . ." *War Diary,* (German) Naval Group West, June 1–30, 1944, OAB.
651 "The assault forces . . ." Adm. Sir Bertram Ramsay, *Despatch,* Supplement to the *London Gazette,* October 7, 1947.
652 "as he listened . . ." *et seq.,* Ryan, p. 129 (Greenwich, Ct: Fawcett, 1960).
652 "General, I believe . . ." *ibid.,* p. 127.
652 "It was not at all . . ." Speidel, *Invasion 1944, op. cit.,* p. 77.
652 "the affair is . . ." Ryan, p. 129.
653 "The German fighter . . ." Price, p. 184.
654 "I had been told . . ." E. Feuchtinger, *History of the 21st Panzer Division from the Time of Its Formation until the Beginning of the Invasion,* February 18, 1947, OCMH Ms. No. B441, EDS, NA.
654 "Anchor holding . . ." Morison, p. 93.
656–58 "a fair number," *et seq., War Diary,* (German) Naval Group West, *op. cit.*
658–59 "definitely the opening . . ." *et seq.,* Rundstedt, *et al.,* Ms. No. B633, *op. cit.*
659–60 "extremely vague," *et seq.,* Ryan, p. 147.
660 "made an ungodly . . ." Morison, p. 94.
661 "At the time . . ." Price, p. 108.
662 "In the main . . ." *War Diary,* (German) Naval Group West, *op. cit.*
662 "fast and lean . . ." American military attaché report on German paratroopers, Cairo, November 14, 1942, in OSS R&A file on Crete, MMR, NA.
662 "north of Carentan," *et seq.,* Maj. Friedrich-August Baron von der Heydte, *Operations of the 6th Parachute Regiment,* Ms. No. B839, EDS, NA.
665 "pursuing," Foot, p. 387.
666 "very widely spaced . . ." Lt. Col. Zeigelman, *History of the 352nd Infantry Division,* OCMH Ms. No. B432, EDS, NA.
666 "shocked and shaken, *et seq.,* Ryan, p. 222.
667 "seriously unbalance . . ." Foot, p. 347.
667 "While the Anglo-Saxon . . ." *et seq.,* Rundstedt, *et al.,* Ms. No. B633, *op. cit.*
668 "My dear Staubwasser," *et seq.,* Staubwasser, Ms. No. B782, *op. cit.;* and Staubwasser interview.
668–69 "So, we're off." *et seq.,* Warlimont, p. 427.

2. THE DECEPTIONS OF D-DAY

Sources

Maj. Kenneth W. Hechler, "The Invasion," an interview with Genfldm Wilhelm Keitel and Genobst Alfred Jodl, Ethint 49, SC; Hechler, "From the Invasion to the Ruhr," "Eastern vs. Western Fronts," "High Level Strategy," a series of interviews with Reichsmarschall Hermann Goering, July 21, 1945, Ethint 30, OCMH; Hechler, "Invasion and Normandy Campaign," an interview with General Jodl, July 31–August 2, 1945, SC; Hechler, "The Invasion," "The Battle of Normandy," "Cherbourg," "Replacement of von Rundstedt," "Normandy Breakthrough and Mortain Counterattack," "Eberbach," "Retreat toward the German Frontier," a series of interviews with General Warlimont, July 19–20, 1945, SC; Relevant documents in the "Harris Report," *op. cit.*

Notes

page
670   "a little rough . . ." Curtis interview.
670   "the chance . . ." *et seq.,* Stagg, p. 125.
670   "Our landings . . ." EPF.
671   "largely by surprise," *et seq.,* JIC appreciation in Chiefs of Staff (British) Brief, War Cabinet Papers, Piece 79, PRO.
671   ". . . Allied naval forces . . ." SHAEF Psychological Warfare Division, Plans in Support of Overlord, April 30, 1944, Record Group 331, MMR, NA.
671–72   "Topflite at 9030." *et seq.,* SHAEF, G3, D-Day Proclamations, in *BBC Warnings to Resistance Groups, op. cit.*
672   "Many thanks . . ." *et seq.,* Gubbins interview.
674   "the greatest . . ." *Daily Mail,* London, June 7, 1944.
674–75   "I have received . . ." *et seq.,* An essay by William Barkley, Gallery Correspondent, *Daily Express,* London, June 7, 1944.
675   "a mighty endeavor," *et seq., New York Times,* June 7, 1944.
675   "The supreme battle . . ." *et seq., The Times,* London, June 7, 1944.
676   "de Gaulle's address . . ." Staubwasser interview.
676   "obliged to . . ." *et seq.,* Delmer, *The Counterfeit Spy,* pp. 183–84.
676   "flaming fury," *et seq., ibid.,* pp. 184–85.
677   "This was the time . . ." Wilmot, p. 287.
678   "There was," *et seq.,* Wingate interview.

3. SWORD AND STRATAGEM

Sources

Letter, Maj. Gen. Harry J. Maloney to Gen. Omar N. Bradley, Subject: Loss of two U.S. Corps operational orders, January 25, 1949, in Geog. M. France 314.4 (Normandy), OCMH; German Summary of U.S. 7th Corps order captured in Normandy, EDS, OCMH; U.S. 5th and 7th Corps operational orders with annexes, OCMH; Oberstleutnant Ziegelman, *Additional Information About the Operational Plan of 5 (US) Corps Captured on June 7, 1944, in the Sector of the 352nd Infantry Division,* September 3, 1947, OCMH Ms. No. B636,

EDS, NA; An Account of the Operations of (British) 2nd Army in Europe, copy of Gen. Sir Miles Dempsey, IWM; 12th Army Group, G2, Report of the Air Effects Committee, Frankfurt, 1945.

Notes

page
679   "considerable anxiety," Ellis, p. 217.
679   "hung like a vulture . . ." Wilmot, citing Churchill, p. 293.
680   "the entire scheme . . ." *et seq.*, Blumentritt, *et al., The Capture of U.S. 5th Corps Operational Orders,* OCMH Ms. No. B637, EDS, NA.
681   "effectively cut off . . ." Scott interview.
681   "invaluable respite," *et seq.*, Wilmot, pp. 298–99.
682   "handle any eventuality . . ." Marshall, Note for Conference with General Brooke, EPF.
682   "general harassing . . ." SHAEF 17240/17/Ops (a), June 7, 1944, in *BBC Warnings to Resistance Groups, op. cit.*
683   "Paradise," Plan Paradise, in SHAEF SGS 381, *Fortitude, op. cit.*
683   "unsatisfactory . . ." *et seq.*, "Sunday Punch in Normandy," After-Action Report of the U.S. 8th Air Force, OUP, MMR, NA; and G2 (Air) 12th Army Group, "Effect of Air Power on Military Operations," in the private collection of General E. L. Sibert.
684–85 "with my own eyes . . ." *et seq.*, Wingate interview.
685   "on Hitler's desk . . ." Bevan interview.
685   "I transmit . . ." Wingate interview.
685   "In all probability . . ." *et seq.*, Staubwasser, Ms. No. B782, *op. cit.*
685   "active and bold . . ." Hodgson, R Study, *op. cit.*
686   "present your points . . ." Delmer, *The Counterfeit Spy,* p. 16.
686   "After a personal . . ." *ibid.*, p. 18.
687   "heavy with tension . . ." *et seq.*, Wingate interview.

4. THE FRENCH REVOLT

Sources

SOE Monthly Progress Reports to SHAEF for May, June, July, August 1944, CIAP; Capt. J. Kerneval, "Report of Jed Team Felix on Operations 7 July–23 August 1944," CIAP; Lt. S. R. Trumps, OSS, "Report of Jed Team Ronald on Operations," CIAP; Capt. R. Marchant, R. Pariselle, "Reports of Jed Team Hillary on Operations," CIAP; *War Diary*, (German) Inspectorate of the Armistice Commission, CIAP; Brig. Gen. A. S. Nevins, Chief Operations Section, SHAEF, "D-Day Propaganda to French," June 17, 1944, in *BBC Warnings to Resistance Groups, op. cit.* Michel de Galzain, *"Le Bal du Ciel,"* a monograph provided by the Mairie, Vannes, Brittany, CIAP; SFHQ, London, "9th (May 1944), 10th (June 1944), 11th (July 1944) Reports of Operations to SHAEF," CIAP; Sgt. O. A. Brown, Royal Armoured Corps (on detachment to Team Quinine), "Quinine Radio Report," CIAP; Capt. J. E. Tonkin, "Bulbasket Report," CIAP; HQ SAS Troops, "Operations in Brittany," Report to the B.G.S. 21st Army Group, August 21, 1944, CIAP; C. B. MacDonald, "France 1940–1944," Working Paper for the Special Operations Research Office,

Washington, D.C., 1968; 3rd French Paratroop Battalion, "Report of Cooney Operations," circa August 1944, CIAP.

Notes

page
690 "We would have . . ." Staubwasser interview.
691 "have far . . ." *et seq.,* Lt. Gen. F. A. M. Browning, Commander, Airborne Troops, 21st Army Group to Headquarters 21st Army Group, "Progress Report SAS Operations 5–20 June 1944" June 22, 1944, CIAP.
692 "one sacred duty . . ." *et seq.,* FBIS Survey for period June 6–July 6, 1944, FCC, NA.
692 "methods of manipulation," *et seq.,* "Cover and Deception, Definition and Procedure," the "Harris Report," *op. cit.*
693 "provocateurs . . ." *et seq.,* Broadcast transcript in SAS Brittany file, CIAP.
694 "assisted by . . ." Capt. Paul Aguirec, "Report on Jed Team Frederick on Operations 9 June–27 August 1944," CIAP.
694 "There was . . ." *et seq.,* Capitaine Jules Leblond, "Report on Operations of 4th French Parachute Battalion and on the Present Situation in Brittany, 6 June–13 July 1944," CIAP.
694 "Without our knowledge . . ." Aguirec report, *op. cit.*
695 "I did not want . . ." Leblond report, *op. cit.*
696 "surprised . . ." Roger Le Hyaric, *"Les patriotes de Brétagne,"* a monograph provided by the Mairie, Vannes, Brittany, CIAP.
696 "Dingson under attack . . ." Capt. P. Cyr (US), "Report on Operations of Jed Team George," CIAP.
696 "unknown Germans." Maj. O. A. J. Cary Elwes, "Report of Operations of 'Operation Lost' in Brittany," CIAP.
699 "some dozen . . ." Maj. T. MacPherson, "Report of Operations of Team Quinine," CIAP.
700 "secured the best . . ." Foot, p. 404 ff.
700 "The enemy were . . ." Capt. C. S. S. Burt, "Report of Operations of Team Dickens," CIAP.
701 "blood and ashes," *et seq.,* Cookridge, p. 340.
701 "the most horrible . . ." *ibid.,* p. 341.
701–2 "so thoroughly mauled . . ." *et seq.,* Foot, p. 398.
702 "The extra . . ." *ibid.,* p. 397.

5. ROMMEL

Sources

HQ USFET, Public Relations Division, "20th July and Rommel," USFET Release 282, September 4, 1945, CIAP; Drew Middleton, "The War as Rommel Fought It," *New York Times Book Review,* May 17, 1953; 2nd Panzer Division, *Bericht über Rückkehr der 2 DRK—Schwesterngruppe aus amerik, Gefangenschaft an die 2 Pz Div. nachrichtl.,* MIRS/W 1044, EDS, NA; PWD, Report of Transfer of Red Cross Nurses, September 21, 1944, HI; Intelligence Section, Office of the Director of Operations and Intelligence, MAAFHQ, *Operation Hellhound,* Record Group 331, AFHQ microfilm, WNRC.

Notes

page
704   "one terrible . . ." *et seq.*, Rommel, p. 496.
704   "My functions . . ." *ibid.*, p. 495.
705   "every two or three . . ." *et seq.*, Staubwasser, Ms. No. B782, *op. cit.;* and Staubwasser interview.
706   "unbelievable courage . . ." *et seq.*, Speidel, Ms. No. B720, *op. cit.*
706–7 "Rommel was under . . ." Speidel, Ms. No. B721, *op. cit.*
707   "hardly be restrained . . ." *et seq.*, Dr. Walter Bargatzky, "Personal Recollections of the 20th of July 1944 Insurrectionary Movement in France," Baden-Baden, October 20, 1945, HI.
707–8 "one more chance," *et seq.*, Speidel, Ms. No. B721, *op. cit.*
709   "The present positions . . ." Hodgson, R Study, *op. cit.*
709   "I shall be next." Staubwasser interview.
709–10 "Rommel himself . . ." *et seq.*, Speidel, *Invasion 1944, op. cit.*, p. 105.
710   "trustworthy . . ." Bargatzky, *op. cit.*
710   *"Achtung"* German 47th Corps HQ, *Gespräch zwischen deutscher Kommandostelle und einer amerikanischen Dienststelle am 2/7/44, Beginn 14:00 Uhr,* Mirs/W 1043, EDS, NA.
711   "Hello," *et seq.*, U.S. 1st Infantry Division AA Report, "Transfer of Red Cross Nurses," with G2 Annexes, OCMH.
712   "With the knowledge . . ." Wheeler-Bennett, *Nemesis of Power,* pp. 631–32.
712   "The situation . . ." *et seq.*, Rommel, pp. 486–87.
712–13 "Staubwasser . . ." *et seq.*, Staubwasser interview.
714–15 *"Je cherche . . ."* *et seq.*, Operation Houndsworth, Operational and (Fraser) Personal File, CIAP.
715–16 "From HOUNDSWORTH . . ." *et seq.*, Operation Houndsworth, Signals File, made available to the author by private sources.
717, 718 "kill or kidnap . . ." *et seq.*, SAS Brigade Operation Instruction No. 32, Operation Gaff—OC 2 SAS Regiment, HQ SAS Tps/TSB/5/G, with annexes, CIAP.

6. THE V1

Sources

U.S. General Board Reports on V1 and V2, 1945–47, MMR, NA; War Cabinet and Chiefs of Staff files 1944, PRO; U.S. Navy, Report of the Disappearance of Lt. (jg.) J. Kennedy, USN, OAB.

Notes

page
719   "Not v. . . ." Dilks, p. 639.
720   "exuberantly . . ." *et seq.*, Irving, *The Mare's Nest*, p. 234.
720   "all possible measures . . ." *et seq.*, *ibid.*, p. 236.
720   "The congregation . . ." Flower and Reeves, pp. 584–85.
721   "whose modern steel . . ." Churchill, *The Second World War,* Vol. 6, p. 37.

page
721 "grating roar . . ." *et seq.,* Longmate, *How We Lived Then, op. cit.,* p. 490.
722 "finding it . . ." *et seq.,* Parkinson, pp. 326–27.
724 ". . . we knew . . ." Masterman, p. 122.
725 "News . . ." *ibid.,* p. 171.
725 "M.I.5 was not . . ." Irving, *The Mare's Nest,* p. 257.
726–27 "At their meeting . . ." *et seq.,* War Cabinet Paper, Secretary's Standard [i.e., Sensitive] File, COS 1944, PRO.
727 ". . . the possibility . . ." Parkinson, p. 342.

7. GOODWOOD

Sources

SHAEF G2 (CI), Counter-Intelligence Digests, September–October 1944, in 6th Army Group G2 Records, MMR, NA; G2 Section, FUSAG, Policy Book for CI Branch, date uncertain, CIAP; G2 12th Army Group, CI Organization and Operations, date uncertain, CIAP; U.S. 1st Army, *Report of Operations,* Vols. 1–12, OCMH; General E. L. Sibert, G2 12th Army Group and G2 FUSAG, notes for National War College lectures, dates uncertain, CIAP; Exhibit 4: "Use of Intelligence in Cover and Deception," and Exhibit 6: "Fortitude South II (Rosebud)," in the "Harris Report," *op. cit.;* WDGS, "Biography of Lesley James McNair," OCMH; CSDIC, Interview with Count Helldorf, PW Paper 12, August 4, 1944, CIAP; Lt. Col. H. P. Persons, Instructor, Command and General Staff College, "St.-Lô Breakthrough," *Military Review,* March 1951; Interrogation of Robert v. Mendelssohn, OUP, handwritten on H.M. Government note paper, undated, CIAP.

Notes

page
729 "prevent the operation . . ." *et seq.,* GSI (b), HQ 21st Army Group, Detailed Counter-Intelligence Instruction No. 1, May 5, 1944, CIAP.
730 "Even if the . . ." Harrison, p. 426.
730 "The demolition . . ." *ibid.,* p. 441.
731 "Over a stretch . . ." Blumenson, *Breakout and Pursuit,* p. 176.
731–33 "the most monstrous . . ." *et seq.,* Hodgson, R Study, *op. cit.*
734 "directed the tactical . . ." Blumenson, *Breakout and Pursuit,* p. 9.
736 ". . . you felt . . ." *ibid.,* p. 428.
736 "the Allies' secret weapon," *et seq., ibid.,* p. 478.
736 "Patton has lost . . ." SHAEF SGS 381, *Fortitude, op. cit.*
736 "obsessed with the . . ." Delmer, *The Counterfeit Spy,* p. 226.
737 "for immoral purposes," HQ Advance Section, Communications Zone, ETO, U.S. Army, Office of the Staff of the Judge Advocate General, Record of Trial by General Court Martial of Pfc. ——— . . . Pvt. ———, August 6, 1944, Clerk of the Court, JAG, U.S. Army, Washington, D.C.
738 "he was white . . ." Curtis interview.
738 "revealed," *et seq.,* Delmer, *The Counterfeit Spy,* p. 227.
739 "an emissary . . ." *et seq.,* Gehlen, p. 99.
739 ". . . it is the duty . . ." *ibid.,* p. 103.

page
740   "made contact . . ." CSDIC (UK) Report, Interrogation of Oberst-
        leutnant Arntz, SIR 1610, April 11, 1945, CIAP.
741   "arrange a channel . . ." Liss interview.
740   "So far as His . . ." *Hansard*, July 6, 1944.
741   "their Nazi taskmasters," *et seq.*, Charles Eade (comp.), *The Dawn
        of Liberation, War Speeches by the Rt. Hon. Winston S. Churchill*,
        London: Cassell, 1945.
741   "that the next . . ." "Germany: Nazi Opposition Reports Prog-
        ress," Document L89970, July 18, 1944, OSS German Section,
        MMR, NA.
741   "In reviewing . . ." Dulles, *Germany's Underground*, pp. 140–41.
743   "to prove . . ." Wheeler-Bennett, citing Tresckow, *Nemesis of
        Power*, p. 627.
744   "I saw a tank officer . . ." Detmar H. Finke, U.S. Army Archivist,
        Attack on Field Marshal Rommel, Medical Report, a letter to Dr.
        R. A. Davis, Department of Surgery, Northwestern University,
        Chicago, May 8, 1958.
744   "Rommel was in fact . . ." *et seq.*, Speidel, Ms. No. B721, *op. cit.*
745   "we [the air forces] . . ." ED, July 20, 1944.
745   "had the makings . . ." Ellis, p. 353.
745   "Monty . . ." Dilks, p. 649.

        8. JULY 20, 1944

Sources

Gen. Günther Blumentritt, *Three Marshals, National Character, and the
July 20th Complex*, February 15, 1947, Ms. No. B344, OCMH; Standartenführer Kopkow (member of Gestapo investigation team), Account of the Plot
of July 20th, an interrogation report, OUP but presumed MI-6 or BAOR G2
service in origin, undated, but circa 1946, CIAP; CSDIC (WEA), Report on
Heinz Lorenz, BOAR/Int/B3/PF582, November 20, 1945, CIAP; Fabian von
Schlabrendorff, Answers to Questionnaire re 20th July, MI-6 in origin, undated, unsigned typescript, CIAP; CSDIC (UK), Report of Conversation between General der Flieger Bodenschatz and an RAF Officer, SRGG 1219 (C),
undated but immediately postwar, CIAP; MI-6 Report 1583, "Eyewitness Account of 20th July: PW from F. U. Grenadier Regiment on Guard Outside the
Hut at Rastenburg," unsigned, undated, CIAP; Nicholas Count von Below,
Interrogation Report, "Events at Führerhauptquartier," marked 032/Case No.
0279, OUP but presumed MI-6, undated, unsigned, CIAP; Sgt. A. Croy,
Civilian Interrogation Camp, BAOR, Secret Documents left by Canaris in the
care of Frau von Haase, to the CO, Documents Section, GSI (b), BAOR,
November 27, 1949, CIAP; B. H. Liddell Hart, 3rd Interrogation of General
Blumentritt, OUP, presumed GSI (b), BAOR, CIAP; CSDIC (UK), Report of
Conversation between General Blumentritt and a British Army Officer, June 7,
1945, SRGG 129 (C), CIAP; Dr. Georg Kiesell, *Das Attentat des 20 Juli 1944
und seine Hintergruende*, Description of Gestapo activity following assassination attempt by a leading member of the RSHA Amt IV, OUP, CIAP; Toten-
tafel, a list of names, ranks, dates of execution, addresses of next-of-kin, situation
of surviving dependents, of 130 people shot or otherwise executed in connection
with July 20, 1944, OUP, CIAP; Baronin Funck (*née* Frau M. von Haase),

"The Growing of the Opposition Until July 20, 1944," November 26, 1945, OUP, but presumed British G2, CIAP; Gen. Georg Thomas, *Gedanken und Ereignisse, Aufzeichnung vom July 20, 1944*, FC; MI-14, War Office, London, Report of Executions at the Plötzensee, OUP, CIAP; Notes of an Interview between B. H. Liddell Hart and Gen. Rohricht (GOC 59th Corps) concerning the association of Rundstedt and Kluge with conspiracies and bomb plot, undated, OUP but presumed British G2 in origin, CIAP; Interrogation of Field Marshal Gerd von Rundstedt by Liddell Hart on events of July 20, 1944, OUP, CIAP; Walter Huppenkothen, Interrogation Report, USFET/CIC, July 20, 1944, including British questionnaire, dated May 17, 1946, CIAP; Martin Bormann, Report of July 20, 1944, Rundschreiben Nr. 155/44, undated, HI; Walter Schellenberg, MI-6 Interrogation concerning July 20, "Hansen und Canaris," undated, handwritten document, CIAP; Extracts from the diary of Dr. Erwin Giessing, ENT specialist who treated Hitler just after attentat, OUP, undated, CIAP.

Notes

page

748   "indirect hints," Schellenberg, MI-6 interrogation, *op. cit.*
748   "cross between . . ." Payne, p. 433.
749–50 "I will leave . . ." *et seq.*, Wheeler-Bennett, *Nemesis of Power*, pp. 640–41.
750   "I am not . . ." CSDIC (UK) Report, Interrogation of Oberstleutnant Arntz, *op. cit.*
751   "Duce, an infernal . . ." *et seq.*, Deakin, p. 708.
751   "I was standing . . ." *et seq.*, Payne, p. 511.
751   "continuous fire . . ." Irving, *The Mare's Nest*, p. 260.
752   "the treatment . . ." A remark made to Gen. Jodl, reported in *Besprechung der Führer* for July 31, 1944, OCMH.
752   "At five o'clock . . ." A conversation between SS Gen. Eugen Dollmann and SS Gen. Georg Elling, CSDIC Report CMF/X 194, July 22, 1945, CIAP.
753–55 "still suffering . . ." *et seq.*, John memorandum, *op. cit.*
756–57 "It's starting! . . ." *et seq.*, Gisevius, pp. 533–35.
757   "We shall need . . ." *et seq.*, John memorandum, *op. cit.*
757   "a spirited speech . . ." GSI (b) 21 Army Group, Interrogation Report of Otto Werth, late Wachtmeister im Nachrichtendienst, August 23, 1945, BA/907/Int, CIAP.
758   "just in case," Speer, p. 490.
758   "Goebbels seemed . . ." *et seq., ibid.*, p. 492.
759   "Do you recognize . . ." *et seq.*, Gisevius, p. 556.
759   ". . . from the telephone . . ." John memorandum, *op. cit.*
758–59 "Kluge, I now . . ." *et seq.*, Gisevius, p. 551.
760   "You're crazy . . ." MI-6 interrogation record of an unnamed German doctor with the battalion, CIAP.
760–61 "In totally . . ." *et seq.*, Speer, p. 493.
761–62 *"Beck:* I have . . ." *et seq.*, Gisevius, pp. 563–64.
762   "a massive shadow . . ." Speer, p. 495.
763   ". . . von Kluge . . ." Document L42251, August 17, 1944, OSS German Section, MMR, NA.
763   "Good heavens!" Colvin, *Master Spy*, p. 236.

page
763   "If they . . ." Speer, p. 496.
764   "None of those . . ." Schramm, p. 31.
764   "mad," *et seq., ibid.,* p. 32.
764   "line in the . . ." *et seq.,* Hodgson, R Study, *op. cit.*
765   "I must first . . ." Schramm, p. 46.
765   "Between 7:30 . . ." *ibid.,* p. 50.
765   "Kluge turned . . ." CSDIC Report SRGG 1347, "A Conversation Between General Eberbach and General Blumentritt," *op. cit.*
765   ". . . it was natural . . ." Schramm, p. 51.
766   "Find out what . . ." *et seq., ibid.,* p. 52.
766   "bungled business," *ibid.,* p. 54.
766   "You know . . ." *et seq., ibid.,* p. 55.
766   "Field Marshal . . ." Schramm, p. 59.
767   "This is the . . ." CSDIC Report SRGG 1347, *op. cit.*
767   "(He) felt . . ." Schramm, p. 60.
767   "Then Stuelpnagel . . ." *et seq.,* CSDIC Report SRGG 1347, *op. cit.*
767–68   "You must get . . ." *et seq.,* Schramm, p. 64.
768   "To the Führer . . ." *et seq.,* Hodgson, R Study, *op. cit.*
768   "One of Eisenhower's . . ." Curtis interview.
769   "an acid grin," *et seq., New York Times,* July 24, 1944.
769   "exhilarating," G2 estimate, July 24, 1944, in First United States Army Report of Operations, OCMH.
769   "I never saw . . ." R. Harris Smith, p. 221.

9. THE BREAKOUT

Sources

OB-West War Diary *Anlagen* July–August 1944, EDS, NA; U.S. 30th Infantry Division, *Workhorse of the Western Front,* Unit History Collection, OCMH; Col. T. J. Crystal, U.S. 19th Corps G2, "Reports," in the Crystal Collection, HI; History of the (U.S.) 120th Infantry Regiment, Unit History Collection, OCMH; U.S. 8th Air Force, "Report of Operation 494," Albert F. Simpson Library, MAFB; U.S. 1st Army, *Report of Operations,* Vol. 1, OCMH; U.S. 3rd Army, *Report of Operations,* Army and Navy Club Library, Washington, D.C.; Brig. R. W. MacLeod, "Report of Operations in Brittany as at 16 July 1944," CIAP; Captain S. J. Knerly, "Report of Operations of Jed Team Gerald, 7 July–23 August 1944," CIAP; Scipion (code name), "Report of Operations of Jed Team Hugh," undated, CIAP; Maj. J. V. Summers, "Report of Operations of Jed Team Horace on Operations in Brittany 17 July–15 September 1944," CIAP; Maj. B. J. Cliffe, "Report on Visit to 1 SAS Regiment in France," October 2, 1944, CIAP; Capt. J. H. Cox, "Report of Operations of Jed Team Ivor," CIAP; Senior Intelligence Officer, Combined Operations Headquarters, "Brittany and Lucky Strike," May 14, 1944, CIAP; Capt. Bennett, "Report of Operations of Jed Team Daniel," August 14, 1944; Brig. R. W. MacLeod, "Report on Visit to Southern Morbihan," August 19, 1944, CIAP; Director of Tactical Investigation, War Office, *SAS/SOE Operations in Brittany,* CIAP; Director of Tactical Investigation, War Office, *Organisation and Development of Resistance in Brittany,* October 12, 1944, CIAP; Gen. Koenig, EMMFFI missions, *Aloes, Muguet, Lilal, Oeille, Héliotrope, Violette,* with intelligence and communications annexes, CIAP; *le Général de Corps d'Armée Koenig, Commandant des Forces Françaises de l'Intérieur, ordre à Commandant Bourgoin,*

Commandant le 4e Bataillon SAS, 90, Londres, le 1er Août 1944, CIAP; Gen. Fritz Bayerlein, 21st Panzer Division, Ms. No. A902, OCMH.

Notes

page

770 "I can report . . ." *et seq.,* Hodgson, R Study, *op. cit.*
771 "Anyone who . . ." Payne, p. 519.
771 ". . . the deep distrust . . ." Guderian, p. 272.
772 "And now came . . ." Rundstedt, *et al.,* Ms. No. B633, *op. cit.*
772–73 "marked increase . . ." *et seq.,* Staubwasser, Ms. No. B782, *op. cit.*
773 "Without any doubt . . ." Hodgson, R Study, *op. cit.*
773 "an orchestra . . ." Blumenson, *Breakout and Pursuit,* p. 238.
774 "the bombardment . . ." *ibid.,* p. 240.
774 "rushed dementedly . . ." *et seq.,* Bayerlein, Ms. No. A902, *op. cit.*
774 "I have learned . . ." Delmer, *The Counterfeit Spy,* p. 235.
775–76 *"eine Riesensauerei," et seq.,* Hodgson, R Study, *op. cit.*
776 "Paris and the Seine . . ." EPF.
776 "hasten the end . . ." Pogue study, *op. cit.*
777 "Only discipline . . ." *et seq.,* G2 Report, July 31, 1944, in U.S. 1st Army, *Report of Operations, op. cit.*
778 "received a cavalry mission . . ." Blumenson, *Breakout and Pursuit,* p. 370.
778 "a terrible . . ." Foot, citing Eisenhower, p. 408.
779 "They were all . . ." "Report of Operations of Jed Team Giles," *op. cit.*
780 "French people . . ." *et seq.,* Radio France, Call to Breton Insurrection, 0700, August 6, 1944, in *BBC Warnings to Resistance Groups, op. cit.*
782 "in the interests . . ." *et seq.,* SFHQ September Report to Supreme Commander, CIAP.
783 "We regret . . ." "Report of Operations of Jed Team Giles," *op. cit.*

10. GÖTTERDÄMMERUNG

Sources

U.S. V Corps in the ETO, OCMH; Capt. Martin Blumenson, "The Mortain Counterattack," *Army,* 8 (July 1958): 30–38; Count G. von Schwerin, "The 116th Panzer Division," unnumbered U.S. Army interrogation report, OCMH; Gen. Walter Warlimont, *Circumstances of the 20th July 1944 Attempt, op. cit.;* *Günther von Kluge, deutscher Generalfeldmarschall,* ME-KI (v. Kluge+) 2.11.1963 137*** Aus: Internat.: Biograph Munzingerarchiv, Lieferung 44/63, CIAP; Blumentritt, *von Kluge on 15 August 1944,* Ms. No. B034, OCMH; German Army, Form 202, "von Kluge, Günther," OCMH; Martin Bormann, "File on Kluge," OCMH; Heinz Eberbach, Ms. No. A922, OCMH; MIRS London, Kluge to Hitler, Letter, August 18, 1944, CIAP.

Notes

page

784 "The decision . . ." Hodgson, R Study, *op. cit.*
784 "to make quite . . ." Winterbotham, *The Ultra Secret,* p. 149.
785 "absolutely copper-bottom . . ." Winterbotham interview.

page
785   ". . . an attack . . ." Hodgson, R Study, *op. cit.*
785   "Now the vital . . ." Winterbotham, *The Ultra Secret,* pp. 149–50.
785   "Kluge staked . . ." *ibid.,* p. 151.
786   "With a heavy . . ." U.S. 30th Infantry Division, *Workhorse of the Western Front, op. cit.*
787   "We didn't expect . . ." *et seq.,* Hodgson, R Study, *op. cit.*
788–89   "display of weakness . . ." *et seq.,* "Tactical Operation B," Folder 15, the "Harris Report," *op cit.*
790   "Hundreds of men . . ." R. M. Wingfield, *The Only Way Out,* London: Hutchinson, 1945, p. 27.
791   "August 15th . . ." HQ USFET, Information Control Division, Intelligence Section, "Transcript of Fragments of Hitler's Conference of August 31, 1944, at the Wolfsschanze, Westphal and Krebs Present," CIAP.
791   "Hitler was desperate . . ." Guderian, p. 296.
791   "Field Marshal von Kluge . . ." HQ USFET, "Transcript of Hitler's conference of August 31, 1944," *op. cit.*
792   *"The Road to Avranches . . ."* *et seq., Time,* June 25, 1945.
792   "a futile attempt . . ." Dulles, *Germany's Underground,* p. 188 ff.
792   "in charge of . . ." *et seq.,* OSS Interoffice Memo, "German Economic Agent Seeks Allied Contacts in Lisbon," L Document 42255, August 11, 1944, based upon OSS Official Despatches, Lisbon, August 7 and 8, 1944, MMR, NA.
793   "The Commander-in-Chief . . ." Hodgson, R Study, *op. cit.*
793–94   "Here at Avranches . . ." *et seq.,* Rundstedt *et al.,* Ms. B633, *op. cit.*
794   "Should the new . . ." Hodgson, R Study, *op. cit.*
795   "Get everything . . ." Schramm, p. 205.

EPILOGUE

Sources

CIC/CCS Intelligence Reports for June–December 1944, MMR, NA; Theater Intelligence Section Martian Report 87, Annex V1, "Plans for the Evacuation of German Troops by Rail from France," of uncertain date but promulgated no later than March 31, 1944, OPD, WDGS files, Overlord Section, MMR, NA; Dr. Louis de Jong, Director of the Netherlands State Institute for War Documentation, Amsterdam, "Report prepared for the Second International Conference on the History of the European Resistance, 1939–1945, Milan 26/29 March 1961," HI; Angus McLean Thuermer, letter to the publisher concerning the capture of the Enigma keys at Brest; Minutes, Committee of Three, June 5, 1945, "Top Secret Ultra," in Assistant Scretary of War Safe File 334.8, Record Group 107, MMR, NA.

Notes

page
796   "Two-and-a-half . . ." SHAEF G2 report, August 23, 1944, in SHAEF Record Group 331, MMR, NA.
797   "vital importance . . ." *et seq.,* Loewenheim, *et al.,* pp. 603–6.
798   "thief on the cross . . ." Zimmermann and Jacobsen, *Germans against Hitler, 20 July 1944, op. cit.*

page
798   "Now everyone . . ." Schlabrendorff, p. 157.
798   "My functions . . ." *et seq.,* Manfred Rommel, monograph, in Rommel, p. 495.
799   "I have just . . ." *et seq., ibid.,* p. 503.
799   "Accept my . . ." *ibid.,* p. 505.
799   "The Führer . . ." Desmond Young, p. 222.
799–800   "von Kluge's participation . . ." *et seq.,* War Department Historical Commission Report, "Field Marshal von Kluge and the Plot of 20th July 1944," prepared by Lt. Col. O. J. Hale, SC.
802   "in particular . . ." John, p. 312.
803   "a very, very . . ." *et seq.,* Ryan, *A Bridge Too Far,* New York: Simon & Schuster, 1974, p. 65.
803   "psychopath," *et seq., ibid.,* p. 76.
803   "Montgomery was . . ." Bradley interview.
804   "We wanted no . . ." Wingate interview.
804   "achieved a degree . . ." Eisenhower Report, *op. cit.*
804   "remarkably effective," *et seq.,* Eisenhower to Marshall, July 6, 1944, in SHAEF 370.2, *Fortitude,* MMR, NA.
804   "Operation Fortitude . . ." HQ 12th Army Group, Bradley to Eisenhower, Cover and Deception, European Theater of Operations, 18 November 1944, in SHAEF 370.2, *Fortitude, op. cit.*
805   "entered deception operations . . ." *et seq.,* "Appreciation of Deception in the European Theater," in the "Harris Report," *op. cit.*
805   "the service . . ." Wingate interview.
806   "as to what . . ." *et seq.,* Overlord file of the U.S. Military Mission to Moscow, a copy of a letter from "Bolton" to Col. J. H. Bevan, July 19, 1944, MMR, NA.
807   "happy and handy . . ." Foot, p. 419.
807   "express my great . . ." *ibid.,* p. 442.
807   "amateurish . . ." Webster, Vol. 3, p. 88.
808   "40 years . . ." Dunderdale interview.
809   "like shooting . . ." Blumenson, *Breakout and Pursuit,* p. 683.
809   "These potential . . ." *ibid.,* p. 684.
810   "apparent inability . . ." *et seq.,* OSS, R&A Report No. 2947, "Prince Bernhard, The Future Prince Consort of the Netherlands, an examination of the personal history, character and constitutional position," March 30, 1945, MMR, NA.
810   "an important agent," *et seq.,* SHAEF Counter-Intelligence Report No. 4, November 10, 1944, in 6th Army Group CI file, MMR, NA.
812   "wished to make . . ." *et seq.,* Charles Mee, *Meeting at Potsdam,* New York: M. Evans, 1975, p. 83.
812–13   ". . . the Japanese . . ." *et seq.,* Operations Division, WDGS, "Ultra: The 'Starts' File," Executive 17, Item B, Record Group 165, Records of the WDGSS, MMR, NA.
813   "handed back . . ." Winterbotham, *The Ultra Secret,* p. 186.
814   "I am forced . . ." Report of the death of A. M. Turing, *Wilmslow County Express,* Cheshire, U.K., June 10, 1954, obtained by Mrs. G. M. Barry.
814   "witless, upperclass . . ." Winterbotham interview.
815   "Stewart Graham . . ." Menzies's death certificate, Somerset House, London, CIAP.

page
815 "Dear General Menzies," Eisenhower to Menzies, in Eisenhower-Menzies file, EL.
816 "Canaris was never . . ." *et seq.,* Menzies interview.
817 "from Canaris." Trevor-Roper interview.
817–18 "Somehow I felt . . ." *et seq.,* Schellenberg, p. 410.
818 "important military . . ." Bartz, p. 163.
819 "I . . . die . . ." Colvin, *Master Spy,* p. 248.
820 "belonged to the . . ." Zimmermann and Jacobsen, *Germans against Hitler, 20 July 1944, op. cit.,* p. 64.
820 "D-Day was one . . ." Charles V. P. von Luttichau, a note to the author, May 1975.
821 "But what . . ." *New York Times,* November 30, 1974.

AUTHOR'S NOTE

Notes

page
825 "be given access . . ." *et seq.,* CCS 334, Record Group 218, Records of the USJCS, and JCS 385, MMR, NA.
826 "Appropriate departments . . ." OPD 311.5, MMR, NA.
826 "The existence of . . ." *et seq.,* CCS 334, Record Group 218, Records of the USJCS, and JCS 385, MMR, NA.
826 "tried his . . ." *et seq.,* Cornwall-Jones to JSC, April 17, 1946, including "Information Concerning General Patton," undated, CCS 201, "Patton, General," Record Group 218, Records of the USJCS, MMR, NA.

Bibliography

Alanbrooke, Viscount. *Diaries*. Edited by Sir Arthur Bryant. 2 vols. London: Collins, 1957–59.

Alexander of Tunis, Earl. *Memoirs, 1940–45*. Edited by J. North. London: Cassell, 1962.

Alsop, Stewart, and Braden, Thomas. *Sub Rosa: The OSS and American Espionage*. New York: Harcourt, Brace & World, 1964.

Ambrose, Stephen E. *The Supreme Commander: The War Years of General Dwight D. Eisenhower*. New York: Doubleday, 1970.

Amort, C., and Jedlicka, M. *The Canaris File*. Translated by M. Parker and R. Gheysens. London: Wingate, 1970.

Armstrong, Anne. *Unconditional Surrender*. New Brunswick, N.J.: Rutgers Univ. Press, 1961.

Aron, Robert. *De Gaulle Before Paris: The Liberation of France, June–August 1944*. Translated by Humphrey Hare. New York: Putnam, 1962.

———. *France Reborn: The History of the Liberation, June 1944–May 1945*. Translated by Humphrey Hare. New York: Scribners, 1964.

Aster, Sidney. *1939: The Making of the Second World War*. New York: Simon & Schuster, 1974.

Astley, Joan Bright. *The Inner Circle*. London: Hutchinson, 1971.

Attlee, Clement R. *As It Happened*. London: Heinemann, 1954.

Avon, The Earl of. *The Eden Memoirs*. London: Cassell, 1960–1965. Vol. 3, *The Reckoning*, 1965.

Barkas, G. *The Camouflage Story*. London: Cassell, 1952.

Bartz, K. *The Downfall of the German Secret Service*. Translated by E. Fitzgerald. London: Kimber, 1956.

Bazna, Elyesa. *I Was Cicero*. Translated by Eric Mosbacher. New York: Harper & Row, 1962.

Bekker, Cajus. *The Luftwaffe War Diaries*. New York: Doubleday, 1968.

Belgium, The Official Account of What Happened, 1939–40. Published for the Belgium Ministry of Foreign Affairs, New York, 1941.

Bernstein, Jeremy. *The Analytical Engine: Computers—Past, Present and Future*. New York: Random House, 1963.

Bertrand, G. *Enigma ou le Plus Grande Enigme de la Guerre 1939–1945*. Paris: Librairie Plon, 1973.

Best, S. P. *The Venlo Incident.* London: Hutchinson, 1950.

Bethge, Eberhard. *Dietrich Bonhoeffer.* London: Collins, 1970.

Birse, Arthur H. *Memoirs of an Interpreter.* New York: Coward, McCann, 1967.

Bleicher, Hugo. *Colonel Henri's Story.* Translated by Ian Colvin. London: Kimber, 1954.

Blumenson, Martin. *Breakout and Pursuit.* Washington, D.C.: Department of the Army, 1961.

————. *Anzio: The Gamble That Failed.* Philadelphia: Lippincott, 1963.

————. *The Patton Papers 1940–1945.* Boston: Houghton Mifflin, 1974.

Bonhoeffer, Dietrich. *Letters and Papers from Prison.* Rev. ed. Edited by Eberhard Bethge. New York: Macmillan, 1967.

Boveri, Margaret. *Treason in the 20th Century.* Translated by Jonathan Steinberg. New York: Putnam, 1963.

Bradley, Omar N. *A Soldier's Story.* New York: Henry Holt, 1951.

Brickhill, P. *The Dam Busters.* War Classics Series. London: Evans, 1966.

Buckley, Christopher. *Norway; The Commandos; Dieppe.* Popular Military History series. London: HMSO, 1951.

Buckmaster, Maurice J. *Specially Employed.* London: Batchworth, 1952.

Bulloch, John. *M.I. 5.* London: Barker, 1963.

Bullock, Alan. *Hitler—A Study in Tyranny.* Rev. ed. New York: Harper & Row, 1963.

Butcher, Harry. *My Three Years with Eisenhower.* New York: Simon & Schuster, 1946.

Campbell, James. *The Bombing of Nuremberg.* New York: Doubleday, 1974.

Carré, M.-L. *I Was The "Cat."* Translated by M. Savill. London: Four Square Books, 1961.

Carroll, Wallace. *Persuade or Perish.* New York: Houghton Mifflin, 1948.

Catton, Bruce. *The War Lords of Washington.* New York: Harcourt Brace, 1948.

Churchill, Right Hon. Winston S. *The Great War.* 3 vols. London: George Newnes, 1933.

————. *The Second World War.* 6 vols. London: Cassell, 1948–54.

Ciano, Galeazzo. *The Ciano Diaries, 1939–1943.* New York: H. Fertig, 1973.

Clark, Alan. *Barbarossa: The Russian-German Conflict, 1941–1945.* New York: Morrow, 1965.

Clark, Mark W. *Calculated Risk.* New York: Harper & Bros., 1950.

Cline, Ray S. *Washington Command Post: The Operations Division.* Washington, D.C.: Department of the Army, 1951.

Collier, Basil. *The Defence of the United Kingdom.* London: HMSO, 1957.

Collier, Richard. *Ten Thousand Eyes.* New York: Dutton, 1958.

Collins, Larry, and Lapierre, Dominique. *Is Paris Burning?* London: Gollancz, 1965.

Colvin, Ian. *Master Spy.* New York: McGraw-Hill, 1951.

————. *Vansittart in Office: The Origins of World War II.* London: Gollancz, 1965.

Combined Operations Command. *Combined Operations. Great Britain.* New York: Macmillan, 1943.

Connell, J. *Auchinleck: A Critical Biography.* London: Cassell, 1959.

————. *Wavell.* Edited by M. Roberts. 2 vols. London: Collins, 1969.

Cookridge, E. H. *Inside S.O.E.* London: Barker, 1966.

Cookson, John, and Nottingham, Judith. *A Survey of Chemical and Biochemical Warfare.* London: Sheed & Ward, 1969.

Craig, Gordon A., and Gilbert, Felix, eds. *The Diplomats 1919–1939*. 2 vols. Princeton, N.J.: Princeton Univ. Press, 1953.

Craven, Wesley F., and Cate, James L., eds. *The Army Air Forces in World War II*. 6 vols. Chicago: Univ. of Chicago Press, 1949–58. Vol. 3, *Europe: Argument to VE Day, January 1944 to May 1945*, 1951.

Cretzianu, A. *The Lost Opportunity*. London: Cape, 1957.

Cunningham, Andrew B. *A Sailor's Odyssey*. New York: Dutton, 1951.

Dalton, Hugh. *Memoirs*. London: Muller, 1953–62. Vol. 2, *The Fateful Years*, 1957.

Dansette, A. *Histoire de la Liberation de Paris*. Paris: Fayard, 1959.

Deacon, R. *A History of the British Secret Service*. London: Muller, 1969.

Deakin, F. W. *The Brutal Friendship: Mussolini's Last Years*. London: Weidenfeld & Nicolson, 1962.

Deane, John R. *The Strange Alliance: The Story of Our Efforts at Wartime Cooperation with Russia*. New York: Viking, 1947.

De Gaulle, Charles. *Appels et Discours, 1940–1944*. Published clandestinely, 1944.

———. *War Memoirs*. 3 vols. New York: Simon & Schuster, 1958–1960.

De Guingand, Sir Francis W. *Operation Victory*. New York: Scribners, 1947.

———. *Generals at War*. London: Hodder & Stoughton, 1964.

De Launay, J., ed. *European Resistance Movements, 1939–1945: In English, French and German*. 2 vols. London: Pergamon, 1960–64.

Delmer, Sefton. *Black Boomerang*. New York: Viking, 1962.

———. *The Counterfeit Spy*. New York: Harper & Row, 1971.

Dennett, Raymond, and Johnson, J. E., eds. *Negotiating with the Russians*. Boston: World Peace Foundation, 1951.

Deutsch, Harold C. *The Conspiracy Against Hitler in the Twilight War*. Bloomington, Minn.: Univ. of Minnesota Press, 1968.

Dewavrin, André. *Souvenirs*. Paris: Librairie Plon, 1951.

Dilks, David, ed. *The Diaries of Sir Alexander Cadogan 1938–1945*. New York: Putnam, 1972.

Doenitz, Karl. *Memoirs*. London: Weidenfeld & Nicolson, 1959.

Dourlein, Peter. *Inside North Pole*. London: Kimber, 1953.

Dulles, Allen W. *The Craft of Intelligence*. New York: Harper & Row, 1963.

———. *Germany's Underground*. London: Macmillan, 1947.

———. *The Secret Surrender*. New York: Harper & Row, 1966.

Dupuy, Richard E., and Dupuy, Trevor N. *The Encyclopedia of Military History*. London: Macdonald, 1970.

———. *The Military Heritage of America*. New York: McGraw-Hill, 1956.

Ehrlich, B. *The French Resistance*. London: Chapman and Hall, 1966.

Ehrman, J. *Grand Strategy, August 1943–September 1944*. London: HSMO, 1956.

Eisenhower, Dwight D. *Crusade in Europe*. New York: Avon, 1968.

———. *General Eisenhower on the Military Churchill: A Conversation with Alastair Cooke*. New York: Norton, 1970.

———. *The Papers of Dwight David Eisenhower: The War Years*. Edited by Alfred D. Chandler, Jr. 5 vols. Baltimore: Johns Hopkins Press, 1970.

Ellis, L. F., and Warhurst, A. E. *Victory in the West*. Vol. 1. United Kingdom Military History series. London: HMSO, 1962.

Ellsberg, Edward. *The Far Shore*. New York: Dodd, Mead, 1960.

Essame, Hubert, and Belfield, E. M. G. *Normandy Bridgehead*. New York: Ballantine, 1970.

Farago, Ladislas. *The Broken Seal: "Operation Magic" and the Secret Road to Pearl Harbor*. New York: Random House, 1967.

————. *The Game of the Foxes: The Untold Story of German Espionage in the United States and Great Britain during World War II*. New York: McKay, 1971.

————. *Patton—Ordeal and Triumph*. New York: Obolensky, 1964.

Farran, R. *Winged Dagger: Adventures on Special Service*. London: Collins, 1948.

Feis, H. *Churchill, Roosevelt, Stalin: The War They Waged and the Peace They Sought*. Princeton, N.J.: Princeton Univ. Press, 1957.

Fergusson, Bernard. *The Watery Maze: The Story of Combined Operations*. New York: Holt, Rinehart and Winston, 1961.

First Infantry Division, U.S. Army. *Danger Forward, A History with Introduction by Hanson W. Baldwin*. U.S.: Albert Love Enterprises, 1947.

Fitzgibbon, Constantine. *The Shirt of Nessus*. New York: Norton, 1957.

Fleming, Peter. *Operation Sea Lion*. New York: Simon & Schuster, 1957.

Flicke, W. F. *Rote Kapelle*. Düsseldorf: Hilden, 1949.

————. *War Secrets in the Ether*. 2 vols. Washington, D.C.: National Security Agency, 1954.

Flower, Desmond, and Reeves, James, eds. *The Taste of Courage: The War 1939–45*. New York: Harper & Bros., 1960.

Foot, M. R. D. *S.O.E. In France*. London: HMSO, 1966.

Foote, Alexander [pseud.]. *Handbook for Spies*. New York: Doubleday, 1949.

Ford Corey. *Donovan of OSS*. Boston: Little, Brown, 1970.

Ford, Corey, and McBain, Alastair. *Cloak and Dagger: The Secret Story of OSS*. New York: Random House, 1946.

Forrestal, James. *Diaries*. Edited by Walter Millis. New York: Viking, 1951.

Frank, Owen. *The Eddie Chapman Story*. London: Wingate, 1953.

Frank, Wolfgang. *The Sea Wolves*. Translated by R. O. B. Long. New York: Rinehart, 1955.

Freidin, Seymour, and Richardson, William, eds. *The Fatal Decisions*. Translated by Constantine Fitzgibbon. New York: Sloane, 1956.

Fuller, J. F. C. *The Second World War, 1939–1945: A Strategical and Tactical History*. New York: Duell, Sloane & Pearce, 1949.

Fuller, Jean Overton. *Born for Sacrifice*. London: Pan, 1957.

————. *Double Webs*. New York: Putnam, 1958.

————. *Madeleine*. London: Gollancz, 1952.

————. *The Starr Affair*. London: Gollancz, 1954.

Funk, Arthur L. *Charles de Gaulle: The Crucial Years, 1943–44*. Norman, Okla.: Univ. of Oklahoma Press, 1959.

Galland, Adolf. *The First and the Last: The German Fighter Force in World War II*. Translated by M. Savill. London: Methuen, 1955.

Garby-Czerniawski, Roman. *The Big Network*. London: Ronald, 1961.

Garlinski, J. *Poland, S.O.E. and the Allies*. Translated by P. Stevenson. London: Allen & Unwin, 1969.

Gehlen, Reinhard. *The Service: The Memoirs of General Reinhard Gehlen*. Translated by David Irving. New York: World, 1972.

Gilbert, Felix. *Hitler Directs His War*. New York: Oxford Univ. Press, 1950.

Gisevius, H. B. *To the Bitter End*. Translated by R. and C. Winston. London: Cape, 1948.

Giskes, H. J. *London Calling North Pole*. London: Kimber, 1953.

Goebbels, Joseph. *Diaries, 1942–1943.* Edited and translated by Louis P. Lochner. New York: Doubleday, 1948.

Goerlitz, Walter. *History of the German General Staff, 1657–1945.* Translated by Brian Battershaw. New York: Praeger, 1953.

Gordon, David L., and Dangerfield, R. J. *The Hidden Weapon: The Story of Economic Warfare.* New York: Harper & Bros., 1947.

Grunberger, Richard. *The Twelve-Year Reich: A Social History of Nazi Germany, 1933–1945.* New York: Holt, Rinehart and Winston, 1971.

Guderian, Heinz. *Panzer Leader.* New York: Ballantine, 1972.

Guillaume, P. *La Sologne au Temps de l'Heroisme et de la Traison.* Orleans: Imprimerie Nouvelle, 1950.

Hagen, Louis. *The Secret War for Europe.* New York: Stein & Day, 1969.

Halder, H. *Hitler as Warlord.* Translated by P. Findlay. London: Putnam & Co., 1950.

Harris, L. H. *Signal Venture.* Aldershot, U. K.: Gale and Polden, 1951.

Harrison, Gordon A. *Cross-Channel Attack.* Washington, D.C.: Department of the Army, 1951.

Hassell, Ulrich von. *The Von Hassell Diaries, 1938–1944.* 1947. Reprint. Westport, Conn.: Greenwood Press, 1971.

Hassett, William D. *Off the Record with F.D.R., 1942–1945.* New Brunswick, N.J.: Rutgers University Press, 1958.

Haukelid, Knut. *Skis Against the Atom.* Translated by Lyon. London: Kimber, 1954.

Hayn, F. *Die Invasion.* Heidelberg: Vowinckel, 1954.

Henderson, Sir N. *Failure of a Mission.* London: Hodder & Stoughton, 1940.

Herington, John. *Air Power Over Europe, 1944–1945.* Canberra: Australian War Memorial, 1963.

Hislop, J. *Anything But A Soldier.* London: Michael Joseph, 1965.

Hitler, Adolph. *Hitler's Secret Conversations, 1941–1944.* New York: Farrar, Straus and Young, 1953.

Hoegner, W. *Der Schwierige Aussenseiter.* Munich: Isar Verlag, 1959.

Hoettl, Wilhelm. *The Secret Front: The Story of Nazi Political Espionage.* Translated by R. H. Stevens. New York: Praeger, 1954.

Höhne, H. *The Order of the Death's Head: The Story of Hitler's SS.* Translated by R. Barry. London: Secker & Warburg, 1969.

Höhne, Heinz, and Zolling, Hermann. *The General Was A Spy: The Truth about General Gehlen and His Spy Ring.* New York: Coward, McCann & Geoghegan, 1972.

Howarth, P., ed. *Special Operations.* London: Routledge, 1955.

Hull, Cordell. *Memoirs.* New York: Macmillan, 1948.

Hunt, Sir. David. *A Don at War.* London: Kimber, 1966.

Hyde, H. M. *Cynthia.* London: Hamish Hamilton, 1966.

———. *Room 3603: The Story of the British Intelligence Center in New York During World War II.* New York: Farrar, Straus, 1952.

Ingersoll, R. *Top Secret.* New York: Harcourt Brace, 1946.

International Military Tribunal. *The Trial of the Major War Criminals before the International Military Tribunal, Nuremberg, 14 November 1945–1 October 1946.* London: HMSO, 1947–49.

Irving, David. *The German Atomic Bomb.* New York: Simon & Schuster, 1968.

———. *The Mare's Nest.* Boston: Little, Brown, 1965.

Jackson, W. G. F. *The Battle for Italy.* British Battles series. London: Batsford, 1967.

James, Clifton. *I Was Monty's Double.* London: Rider, 1954.

John, Otto. *Twice Through the Lines.* Translated by R. H. Barry. Harper & Row, 1973.

Joslen, H. F. ed. *Orders of Battle: 1939–1945.* Vol. 1. United Kingdom Military History series. London: HMSO, 1960.

Kahn, David. *The Codebreakers.* New York: Macmillan, 1967.

Kallay, Miklos. *Hungarian Premier: A Personal Account of a Nation's Struggle in the Second World War.* New York: Columbia Univ. Press, 1954.

Kennedy, Sir John. *The Business of War.* London: Hutchinson, 1957.

Kimche, J. *Spying for Peace.* London: Weidenfeld & Nicolson, 1961.

King, Ernest Joseph, and Whitehill, W. M. *Fleet Admiral King.* New York: Norton, 1952.

Kirkpatrick, Lyman B. *The Real CIA.* New York: Macmillan, 1968.

Knatchbull-Hugessen, Sir H. *Diplomat in Peace and War.* London: John Murray, 1949.

Kramarz, J. *Stauffenberg—The Life and Death of an Officer.* Translated by R. H. Barry. London: Deutsch, 1967.

Langelaan, G. *Knights of the Floating Silk.* London: Hutchinson, 1959.

Leahy, W. *I Was There.* New York: Whittlesey, 1950.

Leasor, J. *War at the Top.* London: Michael Joseph, 1959.

Lee, Asher. *Blitz on Britain.* London: Four Square, 1960.

Lerner, Daniel. *Psychological Warfare Against Nazi Germany: The Skywar Campaign D-Day to VE-Day.* Cambridge, Mass.: MIT Press, 1971.

Leverkuehn, P. *German Military Intelligence.* Translated by R. H. Stevens and Constantine Fitzgibbon. London: Weidenfeld & Nicolson, 1954.

Lewin, Ronald. *Rommel as Military Commander.* Military Commanders series. London: Batsford, 1969.

Liddell Hart, B. H. "The Military Strategist," in A. J. P. Taylor, *Churchill Revised.* New York: Dial Press, 1969.

————. *The German Generals Talk.* New York: Morrow, 1948.

————. *History of the Second World War.* 2 vols. New York: Putnam, 1972.

Livry-Level, P. *Missions dans la RAF.* Caen: Ozanne, 1951.

Loewenheim, Francis W., et al. *Roosevelt and Churchill: Their Secret Wartime Correspondence.* New York: Saturday Review Press, 1975.

Lomax, Sir John. *The Diplomatic Smuggler.* London: Barker, 1965.

Longmate, Norman. *If Britain Had Failed.* New York: Stein & Day, 1974.

MacCloskey, Monro. *Secret Air Missions.* New York: Richards Rosen, 1966.

MacDonald, Charles B. *The Mighty Endeavor: American Armed Forces in the European Theater in World War 2.* New York: Oxford Univ. Press, 1969.

McKee, Alexander. *Last Round Against Rommel: Battle of the Normandy Beachhead.* New York: New American Library, 1964.

McLachlan, Donald. *Room 39: A Study in Naval Intelligence.* New York: Atheneum, 1968.

Macmillan, Harold. *The Blast of War, 1939–1945.* New York: Harper & Row, 1967.

Maiskii, Ivan. *Memoirs of a Soviet Ambassador; The War: 1939–1943.* Translated by Andrew Rothstein. New York: Scribners, 1968.

Majdalany, Frederick. *The Battle of El Alamein: Fortress in the Sand.* New York: Lippincott, 1965.

————. *The Fall of Fortress Europe.* Crossroads of World History series. New York: Doubleday, 1968.

Manvell, Roger. *Conspirators.* New York: Ballantine, 1971.

Manvell, Roger, and Fraenkel, Heinrich. *The Canaris Conspiracy.* London: Heinemann, 1969.

————. *Himmler.* New York: Paperback Library, 1972.

Marshall, George C. *Reports to the Secretary of War.* Washington, D.C.: Government Printing Office, 1943, 1945.

Marshall, Samuel L. A. *Night Drop: The American Airborne Invasion of Normandy.* Boston: Little, Brown, 1962.

Martienssen, A. *Hitler and His Admirals.* London: Secker & Warburg, 1948.

Maser, Werner. *Hitler's Letters and Notes.* Translated by Arnold Pomerance. New York: Harper & Row, 1974.

Mason, David. *U-Boat: The Secret Menace.* New York: Ballantine, 1968.

Masterman, J. C. *The Double-Cross System in the War of 1939–1945.* New Haven: Yale Univ. Press, 1972.

Matloff, Maurice, and Snell, Edwin M. *Strategic Planning for Coalition Warfare, 1941–1942.* Washington, D.C.: Department of the Army, 1953.

————. *Strategic Planning for Coalition Warfare, 1943–1944.* Washington, D.C.: Department of the Army, 1959.

Medlicott, William Norton. *The Economic Blockade.* 2 vols. History of the Second World War: United Kingdom Civil series. London: HMSO, 1952.

Michel, Henri. *Jean Moulin l'Unificateur.* Paris: Hachette, 1964.

————. *The Shadow War: European Resistance, 1939–1945.* New York: Harper & Row, 1973.

Middlebrook, Martin. *The Nuremberg Raid.* New York: Morrow, 1974.

Millar, George. *Horned Pigeon.* London: Heinemann, 1946.

Moll, Otto E. *Die deutschen Generalfeldmarschälle, 1939–1945.* Rostatt/Baden: Pabel Verlag, 1961.

Montagu, Ewen. *The Man Who Never Was.* War Classics series. London: Evans, 1966.

Montgomery, Viscount. *Normandy to the Baltic.* London: Hutchinson, 1947.

————. *The Memoirs of Field Marshal Lord Montgomery.* Cleveland: World, 1958.

Moran, Lord. *Churchill: Taken from the Diaries of Lord Moran.* New York: Houghton Mifflin, 1966.

Morgan, Sir F. *Overture to Overlord.* London: Hodder & Stoughton, 1950.

Morison, Samuel E. *The History of United States Naval Operations in World War II.* 14 vols. Boston: Little, Brown, 1947–1962. Vol. 11, *The Invasion of France and Germany, 1944–1945,* 1957.

Mosley, Leonard. *The Cat and the Mice.* New York: Harper & Bros., 1959.

Moyzisch, L. C. *Operation Cicero.* Translated by H. Fraenkel and Constantine Fitzgibbon. London: Wingate, 1950.

Munro, Ross. *Gauntlet to Overlord: The Story of the Canadian Army.* Toronto: Macmillan, 1946.

Neave, Airey. *Saturday at M.I.9: A History of Underground Escape Lines in Northwest Europe in 1940–1945.* London: Hodder & Stoughton, 1969.

Nelson, O. L. "National Security and the General Staff." Washington, D.C. *Infantry Journal,* 1946.

Nicholas, E. *Death Be Not Proud.* London: Cresset, 1958.

Norman, Albert. *Operation Overlord, The Design and Reality: The Allied In-*

vasion of Western Europe. Harrisburg, Pennsylvania: The Military Service Publishing Co., 1952.

O'Connor, Raymond G. *Diplomacy for Victory: FDR and Unconditional Surrender.* Norton Essays in American History series. New York: Norton, 1971.

Olden, Rudolf. *Hitler.* Translated by Walter Ettinghausen. New York: Covici-Friede, 1936.

O'Neill, Robert J. *The German Army and the Nazi Party, 1933–1939.* London: Cassell, 1966.

Page, Bruce, *et al. The Philby Conspiracy.* New York: Doubleday, 1968.

Papen, Franz von. *Memoirs.* Translated by Brian Connell. New York: Dutton, 1952.

Parker, T. W., and Thompson, W. J. "Conquer. The Story of the Ninth Army, 1944–1945," Washington, D.C. *Infantry Journal,* 1947.

Parkinson, Roger. *A Day's March Nearer Home.* New York: McKay, 1974.

Pash, Boris. *The Alsos Mission.* New York: Award, 1969.

Patton, George S., Jr. *War As I Knew It.* Boston: Houghton Mifflin, 1947.

Payne, Robert. *The Life and Death of Adolf Hitler.* New York: Praeger, 1973.

Pendar, Kenneth. *Adventure in Diplomacy: Our French Dilemma.* New York: Dodd, Mead, 1945.

Philby, Kim. *My Silent War.* New York: Grove, 1968.

Phillips, William. *Ventures in Diplomacy.* Boston: Beacon, 1953.

Pinto, Oreste. *Friend or Foe?* New York: Putnam, 1954.

Piquet-Wicks, E. *Four in the Shadows.* London: Jarrolds, 1957.

Playfair, I. S. O. *et al. The Mediterranean and the Middle East.* 3 vols. London: HMSO, 1954–1960.

Pogue, Forrest C. *George C. Marshall.* 3 vols. [to date]. New York: Viking, 1963–.

————. *The Supreme Command.* Washington, D.C.: Department of the Army, 1954.

Popov, Dusko. *Spy-Counterspy.* New York: Grosset & Dunlap, 1974.

Price, Alfred. *Instruments of Darkness.* London: Kimber, 1967.

Robertson, Terence. *Dieppe: The Shame and the Glory.* London: Hutchinson, 1963.

Roosevelt, Elliott. *As He Saw It.* New York: Duell, Sloane & Pearce, 1946.

Rommel, Erwin. *The Rommel Papers.* Edited by B. H. Liddell Hart. Translated by Paul Findlay. New York: Harcourt, 1953.

Root, Waverly. *Secret History of the War.* 3 vols. New York: Scribners, 1945–46.

Roskill, S. W. *The War at Sea, 1939–1945.* 3 vols. London: HMSO, 1954–56.

Rothfels, Hans. *The German Opposition to Hitler.* Translated by L. Wilson. London: Wolff, 1961.

Rowan, Richard W., and Deindorfer, Robert G. *The Secret Service: Thirty-three Centuries of Espionage.* New York: Hawthorn, 1967.

Royal Air Force, 1939–1945. 3 vols. London: HMSO, 1953–54.

Royal Institute of International Affairs. *Chronology of the Second World War.* London: Royal Institute of International Affairs, 1947.

Rozek, Edward J. *Allied Wartime Diplomacy: A Pattern in Poland.* New York: Wiley, 1958.

Ruge, F. *Sea Warfare, 1939–1945: A German Viewpoint.* Translated by M. D. Saunders. London: Cassell, 1957.

Ryan, Cornelius. *The Longest Day.* London: Gollancz, 1960.

Sampson, Anthony. *Anatomy of Britain.* New York: Harper & Row, 1962.

Saunders, H. St. George. *The Red Beret.* London: Michael Joseph, 1950.

Schellenberg, Walter. *The Schellenberg Memoirs.* London: Deutsch, 1956.

Schlabrendorff, Fabian von. *The Secret War Against Hitler.* Translated by H. Simon. London: Hodder & Stoughton, 1966.

Schramm Percy. *Hitler: The Man and the Military Leader.* Translated by Donald S. Detwiler. Chicago: Watts, 1971.

Schramm, Ritter von. *Conspiracy Among Generals.* Translated by R. T. Clark. London: Allen & Unwin, 1956.

Schulze-Gaevernitz, Gero von, ed. *They Almost Killed Hitler; Based on the Personal Account of Fabian von Schlabrendorff.* New York: Macmillan, 1947.

Sherwood, Robert E. *Roosevelt and Hopkins: An Intimate History.* New York: Harper & Bros., 1948.

Shirer, William L. *Collapse of the Third Republic: An Inquiry into the Fall of France in 1940.* New York: Pocket Books, 1971.

————. *The Rise and Fall of the Third Reich: A History of Nazi Germany.* London: Secker & Warburg, 1960.

Shulman, Milton. *Defeat in the West.* London: Secker & Warburg, 1947.

Smith, Gaddis. *American Diplomacy During the Second World War, 1941–1945.* New York: Wiley, 1965.

Smith, R. Harris. *OSS: The Secret History of America's First Central Intelligence Agency.* Berkeley: Univ. of California Press, 1972.

Smyth, Howard M., and Garland, Albert N. *Sicily and the Surrender of Italy.* Washington, D.C.: Department of the Army, 1965.

Snell, John L. *Illusion and Necessity: The Diplomacy of Global War, 1939–1945.* Boston: Houghton Mifflin, 1963.

Soustelle, Jacques. *Envers et Contre Tout.* 2 vols. Paris: Laffont, 1947–50.

Soviet Commission on Foreign Diplomatic Documents, Correspondence Between the Chairman of the Council of Ministers of the USSR and the Presidents of the USA and the Prime Minister of Great Britain During the Great Patriotic War of 1941–1945. Moscow: Foreign Languages Publishing House, 1957.

Spears, Edward. *Assignment to Catastrophe.* 2 vols. London: Heinemann, 1954.

Speer, Albert. *Inside the Third Reich: Memoirs of Albert Speer.* New York: Avon, 1970.

Stacey, C. P. *Canada's Battle in Normandy: The Canadian Army's Share in the Operations 6 June–1 September 1944.* Ottawa: The King's Printer, 1946.

————. *Official History of the Canadian Army in World War II.* Ottawa: The Queen's Printer. Vol. 3, *The Victory Campaign Operations in North-West Europe, 1944–45,* 1960.

Stagg, J. M. *Forecast for Overlord.* New York: Norton, 1972.

Stanford, Alfred Boller. *Force Mulberry.* New York: Morrow, 1951.

Stettinius, Edward R. *Roosevelt and the Russians: The Yalta Conference.* Edited by Walter Johnson. New York: Doubleday, 1949.

Stimson, Henry L., and Bundy, McGeorge. *On Active Service in Peace and War.* New York: Harper & Bros., 1948.

Strawson, John. *Hitler as Military Commander.* Military Commander series. London: Batsford, 1971.

Strong, Sir Kenneth W. D. *Intelligence at the Top: Recollections of an Intelligence Officer.* New York: Doubleday, 1969.

Strutton, B., and Pearson, M. *The Secret Invaders.* London: Hodder & Stoughton, 1958.

Sweet-Escott, B. *Baker Street Irregular.* London: Methuen, 1965.

Sykes, Christopher. *Troubled Loyalty.* London: Collins, 1968.

Taylor, Telford. *Sword and Swastika: Generals and Nazis in the Third Reich.* New York: Simon & Schuster, 1952.

Templewood, Viscount. *Ambassador on Special Mission.* London: Collins, 1946.

Thompson, G. R., and Harris, D. R. *The Signal Corps: The Outcome.* Washington, D.C.: Department of the Army, 1966.

Thompson, R. W. *D-Day: Spearhead of Invasion.* London: Purnell's, 1968.

Tickell, J. *Moon Squadron.* London: Wingate, 1956.

Tompkins, Peter. *Italy Betrayed.* New York: Simon & Schuster, 1966.

Toynbee, Arnold, ed. *Hitler's Europe: Survey of International Affairs, 1939–1946.* Oxford: Oxford Univ. Press, 1954.

Toynbee, A. J., and Toynbee, V. M., eds. *The War and the Neutrals.* Oxford: Oxford Univ. Press, 1956.

Trevor-Roper, Hugh R., ed. *Hitler's War Directives, 1939–1945.* New York: Holt, Rinehart and Winston, 1965.

Truman, Harry S. *Memoirs.* 2 vols. New York: Doubleday, 1958.

Turing, S. *Alan M. Turing.* Cambridge: Heffer, 1959.

U.S., Chief of Counsel for Prosecution of Axis Criminality. *Nazi Conspiracy and Aggression.* 8 vols. Washington, D.C.: Government Printing Office, 1946–47. Supplements A and B. 2 vols. 1947–48.

U.S., Department of the Army, Army Forces, Far East. *Operational History of Naval Communications: December 1941–August 1945.* Washington, D.C.: Office of the Chief of Military History, no date.

U.S., Department of the Army, Seventh Army. *The Seventh Army in France and Germany, 1944–1945.* 3 vols. Heidelberg: Seventh Army, 1946.

U.S., Department of State. *Foreign Relations of the United States, 1943, Europe.* Washington, D.C.: Government Printing Office, 1964.

Verrier, Anthony. *The Bomber Offensive.* New York: Macmillan, 1968.

Vomecourt, Phillipe de. *Who Lived to See the Day.* London: Hutchinson, 1961.

Walker, David E. *Lunch With A Stranger.* London: Wingate, 1957.

Ward, Irene. *F.A.N.Y. Invicta.* London: Hutchinson, 1955.

Warlimont, Walter. *Inside Hitler's Headquarters, 1939–45.* Translated by R. H. Barry. New York: Praeger, 1966.

Watson-Watt, Sir Robert. *The Pulse of Radar.* New York: Dial, 1959.

Webb, A. M., ed. *The Natzweiter Trial.* War Crimes Trials series. London: Hodge, 1949.

Webster, Sir Charles. *The Strategic Air Offensive Against Germany, 1939–1945.* 4 vols. London: HMSO, 1961.

Weizsäcker, E. *Memoirs.* London: Gollancz, 1951.

Werth, A. *Russia at War, 1941–45.* London: Barrie and Rockcliff, 1964.

Westphal, S. *The German Army in the West.* London: Cassell, 1952.

Wheeler-Bennett, John W. *Munich, Prologue to Tragedy.* New York: Duell, Sloan & Pearce, 1948.

———. *The Nemesis of Power: The German Army in Politics, 1918–1945.* London: Macmillan, 1953.

———, ed. *Action This Day.* London: Macmillan, 1968.

Whitehead, Donald. *The FBI Story: A Report to the People.* New York: Random House, 1956.

Whiting, Charles. *Patton*. New York: Ballantine, 1971.

Wiener, Jan G. *The Assassination of Heydrich*. New York: Pyramid, 1969.

Wighton, C. *Pinstripe Saboteur*. London: Collins, 1952.

Williams, Mary H. *Chronology, 1941–1945*. Washington, D.C.: Department of the Army, 1960.

Wilmot, Chester. *The Struggle for Europe*. London: Collins, 1952.

Wilson, Field Marshal Lord. *Reports by the Supreme Allied Commander, Mediterranean, to the Combined Chiefs of Staff, Washington, D.C.* London: HMSO, 1946–48.

Wingate, Sir Ronald. *Not In The Limelight*. London: Hutchinson, 1959.

Winterbotham, Frederick W. *Secret and Personal*. London: Kimber, 1969.

———. *The Ultra Secret*. New York: Harper & Row, 1974.

Wiskemann, Elizabeth. *The Rome-Berlin Axis*. London: Collins, 1969.

Woollcombe, R. *The Campaigns of Wavell, 1939–1943*. London: Cassell, 1959.

Woodward, E. L. *British Foreign Policy in the Second World War*. United Kingdom Military History series. London: HMSO, 1962.

Wright, Robert. *Dowding and the Battle of Britain*. London: Macdonald, 1969.

Wrinch, P. N. *The Military Strategy of Winston Churchill*. Brookline, Mass.: Boston University Press, 1961.

Young, Desmond. *Rommel, the Desert Fox*. New York: Harper & Bros., 1950.

Young, Gordon. *Cat With Two Faces*. New York: Putnam, 1957.

Young, Kenneth. *Churchill and Beaverbrook: A Study in Friendship and Politics*. London: Eyre & Spottiswoode, 1966.

Zeller, Eberhard. *The Flame of Freedom: The German Struggle Against Hitler*. Translated by R. P. Heller and D. R. Masters. London: Wolff, 1967.

Ziemke, Earl F. *Stalingrad to Berlin: The German Defeat in the East*. Washington, D.C.: Department of the Army, 1968.

Index

Abetz, Otto, 767
Abwehr, 138
  agents, 216, 217, 218; defections, 401,
    455–56; *see also* XX-Committee,
    double agents; individual countries
    below
  A-Net, 197
  Belgium, 206
  "Belinda," 302, 456
  Brandenburg Division, 222, 304
  codes and ciphers: American "Black
    Code," 101–02, 104, 116, 120–21;
    based on books, 105, 106, 108–09,
    110, 111, 478, 485; Enigma and
    "Ultra" intercepts, 21, 200, 401,
    438, 486, 491; Madrid special code
    obtained by British, 482–83
  communications, control of, 201
  Czechoslovakia, 217–19, 220, 222,
    223,228
  Department Z, 180; *see also* Oster,
    Col. Hans
  Dieppe raid, knowledge of, 85–86
  "Donar," 337
  Egypt, 217, 218; Kondor mission,
    104–13 *passim,* 116, 471
  England, 154, 170, 275; *see also* MI-6
    below; XX-Committee, double
    agents
  foreign agents kept out of Germany,
    217
  France, 217, 332, 334, 336, 337,
    485–86
  and Gestapo, 180, 199, 221, 302;
    arrests by, 288, 301–05 *passim,* 307,
    455, 586

Abwehr (*cont'd*)
  Hitler's personal files in possession of,
    166, 180
  Iraq, 52, 217
  Ireland, 210–12
  Italian campaign, 419–20
  lipreading by deaf-mutes, 203
  "Lisbon Report," 199–200, 314, 364,
    455, 586
  and MI-6, 6, 14, 52, 140, 154–56, 178,
    206, 481; *see also* MI-6, Germans
  microphotography, 485, 488
  Morocco, 52, 212, 213
  Netherlands, 810
  "Operation 7," 302, 303
  Pearl Harbor, interest in, 60–61
  "playing cards," 303
  Persia, 52, 217, 218
  Portugal, 60, 314, 456, 471, 482, 486,
    488, 489, 490, 491, 606
  and SD, 141, 158, 180, 198, 217, 221,
    222–23, 288, 302, 303, 304, 305,
    334, 497; reorganization by, 454–58
    passim, 472, 480, 490, 497–98; *see*
    also Amt Mil
  "Sealion," 207–12 *passim*
  secret ink and secret writing, 208, 478,
    479, 484–85, 486, 488, 490
  Spain, 21, 52, 60, 153, 212–16 *passim,*
    234, 282, 285–86, 481–85 *passim,*
    611, 673–74, 676–77, 685, 686
  Sweden, 217, 402, 456, 470–72, 542
  Turkey, 216, 217, 218, 401, 455–56
  U.S., 6, 101–02, 227, 275, 478–80
  Vatican *see* Mueller, Dr. Josef
  Yugoslavia, 218, 487, 488